Biopsychology

Biopsychology

THIRD EDITION

John P. J. Pinel

University of British Columbia

ALLYN AND BACON

Boston   London   Toronto   Sydney   Tokyo   Singapore

Vice President, Social Sciences:
Sean Wakely

Series Editor:
Carolyn Merrill

Series Editorial Assistant:
Jennifer Normandin

Vice President, Marketing:
Joyce Nilsen

Composition and Prepress Buyer:
Linda Cox

Manufacturing Buyer:
Megan Cochran

Cover Administrator:
Linda Knowles

Cover Designer:
Studio Nine

Editorial-Production Manager:
Elaine Ober

Copyeditor:
Naples Production Services

Editorial Production Services:
Schneck-DePippo Graphics

Illustrators:
William C. Ober, Claire W. Garrison, Mark Lefkowitz,
Schneck-DePippo Graphics, Illustrious Interactive,
Academy Artworks, LM Graphics
Leo Harrington, Phil Oliver, Adrienne Lehmann

Art and Design Management:
Schneck-DePippo Graphics/Electronic Supervision Phil Oliver

Library of Congress Cataloging-in-Publication Data

Pinel, John P. J.
    Biopsychology / John P. J. Pinel. -- 3rd ed.
      p. cm.
    Includes biobliographical references and index.
    ISBN 0-205-18445-6 (alk. paper)
    1. Psychobiology.   I. Title.
QP360.P463 1997   96-15823
152--dc20   CIP

To my surrogate parents,

Pearl and Harold Pinel

and Eileen and Bob Peake

Brief Contents

Chapter 1   Biopsychology as a Neuroscience   1

Chapter 2   Evolution, Genetics, and Experience: Asking the Right Questions about the Biology of Behavior   19

Chapter 3   The Anatomy of the Nervous System   49

Chapter 4   Neural Conduction and Synaptic Transmission   80

Chapter 5   What Biopsychologists Do: The Research Methods of Biopsychology   105

Chapter 6   Human Brain Damage and Animal Models   130

Chapter 7   The Visual System: From Eye to Cortex   150

Chapter 8   Mechanisms of Perception   179

Chapter 9   The Sensorimotor System   208

Chapter 10   The Biopsychology of Eating and Drinking   234

Chapter 11   Hormones and Sex   268

Chapter 12   Sleep, Dreaming, and Circadian Rhythms   295

Chapter 13   Drug Addiction and Reward Circuits in the Brain   323

Chapter 14   Memory and Amnesia   350

Chapter 15   Neuroplasticity: Development, Learning, and Recovery from Brain Damage   378

Chapter 16   Lateralization, Language, and the Split Brain   410

Chapter 17   Biopsychology of Emotion, Stress, and Mental Illness   437

Contents

Preface   xix

CHAPTER 1

Biopsychology as a Neuroscience   1

1.1   What is Biopsychology?   3

1.2   What Is the Relation between
Biopsychology and the Other Disciplines
of Neuroscience?   4

1.3   What Types of Research Characterize the
Biopsychological Approach?   5
Human and Nonhuman Subjects   5
Experiments and Nonexperiments   5
Pure and Applied Research   8

1.4   What Are the Divisions of
Biopsychology?   8
Physiological Psychology   8
Psychopharmacology   9
Neuropsychology   9
Psychophysiology   10
Comparative Psychology   11

1.5   Converging Operations: How Do
Biopsychologists Work Together?   11

1.6   Scientific Inference: How Do
Biopsychologists Study the
Unobservable?   12

1.7   What is Bad Science, and How Do You
Spot It?   14

Conclusion   17
Food for Thought   17

Key Terms   17
Additional Reading   18

CHAPTER 2

Evolution, Genetics, and Experience: Asking the Right Questions about the Biology of Behavior   19

2.1   Thinking about the Biology of Behavior:
From Dichotomies to Relations and
Interactions   20
Is It Physiological or Is It Psychological?   20
Is It Inherited or Is It Learned?   20
Problems with Thinking about the Biology of
Behavior in Terms of Traditional
Dichotomies   21

2.2   Human Evolution   23
Evolution and Behavior   26
Course of Human Evolution   27
Evolution of the Human Brain   30
Conclusion   31

2.3   Fundamental Genetics   32
Mendelian Genetics   32
Chromosomes, Reproduction, and Linkage   34
Sex Chromosomes and Sex-Linked Traits   35
Chromosome Structure and Replication   37
The Genetic Code and Gene Expression   38
Human Genome Project   39

2.4   Behavioral Development: The Interaction of
Genetic Factors and Experience   42
Selective Breeding of "Maze-Bright" and
"Maze-Dull" Rats   42

Phenylketonuria: A Single-Gene Metabolic Disorder   43

Development of Birdsong   44

2.5   The Genetics of Human Psychological Differences   45

Development of the Individual versus Development of Differences among Individuals   46

Minnesota Study of Twins Reared Apart   46

Conclusion   48

Food for Thought   48

Key Terms   48

Additional Reading   48

CHAPTER 3

The Anatomy of the Nervous System   49

3.1   General Layout of the Nervous System   50

Divisions of the Nervous System   50

Meninges, Ventricles, and Cerebrospinal Fluid   52

Blood-Brain Barrier   53

3.2   Cells of the Nervous System   54

Anatomy of Neurons   54

Supportive Cells of the Nervous System: Glial Cells and Satellite Cells   58

3.3   Neuroanatomical Techniques and Directions   58

Neuroanatomical Techniques   58

3.4   Spinal Cord   64

3.5   The Five Major Divisions of the Brain   65

3.6   Major Structures of the Brain   66

Myelencephalon   66

Metencephalon   67

Mesencephalon   68

Diencephalon   68

Telencephalon   70

Conclusion   77

Food for Thought   78

Key Terms   79

Additional Reading   79

CHAPTER 4

Neural Conduction and Synaptic Transmission   80

4.1   The Neuron's Resting Membrane Potential   81

Recording the Membrane Potential   81

Resting Membrane Potential   82

The Ionic Basis of the Resting Potential   82

4.2   Generation and Conduction of Postsynaptic Potentials   85

4.3   Integration of Postsynaptic Potentials and Generation of Action Potentials   86

4.4   Conduction of Action Potentials   88

Ionic Basis of Action Potentials   88

Refractory Periods   89

Conduction of Action Potentials   89

Conduction in Myelinated Axons   90

The Velocity of Axonal Conduction   90

Conduction in Neurons without Axons   91

4.5   Synaptic Transmission: Chemical Transmission of Signals from One Neuron to Another   91

Structure of Synapses   91

Synthesis, Packaging, and Transport of Neurotransmitter Molecules   92

Release of Neurotransmitter Molecules   93

The Activation of Receptors by Neurotransmitter Molecules   94

Reuptake, Enzymatic Degradation, and Recycling   96

4.6   The Neurotransmitters   97

Amino Acid Neurotransmitters   97

Monoamine Neurotransmitters   97

Soluble-Gas Neurotransmitters   98

Acetylcholine   98

Neuropeptides   98

4.7 Pharmacology of Synaptic Transmission 99
How Drugs Influence Synaptic
Transmission 100
Psychoactive Drugs: Four Examples 101

Conclusion 103
Food for Thought 103
Key Terms 103
Additional Reading 104

CHAPTER 5

What Biopsychologists Do: The Research Methods of Biopsychology 105

PART 1

Methods of Studying the Nervous System 106

5.1 Methods of Visualizing the Living Human Brain 106
Contrast X-Rays 106
X-Ray Computed Tomography 107
Magnetic Resonance Imaging 107
Positron Emission Tomography 108
Functional MRI 109

5.2 Recording Human Psychophysiological Activity 109
Scalp Electroencephalography 109
Muscle Tension 110
Eye Movement 111
Skin Conductance 112
Cardiovascular Activity 112

5.3 Invasive Physiological Research Methods 113
Stereotaxic Surgery 114
Lesion Methods 114
Electrical Stimulation 116
Invasive Electrophysiological Recording
Methods 117

5.4 Pharmacological Research Methods 117
Routes of Drug Administration 117
Selective Chemical Lesions 117
Measuring Chemical Activity of the
Brain 118
Locating Neurotransmitters and Receptors in
the Brain 118

PART 2

Behavioral Research Methods of Biopsychology 120

5.5 Neuropsychological Testing 121
Neuropsychological Testing 121
Tests of General Intelligence 121
Tests of Language Lateralization 121
Tests of Memory 121
Tests of Language 123
Tests of Perceptual-Motor Function 123

5.6 Behavioral Methods of Cognitive Neuroscience 124

5.7 Biopsychological Paradigms of Animal Behavior 125
Paradigms for Assessment of Species-Common
Behaviors 125
Traditional Conditioning Paradigms 126
Seminatural Animal Learning Paradigms 127

Conclusion 128
Food for Thought 129
Key Terms 129
Additional Reading 129

CHAPTER 6

Human Brain Damage and Animal Models 130

6.1 Causes of Brain Damage 131
Brain Tumors 131
Cerebrovascular Disorders 132
Closed-Head Injuries 134
Infections of the Brain 135

Neurotoxins 136
Genetic Factors 136

6.2 Neuropsychological Diseases 137
Epilepsy 137
Parkinson's Disease 140
Huntington's Disease 140
Multiple Sclerosis 142
Alzheimer's Disease 143

6.3 Animal Models of Human Neuropsychological Diseases 144
Kindling Model of Epilepsy 145
Amphetamine Model of Schizophrenia 146
MPTP Model of Parkinson's Disease 147

Conclusion 148
Food for Thought 148
Key Terms 148
Additional Readings 149

Complex Cortical Cells 167
Columnar Organization of Primary Visual Cortex 168
Spatial-Frequency Theory 170

7.5 Seeing Color 172
Component and Opponent Processing 172
Color Constancy and the Retinex Theory 174

Conclusion 177
Food for Thought 177
Key Terms 178
Additonal Reading 178

CHAPTER 7

The Visual System: From Eye to Cortex   150

7.1 Light Enters the Eye and Reaches the Retina 151

7.2 The Retina and Translation of Light into Neural Signals 154
Cone and Rod Vision 155
Eye Movement 158
Visual Transduction: The Conversion of Light to Neural Signals 159

7.3 From Retina to Primary Visual Cortex 161
Retinotopic Organization 161
The M and P Pathways 161

7.4 Seeing Edges 163
Lateral Inhibition and Contrast Enhancement 163
Receptive Fields of Visual Neurons 165
On-Center Cells and Off-Center Cells 166
Simple Cortical Cells 167

CHAPTER 8

Mechanisms of Perception   179

8.1 Principles of Sensory System Organization 180
Hierarchical Organization 180
Functional Segregation 181
Parallel Processing 182
The Current Model of Sensory System Organization 182

8.2 Cortical Mechanisms of Vision 183
Scotomas and Completion 183
Blindsight: Seeing without Consciousness 184
Perception of Subjective Contours 185
Functional Segregation in Visual Cortex: The Dorsal and Ventral Streams 185
Visual Agnosia 187

8.3 Audition 188
The Ear 189
From the Ear to the Primary Auditory Cortex 190
Primary Auditory Cortex 191
Sound Localization 191
Effects of Auditory Cortex Damage 192

8.4 Somatosensation: Touch and Pain 193
Cutaneous Receptors 193
Dermatomes 194
The Two Major Ascending Somatosensory Pathways 194

Cortical Areas of Somatosensation   195

Effects of Damage to the Primary Somatosensory Cortex   196

Somatosensory Agnosias   197

The Paradoxes of Pain   198

Phantom Limbs   200

8.5   The Chemical Senses: Smell and Taste   201

Olfactory System   201

Gustatory System   203

Brain Damage and the Chemical Senses   204

8.6   Selective Attention   205

Conclusion   206

Food for Thought   206

Key Terms   207

Additional Reading   207

CHAPTER 9

The Sensorimotor System   208

9.1   Three Principles of Sensorimotor Function   209

The Sensorimotor System Is Hierarchically Organized   209

Motor Output Is Guided by Sensory Input   210

Learning Changes the Nature and Locus of Sensorimotor Control   210

A General Model of Sensorimotor System Function   211

9.2   Sensorimotor Association Cortex   211

Posterior Parietal Association Cortex   211

Dorsolateral Prefrontal Association Cortex   212

9.3   Secondary Motor Cortex   214

Supplementary Motor Area   215

Premotor Cortex   215

9.4   Primary Motor Cortex   216

9.5   Cortical Blood Flow Studies: A Recap of the Sensorimotor Areas of the Human Cerebral Cortex   217

9.6   Cerebellum and Basal Ganglia   219

Cerebellum   219

Basal Ganglia   219

9.7   Descending Motor Pathways

Dorsolateral Corticospinal Tract and Dorsolateral Corticorubrospinal Tract   221

Ventromedial Corticospinal Tract and Ventromedial Cortico-Brainstem-Spinal Tract   221

The Two Dorsolateral Motor Pathways and the Two Ventromedial Motor Pathways Compared   222

9.8   Sensorimotor Spinal Circuits   224

Muscles   224

Receptor Organs of Tendons and Muscles   225

Stretch Reflex   226

Withdrawal Reflex   228

Reciprocal Innervation   229

Recurrent Collateral Inhibition   230

Walking: A Complex Sensorimotor Reflex   230

9.9   Central Sensorimotor Programs   231

Conclusion   232

Food for Thought   233

Key Terms   233

Additional Reading   233

CHAPTER 10

The Biopsychology of Eating and Drinking   234

PART 1

Hunger, Eating, and Body Weight Regulation   235

10.1   Digestion and Energy Flow   235

10.2   Theories of Hunger and Eating: Set Points versus Positive Incentives   239

Nature of Set-Point Theories   239

Glucostatic and Lipostatic Set-Point Theories of Hunger and Eating   239

Problems with Set-Point Theories of Hunger and Eating   240

Positive-Incentive Theory   240

10.3 Factors That Determine What, When, and How Much We Eat 241

Factors That Determine What We Eat 241

Factors That Influence When We Eat 242

Factors That Influence How Much We Eat 242

10.4 Neural Mechanisms of Hunger and Satiety 244

Role of Blood Glucose Levels in Hunger and Satiety 244

Role of Hypothalamic Mechanisms in Hunger and Satiety 245

Role of the Gastrointestinal Tract in Satiety 248

Gut Satiety Peptides 248

10.5 Body Weight Regulation: Set Points versus Settling Points 250

Regulation of Body Fat by Changes in the Efficiency of Energy Utilization 250

Set Points and Settling Points in Weight Control 251

PART 2

Thirst, Drinking, and Body Fluid Regulation 254

10.6 Regulation of the Body's Fluid Resources 254

Intracellular and Extracellular Fluid Compartments 254

The Kidneys: Regulation of Water and Sodium Levels 254

10.7 Deprivation-Induced Drinking: Cellular Dehydration and Hypovolemia 255

Cellular Dehydration and Thirst 255

Hypovolemia and Thirst 257

Effects of Antidiuretic Hormone 258

Angiotensin II and Drinking 258

Drinking Produced by Naturally Occurring Water Deficits 260

10.8 Spontaneous Drinking: Drinking in the Absence of Water Deficits 261

Flavor 261

Food 261

Learning 261

10.9 Drinking and Satiety 261

Drinking and Sensory-Specific Satiety 262

PART 3

Disorders of Consumption 263

10.10 Obesity 265

10.11 Anorexia Nervosa 265

Conclusion 266
Food for Thought 266
Key Terms 267
Additional Reading 267

CHAPTER *11*

Hormones and Sex 268

The Men-Are-Men and Women-Are-Women Attitude 269

11.1 The Neuroendocrine System 269

Glands 269

Hormones 269

Gonads 270

Sex Steroids 270

Hormones of the Pituitary 271

Female Gonadal Hormone Levels Are Cyclic, Male Gonadal Hormone Levels Are Steady 272

Neural Control of the Pituitary 272

Control of the Anterior and Posterior Pituitary by the Hypothalamus 273

Discovery of Hypothalamic Releasing Hormones 273

Feedback in the Neuroendocrine System 274

Pulsatile Hormone Release 275

A Summary Model of Gonadal Endocrine Regulation 275

11.2 Hormones and Sexual Development 275

Fetal Hormones and the Development of Reproductive Organs 275

Development of Sex Differences in the Brain 278

Perinatal Hormones and Behavioral
Development   279

Puberty: Hormones and the Development of
Secondary Sex Characteristics   280

Three Cases of Exceptional Human Sexual
Development   282

11.3   Effects of Gonadal Hormones on
Adults   285

Male Reproduction-Related Behavior and
Testosterone   285

Female-Reproduction-Related Behavior and
Gonadal Hormones   286

Anabolic Steroid Abuse   287

11.4   The Hypothalamus and Sexual
Behavior   288

Structural Differences between the
Male Hypothalamus and the Female
Hypothalamus   288

The Hypothalamus and Male Sexual
Behavior   288

The Hypothalamus and Female Sexual
Behavior   290

11.5   Sexual Orientation, Hormones, and
the Brain   291

Sexual Orientation, Genes, and
Hormones   291

Is There a Difference in the Brains of
Homosexuals and Heterosexuals?   292

Conclusion   293
Food for Thought   293
Key Terms   293
Additional Reading   294

CHAPTER *12*

Sleep, Dreaming, and Circadian
Rhythms   295

12.1   The Physiological and Behavioral
Correlates of Sleep   296

The Three Standard Psychophysiological
Measures of Sleep   296

Four Stages of Sleep EEG   297

12.2   REM Sleep and Dreaming   299

Testing Common Beliefs about Dreaming   299

The Interpretation of Dreams   300

Lucid Dreams   300

12.3   Why Do We Sleep?   301

Recuperation and Circadian Theories   301

12.4   Circadian Sleep Cycles   302

Free-Running Circadian Sleep-Wake
Cycles   302

Jet Lag and Shift Work   303

12.5   Effects of Sleep Deprivation   304

Sleep-Deprivation Studies in Humans   304

Sleep-Deprivation Studies in Laboratory
Animals   306

REM-Sleep Deprivation   307

12.6   Recuperation and Circadian Theories of
Sleep Combined   308

12.7   Neural Mechanisms of Sleep   310

Reticular Activating System Theory of
Sleep   310

Three Important Discoveries about the Neural
Basis of Sleep   310

Brain Areas That Have Been Implicated in
Sleep and Dreaming   312

12.8   The Circadian Clock: Neural
Mechanisms   314

Location of the Circadian Clock in the
Suprachiasmatic Nuclei   314

Genetics of Circadian Rhythms   315

Mechanisms of Entrainment   316

12.9   Hypnotic and Antihypnotic Drugs   317

Hypnotic Drugs   317

Antihypnotic Drugs   317

Endogenous Sleep Factors   317

12.10   Sleep Disorders   318

Insomnia   318

Hypersomnia   319

REM-Sleep-Related Disorders   319

12.11   The Effects of Sleep Reduction   320

Conclusion   321
Food for Thought   322
Key Terms   322
Additional Reading   322

CHAPTER 13

Drug Addiction and Reward Circuits in the Brain   323

13.1   Basic Principles of Drug Action   324
Drug Administration and Absorption   324
Penetration of the Central Nervous System by Drugs   325
Mechanisms of Drug Action   325
Drug Metabolism and Elimination   325
Drug Tolerance   325
Drug Withdrawal Effects and Physical Dependence   326
Addiction: What Is It?   327

13.2   Role of Learning in Drug Tolerance and Drug Withdrawal Effects   327
Contingent Drug Tolerance   327
Conditioned Drug Tolerance   328
Conditioned Withdrawal Effects   330

13.3   Five Commonly Abused Drugs   331
Tobacco   331
Alcohol   332
Marijuana   333
Cocaine   335
The Opiates: Heroin and Morphine   336
Comparison of the Hazards of Tobacco, Alcohol, Marijuana, Cocaine, and Heroin   338
The Drug Dilemmas: Striking the Right Balance   338

13.4   Biopsychological Theories of Addiction   340
Physical-Dependence Theories of Addiction   340
Positive-Incentive Theories of Addiction   340

13.5   Reward Circuits in the Brain   341
Intracranial Self-Stimulation: Fundamental Characteristics   341
The Mesotelencephalic Dopamine System and Intracranial Self-Stimulation   343
The Mesotelencephalic Dopamine System and Natural Motivated Behaviors   345

13.6   Neural Mechanisms of Addiction   346
Evidence of the Involvement of the Mesotelencephalic Dopamine System in Drug Addiction   346

Conclusion   347
Food for Thought   348
Key Terms   349
Additional Reading   349

CHAPTER 14

Memory and Amnesia   350

14.1   Amnesic Effects of Bilateral Medial Temporal Lobectomy: The Case of H.M.   351
Early Theories of Memory Storage   351
Bilateral Medial Temporal Lobectomy   352
H.M.'s Postsurgery Memory Deficits   353
Formal Assessment of H.M.'s Anterograde Amnesia   354
Scientific Contributions of H.M.'s Case   356
The Case of R.B.: Hippocampal Damage and Medial Temporal Lobe Amnesia   358

14.2   Amnesia of Korsakoff's Syndrome   359
Medial Diencephalic Damage and Korsakoff Amnesia   359
The Cases of N.A. and B.J.   360

14.3   Memory Deficits Associated with Prefrontal Cortex Damage   360

14.4   Amnesia of Alzheimer's Disease   361

14.5   Amnesia after Concussion   362
Electroconvulsive Shock and Gradients of Retrograde Amnesia   362

14.6   Neuroanatomy of Object-Recognition Memory   366
Monkey Model of Object-Recognition Amnesia: The Nonrecurring-Items Delayed Nonmatching-to-Sample Test   366
Early Monkey Studies of Medial Temporal Lobe Damage and Object-Recognition Amnesia   367

Rat Model of Object-Recognition Amnesia: The Nonrecurring-Items Delayed Nonmatching-to-Sample Test   368

Neuroanatomical Basis of the Object-Recognition Deficits Resulting from Medial Temporal Lobectomy   369

Ischemia-Produced Brain Damage and Object-Recognition Deficits   369

14.7   Hippocampus and Memory for Space   372

14.8   Memory Structures of the Brain   374

Rhinal Cortex   374

Hippocampus   374

Amygdala   374

Inferotemporal Cortex   374

Cerebellum   375

Prefrontal Cortex   375

Mediodorsal Nucleus   376

Basal Forebrain   376

Conclusion   376

Food for Thought   376

Key Terms   377

Additional Reading   377

CHAPTER *15*

Neuroplasticity: Development, Learning, and Recovery from Brain Damage   378

15.1   Phases of Neural Development   379

Induction of the Neural Plate   379

Neural Proliferation   380

Migration and Aggregation   380

Axon Growth and Synapse Formation   381

Neuron Death and Synapse Rearrangement   384

15.2   Effects of Experience on Neural Development   387

15.3   Neural Bases of Learning and Memory in Simple Systems   388

Learning in the Aplysia Gill-Withdrawal Reflex Circuit   388

Long-Term Potentiation in Mammalian Hippocampus   393

15.4   Neural Degeneration, Regeneration, and Reorganization   398

Neural Degeneration   398

Neural Regeneration   398

Neural Reorganization   400

15.5   Neurotransplantation in the Brain   403

Modern Era of Research on Neurotransplantation   404

Promotion of Regeneration with Brain Transplants   406

Transplantation of Brain Replacement Parts   406

Conclusion   408

Food for Thought   408

Key Terms   409

Additional Reading   409

CHAPTER *16*

Lateralization, Language, and the Split Brain   410

16.1   Lateralization of Function: Methods and Basic Findings   412

Aphasia, Apraxia, and Left-Hemisphere Damage   412

Tests of Language Lateralization   412

Speech Laterality and Handedness   414

Sex Differences in Brain Lateralization   414

16.2   The Split Brain   415

Groundbreaking Experiment of Myers and Sperry   415

Commissurotomy in Human Epileptics   417

Evidence That the Hemispheres of Split-Brain Patients Function Independently   418

Cross-Cuing   419

Learning Two Things at Once   419

The Z Lens   420

16.3 Differences between the Left and Right Hemispheres 421

Demise of the Theory of Left-Hemisphere Dominance 421

Statistical versus All-or-None Hemispheric Differences 422

Neuroanatomical Asymmetries 423

Theories of Cerebral Asymmetry 423

16.4 Cortical Localization of Language 425

Historic Antecedents of the Wernicke-Geschwind Model 425

Wernicke-Geschwind Model 426

Evaluation of the Wernicke-Geschwind Model 428

Effects of Brain Damage on Language-Related Abilities 428

Cortical Stimulation and Localization of Language 430

Parallel Processing of Language: Evidence from Dyslexia 432

PET Scans during Language-Related Activities 433

Conclusion 436
Food for Thought 436
Key Terms 436
Additional Reading 436

CHAPTER *17*

Biopsychology of Emotion, Stress, and Mental Illness 437

17.1 Biopsychology of Emotion 438

Early Progress in the Biopsychological Study of Emotion 438

Emotions and the Autonomic Nervous System 441

Emotions and Facial Expression 442

Effects of Cortical Damage on Human Emotion 444

17.2 Fear, Defense, and Aggression 445

Types of Aggressive and Defensive Behaviors 445

Aggression and Testosterone 447

Neural Mechanisms of Conditioned Fear 448

Human Aggression, the Amygdala, and Psychosurgery 449

17.3 Stress and Health 449

The Stress Response 450

Stress and Gastric Ulcers 450

Psychoneuroimmunology: Stress and Infections 451

17.4 Schizophrenia 455

Causal Factors in Schizophrenia 455

Discovery of the First Antischizophrenic Drugs 456

Dopamine Theory of Schizophrenia 456

Current Research on the Neural Basis of Schizophrenia 458

17.5 Affective Disorders: Depression and Mania 459

Causal Factors in Affective Disorders 460

Discovery of Antidepressant Drugs 460

Neural Mechanisms of Depression 461

17.6 Anxiety Disorders 463

Pharmacological Treatment of Anxiety Disorders 463

Animal Models of Anxiety 464

Neural Bases of Anxiety Disorders 464

Conclusion 464
Food for Thought 465
Key Terms 465
Additional Reading 465

Epilogue 467
Appendices 469
References 479
Indexes 535

Preface

The third edition of *Biopsychology* is a clear, engaging introduction to current biopsychological theory and research. It is intended for use as a primary text in one- or two-semester courses in biopsychology—variously entitled *Biopsychology, Physiological Psychology, Brain and Behavior, Psychobiology, Behavioral Neuroscience,* or *Behavioral Neurobiology.*

The defining feature of *Biopsychology* is its unique combination of cutting-edge biopsychological science and personal, reader-oriented discourse. It is a textbook that is remarkably "untextbooklike." Rather than introducing biopsychology in the usual textbook fashion, it weaves the fundamentals of biopsychology together with clinical case studies, social issues, personal implications, and humorous anecdotes. It is like a friendly mentor who speaks directly to the reader and enthusiastically relates recent advances in biopsychological science.

The personality of *Biopsychology* is more than mere window dressing. Because its engaging pedagogical approach facilitates the acquisition and retention of information, *Biopsychology* delivers more cutting-edge biopsychology, more insight, and more enjoyment for less effort.

Writing this preface is the final step in my preparation of this edition. It marks the end of a year in which I have dedicated myself to further strengthening *Biopsychology*'s strong points, dealing with areas needing improvement, and keeping it abreast of important advances in the field. The following sections of this preface describe the major features of this edition.

Features That Have Carried Over From Previous Editions

The following are features of the first two editions of *Biopsychology* that have been maintained and strengthened in this edition.

An emphasis on behavior   In many biopsychological textbooks, the coverage of neurophysiology, neurochemistry, and neuroanatomy subverts the coverage of behavioral research. In contrast, *Biopsychology* gives top billing to

behavior: It stresses that neuroscience is a team effort and that the unique contribution made by biopsychologists to this team effort is their behavioral expertise.

A broad definition of biopsychology   Biopsychology is the study of the biology of behavior. Accordingly, *Biopsychology* covers more than the neural mechanisms of behavior; it also deals with the evolution, genetics, and adaptiveness of behavioral processes.

Extensive coverage of clinical and human research   *Biopsychology* provides more than the customary coverage of clinical case studies and research on human subjects. One of *Biopsychology*'s dominant themes is that diversity is an important feature of biopsychological research: that major advances in biopsychological science often result from the convergence of pure and applied research and from the convergence of research involving human and nonhuman subjects.

A focus on the scientific method   *Biopsychology* emphasizes important, but frequently misunderstood, points about the scientific method. The following are three of them: (1) The scientific method is a means of answering questions that is as applicable to daily life as it is to the laboratory. (2) The scientific method is fun—it is basically the same method that is used by detectives to solve crimes. (3) Widely accepted scientific theories are current best estimates, not statements of absolute fact.

An integrative approach   Some biopsychology texts have taken the modular approach, dispensing biopsychology as a series of brief independent subject modules. In contrast, *Biopsychology*'s approach is integrative. It creates a strong fabric of research findings and ideas by weaving together related subject areas and research findings into chapters of intermediate length.

An emphasis on personal and social relevance   Several chapters of *Biopsychology*—particularly those on eating, sleeping, sex, and drug addiction—carry strong personal and social messages. In these chapters, students are encouraged to consider the relevance of biopsychological research to their lives outside the classroom.

Wit and enthusiasm   An important element of biopsychology is missing from most biopsychology texts. In my experience, biopsychology laboratories are places of enthusiasm, dedication, and good humor. *Biopsychology* communicates these important aspects of "biopsychological life".

Features New to This Edition

The following are features of this edition of *Biopsychology* that were not in the first two editions.

New references   Biopsychology is one of the most rapidly progressing fields of science. This edition of *Biopsychology* has kept abreast of recent developments; it contains approximately 500 references to articles that have been published since the last edition.

New figures and illustrations   The art and design of *Biopsychology* have been thoroughly revised and upgraded. The improved art and design have greatly increased *Biopsychology*'s overall attractiveness and emotional impact, but the improvements have not been merely cosmetic. The artwork in this edition of *Biopsychology* is without pedagogical peer: Each illustration has been meticulously conceptualized and designed to clarify and reinforce the writing without introducing extraneous information or nagging inconsistencies.

Chapter reorganization   With the exception of Chapter 1, all chapters have been subjected to substantial revision. Most notable in this respect are Chapter 10 (Biopsychology of Eating and Drinking) and Chapter 17 (Biopsychology of Emotion, Stress, and Mental Illness). Both chapters have new central themes that increase their clarity, cohesiveness, and impact. Chapter 10 is organized around common misconceptions about hunger, eating, and weight regulation and how these misconceptions have been debunked by modern biopsychological research. Chapter 17 is organized around the role of stress and anxiety in the etiology of psychiatric disorders.

New topics   The following are some of the topics that are either new to this edition of *Biopsychology* or have received improved coverage:

- human genome project
- mechanisms of gene expression
- structure of the neocortex
- anatomy of neural cell membranes
- ion channels
- receptor subtypes

- second messengers
- functional MRI
- cognitive neuroscience
- role of excitatory amino acids in brain damage
- Alzheimer's disease
- retinex theory of vision
- magnocellular and parvocellular divisions of the visual system
- parallel processing in the brain
- weight regulation
- eating disorders
- sexual orientation and the hypothalamus
- interpretation of dreams
- sleep disorders
- genetics of circadian cycles
- rhinal cortex and object-recognition memory
- hippocampus and memory for spatial location
- neuroplasticity and second messengers
- neurotransplantation as a treatment for Parkinson's disease
- dyslexia and brain damage
- testosterone and human aggression
- conditioned fear and the amygdala
- psychoneuroimmunology
- serotonin-reuptake inhibitors and depression

Marginal definitions   New to this edition are marginal definitions. The first time that a particular key term appears in a chapter it appears both in bold print in the text, and with its definition located on the same spread on a blue background. The marginal definitions are designed to improve comprehension and to serve as vehicles for review.

Learning Aids

Biopsychology has four features that are expressly designed to help students learn and remember the material:

- boldfaced **key terms** and their **marginal definitions**—additional key terms of less importance appear in italics;
- **study exercises** that occur in the chapters at key transition points, where students can benefit most

from pausing to consolidate preceding material before continuing;

- **food-for-thought discussion questions** at the end of each chapter;

- **appendices,** which serve as convenient sources of important information that is too detailed for many beginning students of biopsychology (*e.g.,* the anatomy of the cranial nerves).

Ancillary Materials Available With Biopsychology

The test bank and instructor's manual for this edition of *Biopsychology* were skillfully prepared by Marie Fox of the Metropolitan State College of Denver.

Test bank   The test bank for this edition of *Biopsychology* comprises more than 2,000 multiple-choice questions. The difficulty of each item is rated—easy, moderate, or difficult—to assist instructors with their test construction.

Instructor's manual   The instructor's manual for *Biopsychology* includes a set of lecture notes and a set of overhead transparency masters. Notes for two one-hour lectures complement each chapter of the text, and there are two or three overhead masters for each lecture. The lecture notes are printed on the left side of each page, and the right side is left blank for each instructor to add customizing notes. The instructor's manual is available on disk.

Study guide   Each chapter of the study guide prepared by Michael Mana of Chatham College includes three sections. Section I is composed of "jeopardy" study items—named after the popular television quiz show. The jeopardy study items are arranged in two columns: questions on the left and answers on the right. Sometimes there is nothing in the space to the right of a question, and the student's task is to write the correct answer. Sometimes there is nothing in the space to the left of an answer, and the student's task is to write in the correct question. Once the jeopardy study items are completed, the student has a list of questions and answers that summarize the main points of the chapter, conveniently arranged for bidirectional studying.

Section II of each chapter is composed of essay study questions. Spaces are provided for the student to write outlines of the correct answers to each question. The essay study questions encourage students to consider general issues.

Section III of each chapter is a practice examination. Students are advised to use their results on the practice examination to guide the final stages of their preparation for in-class examinations.

Biopsychology video   Instructors who adopt *Biopsychology* can obtain a 60-minute biopsychology video on videotape or laserdisc. Based on the *Films for the Humanities* series, this video provides students with glimpses of important biopsychological phenomena such as sleep recording, growing axons, memory testing in monkeys, the formation of synapses, gender differences in brain structure, human amnesic patients, rewarding brain stimulation, and brain scans.

Additional ancillary materials are also available to intructors. Please consult with your local Allyn and Bacon representative for details.

Acknowledgments

I wrote *Biopsychology,* but Maggie Edwards made important contributions to all other aspects of the manuscript preparation. Her role in the preparation of the art warrants special acknowledgment. Users of this book will come to recognize that its illustrations are special: The illustrations are so finely attuned to the writing that it appears as if the author must be a talented designer who designed them himself—but I'm not, and I didn't. The illustrations were all designed by Maggie after extensive discussion, debate, and, in some cases, argument with me. You see, Maggie is a professional artist with an extensive background in psychology who also happens to be my partner in life. Maggie took a year from her own successful career to help me achieve a level of illustration that is normally out of reach of writers who are not lucky enough to share their lives with such a talented and dedicated person. I thank her on behalf of the many students who will benefit from her contribution.

Allyn and Bacon did a remarkable job of producing this book. They shared my dream of a textbook that meets the highest standards of pedagogy but is still personal, attractive, and enjoyable. Thank you to Bill Barke, Sean Wakely, and the other executives at Allyn and Bacon for having faith in *Biopsychology* and providing the financial and personal support necessary for it to stay at the forefront of its field. Thank you also to the people who made it all happen: to Jo-Anne Naples, Jennifer Normandin, Deborah Schneck, Kathy Smith, and Linda Knowles. A special thank you goes to Elaine Ober for coordinating the entire production effort—an excruciatingly difficult and often thankless job.

I thank the following biopsychology instructors for providing Allyn and Bacon with reviews of *Biopsychology.* Their comments led to significant improvements in this edition.

Marie Banich, University of Illinois
Robert Blanchard, University of Hawaii at Manoa
Peter C. Brunjes, University of Virginia
Leo Chalupa, University of California at Davis
Carl Erickson, Duke University

Stanley Finger, Washington University
Mary Gotch, Solano Community College
Kenneth Guttman, Citrus College
Jon Kaas, Vanderbilt University
Richard King, University of North Carolina at Chapel Hill
Kenneth Kleinman, Southern Illinois University
Charles Kuttcher, Syracuse University
Frederick Maxwell, Southern Missouri State University
Lin Myers, California State University at Stanislaus
James Pierce, Purdue University at Calumet
Martin Sarter, The Ohio State University
Charles Weaver, Baylor University

One person who made an important contribution to *Biopsychology* is not a biopsychologist at all. He is Tom Jenkyns of the Department of Mathematics, Brock University. Tom read the second edition of *Biopsychology* out of interest because it was written by a high school friend whom he had not seen many years. To be helpful, Tom provided me with page upon page of thoughtful comments and criticisms, many of which are reflected in this edition. Thank you Tom; I am pleased to still be counted among your friends.

Finally, I would like to thank the many students who have sent me letters of friendship and encouragement.

To the Student

In the 1960s, I was, in the parlance of the times, "turned on" by an undergraduate course in biopsychology. I could not imagine anything more interesting than a field of science dedicated to studying the relation between psychological processes and the brain. My initial fascination led to a long career as a student, researcher, and teacher of biopsychological science. *Biopsychology* is my attempt to share this fascination with you.

I have tried to make *Biopsychology* a different kind of textbook, a textbook that includes clear, concise, and well-organized explanations of the key points but is still interesting to read—a book from which you might suggest a suitable chapter to an interested friend or relative. To accomplish this goal, I thought about what kind of textbook I would have liked when I was a student, and I decided immediately to avoid the stern formality and ponderous style of conventional textbook writing.

I wanted *Biopsychology* to have a relaxed and personal style. In order to accomplish this, I imagined that you and I were chatting as I wrote, and that I was telling you—usually over a glass of something—about the interesting things that go on in the field of biopsychology. Imagining these chats kept my writing from drifting back into conventional "textbookese," and it never let me forget that I was writing this book for you, the student.

I hope that *Biopsychology* teaches you much, and that reading it generates in you the same personal feeling that writing it did in me. If you are so inclined, I welcome your comments and suggestions. You can contact me at the Department of Psychology, University of British Columbia, Vancouver, B.C., Canada, V6T 1Z4 (jpinel@cortex.psych.ubc.ca).

Biopsychology

CHAPTER 1

Biopsychology as a Neuroscience

1.1 What Is Biopsychology?

1.2 What Is the Relation between Biopsychology and the Other Disciplines of Neuroscience?

1.3 What Types of Research Characterize the Biopsychological Approach?

1.4 What Are the Divisions of Biopsychology?

1.5 Converging Operations: How Do Biopsychologists Work Together?

1.6 Scientific Inference: How Do Biopsychologists Study the Unobservable?

1.7 What Is Bad Science, and How Do You Spot It?

The appearance of the human brain is far from impressive (see Figure 1.1). The human brain is a squishy, wrinkled, walnut-shaped hunk of tissue weighing about 1.3 kilograms. It looks more like something that you might find washed up on a beach than like one of the wonders of the world—which it surely is. Despite its disagreeable external appearance, the human brain is an amazingly intricate network of **neurons** (cells that receive and transmit electrochemical signals). Contemplate for a moment the complexity of your own brain's neural circuits. Consider the 100 billion neurons in complex array, the estimated 100 trillion connections among them, and the almost infinite number of paths that neural signals can follow through this morass.

The complexity of the human brain is hardly surprising, considering what it can do. An organ capable of creating a Mona Lisa, an artificial limb, and a supersonic aircraft; of traveling to the moon and to the depths of the sea; and of experiencing the wonders of an alpine sunset, a newborn infant, and a reverse slam dunk must be complex. Paradoxically, **neuroscience** (the scientific study of the nervous system) may prove to be the brain's ultimate challenge: Does the brain have the capacity to understand something as complex as itself?

Neuroscience comprises several related disciplines. The primary purpose of this chapter is to introduce you to one of them: biopsychology. Each of this chapter's seven sections characterizes biopsychology from a different perspective.

Before you proceed to the body of this chapter, I would like to introduce you to the case of Jimmie G. Biopsychologists have learned much about the brain from the study of human victims of brain damage—and you will too. But it is important that you do not grow insensitive to their personal tragedy. Jimmie G. introduces you to it.

[In 1975] Jimmie was a fine-looking man, with a curly bush of grey hair, a healthy and handsome forty-nine-year-old. He was cheerful, friendly, and warm.

"Hiya, Doc!" he said. "Nice morning! Do I take this chair here?" ... He spoke of the houses where his family had lived.... He spoke of school and school days, the friends he'd had, and his special fondness for mathematics and science ... he was seventeen, had just graduated from high school when he was drafted in 1943.... He remembered the names of the various submarines on which he had served, their missions, where they were stationed, the

Figure 1.1 The human brain, which looks more like something that you might find washed up on a beach than like one of the wonders of the world.

names of his shipmates.... But there for some reason his reminiscences stopped....

...I was very struck by the change of tense in his recollections as he passed from his school days to his days in the navy. He had been using the past tense, but now used the present ...

A sudden, improbable suspicion seized me.

"What year is this, Mr. G.?" I asked, concealing my perplexity under a casual manner.

"Forty-five, man. What do you mean?" He went on, "We've won the war, FDR's dead, Truman's at the helm. There are great times ahead."

"And you, Jimmie, how old would you be?" ...

"Why, I guess I'm nineteen, Doc. I'll be twenty next birthday."

Looking at the grey-haired man before me, I had an impulse for which I have never forgiven myself ...

"Here," I said, and thrust a mirror toward him. "Look in the mirror and tell me what you see." ...

He suddenly turned ashen and gripped the sides of the chair. "Jesus Christ," he whispered. "Christ, what's going on? What's happened to me? Is this a nightmare? Am I crazy? Is this a joke?"—and he became frantic, panicked....

...I stole away, taking the hateful mirror with me.

Two minutes later I re-entered the room.... "Hiya, Doc!" he said. "Nice morning! You want to talk to me—do I take this chair here?" There was no sign of recognition on his frank, open face.

"Haven't we met before, Mr. G.?" I asked casually.

"No, I can't say we have. Quite a beard you got there. I wouldn't forget you, Doc!"...

..."Where do you think you are?"

"I see these beds, and these patients everywhere. Looks like a sort of hospital to me. But hell, what would I be doing in a hospital—and with all these old people, years older than me.... Maybe I *work* here.... If I don't work here, I've been *put* here. Am I a patient, am I sick and don't know it, Doc? It's crazy, it's scary."...

On intelligence testing he showed excellent ability. He was quick-witted, observant, and logical, and had no difficulty solving complex problems and puzzles—no difficulty, that is, if they could be done quickly. If much time was required, he forgot what he was doing....

Homing in on his memory, I found an extreme and extraordinary loss of recent memory—so that whatever was said or shown to him was apt to be forgotten in a few seconds' time. Thus I laid out my watch, my tie, and my glasses on the desk, covered them, and asked him to remember these. Then, after a minute's chat, I asked him what I had put under the cover. He remembered none of them—or indeed that I had even asked him to remember. I repeated the test, this time getting him to write down the names of the three objects; again he forgot, and when I showed him the paper with his writing on it he was astounded ...

"What is this?" I asked, showing him a photo in the magazine I was holding.

"It's the moon," he replied.

"No, it's not," I answered. "It's a picture of the earth taken from the moon."

"Doc, you're kidding! Someone would've had to get a camera up there! ... how the hell would you do that?"...

He was becoming fatigued, and somewhat irritable and anxious, under the continuing pressure of anomaly and contradiction, and their fearful implications... And I myself was wrung with emotion—it was heartbreaking ... to think of his life lost in limbo, dissolving.

He is, as it were ... isolated in a single moment of being, with a moat ... of forgetting all round him... He is a man without a past (or future), stuck in a constantly changing, meaningless moment. (pp. 22–28)[1]

Remember Jimmie G.; you will encounter him later in this chapter.

1.1 What Is Biopsychology?

Biopsychology is the scientific study of the biology of behavior—see Dewsbury (1991). Some refer to this field as *psychobiology* or *behavioral biology* or *behavioral neuroscience,* but I prefer the term *biopsychology* because it denotes a biological approach to the study of psychology rather than a psychological approach to the study of biology: Psychology commands center stage in this text. *Psychology* is the scientific study of behavior—the scientific study of all overt activities of the organism as well as all the internal processes that are presumed to underlie them (e.g.,

learning, memory, motivation, perception, and emotion).

The study of the biology of behavior has a long history, but biopsychology did not coalesce into a major neuroscientific discipline until this century. Although it is not possible to specify the exact date of biopsychology's birth, the publication of the *Organization of Behavior* in 1949 by D. O. Hebb played a key role in its emergence (see Milner, 1993; Milner & White, 1987). In his book, Hebb (see Figure 1.2) developed the first comprehensive theory of how complex psychological phenomena, such as perceptions, emotions, thoughts, and memories, might be produced by brain activity. Hebb's theory did much to discredit the view that psychological functioning is too complex to have its roots in the physiology and chemistry of the brain. Hebb based his theory on experiments involving both humans and laboratory animals, on clinical case studies, and on logical arguments developed from his own insightful observations of daily life. This eclectic approach has become a hallmark of biopsychological inquiry.

In comparison to physics, chemistry, and biology, biopsychology is an infant—a raucous, healthy, rapidly growing infant, but nonetheless an infant. In this book, you will reap the benefits of biopsychology's youth. Because biopsychology does not have a long and complex history, you will be able to move directly to the excitement of current research.

Figure 1.2 D. O. Hebb. (Photograph courtesy of McGill University.)

[1] From *The Man Who Mistook His Wife for a Hat and Other Clinical Tales* (pp. 22–28) by Oliver Sacks. Copyright © 1970, 1981, 1983, 1984, 1985 by Oliver Sacks. Reprinted by permission of Summit Books, a division of Simon & Schuster, Inc.

Neurons. Cells of the nervous system that are specialized for receiving and transmitting electrochemical signals.

Neuroscience. The scientific study of the nervous system.

Biopsychology. The scientific study of the biology of behavior.

Neuroscience is a team effort, and biopsychologists are important members of the team. This section further defines biopsychology by discussing its relation to other neuroscientific disciplines.

Biopsychologists are neuroscientists who bring to their research a knowledge of behavior and of the methods of behavioral research. It is their behavioral orientation and expertise that is their unique contribution to neuroscience. You will be able to better appreciate the importance of this contribution if you consider that the ultimate purpose of the nervous system is to produce and control behavior.

Biopsychology is an integrative discipline. Biopsychologists draw together knowledge from the other neuroscientific disciplines and apply it to the study of behavior. The following are a few of the disciplines of neuroscience that are particularly relevant to biopsychology:

Neuroanatomy. The study of the structure of the nervous system (see Chapter 3).

Neurochemistry. The study of the chemical bases of neural activity (see Chapter 4).

Neuroendocrinology. The study of interactions between the nervous system and the endocrine system (see Chapters 11 and 17).

Neuropathology. The study of nervous system disorders (see Chapter 6).

Neuropharmacology. The study of the effects of drugs on neural activity (see Chapters 4, 13, and 17).

Neurophysiology. The study of the functions and activities of the nervous system (see Chapter 4).

Recently, I assessed biopsychology's contribution to neuroscience by recording the departmental affiliation of a random sample of neuroscientists selected from the membership directory of the **Society for Neuroscience**, a major international association of neuroscientists. The results are presented in Table 1.1. Clearly, the contribution of biopsychology to neuroscience is substantial; about 16 percent of the members of the society listed psychology as their primary departmental affiliation. A published analysis of the graduate-student members of the Society of Neuroscience suggests that biopsychology's major contribution to neuroscience is likely to continue (Davis et al., 1988)—see Figure 1.3.

TABLE 1.1

Departmental Affiliations of Members of the Society for Neuroscience

Departmental Affiliation	Percentage of Sample
Psychology	16.1
Physiology	14.3
Pharmacology	12.5
Biology	11.2
Anatomy	11.2
Neurology	6.7
Psychiatry	5.8
Neuroscience/Neurobiology	5.3
Neurosurgery	3.1
Pathology	3.1
Veterinary Medicine	1.8
Others	8.9
	100.0

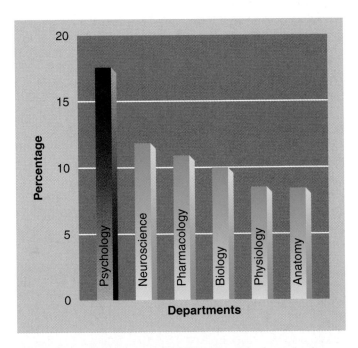

Figure 1.3 The departmental affiliation of graduate-student members of the Society for Neuroscience. Only academic departments contributing over 5% of the graduate-student members are listed. (Adapted from Davis et al., 1988.)

Another way to define biopsychology is to describe how biopsychologists do their research. To characterize the diversity of biological research, this section discusses three major dimensions along which biopsychological research varies. Biopsychological research can involve either human or nonhuman subjects; it can take the form of either formal experiments or nonexperimental studies; and it can be either pure or applied.

Human and Nonhuman Subjects

Both human and nonhuman animals are the subject of biopsychological research. Of the nonhumans, rats are the most common subjects; however, mice, cats, dogs, and nonhuman primates are also widely studied.

Humans have several advantages as experimental subjects: They can follow instructions, they can report their subjective experiences, and their cages are easier to clean. Of course, I am joking about the cages, but the joke does serve to draw attention to one advantage that humans have over other species of experimental subjects: Humans are often cheaper. Because only the highest standards of animal care are acceptable, the cost of maintaining an animal laboratory can be prohibitive for all but the most well-funded researchers.

Of course, the greatest advantage that humans have as subjects in a field aimed at understanding the intricacies of human brain function is that they have human brains. In fact, you might wonder why biopsychologists would bother studying nonhuman subjects at all. The answer lies in the evolutionary continuity of the brain. The brains of humans differ from the brains of other mammals primarily in their overall size and the extent of their cortical development. In other words, the differences between the brains of humans and those of related species are more quantitative than qualitative, and thus many of the principles of human brain function can be derived from the study of nonhumans (see Kolb & Whishaw, 1990).

Nonhuman animals have three advantages as subjects in biopsychological research. The first is that the brains and behavior of nonhuman subjects are more simple than those of human subjects. Hence, the study of nonhuman species is often more likely to reveal basic principles of brain-behavior interaction. The second is that insights frequently arise from a **comparative approach**, the study of biological processes by comparison of different species. For example, comparing the behavior of species that do not have a cerebral cortex with the behavior of species that do can provide valuable clues about cortical function. The third is that it is possible to conduct research on laboratory animals that, for ethical reasons, is not possible on human subjects. This is not to say that the study of nonhuman animals is not governed by a strict code of ethics—it is—but there are fewer ethical constraints on the study of laboratory species than on the study of humans.

In my experience, most biopsychologists display considerable concern for their subjects whether they are of their own species or not; however, ethical issues are not left to the discretion of the individual researcher. All biopsychological research, whether it involves human or nonhuman subjects, is regulated by independent committees according to strict ethical guidelines: "Researchers cannot escape the logic that if the animals we observe are reasonable models of our own most intricate actions, then they must be respected as we would respect our own sensibilities" (Ulrich, 1991, p. 197).

Experiments and Nonexperiments

Biopsychological research involves both experiments and nonexperimental studies. Nonexperimental studies include quasiexperimental studies and case studies.

Experiments The experiment is the method used by scientists to find out what causes what, and as such, it is almost single-handedly responsible for our modern way of life. It is paradoxical that a method capable of such complex feats is itself so simple. To conduct an experiment involving living subjects, the experimenter first designs two or more conditions under which the subjects will be tested.

Neuroanatomy. The study of the structure of the nervous system.

Neurochemistry. The study of the chemical bases of neural activity.

Neuroendocrinology. The study of the interactions between the nervous system and the endocrine system.

Neuropathology. The study of nervous system disorders.

Neuropharmacology. The study of the effects of drugs on neural activity.

Neurophysiology. The study of the functions and activities of the nervous system.

Society for Neuroscience. A major international association of neuroscientists.

Comparative approach. The study of biological processes by comparison of different species.

Usually, a different group of subjects is tested under each condition (**between-subjects design**), but sometimes it is possible to test the same group of subjects under each condition (**within-subjects design**). The experimenter assigns the subjects to conditions, administers the treatments, and measures the outcome in such a way that there is only one relevant difference between the conditions that are being compared. This difference between the conditions is called the **independent variable**. The variable that is measured by the experimenter to assess the effect of the independent variable is called the **dependent variable**.

Why is it critical that there be no differences between conditions other than the independent variable? The reason is that when there is more than one difference that could affect the dependent variable, it is difficult to determine whether it was the independent variable or the unintended difference—called a **confounded variable**—that led to the observed effects on the dependent variable. Although the experimental method is conceptually simple, eliminating all confounded variables can be quite difficult. Readers of research papers must be constantly on the alert for confounded variables that have gone unnoticed by the experimenters themselves.

An experiment by Lester and Gorzalka (1988) illustrates the experimental method in action. The experiment was a demonstration of the Coolidge effect. The **Coolidge effect** is the fact that a copulating male who becomes incapable of continuing to copulate with one sex partner can often recommence copulating with a new sex partner (see Figure 1.4). Before your imagination starts running wild, I should mention that the subjects in Lester and Gorzalka's experiment were hamsters, not students from the undergraduate subject pool.

Lester and Gorzalka argued that the Coolidge effect had not been demonstrated in females because it is more difficult to conduct well-controlled Coolidge-effect experiments in females—not because females do not display a Coolidge effect. The confusion, according to Lester and Gorzalka, stemmed from the fact that the males of most mammalian species become sexually fatigued more readily than do the females. As a result, attempts to demonstrate the Coolidge effect in females are often confounded by the fatigue of the males. When, in the midst of copulation, a female is provided with a new sex partner, the increase in her sexual receptivity could be either a legitimate Coolidge effect or a reaction to the greater vigor of the new male. Because female mammals usually display little sexual fatigue, this confounded variable is not a serious problem in demonstrations of the Coolidge effect in males.

Lester and Gorzalka devised a clever procedure to control for this confounded variable. At the same time that a female subject was copulating with one male (the familiar male), the other male to be used in the test (the unfamiliar male) was copulating with another female. Then, both males were given a rest while the female was copulating with a third male. Finally, the female subject was tested with either the familiar male or the unfamiliar male. The

dependent variable was the amount of time that the female displayed **lordosis** (the arched-back, rump-up, tail-diverted posture of female rodent sexual receptivity) during each sex test. As Figure 1.5 illustrates, the females responded more vigorously to the unfamiliar males than they did to the familiar males during the third test, despite the fact that both the unfamiliar and familiar males were equally fatigued and both mounted the females with equal vigor. This experiment illustrates the importance of good experi-

Figure 1.4 President Calvin Coolidge and Mrs. Grace Coolidge. Many students think that the Coolidge effect is named after a biopsychologist named Coolidge. It is named after President Calvin Coolidge of whom the following story is told. (If the story isn't true, it should be.) During a tour of a poultry farm, Mrs. Coolidge inquired of the farmer how his farm managed to produce so many eggs with such a small number of roosters. The farmer proudly explained that his roosters performed their duty dozens of times each day.

"Perhaps you could point that out to Mr. Coolidge," replied the first lady in a pointedly loud voice.

The President, overhearing the remark, asked the farmer, "Does each rooster service the same hen each time?"

"No," replied the farmer, "there are many hens for each rooster."

"Perhaps you could point that out to Mrs. Coolidge," replied the President.

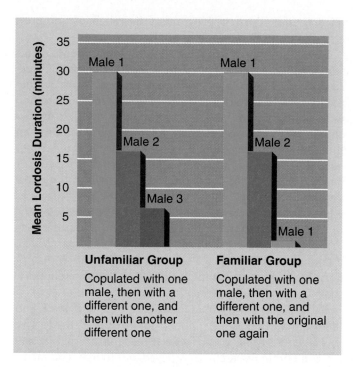

Figure 1.5 The experimental design and results of Lester and Gorzalka (1988). On the third test, the female hamsters were more sexually receptive to unfamiliar males than they were to the males with which they had copulated on the first test.

revealed extensive brain damage. Although this quasiexperimental study seems like an experiment, it is not. Because the subjects themselves decided which group they would be in—by drinking alcohol or not—the researchers had no means of ensuring that alcohol consumption was the only variable that distinguished the two groups. Can you think of differences other than alcohol consumption that could reasonably be expected to exist between a group of alcoholics and a group of abstainers—differences that could have contributed to the neuroanatomical or intellectual differences that were observed between them? There are several. For example, alcoholics as a group tend to be more poorly educated, more prone to accidental head injury, more likely to use other drugs, and more likely to have poor diets. Accordingly, quasiexperimental studies have revealed that alcoholics tend to have more brain damage than nonalcoholics, but they have not proved why.

Have you forgotten Jimmie G.? He was a product of long-term alcohol consumption.

Case studies Studies that focus on a single case or subject are called **case studies**. Because they focus on a single case, they often provide a more in-depth picture than that provided by an experiment or a quasiexperimental study, and they are an excellent source of testable hypotheses. On the

mental design as well as a theme of Chapter 11: that males and females are more similar than most people appreciate.

Quasiexperimental studies It is not possible for biopsychologists to bring the experimental method to bear on all problems of interest to them. There are frequently physical or ethical impediments that make it impossible to assign subjects to particular conditions or to administer the conditions once the subjects have been assigned to them. For example, experiments on the causes of brain damage in human alcoholics are not feasible because it would not be ethical to assign a subject to a condition that involves years of alcohol consumption. (Some of you may be more concerned about the ethics of assigning subjects to a control condition that involves years of sobriety.) In such prohibitive situations, biopsychologists conduct **quasiexperimental studies**—studies of groups of subjects who have been exposed to the conditions of interest in the real world. These studies have the appearance of experiments, but they are not true experiments because potential confounded variables have not been controlled—for example, by the random assignment of subjects to conditions.

In one quasiexperimental study, a team of researchers compared 100 detoxified male alcoholics from an alcoholism treatment unit with 50 male nondrinkers obtained from various sources (Acker et al., 1984). The alcoholics as a group performed more poorly on various tests of perceptual, motor, and cognitive ability; and their brain scans

Between-subjects design. An experimental design in which a different group of subjects is tested under each condition.

Within-subjects design. An experimental design in which the same subjects are tested under each condition.

Independent variable. The difference between experimental conditions that is arranged by the experimenter.

Dependent variable. The variable measured by the experimenter—the variable that is affected by the independent variable.

Confounded variable. An unintended difference between the conditions of an experiment that could have affected the independent variable.

Coolidge effect. The fact that a copulating male who becomes incapable of continuing to copulate with one sex partner can often recommence copulating with a new sex partner.

Lordosis. The arched-back, rump-up, tail-diverted posture of female rodent sexual receptivity.

Quasiexperimental studies. Studies that have the appearance of experiments but are not true experiments because potential confounded variables have not been controlled.

Case studies. Studies that focus on a single case or subject.

other hand, a major problem with case studies is their **generalizability**—the degree to which their results can be applied to other cases. Because humans differ from one another in both brain function and behavior, it is important to be skeptical of any biopsychological theory based entirely on a few case studies.

Pure and Applied Research

Biopsychological research can be either pure or applied. Pure and applied research differ in a number of respects, but they are distinguished less by their own attributes than by the motives of the individuals involved in their pursuit. **Pure research** is research motivated primarily by the curiosity of the researcher—it is done solely for the purpose of acquiring knowledge. In contrast, **applied research** is research intended to bring about some direct benefit to humankind.

Many scientists believe that pure research will ultimately prove to be of more practical benefit than applied research. Their view is that applications flow readily from an understanding of basic principles and that attempts to move directly to application without first gaining a basic understanding are shortsighted. Of course, it is not necessary for a research project to be completely pure or completely applied; many research programs have elements of both approaches.

One important difference between pure and applied research is that pure research is more vulnerable to the vagaries of political regulation because politicians and the voting public have difficulty understanding why research of no immediate practical benefit should be supported. If the decision were yours, would you be willing to grant hundreds of thousands of dollars to support the study of squid *motor neurons* (neurons that control muscles), learning in recently hatched geese, the activity of single nerve cells in the visual systems of monkeys, the *hypothalamic hormones* (hormones released by the hypothalamus) of pigs and sheep, or the function of the *corpus callosum* (the large neural pathway that connects the left and right halves of the brain)? Which, if any, of these projects would you consider worthy of support? Each of these seemingly esoteric projects was supported, and each earned a Nobel Prize for its author.

Table 1.2 lists the Nobel Prizes awarded for research on the brain and behavior. The purpose of this list is to give you a general sense of the official recognition that behavioral and brain research has received, not to have you memorize the list. You will learn later in the chapter that when it comes to evaluating science, the Nobel committee has been far from infallible.

1.4   What Are the Divisions of Biopsychology?

As you have just learned, biopsychologists conduct their research in a variety of fundamentally different ways. Biopsychologists who take the same approaches to their research tend to publish their research in the same journals, attend the same scientific meetings, and belong to the same professional societies. The particular approaches to biopsychology that have flourished and grown have gained wide recognition as separate divisions of biopsychological research. The purpose of this section of the chapter is to give you a clearer sense of biopsychology and its diversity by describing five of its major divisions: (1) physiological psychology, (2) psychopharmacology, (3) neuropsychology, (4) psychophysiology, and (5) comparative psychology. For simplicity, they are presented as distinct approaches; but there is much overlap among them, and many biopsychologists regularly follow more than one approach.

Physiological Psychology

Physiological psychology is the division of biopsychology that studies the neural mechanisms of behavior through the direct surgical, electrical, and chemical manipulation of the brain in controlled experiments. The subjects of physiological psychology research are almost always laboratory animals, because the focus on direct brain manipulation and controlled experiments precludes the use of human subjects in most instances. There is also a tradition of pure research

Generalizability. The degree to which the results of a study can be applied to other individuals or situations.

Pure research. Research motivated primarily by the curiosity of the researcher.

Applied research. Research that is intended to bring about some direct benefit to humankind.

Physiological psychology. The division of biopsychology that studies the neural mechanisms of behavior by directly manipulating the nervous systems of nonhuman animal subjects in controlled experiments.

Psychopharmacology. The division of biopsychology that studies the effects of drugs on the brain and behavior.

Neuropsychology. The division of biopsychology that studies the psychological effects of brain damage in human patients.

Cerebral cortex. The layer of neural tissue covering the cerebral hemispheres of humans and other mammals.

in physiological psychology; the emphasis is usually on research that contributes to the development of theories of the neural control of behavior rather than on research that is of immediate practical benefit.

Psychopharmacology

Psychopharmacology is similar to physiological psychology, except that it focuses on the manipulation of neural activity and behavior with drugs. In fact, many of the early psychopharmacologists were simply physiological psychologists who moved into drug research, and many of today's biopsychologists identify closely with both approaches. However, the study of the effects of drugs on the brain and behavior has become so specialized that psychopharmacology is widely regarded as a separate discipline.

A substantial portion of psychopharmacological research is applied research (see Brady, 1993). Although drugs are frequently used by psychopharmacologists to study the basic principles of brain-behavior interaction, the purpose of many psychopharmacological experiments is to develop therapeutic drugs (see Chapter 17) or to reduce drug abuse (see Chapter 13). Psychopharmacologists study the effects of drugs on laboratory species—and on humans, if the ethics of the situation permits it (see Meltzer, 1987).

Neuropsychology

Neuropsychology is the study of the psychological effects of brain damage in human patients. Obviously, human subjects cannot ethically be exposed to experimental treatments that endanger normal brain function. Consequently, neuropsychology deals almost exclusively with case studies and quasiexperimental studies of patients with brain damage resulting from disease, accident, or neurosurgery. The outer layer of the cerebral hemispheres—the **cerebral cortex**—is most likely to be damaged by accident or surgery; this is one reason why neu-

TABLE 1.2

Nobel Prizes Awarded for Studies of the Nervous System or Behavior

Nobel Winner	Date	Accomplishment
Ivan Pavlov	1902	Research on the physiology of digestion
Camillio Golgi and Ramón y Cajal	1906	Research on the structure of the nervous system
Charles Sherrington and Edgar Adrian	1932	Discoveries about the functions of neurons
Henry Dale and Otto Loewi	1936	Discoveries about the transmission of nerve impulses
Joseph Erlanger and Herbert Gasser	1944	Research on the functions of single nerve fibers
Walter Hess	1949	Research on the role of the brain in controlling behavior
Egas Moniz	1949	Development of prefrontal lobotomy for the treatment of psychosis
Georg von Békésy	1961	Research on the auditory system
John Eccles, Alan Hodgkin, and Andrew Huxley	1963	Research on the ionic basis of neural transmission
Ragnor Granit, Haldan Hartline, and George Wald	1967	Research on the chemistry and physiology of the visual system
Bernard Katz, Ulf von Euler, and Julius Axelrod	1970	Discoveries related to the mechanisms of synaptic transmission
Karl Von Frisch, Konrad Lorenz, and Nikolaas Tinbergen	1973	Studies of animal behavior
Roger Guillemin and Andrew Schally	1977	Discoveries related to hormone production by the brain
Herbert Simon	1979	Research on human cognition
Roger Sperry	1981	Research on the differences between the two cerebral hemispheres
David Hubel and Torsten Wiesel	1981	Research on information processing in the visual system
Rita Levi-Montalcini and Stanley Cohen	1986	Discovery and study of nerve and epidermal growth factors

ropsychology has focused on this important part of the human brain.

Neuropsychology is the most applied of the biopsychological subdisciplines; the neuropsychological assessment of human patients, even when part of a program of pure research, is always done with an eye toward benefiting them in some way. Neuropsychological tests facilitate diagnosis and thus help the attending physician prescribe effective treatment (see Benton, 1994). They can also be an important basis for patient care and counseling; Kolb and Whishaw (1990) have described such an application:

> Mr. R., a 21-year-old left-handed man, struck his head on the dashboard in a car accident 2 years prior to our seeing him. He was unconscious for a few minutes after the accident but other than a cut on the right side of his forehead and amnesia for the period just before and after the accident, Mr. R. appeared none the worse for his mishap. Prior to his accident Mr. R. was an honor student at a university, with plans to attend professional or graduate school. However, a year after the accident he had become a mediocre student who had particular trouble completing his term papers on time, and although he claimed to be studying harder than he had before the accident, his marks had fallen drastically in courses requiring memorization. He was referred for a neurological exam by his family physician, but it proved negative and an EEG and a CT scan failed to demonstrate any abnormality. He was referred to us for neuropsychological assessment, which revealed several interesting facts.
>
> First, Mr. R. was one of about one-third of left-handers whose language functions are represented in the right rather than left hemisphere. This discovery was significant not only in interpreting his difficulties but also in the event that Mr. R. should ever require neurosurgery, since the surgeon would want to respect the speech zones of the neocortex. In addition, although Mr. R. had a superior IQ, his verbal memory and reading speed were only low-average, which is highly unusual for a person of his intelligence and education. These deficits indicated that his right temporal lobe may have been slightly damaged in the car accident, resulting in an impairment of his language skills. On the basis of our neuropsychological investigation we were able to recommend vocations to Mr. R. that did not require superior verbal memory skills, and he is currently studying architecture. (p. 128)[2]

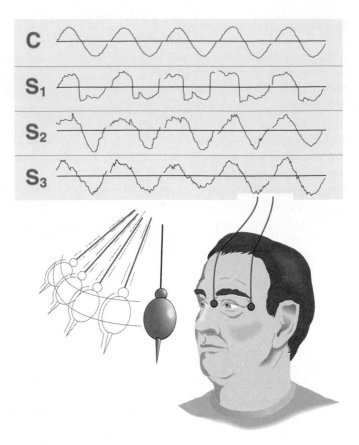

Figure 1.6 Visual tracking of a pendulum by a normal control subject (top) and three schizophrenics. (Adapted from "Features That Distinguish the Smooth-Pursuit Eye-Tracking Performance of Schizophrenic, Affective-Disorder, and Normal Individuals" by W. G. Iacono and W. G. R. Koenig, 1983, *Journal of Abnormal Psychology, 92,* p. 39. Copyright 1983 by the American Psychological Association. Reprinted by permission.

Psychophysiology

Psychophysiology is the division of biopsychology that studies the relation between physiological activity and psychological processes in human subjects (see Andreassi, 1989). Because the subjects of psychophysiological research are human, psychophysiological recording procedures are typically noninvasive; that is, the physiological activity is recorded from the surface of the body. The usual measure of brain activity is the scalp **electroencephalogram** (EEG). Other common psychophysiological measures are muscle tension, eye movement, and several types of autonomic nervous system activity (e.g., heart rate, blood pressure, pupil dilation, and electrical conductance of the skin). The

autonomic nervous system is the division of the nervous system that regulates the body's inner environment.

Most psychophysiological research focuses on understanding the physiology of psychological processes, such as attention, emotion, and information processing, but there have also been a number of interesting clinical applications of the psychophysiological method (see Iacono, 1985). For example, psychological experiments have indicated that schizophrenics have difficulty smoothly tracking a moving object such as a pendulum (Iacono & Koenig, 1983)—see Figure 1.6.

Comparative Psychology

Although most biopsychologists study the neural mechanisms of behavior, there is more to biopsychology than this. As Dewsbury (1991) asserted:

To make sure that you understand the distinctions among the five biopsychological approaches, fill in each of the following blanks. If you have difficulty, review the preceding section before continuing.

1. A biopsychologist who studies the memory deficits of human patients with brain damage would likely identify with the division of biopsychology termed _____.

2. Psychologists who study the physiological correlates of psychological processes by recording physiological signals from the surface of the human body are often referred to as

_____.

3. The biopsychological research of

_____ frequently involves the direct manipulation or recording of the neural activity of laboratory animals by various invasive surgical, electrical, and chemical means.

4. The division of biopsychology that focuses on the study of the effects of drugs on behavior is often referred to as _____.

5. _____

are biopsychologists who study the genetics, evolution, and adaptiveness of behavior by using the comparative method.

The "biology" in "psychobiology" should include the whole-animal approaches of ethology, ecology, evolution ... as well as the latest in physiological methods and thought.... The "compleat psychobiologist" should use whatever explanatory power can be found with modern physiological techniques, but never lose sight of the problems that got us going in the first place: the integrated behavior of whole, functioning, adapted organisms. (p. 198)

The division of biopsychology that deals generally with the biology of behavior, rather than specifically with the neural mechanisms of behavior, is **comparative psychology**. Comparative psychologists compare the behavior of different species and focus on the genetics, evolution, and adaptiveness of behavior (see Timberlake, 1993). Historically, comparative psychologists have focused on the experimental investigation of animal behavior in controlled laboratory environments. However, modern comparative psychology also encompasses **ethological research**—the study of animal behavior in its natural environment.

Psychophysiology. The division of biopsychology that studies the relation between physiological activity and psychological processes in human subjects by noninvasive recording.

Electroencephalogram (EEG). A measure of the general electrical activity of the brain, often recorded through the scalp.

Autonomic nervous system. The division of the nervous system that regulates the body's inner environment.

Comparative psychology. The division of biopsychology that studies the evolution, genetics, and adaptiveness of behavior, often by using the comparative method.

Ethological research. The study of animal behavior in its natural environment.

The answers are (1) neuropsychology, (2) psychophysiologists, (3) physiological psychologists, (4) psychopharmacology, and (5) comparative psychologists.

1.5 Converging Operations: How Do Biopsychologists Work Together?

Because none of the five biopsychological approaches to research is without its shortcomings, major biopsychological issues are rarely resolved by a single experiment or even

by a single series of experiments taking the same general approach. Progress is most rapid when different approaches are focused on a single problem in such a way that the strengths of one approach compensate for the weaknesses of the others; this is called **converging operations**.

Consider, for example, the relative strengths and weaknesses of neuropsychology and physiological psychology in the study of the psychological effects of damage to the human cerebral cortex. In this instance, the strength of the neuropsychological approach is that it deals directly with human patients; its weakness is that its focus on human patients precludes experiments. In contrast, the strength of the physiological approach is that it can bring the power of the experimental method and neuroscientific technology to bear on the question through research on nonhuman animals; its weakness is that the relevance of research on laboratory animals to human neuropsychological deficits is always open to question. Clearly these two approaches complement each other well; together they can answer questions that neither can answer individually.

To examine converging operations in action, let's return to the case of Jimmie G. The neuropsychological disorder from which Jimmie G. suffered was first described in the late 1800s by S. S. Korsakoff, a Russian physician, and subsequently became known as **Korsakoff's syndrome**. The primary symptom of Korsakoff's syndrome is severe memory loss, which is made all the more heartbreaking—as you have seen in Jimmie G.'s case—by the fact that its sufferers are often otherwise quite capable. Because Korsakoff's syndrome commonly occurs in alcoholics, it was initially believed to be a direct consequence of alcohol-produced brain damage. This conclusion proved to be a good illustration of the inadvisability of basing causal conclusions on quasiexperimental research. Subsequent research showed that Korsakoff's syndrome is caused by the brain damage associated with *thiamin* (vitamin B1) *deficiency*—see Butterworth, Kril, and Harper (1993) and Lishman (1990).

The first support for the thiamin-deficiency interpretation of Korsakoff's syndrome came from the discovery of the syndrome in malnourished persons who consumed little or no alcohol. Additional support came from experiments in which thiamin-deficient rats were compared with otherwise identical groups of control rats. The thiamin-deficient rats displayed memory deficits and patterns of brain damage similar to those observed in human alcoholics (Knoth & Mair, 1991; Mair, Knoth, et al., 1991; Mair, Otto, et al., 1991). Alcoholics often develop Korsakoff's syndrome because most of their caloric intake comes in the form of alcohol, which lacks vitamins, and because alcohol interferes with the metabolism of what little thiamin they do consume (Rindi, 1989). However, alcohol has been shown to accelerate the development of brain damage in thiamin-deficient rats (Zimitat et al., 1990). The point of all this (in case you have forgotten) is that progress in biopsychology typically comes from converging operations—in this case, from the convergence of neuropsychological case studies, quasiexperiments on human subjects, and controlled experiments on laboratory animals. The strength of biopsychology lies in its diversity.

So what has all this research done for Jimmie G. and others like him? Today, alcoholics are often counseled to stop drinking and are treated with massive doses of thiamin. The thiamin limits the development of further brain damage and often leads to a slight improvement in the patient's condition; but unfortunately, brain damage, once produced, is permanent. In some parts of the world, the fortification of alcoholic beverages with thiamin is being seriously considered (Wodak, Richmond, & Wilson, 1990). What do you think of this plan?

1.6 Scientific Inference: How Do Biopsychologists Study the Unobservable?

Scientific inference is the fundamental method of biopsychology and of many other sciences—it is what makes being a biopsychologist fun. This section provides further insight into the nature of biopsychology by defining, illustrating, and discussing scientific inference.

The scientific method is a system of finding out things by careful observation, but many of the processes studied by scientists cannot be observed. For example, scientists use *empirical* (observational) *methods* to study ice ages, gravity, evaporation, electricity, and nuclear fission—none of which can be directly observed; their effects can be observed, but the processes themselves cannot. Biopsychology is no different from other sciences in this respect. One of its main goals is to characterize, through empirical methods, the unobservable processes by which the nervous system controls behavior.

The empirical method that biopsychologists and other scientists use to study the unobservable is called **scientific inference**. The scientists carefully measure key events that they can observe and then use these measures as a basis for logically inferring the nature of events that they cannot observe. Like a detective carefully gathering clues from which to recreate an unwitnessed crime, a biopsychologist carefully gathers relevant measures of behavior and neural activity from which to infer the nature of the neural processes that regulate behavior. The fact that the neural mechanisms of behavior cannot be directly observed and must be studied through scientific inference is what makes biopsychological research such a challenge—and, as I said before, so much fun.

To illustrate scientific inference, I have selected a research project in which you can participate. By making a few simple observations about your own visual abilities under different conditions, you will be able to discover how

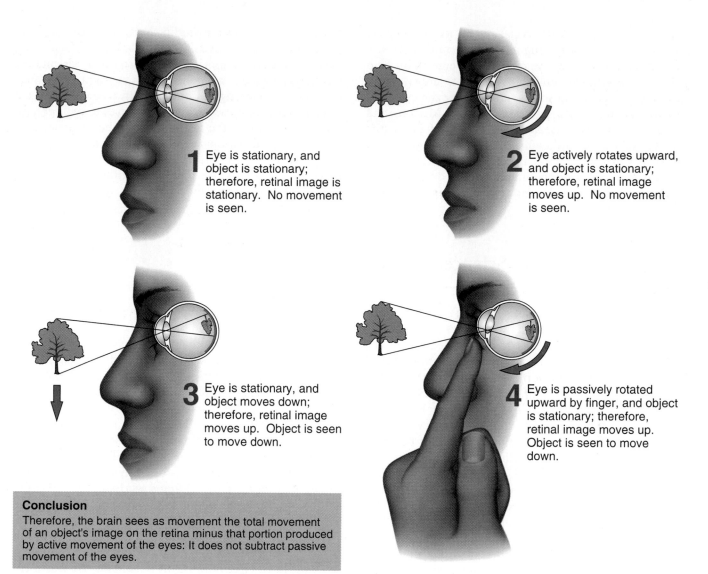

1 Eye is stationary, and object is stationary; therefore, retinal image is stationary. No movement is seen.

2 Eye actively rotates upward, and object is stationary; therefore, retinal image moves up. No movement is seen.

3 Eye is stationary, and object moves down; therefore, retinal image moves up. Object is seen to move down.

4 Eye is passively rotated upward by finger, and object is stationary; therefore, retinal image moves up. Object is seen to move down.

Conclusion
Therefore, the brain sees as movement the total movement of an object's image on the retina minus that portion produced by active movement of the eyes: It does not subtract passive movement of the eyes.

Figure 1.7 The perception of motion under four different conditions.

your brain translates the movement of images on your retinas into perceptions of movement. One feature of the mechanism is immediately obvious. Hold your hand in front of your face, and then move its image across your retinas by moving your eyes, by moving your hand, or by moving both at once. You will notice that only those movements of the retinal image that are produced by the movement of your hand are translated into the sight of motion; movements of the retinal image that are produced by your own eye movements are not. Obviously, there must be a part of your brain that monitors the movements of your retinal image and subtracts from the total those image movements that are produced by your own eye movements, leaving the remainder to be perceived as motion.

Now, let's try to characterize the nature of the information about your eye movements that is used by your brain in its perception of motion (see Bridgeman, van der Heijden, & Velichkovsky, 1994). Try the following. Shut one eye; then rotate your other eye slightly upward by gently pressing on your lower eyelid with your fingertip. What do you see? You see all of the objects in your visual field mov-

ing downward. Why? It seems that the brain mechanism that is responsible for the perception of motion does not consider eye movement per se. It considers only those eye movements that are actively produced by neural signals from the brain to the eye muscles, not those that are passively produced by external means (e.g., by your finger). Thus when your eye was moved passively, your brain assumed that it had remained still and attributed the movement of your retinal image to the movement of objects in your visual field (see Figure 1.7).

Converging operations. The use of several research approaches to solve a single problem.

Korsakoff's syndrome. A neuropsychological disorder that is common in alcoholics, the primary symptom of which is a disturbance of memory.

Scientific inference. The logical process by which observable events are used to infer the properties of unobservable events.

It is possible to trick the visual system in the opposite way; instead of the eyes being moved when no active signals have been sent to the eye muscles, the eyes can be held stationary despite the brain's attempts to move them. Because this experiment involves paralyzing the eye muscles, you cannot participate. Hammond, Merton, and Sutton (1956) injected the active ingredient of *curare*, the paralytic substance with which some South American natives coat their blow darts, into the eye muscles of their subject—who was Merton himself. What do you think Merton saw when he tried to move his eyes? He saw the stationary visual world moving in the same direction as his attempted eye movements. If a visual object is focused on part of your retina and it stays focused there despite the fact that you have moved your eyes to the right, it too must have moved to the right. Consequently, when Merton sent signals to his eye muscles to move his eyes to the right, his brain assumed that the movement had been carried out, and it perceived stationary objects as moving to the right. The point of this example is that biopsychologists can learn much about the activities of the brain without being able to directly observe them—and so can you.

1.7 What Is Bad Science, and How Do You Spot It?

Scientists, like other people, make mistakes; and biopsychologists are no exception. In fact, two features of biopsychological inquiry make it particularly susceptible to error. The first is that biopsychological research has such a wide appeal that it invites the participation of those who have had little or no experience with its complexities. The second is that it is often difficult to be objective when studying biopsychological phenomena. Whether we realize it or not, we all have many preconceptions about the brain and behavior ingrained in our thinking. Accordingly, this, the final section of the chapter, completes the task of defining biopsychology by discussing two of its most egregious errors.

You might wonder why a book about biopsychology would dwell, even momentarily, on errors in biopsychological research. There are two reasons. One reason is that understanding biopsychology's errors provides important insights into what biopsychology is—the standards and methods of a discipline frequently grow out of its mistakes. The other reason is that an understanding of biopsychology's errors will help you to become a better consumer of biopsychological science—it will imbue you with an appropriate degree of skepticism and the skills necessary to evaluate for yourself the validity of various claims. In other words, one purpose of this final section of Chapter 1 is to improve your BS detection skills—*BS*, of course, stands for bad science. Following are two examples of biopsychological analysis that are seriously flawed.

CASE 1

José Delgado demonstrated to a group of newspaper reporters a remarkable new procedure for controlling aggression. Delgado strode into a Spanish bull ring carrying only a red cape and a small radio transmitter. With the transmitter, he could activate a battery-powered stimulator that had previously been mounted on the horns of the other inhabitant of the ring. As the raging bull charged, Delgado calmly activated the stimulator and sent a weak train of electrical current from the stimulator through an electrode that had been implanted in the caudate nucleus deep in the bull's brain. The bull immediately veered from its charge. After a few such interrupted charges, the bull stood tamely as Delgado swaggered about the ring. According to Delgado, this demonstration marked a significant scientific breakthrough—the discovery of a caudate taming center and the fact that stimulation of this structure could eliminate aggressive behavior, even in bulls specially bred for their ferocity.

To those present at this carefully orchestrated event and to most of the millions who subsequently read about it, Delgado's conclusion was compelling. Surely, if caudate stimulation could stop the charge of a raging bull, the caudate must be a taming center. It was even suggested that caudate stimulation through implanted electrodes might be an effective treatment for human psychopaths. What do you think?

Analysis of Case 1

The fact of the matter is that Delgado's demonstration provided little or no support for his conclusion. It should have been obvious to anyone who did not get caught up in the provocative nature of Delgado's media event that there are numerous ways in which brain stimulation can abort a bull's charge, most of which are more simple, and thus more probable, than the one suggested by Delgado. For example, the stimulation may have simply rendered the bull confused, dizzy, nauseous, sleepy, or temporarily blind rather than nonaggressive; or the stimulation could have been painful. Clearly, any observation that can be interpreted in so many different ways provides little support for any one interpretation. When there are several possible interpretations for a behavioral observation, the rule is to give precedence to the simplest one; this rule is called **Morgan's Canon**. The following comments of Valenstein (1973) provide a reasoned view of Delgado's demonstration:

Actually there is no good reason for believing that the stimulation had any direct effect on the bull's aggressive tendencies. An examination of the film record makes it apparent that the charging bull was stopped because as long as the stimulation was on it was forced to turn around in the same direction continuously. After examining the film, any scientist with knowledge in this field could conclude only that the stimulation had been activating a neural pathway controlling movement. (p. 98)

... he [Delgado] seems to capitalize on every individual effect his electrodes happen to produce and presents little, if any, experimental evidence that his impression of the underlying cause is correct. (p. 103)

... his propensity for dramatic, albeit ambiguous, demonstrations has been a constant source of material for those whose purposes are served by exaggerating the omnipotence of brain stimulation. (p. 99)

CASE 2

In 1949, Dr. Egas Moniz was awarded the Nobel Prize in Physiology and Medicine for the development of **prefrontal lobotomy**—a surgical procedure in which the connections between the prefrontal lobes and the rest of the brain are cut—as a treatment for mental illness. The **prefrontal lobes** are the large areas, left and right, at the very front of the brain (see Figure 1.8). Moniz's discovery was based on the report that

Right prefrontal lobe

Left prefrontal lobe

Figure 1.8 The left and right prefrontal lobes, whose connections to the rest of the brain are disrupted by prefrontal lobotomy.

Becky, a chimpanzee that frequently became upset when she made errors during the performance of a food-rewarded task, did not do so following the creation of a large *bilateral lesion* (an area of damage to both sides of the brain) of her prefrontal lobes. After hearing about this isolated observation at a scientific meeting in 1935, Moniz persuaded neurosurgeon Almeida Lima to operate on a series of psychiatric patients; Almeida cut out six large cores of prefrontal tissue with a surgical device called a **leucotome** (see Figure 1.9 on page 16).

Following Moniz's claims that prefrontal surgery was therapeutically successful and had no significant side effects, there was a rapid proliferation of various forms of prefrontal psychosurgery (see O'Callaghan & Carroll, 1982; Valenstein, 1980, 1986). One such variation was **transorbital lobotomy**, which was developed in Italy and then was popularized in the United States by Walter Freeman in the late 1940s. It involved inserting an ice-pick-like device under the eyelid, driving it through the orbit (the eye socket) with a few taps of a mallet, and pushing it into the frontal lobes, where it was waved back and forth to sever the connections between the prefrontal lobes and the rest of the brain (see Figure 1.10 on page 16). This operation was frequently performed in the surgeon's office.

Analysis of Case 2

Incredible as it may seem, Moniz's program of psychosurgery was largely based on the observation of a single chimpanzee in a single situation, thus displaying a complete lack of appreciation for the diversity of brain and behavior, both within and between species. No program of psychosurgery should ever be initiated without a thorough assessment of the effects of the surgery on a large sample of subjects from various nonhuman mammalian species.

Morgan's Canon. The rule that the simplest possible interpretation for a behavioral result should be given precedence.

Prefrontal lobotomy. A surgical procedure in which the connections between the prefrontal lobes and the rest of the brain are cut as a treatment for mental illness.

Prefrontal lobes. The large areas, left and right, at the very front of the brain.

Leucotome. Any one of the various surgical devices used for performing lobotomies—*leucotomy* is another word for lobotomy.

Transorbital lobotomy. A prefrontal lobotomy performed with a cutting instrument inserted through the orbit or eye socket.

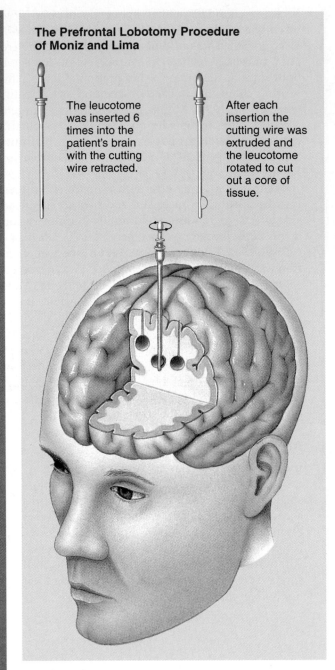

The Prefrontal Lobotomy Procedure of Moniz and Lima

The leucotome was inserted 6 times into the patient's brain with the cutting wire retracted.

After each insertion the cutting wire was extruded and the leucotome rotated to cut out a core of tissue.

Figure 1.9 A prefrontal lobotomy procedure that was developed by Moniz and Lima.

A second major weakness in the scientific case for prefrontal psychosurgery was the failure of Moniz and others to carefully evaluate the consequences of the surgery in the first patients to undergo the operation. The early reports that the operation was therapeutically successful were based on the impressions of the individuals who were the least objective—the physicians who had prescribed the surgery. Patients were frequently judged as improved if they were more man-

Figure 1.10 The transorbital procedure for performing prefrontal lobotomy.

ageable, and little effort was made to evaluate more important aspects of their psychological adjustment or to document the existence of adverse side effects.

Eventually, it became clear that prefrontal lobotomies are of little therapeutic benefit and that they produce a wide range of undesirable side effects, such as amorality, lack of foresight, emotional unresponsiveness, epilepsy, and urinary incontinence. This led to the abandonment of frontal lobotomy in many parts of the world—but not before over 40,000 patients had been lobotomized in the United States alone. Moreover, prefrontal lobotomies continue to be performed in some countries. Some regard the fundamentals of scientific protocol as unnecessary obstacles in the path of patients seeking treatment and therapists striving to provide it. However, the practice of prefrontal lobotomy should caution us against abandoning science for expediency. Only by observing the rules of science can scientists protect the public from bogus scientific claims (Carroll, 1984).

There is a somber postscript to this story. Moniz was shot by one of his patients. The bullet became lodged in his spine, rendering him *paraplegic* (paralyzed below the waist).

CONCLUSION

The general purpose of this chapter was to define *biopsychology* and to whet your appetite for more of it. Biopsychology was characterized from seven different perspectives, each corresponding to a section of the chapter. First, you learned that biopsychology is the study of the biology of behavior (1.1), that biopsychology is a major discipline of neuroscience (1.2), that biopsychological research is conducted in a variety of different ways (1.3), and that biopsychology comprises five fundamentally different divisions: physiological psychology, psychopharmacology, neuropsychology, psychophysiology, and comparative psychology (1.4). Then, you were introduced to two important principles of biopsychological research: converging operations (1.5) and scientific inference (1.6). Finally, you were provided with two examples of bad biopsychology, which illustrated the importance of adhering to the fundamental principles of scientific inquiry and of greeting claims of major scientific breakthroughs with a healthy degree of skepticism (1.7).

You are about to enter a world of amazing discoveries and intriguing ideas: the world of biopsychology. I hope that your brain enjoys learning about itself.

FOOD FOR THOUGHT

1. Chapter 1 tells you in general conceptual terms what biopsychology is. Another, and perhaps better, way of defining biopsychology is to describe what biopsychologists do. Ask your instructor what she or he did to become a biopsychologist and what she or he does each workday. I think that you will be surprised. Is your instructor predominantly a physiological psychologist, a psychopharmacologist, a neuropsychologist, a psychophysiologist, or a comparative psychologist?

2. What ethical considerations should guide biopsychological research on nonhuman animals? How should these ethical considerations differ from those that should guide biopsychological research on humans? See the chapter's Additional Readings section.

3. In retrospect, the entire prefrontal lobotomy episode is shocking. How could physicians, who are generally intelligent, highly educated, and dedicated to helping their patients, participate in such a travesty? How could somebody win a Nobel Prize for developing a form of surgery that left over 40,000 mental cripples in the United States alone? Why did this happen? Could it happen today?

KEY TERMS

Neurons *(p. 2)*
Neuroscience *(p. 2)*
Biopsychology *(p. 3)*
Neuroanatomy *(p. 4)*
Neurochemistry *(p. 4)*
Neuroendocrinology *(p. 4)*
Neuropathology *(p. 4)*
Neuropharmacology *(p. 4)*
Neurophysiology *(p. 4)*
Society for Neuroscience *(p. 4)*
Comparative approach *(p. 5)*
Between-subjects design *(p. 6)*

Within-subjects design *(p. 6)*
Independent variable *(p. 6)*
Dependent variable *(p. 6)*
Confounded variable *(p. 6)*
Coolidge effect *(p. 6)*
Lordosis *(p. 6)*
Quasiexperimental studies *(p. 7)*
Case studies *(p. 7)*
Generalizability *(p. 8)*
Pure research *(p. 8)*
Applied research *(p. 8)*

Physiological psychology *(p. 8)*
Psychopharmacology *(p. 9)*
Neuropsychology *(p. 9)*
Cerebral cortex *(p. 9)*
Psychophysiology *(p. 10)*
Electroencephalogram *(p. 10)*
Autonomic nervous system *(p. 10)*
Comparative psychology *(p. 11)*
Ethological research *(p. 11)*

Converging operations *(p. 12)*
Korsakoff's syndrome *(p. 12)*
Scientific inference *(p. 12)*
Morgan's Canon *(p. 14)*
Prefrontal lobotomy *(p. 15)*
Prefrontal lobes *(p. 15)*
Leucotome *(p. 15)*
Transorbital lobotomy *(p. 15)*

ADDITIONAL READING

Each of the following books provides an excellent introduction to one of the five biopsychological subdisciplines:

Andreassi, J. L. (1989). *Psychophysiology: Human behavior and physiological response.* Hillsdale, NJ: Erlbaum.

Carlson, N. R. (1991). *Physiology of behavior* (4th ed.). Boston: Allyn & Bacon.

Dewsbury, D. A. (1990). *Contemporary issues in comparative psychology.* Sunderland, MA: Sinauer.

Kolb, B., & Whishaw, I. Q. (1990). *Fundamentals of human neuropsychology* (3rd ed.). New York: Freeman.

McKim, W. A. (1986). *Drugs and behavior: An introduction to behavioral pharmacology.* Englewood Cliffs, NJ: Prentice-Hall.

This book provides an excellent overview of the topic of psychosurgery:

Valenstein, E. S. (1986). *Great and desperate cures: The rise and decline of psychosurgery and other radical treatments for mental illness.* New York: Basic Books.

The following article is a good discussion of what biopsychology is and how it is related to the other neurosciences:

Davis, H. P., Rosenzweig, M. R., Becker, L. A., & Sather, K. J. (1988). Biological psychology's relationships to psychology and neuroscience. *American Psychologist, 43,* 359–371.

This article argues convincingly that biopsychology is more than the study of the neural basis of behavior:

Dewsbury, D. A. (1991). Psychobiology. *American Psychologist, 46,* 198–205.

The following articles deal with the ethics of research on nonhuman animals:

National Institutes of Health (1985). *NIH guide for the care and use of laboratory animals* (Publication No. 85–23, (rev. 1985). Bethesda, MD: Author.

Miller, N. E. (1991). Commentary on Ulrich: Need to check truthfulness of statements by opponents of animal research. *Psychological Science, 6,* 422–424.

Ulrich, R. E. (1991). Commentary: Animal rights, animal wrongs, and the question of balance. *Psychological Science, 2,* 197–201.

Evolution, Genetics, and Experience: Asking the Right Questions about the Biology of Behavior

2.1 Thinking about the Biology of Behavior:
From Dichotomies to Relations and Interactions

2.2 Human Evolution

2.3 Fundamental Genetics

2.4 Behavioral Development: The Interaction of
Genetic Factors and Experience

2.5 The Genetics of Human Psychological Differences

We all tend to think about things in ways that have been ingrained in us by our **Zeitgeist** (pronounced "ZYTE-gyste"), the general intellectual climate of our culture. That is why this is a particularly important chapter for you. You see, you are the intellectual product of a Zeitgeist that promotes ways of thinking about the biological bases of behavior that are inconsistent with the facts. The primary purpose of this chapter is to help you bring your thinking about the biology of behavior in line with modern biopsychological science.

Most textbook chapters focus on answers. This chapter focuses on questions—the questions that people tend to ask about the biology of behavior. It tries to teach you to ask the right questions about the biology of behavior by describing why biopsychologists have abandoned traditional questions in favor of more insightful alternatives. Asking the right questions is the first step toward getting the right answers.

2.1 Thinking about the Biology of Behavior: From Dichotomies to Relations and Interactions

We tend to ignore the subtleties, inconsistencies, and complexities of our existence and to think in terms of simple, mutually exclusive dichotomies: right-wrong, good-bad, attractive-unattractive, and so on. The allure of this way of thinking is its simplicity.

The tendency to think about behavior in terms of dichotomies is illustrated by two kinds of questions that people commonly ask about behavior: (1) Is it physiological or is it psychological? (2) Is it inherited or is it learned? Both questions have proved to be misguided; yet they are among the most common kinds of questions asked in biopsychology classrooms. That is why I am dwelling on them here.

Is It Physiological or Is It Psychological?

The idea that human processes fall into one of two categories, physiological or psychological, grew out of a 17th-century conflict between science and the Roman Church. For much of the history of Western civilization, truth was whatever was decreed to be true by the Church. Then, in about 1400, things started to change. The famines, plagues, and marauding armies that had repeatedly swept Europe during the dark and middle ages subsided, and interest turned to art, commerce, and scholarship—this was the period of the *Renaissance*, or rebirth (1400 to 1700). Some Renaissance scholars were not content to follow the dictates of the Church; instead, they started to study things directly by observing them—and so it was that science was born.

Much of the scientific knowledge that accumulated during the Renaissance was at odds with Church dogma. However, the conflict was resolved by the prominent French philosopher René Descartes (pronounced "day CART"). Descartes (1596–1650) proposed a philosophy that gave one part of the universe to science and the other part to the Church. He argued that the universe is composed of two elements: (1) physical matter, which behaves according to the laws of nature and is thus a suitable object of scientific investigation; and (2) the human mind (soul or spirit), which lacks physical substance, controls human behavior, obeys no natural laws, and is thus the appropriate purview of the Church. The human body, including the brain, was assumed to be entirely physical, and so were nonhuman animals.

Cartesian dualism, as Descartes's philosophy became known, was sanctioned by the Roman Church, and so the idea that the human brain and the mind are separate entities became widely accepted. It has survived to this day, despite the intervening centuries of scientific progress. Most people now understand that human behavior has a physiological basis, but many still cling to the dualistic assumption that there is a category of human activity that somehow transcends the human brain.

Is It Inherited or Is It Learned?

The tendency to think in terms of dichotomies extends to the way people think about the development of behavioral capacities. For centuries, scholars have debated whether humans and other animals inherit their behavioral capacities or whether they acquire them through learning. This issue is commonly referred to as the **nature-nurture issue.**

Most of the early North American experimental psychologists were totally committed to the nurture (learning) side of the nature-nurture issue. The degree of this commitment is illustrated by the oft-cited words of John B. Watson, the father of *behaviorism*:

> We have no real evidence of the inheritance of [behavioral] traits. I would feel perfectly confident in the ultimately favorable outcome of careful upbringing of a healthy, well-formed baby born of a long line of crooks, murderers and thieves, and prostitutes. Who has any evidence to the contrary?
>
> …Give me a dozen healthy infants, well-formed, and my own specified world to bring them up in and I'll guarantee to take any one at random and train him to become any type of specialist I might select—doctor, lawyer, artist, merchant-chief and, yes even beggar-man and thief (Watson, 1930, pp. 103–104)

At the same time that experimental psychology was taking root in North America, **ethology**—the study of animal behavior in the wild—was becoming the dominant approach to the study of behavior in Europe. European ethology, in contrast to North American experimental psychology, focused on the study of **instinctive behaviors**—behaviors that occur in all like members of a species, even when there seems to have been no opportunity for them to have been learned; and it emphasized the role of nature, or inherited factors, in behavioral development. For example, Tinbergen and Perdeck (1950) studied the tendency of newly hatched herring-gull chicks to peck at the red dot on the bills of their parents, which caused the parents to regurgitate a yummy meal of half-digested fish. Because instinctive behaviors do not seem to be learned, the early ethologists assumed that they are inherited. They were wrong, but then so were the early psychologists.

Problems with Thinking about the Biology of Behavior in Terms of Traditional Dichotomies

The physiological-or-psychological and nature-or-nurture questions are based on incorrect ways of thinking about the biology of behavior, and a new generation of questions is directing the current boom in biopsychological research. What is wrong with these old ways of thinking about the biology of behavior, and what are the new ways?

Physiological-or-psychological thinking runs into difficulty
Not long after Descartes's mind-brain dualism was officially sanctioned by the Roman Church, it started to come under public attack.

> In 1747, Julien Offroy de la Mettrie anonymously published a pamphlet that scandalized Europe.... La Mettrie fled to Berlin, where he was forced to live in exile for the rest of his life. His crime? He had argued that thought was

produced by the brain—a dangerous assault, in the eyes of his contemporaries....Not for the last time, the science of human mind had outgrown human imagination. (Corsi, 1991, cover)

Although many people still believe that there is a purely psychological category of human activity that transcends the human brain, two kinds of evidence indicate otherwise. First, numerous studies have shown that even the most complex psychological processes (e.g., memory, emotion, and self-awareness) can be modified by damage to or stimulation of the higher regions of the brain (see Kosslyn & Andersen, 1992). Second, some nonhuman species have been found to possess abilities that were once assumed to be purely psychological and thus purely human (see Cheney & Seyfarth, 1992). The following two quotations illustrate these two kinds of evidence; both quotations deal with the study of self-awareness.

The first quotation describes Oliver Sacks's (1985) case of "the man who fell out of bed."[1] He was suffering from **asomatognosia,** a deficiency in the awareness of parts of one's own body. Asomatognosia typically involves the left side of the body and usually results from damage to the *right parietal lobe* (see Figure 2.1 on page 22). The second quotation describes G. G. Gallup's (1983) demonstrations of self-awareness in chimpanzees (see Parker, Mitchell, & Boccia, 1994; and Figure 2.2 on page 22)[2]

> He had felt fine all day, and fallen asleep towards evening. When he woke up he felt fine too, until he moved in the bed. Then he found, as he put it "someone's leg" in the bed—*a severed human leg,* a horrible thing! He was stunned, at first, with amazement and disgust....[Then] he had a brainwave....Obviously one of the nurses ... had stolen into the Dissecting Room and nabbed a leg, and then slipped it under his bedclothes as a joke....*When he threw it out of bed, he somehow came after it—and now it was attached to him.*
> "Look at it!" he cried...."Have you ever seen such a creepy, horrible thing?"...
> "Easy!" I said. "Be calm! Take it easy!"...
> "...why..." he asked irritably, belligerently.
> "Because it's *your* leg," I answered. "Don't you know your own leg?"...
> ..."Ah Doc!" he said. "You're fooling me! You're in cahoots with that nurse."...
> "Listen," I said. "I don't think you're well. Please allow us to return you to bed. But I want to ask you one final ques-

Zeitgeist. The general intellectual climate of a culture.

Cartesian dualism. The philosophical position of Descartes, who argued that the universe is composed of two elements: physical matter and the human mind.

Nature-nurture issue. The debate about the relative contributions of nature (genes) and nurture (experience) to the behavioral capacities of individuals.

Ethology. The study of the behavior of animals in their natural environments.

Instinctive behaviors. Behaviors that occur in all like members of a species, even when there seems to have been no opportunity for them to have been learned.

Asomatognosia. A deficiency in awareness of one's own body that is produced by brain damage.

---

[1]From *The Man Who Mistook His Wife for a Hat and Other Clinical Tales* (pp. 53–55) by Oliver Sacks, 1985. New York: Summit Books. Copyright © 1970, 1981, 1983, 1984, 1985 by Oliver Sacks. Reprinted by permission of Summit Books, a division of Simon & Schuster, Inc.

[2]From *Toward a Comparative Psychology of Mind* (pp. 474–477) by G. G. Gallup, Jr. In R. L. Mellgren, ed., *Animal Cognition and Behavior.* Amsterdam: North-Holland Publishing Co. Copyright © 1983. Reprinted by permission of North-Holland Publishing Co. and G. G. Gallup, Jr.

Right parietal lobe

Figure 2.1 Asomatognosia typically involves damage to the right parietal lobe.

An organism is self-aware to the extent that it can be shown capable of becoming the object of its own attention....One way to assess an organism's capacity to become the object of its own attention is to confront it with a mirror.

...I gave a number of group-reared, preadolescent chimpanzees individual exposure to themselves in mirrors....Invariably, their first reaction to the mirror was to respond as if they were seeing another chimpanzee.... After about two days, however, ... they ... started to use the mirror to groom and inspect parts of their bodies they had not seen before, and progressively began to experiment with the reflection by making faces, looking at themselves upside down, and assuming unusual postures while monitoring the results in the mirror....

So in an attempt to provide a more convincing demonstration of self-recognition, I devised an unobtrusive and more rigorous test....[E]ach chimpanzee was anesthetized. ... I carefully painted the uppermost portion of an eyebrow ridge and the top half of the opposite ear with a bright red, odorless, alcohol soluble dye....

Following recovery from anesthesia ... the mirror was then reintroduced as an explicit test of self-recognition. Upon seeing their painted faces in the mirror, all the chimpanzees showed repeated mark-directed responses, consisting of attempts to touch and inspect marked areas on their eyebrow and ear while watching the image. In addition, there was over a three-fold increase in viewing time....Several chimpanzees also showed noteworthy attempts to visually examine and smell the fingers which had been used to touch these facial marks. I suspect that you would respond pretty much the same way, if upon awakening one morning you saw yourself in the mirror with red spots on your face. (Gallup, 1983, pp. 474–477)

tion. If this—this thing—is *not* your left leg ... then where is your own left leg?"

Once more he became pale—so pale that I thought he was going to faint. "I don't know," he said. "I have no idea. It's disappeared. It's gone. It's nowhere to be found." (Sacks, 1985, pp. 53–55)

• • •

Figure 2.2 The reactions of chimpanzees to their own images indicate that they are self-aware. In this photo, the chimpanzee is reacting to the bright red, odorless dye that was painted on its eyebrow ridge while it was anesthetized. (Photograph by Donna Bierschwale, courtesy of the New Iberia Research Center.)

Nature-or-nurture thinking runs into difficulty The history of nature-or-nurture thinking can be summed up by paraphrasing Mark Twain: "Reports of its death have been greatly exaggerated." Each time it has been discredited, it has resurfaced in a slightly modified form. First, factors other than genetics and learning were shown to influence behavioral development; factors such as the fetal environment, nutrition, stress, and sensory stimulation also proved to be influential. This led to a broadening of the concept of nurture to include a variety of experiential factors in addition to learning. In effect, it changed the nature-or-nurture dichotomy from "genetic factors or learning" to "genetic factors or experience."

Next, it was argued convincingly that behavior always develops under the combined control of both nature and nurture (e.g., Johnston, 1987), not under the control of one or the other. Faced with this discovery, many people merely substituted one kind of nature-nurture thinking for another. They stopped asking, "Is it genetic or is it the result of experience?" and started asking, "How much of it is genetic and how much of it is the result of experience?"

Like earlier versions of the nature-nurture question, the how-much-of-it-is-genetic-and-how-much-of-it-is-the-result-of-experience version is fundamentally flawed. The problem is that it is based on the premise that genetic factors and experiential factors combine in an additive fashion—that a behavioral capacity, such as intelligence, is created through the combination of so many parts of genetics and so many parts of experience. Once you learn more about how genetic factors and experience interact, you will better appreciate the folly of this assumption. For the time being, however, let me illustrate its weakness with a metaphor embedded in an anecdote:

> One of my students told me that she had read that intelligence was one-third genetic and two-thirds experience, and she wondered whether this was true. She must have been puzzled when I began my response by describing an alpine experience. "I was lazily wandering up a summit ridge when I heard an unexpected sound. Ahead, with his back to me, was a young man sitting on the edge of a precipice, blowing into a peculiar musical instrument. I sat down behind him on a large sun-soaked rock, ate my lunch, and shared his experience with him. Then, I got up and wandered back down the ridge, leaving him undisturbed."

I put the following question to my student: "If I wanted to get a better understanding of this music, would it be reasonable for me to begin by asking how much of it came from the musician and how much of it came from the instrument?"

"That would be dumb," she said. "The music comes from both; it makes no sense to ask how much comes from the musician and how much comes from the instrument. Somehow the music results from the interaction of the two together. You would have to ask about the interaction."

"That's exactly right," I said. "Now, do you see why…"

"Don't say any more," she interrupted. "I see what you're getting at. Intelligence is the product of the interaction of genes and experience, and it is dumb to try to find how much comes from genes and how much comes from experience."

"And the same is true of any other behavioral trait," I added.

Several days later, the student strode into my office, reached into her pack, and pulled out a familiar object. "I believe that this is your mystery musical instrument," she said. "It's a Peruvian panpipe." She was right … again.

A model of the biology of behavior So far in this section, you have learned why people tend to think about the biology of behavior in terms of dichotomies, and you have learned some of the reasons why this way of thinking is inappropriate. Now, let's look at the way of thinking about the biology of behavior that has been adopted by many biopsychologists (see Kimble, 1989). It is illustrated in Figure 2.3 on page 24. Like other powerful ideas, it is simple and logical. This five-stage model boils down to the single premise that all behavior is the product of interactions among three factors: (1) the organism's genetic endowment, which is a product of its evolution; (2) its experience; and (3) its perception of the current situation. Please examine the model carefully, and consider its implications.

The next three sections of this chapter deal with three elements of this model of behavior: evolution, genetics, and the interaction of genetics and experience in behavioral development. The final section deals with the genetics of human psychological differences.

2.2 Human Evolution

Modern biology began in 1859 with the publication of Charles Darwin's *On the Origins of Species*. In this monumental work, Darwin described his theory of evolution—the single most influential theory in the biological sciences. Darwin was not the first to suggest that species **evolve** (undergo gradual orderly change) from preexisting species; but he was the first to amass a large body of supporting evidence, and he was the first to suggest how evolution occurs.

Evolve. To undergo gradual orderly change.

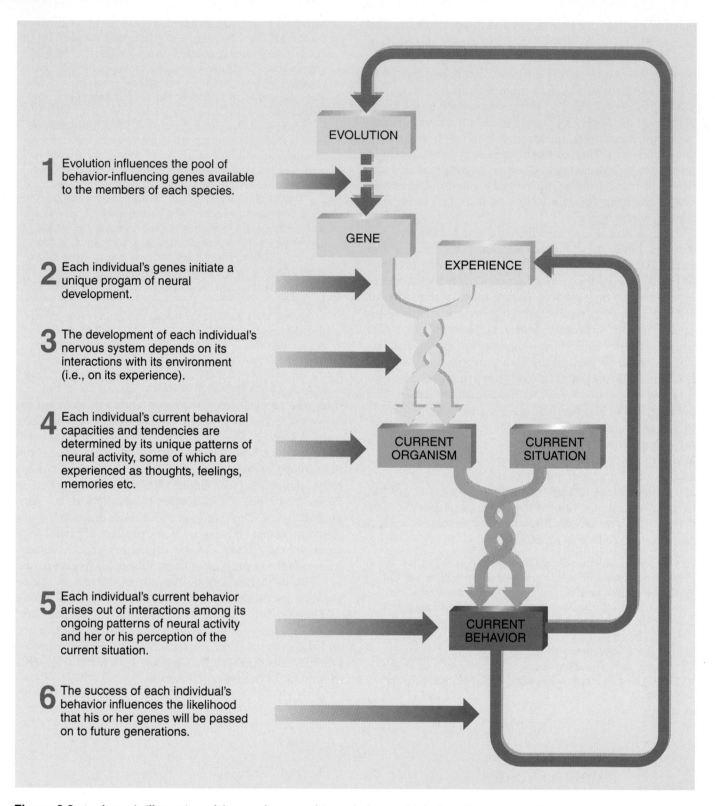

1 Evolution influences the pool of behavior-influencing genes available to the members of each species.

2 Each individual's genes initiate a unique progam of neural development.

3 The development of each individual's nervous system depends on its interactions with its environment (i.e., on its experience).

4 Each individual's current behavioral capacities and tendencies are determined by its unique patterns of neural activity, some of which are experienced as thoughts, feelings, memories etc.

5 Each individual's current behavior arises out of interactions among its ongoing patterns of neural activity and her or his perception of the current situation.

6 The success of each individual's behavior influences the likelihood that his or her genes will be passed on to future generations.

EVOLUTION

GENE

EXPERIENCE

CURRENT ORGANISM

CURRENT SITUATION

CURRENT BEHAVIOR

Figure 2.3 A schematic illustration of the way that many biopsychologists think about the biology of behavior.

Darwin presented three kinds of evidence to support his assertion that species evolve: (1) He documented the evolution of fossil records through progressively more recent geological layers. (2) He described striking structural simi-larities among living species (e.g., a human's hand, a bird's wing, and a cat's paw), which suggested that they had evolved from common ancestors. (3) He pointed to the major changes that had been brought about in domestic

Fossil records change systematically through geological layers. Illustrated here is the evolution of the hominid skull.

Major changes have been created in domestic plants and animals by programs of selective breeding.

Evolution has been observed in progress. For example, an 18-month drought on one of the Galapagos Islands left only large, difficult-to-eat seeds and increased the beak size in one species of finch.

There are striking structural similarities among diverse living species (e.g., between a human arm and a bat's wing).

Figure 2.4 Four kinds of evidence supporting the theory that species evolve.

plants and animals by programs of selective breeding. However, the most convincing evidence of evolution comes from direct observations of evolution in progress. For example, Grant (1991) observed evolution of the finches of the Galápagos Islands—a population studied by Darwin himself—after only a single season of drought. Figure 2.4 illustrates these four kinds of evidence.

Darwin argued that evolution occurs through **natural selection.** He pointed out that the members of each species vary greatly in their structure, physiology, and behavior, and that the heritable traits that are associated with high rates of survival and reproduction are the most likely ones to be passed on to future generations. He argued that natural selection, when repeated generation after generation, leads to the evolution of species that are better adapted to surviving and reproducing in their particular environmental niche. Darwin called this process *natural selection* to emphasize its similarity to the artificial selective breeding practices employed by breeders of domestic animals. Just as horse breeders create faster horses by selectively breeding the fastest of their existing stock, nature creates fitter animals by selectively breeding the fittest. **Fitness,** in the Darwinian sense, is the ability of an organism to survive and contribute its genes to the next generation.

The theory of evolution was at odds with the various dogmatic views that were embedded in the 19th-century

Natural selection. The idea that heritable traits that are associated with high rates of survival and reproduction are preferentially passed on to future generations.

Fitness. The ability of an organism to survive and contribute its genes to the next generation.

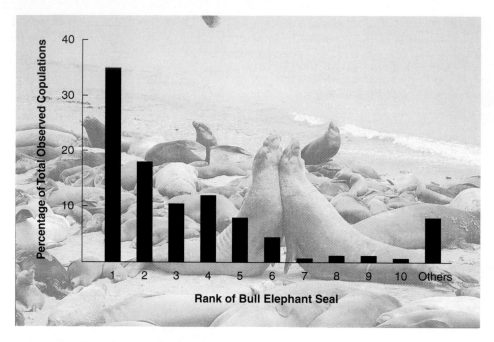

Figure 2.5 Two massive bull elephant seals challenging one another. Dominant bull elephant seals copulate more frequently than those that are lower in the dominance hierarchy. (Adapted from McCann, 1981.)

is established, hostilities diminish because the low-ranking males learn to avoid or quickly submit to the dominant males. Because most of the fighting goes on between males competing for positions high in the social hierarchy, low-ranking males fight little; hence the lower levels of the hierarchy tend to be only vaguely recognizable.

Why is social dominance an important factor in evolution? The reason is that dominant males copulate more than nondominant males and thus are more effective in passing on their characteristics to future generations. McCann (1981) studied the effect of social dominance on the rate of copulation in 10 bull elephant seals that cohabited the same breeding beach. Figure 2.5 illustrates how these massive animals challenge each other by raising themselves to full height and pushing chest to chest. Usually, the smaller of the two backs down; if it does not, a vicious neck-biting battle ensues. McCann found that the dominant male accounted for about 37% of the copulations during the study, whereas poor number 10 accounted for only about 1% (see Figure 2.5).

Courtship display An intricate series of courtship displays precedes copulation in many species (see Figure 2.6). The male approaches the female and signals his interest. His signal (which may be olfactory, visual, auditory, or tactual) may elicit a signal in the female, which may elicit another response in the male, and so on until copulation ensues. But copulation is unlikely to occur if one of the pair fails to react appropriately to the signals of the other.

Zeitgeist, so it met with initial resistance. Although traces of this resistance still exist, virtually none comes from people who understand the evidence:

> Evolution by natural selection meets no significant opposition within biological science. The principle of natural selection has a logical necessity to it; indeed, some have argued that it is a tautology rather than an empirical law ... [S]ubsequent development of biology in major new areas like genetics and biochemistry has only reinforced Darwin's conclusion that the facts make a belief in the theory of evolution by natural selection "inescapable." (Daly & Wilson, 1983, p. 7)

Evolution and Behavior

Some behaviors play an obvious role in evolution. For example, the ability to find food, avoid predation, and defend one's young obviously increase an animal's ability to pass on its genes to future generations. Other behaviors play a role that is less obvious but no less important; two examples are social dominance and courtship display.

Social dominance The males of many social species establish a stable *hierarchy of social dominance* through combative encounters with other males. In some species, these encounters often involve physical damage; in others, they involve mainly posturing and threatening until one of the two combatants backs down. The dominant male usually wins encounters with all other males of the group; the number 2 male usually wins encounters with all males except the dominant male; and so on down the line. Once a hierarchy

Figure 2.6 A courtship display of the male great frigatebird.

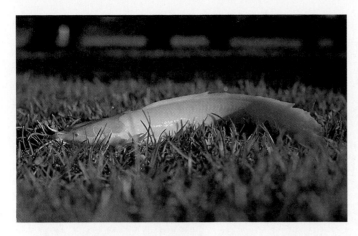

Figure 2.7 Florida walking catfish, which travel on land by propelling themselves with their fins.

Courtship displays are thought to promote the evolution of new species. Let me explain. A **species** is a group of organisms that is reproductively isolated from other organisms; that is, the members of one species can produce fertile offspring only by mating with members of the same species. A new species begins to branch off from an existing species when some barrier discourages breeding between a subpopulation of the existing species and the remainder of the species. Once such a reproductive barrier forms, the subpopulation evolves independently of the remainder of the species until cross-fertilization becomes impossible.

The reproductive barrier may be geographic; for example, a few birds may fly together to an isolated island, where many generations of their offspring breed among themselves and evolve into a separate species. Alternatively—to get back to the main point—the reproductive barrier may be behavioral. A few members of a species may develop different courtship displays, and these may form a reproductive barrier between themselves and the rest of their **conspecifics** (members of the same species).

Course of Human Evolution

By studying fossil records and comparing current species, we humans have looked back in time and pieced together the evolutionary history of our species—although some of the details are still controversial. Human evolution, as it is currently understood, is summarized in this section.

Evolution of vertebrates Single-cell water-dwelling organisms first appeared on earth about 600 million years ago. About 150 million years later, the first chordates evolved. **Chordates** (pronounced "KOR dates") are animals with dorsal nerve cords (large nerves that run along the center of the back, or *dorsum*); they are 1 of the 20 or so large categories, or *phyla* (pronounced "FY la"), into which zoologists group animal species. The first chordates with spinal bones to protect their dorsal nerve cords evolved

about 25 million years later. The spinal bones are called *vertebrae* (pronounced "VERT eh bray"), and the chordates that possess them are called **vertebrates.** The first vertebrates were primitive bony fishes. Today, there are seven classes of vertebrates: three classes of fishes, plus amphibians, reptiles, birds, and mammals.

Evolution of amphibians About 410 million years ago, the first bony fishes ventured out of the water. Fishes that could survive on land for brief periods of time had two great advantages: They could escape from stagnant pools to nearby fresh water, and they could take advantage of terrestrial food sources (see Figure 2.7). The advantages of life on land were so great that natural selection transformed the fins and gills of bony fishes to legs and lungs, respectively—and so it was that the first **amphibians** evolved about 400 million years ago. Amphibians (e.g., frogs, toads, and salamanders) in their larval form must live in the water; only adult amphibians can survive on land.

Evolution of reptiles About 300 million years ago, reptiles (e.g., lizards, snakes, and turtles) evolved from amphibians. Reptiles were the first vertebrates to lay shell-covered eggs and to be covered by dry scales. Both of these adaptations reduced the reliance of reptiles on watery habitats. A reptile does not have to spend the first stage of its life in the watery environment of a pond or lake; instead it spends the first stage of its life in the watery environment of a shell-covered egg. And once hatched, a reptile can live far from water because its dry scales greatly reduce water loss through its water-permeable skin.

Evolution of mammals About 180 million years ago, during the height of the age of dinosaurs, a new class of vertebrates evolved from one line of small reptiles. The females of this new class fed their young with secretions from special glands called *mammary glands*, and thus the members of this line are called **mammals** after these glands. Eventually, mammals stopped laying eggs; instead, the females nurtured their young in the watery environment of their bodies until the young were mature enough to be

Species. A group of organisms that is reproductively isolated from other organisms; the members of one species cannot produce fertile offspring by mating with members of other species.

Conspecifics. Members of the same species.

Chordates. Animals with dorsal nerve chords.

Vertebrates. Chordates that possess spinal bones.

Amphibians. Species that spend their larval phase in water and their adult phase on land.

Mammals. Species whose young are fed from mammary glands.

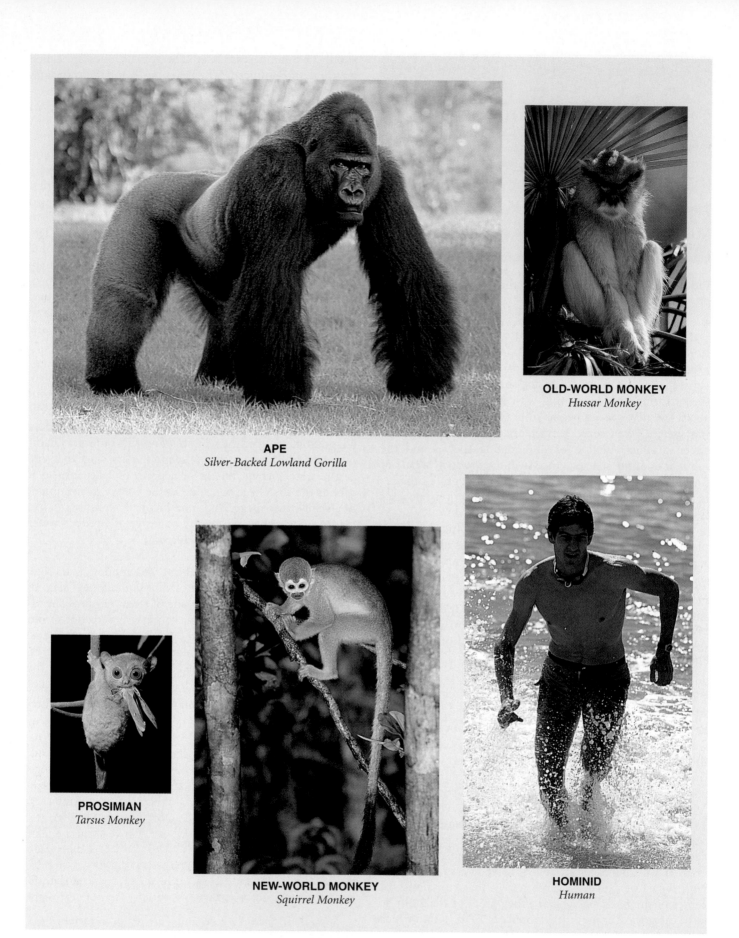

APE
Silver-Backed Lowland Gorilla

OLD-WORLD MONKEY
Hussar Monkey

PROSIMIAN
Tarsus Monkey

NEW-WORLD MONKEY
Squirrel Monkey

HOMINID
Human

Figure 2.8 Examples of the five different families of primates.

Chapter 2   Evolution, Genetics, and Experience

born. The *duck-billed platypus* is one surviving mammalian species that lays eggs.

Spending the first stage of life inside one's mother proved to have considerable survival value; it provided the long-term security and environmental stability necessary for complex programs of development to unfold. Today, there are 14 different orders of mammals. The one to which we belong is the order **primates.** We humans—in our usual humble way—named our order after the Latin *primus,* which means "first" or "foremost." There are five families of primates: prosimians, New-World monkeys, Old-World monkeys, apes, and hominids. Examples of the five primate families appear in Figure 2.8.

Apes (gibbons, orangutans, gorillas, and chimpanzees) are thought to have evolved from a line of Old-World monkeys. Like Old-World monkeys, apes have long arms and grasping hind feet that are specialized for arboreal travel, and they have opposable thumbs that are not long enough to be of much use for precise manipulation (see Figure 2.9). Unlike Old-World monkeys, apes have no tails and can walk upright for short distances. Chimpanzees are the closest living relatives of humans; approximately 99% of the genetic material is identical in the two species (see O'Neill, Murphy, & Gallagher, 1994).

Emergence of humankind The **hominids** are the family of primates that includes humans; it is composed of two genera (the plural of *genus*): *Australopithecus* and *Homo* (*Homo erectus* and *Homo sapiens*). However, humans (*Homo sapiens*) are the only surviving hominid species.

The fossil and genetic evidence suggests that the Australopithecines evolved about 6 million years ago in East Africa from a line of apes (*australo* means "southern," and *pithecus* means "ape")—from the same line of apes that evolved into chimpanzees in West Africa (see Coppens, 1994). Several species of *Australopithecus* are thought to have roamed the plains of Africa in small groups for about 5 million years before becoming extinct. Australopithecines were only about 1.3 meters (4 feet) tall, and they had small brains; but analysis of their pelvis and leg bones indicates that their posture was as upright as yours or mine. Any doubts about their upright posture were erased by the

Human   **Chimpanzee**

Figure 2.9 A comparison of the feet and hands of a human and a chimpanzee.

discovery of the fossilized footprints pictured in Figure 2.10 on page 30.

The first *Homo* species, **Homo erectus,** is thought to have evolved from a species of *Australopithecus* about 1.5 million years ago. It was so named because of the incorrect initial assumption that its predecessors were stooped. The most distinctive feature of the *Homo erectus* skull is its large brain cavity (about 850 cubic centimeters), larger than that of *Australopithecus* (about 500 cc), but smaller than that of modern humans (about 1,350 cc). *Homo erectus* used fire and tools (see Susman, 1994) and coexisted in Africa with *Australopithecus* for about 2 million years, until *Australopithecus* died out. *Homo erectus* spread through Europe and Asia.

About 200,000 years ago, *Homo erectus* was gradually replaced in the fossil record by modern humans (*Homo sapiens*). Paradoxically, although the big three human

---

Primates. One of 14 different orders of mammals; there are five families of primates: prosimians, New-World monkeys, Old-World monkeys, apes, and hominids.

Hominids. The family of primates that includes *Homo sapiens* (humans), *Homo erectus,* and *Australopithecus.*

Homo erectus. The first *Homo* species, thought to have evolved from *Australopithecus* about 1.5 million years ago and to have evolved into *Homo sapiens* about 200,000 years ago.

attributes—big brain, upright posture, and free hands with a workable opposing thumb—have been with us for hundreds of thousands of years, most human accomplishments are of recent origin. Artistic artifacts (e.g., wall paintings and carvings) did not appear until 25,000 years ago; ranching and farming were not established until 10,000 years ago, and writing did not appear until 3,000 years ago.

Figure 2.11 illustrates the main branches of vertebrate evolution. As you examine it, remember that fewer than 1% of all known species are still in existence, that evolution does not proceed in a straight line toward some optimal design (metaphorically, evolution is a bush, not a ladder), and that we humans have little reason to claim evolutionary supremacy—we are the last surviving species of a family (hominids) that has existed for only a blip of evolutionary time.

Evolution of the Human Brain

Early research on the evolution of the human brain focused on size. This research was stimulated by the assumption that brain size and intellectual capacity are closely related —an assumption that ran into two problems. First, it was shown that modern humans, whom modern humans believe to be the most intelligent of all creatures, do not have the biggest brains. At 1,350 grams, humans rank far behind whales and elephants, whose brains weigh between 5,000 and 8,000 grams (Harvey & Krebs, 1990). Second, the brains of deceased intellectuals (e.g., Einstein) were found to be no match for their gigantic intellects. Healthy adult human brains vary greatly in size—between about 1,000 and 2,000 grams—but there is no clear relationship between brain size and intelligence.

One obvious problem in relating brain size to intelligence is the fact that larger animals tend to have larger brains, presumably because larger bodies require more brain tissue to control and regulate them. Thus the fact that large men tend to have larger brains than small men, that men tend to have larger brains than women, and that elephants have larger brains than humans does not suggest

Figure 2.10 Fossilized footprints of Australopithecine hominids who strode across African volcanic ash about 3.6 million years ago. They left a 70-meter trail, which was discovered in 1978. There were two adults and a child; the child walked in the footsteps of the adults.

Brain stem. The part of the brain on which the cerebral hemispheres rest; in general, it regulates reflex activities that are critical for survival (e.g., heart rate and respiration).

Cerebrum. The portion of the brain that sits on the brain stem; in general, it plays a role in complex adaptive processes (e.g., learning, perception, and motivation).

Convolutions. Folds on the surface of the cerebral hemispheres.

anything about the relative intelligence of these populations. This has led to the proposal that brain weight expressed as a percentage of total body weight might be a better measure of intellectual capacity. This measure allows humans (2.33%) to take their rightful place ahead of elephants (0.20%), but it also allows both humans and elephants to be surpassed by that intellectual giant of the animal kingdom, the shrew (3.33%).

A more reasonable approach to the study of brain evolution has been to compare the evolution of different brain regions. For example, it has been informative to consider

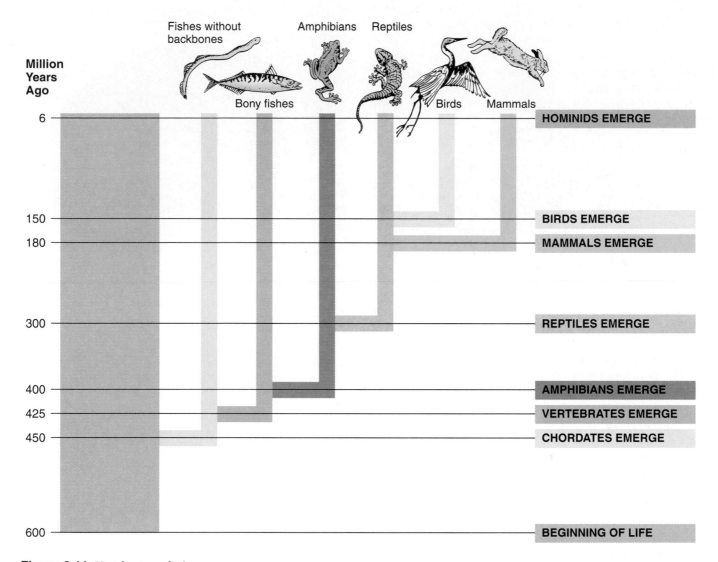

Figure 2.11 Vertebrate evolution.

the evolution of the **brain stem** separately from the evolution of the **cerebrum** (cerebral hemispheres). In general, the brain stem regulates reflex activities that are critical for survival (e.g., heart rate, respiration, and blood glucose level), whereas the cerebrum is involved in more complex adaptive processes such as learning, perception, and motivation.

Figure 2.12 on page 32 is a schematic representation of the relative size of the brain stems and cerebrums of several species that are living ancestors of species from which humans evolved. This figure makes three important points about the evolution of the human brain. The first is that it has increased in size during evolution; the second is that most of the increase in size has occurred in the cerebrum; and the third is that there has been an increase in the number of **convolutions**—folds on the cerebral surface—which

has greatly increased the volume of the cerebral cortex (the outermost layer of cerebral tissue).

More significant than the differences among the brains of various related species are the similarities. All brains are constructed of neurons, and the neural structures that compose the brains of one species can almost always be found in the brains of related species. For example, the brains of humans, monkeys, rats, and mice contain the same gross structures.

Conclusion

In this section, you have been confronted by two indisputable facts of life: (1) that we humans, like other living animals, are the cumulative products of 600 million years

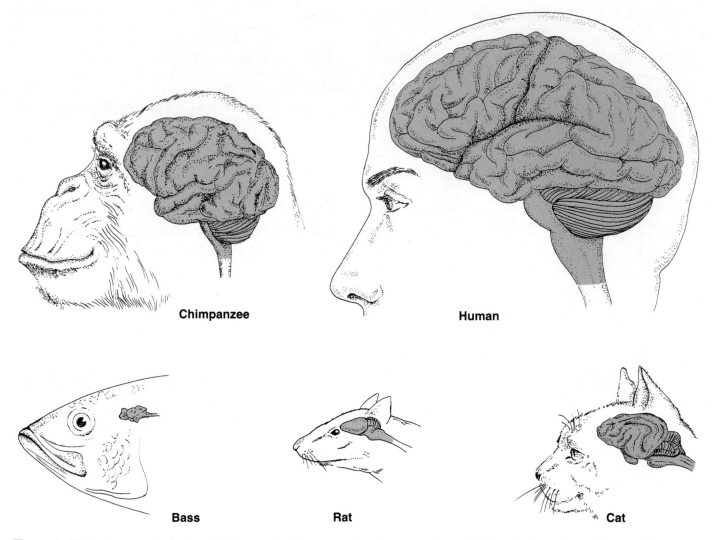

Figure 2.12 The brains of animals of different evolutionary age. Cerebrums are shown in beige; brain stems are shown in blue.

of adaptation; and (2) that we humans are related to all other animal species—in some cases more closely than we like to admit. These two truths are foundations on which two approaches to biopsychological research rest. Biopsychologists often study behavior and neural mechanisms by considering their adaptability and the environmental pressures that led to their evolution—this is called the **functional approach.** And biopsychologists often try to learn about the behaviors and neural mechanisms of one species, usually humans, by studying the behaviors and neural mechanisms of related species—this is called the **comparative approach.**

2.3 Fundamental Genetics

Darwin did not understand two of the key facts on which his theory of evolution was based. He did not understand why conspecifics differ from one another, and he did not understand how anatomical, physiological, and behavioral characteristics are passed from parent to offspring. While Darwin puzzled over these questions, there was an unread manuscript in his files that contained the answers. It had been sent to him by an unknown Augustinian monk, Gregor Mendel. Unfortunately for Darwin (1809–1882) and for Mendel (1822–1884), the significance of Mendel's research was not recognized until the early part of this century, well after both of their deaths.

Mendelian Genetics

Mendel studied inheritance in pea plants. In designing his experiments, he made two wise decisions. He decided to study dichotomous traits, and he decided to begin his experiments by crossing the offspring of true-breeding lines. **Dichotomous traits** are traits that occur in one form or the other, never in combination. For example, seed color is a dichotomous pea plant trait: Every pea plant has either brown seeds or white seeds. **True-breeding lines** are breeding lines in which interbred members always produce offspring with the same trait (e.g., brown seeds), generation after generation.

In one of his early experiments, Mendel studied the inheritance of seed color: brown or white. He began by cross breeding the offspring of a line of pea plants that had bred true for brown seeds with the offspring of a line of pea plants that had bred true for white seeds. The offspring of this cross all had brown seeds. Then Mendel bred these first-generation offspring with one another, and he found that about three-quarters of the resulting second-generation offspring had brown seeds and about one-quarter had white seeds. Mendel repeated this experiment many times with various pairs of dichotomous pea plant traits, and each time the result was the same. One trait, which Mendel called the **dominant trait,** appeared in all of the first-generation offspring; the other trait, which he called the **recessive trait,** appeared in about one-quarter of the second-generation offspring. Mendel would have obtained a similar result if he had conducted an experiment with true-breeding lines of brown-eyed (dominant) and blue-eyed (recessive) humans.

The results of Mendel's experiment challenged the central premise upon which all previous ideas about inheritance had rested: that offspring inherit the traits of their parents. Somehow, the recessive trait (white seeds) was passed on to one-quarter of the second-generation pea plants by first-generation pea plants that did not themselves possess it. An organism's observable traits are referred to as its **phenotype**; the traits that it can pass on to its offspring through its genetic material are referred to as its **genotype.**

Mendel devised a theory to explain his results. It comprised four ideas. First, Mendel proposed that there are two kinds of inherited factors for each dichotomous trait—for example, that a brown-seed factor and a white-seed factor control seed color. Today, we call each inherited factor a gene. Second, Mendel proposed that each organism possesses two genes for each of its dichotomous traits; for example, each pea plant possesses either two brown-seed genes, two white-seed genes, or one of each. Organisms that possess two identical genes for a trait are said to be **homozygous** for that trait; those that possess two different genes for a trait are said to be **heterozygous** for that trait. Third, Mendel proposed that one of the two kinds of genes for each dichotomous trait dominates the other in heterozygous organisms. For example, pea plants with a brown-seed gene and a white-seed gene always have brown seeds because the brown-seed gene always dominates the white-seed gene. And fourth, Mendel proposed that for each trait each organism randomly inherits one of its "father's" two factors and one of its "mother's" two factors. Figure 2.13 illustrates how Mendel's theory accounts for the result of his experiment on the inheritance of seed color in pea plants.

Functional approach. The study of behavior and neural mechanisms by consideration of their adaptiveness and of the environmental pressures that led to their evolution.

Comparative approach. Learning about behaviors and neural mechanisms (or about other biological processes) by comparing species.

Dichotomous traits. Traits that occur in one form or the other, never in combination.

True-breeding lines. Breeding lines in which interbred members always produce offspring with the same trait, generation after generation.

Dominant trait. The trait of a dichotomous pair that is expressed in the phenotypes of heterozygous individuals.

Recessive trait. The trait of a dichotomous pair that is not expressed in the phenotype of heterozygous individuals.

Phenotype. An organism's observable traits.

Genotype. The traits that an organism can pass on to its offspring in its genetic material.

Gene. A unit of inheritance; for example, the section of a chromosome that controls the synthesis of one protein.

Homozygous. Possessing two identical genes for a particular trait.

Heterozygous. Possessing two different genes for a particular trait.

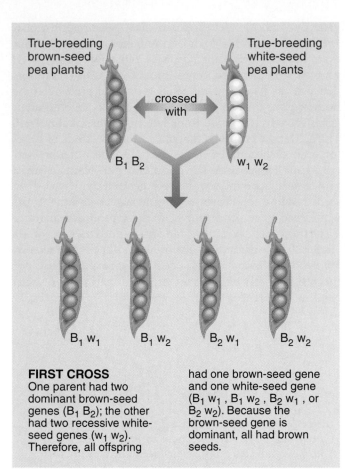

True-breeding brown-seed pea plants

crossed with

True-breeding white-seed pea plants

B_1 B_2

w_1 w_2

B_1 w_1 B_1 w_2 B_2 w_1 B_2 w_2

FIRST CROSS
One parent had two dominant brown-seed genes (B_1 B_2); the other had two recessive white-seed genes (w_1 w_2). Therefore, all offspring had one brown-seed gene and one white-seed gene (B_1 w_1 , B_1 w_2 , B_2 w_1 , or B_2 w_2). Because the brown-seed gene is dominant, all had brown seeds.

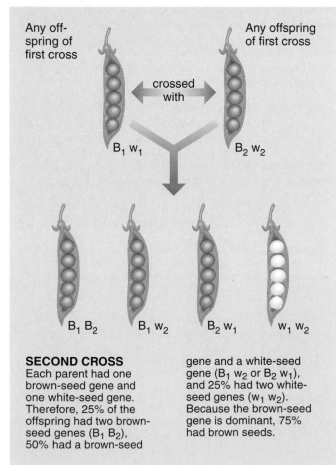

Any off-spring of first cross

crossed with

Any offspring of first cross

B_1 w_1

B_2 w_2

B_1 B_2 B_1 w_2 B_2 w_1 w_1 w_2

SECOND CROSS
Each parent had one brown-seed gene and one white-seed gene. Therefore, 25% of the offspring had two brown-seed genes (B_1 B_2), 50% had a brown-seed gene and a white-seed gene (B_1 w_2 or B_2 w_1), and 25% had two white-seed genes (w_1 w_2). Because the brown-seed gene is dominant, 75% had brown seeds.

Figure 2.13 How Mendel's theory accounts for the results of his experiment on the inheritance of seed color in pea plants.

Chromosomes, Reproduction, and Linkage

It was not until the early 1900s that genes were found to be located located on **chromosomes**—the threadlike structures in the *nucleus* of each cell. Chromosomes occur in matched pairs, and each species has a characteristic number of pairs in each of its body cells; humans have 23 pairs. The two genes that control each trait are situated at the same locus, one on each chromosome of a particular pair.

The process of cell division that produces **gametes** (egg cells and sperm cells) is called **meiosis** (pronounced "MY-oh-sis"). In meiosis, the chromosomes divide, and one chromosome of each pair goes to each of the two gametes that results from the division. As a result, each gamete has only half the usual number of chromosomes (23 in humans); and when a sperm cell and an egg cell combine during fertilization (see Figure 2.14), a **zygote** (a fertilized egg cell) with the full complement of chromosomes is produced. All other cell division in the body occurs by **mitosis** (pronounced "MY-toe-sis"). Just prior to mitotic division, the number of chromosomes doubles so that when the division occurs, both daughter cells end up with the full complement of chromosomes. Figure 2.15 on page 36 illustrates meiosis, fertilization, and mitosis.

Meiosis accounts for much of the genetic diversity within each species. In humans, for example, each meiotic division produces two gametes; each gamete contains 1 chromosome from each of the 23 pairs contained in each body cell. Because each of the 23 pairs is randomly sorted into the two gametes, each human can produce gametes with 2^{23} (8,388,608) different combinations of chromosomes.

The first comprehensive study of **linkage** was published in 1915 by Morgan and his colleagues. They found that there are four different clusters of fruit fly genes. If the gene for one trait in a cluster was inherited from one parent, that fruit fly had a higher probability (greater than 0.5) of inheriting genes for other traits in the cluster from the same parent. Because fruit flies have four pairs of chromosomes, Morgan and his colleagues concluded that linkage occurs between traits that are encoded on the same chromosome. They were correct; in every species in which linkage has been assessed, the number of clusters of linked traits has been found to equal the number of pairs of chromosomes.

If genes are passed from generation to generation on chromosomes, why are the genes on the same chromosome not always inherited together? The linkage between pairs of genes on a single chromosome varies from almost complete (close to 1.0) to just above chance (just over 0.5).

Figure 2.14 Fertilization. A sperm cell attaches itself to the surface of an egg cell.

somes, X and Y, and the two look different and carry different genes. Female mammals have two X chromosomes, and male mammals have an X and a Y. Traits that are influenced by genes on the sex chromosomes are referred to as **sex-linked traits.** Virtually all sex-linked traits are controlled by genes on the X chromosome because the Y chromosome is small and carries few genes other than those that cause an individual to develop into a male.

Traits that are controlled by genes on the X chromosome occur more frequently in one sex than the other. If the trait is dominant, it occurs more frequently in females. Females have twice the chance of inheriting the dominant gene because they have twice the number of X chromosomes. In contrast, recessive sex-linked traits occur more frequently in males. The reason is that recessive sex-linked traits are manifested only in females who possess two of the recessive genes—one on each of their X chromosomes—whereas the traits are manifested in all males who possess the gene because they have only one X chromosome. The classic example of a recessive sex-linked trait is color blindness. Because the color blindness gene is quite rare, females almost never inherit two of them and thus almost never possess the disorder; in contrast, every male who possesses one color blindness gene is color-blind.

Morgan and his colleagues proposed that **crossing over** provided the solution to the puzzle of partial linkage. Figure 2.16 on page 37 illustrates how crossing over works. During the first stage of meiosis, after the chromosomes have replicated, they line up in their pairs. Then they usually cross over one another at random points, break apart at the points of contact, and exchange sections of chromosome. As a result, parents rarely pass on intact chromosomal clusters of genes to their children. Each of your gametes contains chromosomes that are unique spliced-together combinations of chromosomes inherited from your mother and father.

The phenomenon of crossing over is important for two reasons. First, by ensuring that chromosomes are not passed intact from generation to generation, crossovers increase the diversity of the species; in a sense, crossing over shuffles the genetic deck before the chromosomes are randomly dealt out to the next generation. Second, the study of crossovers has been one of the major means by which geneticists have been able to construct **gene maps** for many species. Because each crossover occurs at a random point along the length of a chromosome, the degree of linkage between two genes indicates how close they are together on the chromosome. Crossovers rarely occur between adjacent genes, and they frequently occur between genes at opposite ends of a chromosome.

Sex Chromosomes and Sex-Linked Traits

There is one exception to the rule that chromosomes always come in matched pairs. That exception is the **sex chromosomes**—the pair of chromosomes that determines an individual's sex. There are two types of sex chromo-

Chromosomes. Threadlike genetic structures in the cell nucleus; each chromosome is a DNA molecule.

Gametes. Egg cells and sperm cells.

Meiosis. The process of cell division that produces cells (e.g., egg cells and sperm cells) with half the chromosomes of the parent cell.

Zygote. A fertilized egg cell.

Mitosis. The process of cell division that produces cells with the same number of chromosomes as the parent cell.

Linkage. The tendency for traits that are encoded on the same chromosome to be inherited together.

Crossing over. The exchange of sections between pairs of chromosomes during the first stage of meiosis.

Gene maps. Maps that indicate the relative positions of genes along a chromosome.

Sex chromosomes. The pair of chromosomes that determine an individual's sex: XX for a female and XY for a male.

Sex-linked traits. Traits that are influenced by genes on the sex chromosomes.

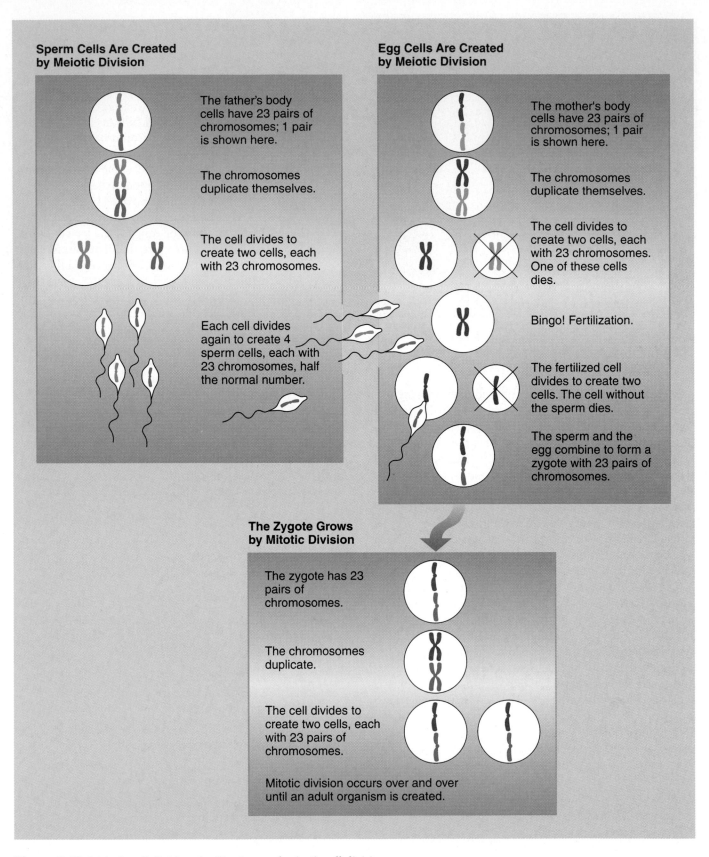

Sperm Cells Are Created by Meiotic Division

The father's body cells have 23 pairs of chromosomes; 1 pair is shown here.

The chromosomes duplicate themselves.

The cell divides to create two cells, each with 23 chromosomes.

Each cell divides again to create 4 sperm cells, each with 23 chromosomes, half the normal number.

Egg Cells Are Created by Meiotic Division

The mother's body cells have 23 pairs of chromosomes; 1 pair is shown here.

The chromosomes duplicate themselves.

The cell divides to create two cells, each with 23 chromosomes. One of these cells dies.

Bingo! Fertilization.

The fertilized cell divides to create two cells. The cell without the sperm dies.

The sperm and the egg combine to form a zygote with 23 pairs of chromosomes.

The Zygote Grows by Mitotic Division

The zygote has 23 pairs of chromosomes.

The chromosomes duplicate.

The cell divides to create two cells, each with 23 pairs of chromosomes.

Mitotic division occurs over and over until an adult organism is created.

Figure 2.15 Meiotic cell division, fertilization, and mitotic cell division.

During meiosis, homologous chromosomes line up parallel to each other.

Then, they replicate their genetic materal.

Next, one chromosome crosses over the other chromosome

The crossed-over chromosomes break apart at the crossover and exchange segments.

Crossing over shuffles the genetic material; it is why not all the genes on a chromosome are not always inherited together.

Figure 2.16 Crossing over.

Chromosome Structure and Replication

Each chromosome is a double-stranded molecule of **deoxyribonucleic acid (DNA).** Each strand is a sequence of **nucleotide bases** attached to a chain of *phosphate* and *deoxyribose*; there are four nucleotide bases: *adenine, thymine, guanine,* and *cytosine.* It is the sequence of these bases on each chromosome that constitutes the genetic code—just as the sequence of letters constitutes the code of our language.

The two strands that compose each chromosome are coiled around each other and bonded together by the attraction of adenine for thymine and guanine for cytosine. This specific bonding pattern has an important consequence: The two strands that compose each chromosome are exact complements of each other. For example, the sequence of adenine, guanine, thymine, cytosine, and guanine on one strand is always attached to the complementary sequence of thymine, cytosine, adenine, guanine, and

Deoxyribonucleic acid (DNA). Double-stranded, coiled molecules of genetic material; chromosomes.

Nucleotide bases. A class of molecules that includes adenine, thymine, guanine, and cytosine—the constituents of the genertic code.

Adenine and thymine bind

Guanine and cytosine bind

Figure 2.17 A schematic illustration of the structure of a DNA molecule. Notice the complementary binding of nucleotide bases: thymine to adenine, and guanine to cytosine.

cytosine on the other. Figure 2.17 illustrates the structure of DNA. Figure 2.18 on page 38 is a computer enhancement of the surface of several DNA molecules.

Figure 2.18 A computer-coded image of the surface of a DNA molecule.

components of their structure. All the cells in the body (e.g., brain cells, hair cells, and bone cells) contain exactly the same structural genes. How then do different kinds of cells develop? The answer lies in another category of genes, the **operator gene.** Each operator gene controls a structural gene or a group of related structural genes; its function is to determine whether or not each of its structural genes initiates the synthesis of a protein (i.e., whether or not the structural gene will be expressed).

The control of **gene expression** by operator genes is an important process because it determines how a cell will develop and how it will function once it reaches maturity. Operator genes are like switches; and like switches, they can be regulated in two ways. Some operator genes are normally off, and they are regulated by **DNA-binding proteins** that turn them on; others are normally on, and they are reg-

Replication is a critical process of the DNA molecule. Without it, mitotic cell division would not be possible. Figure 2.19 illustrates how DNA replication works. The two strands of DNA start to unwind. Then the exposed nucleotide bases on each of the two strands attract loose complementary bases from the fluid of the nucleus. Thus, when the unwinding is complete, two double-stranded DNA molecules, both of which are identical to the original, have been created.

Chromosome replication does not always go according to plan; there may be errors. Sometimes, these errors are gross errors. For example, in *Down syndrome,* which you will learn about in Chapter 6, there is an extra chromosome in each cell. But more commonly, errors in duplication take the form of **mutations**—accidental alterations in individual genes. In most cases, mutations disappear from the genetic pool within a few generations because the organisms that inherit them are less fit. However, in rare instances, mutations increase fitness and in so doing contribute to the evolution of the species.

The Genetic Code and Gene Expression

There are several different kinds of genes. The most prevalent are the **structural genes**—genes that contain the information necessary for the synthesis of a single protein. **Proteins** are long chains of **amino acids** that control the physiological activities of cells and are important

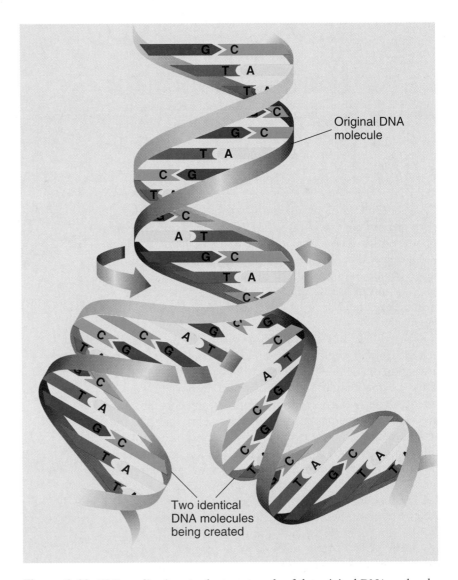

Original DNA molecule

Two identical DNA molecules being created

Figure 2.19 DNA replication. As the two strands of the original DNA molecule unwind, the nucleotide bases on each strand attract loose complementary bases. Once the unwinding is complete, two DNA molecules, each identical to the first, have been created.

ulated by DNA-binding proteins that turn them off. Many of the DNA-binding proteins that control operator genes are activated by signals received by the cell from its environment. This, then, is a major mechanism by which experience interacts with genes to influence development.

The expression of a structural gene begins when it is activated by its operator gene. The process is illustrated in Figure 2.20 on page 40. First, the small section of the chromosome that contains the structural gene unravels, and the unraveled section of one of the DNA strands serves as a template for the transcription of a short strand of **ribonucleic acid (RNA).** RNA is like DNA except that it has uracil bases instead of thymine bases and a phosphate and ribose backbone instead of a phosphate and deoxyribose backbone. The strand of transcribed RNA is called **messenger RNA** because it carries the genetic code from the nucleus of the cell. Once it has left the nucleus, the messenger RNA attaches itself to one of the many **ribosomes** in the cell's *cytoplasm* (the clear inner fluid of the cell). The ribosome then moves along the strand of messenger RNA, translating the genetic code as it proceeds.

Each group of three consecutive nucleotide bases along the messenger RNA strand is called a **codon.** Each codon instructs the ribosome to add 1 of the 20 different kinds of amino acids to the protein that it is constructing; for example, the sequence guanine-guanine-adenine instructs the ribosome to add the amino acid glycine. Each kind of amino acid is carried to the ribosome by molecules of **transfer RNA**; and as the ribosome reads a codon, it attracts a transfer RNA molecule that is attached to the appropriate amino acid. The ribosome reads codon after codon and adds amino acid after amino acid until it reaches a codon that tells it the protein is complete, whereupon the completed protein is released into the cytoplasm. Thus, the process of gene expression involves two phases: the *transcription* of the DNA base-sequence code to an RNA base-sequence code and the *translation* of the RNA base-sequence code into a sequence of amino acids.

Human Genome Project

Arguably, the most ambitious scientific project of all time began in 1990. Known as the **human genome project,** it is a loosely knit collaboration of major research institutions and individual research teams in many different countries. Its primary goal is the construction of a detailed physical map of each of the human chromosomes (see Cox et al., 1994) to facilitate the identification of the approximately 200,000 genes in the human genome (Capecchi, 1994).

The mapping is done as follows. First, samples of the chromosome of interest are exposed to enzymes that break them into many small segments. Next, the segments are cloned so that the researchers will have an unlimited supply of each. Then, the segments are exposed to chemical markers that uniquely label specific loci along their length. Finally, the patterns of markers on the segments are exam-

ined in an effort to locate identical patterns on two segments—an indication that they are overlapping segments of the same chromosome. Once a chromosome is physically mapped, banks of short cloned DNA segments of known location along the chromosome will be available to scientists interested in studying them.

The immediate goal of the human genome project is to develop physical maps of the human genome that involve at least 30,000 equally spaced unique landmarks. With the large number of geneticists participating in the project, this task will almost certainly be accomplished by the turn of the century. An ancillary goal of the project is to map the mouse genome (see Ringwald et al., 1994); the mouse is the favorite mammalian subject of genetic research.

The physical mapping of the human and mouse genomes will provide genetic materials, knowledge, and techniques

Replication. The process by which the DNA molecule duplicates itself.

Mutations. Abnormal genes that are created by accidents of chromosome duplication.

Structural genes. Genes that contain the information required for the synthesis of a particular protein.

Proteins. Long chains of amino acids.

Amino acids. The chemical elements from which proteins are synthesized.

Operator gene. A short segment of DNA that determines whether or not messenger RNA will be transcribed from adjacent structural genes.

Gene expression. The production of the protein specified by a particular gene.

DNA-binding proteins. Proteins that bind to DNA molecules and in so doing either induce or block gene expression.

Ribonucleic acid (RNA). A molecule that is similar to DNA except that it has uracil nucleotide bases and a phosphate and ribose backbone.

Messenger RNA. The strands of RNA that are transcribed from DNA and direct the synthesis of proteins.

Ribosome. A structure in the cytoplasm that reads the genetic code from strands of messenger RNA.

Codon. A group of three consecutive nucleotide bases on a DNA molecule; each codon specifies the particular amino acid that is to be added to an amino acid chain during protein synthesis.

Transfer RNA. Molecules of RNA that carry amino acids to ribosomes during protein synthesis; each kind of amino acid is carried by a different kind of transfer RNA molecule.

Human genome project. The international effort to construct a detailed physical map of the human chromosomes.

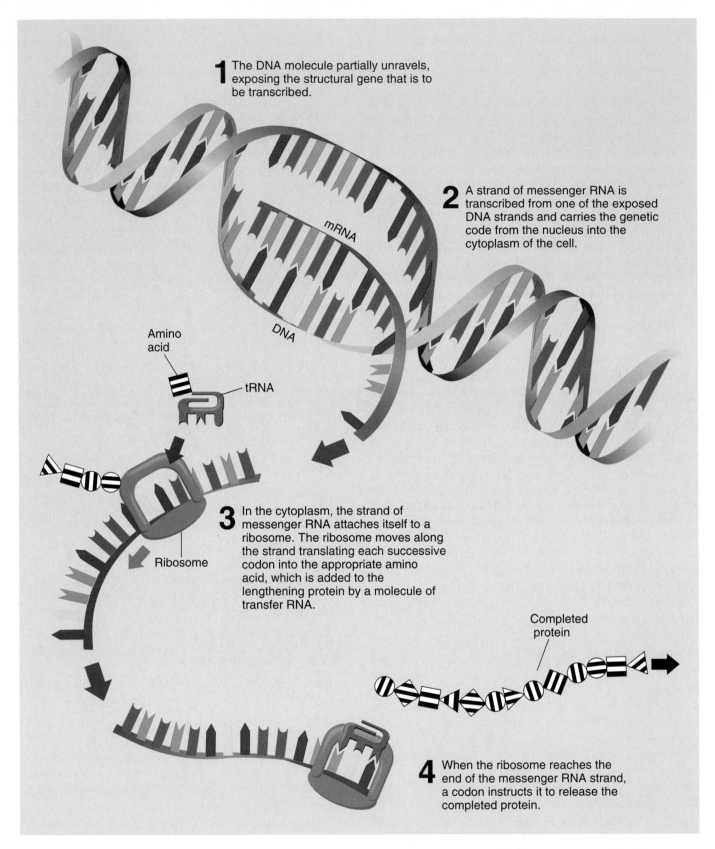

1 The DNA molecule partially unravels, exposing the structural gene that is to be transcribed.

2 A strand of messenger RNA is transcribed from one of the exposed DNA strands and carries the genetic code from the nucleus into the cytoplasm of the cell.

mRNA

DNA

Amino acid

tRNA

3 In the cytoplasm, the strand of messenger RNA attaches itself to a ribosome. The ribosome moves along the strand translating each successive codon into the appropriate amino acid, which is added to the lengthening protein by a molecule of transfer RNA.

Ribosome

Completed protein

4 When the ribosome reaches the end of the messenger RNA strand, a codon instructs it to release the completed protein.

Figure 2.20 Gene expression: transcription of a section of DNA into a complementary strand of messenger RNA, then the translation of the messenger RNA strand into a protein.

This is a good point at which to pause and consolidate what you have learned so far in this chapter. Fill in the following blanks with the most appropriate terms from the first three sections of the chapter. The correct answers are provided at the bottom of this page. Before proceeding, review material related to your errors and omissions.

1. The _____ side of the nature-nurture controversy is that all behavior is learned.

2. Physiological-or-psychological thinking was given official recognition in the 1600s when the Roman Church sanctioned _____ _____.

3. In the Darwinian sense, _____ refers to the ability of an organism to survive and produce large numbers of fertile offspring.

4. A _____ is a group of reproductively isolated organisms.

5. Mammals are thought to have evolved from _____ about 180 million years ago.

6. There are five different families of primates: prosimians, New-World monkeys, Old-World monkeys, _____, and _____.

7. _____ are the closest living relatives of humans; they have 99% of the same genetic material.

8. The first hominids were _____.

9. An organism's observable traits are its _____; the traits that it can pass to its offspring through its genetic material are its _____.

10. The degree of _____ between two genes is a measure of how close they are together on a chromosome.

11. Each structural gene contains the information for the production of a single _____.

12. Structural genes are turned off or on by _____ genes.

13. The massive international effort to physically map human chromosomes is known as the _____ project.

necessary for rapid progress in the diagnosis, treatment, and prevention of genetically based disorders. It will also be a boon to behavioral scientists interested in the contributions of genes to normal behavioral variation. Much of this progress will be realized during your lifetime: What once seemed the stuff of science fiction is within our grasp.

The answers are (1) nurture, (2) Cartesian dualism, (3) fitness, (4) species, (5) reptiles, (6) apes and hominids, (7) chimpanzees, (8) Australopithecines, (9) phenotype, genotype, (10) linkage, (11) protein, (12) operator, (13) human genome.

Behavioral Development: The Interaction of Genetic Factors and Experience

This section of the chapter provides three classic examples of how genetic factors and experience interact to direct behavioral ontogeny. **Ontogeny** is the development of individuals through their life span. **Phylogeny,** in contrast, is the evolutionary development of species through the ages.

Selective Breeding of "Maze-Bright" and "Maze-Dull" Rats

You have already learned in this chapter that nature-or-nurture thinking dominated the study of behavior during the first half of this century and that most psychologists of that era assumed that behavior develops largely through learning. Tryon (1934) undermined this assumption by showing that behavioral traits can be selectively bred.

Tryon focused his selective-breeding experiments on the very behavior that had been the focus of early psychologists in their investigations of learning: the maze running of laboratory rats. Tryon began by training a large heterogeneous group of laboratory rats to run a complex maze; the rats received a food reward when they reached the goal box. Tryon then mated the females and males that least frequently entered incorrect alleys during training—he referred to these rats as *maze-bright.* And he bred the females and males that most frequently entered incorrect alleys during training—he referred to these rats as *maze-dull.*

When the offspring of the maze-bright and of the maze-dull rats matured, their maze-learning performance was assessed. Then, the brightest of the maze-bright offspring were mated with one another and so were the dullest of the maze-dull offspring. This selective breeding procedure was continued for 21 generations, and the descendants of Tryon's original strains are available today to those interested in studying them. By the 8th generation, there was almost no overlap in the maze-learning performance of the two strains. With a few exceptions, the worst of the maze-bright strain made fewer errors than the best of the maze-dull strain (see Figure 2.21).

To control for the possibility that good maze-running performance was somehow being passed from parent to off-spring through learning, Tryon used a *cross-fostering control procedure*: He tested maze-bright offspring that had been reared by maze-dull parents and maze-dull offspring that had been reared by maze-bright parents. However, the offspring of maze-bright rats made few errors even when they were reared by maze-dull rats, and the offspring of maze-dull rats made many errors even when they were reared by maze-bright rats.

Since Tryon's seminal selective-breeding experiments, many behavioral traits have been selectively bred. Among them are open-field activity in mice, susceptibility to alcohol-induced sleep in mice, susceptibility to alcohol-withdrawal seizures in mice, nest building in mice, avoidance learning in rats, and mating in fruit flies. Indeed, it appears that any measurable behavioral trait that varies among members of a species can be selectively bred.

An important general point made by studies of selective breeding is that selective breeding based on one behavioral trait usually brings a host of other behavioral traits along

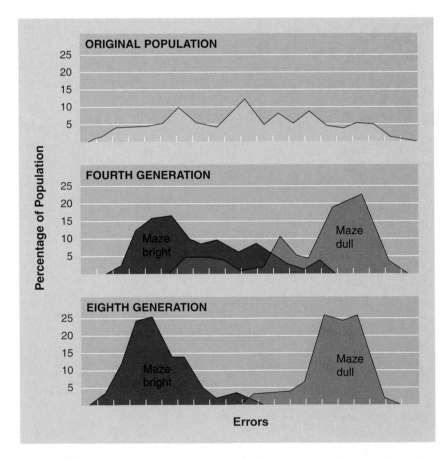

Figure 2.21 Selective breeding of maze-bright and maze-dull strains of rats by Tryon (1934).

with it. This indicates that the behavioral trait used as the criterion for selective breeding is not the only behavioral trait that is influenced by the genes segregated by the breeding. Thus, in order to characterize the behavioral function of the segregated genes, it is necessary to compare the performance of the selectively bred strains on a variety of tests. For example, Searle (1949) compared maze-dull and maze-bright rats on 30 different behavioral tests and found that they differed on many of them; the pattern of differences suggested that the maze-bright rats were superior maze learners not because they were more intelligent but because they were less emotional.

Selective-breeding studies have proved that genes influence the development of behavior. This conclusion in no way implies that experience does not. This point was clearly illustrated by Cooper and Zubek (1958) in a classic study of maze-bright and maze-dull rats. The researchers reared maze-bright and maze-dull rats in one of two environments: (1) an impoverished environment (a barren wire-mesh group cage) or (2) an enriched environment (a wire-mesh group cage that contained tunnels, ramps, visual displays, and other objects designed to stimulate interest). When the maze-dull rats reached maturity, they made significantly more errors than the maze-bright rats only if they had been reared in the impoverished environment (see Figure 2.22). Apparently, enriched early environments can overcome the negative effects of disadvantaged genes. Indeed, rats reared in enriched environments develop thicker cerebral cortexes than those reared in impoverished environments (Bennett et al., 1964).

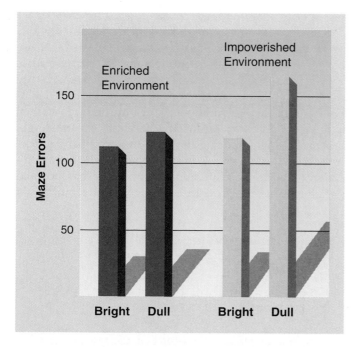

Figure 2.22 Maze-dull rats did not make significantly more errors than maze-bright rats when they were both reared in an enriched environment (Cooper & Zubek, 1958).

Phenylketonuria: A Single-Gene Metabolic Disorder

In contrast to what you might expect, it is often easier to understand the genetics of a behavioral disorder than it is to understand the genetics of normal behavior. The reason is that many genes influence the development of a normal behavioral trait, but it often takes only one abnormal gene to screw it up (see Plomin, Owen, & McGuffin, 1994). A good example of this point is the neurological disorder **phenylketonuria (PKU)**.

PKU was discovered in 1934 when a Norwegian dentist, Asbjörn Fölling, noticed a peculiar odor in the urine of his two mentally retarded children. He correctly assumed that the odor was related to their disorder, and he had their urine analyzed. High levels of **phenylpyruvic acid** were found in both samples. Spurred on by his discovery, Fölling identified other retarded children who had abnormally high levels of urinary phenylpyruvic acid, and he concluded that this subpopulation of retarded children was suffering from the same disorder. In addition to mental retardation, the symptoms of PKU include vomiting, seizures, hyperactivity, and hyperirritability.

The pattern of transmission of PKU through the family trees of afflicted individuals indicates that it is transmitted by a single gene mutation. About 1 in 100 people of European descent carry the PKU gene; but because the gene is recessive, PKU develops only in homozygous individuals (those who inherit a PKU gene from both their mother and their father). In the United States, about 1 in 10,000 white infants is born with PKU; the incidence is much lower among black infants.

The biochemistry of PKU turned out to be reasonably straightforward. PKU homozygotes lack *phenylalanine hydroxylase*, an enzyme that is required for the conversion of the amino acid *phenylalanine* to *tyrosine*. As a result, phenylalanine accumulates in the body; and levels of *dopamine*, a neurotransmitter normally synthesized from tyrosine, are low. The consequence is abnormal brain development.

Like other behavioral traits, the behavioral symptoms of PKU result from an interaction between genetic and environmental factors: between the PKU gene and diet.

Ontogeny. The development of individuals through their life span.

Phylogeny. The evolutionary development of species.

Phenylketonuria (PKU). A neurological disorder whose symptoms are vomiting, seizures, hyperactivity, hyperirritability, mental retardation, and high levels of phenylpyruvic acid in the urine.

Phenylpyruvic acid. A substance that is found in abnormally high concentrations in the urine of those suffering from phenylketonuria.

Accordingly, in most modern hospitals, the blood of each newborn infant is routinely screened for a high phenylalanine level. If the level is high, the infant is immediately placed on a special phenylalanine-reduced diet; this diet reduces both the amount of phenylalanine in the blood and the development of mental retardation. The timing of the treatment is extremely important. The phenylalanine-reduced diet does not significantly reduce the development of mental retardation in PKU homozygotes unless it is initiated within the first few weeks of life; conversely, the restriction of phenylalanine in the diet is usually relaxed in late childhood, with few obvious adverse consequences. The period of development, usually early in life, during which a particular experience must occur to have a major effect on development is its **sensitive period.**

Diamond and her colleagues (e.g., Herzberg & Diamond, 1993) recently shed new light on the treatment of PKU and on the nature of the disorder. First, they showed that early application of the standard phenylalanine-reduced diet reduces, but does not prevent, the development of cognitive deficits. PKU children on the special diet performed more poorly than healthy children on several tests of cognitive ability. This finding is consistent with the fact that the blood levels of phenylalanine in PKU children on the standard phenylalanine-reduced diets tend to remain above normal. The cognitive deficits observed by Diamond and her colleagues (e.g., deficits in the ability to inhibit inappropriate responses) suggests prefrontal lobe damage. Diamond recommended putting all PKU children with elevated phenylalanine levels on stricter phenylalanine-reduced diets, and she suggested that the therapeutic potential of drugs that elevate prefrontal dopamine levels be quickly assessed.

Development of Birdsong

In the spring, the songs of male songbirds threaten conspecific male trespassers and attract potential mates. The males of each species sing similar songs that are readily distinguishable from the songs of other species (see Marler & Nelson, 1992), and there are recognizable local dialects within each species (see King & West, 1990).

Studies of the ontogenetic development of birdsong suggest that birdsong develops in two phases (see Marler, 1991; Nottebohm, 1991). The first phase, called the **sensory phase,** begins several days after hatching. Although the young birds do not sing during this phase, they form memories of the adult songs they hear—usually sung by their own male relatives—which later guide the development of

Figure 2.23 Male zebra finches (age-limited song learners) and male canaries (open-ended song learners) are common subjects of research on birdsong development. (Illustration kindly provided by *Trends in Neuroscience*; original photograph by Arturo Alvarez-Buylla.)

their own singing. The young males of many songbird species are genetically prepared to acquire the songs of their own species during the sensory phase. They cannot readily acquire the songs of other species; nor can they acquire the songs of their own species if they do not hear them during the sensory phase (see Petrinovich, 1990). Males who do not hear the songs of their own species early in their lives may later develop a song, but it is likely to be highly abnormal with only a few recognizable features of their species' mature songs.

The second phase of birdsong development, the **sensorimotor phase,** begins when the juvenile males begin to twitter *subsongs* (the immature songs of young birds), usually when they are several months old. During this phase, the rambling vocalizations of subsongs are gradually refined until they resemble the songs of the birds' earlier adult tutors. Auditory feedback is necessary for the development of singing during the sensorimotor phase; unless the young birds are able to hear themselves sing, their subsongs do not develop into adult songs. However, once stable adult song has crystallized, songbirds are much less

Sensitive period. The period of development during which a particular experience must occur to have a major effect on development.

Sensory phase. The first of the two phases of birdsong development, during which young birds do not sing but form memories of the adult songs they hear.

Sensorimotor phase. The second of the two phases of birdsong development, during which juvenile birds progress from subsong to adult song.

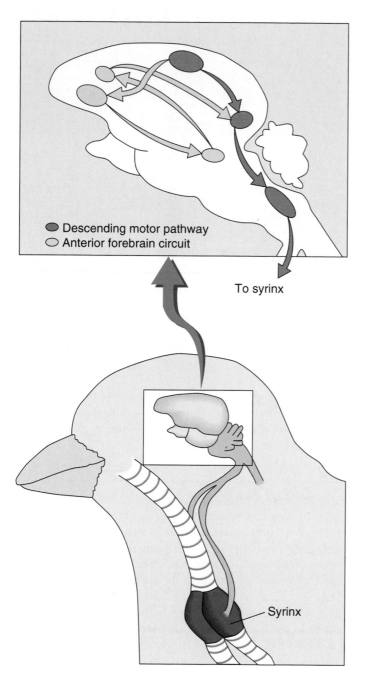

Figure 2.24 The neural circuit responsible for the production and learning of song in the male canary.

Descending motor pathway
Anterior forebrain circuit

To syrinx

Syrinx

dependent on hearing for normal song production; the disruptive effects of deafening on adult song are usually less severe, and they require several months to be fully realized (Nordeen & Nordeen, 1992).

When it comes to the retention of their initial crystallized adult songs, there are two common patterns among songbird species. Most songbird species, such as the widely studied zebra finches and white-crowned sparrows, are *age-limited learners*; in these species, adult songs, once crystallized, remain unchanged for the rest of the birds' lives. In contrast, some species are *open-ended learners*; they are able to add new songs to their repertoire throughout their lives. For example, at the end of each mating season, male canaries return from a period of stable song to a period of plastic song—a period during which they can add new songs for the next mating season. Male zebra finches (age-limited learners) and male canaries (open-ended learners) are shown in Figure 2.23.

Figure 2.24 is a simplified version of the neural circuit that controls birdsong in the canary. It has two major components: the descending motor pathway and the anterior forebrain pathway. The *descending motor pathway* descends from the high vocal center on each side of the brain to the *syrinx* (voice box) on the same side; it mediates song production. The *anterior forebrain pathway* mediates song learning (Doupe, 1993; Vicario, 1991).

The canary song circuit is remarkable in four respects (Nottebohm, 1991). First, the left descending motor circuit plays a more important role in singing than the right descending motor circuit (which duplicates the left-hemisphere dominance for language in humans). Second, the high vocal center is four times larger in male canaries than in females. Third, each spring, as the male canary prepares its new repertoire of songs for the summer seduction, the song-control structures of its brain double in size, only to shrink back in the fall; this springtime burst of brain growth and singing is triggered by elevated levels of the hormone testosterone that result from the increasing daylight. Fourth, the seasonal increase in size of the song-control brain structures results from the growth of new neurons, not from an increase in the size of existing ones—a result that is remarkable because the growth of new neurons in adult vertebrates was until recently assumed to be impossible.

2.5 The Genetics of Human Psychological Differences

So far, this chapter has focused on three topics—human evolution, genetics, and the interaction of genetics and experience in psychological development. All three topics converge on one fundamental question: Why are we the way we are? You have learned that each of us is a product of gene-experience interactions and that the effects of genes and experience on individual development are inseparable—

remember the metaphor of the musical mountaineer and the panpipe. In view of the fact that I have emphasized these points at every opportunity throughout the chapter, I am certain that you appreciate them by now. However, I am raising them again one last time because this final section of the chapter focuses on a developmental issue that is fundamentally different from the ones that we have been discussing.

Development of the Individual versus Development of Differences among Individuals

So far, this chapter has dealt with the development of the individual. The remainder of the chapter deals with the development of differences among individuals. In the development of the individual, the effects of genes and experience are inseparable. In the development of differences among individuals, they are separable. This distinction is extremely important, but it confuses many people. Let me return to the mountaineer-and-panpipe metaphor to explain it.

The music of an individual panpipe musician is the product of the interaction of the musician and the panpipe, and it is nonsensical to ask what proportion of the music is produced by the musician and what proportion by the panpipe. However, if we measured the panpipe playing of a large sample of subjects, we could statistically estimate the degree to which the differences among them in the quality of their music resulted from differences in the subjects themselves as opposed to differences in their instruments. For example, if we selected 100 Peruvians at random and gave each a test on a professional-quality panpipe, we would likely find that most of the variation in the quality of the music resulted from differences in the subjects, some being experienced players and some never having played before. In the same way, behavioral geneticists measure a behavioral attribute of a group of subjects (e.g., the IQ of human subjects) and ask what proportion of the variation among the subjects resulted from genetic differences as opposed to experiential differences.

To assess the relative contributions of genes and experience to the development of differences in psychological attributes, behavioral geneticists study individuals of varying genetic similarity. For example, they often compare **identical twins** (monozygotic twins), who developed from the same zygote and thus are genetically identical, with **fraternal twins** (dizygotic twins), who developed from two zygotes and thus are no more similar than any pair of siblings. Studies of identical and fraternal twins who have been separated at infancy by adoption are particularly informative about the relative contributions of genetics and experience to differences in human psychological develop-

Figure 2.25 The average correlations between the intelligence quotients of identical twins in the Minnesota study.

ment (see Segal, 1993). The most extensive of such studies is the Minnesota Study of Twins Reared Apart (see Bouchard et al., 1990; Bouchard, 1994).

Minnesota Study of Twins Reared Apart

The Minnesota Study of Twins Reared Apart involved 59 pairs of identical twins and 47 pairs of fraternal twins who had been reared apart, as well as many pairs of identical and fraternal twins who had been reared together. Their ages ranged from 19 to 68 years. Each twin was brought to the University of Minnesota for approximately 50 hours of testing, which focused on the assessment of intelligence and personality. Would the identical twins reared apart prove to be similar because they were genetically identical, or would they prove to be different because they had been brought up in different family environments?

The identical twins proved to be similar in both intelligence and personality, whether they had been reared together or apart. For example, the average correlation between the intelligence quotients (IQs) of identical twins on the Wechsler Adult Intelligence Scale was about 0.85 for those who had been reared together and about 0.70 for those who had been reared apart (see Figure 2.25); the correlations for fraternal twins have not yet been published. The high correlation coefficients for identical twins indicate that genetic differences were major contributing factors to the observed differences between the subjects' IQs, but the fact that the correlations were not 1.00 indicates that differences in experience also contributed to the IQ differences in the study.

The results of the Minnesota study have been widely disseminated by the popular press. Unfortunately, the mean-

Identical twins. Twins that develop from the same zygote and are thus genetically identical; monozygotic twins.

Fraternal twins. Twins that develop from different zygotes and thus are no more likely to be similar than any pair of siblings; dizygotic twins.

Heritability estimate. An estimate of the proportion of variability occurring in a particular trait in a particular study that resulted from the genetic variation among the subjects in that study.

Chapter 2   Evolution, Genetics, and Experience

ing of the results has often been distorted. Sometimes, the misrepresentation of science by the popular press does not matter—at least not much. This is not one of those times. People's misbeliefs about the origins of human intelligence and personality are often translated into inappropriate and discriminatory social attitudes and practices. The news story "Twins Prove Intelligence and Personality Inherited" illustrates how the results of the Minnesota study have been presented to the public.

This story is misleading in four ways. You should have no difficulty spotting the first; it oozes nature-or-nurture thinking and all of the misconceptions associated with it. Second, by focusing on the similarities of Bob and Bob, the story cre-

The Minnesota Signal, Tuesday, November 19

Twins prove intelligence and personality inherited

Bob and Bob don't know each other. But they were born on the same day, graduated with engineering degrees in the same year, and both married teachers named Brenda. They both wear glasses, have mustaches, and smoke a pipe.

Bob and Bob are 38-year old identical twins who were separated by adoption shortly after birth.

Dr. Thomas Bouchard and his colleagues recently brought Bob and Bob and 55 other pairs of genetically identical twins reared apart to the University of Minnesota.

Each twin underwent 50 hours of intensive psychological testing.

Dr. Bouchard found that the pairs of twins were almost identical in their intelligence and personality, despite having been reared by different families.

These findings are spearheading a psychological revolution.

They show that intelligence and personality are mostly genetic rather than being the result of experience, as thought by most psychologists.

The heritability estimates for IQ were found to be 70.

Nancy Baynes, chairperson of the school board, when contacted said, "We will certainly be discussing the implications of these important findings at our next meeting."

ates the impression that Bob and Bob (and the other monozygotic pairs of twins reared apart) are virtually identical. They are not. It is easy to come up with a long list of similarities between any two people if one asks them enough questions and ignores the dissimilarities. Third, the story creates the impression that the results of the Minnesota study are revolutionary. On the contrary, the importance of the Minnesota study lies mainly in the fact that it constitutes a particularly thorough confirmation of the results of previous adoption studies (see Plomin, 1990). Fourth, the story creates the false impression that the results of the Minnesota study make some general point about the relative contributions of genes and experience to the development of intelligence and personality in individuals. It does not, and neither does any other adoption study. Bouchard and his colleagues estimated the heritability of IQ to be 0.70, but they did not conclude that IQ is 70% genetic. A **heritability estimate** is an estimate of the proportion of variability occurring in a particular trait in a particular study that resulted from the genetic variation in that study. Thus heritability estimates tell us about the contribution of genetic differences to phenotypic differences among subjects; they have nothing to say about the relative contributions of genes and experience to the development of individuals.

The magnitude of a study's heritability estimate depends on the amount of genetic and environmental variation from which it was calculated, and it cannot be applied to other kinds of situations. For example, in the Minnesota study, there was relatively little environmental variation. All subjects were raised in industrialized countries (e.g., Great Britain, Canada, and the United States) by parents who could meet the strict standards required for adoption. Accordingly, most of the variation in the subjects' intelligence and personality resulted from genetic variation. If the twins had been separately adopted by European royalty, African Bushmen, Hungarian Gypsies, Los Angeles rap stars, London advertising executives, and Argentinian army officers, the resulting heritability estimates for IQ and personality would likely have been much lower. Bouchard et al. emphasize this point in their papers. Still, selective-breeding studies in laboratory animals and twin studies in humans have revealed no psychological differences that do not have a significant genetic component.

A commonly overlooked point about the role of genetic factors in the development of human psychological differences is that genetic differences promote psychological differences by influencing experience (see Plomin & Neiderhiser, 1992). At first, this statement seems paradoxical because we have been conditioned to think of genes and experience as separate developmental influences. However, there is now ample evidence that individuals of similar genetic endowment tend to seek out similar environments and experiences. For example, individuals whose genetic endowments promote aggression are likely to become involved in aggressive activities (e.g., football or competitive fighting), and these experiences are likely to further contribute to the development of aggressive tendencies.

CONCLUSION

In this chapter, you first learned how to think productively about the biology of behavior. You learned that biopsychologists have rejected conventional physiological-or-psychological and nature-or-nurture dichotomies in favor of more enlightened alternatives. They view all behavior and the psychological processes that underlie it as products of neural activity shaped by the interaction among genes, which are the products of evolution, experience, and the current situation (2.1). Then, you learned about the course of human evolution (2.2), about fundamental genetics (2.3), and about the interaction of genetic factors and experience in behavioral development (2.4). Finally, you learned about the genetics of human intellectual and personality differences (2.5).

FOOD FOR THOUGHT

1. Nature-or-nurture thinking about intelligence is sometimes used as an excuse for racial discrimination. How can the interactionist approach, which has been championed in this chapter, be used as a basis for arguing against discriminatory practices?

2. Imagine that you are a biopsychology instructor. One of your students asks you whether depression is physiological or psychological. What would you say?

3. Modern genetics can prevent the tragedy of a life doomed by heredity; embryos can now be screened for some genetic diseases. But what constitutes a disease? Should genetic testing be used to select a child's characteristics? If so, what characteristics?

KEY TERMS

Zeitgeist (p. 20)
Cartesian dualism (p. 20)
Nature-nurture issue (p. 20)
Ethology (p. 21)
Instinctive behaviors (p. 21)
Asomatognosia (p. 21)
Evolve (p. 23)
Natural selection (p. 25)
Fitness (p. 25)
Species (p. 27)
Conspecifics (p. 27)
Chordates (p. 27)
Vertebrates (p. 27)
Amphibians (p. 27)
Mammals (p. 27)
Primates (p. 29)
Hominids (p. 29)
Homo erectus (p. 29)

Brain stem (p. 30)
Cerebrum (p. 30)
Convolutions (p. 31)
Functional approach (p. 32)
Comparative approach (p. 32)
Dichotomous traits (p. 32)
True-breeding lines (p. 32)
Dominant trait (p. 33)
Recessive trait (p. 33)
Phenotype (p. 33)
Genotype (p. 33)
Gene (p. 33)
Homozygous (p. 33)
Heterozygous (p. 33)
Chromosomes (p. 34)
Gametes (p. 34)
Meiosis (p. 34)
Zygote (p. 34)

Mitosis (p. 34)
Linkage (p. 34)
Crossing over (p. 35)
Gene maps (p. 35)
Sex chromosomes (p. 35)
Sex-linked traits (p. 35)
Deoxyribonucleic acid (DNA) (p. 37)
Nucleotide bases (p. 37)
Replication (p. 38)
Mutations (p. 38)
Structural genes (p. 38)
Proteins (p. 38)
Amino acids (p. 38)
Operator gene (p. 38)
Gene expression (p. 38)
DNA-binding proteins (p. 38)

Ribonucleic acid (RNA) (p. 39)
Messenger RNA (p. 39)
Ribosomes (p. 39)
Codon (p. 39)
Transfer RNA (p. 39)
Human genome project (p. 39)
Ontogeny (p. 42)
Phylogeny (p. 42)
Phenylketonuria (PKU) (p. 43)
Phenylpyruvic acid (p. 43)
Sensitive period (p. 44)
Sensory phase (p. 44)
Sensorimotor phase (p. 44)
Identical twins (p. 46)
Fraternal twins (p. 46)
Heritability estimate (p. 47)

ADDITIONAL READING

The following articles focus on current issues in the study of human evolution:

Coppens, Y. (1994, May). East side story: The origin of humankind. *Scientific American, 270,* 88–95.

Thorne, A. G., & Wolpoff, M. H. (1992, April). The multiregional evolution of humans. *Scientific American, 266,* 76–83.

Wilson, A. C., & Cann, R. L. (1992, April). The recent African genesis of humans. *Scientific American, 266,* 68–73.

For those interested in evolution and its implications, the essays of Stephen J. Gould are enjoyable and informative—a tough combination to beat. The following is one of several recent collections:

Gould, S. J. (1991). *Bully for brontosaurus.* New York: Norton.

The following text provides an excellent introduction to the field of human behavioral genetics:

Plomin, R. (1990). *Nature and nurture: An introduction to human behavioral genetics.* Pacific Grove, CA: Brooks/Cole.

The following articles straighten out some common misconceptions about the biology of behavior:

Dewsbury, D. A. (1989). Comparative psychology, ethology, and animal behavior. *Annual Review of Psychology, 40,* 581–602.

Johnston, T. D. (1987). The persistence of dichotomies in the study of behavioral development. *Developmental Review, 7,* 149–182.

3

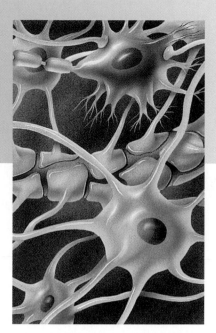

The Anatomy of
the Nervous System

3.1　General Layout of the Nervous System

3.2　Cells of the Nervous System

3.3　Neuroanatomical Techniques and Directions

3.4　Spinal Cord

3.5　The Five Major Divisions of the Brain

3.6　Major Structures of the Brain

In order to understand what the brain does, it is essential to understand what it is—to know the names and locations of its major parts and how they are connected to one another. This chapter introduces you to these fundamentals of brain anatomy.

Before you begin this chapter, I want to apologize for the lack of foresight displayed by early neuroanatomists in their choice of names for neuroanatomical structures—but, then, how could they have anticipated that Latin and Greek, universal languages of the educated in their day, would not be compulsory university fare in the 1990s? To help you, I have provided the literal English meanings of many of the neuroanatomical terms, and I have kept this chapter as brief and to the point as possible by covering only the most important structures. Still, there is no denying that this chapter will require extra effort. I can assure you, however, that it is effort well expended. Knowledge of your brain's basic structure is the necessary first step in understanding its psychological functions.

3.1   General Layout of the Nervous System

Divisions of the Nervous System

The vertebrate nervous system is composed of two divisions: the central nervous system and the peripheral nervous system (see Figure 3.1). The **central nervous system (CNS)** is the division of the nervous system that is located within the skull and spine. The **peripheral nervous system (PNS)** is the division that is located outside the skull and spine.

The central nervous system is composed of two divisions: the brain and the spinal cord. The *brain* is the part of the CNS that is located in the skull; the *spinal cord* is the part that is located in the spine.

The peripheral nervous system is also composed of two divisions: the somatic nervous system and the autonomic nervous system. The **somatic nervous system (SNS)** is the

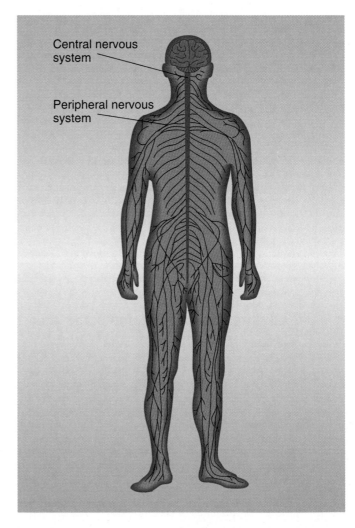

Figure 3.1 The human central nervous system (CNS) and peripheral nervous system (PNS). The CNS is represented in red; the PNS in blue.

Central nervous system

Peripheral nervous system

Central nervous system (CNS). The portion of the nervous system within the skull and spine.

Peripheral nervous system (PNS). The portion of the nervous system outside the skull and spine.

Somatic nervous system (SNS). The part of the peripheral nervous system that interacts with the external environment.

Afferent nerves. Nerves that carry sensory signals to the central nervous system; sensory nerves.

Efferent nerves. Nerves that carry motor signals from the central nervous system to the skeletal muscles or internal organs.

Autonomic nervous system (ANS). The part of the peripheral nervous system that participates in the regulation of the body's internal environment.

Sympathetic nerves. Nerves of the autonomic nervous system whose activity tends to mobilize energy resources and prepare the body for action.

Parasympathetic nerves. Nerves of the autonomic nervous system whose activity tends to conserve the body's energy resources.

Cranial nerves. The 12 pairs of nerves extending from the brain (e.g., the optic nerves, the olfactory nerves, and the vagus nerves).

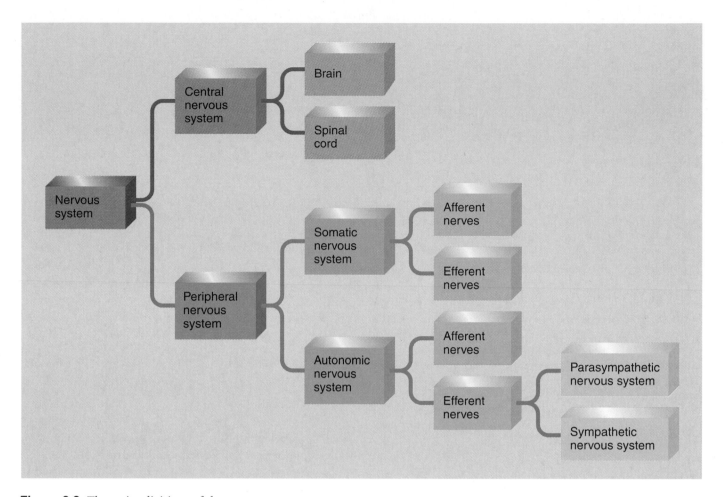

Figure 3.2 The major divisions of the nervous system.

part of the PNS that interacts with the external environment. It is composed of **afferent nerves** that carry sensory signals from the skin, skeletal muscles, joints, eyes, ears, etc. to the central nervous system and **efferent nerves** that carry motor signals from the central nervous system to the skeletal muscles. The **autonomic nervous system (ANS)** is the part of the peripheral nervous system that participates in the regulation of the internal environment. It is composed of afferent nerves that carry sensory signals from internal organs to the CNS and efferent nerves that carry motor signals from the CNS to internal organs. You will not confuse the terms *afferent* and *efferent* if you remember that many words that involve the idea of going toward something—in this case, going toward the CNS—begin with an *a* (e.g., advance, approach, arrive) and that many words that involve the idea of going away from something begin with an *e* (e.g., exit, embark, escape).

The autonomic nervous system has two kinds of efferent nerves: sympathetic nerves and parasympathetic nerves. In general, the **sympathetic nerves** stimulate, organize, and mobilize energy resources to deal with threatening situations (see Jänig & McLachlan, 1992), whereas the **parasympathetic nerves** act to conserve energy. Most autonomic organs receive both sympathetic and parasympathetic input; thus their activities are controlled by the relative levels of sympathetic and parasympathetic activity. In general, sympathetic activity is indicative of psychological arousal; that is why indexes of sympathetic activity (e.g., increased heart rate, blood pressure, and perspiration) are the basis of the lie detector test. The location of sympathetic and parasympathetic fibers is illustrated in Appendix I. (Ask your instructor if you are responsible for material in the appendixes or if you should use them just for reference.)

Most of the nerves of the peripheral nervous system project from the spinal cord, but there are 12 pairs of exceptions: the 12 pairs of **cranial nerves,** which project from the brain. They are numbered in sequence from front to back. The cranial nerves include purely sensory nerves such as the olfactory nerves (I) and the optic nerves (II), but most contain both sensory and motor fibers. The longest cranial nerves are the vagus nerves (X), which contain motor and sensory fibers traveling to and from the gut. The 12 pairs of cranial nerves and their targets are illustrated in Appendix II; their functions are listed in Appendix III.

Figure 3.2 summarizes the major divisions of the nervous system. Notice that the nervous system is a system of twos.

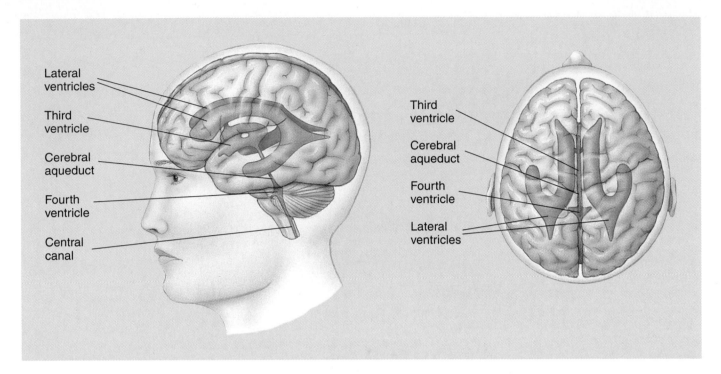

Labels on left (lateral view):
Lateral ventricles
Third ventricle
Cerebral aqueduct
Fourth ventricle
Central canal

Labels on right (superior view):
Third ventricle
Cerebral aqueduct
Fourth ventricle
Lateral ventricles

Figure 3.3 The cerebral ventricles.

Meninges, Ventricles, and Cerebrospinal Fluid

The brain and spinal cord (the CNS) are the most protected organs in the body. They are encased in bone and covered by three protective membranes, the three **meninges** (pronounced "MEN in gees"). The outer *menynx* (which, believe it or not, is the singular of *meninges*) is a tough membrane called the **dura mater** (tough mother). Immediately inside the dura mater is the fine **arachnoid membrane** (spider-web-like membrane). Beneath the arachnoid membrane is a space called the **subarachnoid space,** which contains many large blood vessels and cerebrospinal fluid;

then comes the innermost menynx, the delicate **pia mater** (pious mother), which adheres to the surface of the CNS.

Also protecting the CNS is the **cerebrospinal fluid (CSF),** which fills the subarachnoid space, the central canal of the spinal cord, and the cerebral ventricles of the brain. The **central canal** is a small central channel that runs the length of the spinal cord; the **cerebral ventricles** are the four large internal chambers of the brain: the two lateral ventricles, the third ventricle, and the fourth ventricle (see Figure 3.3). The cerebrospinal fluid supports and cushions the brain. These functions are all too apparent to patients who have had some of their cerebrospinal fluid drained away; they suffer raging headaches and experience stabbing pain each time they jerk their heads.

Meninges. The three protective membranes that cover the brain and spinal cord.

Dura mater. The tough outer menynx.

Arachnoid membrane. The menynx that is located between the dura mater and the pia mater and has the appearance of a gauzelike spider web.

Subarachnoid space. The space beneath the arachnoid membrane; it contains many large blood vessels and cerebrospinal fluid.

Pia mater. The delicate, innermost menynx.

Cerebrospinal fluid (CSF). The colorless fluid that fills the subarachnoid space, the central canal, and the cerebral ventricles.

Central canal. The small CSF-filled passage that runs the length of the spine.

Cerebral ventricles. The four CSF-filled internal chambers of the brain: the two lateral ventricles, the third ventricle, and the fourth ventricle.

Choroid plexuses. The networks of capillaries that protrude into the ventricles and continuously produce cerebrospinal fluid.

Cerebral aqueduct. The narrow channel that connects the third and fourth ventricles.

Blood-brain barrier. The mechanism that keeps certain toxic substances in the blood from penetrating cerebral neural tissue.

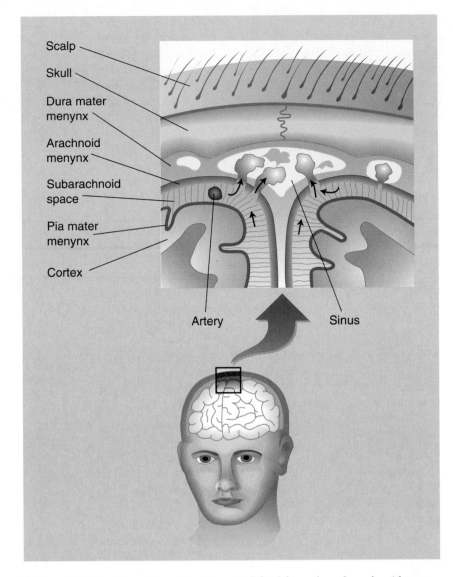

Scalp

Skull

Dura mater
menynx

Arachnoid
menynx

Subarachnoid
space

Pia mater
menynx

Cortex

Artery

Sinus

Figure 3.4 The absorption of cerebrospinal fluid from the subarachnoid space (blue) into a major sinus. Note the three meninges.

Cerebrospinal fluid is continuously produced by the **choroid plexuses**—networks of small blood vessels that protrude into the ventricles from their pia mater lining (see Spector & Johanson, 1989). The excess CSF fluid is continuously absorbed from the subarachnoid space into large blood-filled spaces, or *sinuses,* which run through the dura mater and drain into the large jugular veins of the neck. Figure 3.4 illustrates the absorption of cerebrospinal fluid from the subarachnoid space into the large sinus that runs along the top of the brain between the two cerebral hemispheres.

Occasionally, the flow of cerebrospinal fluid is blocked by a tumor near one of the narrow channels that link the ventricles—for example, near the **cerebral aqueduct,** which connects the third and fourth ventricles. The resulting buildup of fluid in the ventricles causes the walls of the ventricles, and thus the entire brain, to expand, producing

a condition called *hydrocephalus* (water head). Hydrocephalus is treated by draining the excess fluid from the ventricles and trying to remove the obstruction.

Blood-Brain Barrier

The brain is a finely tuned electrochemical organ whose function can be severely disturbed by the introduction of certain kinds of chemicals. Fortunately, there is a mechanism that impedes the passage of many toxic substances from the blood into the brain: the **blood-brain barrier.** This barrier is a consequence of the special structure of cerebral blood vessels. In the rest of the body, the cells that compose the walls of blood vessels are loosely packed; as a result, most molecules pass readily through them into surrounding tissue. In the brain, however, the cells of the blood vessel walls are tightly packed, thus forming a barrier to the passage of many molecules—particularly proteins and other large molecules (see Goldstein & Betz, 1986).

The blood-brain barrier does not impede the passage of all large molecules. Some large molecules that are critical for normal brain function (e.g., glucose) are actively transported through cerebral blood vessel walls. Also, the blood vessel walls in some areas of the brain allow certain large molecules to pass through them unimpeded; for example, sex hormones, which have difficulty permeating some parts of the brain, readily enter parts of the brain involved in sexual behavior. The degree to which psychoactive drugs influence psychological processes depends on the ease with which they penetrate the blood-brain barrier.

3.2   Cells of the Nervous System

The cells of the nervous system are of two fundamentally different types: neurons and supportive cells. Their anatomy is discussed in the following two subsections.

Anatomy of Neurons

Neurons are cells that are specialized for the reception, conduction, and transmission of electrochemical signals. They come in an incredible variety of shapes and sizes; however, many are similar to the one illustrated in Figures 3.5 and 3.6.

External anatomy of neurons   Figure 3.5 is an illustration of the major external features of a typical neuron. For your convenience, the definition of each feature is included in the illustration.

Multipolar neuron. A neuron with more than two processes emanating from its cell body.

Unipolar neuron. A neuron with one process emanating from its cell body.

Bipolar neuron. A neuron with two processes extending from its cell body.

Interneurons. Neurons whose processes are contained within a single brain structure; neurons with short axons or no axons at all.

Nucleus. The large spherical structure of the cell body that contains the DNA; also, a cluster of neuronal cell bodies in the central nervous system.

Ganglia. Clusters of neuronal cell bodies in the peripheral nervous system.

Tracts. Bundles of axons in the central nervous system.

Nerves. Bundles of axons in the peripheral nervous system.

Internal anatomy of neurons   Figure 3.6 is an illustration of the major internal features of a typical neuron. For your convenience, the definition of each feature is included in the illustration.

Neuron cell membrane   The neuron cell membrane is composed of a *lipid bilayer*—two layers of fat molecules (see Figure 3.7). Embedded in the lipid bilayer are numerous protein molecules that are the basis of many of the cell membrane's functional properties. Some membrane proteins are *channel proteins,* through which certain molecules can pass, others are *signal proteins,* which transfer a signal to the inside of the neuron when particular molecules bind to their exterior.

Classes of neurons   Figure 3.8 illustrates a way of classifying neurons that is based on the number of processes emanating from their cell bodies. A neuron with more than two processes extending from its cell body is classified as a **multipolar neuron**; most neurons are multipolar. A neuron with one process extending from its cell body is classified as a **unipolar neuron,** and a neuron with two processes extending from its cell body is classified as a **bipolar neuron.** Neurons with short axons or no axons at all are called **interneurons**; their function is to integrate the neural activity within a single brain structure, not to conduct signals from one structure to another.

In general, there are two kinds of gross neural structures in the nervous system: those composed primarily of cell bodies and those composed primarily of axons. In the central nervous system, clusters of cell bodies are called **nuclei** (singular *nucleus*); in the peripheral nervous system, they are called **ganglia** (singular *ganglion*). (Note that the word *nucleus* has two different meanings; it is a structure in the neuron cell body and a cluster of cell bodies in the CNS.) In the central nervous system, bundles of axons are called **tracts**; in the peripheral nervous system, they are called **nerves.**

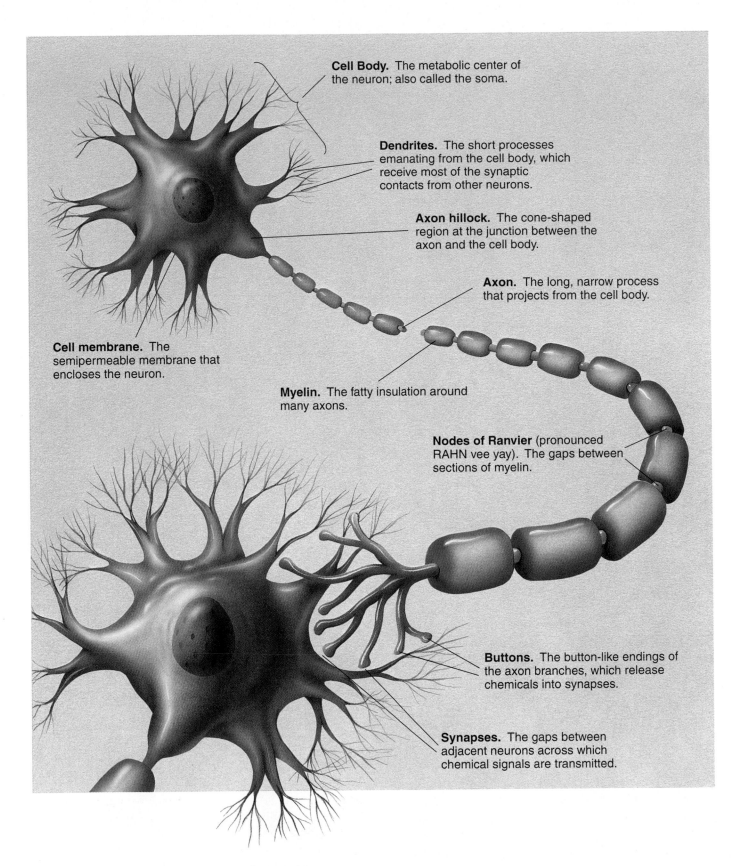

Cell Body. The metabolic center of the neuron; also called the soma.

Dendrites. The short processes emanating from the cell body, which receive most of the synaptic contacts from other neurons.

Axon hillock. The cone-shaped region at the junction between the axon and the cell body.

Axon. The long, narrow process that projects from the cell body.

Cell membrane. The semipermeable membrane that encloses the neuron.

Myelin. The fatty insulation around many axons.

Nodes of Ranvier (pronounced RAHN vee yay). The gaps between sections of myelin.

Buttons. The button-like endings of the axon branches, which release chemicals into synapses.

Synapses. The gaps between adjacent neurons across which chemical signals are transmitted.

Figure 3.5 The major external features of a typical neuron.

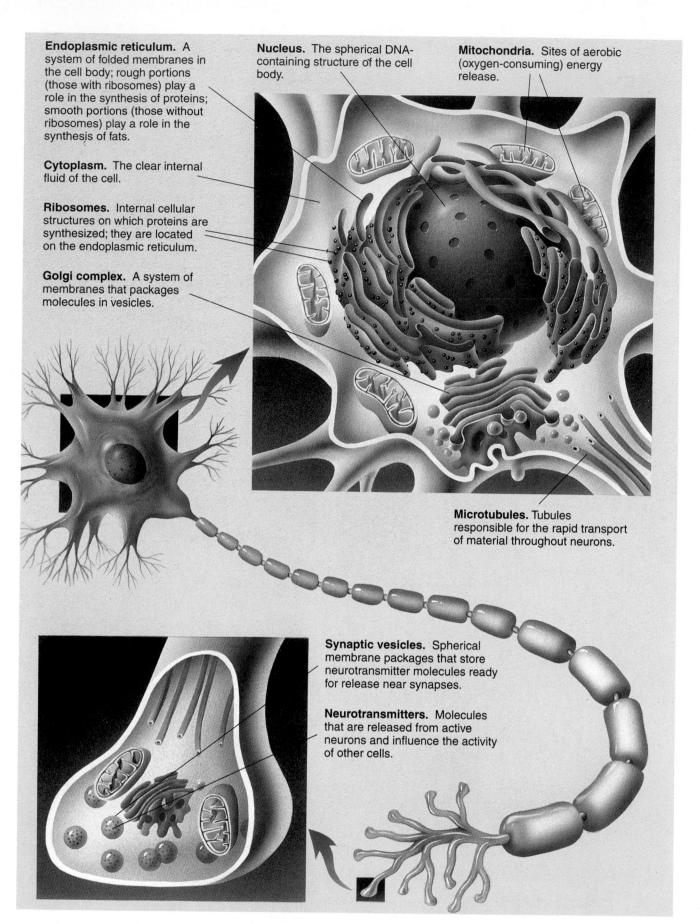

Endoplasmic reticulum. A system of folded membranes in the cell body; rough portions (those with ribosomes) play a role in the synthesis of proteins; smooth portions (those without ribosomes) play a role in the synthesis of fats.

Cytoplasm. The clear internal fluid of the cell.

Ribosomes. Internal cellular structures on which proteins are synthesized; they are located on the endoplasmic reticulum.

Golgi complex. A system of membranes that packages molecules in vesicles.

Nucleus. The spherical DNA-containing structure of the cell body.

Mitochondria. Sites of aerobic (oxygen-consuming) energy release.

Microtubules. Tubules responsible for the rapid transport of material throughout neurons.

Synaptic vesicles. Spherical membrane packages that store neurotransmitter molecules ready for release near synapses.

Neurotransmitters. Molecules that are released from active neurons and influence the activity of other cells.

Figure 3.6 The major internal features of a typical neuron.

Chapter 3   The Anatomy of the Nervous System

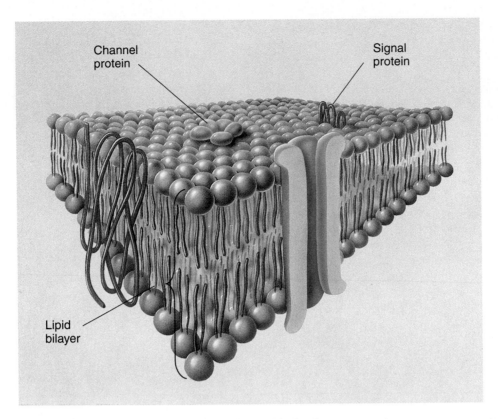

Figure 3.7 The cell membrane: A lipid bilayer with signal proteins and channel proteins embedded in it.

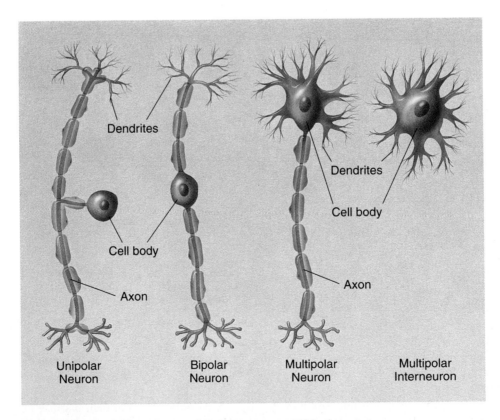

Figure 3.8 A unipolar neuron, a bipolar neuron, a multipolar neuron, and an interneuron.

Supportive Cells of the Nervous System: Glial Cells and Satellite Cells

Neurons are not the only cells in the nervous system. In the central nervous system, they are provided with physical and functional support by **glial cells;** in the peripheral nervous system, they are provided with physical and functional support by **satellite cells.** Among their many supportive functions, glial cells and satellite cells form a physical matrix that holds neural circuits together (*glia* means "glue") and they absorb dead cells and other debris.

The largest glial cells are called **astroglia,** or **astrocytes** (see Chan-Ling & Stone, 1991; Kimelberg & Norenberg, 1989), because they are star-shaped (*astron* means "star"). The armlike processes of astroglia cover the outer surface of blood vessels that course through the brain; they also contact neuron cell bodies. Accordingly, astroglia are thought to play a role in the passage of chemicals from the blood into neurons (see Figure 3.9).

Oligodendroglia, or **oligodendrocytes,** are another class of glial cells; they send out processes that wrap around the axons of some neurons of the central nervous system. These processes are rich in *myelin,* a fatty insulating substance; and the myelin sheaths that they form increase the speed and efficiency of axonal conduction. A similar function is performed by **Schwann cells** (a class of satellite cells) in the peripheral nervous system. Oligodendroglia and Schwann cells are illustrated in Figure 3.10. Notice that each Schwann cell constitutes one myelin segment, whereas each oligodendroglia cell constitutes several. Another important difference between Schwann cells and oligodendroglia is that only Schwann cells can guide axonal *regeneration* (regrowth) after damage. That is why there is normally little axonal regeneration in the mammalian CNS.

3.3 Neuroanatomical Techniques and Directions

The major problem in visualizing neurons is not their minuteness. The major problem is that neurons are so tightly packed and their axons and dendrites so intricately intertwined that looking through a microscope at unprepared neural tissue reveals almost nothing about them. The key to the study of neuroanatomy lies in preparing neural tissue in a variety of ways, each of which permits a clear view of a different aspect of neural structure, and then combining the knowledge obtained from each of the preparations. This section of the chapter first describes a few of the most common neuroanatomical techniques, then explains the system of directions that neuroanatomists use to describe the location of structures in vertebrate nervous systems.

Neuroanatomical Techniques

Golgi stain   The greatest blessing to befall neuroscience in its early years was the accidental discovery of the **Golgi stain** by Camillo Golgi (pronounced "GOLE-gee"), an Italian physician, in the early 1870s. Golgi was trying to stain the meninges by exposing a block of neural tissue to potassium dichromate and silver nitrate, when he noticed an amazing thing. For some unknown reason, the silver chromate created by the chemical reaction invaded a few neurons in each slice of tissue and stained each invaded neuron entirely black. This discovery made it possible to see individual neurons for the first time, although only in silhouette (see Figure 3.11). Stains that totally dye all neurons on a slide reveal nothing of their structure because the neurons are so tightly packed.

Nissl stain   Although the Golgi stain permits an excellent view of the silhouettes of the few neurons that take up the stain, it provides no indication of the number of neurons in an area or the nature of their inner structure. The first neural staining procedure to overcome these shortcomings was the **Nissl stain,** which was developed by Franz Nissl, a German psychiatrist, in the 1880s. The most common dye used in the Nissl method is cresyl violet. Cresyl violet and other Nissl dyes penetrate all cells on a slide, but

---

Glial cells. The supportive cells of the central nervous system.

Satellite cells. The supportive cells of the peripheral nervous system.

Astroglia (astrocytes). Large, star-shaped glial cells that provide a supportive matrix for neurons in the central nervous system and are thought to play a role in the transfer of molecules from blood to CNS neurons.

Oligodendroglia (oligodendrocytes). Glial cells that myelinate axons of the central nervous system.

Schwann cells. Satellite cells whose myelin-rich processes wrap around axons in the peripheral nervous system.

Golgi stain. A neural stain that completely darkens a few of the neurons in each slice of tissue, thereby revealing their silhouettes.

Nissl stain. A neural stain that has an affinity for structures of neural cell bodies.

Figure 3.9 Astrocytes. Astrocytes have an affinity for blood vessels, and they form a supportive matrix for neurons. The photograph is of brain tissue stained with a glial stain; the unstained channels are blood vessels. The illustration shows how the feet of astrocytes cover blood vessels and contact neurons. (Photograph courtesy of T. Chan-Ling.)

Myelination in the Peripheral Nervous System

Myelination in the Central Nervous System

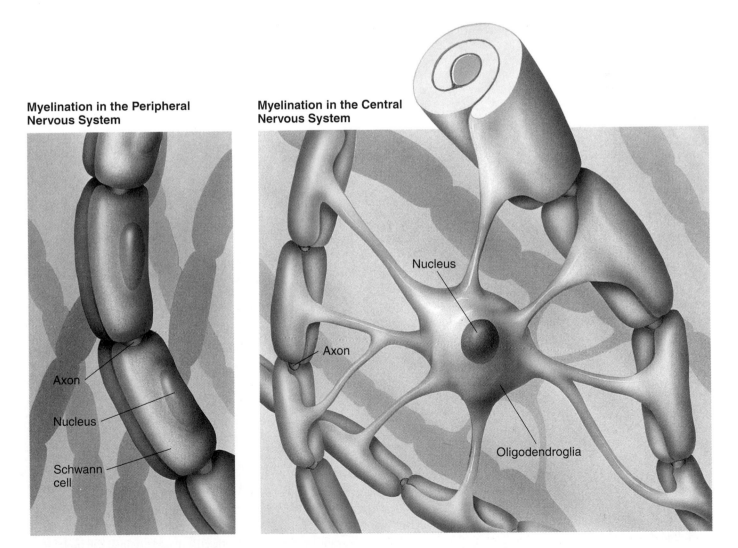

Nucleus

Axon

Axon

Nucleus

Schwann cell

Oligodendroglia

Figure 3.10 The myelination of CNS axons by an oligodendrocyte and the myelination of PNS axons by Schwann cells.

Figure 3.11 Neural tissue that has been stained by the Golgi method. Because only a few neurons take up the stain, their silhouettes are revealed in great detail but their internal details are invisible. Usually, only part of a neuron is captured in a single slice. (Ed Reschke © Peter Arnold, Inc.)

they bind effectively only to structures in neuron cell bodies. Thus one can estimate the number of cell bodies in an area by counting the number of Nissl-stained dots. Figure 3.12 is a photograph of a slice of brain tissue stained with cresyl violet. Notice that only the layers composed mainly of neuron cell bodies are densely stained.

Electron microscopy A neuroanatomical technique that provides information about the details of neuronal structure is **electron microscopy** (pronounced "my-CROSS-cuh-pee"). Because of the nature of light, the limit of magnification in light microscopy is about 1,500 times, a level of magnification that is insufficient to reveal the fine anatomical details of neurons. Greater detail can be obtained by first coating thin slices of neural tissue with an electron-absorbing substance that is taken up by different parts of neurons to different degrees, then passing a beam of electrons through the tissue onto a photographic film. The result is an *electron micrograph,* which captures neuronal structure in exquisite detail (see Figure 4.12). A *scan-*

ning electron microscope provides spectacular electron micrographs in three dimensions (see Figure 3.13), but is not capable of as much magnification as a conventional electron microscope.

Myelin stains The first stains specifically developed for studying axons were **myelin stains**—stains that selectively dye the sheaths of myelinated axons. Figure 3.14 is a myelin-stained coronal section of the human brain. Notice that the subcortical white matter, which is composed largely of myelinated axons, is stained, while the cerebral cortex and various subcortical nuclear groups are not. Although myelin stains are useful for visualizing myelinated areas of the CNS, they are not very useful for tracking the pathways of individual axons—for three reasons. First, the stains are of no use in tracking unmyelinated axons. Second, because the initial segment and terminal branches of myelinated axons are not myelinated, the stains cannot reveal exactly where a myelinated axon originates or where it terminates. Third, because all myelinated axons are stained indiscriminately, once a myelinated axon becomes intermingled with others, it is impossible to trace it

Figure 3.12 A Nissl-stained section (slice) of the mouse hippocampus, a structure that plays an important role in learning and memory. Notice the densely stained cell body layers. (Courtesy of Jerold J. M. Chun, M.D., Ph.D.)

Electron microscopy. A technique used to study the fine details of cellular structure.

Myelin stains. Stains that selectively dye the sheaths of myelinated axons.

Figure 3.13 A color-enhanced scanning electron micrograph of a neuron cell body (green) studded with terminal buttons (orange). Each neuron receives numerous synaptic contacts. (Courtesy of Jerold J. M. Chun, M.D., Ph.D.)

through a series of slices. Modern neuroanatomical tracing techniques circumvent these problems.

Neuroanatomical tracing techniques Neuroanatomical tracing techniques are of two types: anterograde (forward) tracing methods and retrograde (backward) tracing methods. *Anterograde tracing methods* are used when an investigator wants to trace the paths of axons projecting away from cell bodies located in a particular area. The investigator injects into the area one of several chemicals commonly used for anterograde tracing—chemicals that are taken up by cell bodies and then transported forward along their axons to their terminal buttons. After a few days, the brain is removed and sliced; the slices are then treated to reveal the locations of the injected chemical. *Retrograde tracing methods* work in reverse; they are used when an investigator wants to trace the paths of axons projecting into a particular area. The investigator injects into the area one of several chemicals commonly used for retrograde tracing—chemicals that are taken up by terminal buttons and then transported backward along their axons to their cell bodies. After a few days, the brain is removed

Figure 3.14 A myelin-stained section of the human brain. Notice that the white matter is stained black but that the cortex and other nuclear groups are relatively unstained. (From *Fundamental Neuroanatomy* by Walle J. H. Nauta and Michael Feirtag. Copyright © 1986 W. H. Freeman and Company. Reprinted with permission.)

Figure 3.15 Retrograde tracing. Injection of a red fluorescent dye (rhodamine dextrans) into one visual cortex of a cat was taken up by neural buttons in the area and transported back to their cell bodies. In this section, stained red are the neural cell bodies in the contralateral visual cortex whose axons projected via the corpus callosum to the site of the injection. (Courtesy of Joanne Matsubara, Department of Ophthalmology, University of British Columbia.)

positions of various body surfaces are the same in humans as they are in more typical, non-upright vertebrates. Specifically, notice that the top of the human head and the back of the human body are both referred to as *dorsal* even though they are in different directions, and the bottom of the human head and the front of the human body are both referred to as *ventral* even though they are in different directions (see Figure 3.17). To circumvent this complication, the terms **superior** and **inferior** are often used to refer to the top and bottom of the primate head, respectively.

In the next few pages, you will be seeing drawings of sections (slices) of the brain cut in one of three different planes: **horizontal sections, frontal** (also termed *coronal*) **sections,** and **sagittal sections.** These three planes are illustrated in Figure 3.18. A section cut down the center of the brain, between the two hemispheres, is called a *midsagittal section.* A section cut at a right angle to any long, narrow structure, such as the spinal cord or a nerve, is called a **cross section.**

and sliced; the slices are then treated to reveal the locations of the injected chemical (see Figure 3.15).

Directions in the Vertebrate Nervous System Directions in the vertebrate nervous system are described in relation to the orientation of the spinal cord. This system is straightforward for most vertebrates, as Figure 3.16 indicates. The vertebrate nervous system has three axes: anteriorposterior, dorsal-ventral, and medial-lateral. First, **anterior** means toward the nose end (the anterior end), and **posterior** means toward the tail end (the posterior end); these same directions are sometimes referred to as *rostral* and *caudal,* respectively. Second, **dorsal** means toward the surface of the back or the top of the head (the dorsal surface), and **ventral** means toward the surface of the chest or the bottom of the head (the ventral surface). Third, **medial** means toward the midline of the body, and **lateral** means away from the midline toward the body's lateral surfaces.

We humans complicate this simple three-axis (anterior-posterior, ventral-dorsal, medial-lateral) system of neuroanatomical directions by insisting on walking around on our hind legs, thus changing the orientation of our brains in relation to our spines. You can save yourself a lot of confusion if you remember that the system of vertebrate neuroanatomical directions was adapted for use in humans in such a way that the terms used to describe the

Anterior. Toward the nose end of a vertebrate.

Posterior. Toward the tail end of a vertebrate, or toward the back of the head.

Dorsal. Toward the surface of the back of a vertebrate, or toward the top of the head.

Ventral. Toward the stomach surface of a vertebrate, or toward the bottom of the head.

Medial. Toward the midline of the body.

Lateral. Away from the midline of the body and toward the body's lateral surfaces.

Superior. Toward the top of the primate brain.

Inferior. Toward the bottom of the primate brain.

Horizontal sections. Any slices of brain tissue cut in a plane that is parallel to the top of the brain.

Frontal sections. Any slices of brain tissue cut in a plane that is parallel to the face; also termed *coronal section.*

Sagittal sections. Any slices of brain tissue cut in a plane that is parallel to the side of the brain.

Cross section. A section cut at a right angle to any long narrow structure.

Figure 3.16 Anatomical directions in a representative vertebrate.

Figure 3.17 Anatomical directions in a human. Notice that the directions in the cerebral hemisphere are rotated by 90° because of the unconventional upright posture of humans.

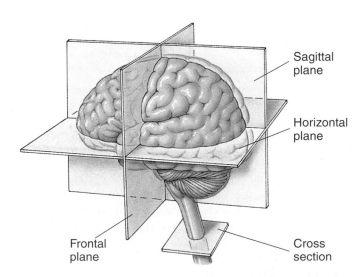

Figure 3.18 Horizontal, frontal (coronal), and sagittal planes in the human brain and a cross section of the human spinal cord.

To test your comprehension and retention of the first three sections of this chapter, draw a line between each term in column 1 and the appropriate phrase in column 2.

The correct answers are provided at the bottom of this page. Before proceeding, review material related to your incorrect answers.

1. Autonomic nervous system	a. Packets of neurotransmitter molecules
2. Cerebral aqueduct	b. PNS minus the somatic nervous system
3. Axon hillock	c. Connects the 3rd and 4th ventricles
4. Dorsal	d. Stains cell bodies
5. Cell membrane	e. Top of a vertebrate's head
6. Cranial nerves	f. Outer menynx
7. Superior or dorsal	g. Between the cell body and axon
8. Cell body	h. Contains the nucleus of a neuron
9. Synaptic vesicles	i. Olfactory, visual, and vagus
10. Oligodendroglia	j. Myelinate CNS axons
11. Nissl	k. A slice down the center of the brain
12. Dura mater	l. Top of the primate head
13. Midsagittal section	m. Silhouette
14. Golgi	n. Lipid bilayer

3.4 Spinal Cord

In the first three sections of this chapter, you learned about the divisions of the nervous system, the cells that compose it, and some of the neuroanatomical techniques that are used to study it. This section begins your ascent of the human CNS by focusing on the spinal cord. The final two sections of the chapter focus on the brain.

In cross section, it is apparent that the spinal cord comprises two different areas (see Figure 3.19): an inner H-shaped core of gray matter and a surrounding area of white matter. *Gray matter* is composed largely of cell bodies and unmyelinated interneurons, whereas *white matter* is composed largely of myelinated axons. (It is the myelin that gives the white matter its glossy white sheen.) The two dorsal arms of the spinal gray matter are called the **dorsal horns,** and the two ventral arms are called the **ventral horns.**

Pairs of *spinal nerves* are attached to the spinal cord— one on the left and one on the right—at 31 different levels of the spine. As Figure 3.19 shows, each of these 62 spinal nerves divides as it nears the cord, and its axons are joined to the cord via one of two roots: the *dorsal root* or the *ventral root.*

The answers to the preceding exercise are the following: (1) b, (2) c, (3) g, (4) e, (5) k, (6) i, (7) l, (8) h, (9) a, (10) j, (11) d, (12) f, (13) e, (14) m.

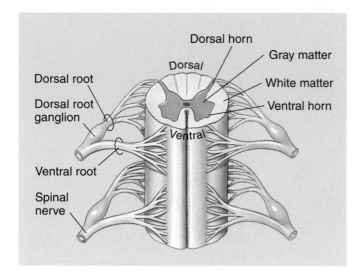

Figure 3.19 The dorsal and ventral roots of the spinal cord.

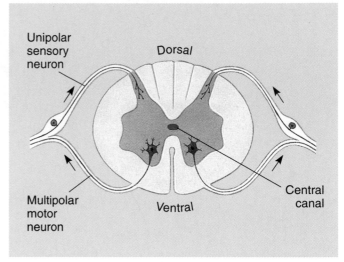

Figure 3.20 A schematic cross section of the spinal cord.

All dorsal root axons are sensory (afferent) unipolar neurons with their cell bodies grouped together just outside the cord to form the *dorsal root ganglia*. Many of their synaptic terminals are in the dorsal horns of the spinal gray matter (see Figure 3.20). In contrast, the neurons of the ventral root are motor (efferent) multipolar neurons with their cell bodies in the ventral horns. Those that are part of the somatic nervous system project to skeletal muscles; those that are part of the autonomic nervous system project to ganglia, where they synapse on neurons that in turn project to internal organs (heart, stomach, liver, etc.). See Appendix I.

3.5 The Five Major Divisions of the Brain

A necessary step in learning to live in an unfamiliar city is learning the names and locations of its major neighborhoods or districts. Those who possess this information can easily communicate the general location of any destination in the city. This section of the chapter introduces you to the five "neighborhoods," or divisions, of the brain—for much the same reason.

To understand why the brain is considered to be composed of five divisions, it is necessary to understand its early development. In the vertebrate embryo, the tissue that eventually develops into the CNS is recognizable as a fluid-filled tube (see Figure 3.21). The first indications of the developing brain are three swellings that occur at the ante-rior end of this tube. These three swellings eventually develop into the adult *forebrain, midbrain,* and *hindbrain.*

Before birth, the initial three swellings in the neural tube become five (see Figure 3.21). This occurs because the fore-brain swelling grows into two different swellings, and so does the hindbrain swelling. From anterior to posterior, the five swellings that compose the developing brain at birth are the *telencephalon,* the *diencephalon,* the *mesencephalon* (or midbrain), the *metencephalon,* and the *myelencephalon* (encephalon means "within the head"). These swellings ultimately develop into the five divisions of the adult brain. As a student, I memorized their order by remembering that the *tel*encephalon is on the *top* and that the other four divisions are arrayed below it in alphabetical order.

Figure 3.22 illustrates the locations of the telencephalon, diencephalon, mesencephalon, metencephalon, and mye-lencephalon in the adult human brain. Notice that in humans, as in other higher vertebrates, the telencephalon (the left and right *cerebral hemispheres*) undergoes the greatest growth during development. The other four divisions of the brain are often referred to collectively as the **brain stem**—the stem on which the cerebral hemispheres sit. The myelencephalon is often referred to as the medulla.

Dorsal horns. The two dorsal arms of the spinal gray matter.

Ventral horns. The two ventral arms of the spinal gray matter.

Brain stem. The myelencephalon, the metencephalon, the mesencephalon, and the diencephalon.

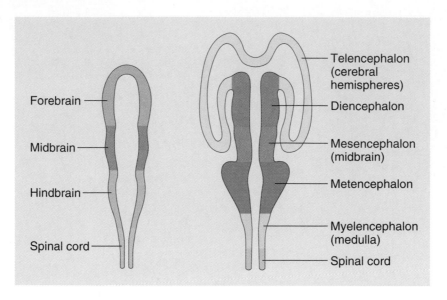

Figure 3.21 The early development of the mammalian brain as illustrated in schematic horizontal sections. Compare with the adult human brain in Figure 3.22.

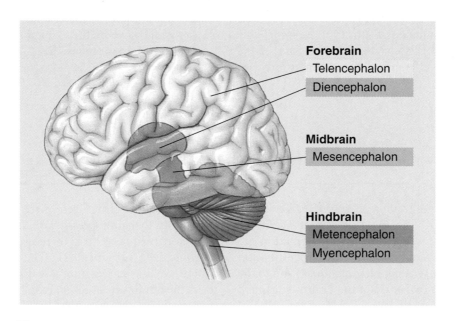

Figure 3.22 The divisions of the adult human brain.

3.6   Major Structures of the Brain

Now that you have learned the five major divisions of the brain, it is time to introduce you to their major structures. This section of the chapter begins its survey of brain structures in the myelencephalon, then ascends through the other divisions to the telencephalon. Rather than being defined in the blue key term boxes, the boldfaced brain structures introduced in this section are defined by Figure 3.32 at the end of the section.

Myelencephalon

Not surprisingly, the **myelencephalon** (or **medulla**), the most posterior division of the brain, is composed largely of tracts carrying signals between the rest of the brain and the body. An interesting part of the myelencephalon from a psychological perspective is the **reticular formation** (see Figure 3.23). It is a complex network of about 100 tiny

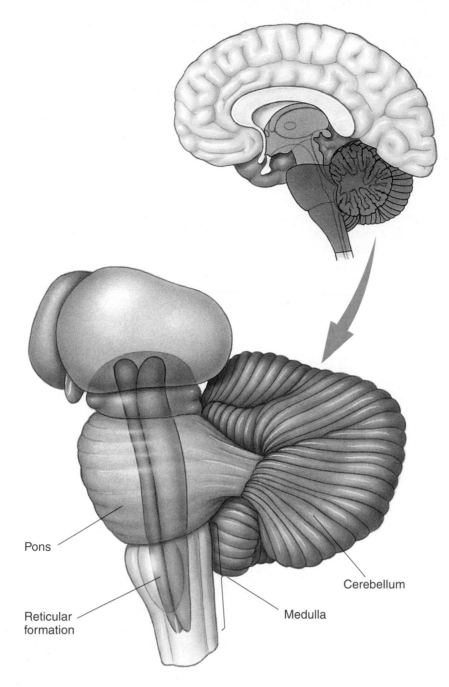

Figure 3.23 Structures of the human myelencephalon (medulla) and metencephalon.

nuclei that occupies the central core of the brain stem from the posterior boundary of the myelencephalon to the anterior boundary of the midbrain. It is so named because of its netlike appearance (*reticulum* means "little net"). Sometimes, the reticular formation is referred to as the *reticular activating system* because parts of it seem to play a role in arousal. The various nuclei of the reticular formation are involved in a variety of functions, however—including sleep, attention, movement, the maintenance of muscle tone, and various cardiac, circulatory, and respiratory reflexes. Accordingly, referring to this collection of nuclei as a system can be misleading.

Metencephalon

The **metencephalon,** like the myelencephalon, houses many ascending and descending tracts and part of the reticular formation. These structures create a bulge, called the **pons,** on the brain stem's ventral surface. The pons is one major division of the metencephalon; the other is the cerebellum ("little brain")—see Figure 3.23. The **cerebellum** is the large, convoluted structure on the brain stem's dorsal surface. It is an important sensorimotor structure; cerebellar damage eliminates the ability to precisely control one's movements and to adapt them to changing conditions.

Mesencephalon

The **mesencephalon,** like the metencephalon, has two divisions. The two divisions of the mesencephalon are the tectum and the tegmentum (see Figure 3.24). The **tectum** ("roof") is the dorsal surface of the midbrain. In mammals, the tectum is composed of two pairs of bumps, the *colliculi* ("little hills"). The posterior pair, called the **inferior colliculi,** have an auditory function; the anterior pair, called the **superior colliculi,** have a visual function. In lower vertebrates, the function of the tectum is entirely visual, thus the tectum is referred to as the *optic tectum.*

The **tegmentum** is the division of the mesencephalon ventral to the tectum. In addition to the reticular formation and tracts of passage, the tegmentum contains three colorful structures that are of particular interest to biopsy-chologists: the periaqueductal gray, the substantia nigra, and the red nucleus (see Figure 3.24). The **periaqueductal gray** is the gray matter situated around the **cerebral aqueduct,** the duct connecting the third and fourth ventricles; it is of special interest because of its role in mediating the analgesic (pain-reducing) effects of opiate drugs. The **substantia nigra** ("black substance") and the **red nucleus** are both important components of the sensorimotor system.

Diencephalon

The **diencephalon** is composed of two structures: the thalamus and the hypothalamus (see Figure 3.25). The **thalamus** is the large, two-lobed structure that constitutes the top of the brain stem. One lobe sits on each side of the

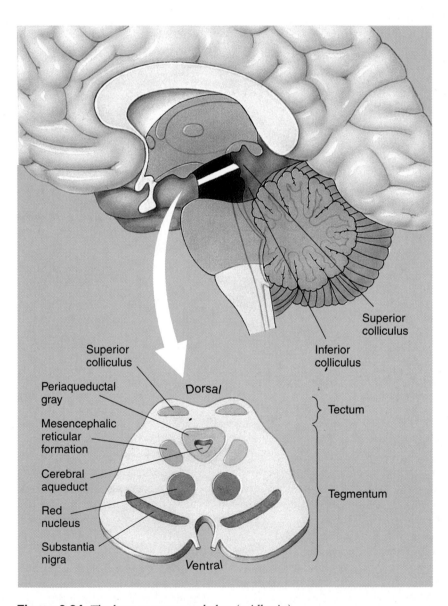

Figure 3.24 The human mesencephalon (midbrain).

Right
thalamus

Bands of
myelinated
axons

Left
thalamus

Cerebellum

Hypothalamus

Figure 3.25 The human diencephalon.

third ventricle, and the two lobes are joined by the **massa intermedia,** which runs through the ventricle. Visible on the surface of the thalamus are white *lamina* (layers) that are composed of myelinated axons.

The thalamus comprises many different pairs of nuclei, most of which project to the cortex. Some are *sensory relay nuclei*—nuclei that receive signals from sensory receptors, process them, and then transmit them to the appropriate areas of sensory cortex. For example, the **lateral geniculate nuclei,** the **medial geniculate nuclei,** and the **ventral posterior nuclei** are important relay stations in the visual, auditory, and somatosensory systems, respectively (see Figure 3.25). The various thalamic nuclei are illustrated in Appendix IV.

The **hypothalamus** is located just below the anterior thalamus (*hypo* means "below")—see Figure 3.26. It plays an important role in the regulation of several motivated behaviors. It exerts its effects in part by regulating the release of hormones from the **pituitary gland,** which dangles from it on the ventral surface of the brain. The literal meaning of *pituitary gland* is "snot gland"; it was discov-

ered in a gelatinous state behind the nose of an unembalmed cadaver and was incorrectly assumed to be the main source of nasal mucus.

In addition to the pituitary gland, two other structures appear on the inferior surface of the hypothalamus: the optic chiasm and the mammillary bodies (see Figure 3.26). The **optic chiasm** is the point at which the *optic nerves* from each eye come together. The X-shape is created because some of the axons of the optic nerve **decussate** (cross over to the other side of the brain) via the optic chiasm. The decussating fibers are said to be **contralateral** (projecting from one side of the body to the other), and the nondecussating fibers are said to be **ipsilateral** (staying on the same

Decussate. To cross over to the other side of the brain.

Contralateral. Projecting from one side of the body to the other.

Ipsilateral. On the same side of the body.

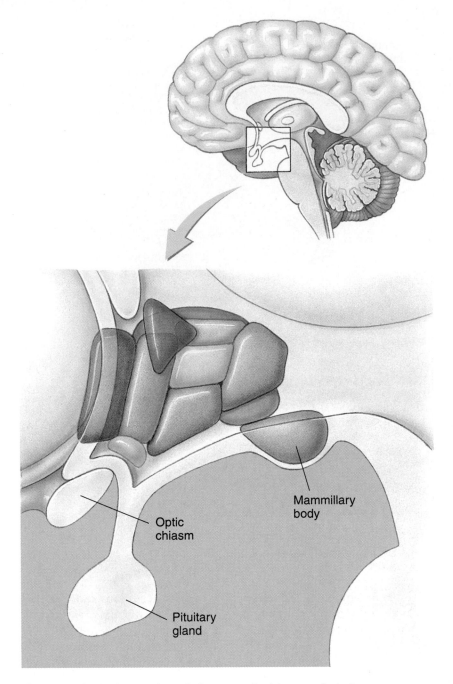

Figure 3.26 The human hypothalamus, optic chiasm, and pituitary.

side of the body). The **mammillary bodies** are a pair of spherical hypothalamic nuclei located on the inferior surface of the hypothalamus, just behind the pituitary. The mammillary bodies and the other nuclei of the hypothalamus are illustrated in Appendix V.

Telencephalon

The **telencephalon** is the largest division of the human brain, and it mediates its most complex functions. It initiates voluntary movement, interprets sensory input, and mediates complex cognitive processes such as learning, speaking, and problem solving.

Cerebral cortex The cerebral hemispheres are covered by a layer of tissue called the **cerebral cortex** (cerebral bark). In humans, the cerebral cortex is deeply convoluted (furrowed)—see Figure 3.27. The convolutions have the effect of increasing the amount of cerebral cortex without increasing the overall volume of the brain. Not all mammals have convoluted cortexes; most mammals are *lissencephalic* (smooth-brained). It was once believed that the degree of cortical convolution determined a species'

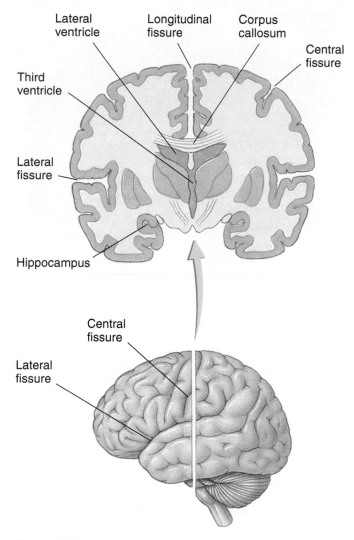

Figure 3.27 The major fissures of the human cerebral hemispheres.

Labels in figure:
Lateral ventricle
Longitudinal fissure
Corpus callosum
Central fissure
Third ventricle
Lateral fissure
Hippocampus
Central fissure
Lateral fissure

intellectual capacities; however, the degree of convolution appears to be related more to body size. Every large mammal has a deeply convoluted cortex.

The large furrows in a convoluted cortex are called **fissures,** and the small ones are called **sulci** (singular *sulcus*). The ridges between fissures and sulci are called **gyri** (singular *gyrus*). It is apparent in Figure 3.27 that the cerebral hemispheres are almost completely separated by the largest of the fissures: the **longitudinal fissure.** The cerebral hemispheres are directly connected by only a few tracts spanning the longitudinal fissure; these hemisphere-connecting tracts are called **cerebral commissures.** The largest cerebral commissure, the **corpus callosum,** is clearly visible in Figure 3.27.

As Figure 3.28 indicates, the two major landmarks on the lateral surface of each hemisphere are the **central fissure** and the **lateral fissure.** These fissures partially divide each hemisphere into four lobes: the **frontal lobe,** the **parietal lobe** (pronounced "pa RYE e tal"), the **temporal lobe,** and the **occipital lobe** (pronounced "ok SIP i tal"). Among the largest gyri are the **precentral gyri,** which contain motor cortex; the **postcentral gyri,** which contain somatosensory (body-sensation) cortex; and the **superior temporal gyri,** which contain auditory cortex. The function of occipital cortex is entirely visual.

About 90 percent of human cerebral cortex is **neocortex** (new cortex); that is, it is six-layered cortex of relatively recent evolution. By convention, the layers of neocortex are numbered I through VI, starting at the surface. Figure 3.29 illustrates two adjacent sections of neocortex. One has been stained with a Nissl stain to reveal the number and shape of its cell bodies; the other has been stained with a Golgi stain to reveal the silhouettes of a small number of its neurons.

Three important characteristics of neocortex anatomy are apparent from the sections in Figure 3.29. First, it is apparent that there are two fundamentally different kinds of cortical

Longitudinal
fissure

Precentral
gyrus

Central
fissure

Postcentral
gyrus

Lateral
fissure

Superior
temporal
gyrus

Cerebellum

Frontal
lobe

Parietal
lobe

Temporal
lobe

Occipital
lobe

Figure 3.28 The lobes of the cerebral hemispheres.

neurons: pyramidal (pyramid-shaped) cells and stellate (star-shaped) cells. **Pyramidal cells** are large multipolar neurons with pyramid-shaped cell bodies, a large dendrite called an *apical dendrite* that extends from the apex of the pyramid straight towards the cortex surface, and a very long axon. In contrast, **stellate cells** are small star-shaped interneurons (neurons with short axons). Second, it is apparent that the six layers of neocortex differ from one anoth-er in terms of the size and density of their cell bodies and the relative proportion of pyramidal and stellate cell bodies that they contain. Third, it is apparent that many long axons and dendrites course vertically (i.e., at right angles to the cortical layers) through the neocortex. This vertical flow of information is the basis of the neocortex's **columnar organization;** neurons in a given vertical column of neocortex form a mini circuit that performs a single function.

Chapter 3   The Anatomy of the Nervous System

Nissl Stained Neocortex

Stellate cell

Pyramidal cell

WHITE MATTER

Golgi Stained Neocortex

WHITE MATTER

1   Axons and dendrites; few cell bodies.

2   Densely packed stellate cells; a few small pyramidal cells.

3   Loosely packed stellate cells; intermediate sized pyramidal cells.

4   Bands of densely packed stellate cells; no pyramidal cells.

5   Very large pyramidal cells; a few loosely packed stellate cells.

6   Pyramidal cells of various sizes; loosely packed stellate cells.

  Myelinated pyramidal cell axons; few cell bodies.

Figure 3.29   The six layers of neocortex. (Adapted from Rakic, 1979.)

A fourth important characteristic of neocortex anatomy is not apparent in Figure 3.29: Although all neocortex is six-layered, there are variations in the layers from area to area. For example, because the stellate cells of layer IV are specialized for receiving sensory signals from the thalamus, layer IV is extremely thick in areas of sensory cortex. Con-versely, because the pyramidal cells of layer V conduct signals from the neocortex to the brain stem and spinal cord, layer V is extremely thick in areas of motor cortex.

The **hippocampus** is one important area of cortex that is not neocortex—it has only three layers. The hippocampus is located at the medial edge of the cerebral cortex as it folds back on itself in the medial temporal lobe (see Figure 3.27). This folding produces a shape that is, in cross section, somewhat reminiscent of a sea horse (*hippocampus* means "sea horse").

The limbic system and the basal ganglia   Although much of the subcortical portion of the telencephalon is taken up by axons projecting to and from the neocortex, there are several large subcortical nuclear groups. Some of them are considered to be part of either the *limbic system* or the *basal ganglia motor system*. Don't be misled by the word *system* in these contexts; it implies a level of certainty that is unwarranted. It is not entirely clear exactly what

Pyramidal cells. Large cortical multipolar neurons with a pyramid-shaped cell body, an apical dendrite, and a long axons.

Stellate cells. Small star-shaped cortical interneurons with short axons.

Columnar organization. The functional organization of the neocortex in vertical columns; the cells in each column form a mini circuit that performs a single function.

these hypothetical systems do, exactly which structures should be included in them, or even whether it is appropriate to view them as unitary systems. Nevertheless, if not taken too literally, the concepts of *limbic system* and *basal ganglia motor system* provide a useful means of conceptualizing the organization of the subcortex.

The **limbic system** is a circuit of midline structures that circle the thalamus (*limbic* means "ring"). The limbic system is involved in the regulation of motivated behaviors—including the four *F*s of motivation: fleeing, feeding, fighting, and sexual behavior. (This joke is as old as biopsychology itself, but it is a good one.) In addition to several structures about which you have already read (e.g., the mammillary bodies and the hippocampus), major structures of the limbic system include the amygdala, the fornix, the cingulate cortex, and the septum.

Let's begin tracing the limbic circuit (see Figure 3.30) at the **amygdala**—the almond-shaped nucleus in the anterior temporal lobe (*amygdala* means "almond"). Posterior to the amygdala is the hippocampus, which runs beneath the thalamus in the medial temporal lobe. Next in the ring are the **cingulate cortex** and the **fornix.** The cingulate cortex is the large area of neocortex in the **cingulate gyrus** on the medial surface of the cerebral hemispheres, just superior to the corpus callosum; it encircles the dorsal thalamus (*cingulate* means "encircling"). The fornix, the major tract of the limbic system, also encircles the dorsal thalamus; it leaves the dorsal end of the hippocampus and sweeps forward in an arc coursing along the superior surface of the third ventricle and terminating in the septum and mammillary bodies (*fornix* means "arc"). The **septum** is a midline nucleus that is located at the anterior tip of the cingu-

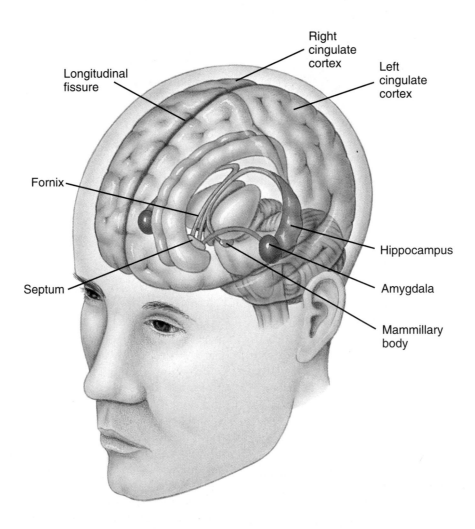

Figure 3.30 The major structures of the limbic system: amygdala, hippocampus, cingulate cortex, fornix, septum, and mammillary body.

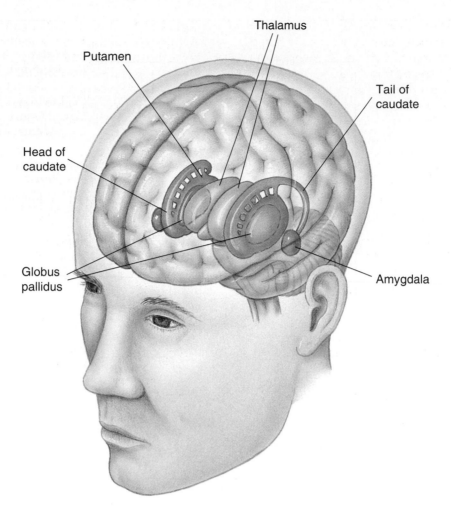

Putamen

Thalamus

Tail of
caudate

Head of
caudate

Globus
pallidus

Amygdala

Figure 3.31 The basal ganglia: amygdala, striatum (caudate plus putamen), and globus pallidus.

late cortex. Several tracts connect the septum and mammillary bodies with the amygdala and hippocampus, thereby completing the limbic ring.

The **basal ganglia** are illustrated in Figure 3.31. As we did with the limbic system, let's begin our examination of the basal ganglia with the amygdala (pronounced "a MIG dah lah"), which is considered to be part of both systems. Sweeping out of each amygdala, first in a posterior direction and then in an anterior direction, is the long tail-like **caudate** nucleus (*caudate* means "tail-like"). Each caudate nucleus forms an almost complete circle; in its center, connected to it by a series of fiber bridges, is the **putamen** (pronounced "pew TAY men"). Together, the caudate nucleus and putamen, which both have a striped appearance, are known as the **striatum** ("striped structure"). The remaining structure of the basal ganglia is the pale circular structure known as the **globus pallidus** ("pale globe"). The globus pallidus is located medial to the putamen, between the putamen and the thalamus.

The basal ganglia play a major role in the performance of voluntary motor responses. Of particular interest is a pathway that projects to the striatum from the substantia nigra of the midbrain. *Parkinson's disease,* a disorder that is characterized by rigidity, tremors, and poverty of voluntary movement, is associated with the deterioration of this pathway.

Figure 3.32 summarizes the major brain structures—those that have appeared in boldface.

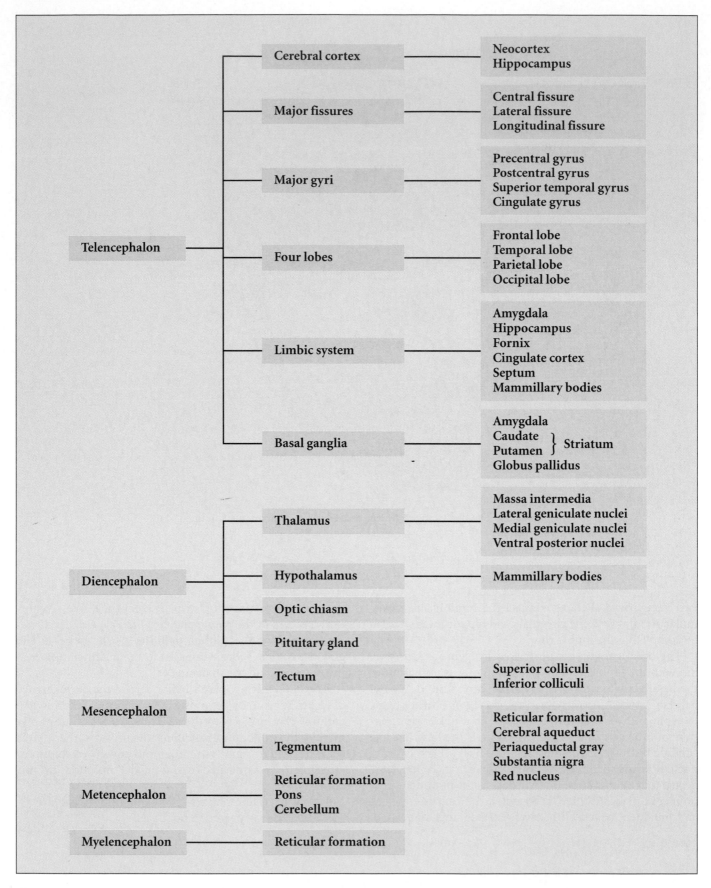

Figure 3.32 Summary of major brain structures. This is a diagram of brain anatomy key terms. It contains all the brain anatomy key terms that appear in boldface in this chapter.

If you have not previously studied the gross anatomy of the brain, your own brain is probably straining under the burden of new terms. It is time to pause and assess your progress. Test your knowledge of the brain by labeling the following midsagittal view of a human brain. The correct answers are provided at the bottom of the page. Before proceeding, review material related to your errors and omissions. Notice Figure 3.32; it includes all the brain structures that have appeared in this chapter in bold type, and thus it is an excellent vehicle for review.

1. _____ lobe
2. _____ gyrus
3. _____
4. _____
5. _____
6. _____
7. _____ colliculus
8. _____ body
9. _____
10. _____ ventricle
11. _____
12. _____
13. _____
14. _____

CONCLUSION

The first three sections of this chapter introduced you to the general layout of the nervous system (3.1), to the cells that compose it (3.2), and to the neuroanatomical techniques that are used to study it (3.3). The final three sections introduced you to the names and locations of the central nervous system's major structures: First, you learned about the structures of the spinal cord (3.4); then you learned about the brain's five major divisions (3.5);

and finally, you learned about the brain's major nuclei and tracts (3.6).

Figure 3.33 concludes this chapter for reasons that too often get lost in the shuffle of neuroanatomical terms and technology. I have included it here to illustrate the beauty of the brain and the art of those who study its structure. I hope you are inspired by it. I wonder what ideas these neural circuits once contained.

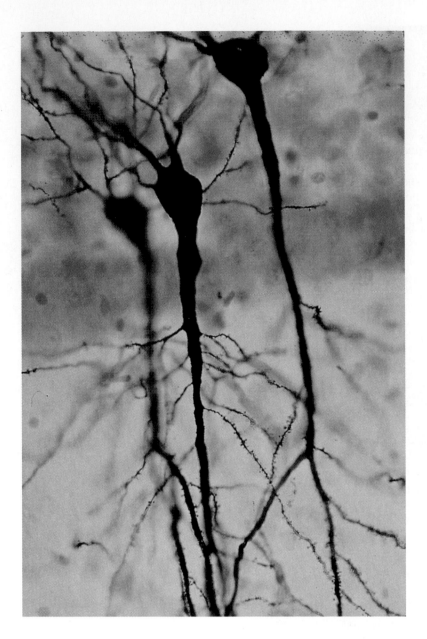

Figure 3.33 The art of neuroanatomical staining. These pyramidal cells were stained with a Golgi stain and then with a Nissl stain. Clearly visible are the pyramid-shaped cell bodies and apical dendrites of the pyramidal cells. Each pyramidal cell has a long, narrow axon; here they project off the bottom of the slide. (Courtesy of Miles Herkenham, Unit of Functional Neuroanatomy, National Institute of Mental Health, Bethesda, MD.)

FOOD FOR THOUGHT

1. Which of the following extreme positions do you think is closer to the truth? (a) The primary goal of all psychological research should be to relate psychological phenomena to the anatomy of neural circuits. (b) Psychologists should leave the study of neuroanatomy to neuroanatomists.

2. Perhaps the most famous mistake in the history of biopsychology was made by Olds and Milner (see Chapter 13). They botched an electrode implantation, and the tip of the stimulation electrode ended up in an unknown structure in the brain of a rat. When they subsequently tested the effects of electrical stimulation of this unknown structure, they made a fantastic discovery: The rat seemed to find the brain stimulation extremely pleasurable. In fact, the rat would press a lever for hours at an extremely high rate if every press produced a brief stimulation to its brain through the electrode. If you had accidentally stumbled on this intracranial self-stimulation phenomenon, what neuroanatomical procedures would you have used to identify the stimulation site and the neural circuits involved in the pleasurable effects of the stimulation?

KEY TERMS

Central nervous system
(CNS) *(p. 50)*
Peripheral nervous system
(PNS) *(p. 50)*
Somatic nervous system
(SNS) *(p. 50)*
Afferent nerves *(p. 51)*
Efferent nerves *(p. 51)*
Autonomic nervous system
(ANS) *(p. 51)*
Sympathetic nerves *(p. 51)*
Parasympathetic nerves
(p. 51)
Cranial nerves *(p. 51)*
Meninges *(p. 52)*
Dura mater *(p. 52)*
Arachnoid membrane
(p. 52)
Subarachnoid space *(p. 52)*
Pia mater *(p. 52)*
Cerebrospinal fluid (CSF)
(p. 52)
Central canal *(p. 52)*
Cerebral ventricles *(p. 52)*
Choroid plexuses *(p. 53)*
Cerebral aqueduct *(p. 53)*
Blood-brain barrier *(p. 53)*
Multipolar neuron *(p. 54)*
Unipolar neuron *(p. 54)*
Bipolar neuron *(p. 54)*
Interneurons *(p. 54)*
Nucleus *(p. 54)*
Ganglia *(p. 54)*
Tracts *(p. 54)*
Nerves *(p. 54)*
Dendrites *(p. 55)*

Cell body *(p. 55)*
Axon hillock *(p. 55)*
Axon *(p. 55)*
Buttons *(p. 55)*
Cell membrane *(p. 55)*
Myelin *(p. 55)*
Nodes of Ranvier *(p. 55)*
Synapses *(p. 55)*
Endoplasmic reticulum
(p. 56)
Mitochondria *(p. 56)*
Nucleus *(p. 56)*
Cytoplasm *(p. 56)*
Ribosomes *(p. 56)*
Golgi complex *(p. 56)*
Microtubules *(p. 56)*
Synaptic vesicles *(p. 56)*
Neurotransmitters *(p. 56)*
Glial cells *(p. 58)*
Satellite cells *(p. 59)*
Astroglia (astrocytes)
(p. 59)
Oligodendroglia
(oligodendrocytes)
(p. 59)
Schwann cells *(p. 59)*
Golgi stain *(p. 59)*
Nissl stain *(p. 59)*
Electron microscopy *(p. 60)*
Myelin stains *(p. 60)*
Anterior *(p. 62)*
Posterior *(p. 62)*
Dorsal *(p. 62)*
Ventral *(p. 62)*
Medial *(p. 62)*
Lateral *(p. 62)*

Superior *(p. 62)*
Inferior *(p. 62)*
Horizontal sections *(p. 62)*
Frontal sections *(p. 62)*
Sagittal sections *(p. 62)*
Cross sections *(p. 62)*
Dorsal horns *(p. 64)*
Ventral horns *(p. 64)*
Brain stem *(p. 65)*
Myelencephalon *(p. 66)*
Reticular formation *(p. 66)*
Metencephalon *(p. 67)*
Pons *(p. 67)*
Cerebellum *(p. 67)*
Mesencephalon *(p. 68)*
Tectum *(p. 68)*
Inferior colliculi *(p. 68)*
Superior colliculi *(p. 68)*
Tegmentum *(p. 68)*
Periaqueductal gray *(p. 68)*
Cerebral aqueduct *(p. 68)*
Substantia nigra *(p. 68)*
Red nucleus *(p. 68)*
Diencephalon *(p. 68)*
Thalamus *(p. 68)*
Massa intermedia *(p. 69)*
Lateral geniculate nuclei
(p. 69)
Medial geniculate nuclei
(p. 69)
Ventral posterior nuclei
(p. 69)
Hypothalamus *(p. 69)*
Pituitary gland *(p. 69)*
Optic chiasm *(p. 69)*
Decussate *(p. 69)*

Contralateral *(p. 69)*
Ipsilateral *(p. 69)*
Mammillary bodies *(p. 70)*
Telencephalon *(p. 70)*
Cerebral cortex *(p. 70)*
Fissures *(p. 71)*
Gyri *(p. 71)*
Longitudinal fissure *(p. 71)*
Central fissure *(p. 71)*
Lateral fissure *(p. 71)*
Frontal lobe *(p. 71)*
Parietal lobe *(p. 71)*
Temporal lobe *(p. 71)*
Occipital lobe *(p. 71)*
Precentral gyri *(p. 71)*
Postcentral gyri *(p. 71)*
Superior temporal gyri
(p. 71)
Neocortex *(p. 71)*
Pyramidal cells *(p. 72)*
Stellate cells *(p. 72)*
Columnar organization
(p. 72)
Hippocampus *(p. 73)*
Limbic system *(p. 74)*
Amygdala *(p. 74)*
Cingulate cortex *(p. 74)*
Fornix *(p. 74)*
Cingulate gyrus *(p. 74)*
Septum *(p. 74)*
Basal ganglia *(p. 75)*
Caudate *(p. 75)*
Putamen *(p. 75)*
Striatum *(p. 75)*
Globus pallidus *(p. 75)*

ADDITIONAL READING

I recommend the following three books for those interested in learning more about neuroanatomy. The first is a wonderfully illustrated historical introduction to the brain; the second is a particularly clear neuroanatomy text; and the third is a classic collection of neuroanatomical illustrations:

Corsi, P. (1991). *The enchanted loom: Chapters in the history of neuroscience.* New York: Oxford University Press.

Nauta, W. J. H., & Feirtag, M. (1986). *Fundamental neuroanatomy.* New York: Freeman.

Netter, F. H. (1962). The CIBA collection of medical illustrations: Vol. 1. The nervous system. New York: CIBA.

4

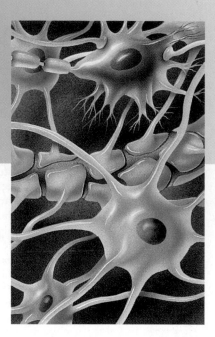

Neural Conduction and Synaptic Transmission

4.1 The Neuron's Resting Membrane Potential

4.2 Generation and Conduction of Postsynaptic Potentials

4.3 Integration of Postsynaptic Potentials and Generation of Action Potentials

4.4 Conduction of Action Potentials

4.5 Synaptic Transmission: Chemical Transmission of Signals from One Neuron to Another

4.6 The Neurotransmitters

4.7 Pharmacology of Synaptic Transmission

Chapter 3 introduced you to the anatomy of neurons. This chapter introduces you to their function—it is a chapter about how neurons conduct and transmit electrochemical signals. It begins with a description of how signals are generated in resting neurons; then it follows the signals as they are conducted through neurons and transmitted across synapses to other neurons.

The Lizard will help you appreciate why a knowledge of neural conduction and synaptic transmission is an integral part of biopsychology. *The Lizard* is the title of a case study of a patient with Parkinson's disease, Roberto Garcia d'Orta:

> "I have become a lizard," he began. "A great lizard frozen in a dark, cold, strange world."
>
> His name was Roberto Garcia d'Orta. He was a tall thin man in his sixties, but like most patients with Parkinson's disease, he appeared to be much older than his actual age. Not many years before, he had been an active, vigorous business man. Then it happened—not all at once, not suddenly, but slowly, subtly, insidiously. Now he turned like a piece of granite, walked in slow shuffling steps, and spoke in a monotonous whisper.
>
> What had been his first symptom?
>
> A tremor.
>
> Had his tremor been disabling?
>
> "No," he said. "My hands shake worse when they are doing nothing at all"—a symptom called tremor-at-rest.
>
> The other symptoms of Parkinson's disease are not quite so benign. They can change a vigorous man into a lizard. These include rigid muscles, a marked poverty of spontaneous movements, difficulty in starting to move, and slowness in executing voluntary movements once they have been initiated.
>
> The term "reptilian stare" is often used to describe the characteristic lack of blinking and the widely opened eyes gazing out of a motionless face, a set of features that seems more reptilian than human. Truly a lizard in the eyes of the world.
>
> What was happening in Mr. d'Orta's brain? A small group of nerve cells called the *substantia nigra* (black substance) were unaccountably dying. These neurons make a particular chemical neurotransmitter called dopamine, which they deliver to another part of the brain, known as the striatum. As the cells of the substantia nigra die, the amount of dopamine they can deliver goes down. The striatum helps control movement, and to do that normally, it needs dopamine. (Paraphrased from Klawans, 1990, pp. 53–57)[1]

Dopamine is not an effective treatment for Parkinson's disease because it does not readily penetrate the blood-brain barrier. However, knowledge of dopaminergic transmission has led to the development of an effective treatment: L-DOPA, the chemical precursor of dopamine, which readily penetrates the blood-brain barrier and is converted to dopamine once inside the brain.

Mr. d'Orta's neurologist prescribed L-DOPA, and it worked. He still had a bit of tremor; but his voice became stronger, his feet no longer shuffled, his reptilian stare faded away, and he was once again able to perform with ease many of the activities of daily life (e.g., eating, bathing, writing, speaking, and even making love with his wife). Mr. d'Orta had been destined to spend the rest of his life trapped inside a body that was becoming increasingly difficult to control, but his life sentence was repealed.

Keep Mr. d'Orta in mind as you read this chapter. His situation will remind you that normal neural activity is necessary for normal psychological activity, and it will serve as an example of the potential clinical benefits of understanding neural function. A knowledge of neural conduction and synaptic transmission is a major asset for any psychologist; it is a must for any biopsychologist.

4.1 The Neuron's Resting Membrane Potential

One key to understanding neural function is the **membrane potential,** the difference in electrical charge between the inside and the outside of a cell.

Recording the Membrane Potential

To record a neuron's membrane potential, it is necessary to position the tip of one electrode inside the neuron and the tip of another electrode outside the neuron in the extracellular fluid. Although the size and shape of the extracellular electrode are not critical, it is paramount that the tip of the intracellular electrode be fine enough to pierce the neural membrane without severely damaging it. The tips of intracellular **microelectrodes,** as they are called, are less than one thousandth of a millimeter in diameter—much too small to be seen by the naked eye.

To construct a microelectrode (see Figure 4.1), a fine glass tube is melted in the center and then suddenly pulled apart by an automated *microelectrode puller.* The infinitesimally small, but still hollow, point at which the tube separates serves as the electrode tip. The tube is then filled with

---

> **Membrane potential.** The difference in electrical charge between the inside and the outside of a cell.
>
> **Microelectrodes.** Extremely fine recording electrodes, which are used for intracellular recording.

---

[1]Paraphrased from *Newton's Madness: Further Tales of Clinical Neurology* by Harold L. Klawans. New York: Harper & Row, © Harold Klawans, 1990.

Figure 4.1 The construction of a microelectrode. The point of the microelectrode is invisible to the naked eye, so fine that it can penetrate a neuron without seriously damaging it.

(a) Heating the fine glass tube

(b) Pulling the electrode

(c) Filling it with saline

(d) Inserting the wire and sealing the end

a concentrated salt solution through which neural signals can be recorded. The construction of the microelectrode is completed by inserting a wire into the solution through the larger end and sealing it. The solution does not leak from the electrode tip because the opening is too small.

One method of recording a membrane potential is to connect the intracellular and extracellular electrodes by wires to an **oscilloscope**—a device that displays differences in the electrical potential at the two electrodes over time. The differences are displayed as vertical displacements of a glowing spot that sweeps across a fluorescent screen. Because the spot on an oscilloscope screen is produced by a beam of electrons, which has little inertia to overcome, an oscilloscope can accurately display even the most rapid changes in membrane potential. Figure 4.2 illustrates how a membrane potential is recorded on an oscilloscope.

Resting Membrane Potential

When both electrode tips are in the extracellular fluid, the voltage difference between them is zero. However, when the tip of the intracellular electrode is inserted into a neuron, a steady potential of about –70 millivolts (mV) is registered

on the oscilloscope screen. This indicates that the potential inside the resting neuron is about 70 mV less than that outside the neuron. This steady membrane potential of about –70 mV is called the neuron's **resting potential.** In its resting state, with the -70 mV charge built up across its membrane, a neuron is said to be *polarized.*

The Ionic Basis of the Resting Potential

Why are resting neurons polarized? Like all salts in solution, the salts in neural tissue separate into positively and negatively charged particles called **ions.** The resting potential results from the fact that the ratio of negative to positive charges is greater inside the neuron than outside. Why this unequal distribution of charges occurs can be understood in terms of the interaction of four factors: two forces that act to distribute ions equally throughout the intracellular and extracellular fluids of the nervous system and two features of the neural membrane that counteract these homogenizing forces.

The first of the two homogenizing forces is *random motion.* The ions in neural tissue are in constant random motion, and particles in random motion tend to become evenly distributed because they are more likely to move down their *concentration gradients* than up them; that is, they are more likely to move from areas of high concentration to areas of low concentration than vice versa. The second force that promotes the even distribution of ions is *electrostatic pressure.* Any accumulation of charges, positive or negative, in one area tends to be dispersed by the repulsion of like charges in the vicinity and the attraction of opposite charges concentrated elsewhere.

Despite the continuous homogenizing effects of random movement and electrostatic pressure, no single class of ions

Oscilloscope. A device used for recording membrane potentials.

Resting potential. The steady membrane potential of a neuron at rest, usually about –70 mV.

Ions. Positively or negatively charged particles.

Ion channels. Pores in membranes through which specific ions pass.

Chapter 4   Neural Conduction and Synaptic Transmission

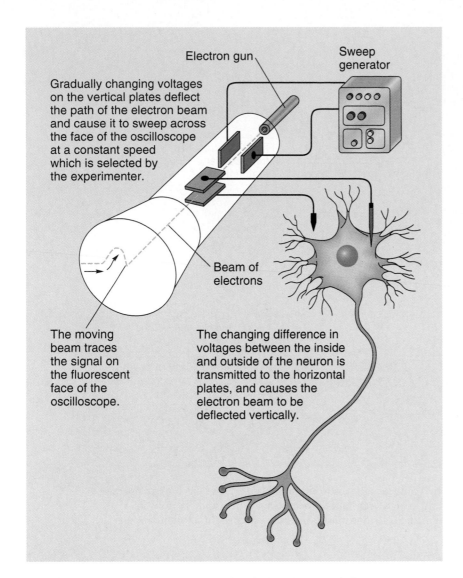

Gradually changing voltages on the vertical plates deflect the path of the electron beam and cause it to sweep across the face of the oscilloscope at a constant speed which is selected by the experimenter.

Electron gun

Sweep generator

Beam of electrons

The moving beam traces the signal on the fluorescent face of the oscilloscope.

The changing difference in voltages between the inside and outside of the neuron is transmitted to the horizontal plates, and causes the electron beam to be deflected vertically.

Figure 4.2 How a membrane potential is displayed on an oscilloscope.

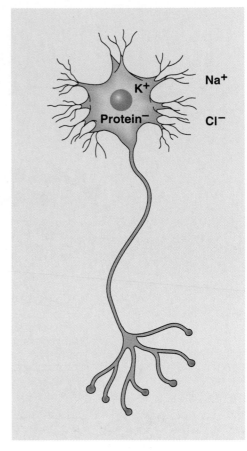

Figure 4.3 In its resting state, more Na$^+$ and Cl$^-$ ions are outside the resting neuron than inside, and more K$^+$ ions and protein$^-$ ions are inside the neuron than outside.

is distributed equally on the two sides of the neural membrane. Four kinds of ions contribute significantly to the resting potential: sodium ions (Na$^+$), potassium ions (K$^+$), chloride ions (Cl$^-$), and various negatively charged protein ions. The concentration of both Na$^+$ and Cl$^-$ ions is greater outside a resting neuron than inside, whereas K$^+$ ions are more concentrated on the inside. The negatively charged protein ions are synthesized inside the neuron and, for the most part, they stay there. See Figure 4.3. By the way, the symbols for sodium and potassium were derived from their Latin equivalents: *natrium* (Na$^+$) and *kalium* (K$^+$), respectively.

Two properties of the neural membrane are responsible for the unequal distribution of Na$^+$, K$^+$, Cl$^-$, and protein ions in resting neurons. One of these properties is passive, that is, it does not involve the consumption of energy. The other is active and does involve the consumption of energy. The passive property of the neural membrane that con-

tributes to the unequal disposition of ions is its differential permeability to Na$^+$, K$^+$, Cl$^-$, and protein ions. In resting neurons, K$^+$ and Cl$^-$ ions pass readily through the neural membrane, Na$^+$ ions pass through it with difficulty, and the negatively charged protein ions do not pass through it at all. Ions pass through the neural membrane at specialized pores called **ion channels,** each of which is specialized for the passage of particular ions.

In the 1950s, the classic experiments of neurophysiologists Alan Hodgkin and Andrew Huxley provided the first evidence that an energy-consuming process is involved in the maintenance of the resting potential. Hodgkin and Huxley began by wondering why the high extracellular concentrations of Na$^+$ and Cl$^-$ ions and the high intracellular concentration of K$^+$ ions were not eliminated by pressure for them to move down their concentration gradients to the side of lesser concentration. Could the electrostatic pressure of -70 mV across the membrane be the counter-

Figure 4.4 The passive and active forces that influence the distribution of Na⁺, K⁺, and Cl⁻ ions across the neural membrane. Passive forces continuously drive K⁺ ions out of the resting neuron and Na⁺ ions in; therefore, K⁺ ions must be actively pumped in and Na⁺ ions must be actively pumped out to maintain the resting equilibrium.

acting force that maintained the unequal distribution of ions? To answer this question, Hodgkin and Huxley calculated for each of the three ions the electrostatic charge that would be required to offset the pressure for them to move down their concentration gradients.

For Cl⁻ ions, this calculated electrostatic charge was −70 mV, the same as the actual resting potential. Hodgkin and Huxley thus concluded that when neurons are at rest, the unequal distribution of Cl⁻ ions across the neural membrane is maintained in equilibrium by the balance between the 70 mV force driving Cl⁻ ions down their concentration gradient into the neuron and the 70 mV of electrostatic pressure driving them out.

The situation turned out to be different for the K⁺ ions. Hodgkin and Huxley calculated that 90 mV of electrostatic pressure would be required to keep intracellular K⁺ ions from moving down their concentration gradient and leaving the neuron—some 20 mV more than the actual resting potential.

In the case of Na⁺ ions, the situation was much more extreme because the forces of both the concentration gradient and the electrostatic gradient act in the same direc-

tion. In the resting neuron, the concentration of Na⁺ ions outside the neuron creates 50 mV of pressure for Na⁺ ions to move down their concentration gradient into the neuron, which is added to the 70 mV of electrostatic pressure

Sodium-potassium pumps. Active transport mechanisms that pump Na⁺ ions out of neurons and K⁺ ions in.

Depolarize. To decrease the membrane potential.

Hyperpolarize. To increase the membrane potential.

Excitatory postsynaptic potentials (EPSPs). Graded postsynaptic depolarizations, which increase the likelihood that an action potential will be generated.

Inhibitory postsynaptic potentials (IPSPs). Graded postsynaptic hyperpolarizations, which decrease the likelihood that an action potential will be generated.

Graded responses. Responses whose magnitude is related to the magnitude of the stimuli.

for them to move in the same direction. Thus a whopping total of 120 mV of pressure is trying to force Na$^+$ ions into resting neurons.

Subsequent experiments confirmed Hodgkin and Huxley's calculations. They showed that K$^+$ ions are continuously being driven out of resting neurons by the 20 mV of pressure and that, despite the high resistance of the cell membrane to the passage of Na$^+$ ions, the Na$^+$ ions are continuously being driven in by the 120 mV of pressure. Why, then, do the intracellular and extracellular concentrations of Na$^+$ and K$^+$ remain constant in resting neurons? Hodgkin and Huxley discovered that there are active mechanisms in the cell membrane to counteract the *influx* (inflow) of Na$^+$ ions by pumping Na$^+$ ions out as rapidly as they leak in and to counteract the *efflux* (outflow) of K$^+$ ions by pumping K$^+$ ions in as rapidly as they leak out. Figure 4.4 summarizes Hodgkin and Huxley's findings and conclusions.

It was subsequently discovered that the transport of Na$^+$ ions out of neurons and the transport of K$^+$ ions into them are not independent processes. Sodium and potassium transport is performed by energy-consuming transport mechanisms in the cell membrane that continually exchange three Na$^+$ ions inside the neuron for two K$^+$ ions outside. These mechanisms are commonly referred to as **sodium-potassium pumps.**

Table 4.1 summarizes the major factors that are responsible for maintaining the differences between the intracellular and extracellular concentrations of Na$^+$, K$^+$, and Cl$^-$ ions in resting neurons. These differences plus the negatively charged protein ions, which are trapped inside the neuron, are largely responsible for the resting membrane potential.

Now that you understand these basic properties of the resting neuron, you are prepared to consider how neurons respond to input.

TABLE 4.1

The Factors Responsible for Maintaining the Differences in the Intracellular and Extracellular Concentrations of Na$^+$, K$^+$, and Cl$^-$ Ions in Resting Neurons

Na$^+$	Na$^+$ ions are driven into the neuron by both the high concentration of Na$^+$ ions outside the neuron and the negative internal resting charge of -70 mV. However, the membrane is resistant to the passive diffusion of Na$^+$, and the sodium-potassium pump is thus able to maintain the high external concentration of Na$^+$ ions by pumping them out at the same slow rate as they leak in.
K$^+$	K$^+$ ions are driven out of the neuron by their high internal concentration, although this pressure is partially offset by the internal negative charge. Despite the minimum pressure for the K$^+$ ions to leave the neuron, they do so at a substantial rate because the membrane offers little resistance to their passage. To maintain the high internal concentration of K$^+$ ions, mechanisms in the cell membrane pump K$^+$ ions into neurons at the same rate as they diffuse out.
Cl$^-$	There is little resistance in the neural membrane to the passage of Cl$^-$ ions. Thus Cl$^-$ ions are readily forced out of the neuron by the negative internal charge. As chloride ions begin to accumulate on the outside, there is increased pressure for them to move down their concentration gradient back into the neuron. When the point is reached where the electrostatic pressure for Cl$^-$ ions to move out of the neuron is equal to the pressure for them to move back in, the distribution of Cl$^-$ ions is held in equilibrium. This point of equilibrium occurs at -70 mV.

4.2 Generation and Conduction of Postsynaptic Potentials

When neurons fire, they release from their terminal buttons chemicals called *neurotransmitters,* which diffuse across the synaptic clefts and interact with specialized receptor molecules on the receptive membranes of the next neurons in the circuit. When neurotransmitter molecules bind to postsynaptic receptors, they typically have one of two effects, depending on the structure of both the neurotransmitter and the receptor in question. They may **depolarize** the receptive membrane (decrease the resting membrane potential—from -70 to -67 mV, for example) or they may **hyperpolarize** it (increase the resting membrane potential—from -70 to -72 mV, for example).

Postsynaptic depolarizations are called **excitatory postsynaptic potentials (EPSPs)** because, as you will soon learn, they increase the likelihood that the neuron will fire. Postsynaptic hyperpolarizations are called **inhibitory postsynaptic potentials (IPSPs)** because they decrease the likelihood that the neuron will fire. Both EPSPs and IPSPs are **graded responses.** This means that the amplitudes of EPSPs and IPSPs are proportional to the intensity of the signals that elicit them; weak signals elicit small postsynaptic potentials and strong signals elicit large ones.

EPSPs and IPSPs travel passively from their sites of generation at synapses, usually on the dendrites or cell body, in much the same way that electrical signals travel through a cable. Accordingly, the transmission of postsynaptic potentials has two important characteristics. First, it is rapid—so rapid that it can be assumed to be instantaneous for most purposes. It is important not to confuse the duration of EPSPs and IPSPs with their rate of transmission; although the duration of EPSPs and IPSPs varies considerably, all postsynaptic potentials, whether brief or enduring, are transmitted at great speed. Second, the transmission of EPSPs and IPSPs is *decremental*; EPSPs and IPSPs decrease in amplitude as they travel through the neuron, just as a sound wave grows fainter as it travels through air.

<table>
<tr><td>**4.3**</td><td></td></tr>
</table>

4.3 Integration of Postsynaptic Potentials and Generation of Action Potentials

The postsynaptic potentials created at a single synapse typically have little effect on the firing of the postsynaptic neuron. The receptive areas of most neurons are covered with thousands of synapses, and whether or not a neuron fires is determined by the net effect of their activity. More specifically, whether or not a neuron fires depends on the balance between the excitatory and inhibitory signals reaching its **axon hillock**—the conical structure at the junction between the cell body and the axon.

The graded EPSPs and IPSPs created by the action of neurotransmitters at particular receptive sites on the neural membrane are conducted instantly and decrementally to the axon hillock. If the sum of the depolarizations and hyperpolarizations reaching the axon hillock at any time is sufficient to depolarize the membrane to a level referred to as its **threshold of excitation**—usually about –65 mV—an action potential is generated at the axon hillock. The **action potential (AP)** is a massive momentary—about 1 millisecond—reversal of the membrane potential from about –70 to about +50 mV. Unlike postsynaptic potentials, action

Axon hillock. The conical structure at the junction between the axon and cell body, where action potentials are normally generated.

Threshold of excitation. The level of depolarization at the axon hillock necessary to generate an action potential, usually about –65 mV.

Action potential (AP). The firing of a neuron; a massive momentary change in the membrane potential from about –70 mV to about +50 mV.

All-or-none responses. Responses that are not graded; responses that occur full-blown or not at all.

Integration. Adding or combining a number of individual signals into one overall signal.

Spatial summation. The integration of signals that occur at different sites on the neuron.

Temporal summation. The integration of neural signals that begin at different times on the same neuron.

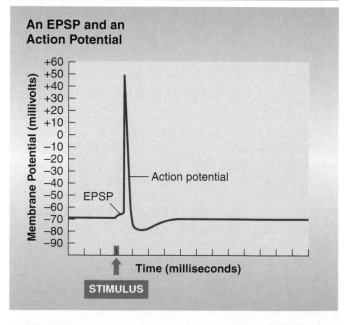

Figure 4.5 An EPSP, an IPSP, and an EPSP followed by an AP.

Chapter 4   Neural Conduction and Synaptic Transmission

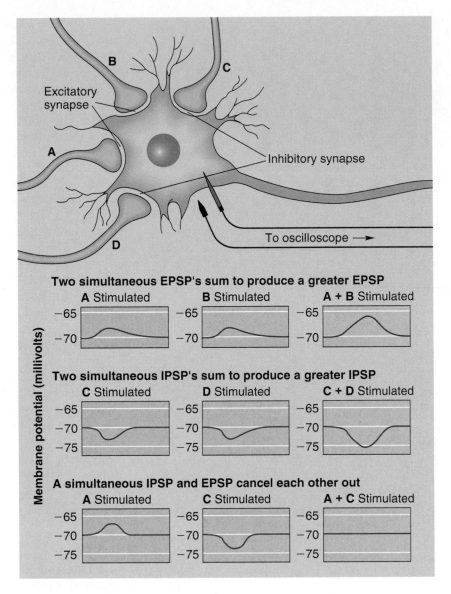

Figure 4.6 The three possible combinations of spatial summation.

potentials are not graded responses; their magnitude is not related in any way to the intensity of the stimuli that elicit them. To the contrary, they are **all-or-none responses**; that is, they either occur full-blown or do not occur at all. See Figure 4.5 for an illustration of an EPSP, an IPSP, and an AP.

In effect, each multipolar neuron adds together all the graded excitatory and inhibitory postsynaptic potentials reaching its axon hillock and decides to fire or not to fire on the basis of their sum. Adding or combining a number of individual signals into one overall signal is called **integration.** Neurons integrate incoming signals in two ways: over space and over time.

Figure 4.6 illustrates the three possible combinations of **spatial summation.** It shows how local EPSPs that are produced simultaneously on different parts of the receptive membrane sum to form a greater EPSP, how simultaneous IPSPs sum to form a greater IPSP, and how simultaneous EPSPs and IPSPs sum to cancel each other out.

Figure 4.7 illustrates **temporal summation.** It shows how postsynaptic potentials produced in rapid succession at the same synapse sum to form a greater signal. The reason that stimulations of a neuron can summate over time is that the postsynaptic potentials they produce often outlast them. Thus, if a particular synapse is activated and then activated again before the original postsynaptic potential has completely dissipated, the effect of the second stimulus will be superimposed on the lingering postsynaptic potential produced by the first. Accordingly, it is possible for a brief subthreshold excitatory stimulus to fire a neuron if it is administered twice in rapid succession. In the same way,

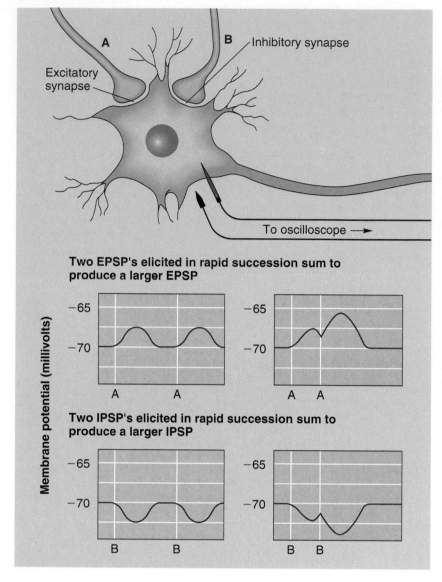

Two EPSP's elicited in rapid succession sum to produce a larger EPSP

Two IPSP's elicited in rapid succession sum to produce a larger IPSP

Figure 4.7 The two possible combinations of temporal summation.

an inhibitory synapse activated twice in rapid succession can produce a greater IPSP than that produced by a single stimulation.

Each neuron continuously integrates signals over both time and space as it is continually bombarded with stimuli through the thousands of synapses covering its dendrites and cell body. Remember that although schematic diagrams of neural circuitry rarely include neurons with more than a few representative synaptic contacts, most neurons receive thousands of synaptic contacts. The location of a synapse on a receptive membrane is an important factor in determining its potential to influence neural firing. Because EPSPs and IPSPs are transmitted decrementally, synapses near the axon hillock trigger zone have the most influence on the firing of the neuron.

In some ways, the firing of a neuron is like the firing of a gun. Both are all-or-none reactions triggered by graded responses. As a trigger is squeezed, it gradually moves back until it causes the gun to fire; as a neuron is stimulated, it becomes less polarized until the threshold of excitation is reached and the neuron fires. Furthermore, the firing of a gun and neural firing are both all-or-none events. Just as squeezing a trigger harder does not make the bullet travel faster or farther, stimulating a neuron more intensely does not increase the speed or amplitude of the resulting action potential.

4.4 Conduction of Action Potentials

Ionic Basis of Action Potentials

How are action potentials produced, and how are they conducted through the neuron? The answer to both questions is basically the same: through the action of **voltage-activated ion channels**—ion channels that open or close in response to changes in the voltage of the membrane potential.

Recall that the membrane potential of a neuron at rest is relatively constant despite the great pressure for Na^+ ions to flow into the cell. This is because the resting membrane is relatively impermeable to Na^+ ions and because those few that leak in are pumped out. But things suddenly change

when the membrane potential at the axon hillock is reduced to the threshold of excitation. The voltage-activated sodium channels in the hillock membrane open wide, and Na^+ ions rush in, suddenly driving the membrane potential from about −70 to about +50 mV. The rapid change in the membrane potential that is associated with the *influx* of Na^+ ions then triggers the opening of voltage-activated potassium channels. At this point, K^+ ions near the membrane are driven out of the cell through these channels—first by their relatively high internal concentration and then, when the action potential is near its peak, by the positive internal charge. After about 1 millisecond, the sodium channels close. This marks the end of the *rising phase* of the action potential and the beginning of *repolarization* by the continued efflux of K+ ions. Once repolarization has been achieved, the potassium channels gradually close. Because they close gradually, too many K+ ions flow out of the neuron, and it is left hyperpolarized for a brief period of time. Figure 4.8 illustrates the timing of the opening and closing of the sodium and potassium channels during an action potential.

Figure 4.8 The opening and closing of voltage-activated sodium and potassium channels during the three phases of the action potential: rising phase, repolarization, and hyperpolarization.

The number of ions that flow through the membrane during an action potential is extremely small in relation to the total number inside and around the neuron. The action potential involves only those ions right next to the membrane. Therefore, a single action potential has little effect on the relative concentrations of various ions inside and outside the neuron, and the resting ion concentrations next to the membrane are rapidly reestablished by the random movement of ions. The sodium-potassium pump plays only a minor role in the reestablishment of the resting potential.

Refractory Periods

There is a brief period of about 1 to 2 milliseconds after the initiation of an action potential during which it is impossible to elicit a second one. This period is called the **absolute refractory period.** The absolute refractory period is followed by the **relative refractory period**—the period during which it is possible to fire the neuron again, but only by applying higher-than-normal levels of stimulation. The end of the relative refractory period is the point at which the amount of stimulation necessary to fire a neuron returns to baseline.

The refractory period is responsible for two important characteristics of neural activity. First, it is responsible for the fact that action potentials normally travel along axons in only one direction. Because the portions of an axon over which an action potential has just traveled are left momentarily refractory, an action potential cannot reverse direction. Second, it is responsible for the fact that the rate of neural firing is related to the intensity of the stimulation. If a neuron is subjected to a high level of continual stimulation, it fires and then fires again as soon as its absolute refractory period is over—a maximum of about 1,000 times per second. However, if the level of stimulation is of an intensity just sufficient to fire the neuron when it is at rest, the neuron does not fire again until both the absolute

and the relative refractory periods have run their course. Intermediate levels of stimulation produce intermediate rates of neural firing.

Conduction of Action Potentials

The conduction of action potentials along an axon differs from the conduction of EPSPs and IPSPs in two important ways. First, the conduction of action potentials along an axon is *nondecremental*; action potentials do not grow weaker as they travel along the axonal membrane. Second, action potentials are conducted more slowly than postsynaptic potentials.

The reason for these two differences is that the conduction of EPSPs and IPSPs is passive, whereas the axonal conduction of action potentials is largely active. Once an action potential has been generated at the axon hillock, it travels passively along the axonal membrane to the adjacent voltage-activated sodium channels, which have yet to

Voltage-activated ion channels. Ion channels that open and close in response to changes in the membrane potential.

Absolute refractory period. A brief period (typically 1 to 2 milliseconds) after the initiation of an action potential during which it is impossible to elicit another action potential in the same neuron.

Relative refractory period. A period after the absolute refractory period during which a higher-than-normal amount of stimulation is necessary to make a neuron fire.

open. The arrival of the electrical signal opens these channels, thereby allowing Na^+ ions to rush into the neuron and generate a full-blown action potential on this portion of the membrane. This signal is then conducted passively to the next sodium channels, where another action potential is actively triggered. These events are repeated again and again until a full-blown action potential is triggered in the terminal buttons.

However, because the ion channels on the axonal membrane are so close together, it is usual to think of axonal conduction as a single wave of excitation spreading actively at a constant speed along the axon, rather than as a series of discrete events.

The wave of excitation triggered by the generation of an action potential on the hillock membrane also spreads back through the cell body and dendrites of the neuron. However, because the sodium channels of the cell body and dendrites are not voltage-activated, the conduction of action potentials back through the cell body and dendrites is passive.

The following analogy may help you appreciate the major characteristics of axonal conduction. Consider a row of mouse traps on a wobbly shelf, all of them set and ready to be triggered. Each trap stores energy by holding back its striker against the pressure of the spring, in the same way that each sodium channel stores energy by holding back Na^+ ions, which are under pressure to move down their concentration and electrostatic gradients into the neuron. When the first trap in the row is triggered, the vibration is transmitted passively through the shelf and the next trap is sprung—and so on down the line.

The nondecremental nature of action potential conduction is readily apparent from this analogy; the last trap on the shelf strikes with no less intensity than did the first. This analogy also illustrates the refractory period: A trap cannot respond again until it has been reset, just as a section of axon cannot fire again until it has been repolarized. Furthermore, the row of traps can transmit in either direction, just like an axon. If electrical stimulation of sufficient intensity is applied to the terminal end of an axon, an action potential will be generated and will travel along the axon back to the cell body; this is called **antidromic conduction.** Axonal conduction in the natural direction—from cell body to terminal buttons—is called **orthodromic conduction.**

Conduction in Myelinated Axons

In Chapter 3, you learned that the axons of many neurons are insulated from the extracellular fluid by segments of fatty tissue called *myelin.* In myelinated axons, ions can pass through the axonal membrane only at the **nodes of Ranvier**—the gaps between adjacent myelin segments. How, then, are action potentials transmitted in myelinated axons?

When an action potential is generated at the axon hillock of a myelinated axon, the signal is conducted passively—that is, instantly and decrementally—along the first segment of myelin to the first node of Ranvier. Although the signal is somewhat diminished by the time it reaches the first node, it is still strong enough to open the voltage-activated sodium channels at the node and to generate another full-blown action potential. This action potential is conducted passively to the next node, where another full-blown action potential is elicited, and so on.

Myelination increases the speed of axonal conduction. Because conduction along the myelinated segments of the axon is passive, it occurs instantly, and the signal thus "jumps" down the axon from node to node. There is, of course, a slight delay at each node of Ranvier while the action potential is actively generated, but the conduction in myelinated axons is still much faster than in unmyelinated axons, in which passive conduction plays a less prominent role. The transmission of action potentials in myelinated axons is called **saltatory conduction** (*saltare* means "to skip or jump").

The Velocity of Axonal Conduction

At what speed are action potentials conducted along an axon? The answer to this question depends on two properties of the axon. Conduction is faster in large-diameter axons, and—as you have just learned—it is faster in those that are myelinated. Mammalian *motor neurons* (neurons that synapse on skeletal muscles) are large and myelinated; thus they can conduct at speeds of up to 100 meters per second (about 224 miles per hour). In contrast, small, unmyelinated axons conduct action potentials at about 1 meter per second.

Antidromic conduction. Axonal conduction opposite to the normal direction; conduction from axon terminals back toward the cell body.

Orthodromic conduction. Axonal conduction in the natural direction; conduction from the cell body toward the terminal buttons.

Nodes of Ranvier. The gaps in axonal myelin.

Saltatory conduction. Conduction of an action potential from node to node down a myelinated axon.

Dendritic spines. Specialized dendritic buds on which axodendritic synapses often occur.

Presynaptic inhibition. A form of inhibition that selectively reduces a neuron's responsiveness to specific synaptic input; it is mediated by excitatory axoaxonal synapses.

Postsynaptic inhibition. A form of inhibition that reduces a neuron's responsiveness to all excitatory synaptic inputs.

Conduction in Neurons without Axons

Action potentials are the means by which axons conduct all-or-none signals nondecrementally over relatively long distances. Thus, to keep what you have just learned about action potentials in perspective, it is important for you to remember that many neurons in the mammalian brain do not have axons and thus do not display action potentials. Neural conduction in such *interneurons* is entirely by graded, decrementally conducted potentials.

4.5 Synaptic Transmission: Chemical Transmission of Signals from One Neuron to Another

You have learned in this chapter how postsynaptic potentials are generated on the receptive membrane of resting neurons, how these graded potentials are conducted passively to the axon hillock, how the sum of these graded potentials can trigger action potentials, and how these all-or-none potentials are actively conducted down the axon to the terminal buttons. In the remaining sections of this chapter, you will learn how action potentials arriving at terminal buttons trigger the release of neurotransmitters into synapses and how neurotransmitters carry signals to other cells. This section provides an overview of five aspects of synaptic transmission: (1) the structure of synapses; (2) the synthesis, packaging, and transport of neurotransmitter molecules; (3) the release of neurotransmitter molecules; (4) the activation of receptors by neurotransmitter molecules; and (5) the reuptake, enzymatic degradation, and recycling of neurotransmitter molecules.

Structure of Synapses

Most communication among neurons occurs across synapses such as the one illustrated in Figure 4.9. Neurotransmitter molecules are released from buttons into synaptic clefts, where they induce EPSPs or IPSPs in other neurons by binding to receptors in their postsynaptic membranes. The synapses featured in Figure 4.9 are *axodendritic synapses*—synapses of axon terminal buttons on dendrites. Many axodendritic synapses terminate on **dendritic spines** (see Figure 3.33)—small synaptic buds that cover the surfaces of many dendrites (see Harris & Kater, 1994). Also common are *axosomatic synapses*—synapses of axon terminal buttons on *somas* (cell bodies).

Although axodendritic and axosomatic synapses are the most common synaptic arrangements, there are several other kinds. For example, there are *dendrodendritic synapses*, which are interesting because they are often capable of transmission in either direction; and there are *axoaxonal synapses*, which are interesting because some of them mediate presynaptic inhibition (see Rudomin, 1990). **Presynaptic inhibition** is compared with **postsynaptic inhibition** in Figure 4.10.

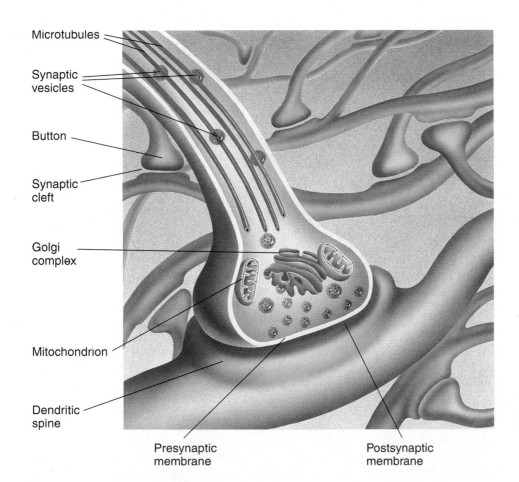

Microtubules
Synaptic vesicles
Button
Synaptic cleft
Golgi complex
Mitochondrion
Dendritic spine
Presynaptic membrane
Postsynaptic membrane

Figure 4.9 The anatomy of a typical synapse.

The synapses depicted in Figure 4.9 are **directed synapses**—synapses at which the site of neurotransmitter release and the site of neurotransmitter reception are in close proximity. This is a common arrangement, but there are also many nondirected synapses in the nervous system. **Nondirected synapses** are synapses at which the site of release is at some distance from the site of reception (see Agnati, Bjelke, & Fuxe, 1992). One type of nondirected synapse is depicted in Figure 4.11. In this type of arrangement, neurotransmitter molecules are released from a series of varicosities along the axon and its branches and thus are widely dispersed to surrounding targets. These synapses are often referred to as *string-of-beads synapses* because of their appearance.

Synthesis, Packaging, and Transport of Neurotransmitter Molecules

Neurotransmitter molecules are of two basic types: small and large (see Matteoli & DeCamilli, 1991). The molecules of most neurotransmitters are small; only the peptide neurotransmitters are large. **Peptides** are amino acid chains that are composed of 10 or fewer amino acids; in effect, they are short proteins.

Small-molecule neurotransmitters are typically synthesized in the cytoplasm of the button and packaged in **synaptic vesicles** by the button's **Golgi complex** (Miller & Heuser, 1984). Once filled with neurotransmitter, the vesicles are stored in clusters right next to the presynaptic membrane. In contrast, peptide neurotransmitters, like other proteins, are synthesized in the cytoplasm of the cell body by *ribosomes*; then they are packaged in vesicles by the cell body's Golgi complex and transported by *micro-tubules* to the terminal buttons at a rate of about 40 centimeters per day (see Vallee & Bloom, 1991). The vesicles that contain large-molecule neurotransmitters are larger

Postsynaptic Inhibition

Excitatory synapse

A

B

C

Inhibitory synapse

In postsynaptic inhibition, **B** inhibits the excitatory effects of **A** or any other excitatory neuron synapsing on **C** by hyperpolarizing **C**.

Presynaptic Inhibition

Excitatory synapse

A

B

C

Excitatory synapse

In presynaptic ihibition, **B** inhibits the excitatory effects of **A** on **C** by partially depolarizing the button of **A**, so that action potentials traveling down **A** release less neurotransmitter onto **C**. Notice that presynaptic inhibition occurs in the absence of inhibitory neurotransmitters or IPSPs.

Figure 4.10 Presynaptic and postsynaptic inhibition.

than those that contain small-molecule neurotransmitters, and they do not congregate as closely as the other vesicles to the presynaptic membrane (see Thureson-Klein & Klein, 1990).

It may have escaped your notice that the button illustrated in Figure 4.9 contains synaptic vesicles of two sizes. This means that it contains two neurotransmitters: a peptide neurotransmitter in the larger vesicles and a small-molecule neurotransmitter in the smaller vesicles. It was once believed that each neuron synthesizes and releases only one neurotransmitter, but it is now clear that many neurons contain two neurotransmitters—a situation that is referred to as **coexistence.** So far, all documented cases of coexistence have involved one small-molecule neurotransmitter and one peptide neurotransmitter (see Jung & Scheller, 1991).

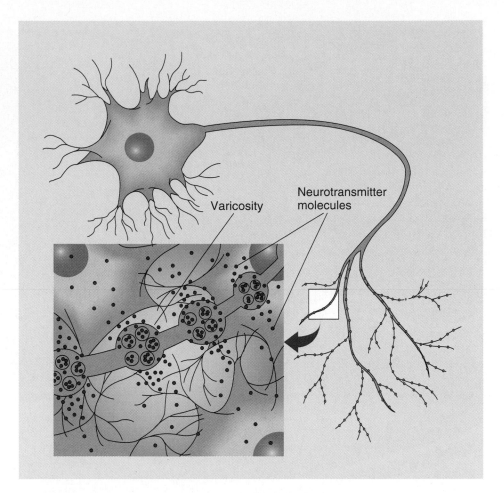

Figure 4.11 Nondirected neurotransmitter release. Some neurons release neurotransmitter molecules diffusely from varicosities along the axon and its branches.

Release of Neurotransmitter Molecules

Exocytosis—the process of neurotransmitter release—is illustrated in Figure 4.12 on page 94. When a neuron is at rest, synaptic vesicles that contain small-molecule neurotransmitters congregate next to sections of the presynaptic membrane that are particularly rich in *calcium channels* (Robitaille, Adler, & Charlton, 1990). When stimulated by action potentials, the voltage-activated calcium channels open and Ca^{++} ions enter the button. The entry of the Ca^{++} ions causes the synaptic vesicles to fuse with the presynaptic membrane and empty their contents into the synaptic cleft.

The exocytosis of small-molecule neurotransmitters differs from the exocytosis of peptide neurotransmitters in one important respect. Small-molecule neurotransmitters are typically released in a pulse each time an action potential triggers a momentary influx of Ca^{++} ions through the presynaptic membrane; in contrast, peptide neurotransmitters are typically released gradually in response to general increases in the level of intracellular Ca^{++} ions, such as might occur during a general increase in the rate of neuron firing (DeCamilli & Jahn, 1990).

Directed synapses. Synapses at which the site of neurotransmitter release and the receptor sites on the postsynaptic membrane are in close proximity.

Nondirected synapses. Synapses at which the site of neurotransmitter release and the target site are not close together.

Peptides. Short chains of amino acids, some of which function as neurotransmitters.

Synaptic vesicles. Small spherical membranes that store neurotransmitter molecules and release them into the synaptic cleft.

Golgi complex. Structures in the cell bodies and buttons of neurons that package neurotransmitters and other molecules in vesicles.

Coexistence. The presence of more than one neurotransmitter in the same neuron.

Exocytosis. The process of releasing a neurotransmitter.

Figure 4.12 Schematic and photographic illustrations of exocytosis. (The photomicrograph was reproduced from J. E. Heuser et al., *Journal of Cell Biology*, 1979, *81*, 275–300 by copyright permission of The Rockefeller University Press.)

The Activation of Receptors by Neurotransmitter Molecules

Once released, neurotransmitter molecules produce signals in postsynaptic neurons by binding to their **receptors** (see Changeux, 1993). Each receptor is a protein that contains binding sites for only particular neurotransmitters; thus a particular neurotransmitter can influence only those cells that have receptors for it.

It was initially assumed that there would be only one type of receptor for each neurotransmitter, but this has not proved to be the case. As more receptors have been identified, it has become clear that most neurotransmitters bind to several different types of receptors. The different types of receptors to which a particular neurotransmitter can bind are

Receptors. Protein molecules that initiate a reaction in the postsynaptic cell when neurotransmitters bind to them.

Receptor subtypes. The different types of receptors to which a single neurotransmitter can bind.

Ion-channel linked receptors. Receptors that are components of chemically activated ion channels; the binding of a neurotransmitter to the receptor typically opens or closes the channel.

Chemically activated ion channels. Ion channels that are opened or closed by the binding of molecules to their receptors.

G-protein linked receptors. Receptors that when activated trigger the release into the cell of a subunit of a G protein.

Second messenger. A molecule created in the cytoplasm of a postsynaptic cell in response to the activation of G-protein linked receptors; once created, a second messenger can influence the postsynaptic cell in a variety of ways.

An Ion-Channel Linked Receptor

Ion

Neurotransmitter

Receptor

Closed
Ion
Channel

Some neurotransmitter molecules bind to receptors on ion channels. When a neurotransmitter molecule binds to an ion-channel linked receptor the channel opens (as in this case) or closes, thereby altering the flow of ions into or out of the neuron.

A G-Protein Linked Receptor

Neurotransmitter

Receptor

G-Protein

Some neurotransmitter molecules bind to receptors on membrane signal proteins that are linked to G-proteins. When a neurotransmitter molecule binds to a G-protein linked receptor, a subunit of the G-protein breaks off into the neuron and either binds to an ion channel or stimulates the synthesis of a second messenger.

Figure 4.13 Ion-channel linked receptors and G-protein linked receptors.

fundamentally different ways, depending on whether the receptor is ion-channel linked (Changeux, 1993) or G-protein linked (Linder & Gilman, 1992)—see Figure 4.13. **Ion-channel linked receptors** are linked to **chemically activated ion channels** in the postsynaptic membrane. When a neurotransmitter binds to an ion-channel linked receptor, the ion channel usually opens or closes, thereby inducing an immediate postsynaptic potential. For example, in some neurons, EPSPs (depolarizations) occur because the neurotransmitter opens sodium channels, thereby increasing the flow of Na^+ ions into the neuron. In contrast, IPSPs (hyperpolarizations) often occur because the neurotransmitter opens potassium channels or chloride channels, thereby increasing the flow of K^+ ions out of the neuron or the flow of Cl^- ions into it, respectively.

G-protein linked receptors are more prevalent than ion-channel linked receptors, and their effects are slower to develop, longer-lasting, more diffuse, and more varied (see Linder & Gilman, 1992). There are many different kinds of G-protein linked receptors, but each is a protein chain that winds its way in and out of the cell, spanning the cell membrane seven times in the process; and each is located next to a *G protein* (a guanine-sensitive protein)—see Figure 4.13.

When a neurotransmitter binds to a G-protein linked receptor, a subunit of the adjacent G protein breaks away. Then, one of two things happens, depending on the particular G protein: The subunit may move along the inside surface of the membrane and bind to a nearby ion channel, thereby inducing an EPSP or IPSP (see Clapham, 1994); or it may trigger the synthesis of a chemical called a **second messenger** (neurotransmitters are considered to be the *first messengers*). Once created, a second messenger diffuses through the cytoplasm and does one of three things: It binds to ion channels, thereby inducing an EPSP or an IPSP; it directly influences the metabolic activities of the cell; or it enters the nucleus and binds to the DNA, thereby influencing gene expression. Thus, although a common consequence of a neurotransmitter binding to a receptor is a brief EPSP or IPSP, neurotransmitters can also have radical long-term effects via second messengers.

Differences between small-molecule and peptide neurotransmitters in patterns of release and receptor binding suggest that these neurotransmitters serve different functions.

called the **receptor subtypes** for that neurotransmitter. The various receptor subtypes for a neurotransmitter are typically located in different brain areas, and they typically respond to the neurotransmitter in different ways. Thus, one advantage of receptor subtypes is that they enable a neurotransmitter to transmit different kinds of messages to different parts of the brain (see Schofield, Shivers, & Seeburg, 1990).

The binding of a neurotransmitter to one of its receptor subtypes can influence a postsynaptic neuron in one of two

Small-molecule neurotransmitters tend to be released into directed synapses and to activate either ion-channel linked receptors or G-protein linked receptors that act directly on ion channels. In contrast, peptides tend to be released diffusely and to bind to G-protein linked receptors that act through second messengers. Consequently, the function of small-molecule neurotransmitters appears to be the transmission of rapid, brief excitatory or inhibitory messages to adjacent cells; and the function of peptide neurotransmitters appears to be the transmission of slow, diffuse, long-lasting signals.

One type of G-protein linked receptors—autoreceptors—warrants special mention. **Autoreceptors** are G-protein linked receptors that have two unconventional characteristics: They bind their neuron's own neurotransmitter molecules; and they are located on the presynaptic, rather than the postsynaptic, membrane. Their usual function is to monitor the number of neurotransmitter molecules in the synapse and to reduce subsequent release when the levels are high.

Reuptake, Enzymatic Degradation, and Recycling

If nothing intervened, a neurotransmitter molecule would remain active in the synapse, in effect clogging that channel of communication. However, two mechanisms terminate synaptic messages and keep that from happening. These message-terminating mechanisms are **reuptake** and **enzymatic degradation** (see Figure 4.14).

Reuptake is the more common of the two deactivating mechanisms. The majority of neurotransmitters, once released, are almost immediately drawn back into the presynaptic buttons (see Clements et al., 1992), repackaged in vesicles by the Golgi complex, and rereleased—over and over again.

In contrast, other neurotransmitters are degraded (broken apart) in the synapse by **enzymes**—chemicals that stimulate or inhibit chemical reactions without directly participating in them. For example, *acetylcholine,* one of the

Autoreceptors. Receptors, often on the presynaptic membrane, that are sensitive to a neuron's own neurotransmitter.

Reuptake. The more common of the two mechanisms for deactivating a released neurotransmitter.

Enzymatic degradation. The breakdown of chemicals by enzymes—one of the two mechanisms for deactivating released neurotransmitters.

Enzymes. Chemicals that stimulate or inhibit chemical reactions without directly participating in them.

Acetylcholinesterase. The enzyme that breaks down acetylcholine.

Two Mechanisms of Neurotransmitter Deactivation

Reuptake

Deactivating Enzymes

Figure 4.14 The two mechanisms of terminating neurotransmitter action in the synapse: reuptake and enzymatic degradation.

few neurotransmitters for which enzymatic degradation is the main mechanism of synaptic deactivation, is broken down by the enzyme **acetylcholinesterase.** Many of the break-down products of enzymatic degradation are reabsorbed by the presynaptic button and used in the synthesis of more neurotransmitter molecules.

Neurons also recycle their synaptic vesicles (see Jahn & Südhof, 1994). This is why terminal buttons do not grow steadily bigger as multitudes of vesicles keep adding themselves to the presynaptic membrane during exocytosis. Bits of button membrane continually break off into the button cytoplasm from the region near its boundary with its axon branch. Once in the button cytoplasm, the bits of button membrane are recycled by the resident Golgi complex into small synaptic vesicles.

Now that you understand the basics of neurotransmitter function, let's take a look at some of the neurotransmitter substances. There are four classes of small-molecule neurotransmitters: the *amino acids,* the *monoamines,* the recently discovered *soluble gases,* and *acetylcholine.* In addition, there is the one class of large-molecule neurotransmitters: the *neuropeptides.* Most neurotransmitters produce either excitation or inhibition, not both; but a few produce excitation when they bind to some of their receptor subtypes and inhibition when they bind to others. All of the neurotransmitter classes and individual neurotransmitters that appear in this section in bold print are defined in Figure 4.17 at the end of this section rather than appearing in margin definitions.

Figure 4.15 String-of-beads noradrenergic nerve fibers in rat cerebellar cortex. The bright beaded structures represent sites in these multiply-branched axons where the monoamine neurotransmitter norepinephrine is stored in high concentration and released into the surrounding extracellular fluid. (Courtesy of Floyd E. Bloom, M.D., The Scripps Research Institute, La Jolla California.)

Amino Acid Neurotransmitters

The neurotransmitters in the vast majority of fast-acting, directed synapses in the central nervous system are **amino acids**—the molecular building blocks of proteins. Four amino acids have proved to be neurotransmitters to the satisfaction of most experts: **glutamate, aspartate, glycine, and gamma-aminobutyric acid (GABA).** The first three are common in the proteins we consume, whereas GABA is synthesized by a simple modification of the structure of glutamate. Glutamate is the most prevalent excitatory neurotransmitter in the mammalian central nervous system; GABA is the most prevalent inhibitory neurotransmitter.

Monoamine Neurotransmitters

Monoamines are another class of small-molecule neurotransmitters. Each is synthesized from a single amino acid—hence the name *monoamine* (one amine). Monoamine neurotransmitters are slightly larger than amino acid neurotransmitters, and their effects tend to be more diffuse. The monoamines are present in small groups of neurons whose cell bodies are, for the most part, located in the brain stem. These neurons often have highly branched axons with many *varicosities* (string-of-beads axons), from which monoamine neurotransmitters are diffusely released into the extracellular fluid (see Figures 4.15 and 4.11).

There are four monoamine neurotransmitters: **dopamine, norepinephrine, epinephrine,** and **serotonin.** They are subdivided into two groups, **catecholamines** and **indolamines,** on the basis of their structure. Dopamine, norepinephrine, and epinephrine are catecholamines. Each is synthesized from the amino acid *tyrosine.* Tyrosine is converted to *L-DOPA,* which in turn is converted to dopamine. Neurons that release norepinephrine have an extra enzyme (one that is not present in dopaminergic neurons), which converts the dopamine in them to norepinephrine. Similarly, neurons that release epinephrine have all the enzymes present in neurons that release norepinephrine, along with an extra enzyme that converts norepinephrine to epinephrine (see Figure 4.16). In contrast to the other monoamines, *serotonin* (also called *5-hydroxytryptamine,* or *5-HT*) is synthesized from the amino acid *tryptophan* and is classified as an indolamine.

Neurons that release norepinephrine are called *noradrenergic;* those that release epinephrine are called *adrenergic.* There are two reasons for this naming. One is that epinephrine and norepinephrine used to be called *adrenaline* and *noradrenaline,* respectively, by many scientists, until a drug company registered *adrenaline* and *noradrenaline* as brand names. The other reason will become apparent to you if you try to say *norepinephrinergic.*

Soluble-Gas Neurotransmitters

Another class of small-molecule neurotransmitters, the **soluble gases,** has only recently been discovered; so far, the class includes **nitric oxide** (see Madison, 1994; Snyder & Bredt, 1992) and **carbon monoxide** (Verma et al., 1993). The soluble gases do not act like the other neurotransmitters. They are produced in the neural cytoplasm; and once produced, they immediately diffuse through the cell membrane into the extracellular fluid and then into nearby cells. They easily pass through cell membranes because they are soluble in lipids. Once in other cells, they stimulate the production of a second messenger and are immediately broken down. They are difficult to study because they exist for only a few seconds.

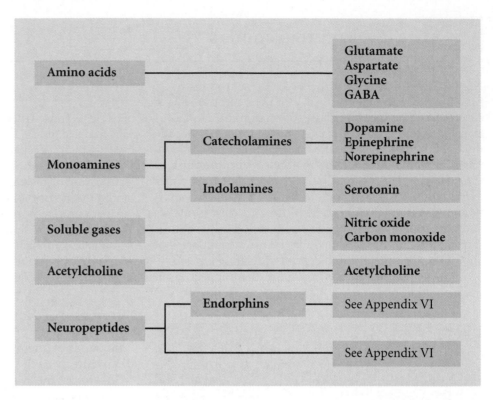

Figure 4.17 Classes of neurotransmitters and the particular neurotransmitters that are introduced in this chapter. This diagram contains all the neurotransmitter classes and all the neurotransmitters that appear in bold face in this chapter, and thus it substitutes for their key term definitions.

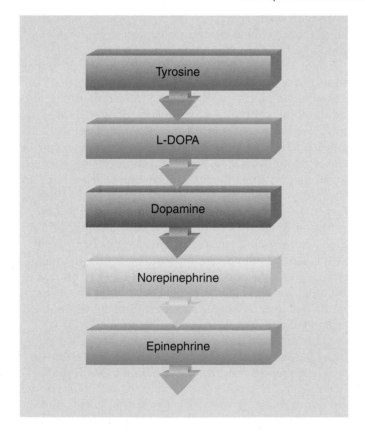

Figure 4.16 The steps in the synthesis of catecholamines from tyrosine.

Acetylcholine

Acetylcholine (Ach) is a small-molecule neurotransmitter that is in one major respect like a professor who is late for lecture: It is in a class by itself. It is created by adding an *acetyl group* to a *choline molecule.* Acetylcholine is the neurotransmitter at neuromuscular junctions, at many of the synapses in the autonomic nervous system, and at synapses throughout the central nervous system. As you learned in the last section, acetylcholine is broken down in the synapse by the enzyme *acetylcholinesterase.* Neurons that release acetylcholine are said to be *cholinergic.*

Neuropeptides

About 50 or so peptides currently qualify as neurotransmitters or putative neurotransmitters (see Appendix VI). A *putative neurotransmitter* is a suspected neurotransmitter—one for which the evidence is strong but not yet unequivocal.

Peptides that play a role in neurotransmission are referred to as **neuropeptides.** Among the most interesting neuropeptides are the **endorphins;** endorphins are endogenous opiates (literally, opiumlike chemicals that are produced within the body). The existence of endorphins was first suggested by the discovery that opiate drugs (e.g., opi-

To review the neurotransmitters to which you have just been introduced, fill in the blanks in the following paragraph. The correct answers are provided at the bottom of this page. Before proceeding, review material related to your errors and omissions.

Amino acids are the neurotransmitters in the vast

majority of (1) _____-acting,

directed synapses. Four amino acids are widely

recognized neurotransmitters:

(2) _____,

(3) _____,

(4) _____, and

(5) _____. In contrast to the

amino acid neurotransmitters, the

(6) _____ are small-molecule

neurotransmitters with slower, more diffuse effects;

they belong to one of two categories:

(7) _____ or indolamines.

Belonging to the former category are epinephrine,

(8) _____, and

(9) _____;

(10) _____ is the only

neurotransmitter belonging to the latter category.

The neuropeptides, which are short chains of

(11) _____, are the only class of

large-molecule neurotransmitters.

(12) _____, the neurotransmitter

at neuromuscular junctions, is a neurotransmitter in

a class by itself. (13) Finally, there are the recently

discovered _____ neurotransmit-

ters, nitric oxide and carbon monoxide.

um, morphine, and heroin) bind to receptors in the brain (Pert, Snowman, & Snyder, 1974); presumably, there would not be receptors in the brain for substances that are not themselves produced by the body. This suggestion was subsequently confirmed by the discovery of several different endorphins and several subtypes of the endorphin receptor. Endorphins activate neural systems that produce *analgesia* (pain supression) and neural systems that mediate (underlie) the experience of pleasure. These effects are presumably why opiate drugs are so addictive.

Neuropeptides are often referred to as neuromodulators. A *neuromodulator* is a chemical transmitter that does not itself induce signals in other cells; instead, it adjusts the sensitivity of populations of cells to the excitatory and inhibitory signals at fast-acting directed synapses. The concept of neuromodulation is an important one, and there is evidence that some neuropeptides act as neuromodulators under some conditions. However, at present, the evidence does not warrant indiscriminately referring to all neuropeptides as neuromodulators.

Figure 4.17 summarizes the neurotransmitters that were introduced in this section.

The answers are (1) fast; (2, 3, 4, 5) glutamate, aspartate, glycine, and GABA, in any order; (6) monoamines; (7) catecholamines; (8, 9) norepinephrine and dopamine in either order; (10) serotonin; (11) amino acids; (12) Acetylcholine; and (13) soluble gas.

4.7 Pharmacology of Synaptic Transmission

The more neuroscientists have discovered about synaptic transmission, the more it has been possible for them to develop drugs to modify it in specific ways. The study of the effects of such drugs on psychological processes is currently one of the most productive areas of biopsychological research. The psychological effects of transmission-altering drugs have told us a great deal about the neural bases of psychological processes. Also, as you have already seen in this chapter, they have led to the development of effective pharmacologic treatments for psychological disorders—recall the improvement of Roberto Garcia d'Orta. This section completes the chapter by explaining some of the ways drugs influence psychological processes through their effects on synaptic transmission.

Drugs have two fundamentally different kinds of effects on synaptic transmission: They facilitate it or they inhibit it. Drugs that facilitate the effects of a particular neurotransmitter are said to be **agonists** of that neurotransmitter. Drugs that inhibit the effects of a particular neurotransmitter are said to be its **antagonists.**

How Drugs Influence Synaptic Transmission

Although the synthesis, release, and action of neurotransmitters vary somewhat from neurotransmitter to neurotransmitter, the following seven general processes are common to most: (1) synthesis of the neurotransmitter, (2) storage in vesicles, (3) breakdown in the cytoplasm of any neurotransmitter that leaks from the vesicles, (4) exocytosis, (5) inhibitory feedback via autoreceptors, (6) activation of postsynaptic receptors, and (7) deactivation. Fig-

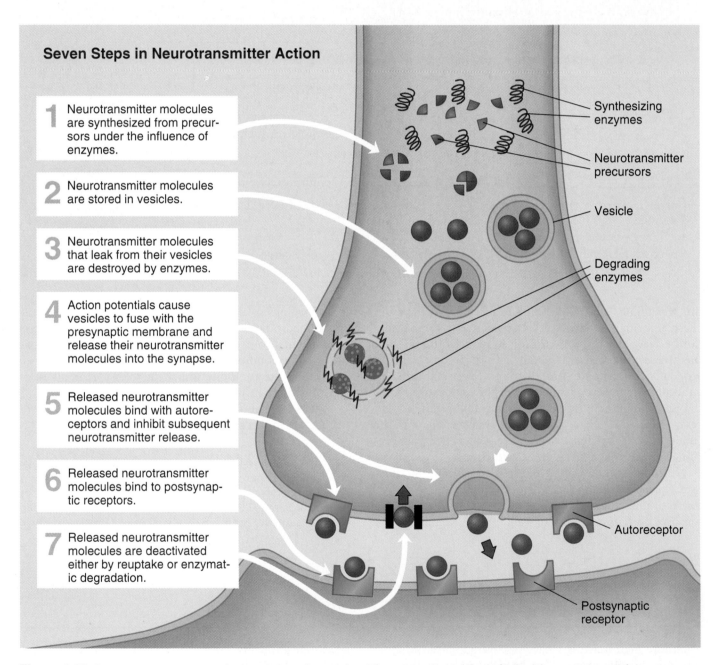

Seven Steps in Neurotransmitter Action

1 Neurotransmitter molecules are synthesized from precursors under the influence of enzymes.

2 Neurotransmitter molecules are stored in vesicles.

3 Neurotransmitter molecules that leak from their vesicles are destroyed by enzymes.

4 Action potentials cause vesicles to fuse with the presynaptic membrane and release their neurotransmitter molecules into the synapse.

5 Released neurotransmitter molecules bind with autoreceptors and inhibit subsequent neurotransmitter release.

6 Released neurotransmitter molecules bind to postsynaptic receptors.

7 Released neurotransmitter molecules are deactivated either by reuptake or enzymatic degradation.

Synthesizing enzymes

Neurotransmitter precursors

Vesicle

Degrading enzymes

Autoreceptor

Postsynaptic receptor

Figure 4.18 Seven common processes in neurotransmitter action. The processes are (1) synthesis, (2) storage in vesicles, (3) breakdown of any neurotransmitter leaking from the vesicles, (4) exocytosis, (5) inhibitory feedback via autoreceptors, (6) activation of postsynaptic receptors, and (7) deactivation.

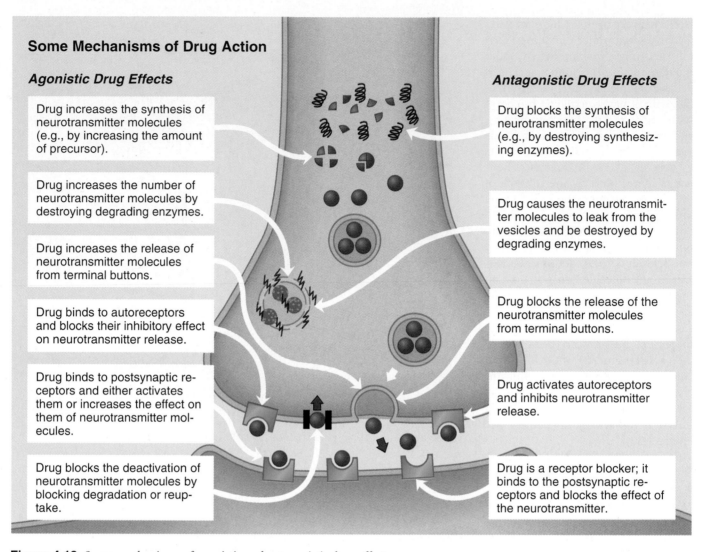

Some Mechanisms of Drug Action

Agonistic Drug Effects

Drug increases the synthesis of neurotransmitter molecules (e.g., by increasing the amount of precursor).

Drug increases the number of neurotransmitter molecules by destroying degrading enzymes.

Drug increases the release of neurotransmitter molecules from terminal buttons.

Drug binds to autoreceptors and blocks their inhibitory effect on neurotransmitter release.

Drug binds to postsynaptic receptors and either activates them or increases the effect on them of neurotransmitter molecules.

Drug blocks the deactivation of neurotransmitter molecules by blocking degradation or reuptake.

Antagonistic Drug Effects

Drug blocks the synthesis of neurotransmitter molecules (e.g., by destroying synthesizing enzymes).

Drug causes the neurotransmitter molecules to leak from the vesicles and be destroyed by degrading enzymes.

Drug blocks the release of the neurotransmitter molecules from terminal buttons.

Drug activates autoreceptors and inhibits neurotransmitter release.

Drug is a receptor blocker; it binds to the postsynaptic receptors and blocks the effect of the neurotransmitter.

Figure 4.19 Some mechanisms of agonistic and antagonistic drug effects.

ure 4.18 illustrates these seven processes, and Figure 4.19 illustrates the ways that agonistic and antagonistic drugs influence them. For example, some antagonistic drugs, called **receptor blockers,** bind to postsynaptic receptors without activating them and, in so doing, block the access of the usual neurotransmitter.

Psychoactive Drugs: Four Examples

You will encounter many psychoactive drugs, their psychological effects, and their mechanisms of action in future chapters. Here are four examples: two agonists, cocaine and the benzodiazepines; and two antagonists, atropine and curare.

Cocaine   **Cocaine** is a potent catecholamine agonist that is highly addictive. It increases the activity of both dopamine and norepinephrine by blocking their reuptake from the synapse into the presynaptic button. Accordingly, when

there are high levels of cocaine in the brain, molecules of dopamine and norepinephrine, once released into the synapse, continue to activate postsynaptic receptors because their primary method of deactivation has been blocked. This produces a variety of psychological effects, including euphoria, loss of appetite, and insomnia. It is also responsible for the addictive potential of cocaine (see Chapter 13).

Agonists. Drugs that facilitate the effects of a particular neurotransmitter.

Antagonists. Drugs that inhibit the effects of a particular neurotransmitter.

Receptor blockers. Antagonistic drugs that bind to postsynaptic receptors without activating them and block the access of the usual neurotransmitter.

Cocaine. A potent catecholamine agonist that is highly addictive.

Benzodiazepines *Chlordiazepoxide* (marketed under the name *Librium*) and *diazepam* (marketed under the name *Valium*) belong to a class of drugs called benzodiazepines. **Benzodiazepines** have *anxiolytic* (anxiety-reducing), *sedative* (sleep-inducing), and *anticonvulsant* effects. They appear to exert their anxiolytic effects by serving as GABA agonists. Benzodiazepines bind to one subtype of the GABA receptor, the ion-channel linked GABA$_A$ receptor (see Macdonald & Olsen, 1994), but they do not exert their agonistic effect by mimicking GABA's actions. Benzodiazepine molecules do not bind to the GABA$_A$ receptor at the same site at which GABA molecules bind. Instead they bind to another part of the molecule; and by so doing, they increase the binding of GABA molecules to the receptor and thus increase GABA's inhibitory effects by increasing the influx of chloride ions, thus hyperpolarizing the neuron (see Figure 4.20).

In view of the anxiolytic and anticonvulsant effects of benzodiazepines, it is not surprising that benzodiazepine binding sites are particularly dense in the *amygdala,* a structure known to play a role in emotion and in the propagation of seizures. The fact that there are benzodiazepine binding sites on the GABA$_A$ receptor suggests that the brain may produce its own benzodiazepinelike chemical. But despite a concerted effort, an endogenous benzodiazepine has yet to be identified.

Atropine Many of the drugs that are used in research and in medicine are extracts of plants that have long been used for medicinal and recreational purposes. For example, in the time of Hippocrates, the Greeks consumed extracts of the belladonna plant to treat stomach ailments and to make themselves more attractive. Greek women believed that its pupil-dilating effects enhanced their beauty (*belladonna* means "beautiful lady"). **Atropine** is the active ingredient of belladonna. It is a receptor blocker that exerts its antagonist effect by binding to a subtype of acetylcholine receptors called *muscarinic receptors,* thereby blocking the effects of acetylcholine on them. The disruptive effect of high doses of atropine on memory was one of the earliest clues that cholinergic mechanisms play an important role in memory (see Chapter 14).

Curare South American Indians have long used **curare**—an extract of a certain class of woody vines—to kill their game and occasionally their enemies. Like atropine, curare is a receptor blocker at cholinergic synapses, but it acts at a different subtype of acetylcholine receptors: *nicotinic receptors.* By binding to nicotinic receptors, curare blocks transmission at **neuromuscular junctions,** thus paralyzing its recipients and killing them by blocking their respiration. You may be surprised, then, to learn that the active ingredient of curare is sometimes administered to human patients during surgery to ensure that patients' muscles do not contract during an incision. When curare is used for this purpose, the patient's breathing must be artificially maintained by a respirator.

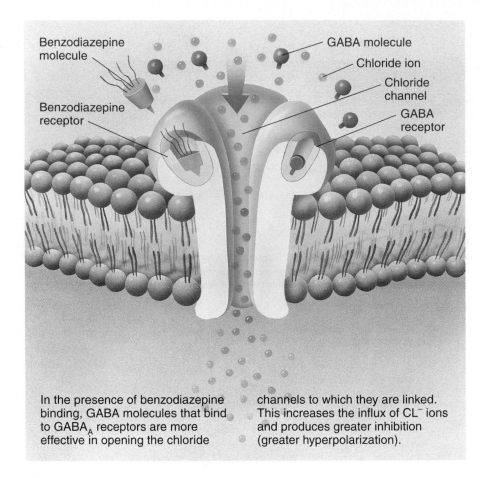

Figure 4.20 The GABA$_A$-benzodiazepine receptor complex.

Labels: Benzodiazepine molecule; Benzodiazepine receptor; GABA molecule; Chloride ion; Chloride channel; GABA receptor.

In the presence of benzodiazepine binding, GABA molecules that bind to GABA$_A$ receptors are more effective in opening the chloride channels to which they are linked. This increases the influx of CL⁻ ions and produces greater inhibition (greater hyperpolarization).

Benzodiazepines. A class of GABA agonists with anxiolytic, sedative, and anticonvulsant properties.

Atropine. A receptor blocker at muscarinic cholinergic synapses.

Curare. A blocker of nicotinic cholinergic synapses that produces paralysis by blocking transmission at neuromuscular junctions.

Neuromuscular junctions. The synapses of a motor neuron on a muscle.

You are likely wondering about the differences between muscarinic and nicotinic receptors and about the significance of their names. The existence of these cholinergic receptor subtypes was inferred from the discovery that some of the receptors to which acetylcholine binds also bind to *muscarine*, whereas others bind to *nicotine*.

Conclusion

The function of the nervous system, like the function of any circuit, depends on how signals are transmitted through it. Accordingly, an understanding of the basic principles of neural conduction and synaptic transmission is a prerequisite to the study of the neural bases of behavior. This chapter has introduced you to these basic principles. First, you learned why neurons in their resting state have a charge, called the resting potential, built up across their cell membranes (4.1). Then, you learned about the excitatory and inhibitory signals that are conducted from postsynaptic membranes to the axon hillock (4.2), where they elicit action potentials if their integrated value exceeds the threshold of excitation (4.3). Next, the conduction of action potentials along myelinated and unmyelinated axons was described (4.4). The final three sections of the chapter dealt with synaptic transmission: how signals are transmitted from one neuron to another by chemical neurotransmitters (4.5), the various classes of chemical neurotransmitters (4.6), and the ways in which drugs influence synaptic transmission (4.7). *The Lizard*, the story of Roberto Garcia d'Orta, was the glue that held this chapter together; it demonstrated the relevance of neural conduction and synaptic transmission to the study of psychological function.

FOOD FOR THOUGHT

1. Just as computers operate on binary (yes-no) signals, the all-or-none action potential is the basis of neural communication. The human brain is thus nothing more than a particularly complex computer. Discuss.

2. How have the findings described in this chapter changed your understanding of brain function?

3. Why is it important for biopsychologists to understand neural conduction and synaptic transmission? Is it important for all psychologists to have such knowledge? Discuss.

KEY TERMS

Membrane potential *(p. 81)*
Microelectrodes *(p. 81)*
Oscilloscope *(p. 82)*
Resting potential *(p. 82)*
Ions *(p. 82)*
Ion channels *(p. 83)*
Sodium-potassium pumps *(p. 85)*
Depolarize *(p. 85)*
Hyperpolarize *(p. 85)*
Excitatory postsynaptic potentials (EPSPs) *(p. 85)*
Inhibitory postsynaptic potentials (IPSPs) *(p. 85)*
Graded responses *(p. 85)*
Axon hillock *(p. 86)*
Threshold of excitation *(p. 86)*
Action potential (AP) *(p. 86)*
All-or-none responses *(p. 87)*
Integration *(p. 87)*
Spatial summation *(p. 87)*
Temporal summation *(p. 87)*

Voltage-activated ion channels *(p. 88)*
Absolute refractory period *(p. 89)*
Relative refractory period *(p. 89)*
Antidromic conduction *(p. 90)*
Orthodromic conduction *(p. 90)*
Nodes of Ranvier *(p. 90)*
Saltatory conduction *(p. 90)*
Dendritic spines *(p. 91)*
Presynaptic inhibition *(p. 91)*
Postsynaptic inhibition *(p. 91)*
Directed synapses *(p. 92)*
Nondirected synapses *(p. 92)*
Peptides *(p. 92)*
Synaptic vesicles *(p. 92)*
Golgi complex *(p. 92)*
Coexistence *(p. 93)*

Exocytosis *(p. 93)*
Receptors *(p. 94)*
Receptor subtypes *(p. 95)*
Ion-channel linked receptors *(p. 95)*
Chemically activated ion channels *(p. 95)*
G-protein linked receptors *(p. 95)*
Second messenger *(p. 95)*
Autoreceptors *(p. 96)*
Reuptake *(p. 96)*
Enzymatic degradation *(p. 96)*
Enzymes *(p. 96)*
Acetylcholinesterase *(p. 96)*
Amino acids *(p. 97)*
Glutamate *(p. 97)*
Asparate *(p. 97)*
Glycine *(p. 97)*
Gamma-aminobutyric acid (GABA) *(p. 97)*

Monoamines *(p. 97)*
Dopamine *(p. 97)*
Norepinephrine *(p. 97)*
Epinephrine *(p. 97)*
Serotonin *(p. 97)*
Catecholamines *(p. 97)*
Indolamines *(p. 97)*
Soluble gases *(p. 98)*
Nitric oxide *(p. 98)*
Carbon monoxide *(p. 98)*
Acetylcholine *(p. 98)*
Neuropeptides *(p. 98)*
Endorphins *(p. 98)*
Agonists *(p. 100)*
Antagonists *(p. 100)*
Receptor blocker *(p. 101)*
Cocaine *(p. 101)*
Benzodiazepines *(p. 102)*
Atropine *(p. 102)*
Curare *(p. 102)*
Neuromuscular junctions *(p. 102)*

ADDITIONAL READING

For a systematic introduction to neural conduction and synaptic transmission that is much more detailed than that provided by this chapter, the following text is hard to beat:

Kandel, E. R., & Schwartz, J. H. (Eds.) (1991). *Principles of neural science* (2d ed.). New York: Elsevier.

Scientific American is one of the few scientific journals that can be purchased at your local news stand. It specializes in making the research of the world's greatest scientists accessible to the educated public in beautifully illustrated, well-written articles. The following are several that are relevant to this chapter:

Changeux, J. P. (1993, November). Chemical signaling in the brain. *Scientific American, 269*, 58–62.

Dunant, Y., & Israël, M. (1985, April). The release of acetylcholine. *Scientific American, 252*, 58–66.

Gottlieb, D. I. (1988, February). GABAergic neurons. *Scientific American, 258*, 82–89.

Linder, M. E., & Gilman, A. G. (1992, July). G proteins. *Scientific American, 267*, 56–65.

Neher, E., & Sakmann, B. (1992, March). The patch clamp technique. *Scientific American, 266*, 44–51.

Snyder, S. H. (1985, October). The molecular basis of communication between cells. *Scientific American, 253*, 132–141.

Snyder, S. H., & Bredt, D. S. (1992, May). Biological roles of nitric oxide. *Scientific American, 266*, 68–77.

The following book provides a thorough overview of neurotransmitters, drugs, and neuropsychological disorders:

Strange, P. G. (1992). *Brain biochemistry and brain disorders*. New York: Oxford University Press.

What Biopsychologists Do: The Research Methods of Biopsychology

Part 1 Methods of Studying the Nervous System

5.1   Methods of Visualizing the Living Human Brain

5.2   Recording Human Psychophysiological Activity

5.3   Invasive Physiological Research Methods

5.4   Pharmacological Research Methods

Part 2 Behavioral Research Methods of Biopsychology

5.5   Neuropsychological Testing

5.6   Behavioral Methods of Cognitive Neuroscience

5.7   Biopsychological Paradigms of Animal Behavior

Chapters 1 and 2 introduced you to the general interests, ideas, and approaches that characterize biopsychology. In Chapters 3 and 4, your introduction to biopsychology was temporarily curtailed while background material in neuro-anatomy, neurophysiology, and neurochemistry was presented. This chapter gets down to the nitty-gritty of biopsychology; it describes the specific day-to-day activities of the biopsychology laboratory. It is intended to sharpen your understanding of biopsychology by describing how biopsychologists do their research.

The organization of this chapter reflects biopsychology's intrinsic duality. The chapter has two major parts: one dealing with methods of studying the nervous system and the other dealing with methods of studying behavior.

Part 1   Methods of Studying the Nervous System

5.1   Methods of Visualizing the Living Human Brain

Prior to the early 1970s, biopsychological research was impeded by the inability to obtain images of the organ of primary interest: the living human brain. Conventional X-ray photography is next to useless for this purpose. For an X-ray photograph to be taken, an X-ray beam is passed through an object and then onto a photographic plate. Each of the molecules through which the beam passes absorbs some of the radiation; thus only the unabsorbed portions of the beam reach the photographic plate. X-ray photography is therefore effective in characterizing internal structures that differ substantially from their surroundings in the degree to which they absorb X-rays—for example, a revolver in a suitcase full of clothes or a bone in flesh. However, by the time an X-ray beam has passed through the numerous overlapping structures of the brain, which differ only slightly from one another in their ability to absorb X-rays, it carries little information about the shape of the individual structures through which it has passed.

Contrast X-Rays

Although conventional X-ray photography is next to useless for visualizing the brain itself, it has long been used to visualize two compartments within the brain: the cerebral ventricular system and the cerebral circulatory system. The visualization is done with **contrast X-ray techniques**—X-ray techniques that involve the injection of a substance that effectively absorbs X-rays (a *radio-opaque substance*) into one of the compartments. This injection heightens the contrast between the compartment and the surrounding brain tissue.

One contrast X-ray technique, **pneumoencephalography**, involves temporarily replacing some of the cerebro-

Contrast X-ray techniques. X-ray techniques that involve the injection of a radio-opaque substance into structures to make them visible on an X-ray photograph.

Pneumoencephalography. A contrast X-ray technique that involves temporarily replacing some of the cerebrospinal fluid with air.

Cerebral angiography. A contrast X-ray technique for visualizing the cerebral circulatory system by infusing a radio-opaque dye through a cerebral artery.

Computed tomography (CT). A computer-assisted X-ray procedure that can be used to visualize the brain and other inner parts of the living body.

Magnetic resonance imaging (MRI). A procedure in which high-resolution images of the structures of the living brain are constructed from the measurement of waves that hydrogen atoms emit when they are activated by radio-frequency waves in a magnetic field.

Figure 5.1 A cerebral angiogram of a healthy subject.

spinal fluid with air. Because air is radio-opaque, the ventricles and fissures of the brain are clearly visible in the subsequent contrast X-ray photograph, which is called a *pneumoencephalogram*. A local deformation of a ventricle or a fissure may indicate the location of a tumor, and a general increase in the size of the ventricles and fissures is indicative of diffuse brain *atrophy* (degeneration).

Another contrast X-ray technique is **cerebral angiography**—a procedure for visualizing the cerebral circulatory system by infusing a radio-opaque dye through a cerebral artery during X-ray photography (see Figure 5.1). Cerebral angiograms are most useful for localizing vascular damage, but the displacement of blood vessels from their normal position can indicate the location of a tumor.

X-Ray Computed Tomography

In the early 1970s, the study of the living human brain was revolutionized by the introduction of computed tomography. **Computed tomography (CT)** is a computer-assisted X-ray procedure that can be used to visualize the brain and other internal structures of the living body. During cerebral computed tomography, the neurological patient lies with his or her head positioned in the center of a large cylinder, as depicted in Figure 5.2. On one side of the cylinder is an X-ray tube that projects an X-ray beam through the head to an X-ray detector mounted on the other side. The X-ray tube and detector automatically rotate around the head of the patient at one level of the brain, taking many individual X-ray photographs as they rotate. The meager information

Figure 5.3 A CT scan. Notice the tumor in the left frontal lobe (by convention, posterior is toward the bottom of the scan).

in each X-ray photograph is combined by a computer to generate a CT scan of one horizontal section of the brain (see Figure 5.3). Then, the X-ray tube and detector are moved along the axis of the patient's body to another level of the brain, and the process is repeated. Scans of eight or nine horizontal brain sections are typically obtained from a patient; combined, they provide a three-dimensional representation of the brain.

Magnetic Resonance Imaging

The success of computed tomography stimulated the development of other techniques for obtaining images of the inside of the living body. Among these techniques is **magnetic resonance imaging (MRI)**—a procedure in which high-resolution images are constructed from the measurement of

Figure 5.2 Cerebral computed tomography (CT).

X-ray source

X-ray detector

Figure 5.4 A color-enhanced sagittal MRI scan.

Figure 5.6 Functional MRI. Functional MRI provides a three-dimensional image of the brain, with areas of heightened activity indicated in color. This particular image is a brain in the control condition, thus no areas of heightened activity are shown. (Courtesy of Bruce Forster, Radiology Department, and Robert Hare, Psychology Department, University of British Columbia. Research funded by the British Columbia Medical Services Foundation.)

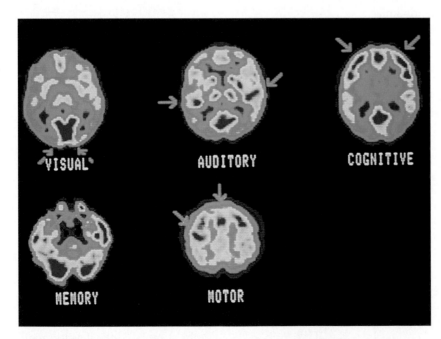

Figure 5.5 A series of PET scans. Each scan is a horizontal section recorded during a different psychological activity. Areas of high activity are indicated by reds and yellows. For example, notice the high level of activity in the visual cortex of the occipital lobe when the subject scanned a visual display. (From "Positron Tomography: Human Brain Function and Biochemistry" by Michael E. Phelps and John C. Mazziotta, *Science, 228* [9701], May 17, 1985, p. 804. Copyright 1985 by the AAAS. Reprinted by permission. Courtesy of Drs. Michael E. Phelps and John Mazziotta, UCLA School of Medicine.)

waves that hydrogen atoms emit when they are activated by radio-frequency waves in a magnetic field. MRI provides clearer images of the brain than does CT (see Moonen et al., 1990). A color-coded MRI scan of the brain is illustrated in Figure 5.4.

Positron Emission Tomography

Positron emission tomography (PET) is a recently developed brain-imaging technique that has been widely used in biopsychological research because it provides images of brain activity rather than brain structure. In one common version of PET, radioactive **2-deoxyglucose (2-DG)** is injected into the patient's *carotid artery* (an artery of the neck that feeds the ipsilateral cerebral hemisphere). Because of its similarity to glucose, the primary metabolic fuel of the brain, 2-deoxyglucose is rapidly taken up by active (energy-consuming) neurons. However, unlike glucose, 2-deoxyglucose cannot be metabolized; it thus accumulates in active neurons until it can be gradually broken down and released.

PET provides images of the levels of radioactivity in various parts of the brain. Thus,

Chapter 5   What Biopsychologists Do

if a PET scan is taken of a patient who engages in an activity, such as reading, for about 1 minute after the 2-DG injection, the resulting scan will indicate the areas of the brain that were most active during the activity (see Figure 5.5).

Another PET procedure takes advantage of the fact that there is an increase in blood flow to active areas of the brain because active neurons often release *nitric oxide,* a vasodilator (Iadecola, 1993). Accordingly, if radioactive water is injected into the brain's circulatory system as the subject engages in some activity, the PET scan will indicate the areas in which blood flow is increased during the activity (see Raichle, 1994).

Functional MRI

Recently, MRI technology has been applied with great success to the measurement of brain activity (e.g., Belliveau et al., 1991). **Functional MRI** produces images of the increase in oxygen (blood) flow to active areas of the brain (see Figure 5.6). It has four advantages over PET: (1) Nothing has to be injected into the subject, (2) it provides both structural and functional information in the same image, (3) its spatial resolution is better, and (4) it can monitor changes in real time, rather than requiring the minute or so for a single measurement that PET needs.

5.2   Recording Human Psychophysiological Activity

In psychophysiological studies of human subjects, physiological activity is usually recorded from the surface of the body. This section of the chapter describes five of the most widely studied psychophysiological measures: one measure of brain activity (the scalp EEG), two measures of somatic nervous system activity (muscle tension and eye movement), and two measures of autonomic nervous system activity (skin conductance and cardiovascular activity).

Scalp Electroencephalography

The *electroencephalogram (EEG)* is a gross measure of the electrical activity of the brain. It is recorded through large electrodes by a device called an *electroencephalograph (EEG machine),* and the technique is called **electroencephalography.** In EEG studies of human subjects, each channel of EEG activity is usually recorded between two disk-shaped electrodes, about half the size of a dime, that are taped to the scalp. In *bipolar recording,* both electrodes are placed over active sites. In *monopolar recording,* one of the two electrodes is placed over the target site and the other is attached to the subject at a point of relative electrical silence—for example, an earlobe.

The scalp EEG signal reflects the sum of electrical events throughout the head. These events include action potentials and postsynaptic potentials, as well as electrical signals from the skin, muscles, blood, and eyes. Thus the utility of the scalp EEG does not lie in its ability to provide an unclouded view of neural activity. Its value as a research and diagnostic tool rests on the fact that some EEG wave forms are associated with particular states of consciousness or particular types of cerebral pathology. For example, **alpha waves** are regular 8-to-12-per-second high-amplitude waves that are associated with relaxed wakefulness. A few examples of EEG wave forms and their psychological correlates are presented in Figure 5.7.

Because EEG signals decrease in amplitude as they spread from their source, a comparison of signals recorded from various sites on the scalp can sometimes indicate the origin of particular waves. This is why it is usual to record EEG activity from many sites simultaneously (see Figure 5.8).

In some cases, psychophysiologists are more interested in the EEG waves that accompany certain psychological events than they are in the background EEG signal. These accompanying EEG waves are generally referred to as **event-related potentials (ERPs).** One commonly studied type of event-related potential is the **sensory evoked potential**—the change in the cortical EEG signal that is elicited by the momentary presentation of a sensory stimulus. As Figure

Positron emission tomography (PET). A technique for visualizing the activity in the brain by measuring the accumulation of radioactive 2-deoxyglucose (2-DG) or radioactive water in the various regions of the brain.

2-deoxyglucose (2-DG). A substance similar to glucose that is taken up by active neurons and accumulates in them because, unlike glucose, it cannot be used by neurons as a source of energy.

Functional MRI. A magnetic resonance imaging technique for measuring brain activity.

Electroencephalography. A procedure for recording the gross electrical activity of the brain through large electrodes, which in humans are usually taped to the surface of the scalp.

Alpha waves. Regular 8-to-12-per-second high-amplitude cortical EEG waves that typically occur during relaxed wakefulness.

Event-related potentials (ERPs). The EEG waves that regularly accompany certain psychological events.

Sensory evoked potential. A change in the electrical activity of the brain that is elicited by the momentary presentation of a sensory stimulus.

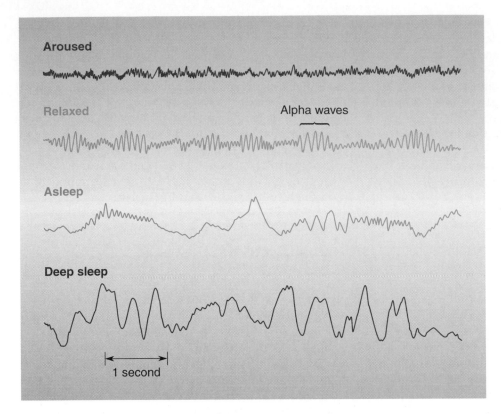

Aroused

Relaxed

Alpha waves

Asleep

Deep sleep

1 second

Figure 5.7 Some typical electroencephalograms and their psychological correlates.

5.9 illustrates, the cortical EEG that follows a sensory stimulus has two components: the response to the stimulus (the signal) and the ongoing background EEG activity (the noise). The *signal* is the part of any recording that is of interest; the *noise* is the part that isn't. The problem in recording sensory evoked potentials is that the noise of the background EEG is often so great that the sensory evoked potential is masked. Measuring a sensory evoked potential can be like measuring a whisper at a rock concert.

A method used to reduce the noise of the background EEG is **signal averaging.** First, a subject's response to a stimulus, such as a click, is recorded many—let's say 1,000—times. Then, a computer identifies the millivolt value of each of the 1,000 traces at their starting points (i.e., at the click) and calculates the mean of these 1,000 scores. Next, it considers the value of each of the 1,000 traces 1 millisecond (msec) from their start, for example, and calculates the mean of these values. It repeats this process at the 2-msec mark, the 3-msec mark, and so on. When these averages are plotted, the average response evoked by the click is more apparent because the random background EEG is canceled out by the averaging. See Figure 5.9, which illustrates the averaging of an auditory evoked potential.

The analysis of *average evoked potentials (AEPs)* focuses on the various peaks or waves in the averaged signal. Each wave is characterized by its direction, positive or negative, and by its latency. For example, the **P300 wave** illustrated in Figure 5.10 is the positive wave that occurs about 300 msec

after a momentary stimulus that has considerable meaning for the subject (Sutton & Ruchkin, 1984). In contrast, the small waves recorded in the first few milliseconds after a stimulus are not influenced by the meaning of the stimulus. These small waves are called **far-field potentials** because, although they are recorded from the scalp, they originate in the sensory nuclei of the brain stem (Vaughan & Arezzo, 1988).

Muscle Tension

Each skeletal muscle is composed of millions of threadlike muscle fibers. Each muscle fiber contracts in an all-or-none fashion when activated by the motor neuron that innervates it. At any given time, a few fibers in each resting muscle are likely to be contracting, thus maintaining the overall tone (tension) of the muscle. Movement results when a large number of fibers contract at the same time. However, tension of stationary muscles is a commonly employed measure of a person's psychological arousal.

Figure 5.8 Electroencephalography. It is usual to simultaneously record EEG signals from many pairs of scalp electrodes.

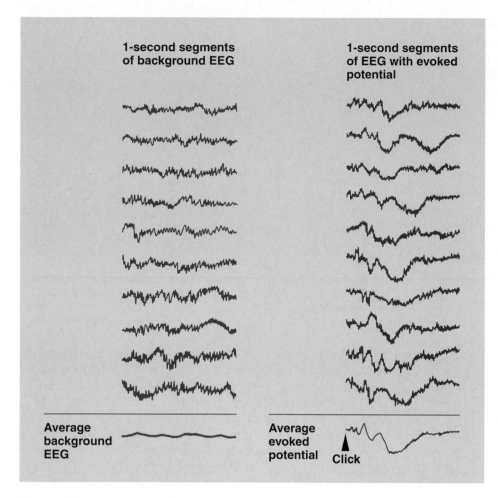

1-second segments of background EEG

1-second segments of EEG with evoked potential

Average background EEG

Average evoked potential   Click

Figure 5.9 The averaging of an auditory evoked potential. Averaging increases the signal-to-noise ratio.

Electromyography is the usual procedure for measuring muscle tension. The resulting record is called an *electromyogram (EMG)*. EMG activity is usually recorded between two electrodes taped to the surface of the skin over the muscle of interest. An EMG record is presented in

Figure 5.11. You will notice from this figure that the main correlate of an increase in muscle contraction is an increase in the amplitude of the EMG signal, which reflects the number of fibers contracting at any one time.

Most psychophysiologists do not work with raw EMG signals; they convert them instead to a more workable form by a process called *signal integration*. The signal is fed into a computer that calculates the total amount of EMG spiking per unit of time—in consecutive 0.1-second intervals, for example. The total EMG activity per unit of time is then plotted. The result is a smooth curve, the amplitude of which is a simple, continuous measure of the level of muscle tension over time (see Figure 5.11).

Eye Movement

The electrophysiological technique for recording eye movements is called **electrooculography,** and the resulting record is called an *electrooculogram (EOG)*. Electrooculography is based on the fact that there is a steady potential difference between the front (positive) and back (negative) of the eyeball. Because of this steady potential, when the eye moves, a change in the electrical potential can be recorded between electrodes placed around the eye. It is

Signal averaging. A method of increasing the signal-to-noise ratio by reducing background noise.

P300 wave. The positive EEG wave that usually occurs about 300 msec after a momentary stimulus that has considerable meaning for the subject.

Far-field potentials. EEG signals recorded in an attenuated form at a distance far from their source—for example, brain stem potentials recorded from the scalp.

Electromyography. A procedure for recording the gross electrical discharges of muscles.

Electrooculography. A procedure for recording eye movements through electrodes placed around the eye.

Far-field potentials

Meaningful click   200   400   600

P300

Time (milliseconds)

Figure 5.10 An average auditory evoked potential. Notice the P300 wave. This wave occurs only if the stimulus has meaning for the subject; in this case, the click signals the imminent delivery of a reward. By convention, positive EEG waves are always shown as downward deflections.

usual to record EOG activity between two electrodes placed on each side of the eye to measure its horizontal movements and between two electrodes placed above and below the eye to measure its vertical movements (see Figure 5.12).

Skin Conductance

Emotional thoughts and experiences are associated with increases in the ability of the skin to conduct electricity. The two most commonly employed indexes of *electrodermal activity* are the **skin conductance level (SCL)** and the **skin conductance response (SCR).** The SCL is a measure of the background level of skin conductance that is associated with a particular situation, whereas the SCR is a measure of the transient changes in skin conductance that are associated with discrete experiences.

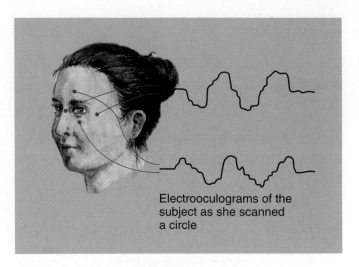

Electrooculograms of the subject as she scanned a circle

Figure 5.12 The typical placement of electrodes around the eye for electrooculography. The two electrooculogram traces were recorded as the subject scanned a circle.

The physiological bases of skin conductance changes are not fully understood, but there is considerable evidence implicating the sweat glands. Although the main function of sweat glands is to cool the body, these glands tend to become active in emotional situations. Sweat glands are distributed over most of the body surface; but, as you are almost certainly aware, those of the hands, feet, armpits, and forehead are particularly responsive to emotional stimuli. Few young lovers have escaped the dreaded duo of clammy hands and hircismus. (I recommend *Mrs. Byrne's Dictionary of Unusual, Obscure, and Preposterous Words* for those of you who collect unusual words such as *hircismus* which, by the way, means "underarm odor.")

Cardiovascular Activity

The presence in our language of phrases such as *chicken-hearted, white with fear,* and *blushing bride* indicates that modern psychophysiologists were not the first to recognize the relationship between *cardiovascular activity* and emo-

Raw EMG signal

Integrated EMG signal

Figure 5.11 The relation between a raw EMG signal and its integrated version. The subject tensed the muscle beneath the electrodes and then gradually relaxed it.

Skin conductance level (SCL). The steady level of skin conductance associated with a particular situation.

Skin conductance response (SCR). The transient change in skin conductance associated with a brief experience.

Electrocardiogram (ECG or EKG). A recording of the electrical activity of the heart.

Hypertension. Chronically high blood pressure.

Plethysmography. Measuring changes in the volume of blood in a part of the body.

tion. The cardiovascular system has two parts: the blood vessels and the heart. It is a system for distributing oxygen and nutrients to the tissues of the body, removing metabolic wastes, and transmitting chemical messages. Three different measures of cardiovascular activity are frequently employed in psychophysiological research: heart rate, arterial blood pressure, and local blood volume.

Heart rate   The electrical signal that is associated with each heartbeat can be recorded through electrodes placed on the chest. The recording is called an **electrocardiogram** (abbreviated either **ECG,** for obvious reasons, or **EKG,** from the original German). The average resting heart rate of a healthy adult is about 70 beats per minute, but it increases abruptly at the sound, or thought, of a dental drill.

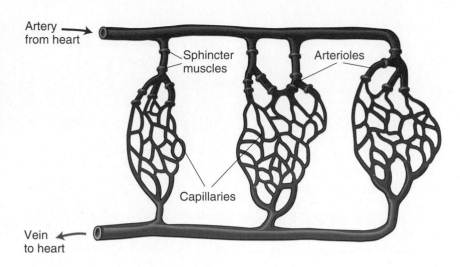

Figure 5.13 An illustration of the parallel structure of the circulatory system. This parallel structure permits blood flow to particular parts of the body to be increased or decreased by the contraction or relaxation of various arteriole sphincters.

Blood pressure   Measuring arterial blood pressure involves two independent measurements: a measurement of the peak pressure during the periods of heart contraction, the *systoles,* and a measurement of the minimum pressure during the periods of relaxation, the *diastoles.* Blood pressure is usually expressed as a ratio of systolic over diastolic blood pressure in millimeters of mercury (mmHg). The normal resting blood pressure for an adult is about 130/70 mmHg. A chronic blood pressure of more than 140/90 mmHg is viewed as a serious health hazard and is called **hypertension.**

You have likely had your blood pressure measured with a *sphygmomanometer*—a crude device composed of a hollow cuff, a rubber bulb for inflating it, and a pressure gauge for measuring the pressure in the cuff (*sphygmos* means "pulse"). The methods used to measure blood pressure in modern psychophysiological research are fully automated (see Linden & Estrin, 1988).

Blood volume   Changes in the volume of blood in particular parts of the body are associated with psychological events. The best-known example of such a change is the engorgement of the genitals that is associated with sexual arousal in both males and females. **Plethysmography** refers to the various techniques for measuring changes in the volume of blood in a particular part of the body (*plethysmos* means "an enlargement").

One method of measuring these changes is to record the volume of the target tissue by wrapping a strain gauge around it. Although this method has utility in measuring blood flow in fingers, or in similarly shaped organs, the possibilities for employing it are somewhat restricted. Another plethysmographic method is to shine a light through the tissue under investigation and to measure the amount of the light that is absorbed by it. The more blood there is in a structure, the more light it will absorb.

Changes in the amounts of blood in particular parts of the body (including the brain) can occur because the cardiovascular system is connected in parallel (see Figure 5.13), rather than being a single closed loop of vessels. The selective distribution of blood to various tissues is accomplished by the activity of *sphincter muscles* (muscles whose contraction closes a body channel) in the walls of the *arterioles* (small arteries). Constriction of particular arterioles reduces the blood flowing to areas of the body supplied by them, whereas dilation increases it.

5.3   Invasive Physiological Research Methods

Efforts to study brain-behavior relations in human subjects are impeded by the necessity of adhering to lines of research that involve no direct interaction with the organ of interest: the brain. We turn now from a consideration of the *noninvasive techniques* employed in research on living human brains to a consideration of more direct techniques. This section introduces some of the physiological methods commonly employed in biopsychological studies of laboratory animals.

Most physiological techniques used in biopsychological research on laboratory animals fall into one of three categories: lesion methods, electrical stimulation methods, and invasive recording methods. Each of these three methods is discussed in this section of the chapter, but it begins with a description of *stereotaxic surgery.*

Stereotaxic Surgery

Stereotaxic surgery is the first step in many biopsychological experiments. *Stereotaxic surgery* is the means by which experimental devices are precisely positioned in the depths of the brain. Two things are required in stereotaxic surgery: an atlas to provide directions to the target site and an instrument for getting there.

The **stereotaxic atlas** is used to locate brain structures in much the same way that a geographic atlas is used to locate geographic landmarks. There is, however, one important difference. In contrast to the surface of the earth, which has only two dimensions, the brain has three. Accordingly, the brain is represented in a stereotaxic atlas by a series of individual maps, one per page, each representing the structure of a single, two-dimensional frontal brain slice. In stereotaxic atlases, all distances are given in millimeters from a designated reference point. In some rat atlases, the reference point is **bregma**—the point on top of the skull where two of the major *sutures* (seams in the skull) intersect.

The **stereotaxic instrument** has two parts: a *head holder,* which firmly holds each subject's brain in the prescribed position and orientation; and an *electrode holder,* which holds the device to be inserted. The electrode holder can be moved in three dimensions—anterior-posterior, dorsal-ventral, or lateral-medial—by a system of precision gears. The implantation by stereotaxic surgery of an electrode in the amygdala of a rat is illustrated in Figure 5.14.

Lesion Methods

Those of you with an unrelenting drive to dismantle objects to see how they work will appreciate the lesion method. In this method, a part of the brain is removed, damaged, or destroyed; then, the behavior of the subject is carefully assessed in an effort to determine the functions of the lesioned structure. Four types of lesions are discussed

1 The atlas indicates that the amygdala target site is 2.8 mm posterior to bregma, 4.5 mm lateral, and 8.5 mm ventral. (drawn from Paxinos & Watson, 1982).

2 A hole is drilled 2.8 mm posterior to bregma and 4.5 lateral to it. Then, the electrode holder is positioned over the hole, and the electrode is lowered 8.5 mm through the hole.

3 The electrode is anchored to the skull by letting dental acrylic harden around the electrode connector and several stainless steel skull screws.

Figure 5.14 Stereotaxic surgery: Implanting an electrode in the rat amygdala.

here: aspiration lesions, radio-frequency lesions, knife cuts, and cryogenic blockade.

Aspiration lesions When a lesion is to be made in an area of cortical tissue that is accessible to the eyes and instruments of the surgeon, **aspiration** is frequently the method of choice. The cortical tissue is drawn off by suction through a fine-tipped hand-held glass pipette. Because the underlying white matter is slightly more resistant to suction than the cortical tissue itself, a skilled surgeon can delicately peel off the layers of cortical tissue from the surface of the brain, leaving the underlying white matter and major blood vessels undamaged.

Radio-frequency lesions Subcortical lesions are most frequently made by passing *radio-frequency current* (high-frequency current) through the target tissue from the tip of a stereotaxically positioned electrode. It is the heat from the current that destroys the tissue. The size and shape of the lesion are determined by the duration and intensity of the current and the configuration of the electrode tip.

Knife cuts Cutting or sectioning is used to eliminate conduction in a nerve or tract. A tiny, well-placed cut can unambiguously accomplish this task without producing extensive damage to surrounding tissue. How does one insert a knife into the brain to make a cut without severely damaging the overlying tissue? The method is depicted in Figure 5.15.

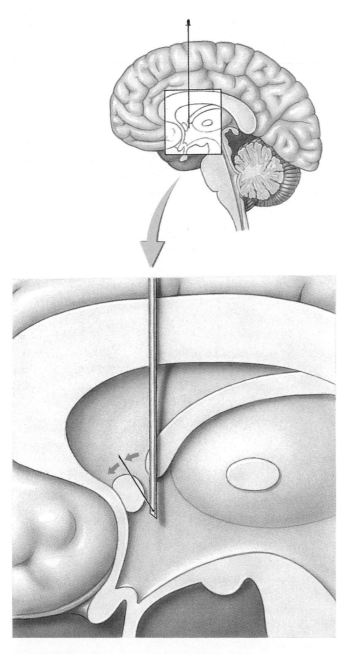

Figure 5.15 A device for performing subcortical knife cuts. The device is stereotaxically positioned in the brain; then, the blade swings out to make the cut. Here we see the anterior commissure being sectioned.

Figure 5.16 A cryoprobe. The cryoprobe is implanted in the brain; then, the brain area at the uninsulated tip of the cryoprobe is cooled while the effects on behavior are assessed. Cryoprobes are slender so that they can be implanted in the brain without causing substantial damage; they are typically constructed of hypodermic tubing.

Cryogenic blockade An alternative to destructive lesions is **cryogenic blockade.** When coolant is pumped through an implanted *cryoprobe*, such as the one depicted in Figure 5.16, neurons near the tip are cooled until they stop firing. The temperature is maintained above the freezing level so there is no structural damage. Then, when the tissue is allowed to warm up, normal neural activity returns. A cryogenic blockade is functionally similar to a lesion in that it eliminates the contribution of a particular area of the brain to the ongoing behavior of the subject.

Stereotaxic atlas. A three-dimensional map of the brain that is used to determine coordinates for stereotaxic surgery.

Bregma. A landmark on the surface of the skull that is commonly used as a reference point in stereotaxic surgery on rats.

Stereotaxic instrument. A device for performing stereotaxic surgery, composed of two parts: a head holder and an electrode holder.

Aspiration. A lesion technique in which tissue is drawn off by suction through the tip of a glass pipette.

Cryogenic blockade. The temporary elimination of neural activity in an area of the brain by cooling the area with a cryoprobe.

This is why cryogenic blockades are sometimes referred to as *reversible lesions*. Reversible lesions can also be produced with microinjections of local anesthetics into the brain.

Interpreting lesion effects   Before you leave this section on lesions, a word of caution is in order. Lesion effects are deceptively difficult to interpret. Because the structures of the brain are small, convoluted, and tightly packed together, even a highly skilled surgeon cannot completely destroy a structure without producing significant damage to adjacent structures. There is, however, an unfortunate tendency to lose sight of this fact. For example, a lesion that leaves major portions of the amygdala intact and damages an assortment of neighboring structures comes to be thought of simplistically as an *amygdala lesion.* Such an apparently harmless abstraction can be misleading. If you believe that all lesions referred to as amygdala lesions involve no other tissue, you will incorrectly attribute all of the behavioral effects of such lesions to amygdala damage; conversely, if you believe that all so-called amygdala lesions involve the entire amygdala, you will incorrectly conclude that the amygdala does not participate in behaviors uninfluenced by the lesion.

Electrical Stimulation

Clues about the function of a neural structure can be obtained by stimulating it electrically. Electrical brain stimulation is usually delivered across the two tips of a *bipolar electrode*—two insulated wires wound tightly together and cut at the end. Weak pulses of current produce an immediate increase in the firing of neurons near the tip of the electrode.

Electrical stimulation of the brain is an important biopsychological research tool because it often has behavioral effects. It can elicit a number of species-common behavioral sequences, including eating, drinking, attacking, copulating, and sleeping. The particular behavioral response that is elicited depends on the location of the electrode tip, the parameters of the current, and the test environment in which the stimulation is administered. Electrical stimulation of a particular brain structure usually has behavioral effects that are opposite to those produced by a lesion to the same structure.

Figure 5.17 Four methods of recording electrical activity of the nervous system.

An Intracellular Unit Recording
An intracellular microelectrode records the membrane potential from one neuron as it fires.

An Extracellular Unit Recording
An extracellular microelectrode records the electrical disturbance that is created each time that an adjacent neuron fires.

A Multiple Unit Recording
A small electrode records the action potentials of many nearby neurons. These are added up and plotted. In this example, firing in the area of the electrode tip gradually declined and then suddenly increased.

An Invasive EEG Recording
A large implanted electrode picks up general changes in electrical brain activity. The EEG signal is not related to neural firing in any obvious way.

Invasive Electrophysiological Recording Methods

This section describes four invasive electrophysiological recording methods: intracellular unit recording, extracellular unit recording, multiple-unit recording, and invasive EEG recording. See Figure 5.17 for an example of each method.

Intracellular unit recording   A method discussed at length in Chapter 4, *intracellular unit recording* provides a moment-by-moment record of the graded fluctuations in one neuron's membrane potential. Most experiments using this recording procedure are performed on chemically immobilized animals because it is next to impossible to keep the tip of a microelectrode positioned inside a neuron of a freely moving animal.

Extracellular unit recording   It is possible to record the action potentials of a neuron through a microelectrode whose tip is positioned in the extracellular fluid next to it. Each time the neuron fires, a blip is recorded on the oscil-loscope. Accordingly, *extracellular unit recording* provides a record of the firing of a neuron, but no information about the neuron's membrane potential. It is difficult, but not impossible, to record extracellularly from a single neuron in a freely moving animal without the electrode tip shifting away from the neuron.

Multiple-unit recording   In *multiple-unit recording,* the electrode tip is larger than that of a microelectrode; thus it picks up signals from many neurons. (The larger the electrode, the more neurons contribute to the signal.) The action potentials picked up by the electrode are fed into an integrating circuit, which adds them together. A multiple-unit recording is a graph of the total number of recorded action potentials per unit of time (e.g., per 0.1 second).

Invasive EEG recording   In laboratory animals, EEG signals are recorded through large implanted electrodes rather than through scalp electrodes. Cortical EEG signals are frequently recorded through stainless steel skull screws, whereas subcortical EEG signals are typically recorded through stereotaxically implanted wire electrodes.

5.4   Pharmacological Research Methods

The major research strategy of psychopharmacology is to administer drugs that either increase or decrease the effects of particular neurotransmitters and to observe the behavioral consequences. You learned in the preceding chapter how *agonists* and *antagonists* affect neurotransmitter systems. Described here are the various routes of drug administration, several methods of using chemicals to make selective brain lesions, and three methods of measuring the chemical activity of the brain that are particularly useful in biopsychological research.

Routes of Drug Administration

In most psychopharmacological experiments, drugs are administered in one of the following ways: (1) They are fed to the subject; (2) they are injected through a tube into the stomach (*intragastrically*); or (3) they are injected hypodermically into the peritoneal cavity of the abdomen (*intraperitonally, IP*), into a large muscle (*intramuscularly, IM*), into the fatty tissue beneath the skin (subcutaneously, SC), or into a large surface vein (*intravenously, IV*). A problem with these peripheral routes of administration is that many drugs do not readily pass through the blood-brain barrier. To overcome this problem, drugs can be injected in small amounts through a fine, hollow needle, called a **cannula,** that has been stereotaxically implanted in the brain.

Selective Chemical Lesions

The effects of surgical, electrolytic, and cryogenic lesions are frequently difficult to interpret because they affect all neurons in the target area. In some cases, it is possible to make more selective lesions by injecting **neurotoxins** (neural poisons) that have an affinity for certain components of the nervous system. There are many selective neurotoxins. For example, when *kainic acid* and *ibotenic acid* are administered by microinjection, they are preferentially taken up by cell bodies at the tip of the cannula and destroy those neurons, while leaving neurons with axons passing through the area largely unscathed. Another widely used selective neurotoxin is *6-hydroxydopamine (6-OHDA)*. It is taken up only by those neurons that release the neurotransmitters *norepinephrine* or *dopamine*; it leaves other neurons at the injection site undamaged.

Cannula. A fine tube, such as a hypodermic needle, that is implanted in the body for the purpose of introducing or extracting substances.

Neurotoxins. Neural poisons.

Measuring Chemical Activity of the Brain

There are many procedures for measuring the chemical activity of the brains of laboratory animals (see Westerink & Justice, 1991). Three that have proved particularly useful in biopsychological research are the 2-deoxyglucose technique, cerebral dialysis, and in vivo voltammetry.

2-deoxyglucose technique The *2-deoxyglucose (2-DG)* technique entails placing an animal that has been injected with radioactive 2-DG in a test situation in which it engages in the behavior of interest. Because 2-DG is similar in structure to glucose—the brain's main source of energy—neurons active during the test absorb it at a high rate, but do not metabolize it. After the subject engages in the behavior, it is killed and its brain is removed and sliced. The slices are then subjected to **autoradiography** (see Figure 5.18); they are coated with a photographic emulsion, stored in the dark for a few days, and then developed much like film. Areas of the brain that absorbed high levels of the radioactive 2-DG during the test appear as black spots on the slides. The density of the spots in various regions of the brain can then be color coded.

Cerebral dialysis The extracellular concentration of specific neurochemicals can be measured in behaving animals by **cerebral dialysis** (see Robinson & Justice, 1991). (Most other techniques for measuring neurochemicals require that the animals be killed so samples can be extracted.) Cerebral dialysis involves implanting in the brain a fine tube with a short semipermeable section. The semipermeable section is positioned in the brain structure of interest so the extracellular chemicals from the structure will diffuse into the tube. Once in the tube, they are carried by a solution flowing through it directly to an automated *chromatograph*—a device for measuring the chemical constituents of liquids and gases.

In vivo voltammetry Another technique for recording the extracellular concentration of neurochemicals in behaving animals is **in vivo voltammetry** (see Blaha et al., 1990; Blaha & Jung, 1991). This is a technique for inferring the changes in the extracellular concentration of specific chemicals at the tip of a carbon-based electrode from changes in the flow of current as the voltage across the electrode is gradually increased. It takes advantage of the fact that some chemicals are oxidized at characteristic current intensities, thus releasing a flow of electrons. In vivo voltam-

metry has been used most extensively to measure the release of *dopamine.*

Locating Neurotransmitters and Receptors in the Brain

A key step in trying to understand the psychological function of a particular neurotransmitter or receptor is finding out where it is located in the brain. Two of the techniques available for this purpose are immunocytochemistry and in situ hybridization. Each involves exposing brain slices to a labeled ligand of the molecule under investigation. The **ligand** of a molecule is another molecule that binds to it.

Immunocytochemistry When a foreign protein (an *antigen*) is injected into an animal, the animal creates *antibodies* that bind to it and then help the body remove or destroy it; this is known as the body's *immune reaction.* Neurochemists have created stocks of antibodies to most of the brain's peptide neurotransmitters and receptors. **Immunocytochemistry** is a procedure for locating particular neuroproteins in the brain by labeling antibodies to the neuroproteins with a dye or radioactive element and then exposing slices of brain tissue to the labeled antibod-

Figure 5.18 The 2-deoxyglucose technique. The accumulation of radioactivity in three frontal sections taken from the brain of a Richardson's ground squirrel. The subject was injected with radioactive 2-deoxyglucose; then, for 45 minutes it viewed brightly illuminated black and white stripes through its left eye while its right eye was covered. Because the ground squirrel visual system is largely crossed, most of the radioactivity accumulated in the visual structures of the right hemisphere (the hemisphere on your right). (Courtesy of Rod Cooper, Department of Psychology, University of Calgary.)

Figure 5.19 Immunocytochemistry. This section through the cat visual cortex reveals GABAergic inhibitory interneurons that have taken up the antibody for GABA. (Courtesy of Joanne Matsubara, Department of Ophthalmology, University of British Columbia.)

ies (see Figure 5.19). Regions of dye or radioactivity accumulation in the brain slices mark the locations of the target neuroprotein.

Because all enzymes are proteins and because only those neurons that release a particular neurotransmitter are likely to contain all the enzymes required for its synthesis, immunocytochemistry can be used to locate neurotransmitters that are not peptides. This is done by exposing brain slices to labeled antibodies that bind to enzymes located in only those neurons that contain the neurotransmitter of interest (see Figure 5.20).

In situ hybridization Another technique for locating peptides and other proteins in the brain is **in situ hybridization.** This technique takes advantage of the fact that all peptides and proteins are transcribed from sequences of

Figure 5.20 Immunocytochemistry. This section through the rat substantia nigra reveals dopaminergic neurons that have taken up the antibody for tyrosine hydroxylase, the enzyme that converts tyrosine to L-DOPA. (Courtesy of Mark Klitenick and Chris Fibiger, Department of Psychiatry, University of British Columbia.)

Figure 5.21 In situ hybridization. This color-coded frontal section through the rat brain reveals high concentrations of mRNA expression for the endorphin preproenkephalon in the striatum. In this illustration, the lowest levels (in red and yellow) indicate the highest concentrations. (Courtesy of Ningning Guo and Chris Fibiger, Department of Psychiatry, University of British Columbia.)

nucleotide bases on strands of messenger RNA (see Chapter 2). The nucleotide base sequences that direct the synthesis of many neuroproteins have been identified, and hybrid strands of mRNA with the complementary base sequences have been artificially created. In situ hybridization (see Figure 5.21) involves the following steps. First,

Autoradiography. The technique of photographically developing brain slices that have been exposed to a radioactively labeled substance such as 2-DG so that regions of high uptake are visible on the brain slices.

Cerebral dialysis. A method for recording changes in brain chemistry in behaving animals; a tube with a short semipermeable section is implanted in the brain and extracellular neurochemicals are continuously drawn off for analysis through the semipermeable section.

In vivo voltammetry. A procedure for inferring the changes in the extracellular concentration of specific chemicals at the tip of a carbon-based electrode from changes in the flow of current as the voltage across the electrode is gradually increased.

Ligand. A molecule that binds to the molecule under investigation.

Immunocytochemistry. A procedure for locating particular proteins in the brain by labeling antibodies to the neuroproteins with a dye or radioactive element and then exposing slices of brain tissue to the labeled antibodies.

In situ hybridization. A technique for locating particular proteins in the brain: Hybrid molecules that bind to the mRNA that directs the synthesis of the target protein are synthesized; then these hybrid ligands are labeled, and brain slices are exposed to them.

We turn now from the methods used by biopsychologists to study the nervous system to those that deal with the behavioral side of biopsychology. As we progress through this section of the chapter, it will become apparent that a fundamental difference between behavior and the nervous system is reflected in the nature of the methods used in their investigation. This difference is one of visibility. The nervous system and its activities are not ordinarily observable, whereas behavior is continuously on display in all its diversity and complexity. In essence, behavior is the overt expression of covert neural activity.

Because of the inherent invisibility of neural activity, the primary objective of the methods used in its investigation is to render the unobservable observable. In contrast, the

The answers (1) computed tomography, (2) magnetic resonance imaging, (3) positron emission tomography, (4) 2-deoxyglucose, (5) electroencephalogram, (6) event-related potential, (7) average evoked potential, (8) electromyogram, (9) electrooculogram, (10) skin conductance level, (11) skin conductance response, (12) electrocardiogram, (13) electrocardiogram, (14) intraperitoneal, (15) intramuscular, (16) intravenous, (17) subcutaneous, and (18) 6-hydroxydopamine.

major objectives of behavioral research methods are to control, to simplify, and to objectify. A single set of such procedures developed for the investigation of a particular behavioral phenomenon is commonly referred to as a **behavioral paradigm.** Each behavioral paradigm normally

Part 2: The Behavioral Research Methods of Biopsychology

hybrid RNA strands with the base sequence complementary to the mRNA that directs the synthesis of the target neuroprotein are obtained. Next, the hybrid RNA strands are labeled with a dye or radioactive element. Finally, when

brain slices are exposed to the labeled hybrid RNA strands; they bind to the complementary mRNA strands, thus marking the location of neurons that release the target neuroprotein.

SELF TEST

The research methods of biopsychology illustrate a psychological disorder suffered by many scientists. I call it "unabbreviaphobia"—the fear of leaving any term unabbreviated. As a means of reviewing Part I of this chapter, write out the following abbreviations in full.

1. CT: _____

2. MRI: _____

3. PET: _____

4. 2-DG: _____

5. EEG: _____

6. ERP: _____

7. AEP: _____

8. EMG: _____

9. EOG: _____

10. SCL: _____

11. SCR: _____

12. ECG: _____

13. EKG: _____

14. IP: _____

15. IM: _____

16. IV: _____

17. SC: _____

18. 6-OHDA: _____

comprises a method for producing the behavioral phenomenon under investigation and a method for objectively measuring it.

There is an unfortunate tendency to underestimate both the critical role that effective behavioral paradigms play in the progress of neuroscience and the ingenuity and effort required to develop them. Perhaps this is a consequence of behavior's visibility—we all seem to undervalue the familiar. Do not make this mistake! Remember that behavior is the ultimate manifestation of nervous system activity. In the final analysis, the purpose of all neural activity is the production of behavior. Studying it is no simple matter (see Jacobs et al., 1988; Whishaw, Kolb, & Sutherland, 1983).

5.5 Neuropsychological Testing

A patient suspected of suffering from some sort of nervous system dysfunction is usually sent to a *neurologist*. However, neurological examinations typically focus on sensory and motor function; they rarely reveal subtle changes in emotional, motivational, or intellectual function. This is the domain of the *neuropsychologist*.

Because of the diversity and complexity of psychological function, a thorough neuropsychological assessment requires several hours, spread over 2 or 3 days. As a result, neuropsychological testing is seldom prescribed. This is unfortunate.

Neuropsychological tests are normally administered (1) to serve as a basis for diagnosis, particularly in cases in which brain imaging, EEG, and neurological testing have proved equivocal; (2) to serve as a basis for counseling and caring for neurological patients; or (3) to evaluate the effectiveness of treatment. This section introduces some of the tests that are commonly employed in the neuropsychological assessment of general intelligence, language lateralization, memory, language, and perceptual-motor function.

Tests of General Intelligence

Most neuropsychological assessments begin with a so-called intelligence test such as the **Wechsler Adult Intelligence Scale (WAIS).** The overall intelligence quotient (IQ) is a notoriously poor measure of brain damage. However, a skilled neuropsychologist can sometimes draw inferences about a patient's neuropsychological dysfunction from the pattern of deficits on the various subtests. For example, low scores on subtests of verbal ability tend to be associated with left hemisphere damage, whereas right hemisphere damage tends to reduce scores on performance subtests. The 11 subtests of the WAIS are illustrated in Table 5.1.

Tests of Language Lateralization

It is usual for one hemisphere to participate more than the other in language-related activities. In most people, the left hemisphere is dominant for language; but in some, the right hemisphere is dominant. Two tests are commonly used to identify the dominant language hemisphere: the sodium amytal test (Wada, 1949) and the dichotic listening test (Kimura, 1973).

The **sodium amytal test** involves injecting the anesthetic sodium amytal into either the left or right carotid arteries of the neck. This temporarily anesthetizes the ipsilateral hemisphere while leaving the contralateral hemisphere largely unaffected. Several tests of language function are quickly administered while the ipsilateral hemisphere is anesthetized. Later, the process is repeated for the other side of the brain. When the injection is on the side dominant for language, the patient is completely mute for about 2 minutes. When the injection is on the nondominant side, there are only a few minor speech problems. Because the sodium amytal test is invasive, it can be administered only for medical reasons—usually to determine the dominant language hemisphere prior to brain surgery.

In the standard version of the **dichotic listening test,** sequences of spoken digits are presented to subjects through stereo headphones. Three digits are presented to one ear at the same time that three different digits are presented to the other ear. Then the subjects are asked to report as many of the six digits as they can. Kimura found that subjects correctly report more of the digits heard by the ear contralateral to their dominant hemisphere for language, as determined by the sodium amytal test.

Tests of Memory

Brain damage can disrupt some aspects of memory while leaving other aspects of memory unaffected. Thus a variety of tests are needed to properly assess the memory deficits of

Behavioral paradigm. A single set of procedures developed for the investigation of a particular behavioral phenomenon.

Wechsler Adult Intelligence Scale (WAIS). A widely used test of general intelligence.

Sodium amytal test. A test involving the anesthetization of first one hemisphere and then the other to determine which hemisphere plays the dominant role in language.

Dichotic listening test. A test of language lateralization in which patients simultaneously hear two different sequences of digits, one sequence in each ear.

TABLE 5.1

The 11 Subtests of the Wechsler Adult Intelligence Scale (WAIS)

Verbal Subtests

Information Read to the subject are 29 questions of general information—for example: "Who was the president of the United States during the Civil War?"

Digit-span Three digits are read to the subject at 1-second intervals, and the subject is asked to repeat them in the same order. Two trials are given at three digits, four digits, five digits, and so on until the subject fails both trials at one level.

Vocabulary The subject is asked to define a list of 35 words ranging in difficulty from *bed* to *tirade*.

Arithmetic The subject is presented with 14 arithmetic questions and must answer them without the benefit of pencil and paper.

Comprehension The subject is asked 16 questions that test the ability to understand general principles—for example: "Why should people pay taxes?"

Similarities The subject is presented with pairs of items and is asked to explain how the items in each pair are similar.

Performance Subtests

Picture-completion The subject must identify the important part missing from 20 drawings—for example, a door with no doorknob.

Picture-arrangement The subject is presented with 10 sets of cartoon drawings and is asked to arrange each set so it will tell a sensible story.

Block-design The subject is presented with blocks that are red on two sides, white on two sides, and half red and half white on the other two. The subject is shown pictures of nine patterns and is asked to duplicate them by arranging the blocks appropriately.

Object-assembly The subject is asked to put together the pieces of four jigsaw puzzles to form familiar objects.

Digit-symbol The subject is presented with a key that matches each of a series of symbols with a different digit. On the lower part of the page is a series of digits, and the subject is given 90 seconds to write the correct symbol next to as many digits as possible.

Figure 5.22 The Wisconsin Card Sorting Test. This woman is just starting the test; in front of which of the four test cards should she place her first card? She must guess until she can learn which principle—color, shape, or number—should guide her sorting.

neurological patients. It is common to begin by generally assessing memory for current and past information. (Where are you? What day is it? Who are the Beatles?). Some neurological patients, such as Jimmie G. from Chapter 1, have relatively normal memory for remote information while having almost total amnesia for recent information.

Short-term memory is typically assessed with a **digit-span test** (see Table 5.1). A patient's digit span is the longest sequence of random digits that can be correctly repeated 50% of the time. Most people have a digit span of 7.

Another widely used test of memory is the **Wisconsin Card Sorting Test** (see Figure 5.22). On each Wisconsin card is either one symbol or two, three, or four identical symbols. The symbols are all either triangles, stars, circles, or crosses; and they are all either red, green, yellow, or blue. At the beginning of the test, the patient is confronted with four stimulus cards that differ from one another in form, color, and number. The task is to correctly sort cards from a deck into piles in front of the stimulus cards. However, the patient does not know whether to sort by form, by color, or by number. The patient begins by guessing and is told after each card has been sorted whether it was sorted correctly or incorrectly. At first, the task is to learn to sort by color. But as soon as the patient makes several consecutive correct responses, the sorting principle is changed to shape or number without any indication other than the fact that responses based on color become incorrect. Thereafter, each time a new sorting principle is learned, the principle is changed.

The Wisconsin Card Sorting Test is sensitive to *frontal-lobe damage*. Patients with damage to their frontal lobes often continue to sort on the basis of one sorting principle for 100 or more trials after it has become incorrect. They seem to have great difficulty learning and remembering that previously appropriate guidelines for effective behavior are no longer appropriate.

Tests of Language

Language is one of the most complex human abilities. Consequently, it is usual to administer a brief screening test of language abilities and to follow it up with more extensive testing if deficits are revealed by the initial screening. One screening test for language-related problems is the **token test.** Twenty tokens of two different shapes (squares and circles), two different sizes (large and small), and five different colors (white, black, yellow, green, and red) are placed on a table in front of the subject. The test begins with the examiner reading simple instructions—for example, "Touch a red square" and the subject trying to follow them. Then, the test progresses to more difficult instructions, such as "Touch the small, red circle and then the large, green square." Finally, the subject is asked to read the instructions aloud and then follow them.

Tests of Perceptual-Motor Function

Most patients who are referred for neuropsychological testing will already have had their basic sensorimotor abilities evaluated by a neurologist. The neurologist will have assessed their ability to detect the presence of simple stimuli and their ability to control each major voluntary muscle of the body. In addition, the neurologist will have evaluated basic aspects of sensorimotor coordination by checking the status of various reflexes (e.g., pupillary and knee-jerk reflexes) and of various reflexively regulated voluntary behaviors (e.g., walking and balancing). However, it is not un-

common for brain-damaged patients to perform perfectly on such tests and yet have severe deficits on neuropsychological tests of complex perceptual-motor function.

Two neuropsychological tests of sensorimotor function are the *block-design subtest* of the WAIS (see Table 5.1) and the Rey-Osterrieth Complex Figure Test. Both are tests of visuospatial ability. In the **Rey-Osterrieth Complex Figure Test,** the subject's task is simply to copy the Rey-Osterrieth figure onto a sheet of paper with a pencil, a task that is no problem for normal subjects. Patients with damage to the right hemisphere tend to copy all of the details but link them together inappropriately; those with damage to the left hemisphere tend to get the overall configuration correct but omit the details. Asking a subject to draw the figure from memory is a means of assessing nonverbal memory. Figure 5.23 illustrates the performance on the block-design test and the Rey-Osterrieth Complex Figure Test of a subject who suffered a stroke in the right hemisphere (Goodglass & Kaplan, 1979).

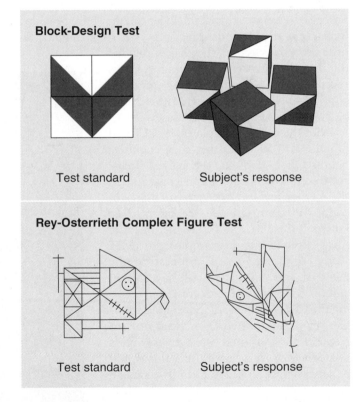

Block-Design Test

Test standard   Subject's response

Rey-Osterrieth Complex Figure Test

Test standard   Subject's response

Figure 5.23 The performance of a patient with right-hemisphere damage on the block-design and Rey-Osterrieth Complex Figure tests. In the usual version of these tests, the patient responds with the test standards in full view. (Test standards are from *Wechsler Adult Intelligence Scale.* Copyright © 1955 by The Psychological Corporation. Reproduced by permission. All rights reserved. Subject's responses are from H. Goodglass and E. Kaplan, "Assessment of Cognitive Functions in the Brain Injured Patient," in M. Gazzaniga (Ed.), *Handbook of Behavioral Neurobiology,* Vol. 2 (p. 20). New York, Plenum Publishing Corporation, 1979. Copyright 1982 by Plenum Publishing Corporation. Reprinted with permission.)

Digit-span test. A classic test of verbal short-term memory that assesses the ability of subjects to repeat sequences of random digits.

Wisconsin Card Sorting Test. A neuropsychological test that evaluates a patient's ability to remember that previously learned rules of behavior are no longer effective and to learn to respond to new rules.

Token test. A preliminary test of language deficits that involves following verbal instructions to touch or move tokens of different colors and shapes.

Rey-Osterrieth Complex Figure Test. A neuropsychological test of complex visuospatial ability.

Cognitive neuroscience is an interdisciplinary field of research that focuses on the study of the neural bases of cognition (thinking). It is a product of the combined expertise of three major groups of scientists: cognitive psychologists, computer scientists, and neuroscientists. The field is predicated on two related premises (see Posner & Raichle, 1994). The first premise is that each complex cognitive process results from the combined activity of simple cognitive processes called **constituent cognitive processes.** The second premise is that each constituent cognitive process is mediated by neural activity in a particular area of the brain. One of the main goals of cognitive neuroscience is to identify the parts of the brain that mediate various constituent cognitive processes.

Computer scientists have made two important contributions to the cognitive neuroscience team effort. First, by developing computer models of complex cognitive processes (e.g., of artificial intelligence), they have provided indications of how constituent processes might interact to produce them. Second, they have provided the computer expertise that has fueled the recent development of techniques for applying PET and functional MRI technology to cognitive neuroscience research.

With the central role played by PET and functional MRI in cutting-edge cognitive neuroscience research, the **paired-image subtraction technique** has become one of the key behavioral research methods in cognitive neuroscience research (see Posner & Raichle, 1994). Let me illustrate this technique with an example from a PET study of single-word processing by Petersen and colleagues (1988). Petersen and his colleagues were interested in locating the parts of the brain that enable a subject to make a word association (to respond to a printed word by saying a related word). You might think this would be an easy task to accomplish by having a subject perform a word-association task while a PET image of the subject's brain is recorded. The problem with this approach is that many parts of the brain that would be active during the test period would have nothing to do with the constituent cognitive process of forming a word association; much of the activity recorded would be associated with other processes such as seeing the words, reading the words, and speaking. The paired-image subtraction technique was developed to deal with this problem.

The paired-image subtraction technique involves obtaining PET or functional MRI images during several different cognitive tasks. Ideally, the tasks are designed so that pairs of them differ from each other in terms of only a single constituent cognitive process. Then, the brain activity associated with that process can be estimated by subtracting the activity in the image associated with one of the two tasks from the activity in the image associated with the other. For example, in one of the tasks in the Petersen et al. study, subjects spent a minute reading aloud printed nouns as they appeared on a screen; in another, they observed the same nouns on the screen but responded to each of them by saying aloud an associated verb (e.g., *truck, drive*). Then, Petersen and his colleagues subtracted the activity in the images that they recorded during the two tasks to obtain a *difference image.* The difference image illustrated the areas of the brain that were specifically involved in the constituent cognitive process of forming the word association; the activity associated with fixating on the screen, seeing

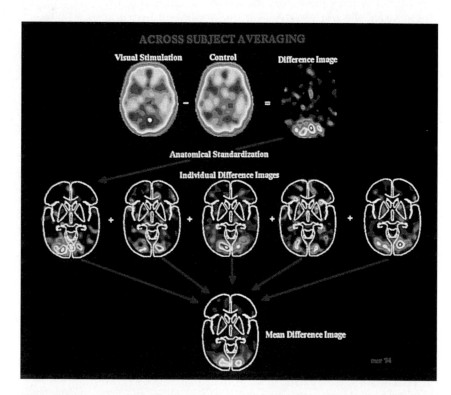

Figure 5.24 The paired-image subtraction technique, which is commonly employed in cognitive neuroscience. Here we see that the brain of the subject is generally active when the subject looks at a flickering checkerboard pattern (stimulation condition). However, if the activity that occurred when the subject stared at a blank screen is subtracted, it becomes apparent that the perception of the flashing checkerboard pattern was associated with an increase in activity in the occipital lobe. The individual difference images of five subjects were averaged to produce the ultimate mean difference image. (PET scans courtesy of Marcus Raichle, Mallindkrodt Institute of Radiology, Washington University Medical Center.)

the nouns, saying the words, and so on was eliminated by the subtraction (see Figure 5.24).

Another problem involved in using PET and functional MRI to locate constituent cognitive processes is the *noise* associated with random cerebral events that occur during the test—for example, thinking about a sudden pang of hunger, noticing a fly on the screen, or wondering whether the test will last much longer. The noise created by such events can be significantly reduced with a technique discussed earlier in this chapter: *signal averaging*. By averaging the difference images obtained from repetitions of the same tests, the researchers can greatly increase the *signal-to-noise ratio*. It is standard practice to average the images obtained from several subjects; the resulting averaged difference image emphasizes areas of activity that are common to most of the subjects and deemphasizes areas of activity that are peculiar to a few of them (see Figure 5.24).

5.7   Biopsychological Paradigms of Animal Behavior

Noteworthy examples of the behavioral paradigms used to study the biopsychology of laboratory species are provided here under three headings: (1) paradigms for the assessment of species-common behaviors, (2) traditional conditioning paradigms, and (3) seminatural animal learning paradigms. In each case, the focus is on methods used to study the behavior of the laboratory rat, the most common subject of biopsychological research.

Paradigms for Assessment of Species-Common Behaviors

Many of the behavioral paradigms that are used in biopsychological research are used to study species-common behaviors. **Species-common behaviors** are those that are displayed by virtually all members of a species, or at least by all those of the same age and sex. Commonly studied species-common behaviors include grooming, swimming, eating, drinking, copulating, fighting, and nest building. Described here are the open-field test, tests of aggressive and defensive behavior, and tests of sexual behavior.

Open-field test   In the **open-field test** the subject is placed in a large, barren chamber, and its activity is recorded. It is usual to measure general activity either with an automated activity recorder or by drawing lines on the floor of the chamber and counting the number of line-crossings during the test. It is also common in the open-field test to count the number of *boluses* (pieces of excrement) that were dropped by an animal during the test. Low activity scores and high bolus counts are frequently used as indicators of fearfulness. Fearful rats are highly **thigmotaxic**; that is, they rarely venture away from the walls of the test chamber and rarely engage in such activities as rearing and grooming. Rats are often fearful when they are first placed in a strange open field, but this fearfulness declines with repeated exposure to the same open field.

Tests of aggressive and defensive behavior   Typical patterns of aggressive and defensive behavior can be observed and measured during combative encounters between the dominant male rat of an established colony and a small-er male intruder (see Blanchard & Blanchard, 1988). This is called the **colony-intruder paradigm.** The behaviors of the dominant male are considered to be aggressive and those of the hapless intruder defensive. The dominant male of the colony (the *alpha male*) moves sideways toward the intruder, with its hair erect. When it nears the intruder, it tries to push the intruder off balance and to deliver bites to its back and flanks. The defender tries to protect its back and flanks by rearing up on its hind legs and pushing the attacker away with its forepaws or by rolling onto its back. Thus piloerection, lateral approach, and flank- and back-biting indicate conspecific aggression in the rat; freezing, boxing (rearing and pushing away), and rolling over indicate defensiveness.

Cognitive neuroscience. An approach to studying the neural bases of cognitive processes that involves a collaboration between cognitive psychologists, computer scientists, and neuroscientists.

Constituent cognitive processes. Simple cognitive processes that combine to produce complex cognitive processes.

Paired-image subtraction technique. Using PET and functional MRI to locate constituent cognitive processes in the brain by producing an image of the difference in brain activity associated with two cognitive tasks that differ in terms of a single constituent cognitive process.

Species-common behaviors. Behaviors that are displayed in the same manner by virtually all like members of a species.

Open-field test. Scoring the behavior of an animal in a large, barren chamber.

Thigmotaxic. Tending to stay near the walls of an open field.

Colony-intruder paradigm. A paradigm for the study of aggressive and defensive behavior in male rats; a small male intruder rat is placed in an established colony in order to study the aggressive responses of the colony's alpha male and the defensive responses of the intruder.

Some tests of rat defensive behavior assess reactivity to the experimenter rather than to another rat. The test developed by Albert (e.g., Albert et al., 1991) is an example. The rat is confronted in the test box by a sequence of test stimuli: a pencil held in front of its nose, a tap on its back with a pencil, a poke in its side with a pencil, a gloved hand held in front of its nose, a gloved hand grasping its tail, and a hand held around its abdomen. The response to each stimulus is rated on a scale from 0 (no response) to 3 (defensive attack). Rats with bilateral *septal lesions* are notoriously reactive to these stimuli.

The **elevated plus maze** is a test of defensiveness that is commonly used to study the *anxiolytic* (antianxiety) effects of drugs in rats. It is a four-armed plus-sign-shaped maze that is typically mounted 50 centimeters above the floor. Two of the arms of the maze have sides, and two do not. The measure of defensiveness, or anxiety, is the proportion of time the rats spend in the protected closed arms rather than on the exposed arms. Anxiolytic drugs such as the *benzodiazepines* significantly increase the proportion of time that rats spend on the open arms (see Pellow et al., 1985).

Tests of sexual behavior   Most attempts to study the physiological bases of rat sexual behavior have focused on the copulatory act itself. The male mounts the female from behind and clasps her hindquarters. If the female is receptive, she responds by assuming the **lordosis** posture; that is, she sticks her hindquarters in the air, she bends her back in a U, and she deflects her tail to the side. During some mounts, the male inserts his penis into the female's vagina; this act is called **intromission.** After intromission, the male dismounts by jumping backwards. He then returns a few seconds later to mount and intromit once again. Following about 10 such cycles of mounting, intromitting, and dismounting, the male mounts, intromits, and **ejaculates** (ejects his sperm).

Three common measures of male rat sexual behavior are the number of mounts required to achieve intromission, the number of intromissions required to achieve ejaculation, and the interval between ejaculation and the reinitiation of mounting. The most common measures of female rat sexual behavior are the **lordosis quotient** (the proportion of mounts that elicit lordosis) and the degree of back bending during lordosis.

Traditional Conditioning Paradigms

Learning paradigms play a major role in biopsychological research for three reasons. The first is that learning is a phenomenon of primary interest to psychologists. The second is that learning paradigms provide an effective technology for producing and controlling animal behavior. Because animals cannot follow instructions from the experimenter, it is often necessary to train them to behave in a fashion consistent with the goals of the experiment. The third rea-

son is that it is possible to infer much about the sensory, motor, motivational, and cognitive state of an animal from its ability to learn various tasks and to perform various learned responses.

If you have taken a previous course in psychology, you will likely be familiar with the Pavlovian and operant conditioning paradigms. In the **Pavlovian conditioning paradigm,** the experimenter pairs an initially neutral stimulus called a *conditional stimulus* (e.g., a tone or a light) with an *unconditional stimulus* (e.g., meat powder)—a stimulus that elicits an *unconditional* (reflexive) *response* (e.g., salivation). As a result of these pairings, the conditional stimulus eventually acquires the capacity, when administered alone, to elicit a *conditional response* (e.g., salivation)—a response that is often, but not always, similar to the unconditional response.

In the **operant conditioning paradigm,** the rate at which a particular voluntary response (such as a lever press) is emitted is increased by *reinforcement* or decreased by *punishment.* One of the most widely used operant con-

Elevated plus maze. A test of defensiveness or anxiety in rats that assesses the tendency of rats to avoid the two open arms of an elevated plus-sign-shaped maze.

Lordosis. The female rat's rump-up, tail-to-the-side posture of sexual receptivity.

Intromission. Insertion of the penis into the vagina.

Ejaculates. Ejects sperm.

Lordosis quotient. The proportion of mounts that produce lordosis.

Pavlovian conditioning paradigm. A paradigm in which the experimenter pairs an initially neutral stimulus (conditional stimulus) with a stimulus (unconditional stimulus) that elicits a reflexive response (unconditional response); after several pairings, the neutral stimulus elicits a response (conditional response).

Operant conditioning paradigm. A paradigm in which the rate of a particular voluntary response is increased by reinforcement or decreased by punishment.

Self-stimulation paradigm. A paradigm in which animals press a lever to administer reinforcing electrical stimulation to their own brains.

Drug self-administration paradigm. An operant conditioning paradigm in which animals press a lever to administer reinforcing drugs to themselves.

Conditioned taste aversion. The aversion developed by animals to tastes that have been followed by illness.

Radial arm maze. A maze in which several arms radiate out from a central starting chamber; it is commonly used to study spatial learning in rats.

ditioning paradigms in biopsychology is the self-stimulation paradigm. In the **self-stimulation paradigm,** animals press a lever to administer reinforcing electrical stimulation to certain "pleasure centers" in their brains (e.g., Phillips & Fibiger, 1989; Stellar, 1990). Another operant conditioning paradigm that is widely used in biopsychology is the **drug self-administration paradigm,** in which animals inject drugs into themselves through implanted cannulas by pressing a lever (e.g., Mello et al., 1989).

Seminatural Animal Learning Paradigms

In addition to Pavlovian and operant conditioning paradigms, biopsychologists use animal learning paradigms that have been specifically designed to mimic situations that an animal might encounter in its natural environment. Among these "seminatural" animal learning paradigms are the conditioned taste aversion, radial arm maze, Morris water maze, and conditioned defensive burying paradigms.

Conditioned taste aversion
The 1950s was a time of sock hops, sodas at Al's, crewcuts, and drive-in movies. In the animal-behavior laboratory, it was a time of lever presses, key pecks, and shuttles made in response to flashing lights, tones, and geometric patterns. Then, along came rock 'n roll, and along came the conditioned taste aversion paradigm. Things have not been the same since.

Conditioned taste aversion is the aversion developed by animals to tastes whose consumption has been followed by illness (see Garcia & Koelling, 1966). In the standard conditioned taste aversion experiment, rats receive an *emetic* (a nausea-inducing drug) after they consume a food with an unfamiliar taste. On the basis of this single conditioning trial, the rats subsequently avoid the taste.

The ability of rats to readily learn the relationship between a particular taste and subsequent illness unquestionably increases their chances of survival in their natural environment, where potentially edible substances are not routinely screened by government agencies. Rats and many other animals are *neophobic* (afraid of new things); thus, when they first encounter a new food, they consume it in only small quantities. If they subsequently become ill, they will not consume it again. Conditioned aversions also develop to familiar tastes, but these typically require more than a single trial to be learned.

Humans also develop conditioned taste aversions. Cancer patients have been reported to develop aversions to foods consumed before nausea-inducing chemotherapy (Bernstein & Webster, 1980). Many of you will be able to testify on the basis of personal experience about the effectiveness of conditioned taste aversions. I still have vivid memories of a long-ago batch of laboratory punch that I overzealously consumed after eating two pieces of blueberry pie. But that is another story—albeit a particularly colorful one.

Research on conditioned taste aversion challenged three principles of learning (see Revusky & Garcia, 1970) that had grown out of research on traditional operant and Pavlovian conditioning paradigms. First, it challenged the view that animal conditioning is always a gradual step-by-step process; robust taste aversions can be established in only a single trial. Second, it showed that *temporal contiguity* is not essential for conditioning; rats acquire taste aversions even when they do not become ill until several hours after eating. Third, it challenged the *principle of equipotentiality* —the view that conditioning proceeds in basically the same manner regardless of the particular stimuli and responses under investigation. Rats appear to be particularly well prepared to learn associations between tastes and illness; it is only with difficulty that they learn relations between the color of food and nausea or between taste and footshock.

Radial arm maze
The radial arm maze taps the well-developed spatial abilities of rodents. The survival of rats in the wild depends on their ability to navigate quickly and accurately through their environment and to learn which locations in it are likely to contain food and water. This task is much more complex for a rodent than it is for us. Most of us obtain food from locations where the supply is continually replenished; we go to the market confident that we will find enough food to satisfy our needs. In contrast, the foraging rat must learn, and retain, a complex pattern of spatially coded details. It must not only learn where morsels of food are likely to be found but must also remember which of these sites it has recently stripped of their booty so as not to revisit them too soon. Designed by Olton and Samuelson (1976) to study these spatial abilities, the **radial arm maze** (see Figure 5.25) is an array of arms— usually eight or more—radiating from a central starting area. At the end of each arm is a food cup, which may or may not be baited, depending on the purpose of the experiment.

Figure 5.25 A radial arm maze.

In one version of the radial arm maze paradigm, rats are placed each day in a radial arm maze that has the same arms baited each day. After a few days of experience, rats rarely visit unbaited arms at all, and they rarely visit baited arms more than once in the same day—even when control procedures make it impossible for them to recognize odors left during previous visits to an arm or to make their visits in a systematic sequence. Because the arms are identical, rats must orient themselves in the maze with reference to external room cues; thus their performance can be disrupted by rotation of the maze or by changes in the appearance of the room.

Figure 5.26 A rat burying a test object from which it has just received a single mild shock. (Photograph by Jack Wong.)

Morris water maze Another seminatural learning paradigm that has been designed to study the spatial abilities of rats is the **Morris water maze** (Morris, 1981). The rats are placed in a circular, featureless pool of cool milky water, in which they must swim until they discover the escape platform—which is invisible just beneath the surface of the water. The rats are allowed to rest on the platform before being returned to the water for another trial. Despite the fact that the starting point is varied from trial to trial, the rats learn after only a few trials to swim directly to the platform, presumably by using spatial cues from the room as a reference. The Morris water maze has proved extremely useful for assessing the navigational skills of lesioned or drugged animals (e.g., Kolb, 1989).

Conditioned defensive burying Yet another seminatural learning paradigm that is useful in biopsychological research is the conditioned defensive burying paradigm (e.g., Pinel & Mana, 1989; Pinel & Treit, 1978). In the **conditioned defensive burying paradigm,** rats receive a single aversive stimulus (e.g., a shock, airblast, or noxious odor) from an object mounted on the wall of the chamber just above the floor, which is littered with bedding material. After a single trial, almost every rat learns that the test object is a threat and responds by spraying bedding material at the test object with its head and forepaws (see Figure 5.26). This response has been termed *conditioned defensive burying* because many subjects completely cover the source of aversive stimulation during the test period. Treit has shown that antianxiety drugs reduce the amount of conditioned defensive burying and has used the paradigm to study the neurochemistry of anxiety (e.g., Treit, 1987). The burying response does not develop normally in rats that have been reared in cages with wire-mesh floors rather than bedding-covered floors (Pinel et al., 1989).

Morris water maze. A pool of milky water with a goal platform invisible just beneath its surface; it is used to study the ability of rats to learn spatial locations.

Conditioned defensive burying paradigm. A paradigm in which rodent subjects respond to the source of an aversive stimulation by spraying material at it.

Conclusion

This chapter has introduced you to the research methods of biopsychology. In Part 1—the brain half of the chapter—you learned about methods of visualizing the living human brain (5.1); about noninvasive methods of recording human physiological activity (5.2); about invasive lesion, stimulation, and recording methods that are used in biopsychological research on laboratory animals (5.3); and about pharmacological research methods that are used in biopsychological research (5.4). In Part 2—the behavior half of the chapter—you learned about neuropsychological testing (5.5); behavioral research methods of cognitive neuroscience (5.6); and biopsychological paradigms of animal behavior (5.7).

Before you leave the chapter, you need to appreciate that to be effective these methods must be used together. Seldom, if ever, is an important biopsychological issue resolved by a single set of methods. The reason for this is that neither the methods used to manipulate the brain nor the methods used to assess the behavioral consequences of these manipulations are totally selective; there are no methods of manipulating the brain that change only a single aspect of brain function, and there are no measures of behavior that reflect only a single psychological process. Accordingly, lines of research that use a single set of methods can often be interpreted in more than one way and thus cannot provide unequivocal evidence for any one interpretation. Typically, important research questions are resolved only when several methods are brought to bear on a single problem in such a way that all interpretations but one can be ruled out. This approach, as you learned in Chapter 1, is called *converging operations*.

FOOD FOR THOUGHT

1. The current rate of progress in the development of new and better brain scanning devices will soon render behavioral tests of brain damage obsolete. Discuss.

2. You are taking a physiological psychology laboratory course, and your instructor gives you two rats: one rat with a lesion in an unknown structure and one normal rat. How would you test the rats to determine which has the lesion? How would your approach differ from what you might use to test a human patient suspected of having brain damage?

KEY TERMS

Contrast X-ray techniques (p. 106)
Pneumoencephalography (p. 106)
Cerebral angiography (p. 107)
Computed tomography (CT) (p. 107)
Magnetic resonance imaging (MRI) (p. 108)
Positron emission tomography (PET) (p. 108)
2-deoxyglucose (2-DG) (p. 109)
Functional MRI (p. 109)
Electroencephalography (p. 109)
Alpha waves (p. 109)
Event-related potentials (ERPs) (p. 109)
Sensory evoked potential (p. 109)
Signal averaging (p. 110)

P300 wave (p. 110)
Far-field potentials (p. 110)
Electromyography (p. 111)
Electrooculography (p. 111)
Skin conductance level (SCL) (p. 112)
Skin conductance response (SCR) (p. 112)
Electrocardiogram (ECG or EKG) (p. 113)
Hypertension (p. 113)
Plethysmography (p. 113)
Stereotaxic atlas (p. 114)
Bregma (p. 114)
Stereotaxic instrument (p. 114)
Aspiration (p. 114)
Cryogenic blockade (p. 115)
Cannula (p. 117)
Neurotoxins (p. 117)
Autoradiography (p. 118)
Cerebral dialysis (p. 118)
In vivo voltammetry (p. 118)
Ligand (p. 118)

Immunocytochemistry (p. 118)
In situ hybridization (p. 119)
Behavioral paradigm (p. 120)
Wechsler Adult Intelligence Scale (WAIS) (p. 121)
Sodium amytal test (p. 121)
Dichotic listening test (p. 121)
Digit-span test (p. 122)
Wisconsin Card Sorting Test (p. 122)
Token test (p. 123)
Rey-Osterrieth Complex Figure Test (p. 123)
Cognitive neuroscience (p. 124)
Constituent cognitive processes (p. 124)
Paired-image subtraction technique (p. 124)
Species-common behaviors (p. 125)

Open-field test (p. 125)
Thigmotaxic (p. 125)
Colony-intruder paradigm (p. 125)
Elevated plus maze (p. 126)
Lordosis (p. 126)
Intromission (p. 126)
Ejaculates (p. 126)
Lordosis quotient (p. 126)
Pavlovian conditioning paradigm (p. 126)
Operant conditioning paradigm (p. 126)
Self-stimulation paradigm (p. 127)
Drug self-administration paradigm (p. 127)
Conditioned taste aversion (p. 127)
Radial arm maze (p. 127)
Morris water maze (p. 128)
Conditioned defensive burying paradigm (p. 128)

ADDITIONAL READING

The following are provocative discussions of two behavioral testing strategies:

Jacobs, W. J., Blackburn, J. R., Buttrick, M., Harpur, T. J., Kennedy, D., Mana, M. J., MacDonald, M. A., McPherson, L. M., Paul, D., & Pfaus, J. G. (1988). Observations. *Psychobiology, 16,* 3–19.

Whishaw, I. Q., Kolb, B., & Sutherland, R. J. (1983). The analysis of behavior in the laboratory rat. In T. E. Robinson (Ed.), *Behavioral approaches to brain research.* New York: Oxford University Press.

An interesting, colorful, and simple introduction to modern brain-imaging techniques and the emerging field of cognitive neuroscience is provided by the following book:

Posner, M. I., & Raichle, M. E. (1994). *Images of the mind.* New York: Scientific American Library.

6

Human Brain Damage and Animal Models

6.1 Causes of Brain Damage

6.2 Neuropsychological Diseases

6.3 Animal Models of Human Neuropsychological Diseases

The study of the psychological effects of human brain damage has two major goals: the furtherance of our understanding of the normal psychological functions of the human brain and the development of effective strategies for the treatment of neuropsychological disorders. This chapter is an introduction to the topic of human brain damage that focuses on both of these goals.

The first section of this chapter describes common causes of human brain damage; the second section describes several major neuropsychological disorders; and the third, and final, section discusses the investigation of human neuropsychological disorders through the study of animal models. But first sublieutenant L. Zasetsky introduces you to the personal tragedy that underlies the academic discourse that follows.

Zasetsky suffered a bullet wound to his left parietal and occipital lobes, and his life was irrevocably changed. A. R. Luria, an eminent Soviet neuropsychologist, documented Zasetsky's struggle to regain his mental faculties in *The Man With a Shattered World* (1972). Following is a paraphrased description from this book of Luria's first meeting with Zasetsky:

I first met Zasetsky 3 months after he had been wounded. I was struck by how young he looked. When I asked him how he was feeling, he shyly replied, "Okay." But my further questioning only confused him. He had difficulty understanding my questions, but even when he did, he had difficulty answering. Each question initiated a frantic struggle to come up with the right words.

"What town are you from?"
"At home ... there's ... I want to write ... but just can't."
"Do you have any relatives?"
"There's ... my mother ... and also—what do you call them?"
"Try reading this," I suggested.
"What's this? ... No, I don't know ... don't understand ... what is this?"

"All right, then," I said. "Try to write your name." He awkwardly picked up the pencil, by the wrong end at first. He was shocked to discover that he couldn't form a single letter. The truth was becoming apparent to him. Somehow he had become illiterate.

"Well, then, take a look at this picture and tell me what you see."
"Over here there's ... he's ... he's sitting. And this one here is ... is ... And there's this ... I don't know! Certainly is something there, but ... but what's it called?"
"Could you raise your right hand?"
"Right? Right? ... Left? No, I don't know ... What does right mean?, ... Or left? ... No, I can't."

When I asked him to list the months of the year, he did it with ease and was reassured. But when I asked him what season comes before winter, he became confused again.

"Before winter? After winter? ... Summer? ... Or something! No, I can't get it."

In the years to come, Zasetsky's verbal abilities improved somewhat, and I learned more about his problems. He had great difficulty gauging the spatial relationships among objects; he could often not locate parts of his own body; he would often be unaware of the right side of things that he was looking at; and he had difficulty remembering recent events, although many of his memories of childhood returned.

His response to nature, however, was as keen as ever; he enjoyed the singing of the birds and the beauty of the lake. And oh how he wanted to accomplish what was asked of him. Each failure renewed his sense of loss. What type of brain injury had damaged some of his faculties but left others intact? His grasp of his immediate world, his will, and his desire to accomplish and experience had all been spared—enough had been spared to enable him to experience the anguish of his every failure and shortcoming.

Remember Zasetsky and his struggle; you will encounter them again, later in the book.

6.1 Causes of Brain Damage

This section of the chapter provides an introduction to six causes of brain damage: brain tumors, cerebrovascular disorders, closed-head injuries, infections of the brain, neurotoxins, and genetic factors.

Brain Tumors

A **tumor** or **neoplasm** (literally, "new growth") is a mass of cells that grows independently of the rest of the body. In other words, it is a cancer.

About 20% of tumors found in the human brain are **meningiomas** (see Figure 6.1)—tumors that grow between the *meninges*, the three membranes that cover the central nervous system. All meningiomas are **encapsulated tumors**—tumors that grow within their own membrane. As a result, they are particularly easy to identify on a CAT scan, they can influence the function of the brain only by

Tumor (neoplasm). A mass of cells that grows independently of the rest of the body.

Meningiomas. Tumors that grow between the meninges.

Encapsulated tumors. Tumors that grow within their own membrane.

Figure 6.1 A meningioma. (Courtesy of Kenneth Berry, Head of Neuropathology, Vancouver General Hospital.)

the pressure they exert on surrounding tissue, and they are almost always **benign tumors**—tumors that are surgically removable with little risk of further growth in the body.

Unfortunately, encapsulation is the exception rather than the rule when it comes to brain tumors. With the exception of meningiomas, most brain tumors are infiltrating. **Infiltrating tumors** are those that grow diffusely through surrounding tissue. As a result, they are usually **malignant tumors**; it is difficult to remove them completely, and any cancerous tissue that remains after surgery continues to grow.

About 10% of brain tumors do not originate in the brain. They grow from infiltrating tumor fragments carried to the brain by the bloodstream from some other part of the body. (The brain is a particularly fertile ground for tumor growth.) These tumors are called **metastatic tumors**; *metastasis* refers to the transmission of disease from one organ to another. Most metastatic brain tumors originate as cancers of the lungs. Obviously, the chance of recovering from a cancer that has already attacked two or more separate sites is slim at best. Figure 6.2 illustrates the ravages of metastasis.

Infiltrating brain tumors are usually untreatable, but there is reason for optimism. Tumor growth results from the dysfunction of mechanisms that regulate normal cell division and growth. It has been discovered that normal cells contain *tumor suppressor genes*, which become dysfunctional during the growth of certain types of tumors. Efforts to understand and treat tumor growth are currently focusing on these genes (see Sager, 1989; Weinberg, 1991).

Cerebrovascular Disorders

Strokes are sudden-onset cerebrovascular disorders that cause brain damage. Two types of cerebrovascular disorders lead to strokes: cerebral hemorrhage and cerebral ischemia (pronounced "iss-KEEM-ee-a"). In the United States, stroke is the third leading cause of death and the

Figure 6.2 Multiple metastatic brain tumors. The arrows indicate some of the more advanced areas of metastatic tumor development.

most common cause of adult disability. Common consequences of stroke are amnesia, aphasia (language difficulties), paralysis, and coma (see Zivin & Choi, 1991).

Cerebral hemorrhage   **Cerebral hemorrhage** means "bleeding in the brain." It occurs when a cerebral blood vessel ruptures and blood seeps into the surrounding neural tissue and damages it.

Bursting aneurysms are a common cause of intracerebral hemorrhage. An **aneurysm** is a pathological balloon-like dilation that forms in the wall of a blood vessel at a point where the elasticity of the vessel wall is defective. They can be **congenital** (present at birth) or can result from exposure to vascular poisons or infection. Individuals who have aneurysms should make every effort to avoid high blood pressure.

Cerebral ischemia   **Cerebral ischemia** is a disruption of the blood supply to an area of the brain.

The three main causes of cerebral ischemia are thrombosis, embolism, and arteriosclerosis. In **thrombosis**, a plug

Figure 6.3 An angiogram that illustrates narrowing of the carotid artery (see arrow), the main pathway of blood to the brain. Compare this angiogram with the normal angiogram in Figure 5.1.

Benign tumors. Tumors that are surgically removable with little risk of further growth in the body.

Infiltrating tumors. Tumors that grow diffusely through surrounding tissue.

Malignant tumors. Tumors that cannot be surgically removed without continued growth in the body.

Metastatic tumors. Tumors that originate in one organ and spread to another.

Strokes. Sudden-onset cerebrovascular disorders that cause brain damage.

Cerebral hemorrhage. Bleeding in the brain.

Aneurysm. A pathological balloonlike dilation that forms in the wall of a blood vessel at a point where the elasticity of the vessel wall is defective.

Congenital. Present at birth.

Cerebral ischemia. A disruption of blood supply to an area of the brain.

Thrombosis. The blockage of blood flow by a plug (a thrombus) at the site of its formation.

Embolism. The blockage of blood flow in a smaller blood vessel by a plug that was formed in a larger blood vessel and carried by the bloodstream to the smaller one.

Arteriosclerosis. A condition in which blood vessels are blocked by the accumulation of fat deposits in the vessel walls.

Glutamate. The brain's most prevalent exitatory neurotransmitter, whose excessive release causes much of the brain damage resulting from cerebral ischemia.

---

called a *thrombus* is formed and blocks blood flow at the site of its formation. A thrombus may be composed of a blood clot, fat, oil, an air bubble, tumor cells, or any combination thereof. **Embolism** is similar except that the plug, called an *embolus* in this case, is carried by the blood from a larger vessel, where it was formed, to a smaller one, where it becomes lodged; in essence, an embolus is just a thrombus that has taken a trip. In **arteriosclerosis,** the walls of blood vessels thicken and the channels narrow, usually as the result of fat deposits; this narrowing can eventually lead to complete blockage of the blood vessels. The *angiogram* in Figure 6.3 illustrates partial blockage of one carotid artery.

Paradoxically, some of the brain's own neurotransmitters, specifically the *excitatory amino acids,* play a key role in the development of stroke-related brain damage (see Beal, 1992; Choi, 1992; and Coyle & Puttfarcken, 1993). It was once assumed—quite reasonably—that the disruption of the oxygen and glucose supply was the key causal factor in stroke-related brain damage; however, it now appears that much of the brain damage associated with stroke is a consequence of excessive glutamate release. **Glutamate**, is an amino acid, the brain's most prevalent excitatory neurotransmitter.

Here is how this mechanism is thought to work (see Rothman, 1994; and Zivin & Choi, 1991). After a blood vessel becomes blocked, many of the blood-deprived neurons become overactive and release excessive quantities of glutamate. The excessive glutamate in turn overactivates glutamate receptors in the membranes of postsynaptic neurons. Then, the overactivity of the postsynaptic glutamate receptors allows large numbers of Na$^+$ and Ca^{++} ions to enter the postsynaptic neurons. The glutamate receptors that are most involved in this reaction are the **NMDA (N-methyl-D-aspartate) receptors.** The excessive internal concentrations of Na$^+$ and Ca^{++} ions affect the postsynaptic neurons in two ways: They trigger the release of excessive amounts of glutamate from them, thus spreading the toxic cascade to yet other neurons; and they trigger a sequence of reactions that ultimately kills the postsynaptic neurons. (See Figure 6.4.)

An exciting implication of the discovery that excessive glutamate release causes much of the brain damage associated with stroke is the possibility of preventing stroke-related brain damage by blocking the glutaminergic cascade. Indeed, it has already been shown that *NMDA receptor blockers* administered immediately after a stroke can substantially reduce the subsequent development of brain damage in experimental animals (e.g., Kaku, Giffard, & Choi, 1993; Olney et al., 1991). The search is now on for an NMDA receptor blocker that is safe for use in human stroke victims (see Zivin & Choi, 1991).

Closed-Head Injuries

It is not necessary for the skull to be penetrated for the brain to be seriously damaged. In fact, any blow to the head should be treated with extreme caution, particularly when confusion, sensorimotor disturbances, or loss of consciousness ensue. Brain injuries produced by blows that do not penetrate the skull are called *closed-head injuries.*

Contusions are closed-head injuries that involve damage to the cerebral circulatory system. Such damage produces internal hemorrhaging, which results in a hematoma. A **hematoma** is a localized collection of clotted blood in an organ or tissue—in other words, a bruise.

It is paradoxical that the very hardness of the skull, which protects the brain from penetrating injuries, is the major factor in the development of contusions. Contusions from closed-head injuries

occur when the brain slams against the inside of the skull. As Figure 6.5 illustrates, blood from such injuries can accumulate in the *subdural space*—the space between the dura mater and arachnoid membrane—and severely distort the surrounding neural tissue.

It may surprise you to learn that contusions frequently occur on the side of the brain opposite the side struck by a blow. The reason for such so-called **contrecoup injuries** is that the blow causes the brain to strike the inside of the skull on the other side of the head.

When there is a disturbance of consciousness following a blow to the head and there is no evidence of a contusion

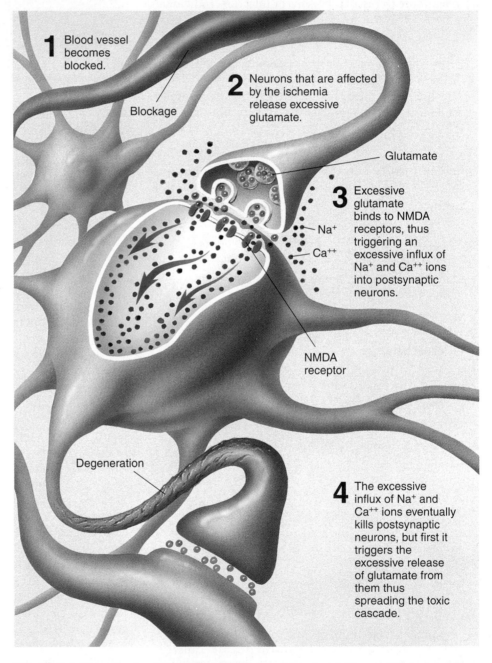

1 Blood vessel becomes blocked.

Blockage

2 Neurons that are affected by the ischemia release excessive glutamate.

Glutamate

3 Excessive glutamate binds to NMDA receptors, thus triggering an excessive influx of Na$^+$ and Ca^{++} ions into postsynaptic neurons.

Na$^+$

Ca^{++}

NMDA receptor

Degeneration

4 The excessive influx of Na$^+$ and Ca^{++} ions eventually kills postsynaptic neurons, but first it triggers the excessive release of glutamate from them thus spreading the toxic cascade.

Figure 6.4 The cascade of events by which the stroke-induced release of glutamate kills neurons.

Figure 6.5 A CAT scan of a subdural hematoma. Notice that the subdural hematoma has displaced the left lateral ventricle.

Bacterial infections When bacteria infect the brain, they often lead to the formation of *cerebral abscesses*—pockets of pus in the brain. They also often attack and inflame the meninges, creating a disorder known as **meningitis.** Penicillin and other antibiotics are no panacea for bacterial brain infections. They can eliminate the infection, but they cannot reverse brain damage that has already been produced.

Syphilis is one bacterial brain infection you have likely heard about. Syphilis bacteria are passed from infected to noninfected individuals through contact with genital sores. The infecting bacteria then go into a dormant stage for several years before they become virulent and attack many parts of the body, including the brain. The syndrome of insanity and dementia that results from a syphilitic infection is called **general paresis.**

Syphilis has a particularly interesting history (see Klawans, 1990). The first Europeans to visit America stripped the natives of their gold and left smallpox in return. But the deal was not totally one-sided; the booty carried back to Europe by Columbus's sailors and the adventurers that followed included a cargo of syphilis bacteria. Until then, syphilis had been restricted to the Americas, but it was quickly distributed to the rest of the world.

Viral Infections There are two types of viral infections of the nervous system—neurotropic and pantropic.

or other structural damage, the diagnosis is **concussion.** It is commonly assumed that concussions entail a temporary disruption of normal cerebral function with no long-term damage. However, the punch-drunk syndrome suggests otherwise. The **punch-drunk syndrome** is the **dementia** (general intellectual deterioration) and cerebral scarring that is observed in boxers and other individuals who experience repeated concussions. If there were no damage associated with a single concussion, the effects of many concussions could not summate to produce severe damage. One of the most dangerous aspects of concussion is the complacency with which it is regarded. Flippant references to it, such as "having one's bell rung," do little to communicate its hazards.

Infections of the Brain

An invasion of the brain by microorganisms is a *brain infection,* and the resulting inflammation is **encephalitis.** There are two common types of brain infections: bacterial infections and viral infections.

NMDA (N-methyl-D-aspartate) receptors. Glutamate receptors that play a key role in the development of stroke-induced brain damage.

Contusions. Closed-head injuries that involve bleeding.

Hematoma. A bruise.

Contrecoup injuries. Contusions that occur on the side of the brain opposite to the side of a blow.

Concussion. The situation in which there is a disturbance of consciousness following a blow to the head with no cerebral bleeding or obvious structural damage.

Punch-drunk syndrome. The psychological disturbances that result from repeated concussions.

Dementia. General intellectual deterioration.

Encephalitis. The inflammation associated with brain infection.

Meningitis. Inflammation of the meninges, usually caused by bacterial infection.

General paresis. The insanity and intellectual deterioration resulting from syphilitic infection.

Neurotropic infections have a particular affinity for neural tissue. **Pantropic infections** attack neural tissue but not preferentially.

Rabies, which is usually transmitted through the bite of a rabid animal, is a well-known example of a neurotropic viral infection. The fits of rage caused by the virus's effects on the brain increase the probability that rabid animals that normally attack by biting (e.g., dogs, cats, raccoons, bats, and mice) will spread the disorder. Although the effects of the rabies virus on the brain are ultimately lethal, the virus does have one redeeming feature: It does not usually attack the brain for at least a month after it has been contracted, thus allowing time for a preventive vaccination.

The *mumps* and *herpes* viruses are common examples of pantropic viruses. They typically attack other tissues of the body, but they can spread into the brain—with dire consequences.

Neurotoxins

The nervous system can be damaged by exposure to any one of a variety of toxic chemicals, which can enter general circulation from the gastrointestinal tract, from the lungs, or through the skin. For example, heavy metals such as mercury and lead can accumulate in the brain and permanently damage it, producing a **toxic psychosis** (chronic insanity produced by a neurotoxin). Have you ever wondered why Alice in Wonderland's Mad Hatter was a mad hatter and not a mad something else? In 18th- and 19th-century England, hatmakers were commonly driven mad by the *mercury* employed in the preparation of the felt used to make hats. In a similar vein, the word *crackpot* originally referred to the toxic psychosis observed in people—primarily the British poor—who steeped their tea in cracked ceramic pots with *lead* cores.

Sometimes, the very drugs used to treat neurological disorders prove to have toxic effects. Some of the antipsychotic drugs introduced in the early 1950s provide an example of distressing scope. By the late 1950s, millions of psychotic patients were being maintained on these drugs. However, the initial enthusiasm for these drugs was tempered by the discovery that many of the patients eventually developed a motor disorder termed **tardive dyskinesia (TD).** Its primary symptoms are involuntary smacking and sucking movements of the lips, thrusting and rolling of the tongue, lateral jaw movements, and puffing of the cheeks. Unfortunately, tardive dyskinesia is not responsive to treatment. Once it has developed, even lowering the dose of the offending drug does not help; in fact, it sometimes makes the symptoms worse. Safer antipsychotic drugs have now been developed.

Brain damage from the neurotoxic effects of recreational drugs is also a serious problem. You learned in Chapter 1 that alcohol produces brain damage through a combination of its direct toxic effects and its effects on thiamin metabolism. Do you remember the case of Jimmie G.? You will learn more about the neurotoxic effects of recreational drugs in Chapter 13.

Some neurotoxins are *endogenous* (produced by the patient's own body). For example, the body can produce antibodies that can cause various types of disorders by attacking components of the nervous system (see Newsom-Davis & Vincent, 1991). Multiple sclerosis, an example of such an *autoimmune disorder,* is a consequence of antibodies that attack their body's own myelin. It is described in detail later in the chapter.

Genetic Factors

Normal human cells have 23 pairs of chromosomes; however, sometimes accidents of cell division occur, and the fertilized egg ends up with an abnormal chromosome or with an abnormal number of normal chromosomes. Then, as the fertilized egg divides and redivides, these chromosomal anomalies are duplicated in every cell of the body.

A common example of a disorder caused by such a genetic accident is **Down syndrome,** which occurs in 0.15% of all live births. This syndrome is associated with an extra chromosome in pair 21. The consequences of the superfluous chromosome are unfortunate. In addition to a characteristic disfigurement—flattened skull and nose, folds of skin over the inner corners of the eyes, and short fingers (see Figure 6.6)—intellectual development is retarded, and there are often serious medical complications. The probability of giving birth to a child with Down syndrome increases with advancing maternal age.

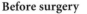

Before surgery   **After surgery**

Figure 6.6 A child with Down syndrome before and after plastic surgery. The purpose of these photographs is not to promote cosmetic surgery but to challenge our culture's reaction to patients with Down syndrome. The little girl on the left and the little girl on the right are the same girl; they deserve the same respect and consideration. (Courtesy of Kenneth E. Salyer, Director, International Craniofacial Institute.)

Few neuropsychological diseases of genetic origin are the result of faulty chromosomal duplication. Most are caused by abnormal recessive genes that are passed from parent to offspring. (In Chapter 2, you learned about one such disorder, *phenylketonuria*.) Inherited neuropsychological disorders are rarely associated with faulty dominant genes because dominant genes that disturb neuropsychological function tend to be eliminated from the gene pool—every individual who carries one is at a major survival and reproductive disadvantage. In contrast, individuals who inherit one abnormal recessive gene do not develop the disorder, and the gene is likely to be passed on to future generations; only individuals who inherit two of these genes are affected.

There are, however, two situations in which neurological disorders are associated with dominant genes. One is the case in which an abnormal dominant gene manifests itself only in rare environmental circumstances. The other is the case in which an abnormal dominant gene is not expressed until the individual is well past puberty. The gene for Huntington's disease is of this type. (Huntington's disease will be described in detail later in the chapter.)

Rapid progress is being made in locating and characterizing the faulty genes that underlie some neuropsychological disorders. Once this goal is achieved, it will open up a variety of new treatment and prevention strategies, such as splicing in healthy genes to replace faulty ones and developing specific DNA-binding proteins that can enter neurons and block the expression of faulty genes.

6.2 Neuropsychological Diseases

The preceding section focused on the causes of neuropsychological diseases. This section focuses on the neuropsychological diseases themselves.

It is not always easy to decide whether an individual has a neuropsychological disease. Is an individual who performs poorly on intelligence tests, sleeps longer than most, or displays aggressive behavior in inappropriate contexts suffering from a disorder of the brain, or does the person simply represent the extreme of normal biological function?

The problem of *differential diagnosis*—of deciding which particular neural disorder a patient has—is even more thorny. Each neuropsychological patient displays a unique array of complex behavioral symptoms—no two neuropsychological patients display exactly the same pattern of symptoms. Physicians and scientists search for clusters of neuropsychological symptoms that tend to occur together. When they identify a recurring cluster, they coin a term for it. This term and the cluster of symptoms it represents come to be thought of as a neuropsychological disease. The assumptions on which this approach is based are that all patients with a particular cluster of symptoms will prove to have the same underlying neural pathology and that the pathology will prove in each case to have the same causes. These assumptions do not always turn out to be correct. As more is found out about patients with a particular cluster of neuropsychological symptoms, it is usually necessary to redefine the disorder—by excluding some cases, including others, or dividing the disorder into subtypes. The more that is known about the causes and neural bases of a neuropsychological disorder, the more accurately it can be diagnosed; and the more accurately it can be diagnosed, the more readily its causes and neural bases can be identified.

Epilepsy, Parkinson's disease, Huntington's disease, multiple sclerosis, and Alzheimer's disease are the neuropsychological diseases that are discussed in this section.

Epilepsy

The primary symptom of **epilepsy** is the epileptic seizure, but not all persons who suffer seizures are considered to have epilepsy. It is not uncommon for otherwise healthy persons to have a seizure during temporary illness or following exposure to a convulsive agent. The label *epilepsy* is applied to only those patients whose seizures appear to be generated by their own chronic brain dysfunction. About 1% of the population are diagnosed as epileptic at some point in their lives.

In view of the fact that epilepsy is characterized by epileptic seizures—or, more accurately, by spontaneously recurring epileptic seizures—you might think that the task of diagnosing epilepsy would be an easy one. But you would be wrong. The task is made difficult by the diversity and complexity of epileptic seizures. You are probably

Neurotropic infections. Viral infections that have a particular affinity for neural tissue.

Pantropic infections. Viral infections that can infect brain tissue, but have no preference for it.

Toxic psychosis. Psychiatric disturbance that is caused by exposure to toxic chemicals.

Tardive dyskinesia (TD). A motor disorder that results from chronic use of certain antipsychotic drugs.

Down syndrome. A disorder associated with the presence of an extra chromosome in pair 21, resulting in disfigurement and mental retardation.

Epilepsy. A neurological disorder characterized by spontaneously recurring seizures.

familiar with seizures that take the form of **convulsions** (motor seizures); these often involve tremors (*clonus*), rigidity (*tonus*), and loss of both balance and consciousness. But many seizures do not take this form; instead, they involve subtle changes of thought, mood, or behavior that are not easily distinguishable from normal ongoing activity. In such cases, the diagnosis of epilepsy rests heavily on electroencephalographic evidence.

Figure 6.7 EEG activity before, during, and after a clonic convulsion.

The value of scalp electroencephalography in suspected cases of epilepsy stems from the fact that epileptic seizures are associated with bursts of high-amplitude EEG spikes, which are often apparent in the scalp EEG during an attack (see Figure 6.7), and from the fact that individual spikes often punctuate the scalp EEGs of epileptics between attacks. Although the observation of spontaneous epileptic discharges is incontrovertible evidence of epilepsy, the failure to observe them does not always mean that the patient is not epileptic. It could mean that the patient is epileptic but did not happen to experience epileptic discharges during the test or that epileptic discharges did occur during the test but were not recorded through the scalp electrodes.

Some epileptics experience peculiar psychological changes just before a convulsion. These changes, called **epileptic auras,** may take many different forms—for example, a bad smell, a specific thought, a vague feeling of familiarity, a hallucination, or a tightness of the chest. Epileptic auras are important for two reasons. First, the nature of the auras provides clues concerning the location of the epileptic focus. Second, because the epileptic auras experienced by a particular patient are often similar from attack to attack, they warn the patient of an impending convulsion. For most people, the warning is an advantage; but for some it can become an experience of dread, as the normal parts of their brains struggle to keep in touch with reality.

Once an individual has been diagnosed as epileptic, it is usual to assign the epilepsy to one of two general categories—*partial epilepsy* or *generalized epilepsy*—and then to one of their respective subcategories. The various seizure types are so different from one another that there are many who believe that epilepsy is best viewed not as a single disease but as a number of different, but related, diseases. Supporting this view is the fact that epilepsy has no single cause; almost any kind of brain disturbance can cause seizures. The diagnosis of the two general categories of eilepsy depends on which of the two types of seizures—partial or generalized—is more prevalent.

Partial seizures   A **partial seizure** is a seizure that does not involve the entire brain. For reasons unknown, the epileptic neurons at a focus begin to discharge together in bursts, and it is this synchronous bursting of neurons (see Figure 6.8) that produces epileptic spiking in the EEG. The synchronous activity may stay restricted to the focus until the seizure is over, or it may spread to healthy areas of the brain—but, in the case of partial seizures, not to the entire brain. The specific behavioral symptoms of a partial epileptic seizure depend on where the disruptive discharges begin and into what structures they spread. Because partial seizures do not involve the entire brain, they are not usually accompanied by a total loss of consciousness or equilibrium.

There are two major categories of partial seizures: simple and complex. **Simple partial seizures** are partial seizures whose symptoms are primarily sensory or motor or both; they are sometimes called *Jacksonian seizures* after the famous 19th-century neurologist Hughlings Jackson. As the epileptic discharges spread through the sensory or motor areas of the brain, the symptoms spread systematically through the body.

In contrast, **complex partial seizures** are usually restricted to the temporal lobes, and those who experience them are said to have *temporal lobe epilepsy*. Complex partial seizures typically begin with an aura, which may develop into a psychomotor attack. In a **psychomotor attack,** the patient engages in compulsive, repetitive, simple behaviors commonly referred to as *automatisms* (e.g., doing and undoing a button) or in more complex behaviors that appear almost normal. The diversity of psychomotor attacks is illustrated by the following four cases reported by Lennox (1960):

Figure 6.8 The bursting of an epileptic neuron, recorded by extracellular unit recording.

A war veteran subject to many automatisms read in the newspaper about a man who had embraced a woman in a park, followed her into a women's toilet, and then boarded a bus. From the description given, he realized he was the man.

One morning a doctor left home to answer an emergency call from the hospital and returned several hours later, a trifle confused, feeling as though he had experienced a bad dream. At the hospital he had performed a difficult … [operation] with his usual competence, but later had done and said things deemed inappropriate.

A young man, a music teacher, when listening to a concert, walked down the aisle and onto the platform, circled the piano, jumped to the floor, did a hop, skip, and jump up the aisle, and regained his senses when part way home. He often found himself on a trolley [bus] far from his destination.

A man in an attack went to his employer and said, "I have to have more money or [I] quit." Later, to his surprise, he found that his salary had been raised. (pp. 237–238)

Although patients appear to be conscious throughout their psychomotor attacks, they usually have little or no subsequent recollection of them. About half of all cases of epilepsy are of the complex partial variety—the temporal lobes are particularly susceptible to epileptic discharges.

Convulsions. Motor seizures.

Epileptic auras. Psychological symptoms that precede the onset of a convulsion.

Partial seizures. Seizures that do not involve the entire brain.

Simple partial seizures. Partial seizures in which the symptoms are primarily sensory or motor or both.

Complex partial seizures. Seizures that are characterized by various complex psychological phenomena and are thought to result from temporal lobe discharges.

Psychomotor attack. An epileptic attack in which the patient engages in compulsive behaviors that, although inappropriate, have the appearance of normal behaviors.

Generalized seizures. Seizures that involve the entire brain.

Grand mal seizure. A seizure whose symptoms are loss of consciousness, loss of equilibrium, and a violent tonic-clonic convulsion.

Hypoxia. Shortage of oxygen in the blood.

Petit mal seizure. A generalized seizure that is characterized by a disturbance of consciousness and a 3-per-second spike-and-wave EEG discharge.

3-per-second spike-and-wave discharge. The characteristic EEG of the petit mal seizure.

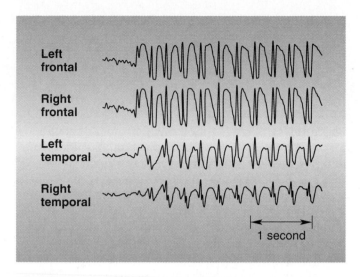

Figure 6.9 The bilaterally symmetrical, 3-per-second spike-and-wave EEG discharge that is associated with petit mal epileptic attacks.

Generalized seizures Generalized seizures are seizures that involve the entire brain. Some begin as focal discharges that gradually spread through the entire brain. In other cases, the discharges seem to begin almost simultaneously in all parts of the brain. Such sudden-onset generalized seizures may result from diffuse pathology or may begin focally in a structure, such as the thalamus, that projects to many parts of the brain.

Like partial seizures, generalized seizures occur in many forms. One is the **grand mal** (literally "big trouble") **seizure.** The primary symptoms of a grand mal seizure are loss of consciousness, loss of equilibrium, and a violent *tonic-clonic convulsion*—a convulsion involving both tonus and clonus. Tongue biting, urinary incontinence, and *cyanosis* (turning blue from excessive extraction of oxygen from the blood during the convulsion) are common manifestations of grand mal convulsions. The **hypoxia** (shortage of oxygen) that accompanies a grand mal convulsion can itself cause brain damage, which is likely mediated by the excessive release of excitatory amino acids.

A second major category of generalized seizure is the **petit mal** (literally "small trouble") **seizure.** Petit mal seizures are not associated with convulsions; their primary behavioral symptom is the *petit mal absence*—a disruption of consciousness that is associated with a cessation of ongoing behavior, a vacant look, and sometimes fluttering eyelids. The EEG of a petit mal seizure is different from that of other seizures; it is a bilaterally symmetrical **3-per-second spike-and-wave discharge** (see Figure 6.9). Petit mal seizures are most common in children, and they frequently cease at puberty. They often go undiagnosed; thus children with petit mal epilepsy are sometimes considered to be "daydreamers" by their parents and teachers and "space cadets" by their playmates.

Although there is no cure for epilepsy, the frequency and severity of seizures can often be reduced by anticonvulsant medication. Brain surgery is prescribed only in life-threatening situations.

Parkinson's Disease

Parkinson's disease is a movement disorder of adulthood that affects about 0.5% of the population. Its initial symptoms are mild—perhaps no more than a slight stiffness or tremor of the fingers—but they inevitably increase in severity with advancing years. The most common symptoms of the full-blown disorder are a tremor that is pronounced during inactivity but not during voluntary movement or sleep, muscular rigidity, difficulty initiating movement, slowness of movement, and a masklike face. There is typically little or no intellectual impairment. Parkinson's disease victims are normal-thinking people trapped inside bodies they cannot control. Do you remember from Chapter 4 the case of the "lizard"—Roberto Garcia d'Orta?

Like epilepsy, Parkinson's disease seems to have no single cause; faulty genes, brain infections, strokes, tumors, traumatic brain injury, and neurotoxins have all been implicated in specific cases. However, in the majority of cases, no cause is obvious and there is no family history of the disorder (see Calne et al., 1987).

Parkinson's disease is associated with degeneration of the **substantia nigra**—the midbrain nucleus whose neurons project via the **nigrostriatal pathway** to the **striatum** of the basal ganglia. The neurotransmitter of substantia nigra neurons is *dopamine,* and there is almost a total lack of dopamine in the substantia nigras and striatums of long-term Parkinson's patients.

As you saw in the case of d'Orta, the symptoms of Parkinson's disease can be alleviated by injections of **L-DOPA**—the chemical from which dopamine is synthesized. However, L-DOPA is rarely a permanent solution; it typically becomes less and less effective with use, until its side effects outweigh its benefits. This is exactly what happened to d'Orta. L-DOPA therapy did give him a 3-year respite from his disease, but ultimately it became totally ineffective. His prescription was then changed to a dopamine agonist, and again his condition improved—but again the improvement was only temporary. You will return to d'Orta's roller-coaster case in Chapter 15, which will describe how, as a last resort, dopamine-releasing cells were transplanted into d'Orta's brain.

Huntington's Disease

Like Parkinson's disease, **Huntington's disease** is a progressive disorder of motor function; unlike Parkinson's disease, it is rare, it has a strong genetic basis, and it is always associated with severe dementia. At first, the motor symptoms of Huntington's disease take the form of increased fidgetiness; but they slowly grow worse, until the behavior of the patient is characterized by the incessant involuntary performance of a variety of rapid, complex, jerky movements that involve entire limbs rather than individual muscles. Huntington's disease is sometimes called *Huntington's chorea* because the twisting, writhing, grimacing movements displayed by some Huntington's patients have a dancelike quality. (*Chorea* means "dance," as in *chorus line* and *choreography.*)

Huntington's disease is passed from generation to generation by a single dominant gene; thus all of the individuals carrying the gene develop the disorder, as do about half their offspring. The Huntington's gene is readily passed from parent to child because the first symptoms of the disease do not appear until the parent is well past the peak reproductive years (at about age 40). There is no cure; and death occurs approximately 15 years after the appearance of the first symptoms. Autopsy reveals general shrinkage of the brain and gross degeneration of the striatum and cerebral cortex.

If one of your parents were to develop Huntington's disease, the chance would be 50/50 that you too would develop it. If you were in such a situation, would you want to know whether or not you would suffer the same fate? Medical geneticists have discovered the location of the lethal Huntington's gene (see Wexler, Rose, & Housman, 1991). They have also developed a test that can tell relatives of Huntington's patients whether they too are carrying the gene (Gilliam, Gusella, & Lehrach, 1987; Martin, 1987). Some choose to take the test, and some do not. One advantage of the test is that it permits the relatives of Huntington's patients who have not inherited the gene to have children without the fear of passing on the disorder.

Much of the early research on Huntington's disease was aimed at tracing the family trees of those with the disorder. The first recorded cases of the disease occured in 1630 in the town of Bures, England (Vessie, 1932). At that time, afflicted individuals were judged to be witches and were executed. Many North American cases of Huntington's disease can be traced to two families who fled Bures. Once in

---

Parkinson's disease. A movement disorder that is associated with degeneration of dopaminergic neurons in the nigrostriatal pathway.

Substantia nigra. The dopaminergic midbrain nucleus that degenerates in cases of Parkinson's disease.

Nigrostriatal pathway. The pathway along which axons from the substantia nigra project to the striatum.

Striatum. The structure of the basal ganglia that is the terminal of the dopaminergic nigrostriatal pathway.

L-DOPA. The chemical precursor of dopamine, which is used in the treatment of Parkinson's disease.

Huntington's disease. A progressive disorder of motor and intellectual function that is produced in adulthood by a dominant gene.

North America, these unfortunates were dealt with more humanely: Only one of them was hanged. In the last few decades, the prevalence of Huntington's disease has declined as a result of genetic counseling.

Shortly after the first edition of this textbook appeared in print, I received this letter, which I have altered slightly to protect the identity of its author and his family. It speaks for itself.

Mr. Walter S. Miller
1500 N. Severn-Langdon Rd.
Manchester, Connecticut 22022
Z9/900-854

==

August 5, 1991

Dr. John P. J. Pinel
Department of Psychology
University of British Columbia
Vancouver, B.C. Canada V6T.,1Y7.

Dear Dr. Pinel:

I am worried about my children and their future. In fact, I am worried sick. After reading your book I feel that you are my friend and I have nowhere else to turn.

My wife came down with Huntington's disease 7 years ago, and today she can't walk or take care of herself. I have three young children. Where can I take them to see if they have inherited my wife's infected cells? I am presently incarcerated, which adds to my psychological pain. I look to be released soon, and could take my wife and kids just about any wheres to find help and get answers.

Any kind of advice that you could give us would be greatly appreciated by me and my family. I wish to thank you for any assistance that you can give.

God bless you and give you and yours His love and peace! I remain with warmest personal regards.

Very truly yours,

Walter S. Miller

Walter S. Miller

WSM:

THE UNIVERSITY OF BRITISH COLUMBIA

Department of Psychology
2136 West Mall
Vancouver, B.C. Canada V6T 1Z4
Tel: (604) 822-2755
Fax: (604) 822-6923

November 25, 1991

Mr. Walter S. Miller
1500 N. Severn-Langdon Road
Manchester, Connecticut 22022
U.S.A.

Dear Mr. Miller:

I was saddened to learn of your unhappy state of affairs. In requesting my advice, I hope that you understand that I am a scientist, not a physician. In any case, the following is my assessment.

If your wife does in fact have Huntington's disease and not some other neurological disorder, each of your children has a 50/50 chance of developing Huntington's disease in adulthood. I am sure that you are aware that there is currently no cure.

I advise you to seek the advice of a local neurologist, who can explain your options to you and provide you with the advice and support that you sorely need. You must decide whether or not to subject your children to the tests that are required to determine whether or not they are carrying the Huntington's gene. One option would be to wait for your children to reach legal age and then allow them to make the decision for themselves. Some people whose parents develop Huntington's disease decide to take the test; others decide not to. In either case, it is extremely important for them not to risk passing on the Huntington's gene to future generations.

I am sorry that I cannot provide you with a more optimistic assessment, but your children's situation is too serious for me to be less than totally frank. Again, please consult a neurologist as soon as possible.

Do not lose hope. There is a chance (1/8) that none of your children is carrying the Huntington's gene. I wish you, your wife, and your children good fortune.

Cordially,

John P. J. Pinel
Professor

Multiple Sclerosis

Multiple sclerosis (MS), a progressive disease of CNS myelin, typically begins in early adult life. First, there are microscopic areas of degeneration on myelin sheaths; but eventually there is a breakdown of both the myelin and the associated axons, along with the development of many areas of hard scar tissue (*sclerosis* means "hardening"). Figure 6.10 illustrates degeneration in the white matter of a patient with multiple sclerosis.

Diagnosing multiple sclerosis is difficult because the nature of the disorder depends on the number, size, and position of the sclerotic lesions. Furthermore, in some cases there are lengthy periods of remission (up to 2 years), during which the patient seems almost normal; but these are merely oases in the cruel progression of the disorder. Common symptoms of advanced multiple sclerosis are urinary incontinence, visual disturbances, muscular weakness, numbness, tremor, and **ataxia** (loss of motor coordination).

Epidemiological studies of multiple sclerosis have provided evidence of the environmental and genetic factors that influence its development (McDonald, 1984). **Epidemiology** is the study of the various factors, such as diet, geographic location, age, sex, and race, that influence the distribution of a disease in the general population.

Evidence that environmental factors influence the development of multiple sclerosis comes from the finding that the incidence of multiple sclerosis is far greater in people who spent their childhood in a cool climate, even if they subsequently moved to a warm climate. In contrast, evidence of genetic involvement comes from the finding that multiple sclerosis is rare among certain groups, such as gypsies and Asians, even when they live in environments in which the incidence of the disease is high in other groups. Further evidence of a genetic factor in multiple sclerosis comes from comparisons of the concordance of the disease

Figure 6.11 Amyloid plaques (stained blue; see arrows) in the brain of a patient with Alzheimer's disease.

in *monozygotic* (identical) twins (about 36%) and *dizygotic* (fraternal) twins (about 12%). (See, for example, Currier & Eldridge, 1982; McFarland et al., 1984.)

A model of multiple sclerosis can be induced in laboratory animals by injecting them with myelin and a preparation that stimulates the body's immune reaction (see Wekerle, 1993). Because the resulting disorder, which is termed **experimental autoimmune encephalomyelitis,** is similar in some respects to multiple sclerosis, it has led to the view that multiple sclerosis results from a faulty immune reaction that attacks the body's own myelin as if it were a foreign substance (see Allegretta, Nicklas, Sriram, & Albertini, 1990). Many researchers believe that this faulty *autoimmune reaction* is the result of a slow-acting infection contracted early in life.

Figure 6.10 Areas of sclerosis (see arrows) in the white matter of a patient with MS.

Alzheimer's Disease

Alzheimer's disease is the most common cause of *dementia* (Wurtman, 1985). It sometimes appears in individuals as young as 40, but the likelihood of its manifestation becomes greater with advancing years. About 3% of the general population over the age of 65 suffer from the disease, and the proportion is about 10% in those over 85.

Alzheimer's disease is progressive. Its early stages are characterized by depression and a general decline in cognitive ability; its intermediate stages are marked by irritability, anxiety, and deterioration of speech; and in its advanced stages, the patient deteriorates to the point that even simple responses such as swallowing and controlling the bladder are difficult. Alzheimer's disease is terminal.

Because Alzheimer's disease is not the only cause of severe dementia, it cannot be diagnosed with certainty on the basis of its behavioral symptoms—definitive diagnosis of Alzheimer's disease must await autopsy. The two defining characteristics of the disease are neurofibrillary tangles and amyloid plaques. *Neurofibrillary tangles* are threadlike tangles of protein in the neural cytoplasm, and *amyloid plaques* are clumps of scar tissue composed of degenerating neurons and a protein called **amyloid.** In addition, there is substantial neuron loss. The presence of amyloid plaques in the brain of a patient who died of Alzheimer's disease is illustrated in Figure 6.11.

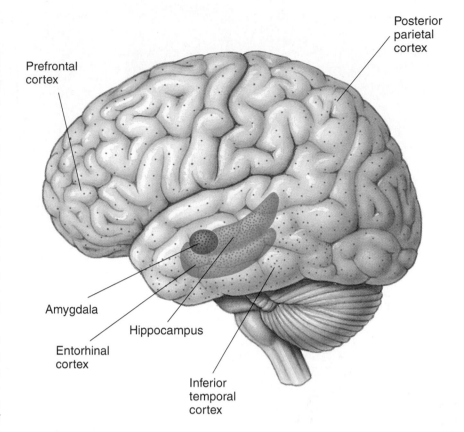

Figure 6.12 The typical distribution of neurofibrillary tangles and amyloid plaques in the brains of patients with advanced Alzheimer's disease. (Based on Selkoe, 1991, and Goedert, 1993.)

Although neurofibrillary tangles (see Goedert, 1993), amyloid plaques (see Selkoe, 1991), and neuron loss (see O'Banion, Coleman, & Callahan, 1994) tend to occur throughout the brains of Alzheimer's patients, they are more prevalent in some areas than others. For example, they are particularly prevalent in medial temporal lobe structures such as the *entorhinal cortex, amygdala,* and *hippocampus*—all structures that are involved in various aspects of memory. And on the lateral surface of the cerebral hemispheres, they are most prevalent in the inferior temporal cortex, posterior parietal cortex, and prefrontal cortex—all areas that mediate complex cognitive functions. (See Figure 6.12.)

There is a major difficulty in studying the genetics of Alzheimer's disease: Its carriers often die of natural causes before their Alzheimer's symptoms can be manifested. Nevertheless, it is now clear that Alzheimer's disease does have a major genetic component. People with an Alzheimer's victim in their immediate family have a 50% chance of being stricken by the disease if they survive into their 80s and 90s (Breitner, 1990).

The discovery that Alzheimer's disease has a genetic component has triggered a search for an Alzheimer's gene. One group of investigators (Goate et al., 1991) has located a gene mutation on chromosome 21 that is associated

---

Multiple sclerosis (MS). A progressive disease of the CNS myelin.

Ataxia. Loss of motor coordination.

Epidemiology. The study of factors that influence the distribution of a disease in the general population.

Experimental autoimmune encephalomyelitis. A model of multiple sclerosis that can be induced in laboratory animals by injecting them with myelin and a preparation that stimulates the body's immune system.

Alzheimer's disease. The major cause of dementia in old age, characterized by neurofibrillary tangles, amyloid plaques, and neuron loss.

Amyloid. A protein that is found in clumps of degenerating neurons in Alzheimer's patients.

Test your knowledge of neuropsychological disorders by filling in the following blanks. The correct answers are provided at the bottom of this page. Before proceeding, review material related to your errors and omissions.

1. The two major categories of epileptic seizures are

   _____ and

   _____ seizures.

2. The disorder characterized by tremor at rest is

   _____.

3. _____ is passed from

   generation to generation by a single dominant

   gene.

4. Parkinson's disease is associated with degeneration

   in the _____

   dopamine pathway.

5. Experimental autoimmune encephalomyelitis is

   an animal model of _____

   _____.

6. The most common cause of dementia is

   _____.

7. _____ attacks are

   complex partial seizures that are similar in many

   respects to normal behavior.

8. Alzheimer's disease is associated with

   _____ syndrome.

9. Two major neuropathological symptoms of

   Alzheimer's disease are

   _____ tangles and

   _____ plaques.

with an early-onset form of Alzheimer's disease that is running through several families. It makes sense that the disease would be caused by a defect on chromosome 21: The gene responsible for the production of amyloid is on that chromosome; and many Down patients, who have an extra chromosome 21, develop Alzheimer's disease in adulthood. However, in some families, the early-onset form of the disorder is linked to a mutation on chromosome 14 (Schellenberg et al., 1992); and in some families, the more usual late-onset form of the disorder is linked to a mutation on chromosome 19 (Corder et al., 1993). Collectively, these results suggest that Alzheimer's disease is not a unitary disorder with a single genetic cause (see Tanzi, 1991).

6.3 Animal Models of Human Neuropsychological Diseases

The first two sections of this chapter focused on neuropsychological diseases and their causes, but they also provided some glimpses into the ways in which researchers have attempted to solve the many puzzles of neurological dysfunction. This section focuses on one of these ways: the experimental investigation of animal models. Because the laboratory experimentation necessary to identify the neuropathological basis of human neuropsychological disorders is seldom possible on the patients themselves, animal models of the disorders play a particularly important role in their investigation.

Three types of animal models are used in medical research: homologous, isomorphic, and predictive (Kornet-

The answers are (1) partial and generalized, in either order, (2) Parkinson's disease, (3) Huntington's disease, (4) nigrostriatal, (5) multiple sclerosis, (6) Alzheimer's disease, (7) Psychomotor, (8) Down, and (9) neurofibrillary and amyloid.

sky, 1977). **Homologous animal models** are disorders in animals that duplicate human disorders in every respect; the *etiology* (causes), symptoms, and prognosis of a homologous model resemble those of the human disorder. **Isomorphic animal models** resemble human disorders, but are artificially produced in the laboratory in a way that does not reflect normal etiology. Finally, **predictive animal models** do not resemble the human disorders but are of value in predicting some aspects of the disorders, such as their response to various drugs.

In a sense, the three types of animal models represent a hierarchy. A predictive model enables one to make certain predictions about the disorder it models. An isomorphic model permits predictions and the study of underlying mechanisms and homologous model serves as a basis for studying all aspects of a disorder, including its causes. Accordingly, to understand a model's potential uses and limitations, it is important to recognize which type of model it is.

It is difficult to judge how closely animal models mirror neuropsychological disorders because we do not fully understand the causes and mechanisms of the disorders. It is clear, however, that even the best animal models of neuropsychological disorders display only some of the features of the disorders that they are modeling. Consequently, animal models must be employed with caution. Studying an animal model is like exploring a section of an unknown maze. One enters an unfamiliar section with little more than a hope that its exploration will prove fruitful, and it is only after each of its arms has been carefully explored that it is possible to know whether the decision to enter the section was wise. In the same way, it is not possible to evaluate the numerous animal models of neuropsychological dysfunction that are currently under investigation until each has been thoroughly explored. Surely, only a few animal models will lead toward the goals of understanding and prevention, but only time and effort can tell which ones these are.

Completing this chapter is a discussion of three animal models that are currently the focus of intensive investigation: the kindling model of epilepsy, the amphetamine model of schizophrenia, and the MPTP model of Parkinson's disease.

Kindling Model of Epilepsy

In 1969, Goddard, McIntyre, and Leech delivered one mild electrical stimulation per day to rats through implanted amygdalar electrodes. There was no behavioral response to the first few stimulations, but soon each stimulation began to elicit a convulsive response. The first convulsions were mild, involving only a slight tremor of the face. However, with each subsequent stimulation, the elicited convulsions became more generalized, until each convulsion involved the entire body. Each of these fully generalized kindled convulsions in rats was characterized by the following pro-

gression of symptoms: facial tremor, rhythmic jaw movements, rhythmic head nodding, forelimb clonus, rearing up on the hind legs, and falling (e.g., Racine, 1972; 1978). This progressive development and intensification of convulsions elicited by a series of periodic brain stimulations became known as the **kindling phenomenon.**

Although kindling is most frequently studied in rats subjected to repeated amygdalar stimulation, it is a remarkably general phenomenon. For example, kindling has been reported in mice (Leech & McIntyre, 1976), rabbits (Tanaka, 1972), cats (Adamec, 1990), dogs (Wauquier, Ashton, & Melis, 1979), and various primates (Wada, 1990a). Moreover, kindling can be produced by the repeated stimulation of many brain sites other than the amygdala, and it can be produced by the repeated application of initially subconvulsive doses of convulsive chemicals (Cain, 1986; Mori & Wada, 1990; Post et al., 1990).

There are many interesting features of kindling (see Racine & Burnham, 1984; Wada, 1990b), but two warrant emphasis. The first is that the neural changes underlying kindling are permanent. A subject that has been kindled and then left unstimulated for several months still responds to each low-intensity stimulation with a generalized convulsion (Goddard et al., 1969; Wada & Sato, 1974). The second is that kindling is produced by distributed, as opposed to massed, stimulations. If the intervals between successive stimulations are shorter than an hour or two, it usually requires many more stimulations to kindle a subject; and under normal circumstances, no kindling at all occurs at intervals of less than about 20 minutes (Racine et al., 1973).

Much of the interest in kindling stems from the fact that it models epilepsy in two ways. First, the convulsions elicited in kindled animals are similar in many respects to those observed in some types of human epilepsy. Second, the kindling phenomenon itself is comparable to the **epileptogenesis** (the development, or genesis, of epilepsy) that can

---

Homologous animal models. Disorders in animals that duplicate human disorders in every respect.

Isomorphic animal models. Disorders in animals that resemble human disorders, but are artificially produced in the laboratory.

Predictive animal models. Animal models that do not resemble the human disorders in key respects but are of value in predicting some aspect of the disorders.

Kindling phenomenon. The progressive development and intensification of convulsions elicited by a series of periodic low-intensity stimulations—most commonly by daily electrical stimulations to the amygdala.

Epileptogenesis. Development of epilepsy.

follow a head injury: Some individuals who at first appear to have escaped serious injury after a blow to the head begin to experience convulsions a few weeks later, and these convulsions sometimes begin to recur more and more frequently and with greater and greater intensity.

Many studies have been conducted in order to determine which drugs block the kindling of motor convulsions and which block the elicitation of convulsions in animals that have already been kindled (e.g., Pinel, Kim, & Mana, 1990). The study of Racine, Livingston, and Joaquin (1975) is a particularly good example of this type of study. In this study, an anticonvulsant commonly used in the treatment of human epileptics, *diphenylhydantoin* (Dilantin), blocked convulsions elicited in kindled rats by neocortical stimulation but not those elicited by amygdalar stimulation. Conversely, another commonly used anticonvulsant, *diazepam* (Valium), blocked kindled convulsions elicited by amygdalar stimulation, but had no effect on neocortical kindled convulsions. These findings suggest that the response of human epileptics to various anticonvulsant drugs may depend on the location of the epileptic focus.

It must be stressed that the kindling model as it is applied in most laboratories is not isomorphic. You will recall from earlier in this chapter that epilepsy is a disease in which epileptic attacks recur spontaneously; in contrast, kindled convulsions are elicited. However, a model that overcomes this shortcoming has been developed in several species. If subjects are kindled for a very long time—about 300 stimulations in rats—a syndrome can be induced that is truly epileptic, in the sense that the subjects begin to display spontaneous seizures and continue to display them even after the regimen of stimulation is curtailed (e.g., Pinel, 1981; Shouse et al., 1990; Wada, Sato, & Corcoran, 1974).

Amphetamine Model of Schizophrenia

Amphetamine abuse can lead to a syndrome called **amphetamine psychosis,** which is similar in many respects to schizophrenia; the abuse of other stimulant drugs (e.g., cocaine) can have a similar effect. The symptoms of amphetamine psychosis include compulsive pacing, continual touching and picking of the face and extremities, repeated assembling and disassembling of objects, distortion of time and space, extreme reactivity to perceived threat, olfactory and tactile hallucinations, and paranoia. Once individuals displaying amphetamine psychosis stop taking the drug, these symptoms dissipate in a day or two. However, residual delusions and mannerisms frequently persist long after amphetamine abuse has stopped, and a full-blown psychotic episode can sometimes be reinstated by a single dose of the drug after a long period of abstinence (Bell, 1973). Amphetamines and other stimulants have been found to exacerbate the schizophrenic symptoms of psychotic patients (Janosky, Huey, & Storms, 1977), and antischizophrenic drugs have been shown to counteract the symp-

toms of amphetamine psychosis (Angrist, Rotrosen, & Gershon, 1980).

Although the behavioral effects of amphetamines are not the same in each species, in mammals there is always a general increase in locomotor activity (pacing) and other repetitive, apparently functionless, behaviors (e.g., Haber, Barchas, & Barchas, 1981). Because these so-called *behavioral stereotypies* resemble behaviors that are commonly associated with amphetamine psychosis in humans, they have been widely used as an animal model of human schizophrenia. Following is a description of the amphetamine-induced open-field behavior of the rat:

> Doses that range from 0.3 to 1.5 mg/kg (*d*-amphetamine injected subcutaneously) produce an increase in forward locomotion.... This ambulation persists for approximately 40 to 90 minutes, depending on the dose, and is followed by a period of sleep. Administration of higher doses elicits a multiphasic response pattern that consists of early and late phases of ambulation, and an intermediate phase of focused stereotypy during which locomotion is absent. The focused stereotypy phase is characterized by sniffing, repetitive head and limb movements, and oral behaviors (e.g., licking, biting and/or gnawing) expressed over a small area of the cage floor. Although these behaviors are most prominent during the focused stereotypy phase, they may appear intermittently during other phases of the drug response. The time course of each phase is dose-dependent: with increasing doses, the initial locomotor phase decreases in duration as the animal spends progressively more time in focused stereotypy and in the last phase of locomotion. In fact, at doses of 5.0 to 10.0 mg/kg the total duration of the response may exceed 5 or 6 hours before the animal goes to sleep. (Rebec & Bashore, 1984, p. 154)

Because many of the drugs effective in the treatment of human schizophrenia attenuate the *stereotypies* induced in laboratory animals by amphetamines, the amphetamine model has been widely used to assess the efficacy of various antischizophrenic drugs and to study their mechanisms of action. However, Rebec and Bashore (1984) have argued that progress in this area of research has been impeded by the lack of precise behavioral assessment. Most investigators lump the complex behavioral changes observed during

Amphetamine psychosis. A psychotic state produced by amphetamine abuse that is similar to schizophrenia.

MPTP. A neurotoxin that produces a disorder in primates that is similar to Parkinson's disease.

Deprenyl. A monoamine oxidase inhibitor that has been shown to retard the development of Parkinson's disease.

Monoamine oxidase (MAO) inhibitor. A drug that increases the activity of monoamine neurotransmitters by inhibiting monoamine oxidase—an enzyme in neurons that breaks down monoamines.

the course of a test into one or two scores—for example, a single measure of locomotor activity and a single measure of stereotypy. Rebec and Bashore, however, contend that a more selective behavioral approach is warranted. They have offered the following lines of evidence in support of their contention:

1. Some of the behavioral symptoms of amphetamine psychosis in humans occur in individuals who chronically use amphetamine but do not become psychotic.

2. Although amphetamine psychosis typically occurs only after long-term amphetamine abuse, some of the behavioral effects of amphetamines in laboratory animals, such as the oral stereotypies (licking and biting), actually decline with repeated exposure.

3. Some clinically effective antischizophrenic agents block some of the stereotypical behaviors elicited in animals by amphetamine but leave others, such as the oral stereotypies, unaffected (Costall & Naylor, 1977; Iversen & Koob, 1977).

On the basis of the preceding observations, Rebec and Bashore have concluded that the amphetamine-produced locomotion, but not oral stereotypy, models amphetamine psychosis; and they have stressed the need for careful and independent assessment of each of the behavioral aspects of the amphetamine model.

MPTP Model of Parkinson's Disease

The preeminent animal model of Parkinson's disease grew out of an unfortunate incident that occured in the early 1980s:

> Parkinson's disease . . . rarely occurs before the age of 50. It was somewhat of a surprise then to see a group of young drug addicts at our hospital in 1982 who had developed symptoms of severe and what proved to be irreversible parkinsonism. The only link between these patients was the recent use of a new "synthetic heroin." They exhibited virtually all of the typical motor features of Parkinson's disease, including the classic triad of bradykinesia (slowness of movement), tremor and rigidity of their muscles. Even the subtle features, such as seborrhea (oiliness of the skin) and micrographia (small handwriting), that are typical of Parkinson's disease were present. After tracking down samples of this substance, the offending agent was tentatively identified as 1-methyl-4-phenyl-1,2,3,6-tetrahydropyridine or **MPTP**. . . . After nearly two and a half years, there has been no sign of remission, and most are becoming increasingly severe management problems. (Langston, 1985, p. 79)

Researchers immediately tried to turn the misfortune of these few to the advantage of many by developing a much-needed animal model of Parkinson's disease (Langston, 1986). It was quickly established that nonhuman primates respond like humans to MPTP (Burns et al., 1983; Lang-

ston et al., 1984), but attempts to develop a rodent model have been less successful. Rodents treated with MPTP develop some mild symptoms of Parkinson's disease, but the symptoms do not persist for more than a few weeks (Duvoisin et al., 1986).

The brains of primates exposed to MPTP have cell loss to the substantia nigra similar to that observed in the brains of Parkinson's patients. Considering that the substantia nigra is the major source of the brain's dopamine, it is not surprising that the level of dopamine is greatly reduced in both the MPTP model and in the naturally occurring disorder. However, it is curious that in a few monkeys MPTP produces a major depletion of dopamine without producing any gross motor symptoms (Taylor et al., 1990).

The development of the MPTP animal model has already started to benefit patients with Parkinson's disease. For example, it was discovered that **deprenyl,** a monoamine agonist, blocks the effects of MPTP in an animal model. Deprenyl is a **monoamine oxidase (MAO) inhibitor;** that is, it increases the level of dopamine and other monoamines by inhibiting the activity of *monoamine oxidase*—an enzyme in monoaminergic neurons that breaks down any monoamine molecules that are not stored in vesicles. It was subsequently shown that deprenyl administered to early Parkinson's patients greatly retards the progression of the disease (Tetrud & Langston, 1989)—see Figure 6.13.

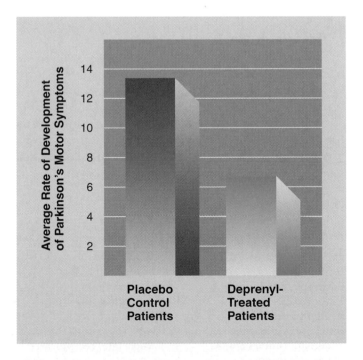

Figure 6.13 Average rate of motor symptom development in early Parkinson's patients treated with deprenyl (a monoamine oxidase inhibitor) or with a placebo. Deprenyl slowed the progression of the disease by 50%. (Based on Tetrud and Langston, 1989.)

Conclusion

This chapter began with the case history of sublieutenant Zasetsky, a man with a shattered world. Then, it discussed the causes of brain damage (6.1), common neuropsychological diseases (6.2), and animal models of these diseases (6.3). The following case history of a 30-year-old woman who was poisoned by MPTP (Ballard, Tetrud, & Langston, 1985) completes the circle:

> During the first 4 days of July 1982, ... [she] used 4½ grams of a "new synthetic heroin." The substance was injected IV [intravenously] three or four times daily and caused a burning sensation at the site of injection....
>
> She had brief auditory hallucinations and visual distortions with larger doses. After 3 days of use, she felt "weak" and "slow," but used the drug for another day. Four days later, she was described by family as sitting quietly without moving all day, staring into space "like a zombie." She later said that she felt fully alert during this period and was aware of the environment, but had difficulty initiating speech and could move only with great effort. She also noted intermittent "shaking" of the left arm. Her family provided total care for her, including all dressing, feeding, and bathing.
>
> On July 21, 1982, she was admitted to our neurobehavioral unit. She had the appearance of a "wax doll," sitting immobile with head and arms held in flexion. General examination [revealed] ... facial seborrhea [oiliness] ..., a breakdown of horizontal smooth [visual] pursuit, ... infrequent blinking, continuous drooling, ... and difficulty initiating speech. Tongue protrusion was slow, limited to about 1 cm. Voluntary movements were profoundly slowed. Left to herself, she remained motionless.... A resting tremor of 5 to 6 Hz in the right hand and foot disappeared on volitional movement.... She could not rise from a chair without assistance. Gait was shuffling, with small steps, loss of associated movement ... and loss of postural reflexes. Sensation was normal. The remainder of the neurologic examination was normal, including mental status....
>
> After 2 years of treatment, there has been no improvement in her parkinsonism, and she has suffered a variety of therapeutic complications. (pp. 949–951)[1]

Before leaving this chapter, pause for a moment to contemplate the plight of this woman, of Roberto Garcia d'Orta, and of others who suffer from advanced Parkinson's disease or MPTP poisoning. These are intelligent, alert, sensitive people—people just like you—who are trapped inside bodies that do not work. Also contemplate the plight of Alzheimer's patients with severe dementia. Which is worse?

---

[1]From "Permanent Human Parkinsonism Due to 1-methyl-4-phenyl-1,2,3,6-tetrahydropyridine (MPTP): Seven Cases" by P. A. Ballard, J. W. Tetrud, and J. W. Langston, 1985, *Neurology, 35*, 949–956. Reprinted by permission.

FOOD FOR THOUGHT

1. An epileptic is brought to trial for assault. The lawyer argues that her client is not a criminal and that the assaults in question were psychomotor attacks. She points out that her client takes her medication faithfully, but that it does not help. The prosecution lawyer argues that the defendant has a long history of violent assault and must be locked up. What do you think that the judge should do?

2. Describe a bizarre incident you have observed that you think in retrospect might have been a psychomotor or petit mal attack.

3. The more that is known about a disorder, the easier it is to diagnose; and the more accurately that it can be diagnosed, the easier it is to find things out about it. Explain and discuss.

KEY TERMS

Tumor (neoplasm) *(p. 131)*
Meningiomas *(p. 131)*
Encapsulated tumors *(p. 131)*
Benign tumors *(p. 132)*
Infiltrating tumors *(p. 132)*
Malignant tumors *(p. 132)*
Metastatic tumors *(p. 132)*
Strokes *(p. 132)*
Cerebral hemorrhage *(p. 133)*
Aneurysm *(p. 133)*
Congenital *(p. 133)*

Cerebral ischemia *(p. 133)*
Thrombosis *(p. 133)*
Embolism *(p. 133)*
Arteriosclerosis *(p. 133)*
Glutamate *(p. 133)*
NMDA (N-methyl-D-aspartate) receptors *(p. 134)*
Contusions *(p. 134)*
Hematoma *(p. 134)*
Contrecoup injuries *(p. 134)*
Concussion *(p. 135)*

Punch-drunk syndrome *(p. 135)*
Dementia *(p. 135)*
Encephalitis *(p. 135)*
Meningitis *(p. 135)*
General paresis *(p. 135)*
Neurotropic infections *(p. 136)*
Pantropic infections *(p. 136)*
Toxic psychosis *(p. 136)*
Tardive dyskinesia (TD) *(p. 136)*
Down syndrome *(p. 136)*

Epilepsy *(p. 137)*
Convulsions *(p. 138)*
Epileptic auras *(p. 138)*
Partial seizures *(p. 138)*
Simple partial seizures *(p. 138)*
Complex partial seizures *(p. 138)*
Psychomotor attack *(p. 138)*
Generalized seizures *(p. 139)*
Grand mal seizure *(p. 139)*
Hypoxia *(p. 139)*
Petit mal seizure *(p. 139)*

3-per-second spike-and-
wave discharge *(p. 139)*
Parkinson's disease *(p. 140)*
Substantia nigra *(p. 140)*
Nigrostriatal pathway
(p. 140)
Striatum *(p. 140)*
L-DOPA *(p. 140)*
Huntington's disease *(p. 140)*

Multiple sclerosis (MS)
(p. 142)
Ataxia *(p. 142)*
Epidemiology *(p. 142)*
Experimental autoimmune
encephalomyelitis
(p. 142)
Alzheimer's disease *(p. 143)*

Amyloid *(p. 143)*
Homologous animal models
(p. 145)
Isomorphic animal models
(p. 145)
Predictive animal models
(p. 145)
Kindling phenomenon
(p. 145)

Epileptogenesis *(p. 145)*
Amphetamine psychosis
(p. 146)
MPTP *(p. 147)*
Deprenyl *(p. 147)*
Monoamine oxidase (MAO)
inhibitor *(p. 147)*

ADDITIONAL READING

I strongly recommend the following two books, both of which are collections of entertaining personal essays about neuropsychological patients:

Klawans, H. L. (1990). *Newton's madness: Further tales of clinical neurology.* New York: Harper & Row.

Sacks, O. (1985). *The man who mistook his wife for a hat and other clinical tales.* New York: Summit Books.

7

The Visual System: From Eye to Cortex

7.1 Light Enters the Eye and Reaches the Retina

7.2 The Retina and Translation of Light into Neural Signals

7.3 From Retina to Primary Visual Cortex

7.4 Seeing Edges

7.5 Seeing Color

This chapter is about the visual system. Most people think their visual system has evolved to respond as accurately as possible to the patterns of light that enter their eyes. They recognize the obvious limitations in their visual system's accuracy, of course; and they appreciate those curious instances, termed *visual illusions,* in which it is "tricked" into seeing things the way they aren't. But such shortcomings are generally regarded as minor imperfections in a system that responds as faithfully as possible to the external world.

Despite its intuitive appeal, this way of thinking about the visual system is wrong. The visual system does not produce an accurate internal copy of the external world. It does much more. From the tiny, distorted, upside-down, two-dimensional retinal images projected upon the visual receptors lining the backs of our eyes, the visual system creates an accurate, richly detailed, three-dimensional perception that is—and this is the really important part—in some respects even better than the external reality from which it was created.

Regardless of what you may have heard to the contrary, what you see is not necessarily what you get. One of my primary goals in this chapter is to help you recognize and appreciate the inherent creativity of your own visual system.

This chapter is composed of five sections. The first three sections take you on a journey from the external visual world to the visual receptors of the retina, and from there over the major visual pathway to the primary visual cortex. The last two sections describe how the neurons of the visual system mediate the perception of two particularly important features of the visual world: edges and color.

You will learn in this chapter how understanding the visual system requires the integration of two types of research: (1) research that probes the visual system with sophisticated neuroanatomical, neurochemical, and neurophysiological techniques; and (2) research that focuses on the assessment of what we see. Both types of research receive substantial coverage, but it is the second that provides you with a unique educational opportunity: the opportunity to participate in the very research you are studying. Throughout this chapter, you are encouraged to participate in demonstrations designed to give you a taste of the excitement of scientific discovery and to illustrate the relevance of what you are learning in this chapter to life outside its pages.

7.1 Light Enters the Eye and Reaches the Retina

Everybody knows that cats, owls, and other nocturnal animals can see in the dark. Right? Wrong! Some animals have special adaptations that allow them to see under very dim illumination, but no animal can see in complete darkness. It is the light reflected into your eyes from the objects around you that is the basis for your ability to see the objects; if there is no light, there is no vision.

You may recall from high-school physics that light can be thought of in two different ways: as discrete particles of energy, called *photons,* traveling through space at about 300,000 kilometers (186,000 miles) per second or as waves of energy. Both theories are useful; in some ways light behaves like a particle, and in others it behaves like a wave. Physicists have learned to live with this nagging inconsistency, and we must do the same.

Light is sometimes defined as waves of electromagnetic energy that are between 380 and 760 nanometers (billionths of a meter) in length (see Figure 7.1). There is nothing special about these wavelengths except that the human visual system responds to them. In

Figure 7.1 The electromagnetic spectrum and the colors associated with the frequencies of the spectrum that are visible to humans.

fact, some animals can see wavelengths that we cannot. For example, rattlesnakes can see *infrared waves,* which are too long for humans to see; as a result, they can see warm-blooded prey in what for us would be complete darkness (Newman & Hartline, 1982). Accordingly, if I were writing this book for rattlesnakes, I would be forced to provide another, equally arbitrary, definition of light.

Wavelength and intensity are two properties of light that are of particular interest—wavelength because it plays an important role in the perception of color, and intensity because it plays an important role in the perception of brightness. The terms *wavelength* and *color* tend to be used interchangeably in everyday speech, and so do *intensity* and *brightness.* For example, we commonly refer to an intense light with a wavelength of 700 nanometers as being a bright red light, when in fact it is our perception of the light, not the light itself, that is bright and red. I know that these distinctions may seem trivial to you now, but I am confident that you will appreciate their importance by the end of the chapter.

The amount of light reaching the retinas is regulated by the donut-shaped bands of contractile tissue, the *irises,* which give our eyes their characteristic blue or brown color (see Figure 7.2). Light enters the eye through the *pupil,* the hole in the iris. The adjustment of pupil size in response to changes in illumination represents a compromise between **sensitivity** (the ability to detect the presence of dimly lit objects) and **acuity** (the ability to see the details of objects). When the level of illumination is high and sensitivity is thus not important, the visual system takes advantage of the situation by constricting the pupils. When the pupils are constricted, the image falling on each retina is sharper and there is a greater *depth of focus*; that is, a greater range of depths are simultaneously kept in focus on the retinas. However, when the level of illumination is too low to adequately activate the receptors, the pupils dilate to let in more light thereby sacrificing acuity and depth of focus.

Behind each pupil is a *lens,* which focuses incoming light on the retina (see Figure 7.3). When we direct our gaze at something near, the tension on the ligaments hold-

Figure 7.2 The human eye. Light enters the eye through the pupil, whose size is regulated by the iris. The iris gives the eye its characteristic brown or blue color.

ing each lens in place is reduced by the contraction of the **ciliary muscles,** and the lens assumes its natural cylindrical shape. (Be alert here: The fact that the tension on the lens is reduced by muscle contraction is counterintuitive.) This increases the ability of the lens to *refract* (bend) light and thus brings close objects into sharp focus. When we focus on a distant object, the ciliary muscles relax and the lens is flattened. The process of adjusting the configuration of the lenses to bring images into focus on the retina is called **accommodation.**

No description of the eyes of vertebrates would be complete without a discussion of their most obvious feature: the fact that they come in pairs. One reason vertebrates have two eyes is that vertebrates have two sides: left and right. By having one eye on each side, which is by far the most common arrangement, vertebrates can see in almost every direction without moving their heads. But then why do some mammals, including humans, have their eyes mounted side by side on the front of their heads? This arrangement sacrifices the ability to see behind so that what is in front can be viewed through both eyes simultaneously—an arrangement that is an important basis for our visual system's ability to create three-dimensional perceptions (to see depth) from two-dimensional retinal images. Why do you think the two-eyes-on-the-front arrangement has evolved in some species but not in others?

The movements of your eyes are coordinated so that each point in your visual world is projected to corresponding points on your two retinas. To accomplish this, your eyes must *converge* (turn slightly inward); convergence is greatest when you are inspecting things that are close. But the positions of the retinal images on your two eyes can never correspond exactly because your two eyes do not

Sensitivity. In vision, the ability to detect the presence of dimly lit objects.

Acuity. The ability to see the details of objects.

Ciliary muscles. The eye muscles that control the lenses.

Accommodation. The process of adjusting the configuration of the lenses to bring images into focus on the retina.

Binocular disparity. The difference between the retinal image of the same object on the two retinas.

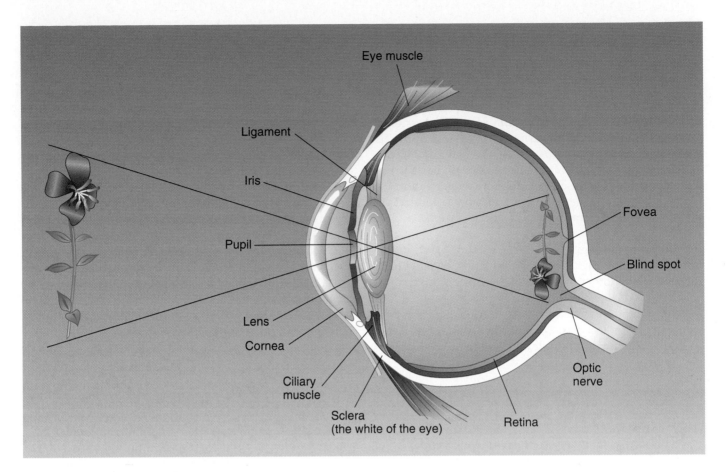

Figure 7.3 A section of the human eye.

view the world from exactly the same position (see the following demonstration). **Binocular disparity**—the difference in the position of the same images on the two retinas—is greater for close objects than for distant objects; therefore your visual system can use the degree of binocular disparity to construct one three-dimensional perception from two two-dimensional retinal images (Julesz, 1986; Trotter et al., 1992).

DEMONSTRATION

The demonstration of binocular disparity and convergence is the first of the demonstrations that punctuate this chapter. If you compare the views from each eye (by quickly closing one eye and then the other) of objects at various distances in front of you—for example, your finger held at different distances—you will notice that the disparity between the two views is greater for closer objects. Now try the mysterious demonstration of

the cocktail sausage. Face the farthest wall (or some other distant object) and bring the tips of your two pointing fingers together at

arm's length in front of you—with your nails away from you, unless you prefer sausages with fingernails. Now, with both eyes open, sight through the notch between your touching fingertips, but focus on the wall. Do you see the cocktail sausage between your fingertips? Where did it come from? To prove to yourself that the sausage is a product of binocularity, make it disappear by shutting one eye. Warning: Do not eat this sausage.

Figure 7.4 illustrates the cellular structure of the retina. Notice the five different layers of cells: **receptors, horizontal cells, bipolar cells, amacrine cells,** and **retinal ganglion cells.** Notice too that the amacrine cells and horizontal cells are specialized for *lateral communication* (communication across the major channels of sensory input). The amacrine and bipolar cells release the inhibitory neurotransmitter GABA; in contrast, the receptors and bipolar cells release the excitatory neurotransmitter glutamate (see Barnstable, 1993).

Also notice in Figure 7.4 that the retina is in a sense inside-out: Light reaches the receptor layer only after passing through the other four layers. Then, once the receptors have been activated, the neural message is transmitted back out through the retinal layers to the retinal ganglion cells, whose axons project across the inside of the retina before gathering together in a bundle and exiting the eyeball. This inside-out arrangement creates two visual problems. One is that the incoming light is distorted by the retinal tissue through which it must pass before reaching the receptors. The other is that for the bundle of retinal ganglion cell axons to leave the eye, there must be a gap in the receptor layer; this gap is called the **blind spot.**

The first of these two problems is minimized by the fovea (see Figure 7.5 on page 156). The **fovea** is an indentation, about 0.33 centimeter in diameter, at the center of the retina; it is the area of the retina that is specialized for high-acuity vision (for seeing fine details). The thinning of the retinal ganglion cell layer at the fovea reduces the distortion of incoming light. The blind spot, the second of the two visual problems created by the inside-out structure of the retina, requires a more creative solution—which is illustrated in the following demonstration.

DEMONSTRATION

First, prove to yourself that you do have an area of blindness that corresponds to your retinal blind spots. Close your left eye and stare directly at the **A** below, trying as hard as you can to not shift your gaze. While keeping the gaze of your right eye fixed on the **A**, hold the book at different distances from you until the black dot to the right of the **A** becomes focused on your blind spot and disappears (at about 20 centimeters, or 8 inches).

Why is there not a black hole in your perception of the world when you look at it with one eye? You will discover the answer by focusing on **B** without moving your eyes while holding the book at the same distance.

Suddenly, the broken line to the right of **B** will become whole. Now focus on **C** at the same distance without moving your eyes. What do you see?

You have just experienced **completion.** The visual system uses information provided by the receptors around the blind spot to fill in the gaps in your retinal images. When the visual system detects a straight bar going into one side of the blind spot and another straight bar leaving the other side, it fills in the missing bit for you; and what you see is a continuous straight bar, regardless of what is actually there. The completion phenomenon is one of the most compelling demonstrations that the visual system does much more than create a faithful copy of the external world.

It is a mistake to think that completion is merely a response to blind spots (see Ramachandran, 1992). Indeed, completion is a fundamental feature of visual system function. When you look at an object, your visual system does not conduct an image of that object from your retina to your cortex. Instead, it extracts key information about the

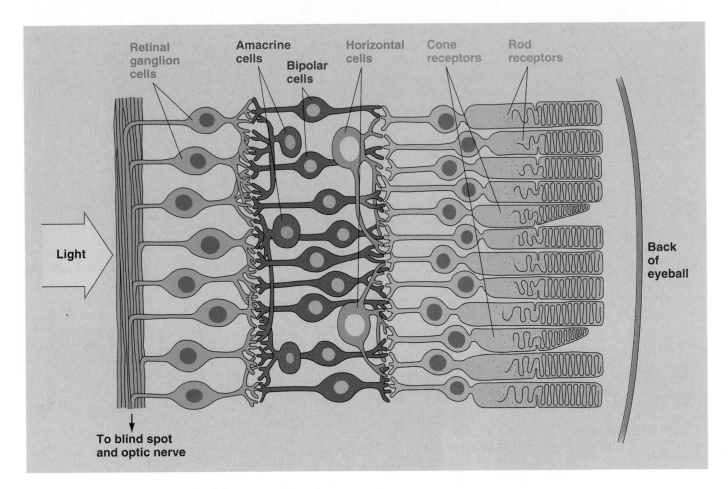

Retinal ganglion cells

Amacrine cells

Bipolar cells

Horizontal cells

Cone receptors

Rod receptors

Light

Back of eyeball

To blind spot and optic nerve

Figure 7.4 The cellular structure of the mammalian retina.

object—primarily information about its edges and their location—and conducts that information to the cortex, where a perception of the entire object is created from that partial information. For example, the color and brightness of large unpatterned surfaces are filled in by a process called *surface interpolation*.

Cone and Rod Vision

You likely noticed in Figure 7.4 that there are two different types of receptors in the human retina: cone-shaped receptors called **cones,** and rod-shaped receptors called **rods** (see Figure 7.6 on page 156). The existence of these two types of receptors puzzled researchers until 1866, when it was first noticed that species active only in the day tend to have cone-only retinas and that species active only at night tend to have rod-only retinas.

Receptors. Cells that are specialized to receive chemical, mechanical, or radiant signals from the environment.

Horizontal cells. A layer of retinal neurons whose function is lateral communication.

Bipolar cells. The cells in the middle layer of the retina.

Amacrine cells. A layer of retinal neurons whose function is lateral communication.

Retinal ganglion cells. The layer of neurons in the retina whose axons leave the eyeball.

Blind spot. The area on the retina where the axons of retinal ganglion cells gather together, penetrate the receptor layer, and leave the eye as the optic nerve.

Fovea. The central indentation of the retina which is specialized for high-acuity vision.

Completion. The visual system's automatic use of information obtained from receptors around a blind spot to create a perception of the missing portion of the retinal image.

Cones. The visual receptors that mediate high-acuity color vision in good lighting.

Rods. The visual receptors that mediate achromatic, low-acuity vision under dim light.

From this observation emerged the **duplexity theory** of vision—the theory that cones and rods mediate different kinds of vision. Cone-mediated vision (**photopic vision**) predominates in good lighting and provides high-acuity (finely detailed) colored perceptions of the world. In dim illumination, there is not enough light to reliably excite the cones, and the more sensitive rod-mediated vision (**scotopic vision**) predominates. However, the sensitivity of scotopic vision is not achieved without cost: Scotopic vision lacks both the detail and the color of photopic vision.

The differences between photopic (cone) and scotopic (rod) vision result in part from a difference in the way the two systems are "wired." As Figure 7.7 illustrates, there is a large difference between the two systems in *convergence*.

Figure 7.6 Cones and rods. The smaller, conical cells are cones; the larger, cylindrical cells are rods.

The output of several hundred rods may ultimately converge on a single retinal ganglion cell, whereas it is not uncommon for a retinal ganglion cell to receive input from only a few cones. As a result, the effects of dim light simultaneously stimulating many rods can summate to influence the firing of a retinal ganglion cell onto which the output of the stimulated rods converges, whereas the effects of the same dim light applied to a sheet of cones cannot summate to the same degree, and the retinal ganglion cells may not respond to the light.

The convergent scotopic system pays for its high degree of sensitivity with a low level of acuity. When a retinal ganglion cell that receives input from hundreds of rods changes its firing, the brain has no way of knowing which portion of the rods contributed to the change. Although a more intense light is required to change the firing of a retinal gan-

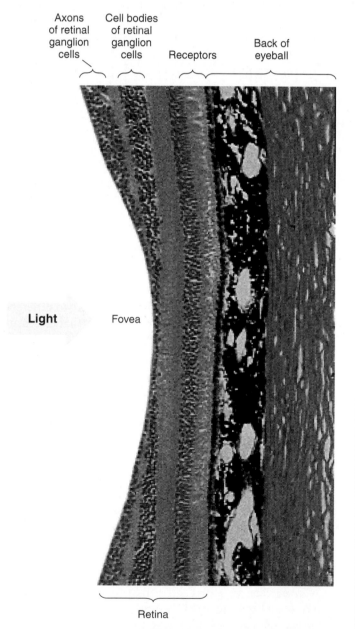

Axons of retinal ganglion cells

Cell bodies of retinal ganglion cells

Receptors

Back of eyeball

Light

Fovea

Retina

Figure 7.5 A section of the retina. The fovea is the indentation at the center of the retina; it is specialized for high-acuity vision.

Duplexity theory. The theory that cones and rods mediate photopic and scotopic vision, respectively.

Photopic vision. Cone-mediated vision, which predominates when lighting is good.

Scotopic vision. Rod-mediated vision, which predominates in dim light.

Nasal hemiretina. The half of each retina next to the nose.

Temporal hemiretina. The half of each retina next to the temple.

Photopic spectral sensitivity curve. The graph of the sensitivity of cone-mediated vision to different wavelengths of light.

Scotopic spectral sensitivity curve. The graph of the sensitivity of rod-mediated vision to different wavelengths of light.

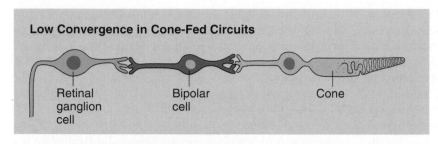

Low Convergence in Cone-Fed Circuits

Retinal ganglion cell   Bipolar cell   Cone

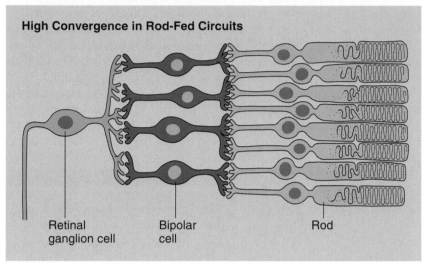

High Convergence in Rod-Fed Circuits

Retinal ganglion cell   Bipolar cell   Rod

Figure 7.7 A schematic representation of the convergence of cones and rods on retinal ganglion cells. There is a low degree of convergence in cone-fed pathways and a high degree of convergence in rod-fed pathways.

brightness. Because our visual systems are not equally sensitive to all wavelengths in the visible spectrum, lights of the same intensity but of different wavelengths can differ markedly in brightness. A graph of the relative brightness of lights of the same intensity presented at different wavelengths is called a *spectral sensitivity* curve.

By far the most important thing to remember about spectral sensitivity curves is that humans and other animals with both cones and rods have two of them: a **photopic spectral sensitivity curve** and a **scotopic spectral sensitivity curve.** The photopic spectral sensitivity of humans is determined by having subjects judge the relative brightness of different wavelengths of light shone on the fovea. Their scotopic spectral sensitivity is determined by asking subjects to judge the relative brightness of different wavelengths of light shone on the periphery of the retina at an intensity too low to activate the few peripheral cones that are located there.

The photopic and scotopic spectral sensitivity curves of human subjects are plotted in Figure 7.9. Notice that under photopic conditions, the visual system is maximally sensitive to wavelengths of about 560 nanometers; thus a light at 500 nanometers would

glion cell that receives signals from cones, when it does react there is less ambiguity about the location of the stimulus that triggered the reaction.

Cones and rods differ in their distribution on the retina. As Figure 7.8 illustrates, there are no rods at all in the fovea, only cones. At the boundaries of the foveal indentation, the proportion of cones declines markedly and there is an increase in the number of rods. The density of rods reaches a maximum at 20° from the center of the fovea. You may be puzzled by the fact that in the periphery of the retina, there are many more rods in the **nasal hemiretina** (the half of each retina next to the nose) than in the **temporal hemiretina** (the half next to the temples). The solution to this puzzle is as plain as the nose on your face. In fact, it is the nose on your face. Because your nose blocks the input of light onto the edges of your temporal hemiretinas, there is less need for receptors there.

Generally speaking, more intense lights appear brighter. However, wavelength also has a substantial effect on the perception of

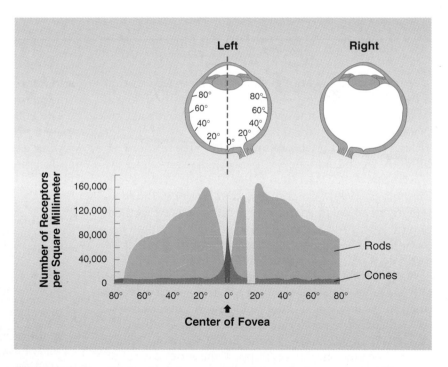

Figure 7.8 The distribution of cones and rods over the human retina. The figure illustrates the number of cones and rods per square millimeter as a function of distance from the center of the fovea. (Adapted from Lindsay & Norman, 1977.)

have to be much more intense than one at 560 nanometers to be seen as equally bright. In contrast, under scotopic conditions, the visual system is maximally sensitive to wavelengths of about 500 nanometers; thus a light of 560 nanometers would have to be much more intense than one at 500 nanometers to be seen as equally bright.

Because of the difference in photopic and scotopic spectral sensitivity, an interesting visual effect can be observed during the transition from photopic to scotopic vision. In 1825, Purkinje described the following occurrence, which has become known as the **Purkinje effect** (pronounced "pur-KIN-gee"). One evening, just before dusk, while Purkinje was walking in his garden, he noticed how bright most of his yellow and red flowers appeared in relation to his blue ones. What amazed him was that just a few hours later the relative brightness of his flowers had somehow been reversed; the entire scene, when viewed at night, appeared only in shades of gray, but most of the blue flowers appeared as brighter grays than did the yellow and red ones. Can you explain this shift in relative brightness by referring to the photopic and scotopic spectral sensitivity curves in Figure 7.9?

Eye Movement

If cones are in fact responsible for mediating high-acuity, color vision under photopic conditions, how can they accomplish their task when most of them are crammed into the fovea? Look around you. What you see is not a few colored details at the center of a grayish scene. You see an expansive, richly detailed, lavishly colored visual world. How can such a perception be the product of a photopic system that, for the most part, is restricted to a few degrees in the center of your visual field? The following demonstration provides a clue.

DEMONSTRATION

Close your left eye, and with your right eye stare at the fixation point ✦ at a distance of about 12 centimeters (4.75 inches) from the page. Be very careful that your gaze does not shift. You will notice when your gaze is totally fixed that it is difficult to see detail and color at 20° or more from the fixation point. Now look at the page without fixing your gaze, and notice the difference that eye movement makes to your vision.

W		F	D	M	E	A	✦
50°		40°	30°	20°	10°	5°	0°

What this demonstration shows is that what we see is determined not just by what is projected on the retina at that instant (e.g., Cumming, 1978). Although we are not aware of it, the eye continually scans the visual field by making a series of brief fixations. About three fixations occur every second, and they are connected by very quick eye movements called **saccades** (Kowler, 1990; Whittaker & Cummings, 1990). The visual system *integrates* (adds together) the foveal images from the preceding few fixations to produce a wide-angled, high-acuity, richly colored perception. It is because of this *temporal integration* that the world does not vanish momentarily each time we blink.

One way of demonstrating the critical role played by eye movement in vision is to study what happens to vision when all eye movement is stopped. However, because of the risks inherent in paralyzing the eye muscles, researchers have taken an alternative approach. Rather than stopping eye movement, they have stopped the primary consequence of eye movement—the movement of the retinal image across the retina. They have accomplished this by projecting test stimuli from a tiny projector mounted on a contact lens. Each time the eye moves, the lens and the pro-

jector move with it; this keeps the retinal image fixed on the same receptors, as if the eye had remained still.

The effect on vision of stabilizing the retinal image is dramatic (e.g., Pritchard, 1961). After a few seconds of viewing, a simple **stabilized retinal image** disappears, leaving a featureless gray field. The movements of the eyes then

Purkinje effect. In intense light, red and yellow wavelengths look brighter than blue or green wavelengths of equal intensity; in dim light, blue and green wavelengths look brighter than red and yellow wavelengths of equal intensity.

Saccades. The rapid movements of the eyes between fixations.

Stabilized retinal image. A retinal image that does not shift across the retina when the eye moves.

Transduction. The conversion of one type of energy to another.

Rhodopsin. The photopigment of rods.

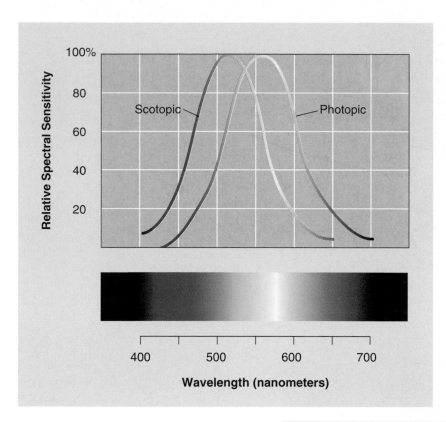

Figure 7.9 Human photopic (cone) and scotopic (rod) spectral sensitivity curves. The peak of each curve has been arbitrarily set at 100%.

Transduction is the conversion of one form of energy to another. *Visual transduction* is the conversion of light to neural signals by the visual receptors. A breakthrough in the study of visual transduction came in 1876, when a red *pigment* (a pigment is any substance that absorbs light) was extracted from the predominantly rod retina of the frog. This pigment had a curious property. When the pigment (which became known as **rhodopsin**), was exposed to continuous intense light, it was bleached (lost its color) and lost its ability to absorb light; but when it was returned to the dark, it regained both its redness and its light-absorbing capacity.

It is now clear that the absorption and bleaching of rhodopsin by light is the first

increase, presumably in an attempt to bring the image back. However, such movements are futile in this situation because the stabilized retinal image simply moves with the eyes. In a few seconds, the stimulus pattern, or part of it, spontaneously reappears, only to disappear once again.

Why do stabilized images disappear? The answer lies in the fact that the neurons of the visual system respond to change rather than to steady input. Most visual system neurons respond vigorously when a stimulus is presented, moved, or terminated; but they respond only weakly to a continuous, unchanging stimulus. Apparently, one function of eye movements is to keep the retinal image moving back and forth across the receptors, thus ensuring that the receptors and the neurons to which they are connected receive a continually changing pattern of stimulation. When a retinal image is stabilized, parts of the visual system stop responding to the image, and it disappears.

- ■ The sensitivity of human vision to different wavelengths under scotopic conditions
- ■ The ability of rhodopsin to absorb different wavelengths of light under scotopic conditions

Figure 7.10 The absorption spectrum of rhodopsin compared with the human scotopic spectral sensitivity curve.

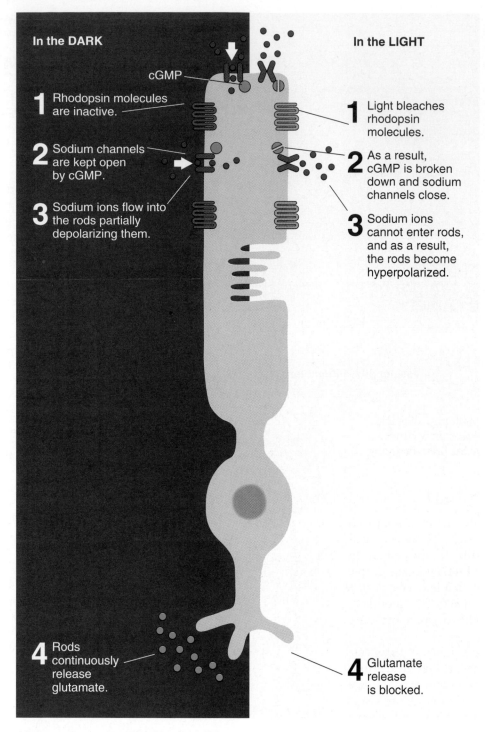

In the DARK

1 Rhodopsin molecules are inactive.

2 Sodium channels are kept open by cGMP.

3 Sodium ions flow into the rods partially depolarizing them.

cGMP

4 Rods continuously release glutamate.

In the LIGHT

1 Light bleaches rhodopsin molecules.

2 As a result, cGMP is broken down and sodium channels close.

3 Sodium ions cannot enter rods, and as a result, the rods become hyperpolarized.

4 Glutamate release is blocked.

Figure 7.11 The inhibitory response of rods to light. When light bleaches rhodopsin molecules, the rods' sodium channels close; as a result, the rods become hyperpolarized and release less glutamate.

step in rod-mediated vision. Evidence comes from demonstrations that the degree to which rhodopsin absorbs light in various situations predicts how humans see under the very same conditions. For example, it has been shown that the degree to which rhodopsin absorbs lights of different wavelengths is related to the ability of humans and other animals with rods to detect the pres-

ence of different wavelengths of light under scotopic conditions. Figure 7.10 on page 159 illustrates the relationship between the **absorption spectrum** of rhodopsin and the human scotopic spectral sensitivity curve. The goodness of the fit leaves little doubt that, in dim light, our sensitivity to various wavelengths is a direct consequence of rhodopsin's ability to absorb them.

Recent research has shown that rhodopsin is a G-protein linked receptor that responds to light rather than to neurotransmitter molecules (see Koutalos & Yau, 1993). Rhodopsin receptors, like other G-protein linked receptors, initiate a cascade of intracellular chemical events when they are activated (see Figure 7.11). When rods are in darkness, an intracellular chemical called *cyclic GMP* (guanosine monophosphate) keeps sodium channels partially opened, thus keeping the rods slightly depolarized and a steady flow of excitatory glutamate neurotransmitter molecules emanating from them. However, when rhodopsin receptors are bleached by light, the resulting cascade of intracellular chemical events deactivates the cyclic GMP; and in so doing, it closes the sodium channels and reduces the release of glutamate. The transduction of light by rods makes an important point: Signals are often transmitted through neural systems by inhibition.

Less is known about the cone photopigments than about rhodopsin. However, their structure and function appear to be similar to those of rhodopsin (see Nathans, 1989).

7.3　From Retina to Primary Visual Cortex

Many pathways in the brain carry visual information. By far the largest and most thoroughly studied visual pathway is the **retina-geniculate-striate pathway,** which conducts signals from the retina to the **primary visual cortex,** or *striate cortex,* via the **lateral geniculate nuclei** of the thalamus. The organization of this retina-geniculate-striate pathway is illustrated in Figure 7.12. Examine it carefully.

The main thing to notice from Figure 7.12 is that all signals from the left visual field reach the right primary visual cortex, either ipsilaterally via the *temporal hemiretina* of the right eye or contralaterally via the *nasal hemiretina* of the left eye—and that the opposite is true of all signals from the right visual field. Each lateral geniculate nucleus has six layers, and each layer receives input from all parts of the contralateral visual field of one eye. Most of the lateral geniculate neurons that project to the primary visual cortex terminate in the lower part of cortical layer IV (see Figure 3.29), producing a characteristic stripe or striation when viewed in cross section—hence the name *striate cortex.*

Retinotopic Organization

The retina-geniculate-striate system is **retinotopic;** each level of the system is organized like a map of the retina. This means that two stimuli presented to adjacent areas of the retina excite adjacent neurons at all levels of the system. The retinotopic layout of the primary visual cortex has a disproportionate representation of the fovea; although the fovea is only a small part of the retina, a relatively large proportion of the primary visual cortex (about 25%) is dedicated to the analysis of its input.

A dramatic demonstration of the retinotopic organization of the primary visual cortex was provided by Dobelle, Mladejovsky, and Girvin (1974). They implanted an array of electrodes in the primary visual cortex of patients who were blind because of damage to their eyes. If electrical current was administered simultaneously through an array of electrodes forming a shape, such as a cross, on the surface of a patient's cortex, the patient reported "seeing" a glowing image of that shape.

The M and P Pathways

Not apparent in Figure 7.12 is the fact that the retina-geniculate-striate system is composed of two largely independent channels of communication. These two channels are most apparent in the lateral geniculate nuclei, where they are spatially segregated. One channel runs through the top four layers of each lateral geniculate nucleus. These layers are called the **parvocellular layers** (or P layers) because they are composed of neurons with small cell bodies (*parvo* means "small"). The other channel runs through the bottom two layers, which are called the **magnocellular layers**

Absorption spectrum. A graph of the ability of a substance to absorb light of different wavelengths.

Retina-geniculate-striate pathway. The major visual pathway from the retina to the striate cortex (primary visual cortex) via the lateral geniculate nuclei of the thalamus.

Primary visual cortex. The area of the cortex that receives direct input from the lateral geniculate nuclei.

Lateral geniculate nucleus. The six-layered thalamic structure that receives input from the retina and transmits its output to the primary visual cortex.

Retinotopic. Laid out according to a map of the retina.

Parvocellular layers. The layers of the lateral geniculate nuclei that are composed of small neurons; the top four layers.

Magnocellular layers. The layers of the lateral geniculate nuclei that are composed of large neurons; the bottom two layers.

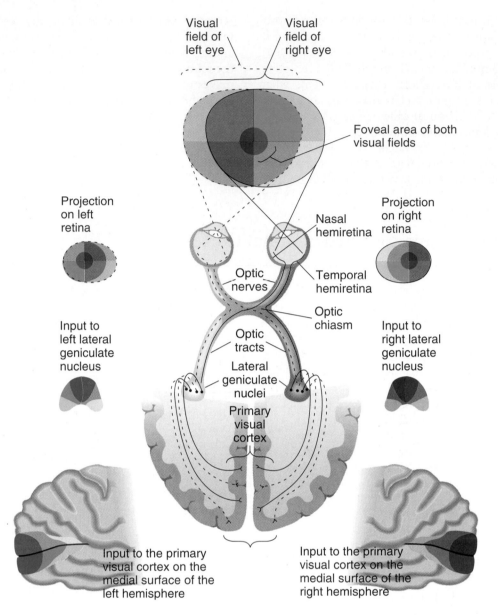

Figure 7.12 The retina-geniculate-striate system: The neural projections from the retinas through the lateral geniculate nuclei to the left and right primary visual cortex (striate cortex). The colors indicate the flow of information from various parts of the receptive fields of each eye to various parts of the visual system. (Adapted from Netter, 1962.)

(or M layers) because they are composed of neurons with large cell bodies (*magno* means "large").

The *P pathway* is composed of the parvocellular neurons of the lateral geniculate nuclei and the retinal ganglion cells that synapse on them. The P pathway neurons, which are in the majority, are particularly responsive to color, to fine pattern details, and to stationary or slowly

moving objects. In contrast, the *M pathway* is composed of the magnocellular neurons of the lateral geniculate nuclei and the retinal ganglion cells that synapse on them. The M pathway neurons are particularly responsive to movement. Cones provide the majority of the input to the P pathway, whereas rods provide the majority of the input to the M pathway.

Before proceeding to the last two sections of the chapter, which describe how the visual system mediates the perception of edges and color, review what you have learned so far about the visual system by filling in the following blanks. Review material related to your errors and omissions.

1. Neural signals are carried from the retina to the lateral geniculate nuclei by the axons of _____ cells.

2. The area of the retina that mediates high-acuity vision is the _____.

3. Cones are the receptors of the _____ system.

4. The photopigment of rods is _____.

5. The most important organizational principle of the retina-geniculate-striate system is that it is laid out _____.

6. The retinal ganglion cells from the nasal hemiretinas decussate via the _____.

7. Evidence that rhodopsin is the scotopic photopigment is provided by the fit between the _____ spectrum of rhodopsin and the scotopic spectral sensitivity curve.

8. The high degree of _____ characteristic of the scotopic system increases its sensitivity but decreases its acuity.

9. The axons of retinal ganglion cells leave the eyeball at the _____.

7.4   Seeing Edges

Edge perception (seeing edges) does not sound like a particularly important topic, but it is. Edges are the most informative features of any visual display because they define the extent and position of the various objects in it. Given the importance of perceiving visual edges and the unrelenting pressure of natural selection, it is not surprising that the visual systems of many species are particularly good at edge perception.

Before considering the visual mechanisms underlying edge perception, it is important to appreciate exactly what a visual edge is. In a sense, a visual edge is nothing: It is merely the place where two different areas of a visual image meet. Thus the perception of an edge is really the perception of a *contrast* between two adjacent areas of the visual field. This section of the chapter reviews the perception of edges (the perception of contrast) between areas that differ from one another in brightness. Color contrast is discussed in the following section.

Lateral Inhibition and Contrast Enhancement

Carefully examine the stripes in Figure 7.13. The intensity graph in the figure indicates what is there—a series of homogeneous stripes of different intensity. But this is not exactly what you see, is it? What you see is indicated in the

The answers are (1) retinal ganglion, (2) fovea, (3) photopic, (4) rhodopsin, (5) retinotopically, (6) optic chiasm, (7) absorption, (8) convergence, and (9) blind spot.

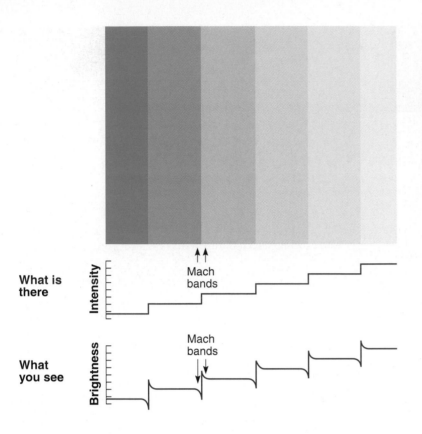

Figure 7.13 Mach bands. The illusory bands visible in this figure are often called Mach bands, but they were in fact discovered by French chemist M. Chevreul in 1890 while he was doing research on textile patterns. The Austrian physicist E. Mach discovered illusory bands in a different figure, but the term *Mach bands* is sometimes used in a general sense—as I have done here—to refer to both his and Chevreul's discovery. (Thanks to David Burr of the Università Degli Studi di Roma for informing me, and now you, of Chevreul's contribution—see Ross, Morrone, & Burr, 1989.)

brightness graph. Adjacent to each edge, the brighter stripe looks brighter than it really is and the darker stripe looks darker than it really is (see the following demonstration). The nonexistent stripes of brightness and darkness running adjacent to the edges are sometimes called *Mach bands*; they enhance the contrast at each edge and make the edge easier to see.

DEMONSTRATION

The Mach band demonstration is so compelling that you may be confused by it. You may think that the Mach bands have been created by the printers of the book, rather than by your own visual system. To prove to yourself that the Mach bands are a creation of your own visual system, view each stripe individually by covering the adjacent ones with two pieces of paper, and you will see at once that each stripe is completely homogeneous. Now take the paper away and the Mach bands will suddenly reappear.

It is important to appreciate that **contrast enhancement** is not something that occurs just in books. Although we are normally unaware of it, every edge we look at is highlighted for us by the contrast-enhancing mechanisms of our nervous systems. Thus our perception of edges is better than the real thing.

The classic studies of the physiological basis of contrast enhancement were conducted on the eyes of an unlikely subject: the *horseshoe crab* (e.g., Ratliff, 1972). The *lateral eyes* of the horseshoe crab are ideal for certain types of neurophysiological research. Unlike mammalian eyes, they are composed of very large receptors, called **ommatidia,** each with its own large axon. The ommatidium axons of each lateral eye are interconnected by a lateral neural network, called the **lateral plexus.**

In order to understand the physiological basis of contrast enhancement in the horseshoe crab, you must know two things. The first is that if a single ommatidium is illuminated, it fires at a rate that is proportional to the intensity of the light striking it; more intense lights produce more firing. The second is that when a receptor fires, it inhibits its neighbors via the lateral plexus; this inhibition is called **lateral inhibition** because it spreads laterally across the array of receptors, or *mutual inhibition* because neighboring receptors inhibit one another. The amount of lateral inhibition produced by a receptor is greatest when it is most intensely illuminated, and it has its greatest effect on its immediate neighbors.

The neural basis of contrast enhancement can be understood in terms of the firing rates of the receptors on each side of an edge, as indicated in Figure 7.14. Notice that the receptor adjacent to the edge on the more intense side (receptor D) fires more than the other intensely illuminated receptors (A, B, C), while the receptor adjacent to the edge on the less-well-illuminated side (receptor E) fires less than the other receptors on that side (F, G, H). Lateral inhibition accounts for these differences. Receptors A, B, and C all fire at the same rate because they are all receiving the same high level of stimulation and the same high degree of lateral inhibition from all their highly stimulated neighbors. Receptor D fires more than A, B, and C because it receives as much stimulation as they do but less inhibition, because many of its neighbors are on the dimmer side of the edge. Now consider the receptors on the dimmer side. Receptors F, G, and H fire at the same rate because they are all being stimulated by the same low level of light and receiving the same low level of inhibition from their neighbors. However, receptor E fires even less because it is receiving the same excitation but more inhibition because many of its immediate neighbors are on the other side of the border in the more intense light. Now that you understand the neural basis of contrast enhancement, take another look at Figure 7.13.

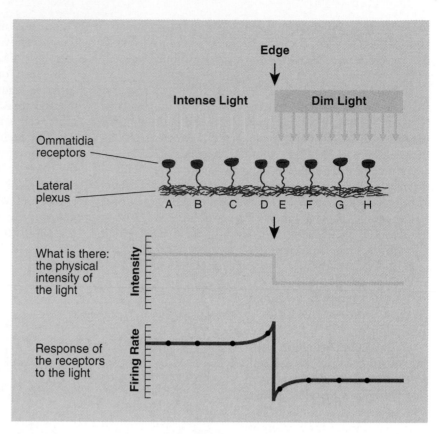

Figure 7.14 How lateral inhibition produces contrast enhancement. (Adapted from Ratliff, 1972.)

Receptive Fields of Visual Neurons

The Nobel-Prize-winning research of Hubel and Wiesel is the fitting climax to this discussion of brightness contrast; the methods of these two researchers have been adopted by a generation of sensory neurophysiologists. The subjects in Hubel and Wiesel's experiments are single neurons in the visual systems of cats and monkeys. The experiments are conducted as follows.

First, the tip of a microelectrode is positioned near a single neuron in the visual area of interest. During testing, eye movements are blocked by *curare* (see Chapter 4), and the images on a screen in front of the subject are focused sharply on the retina by an experimenter using an adjustable lens. The next step in the procedure is to identify the receptive field of the neuron. The **receptive field** of a visual neuron is the area of the visual field within which it is possible for a visual stimulus to influence the firing of that neuron. Visual system neurons tend to be continually active; thus effective stimuli are those that either increase or decrease the rate of firing. The final step in the method is to record the responses of the neuron to various stimuli within its receptive field in order to characterize the types of stimuli that most influence its activity. Then, the electrode is advanced slightly and the entire process of identifying and characterizing the receptive field properties is repeated for another neuron, and then for another, and another, and so on (see Kuffler, 1953). The general strategy involves beginning such studies near the input end of a

Contrast enhancement. The enhancement of the perception of edges.

Ommatidia. The visual receptors of the horseshoe crab.

Lateral plexus. The lateral neural network that interconnects the visual receptors of the horseshoe crab.

Lateral inhibition. Inhibition of adjacent neurons or receptors in a topographic array.

Receptive field. The area (e.g., on the retina) within which it is possible for the appropriate stimulus to influence the firing of the neuron.

sensory system and gradually working up through "higher" and "higher" levels of the system in an effort to understand the increasing complexity of the neural responses at each level.

Hubel and Wiesel (e.g., 1979) used their procedure to study the retina-geniculate-striate system of the monkey. Given the relatively simple circuitry of the pathway from the retina to the primary visual cortex, it is not surprising that many retinal ganglion cells, lateral geniculate neurons, and striate layer IV neurons have similar receptive fields—the parvocellular neurons of the lateral geniculate nuclei terminate in lower layer IV, and the magnocellular neurons terminate just above them, also in lower layer IV. Most of the receptive fields of the neurons at these three levels of the retina-geniculate-striate system are round. Because there is less convergence in foveal circuits, neurons with receptive fields in the foveal area have smaller receptive fields than do those with receptive fields in the periphery.

Many retinal ganglion cells, lateral geniculate cells, and cells in layer IV of the primary visual cortex respond in two different ways to a spot of white light that briefly appears in their receptive field. Depending on where in the field the light appears, the cell displays either "on" firing or "off" firing; that is, it displays an increased rate of firing while the light is on, or it displays a reduced rate of firing while the light is on followed by a burst of firing when it is turned off.

On-Center Cells and Off-Center Cells

The receptive fields of many retinal ganglion cells, lateral geniculate cells, and layer IV primary visual cortex cells fall into one of the two categories illustrated in Figure 7.15: on-center cells and off-center cells. **On-center cells** respond to lights shone in the central region of their receptive fields with "on" firing and to lights shown in the periphery of their receptive fields with inhibition, followed by "off" firing when the light is turned off. **Off-center cells** display the opposite pattern; they respond with inhi-

bition and "off" firing in response to lights in the center of their receptive fields and with "on" firing to lights in the periphery of their receptive fields.

In effect, on-center and off-center cells respond best to contrast. Figure 7.16 illustrates this point. The most effective way to influence the firing rate of an on-center or off-center cell is to maximize the contrast between the center and the periphery of its receptive field by illuminating either the entire center or the entire surround while leaving the other region completely dark. Diffusely illuminating both regions of the receptive field has little effect. Thus Hubel and Wiesel concluded that the function of many neurons in the retina-geniculate-striate system is to respond to the degree of brightness contrast between the two areas of their receptive fields (see Livingstone & Hubel, 1988).

Figure 7.15 The receptive fields of an on-center cell and an off-center cell.

The most effective way of maximizing the firing of an on-center or off-center cell is to completely illuminate either the "on area" or the "off area" of its receptive field:

OFF
ON

LIGHT ON

OFF
ON

LIGHT ON

If both areas of a cell's receptive field are illuminated together, there is little reaction from the cell:

OFF
ON

LIGHT ON

Figure 7.16 The responses of an on-center cell to contrast.

Simple Cortical Cells

Except for the neurons of layer IV, the neurons of the primary visual cortex have receptive field properties that are different from those of retinal ganglion cells and lateral geniculate cells. The receptive fields of most primary visual cortex neurons fall into one of two classes: simple or complex.

Simple cells, like layer IV cells, are unresponsive to diffuse light, and they have receptive fields that can be divided into "on" and "off" regions. The difference is that the borders between the "on" and "off" regions of simple-cell receptive fields are straight lines rather than circles. Several examples of receptive fields of simple cells are presented in Figure 7.17 on page 168. Notice that simple cells respond best to bars of light in a dark field, dark bars in a light field, or single straight edges between dark and light areas. Each simple cell responds maximally only when its preferred straight-edge stimulus is in a particular position and in a particular orientation.

Complex Cortical Cells

Complex cells are more numerous than simple cells. Like simple cells, complex cells respond best to straight-line stimuli in a specific orientation and are unresponsive to diffuse light. However, complex cells differ from simple

cells in three important respects. The first is that they have larger receptive fields. The second is that it is not possible to divide the receptive fields of complex cells into static "on" and "off" regions: A complex cell responds to a particular straight-edge stimulus of a particular orientation regardless of its position within the receptive field of that cell. Thus, if a stimulus (e.g., a 45° bar of light) that produces "on" firing in a particular complex cell is swept across its receptive field, the cell will respond continuously to it as it moves across the field. Many complex cells display a direction preference: They respond more robustly to the movement of a straight line across their receptive fields in a particular direction.

The third way that complex cortical cells differ from simple cortical cells is that many are **binocular.** Virtually all of the simple cortical cells and the neurons of the retina-geniculate-striate pathway are **monocular:** They respond to stimulation of either the right eye or the left eye, but not to both. In contrast, over half the complex cortical cells respond to stimulation of either eye. If the receptive field of a binocular complex cell is measured through one eye and then the other, the two receptive fields turn out to have almost exactly the same position in the visual field, as well as the

On-center cells. Cells that respond to lights shone in the center of their receptive fields with "on" firing and to lights shone in the periphery of their fields with "off" firing.

Off-center cells. Neurons that respond to lights shone in the center of their receptive fields with "off" firing and to lights shone in the periphery of their fields with "on" firing.

Simple cells. Neurons in the visual cortex that respond maximally to straight-edge stimuli in a certain position and orientation.

Complex cells. Neurons in the visual cortex that respond optimally to straight-edge stimuli in a certain orientation in any part of their receptive field.

Binocular. Involving both eyes.

Monocular. Involving only one eye.

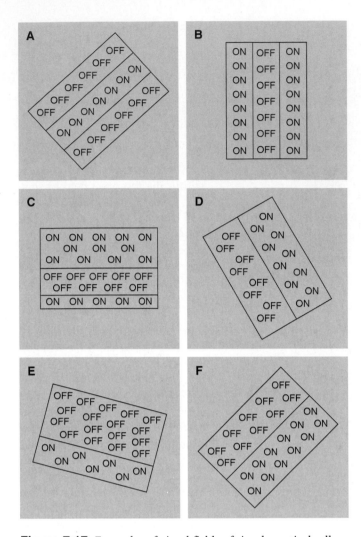

Figure 7.17 Examples of visual fields of simple cortical cells.

same orientation preference. In other words, what you learn about the cell by stimulating one eye is confirmed by stimulating the other. What is more, if the appropriate stimulation is applied through both eyes simultaneously, a binocular cell usually fires more robustly than if only one eye is stimulated.

Over 50% of the binocular cells in the primary visual cortex of the monkey display some degree of ocular dominance; that is, they respond more robustly to stimulation of one eye than they do to the same stimulation of the other. In addition, some binocular cells fire best when the preferred stimulus is presented to both eyes at the same time but in slightly different positions on the two retinas (e.g., Bishop & Pettigrew, 1986). In other words, these cells

Aggregate field. The area encompassing all of the receptive fields of all of the neurons in a given column of visual cortex.

respond to *retinal disparity* and thus likely play a role in depth perception (Ohzawa, DeAngelis, & Freeman, 1990).

Columnar Organization of Primary Visual Cortex

The study of the receptive fields of primary visual cortex neurons has led to two important conclusions. The first conclusion is that the characteristics of the receptive fields of visual cortex neurons are attributable to the flow of signals from neurons with simpler receptive fields to those with more complex fields. Specifically, it seems that signals flow from on-center and off-center cells in lower layer IV to simple cells and from simple cells to complex cells.

The second conclusion is that primary visual cortex neurons are grouped in functional vertical columns; in this context, *vertical* means at right angles to the cortical layers. Much of the evidence for this conclusion comes from studies of the receptive fields of neurons along various vertical and horizontal electrode tracks (see Figure 7.18). If one advances an electrode vertically through the layers of the visual cortex, stopping to plot the receptive fields of many cells along the way, each cell in the column has a receptive field in the same general area of the visual field. The area of the visual field covered by all of the receptive fields of cells in a given column is called the **aggregate field** of that column. Furthermore, all of the cells in a column respond best to straight lines in the same orientation, and those that are monocular or that display ocular dominance are most responsive to stimulation of the same eye. In contrast, if an electrode is advanced horizontally through the tissue, each successive cell encountered is likely to have a receptive field in a slightly different location and to be maximally responsive to straight lines of a slightly different orientation. And during a horizontal electrode pass, the tip passes alternately through areas of left-eye dominance and right-eye dominance.

All of the functional columns in the primary visual cortex that analyze input from one area of the retina are clustered together. Half of a cluster receives input primarily from the left eye, and half receives input primarily from the right eye. Indeed, input from the eyes has been found to enter layer IV independently in alternating patches. The best evidence of this alternating arrangement comes from a study (LeVay, Hubel, & Wiesel, 1975) in which a radioactive amino acid was injected into one eye in sufficient quantities to cross the synapses of the retina-geniculate-striate system and show up in lower layer IV of the primary visual cortex, and to a lesser degree in the layers just above and below it. The alternating patches of radioactivity and nonradioactivity in the autoradiograph in Figure 7.19 indicate alternating patches of input from the two eyes.

All of the clusters of functional columns that analyze input from one area of the retina are thought to include neurons with preferences for straight-line stimuli of various orientations. The columns of orientation specificity

Figure 7.18 The organization of the primary visual cortex: The receptive-field properties of cells encountered along typical vertical and horizontal electrode tracks in the primary visual cortex.

Figure 7.19 The alternation of input into lower layer IV of the primary visual cortex from the left and right eyes. Radioactive amino acids that were injected into one eye were subsequently revealed on autoradiographs of the visual cortex as patches of radioactivity alternating with patches of nonradioactivity. (From "Brain Mechanism of Vision" by D. H. Hubel and T. N. Wiesel. Reprinted by permission of *Scientific American*, vol. 241, p. 151. Copyright © 1979 by Scientific American, Inc.)

Figure 7.20 The columns of orientation specificity in the primary visual cortex of the monkey as revealed by 2-DG autoradiography. (From "Orientation Columns in Macaque Monkey Visual Cortex Demonstrated by the 2-Deoxyglucose Autoradiographic Technique" by D. H. Hubel, T. N. Wiesel, and M. P. Stryker. Reprinted by permission from *Nature,* vol. 269, p. 329. Copyright © 1977 by Macmillan Magazines Ltd.)

were visualized in a study (Hubel, Wiesel, & Stryker, 1977) in which radioactive 2-DG was injected into monkeys that then spent 45 minutes viewing a pattern of vertical stripes moving back and forth. As you know from previous chapters, radioactive 2-DG is taken up by active neurons and accumulates in them, thus identifying the location of neurons that are particularly active during the test period. The autoradiograph in Figure 7.20 reveals the columns of cells in the primary visual cortex that were activated by exposure to the moving vertical stripes. Notice that the neurons in layer IV show no orientation specificity—because they do not respond to straight-line stimuli.

Figure 7.21 summarizes Hubel and Wiesel's theory of how the vertical columns of the primary visual cortex are organized.

Spatial-Frequency Theory

Hubel and Wiesel barely had time to place their Nobel Prizes on their mantel before an important qualification to their theory was proposed. DeValois, DeValois, and their colleagues (see DeValois & DeValois, 1988) proposed that the visual cortex operates on a code of spatial frequency, not on the code of straight lines and edges hypothesized by Hubel and Wiesel.

In support of the **spatial-frequency theory** is the observation that visual cortex neurons respond even more robustly to sine-wave gratings that are placed at specific angles in their receptive fields than they do to bars or edges. A **sine-wave grating** is a set of equally spaced, parallel, alternating light and dark stripes that is created by varying the light across the grating in a sine-wave pattern—see Figure 7.22. Sine-wave gratings differ from one another in frequency (the width of their stripes), amplitude (the magnitude of the difference in intensity between the dark and light stripes), and angle.

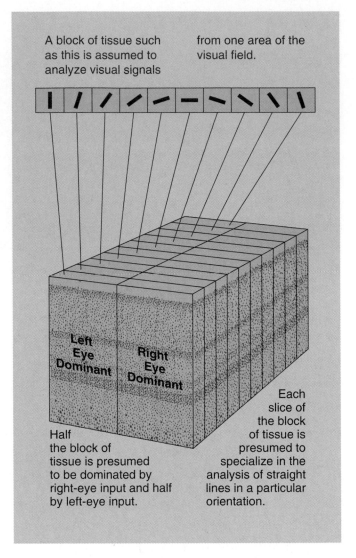

Figure 7.21 Hubel and Wiesel's model of the organization of functional columns in the primary visual cortex.

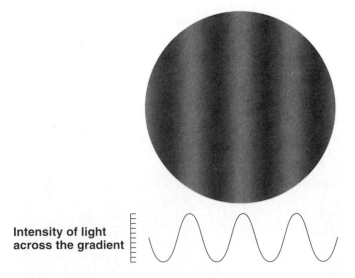

Figure 7.22 A sine-wave grating. (Adapted from DeValois & DeValois, 1988.)

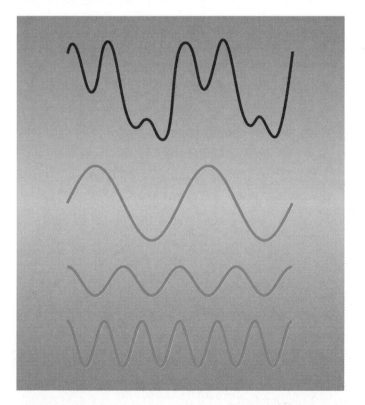

Figure 7.23 A visual stimulus represented by the plotting of changes in the intensity of light along slices running through it. For example, plotted here are the changes in intensity along one slice of a scene that would interest any hungry lion.

The spatial-frequency theory is based on two physical principles. The first is that any visual stimulus can be represented by a plotting of the intensity of light along lines running through it (see Figure 7.23). The second is that any curve, no matter how irregular, can be broken down into constituent sine waves by a mathematical procedure called **Fourier analysis** (see Figure 7.24).

The spatial-frequency theory of visual cortex function (see DeValois & DeValois, 1988) is that each functional module of the visual cortex performs a sort of Fourier analysis on the visual pattern in its receptive field; the neurons in each module are thought to respond selectively to various frequencies and orientations of sine-wave gratings. When all of the visual cortex neurons that are influenced by a particular scene respond together, a perception of the scene is created by the summation of its various constituent sine-wave gratings.

The primary support for the spatial-frequency theory is that primary visual cortex neurons are more responsive to sine-wave gratings than they are to straight lines. Most neurons in the primary visual cortex respond best when a sine-wave grating of a particular frequency is presented at a particular angle in a particular location of the visual field. However, straight-edge stimuli, which have been used in most studies of visual cortex neurons, can readily be translated into component sine-wave gratings of the same orientation. Thus the research on spatial-frequency detection by visual neurons extends and complements previous research rather than refuting it.

Figure 7.24 Any wave can be broken down into component sine waves by Fourier analysis. For example, the complex wave at the top is the sum of the sine waves shown beneath it. (Adapted from DeValois & DeValois, 1988.)

Spatial-frequency theory. The theory that the visual cortex encodes visual patterns in terms of their component sine-wave gratings.

Sine-wave grating. An array of equally spaced, parallel, alternating dark and light stripes that is created by varying the light across the grating in a sine-wave pattern.

Fourier analysis. A mathematical procedure for breaking down a complex wave form (e.g., an EEG signal) into component sine waves of varying frequency.

Color is one of the most obvious qualities of human visual experience. So far in this chapter, we have limited our discussion of vision to the so-called **achromatic colors**: black, white, and gray. Black is experienced when there is an absence of light, the perception of white is produced by an intense mixture of a wide range of wavelengths in roughly equal proportion, and the perception of gray is produced by the same mixture at lower intensities. In this section, we deal with the perception of **chromatic colors**—colors such as blue, green, and yellow. The correct term for chromatic colors is *hues*, but in everyday language they are referred to as colors; and for the sake of simplicity, I will do the same.

What is there about a visual stimulus that determines the color we perceive? To a large degree, the perception of an object's color depends on the wavelengths of light that it reflects into the eye. Figure 7.1 is an illustration of the colors associated with individual wavelengths; however, outside the laboratory, one never encounters objects that reflect single wavelengths. Sunlight and most sources of artificial light contain complex mixtures of most visible wavelengths. Most objects absorb the different wavelengths of light that strike them to varying degrees and reflect the rest. It is the mixture of wavelengths that an object reflects that influences our perception of its color.

With the development and refinement of methods for studying the responses of individual receptors and neurons in the visual system, an impressive amount has been learned in the last two or three decades about how the visual system responds to different wavelengths. However, in some ways, it is even more impressive that the basic mechanisms of color vision were derived in the last century by behaviorial scientists whose research technology was limited to their own ingenuity and observational skills. Through careful observation of the perceptual abilities of their subjects, these scientists were able to infer some of the major features of the physiological basis of color vision.

You have already encountered in this chapter many instances in which scientific gains have resulted from the convergence of behavioral, neurochemical, and neurophysiological research. However, the early advances in the study of the neural basis of color vision occurred long before it was possible to bring modern neurochemical and neurophysiological procedures to bear.

Component and Opponent Processing

The **component theory** (trichromatic theory) of color vision was proposed by Thomas Young in 1802 and refined by Hermann von Helmholtz in 1852. According to this theory, there are three different kinds of color receptors (cones), each with a different spectral sensitivity, and the color of a particular stimulus is presumed to be encoded by the ratio of activity in the three kinds of receptors. Young and Helmholtz derived their theory from the observation that any color of the visible spectrum can be matched by a mixing together of three different wavelengths of light in different proportions. This can be accomplished with any three wavelengths, provided that the color of any one of them cannot be matched by a mixing of the other two. The fact that three is normally the minimum number of different wavelengths necessary to match every color suggested that there were three types of receptors.

Another theory of color vision, the **opponent-process theory** of color vision, was proposed by Ewald Hering in 1878. He suggested that there are two different classes of cells in the visual system for encoding color and another one for encoding brightness. Hering hypothesized that each of the three classes of cells encoded two complementary color perceptions. One class of color-coding cells signaled red by changing its activity in one direction (e.g., hyperpolarization) and signaled red's complementary color, green, by changing its activity in the other direction (e.g., hypopolarization). Another class of color-coding cells was hypothesized to signal blue and its complement, yellow, in the same opponent fashion; and a class of brightness-coding cells was hypothesized to similarly signal both black and white. **Complementary colors** are pairs of colors that produce white or gray when combined in equal measure (e.g., green light and red light).

Hering based his opponent-process theory of color vision on several behavioral observations. One was that the com-

Achromatic colors. Black, white, and gray.

Chromatic colors. The hues—colors such as blue, green, and yellow.

Component theory. The theory that the relative amount of activity produced in three different classes of cones by a light determines its perceived color.

Opponent-process theory. The theory that a receptor or neuron signals one color when it responds in one way (e.g., by increasing its firing rate) and signals its complementary color when it responds in the opposite way (e.g., by decreasing its firing rate).

Complementary colors. Pairs of colors that produce white or gray when combined in equal measure; every color has a complementary color.

Microspectrophotometry. A technique that has been used to measure the absorption spectrum of the photopigment contained in a single visual receptor.

plementary colors blue and yellow cannot exist together; nor can the complementary colors red and green. (There is no such thing as bluish yellow or reddish green.) Another was that the afterimage produced by staring at red is green and vice versa, and the afterimage produced by staring at yellow is blue and vice versa (see the following demonstration).

Have you ever noticed complementary afterimages? To see them, stare at the fixation point in the left panel for 1 minute without moving your eyes; then quickly shift your gaze to the fixation point in the right panel. In the right panel, you will see four squares whose colors are complementary to those in the left panel.

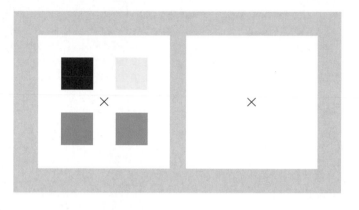

A somewhat misguided debate raged for many years between supporters of the component (trichromatic) and opponent theories of color vision. I say "misguided" because it was fueled more by the adversarial predisposition of scientists than by the incompatibility of the two theories. In fact, research subsequently proved that both color-coding mechanisms coexist in the same visual systems (see Hurlbert, 1991).

It was the development in the early 1960s of **microspectrophotometry**—a technique for measuring the absorption spectrum of the photopigment contained in a single cone—that allowed researchers to confirm the conclusion that had been reached by Young over a century and a half before (e.g., Dartnall, Bowmaker, & Mollon, 1983; MacNichol, 1964; Marks, Dobelle, & MacNichol, 1964; Wald, 1964). They found that there are indeed three different kinds of cones in the retinas of those vertebrates with good color vision, and they found that each of the three has a different photopigment with its own characteristic absorption spectrum. As Figure 7.25 illustrates, some cones are most sensitive to short wavelengths; some are most sensitive to medium wavelengths, and some are most sensitive to long wavelengths.

Although the coding of color by cones operates on a purely component basis, there is evidence of opponent processing of color at all subsequent levels of the retina-

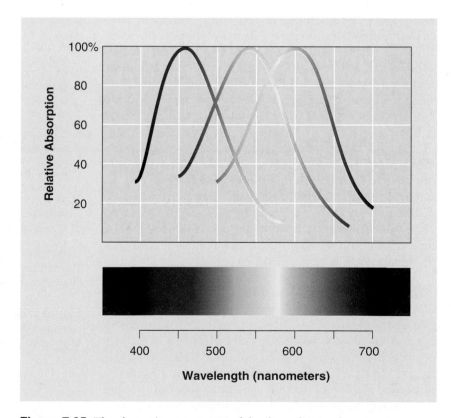

Figure 7.25 The absorption spectrums of the three classes of cones.

geniculate-striate system. The first direct evidence of opponent processing came from a study of bipolar cells in the carp, a fish with excellent color vision (Svaetichin, 1956). Carp bipolar cells respond in one direction (hyperpolarization or depolarization) to red-appearing wavelengths and in the other direction to green-appearing wavelengths. And other retinal cells code both blue-appearing and yellow-appearing wavelengths in the same opponent fashion. Figure 7.26 illustrates a circuit that can translate the component responses of the three types of cones into the red-green and blue-yellow opponent responses of bipolar cells.

Color Constancy and the Retinex Theory

Neither component nor opponent processing can account for the single most important characteristic of color vision: color constancy. **Color constancy** refers to the fact that the perceived color of an object is not a simple function of the wavelengths reflected by it. As I write this at 7:15 on a December morning, it is dark outside, and I am working in my office by the light of a tiny incandescent desk lamp. Later in the morning, when students start to arrive, I turn on my nasty fluorescent office lights; and then, in the afternoon, when the sun has shifted to my side of the building, I turn off the lights and work by natural light. The point is that because these light sources differ markedly in the wavelengths they contain, the wavelengths reflected by various objects in my office—my blue shirt, for example—change substantially during the course of the day. However, although the wavelengths reflected by my shirt change markedly, its color does not. My shirt will be just as blue in midmorning and in late afternoon as it is now. Color constancy is the tendency for an object to stay the same color despite major changes in the wavelengths of light that it reflects.

Although the phenomenon of color constancy is counterintuitive, its advantage is obvious. Color vision improves our ability to tell objects apart in a memorable way so we can respond appropriately to them. However, unreliable distinctions are useless; indeed, they are a hindrance. Our ability to recognize objects would be greatly lessened if their color changed every time there was a major change in illumination (Brou et al., 1986).

Although color constancy is an important feature of our vision, we are normally unaware of it. Under everyday conditions, we have no way of appreciating the major changes that can occur in the wavelengths reflected by an object without the object changing its color. However, in the laboratory, these changes can be controlled and measured. Edwin Land (1977), the inventor of the Polaroid camera, illustrated the nature of color vision in a series of demonstrations in which subjects viewed displays composed of

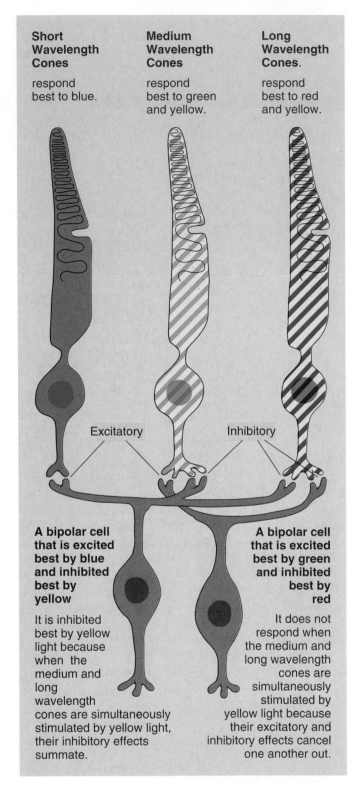

Figure 7.26 A retinal circuit that can translate the component responses of the three types of cones into the red-green and blue-yellow opponent responses of bipolar cells.

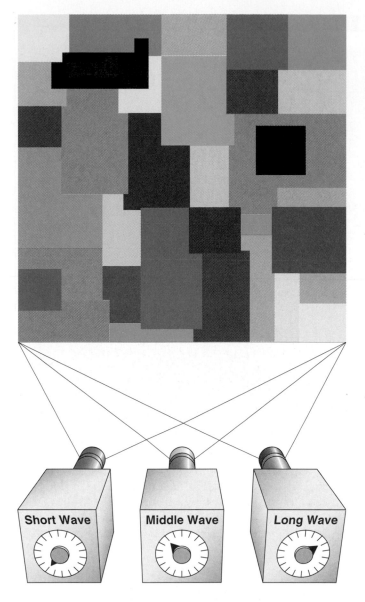

Figure 7.27 Land's (1977) color-vision experiments. Subjects viewed Mondrians that were illuminated by various proportions of three different wavelengths: a short wavelength, a middle wavelength, and a long wavelength.

colored rectangular shapes (see Figure 7.27). These displays are called *Mondrians* because they resemble the paintings of the Dutch master painter Piet Mondrian. Land illuminated each Mondrian with light from three projectors, each of which bathed an entire display with a single wavelength: a short wavelength, a middle wavelength, and a long wavelength.

In one of his demonstrations, Land adjusted the relative amounts of light from the three projectors that were illuminating one Mondrian and the relative amounts of light from the three projectors that were illuminating another. He adjusted them so that the light being reflected by one of the rectangles (let's say a green one) in Mondrian 1 was

exactly the same as the light being reflected by another rectangle (let's say a blue one) in Mondrian 2; he did this by measuring the reflected light with a photometer. The combination of the three wavelengths that was reflected by the green rectangle in Mondrian 1 and the blue rectangle in Mondrian 2 was a combination that was seen as white when viewed as a spot of light in total darkness.

But what color did these wavelengths appear when viewed as part of the Mondrians? All subjects saw the green rectangle in Mondrian 1 as green and the blue rectangle in Mondrian 2 as blue, despite the fact that they were both reflecting exactly the same white wavelengths. Next, without changing the lighting conditions, Land blocked out all parts of the subjects' visual fields except the green and the blue rectangles. Under these conditions, the two rectangles, which were still reflecting exactly the same wavelengths, appeared white.

Land's demonstration makes two important points about color vision. First, the color of objects is not related in any simple way to the wavelengths they reflect. Second, the color of objects depends in some way on the light reflected by surrounding surfaces. How does the visual system produce constant perceptions of an object's color despite wide variations in the wavelengths the object reflects?

According to Land's **retinex theory** of color vision, the color of an object is determined by its *reflectance*—the proportion of light of different wavelengths that a surface reflects. Although the wavelengths of light reflected by a surface change dramatically with changes in illumination, the efficiency with which a surface absorbs each wavelength and reflects the unabsorbed portion does not change. According to the retinex theory, the visual system calculates the reflectance of surfaces, and thus perceives their color, by comparing the ability of adjacent surfaces to absorb light in three different wavelength bands (short, medium, and long), which correspond to the three classes of cones.

The detection of contrast between adjacent areas of the visual field is important in the perception of color. The following demonstration illustrates this point by showing how color constancy can break down when we look at artificial displays that lack sharply defined areas of contrast. Please take the time to experience it; it is an amazing demonstration.

Color constancy. The tendency of an object to appear the same color even when the wavelengths that it reflects change.

Retinex theory. Land's theory that the color of surfaces is determined by their reflectance; with the visual system calculating the reflectance of the surfaces in a scene by comparing the ability of adjacent surfaces to reflect short, medium, and long wavelengths.

The following visual pattern (Brou et al., 1986) illustrates how color constancy can break down when we look at displays that lack sharply defined areas of contrast. Examine it. It may surprise you to learn that the four differently colored hexagons (six-sided figures) are all exactly the same. Although you may have difficulty believing this, you can prove it to yourself by eliminating the effect of the adjacent context. Cut four holes in a piece of paper so that parts of the four hexagons, but not of the rest of the figure, will be visible through them. Place the sheet of paper over the figure and compare the four hexagons. Now do you believe me?

(Courtesy of Jerome Y. Lettvin; photo by Denice Denton and Brad Howland.)

If the perception of color depends on the analysis of contrast between adjacent areas of the visual field, there should be neurons somewhere in the visual system that are responsive to color contrast. And there are. For example, **dual-opponent color cells** in the monkey visual cortex respond with vigorous "on" firing when the center of their circular receptive field is illuminated with one wavelength, such as green, and the surround is simultaneously illuminated with another wavelength, such as red. And the same cells display vigorous "off" firing when the pattern of illumination is reversed—for example, red in the center and green in the surround. In essence, dual-opponent color cells respond to the contrast between wavelengths reflected by adjacent areas of their receptive field.

Dual-opponent color cells. Neurons that respond to the differences in the wavelengths of light stimulating adjacent areas of their receptive field.

Cytochrome oxidase. An enzyme present in particularly high concentrations in the dual-opponent color cells of the visual cortex.

Blobs. Cytochrome oxidase–rich dual-opponent color columns.

A major breakthrough in the understanding of the organization of the primary visual cortex came with the discovery that dual-opponent color cells are not distributed evenly throughout the primary visual cortex (see Zeki, 1993).

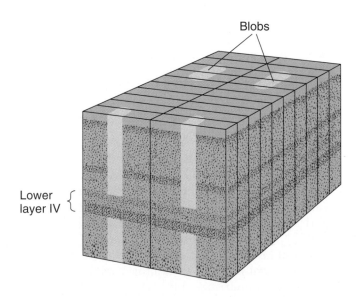

Figure 7.28 Hubel and Livingstone's model of primary visual cortex organization. The blobs are peglike columns that contain dual-opponent color cells.

Livingstone and Hubel (1984) found that these neurons are distributed in the primary visual cortex in peglike columns that penetrate the layers of the primary visual cortex, with the exception of lower layer IV. The neurons in these peglike columns are particularly rich in the mitochondria enzyme **cytochrome oxidase**; thus their distribution in the primary visual cortex can be visualized if one stains slices of tissue with stains that have an affinity for this enzyme.

When a section of striate tissue is cut parallel to the cortical layers and stained in this way, the pegs are seen as "blobs" of stain scattered over the cortex (unless the section is cut from lower layer IV). To the relief of instructors and students alike, the term **blobs** has become the accepted scientific label for peglike, cytochrome oxidase rich dual-opponent color columns. The blobs were found to be located in the middle of ocular dominance columns, which led Hubel and Livingstone to propose the model of primary visual cortex organization illustrated in Figure 7.28 (which is an adaptation of Hubel and Wiesel's original model).

Conclusion

This chapter began by describing the passage of light into the eye to the receptor layer of the retina (7.1). Then, it described the transduction (translation) of light into neural signals (7.2) Next, it followed the transmission of neural signals from the retinal receptors to the primary visual cortex via the retina-geniculate-striate system (7.3). It concluded by discussing the aspects of retina-geniculate-striate system structure and function that influence the perception of brightness contrast (7.4) and color (7.5).

The major theme of this chapter was that vision is a creative process. The retina-geniculate-striate pathway does not conduct intact visual images to the cortex. It conducts, via two major channels (the P channel and the M channel), information about a few critical features of the visual world—for example, information about location, movement, brightness contrast, and color contrast; and from these bits of information, it creates a perception that is better in some respects than the external reality from which it was created. The theme of converging operations pervades much of this book, but the study of the visual system is arguably the single best example of how major insights into the neural bases of psychological processes require the convergence of neuroanatomical, neurochemical, neurophysiological, and behavioral research.

In this chapter, there were opportunities for you to experience first-hand important principles of the visual process. I hope these demonstrations made you more aware of the amazing abilities of your own visual system and the relevance of what you have learned in this chapter to your everyday life.

FOOD FOR THOUGHT

1. In vision, as in photography, one frequently has to sacrifice sharpness (acuity) to increase sensitivity. Discuss.

2. Why is it so important to distinguish between intensity and brightness and between wavelength and color?

3. If you mix equal proportions of red and green light, you get white or gray light, or something close to white or gray light, depending on the exact wavelengths of red and green. However, if you mix equal portions of red and green paint, you get an approximation of black paint. Explain this paradox.

KEY TERMS

Sensitivity *(p. 152)*
Acuity *(p. 152)*
Ciliary muscles *(p. 152)*
Accommodation *(p. 152)*
Binocular disparity *(p. 153)*
Receptors *(p. 154)*
Horizontal cells *(p. 154)*
Bipolar cells *(p. 154)*
Amacrine cells *(p. 154)*
Retinal ganglion cells
(p. 154)
Blind spot *(p. 154)*
Fovea *(p. 154)*
Completion *(p. 154)*
Cones *(p. 155)*
Rods *(p. 155)*
Duplexity theory *(p. 156)*
Photopic vision *(p. 156)*
Scotopic vision *(p. 156)*

Nasal hemiretina *(p. 157)*
Temporal hemiretina
(p. 157)
Photopic spectral sensitivity
curve *(p. 157)*
Scotopic spectral sensitivity
curve *(p. 157)*
Purkinje effect *(p. 158)*
Saccades *(p. 158)*
Stabilized retinal image
(p. 158)
Transduction *(p. 159)*
Rhodopsin *(p. 159)*
Absorption spectrum
(p. 160)
Retina-geniculate-striate
pathway *(p. 161)*
Primary visual cortex
(p. 161)

Lateral geniculate nuclei
(p. 161)
Retinotopic *(p. 161)*
Parvocellular layers *(p. 161)*
Magnocellular layers *(p. 161)*
Contrast enhancement
(p. 164)
Ommatidia *(p. 164)*
Lateral plexus *(p. 164)*
Lateral inhibition *(p. 164)*
Receptive field *(p. 165)*
On-center cells *(p. 166)*
Off-center cells *(p. 166)*
Simple cells *(p. 167)*
Complex cells *(p. 167)*
Binocular *(p. 167)*
Monocular *(p. 167)*
Aggregate field *(p. 168)*
Spatial-frequency theory
(p. 170)

Sine-wave grating *(p. 170)*
Fourier analysis *(p. 171)*
Achromatic colors *(p. 172)*
Chromatic colors *(p. 172)*
Component theory *(p. 172)*
Opponent-process theory
(p. 172)
Complementary colors
(p. 172)
Microspectrophotometry
(p. 173)
Color constancy *(p. 174)*
Retinex theory *(p. 175)*
Dual-opponent color cells
(p. 176)
Cytochrome oxidase
(p. 176)
Blobs *(p. 176)*

ADDITIONAL READING

The best introductory readings for those interested in the biopsychology of perception are *Scientific American* articles. Their large color illustrations are without rival. The following seven articles provide excellent coverage of topics discussed in this chapter:

Brou, P., Sciascia, T. R., Linden, L., & Lettvin, J. Y. (1986, September). The colors of things. *Scientific American, 255,* 84–91.

Hubel, D. H., & Wiesel, T. N. (1979, September). Brain mechanisms of vision. *Scientific American, 241,* 150–162.

Land, E. H. (1977, April). The retinex theory of color vision. *Scientific American, 237,* 108–128.

Nathans, J. (1989, February). The genes for color vision. *Scientific American, 260,* 42–49.

Ramachandran, V. (1992, May) Blind spots. *Scientific American, 266,* 86–91.

Ratliff, F. (1972, June). Contour and contrast. *Scientific American, 226,* 90–101.

Schnapf, J. L., & Baylor, D. A. (1987, April). How photoreceptor cells respond to light. *Scientific American, 256,* 40–47.

The following book is a clear summary of current knowledge about vision and the brain. It is a must for every serious student of the topic:

Zeki, S. (1993). *A vision of the brain.* Oxford: Blackwell Scientific Publications.

For those interested in learning more about the spatial-frequency theory of vision, which I could discuss only briefly in this chapter, I recommend the following book:

DeValois, R. L., & DeValois, K. K. (1988). *Spatial vision.* New York: Oxford University Press.

CHAPTER

8

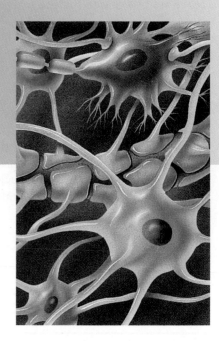

Mechanisms of Perception

8.1 Principles of Sensory System Organization

8.2 Cortical Mechanisms of Vision

8.3 Audition

8.4 Somatosensation: Touch and Pain

8.5 The Chemical Senses: Smell and Taste

8.6 Selective Attention

There are two chapters in this text whose primary focus is sensory: Chapter 7 was the first, and this is the second. Chapter 7 described how visual signals are translated into neural signals by cones and rods, and how these neural signals are conducted by the retina-geniculate-striate system to the primary visual cortex.

This chapter differs from Chapter 7 in two major respects. First, rather than focusing on one sensory system, it discusses all five **exteroceptive sensory systems**—the five sensory systems that interpret stimuli from outside the body: vision, hearing, touch, smell, and taste. Second, rather than focusing on the conduction of sensory signals from receptors to cortex, this chapter focuses on cortical mechanisms and phenomena.

The chapter begins with three general principles of sensory system organization. Then, it returns to the story line initiated in Chapter 7: It returns to the primary visual cortex—the point of entry of visual signals into cortical visual circuits; and it follows these signals as they are subjected to analysis by other areas of visual cortex. Next, the chapter examines the other four exteroceptive sensory systems. It concludes with a discussion of the mechanisms of attention.

The disproportionate coverage of the visual system in Chapters 7 and 8 is not arbitrary. For a variety of reasons, the vast majority of research on sensory systems has focused on the visual system. As a result, far more is known about the visual system than about the other sensory systems, and most current theories of sensory system function are based on visual system research.

8.1 Principles of Sensory System Organization

The sensory areas of the cerebral cortex are of three different types: primary, secondary, and association. The **primary sensory cortex** of a system is the area of sensory cortex that receives most of its input directly from the thalamic relay nuclei of that system. For example, as you learned in Chapter 7, the primary visual cortex is the area of the cerebral cortex that receives most of its input from the lateral geniculate nucleus of the thalamus. The **secondary sensory cortex** of a system is the areas of the sensory cortex that receive most of their input from the primary sensory cortex of that system or from other areas of the secondary sensory cortex of the same system. **Association cortex** is any area of cortex that receives input from more than one sensory system. Most input to areas of association cortex comes via areas of secondary sensory cortex. The interactions among these three types of sensory cortex are characterized by three major principles: hierarchical organization, functional segregation, and parallel processing.

Hierarchical Organization

Sensory systems are characterized by **hierarchical organization.** A *hierarchy* is a system whose members can be assigned to specific levels or ranks in relation to one another. For example, the army is a hierarchical system because all soldiers are ranked with respect to their authority. In the same way, sensory structures are organized in a hierarchy on the basis of the specificity and complexity of their function (see Figure 8.1). As one moves through a sensory system from receptors, to thalamic nuclei, to primary sensory cortex, to secondary sensory cortex, to association cortex, one finds neurons that respond optimally to stimuli of greater and greater specificity and complexity. Each level of a sensory hierarchy receives its input from lower levels and adds another layer of analysis before passing it on up the hierarchy.

The hierarchical organization of sensory systems is apparent from a comparison of the effects of damage to various levels: The higher the level of damage, the more specific and complex the deficit. For example, destruction of a sensory system's receptors produces a complete loss of ability to perceive in that sensory modality (e.g., total blindness or deafness); in contrast, destruction of an area of association or secondary sensory cortex typically produces complex and specific sensory deficits, while leaving fundamental sensory abilities intact. Dr. P., the man who mistook his wife for a hat (Sacks, 1985), displays such a pattern of deficits:

> Dr. P. was a musician of distinction, well-known for many years as a singer ... and as a teacher.... It was obvious within a few seconds of meeting him that there was no trace of dementia [intellectual deterioration].... He was a man of great cul-

Figure 8.1 The hierarchical organization of the sensory systems. The receptors perform the simplest and most general analyses, and the association cortex performs the most complex and specific analyses.

Association Cortex

Secondary Sensory Cortex

Primary Sensory Cortex

Thalamic Relay Nuclei

Receptors

Chapter 8 Mechanisms of Perception

tivation and charm who talked well and fluently, with imagination and humour....

"What seems to be the matter?" I asked him at length.

"Nothing that I know of," he replied with a smile, "but people seem to think that there's something wrong with my eyes."

"But *you* don't recognise any visual problems?"

"No, not directly, but I occasionally make mistakes."...

It was while examining his reflexes ... that the first bizarre experience occurred. I had taken off his left shoe and scratched the sole of his foot with a key—a frivolous-seeming but essential test of a reflex—and then, excusing myself to screw my ophthalmoscope together, left him to put on the shoe himself. To my surprise, a minute later, he had not done this.

"Can I help?" I asked.

"Help what? Help whom?"...

"Your shoe," I repeated. "Perhaps you'd put it on."

He continued to look downwards, though not at the shoe, with an intense but misplaced concentration. Finally his gaze settled on his foot.

"That is my shoe, yes?" Did I mis-hear? Did he mis-see?

"My eyes," he explained, and put his hand to his foot. "This is my shoe, no?"

"No, it is not. That is your foot. *There* is your shoe."

Was he joking? Was he mad? Was he blind? If this was one of his "strange mistakes," it was the strangest mistake I had ever come across.

I helped him on with his shoe (his foot), to avoid further complication.... I resumed my examination. His visual acuity was good; he had no difficulty seeing a pin on the floor....

He saw all right, but what did he see?...

"What is this?" I asked, holding up a glove.

"May I examine it?" he asked, taking it from me.

"A continuous surface," he announced at last, "infolded on itself. It appears to have"—he hesitated—"five outpouchings, if this is the word."

"Yes," I said cautiously. "You have given me a description. Now tell me what it is."

"A container of some sort?"

"Yes," I said, "and what would it contain?"

"It would contain its contents!" said Dr. P., with a laugh. "There are many possibilities. It could be a change purse, for example, for coins of five sizes. It could ..."

"Does it not look familiar? Do you think it might contain, might fit, a part of the body?"

No light of recognition dawned on his face ...

I must have looked aghast, but he seemed to think he had done rather well. There was a hint of a smile on his face. He also appeared to have decided the examination was over and started to look around for his hat. He reached out his hand and took hold of his wife's head, tried to lift it off, to put it on. He had apparently mistaken his wife for a hat! His wife looked as if she was used to such things.[1]

---

[1]From *The Man Who Mistook His Wife for a Hat and Other Clinical Tales* (pp. 7–13) by Oliver Sacks, 1985, New York: Summit Books. Copyright © 1970, 1981, 1983, 1984, 1985 by Oliver Sacks. Reprinted by permission of Summit Books, a division of Simon & Schuster, Inc.

In recognition of the hierarchical organization of sensory systems, psychologists sometimes divide the general process of perceiving into two general phases: sensation and perception. **Sensation** is the process of detecting the presence of stimuli, and **perception** is the higher-order process of integrating, recognizing, and interpreting complete patterns of sensations. Dr. P.'s problem was clearly one of visual perception, not visual sensation.

Functional Segregation

It was once assumed that the primary, secondary, and association areas of a sensory system were each *functionally homogeneous*. That is, it was assumed that all areas of cortex at any given level of a sensory hierarchy acted together to perform the same function. However, recent research has shown that **functional segregation,** rather than functional homogeneity, characterizes the organization of sensory systems. It is now clear that each of the three levels of cerebral cortex in each sensory system—primary, secondary, and association—contains functionally distinct areas that specialize in different kinds of analysis.

Exteroceptive sensory systems. The five sensory systems that interpret stimuli from outside the body: vision, hearing, touch, smell, and taste.

Primary sensory cortex. An area of sensory cortex that receives most of its input directly from the thalamic relay nuclei of one sensory system.

Secondary sensory cortex. Areas of sensory cortex that receive most of their input from the primary sensory cortex of one system or from other areas of secondary cortex of the same system.

Association cortex. Areas of the cortex that receive input from more than one sensory system.

Hierarchical organization. Organization by a series of levels that can be ranked with respect to one another; for example, primary cortex, secondary cortex, and association cortex perform progressively more detailed analyses.

Sensation. The simple process of detecting the presence of stimuli.

Perception. The higher-order process of integrating, recognizing, and interpreting complex patterns of sensations.

Functional segregation. Organization into different areas, each of which performs a different function; for example, in sensory systems, different areas of secondary and association cortex analyze different aspects of the same sensory stimulus.

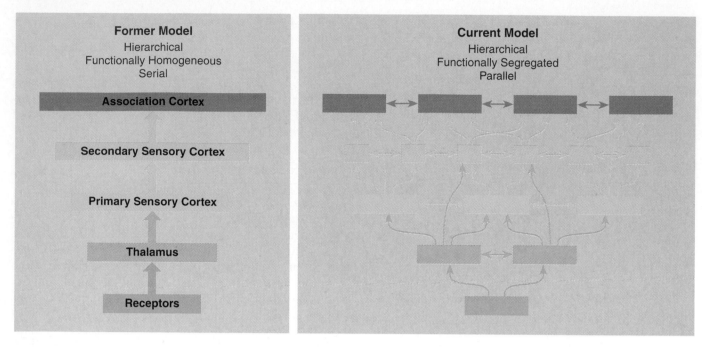

Figure 8.2 Two models of sensory system organization. The former model was hierarchical, functionally homogeneous, and serial; the current model is hierarchical, functionally segregated, and parallel. Not shown in the current model are descending pathways that provide feedback from higher levels to lower levels.

Parallel Processing

It was once believed that the different levels of a sensory hierarchy were connected in a serial fashion. A *serial system* is a system in which information flows among the components over just one pathway, like a string through a strand of beads. However, recent evidence has shown that sensory systems are *parallel systems*—systems in which information flows through the components over multiple pathways. Parallel systems feature **parallel processing**—the simultaneous analysis of a signal in different ways by the multiple parallel pathways of a neural network.

The Current Model of Sensory System Organization

Figure 8.2 summarizes the information in this section of the chapter by illustrating how thinking about the organization of sensory systems has changed. In the 1960s, sensory systems were believed to be hierarchical, functionally homogeneous, and serial. However, four decades of subsequent research have established that sensory systems are hierarchical, functionally segregated, and parallel (see Zeki, 1993a).

Sensory systems are characterized by a division of labor: multiple specialized areas, at multiple levels, interconnected by multiple parallel pathways. Yet, complex stimuli are normally perceived as integrated wholes, not as combinations of independent attributes. How does the brain combine individual sensory attributes to produce integrated perceptions? One possibility is that there is a single area of the cortex at the top of the sensory hierarchy that receives signals from all other areas of the sensory system and puts them together to form perceptions; however, there are no areas of cortex to which all areas of a single sensory system report. It seems, then, that perceptions must be a product of the combined activity of the many cortical areas of each sensory system (see Zeki, 1993a). The various cortical areas of each sensory system are richly interconnected by the major pathways ascending the sensory hierarchy, by minor reciprocal descending pathways (not shown in Figure 8.2), and by a rich web of lateral connections between areas at the same level of the hierarchy.

Parallel processing. The simultaneous analysis of a signal in different ways by the multiple parallel pathways of a neural network.

Prestriate cortex. The area of secondary visual cortex just anterior to the primary visual cortex.

Inferotemporal cortex. The cortex of the inferior temporal lobe, an area of the secondary visual cortex that is involved in object recognition.

Posterior parietal cortex. An area of association cortex that receives input from the visual, auditory, and somatosensory systems and is involved in the perception of spatial location.

Scotoma. An area of blindness in the visual field.

Perimetry test. The procedure used to map scotomas.

All occipital cortex as well as large areas of temporal cortex and parietal cortex are involved in vision (see Figure 8.3). The *primary visual cortex* is located in the posterior region of the occipital lobes, much of it hidden from view in the longitudinal fissure. The *secondary visual cortex* is located in two areas: the prestriate cortex and the inferotemporal cortex. The **prestriate cortex** is the band of tissue in the occipital lobe that surrounds the primary visual cortex. The **inferotemporal cortex** is the cortex of the inferior temporal lobe. Areas of the association cortex that receive visual input are located in several parts of the cerebral cortex, but the largest single area is in the **posterior parietal cortex.**

In keeping with the general hierarchical organization of the sensory cortex, the major flow of visual information is from the primary visual cortex to the secondary visual cortex to the association cortex. As one moves up this visual hierarchy, the neurons have larger receptive fields and the stimuli to which the neurons respond are more specific and complex (see Zeki, 1993b).

Scotomas and Completion

Damage to an area of the primary visual cortex produces a **scotoma**—an area of blindness—in the corresponding area of the contralateral visual field of both eyes (see Figure 7.12). Neurological patients with suspected damage to the primary visual cortex are usually given a **perimetry test.** While the patient's head is held motionless on a chin rest,

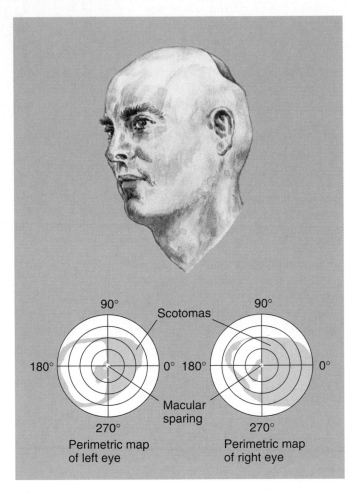

Figure 8.4 The perimetric maps of a subject with a bullet wound in his left primary visual cortex. The scotomas (areas of blindness) are indicated in gray. (Adapted from Teuber, Battersby, & Bender, 1960.)

the patient stares with one eye at a fixation point on a screen. A small dot of light is then flashed on various parts of the screen, and the patient presses a button to record when the dot is seen. Then, the entire process is repeated for the other eye. The result is a map of the visual field of each eye, which indicates any areas of blindness. Figure 8.4 illustrates the perimetric maps of the visual fields of a man with a bullet wound in his left primary visual cortex. Notice the massive scotoma in the right visual field of each eye.

Many patients with extensive scotomas are unaware of their deficits. One of the factors that contributes to this lack of aware-

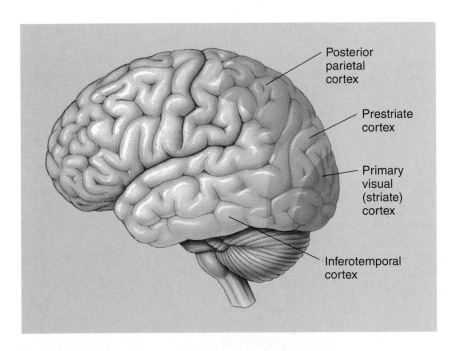

Figure 8.3 The visual areas of the human cerebral cortex.

ness is the phenomenon of **completion** (see Chapter 7). When patients with a scotoma look at a complex figure, part of which lies in their scotoma, they often report seeing a complete image. In some cases, this completion may depend on residual visual capacities in the scotoma; however, completion also occurs in cases in which this explanation can be ruled out. For example, some **hemianopsic** patients (patients with a scotoma that covers half their field of vision) see an entire face when they focus on a person's nose, even when the side of the face in the scotoma has been covered by a blank card.

Consider the completion phenomenon experienced by the esteemed physiological psychologist Karl Lashley (1941), who often developed a large scotoma next to his fovea during a migraine attack (see Figure 8.5):

Lashley's Scotoma   What Lashley saw

Figure 8.5 The completion of a migraine-induced scotoma as described by Karl Lashley.

> Talking with a friend I glanced just to the right of his face wherein his head disappeared. His shoulders and necktie were still visible but the vertical stripes on the wallpaper behind him seemed to extend down to the necktie. It was impossible to see this as a blank area when projected on the striped wallpaper of uniformly patterned surface although any intervening object failed to be seen.

Blindsight: Seeing without Consciousness

Patients who have lost all of their primary visual cortex report being totally blind—which is not surprising. It is surprising, however, that some of these cortically blind patients can perform visually guided tasks, such as grabbing a moving object, all the while claiming to see nothing. Also, if encouraged to guess, they can often reliably indicate the direction of movement, the orientation, and even the identity of objects that they do not consciously see.

The ability of cortically blind subjects to perform visually mediated tasks without conscious awareness of vision is known as **blindsight** (see Corbetta et al., 1990; Cowey & Stoerig, 1991; Stoerig, 1993). If blindsight confuses you, imagine how it confuses people who experience it. Consider, for example, the reactions to blindsight of D.B., a patient who was blind in his left visual field following surgical removal of his right occipital lobe (Weiskrantz et al., 1974):

> Even though the patient had no awareness of "seeing" in his blind [left] field, evidence was obtained that (a) he could reach for visual stimuli [in his left field] with con-

siderable accuracy; (b) could differentiate the orientation of a vertical line from a horizontal or diagonal line; (c) could differentiate the letters "X" and "O". (p. 726)

> Needless to say, he was questioned repeatedly about his vision in his left half-field, and his most common response was that he saw nothing at all.... When he was shown his results [through his good, right-half field] he expressed surprise and insisted several times that he thought he was just "guessing." When he was shown a video film of his reaching and judging orientation of lines, he was openly astonished. (p. 721)

How can subjects with damage to primary visual cortex "see" features of visual stimuli—primarily their location, orientation, and movement—without being aware that they are seeing anything at all? The answer likely lies in the fact that not all visual signals are funneled from subcortical circuits to secondary visual cortex through primary visual cortex; a few parallel tracts ascend directly from subcortical structures into the prestriate area. The current wisdom

Completion. The visual system's automatic use of information obtained from receptors around a scotoma to create a perception of the missing portion of the retinal image.

Hemianopsic. Having a scotoma that covers half their field of vision.

Blindsight. The ability of cortically blind subjects to perform visually mediated tasks without conscious awareness of vision.

Subjective contours. Perceived visual contours that do not exist.

A   B

C

Figure 8.6 Subjective contours. You see the white bar in A and the white triangle in B even though they do not physically exist—they are subjective contours. Your ability to see subjective contours helps you see boundaries between objects of similar brightness, color, and pattern—for example, look at C.

(e.g., Zeki, 1993a) is that the integrity of the primary visual cortex is required for conscious perception, whereas ascending visual pathways that bypass the primary visual cortex carry visual information that can guide behavior without entering conscious awareness (however, see Gazzaniga, Fendrich, & Wessinger, 1994).

Perception of Subjective Contours

Do you recall the theme of the preceding chapter—that our visual perceptions are often better than the physical reality of the visual input? Figure 8.6 illustrates this point (see Spillman & Werner, 1990) by showing that we often see visual contours where none exist. Perceived visual contours that do not exist are called **subjective contours.**

Subjective contours have long been thought to be a product of the highest levels of visual analysis. It was believed that they are a product of the association cortex's efforts to make sense of ambiguous stimuli. However,

recent studies have shown that prestriate neurons (Peterhans & von der Heydt, 1991) and even primary visual cortex neurons (Grosof, Shapley, & Hawken, 1993) respond when subjective contours of the appropriate orientation appear in their receptive fields (see Figure 8.7).

Functional Segregation in Visual Cortex: The Dorsal and Ventral Streams

A major turning point in the understanding of the visual system was the discovery that secondary visual cortex is composed of many different functional areas, each specialized to analyze a different aspect of visual input and each organized to provide a complete map of the retina. Most of the information about these functional areas has come from studies of the responsiveness of monkey cortical neurons to various types of visual stimuli; the neurons in different areas are responsive to different aspects of visual input (e.g., color or movement). For example, in the macaque monkey, there are 31 different visual areas outside primary visual cortex: 24 in secondary visual cortex and 7 in association cortex (Van Essen et al., 1992). These areas are prodigiously interconnected. Anterograde and retrograde tracing studies have identified over 300 interconnecting pathways (Van Essen et al., 1992). Although connections between areas are virtually always reciprocal, the major flow of information is up the hierarchy from more simple to more complex areas.

Figure 8.7 Neurons of the monkey prestriate cortex and primary visual cortex respond to subjective contours of a particular orientation. (Adapted from Peterhans & von der Heydt, 1991.)

Positron emission tomography (PET) has been used to identify various areas of secondary visual cortex in humans (see Kaas, 1992). For example, Zeki and his colleagues used PET to identify an area of human prestriate cortex that seems to be involved in the perception of color and another that seems to be involved in the perception of movement (see Figure 8.8).

As you learned in Chapter 7, visual information enters the primary visual cortex from the lateral geniculate nuclei via the *P pathway*, which carries information about color and fine pattern details, and the *M pathway*, which carries information about movement. In the primary visual cortex, the information from these two pathways is received, combined, and then segregated into multiple pathways that project separately to various areas of secondary visual cortex (see Maunsell, 1992; Merigan & Maunsell, 1993). Ungerleider and Mishkin (1982) were the first to point out that the many pathways over which information flows from the primary visual cortex are organized into two major streams: dorsal and ventral. The **dorsal stream** flows from the primary visual cortex to the dorsal prestriate cortex to the posterior parietal cortex, and the **ventral stream** flows from the primary

Figure 8.9 Information about particular aspects of a visual display flow out of the primary visual cortex over many pathways. The pathways can be grouped into two general streams: dorsal and ventral.

visual cortex to the ventral prestriate cortex to the inferotemporal cortex (Baizer, Ungerleider, & Desimone, 1991)—see Figure 8.9.

Ungerleider and Mishkin (1982) proposed that the dorsal and ventral visual streams perform different visual functions. They suggested that the dorsal stream is involved in the perception of "where" objects are and the ventral stream is involved in the perception of "what" objects are. Some of the evidence in support of this "where" versus "what" theory has come from the comparison of the effects of damage to the dorsal and ventral streams (see Ungerleider & Haxby, 1994). Patients with damage to the posterior parietal cortex often have difficulty reaching accurately for objects that they have no difficulty identifying (Perenin & Vighetto, 1988); conversely, patients with damage to the inferotemporal cortex often have no difficulty reaching accurately for objects that they have difficulty identifying (Farah, 1990).

Goodale and Milner have recently proposed an alternative to the "where" versus "what" theory (Goodale, 1993; Goodale & Milner, 1992; Milner & Goodale, 1993). They have suggested that the key difference between the dorsal and ventral streams is not the kinds of information they carry but the use to which that information is put.

Figure 8.8 An area of the human visual cortex that responds selectively to colored, but not gray, images and another that responds selectively to moving, but not stationary, images. (Adapted from Zeki et al., 1991.)

They suggest that the function of the dorsal stream is to direct behavioral interactions with objects, whereas the function of the ventral stream is to mediate the conscious perception of objects—"how" versus "what." In support of their "how" versus "what" interpretation, Goodale and Milner have pointed out that patients with dorsal damage who have difficulty in picking up objects under visual control can often describe the size, location, shape, and movement of objects in great detail; and conversely, that patients with ventral damage who have difficulty describing the size, location, shape, and movement of objects can often show by the precision of their reaching and grasping behavior that these attributes have been perceived at some level.

Consider the case of D.F., a patient with damage to the prestriate cortex (Goodale et al., 1991). As Goodale and Milner (1992) note:

> Despite her profound inability to recognize the size, shape and orientation of visual objects, DF showed strikingly accurate guidance of hand and finger movements directed at the very same objects. Thus, when she was presented with a pair of rectangular blocks of the same or different dimensions, she was unable to distinguish between them. When she was asked to indicate the width of a single block by means of her index finger and thumb, her matches bore no relationship to the dimensions of the object and showed considerable trial to trial variability. However, when she was asked simply to reach out and pick up the block, the aperture between her index finger and thumb changed systematically with the width of the object, just as in normal subjects. In other words, DF scaled her grip to the dimensions of the objects she was about to pick up, even though she appeared to be unable to "perceive" those dimensions.
>
> A similar dissociation was seen in her responses to the orientation of stimuli. Thus, when presented with a large slot that could be placed in one of a number of different orientations, she showed great difficulty in indicating the orientation either verbally or manually (i.e., by rotating her hand or a hand-held card). Nevertheless, she was as good as normal subjects at reaching out and placing her hand or the card into the slot, turning her hand appropriately from the very onset of the movement. (p. 22)

Visual Agnosia

Agnosia is a failure of recognition (*gnosis* means "to know") that is not attributable to a sensory deficit or to verbal or intellectual impairment. Most cases of agnosia are specific to a particular sensory system; the patient cannot recognize material when it is presented in one sensory modality but can recognize it when it is presented in another.

Visual agnosia is agnosia for visual stimuli; visual agnosics can see visual stimuli, but they don't know what they are. (Recall the case of Dr. P., the man who mistook his wife for a hat.) Visual agnosias are sometimes specific to a particular aspect of visual input and are named accordingly; for example, *movement agnosia, object agnosia,* and *color agnosia* are difficulties in recognizing movement, objects, and colors, respectively. It is presumed that each specific visual agnosia results from damage to a particular area of secondary visual cortex that mediates the recognition of that particular attribute (see Zeki, 1993a).

Prosopagnosia is visual agnosia for faces. It has generated considerable interest because of its theoretical implications (see Damasio, Tranel, & Damasio, 1990). Patients with prosopagnosia have difficulty telling one human face from another; in severe cases, they cannot recognize their own face in a mirror. However, they do not have difficulty recognizing faces as faces or in identifying individual components of faces (e.g., noses, eyes, and ears). Remarkably, prosopagnosics display large skin conductance responses to pictures of familiar faces that they do not consciously recognize (Tranel & Damasio,1985); these responses indicate that the recognition of faces is still occurring at a level of the nervous system that does not involve conscious awareness.

One theory of prosopagnosia is that it results from damage to an area of the visual cortex that is specifically dedicated to the recognition of faces. The main evidence for this view is that patients who have difficulty recognizing faces have little difficulty recognizing other test objects (e.g., a chair, a pencil, or a door). Stop reading for a moment and give this line of evidence some thought: It is seriously flawed. Because prosopagnosics have no difficulty recognizing faces as faces, the fact that they can recognize chairs as chairs, pencils as pencils, and doors as doors is not relevant. The critical question is whether they can recognize which chair, which pencil, and which door. Careful testing of some prosopagnosics has revealed that their recognition deficits are not restricted to faces: A farmer lost his ability to recognize particular cows when he became

Dorsal stream. The group of visual pathways that flows out of the primary visual cortex to the dorsal prestriate cortex to the posterior parietal cortex; according to one theory, its function is the visual perception of an object's location.

Ventral stream. The group of visual pathways that flows out of the primary visual cortex to the ventral prestriate cortex to the inferotemporal cortex; according to one theory, its function is the visual perception of an object's identity.

Agnosia. The inability to recognize sensory stimuli of a particular class that is not attributable to a sensory deficit or to verbal or intellectual impairment.

Visual agnosia. A failure to recognize visual stimuli that is not attributable to sensory, verbal, or intellectual impairment.

Prosopagnosia. Visual agnosia for faces.

prosopagnosic, and a bird watcher lost his ability to distinguish species of birds. Thus prosopagnosics may have a general deficit in distinguishing similar members of complex classes of visual stimuli, the most obvious symptom of which is a difficulty in distinguishing faces (see Gross & Sergent, 1992).

In a few cases, it has been possible to subject the brains of deceased prosopagnosics to histological scrutiny (see Gross & Sergent, 1992). Bilateral damage to the inferior prestriate area and the adjoining portions of the inferotemporal cortex has been found in most of these cases. Consistent with this observation of damage to the ventral stream is the discovery of neurons in the temporal cortex of monkeys that respond selectively to faces (e.g., Gross et al., 1985)—see Figure 8.10.

Figure 8.10 The firing rate of a monkey inferotemporal cortex neuron before, during, and after the presentation of monkey faces at different angles. The profile view (100°) was most effective in increasing the firing rate of this cell. (Adapted from Gross et al., 1985.)

8.3 Audition

The function of the auditory system is the perception of sound—or, more accurately, the perception of objects and events through the sounds that they make (Masterton, 1992). Sounds are vibrations of air molecules that stimulate the auditory system; humans hear only those molecular vibrations between about 20 and 20,000 Hertz (cycles per second). Figure 8.11 illustrates how sounds are commonly recorded in the form of waves and the relation between the physical dimensions of sound vibrations and our perceptions of them. The *amplitude, frequency,* and *complexity* of air molecule vibrations are perceived as *loudness, pitch,* and *timbre,* respectively.

Pure tones (sine wave vibrations) exist only in laboratories and sound recording studios; in real life, sound is always associated with complex patterns of vibrations. For example, Figure 8.12 illustrates the complex sound wave associated with one note of a clarinet. The figure also illustrates that any complex sound wave can be broken down mathematically into a series of sine waves of various

Figure 8.11 The relation between the physical and perceptual dimensions of sound.

Chapter 8   Mechanisms of Perception

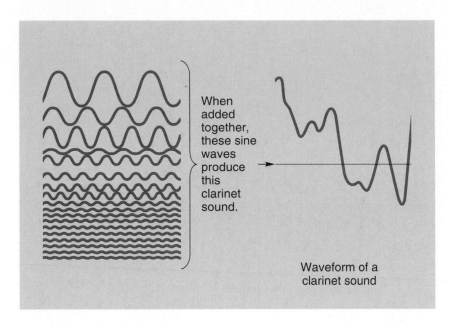

When added together, these sine waves produce this clarinet sound.

Waveform of a clarinet sound

Figure 8.12 The breaking down of a sound—in this case, the sound of a clarinet—into its component sine waves by Fourier analysis. When added together, the sine wave components produce the complex sound wave.

frequencies and amplitudes; these component sine waves produce the original sound when they are added together. As you learned in Chapter 7, *Fourier analysis* is the mathematical procedure for breaking down complex waves into their component sine waves. One theory of audition is that the auditory system performs a Fourier-like analysis of complex sounds in terms of their component sine waves.

The Ear

The ear is illustrated in Figure 8.13. Sound waves travel down the *auditory canal* and cause the **tympanic membrane** (the eardrum) to vibrate. These vibrations are then transferred to the three **ossicles**—the small bones of the middle ear: the *malleus* (the hammer), the *incus* (the anvil), and the *stapes* (the stirrup). The vibrations of the stapes trigger vibrations of the membrane called the **oval window,** which in turn transfers the vibrations to the fluid of the snail-shaped **cochlea** (*kokhlos* means "land snail"). The cochlea is a long, coiled tube with an internal membrane running almost to its tip. This internal membrane is the auditory receptor organ, the **organ of Corti.**

Each pressure change at the oval window travels along the organ of Corti as a wave. The organ of Corti is composed of two membranes: the basilar membrane and the tectorial membrane. The auditory receptors, the **hair cells,** are mounted in the **basilar membrane** and the **tectorial membrane** rests on the hair cells. Accordingly, a deflection of the organ of Corti at any point along its length produces a shearing force on the hair cells at the same point (Corwin & Warchol, 1991). This force stimulates the hair cells and thereby triggers action potentials in axons of the **auditory**

nerve—a branch of the eighth cranial nerve (the *auditory-vestibular nerve*). The vibrations of the cochlear fluid are ultimately dissipated by the *round window,* an elastic membrane in the cochlea wall.

The major principle of cochlear coding is that different frequencies produce maximal stimulation of hair cells at different points along the basilar membrane—with higher frequencies producing greater activation closer to the windows. Thus the many component frequencies that compose each complex sound activate hair cells at many different points along the basilar membrane, and the many signals thus created by a single complex sound are carried out of the ear by many different auditory neurons. Like the cochlea, most other structures of the auditory system are arrayed according to frequency. Thus, in the same way that the organization of the visual system is primarily **retinotopic,** the organization of the auditory system is primarily **tonotopic.**

This brings us to the major unsolved mystery of auditory processing. Imagine yourself in a complex acoustic environment such as a party. The music is playing; people are

Tympanic membrane. The eardrum.

Ossicles. The three small bones of the middle ear: the malleus, the incus, and the stapes.

Oval window. The cochlear membrane that transfers vibrations from the ossicles to the fluid of the cochlea.

Cochlea. The long, coiled structure of the inner ear that houses the organ of Corti and its auditory receptors.

Organ of Corti. The auditory receptor organ, comprising the basilar membrane, the hair cells, and the tectorial membrane.

Hair cells. The receptors of the auditory system.

Basilar membrane. The membrane of the organ of Corti in which the hair cell receptors are embedded.

Tectorial membrane. The cochlear membrane that rests on the hair cells.

Auditory nerve. The branch of the eighth cranial nerve that carries auditory signals from the hair cells in the basilar membrane.

Retinotopic. Organized, like the primary visual cortex, according to a map of the retina.

Tonotopic. Organized, like the primary auditory cortex, according to the frequency of sound.

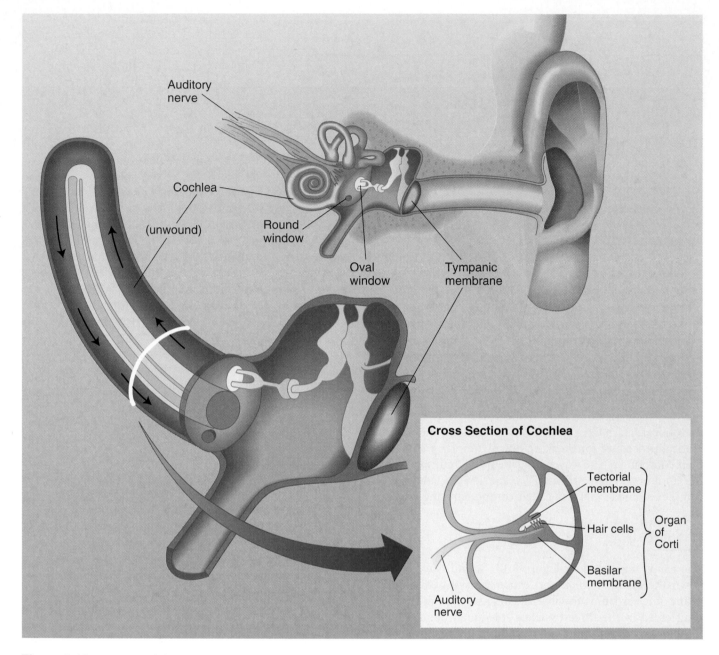

Figure 8.13 Anatomy of the ear.

dancing, eating, and drinking; and numerous conversations are going on around you. Because the component frequencies in each individual sound activate many sites along your basilar membrane, the number of sites simultaneously activated at any one time by the party noises is enormous. But somehow your auditory system manages to sort these individual frequency messages into separate categories and combine them so that you hear each source of complex sounds independently. For example, you hear the speech of the person standing next to you as a separate sequence of sounds, despite the fact that it contains many of the same component frequencies coming from other sources.

Figure 8.13 also shows the **semicircular canals**—the receptive organs of the vestibular system. The **vestibular**

system carries information about the direction and intensity of head movements, which helps us maintain our balance.

From the Ear to the Primary Auditory Cortex

There is no major auditory pathway to the cortex comparable to the retina-geniculate-striate pathway of the visual system. Instead, there is a network of auditory pathways (see Masterton, 1992), some of which are illustrated in Figure 8.14. The axons of each *auditory nerve* synapse in the ipsilateral *cochlear nuclei,* from which many projections

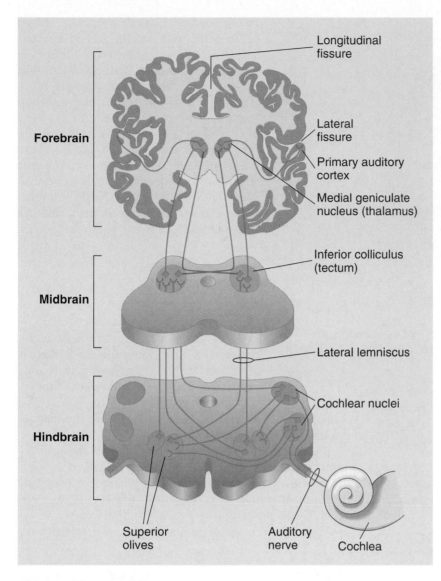

Figure 8.14 Some of the pathways of the auditory system that lead from one ear to the cortex.

nized in functional columns (see Schreiner, 1992): All of the neurons encountered during a vertical microelectrode penetration of the primary auditory cortex (i.e., a penetration at right angles to the cortical layers) respond optimally to sounds in the same frequency range. Second, like the cochlea, the primary auditory cortex is organized tonotopically: More anterior regions of the auditory cortex are responsive to higher frequencies, and more posterior regions are responsive to lower frequencies.

Sound Localization

Localization of sounds in space is mediated by the lateral and medial superior olives, but in different ways. When a sound originates to our left, it reaches the left ear first, and it is louder at the left ear. Some neurons in the *medial superior olives* respond to slight differences in the time of arrival of signals from the two ears, whereas some neurons in the *lateral superior olives* respond to slight differences in the amplitude of sounds from the two ears (see Heffner & Masterton, 1990). In mammals, the medial and lateral superior olives project to the *superior colliculus*. Those layers of the superior colliculus that receive auditory input from the superior olives are laid out according to a map of auditory space (see King & Moore, 1991)—an exception to the usual tonotopic organization of auditory system structures.

Many researchers interested in sound localization have studied barn owls (see

lead to the **superior olives** at the same level. The axons of the olivary neurons project via the *lateral lemniscus* to the **inferior colliculi,** where they synapse on neurons that project to the **medial geniculate nuclei** of the thalamus, which in turn project to the *primary auditory cortex.* Notice that signals from each ear are transmitted to both ipsilateral and contralateral auditory cortex.

Primary Auditory Cortex

In humans, the primary auditory cortex is located in the *lateral fissure* (see Figure 8.15). It is surrounded largely by secondary auditory cortex—there are thought to be about six distinct areas of human secondary auditory cortex.

Two important principles of organization of the primary auditory cortex have been identified. First, like other areas of the cerebral cortex, the primary auditory cortex is orga-

Semicircular canals. The receptive organs of the vestibular system.

Vestibular system. The sensory system that detects changes in the direction and intensity of head movements and that contributes to the maintenance of balance through its output to the motor system.

Superior olives. Medullary nuclei that play a role in sound localization.

Inferior colliculi. The structures of the tectum that receive auditory input from the superior olives and play a role in the localization of sound.

Medial geniculate nuclei. The auditory thalamic nuclei that receive input from the inferior colliculi and project to primary auditory cortex.

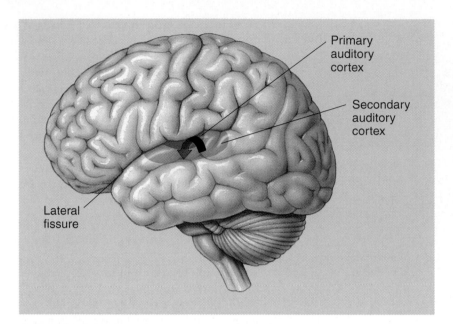

Figure 8.15 Location of the primary and secondary auditory cortex in the temporal cortex. Most of the auditory cortex is hidden in the depths of the lateral fissure.

Figure 8.16). You see, barn owls can locate sounds in space better than any other animal whose hearing has been tested. They are nocturnal hunters and must be able to locate field mice solely by the rustling sounds the mice make in the dark.

The most striking anatomical feature of barn owls is the facial ruff, which is an effective reflector of high-frequency sounds and which accounts, in part, for the owls' remarkable sound-localizing ability. Barn owls locate sounds in the horizontal dimension (horizontal to the top of the head) by comparing the loudness of sounds at the two ears (Konishi, 1993). The ability to locate sounds in the vertical dimension (at a right angle to the top of the head) is not important for most land-dwelling animals, but it is critical for barn owls because they hunt from the air. The facial ruff is the key to their ability to locate sounds in the vertical dimension. The right ear of barn owls is more sensitive to sounds above the horizontal plane because the ruff on the right is directed slightly upward; the left ear is more sensi-

Word deafness. Difficulty in the perception of speech that occurs in the absence of any difficulty in detecting individual sounds.

Glabrous skin. Hairless skin.

Free nerve endings. Cutaneous receptors that are composed of nerve endings without specialized structures on them and that detect cutaneous pain and changes in skin temperature.

Pacinian corpuscles. The largest and most deeply positioned cutaneous receptors, which are sensitive to sudden displacements of the skin.

tive to sounds below the horizontal plane because the ruff on the left is directed slightly downward. This vertical difference is greater for higher frequencies because the ruff reflects higher frequencies more effectively. Accordingly, in order to locate sounds in the vertical dimension, the barn owls' auditory system must compare the intensities detected at each ear for more than one frequency. Barn owls cannot locate single-frequency sounds in vertical space, and they cannot locate complex sounds in vertical space if their ruff has been shaved (Knudsen, 1981).

Effects of Auditory Cortex Damage

Because most human auditory cortex is deep in the lateral fissure, it is rarely destroyed in its entirety; and if it is, there is inevitably extensive damage to surrounding tissue. That is why efforts to understand the effects of auditory cortex damage have relied heavily on comparative experiments (see Berkley & Stebbins, 1990; Phillips, 1989).

Remarkably, complete bilateral lesions of the primary auditory cortex produce no permanent deficits in the ability of most mammalian laboratory species to detect the presence of sounds (e.g., Kavanagh & Kelly, 1988), even when the lesions include secondary auditory cortex. However, such lesions do disrupt the ability to localize brief

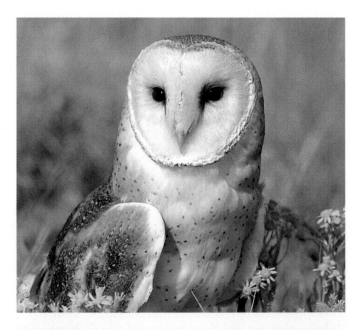

Figure 8.16 A barn owl. Its facial ruff is an important component of an auditory system that allows it to locate mice and other small prey in total darkness.

sounds. For example, Heffner and Heffner (1988) found that monkeys with bilateral auditory cortex lesions could not discriminate between two sounds at different locations in the same *hemifield* (left or right), although they could discriminate between a left sound and a right sound; and Kavanagh and Kelly (1987) found that ferrets with unilateral auditory cortex lesions could not locate sounds in their contralateral hemifield. Humans with large auditory cortex lesions seem to have similar sound localization difficulties (de Renzi, 1982).

In humans, the most obvious long-term consequence of bilateral auditory cortex damage is **word deafness**—diffi-culty in the perception of speech in the absence of deficits in the ability to detect individual sounds; word-deaf patients describe speech sounds as "buzzes" or "static" (Phillips, 1989). The results of several studies indicate that the perceptual deficits of word-deaf patients are not restricted to linguistic sounds (e.g., Auerbach et al., 1982; Yaqub et al., 1988). Such patients have considerable diffi-culty identifying brief sounds of all kinds, and they also have difficulty perceiving the temporal order of brief sounds that are presented in rapid succession. Accordingly, word deafness is but one symptom of a more global audi-tory temporal-processing disorder.

8.4 Somatosensation: Touch and Pain

Somatosensation is a general term that refers to sensations of the body. The somatosensory system is three separate but interacting systems: (1) an *exteroceptive system,* which senses external stimuli that are applied to the skin; (2) a *proprioceptive system,* which monitors information about the position of the body that comes from receptors in the muscles, joints, and organs of balance; and (3) an *interoceptive system,* which provides general information about conditions within the body (e.g., temperature and blood-pressure). This discussion deals almost exclusively with the exteroceptive system, which itself com-prises three somewhat distinct divisions: a divi-sion for perceiving *mechanical stimuli* (touch), one for *thermal stimuli* (temperature), and one for *nociceptive stimuli* (pain).

Cutaneous Receptors

There are several different kinds of receptors in the skin. Figure 8.17 illustrates four that are found in both hairy skin and **glabrous skin**—hairless skin, such as the skin on the palms of your hands. The most simple cutaneous receptors are the **free nerve endings**—neuron endings with no special-ized structures on them which are particularly sensitive to temperature change and pain. The largest and deepest cutaneous receptors are the onionlike **Pacinian corpuscles**; because they adapt rapidly, they respond best to sudden dis-placements of the skin. On the other hand, *Merkel's disks* and *Ruffini endings* both adapt slow-ly, and respond best to gradual skin indentation and gradual skin stretch, respectively.

To appreciate the functional significance of fast and slow receptor adaptation, consider what hap-pens when a constant pressure is applied to the skin. The pressure evokes a burst of firing in all receptors, which corresponds to the sensation of being touched; however, after a few hundred milliseconds, only the slowly adapting receptors remain active, and the quality of the sensation changes. In fact, you are often totally

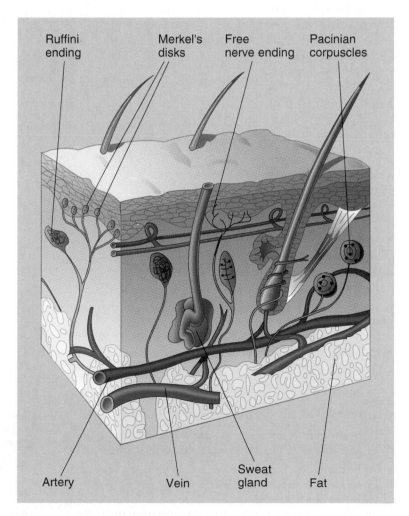

Figure 8.17 Four cutaneous receptors that occur in both hairy and glabrous skin.

unaware of constant skin pressure; for example, you are usually unaware of the feeling of your clothes against your body until you focus attention on it. As a consequence, when you try to identify objects by touch, you manipulate them in your hands so that the pattern of stimulation continually changes. The identification of objects by touch is called **stereognosis.**

Dermatomes

The neural fibers that carry information from cutaneous receptors and other somatosensory receptors gather together in nerves and enter the spinal cord via the *dorsal roots.* The area of the body that is innervated by the left and right dorsal roots of a given segment of the spinal cord is called a **dermatome.** Figure 8.18 is a dermatomal map of the human body. Because there is considerable overlap between adjacent dermatomes, destruction of a single dorsal root typically produces little somatosensory loss.

The Two Major Ascending Somatosensory Pathways

Somatosensory information ascends to the human cortex over two major somatosensory system pathways: the dorsal-column medial-lemniscus system and the anterolateral system. The **dorsal-column medial-lemniscus system** carries information about touch and proprioception. The **anterolateral system** carries information about pain and temperature.

The dorsal-column medial-lemniscus system is illustrated in Figure 8.19. The sensory neurons of this system enter the spinal cord via a dorsal root, ascend ipsilaterally in the **dorsal columns,** and

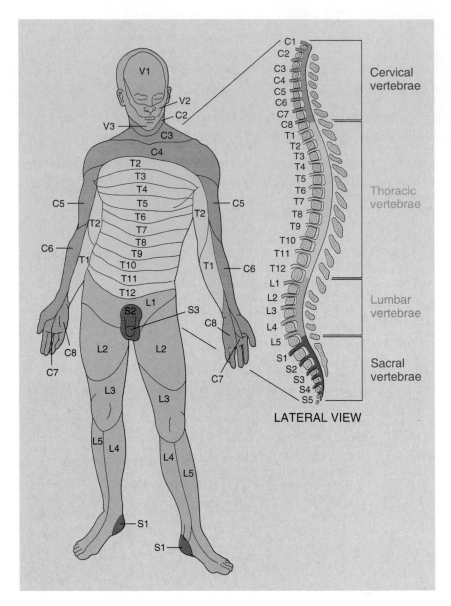

Figure 8.18 The dermatomes of the human body. *S, L, T,* and *C* refer respectively to the *sacral, lumbar, thoracic,* and *cervical* regions of the spinal cord. *V*1, *V*2, and *V*3 stand for the three branches of the trigeminal nerve.

Stereognosis. The identification of objects by touch.

Dermatome. An area of the body that is innervated by the left and right dorsal roots of one segment of the spinal cord.

Dorsal-column medial-lemniscus system. The division of the somatosensory system that ascends in the dorsal portion of the spinal white matter and carries signals related to touch and proprioception.

Anterolateral system. The division of the somatosensory system that ascends in the anterolateral portion of spinal white matter and carries signals related to pain and temperature.

Dorsal columns. The somatosensory tracts that ascend in the dorsal portion of the spinal cord white matter.

Medial lemniscus. The somatosensory pathway between the dorsal column nuclei and the ventral posterior nucleus of the thalamus.

Ventral posterior nucleus. A thalamic relay nucleus in both the somatosensory and gustatory systems.

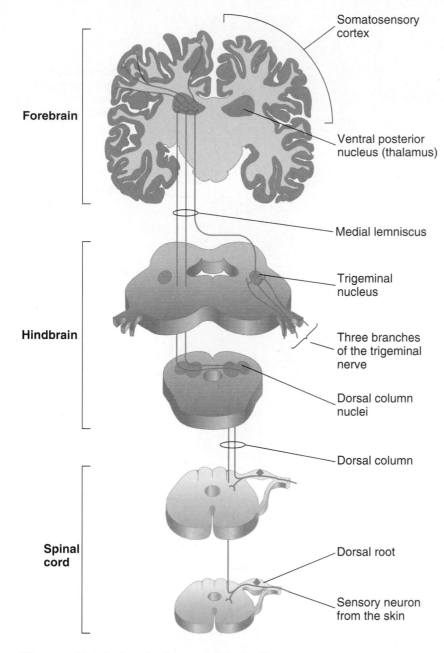

Figure 8.19 The dorsal-column medial-lemniscus system.

Somatosensory cortex

Ventral posterior nucleus (thalamus)

Forebrain

Medial lemniscus

Trigeminal nucleus

Hindbrain

Three branches of the trigeminal nerve

Dorsal column nuclei

Dorsal column

Spinal cord

Dorsal root

Sensory neuron from the skin

in the toes are the longest neurons in the human body.

The anterolateral system is illustrated in Figure 8.20. Most dorsal root neurons of the anterolateral system synapse as soon as they enter the spinal cord. The axons of most of the second-order neurons decussate and then ascend to the brain in the contralateral anterolateral portion of the spinal cord; however, some do not decussate and ascend ipsilaterally. The anterolateral system comprises three different tracts: the *spinothalamic tract,* which projects to the *ventral posterior nucleus* of the thalamus (as does the dorsal-column medial-lemniscus system); the *spinoreticular tract,* which projects to the *reticular formation* (and then to the *parafascicular nuclei* and *intralaminar nuclei* of the thalamus); and the *spinotectal tract,* which projects to the *tectum.* The three branches of the trigeminal nerve carry pain and temperature information from the face to the same thalamic sites. The pain and temperature information that reaches the thalamus is then distributed to SI, SII, the posterior parietal cortex, and other parts of the brain.

Mark, Ervin, and Yakolev (1962) assessed the effects of lesions to the thalamus on the chronic pain of patients in the advanced stages of cancer. Lesions to the ventral posterior nuclei, which receive input from both the spinothalamic tract and the dorsal-column medial-lemniscus system, produced some loss of cutaneous sensitivity to touch, to temperature change, and to sharp pain; but the lesions had no effect on deep, chronic pain. In contrast, lesions of the parafascicular and intralaminar nuclei, both of which receive input from the spinoreticular tract, reduced deep chronic pain without disrupting cutaneous sensitivity.

Cortical Areas of Somatosensation

In 1937, Penfield and his colleagues mapped the primary somatosensory cortex of patients during neurosurgery (see Figure 8.21). Penfield applied electrical stimulation to various sites on the cortical surface; and the patients, who were fully conscious under a local anesthetic, described what they felt. When stimulation was applied to the *postcentral gyrus,* the patients reported somatosensory sensations in various parts of their bodies. When Penfield mapped the relation between each site of stimulation and the part of the body in which the sensation was felt, he discovered that the

synapse in the *dorsal column nuclei* of the medulla. The axons of dorsal column nuclei neurons *decussate* (cross over to the other side of the brain) and then ascend in the **medial lemniscus** to the contralateral **ventral posterior nucleus** of the thalamus. The ventral posterior nuclei also receive input via the three branches of the *trigeminal nerve,* which carry somatosensory information from the contralateral areas of the face. Most neurons of the ventral posterior nucleus project to the *primary somatosensory cortex (SI)*; others project to the *secondary somatosensory cortex (SII)* or the posterior parietal cortex. Neuroscience trivia collectors will almost certainly want to add to their collection the fact that the dorsal column neurons that originate human primary somatosensory cortex (SI) is **somatotopic**—organized according to a map of the body surface. This somatotopic map is commonly referred to as the **somatosensory homunculus** (*homunculus* means "little man").

Evidence of a second somatotopically organized area (SII) was obtained in a similar manner. SII lies just ventral to SI in the postcentral gyrus, much of it extending into the lateral fissure. SII receives much of its input from SI (Pons et al., 1987); but in contrast to SI, whose input is largely contralateral, SII receives substantial input from both sides of the body.

Much of the output of SI and SII goes to the association cortex of the *posterior parietal lobe.* Notice in Figure 8.21 that the somatosensory homunculus is distorted; the greatest proportion of the primary somatosensory cortex is dedicated to receiving input from the parts of the body that are capable of the finest tactual discriminations (e.g., hands, lips, and tongue).

Kaas et al., (1981) found that the primary somatosensory cortex is not a single area as described by Penfield. It is, in fact, four parallel strips, each with a similar, but separate, somatotopic organization. Each strip of primary somatosensory cortex is most sensitive to a different kind of somatosensory input (e.g., to light touch or temperature).

Like the primary visual and auditory cortexes, the primary somatosensory cortex is organized in columns; each neuron in a particular column responds to the same kind of somatosensory stimuli and has a receptive field on the same part of the body. The receptive fields of many neurons in the primary somatosensory cortex, like those of visual system neurons, can be divided into antagonistic excitatory and inhibitory areas. Figure 8.22 on page 198 illustrates the receptive field of a neuron of the primary somatosensory cortex that is responsive to light touch (Mountcastle & Powell, 1959).

Effects of Damage to the Primary Somatosensory Cortex

Like the effects of damage to the primary auditory cortex, the effects of damage to the primary somatosensory cortex

Figure 8.20 The anterolateral system.

Thalamic nuclei (ventral posterior, intralaminar, parafascicular, etc.)

Tectum

Reticular formation

Three branches of trigeminal nerve

Spinothalamic tract

Spinotectal tract

Spinoreticular tract

Forebrain

Midbrain

Hindbrain

Spinal cord

are remarkably mild. Corkin, Milner, and Rasmussen (1970) assessed the somatosensory abilities of patients both before and after unilateral excision of SI for the relief of epilepsy. Following surgery, the patients displayed two minor contralateral deficits: a reduced ability to detect light touch and a reduced ability to identify objects by touch (i.e., a deficit in stereognosis). These deficits were bilateral only in those cases in which the unilateral lesion encroached on SII.

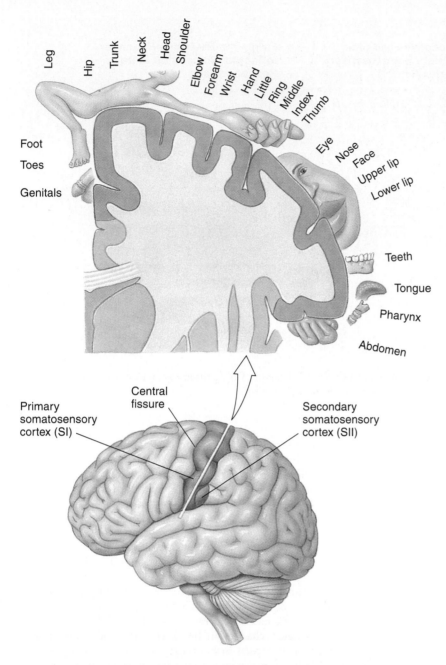

Leg
Hip
Trunk
Neck
Head
Shoulder
Elbow
Forearm
Wrist
Hand
Little
Ring
Middle
Index
Thumb

Foot
Toes
Genitals

Eye
Nose
Face
Upper lip
Lower lip

Teeth
Tongue
Pharynx
Abdomen

Central fissure

Primary somatosensory cortex (SI)

Secondary somatosensory cortex (SII)

Figure 8.21 The location of human primary (SI) and secondary (SII) somatosensory cortex and an illustration of the primary somatosensory homunculus.

extensive damage to the right posterior parietal lobe. You have already encountered one example of asomatognosia in this book, the case of the man who fell out of bed; the case of Klawans's (1990) Aunt Betty is another:

It was time to see Aunt Betty—she wasn't really my aunt, but I grew up thinking that she was. She was my mother's best friend. She had had a stroke in her right hemisphere.

As we walked to her room, one of the medical students described the case. "Left hemiplegia [left-side paralysis]," I was told.

Aunt Betty was lying on her back with her head and eyes turned to the right. "Betty," I called out. Not Aunt Betty, but Betty. I was 37; I'd dropped the "Aunt" long ago—at least 2 years earlier.

I approached her bed from the left, but Aunt Betty did not turn her head or even her eyes to look towards me.

"Hal," she called out. "Where are you?"

I turned her head gently toward me. We talked. It was clear that she had no speech problems, no memory loss, and no confusion. She was as bright as ever. But her eyes still looked to the right as if the left side of her world did not exist.

I picked up her right hand and held it in front of her eyes. "What's this?" I asked.

"My hand, of course," she said with an intonation that suggested what she thought of my question.

"Well then what's this," I said, as I held up her limp left hand where she could see it.

"A hand."

"Whose hand?"

Somatosensory Agnosias

There are two major types of somatosensory agnosia. One is **astereognosia**—the inability to recognize objects by touch. Cases of pure astereognosia—those that occur in the absence of simple sensory deficits—are rare (Corkin et al., 1970). The other type of somatosensory agnosia is **asomatognosia**—the failure to recognize parts of one's own body. Asomatognosia is usually unilateral, affecting only the left side of the body; and it is usually associated with

Somatotopic. Organized, like the primary somatosensory cortex, according to a map of the surface of the body.

Somatosensory homunculus. The somatotopic map that constitutes the primary somatosensory cortex.

Astereognosia. The inability to recognize objects by touch.

Asomatognosia. The failure to recognize parts of one's own body.

"Your hand, I guess," she replied. She seemed genuinely puzzled. I carefully placed her hand on the bed.

"Why have you come to this hospital?" I asked.

"To see you," she replied hesitantly. I could tell that she didn't really know the answer.

"Is there anything wrong with you?"

"No."

"How about your left hand and leg?"

"They're fine," she said. "How are yours?"

"They're fine too," I replied. There was nothing else to do. Aunt Betty was in trouble (pp. 12–14)[2].

As in the case of Aunt Betty, asomatognosia is often accompanied by **anosognosia**—the failure to recognize one's own neurological symptoms. It may also be accompanied by **contralateral neglect**—the tendency not to respond to stimuli that are contralateral to a right-hemisphere injury. You will learn more about contralateral neglect in the next chapter.

Figure 8.22 The receptive field of a neuron of the primary somatosensory cortex. Notice the antagonistic excitatory and inhibitory areas.

The Paradoxes of Pain

A paradox is a logical contradiction. The perception of pain is paradoxical in three respects, which is why I have singled it out for special discussion. The three paradoxes of pain are its adaptiveness, its lack of cortical representation, and the fact that it can be suppressed by descending control.

Adaptiveness of pain One paradox of pain is that an experience that seems in every respect to be so bad is in fact extremely important for our survival. The value of pain is best illustrated by a person who does not experience it:

The best documented of all cases of congenital insensitivity to pain is Miss C., a young Canadian girl who was a student at McGill University in Montreal.... The young lady was highly intelligent and seemed normal in every way except that she had never felt pain. As a child, she had bitten off the tip of her tongue while chewing food, and had suffered third-degree burns after kneeling on a radiator to look out of the window.... She felt no pain when parts of her body

were subjected to strong electric shock, to hot water at temperatures that usually produce reports of burning pain, or to a prolonged ice-bath. Equally astonishing was the fact that she showed no changes in blood pressure, heart rate, or respiration when these stimuli were presented. Furthermore, she could not remember ever sneezing or coughing, the gag reflex could be elicited only with great difficulty, and corneal reflexes (to protect the eyes) were absent. A variety of other stimuli, such as inserting a stick up through the nostrils, pinching tendons, or injections of histamine under the skin—which are normally considered as forms of torture—also failed to produce pain.

Miss C. had severe medical problems. She exhibited pathological changes in her knees, hip, and spine, and underwent several orthopaedic operations. The surgeon attributed these changes to the lack of protection to joints usually given by pain sensation. She apparently failed to shift her weight when standing, to turn over in her sleep, or to avoid certain postures, which normally prevent inflammation of joints....

Miss C. died at the age of twenty-nine of massive infections ... and extensive skin and bone trauma.[3]

Lack of cortical representation of pain The second paradox of pain is that it has no unambiguous cortical representation (see Roland, 1992; Stea & Apkarian, 1992). Removal of SI and SII in humans is not associated with any

---

[2]Paraphrased from *Newton's Madness: Further Tales of Clinical Neurology* by Harold L. Klawans (New York: Harper & Row, 1990).

[3]From *The Challenge of Pain* (pp. 16–17) by Ronald Melzack and Patrick D. Wall, 1982, London: Penguin Books Ltd. Copyright © Ronald Melzack and Patrick D. Wall, 1982.

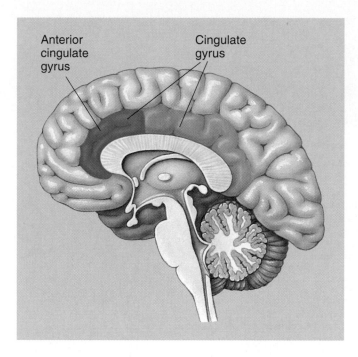

Figure 8.23 Location of anterior cingulate cortex in the cingulate gyrus.

change in the threshold for pain; indeed, *hemispherectomized patients* (patients with one cerebral hemisphere removed) can still perceive pain from both sides of their bodies. Also, no area of the cortex has yet been discovered that results in pain when stimulated or that responds selectively to painful stimuli.

Recently, positron emission tomography (PET) has been applied to the study of the cortical localization of pain (e.g., Talbot et al., 1991). So far, the evidence with respect to pain and various cortical areas has been mixed, with one major exception: PET consistently detects pain-related activation in the **anterior cingulate cortex** (see Figure 8.23). However, it is unlikely that the anterior cingulate cortex is involved in the perception of pain; rather, it seems to be involved in the emotional reaction to painful stimuli and other aversive experiences. After *prefrontal lobotomy,* which typically damages the anterior cingulate cortex and its connections, a patient's threshold for pain is typically unchanged but the emotional reaction to it is much reduced.

Descending pain control   The third paradox of pain is that it, the most compelling of all sensory experiences, can be totally suppressed by cognitive and emotional factors. For example, men participating in a certain religious ceremony swing from ropes attached to giant meat hooks in their backs with little evidence of pain (Kosambi, 1967); severe wounds suffered by soldiers in battle are often associated with little pain (Beecher, 1959); and people injured in life-threatening situations frequently feel no pain until the threat is over.

Melzack and Wall (1965) proposed the **gate-control theory** to account for the ability of cognitive and emotional factors to block the perception of pain. They theorized signals descending from the brain can activate neural gating circuits in the spinal cord to block incoming pain signals.

Three important discoveries led to the identification of the descending pain-control circuit. First was the discovery that electrical stimulation of the **periaqueductal gray (PAG)** has analgesic (pain-blocking) effects: Reynolds (1969) was able to perform abdominal surgery on rats with no analgesia other than that provided by PAG stimulation. Second was the discovery that the PAG and other areas of the brain contain specialized receptors for opiate analgesic drugs such as morphine, which suggested that such analgesic substances might occur naturally in the body: Why else would there be receptors for them? And third was the isolation of several endogenous (internally produced) opiate analgesics, the **endorphins,** which you learned about in Chapter 4 (e.g., Hughs et al., 1975). These three findings together suggested that analgesic drugs and psychological factors might block pain through an endorphin-sensitive circuit that descends from the PAG.

Figure 8.24 illustrates the descending analgesia circuit first hypothesized by Basbaum and Fields (1978); see also Fields and Basbaum (1984). They proposed that the output of the PAG excites the serotonergic neurons of the *raphé nuclei* (a cluster of serotonergic nuclei in the core of the medulla), which in turn project down the dorsal columns of the spinal cord and excite opiate-sensitive interneurons that block incoming pain signals in the dorsal horn.

Evidence in support of Basbaum and Field's hypothetical descending pain-control circuit has come from a variety of sources. For example, microinjection of an opiate antagonist, such as naloxone or naltrexone, into the PAG has

Anosognosia. The failure to recognize one's own neurological symptoms.

Contralateral neglect. A disorder characterized by a tendency not to respond to stimuli that are contralateral to a brain injury.

Anterior cingulate cortex. The cortex of the anterior cingulate gyrus, which is involved in the emotional reaction to painful stimulation.

Gate-control theory. The theory that neural signals that descend from the brain can activate neural gating circuits in the spinal cord to block incoming pain signals.

Periaqueductal gray (PAG). The gray matter around the cerebral aqueduct, which contains opiate receptors and activates a descending analgesia circuit.

Endorphins. Endogenous (internally produced) opiate analgesics.

been found to block the analgesia produced by *systemic injection* (injection into general circulation) of morphine (Yeung & Rudy, 1978); and activation of the raphé nucleus with electrical stimulation has been shown to inhibit pain-sensitive neurons in the dorsal horn of the spinal cord (Oliveras et al., 1974). Moreover, the analgesic effects of morphine and PAG stimulation have been attenuated by sectioning the fibers that descend from the raphé, by lesioning the raphé itself, or by depleting the raphé neurons of their serotonin neurotransmitter (e.g., Basbaum, Clanton, & Fields, 1976). However, the fact that blockage of the PAG-raphé-dorsal-column circuit does not eliminate all analgesic effects (see Terman et al., 1984) suggests that other circuits are also capable of mediating analgesia.

Phantom Limbs

Almost every amputee who has lost an arm or leg continues to feel the presence of the amputated limb; this perception of an amputated limb is referred to as a **phantom limb** (Melzack, 1992). The most striking feature of phantom limbs is their reality. Their existence is so compelling that a patient may try to jump out of bed onto a nonexistent leg or to lift a cup with a nonexistent hand. In most cases, the amputated limb behaves like a normal limb; for example, as an amputee walks, a phantom arm seems to swing back and forth in perfect coordination with the intact arm. However, sometimes an amputee feels that the amputated limb is stuck in a peculiar position:

> One man felt that his phantom arm extended straight out from the shoulder, at a right angle to the body. He therefore turned sideways whenever he passed through doorways, to avoid hitting the wall. Another man, whose phantom arm was bent behind him, slept only on his abdomen or on his side because the phantom got in the way when he tried to rest on his back. (Melzack, 1992, p. 120)

About 50% of amputees experience chronic severe pain in their phantom limbs. A typical complaint is that an amputated hand is clenched so tightly that the fingernails are digging into the palm of the hand. Occasionally, this condition can be treated by having the amputee concentrate on opening the amputated hand. In phantom legs, pain is often felt as a severe cramp or as a flame being applied to the toes. The first published report of phantom

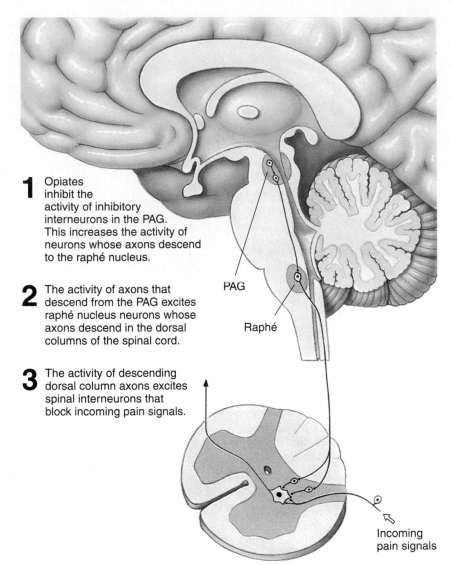

1 Opiates inhibit the activity of inhibitory interneurons in the PAG. This increases the activity of neurons whose axons descend to the raphé nucleus.

2 The activity of axons that descend from the PAG excites raphé nucleus neurons whose axons descend in the dorsal columns of the spinal cord.

3 The activity of descending dorsal column axons excites spinal interneurons that block incoming pain signals.

PAG

Raphé

Incoming pain signals

Figure 8.24 Basbaum and Field's (1978) model of the descending analgesia circuit.

limb pain described the experience of a victim of the American Civil War, who awoke from surgery knowing that his arm had been amputated but not knowing that his legs had been taken as well:

> [I was] suddenly aware of a sharp cramp in my left leg. I tried to get at it . . . with my single arm, but, finding myself too weak, hailed an attendant.

Phantom limb. The vivid perception of an amputated limb.

Flavor. The combined impression of taste and smell.

Pheromones. Odors that are released by an animal and elicit specific patterns of behavior in its conspecifics.

Just rub my calf . . . if you please.

Calf? . . . You ain't got none, pardner. It's took off.

A common explanation of phantom limbs and phantom limb pain is that they result from the irritation of nerves in the stump, which sends signals to those areas of the somatosensory cortex that had received input from the amputated limb prior to amputation. Accordingly, efforts to treat chronic phantom limb pain have involved surgical destruction of various parts of the neural pathway between the stump and the cortex—the peripheral nerves from the stump, the ascending anterolateral tracts, various thalamic relay nuclei—or the somatosensory cortex itself. Unfortunately, none of these surgical interventions has provided more than temporary relief from the pain (see Melzack, 1992)—and none has eliminated the phantom limb.

8.5 The Chemical Senses: Smell and Taste

Olfaction (smell) and *gustation* (taste) are referred to as the chemical senses because their function is to monitor the chemical content of the environment (see Bartoshuk & Beauchamp, 1994). Smell is the response of the olfactory system to airborne chemicals that are drawn by inhalation over receptors in the nasal passages, and taste is the response of the gustatory system to chemicals in the solutions of the oral cavity.

When we are eating, smell and taste act in concert. Molecules of food excite both smell and taste receptors and produce an integrated sensory impression termed **flavor.** The contribution of olfaction to flavor is often underestimated, but you won't make this mistake if you remember that people with no sense of smell have difficulty distinguishing the flavors of apples and onions.

Smell and taste have the dubious distinction of being the least understood of the exteroceptive sensory systems (see Freeman, 1991; Scott & Giza, 1990). One reason is that chemical stimuli are inherently more difficult to control and administer than are lights, tones, and touches. Another is that loss of the ability to smell and taste does not pose many serious health problems for individuals living in societies, such as ours, in which potential foods are screened by government agencies. Be that as it may, the chemical senses have attracted considerable interest in recent years.

Arguably, the single most interesting aspect of the chemical senses is their role in the social lives of many species. The members of many species release **pheromones**—chemicals that influence the behavior of *conspecifics* (members of the same species). For example, Murphy and Schneider (1970) showed that hamster sexual and aggressive behavior is under pheromonal control. Normal male hamsters attacked and killed unfamiliar males that were placed in their colonies, and they mounted and impregnated unfamiliar sexually receptive females; however, male hamsters that were unable to smell the intruders engaged in neither aggressive nor sexual behavior. Murphy and Schneider confirmed the olfactory basis of hamster aggressive and sexual behavior in a particularly devious fashion. They swabbed a male intruder with the vaginal secretions of a sexually receptive female before placing it in an unfamiliar colony; in so doing, they converted it from an object of hamster assassination to an object of hamster lust.

The possibility that humans may release sexual pheromones has received considerable attention because of its financial and recreational potential. There have been several suggestive findings. For example, (1) the olfactory sensitivity of women is greatest when they are ovulating (e.g., Doty et al., 1981); (2) the menstrual cycles of women living together tend to become synchronized (McClintock, 1971); (3) humans—particularly women—can tell the sex of a person from the breath (Doty et al., 1982) or the underarm odor (Schleidt, Hold, & Attili, 1981); and (4) men can judge the stage of a woman's menstrual cycle on the basis of her vaginal odor (Doty et al., 1975). However, there is still no direct evidence that human odors can serve as sex attractants (Doty, 1986). To put it mildly, most subjects did not find the body odors that were employed in the aforementioned studies to be particularly attractive.

Another feature of the chemical senses that has attracted attention is that they are involved in some interesting forms of learning. As you discovered in Chapter 5, animals that suffer from gastrointestinal upset after consuming a particular food develop a *conditioned taste aversion.* Conversely, it has been shown that rats develop preferences for flavors that they encounter in their mother's milk (Galef & Sherry, 1973) or on the breath of conspecifics (Galef, 1989). And adult male rats that were nursed as pups by lemon-scented mothers copulate more effectively with females that smell of lemons (Fillion & Blass, 1986)—a phenomenon that has been aptly referred to as the I-want-a-girl-just-like-the-girl-who-married-dear-old-dad phenomenon (Diamond, 1986).

Olfactory System

Because we can discriminate among thousands of different odors, it has long been assumed that olfaction, like color vision (see Chapter 7), is coded according to component principles—that is, that there are a few primary receptor

Figure 8.25 The olfatory system.

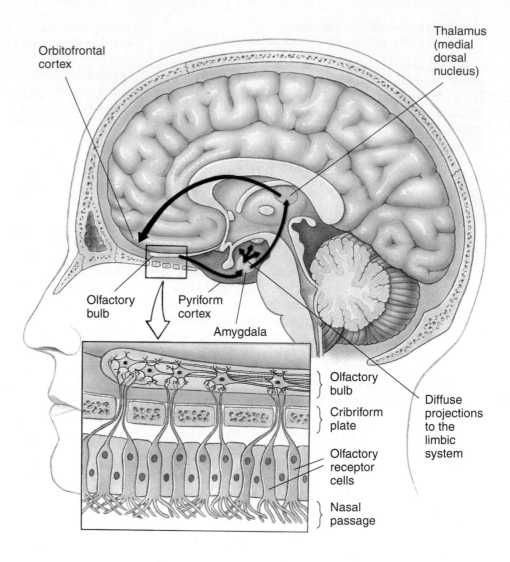

Orbitofrontal cortex

Thalamus (medial dorsal nucleus)

Olfactory bulb

Pyriform cortex

Amygdala

Olfactory bulb

Cribriform plate

Olfactory receptor cells

Nasal passage

Diffuse projections to the limbic system

types and the perception of various odors is produced by different ratios of activity in them. An alternative theory is that the olfactory system is more like the immune system—that is, that there are a multitude of receptor types, each uniquely responsive to a particular chemical. Support for this latter view has come from the recent identification of a family of genes that encodes many hundreds—perhaps thousands—of different kinds of olfactory receptor proteins.

The olfactory system is illustrated in Figure 8.25. The olfactory receptors are located in the upper part of the nose, embedded in a layer of mucus-covered tissue called the **olfactory mucosa.** They have their own axons, which pass through a porous portion of the skull (the *cribriform plate*) and enter the **olfactory bulbs** (the first cranial nerves), where they synapse on neurons that project via the *olfactory tract* to the amygdala and **pyriform cortex**—the area of the medial temporal cortex adjacent to the amygdala. The olfactory system is thus the only sensory system whose signals do not pass through the thalamus before reaching the cerebral cortex.

Two major olfactory pathways leave the amygdala-pyriform area. One projects diffusely to the limbic system, and the other projects via the **medial dorsal nuclei** of the thalamus to the **orbitofrontal cortex**—the area of cortex on the inferior surface of the frontal lobes, next to the orbits,

Olfactory mucosa. The mucous membrane that lines the upper nasal passages and contains the olfactory receptor cells.

Olfactory bulbs. The first cranial nerves, whose output goes primarily to the amygdala and pyriform cortex.

Pyriform cortex. The area of medial temporal cortex that receives direct olfactory input.

Medial dorsal nuclei. The thalamic relay nuclei of the olfactory system.

Orbitofrontal cortex. The cortex of the inferior frontal lobes, which receives olfactory input from the thalamus.

Taste buds. Clusters of taste receptors.

Solitary nucleus. The medullary relay nucleus of the gustatory system.

Figure 8.26 Taste receptors, taste buds, and papillae on the surface of the tongue. Two sizes of papillae are visible in the photogaph; only the larger papillae contain taste buds and receptors.

Surface of Tongue

Papillae

Cross Section of a Papilla

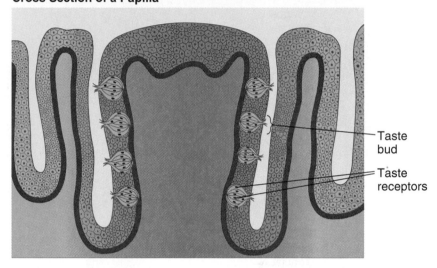

Taste bud

Taste receptors

or eye sockets. The limbic projection is thought to mediate the emotional response to odors; the thalamic-orbitofrontal projection is thought to mediate the conscious perception of odors.

Gustatory System

Taste receptors are found on the tongue and in parts of the oral cavity; they typically occur in clusters of 50 or so called **taste buds.** On the tongue, taste buds are often located around small protuberances called *papillae* (singular: *papilla*). The relation between taste receptors, taste buds, and papillae is illustrated in Figure 8.26. Unlike olfactory receptors, taste receptors do not have their own axons; each neuron that carries impulses away from a taste bud receives input from many receptors.

Psychologically, there are four primary tastes: sweet, sour, bitter, and salty. Consequently, it is commonly assumed that there are four kinds of taste receptors and that the perception of all tastes is a consequence of the relative amounts of activity in these four receptors. Although

this component-processing theory of taste is consistent with some of the data, it is not without its problems. One is that many tastes cannot be created by combinations of the four primaries (Schiffman & Erickson, 1980); another is that there is no evidence that taste receptors come in just four varieties.

The major pathways over which gustatory signals are conducted to the cortex are illustrated in Figure 8.27. Gustatory afferents leave the mouth as part of the *facial* (VII), *glossopharyngeal* (IX), and *vagus* (X) *cranial nerves,* which carry information from the front of the tongue, back of the tongue, and back of the oral cavity, respectively. These fibers all terminate in the **solitary nucleus** of the medulla, where they synapse on neurons that project to the *ventral posterior nucleus* of the thalamus. The gustatory axons of the ventral posterior nucleus project to the *primary gustatory cortex,* which is near the face area of the somatosensory homunculus, and to the *secondary gustatory cortex,* which is hidden from view deep in the lateral fissure. Unlike the projections of other sensory systems, the projections of the gustatory system are primarily ipsilateral.

Figure 8.27 The gustatory system.

Brain Damage and the Chemical Senses

The inability to smell is called **anosmia**; the inability to taste is called **ageusia.** The most common neurological cause of anosmia is a blow to the head that causes a displacement of the brain within the skull and shears the olfactory nerves where they pass through the cribriform plate. Approximately 6% of patients hospitalized for traumatic head injuries are found to have olfactory deficits of some sort (e.g., Zusho, 1983).

In contrast to anosmia, ageusia is rare, presumably because sensory signals from the mouth are carried over three separate pathways. However, ageusia for the anterior two-thirds of the tongue on one side is sometimes observed after damage to the ear on the same side of the body. This is because the branch of the facial nerve (VII) that carries gustatory information from the anterior two-thirds of the tongue passes through the middle ear.

One noteworthy feature of ageusia and anosmia is that they sometimes occur together in neurological patients. This suggests that there is some as yet unidentified area in the brain where olfactory and gustatory information converges.

> **Anosmia.** The inability to smell.
>
> **Ageusia.** The inability to taste.
>
> **Selective attention.** The ability to focus on a small subset of the multitude of stimuli that are being received at any one time.

SELF TEST

Test your knowledge of the anatomy of the sensory systems by completing each sentence with the name of the appropriate sensory system. The correct answers are provided at the bottom of this page. Before proceeding, review material related to your incorrect answers and omissions.

1. The inferotemporal cortex is an area of secondary _____ cortex.

2. The dorsal and ventral streams are part of the _____ system.

3. The primary _____ cortex is tonotopically organized.

4. The inferior colliculi and medial geniculate nuclei are components of the _____ system.

5. The dorsal-column medial-lemniscus system and the anterolateral system are pathways of the _____ system.

6. The ventral posterior nuclei, the intralaminar nuclei, and the parafascicular nuclei are all thalamic nuclei of the _____ system.

7. The periaqueductal gray and the raphé nuclei are involved in blocking the perception of _____.

8. One pathway of the _____ system projects from the amygdala and pyriform cortex, to the medial dorsal nucleus, and then to orbitofrontal cortex.

9. The ventral posterior nuclei are thalamic relay nuclei of both the somatosensory and _____ systems.

10. Unlike the projections of all other sensory systems, the projections of the _____ system are primarily ipsilateral.

8.6 Selective Attention

Selective attention is the ability to focus on only a small subset of the multitude of stimuli that are received by sensory organs at any one time. There are two aspects to selective attention: It improves the perception of the stimuli that are its focus, and it interferes with the perception of the stimuli that are not its focus. For example, if you focus your attention on a potentially important announcement in a noisy airport, your chances of understanding it increase; but your chances of understanding a simultaneous comment from a traveling companion decrease.

Single-cell recording studies have linked selective attention to secondary sensory cortex. For example, when mon-

keys were trained to respond to one visual stimulus and ignore another, the responses of their prestriate and inferotemporal cortex neurons to the target stimulus were increased, whereas the responses to the ignored stimulus were decreased (Moran & Desimone, 1985; Spitzer, Desimone, & Moran, 1988); such changes did not occur in the primary visual cortex. Similarly, when human subjects were asked to watch a test stimulus for subtle changes in either shape, color, or velocity, their ability to perceive the changes in a particular dimension was significantly improved when they attended to that dimension. And when they attended to one dimension, blood flow to the particular area of the secondary visual cortex that specializes in its analysis increased (Corbetta et al., 1990).

The cocktail-party phenomenon makes an important point about the nature of attention. The **cocktail-party phenomenon** is the fact that even when you are focusing so intently on one conversation that you are totally unaware of the content of other conversations going on around you, the mention of your name in one of the other conversations immediately gains access to your consciousness. This phenomenon suggests that your brain can block from consciousness all stimuli except those of a particular kind while still unconsciously monitoring the blocked-out stimuli just in case something comes up that requires attention.

Cocktail-party phenomenon. The ability to unconsciously monitor the contents of one conversation while consciously focusing on another.

CONCLUSION

This chapter began by introducing you to three important principles of sensory system organization (8.1): hierarchical organization, functional segregation, and parallel processing. Then, it reviewed each of the five exteroceptive sensory systems, with an emphasis on cortical function: the visual system (8.2), the auditory system (8.3), the somatosensory system (8.4), and the chemical sensory systems—smell and taste (8.5). It concluded with a brief discussion of selective attention (8.6).

Although the ultimate products of sensory systems are unitary perceptual experiences, the fundamental mechanisms by which the systems produce these unitary experiences are not unitary at all. Each sensory system conducts different aspects of its input over separate parallel pathways through a series of specialized, hierarchically organized structures, each of which performs a different analysis. In healthy persons, these independent neural analyses are ulti-mately reconstituted into compelling unitary experiences, and that is why the nonunitary nature of sensory system function is often most apparent in neuropsychological patients.

In this chapter, you learned much about the function of healthy sensory systems from Dr. P., the visual agnosic who mistook his wife for a hat; from D.B., the man with blindsight; from Karl Lashley, the physiological psychologist who used his scotoma to turn a friend's head into a wallpaper pattern; from D.F., who showed by her accurate reaching that she perceived the size, shape, and orientation of objects that she could not describe; from Aunt Betty, the asomatognosic who lost the left side of her body; from Miss C., the student who felt no pain and died as a result; and from the American Civil War amputee who experienced a leg that he did not have.

FOOD FOR THOUGHT

1. Many amputees who suffer from phantom limb pain receive little or no treatment because "after all, it's all in their heads." Discuss.

2. How has this chapter changed your concept of perception?

3. The theory that there are sensory circuits that directly control behavior and others that mediate conscious perception of the same stimuli has some interesting evolutionary implications. Discuss. Why did consciousness evolve?

KEY TERMS

Exteroceptive sensory systems *(p. 180)*
Primary sensory cortex *(p. 180)*
Secondary sensory cortex *(p. 180)*
Association cortex *(p. 180)*
Hierarchical organization *(p. 180)*
Sensation *(p. 181)*
Perception *(p. 181)*
Functional segregation *(p. 181)*
Parallel processing *(p. 182)*
Prestriate cortex *(p. 183)*
Inferotemporal cortex *(p. 183)*
Posterior parietal cortex *(p. 183)*
Scotoma *(p. 183))*
Perimetry test *(p. 183)*
Completion *(p. 184)*

Hemianopsic patients *(p. 184)*
Blindsight *(p. 184)*
Subjective contours *(p. 185)*
Dorsal stream *(p. 186)*
Ventral stream *(p. 186)*
Agnosia *(p. 187)*
Visual agnosia *(p. 187)*
Prosopagnosia *(p. 187)*
Tympanic membrane *(p. 189)*
Ossicles *(p. 189)*
Oval window *(p. 189)*
Cochlea *(p. 189)*
Organ of Corti *(p. 189)*
Hair cells *(p. 189)*
Basilar membrane *(p. 189)*
Tectorial membrane *(p. 189)*
Auditory nerve *(p. 189)*
Retinotopic *(p. 189)*
Tonotopic *(p. 189)*
Semicircular canals *(p. 190)*
Vestibular system *(p. 190)*

Superior olives *(p. 191)*
Inferior colliculi *(p. 191)*
Medial geniculate nuclei *(p. 191)*
Word deafness *(p. 193)*
Glabrous skin *(p. 193)*
Free nerve endings *(p. 193)*
Pacinian corpuscles *(p. 193)*
Stereognosis *(p. 194)*
Dermatome *(p. 194)*
Dorsal-column medial-lemniscus system *(p. 194)*
Anterolateral system *(p. 194)*
Dorsal columns *(p. 194)*
Medial lemniscus *(p. 195)*
Ventral posterior nucleus *(p. 195)*
Somatotopic *(p. 196)*
Somatosensory homunculus *(p. 196)*
Astereognosis *(p. 197)*
Asomatognosia *(p. 197)*
Anosognosia *(p. 198)*

Contralateral neglect *(p. 198)*
Anterior cingulate cortex *(p. 199)*
Gate-control theory *(p. 199)*
Periaqueductal gray (PAG) *(p. 199)*
Endorphins *(p. 199)*
Phantom limb *(p. 200)*
Flavor *(p. 201)*
Pheromones *(p. 201)*
Olfactory mucosa *(p. 202)*
Olfactory bulbs *(p. 202)*
Pyriform cortex *(p. 202)*
Medial dorsal nuclei *(p. 202)*
Orbitofrontal cortex *(p. 202)*
Taste buds *(p. 203)*
Solitary nucleus *(p. 203)*
Anosmia *(p. 204)*
Ageusia *(p. 204)*
Selective attention *(p. 205)*
Cocktail-party phenomenon *(p. 206)*

ADDITIONAL READING

The following two books provide excellent summaries of recent research on the cortical mechanisms of perception; the first focuses on the visual system, the second on recent PET studies of sensory processing:

Posner, M. I., & Raichle, M. E. (1994). *Images of mind*. New York: Scientific American Library.

Roland, P. E. (1993). *Brain activation*. New York: Wiley.

CHAPTER

9

The Sensorimotor System

9.1 Three Principles of Sensorimotor Function

9.2 Sensorimotor Association Cortex

9.3 Secondary Motor Cortex

9.4 Primary Motor Cortex

9.5 Cortical Blood Flow Studies: A Recap of the Sensorimotor Areas of the Cerebral Cortex

9.6 Cerebellum and Basal Ganglia

9.7 Descending Motor Pathways

9.8 Sensorimotor Spinal Circuits

9.9 Central Sensorimotor Programs

Last evening, while standing in a checkout line at the local market, I furtively scanned the headlines on the prominently displayed magazines—WOMAN GIVES BIRTH TO CAT; FLYING SAUCER LANDS IN CLEVELAND SHOPPING MALL; HOW TO LOSE 20 POUNDS IN 2 DAYS. Then, my mind began to wander, and I started to think about beginning to write this chapter. That is when I began to watch Rhonda's movements and to wonder about the neural system that controlled them. Rhonda was the cashier—the best in the place.

I was struck by the complexity of even her simplest movements. As she deftly transferred a bag of tomatoes to the scale, there was a coordinated adjustment in almost every part of her body. In addition to her obvious finger, hand, arm, and shoulder movements, coordinated movements of her head and eyes tracked her hand to the tomatoes; and there were adjustments in the muscles of her feet, legs, trunk, and other arm, which kept her from lurching forward. The accuracy of these responses suggested that they were guided in part by the patterns of visual, somatosensory, and vestibular change that they produced. The term *sensorimotor* in the title of this chapter formally recognizes the critical contribution of sensory input to guiding motor output.

As my purchases flowed through her left hand, Rhonda registered the prices with her right hand and bantered with Rick, the bagger. I was intrigued by how little of what Rhonda was doing appeared to be under her conscious control. She made general decisions about which items to pick up and where to put them, but she seemed to give no thought to the exact means by which these decisions were carried out. Each of her responses could have been made with an infinite number of different combinations of finger, wrist, elbow, shoulder, and body adjustments; but somehow she unconsciously picked one. The higher parts of her sensorimotor system—perhaps her cortex—seemed to issue conscious general commands to other parts of the system, which unconsciously produced a specific pattern of muscular responses that carried them out.

The automaticity of Rhonda's performance was a far cry from the slow, effortful responses that had characterized her first days at the market. Somehow, experience had integrated her individual movements into smooth sequences and, it seemed to have transferred the movements' control from a mode that involved conscious effort to one that did not.

I was suddenly jarred from my contemplations by a voice. "Sir, excuse me, sir, that will be $18.65," Rhonda said, with just a hint of delight at catching me in mid-daydream. I hastily paid my bill, muttered "thank-you," and scurried out of the market. As I write this, I am smiling both at my own embarrassment and at the thought that Rhonda has unknowingly introduced you to three principles of sensorimotor control that are themes of this chapter: (1) The sensorimotor system is hierarchically organized. (2) Motor output is guided by sensory input. (3) Learning changes the nature and the locus of sensorimotor control.

9.1 Three Principles of Sensorimotor Function

Before getting into the details of the sensorimotor system, let's take a closer look at the three principles of sensorimotor function introduced by Rhonda. You will better appreciate these principles if you recognize that they are the very same principles that govern the operation of a large, efficient company.

The Sensorimotor System Is Hierarchically Organized

The operation of both the sensorimotor system and a large, efficient company is directed by commands that cascade down through the levels of a hierarchy—from the association cortex or the company president (the highest levels)to the muscles or the workers (the lowest levels). Like the orders that are issued from the office of a company president, the commands that emerge from the association cortex specify general goals rather than specific plans of action. Neither the association cortex nor the company president routinely gets involved in the details. The main advantage of this *hierarchical organization* is that the higher levels of the hierarchy are left free to perform more complex functions.

Both the sensorimotor system and large, efficient companies are parallel hierarchical systems (see Fetz, 1993; Kalaska & Crammond, 1992); that is, they are hierarchical systems in which signals flow between levels over multiple paths. This parallel structure is what enables the association cortex or company presidents to exert control over the lower levels of the hierarchy in more than one way. For example, the association cortex may directly inhibit an eyeblink reflex to allow the insertion of a contact lens, and a company president may personally organize a delivery to an important customer.

The sensorimotor and company hierarchies are also characterized by *functional segregation*. That is, each level of the sensorimotor and company hierarchies tends to be composed of different units (neural structures or departments), each of which performs a different function.

In summary, the sensorimotor system—like the sensory systems you read about in the preceding chapter—is a parallel, functionally segregated hierarchical system. The main difference between the sensory systems and the sensorimotor system is the primary direction of information flow. In sensory systems, information mainly flows up through the hierarchy; in the sensorimotor system, information mainly flows down.

Motor Output Is Guided by Sensory Input

Efficient companies continuously monitor the effects of their own activities, and they use this information to fine-tune them. The sensorimotor system does the same. The eyes, the organs of balance, and the receptors in skin, muscles, and joints all monitor the progress of our responses; and they feed their information back into sensorimotor circuits. In most instances, this **sensory feedback** plays an important role in directing the continuation of the responses that produced it. The only responses that are not normally influenced by sensory feedback are *ballistic movements*—brief, all-or-none, high-speed movements, such as swatting a fly.

Behavior in the absence of just one kind of sensory feedback—the feedback that is carried by the somatosensory nerves of the arms—was studied in G.O., a former darts champion. An infection had selectively destroyed the somatosensory nerves of G.O.'s arms (Rothwell et al., 1982). He had great difficulty performing intricate responses such as doing up his buttons or picking up coins, even under visual guidance. Other difficulties resulted from his inability to adjust his motor output in the light of unanticipated external disturbances; for example, he could not keep from spilling a cup of coffee if somebody brushed against him. However, G.O.'s greatest problem was his inability to maintain a constant level of muscle contraction:

> The result of this deficit was that even in the simplest of tasks requiring a constant motor output to the hand, G.O. would have to keep a visual check on his progress. For example, when carrying a suitcase, he would frequently glance at it to reassure himself that he had not dropped it some paces back. However, even visual feedback was of little use to him in many tasks. These tended to be those requiring a constant force output such as grasping a pen whilst writing or holding a cup. Here, visual information was insufficient for him to be able to correct any errors that were developing in the output since, after a period, he had no indication of the pressure that he was exerting on an object; all he saw was either the pen or cup slipping from his grasp. (Rothwell et al., 1982, p. 539)

Figure 9.1 A general model of the sensorimotor system. Notice its hierarchical structure, its functional segregation, its parallel descending pathways, and its feedback circuits.

Many adjustments in motor output that occur in response to sensory feedback are controlled by the lower levels of the sensorimotor hierarchy without the involvement of the higher levels (see Lacquaniti, 1992). In the same way, large companies run more efficiently if the clerks do not have to check with the company president each time they encounter a minor problem.

Learning Changes the Nature and Locus of Sensorimotor Control

When a company is just starting up, each individual decision is made by the company president after careful

Sensory feedback. Sensory signals that are produced by a response and are used to guide the continuation of the response.

Posterior parietal association cortex. The cortex of the posterior parietal lobe, which is thought to receive and integrate the spatial information that guides voluntary behavior.

Frontal eye field. The area of prefrontal cortex that plays a role in the control of eye movements.

consideration. However, as the company develops, many individual actions are coordinated into sequences of prescribed procedures that are routinely carried out by junior executives.

Similar changes occur during sensorimotor learning (see Halsband & Freund, 1993). During the initial stages of motor learning, each individual response is performed under conscious control; then, after much practice, individual responses become organized into continuous integrated sequences of action that flow smoothly and are adjusted by sensory feedback without conscious regulation. If you think for a moment about the sensorimotor skills you have acquired (e.g., typing, swimming, knitting, basketball playing, dancing, piano playing), you will appre-

ciate that the organization of individual responses into continuous motor programs and the transfer of their control to lower levels of the nervous system characterizes most sensorimotor learning.

A General Model of Sensorimotor System Function

Figure 9.1 is a model that illustrates several principles of sensorimotor system function. Notice its hierarchical structure, the functional segregation of the levels (e.g., of secondary motor cortex), the parallel connections between levels, and the numerous feedback pathways.

9.2 Sensorimotor Association Cortex

There are two major areas of sensorimotor association cortex. These are the posterior parietal association cortex and the dorsolateral prefrontal association cortex.

ious areas of *secondary motor cortex,* and to the **frontal eye field**—a small area of prefrontal cortex that controls eye movement (see Figure 9.2).

Posterior Parietal Association Cortex

Before an effective movement can be initiated, certain information is required. The nervous system must know the original positions of the parts of the body that are to be moved, and it must know the positions of any external objects with which the body is going to interact. The **posterior parietal association cortex** plays an important role in integrating these two kinds of information. You learned in Chapter 8 that the posterior parietal cortex is classified as *association cortex* because it receives input from more than one sensory system. It receives information from the three sensory systems that play roles in the localization of the body and external objects in space: the visual system, the auditory system, and the somatosensory system. In turn, much of the output of posterior parietal cortex goes to areas of motor cortex, which are located in the frontal cortex: to *dorsolateral prefrontal association cortex,* to var-

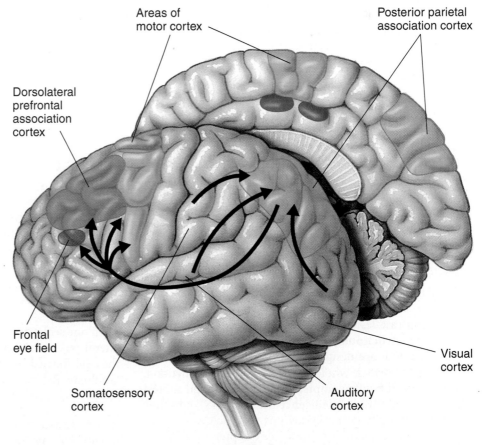

Figure 9.2 The major cortical input and output pathways of the posterior parietal association cortex. Shown are the lateral surface of the left hemisphere and the medial surface of the right hemisphere.

Figure 9.3 A drawing of a 1917 photograph of a patient with constructional apraxia. This war veteran is having difficulty duplicating the stack of blocks on his left. (Drawn from Poppelreuter, 1917.)

Damage to the posterior parietal cortex can result in two movement disorders: apraxia and contralateral neglect. The symptoms of these two disorders confirm the role of the posterior parietal cortex in sensorimotor function.

Apraxia is a disorder of voluntary movement that is not attributable to a simple motor deficit (e.g., not to paralysis or weakness) or to deficits in comprehension or motivation (see Benton, 1985). Remarkably, apraxic patients have difficulty making specific movements when they are requested to do so, but they can readily perform the very same movements when they are not thinking about what they are doing. Although its symptoms are bilateral, apraxia is often caused by unilateral damage to the left posterior parietal lobe. In contrast, lesions of the right posterior parietal lobe produce **constructional apraxia**—a bilateral disruption of movements that are designed to assemble components of an object to form a whole. Patients with constructional apraxia have difficulty completing the block design subtest of the Wechsler Adult Intelligence Scale (WAIS), and they also have difficulty doing jigsaw puzzles, such as those of the WAIS object assembly subtest (see Chapter 5). In Figure 9.3, an illustration drawn from a 1917 photograph, a brain-damaged war veteran is failing a test of constructional apraxia.

Contralateral neglect is a disturbance of the patient's ability to respond to visual, auditory, and somatosensory stimuli on the side of the body contralateral to the side of a brain lesion (see Rafal, 1994). The disturbance is often associated with large lesions of the right posterior parietal lobe (see Weintraub & Mesluam, 1989). For example, Mrs. S. suffered from contralateral neglect after a massive stroke to the posterior portions of her right hemisphere. Like many other neuropsychological patients, she developed ways of dealing with her deficiency:

> She has totally lost the idea of "left", with regard to both the world and her own body. Sometimes she complains that her portions are too small, but this is because she only eats from the right half of the plate—it does not occur to her that it has a left half as well. Sometimes, she will put on lipstick, and make up the right half of her face, leaving the left half completely neglected: it is almost impossible to treat these things, because her attention cannot be drawn to them....

> ... She has worked out strategies for dealing with her [problem]. She cannot look left, directly, she cannot turn left, so what she does is turn right—and right through a circle. Thus she requested, and was given, a rotating wheelchair. And now if she cannot find something which she knows should be there, she swivels to the right, through a circle, until it comes into view.... If her portions seem too small, she will swivel to the right, keeping her eyes to the right, until the previously missed half now comes into view; she will eat this, or rather half of this, and feel less hungry than before. But if she is still hungry, or if she thinks on the matter, and realises that she may have perceived only half of the missing half, she will make a second rotation till the remaining quarter comes into view. (Sacks, 1985, pp. 73–74)[1]

Dorsolateral Prefrontal Association Cortex

The other large area of association cortex that has important sensorimotor functions is the **dorsolateral prefrontal association cortex** (Goldman-Rakic, Bates, & Chafee, 1992). It receives projections from posterior parietal cortex; and it sends projections to areas of *secondary motor cortex,* to *primary motor cortex,* and to the *frontal eye field* (see Figure 9.4).

In one series of experiments, the activity in single dorsolateral prefrontal neurons was recorded in monkeys while they performed an *oculomotor delayed-response task* (see Goldman-Rakic, Bates, & Chafee, 1992). The monkeys

---

[1]From *The Man Who Mistook His Wife for a Hat and Other Clinical Tales* (pp. 73–74) by Oliver Sacks, 1985, New York: Summit Books. Copyright © 1970, 1980, 1983, 1984, 1985 by Oliver Sacks. Reprinted by permission of Summit Books, a division of Simon & Schuster.

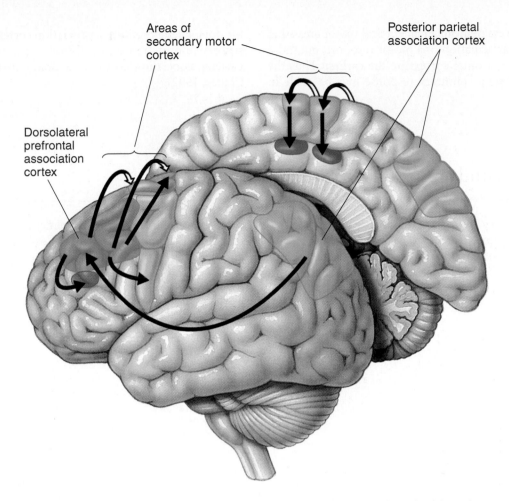

Figure 9.4 The major cortical input and output pathways of the dorsolateral prefrontal association cortex. Shown are the lateral surface of the left hemisphere and the medial surface of the right hemisphere.

were trained to stare at a central fixation point while a target stimulus was flashed somewhere in their visual field; then, after a brief delay, the monkeys were required to look

Apraxia. A loss of the ability to perform voluntary movements upon request.

Constructional apraxia. The inability to perform tests of construction in the absence of primary sensory deficits or general intellectual impairment.

Contralateral neglect. A disturbance of the patient's ability to respond to visual, auditory, and somatosensory stimuli on one side of the body, usually the left side of the body following damage to the right parietal lobe.

Dorsolateral prefrontal association cortex. The area of the prefrontal association cortex that plays a role in the initiation of complex voluntary motor responses.

to where the target stimulus had been in order to earn a reward. Many dorsolateral prefrontal neurons were found to have *memory fields*; that is, many prefrontal neurons increased their firing only when a target stimulus in a particular location disappeared from view, and they maintained the increase until the eye-movement response was performed. On the basis of such observations, it has been suggested that one function of prefrontal association cortex is to provide a mental representation of stimuli to which the subject is going to respond.

In another series of experiments, the activity of dorsolateral prefrontal neurons was recorded while monkeys performed a *delayed matching-to-sample task* (Di Pelligrino & Wise, 1991). The monkeys were briefly shown a sample stimulus; then, after a delay, they were shown the sample and another stimulus. The correct response was to reach for the sample. Some dorsolateral prefrontal units responded to the sensory qualities of the sample both during its presentation and in the delay period—presumably on the basis of signals from posterior parietal cortex. Other prefrontal neurons responded before and during the response. There are neurons in all cortical motor areas that begin to fire in anticipation of a motor response, but those in dorsolateral prefrontal cortex fire the earliest. Thus the decision to initiate a voluntary response may be made in the dorsolateral prefrontal association cortex on the basis of sensory information supplied to it, primarily by posterior parietal association cortex (see Goldman-Rakic, Bates, & Chafee, 1992).

9.3   Secondary Motor Cortex

Areas of **secondary motor cortex** are those that receive much of their input from association cortex and send much of their output to primary motor cortex. Until recently, only two areas of secondary motor cortex were known: the supplementary motor area and the premotor cortex. Both of these large areas are clearly visible on the lateral surface of the frontal lobe, just anterior to the *primary motor cortex*. The **supplementary motor area** wraps over the top of the frontal lobe and extends down its medial surface into the longitudinal fissure, and the **premotor cortex** runs in a strip from the supplementary motor area to the lateral fissure. However, two other areas of the secondary motor cortex—the *cingulate motor areas*—have recently been discovered in the cortex of the cingulate gyrus, just ventral to the supplementary motor area. Figure 9.5 shows the location of the supplementary motor area, the premotor cortex, and the two cingulate motor areas.

The areas of secondary motor cortex are anatomically similar to one another in several respects (see Dum & Strick, 1992). For example, each sends many of its axons to primary motor cortex, each receives axons back from primary motor cortex, each is reciprocally connected to the other areas of secondary motor cortex, each sends axons directly into the motor circuits of the brain stem and spinal cord, and each is **somatotopic**—organized according to a map of the body. There are also two important functional similarities: Electrical stimulation to particular sites within each area of secondary motor cortex results in complex movements of corresponding parts of the body, and neurons in each area of secondary motor cortex respond prior to and during voluntary motor responses.

Research on secondary motor cortex has focused on the supplementary motor area and the premotor cortex. Input to the supplementary motor area is primarily somatosensory, whereas input to the premotor cortex is primarily visual.

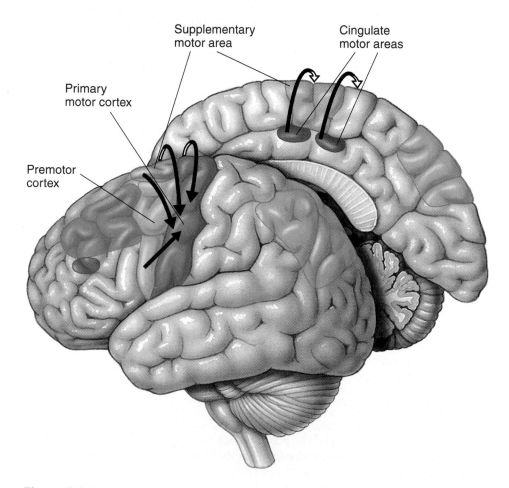

Figure 9.5 Four areas of the secondary motor cortex—the supplementary motor area, the premotor cortex, and the two cingulate motor areas—and their output to the primary motor cortex. Shown are the lateral surface of the left hemisphere and the medial surface of the right hemisphere.

Supplementary Motor Area

Several findings suggest that the function of the supplementary motor area is to program individual movements into coordinated sequences (see Ashe & Urgurbil, 1994; Kurata, 1992). For example, Brinkman (1984) found that monkeys with unilateral lesions of the supplementary motor area had no difficulty making individual reaching and grasping movements of the contralateral arm, hand, and fingers; but they could not organize the individual movements into smooth sequences that would enable them to pick up a peanut. They had particular difficulty coordinating the movements of their two hands (see Figure 9.6).

The supplementary motor area appears to be particularly important during the learning of new motor sequences. Aizawa et al. (1991) found that neurons of the supplementary motor area that typically become more active just prior to a learned arm movement do not show this anticipatory firing once the arm movement has been well learned. Also, supplementary motor neurons respond particularly vigorously before response sequences that are triggered by internal representations in memory rather than by external stimuli (Mushiake, Inase, & Tanji, 1991).

Premotor Cortex

Like the supplementary motor area, the premotor cortex is involved in the preparation for movement. However, in contrast to the supplementary motor area, the premotor cortex programs voluntary movements that are carried out under the guidance of external stimuli rather than by internal representations. The premotor cortex is activated only when sensory information is being used to guide the development of a motor program. For example, in a positron emission tomographic (PET) study of human subjects, the premotor cortex was activated when the subjects made various hand movements in time to a metronome but not when they made the same movements in the absence of any external sensory influence (Colebatch et al., 1991).

Secondary motor cortex. Areas of the cerebral cortex that receive much of their input from association cortex and send much of their output to the primary motor cortex.

Supplementary motor area. The area of the secondary motor cortex that is within and adjacent to the longitudinal fissure.

Premotor cortex. An area of the secondary motor cortex that lies between the supplementary motor area and the lateral fissure.

Somatotopic. Organized according to a map of the surface of the body.

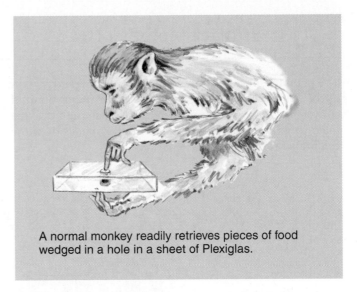

A normal monkey readily retrieves pieces of food wedged in a hole in a sheet of Plexiglas.

A monkey with a unilateral supplementary motor cortex lesion has difficulty coordinating the individual actions necessary to retrieve the food.

Figure 9.6 Illustration of a deficit in bimanual coordination that was produced by a unilateral supplementary motor area lesion. The monkey with the lesion had no difficulty making individual movements, but it could not produce the coordinated sequence of movements required to obtain the food. (Adapted from Brinkman, 1984.)

Premotor cortex neurons have an interesting characteristic. In other regions of the brain, visual receptive fields are *retinocentric*; that is, when the eyes move, the receptive fields move with them, thus maintaining the same retinal location. However, *bimodal cells of the premotor cortex* (premotor neurons that respond to both somatosensory and visual stimuli) have visual receptive fields that move with the contralateral hand (Graziano, Yap, & Gross, 1994). For example, a bimodal premotor neuron might have a visual receptive field that is centered on the contralateral hand regardless of the hand's position or the position of the eyes.

The **primary motor cortex** is located in the *precentral gyrus* of the frontal lobe (see Figure 9.7). It is the major point of convergence of cortical sensorimotor signals, and it is the major point of departure of sensorimotor signals from the cerebral cortex.

In 1937, Penfield and Boldrey mapped the primary motor cortex of conscious human patients during neurosurgery by applying electrical stimulation to various points on the cortical surface and noting which part of the body moved in response to each stimulation. They found that the

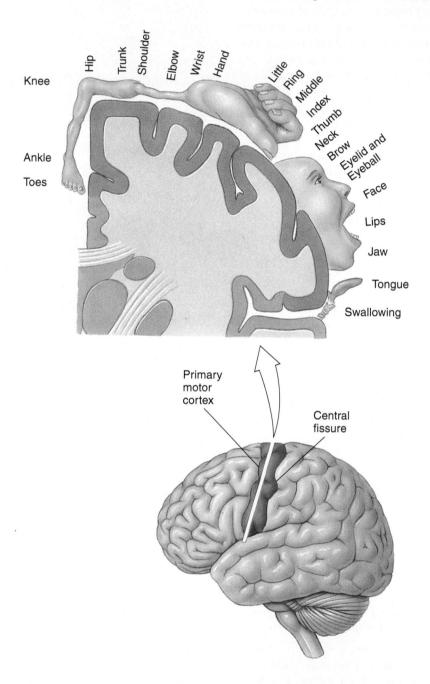

Figure 9.7 The motor homunculus: The somatotopic map of the human primary motor cortex. Stimulation of sites in the primary motor cortex elicits simple movements in the indicated parts of the body. (Adapted from Penfield & Rasmussen, 1950.)

primary motor cortex is somatotopically organized. The somatotopic layout of the human primary motor cortex is commonly referred to as the **motor homunculus** (see Figure 9.7). Notice that most of the primary motor cortex is dedicated to the control of parts of the body that are capable of intricate movements, such as the hands and mouth. More recent research has revealed that in monkeys—and thus presumably in humans—there are two different areas in the primary motor cortex of each hemisphere that control the contralateral hand (see Strick & Preston, 1983).

The somatotopic layout of the primary motor cortex hand area has been studied in detail by recording the activity of single neurons during the movement of individual fingers (Schieber & Hibbard, 1993). The recordings showed that most primary motor cortex finger neurons are involved in the movement of more than a single finger and that there is considerable overlap in the location of neurons that control the various fingers. Thus the control of any individual finger movement depends on the activity of a network of neurons that is widely distributed throughout the primary motor cortex hand area rather than being located in one somatotopically segregated finger area.

Each site in the primary motor cortex controls the movements of a particular group of muscles, and each receives somatosensory feedback, via the somatosensory cortex, from receptors in these muscles and in the joints that they influence. There is one notable exception to this general pattern of feedback. One of the hand areas in the primary motor cortex of each hemisphere receives input from receptors in the skin rather than from receptors in the muscles and joints. Presumably, this adaptation is the basis for the highly developed stereognosic abilities of your hands. Close your eyes, and explore an object with your hands. Notice how **stereognosis**—the process of identifying objects by touch—is based on a complex interplay between motor responses and the somatosensory stimulation produced by them.

Neurons in the arm area of the primary motor cortex fire maximally when the arm reaches in a particular direction; each neuron has a different preferred direction. Georgopoulos et al., (1992) dissociated the direction of force and the direction of movement by applying external forces to monkeys' arms while the arms reached in various directions. The firing of primary motor cortex neurons was correlated with the direction of the resulting movement rather than with the direction of the force that was generated to produce the movement.

Damage to the human primary motor cortex has less effect than you might expect, given that it is the major point of departure of motor fibers from the cerebral cortex. Damage to the primary motor cortex disrupts a patient's ability to move one body part (e.g., one finger) independently of others (see Schieber, 1990); it produces **astereognosia** (deficits in stereognosis); and it reduces the speed, accuracy, and force of a patient's movements. It does not, however, produce paralysis.

9.5 Cortical Blood Flow Studies: A Recap of the Sensorimotor Areas of the Human Cerebral Cortex

The cortical blood flow studies of Roland and his colleagues serve to recap what you have learned in this chapter about the sensorimotor areas of the human cerebral cortex (see Roland, 1993). The rationale for their method is based on the finding that blood flow increases in those regions of the nervous system that are particularly active. To measure regional blood flow in the cortex of conscious human subjects, Roland and his colleagues injected an inert, slightly radioactive chemical, *xenon 133,* into the carotid artery and then measured the accumulation of radioactivity in various parts of the ipsilateral cortex, using a bank of *scintillation counters* placed next to the head.

For each subject, regional cortical blood flow was first measured during a 45-second period of relaxation with eyes shut. Then, 20 minutes later, a second injection was administered; but this time, the subject engaged in some activity

Primary motor cortex. The cortex of the precentral gyrus, which is the major point of departure for motor signals descending from the cortex into lower levels of the sensorimotor system.

Motor homunculus. The somatotopic map in the primary motor cortex.

Stereognosis. The process of identifying objects by touch.

Astereognosia. A difficulty in recognizing objects by touch that is not attributable to a simple sensory deficit or to general intellectual impairment.

Areas activated by a
complex sequence of finger
movements of the right
hand.

Areas activated by just
thinking about performing a
complex sequence of right-
hand finger movements.

Areas activated by making
a series of forceful flexions
with the index finger of the
right hand.

Areas activated by the
performance of a finger
maze test with the right
hand.

Figure 9.8 The regions of the lateral surface of the human left hemisphere that display increases in blood flow during various voluntary activities of the right hand. (Adapted from Roland, 1993).

during the 45-second test period. The output of the scintillation counters was fed into a computer, which assessed the amount of change in each area of the cortex between the baseline resting condition and the test condition.

The results of Roland et al.'s studies are summarized in Figure 9.8, which shows the patterns of regional blood flow that were associated with four different activities of the contralateral hand:

1. The first display shows the areas of increased blood flow that occurred in the left hemisphere during a prescribed sequence of finger movements of the right hand. There was increased blood flow in prefrontal cortex, in the supplementary motor area, in the hand areas of primary motor cortex and primary somatosensory cortex.

2. The second display shows the increases in blood flow in the left hemisphere that occurred when the subjects remained motionless but thought of performing the same prescribed sequence of right-hand finger movements. The increases were restricted to the supplementary motor area.

3. The third display illustrates the left-hemisphere changes that occurred during forceful repeated flexion of one finger of the right hand. There was an increase in blood flow to the hand areas of primary motor and primary somatosensory cortex.

4. The fourth display illustrates the blood flow changes that occurred in the left hemisphere during the performance of a *finger maze test*, during which the subjects, with their eyes shut, moved a finger along a wire grid

in response to verbal instructions from the experimenter (e.g., "move two spaces to the left, move one space forward, move three spaces back," and so on). Finger maze performance was associated with activity increases in posterior parietal cortex, prefrontal cortex, the supplementary motor area, premotor cortex, and the hand areas of primary motor and primary somatosensory cortex.

Roland and his colleagues concluded that the posterior parietal cortex provides sensory information to the supplementary motor area and the premotor cortex, that the sup-plementary motor area and the premotor cortex exert most of their influence through the primary motor cortex, that the supplementary motor area is responsible for developing and executing programs for controlling the sequencing of patterns of motor output, that the premotor cortex modifies existing motor programs on the basis of sensory input, and that the primary motor and somatosensory areas can execute a series of simple repeated movements without the contribution of the association or secondary cortex. On this note, we descend into the subcortical levels of the sensorimotor hierarchy.

9.6 Cerebellum and Basal Ganglia

The cerebellum and the basal ganglia are both important sensorimotor structures (see Figures 3.23 and 3.31), but neither is a major part of the pathway through which signals descend the sensorimotor hierarchy. Instead, both the cerebellum and the basal ganglia interact with different levels of the sensorimotor hierarchy, and in so doing they coordinate and modulate its activities.

Cerebellum

The complexity of the cerebellum is suggested by its structure. Although it constitutes only 10% of the mass of the brain, it contains more than half of its neurons. The cerebellum is thought to receive information about plans of action from the primary and secondary motor cortex, information about descending motor signals from the brain stem motor nuclei, and feedback from motor responses via the somatosensory and vestibular systems. The cerebellum is thought to compare these three sources of input and correct ongoing movements that deviate from their intended course (see Llinás & Welsh, 1993). It has also been suggested that the cerebellum plays important roles in learning and cognition (e.g., Leiner, Leiner, & Dow, 1993), but this suggestion remains controversial (Glickstein, 1992).

The consequences of diffuse cerebellar damage are devastating. The patient loses the ability to precisely control the direction, force, velocity, and amplitude of movements and the ability to adapt patterns of motor output to changing conditions. The person has difficulty maintaining steady postures (e.g., standing), and the attempts to do so frequently lead to tremor. There are also severe disturbances in balance, gait, speech, and the control of eye movement.

Basal Ganglia

The basal ganglia do not contain as many neurons as the cerebellum, but in one sense they are more complex. Unlike the cerebellum, which is organized systematically in lobes, columns, and layers, the basal ganglia are a complex heterogeneous collection of nuclei with an intricate modular internal circuitry (see Graybiel et al., 1994; Mink & Thach, 1993).

The anatomy of the basal ganglia suggests that, like the cerebellum, they perform a modulatory function. They contribute no fibers to descending motor pathways; instead, they are part of neural loops that receive cortical input from various cortical areas and transmit it back via the thalamus to the various areas of motor cortex (see Goldman-Rakic & Selemon, 1990; Middleton & Strick, 1994).

The projections of the basal ganglia to dorsolateral prefrontal association cortex suggest that the basal ganglia may be involved in sensorimotor learning. Support for this view has come from a series of experiments in which the responses of individual *tonically active neurons (TANs)* in the monkey striatum were recorded during Pavlovian conditioning (see Graybiel et al., 1994). The monkeys learned that a click signaled the presentation of fruit juice. At first the clicks had no effect on the monkeys' behavior; but after a series of click-juice pairings, the click elicited licking, even when no fruit juice was subsequently presented. The effects of the clicks on the firing of the TANs parallelled the learning. At first, the clicks had no effect on the firing of the TANs; however, after conditioning, each click produced a brief inhibition of firing. These inhibitory responses disappeared when the monkeys underwent *extinction* (repeated presentations of the clicks with no juice).

Before continuing your descent into the sensorimotor circuits of the spinal cord, review the sensorimotor circuits of the cortex, cerebellum, and basal ganglia by completing the following statements. The correct answers are provided at the bottom of this page. Before proceeding, review material related to your incorrect answers and omissions.

1. Visual, auditory, and somatosensory input converges on the _____ _____ association cortex.

2. A small area of the frontal cortex called the frontal _____ plays a major role in the control of eye movement.

3. Contralateral neglect is often associated with large lesions of the right _____ lobe.

4. The _____ prefrontal cortex seems to play an important role in initiating complex voluntary responses.

5. The secondary motor area that is just dorsal to premotor cortex and is largely hidden from view on the medial surface of each hemisphere is the _____.

6. Most of the direct sensory input to the supplementary motor area comes from the _____ system.

7. Most of the direct sensory input to the premotor cortex comes from the _____ system.

8. The _____ cortex is the main point of departure of motor signals from the cerebral cortex to lower levels of the sensorimotor hierarchy.

9. The foot area of the motor homunculus is in the _____ fissure.

10. Although the _____ constitutes only 10% of the mass of the brain, it contains more than half its neurons.

11. The _____ are part of neural loops that receive input from various cortical areas and transmit it back to various areas of motor cortex via the thalamus.

12. In one experiment, a click conditional stimulus acquired the ability to inhibit tonically active neurons in the monkey _____.

Neural signals are conducted from the primary motor cortex to the motor neurons of the spinal cord over four different pathways. Two pathways descend in the *dorsolateral* region of the spinal cord, and two descend in the *ventromedial* region of the spinal cord.

Dorsolateral Corticospinal Tract and Dorsolateral Corticorubrospinal Tract

One group of axons that descends from the primary motor cortex descends through the *medullary pyramids*—two bulges on the ventral surface of the medulla; then it decussates and continues to descend in the contralateral dorsolateral spinal white matter. This group of axons constitutes the **dorsolateral corticospinal tract.** Most notable among its neurons are the **Betz cells**—extremely large pyramidal neurons of the primary motor cortex. Their axons terminate in the lower regions of the spinal cord on motor neurons that project to the muscles of the legs. They are thought to be the means by which we exert rapid and powerful voluntary control over our legs.

Most axons of the dorsolateral corticospinal pathway synapse on small interneurons of the spinal gray matter, which synapse on the motor neurons of distal muscles of the wrist, hands, fingers, and toes. Primates and the few other mammals that are capable of moving their digits independently (e.g., hamsters and raccoons) have dorsolateral corticospinal tract neurons that synapse directly on digit motor neurons.

A second group of axons that descends from the primary motor cortex synapses in the *red nucleus* of the midbrain. The axons of the red nucleus cells then decussate and descend through the medulla, where some of them terminate in the nuclei of the cranial nerves that control the muscles of the face. The rest continue to descend in the dorsolateral portion of the spinal cord. This pathway is called the **dorsolateral corticorubrospinal tract** (*rubro* refers to the red nucleus). The axons of the dorsolateral corticorubrospinal tract synapse on interneurons that in turn synapse on motor neurons that project to the distal muscles of the arms and legs.

The two divisions of the dorsolateral motor pathway—the direct dorsolateral corticospinal tract and the indirect dorsolateral corticorubrospinal tract—are illustrated schematically in Figure 9.9 on page 222.

Ventromedial Corticospinal Tract and Ventromedial Cortico–Brainstem–Spinal Tract

Just as there are two major divisions of the dorsolateral motor pathway, one direct (the corticospinal tract) and one indirect (the corticorubrospinal tract), there are two major divisions of the ventromedial motor pathway, one direct and one indirect. The direct ventromedial pathway is the **ventromedial corticospinal tract,** and the indirect one—as you might infer from its cumbersome but descriptive name—is the **ventromedial cortico–brainstem–spinal tract.**

The long axons of the ventromedial corticospinal tract descend ipsilaterally from the primary motor cortex directly into the ventromedial areas of the spinal white matter. As each axon of the ventromedial corticospinal tract descends, it branches diffusely and innervates the interneuron circuits in several different spinal segments on both sides of the spinal gray matter.

The ventromedial cortico–brainstem–spinal tract comprises motor cortex axons that feed into a complex network of brain stem structures. The axons of some of the neurons in this complex brain stem motor network then descend bilaterally in the ventromedial portion of the spinal cord. Each side carries signals from both hemispheres, and each neuron synapses on the interneurons of several different spinal cord segments that control the proximal muscles of the trunk and limbs.

What brain stem structures interact with the ventromedial cortico–brainstem–spinal tract? There are four major

Dorsolateral corticospinal tract. The motor tract that leaves the primary motor cortex, descends to the medullary pyramids, decussates, and then descends in the contralateral dorsolateral spinal white matter.

Betz cells. Large pyramidal neurons of the primary motor cortex that synapse directly on spinal motor neurons, mainly in the lower spinal cord.

Dorsolateral corticorubrospinal tract. The descending motor tract that synapses in the red nucleus of the midbrain, decussates, and descends in the dorsolateral spinal white matter.

Ventromedial corticospinal tract. The direct ventromedial motor pathway, which descends ipsilaterally from the primary motor cortex directly into the ventromedial areas of the spinal white matter.

Ventromedial cortico–brainstem–spinal tract. The indirect ventromedial motor pathway, which descends bilaterally from the primary motor cortex to several interconnected brainstem motor structures and then descends in the ventromedial portions of the spinal cord.

Dorsolateral Corticospinal Tract

Medullary
pyramid

Dorsolateral
portion of the
spinal cord

To contralateral
distal limb
muscles

Dorsolateral Corticorubrospinal Tract

To muscles of
contralateral
face

Red nucleus

Nuclei of
cranial nerve
motor neurons

To contralateral
distal limb
muscles

Figure 9.9 The two divisions of the dorsolateral motor pathway: The dorsolateral corticospinal tract and the dorsolateral corticorubrospinal motor tract. The projections from only one hemisphere are shown.

ones: (1) the **tectum,** which receives auditory and visual information about spatial location; (2) the **vestibular nucleus,** which receives information about balance from receptors in the semicircular canals of the inner ear; (3) the **reticular formation,** which, among other things, contains motor programs for complex species-common movements such as walking, swimming, and jumping; and (4) the motor nuclei of the cranial nerves that control the muscles of the face.

The two divisions of the descending ventromedial pathway—the direct ventromedial corticospinal tract and the indirect ventromedial cortico–brainstem–spinal tract—are illustrated in Figure 9.10.

The Two Dorsolateral Motor Pathways and the Two Ventromedial Motor Pathways Compared

The descending dorsolateral and ventromedial pathways are similar in that each is composed of two major tracts, one whose axons descend directly to the spinal cord and the other whose axons synapse in the brain stem on neurons that in turn descend to the spinal cord. However, the two dorsolateral tracts differ from the two ventromedial tracts in two major respects:

Ventromedial Corticospinal Tract

Ventromedial Cortico-Brainstem-Spinal Tract

Vestibular nucleus

Tectum

Motor nuclei of cranial nerves

Reticular formation

Ventromedial portion of the spinal cord

To trunk and proximal limb muscles

To trunk and proximal limb muscles

Figure 9.10 The two divisions of the ventromedial motor pathway: The ventromedial corticospinal tract and the ventromedial cortico–brainstem–spinal tract. The projections from only one hemisphere are shown.

1. The two ventromedial tracts are much more diffuse. Many of their axons innervate interneurons on both sides of the spinal gray matter and in several different segments, whereas the axons of the two dorsolateral tracts terminate in the contralateral half of one segment, sometimes directly on a motor neuron.

2. The motor neurons that are activated by the two ventromedial tracts project to proximal muscles of the trunk and limbs (e.g., shoulder muscles), whereas the motor neurons that are activated by the two dorsolateral tracts project to distal muscles (e.g., finger muscles).

Tectum. The division of the midbrain that comprises the superior and inferior colliculi and receives auditory and visual information about spatial location.

Vestibular nucleus. The brainstem nucleus that receives information about balance from the semicircular canals.

Reticular formation. A complex network of nuclei in the core of the brain stem that contains, among other things, motor programs for complex species-common movements such as walking and swimming.

Because all four of the descending motor tracts originate in the cerebral cortex, they are all presumed to mediate voluntary movement; however, major differences in their routes and destinations suggest that they have different functions. This difference was demonstrated in two experiments that were published by Lawrence and Kuypers in 1968.

In their first experiment, Lawrence and Kuypers (1968a) transected (cut through) the left and right dorsolateral corticospinal tracts of their monkey subjects at the point at which the tracts decussate (i.e., in the medullary pyramids). Following surgery, these monkeys could stand, walk, and climb quite normally; however, their ability to use their limbs for other activities was impaired. For example, their reaching movements were weak and poorly directed, particularly in the first few days following the surgery. Although there was substantial improvement in the monkeys' reaching ability over the ensuing weeks, two other deficits remained unabated. First, the monkeys never regained the ability to move their fingers independently of one another; when they picked up pieces of food, they did so by using all of their fingers as a unit, as if they were glued together. And second, they never regained the ability to release objects from their grasp; as a result, once they picked up a piece of food, they often had to root for it in their hand like a pig rooting for truffles in the ground. In view of this latter problem, it is remarkable that they had no difficulty releasing their grasp on the bars of their cage when they were climbing. This point is important because it shows that the same response performed in different contexts can be controlled by different parts of the central nervous system.

In their second experiment, Lawrence and Kuypers (1968b) made additional transections in the monkeys whose dorsolateral corticospinal tracts had already been transected in their first experiment. The dorsolateral corticorubrospinal tract was transected in one group of these monkeys. The monkeys could stand, walk, and climb after this second transection; but when they were sitting, their arms hung limply by their sides (remember that monkeys normally use their arms for standing and walking). In those few instances in which the monkeys did use an arm for reaching, they used it like a rubber-handled rake—throwing it out from the shoulder and using it to draw small objects of interest back along the floor.

The other group of monkeys in the second experiment had both of their ventromedial tracts transected. In contrast to the first group, these subjects had severe postural abnormalities: They had great difficulty walking or sitting. If they did manage to sit or stand without clinging to the bars of their cages, the slightest disturbance, such as a loud noise, frequently made them fall. Although they had some use of their arms, the additional transection of the two ventromedial tracts eliminated their ability to control their shoulders. When they fed, they did so with elbow and whole-hand movements while their upper arms hung limply by their sides.

What do these experiments tell us about the roles of the various descending sensorimotor tracts in the control of movement? They suggest that the two ventromedial tracts are involved in the control of posture and whole-body movements (e.g., walking and climbing) and that they can exert control over the limb movements involved in such activities. In contrast, both dorsolateral tracts—the corticospinal tract and the corticorubrospinal tract—control the reaching movements of the limbs. This redundancy was presumably the basis for the good recovery of limb movement after the initial lesions of the corticospinal dorsolateral tract. However, only the corticospinal division of the dorsolateral system is capable of mediating independent movements of the digits.

9.8 Sensorimotor Spinal Circuits

Muscles

Motor units are the smallest units of motor activity. Each motor unit comprises a single motor neuron and all of the individual skeletal muscle fibers that it innervates (see Figure 9.11). When the motor neuron fires, all the muscle fibers of its unit contract together. Motor units differ appreciably in the number of muscle fibers they contain; the units with the fewest fibers—those of the fingers and face—permit the highest degree of selective motor control.

A skeletal muscle comprises hundreds of thousands of threadlike muscle fibers bound together in a tough membrane and attached to a bone by a *tendon*. *Acetylcholine,* which is released by motor neurons at *neuromuscular junctions,* activates the **motor end-plate** on each muscle fiber and causes the fiber to contract. All of the motor neurons that innervate the fibers of a single muscle are called its **motor pool.**

Although it is an oversimplification (see Gollinick & Hodgson, 1986), skeletal muscle fibers are often considered to be of two basic types: fast and slow. *Fast muscle fibers,* as you might guess, are those that contract and relax quickly. Although they are capable of generating great force, they fatigue quickly because they are poorly vascularized (which gives them a pale color). In contrast, *slow muscle fibers,* although slower and weaker, are capable of more sustained contraction because they are more richly vascularized (and hence much redder). Muscles have different proportions of fast and slow fibers depending on their function.

ing the number of neurons in its motor pool that are firing, by increasing the firing rates of those that are already firing, or more commonly by a combination of the two.

Receptor Organs of Tendons and Muscles

The activity of skeletal muscles is monitored by two kinds of receptors: Golgi tendon organs and muscle spindles. **Golgi tendon organs** are embedded in the *tendons*, which connect each skeletal muscle to bone; and **muscle spindles** are embedded in the muscle tissue itself. Because of their different locations, Golgi tendon organs and muscle spindles respond to different aspects of muscle contraction. Golgi tendon organs respond to increases in muscle tension (i.e., to the pull of the muscle on the tendon), but they are completely insensitive to changes in muscle length. In contrast, muscle spindles respond to changes in muscle length, but they do not respond to changes in muscle tension.

Under normal conditions, the function of Golgi tendon organs is to provide the central nervous system with information about muscle tension, but they also serve a protective function. When the contraction of a muscle is so extreme that there is a risk of damage, the Golgi tendon

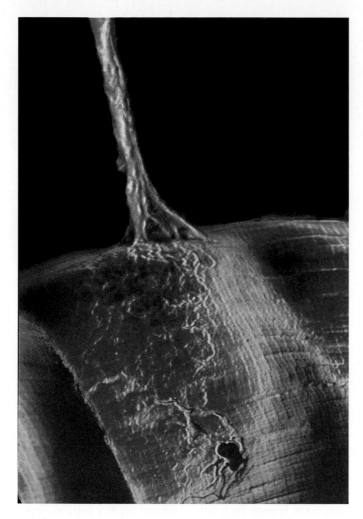

Figure 9.11 An electron micrograph of a motor unit: A motor neuron (pink) and the muscle fibers that it innervates.

Many skeletal muscles belong unambiguously to one of two categories: flexors or extensors. **Flexors** act to bend or flex a joint, and **extensors** act to straighten or extend it. Figure 9.12 illustrates the *biceps* and *triceps*—the flexors and extensors, respectively, of the elbow joint (see Chapter 4). Any two muscles whose contraction produces the same movement, be it flexion or extension, are said to be **synergistic muscles**; those that act in opposition, like the biceps and triceps, are said to be **antagonistic muscles.**

To understand how muscles work, it is important to realize that muscles have elastic, rather than inflexible, cablelike, properties. If you think of an increase in muscle tension as being analogous to an increase in the tension of an elastic band joining two bones, you will appreciate that muscle contraction can be of two types (see Figure 9.13). Excitation of a muscle can increase the tension that it exerts on two bones without shortening and pulling them together; this is termed **isometric contraction.** Or it can shorten and pull them together; this is termed **dynamic contraction.** The tension in a muscle can be increased by increas-

Motor units. All of the muscle fibers that are innervated by a single motor neuron.

Motor end-plate. The receptive area on a muscle fiber at a neuromuscular junction.

Motor pool. All of the motor neurons that innervate the fibers of a given muscle.

Flexors. Muscles that act to bend or flex a joint.

Extensors. Muscles that act to straighten or extend a joint.

Synergistic muscles. Pairs of muscles that produce a movement in the same direction.

Antagonistic muscles. Pairs of muscles that act in opposition.

Isometric contraction. Contraction of a muscle that increases the force of its pull but does not shorten the muscle.

Dynamic contraction. Contraction of a muscle that causes the muscle to shorten.

Golgi tendon organs. Receptors that are embedded in tendons and are sensitive to the amount of tension in the muscles to which their tendons are attached.

Muscle spindles. Receptors that are embedded in muscle tissue and are sensitive to muscle length.

Elbow joint flexion

Biceps
contract

Triceps
extend

Elbow joint extension

Biceps
extend

Triceps
contract

Figure 9.12 The biceps and triceps, which are the flexors and extensors, respectively, of the elbow joint.

organs excite inhibitory interneurons in the spinal cord that cause the muscle to relax.

Figure 9.14 is a schematic diagram of the *muscle-spindle feedback circuit.* Examine it carefully. Notice that each muscle spindle has its own thread-like **intrafusal muscle,** which is innervated by its own **intrafusal motor neuron.** Why would a receptor have its own muscle and motor neuron? The reason becomes apparent when you consider what would happen to a muscle spindle without them. Without its intrafusal motor input, a muscle spindle would fall slack each time its **skeletal muscle (extrafusal muscle)** contracted. In this slack state, the muscle spindle could not do its job, which is to respond to slight changes in extrafusal muscle length. As Figure 9.15 on page 228 illustrates, the intrafusal motor neuron solves this problem by shortening the intrafusal muscle each time the extrafusal muscle becomes shorter, thus keeping enough tension on the mid-

dle, stretch-sensitive portion of the muscle spindle to keep it sensitive to slight changes in the length of the extrafusal muscle.

Stretch Reflex

When the word *reflex* is mentioned, many people think of themselves sitting on the edge of their doctor's examination table having their knees rapped with a little rubber-headed hammer. The resulting leg extension is called the **patellar tendon reflex** (*patella* means "*knee*"). This reflex is a **stretch reflex**—a reflex that is elicited by a sudden external stretching force on a muscle.

When the doctor strikes the tendon of your knee, the extensor muscle running along your thigh is stretched. This initiates the chain of events that is depicted in Figure 9.16

Figure 9.13 Dynamic (left panel) and isometric (right panel) contraction.

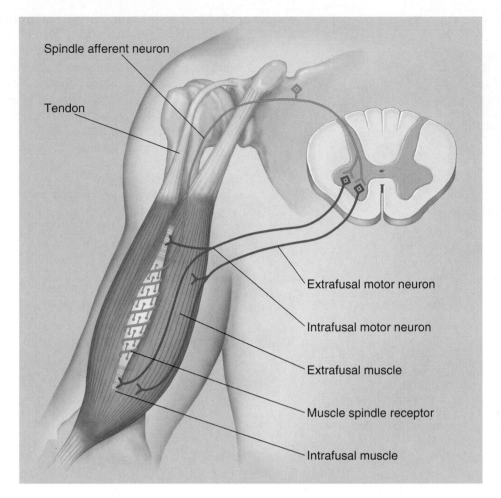

Spindle afferent neuron

Tendon

Extrafusal motor neuron

Intrafusal motor neuron

Extrafusal muscle

Muscle spindle receptor

Intrafusal muscle

Figure 9.14 The muscle-spindle feedback circuit. There are many muscle spindles in each muscle; for clarity, only one muscle spindle is illustrated here.

on page 228. The sudden stretch of the thigh muscle stretches its muscle-spindle stretch receptors, which in turn initiates a volley of action potentials that is carried from the stretch receptors into the spinal cord by **spindle afferent neurons** via the *dorsal root*. This volley of action potentials excites motor neurons in the *ventral horn* of the spinal cord, which respond by sending action potentials back to the muscle whose stretch originally excited them. The arrival of these impulses back at the starting point results in a compensatory muscle contraction and a sudden leg extension.

The method by which the patellar tendon reflex is typically elicited in a doctor's office—that is, by a sharp blow to the tendon of a completely relaxed muscle—is designed to make the reflex readily observable. However, it does little to communicate its functional significance. In real life situations, the function of the stretch reflex is to keep external forces from altering the intended position of the body. When an external force, such as somebody brushing against your arm while you are holding a cup of coffee, causes an unanticipated extrafusal muscle stretch, the muscle-spindle feedback circuit produces an immediate com-

pensatory contraction of the muscle that counteracts the force and keeps you from spilling the coffee—unless, of course, you are wearing your best clothes.

Intrafusal muscle. A threadlike muscle that adjusts the tension on a muscle spindle.

Intrafusal motor neuron. A motor neuron that innervates an intrafusal muscle.

Skeletal muscle (extrafusal muscle). Striated muscle that is attached to the skeleton and is usually under voluntary control.

Patellar tendon reflex. The stretch reflex that is elicited when the patellar tendon is struck.

Stretch reflex. A reflexive counteracting reaction to an unanticipated external stretching force on a muscle.

Spindle afferent neurons. Neurons that carry signals from muscle spindles into the spinal cord via the dorsal root.

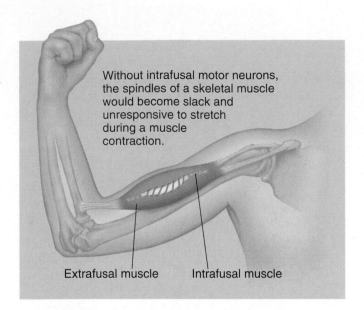

Without intrafusal motor neurons, the spindles of a skeletal muscle would become slack and unresponsive to stretch during a muscle contraction.

Extrafusal muscle   Intrafusal muscle

The function of intrafusal motor neurons is to adjust the length of intrafusal muscles, thus maintaining an appropriate degree of tension on muscle spindles, regardless of the length of the skeletal muscle.

Intrafusal motor neuron

Figure 9.15 The function of intrafusal motor neurons.

The mechanism by which the stretch reflex maintains limb stability is illustrated in Figure 9.17. Examine it carefully because it illustrates two of the principles of sensorimotor system function that are the focus of this chapter: the important role played by sensory feedback in the regulation of motor output and the ability of lower circuits in the motor hierarchy to take care of "business details" without the involvement of higher levels.

Withdrawal Reflex

I am sure that, at one time or another, you have touched something painful—a hot pot, for example—and suddenly pulled back your hand. This is a **withdrawal reflex.** Unlike the stretch reflex, the withdrawal reflex is not *monosynaptic* (Eidelberg, 1987). When a painful stimulus is applied to the hand, the first responses are recorded in the motor neurons of the arm flexor muscles about 1.6 milliseconds later, about the time it takes a neural signal to cross two synapses. Thus the shortest route in the withdrawal-reflex circuit involves one interneuron. Other responses are recorded in the motor neurons of the arm flexor muscles after the initial volley; these responses are triggered by signals that have traveled over multisynaptic pathways—some involving the cortex (see Matthews, 1991). See Figure 9.18 on page 230.

Rap occurs here

The rap on the knee tendon stretches the spindles of the thigh muscle and elicits a burst of firing in their spindle afferents.

Rap occurs here

The burst of firing in the spindle afferents triggers a burst of firing in the thigh muscle motor neurons, which causes the thigh muscle to contract.

Figure 9.16 The elicitation of a stretch reflex. All of the muscle spindles in a muscle are activated during a stretch reflex, but only a single muscle spindle is depicted here.

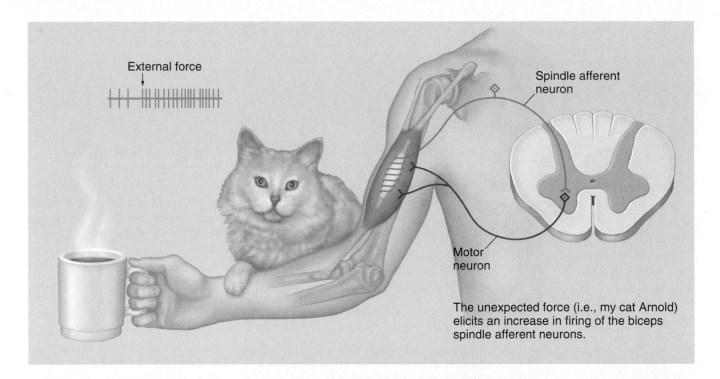

External force

Spindle afferent neuron

Motor neuron

The unexpected force (i.e., my cat Arnold) elicits an increase in firing of the biceps spindle afferent neurons.

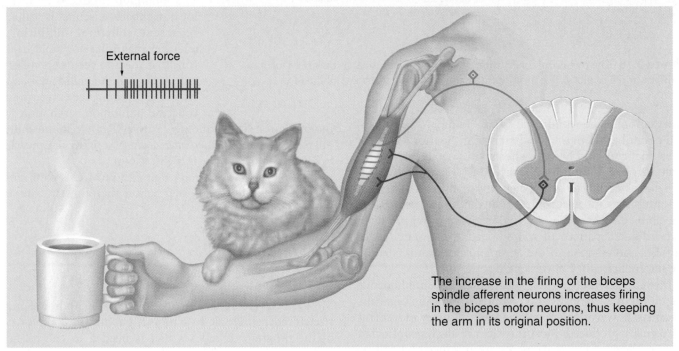

External force

The increase in the firing of the biceps spindle afferent neurons increases firing in the biceps motor neurons, thus keeping the arm in its original position.

Figure 9.17 The automatic maintenance of limb position by the muscle-spindle feedback system.

Reciprocal Innervation

Reciprocal innervation is an important principle of spinal cord circuitry. It refers to the fact that antagonistic muscles are innervated in such a way that when one is contracted, the other relaxes to permit a smooth, unimpeded motor response. Figure 9.18 illustrates the role of reciprocal

Withdrawal reflex. The reflexive withdrawal of a limb when it comes in contact with a painful stimulus.

Reciprocal innervation. The principle of spinal cord circuitry that causes a muscle to automatically relax when a muscle that is antagonistic to it contracts.

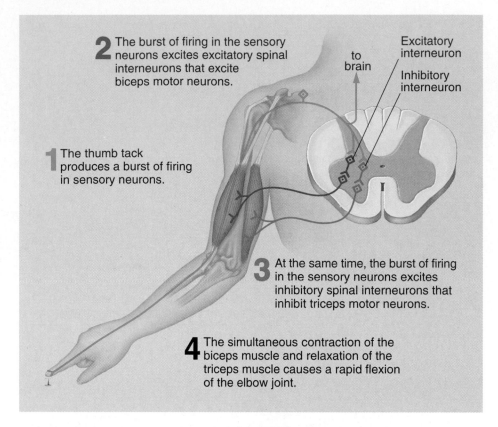

2 The burst of firing in the sensory neurons excites excitatory spinal interneurons that excite biceps motor neurons.

Excitatory interneuron

to brain

Inhibitory interneuron

1 The thumb tack produces a burst of firing in sensory neurons.

3 At the same time, the burst of firing in the sensory neurons excites inhibitory spinal interneurons that inhibit triceps motor neurons.

4 The simultaneous contraction of the biceps muscle and relaxation of the triceps muscle causes a rapid flexion of the elbow joint.

Figure 9.18 The reciprocal innervation of antagonistic muscles in the arm. During a withdrawal reflex, elbow flexors are excited and elbow extensors are inhibited.

innervation in the withdrawal reflex. "Bad news" of a sudden painful event in the hand arrives in the dorsal horn of the spinal cord and has two effects: the signals excite both excitatory and inhibitory interneurons. The excitatory interneurons excite the motor neurons of the elbow flexors; the inhibitory interneurons inhibit the motor neurons of the elbow extensors. Thus a single sensory input produces a coordinated pattern of motor output; the activities of agonists and antagonists are automatically coordinated by the internal circuitry of the spinal cord.

Movements are quickest when there is simultaneous excitation of all agonists and complete inhibition of all antagonists; however, this is not the way voluntary movement is normally produced. Most muscles are always contracted to some degree, and movements are produced by adjustment in the level of relative **cocontraction** between antagonists. Movements that are produced by cocontraction are smooth, and they can be stopped with precision by a slight

Cocontraction. The simultaneous contraction of antagonistic muscles.

Recurrent collateral inhibition. The inhibition of a neuron that is produced by its own activity via a collateral branch of its axon and an inhibitory interneuron.

increase in the contraction of the antagonistic muscles. Moreover, cocontraction insulates us from the effects of unexpected external forces.

Recurrent Collateral Inhibition

Like most workers, muscle fibers and the motor neurons that innervate them need an occasional break; and there are inhibitory neurons in the spinal cord that make sure they get it. Each motor neuron branches just before it leaves the spinal cord, and the branch synapses on a small inhibitory interneuron, which inhibits the very motor neuron from which it receives its input. The inhibition produced by these local feedback circuits is called **recurrent collateral inhibition,** and the small inhibitory interneurons that mediate recurrent collateral inhibition are called *Renshaw cells.* As a consequence of recurrent collateral inhibition, each time a motor neuron fires, it momentarily inhibits itself and shifts the responsibility for the contraction of a particular muscle to other members of the muscle's motor pool.

Figure 9.19 is a summary figure; it illustrates recurrent collateral inhibition and other factors that directly exite or inhibit motor neurons.

Walking: A Complex Sensorimotor Reflex

Most reflexes are much more complex than withdrawal and stretch reflexes. Think for a moment about the complexity of the program of reflexes that is needed to control an activity such as walking. Such a program must integrate visual information from the eyes; somatosensory information from the feet, knees, hips, arms, and so on; and information about balance from the semicircular canals of the inner ears. And it must produce, on the basis of this information, an integrated series of movements that involves the muscles of the trunk, legs, feet, and upper arms. It must also be incredibly flexible; it must be able to adjust its output immediately to changes in the slope of the terrain, to instructions from the brain, or to external forces such as a bag of groceries. Nobody has yet managed to build a robot that can come close to duplicating these feats.

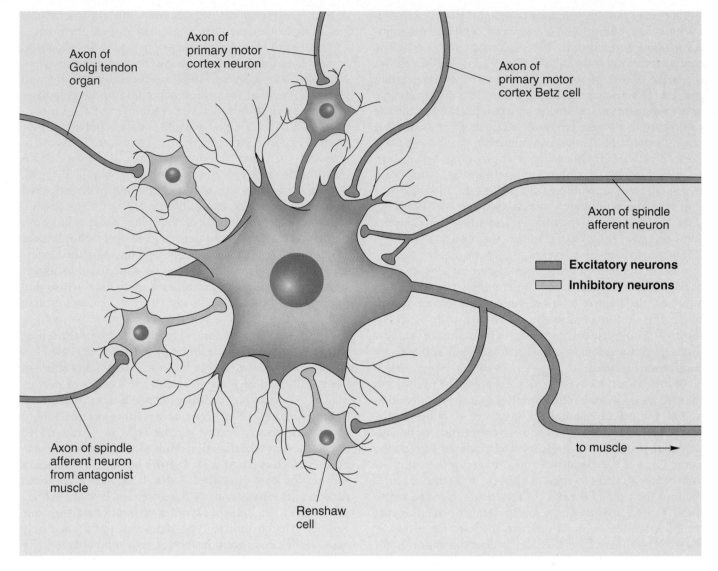

Figure 9.19 The excitatory and inhibitory signals that directly influence the activity of a motor neuron.

Grillner (1985) showed that walking is controlled largely by circuits in the spinal cord. Grillner's subjects were cats whose spinal cords had been separated from their brains by transection. He suspended the cats in a sling over a tread- mill; amazingly, when the treadmill was started so that the cats received sensory feedback of the sort that normally accompanies walking, they began to walk.

<table>
<tr><td>**9.9**</td><td>## Central Sensorimotor Programs</td></tr>
</table>

In this chapter, you have learned that the sensorimotor system is like the hierarchy of a large efficient company. You have learned how the executives—the dorsolateral prefrontal cortex, the supplementary motor area, and the premotor cortex—issue commands based on information supplied to them by the posterior parietal cortex. And you have learned how these commands are forwarded to the managing director (the primary motor cortex) for distrib- ution over four main channels of communication (the two dorsolateral and the two ventromedial spinal motor pathways) to the metaphoric office managers of the sensorimotor hierarchy (the spinal sensorimotor circuits). Finally, you have learned how spinal sensorimotor circuits direct the activities of the workers (the muscles). The major role played by sensory feedback at each stage of the sensorimotor hierarchy has been emphasized throughout.

One theory of sensorimotor function is that the sensorimotor system comprises a hierarchy of **central sensorimotor programs** (see Brooks, 1986; Georgopoulos, 1991). The central sensorimotor program theory suggests that all but the highest levels of the sensorimotor system have certain patterns of activity programmed into them and that complex movements are produced by activating the appropriate combinations of these programs. Accordingly, if your association cortex decides that you might like to look at a magazine, it activates high-level cortical programs that in turn activate lower-level programs—perhaps in your brain stem—for walking, bending over, picking up, and thumbing through. These programs in turn activate specific spinal programs that control the various elements of the sequences and cause your muscles to complete the objective.

Once activated, each level of the sensorimotor system is capable of operating on the basis of current sensory feedback, without the direct control of higher levels. Thus, although the highest levels of your sensorimotor system retain the option of directly controlling your activities, most of the individual responses that you make are performed without direct cortical involvement, and you are barely aware of them.

In much the same way, a company president who wishes to open a new branch office simply issues the command to one of the executives, and the executive responds in the usual fashion by issuing a series of commands to the appropriate people lower in the hierarchy, who in turn do the same. Each of the executives and workers of the company knows how to complete many different tasks and executes them in the light of current conditions when instructed to do so. Good companies have mechanisms for ensuring that the programs of action at different levels of the hierarchy are well coordinated and effective. So does the sensorimotor system; this is the task of the cerebellum and basal ganglia.

How do we get our central motor programs? The results of an important experiment by Fentress (1973) indicate that some fundamental central motor programs are not learned. Fentress showed that adult mice raised from birth without forelimbs still made the patterns of shoulder movements typical of grooming in their species—and that these movements were well coordinated with normal tongue, head, and eye movements. For example, the mice blinked each time they made the shoulder movements that would have swept their forepaws across their eyes. Fentress's study also demonstrated the importance of sensory feedback in the operation of central sensorimotor programs. The fore-limbless mice, deprived of normal tongue-forepaw contact

during face grooming, would often interrupt ostensible grooming sequences to lick a cagemate or even the floor.

Theories of sensorimotor learning emphasize two kinds of processes that influence central motor programs (e.g., Annett, 1985; Johnson, 1984): response chunking and changing the level of control. According to the **response-chunking hypothesis,** practice combines the central control of individual response elements into individual programs that control long sequences (chunks) of behavior. In a novice typist, each response necessary to type a word is individually triggered and controlled; in a skilled typist, sequences of letters are activated as a unit, with a marked increase in speed and continuity.

An important principle of chunking is that chunks can themselves be combined into higher-order chunks. For example, the responses needed to type the individual letters and digits of one's address may be chunked into longer sequences necessary to produce the individual words and numbers, and these chunks may in turn be combined so that the entire address is typed as a unit.

Shifting the level of control to lower levels of the sensorimotor system during training (see Seitz et al., 1990) has two advantages. One is that it frees up the higher levels of the system to deal with more esoteric aspects of performance. For example, skilled pianists can concentrate on interpreting a piece of music because they do not have to consciously focus on pressing the right keys, and skilled secretaries can take dictation while performing other simple mental tasks (Hirst et al., 1980). The other advantage of shifting the level of control is that it permits great speed because different circuits at the lower levels of the hierarchy can act simultaneously without interfering with one another. It is possible to type 120 words per minute only because the circuits responsible for activating each individual key press can become active before the preceding response has been completed (Grudin, 1983; Rummelhart & Norman, 1982).

> **Central sensorimotor programs.** Patterns of activity that are programmed into the sensorimotor system.
>
> **Response-chunking hypothesis.** The hypothesis that practice combines the central sensorimotor programs that control individual responses into programs that control sequences of responses (chunks of behavior).

CONCLUSION

Rhonda began this chapter by illustrating three principles of sensorimotor function (9.1): The sensorimotor system is hierarchically organized, motor output is guided by sensory input, and learning changes the nature and locus of sensorimotor control. The discussion of the sensorimotor system itself began with the two major areas of the sensorimotor association cortex (9.2), the secondary motor cortex (9.3), and the primary motor cortex (9.4). Then, an overview of the functions of the various areas of sensorimotor cortex was provided by the cortical blood flow studies of

Roland and his colleagues (9.5). Next was the introduction to two structures—the cerebellum and the basal ganglia—both of which coordinate activities at different levels of the sensorimotor system rather than participating in the conduction of signals from the cortex to the spinal cord (9.6). Finally, the last three sections of the chapter described the four descending motor pathways (9.7), the sensorimotor circuits of the spinal cord (9.8), and the concept of central sensorimotor programs (9.9).

Recently, I stopped off to pick up a few fresh vegetables and some fish for dinner, and I once again found myself waiting in Rhonda's line. It was the longest line, but I am a creature of habit. This time, I felt rather smug as I watched her. All of the reading and thinking that had gone into the preparation of this chapter had provided me with some new insights into what she was doing and how she was doing it. I wondered whether she appreciated her own finely tuned sensorimotor system as much as I did. Then I hatched my plot—a little test of Rhonda's muscle-spindle feedback system. How would Rhonda's finely tuned sensorimotor system react to a bag that looked heavy but was in fact extremely light? Next time, I would get one of those paper bags at the mushroom counter, blow it up, drop one mushroom in it, and then fold up the top so it looked completely full. I smiled at the thought. But I wasn't the only one smiling. My daydreaming ended abruptly and the smile melted from my face as I noticed Rhonda's extended hand and her amused grin. Will I never learn?

FOOD FOR THOUGHT

1. Both sensorimotor systems and large businesses are complex systems trying to survive in a competitive milieu. It is no accident that they function in similar ways. Discuss.

2. We humans tend to view cortical mechanisms as preeminent, presumably because we are the species with the largest cortexes. However, one might argue from several perspectives that the lower sensorimotor circuits are more important. Discuss.

KEY TERMS

Sensory feedback (p. 210)
Posterior parietal association cortex (p. 211)
Frontal eye field (p. 211)
Apraxia (p. 212)
Constructional apraxia (p. 212)
Contralateral neglect (p. 212)
Dorsolateral prefrontal association cortex (p. 212)
Secondary motor cortex (p. 214)
Supplementary motor area (p. 214)
Premotor cortex (p. 214)

Somatotopic (p. 214)
Primary motor cortex (p. 216)
Motor homunculus (p. 217)
Stereognosis (p. 217)
Astereognosia (p. 217)
Dorsolateral corticospinal tract (p. 221)
Betz cells (p. 221)
Dorsolateral cortico-rubrospinal tract (p. 221)
Ventromedial corticospinal tract (p. 221)
Ventromedial cortico–brain-stem–spinal tract (p. 221)
Tectum (p. 222)
Vestibular nucleus (p. 222)
Reticular formation (p. 222)

Motor units (p. 224)
Motor end-plate (p. 224)
Motor pool (p. 224)
Flexors (p. 225)
Extensors (p. 225)
Synergistic muscles (p. 225)
Antagonistic muscles (p. 225)
Isometric contraction (p. 225)
Dynamic contraction (p. 225)
Golgi tendon organs (p. 225)
Muscle spindles (p. 225)
Intrafusal muscle (p. 226)
Intrafusal motor neuron (p. 226)

Skeletal muscle (extrafusal muscle) (p. 226)
Patellar tendon reflex (p. 226)
Stretch reflex (p. 226)
Spindle afferent neurons (p. 227)
Withdrawal reflex (p. 228)
Reciprocal innervation (p. 229)
Cocontraction (p. 230)
Recurrent collateral inhibition (p. 230)
Central sensorimotor programs (p. 232)
Response-chunking hypothesis (p. 232)

ADDITIONAL READING

For those who are interested in a more detailed introduction to the sensorimotor system, I recommend relevant chapters from the following three books. The first covers the sensorimotor system from a neurophysiological perspective, the second from a neuropsychological perspective, and the third from a cognitive neuroscience perspective:

Kandel, E., & Schwartz, J. H. (1991). *Principles of neural science* (2nd ed.). New York: Elsevier.

Kolb, B., & Whishaw, I. Q. (1990). *Fundamentals of human neuropsychology* (3rd ed.). New York: Freeman.

Roland, P. E. (1993). *Brain activation.* New York: Wiley-Liss.

CHAPTER

10

The Biopsychology of Eating and Drinking

Part 1 Hunger, Eating, and Body Weight Regulation

10.1 Digestion and Energy Flow

10.2 Theories of Hunger and Eating: Set Points versus Positive Incentives

10.3 Factors That Determine What, When, and How Much We Eat

10.4 Neural Mechanisms of Hunger and Satiety

10.5 Body Weight Regulation: Set Points versus Settling Points

Part 2 Thirst, Drinking, and Body Fluid Regulation

10.6 Regulation of the Body's Fluid Resources

10.7 Deprivation-Induced Drinking: Cellular Dehydration and Hypovolemia

10.8 Spontaneous Drinking: Drinking in the Absence of Water Deficits

10.9 Drinking and Satiety

Part 3 Disorders of Consumption

10.10 Obesity

10.11 Anorexia Nervosa

This chapter is about the biopsychology of ingestive behavior. Part 1 deals with hunger, eating, and body weight regulation, Part 2 with thirst and drinking, and Part 3 with disorders of ingestive behavior. The following puzzle illustrates a theme of the chapter: that unintentional, unrecognized assumptions frequently block the way to otherwise obvious solutions.

"It's been a tough day," Slade thought to himself as he held down the brim of his hat with one hand and clutched the collar of his trench coat with the other to protect himself from the biting wind. The star witness had skipped town, and now Boris was on the streets once again, armed and looking for him. Fortunately, Stella, the chief's secretary, had offered him her couch for a few days until things blew over.

As he turned the corner, Slade saw the lights come on in Stella's second-story apartment. Then Stella appeared at the window. Slade sensed immediately that something was wrong. Stella's face was taut and distorted, and the open window exposed her body and the flapping curtains to the full force of the gale. "Damn that Boris," he cursed to himself as he raced up the stairs.

He moved cautiously down the hall toward the sound of Stella's muffled sobs. He paused, drew his revolver, and burst into the apartment. Stella turned and, with a look of terror on her face, fainted into Slade's arms. Then Slade saw the problem; there on the floor by the window lay the body of Freddie the Finn. As Slade examined the body—Freddie's, not Stella's—he noticed the tell-tale signs: the pieces of broken glass scattered around the body, the water on the carpet, and the end table laying on its side beneath the window.

"One of the easiest cases I ever solved," Slade thought, as he attempted to rouse Stella, "a clear case of accidental death by asphyxiation."

Your challenge is to figure out the details of Freddie's death from the clues: How was Slade able to so quickly figure out what had happened? The solution to this puzzle and its relation to the biopsychology of eating and drinking will be explained shortly.

Part 1 Hunger, Eating, and Body Weight Regulation

Eating is a behavior that is of interest to virtually everyone. We all do it, most of us derive great pleasure from it, and for many of us, it becomes a source of serious personal problems. Recent surveys of U.S. adults (see Brownell & Rodin, 1994) indicate that about 30% are significantly overweight, 12% grossly so; that about 45% think they are overweight; and that about 35% are currently dieting. The incidence of obesity is greater in males, but the incidence of dieting is greater in females.

The social impact of obesity on an individual in a society obsessed with slenderness can be devastating, but the health consequences of obesity are the real tragedy. The incidence of diabetes, hypertension, cardiovascular diseases, some cancers, and thus premature death is particularly high among the obese (Bray, 1992). In addition, eating disorders such as *anorexia nervosa* and *bulimia* affect about 3% of the adolescent population, and dieting and food obsessions plague all age groups. The message is clear: At some time in your life, you or somebody you care about will almost certainly suffer from an eating-related disorder.

The major purpose of Part 1 of this chapter is to introduce you to a new way of thinking about hunger, eating, and weight regulation: one that is consistent with the results of recent research and that will help you understand why humans—evolution's most adaptable products—have so much difficulty eating a reasonable diet in the midst of plenty.

10.1 Digestion and Energy Flow

The primary purpose of eating is to supply the body with the energy it needs to survive and function. Accordingly, this section provides a brief overview of the processes of digestion and energy flow.

The *gastrointestinal tract* and the process of digestion are illustrated in Figure 10.1. **Digestion** is the gastrointestinal process of breaking down food and absorbing its constituents into the body. In order to appreciate the basics of digestion, it is useful to consider the body without its protuberances, as a simple living tube with a hole at each end. To supply itself with energy and other nutrients, the tube puts food into one of its two holes—typically the one with

teeth—and passes it along its internal canal so that it can be broken down and partially absorbed from the canal into the body. The leftovers are jettisoned from the other end. Although this is not a particularly appetizing description of eating, it does serve to illustrate that, strictly speaking, food has not been consumed until it has been digested.

> **Digestion.** The process by which food is broken down and absorbed through the lining of the gastrointestinal tract.

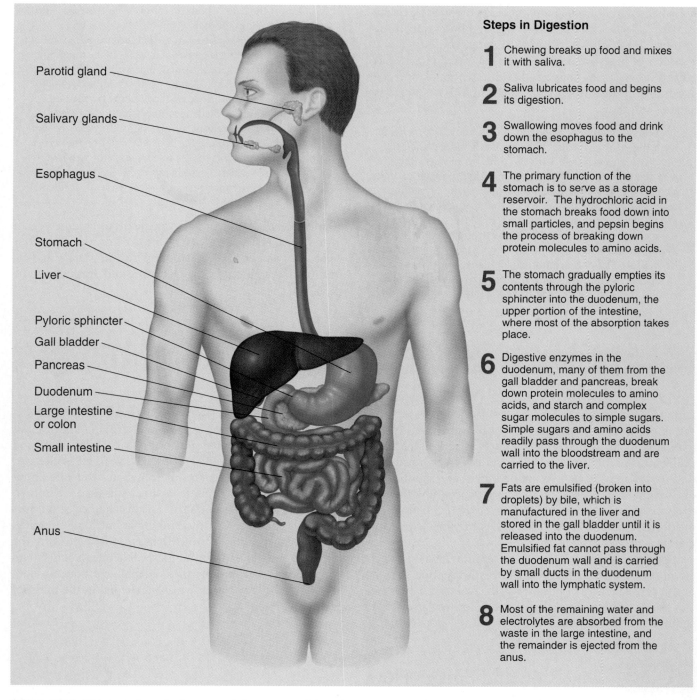

Parotid gland

Salivary glands

Esophagus

Stomach

Liver

Pyloric sphincter

Gall bladder

Pancreas

Duodenum

Large intestine
or colon

Small intestine

Anus

Steps in Digestion

1 Chewing breaks up food and mixes it with saliva.

2 Saliva lubricates food and begins its digestion.

3 Swallowing moves food and drink down the esophagus to the stomach.

4 The primary function of the stomach is to serve as a storage reservoir. The hydrochloric acid in the stomach breaks food down into small particles, and pepsin begins the process of breaking down protein molecules to amino acids.

5 The stomach gradually empties its contents through the pyloric sphincter into the duodenum, the upper portion of the intestine, where most of the absorption takes place.

6 Digestive enzymes in the duodenum, many of them from the gall bladder and pancreas, break down protein molecules to amino acids, and starch and complex sugar molecules to simple sugars. Simple sugars and amino acids readily pass through the duodenum wall into the bloodstream and are carried to the liver.

7 Fats are emulsified (broken into droplets) by bile, which is manufactured in the liver and stored in the gall bladder until it is released into the duodenum. Emulsified fat cannot pass through the duodenum wall and is carried by small ducts in the duodenum wall into the lymphatic system.

8 Most of the remaining water and electrolytes are absorbed from the waste in the large intestine, and the remainder is ejected from the anus.

Figure 10.1 The gastrointestinal tract and the process of digestion.

As a consequence of digestion, energy is delivered to the body in three forms (see Figure 10.1). These forms are (1) **lipids** (fats), (2) **amino acids** (the breakdown products of proteins), and (3) **glucose** (a simple sugar that is the breakdown product of complex *carbohydrates*—that is, of complex starches and sugars).

The body uses energy continuously, but its consumption is intermittent; therefore, it must store energy for use in the intervals between meals. Energy is stored in three forms: *fats, glycogen,* and *proteins*. Most of the body's energy re-

serves are stored as fats, relatively little as glycogen and proteins (see Figure 10.2). Changes in the body weights of adult humans are largely a consequence of changes in the amount of body fat.

Because glycogen, which is largely stored in the liver, is readily converted to glucose—the body's main directly utilizable source of energy—one might expect that glycogen would be the body's preferred mode of energy storage. There are two main reasons that fat, rather than glycogen, is the primary mode of energy storage. One is that a gram bloodstream from the meal is meeting the body's immediate energy needs. The **fasting phase** is the period during which all of the unstored energy from the previous meal has been used and the body is withdrawing energy from its reserves to meet its immediate energy requirements; it ends with the beginning of the next cephalic phase. During periods of rapid weight gain, people often go directly from one absorptive phase into the next cephalic phase, without experiencing an intervening fasting phase.

The flow of energy during the three phases of energy metabolism is controlled by two pancreatic hormones: insulin and glucagon. During the cephalic and absorptive phases, the pancreas releases a great deal of insulin into the bloodstream and very little glucagon. The **insulin** does three things: (1) It promotes the use of glucose as the primary source of energy by the body. (2) It promotes the conversion of bloodborne fuels to forms that can be stored: glucose to glycogen and fat, and amino acids to proteins. (3) It promotes the storage of glycogen in liver and muscle, fat in adipose tissue, and proteins in muscle. Accordingly, the function of insulin during the cephalic phase is to lower the levels of bloodborne fuels, primarily glucose, in anticipation of the impending influx; and its function during the absorptive phase is to minimize the increasing levels of bloodborne fuels by utilizing and storing them.

In contrast to the cephalic and absorptive phases, the fasting phase is characterized by high levels of **glucagon** in the blood and low levels of insulin. Without high levels of insulin, glucose has difficulty entering most body cells;

- Fat in adipose tissue (85%)
- Protein in muscle (14.5%)
- Glycogen in muscle and liver (.5%)

Figure 10.2 Distribution of stored energy in an average person.

of fat can store twice as much energy as a gram of glycogen; the other is that glycogen, unlike fat, attracts and holds substantial quantities of water. Consequently, if your fat calories were all stored as glycogen, you would likely weigh well over 275 kilograms (600 pounds).

There are three phases of *energy metabolism*—the chemical changes by which energy is made available for an organism's use: the cephalic phase, the absorptive phase, and the fasting phase. The **cephalic phase** is the preparatory phase; it often begins with the sight, smell, or even just the thought of food, and it ends when the food starts to be absorbed into the bloodstream. The **absorptive phase** is the period during which the energy absorbed into the

Lipids. Fats.

Amino acids. The breakdown products of proteins.

Glucose. The simple sugar breakdown product of complex starches and sugars; it is the body's primary, directly utilizable source of energy.

Cephalic phase. The metabolic phase during which the body prepares for food that is about to be absorbed.

Absorptive phase. The metabolic phase during which the body is operating on the energy from a recently consumed meal and is storing the excess as body fat, glycogen, and proteins.

Fasting phase. The metabolic phase that begins when energy from the preceding meal is no longer sufficient to meet the immediate needs of the body and during which energy is extracted from fat and glycogen stores.

Insulin. A pancreatic hormone that facilitates the entry of glucose into cells and the conversion of bloodborne fuels to forms that can be stored.

Glucagon. A pancreatic hormone that promotes the release of free fatty acids from adipose tissue and their use as the body's primary fuel.

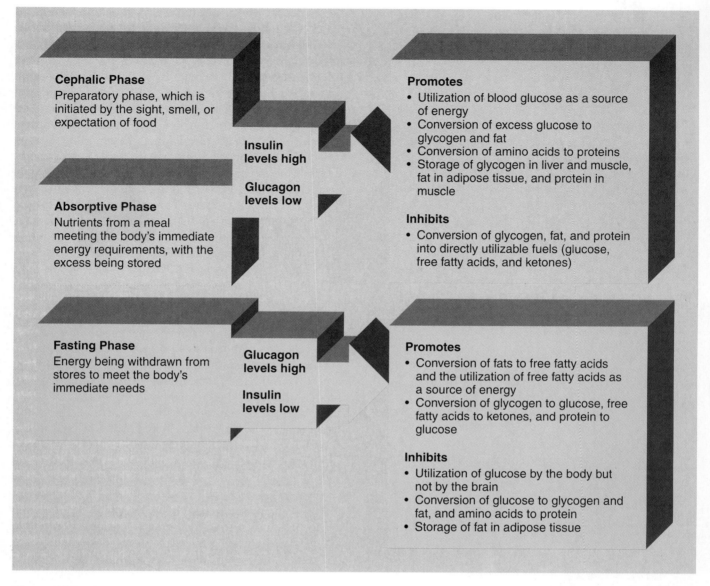

Figure 10.3 The major events associated with the three phases of energy metabolism: The cephalic, absorptive, and fasting phases.

thus glucose stops being the body's primary fuel. In effect, this saves the body's glucose for the brain, because insulin is not required for glucose to enter most brain cells. The low levels of insulin also promote the conversion of glycogen and protein to glucose. (The conversion of protein to glucose is called **gluconeogenesis.**)

On the other hand, the high levels of fasting-phase glucagon promote the release of **free fatty acids** from adipose tissue and their use as the body's primary fuel. The high glucagon levels also stimulate the conversion of free fatty acids to **ketones,** which are used by muscles as a source of energy during the fasting phase. After a prolonged period without food, however, the brain also starts to use ketones, thus further conserving the body's resources of glucose.

Figure 10.3 summarizes the major metabolic events associated with the three phases of energy metabolism.

Gluconeogenesis. The process by which glucose is synthesized from the breakdown products of the body's protein.

Free fatty acids. Released from body fat stores, the main source of the body's energy during the fasting phase.

Ketones. Breakdown products of fat that can be used as a source of energy for the brain when glucose is in short supply.

Negative feedback systems. Systems in which feedback from changes in one direction elicit compensatory effects in the opposite direction.

Homeostasis. The stability of an organism's internal environment.

Theories of Hunger and Eating: Set Points versus Positive Incentives

One of the main impediments faced by students in trying to understand hunger, eating, and body weight regulation is a widely held incorrect assumption about the nature of the system that controls it: the *set-point assumption*. Although it is fundamentally flawed, I am going to focus on it here because it is almost certainly ingrained in your own thinking. You might think it presumptuous of me to assume to know how you think, but I am confident that I do. During the past year, my colleagues and I have studied how people think about their own hunger, eating, and body weight; and we have found the set-point assumption to be prominent in the thinking of almost all of the subjects we have interviewed.

This talk of obstructive implicit assumptions brings us back to the case of Freddie the Finn. Earlier in the chapter, you left Freddie lying in a pool of water and broken glass on the floor of Stella's apartment, and you were warned about the hazards of unrecognized assumptions. If you didn't make the usual mistake of assuming that Freddie was a man from Finland, you likely had little difficulty figuring out that Freddie was Stella's pet fish, whose bowl had been knocked to the floor by the wind blowing through her open window. However, if you did unwittingly fall into the logical trap that I set for you, the experience will have left you with a better appreciation of how easy it is to make incorrect assumptions and how much they can cloud your thinking.

Nature of Set-Point Theories

Most people attribute *hunger* (the motivation to eat) to the presence of an energy deficit, and they view eating as the means by which the energy resources of the body are returned to their appropriate level—that is, to their *energy set point*. Figure 10.4 summarizes this incorrect way of thinking. After a *meal* (a bout of eating), a person's energy resources are thought to be near their set point and to decline thereafter as the body uses energy to fuel its physiological processes. When the level of the body's energy resources falls far enough below the set point, a person becomes motivated by hunger to initiate another meal. The meal continues, according to the set-point assumption, until the energy level returns to its set point and the person feels *satiated* (no longer hungry).

The set-point model of hunger and eating works in much the same way as a thermostat-regulated heating system in a cool climate. The heater increases the house temperature until it reaches its set point (the thermostat setting). This turns off the heat, and then the temperature of the house gradually declines until the decline is large enough to turn the heater back on. All set-point systems have three components: a set-point mechanism, a detector mechanism, and an effector mechanism. The *set-point mechanism* defines the set point, the *detector mechanism* detects deviations from the set point, and the *effector mechanism* acts to eliminate the deviations. For example, the set-point, detector, and effector mechanisms of a heating system are the thermostat, the thermometer, and the heater, respectively.

All set-point systems are **negative feedback systems**—systems in which feedback from changes in one direction elicit compensatory effects in the opposite direction. These systems are common in mammals because they act to defend **homeostasis**—a constant internal environment—which is critical for the mammals' survival.

Glucostatic and Lipostatic Set-Point Theories of Hunger and Eating

In the 1940s and 1950s, researchers working under the assumption that eating is regulated by some type of set-point system speculated about the nature of the regulation. Several researchers suggested that eating is regulated by a system that is designed to maintain a blood glucose set point—the idea being that we become hungry when our

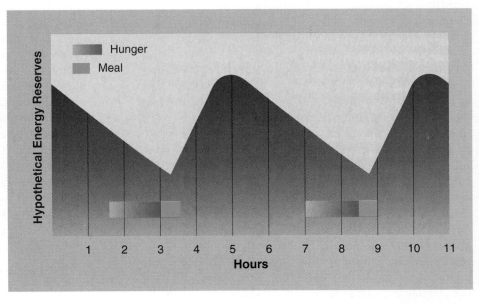

Figure 10.4 The energy set-point view that is the basis of many people's thinking about hunger and eating.

blood glucose levels drop significantly below their set point and that we become satiated when eating returns our blood glucose levels to their set point. Various versions of this theory are referred to as the **glucostatic theory.** It seemed to make good sense that the main purpose of eating is to defend a blood glucose set point because glucose is the brain's primary fuel.

The **lipostatic theory** is another set-point theory that was proposed in various forms in the 1940s and 1950s. According to this theory, every person has a set point for body fat, and deviations from this set point produce compensatory adjustments in the level of eating. The most frequently cited support for the theory is the fact that the body weights of adults stay relatively constant.

The glucostatic and lipostatic theories were viewed as complementary, not mutually exclusive. The glucostatic theory was thought to account for meal initiation and termination, whereas the lipostatic theory was thought to account for long-term regulation. Thus the dominant view in the 1950s was that eating is regulated by the interaction between two set-point systems: a short-term glucostatic system and a long-term lipostatic system. The simplicity of these 1950s theories is appealing. Remarkably, they are still being presented as the latest word in some introductory textbooks; perhaps you have encountered them.

Problems with Set-Point Theories of Hunger and Eating

Set-point theories of hunger and eating have some serious weaknesses. The following are three of them.

First, set-point theories of hunger and eating are inconsistent with basic eating-related evolutionary pressures as we understand them. The major eating-related problem faced by our ancestors was the inconsistency and unpredictability of the food supply. Thus, in order to survive, it was important for them to eat large quantities of good food when it was available so that calories could be banked in the form of body fat. Any ancestor—human or otherwise—that stopped feeling hungry as soon as immediate energy needs were met would not have survived the first hard winter or prolonged drought. For any warm-blooded species to survive under natural conditions, it needs a hunger and eating system that prevents energy deficits, rather than one that merely responds to them once they have developed. From this perspective, it is difficult to imagine how a set-point hunger and feeding system could have evolved in mammals (see Weingarten, 1985).

Second, major predictions of the set-point theories of hunger and eating have been not been confirmed. Early studies seemed to support the set-point theories by showing that large reductions in body fat, produced by starvation, or large reductions in blood glucose, produced by insulin injections, induce increases in eating in laboratory animals. The problem is that reductions of the magnitude needed to reliably induce eating rarely occur naturally. Indeed, as you have already learned in this chapter, approximately 30% of the U.S. population have a significant excess of fat deposits when they begin a meal. Furthermore, baseline blood glucose levels are maintained at nearly constant baseline levels by pancreatic hormones even during the fasting phase (e.g., Smith et al., 1972). Conversely, efforts to reduce meal size by having subjects consume a high-calorie drink just before eating have been largely unsuccessful; indeed, beliefs about the caloric content of a premeal drink influence the size of a subsequent meal more than does its actual caloric content (see Lowe, 1993).

Third, set-point theories of hunger and eating are deficient because they fail to recognize the influence on hunger and eating of such important factors as taste, learning, and social influences. To convince yourself of the importance of these factors, pause for a minute and imagine the sight, smell, and taste of your favorite food. Perhaps it is a succulent morsel of lobster meat covered with melted garlic butter, a piece of chocolate cheesecake, or a plate of sizzling home-made French fries. Are you starting to feel a bit hungry? If the home-made French fries—my personal weakness—were sitting in front of you right now, wouldn't you reach out and have one, or maybe the whole plateful? Have you not on occasion felt discomfort after a large main course, only to polish off a substantial dessert? The usual positive answers to these questions lead unavoidably to the conclusion that hunger and eating are not rigidly controlled by deviations from energy set points. This same point can be demonstrated in laboratory rats by the addition of a small amount of saccharin to their laboratory chow. Saccharin increases the sweetness of the chow without adding calories, and it produces a major increase in both eating and body weight.

Positive-Incentive Theory

The inability of set-point theories to account for the basic phenomena of eating and hunger has led to the development of an alternative theory, a theory that in key respects is opposite to the set-point theories. The central assertion of this new theoretical perspective, commonly referred to as the **positive-incentive theory,** is that humans and other animals are not driven to eat by internal energy deficits but are drawn to eat by the anticipated pleasure of eating. The anticipated pleasure of a behavior is its **positive-incentive value** (see Bolles, 1980; Booth, 1981; Collier, 1980; Rolls, 1981; Toates, 1981).

According to the positive-incentive theory of hunger and eating, the degree of hunger that a person feels depends on the positive-incentive value that eating holds for that person at that particular time. Many factors influence this value; among them are the anticipated taste (flavor) of the food that is likely to be consumed, the amount of time since food was last consumed, the time of day in relation to usual mealtimes, the type and quantity of food in the gut, whether blood glucose levels are within their normal range, and whether other people are present and eating. This partial list illustrates one strength of the positive-incentive theory. Unlike the set-point theories, the positive-incentive theory does not single out one factor as the major determinant of hunger and ignore the others; it acknowledges that many factors interact to determine a person's hunger at any time, and it suggests that this interaction occurs through the influence of these various factors on the positive-incentive value of eating (see Cabanac, 1971). For example, as you have just finished eating a large main course meal, the positive-incentive value of eating most foods is likely to be low; however, the anticipation of the taste of your favorite dessert may still be able to induce you to eat more, especially if others about you are eating it.

In this section of the chapter, you learned that most people tend to think about hunger and eating in terms of set points, you learned that set-point theories of hunger and eating are critically flawed, and you were introduced to the alternative positive-incentive theory. In the sections that follow, you will be introduced to some of the major characteristics of hunger and eating and some of the neural mechanisms that control them. As you progress through these sections, the advantages of the positive-incentive theory over set-point theories should become more apparent.

10.3 Factors That Determine What, When, and How Much We Eat

This section of the chapter describes major factors that determine what we eat, when we eat, and how much we eat.

Factors That Determine What We Eat

Certain tastes have a high positive-incentive value for virtually all members of a species. For example, virtually all humans have a special fondness for sweet, fatty, and salty tastes. This species-typical pattern of human taste preferences is adaptive because in nature sweet and fatty tastes are typically characteristic of high-energy foods that are rich in vitamins and minerals, and salty tastes are characteristic of sodium-rich foods. In contrast, bitter tastes, for which most humans have an aversion, are often associated with toxins. Superimposed on its species-typical taste preferences and aversions, each animal has the ability to learn specific taste preferences and aversions.

Learned taste preferences and aversions Animals learn to prefer tastes that are followed by an infusion of calories, and they learn to avoid tastes that are followed by illness (e.g., Baker & Booth, 1989; Lucas & Sclafani, 1989; Sclafani, 1990). In addition, humans and other animals learn what to eat from their conspecifics. For example, rats learn to prefer flavors that they experience in mother's milk (Galef & Sherry, 1973) and those that they smell on the breaths of other rats (Galef, 1989; Galef, Attenborough, & Whiskin, 1990). In humans, many food preferences are culturally specific—for example, in some cultures various nontoxic insects are considered to be a delicacy.

Learning to eat vitamins and minerals How do animals select a diet that provides all of the vitamins and minerals they need? To answer this question, researchers have studied how dietary deficiencies influence diet selection. Two patterns of results have emerged: one for sodium and one for the other essential vitamins and minerals. When an animal is deficient in sodium, it develops an immediate and compelling preference for the taste of sodium salt (see Rowland, 1990). In contrast, an animal that is deficient in some vitamin or mineral other than sodium must learn to consume foods that are rich in the missing nutrient by experiencing their positive effects; this is because vitamins and minerals other than sodium normally have no detectable taste in food. For example, rats maintained on a diet deficient in *thiamin* (vitamin B_1) develop an aversion to the taste of that diet; and if they are offered two new diets, one deficient in thiamin and one rich in thiamin, they often develop a preference for the taste of the thiamin-rich diet over the ensuing days.

If we, like rats, are capable of learning to select diets that are rich in the vitamins and minerals we need, why are dietary deficiencies so prevalent in our society (see Willett, 1994)? One reason is that, in order to maximize profits, manufacturers produce foods with the tastes that we prefer but with most of the essential nutrients extracted from them. (Even rats prefer chocolate chip cookies to nutritionally complete rat chow.) The second reason is illustrated

Glucostatic theory. The theory that eating is controlled by deviations from a hypothetical blood glucose set point.

Lipostatic theory. The theory that eating is controlled by deviations from a hypothetical body-fat set point.

Positive-incentive theory. The theory that behaviors (e.g., eating and drinking) are motivated by their anticipated pleasurable effects.

Positive-incentive value. The anticipated pleasure involved in the performance of a particular behavior, such as eating a particular food or drinking a particular beverage.

by the classic study of Harris and associates (1933). When thiamin-deficient rats were offered two new diets, one with thiamin and one without, almost all of them learned to eat the complete diet and avoid the deficient one. However, when they were offered ten new diets, only one of which contained the badly needed thiamin, few developed a preference for the complete diet. The number of different substances consumed each day by most people in industrialized societies is immense, and this makes it difficult, if not impossible, for their bodies to learn which foods are beneficial and which are not.

Factors That Influence When We Eat

Collier and his colleagues (see Collier, 1986) found that most mammals choose to eat many small meals each day if they have ready access to a continuous supply of food. Only when there are physical costs involved in initiating meals—for example, having to travel a considerable distance—does an animal opt for a few large meals.

The number of times that humans eat each day is influenced by cultural norms, work schedules, family routines, personal preferences, wealth, and a variety of other factors. However, in contrast to the usual mammalian preference, most people, particularly those living in family groups, tend to eat a few large meals each day at regular times. Interestingly, each person's regular mealtimes are the very same times at which that person is likely to feel most hungry; in fact, many people experience attacks of malaise (headache, nausea, and an inability to concentrate) when they miss a regularly scheduled meal.

Premeal hunger   I am sure that you have experienced attacks of premeal hunger. Subjectively, they seem to provide compelling support for the set-point theories. Your body seems to be crying out: "I need more energy. I cannot function without it. Please feed me." But, as you learned from the case of Freddie the Finn, things are not always the way they seem.

Woods has argued that premeal hunger is not a signal that the body needs energy (see Woods, 1991; Woods & Strubbe, 1994). According to Woods, the key to understanding hunger is to appreciate that eating large meals stresses the body. Before a meal, the body's energy reserves are in reasonable homeostatic balance; then, as a large meal is consumed, there is a massive homeostasis-disturbing influx of fuels into the bloodstream. The body does what it can to defend its homeostasis. At the first indication that a person will soon be eating—for example, when the usual mealtime approaches—the body enters the cephalic phase and takes steps to soften the impact of the impending homeostasis-disturbing influx by releasing insulin into the blood and thus reducing blood glucose. Woods's message is that the strong, unpleasant feelings of hunger that you may experience at mealtimes are not cries from your body for food; they are the sensations of your body's preparations

for the expected homeostasis-disturbing meal. Meal-time hunger is caused by the expectation of food, not by an energy deficit.

As a high school student, I ate lunch at exactly 12:05 every day and was overwhelmed by hunger as the time approached. Now, my eating schedule is different, and I never experience noontime hunger pangs. Have you had a similar experience?

Pavlovian conditioning of hunger   In a clever series of Pavlovian conditioning experiments on laboratory rats, Weingarten (1983, 1984, 1985) provided strong support for the view that hunger is often caused by the expectation of food, not by an energy deficit. During the conditioning phase of one of his experiments, Weingarten presented rats with six meals per day at irregular intervals, and he signaled the impending delivery of each meal with a buzzer-and-light *conditional stimulus*. This conditioning procedure was continued for 11 days. Throughout the ensuing test phase of the experiment, the food was continuously available. Despite the fact that the subjects were never deprived during the test phase, the rats started to eat each time the conditional stimulus was presented—even if they had recently completed a meal.

Factors That Influence How Much We Eat

The motivational state that causes us to stop eating a meal when there is food remaining is **satiety**. Satiety mechanisms play a major role in determining how much we eat.

Sham eating and satiety   Set-point thinking implies that hunger will steadily subside during a meal until the critical energy set point (e.g., a blood glucose set point) is achieved, at which point the meal will be terminated. Strong evidence against this view comes from studies of **sham eating**. In sham-eating experiments, food is chewed and swallowed by the subject; but rather than passing down the sub-

Satiety. The motivational state that terminates a meal.

Sham eating. The experimental protocol in which an animal chews and swallows food, which immediately exits its body through a tube implanted in its esophagus.

Nutritive density. Calories per unit volume of food.

Appetizer effect. The increase in hunger that is produced by the consumption of small amounts of palatable food.

Cafeteria diet. A diet offered to experimental animals that is composed of a wide variety of palatable foods.

Chapter 10   The Biology of Eating and Drinking

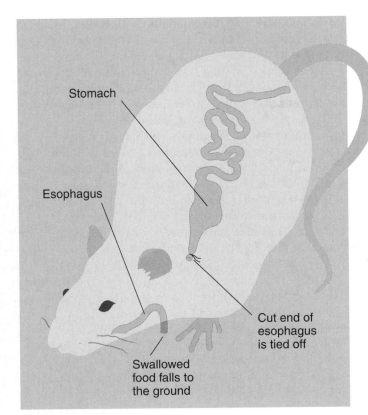

Figure 10.5 The sham-eating preparation.

ject's esophagus into the stomach, it passes out of the body through an implanted tube (see Figure 10.5).

Because sham eating adds no energy to the body, set-point theories predict that all sham-eaten meals should be huge. But this is not the case. Weingarten and Kulikovsky (1989) sham fed rats one of two differently flavored diets: one that the rats had naturally eaten many times before and one that they had never eaten before. The first sham meal of the rats that had previously eaten the diet was the same size as the previously eaten meals of that diet; then, on ensuing days they began to sham eat more and more (see Figure 10.6). In contrast, the rats that were presented with the unfamiliar diet sham ate large quantities right from the start. Weingarten and Kulikovsky concluded that the amount we eat is influenced largely by our previous experience with the particular food's postingestive effects, not by the immediate effect of the food on the body.

Nutritive density   One of the factors that influences the volume of food consumed is its **nutritive density**—calories per unit of volume. The effects of nutritive density have been demonstrated in studies in which laboratory rats have been maintained on a single diet. Once a stable baseline of consumption has been established, the nutritive density of the diet is changed. Many rats learn to adjust the volume of food they consume to keep their caloric intake and body weights relatively constant. However, there are limits to this adjustment: Rats often do not increase their intake suffi-

ciently to maintain their body weights if the nutritive density of their conventional laboratory feed is reduced by more than 50%, and they do not maintain the constancy of their caloric intake if there are major changes in the diet's palatability.

Appetizer effects and social influences on satiety

The next time you attend a dinner party, you may experience two weaknesses of the set-point theory of satiety. If appetizers are served, you will experience the fact that small amounts of food consumed before a meal actually increase hunger rather than reducing it—the **appetizer effect.** Presumably, it occurs because the consumption of a small amount of food is particularly effective in eliciting cephalic-phase responses. Later in the evening, you may experience the suppressive effect on satiety of eating in a group: Redd and de Castro (1992) found that their subjects consumed 60% more when eating with others. Although laboratory rats don't normally attend dinner parties, even they eat more when fed in groups.

Cafeteria diets and sensory-specific satiety   The number of different tastes available at each meal has a major effect on meal size. For example, the effect of offering a laboratory rat a varied diet of highly palatable foods—a **cafeteria diet**—is dramatic. Adults rats that were offered bread and chocolate in addition to their usual laboratory diet increased their average intake of calories by 84%, and after 120 days they had increased their average body weights by 49% (Rogers & Blundell, 1980). The spectacular effects of

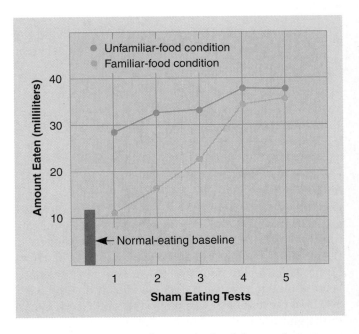

Figure 10.6 Change in the magnitude of sham eating over repeated sham-eating trials. The rats in one group sham ate the same diet they had eaten before the sham-eating phase; the rats in another group sham ate a diet different from the one they had previously eaten. (Adapted from Weingarten, 1990.)

cafeteria diets on consumption and body weight clearly run counter to the idea that satiety is rigidly controlled by internal energy set points.

The effect on meal size of cafeteria diets results from the fact that satiety is to a large degree taste-specific. As you eat one food, the positive-incentive value of all foods declines slightly, but the positive-incentive value of that particular food plummets. As a result, you soon become satiated on that food and stop eating it. However, if another food is offered to you, you will often begin eating again. In one study of **sensory-specific satiety** (Rolls et al., 1981), human subjects were asked to rate the palatability of eight different foods, and then they ate a meal of one of them. After the meal, they were asked to rate the palatability of the eight foods once again, and it was found that their rating of the food they had just eaten had declined substantially more than had their ratings of the other seven foods. Moreover, when the subjects were offered an unexpected second meal, they consumed most of it unless it was the same as the first.

Booth (1981) asked subjects to rate the momentary pleasure produced by the flavor, the smell, the sight, or just the thought of various foods at different times after consuming a large, high-calorie, high-carbohydrate liquid meal. There was an immediate sensory-specific decrease in the palatability of foods of the same or similar flavor as soon as the meal was consumed. This was followed by a general decrease in the palatability of all substances about 30 minutes later. Thus it appears that signals from taste receptors produce an immediate decline in the positive-incentive value of similar tastes and that signals associated with the postingestive consequences of eating produce a general decrease in the positive-incentive value of all foods.

Rolls (1990) suggested that sensory-specific satiety has two kinds of effects. She notes that there are relatively brief effects that influence the selection of foods within a single meal and relatively enduring effects that influence the selection of foods from meal to meal. Some foods seem to be relatively immune to long-lasting sensory-specific satiety; foods such as rice, bread, potatoes, sweets, and green salads can be eaten almost every day with only a slight decline in their palatability (Rolls, 1986).

The phenomenon of sensory-specific satiety has two important consequences. First, it encourages the consumption of a varied diet. If there were no sensory-specific satiety, an animal would tend to eat its preferred food and nothing else, and the result would be malnutrition. Second, sensory-specific satiety encourages animals that have access to a variety of foods to eat a lot; an animal that has eaten its fill of one food will often begin eating again if it encounters a different one. This encourages animals to take full advantage of times of abundance, which are all too rare in nature.

10.4   Neural Mechanisms of Hunger and Satiety

This section of the chapter focuses on the role of blood glucose levels, the hypothalamus, the gastrointestinal tract, and peptides in hunger and satiety.

Role of Blood Glucose Levels in Hunger and Satiety

The experiments of Campfield and Smith (see 1990) have renewed interest in the role of blood glucose levels in hunger and satiety. In a typical Campfield and Smith experiment, rats are housed individually with free access to a mixed diet and water, and blood glucose levels are continually monitored via chronic intravenous catheters. In this situation, baseline blood glucose levels rarely fluctuate by more than a percent or two. However, about 10 minutes before a meal is initiated, the levels suddenly drop by about 8%. Does the finding of Campfield and Smith lend support to the glucostatic theory of hunger? I think not, for two reasons: One is that it is a simple matter to construct a situation in which declines in blood glucose do not precede eating (e.g., Strubbe & Steffens, 1977)—for example, by unexpectedly serving a food with a high positive-incentive value. The second is that the premeal declines in blood glu-

cose observed by Campfield and Smith were likely a response to the animals' intention to start eating, not the other way round. This interpretation is supported by the fact that the declines of premeal blood glucose observed by Campfield and Smith were themselves preceded by an increase in blood insulin levels. The decreases in blood glucose thus did not occur because the animals were running out of energy; the animals lowered their own blood glucose levels by releasing insulin. Also, the suddenness of the drop in blood glucose suggests that the drop was actively produced rather than being a consequence of a gradual decline in the body's energy reserves following the preceding meal (see Figure 10.7). Finally, if the expected meal is not served, blood glucose levels return to their previous homeostatic levels.

The fact that injections of insulin do not reliably induce eating in some experimental subjects unless the injections are sufficiently great to reduce blood glucose levels by 50% (see Rowland, 1981) and the fact that large premeal infusions of glucose often do not suppress eating (see Geiselman, 1987) strongly suggest that glucose deficits are not the primary cause of hunger. However, some results suggest that decreases in blood glucose can contribute to feelings of hunger. For example, Smith and Campfield (1993) induced

Figure 10.7 The meal-related changes in blood glucose levels observed by Campfield and Smith (1986).

with drugs decreases in blood glucose similar to the ones that occur spontaneously prior to meals, and they found that the decreases promoted subsequent food consumption. Conversely, Campfield, Brandon, and Smith (1985) delayed the onset of meals by infusing glucose into the blood of rats at the first sign of a premeal decline in blood glucose.

Role of Hypothalamic Mechanisms in Hunger and Satiety

In the 1950s, experiments on rats seemed to suggest that eating behavior is controlled by two different regions of the hypothalamus: satiety by the **ventromedial hypothalamus (VMH)** and feeding by the **lateral hypothalamus (LH)**. Figure 10.8 on page 246 illustrates the locations of the VMH and the LH in the rat brain.

VMH satiety center   In 1940, it was discovered that large bilateral electrolytic lesions to the ventromedial hypothalamus produce **hyperphagia** (excessive eating) and extreme obesity in rats (Hetherington & Ranson, 1940). This *VMH syndrome* has two different phases: dynamic and static. The **dynamic phase,** which begins as soon as the subject regains consciousness after the operation, is characterized by several weeks of grossly excessive eating and rapid weight gain. However, eventually consumption gradually declines to a level that is just sufficient to maintain a stable level of obesity; this marks the beginning of the **static phase.** Figure 10.9 on page 247 illustrates the weight gain and food intake of an adult rat with bilateral VMH lesions.

The most important feature of the static phase of the VMH syndrome is that the animal "defends" its new body weight. If a rat in the static phase is deprived of food until it has lost a substantial amount of weight, it will increase its intake until the lost weight is regained; conversely, if it is made to gain weight by forced feeding, it will reduce its intake until the excess is lost.

Paradoxically, despite their prodigious levels of consumption, VMH-lesioned rats in some ways seem less hungry than unlesioned controls. Although VMH-lesioned rats eat much more than normal rats when palatable food is readily available, they are less willing to work for it (Teitelbaum, 1957) or to consume it if it is slightly unpalatable (Miller, Bailey, & Stevenson, 1950). Weingarten, Chang, and Jarvie (1983) have shown that the finicky eating of VMH-lesioned rats is a consequence of their obesity, not a primary effect of their lesion; they are no less likely to consume unpalatable food than are unlesioned rats of equal obesity.

LH feeding center   In 1951, Anand and Brobeck reported that bilateral electrolytic lesions to the *lateral hypothalamus* produce **aphagia**—a complete cessation of eating. Even rats that were first made hyperphagic by VMH lesions were rendered aphagic by the addition of LH lesions. Anand and Brobeck concluded that the lateral region of the

Sensory-specific satiety. The fact that the consumption of a particular food produces more satiety for foods of the same taste than for other foods.

Ventromedial hypothalamus (VMH). The area of the hypothalamus that was once thought to be the satiety center.

Lateral hypothalamus (LH). The area of the hypothalamus once thought to be the feeding center.

Hyperphagia. Excessive eating.

Dynamic phase. The first phase of the VMH syndrome, characterized by grossly excessive eating and weight gain.

Static phase. The second phase of the VMH syndrome, during which the grossly obese animal regulates its body weight.

Aphagia. Complete cessation of eating.

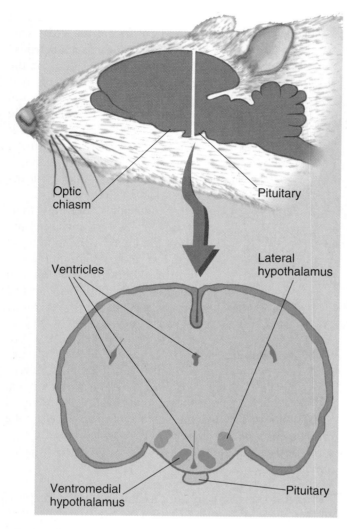

Figure 10.8 The location in the rat brain of the ventromedial hypothalamus and the lateral hypothalamus.

hypothalamus is a feeding center. Teitelbaum and Epstein (1962) subsequently discovered two important features of the *LH syndrome*. First, they found that the aphagia was accompanied by **adipsia**—a complete cessation of drinking. Second, they found that LH-lesioned rats partially recover if they are kept alive by tube feeding. First, they begin to eat wet, palatable foods, such as chocolate chip cookies soaked in milk, and eventually they will eat dry food pellets if water is concurrently available.

Reinterpretation of the effects of VMH and LH lesions The theory of VMH satiety and LH feeding centers became very popular, and it was served up to wave after wave of students as if the evidence for it were unassailable. However, little about it is true.

The theory that the VMH is a satiety center has crumbled in the face of two lines of evidence. One of these lines has shown that the primary role of the hypothalamus is the regulation of energy metabolism, not the regulation of eating. Why, then, do VMH-lesioned animals overeat? The ini-

tial interpretation was that such animals become obese because they overeat; however, the evidence suggests the converse—that they overeat because they become obese. Bilateral VMH lesions increase blood insulin levels, which increases **lipogenesis** (the production of body fat) and decreases **lipolysis** (the breakdown of body fat to utilizable forms of energy)—see Powley et al. (1980). Both are likely to be the result of the increases in insulin levels that occur following the lesion. Because the calories of VMH-lesioned rats are converted to fat at a high rate, the rats must keep eating to ensure that they have enough calories in their blood to meet their immediate energy requirements; they are like misers who run to the bank each time they make a bit of money and deposit it in a savings account from which withdrawals cannot be made. The following four observations support this new interpretation:

1. Insulin levels in the blood are elevated after VMH lesions, even before the rats have been allowed to eat; and the magnitude of this postlesion **hyperinsulinemia** is a good predictor of how obese the rat will eventually become (Hustvedt & Løvø, 1972).

2. Rats with VMH lesions accumulate more fat than do controls, even when they are fed the same amount of food (Han, Feng, & Kuo, 1972; Slaunwhite, Goldman, & Bernardis, 1972).

3. During the day, when normal rats sleep and derive most of their energy from fat stores, VMH-lesioned rats get most of their energy from *gluconeogenesis* (Holm, Hustvedt, & Løvø, 1973).

4. Cutting the branch of the *vagus nerve* that transmits signals from the brain to the pancreas, eliminates the hyperphagia and obesity produced by VMH lesions (Sawchenko et al., 1977).

The second line of evidence that has undermined the theory of a VMH satiety center has shown that many of the effects of VMH lesions are not attributable to VMH damage. A large fiber bundle, the *ventral noradrenergic bundle*, courses past the VMH and is thus inevitably damaged by large electrolytic VMH lesions; in particular, fibers that project from the nearby **paraventricular nuclei** of the hypothalamus are damaged (see Figure 10.10 on page 248). Bilateral lesions of the noradrenergic bundle (e.g., Gold et

Adipsia. Complete cessation of drinking.

Lipogenesis. The production of body fat.

Lipolysis. The breakdown of body fat.

Hyperinsulinemia. A condition in which too much insulin is released into the blood.

Paraventricular nuclei. Hypothalamic nuclei that play a role in eating.

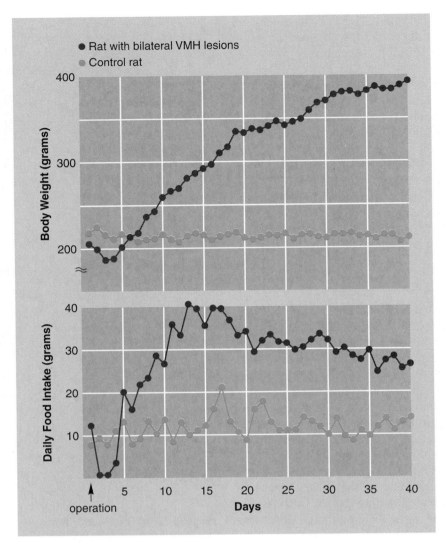

Figure 10.9 Postoperative hyperphagia and obesity in a rat with bilateral VMH lesions. (Adapted from Teitelbaum, 1961.)

al., 1977) or the paraventricular nuclei (Leibowitz, Hammer, & Chang, 1981) produce hyperphagia and obesity similar in several respects to those produced by VMH lesions.

The evidence against the notion of an LH feeding center has come from more thorough analysis of the effects of bilateral LH lesions. Early research focused exclusively on the aphagia and adipsia that are produced by LH lesions, but subsequent research has shown that LH lesions produce a wide range of motor disturbances and a general lack of responsiveness to sensory input (of which food and drink are but two examples). Because the behavioral effects of LH lesions are so general, the notion that the LH is a center specifically dedicated to feeding is untenable.

Although the LH is not a feeding center, Rolls and Rolls (1982) found that it does contain neurons that respond to the positive incentive properties of food rather than to food itself. When monkeys were repeatedly allowed to eat a palatable food, the response of the LH neurons to it declined, although their response to other palatable foods did

not. Furthermore, neurons that responded to the sight of food would come to respond to a neutral stimulus that reliably predicted the presentation of food, and the repeated presentation of a palatable food (e.g., a banana) without the monkey being allowed to eat it eventually rendered that item incapable of producing its usual neural response.

Paraventricular nuclei The finding that the effects of VMH lesions on eating are partially attributable to the destruction of fibers of passage that are connected to the paraventricular nuclei focused attention on the role of these hypothalamic nuclei in eating. It led to the discovery that microinjections of norepinephrine, GABA, neuropeptide Y, galanin peptide, or opioid peptides into the paraventricular nuclei increase eating under various conditions (see Leibowitz, 1992). Norepinephrine, GABA, and neuropeptide Y specifically increase the consumption of carbohydrates by increasing the size, rather than the number, of carbohydrate-rich meals—presumably by attenuating a carbohydrate-related satiety signal. Whereas galanin peptide and opioid peptides specifically increase the size of fat-rich meals—presumably by attenuating a fat-related satiety signal.

The mechanisms by which eating is influenced by microinjections of norepinephrine, GABA, neuropeptide Y, galanin peptides, and opioid peptides into the paraventricular nuclei are still unknown. However, the finding that cutting the branch of the vagus nerve that innervates the pancreas significantly reduces eating stimulated by norepinephrine injections into the paraventricular nucleus suggests that the effects on eating may be secondary to the metabolic effects of the microinjections.

Role of the Gastrointestinal Tract in Satiety

One of the most influential early studies of hunger was published by Cannon and Washburn in 1912. It was a perfect collaboration; Cannon had the ideas, and Washburn had the ability to swallow a balloon. First, Washburn swallowed an empty balloon tied to the end of a thin tube. Then, Cannon pumped some air into the balloon and connected the end of the tube to a water-filled glass U-tube so that Washburn's stomach contractions produced a momentary increase in the level of the water at the other end of the U-tube. Washburn reported a "pang" of hunger each time that a large stomach contraction was recorded (see Figure 10.11).

Cannon and Washburn's finding led to the theory that hunger is the feeling of contractions caused by an empty stomach, whereas satiety is the feeling of stomach distention. However, support for this theory and interest in the role of the gastrointestinal tract in hunger and satiety quickly waned with the discovery that human patients whose stomachs had been surgically removed and whose esophaguses had been hooked up directly to their **duodenums** continued to report feelings of hunger and satiety and continued to maintain their normal body weights by eating more meals of smaller size.

In the 1980s, there was a resurgence of interest in the role of the gastrointestinal tract in eating. It was stimulated by a series of experiments that indicated that the gastrointestinal tract is the source of a satiety signal. For example, Koopmans (1981) transplanted an extra stomach and length of intestine into rats and then joined the major arteries and veins of the implants to the recipients' own circulatory sys-

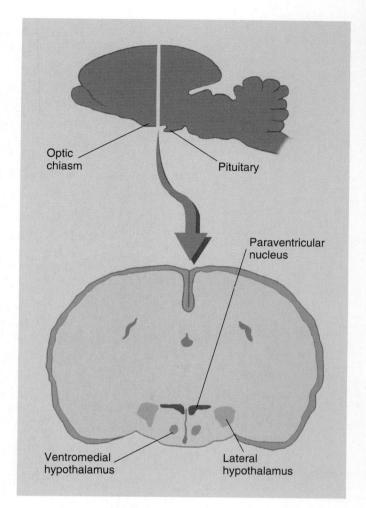

Figure 10.10 Location of the paraventricular nucleus in the rat hypothalamus. Note that the section through the hypothalamus is slightly different than the one in Figure 10.8.

tems (see Figure 10.12 on page 250). Koopmans found that food injected into the transplanted stomach and kept there by a noose around the *pyloric sphincter* decreased eating in proportion to both its caloric content and volume. Because the transplanted stomach had no functional nerves, the gastrointestinal satiety signal had to be reaching the brain through the blood. And because nutrients are not absorbed from the stomach, the bloodborne satiety signal could not have been a nutrient. It had to be some chemical or chemicals that were released from the stomach in response to the caloric value and volume of the food. These gastrointestinal satiety chemicals proved to be *peptides.*

Gut Satiety Peptides

Ingested food interacts with receptors in the gastrointestinal tract and triggers the release of peptides. In 1973, Gibbs, Young, and Smith injected one of these peptides, **cholecystokinin (CCK),** into hungry rats and found that

---

Duodenum. The upper portion of the intestine through which most of the glucose and amino acids are absorbed into the bloodstream.

Cholecystokinin (CCK). A peptide that is released by the gastrointestinal tract and is thought to function as a satiety signal.

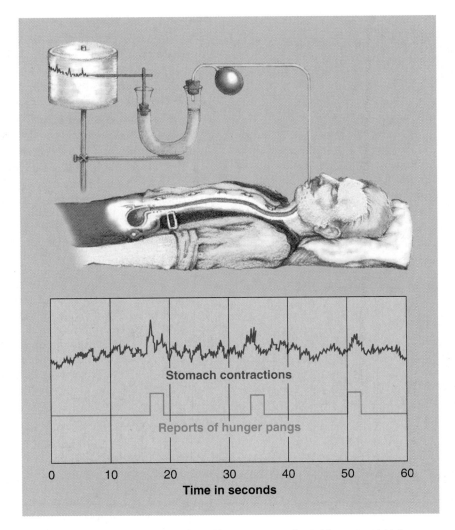

Figure 10.11 The system developed by Cannon and Washburn in 1912 for measuring stomach contractions. They found that large stomach contractions were related to pangs of hunger.

they ate smaller meals. This led to the hypothesis that circulating gut peptides provide the brain with information about the quantity and nature of food in the gastrointestinal tract and that this information plays a role in satiety.

There is now considerable support for the hypothesis that peptides can function as satiety signals (see Leibowitz, 1992). Several gut peptides have been shown to bind to receptors in the brain, and close to a dozen have been reported to reduce food intake (e.g., CCK, bombesin, glucagon, and somatostatin)—see Woods and Gibbs (1989).

It is conceivable that at least part of the inhibitory effect of peptides on eating is indirect—mediated by their effects on peripheral organs (see Weller, Smith, & Gibbs, 1990). For example, McHugh and Moran (1985) have proposed that the inhibitory action of CCK on stomach emptying contributes to its satiety-producing effect. However, Dourish, Rycroft, and Iversen (1989) found that selective antagonists of central nervous system CCK receptors are

100 times more effective in increasing feeding than are selective antagonists of peripheral CCK receptors (see Cooper & Dourish, 1990); and Conover, Collins, and Weingarten (1989) found that CCK reduced food consumption even under conditions in which it did not retard gastric emptying.

Woods and Porte and their colleagues have postulated that insulin plays a role in the regulation of feeding by providing the brain with information about *adiposity* (the amount of body fat). It is true that blood insulin levels are higher in fatter people; still, it is difficult to see how fluctuating levels of blood insulin could provide the brain with information about relatively stable reserves of body fat (Panksepp, 1975). Woods and Porte (1977) suggested how. They found that insulin in the blood penetrates the cerebrospinal fluid at a very slow rate—and thus that the level of insulin in cerebrospinal fluid does not reflect the slight moment-to-moment fluctuations in the level of insulin in

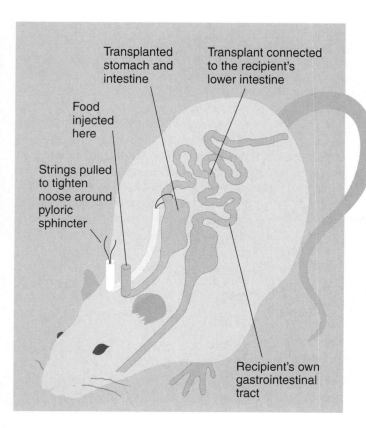

the blood. Accordingly, they suggested that it is the levels of insulin in cerebrospinal fluid that provide the brain with information about levels of fat in the body.

In support of this hypothesis was the discovery of insulin receptors in the hypothalamus and other parts of the brain (Baskin et al., 1983; Porte & Woods, 1981) and the observation that infusing insulin into the lateral ventricles of baboons for 2 to 3 weeks produced a dose-dependent decline of food intake and weight (Woods et al., 1979). At the highest dose, food intake was reduced by close to 75% without altering blood insulin or blood glucose levels (however, see Hannah & Hansen, 1990; Willing, Walls, & Koopmans, 1990).

Figure 10.12 Transplantation of an extra stomach and length of intestine in a rat. Koopmans (1981) implanted an extra stomach and length of intestine in each of his experimental subjects. He then connected the major blood vessels of the implanted stomachs to the circulatory systems of the recipients. Food injected into the extra stomach and kept there by a noose around the pyloric sphincter decreased eating in proportion to its volume and caloric value.

10.5   Body Weight Regulation: Set Points versus Settling Points

Most people we have interviewed about their personal theories of hunger, eating, and weight regulation believe that body weight is regulated by a body-fat set point. They believe that when fat deposits are below a person's set point, a person becomes hungrier and eats more, which results in a return of body-fat levels to that person's set point; and conversely, they believe that when fat deposits are above a person's set point, a person becomes less hungry and eats less, which results in a return of body fat levels to their set point.

The strongest evidence against the set-point view comes from demonstrations of the inability of many humans and other animals to maintain their body weights at healthy levels when highly palatable food is abundantly available and from studies documenting the beneficial effects of *dietary restriction*. The results of experiments on over a dozen different species tell a remarkably consistent story (see Masoro, 1988). In each species, animals whose intake was restricted by 30 to 60% below free-feeding levels became sleeker and healthier, aged more slowly, developed fewer age-related degenerative diseases, and lived longer—25% longer in one study of mice. These results are troubling because most of us live in environments in which highly palatable food is rarely more than a few steps away. Although experiments on dietary restriction have not been conducted in humans, cor-

relational evidence indicates that humans too benefit greatly from it (see Brownell & Rodin, 1994).

Regulation of Body Fat by Changes in the Efficiency of Energy Utilization

The widely held belief that weight is regulated largely by changes in food intake (increases in eating when body weight is low and decreases when it is high) has been contradicted by recent evidence (see Keesey & Powley, 1986). We now know that the body controls its fat levels, to a large degree, by changing the efficiency with which it uses energy. As a person's level of body fat declines, that person starts to use energy resources more efficiently, which limits further weight loss (see Martin, White, & Hulsey, 1991); conversely, weight gain is limited by a progressive decrease in the efficiency of energy utilization. Rothwell and Stock (1982) created a group of obese rats by maintaining them on a cafeteria diet, and they found that the resting level of energy expenditure in these obese rats was 45% greater than in control rats.

This point is illustrated by the progressively declining effectiveness of weight-loss programs. Initially, low-calorie diets produce substantial weight loss. But the rate of weight

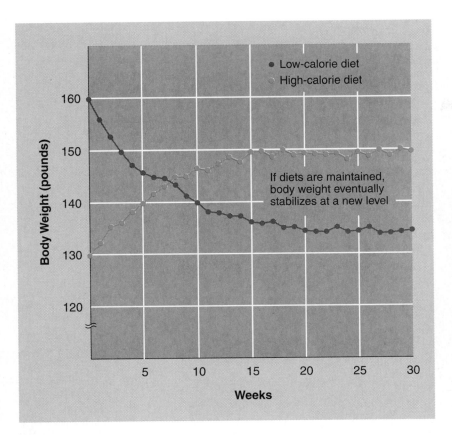

Figure 10.13 The diminishing effect on body weight of a low-calorie diet and a high-calorie diet.

loss diminishes with each successive week on the diet, until an equilibrium is achieved and little or no further weight loss occurs. Most dieters are familiar with this disappointing trend. A similar effect occurs with weight-gain programs (see Figure 10.13).

The mechanism by which the body adjusts the efficiency of its energy utilization in response to its levels of body fat has been termed **diet-induced thermogenesis.** Increases in the levels of body fat produce increases in body temperature, which require additional energy to maintain them—and decreases in the level of body fat have the opposite effects.

Set Points and Settling Points in Weight Control

Although body-fat set-point models can account for the stability of body weight, they have two serious flaws: One is that they are unnecessarily complex; the other is that they are inconsistent with the evidence. Thus many investigators (see Booth, Fuller & Lewis, 1981; Wirtshafter & Davis, 1977) now believe that eating is not part of a system that is designed to defend a body-fat set point. They argue that body weight tends to drift around a natural **settling point**—the level at which the various factors that influence body

weight achieve an equilibrium. The idea is that as body-fat levels increase, changes occur that tend to limit further increases until a balance is achieved between all factors that encourage weight gain and all those that discourage it.

The settling-point model provides a loose kind of homeostatic regulation, without a set-point mechanism or mechanisms to return body weight to a set point. According to the settling-point model, body weight remains stable as long as there are no long-term changes in the factors that influence it; and if there are such changes, their impact is limited by negative feedback. In the settling-point model, the feedback merely limits further changes in the same direction, whereas in the set-point model, negative feedback triggers a return to the set point. (A neuron's resting potential is a well-known biological settling point—see Chapter 4.)

The seductiveness of the set-point theory is attributable in no small part to the existence of the thermostat model, which provides a vivid means of thinking about it. Figure 10.14 is a model that I like to use to think about the settling-point theory. I call it the **leaky-barrel model.** It is an analogy: (1) The amount of water entering the hose is analogous to the amount of food available to the subject; (2) the water pressure at the nozzle is analogous to the positive incentive value of the available food; (3) the amount of water entering the barrel is analogous to the amount of energy consumed; (4) the water level in the barrel is analogous to the level of body fat; (5) the amount of water leaking from the barrel is analogous to the amount of energy being expended; and (6) the weight of the barrel on the hose is analogous to the strength of the satiety signal.

The main advantage of the settling-point theory of body weight regulation over the body-fat set-point theory is that it is more consistent with the data. Another advantage is that in those cases in which both theories make the same prediction, the settling-point theory does so more parsi-

Diet-induced thermogenesis. The homeostasis-defending inceases in body temperature that are associated with increases in body fat.

Settling point. The point at which various factors that influence the level of some regulated function achieve an equilibrium.

Leaky-barrel model. A settling-point model of body-fat regulation.

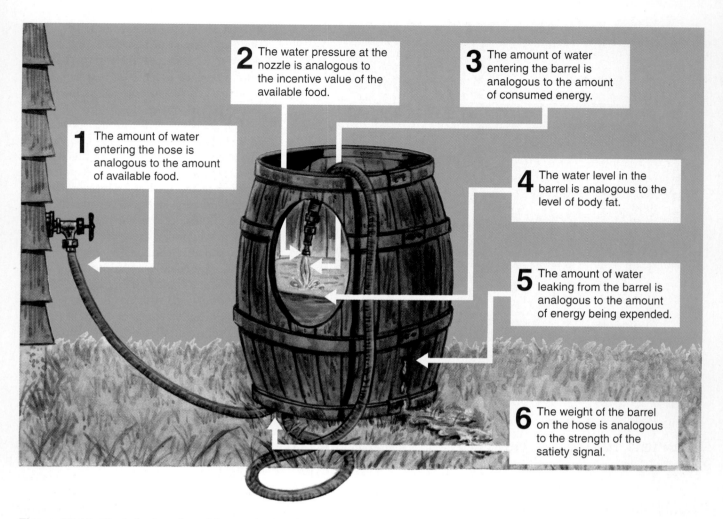

Figure 10.14 The leaky-barrel model: A settling-point model of eating and body weight homeostasis.

1 The amount of water entering the hose is analogous to the amount of available food.

2 The water pressure at the nozzle is analogous to the incentive value of the available food.

3 The amount of water entering the barrel is analogous to the amount of consumed energy.

4 The water level in the barrel is analogous to the level of body fat.

5 The amount of water leaking from the barrel is analogous to the amount of energy being expended.

6 The weight of the barrel on the hose is analogous to the strength of the satiety signal.

moniously—that is, with a simpler mechanism that requires fewer assumptions. Let's use the leaky-barrel model to see how the two theories account for four key facts of weight regulation.

Fact 1: Body weight remains relatively constant in many adult animals. On the basis of this fact, it has been argued that body fat must be regulated around a set point. However, constant body weight does not require, or even imply, a set point. Consider the leaky-barrel model. As water from the tap begins to fill the barrel, the weight of the water in the barrel increases. This increases the amount of water leaking out of the barrel and decreases the amount of water entering the barrel by increasing the pressure of the barrel on the hose. Eventually, this system settles into an equilibrium where the water level stays constant; but because this level is neither predetermined nor actively defended, it is a settling point, not a set point.

Fact 2: Many adult animals experience enduring changes in body weight. Set-point systems are designed to maintain internal constancy in the face of fluctuations of the exter-

nal environment. Thus the fact that many adult animals experience long-term changes in body weight is a strong argument against the set-point theory. In contrast, the set-tling-point theory predicts that when there is an enduring change in one of the parameters that affect body weight—for example, a major increase in the positive-incentive value of available food—body weight will drift to a new settling point.

Fact 3: If a subject's intake of food is reduced, metabolic changes occur that limit the loss of weight; the opposite occurs when the subject overeats. This fact is often cited as evidence for set-point regulation of body weight; however, because the metabolic changes merely limit further weight changes rather than eliminating those that have occurred, they are more consistent with a settling-point model. For example, when water intake in the leaky-barrel model is reduced, the water level in the barrel begins to drop; but the

Lipectomy. The surgical removal of body fat.

Before moving on to Part 2 of the chapter, complete the following review exercise. The correct answers are provided at the bottom of this page. Before proceeding, review material related to your incorrect answers and omissions.

1. The primary function of the _____ is to serve as a storage reservoir for undigested food.

2. Most of the absorption of nutrients into the body takes place through the wall of the _____, or upper intestine.

3. The phase of energy metabolism that is triggered by the expectation of food is the _____ phase.

4. During the absorptive phase, the pancreas releases much _____ into the bloodstream.

5. During the fasting phase, the primary fuel of the body is _____.

6. During the fasting phase, the primary fuel of the brain is _____.

7. The three components of a set-point system are a set-point mechanism, a detector, and an _____.

8. The theory that hunger and satiety are regulated by a blood glucose set point is the _____ theory.

9. The evidence suggests that hunger is a function of the current _____ value of food.

10. The evidence supports a _____ model of body weight regulation rather than a set-point model.

drop is limited by a decrease in leakage and an increase in inflow attributable to the falling water pressure in the barrel. Eventually, a new settling point is achieved, but the reduction in water level is not as great as one might expect because of the loss-limiting changes.

Fact 4: After an individual has lost a substantial amount of weight (by dieting, exercise, or even **lipectomy**—the surgical removal of fat), there is a tendency for the original weight to be regained once the subject returns to the previous eating- and energy-related lifestyle. Although this finding is often offered as irrefutable evidence of a body weight set point, the settling-point theory readily accounts for it. When the water level in the leaky-barrel model is reduced—by temporarily decreasing input (dieting), by temporarily increasing output (exercising), or by scooping out some of the water (lipectomy)—only a temporary drop in the settling point is produced. When the original conditions are reinstated, the water level inexorably drifts back to the original settling point.

Does it really matter whether we think about body weight regulation in terms of set points or settling points—or is it just splitting hairs? It certainly matters to biopsychologists: Understanding that body weight is regulated by a settling-point system helps them better understand and more accurately predict the changes in body weight that are likely to occur in various situations; it also indicates the kinds of physiological mechanisms that are likely to mediate them. And it should matter to you. If the set-point theory is correct, attempting to change your body weight would be a waste of time; you would inevitably be drawn back to your body weight set point. On the other hand, the leaky-barrel model suggests that it is possible to permanently change your body weight by permanently changing any of the factors that influences energy intake and output.

The answers are (1) stomach, (2) duodenum, (3) cephalic, (4) insulin, (5) free fatty acid, (6) glucose, (7) effector, (8) glucostatic, (9) positive-incentive, and (10) settling-point.

Part 2 of the chapter focuses on the biopsychology of thirst, drinking, and body fluid regulation. Most research on drinking is based on the premise that drinking is motivated by a deficit in the body's water resources. Like eating, some drinking is motivated by internal deficits, but most is not.

This part of the chapter begins with an introduction to the regulation of the body's fluid resources. Then, it discusses the regulation of deprivation-induced drinking and drinking in the absence of water deficits.

10.6 Regulation of the Body's Fluid Resources

The body can be thought of as two separate fluid-filled compartments: an intracellular compartment and an extracellular compartment.

Intracellular and Extracellular Fluid Compartments

As Figure 10.15 indicates, about two-thirds of the body's water is inside cells (*intracellular*), and about one-third is outside (*extracellular*). The water found in the extracellular compartment is in the *interstitial fluid* (the fluid in which the cells are bathed), the *blood*, and the *cerebrospinal fluid*.

Normally, the fluids in the intracellular and extracellular body fluid compartments are **isotonic solutions**—solutions of equal concentration to one another. In other words, the proportion of the intracellular fluid that is composed of *solutes* (substances dissolved in a fluid) is normally the same as the proportion of the extracellular fluid that is composed of solutes.

In the isotonic state there is no tendency for the water inside cells to be drawn out of cells, or for water in the interstitial fluid to be drawn into cells. However, if the fluid in one of the compartments is made more concentrated than the other by the addition of solutes to it or by the removal of water from it, the more concentrated fluid draws water from the less concentrated fluid through the cell membranes until the isotonicity of the fluids is reestablished. Conversely, if the concentration of the solution in one of the compartments is decreased by the addition of water to it or by the removal of solutes from it, water is drawn from it into the other compartment. The pressure that draws water from less concentrated solutions (**hypotonic solutions**) through semipermeable membranes into more-concentrated solutions (**hypertonic solutions**) is called **osmotic pressure** (see Figure 10.16).

The Kidneys: Regulation of Water and Sodium Levels

Sodium is the major solute in body fluids. Thus the regulation of water and sodium levels is intimately related. The regulation of the body's water and sodium resources is reasonably straightforward. We normally consume far more water and sodium than we need, and the excess is drawn from the blood and excreted. This is the function of the *kidneys*. Blood enters the kidneys via the *renal arteries*, where various impurities and excess sodium and water are extracted. Blood leaves the kidneys via the *renal veins*, and urine leaves via the *ureters*, which channel the urine to the *bladder* for temporary storage before excretion (see Figure 10.17 on page 256).

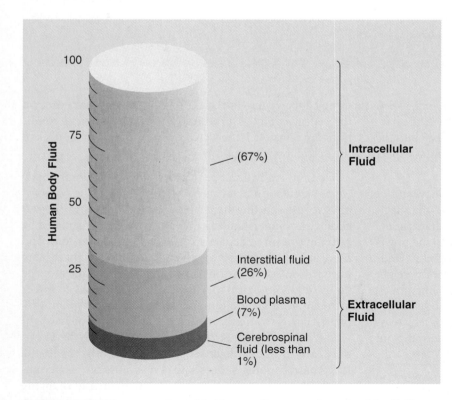

Figure 10.15 The proportion of fluid normally present in each of the fluid compartments of the human body.

Isotonicity

The intracellular and extracellular fluids of the body are normally isotonic to one another; that is, they contain the same concentration of solutes. As a result, there is normally little or no osmotic pressure drawing water into or out of cells.

Hypertonicity

The extracellular fluid is rendered hypertonic to the intracellular fluid by the addition of solutes to the extracellular fluid or by the removal of water from it. This creates an osmotic pressure (see arrow) that draws water out of cells until isotonicity is reestablished.

Hypotonicity

The extracellular fluid is rendered hypotonic to the intracellular fluid by the removal of solutes from the extracellular fluid or by the addition of water to it. This creates an osmotic pressure (see arrow) that draws water into cells until isotonicity is reestablished.

Figure 10.16 Isotonicity, hypertonicity, hypotonicity, and osmotic pressure.

There are approximately 1 million independent functional units, called *nephrons,* in each human kidney (see Figure 10.18 on page 257). Each nephron is a complex tangle of capillaries and tubules. Excess water and sodium pass from the capillaries to the tubules and then to the ureters.

Urination is not the only mechanism of water loss. Significant quantities of water are also lost by perspiration, by respiration, by defecation, and by evaporation through the skin (see Figure 10.19 on page 257).

Regular water consumption is important for our survival because we humans lose water at a high rate and because we have a limited capacity to store excess water. In this sense, drinking is different than eating. Most people can live for weeks without eating, but few can survive more than a few days without water.

10.7 Deprivation-Induced Drinking: Cellular Dehydration and Hypovolemia

When the body's water resources decrease significantly, the body reacts in two ways: Steps are taken to conserve the body's declining water resources, and there are increases in thirst. Two different physiological systems mediate deprivation-induced drinking: one that is sensitive to reductions in intracellular fluid volume and one that is sensitive to reductions in blood volume. A reduction in intracellular fluid volume is called **cellular dehydration** and a reduction in blood volume is called **hypovolemia.**

Cellular Dehydration and Thirst

As the bartenders who supply free salted nuts well know, salt (sodium chloride) makes one thirsty. The thirst produced by salty food is caused by cellular dehydration. Because salt does not readily pass into cells, it accumulates in the extracellular fluid, making it hypertonic and drawing water from cells into the interstitial fluid. Salt consumption has little effect on blood volume.

Isotonic solutions. Solutions that contain the same concentration of solutes as some reference solution.

Hypotonic solutions. Solutions that are less concentrated than some reference solution.

Hypertonic solutions. Solutions that are more concentrated than some reference solution.

Osmotic pressure. The pressure that draws water from a hypotonic solution to a hypertonic solution.

Cellular dehydration. Reduction in intracellular fluid volume.

Hypovolemia. Decreased blood volume.

Cellular dehydration is usually induced in experimental animals through the injection of hypertonic solutions of salt or other solutes that do not readily pass through cell membranes (see Fitzsimons, 1972; Gilman, 1937). It can also be produced by depriving subjects of water. But because water deprivation also reduces the volume of water in the extracellular compartment, researchers interested specifically in the role of cellular dehydration usually study drinking in response to the injection of hypertonic solutions.

Most of the research on cellular dehydration has been aimed at locating the cells in the body that are responsible for detecting it. The cells that detect cellular dehydration are called **osmoreceptors.**

Evidence that osmoreceptors in the brain play a role in drinking comes from studies in which hypertonic solutions have been injected into the *carotid arteries* (arteries of the neck, which carry blood to the brain) of nondeprived animals. In one study, solutions of sodium chloride were bilaterally infused through the carotid arteries of nondeprived dogs at concentrations that increased cerebral osmolarity without having a significant effect on the osmolarity of the body as a whole (Wood, Rolls, & Ramsay, 1977). Figure 10.20 on page 258 shows that the infusions increased the dogs' water consumption during a subsequent 5-minute test and that the amount of water consumed during the test was a function of the concentration of the infused solution.

Four lines of evidence suggest that osmoreceptors that encourage drinking are located in the *lateral preoptic area* of the hypothalamus. First, minute quantities of slightly hypertonic saline injected bilaterally into various sites in the lateral preoptic area (see Figure 10.21 on page 258) elicited drinking in rats (Blass & Epstein, 1971; Andrews et al., 1992) and rabbits (Peck & Novin, 1971). Second, control injections of hypertonic sucrose solutions into the same sites elicited drinking, whereas hypertonic urea injections did not. Sucrose, like sodium chloride, does not readily enter cells and thus draws water out of them, whereas urea readily enters cells and thus has no dehydrating effect. Third, drinking elicited by an injection of sodium chloride into the *peritoneum* (abdominal cavity) was suppressed by the bilateral infusion of small amounts of water directly into sites in the lateral preoptic area (Blass & Epstein, 1971). Fourth, the firing of neurons in the lateral preoptic area increased in proportion to the hypertonicity of solutions of sodium chloride or sucrose injected into the carotid artery (Malmo & Malmo, 1979).

Figure 10.17 The kidneys. Blood enters through the renal arteries; blood and urine exit through the renal veins and ureters, respectively.

There are two mechanisms by which osmoreceptors induce thirst: one direct and one indirect. The direct mechanism is a neural mechanism: Cellular dehydration causes

Osmoreceptors. Receptors sensitive to dehydration.

Antidiuretic hormone (ADH). A hormone released from the posterior pituitary that encourages the conservation of body fluids by decreasing the volume of urine produced by the kidneys also called vasopressin.

Baroreceptors. Blood pressure receptors.

Blood-flow receptors. Receptors that monitor the volume of blood flowing through the kidneys.

Nephrectomized. Having had one's kidneys removed.

Figure 10.18 A nephron. There are approximately 1 million nephrons in each human kidney; each nephron absorbs water, sodium, and waste from the blood.

Blood from renal artery

Blood to renal vein

Urine to ureter

nism is a hormonal mechanism: Cellular dehydration causes osmoreceptors to increase the release of **antidiuretic hormone** (**ADH**) from the posterior pituitary, and the increase in ADH levels triggers a sequence of events that results in conservation of the body's dwindling water resources and an increase in thirst. Different osmoreceptors control the direct and indirect mechanisms of thirst induced by cellular dehydration; intracerebral injections of hypertonic solutions that induce drinking do not always increase ADH levels.

Hypovolemia and Thirst

As noted earlier in this section, in addition to producing cellular dehydration, water deprivation produces hypovolemia—a reduction in blood volume. Hypovolemia, like cellular dehydration, is an important stimulus for thirst. It is selectively induced in experimental animals in one of two ways. One method is to withdraw blood from the subjects; the other is to inject a colloid substance into the peritoneal cavity. *Colloids* are gluelike substances with molecules much too large to pass through cell membranes. Thus colloids injected into the peritoneum stay there and, like sponges,

the hypothalamic osmoreceptors to activate neural circuits that mediate the experience of thirst. The indirect mecha-

draw blood plasma out of the circulatory system by osmotic pressure. Neither bleeding nor colloid injections change the osmolarity of the extracellular fluid; thus they reduce blood volume without producing cellular dehydration.

Hypovolemia is detected by **baroreceptors** (blood pressure receptors) in the wall of the heart and by **blood-flow receptors** (receptors that monitor the volume of blood flow). Evidence suggests that both play a role in hypovolemic thirst. For example, Stricker (1973) implicated the cardiac baroreceptors in hypovolemic drinking by showing that injections of colloid into the peritoneal cavity of rats that had been **nephrectomized**—rats whose kidneys had been removed—caused them to drink. This implicated the cardiac baroreceptors because hypovolemic drinking in kidneyless rats cannot possibly be mediated

Figure 10.19 Sources of water loss from the human body. (Adapted from Guyton, 1987.)

Daily Water Loss (liters)

- Respiration
- Skin
- Feces
- Sweat
- Urine

Normal activity Normal temperature

Normal activity Hot temperature

Heavy exercise Normal temperature

Figure 10.20 Nondeprived dogs began to drink when hypertonic sodium chloride solutions were infused through their carotid arteries. The greater the concentration of the solution, the more they drank. (Adapted from Rolls & Rolls, 1982.)

by receptors in the kidneys. Fitzsimons (1972) implicated the *renal* (kidney) blood-flow receptors by showing that reducing renal blood flow by partially tying off the renal arteries of rats causes them to drink.

When blood volume decreases, both the baroreceptors and the blood-flow receptors trigger changes in the kidneys that increase both thirst and the conservation of the body's water resources. The baroreceptors influence kidney function by increasing the release of ADH; the blood-flow receptors influence kidney function directly.

The mechanisms by which cellular dehydration and hypovolemia increase thirst and elicit physiological reactions that conserve the body's water reserves are outlined in the following paragraphs. They are also illustrated in Figure 10.22.

Effects of Antidiuretic Hormone

Water deprivation causes both the hypothalamic osmoreceptors and the heart baroreceptors to increase the release of antidiuretic hormone from the posterior pituitary. The ADH influences kidney function in two different ways: by reducing the volume of urine produced by the kidneys and by increasing the release of **renin** from the kidneys. The release of renin is also stimulated during water deprivation by the activity of the renal (kidney) blood-flow receptors.

The increase of circulating renin causes the formation in the blood of the peptide hormone **angiotensin II,** and the angiotensin II in turn produces a compensatory increase in blood pressure by constricting the peripheral blood vessels and triggering the release of aldosterone from the adrenal cortexes. **Aldosterone** causes the kidneys to reabsorb much of the sodium that would otherwise have been lost in the urine. The maintenance of high levels of sodium in the

blood is critical for the prevention of further decreases in blood volume; the higher the concentration of sodium in the blood, the more water the blood will retain.

Angiotensin II and Drinking

The discovery that the intraperitoneal injection of kidney extracts causes rats to drink suggested that the kidneys produce a **dipsogen**—a substance that induces drinking. This dipsogen proved to be the peptide angiotensin II, which is synthesized in the blood in response to cellular dehydration or hypovolemia. In many species, infusion of angiotensin II increases drinking without influencing other motivated behaviors (e.g., Fitzsimons & Simons, 1969).

Much of the research on the dipsogenic effect of angiotensin II has been directed at discovering its site of action in the brain. Two early clues focused attention on the

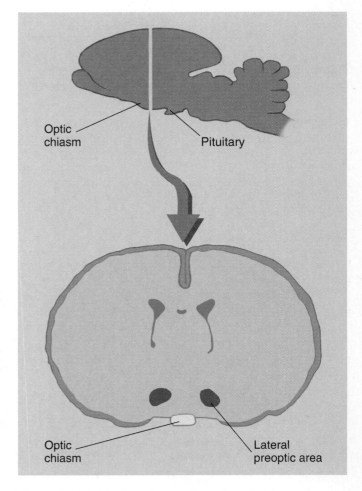

Figure 10.21 The lateral preoptic area—a site into which microinjections of hypertonic solutions elicit drinking in rats.

Chapter 10 The Biology of Eating and Drinking

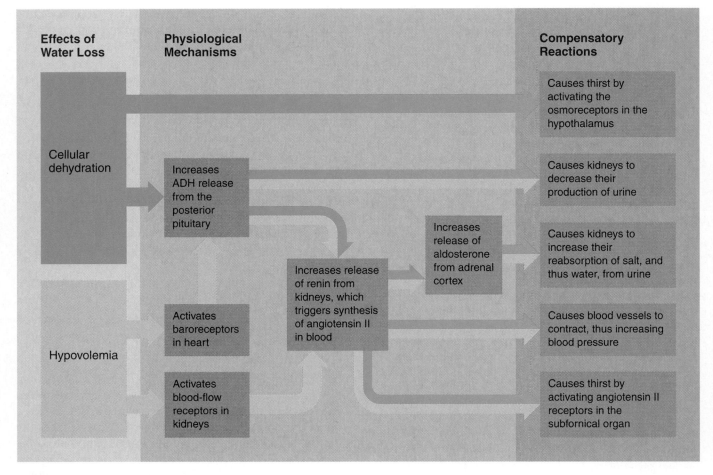

Figure 10.22 The effects of cellular dehydration and hypovolemia.

Effects of Water Loss
- Cellular dehydration
- Hypovolemia

Physiological Mechanisms
- Increases ADH release from the posterior pituitary
- Activates baroreceptors in heart
- Activates blood-flow receptors in kidneys
- Increases release of renin from kidneys, which triggers synthesis of angiotensin II in blood
- Increases release of aldosterone from adrenal cortex

Compensatory Reactions
- Causes thirst by activating the osmoreceptors in the hypothalamus
- Causes kidneys to decrease their production of urine
- Causes kidneys to increase their reabsorption of salt, and thus water, from urine
- Causes blood vessels to contract, thus increasing blood pressure
- Causes thirst by activating angiotensin II receptors in the subfornical organ

subfornical organ (SFO)—the midline structure on the dorsal surface of the third ventricle, just between the openings from the two lateral ventricles (see Figure 10.23 on page 260). The first clue was that the subfornical organ is one of only a small number of sites in the brain that are not protected from angiotensin II exposure by the *blood-brain barrier.* The second clue was that intraventricular infusions of angiotensin II proved to be particularly effective in inducing drinking.

The following four findings subsequently confirmed the hypothesis that the subfornical organ is the site of the angiotensin II receptors that mediate hypovolemic drinking: (1) Microinjections of angiotensin II into the subfornical organ reliably elicit drinking (e.g., Simpson & Routtenberg, 1973). (2) *Saralasin,* a blocker of angiotensin II receptors—blocks the dipsogenic action of intraventricular injections of angiotensin II (Fitzsimons, Epstein, & Johnson, 1978). (3) Destruction of the subfornical organ abolishes the drinking induced by intravenous injection of angiotensin II (Simpson, Epstein, & Camardo, 1978). (4) Neurons in the subfornical organ display dose-dependent increases in firing in response to microinjections of angiotensin II (Phillips & Felix, 1976).

Evidence suggests that systemic blood is not the only source of angiotensin II, that it is also synthesized in the brain. The finding that lesions of the subfornical organ permanently block the ability of bloodborne angiotensin II

Renin. A hormone that is released from the kidneys in response to increasing ADH levels or decreasing signals from cardiac baroreceptors and that stimulates the synthesis of angiotensin II.

Angiotensin II. A peptide dipsogen hormone that is synthesized in the blood in response to either cellular dehydration or hypovolemia.

Aldosterone. The hormone that is released from the adrenal cortexes in response to angiotensin II and that causes the kidneys to reabsorb much of the sodium that would otherwise be lost in the urine.

Dipsogen. A substance that induces drinking.

Subfornical organ (SFO). The midline structure on the dorsal surface of the third ventricle that is the site of the angiotensin II receptors that mediate the dipsogenic effects of angiotensin II.

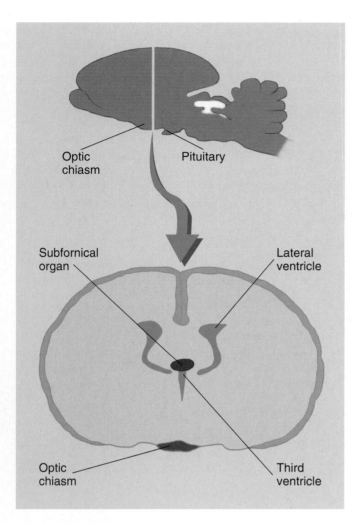

Figure 10.23 The location of the subfornical organ in the rat. It is on the dorsal surface of the third ventricle between the openings to the two lateral ventricles.

Optic chiasm

Pituitary

Subfornical organ

Lateral ventricle

Optic chiasm

Third ventricle

waned since it became apparent that carbachol does not elicit robust drinking responses in laboratory species other than the rat (see Grossman, 1990).

Drinking Produced by Naturally Occurring Water Deficits

As you have just learned in the preceding two subsections, the dipsogenic effects of intracellular and extracellular dehydration are often studied independently of one another. However, because water deprivation simultaneously reduces the water in both the intracellular and extracellular fluid compartments, the key to understanding the drinking that results from naturally occurring water shortages lies in understanding the interaction of the deficits in the two compartments.

Rolls and her colleagues (e.g., Ramsay, Rolls, & Wood, 1977; Rolls, Wood, & Rolls, 1980) have studied the relative effects on drinking of intracellular and extracellular fluid deficits after overnight water deprivation. They injected their water-deprived subjects (rats, dogs, and monkeys) with either water or isotonic saline. The water, because it was hypotonic, was quickly taken up by the dehydrated cells; thus it eliminated the intracellular deficit without substantially influencing the extracellular deficit. Conversely, the saline, because it was isotonic, was not taken up by cells to any significant degree; thus it eliminated the extracellular deficit without substantially influencing the intracellular deficit. The elimination of the intracellular deficit reduced the drinking of the water-deprived subjects by about 75%, and the elimination of the extracellular deficit reduced drinking by about 15% (Rolls & Rolls, 1982).

Where do the systems that detect intracellular and extracellular water deficits converge to produce thirst and drinking? Because large bilateral lesions of the lateral hypothalamus eliminate drinking in response to both cellular dehydration and hypovolemia, "these tissues remain the favored candidates for the zone of convergence of thirst afferents and for their transformation into the urge to drink" (Epstein, 1982, p. 197; see also Grossman, 1990).

to promote drinking suggests that the subfornical organ is the primary mediator of the dipsogenic effect of any angiotensin II in general circulation. However, the fact that lesions of the subfornical organ do not permanently block drinking induced by intraventricular injection of angiotensin II (e.g., Buggy et al., 1975) suggests that brain-produced angiotensin II or its metabolites can activate receptors in the brain that are normally insulated from general circulation by the blood-brain barrier (Epstein, 1987).

The subfornical synapses that mediate drinking in the rat appear to be cholinergic. Injections into the subfornical organ of **carbachol**—an acetylcholine-like drug—elicit drinking in rats (Simpson & Routtenberg, 1974). So do carbachol injections into a variety of other medial diencephalic and limbic structures (e.g., Swanson & Sharpe, 1973). Moreover, systemic or intraventricular injections of *atropine,* a muscarinic acetylcholine antagonist, reduce deprivation-induced drinking in rats (e.g., Block & Fisher, 1970). However, interest in cholinergic thirst circuits has

Carbachol. An acetylcholine agonist that elicits drinking when injected into the subfornical organ of rats.

Spontaneous drinking. Drinking in the absence of fluid deficits; most drinking is spontaneous drinking.

Sham drinking. The experimental protocol in which an animal drinks and swallows a fluid, which immediately exits its body through a tube implanted in its esophagus.

10.8 Spontaneous Drinking: Drinking in the Absence of Water Deficits

Like the study of eating, the study of drinking has until recently focused almost exclusively on deficit-induced consumption. Water deficits are powerful motivators, and understanding how their motivating effects are mediated is important. However, it is also important not to lose sight of the fact that most drinking—like most eating—occurs in the absence of deficits (see Rowland, 1990). Drinking in the absence of fluid deficits is called **spontaneous drinking.**

The fact that drinking regularly occurs in the absence of water deficits suggests that drinking is motivated by the *positive-incentive properties* of potential beverages—that is, that the motivation to drink comes from the anticipated pleasurable effects of the drinking. We tend to prefer drinks that have a pleasurable flavor (e.g., fruit juice, soda, milk) or a pleasurable pharmacologic effect (e.g., beer, coffee, tea)—or, better yet, both. According to the positive-incentive theory of drinking, water deprivation increases the positive-incentive value of virtually all salt-free beverages; after 24 hours of water deprivation, human subjects report that water itself has a pleasant taste (Rolls et al., 1980).

Flavor

The effects of flavor on drinking can be demonstrated by simply adding a bit of saccharin to the water of nondeprived rats. Their water intake skyrockets (Rolls, Wood, & Stevens, 1978). Conversely, there is a substantial decrease in fluid consumption if the palatability of a rat's water supply is reduced by the addition of a small amount of quinine to it. When rats were maintained for 60 days with quinine-adulterated water as their only source of fluid, their fluid intake decreased substantially, but there were no signs of ill health (Nicolaïdis & Rowland, 1975). Like humans, rats with unlimited access to water or other palatable fluids drink far more than they need.

Food

Water is required for the digestion and metabolism of food. Consequently, drinking often occurs in association with eating. Rats, for example, drink about 70% of their total water intake during meals; they drink little when they are food-deprived. Eating-related drinking is greater when the food is dry and when it is protein-rich—proteins draw large amounts of water out of the body into the digestive tract.

The release of insulin, which is associated with food consumption, may be a factor in eating-related drinking. Insulin injections have been shown to increase drinking in both rats (Novin, 1964) and humans (Brime et al., 1991).

Learning

Animals normally drink to prevent water deficits, not just to correct them. They generally drink more water than they need, and they learn to increase their drinking in anticipation of water deficits. Human joggers learn to drink before starting out on a hot day, and rats learn to drink in response to an odor that has been repeatedly paired with a subcutaneous injection of formalin, which induces temporary hypovolemia (Weisinger, 1975).

Fitzsimons and LeMagnen (1969) studied the increased water consumption of rats forced to shift to a high-protein diet. Initially, the increased drinking occurred long after the protein meal was consumed, presumably in response to the hypovolemia it created. But eventually, copious drinking occurred with each meal, rather than after. Apparently, the rats learned to adjust their water intake to prevent the protein-produced dehydration.

10.9 Drinking and Satiety

What terminates a bout of drinking? Set-point theories suggest that it is a return to internal water-resource set points. There are three problems with this idea. The first is that the elimination of water deficits could not possibly be responsible for terminating drinking that is initiated in the absence of water deficits. The second is that even when drinking is triggered by water deprivation, it usually stops before the water has been absorbed into the body from the gastrointestinal tract. The third is that when water or other palatable liquids are readily available, animals drink far more than they need. In one study (Dicker & Nunn, 1957), rats were maintained on a daily water ration that was only about 60% of the amount they consumed when they could drink as much as they wanted to drink; urine excretion was reduced, and the rats remained healthy.

Sham-drinking preparations have been used to study the contribution of oral factors to satiety. In their first post-deprivation bout of **sham drinking,** most animals sham drink an amount that is proportional to the length of the preceding period of water deprivation; longer periods of water deprivation produce more sham drinking (see Blass & Hall, 1976), despite the fact that the water exits the gastrointestinal tract through a fistula before it can be absorbed. This result could reflect the fact that longer periods

Figure 10.24 The saccharin elation effect. Four groups of rats had continuous access to water and a saccharin solution for 8 days. Then, the saccharin solution was withdrawn for 0, 1, 3, or 5 days, but the rats continued to have free access to water. Longer periods of saccharin withdrawal produced greater increases in saccharin drinking once saccharin access was reinstated. (Adapted from Pinel & Rovner, 1977.)

of water deprivation produce greater increases in the positive-incentive value of water.

To what degree do injections of water into the stomach or bloodstream reduce the duration of postdeprivation drinking bouts? In rats, infusions of water directly into the stomach or into the bloodstream reduce deprivation-induced drinking by only 30% of the amount injected (e.g., Rowland & Nicolaïdis, 1976). Remarkably, even total replenishment of an animal's water resources has only a modest inhibitory effect on deprivation-induced drinking. These findings are troublesome for any theory of satiety that is based on the premise that bouts of drinking are terminated by a return to internal fluid set points.

Drinking and Sensory-Specific Satiety

Sensory-specific satiety has a major effect on drinking—as it does on eating. This has been demonstrated in two ways. The first is by showing that animals display less preference for a beverage when it is continuously available than they do for the same beverage when it is only periodically available. For example, Figure 10.24 illustrates a phenomenon known as the **saccharin elation effect**: Rats living with continuous access to water and a saccharin solution consume large amounts of the saccharin solution, but they consume even more of it after the saccharin solution has been withdrawn for several days (e.g., Pinel & Rovner, 1977).

The second way the effect of sensory-specific satiety on drinking has been demonstrated is by showing that animals drink more when they have access to a variety of beverages. For example, Rolls and Wood (cited in Rolls, Wood, & Rolls, 1980) offered nondeprived rats access to water for 1 hour, to water with an artificial flavor added to it for 1 hour, or to water with a different artificial flavor added to it every 15 minutes during the hour. As Figure 10.25 illustrates, the addition of one flavor to the water increased intake by 88%, whereas the availability of four flavors in sequence increased intake by 182%.

Grossly excessive drinking is referred to as *polydipsia*. One method of inducing polydipsia, as you have just seen, is to provide subjects with a variety of palatable beverages. Another is to present a small pellet of food every minute or so to subjects that have continuous access to water (Falk, 1964). In the intervals, the subjects drink huge volumes of water. For example, rats drink about 10 times more than they would if the food were given all at once during the test. This excessive drinking is called **schedule-induced polydipsia.**

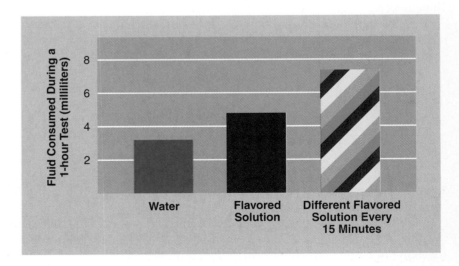

Figure 10.25 The effects of variety on the fluid intake of nondeprived rats during a 1-hour test. The rats in one group had access to water for the 1 hour, the rats in another group had access to flavored water for 1 hour, and the rats in a third group were presented with a different flavor of water every 15 minutes for 1 hour. (Adapted from Rolls, Wood, & Rolls, 1980.)

Chapter 10   The Biology of Eating and Drinking

Before moving on to Part 3 of the chapter, complete the following review exercise. The correct answers are provided at the bottom of this page. Before proceeding, review material related to your incorrect answers and omissions.

1. About two-thirds of the body's water reserves is stored _____ cells.

2. Water is drawn from hypotonic to hypertonic solutions by _____ pressure.

3. Excess water is drawn from the blood by the _____.

4. Cellular dehydration is detected in the lateral preoptic area of the hypothalamus by cells called _____.

5. _____ hormone is a posterior pituitary peptide that decreases urine production.

6. ADH increases the release of _____ from the kidneys.

7. High concentrations of _____ in the blood trigger the formation of angiotensin II.

8. Microinjection of angiotensin II into the _____ elicits drinking.

9. Most drinking in natural situations occurs in the absence of water deficits; such drinking is called _____ drinking.

10. The excessive drinking that is observed when a rat is offered a small pellet of food every minute or so is called schedule-induced _____.

Part 3 Disorders of Consumption

The remainder of the chapter addresses two common disorders of consumption: obesity and anorexia nervosa. So far in this chapter, you have learned to think of consumption in terms of incentive values and settling points, rather than deficits and set points. Will these new ways of thinking provide you with insights into these disorders?

Saccharin elation effect. The increase in saccharin preference that occurs in nondeprived animals following a temporary interruption of access to saccharin solutions.

Schedule-induced polydipsia. Grossly excessive drinking that occurs in animals that receive a small pellet of food every minute or so.

The answers are (1) inside, (2) osmotic, (3) kidneys, (4) osmoreceptors, (5) antidiuretic, (6) renin, (7) renin, (8) subfornical organ, (9) spontaneous, (10) polydipsia.

You have already learned that obesity is currently a major health problem in many parts of the world. What is more distressing is the rate at which the problem is growing; in the United States, for example, its incidence has more than doubled over the last century (see Kuczmarski, 1992). This rapid rate of increase indicates that environmental factors play a significant role in obesity. However, genetic factors also contribute. For example, it was estimated from a sample of U.S. twins that environmental and genetic factors contribute equally to individual differences in body fat in this population (see Price & Gottsman, 1991). Set-point theory is of no help in trying to understand the current epidemic of obesity; according to set-point theory, permanent weight gain should not occur in healthy adults.

Let's begin our analysis of obesity by considering the pressures that have led to the evolution of our eating and weight-regulation systems. During the course of evolution, inconsistent food supplies were one of the main threats to survival. As a result, the fittest individuals were those who preferred high-calorie foods, ate to capacity when food was available, stored as many excess calories as possible in the form of body fat, and used their stores of calories as efficiently as possible. Individuals who did not have these characteristics were unlikely to survive a drought, and so these characteristics were preferentially passed on to future generations.

Augmenting the effects of evolution has been the development of numerous cultural practices and beliefs that promote consumption. For example, in my culture, it is commonly believed that one should eat three meals per day at regular times, whether one is hungry or not; that food should be the focus of most social gatherings; that meals should be served in courses of progressively increasing palatability; and that salt, sweets (e.g., sugar), and fats (e.g., butter) should be added to foods to improve their flavor and thus increase their consumption.

Each of us possesses an eating and weight-regulation system that evolved to deal effectively with periodic food shortages, and many of us live in cultures whose eating-related practices evolved for the same purpose. However, now we live in an environment that differs from our "natural" environment in critical food-related ways. We now live in an environment in which foods of the highest positive-incentive value are readily and continuously available. The consequence is an appallingly high level of consumption.

Why do some people become obese while others living under the same obesity-promoting conditions do not? At a superficial level, the answer is obvious: Those who are obese are those whose energy intake has grossly exceeded their energy output; those who are slim are those whose energy intake has not grossly exceeded their energy output. While this answer provides little insight, it does serve to emphasize that two kinds of individual differences play a role in obesity: those that lead to differences in energy input and those that lead to differences in energy output. Let's consider one example of each kind. First, on the intake side, Rodin (1985) has shown that obese subjects have a larger cephalic-phase insulin response to the sight, sound, and smell of a sizzling steak than do subjects who have never been obese; large cephalic insulin responses are associated with large decreases in blood glucose and high levels of subsequent food consumption. On the output side, people differ markedly from one another in the degree to which they can dissipate excess energy by diet-induced thermogenesis. In a classic study, Rose and Williams (1961) assessed the food intake of subjects of the same sex, weight, age, height, and activity level. They found that it was not uncommon for one member of a pair to be consuming twice as many calories as the other member without gaining more weight than the other.

Figure 10.26 describes the course of the typical dietary weight-loss program. Most weight-loss programs are unsuccessful in the sense that, as predicted by the settling-point model, most of the lost weight is regained once the program is terminated. Clearly, the key to permanent weight loss is a permanent lifestyle change. People who have difficulty controlling their weight may receive some solace by understanding that the tendency to eat large amounts of food, to accumulate body fat, and to use energy efficiently would all be highly adaptive tendencies in a natural environment. It is our current environment that is pathological, not the people with weight problems.

Many people believe that exercise is the most effective method of losing weight; however, several studies have shown that exercise contributes little to weight loss (e.g., Sweeney et al., 1993). One reason is that physical activity normally accounts for only a small proportion of total energy expenditure: About 80% of your energy is used to maintain the resting physiological processes of your body and to digest your food (Calles-Escandon & Horton, 1992). Another reason is that after exercise, many people consume drinks and foods that contain more calories than the relatively small number that were expended during the exercise.

Severe cases of obesity are sometimes treated by wiring the jaw shut to limit consumption to liquid diets, stapling

Anorexia nervosa. An eating disorder that is characterized by a pathological fear of obesity and that results in health-threatening weight loss.

Bulimia nervosa. An eating disorder that is characterized by recurring cycles of fasting, bingeing, and purging without dangerous weight loss.

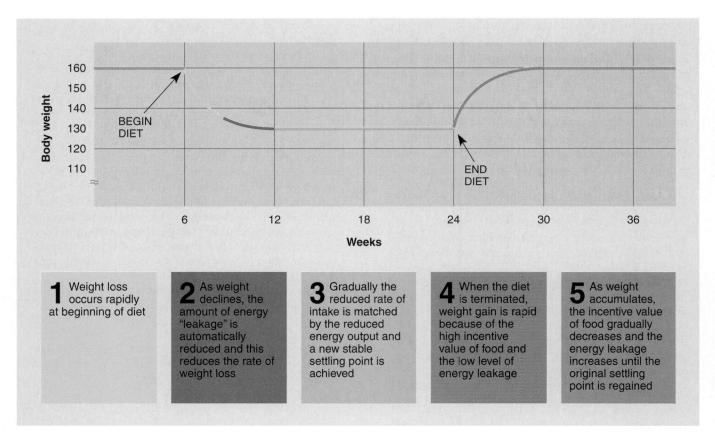

Figure 10.26 The five stages of a typical weight-loss program.

The five stages shown in the figure:

1 Weight loss occurs rapidly at beginning of diet

2 As weight declines, the amount of energy "leakage" is automatically reduced and this reduces the rate of weight loss

3 Gradually the reduced rate of intake is matched by the reduced energy output and a new stable settling point is achieved

4 When the diet is terminated, weight gain is rapid because of the high incentive value of food and the low level of energy leakage

5 As weight accumulates, the incentive value of food gradually decreases and the energy leakage increases until the original settling point is regained

part of the stomach together to reduce the size of meals, or cutting out a section of the duodenum to reduce the absorption of nutrients from the gastrointestinal tract. The main problems with jaw wiring are that some patients do not lose weight on a liquid diet and that those who do typically regain it once the wires are removed. Problems with the other two methods include diarrhea, flatulence, vitamin and mineral deficiencies, and *nimiety*—an unpleasant feeling of excessive fullness (*nimius* means "excessive").

10.11 Anorexia Nervosa

In contrast to obesity, **anorexia nervosa** is a disorder of underconsumption. Anorexics eat so little that they experience health-threatening weight loss; and despite their grotesquely emaciated appearance, they often perceive themselves as fat. About 50% of anorexics periodically engage in binges of eating, which are usually followed by purging with large doses of laxatives or by self-induced vomiting. Individuals who display the cycles of fasting, bingeing, and purging without the extreme weight loss are said to suffer from **bulimia nervosa.**

The incidence of anorexia nervosa among North American student populations is about 2.5%, with the vast majority of sufferers being female. The relatively high incidence of anorexia nervosa in young females suggests that the current societal emphasis on slimness in women may be responsible for many cases; indeed, many cases begin with severe diets. Supporting this theory is the fact that the rates of anorexia nervosa are highest among groups for whom being slim is most strongly advocated; for example, in one study of ballet dancers, the incidence was close to 10% (Szmukler et al, 1985). Unfortunately, there are currently no effective treatments. In one study, only 29% of treated anorexics had shown significant recovery 20 years later. Approximately 15% die from suicide or starvation (Ratnasuriya et al., 1991).

Anorexics are ambivalent about food. On the one hand, they display a higher than normal cephalic-phase insulin response (Broberg & Bernstein, 1989), and they are often preoccupied with the discussion, purchase, and preparation of food. On the other hand, they rarely experience hunger, they are often afraid of gaining weight, they are often disgusted by fatty tastes, and they often feel ill after a meal.

In a society in which obesity is the main disorder of consumption, anorexics are strangely out of step. People who are struggling to eat less have little empathy for those who are refusing to eat. Still, when you stare anorexia in the face, it is difficult not to be touched by it:

> She began by telling me how much she had been enjoying the course and how sorry she was to be dropping out of the university. She was articulate and personable, and her grades were first-class. Her problem was anorexia; she weighed only 82 pounds, and she was about to be hospitalized.
>
> "But don't you want to eat?" I asked naively. "Don't you see that your plan to go to medical school will go up in smoke if you don't eat?"
>
> "Of course I want to eat. I know I am terribly thin—my friends tell me I am. Believe me, I know this is wrecking my life. I try to eat, but I just can't force myself. In a strange way, I am pleased with my thinness."
>
> She was upset, and I was embarrassed by my insensitivity. "It's too bad you're dropping out of the course before we cover the chapter on eating," I said, groping for safer ground.
>
> "Oh, I've read it already," she responded. "It's the first chapter I looked at. It had quite an effect on me; a lot of things started to make more sense. The bit about positive incentives and learning was really good. I think my problem began when food started to lose its positive-incentive value for me—in my mind, I kind of associated food with being fat and all the boyfriend problems I was having. This made it easy to diet, but every once in a while I would get so hungry that I would lose control and eat all of the things that I shouldn't. I would eat so much that I would feel ill. So I would put my finger down my throat and make myself throw up. This made me feel a bit better, and it kept me from gaining weight, but I think it taught my body to associate my favorite foods with illness—kind of a conditioned taste aversion. Now, food has no incentive value for me whatsoever. What do you think of my theory?"
>
> Her insightfulness impressed me; it made me feel all the more sorry that she was going to discontinue her studies.
>
> After a lengthy chat, she got up to leave, and I walked her to the door of my office. I wished her luck and made her promise to come back for a visit. The image of her emaciated body walking down the hallway from my office has stayed with me.

CONCLUSION

Part 1 of this chapter focused on hunger, eating, and body weight regulation. In it, you learned about digestion and energy flow in the body (10.1); about set-point and positive-incentive theories of hunger and eating (10.2); about the factors that influence what, when, and how much we eat (10.3); about the neural mechanisms of hunger and satiety (10.4); and about body weight regulation (10.5). Part 2 of the chapter focused on thirst, drinking, and body fluid regulation. In it, you learned about the regulation of the body's fluid resources (10.6); about the roles of cellular dehydration and hypovolemia in deprivation-induced drinking (10.7); about spontaneous drinking (10.8); and about drinking and satiety (10.9). Lastly, Part 3 of the chapter dealt with two common disorders of consumption: obesity (10.10) and anorexia nervosa (10.11).

This chapter began on an unconventional note, and it ended on another. It began with the puzzle of Freddie the Finn, and it ended with a personal encounter with a student suffering from anorexia nervosa. In between, you learned how modern research on the biopsychology of eating and drinking has revealed the inadequacies of the set-point assumption and has led to the development of ways of thinking about eating and drinking that are more compatible with both experimental findings and personal experience.

FOOD FOR THOUGHT

1. Set-point theories suggest that attempts at permanent weight loss are a waste of time. On the basis of what you have learned in this chapter, design an effective weight-loss program.

2. Most of the dietary problems that people in our society face occur because the conditions in which we live are different from those in which our species evolved. Discuss.

3. There are many parallels between the regulation of eating and drinking. Describe some of them.

4. On the basis of what you have learned in this chapter, develop a feeding program for laboratory rats that would lead to obesity. Compare this program with the eating habits prevalent in those cultures in which obesity is currently a problem.

KEY TERMS

Digestion *(p. 235)*
Lipids *(p. 236)*
Amino acids *(p. 236)*
Glucose *(p. 236)*
Cephalic phase *(p. 237)*
Absorptive phase *(p. 237)*
Fasting phase *(p. 237)*
Insulin *(p. 237)*
Glucagon *(p. 237)*
Gluconeogenesis *(p. 238)*
Free fatty acids *(p. 238)*
Ketones *(p. 238)*
Negative feedback systems
    (p. 239)
Homeostasis *(p. 239)*
Glucostatic theory *(p. 240)*
Lipostatic theory *(p. 240)*
Positive-incentive theory
    (p. 240)

Positive-incentive value
    (p. 240)
Satiety *(p. 242)*
Sham eating *(p. 242)*
Nutritive density *(p. 243)*
Appetizer effect *(p. 243)*
Cafeteria diet *(p. 243)*
Sensory-specific satiety
    (p. 244)
Ventromedial hypothalamus
    (VMH) *(p. 245)*
Lateral hypothalamus (LH)
    (p. 245)
Hyperphagia *(p. 245)*
Dynamic phase *(p. 245)*
Static phase *(p. 245)*
Aphagia *(p. 245)*
Adipsia *(p. 246)*
Lipogenesis *(p. 246)*
Lipolysis *(p. 246)*

Hyperinsulinemia *(p. 246)*
Paraventricular nuclei
    (p. 246)
Duodenum *(p. 248)*
Cholecystokinin (CCK)
    (p. 248)
Diet-induced thermogenesis
    (p. 250)
Settling point *(p. 250)*
Leaky-barrel model *(p. 250)*
Lipectomy *(p. 252)*
Isotonic solutions *(p. 254)*
Hypotonic solutions *(p. 254)*
Hypertonic solutions
    (p. 254)
Osmotic pressure *(p. 254)*
Cellular dehydration *(p. 255)*
Hypovolemia *(p. 255)*
Osmoreceptors *(p. 256)*
Antidiuretic hormone
    (ADH) *(p. 257)*

Baroreceptors *(p. 257)*
Blood-flow receptors
    (p. 257)
Nephrectomized *(p. 257)*
Renin *(p. 258)*
Angiotensin II *(p. 258)*
Aldosterone *(p. 258)*
Dipsogen *(p. 258)*
Subfornical organ (SFO)
    (p. 259)
Carbachol *(p. 260)*
Spontaneous drinking
    (p. 261)
Sham drinking *(p. 261)*
Saccharin elation effect
    (p. 262)
Schedule-induced polydipsia
    (p. 262)
Anorexia nervosa *(p. 265)*
Bulimia nervosa *(p. 265)*

ADDITIONAL READING

The following books and articles provide excellent coverage of current research on eating and drinking:

Brownell, K. D., & Rodin, J. (1994). The dieting maelstrom: Is it possible and advisable to lose weight? *American Psychologist, 49,* 781–791.

Capaldi, E. D., & Powley, T. L. (1990). *Taste, experience, and feeding.* Washington, DC: American Psychological Association.

Grossman, S. P. (1990). *Thirst and sodium appetite: Physiological basis.* New York: Academic Press.

Leibowitz, S. F. (1992). Neurochemical-neuroendocrine systems in the brain controlling macronutrient intake and metabolism. *Trends in Neuroscience, 15,* 491–497.

Martin, J. R., White, B. D., & Hulsey, M. G. (1991). The regulation of body weight. *American Scientist, 79,* 528–541.

Schlundt, D. G., & Johnson, W. G. (1990). *Eating disorders: Assessment and treatment.* Boston: Allyn & Bacon.

Schneider, L. H., Cooper, S. J., & Halmi, K. A. (1989). *The psychology of human eating disorders: Preclinical and clinical perspectives.* New York: New York Academy of Sciences.

Woods, S. C., & Strubbe, J. H. (1994). The psychobiology of meals. *Psychonomic Bulletin & Review, 1,* 141–155.

11

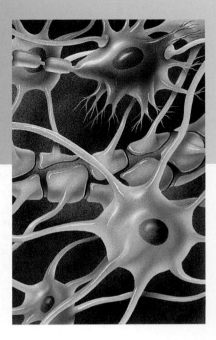

Hormones and Sex

11.1 The Neuroendocrine System

11.2 Hormones and Sexual Development

11.3 Effects of Gonadal Hormones on Adults

11.4 The Hypothalamus and Sexual Behavior

11.5 Sexual Orientation, Hormones, and the Brain

This chapter is about hormones and sex, a topic that fascinates most people. Perhaps it is because we hold our sexuality in such high esteem that we are intrigued by the fact that it is influenced by the secretions of a pair of glands that some regard as unfit topics of conversation. Perhaps it is because we each think of our gender as fundamental and immutable that we are fascinated by the fact that it can be altered with a snip or two and a few hormone injections. Perhaps what fascinates us is the idea that our sex lives might be enhanced by the application of a few hormones. For whatever reason, the topic of hormones and sex is always a hit. Some remarkable things await you in this chapter; let's go directly to them.

Hormones influence sex in two ways: (1) by influencing the development from conception to sexual maturity of the anatomical, physiological, and behavioral characteristics that distinguish one as female or male, and (2) by activating the reproduction-related behavior of sexually mature adults. The *developmental* and *activational* effects of sex hormones are dealt with in the second and third sections of this chapter; the first section prepares you for these topics by introducing the neuroendocrine system. The fourth and fifth sections discuss the role of the hypothalamus in sexual behavior and sexual orientation, respectively.

The Men-Are-Men and Women-Are-Women Attitude

Almost everybody brings to the topic of hormones and sex a piece of excess baggage, the men-are-men and women-are-women attitude—or "mamawawa." This attitude is seductive; it seems so right that we are continually drawn to it without considering alternative views. Unfortunately, it is fundamentally flawed.

The men-are-men and women-are-women attitude is the tendency to think about femaleness and maleness as discrete, mutually exclusive, complementary categories. In thinking about hormones and sex, this general attitude leads one to assume that females have female sex hormones that give them female bodies and make them do female things, and that males have male sex hormones that give them male bodies and make them do male things. Despite the fact that this approach to hormones and sex is totally wrong, its simplicity, symmetry, and comfortable social implications draw us to it. That is why this chapter grapples with it throughout.

11.1   The Neuroendocrine System

This section introduces the general principles of neuroendocrine function by focusing on the glands and hormones that are directly involved in sexual development and behavior. It begins with a few basic facts about hormones, glands, and reproduction; then it describes the line of research that led to our current understanding of neuroendocrine function.

Glands

There are two types of glands: exocrine glands and endocrine glands. **Exocrine glands** (e.g., sweat glands) release their chemicals into ducts, which carry them to their targets, mostly on the surface of the body. **Endocrine glands** (ductless glands) release their chemicals, which are called **hormones,** directly into the circulatory system. Once released by an endocrine gland, a hormone travels via the circulatory system until it reaches the targets on which it normally exerts its effect (e.g., the skin, other endocrine glands, or sites in the nervous system).

The endocrine glands are illustrated in Figure 11.1 on page 272. By convention, only the organs whose primary function is the release of hormones are referred to as endocrine glands. However, other organs (e.g., the stomach, liver, and intestine) also release hormones into general circulation (see Chapter 10), and they are thus, strictly speaking, also part of the endocrine system.

Hormones

Most hormones fall into one of three categories: (1) amino acid derivatives, (2) peptides and proteins, and (3) steroids. **Amino acid derivative hormones** are hormones that are synthesized in a few simple steps from an amino acid molecule; an example is *epinephrine,* which is released from the *adrenal medulla* and synthesized from *tyrosine.* **Peptide hormones** and **protein hormones** are chains of amino acids—peptide hormones being short chains and protein

---

Exocrine glands. Glands that secrete chemicals into ducts which carry them to the surface of the body.

Endocrine glands. Ductless glands that release hormones into the general circulation of the body.

Hormones. Chemicals released by the endocrine system into general circulation.

Amino acid derivative hormones. Hormones that are simple modifications of individual amino acids.

Peptide hormones. Hormones that are short strings of amino acids.

Protein hormones. Hormones that are long strings of amino acids.

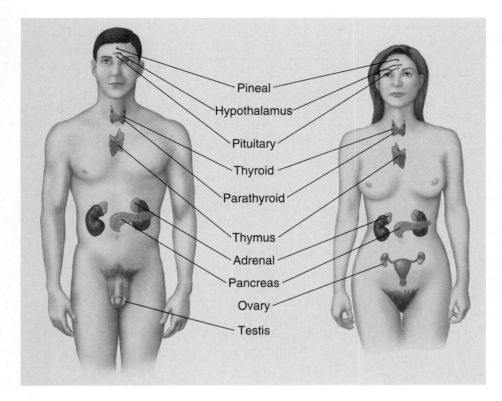

Figure 11.1 The endocrine glands.

Labels (top to bottom): Pineal, Hypothalamus, Pituitary, Thyroid, Parathyroid, Thymus, Adrenal, Pancreas, Ovary, Testis

hormones long chains. **Steroid hormones** are hormones that are synthesized from *cholesterol,* a type of fat molecule.

It is steroid hormones that play the major role in sexual development and behavior, and thus it is steroid hormones that are the focus of this chapter. Most other hormones exert their effects solely by binding to receptors in cell membranes. Steroids too can exert effects in this fashion; but because steroid molecules are small and fat-soluble, they readily penetrate cell membranes. Once inside cells, steroids can bind to receptors in the cytoplasm or nucleus; and by so doing, they can influence gene expression. Consequently, steroid hormones can have particularly diverse and long-lasting effects on cellular function (see Demotes-Mainard, Vernier, & Vincent, 1993; Funder, 1993; Hutchison, 1991).

Gonads

Central to any discussion of hormones and sex are the **gonads**—the male **testes** (pronounced TEST eez) and the female **ovaries** (see Figure 11.1). The primary function of the testes and ovaries is the production of *sperm cells* and *ova,* respectively. After **copulation** (sexual intercourse), a single sperm cell may combine with an *ovum* to form a cell called a **zygote,** which contains all of the information necessary for the growth of a complete adult organism.

With the exception of ova and sperm cells, each cell of the human body has 23 pairs of chromosomes. In contrast, the ova and sperm cells contain only half that number, one member of each of the 23 pairs. Thus, when a sperm cell

fertilizes an ovum, the resulting zygote ends up with the full complement of 23 pairs of chromosomes, one of each pair from the father and one of each pair from the mother.

Of particular interest in the context of this chapter is the pair of chromosomes called the **sex chromosomes,** so named because they contain the genetic programs that direct sexual development. The cells of females have two large **X**-shaped sex chromosomes, called *X chromosomes.* In males, one sex chromosome is an X chromosome, and the other is a small **X**-shaped chromosome called a *Y chromosome.* (There must be a good reason for calling a small **X**-shaped chromosome a Y chromosome, but I don't know what it is.) Consequently, the sex chromosome of every ovum is an X chromosome, whereas half the sperm cells have X chromosomes and half have Y chromosomes. Your gender with all its social, economic, and personal ramifications was determined by which of your father's sperm cells won the dash to your mother's ovum. If a sperm cell with an X sex chromosome won, you are a female; if one with a Y sex chromosome won, you are a male.

Writing this section reminded me of my grade 7 basketball team, "The Nads." The name puzzled our teacher because it was not at all like the names usually favored by pubescent boys—names such as the "Avengers," the "Marauders," and the "Vikings." Her puzzlement ended abruptly at our first game as our fans began to chant their support. You guessed it; "Go Nads, Go! Go Nads, Go!" My 14-year-old spotted-faced teammates and I considered this to be humor of the most mature and sophisticated sort. The teacher didn't.

Sex Steroids

The gonads do more than create sperm and egg cells; they also produce and release hormones. Most people are surprised to learn that the testes and ovaries release the very same hormones. The two main classes of gonadal hormones are **androgens** and **estrogens; testosterone** is the most common androgen, and **estradiol** is the most common estrogen. The fact that ovaries release more estrogens than they do androgens and that testes release more androgens than they do estrogens has led to the common, but misleading, practice of referring to androgens as "the *male* sex hormones" and to estrogens as "the *female* sex hormones." This practice should be avoided because of its men-are-men and women-are-women implication that androgens produce maleness and estrogens produce femaleness. They don't.

The ovaries and testes also release a class of hormones called **progestins.** The most common progestin is **progesterone,** which in females prepares the uterus and the breasts for pregnancy. Its function in males is unclear.

Because the primary function of the **adrenal cortex**—the outer layer of the *adrenal gland* (see Figure 11.1)—is the regulation of glucose and salt levels in the blood, it is not generally thought of as a sex gland. However, in addition to its principal steroid hormones, it does release in small amounts all of the sex steroids that are released by the gonads.

Hormones of the Pituitary

The pituitary gland is frequently referred to as the *master gland* because most of its hormones are tropic hormones. *Tropic hormones* are hormones whose primary function is to influence the release of hormones from other glands (*tropic* is an adjective that describes things that stimulate or change other things). For example, the **gonadotropins** are pituitary tropic hormones that travel through the circulatory system to the gonads, where they stimulate the release of gonadal hormones.

The pituitary gland is really two glands, the posterior pituitary and the anterior pituitary, which fuse during the course of embryological development. The **posterior pituitary** develops from a small outgrowth of hypothalamic tissue that eventually comes to dangle from the *hypothalamus* on the end of the **pituitary stalk** (see Figure 11.2). In contrast, the **anterior pituitary** begins as part of the same embryonic tissue that eventually develops into the roof of the mouth; during the course of development, it pinches off and migrates up to assume its position next to the posterior pituitary. It is the anterior pituitary that releases tropic hormones; thus it is the anterior pituitary in particular, rather than the pituitary in general, that qualifies as the master gland.

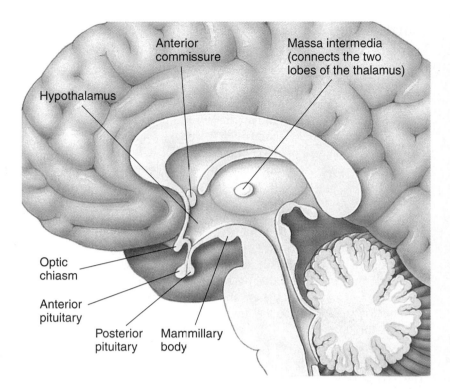

Figure 11.2 A midline view of the posterior and anterior pituitary and surrounding structures.

Steroid hormones. Hormones that are synthesized from cholesterol.

Gonads. The testes and ovaries.

Testes. The male gonads.

Ovaries. The female gonads.

Copulation. Sexual intercourse.

Zygote. The cell formed from the fusion of a sperm cell and an ovum.

Sex chromosomes. The pair of chromosomes (XX or XY) that contain the genetic information that directs sexual development.

Androgens. The class of steroid hormones that includes testosterone.

Estrogens. The class of steroid hormones that includes estradiol.

Testosterone. The most common androgen.

Estradiol. The most common estrogen.

Progestins. The class of gonadal hormones that includes progesterone.

Progesterone. A progestin that prepares the uterus and breasts for pregnancy.

Adrenal cortex. The outer layer of the adrenal gland, which releases gonadal hormones and hormones that regulate the salt and glucose levels of the blood.

Gonadotropins. The anterior pituitary hormones that stimulate the release of hormones from the gonads.

Posterior pituitary. The part of the pituitary gland that contains the terminals of hypothalamic neurons.

Pituitary stalk. The structure connecting the hypothalamus and the pituitary.

Anterior pituitary. The part of the pituitary gland that releases tropic hormones.

Female Gonadal Hormone Levels Are Cyclic, Male Gonadal Hormone Levels Are Steady

The major difference between the endocrine function of women and men is that in women the levels of gonadal and gonadotropic hormones go through a cycle that repeats itself every 28 days or so (see Appendix VII). It is these more-or-less regular hormone fluctuations that control the female **menstrual cycle.** In contrast, human males are, from a neuroendocrine perspective, rather dull creatures; the levels of their gonadal and gonadotropic hormones change little from day to day. An interest in this fundamental difference between females and males was the original stimulus for a particularly fruitful line of experiments.

Because the anterior pituitary is the master gland, many early scientists assumed that an inherent difference between the male and female anterior pituitary was the basis for the difference in their patterns of gonadotropic and gonadal hormone release. However, this hypothesis was discounted by a series of clever transplant studies (Harris & Jacobsohn, 1952). In these studies, a cycling pituitary removed from a mature female rat became a steady-state pituitary when transplanted at a suitable site in a male, and a steady-state pituitary removed from a mature male rat began to cycle once transplanted in a female. What these studies established was that anterior pituitaries are not inherently female (cyclical) or male (steady-state); their patterns of hormone release are controlled by some other part of the body. The master gland seemed to have its own master. Where was it?

Neural Control of the Pituitary

The nervous system was implicated in the control of the anterior pituitary by behavioral research on birds and other animals that breed only during a specific time of the year. It was found that the seasonal variations in the light-dark cycle triggered many of the breeding-related changes in hormone release. If the lighting conditions under which the animals lived were reversed, for example, by having the animals transported across the equator, the breeding seasons were also reversed (Marshall, 1937). Somehow, visual input to the nervous system was controlling the release of tropic hormones from the anterior pituitary.

The search for the particular neural structure that controlled the anterior pituitary turned, naturally enough, to the *hypothalamus,* the structure from which the pituitary is suspended. Hypothalamic stimulation and lesion experiments quickly established that the hypothalamus is the regulator of the anterior pituitary, but how the hypothalamus controls the anterior pituitary remained a mystery. You see, the anterior pituitary, unlike the posterior pituitary, receives no neural input whatsoever from the hypothalamus, or from any other neural structure (see Figure 11.3).

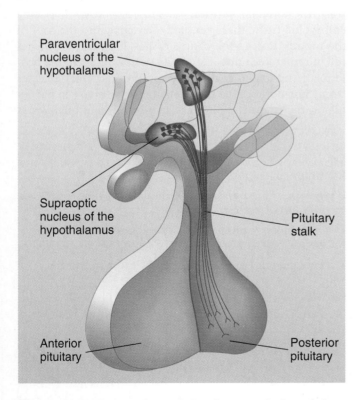

Figure 11.3 The neural connections between the hypothalamus and the pituitary. All neural input to the pituitary goes to the posterior pituitary; the anterior pituitary has no neural connections.

Menstrual cycle. The hormone-regulated cycle in women of follicle growth, egg release, uterus lining build-up, and menstruation.

Vasopressin. One of the two major hormones of the posterior pituitary, which facilitates reabsorption of water by kidneys; also called antidiuretic hormone.

Oxytocin. One of the two major hormones of the posterior pituitary, which in females stimulates contractions of the uterus and the ejection of milk during suckling.

Paraventricular nuclei. One of the two pairs of hypothalamic nuclei in which the hormones of the posterior pituitary are synthesized.

Supraoptic nuclei. One of the two pairs of hypothalamic nuclei in which the hormones of the posterior pituitary are synthesized.

Hypothalamopituitary portal system. The vascular network that carries hormones from the hypothalamus to the anterior pituitary.

Releasing factors. Suspected (hypothesized) hypothalamic releasing hormones that have not yet been isolated.

Inhibitory factors. Hypothalamic hormones thought to regulate anterior pituitary hormones by inhibiting their release.

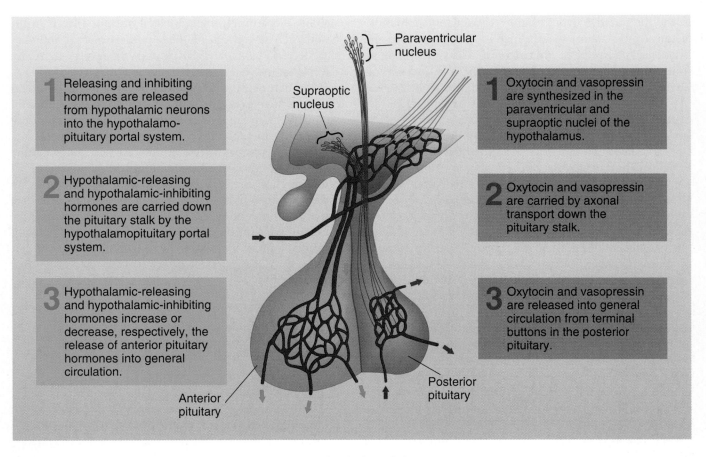

Figure 11.4 Control of the anterior and posterior pituitary by the hypothalamus.

Control of the Anterior and Posterior Pituitary by the Hypothalamus

There are two different mechanisms by which the hypothalamus controls the pituitary: one for the posterior pituitary and one for the anterior pituitary. The two major hormones of the posterior pituitary, **vasopressin** and **oxytocin,** are peptide hormones that are synthesized in the cell bodies of neurons in the **paraventricular nuclei** and **supraoptic nuclei** of the hypothalamus (see Figure 11.3). They are then transported along the axons of these neurons to their terminals in the posterior pituitary and are stored there until the arrival of action potentials causes them to be released into the bloodstream. (Neurons that release hormones into general circulation are called *neurosecretory cells.*) Oxytocin stimulates contractions of the uterus during labor and the ejection of milk during suckling. Vasopressin (also called *antidiuretic hormone*) facilitates the reabsorption of water by the kidneys.

The means by which the hypothalamus controls the release of hormones from the neuron-free anterior pituitary was more difficult to explain. Harris (1955) suggested that the release of hormones from the anterior pituitary was itself regulated by hormones released from the hypothala-

mus. Two findings provided early support for this hypothesis. The first was the discovery of a vascular network, the **hypothalamopituitary portal system,** that seemed well suited to the task of carrying hormones from the hypothalamus to the anterior pituitary. As Figure 11.4 illustrates, a network of hypothalamic capillaries feeds a bundle of portal veins that carries blood down the pituitary stalk into another network of capillaries in the anterior pituitary. (A *portal vein* is a vein that connects one capillary network with another.) The second finding was the discovery that cutting the portal veins of the pituitary stalk disrupts the release of anterior pituitary hormones until the damaged veins regenerate (Harris, 1955).

Discovery of Hypothalamic Releasing Hormones

It was hypothesized that the release of each anterior pituitary hormone is controlled by a different hypothalamic hormone. The putative (hypothesized) hypothalamic hormones that were thought to stimulate the release of anterior pituitary hormones were referred to as **releasing factors.** Those thought to inhibit the release of an anterior pituitary hormone were referred to as **inhibitory factors.** Efforts to isolate the putative hypothalamic releasing and inhibitory factors led to a major breakthrough in 1969. Guilleman and his colleagues isolated **thyrotropin-releasing hormone** from the hypothalamus of sheep, and Schally and his colleagues isolated the same hormone from the hypothalamus of pigs. Thyrotropin-releasing hormone triggers the release of **thyrotropin** from the anterior pituitary, which in turn stimulates the release of hormones from the *thyroid gland.*

It is difficult to appreciate the effort that went into the initial isolation of thyrotropin-releasing hormone. Releasing and inhibiting factors exist in such small amounts that a mountain of hypothalamic tissue is required to extract even minute quantities. For example, Schally (1978) reported that the work of his group required over 1 million pig hypothalami. And where did Schally get such a quantity of pig hypothalami? From Oscar Mayer & Company—where else?

Why would two research teams dedicate over a decade of their lives to accumulate a pitifully small quantity of thyrotropin-releasing hormone? The reason was that it enabled both Guilleman and Schally to determine the chemical composition of thyrotropin-releasing hormone and then to develop methods of synthesizing larger quantities of the hormone for research and clinical use. For their efforts, Guilleman and Schally were awarded Nobel Prizes in 1977.

You may have noticed a change in terminology during the preceding discussion: from *releasing factors* to **releasing hormones.** This shift reflects the usual practice of referring to a hormone as a "factor" or "substance" until it has been isolated and its chemical structure identified.

Schally's and Guilleman's isolation of thyrotropin-releasing hormone confirmed that hypothalamic releasing hormones control the release of hormones from the anterior pituitary and thus provided the major impetus for the isolation and synthesis of several other releasing hormones. Of direct relevance to study of sex hormones was the isolation of **gonadotropin-releasing hormone** by Schally and his group in 1970. This releasing hormone stimulates the release of both of the anterior pituitary's gonadotropins: **follicle-stimulating hormone** (**FSH**) and **luteinizing hormone** (**LH**) (Schally, Kastin, & Arimura, 1971). All releasing hormones, like all tropic hormones, have proven to be peptides.

Feedback in the Neuroendocrine System

The hypothalamus controls the anterior pituitary, and the anterior pituitary in turn controls other endocrine glands; but neuroendocrine regulation is not a one-way street. Circulating hormones often feed back on the very structures that triggered their release: the pituitary, the hypothalamus, and other sites in the brain (see McEwen et al., 1979).

Most of the feedback in the neuroendocrine system is **negative feedback,** whose function is the maintenance of

stability. Accordingly, high gonadal hormone levels in the blood often have effects on the hypothalamus and pituitary that decrease gonadal activity, and low levels often have effects that increase gonadal activity.

Although negative feedback is the rule in the neuroendocrine system, **positive feedback** can also occur; occasionally, increases in the level of a circulating hormone produce further increases, and decreases produce further decreases. For example, just before **ovulation**—the release of a mature ovum from the package of cells, or **follicle,** in which it develops—injection of a small dose of estradiol produces an increase, rather than the usual decrease, in the release of estradiol from the ovary. It does this by stimulating the release of gonadotropin-releasing hormone from the hypothalamus and by increasing the sensitivity of the anterior pituitary to the gonadotropin-releasing hormone that

Thyrotropin-releasing hormone. The hypothalamic hormone that stimulates the release of thyrotropin from the anterior pituitary.

Thyrotropin. The anterior pituitary hormone that stimulates the release of hormones from the thyroid gland.

Releasing hormones. Hypothalamic hormones that stimulate the release of hormones from the anterior pituitary.

Gonadotropin-releasing hormone. The hypothalamic releasing hormone that controls the release of the two gonadotropic hormones from the anterior pituitary.

Follicle-stimulating hormone (FSH). The gonadotropic hormone that stimulates development of ovarian follicles.

Luteinizing hormone (LH). The gonadotropic hormone that causes the developing ovum to be released from its follicle.

Negative feedback. A signal from a change in one direction that results in a compensatory effect in the other direction.

Positive feedback. A signal from a change in one direction that facilitates a further change in the same direction.

Ovulation. The release of the ovum from the follicle in which it develops, which signals the beginning of the fertile period of the menstrual cycle.

Follicle. The package of cells within which each ovum begins its development in the ovary.

Pulsatile hormone release. The typical pattern of hormone release, which occurs in large pulses or surges several times a day.

H-Y antigen. The protein hormone that stimulates the cells of the medullary portion of the primordial gonads to proliferate and develop into testes.

reaches it. It has been suggested that a shift from the usual negative feedback mode to a positive feedback mode may be the key factor in producing the surge in the levels of progesterone and estradiol in the blood of females that is responsible for triggering ovulation (see Appendix VII for details of the hormone fluctuations that occur during the *menstrual cycles* of human females). A similar mechanism has been proposed to account for the surge of gonadal hormones that occurs in both males and females during puberty.

Pulsatile Hormone Release

Hormones tend to be released in pulses (Karsch, 1987); they are discharged several times per day in large surges, which typically last no more than a few minutes. Hormone levels in the blood are regulated by changes in the frequency and duration of the hormone pulses (Reame et al., 1984). One consequence of **pulsatile hormone release** is that there are often large minute-to-minute fluctuations in the levels of circulating hormones (e.g., Koolhaas, Schuurman, & Wiepkema, 1980). Accordingly, when the pattern of human male gonadal hormone release is referred to as steady, it means that there are no major systematic changes in circulating gonadal hormone levels from day to day, not that the levels never vary.

A Summary Model of Gonadal Endocrine Regulation

Figure 11.5 on page 276 is a summary model of the regulation of gonadal hormones. According to this model, the brain controls the release of gonadotropin-releasing hormone from the hypothalamus into the hypothalamopituitary portal system, which carries it to the anterior pituitary. In the anterior pituitary, the gonadotropin-releasing hormone stimulates the release of gonadotropins, which are carried by the circulatory system to the gonads. In response to the gonadotropins, the gonads release androgens, estrogens, and progestins, which feed back onto the pituitary and hypothalamus to regulate subsequent gonadal hormone release.

Armed with this general perspective of neuroendocrine function, you are ready to consider how gonadal hormones direct sexual development (Section 11.2) and activate adult sexual behavior (Section 11.3), and how the hypothalamus influences sexual behavior (Section 11.4) and sexual orientation (Section 11.5).

11.2   Hormones and Sexual Development

You have undoubtedly noticed that humans are *dimorphic*— that they come in two standard models: female and male. This section describes how the development of female and male characteristics is directed by hormones. It concludes with three cases of exceptional sexual development. I am sure you will be intrigued by these three cases, but that is not the only reason why I have chosen to include them. My main reason is expressed by a proverb: The exception proves the rule. Most people think this proverb means that the exception "proves" the rule in the sense that it establishes its truth, but this is nonsense: The truth of a rule is challenged by, not confirmed by, exceptions to it. The word *proof* comes from the Latin *probare,* which means "to test"—as in *proving ground* or printers *proof*—and this is the sense in which it is used in the proverb (Gould, 1980). Hence, the proverb means that the explanation of exceptional cases is a major challenge for any theory. Accordingly, the primary purpose of the three cases of exceptional sexual development that are described at the end of this section is to test the theories presented in it.

Sexual differentiation in mammals begins at fertilization with the production of one of two different kinds of zygotes: either one with an XX (female) pair of sex chromosomes or one with an XY (male) pair. It is the genetic information on these sex chromosomes that normally determines whether development will occur along female or male lines. But be cautious here: Do not fall into the seductive embrace of the men-are-men and women-are-women assumption. Do not begin by assuming that there are two parallel genetic programs for sexual development: one for female development and one for male development. As you are about to learn, sexual development unfolds according to an entirely different principle, one that many males—particularly those who still stubbornly adhere to notions of male preeminence— find unsettling. This principle is that we are all genetically programmed to develop female bodies; genetic males develop male bodies only because their fundamentally female program of development is overruled.

Fetal Hormones and the Development of Reproductive Organs

Gonads   Figure 11.6 on page 277 illustrates the structure of the gonads as they appear 6 weeks after fertilization. Notice that at this stage of development, each fetus, regardless of its genetic sex, has the same pair of structures, called *primordial gonads* (*primordial* means "existing at the beginning"). Each primordial gonad has an outer covering, or *cortex,* which has the potential to develop into an ovary; and each has an internal core, or *medulla,* which has the potential to develop into a testis.

Six weeks after conception, the Y chromosome of the male triggers the synthesis of **H-Y antigen** (see Haqq et al.,

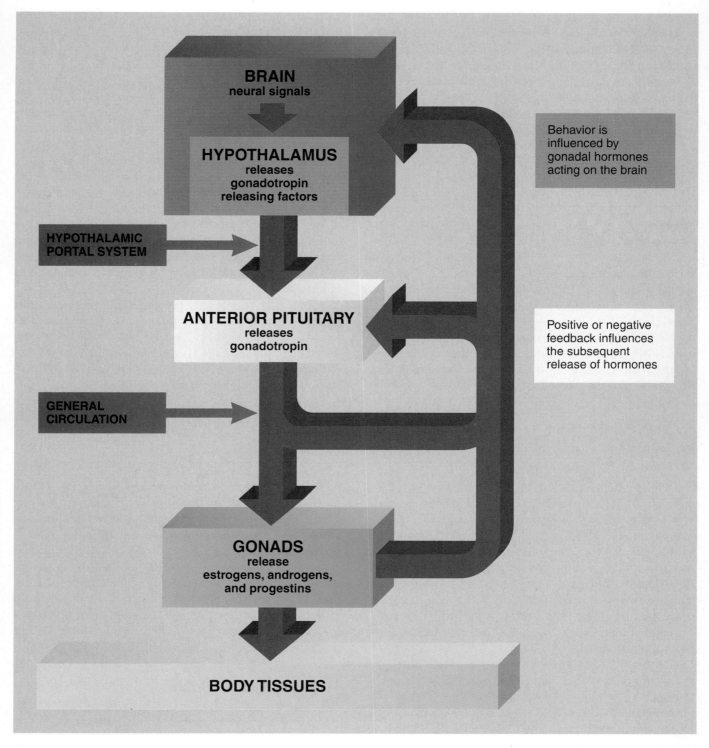

Figure 11.5 The regulation of gonadal hormones: A summary model.

1994), and this protein hormone causes the medulla of each primordial gonad to grow and to develop into a testis. There is no female counterpart of H-Y antigen; in the absence of H-Y antigen, the cortical cells of the primordial gonads automatically develop into ovaries. Accordingly, if H-Y antigen is injected into a genetic female fetus 6 weeks after conception, the result is a genetic female with testes; or if drugs that block the effects of H-Y antigen are injected into a male

fetus, the result is a genetic male with ovaries. Such "mixed-gender" individuals expose in a dramatic fashion the weakness of "mamawawa" thinking (see Crews, 1988).

Internal reproductive ducts Six weeks after fertilization, both males and females have two complete sets of reproductive ducts. They have a male **Wolffian system,** which has the capacity to develop into the male reproduc-

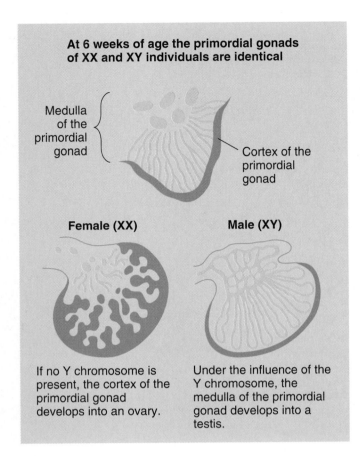

At 6 weeks of age the primordial gonads of XX and XY individuals are identical

Medulla of the primordial gonad

Cortex of the primordial gonad

Female (XX)

Male (XY)

If no Y chromosome is present, the cortex of the primordial gonad develops into an ovary.

Under the influence of the Y chromosome, the medulla of the primordial gonad develops into a testis.

Figure 11.6 The development of an ovary and a testis from the cortex and medulla, respectively, of the primordial gonadal structure that is present 6 weeks after conception.

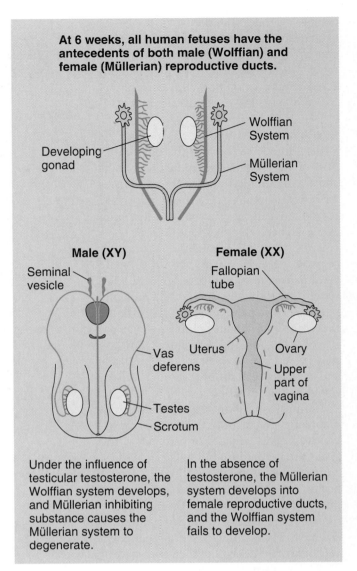

At 6 weeks, all human fetuses have the antecedents of both male (Wolffian) and female (Müllerian) reproductive ducts.

Developing gonad

Wolffian System

Müllerian System

Male (XY)

Seminal vesicle

Vas deferens

Testes

Scrotum

Female (XX)

Fallopian tube

Uterus

Ovary

Upper part of vagina

Under the influence of testicular testosterone, the Wolffian system develops, and Müllerian inhibiting substance causes the Müllerian system to degenerate.

In the absence of testosterone, the Müllerian system develops into female reproductive ducts, and the Wolffian system fails to develop.

Figure 11.7 The development of the internal ducts of the male and female reproductive systems from the Wolffian and Müllerian systems, respectively.

tive ducts (e.g., the *seminal vesicles,* which hold the fluid in which sperm cells are ejaculated; and the *vas deferens,* through which the sperm cells travel to the seminal vesicles). And they have a female **Müllerian system,** which has the capacity to develop into the female ducts (e.g., the *uterus,* the upper part of the *vagina;* and the *fallopian tubes,* through which ova travel from the ovaries to the uterus, where they can be fertilized).

In the third month of male fetal development, the testes secrete testosterone and **Müllerian-inhibiting substance.** As Figure 11.7 illustrates, the testosterone stimulates the development of the Wolffian system, and the Müllerian-inhibiting substance causes the Müllerian system to degenerate and the testes to descend into the **scrotum**—the sac that holds the testes outside the body cavity (Wilson, George, & Griffin, 1981). Because it is testosterone—not the sex chromosomes—that triggers Wolffian development, genetic females who are injected with testosterone during the appropriate fetal period develop male reproductive ducts along with their female ones (Jost, 1972).

The differentiation of the internal ducts of the female reproductive system (see Figure 11.7) is not under the control of ovarian hormones; the ovaries are almost completely inactive during fetal development. The development of

the Müllerian system occurs in any fetus that is not exposed to testosterone during the critical fetal period. Accordingly, normal female fetuses, ovariectomized female fetuses, and orchidectomized male fetuses all develop

Wolffian system. The embryonic precursors of the male reproductive ducts.

Müllerian system. The embryonic precursors of the female reproductive ducts.

Müllerian-inhibiting substance. The testicular hormone that causes the precursors of the female reproductive ducts to degenerate.

Scrotum. The sac that holds the male testes.

female reproductive ducts (Jost, 1972). **Ovariectomy** is the removal of the ovaries, and **orchidectomy** is the removal of the testes (*orchis* means "testicle"). **Gonadectomy,** or *castration*, is the surgical removal of gonads—either ovaries or testes.

External reproductive organs There is a basic difference between the differentiation of the external reproductive organs and the differentiation of the internal reproductive organs (i.e., the gonads and reproductive ducts). As you have just read, every normal fetus develops separate precursors for the male (medulla) and female (cortex) gonads and for the male (Wolffian system) and female (Müllerian system) reproductive ducts; then, only one set, male or female, develops. In contrast, the male and female **genitals**—external reproductive organs—develop from the same precursor. This *bipotential precursor* and its subsequent differentiation are illustrated in Figure 11.8.

In the second month of pregnancy, the bipotential precursor of the external reproductive organs consists of four parts: the glans, the urethral folds, the lateral bodies, and the labioscrotal swellings. Then it begins to differentiate. The *glans* grows into the head of the *penis* in the male or the *clitoris* in the female, the *urethral folds* fuse in the male or enlarge to become the *labia minora* in the female, the *lateral bodies* form the shaft of the penis in the male or the hood of the clitoris in the female, and the *labioscrotal swellings* form the *scrotum* in the male or the *labia majora* in the female.

Like the development of the internal reproductive ducts, the development of the external genitals is controlled by the presence or absence of testosterone. If testosterone is present at the appropriate stage of fetal development, male external genitals develop from the bipotential precursor; if testosterone is not present, the development of the external genitals proceeds along female lines.

Development of Sex Differences in the Brain

The brains of men and women are alike, but they are not identical. The brains of men tend to be, on the average, about 15% larger. Also, in recent years, a number of more subtle anatomical differences have been documented: slight differences in the anatomy of the hypothalamus, corpus callosum, anterior commissure, and thalamus (see Breedlove, 1992). Positron emission tomography (PET)

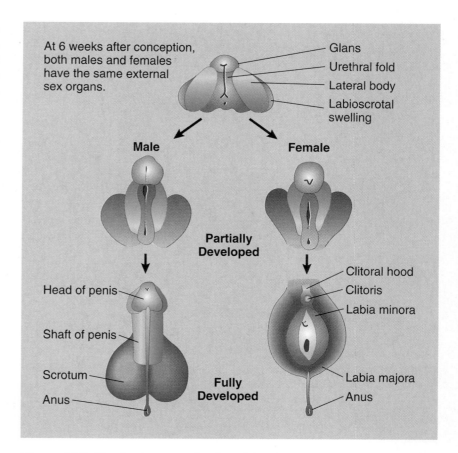

Figure 11.8 The development of male and female external reproductive organs from the same bipotential precursor.

has revealed sex differences in brain function as well; for example, Gur et al. (1995) reported that men tend to have a higher level of baseline metabolic activity in several areas of the temporal lobe and limbic system, whereas women tend to have higher baseline activity in the cingulate gyrus. Presumably, some of these differences are related to differences in sexual behavior, whereas others are related to differences in cognitive and emotional function; but at the present time, the functional significance of cerebral sex differences remains a matter of conjecture.

How do sex differences in the brain develop? Most of our current understanding of the sexual differentiation of the human brain has come from experiments on rats. Rats are useful subjects for the study of brain development because they are born just 22 days after conception. At 22 days after conception, the period during which hormones can influence their genital development is largely over, but the period during which hormones can influence their brain development is just beginning. Accordingly, it is easy to study the effects of hormones on brain development, unconfounded by their effects on genital development.

Perinatal androgens and brain differentiation Most of the early experiments on the development of sex differences in the brain focused on the factors that control the

Chapter 11 Hormones and Sex

development of the steady and cyclic patterns of gonadotropin release in females and males, respectively. The seminal experiments were conducted by Pfeiffer in 1936. In his experiments, some neonatal rats (males and females) were gonadectomized and some were not, and some received gonad transplants (ovaries or testes) and some did not.

Remarkably, Pfeiffer found that gonadectomizing neonatal rats of either genetic sex caused them to develop into adults with the female cyclic pattern of gonadotropin release. In contrast, transplantation of testes into gonadectomized or intact female neonatal rats caused them to develop into adults with the steady male pattern of gonadotropin release. Transplantation of ovaries had no effect on the pattern of hormone release. Pfeiffer concluded that the female cyclic pattern of gonadotropin release develops unless the preprogrammed female cyclicity is overridden by testosterone during perinatal development (see Harris & Levine, 1965).

Pfeiffer incorrectly concluded that the presence or absence of testicular hormones in neonatal rats influenced the development of the pituitary because he was not aware of what we know today: that the release of gonadotropins from the anterior pituitary is controlled by the hypothalamus. Once this was discovered, it became apparent that Pfeiffer's experiments had provided the first evidence of the role of perinatal (around the time of birth) androgens in the sexual differentiation of the hypothalamus. Several other differences between male and female brains have been shown to be under similar hormonal control: The presence of perinatal testosterone leads to the development of male brain characteristics; its absence leads to the development of female brain characteristics, regardless of genetic sex (see Gorski, 1985).

Aromatization and brain differentiation

All gonadal and adrenal sex hormones are steroid hormones, which are all derived from *cholesterol*. Because all steroid hormones have similar structures, they are readily converted from one to the other. For example, the addition of a simple benzene ring to a testosterone molecule changes it to estradiol; this process is called **aromatization.**

There is good evidence that aromatization is a critical step in the masculinization of the brain by testosterone in some species. According to this theory, perinatal testosterone does not directly masculinize the brain; the brain is masculinized by estradiol that has been aromatized from perinatal testosterone. Although the idea that estradiol— the alleged female hormone—masculinizes the brain is counterintuitive, there is strong evidence for it in several species. In the rat, for example, (1) the enzyme that is necessary for aromatization of testosterone is present in neonates (Selmanoff et al., 1977); (2) neonatal injections of estradiol masculinize the brain (Gorski, 1971); (3) **dihydrotestosterone**—an androgen that cannot be converted to estrogen—has no masculinizing effect on the brain

(Whalen & Rezek, 1974); and (4) agents that block the aromatization of testosterone (McEwen et al., 1977) or block estrogen receptors (Booth, 1977) interfere with the masculinizing effects of testosterone on the brain.

How do genetic females keep from being masculinized by the mother's estradiol, which circulates through the fetal blood supply (Ojeda, Kalra, & McCann, 1975)? In the rat, alpha fetoprotein is the answer. **Alpha fetoprotein** is present in the blood of rats during the perinatal period (Plapinger, McEwen, & Clemens, 1973), and it deactivates circulating estradiol by binding to it. How, then, does estradiol masculinize the brain of the male fetus in the presence of the deactivating effects of alpha fetoprotein? Because testosterone is immune to alpha fetoprotein, it can travel unaffected from the testes to the brain, where it enters cells and is converted there to estradiol. The estradiol is not broken down in the brain because alpha fetoprotein does not readily penetrate the blood-brain barrier.

In humans, female fetuses are protected from the masculinizing effects of the mother's estrogens by a *placental barrier*. Unfortunately, this barrier is not as effective against synthetic estrogens (e.g., *diethylstilbestrol*). As a result, the female offspring of mothers who have been exposed to synthetic estrogens while pregnant may display a variety of male characteristics (see McEwen, 1983).

Perinatal Hormones and Behavioral Development

In view of the fact that perinatal hormones influence the development of the brain, it should come as no surprise that they also influence the development of behavior. Most of the research on hormones and behavioral development has focused on the role of perinatal hormones in the development of sexually dimorphic copulatory behaviors in laboratory animals (Feder, 1981, 1984).

Phoenix and colleagues (1959) were among the first to demonstrate that the perinatal injection of testosterone

Ovariectomy. The removal of the ovaries.

Orchidectomy. The removal of the testes.

Gonadectomy. The surgical removal of the gonads (testes or ovaries); castration.

Genitals. The external reproductive organs.

Aromatization. The chemical process by which testosterone is converted to estradiol.

Dihydrotestosterone. An androgen that cannot be aromatized to estrogen.

Alpha fetoprotein. The protein present in the blood of perinatal rats that deactivates circulating estradiol by binding to it.

masculinizes and **defeminizes** a genetic female's adult copulatory behavior. First, they injected pregnant guinea pigs with testosterone. Then, when the litters were born, they ovariectomized the female offspring. Finally, when these ovariectomized female guinea pigs reached maturity, they injected them with testosterone and assessed their copulatory behavior. Phoenix and his colleagues found that the females that had been exposed to perinatal testosterone displayed much more malelike mounting behavior in response to testosterone injections in adulthood than did adult females that had not been exposed to perinatal testosterone. And when as adults they were injected with progesterone and estradiol and mounted by males, they displayed less **lordosis**—the intromission-facilitating arched-back posture of female rodent receptivity.

In a study complementary to that of Phoenix et al., Grady, Phoenix, and Young (1965) found that the lack of early exposure of male rats to testosterone both **feminizes** and **demasculinizes** their copulatory behavior as adults. Male rats castrated shortly after birth failed to display the normal male copulatory pattern of mounting, **intromission** (penis insertion), and **ejaculation** (ejection of sperm) when they were treated with testosterone and given access to a sexually receptive female; and when they were injected with estrogen and progesterone as adults, they exhibited more lordosis than did uncastrated controls. The aromati-

zation of perinatal testosterone to estradiol seems to be important for both the defeminization and the masculinization of rodent copulatory behavior (Goy & McEwen, 1980; Shapiro, Levine, & Adler, 1980).

Most of the research on hormones and behavioral development has focused on the copulatory act itself. As a result, we know relatively little about the role of hormones in the development of **proceptive behaviors** (solicitation behaviors) and in the development of gender-related behaviors that are not directly related to reproduction. However, testosterone has been reported to disrupt the proceptive hopping, darting, and ear wiggling of receptive female rats (Fadem & Barfield, 1981); to increase the aggressiveness of female mice (Edwards, 1969); to disrupt the maternal behavior of female rats (Ichikawa & Fujii, 1982); and to increase rough social play in female monkeys (Goy, 1970) and rats (Meaney & Stewart, 1981).

In thinking about hormones and behavior, it is important to remember that feminizing and demasculinizing effects do not always go together; nor do defeminizing and masculinizing effects. Hormone treatments can enhance or disrupt female behavior without affecting male behavior, and vice versa.

Puberty: Hormones and the Development of Secondary Sex Characteristics

During childhood, levels of circulating gonadal hormones are low, reproductive organs are immature, and males and females differ little in general appearance. This period of developmental quiescence ends abruptly with the onset of *puberty*—the transitional period between childhood and adulthood during which fertility is achieved, the adolescent growth spurt occurs, and the secondary sex characteristics develop. **Secondary sex characteristics** are those features other than the reproductive organs that distinguish sexually mature men and women. The body changes that occur during puberty are illustrated in Figure 11.9; you are undoubtedly familiar with at least half of them.

Puberty is associated with an increase in the release of hormones by the anterior pituitary. The increase in the release of **growth hormone**—the only anterior pituitary hormone that does not have an endocrine gland as its primary target—acts directly on bone and muscle tissue to produce the pubertal growth spurt. Increases in gonadotropic hormone and **adrenocorticotropic hormone** release cause the gonads and adrenal cortex to increase their release of gonadal and adrenal hormones, which in turn initiate the maturation of the genitals and the development of secondary sex characteristics.

The general principle guiding normal pubertal sexual maturation is a simple one: In pubertal males, androgen levels are higher than estrogen levels, and masculinization is the result; in pubertal females, estrogen predominates, and the result is feminization. Individuals castrated prior

---

Masculinizes. Enhances or produces male characteristics.

Defeminizes. Suppresses or disrupts female characteristics.

Lordosis. The intromission-facilitating, arched-back, tail-to-the-side posture of female rodent receptivity.

Feminizes. Enhances or produces female characteristics.

Demasculinizes. Suppresses or disrupts male characteristics.

Intromission. Insertion of the penis into the vagina.

Ejaculation. Ejection of sperm.

Proceptive behaviors. Behaviors that serve to attract the sexual advances of the other sex.

Secondary sex characteristics. Structural features, other than the reproductive organs, that distinguish men from women.

Growth hormone. The anterior pituitary hormone that acts directly on bone and muscle tissue to produce the pubertal growth spurt.

Adrenocorticotropic hormone. The anterior pituitary hormone that causes the adrenal cortex to release its hormones.

Androstenedione. The adrenal androgen that triggers the growth of pubic and axillary hair in human females.

Chapter 11 Hormones and Sex

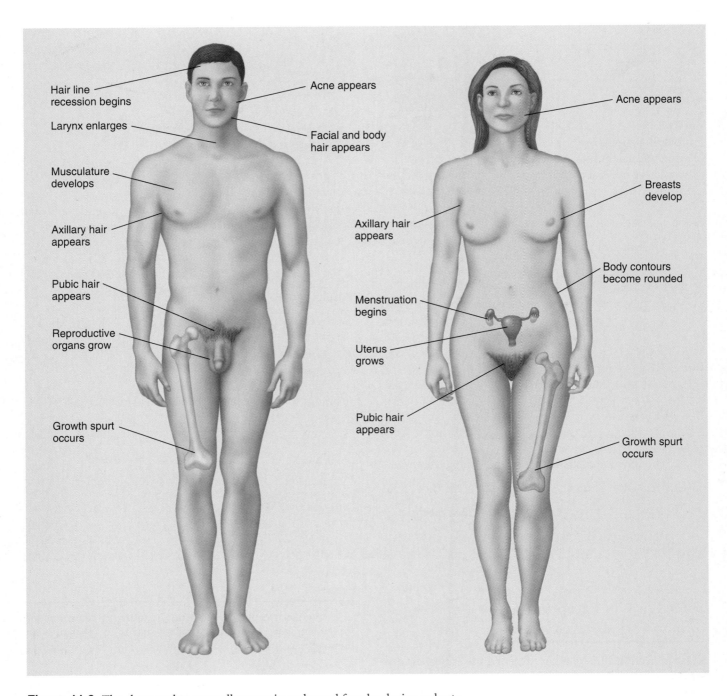

Figure 11.9 The changes that normally occur in males and females during puberty.

Labels (male figure):
- Hair line recession begins
- Larynx enlarges
- Musculature develops
- Axillary hair appears
- Pubic hair appears
- Reproductive organs grow
- Growth spurt occurs
- Acne appears
- Facial and body hair appears

Labels (female figure):
- Acne appears
- Breasts develop
- Axillary hair appears
- Body contours become rounded
- Menstruation begins
- Uterus grows
- Pubic hair appears
- Growth spurt occurs

to puberty do not become sexually mature unless they receive replacement injections of androgen or estrogen.

But even during puberty, its only major stage of relevance, the men-are-men and women-are-women assumption stumbles badly. You see, **androstenedione,** an androgen that is released primarily by the adrenal cortex, is normally responsible for the growth of pubic hair and *axillary hair* (underarm hair) in females. It is hard to take seriously the practice of referring to androgens as "male hormones" when one of them is responsible for the development of the female pattern of pubic hair growth. The male pattern is a pyramid and the female pattern is an inverted pyramid (see Figure 11.9).

Do you remember how old you were when you started to go through puberty? In most North American and European countries, puberty begins at about 11 years of age for girls and 12 for boys. I am sure that you would have been unhappy if you had not started puberty until you were 15 or 16, but this was the norm in North America and Europe just a century and a half ago. Presumably, this 4-year acceleration of puberty has resulted from an improvement in dietary, medical, and socioeconomic conditions.

Before proceeding to a consideration of three cases of exceptional human sexual development, review the basics of normal development by completing the following exercise.

1. Six weeks after conception, the Y chromosome of the human male triggers the production of

   _____.

2. In the absence of H-Y antigen, the cortical cells of the primordial gonads develop into

   _____.

3. In the third month of male fetal development, the testes secrete testosterone and

   _____ substance.

4. The hormonal factor that triggers the development of the human Müllerian system is the lack of

   _____ around the

   third month of fetal development.

5. The scrotum and the

   _____ develop from

   the same bipotential precursor.

6. The female pattern of cyclic

   _____ release from

   the anterior pituitary develops in adulthood unless androgens are present in the body during the perinatal period.

7. It has been hypothesized that perinatal testosterone must first be changed to estrogen before it can masculinize the male rat brain. This is called the _____ hypothesis.

8. _____ is normally responsible for pubic and axillary hair growth in human females during puberty.

Three Cases of Exceptional Human Sexual Development

So far in Section 11.2, you have learned the "rules" according to which hormones influence sexual development. Now, three exceptions are offered to "prove" (to test) these rules.

Androgenic insensitivity syndrome. The developmental disorder of genetic males in which an insensitivity to androgens causes them to develop female bodies.

Adrenogenital syndrome. A disorder characterized by a decrease in the release of the hormone cortisol from the adrenal cortex, which results in the production of high levels of adrenal androgens and masculinizes the bodies of genetic females.

The answers are (1) H-Y antigen, (2) ovaries, (3) Müllerian-inhibiting, (4) androgens (or testosterone), (5) labia majora, (6) gonadotropin, (7) aromatization, and (8) androstenedione.

CASE 1

Androgenic Insensitivity Syndrome: The Case of Anne S.

Anne S., an attractive 26-year-old female, sought treatment for two sex-related disorders: lack of menstruation and pain during sexual intercourse (Jones & Park, 1971). She sought help because she and her husband of 4 years had been trying without success to have children, and she correctly surmised that her lack of a menstrual cycle was part of the problem. A physical examination revealed that Anne was a healthy young woman. Her only readily apparent peculiarity was the sparseness and fineness of her pubic and axillary hair. Examination of her external genitals revealed no abnormalities; however, there were some problems with her internal genitals. Her vagina was only 4 centimeters long, and her uterus was underdeveloped.

At the start of this chapter, I said that you would encounter some amazing things, and the diagnosis of Anne's case certainly qualifies as one of them. Anne's doctors concluded that she was a man. No, this is not a misprint; they concluded that Anne, the attractive young housewife, was in fact Anne, the happily married man. Three lines of evidence supported this diagnosis. First, analysis of cells scraped from the inside of Anne's mouth revealed that they were of the male XY type. Second, a tiny incision in Anne's abdomen, which enabled Anne's physicians to look inside, revealed a pair of internalized testes but no ovaries. Finally, hormone tests revealed that Anne's hormone levels were those of a male.

Anne suffers from **androgenic insensitivity syndrome**; all of her symptoms stem from the fact that her body lacks the ability to respond to androgens. During development, Anne's testes released normal amounts of androgens for a male, but her body could not respond to them, and her development thus proceeded as if no androgens had been released. Her external genitals, her brain, and her behavior developed along preprogrammed female lines, without the effects of androgens to override the female program, and her testes could not descend from her body cavity with no scrotum for them to descend into. Furthermore, Anne did not develop normal internal female reproductive ducts because, like other genetic males, her testes released Müllerian-inhibiting substance; that is why her vagina was short and her uterus undeveloped. At puberty, Anne's testes released enough estrogens to feminize her body in the absence of the counteracting effects of androgens; however, adrenal androstenedione was not able to stimulate the growth of pubic and axillary hair.

Money and Ehrhardt (1972) studied the psychosexual development of 10 androgen-insensitive patients and concluded that the placidity of their childhood play, their goals, their fantasies, their sexual behavior, and their maternal tendencies—several had adopted children—all "conformed to the idealized stereotype of what constitutes femininity in our culture" (p. 112). Apparently, without the masculinizing effects of androgens, infants who look like females and are raised as females come to think and act like females—even when they are genetic males.

An interesting issue of medical ethics is raised by the androgenic insensitivity syndrome. Many people believe that physicians should always disclose all relevant findings to their patients. If you were Anne's physician, would you tell her that she is a man? Would you tell her husband? Anne's vagina was surgically enlarged, she was counseled to consider adoption, and, as far as I know, she is still happily married and unaware of her genetic sex.

CASE 2

Adrenogenital Syndrome

The **adrenogenital syndrome** is characterized by a deficit in the release of the hormone *cortisol* from the adrenal cortex, which results in adrenal hyperactivity and the excessive release of adrenal androgens. This has little effect on the development of males, other than accelerating the onset of puberty, but it has major effects on the development of genetic females. Females who suffer from the adrenogenital syndrome are usually born with an enlarged clitoris and partially fused labia, as Figure 11.10 illustrates. Their internal ducts are usually normal because the adrenal androgens are released too late to stimulate the development of the Wolffian system.

If the adrenogenital syndrome is diagnosed in a female at birth, the abnormalities of the external genitals are surgically corrected, and cortisol is administered to reduce the levels of circulating adrenal androgens. Following early treatment, adrenogenital females grow up to be physically normal except that the onset of menstruation is likely to be later than normal. Thus they provide an excellent opportunity to study the effects of fetal androgen exposure on psychosexual development.

Adrenogenital teenage girls who have been treated with cortisol typically display a high degree of tomboy-

Figure 11.10 Genetic female babies with the andrenogenital syndrome displaying varying degrees of clitoral enlargement and labial fusion. The baby on your right has been surgically treated. Source: Courtesy John Money, Ph.D. First published in *Johns Hopkins Medical Journal, 122* (1968), 160–167.

ishness and little interest in maternity (e.g., Ehrhardt, Epstein, & Money, 1968). They prefer boys' clothes, play mainly with boys, show little interest in handling babies, and tend to daydream about future careers rather than motherhood. It is important not to lose sight of the fact that many teenage girls in our culture display similar characteristics—and why not? Accordingly, the behavior of treated adrenogenital females, although perhaps tending toward the masculine, is well within the range considered normal by the current standards of our culture.

The most interesting questions about the development of females with adrenogenital syndrome concern their romantic and sexual preferences. They seem to lag behind normal females in dating and marriage—perhaps because of the delayed onset of their menstrual cycle—but in other respects their sexual interests appear normal. Most are heterosexual, although there is a tendency toward bisexuality (Ehrhardt & Meyer-Bahlburg, 1981; Money, Schwartz, & Lewis, 1984).

Prior to the development of cortisol therapy in 1950, genetic females with adrenogenital syndrome were left untreated. Some were raised as boys and some as girls, but the direction of their pubertal development was unpredictable. In some cases, adrenal androgens predominated and masculinized their bodies; in others, ovarian estrogens predominated and feminized their bodies. Thus some who were raised as girls were transformed at puberty into men, and some who were raised as boys were transformed into women. Money and Ehrhardt (1972, pp. 158–160) described two cases in which the sex of an untreated androgenital child was ostensibly changed at puberty—with devastating emotional consequences.

One androgenital child was referred to Money and Ehrhardt (1972) for treatment at the age of 12:

> At birth, her external genitals were somewhat ambiguous, but she was raised as a female without incident until puberty. At puberty, her sudden masculinization was the subject of great distress, both for her and her parents. Treatment involved surgical enlargement of her vagina, removal of her large clitoris, and the initiation of [hormone] therapy, which suppressed androgen release and allowed her ovarian estrogens to feminize her body. She became an attractive young woman. Narrow hips and mildly short stature remained unchanged, as the *epiphyses* [the ends of bones, where bone growth takes place] of the bones had already fused under the influence of precocious masculinization. These two signs alone remained as reminders of the past, except for a small amount of coarse facial hair, requiring removal by electrolysis. The voice was husky, but so used as to be not mistaken as masculine.... The capacity for orgasm was not lost. The proof came fifteen years later, upon establishment of a sexual relationship and marriage. (p. 157)

Sex Reassignment of a Twin with Ablatio Penis

One of the most famous cases in the literature on sexual development is that of a male identical twin whose penis was accidentally destroyed during circumcision at the age of 7 months. Because there was no satisfactory way of surgically replacing the lost penis, a widely respected expert in such matters, John Money, recommended that the boy be castrated, that an artificial vagina be created, that the boy be raised as a girl, and that estrogen be administered at puberty to feminize the body. After a great deal of consideration and anguish, the parents followed Money's advice.

Money's (1975) report of this case of **ablatio penis** has been influential. It has been seen by some as the ultimate test of the *nature-nurture controversy* (see Chapter 2) with respect to the development of sexual identity and behavior. It seemed to pit the masculinizing effects of male genes and male hormones against the effects of being reared as a female. And the availability of a genetically identical control subject, the twin brother, made the case all the more interesting.

According to Money, the outcome of this case comes down strongly on the side of the *social-learning theory* of sexual identity. Money reported in 1975, when the patient was 12, that "she" had developed as a normal female, thus confirming his prediction that being raised as a girl would override the masculinizing effects of male genes and early androgens. Because it is such an interesting case, Money's description of it has been featured in many textbooks and in many television, magazine, and newspaper stories, each time carrying with it the message that the sexual identity and sexual behavior of men and women is largely a matter of upbringing.

In 1980, a British news team that was preparing a report on the case discovered that several psychiatrists had examined the child in 1976, when she was 13, and had reached a conclusion that conflicted with Money's. Their conclusion was that she was having significant psychological problems, including considerable ambivalence toward the female role. She refused to draw pictures of females, she aspired to occupations that are commonly regarded as masculine (e.g., auto mechanic), and her masculine gait was the object of scorn from classmates, who referred to her as "cave woman." Clearly, things were not as cut-and-dried as Money's 1975 report had made them out to be.

> It is scientifically regrettable that so much of a theoretical and philosophical superstructure has been built on the supposed results of a single, uncontrolled and unconfirmed case. It is further regrettable that we here in the United States had to depend for a clinical follow-up by a British investigative journalist team for a case originally and so prominently reported in the

American literature. The issues raised by this case are too important to be settled by the media. For scientific and medical reasons, a full updated scientific report on both twins is called for and hopefully will be forthcoming from the team presently associated with this case.... It is further hoped that this particular case will be resolved to the best interest of the particular twin and family involved. The twin should be allowed to truly express any desired sexual identity with familial, social, and medical support. (Diamond, 1982, pp. 184–185)

Do current theories of hormones and sexual development pass the test of these three exceptional cases? I think so. Current theories increase our understanding of each of the three cases, and they provide an effective basis for prescribing treatment. Moreover, because each of the three people is male in some respects and female in others, each case is a serious challenge to the men-are-men and women-are-women assumption.

11.3   Effects of Gonadal Hormones on Adults

Once an individual reaches sexual maturity, gonadal hormones begin to play a role in activating reproductive behavior. These activational effects are the focus of this section, which has three parts. The first deals with the role of hormones in activating the reproduction-related behavior of men. The second deals with the role of hormones in activating the reproduction-related behavior of women. And the third deals with the epidemic of anabolic steroid use by athletes and body builders.

Male Reproduction-Related Behavior and Testosterone

The important role played by gonadal hormones in the activation of male sexual behavior is clearly demonstrated by the asexualizing effects of orchidectomy. Bremer (1959) reviewed the cases of 157 orchidectomized Norwegians. Many had committed sex-related offenses and had agreed to castration to reduce the length of their prison terms.

Two important generalizations can be drawn from Bremer's study. The first is that orchidectomy leads to a reduction in sexual interest and behavior; the second is that the rate and degree of the loss is variable. According to Bremer, about half the men became completely asexual within a few weeks of the operation; others quickly lost their ability to achieve an erection but continued to experience some sexual interest and pleasure; and a few continued to copulate successfully, although somewhat less enthusiastically, for the duration of the study. There were also body changes: a reduction of hair on the trunk, extremities, and face; the deposition of fat on the hips and chest; a softening of the skin; and a reduction in strength. Of the 102 sex offenders in the study, only 3 were reconvicted of sex offenses. Accordingly, Bremer recommended castration as an effective treatment of last resort for male sex offenders.

Why do some men remain sexually active for months after orchidectomy, despite the fact that testicular hormones are cleared from their bodies within days? It has been suggested that adrenal androgens may play some role in the maintenance of sexual activity in some castrated

men, but there is no direct evidence for this hypothesis (Davidson, Kwan, & Greenleaf, 1982). Alternatively, it has been suggested that *endorphins* may play a role in maintaining the sexual interest of castrated men; Miller and Baum (1987) showed that *naloxone*, an opiate antagonist, further reduced the sexual motivation and behavior of castrated male rats.

Orchidectomy, in one fell swoop—or, to put it more precisely, in two fell swoops—removes a pair of glands that release many hormones. Because testosterone is the major testicular hormone, the major symptoms of orchidectomy have been generally attributed to the loss of testosterone, rather than to the loss of some other testicular hormone or to some nonhormonal consequence of the surgery. The therapeutic effects of **replacement injections** of testosterone have confirmed this assumption.

The very first case report of the effects of testosterone replacement therapy was that of a 38-year-old World War I veteran, who was castrated in 1918 at the age of 19 by a shell fragment that removed his testes but left his penis undamaged:

His body was soft; it was as if he had almost no muscles at all; his hips had grown wider and his shoulders seemed narrower than when he was a soldier. He had very little drive....

Just the same this veteran had married, in 1924, and you'd wonder why, because the doctors had told him he would surely be **impotent** [unable to achieve an erection].... he made some attempts at sexual intercourse "for his wife's satisfaction" but he confessed that he had been unable to satisfy her at all....

Dr. Foss began injecting it [testosterone] into the feeble muscles of the castrated man in good stiff doses [I assume this pun was intended]....

Ablatio penis. Accidental destruction of the penis.

Replacement injections. Injections of a hormone whose natural release has been curtailed by the removal of the gland that normally releases it.

Impotent. Unable to achieve a penile erection.

After the fifth injection, erections were rapid and prolonged.... But that wasn't all. During twelve weeks of treatment he had gained eighteen pounds, and all his clothes had become too small. Originally, he wore fourteen-and-a-half inch collars. Now fifteen-and-a-half were too tight.... testosterone had resurrected a broken man to a manhood he had lost forever. (de Kruif, 1945, pp. 97–100)

Since this first clinical trial, testosterone has breathed sexuality into the lives of many men. Testosterone does not, however, eliminate the *sterility* (inability to reproduce) of males who lack functional testes.

The fact that testosterone is necessary for male sexual behavior has led to two assumptions: (1) that the level of a man's sexuality is a function of the amount of testosterone he has in his blood, and (2) that a man's sex drive can be increased by increasing his testosterone levels. Both assumptions are incorrect.

Sex drive and testosterone levels are uncorrelated in healthy men, and testosterone injections do not increase their sex drive. It seems that each healthy male has far more testosterone than is required to activate the neural circuits that produce his sexual behavior and that having more than the minimum is of no advantage in this respect (Sherwin, 1988). An experiment by Grunt and Young (1952) clearly illustrates this point. First, Grunt and Young rated the sexual behavior of each of the male guinea pigs in their experiment. Then, on the basis of the ratings, the researchers divided the male guinea pigs into three experimental groups: low, medium, and high sex drive. Following castration, the sexual behavior of all of the guinea pigs fell to negligible levels within a few weeks (see Figure 11.11), but it recovered after the initiation of a series of testosterone replacement injections. The important point is that although each subject received the same, very large replacement injections of testosterone, the injections simply returned each to its previous level of copulatory activity. The conclusion is clear: With respect to the effects of testosterone on sexual behavior, more is not necessarily better.

Dihydrotestosterone, a nonaromatizable androgen, has failed to reactivate the copulatory behavior of castrated male rats in several studies (see MacLusky & Naftolin, 1981). This suggests that in male rats the activational effects of testosterone on sexual behavior may be produced by estradiol that has been aromatized from the testoster-

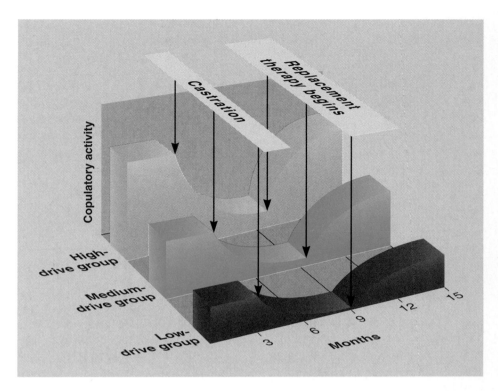

Figure 11.11 The sexual behavior of male guinea pigs with low, medium, and high sex drive. Sexual behavior was disrupted by castration and returned to its original level by very large replacement injections of testosterone. (Adapted from Grunt & Young, 1952.)

one. However, dihydrotestosterone has proved effective in activating sexual behavior in orchidectomized primates (e.g., Davidson, Kwan, & Greenleaf, 1982).

Female Reproduction-Related Behavior and Gonadal Hormones

Sexually mature female rats and guinea pigs display 4-day cycles of gonadal hormone release. There is a gradual increase in the secretion of estrogen by the developing follicle in the 2 days prior to ovulation, followed by a sudden surge in progesterone as the egg is released. These surges of estrogen and progesterone initiate **estrus**—a period of 12 to 18 hours during which the female is *fertile, receptive* (likely to assume the lordosis posture when mounted), *proceptive*

Estrus. The portion of the estrous cycle characterized by fertility and sexual receptivity (*estrus* is a noun and *estrous* an adjective).

Estrous cycle. The cycle of sexual receptivity and nonreceptivity displayed by many female mammals.

Anabolic steroids. Steroid drugs that are similar to testosterone and have powerful anabolic (growth-promoting) effects.

(likely to engage in behaviors that serve to attract the male), and *sexually attractive* (smelling of chemicals that attract males). The close relation between the cycle of hormone release and the **estrous cycle**—the cycle of sexual receptivity—in female rats and guinea pigs and in many other mammalian species suggests that female sexual behavior in these species is under hormonal control. The effects of ovariectomy confirm this conclusion; ovariectomy produces a rapid decline of both proceptive and receptive behaviors. Furthermore, estrus can be induced in ovariectomized rats and guinea pigs by an injection of estrogen followed a day and a half later by an injection of progesterone.

Women are not at all like female rats and guinea pigs when it comes to the hormonal control of their sexual behavior. The sexual motivation and sexual behavior of women are not inextricably linked with their menstrual cycles (see Sanders & Bancroft, 1982), and ovariectomy has surprisingly little effect (e.g., Martin, Roberts, & Clayton, 1980). Ovariectomy does decrease the vaginal lubrication of women, which can interfere with intercourse if a commercial lubricant is not used, but there is typically little or no associated decline in sexual motivation (Dennerstein & Burrows, 1982). Estrogen replacement therapy replenishes the vaginal lubrication.

There is evidence that the sex drive of women is under the control of androgens, not estrogens (see Sherwin, 1988). According to this theory, enough androgen is released from the human adrenal glands to maintain the sexual motivation of women after their ovaries have been removed. Support for this androgen theory of human female sexuality has come from three sources.

1. Experiments in nonhuman female primates. Replacement injections of testosterone, but not estradiol, increased the proceptivity of ovariectomized and adrenalectomized rhesus monkeys (see Everitt & Herbert, 1972; Everitt, Herbert, & Hamer, 1971).

2. Correlational studies in healthy women. Various measures of sexual motivation were correlated with testosterone levels but not with estradiol levels (see Bancroft et al., 1983; Morris et al., 1987).

3. Clinical studies of women following *hysterectomy* (surgical removal of the internal reproductive organs). Replacement injections of testosterone, but not of estradiol, increased their sexual motivation (see Sherwin, 1985; Sherwin, Gelfand, & Brender, 1985).

Anabolic Steroid Abuse

Anabolic steroids are steroids, such as testosterone, that have *anabolic* (growth-promoting) effects. Testosterone itself is not very useful as an anabolic drug because it is broken down soon after injection and because it has undesirable side effects. Chemists have managed to synthesize a number of potent anabolic steroids that are long-acting,

but they have not managed to synthesize one that does not have side effects.

We are currently in the midst of an epidemic of anabolic steroid abuse. Many competitive athletes and body builders are self-administering appallingly large doses to increase their muscularity and strength, but the problem is much more extensive than this. In recent years, the cosmetic use of steroids by young males has reached epidemic proportions.

Do anabolic steroids really increase the muscularity and strength of the athletes who use them? Initially, the athletes said yes and the scientists said no. The athletes were right. The early scientific studies, although well designed, involved doses of steroids much smaller than those that were being used by most athletes—in part because of the concern of the experimenters for the welfare of their subjects. On the basis of these early studies, it was concluded that anabolic steroids do not improve athletic performance. However, more recent studies, in which larger doses of anabolic steroids have been administered for longer periods of time, have proved their efficacy (see Haupt & Rovere, 1984). In fact, many athletes believe that it is impossible to compete successfully at the highest levels of their sports without an anabolic steroid boost. It is difficult to ignore the successes of steroid users such as the gentleman pictured in Figure 11.12.

It is the sex-related side effects of anabolic steroids that are of primary relevance here. However, it has proved extremely difficult to document these effects because the use

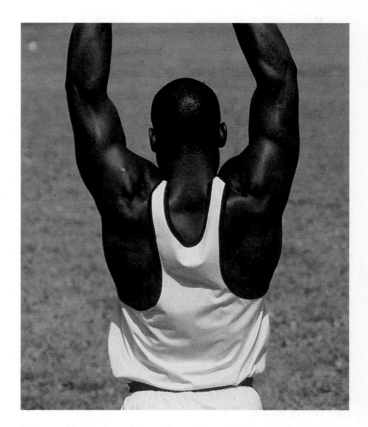

Figure 11.12 An athlete who used anabolic steroids to augment his training program.

of anabolic steroids without prescription is illegal in many parts of the world.

Nevertheless, there is general agreement (Goldman, 1984; Haupt & Revere, 1984; Wilson & Griffin, 1980) that people who take high doses of anabolic steroids risk the following sex-related side effects. In men, the negative feedback from high levels of anabolic steroids reduces gonadotropin release; this leads to a reduction in testicular activity, which can result in *testicular atrophy* (wasting away of the testes) and sterility. *Gynecomastia* (breast growth in men) can also occur, presumably as the result of the aromatization of anabolic steroids to estrogens. In women, anabolic steroids can produce *amenorrhea* (cessation of menstruation), sterility, *hirsutism* (excessive growth of body hair), growth of the clitoris, development of a masculine body shape, baldness, and deepening and coarsening of the voice:

> The most popular story of the 1976 Montreal Olympics involved the success of East German women swimmers. When asked why so many of their women had deep voices,

an East German coach replied, "We have come here to swim, not sing." (*New York Times,* quoted in Goldman, 1984, p. 19)

Both men and women who use anabolic steroids can suffer muscle spasms, muscle pains, blood in the urine, acne, general swelling from the retention of water, bleeding of the tongue, nausea, vomiting, and a variety of psychotic behaviors, including fits of depression and anger (Pope & Katz, 1987). Oral anabolic steroids produce cancerous liver tumors.

The side effects of anabolic steroid abuse make two important points about hormones and sex. The first is that testosteronelike substances do not produce increases in the sexual motivation and behavior of people with testosterone levels in the normal range. The second is that the effects of hormones on the structure of the human body are not restricted to critical prenatal and pubertal periods. Although there are periods in one's life when hormones (or other agents or experiences) have a particularly great effect on development, they can also influence development outside these periods when administered in high doses.

11.4 The Hypothalamus and Sexual Behavior

Many parts of the brain are involved in mammalian sexual behavior. However, the discovery that gonadotropin release is controlled by the hypothalamus focused the study of the neural bases of sexual behavior on this structure.

Structural Differences between the Male Hypothalamus and the Female Hypothalamus

You have already learned that the male hypothalamus and the female hypothalamus are functionally different in their control of anterior pituitary hormones (steady versus cyclic release, respectively). In the 1970s, structural differences between the male and female hypothalamus were discovered in rats (Raisman & Field, 1971). Most notably, Gorski and his colleagues (1978) discovered a nucleus in the **medial preoptic area** of the rat hypothalamus that was several times larger in males (see Figure 11.13). They called this nucleus the **sexually dimorphic nucleus.**

At birth, the sexually dimorphic nuclei of male and female rats are the same size. In the first few days after birth, the male sexually dimorphic nuclei grow at a high rate and the female sexually dimorphic nuclei do not. The growth of the male sexually dimorphic nuclei is triggered by estradiol, which has been aromatized from testosterone (see McEwen, 1987). Accordingly, castrating day-old (but not 4-day-old) male rats significantly reduces the size of their sexually dimorphic nuclei as adults, whereas injecting

neonatal (newborn) female rats with testosterone significantly increases the size of theirs (Gorski, 1980)—see Figure 11.14 on page 290. The size of a male rat's sexually dimorphic nuclei is correlated with the rat's level of sexual activity (Anderson et al., 1986). Although the overall size of the sexually dimorphic nuclei diminishes only slightly in male rats that are castrated in adulthood, specific areas of the nucleus do display significant degeneration (Bloch & Gorski, 1988).

Since the discovery of the sexually dimorphic nuclei in rats, sex differences in hypothalamic anatomy have been identified in other species (see Witelson, 1991). In humans, for example, there are nuclei in the preoptic (Swaab & Fliers, 1985) and anterior (Allen et al., 1989) regions of the hypothalamus that are substantially larger in men than women. The gender difference in human preoptic anatomy is not apparent in children who are less than 2 years old (Hofman & Swaab, 1989).

The Hypothalamus and Male Sexual Behavior

The medial preoptic area of the hypothalamus plays a key role in male sexual behavior. Destruction of the entire area abolishes sexual behavior in the males of many species, and selective destruction of the sexually dimorphic nuclei has been shown to reduce the sexual behavior of male rats (De

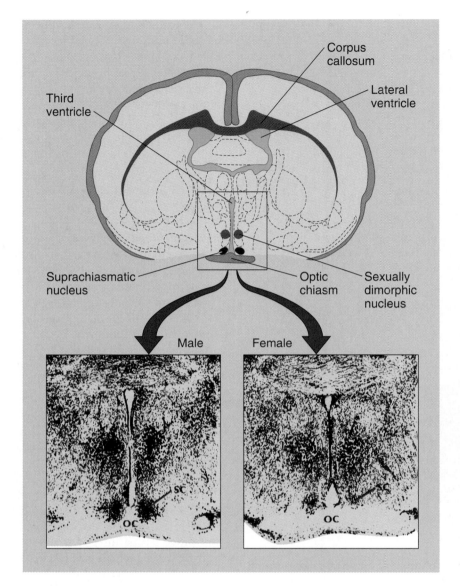

Figure 11.13 Nissl-stained coronal sections through the preoptic area of male and female rats. The sexually dimorphic nuclei (indicated by the arrows) are larger in male rats than in female rats. (Adapted from Gorski et al., 1978.)

Jonge et al., 1989; Turkenburg et al., 1988). In contrast, medial preoptic area lesions have no effect on female sexual behavior, but they do eliminate the mounting behavior that is occasionally observed in female rats (Singer, 1968). Thus bilateral medial preoptic lesions appear to abolish

Medial preoptic area. The area of the hypothalamus that includes the sexually dimorphic nuclei and that plays a key role in the control of male sexual behavior.

Sexually dimorphic nucleus. The nucleus in the medial preoptic area of rats that is larger in males than in females.

male copulatory behavior in both sexes. On the other side of the coin, electrical stimulation of the medial preoptic area elicits copulatory behavior in male rats (Malsbury, 1971), and copulatory behavior can be reinstated in castrated male rats by medial preoptic implants of testosterone (Davidson, 1980).

It is not clear why males with medial preoptic lesions stop copulating. These males vigorously approach and investigate receptive females, and they make clumsy attempts to mount them (e.g., Malsbury & Pfaff, 1974; Powers, Newman, & Bergondy, 1987). They seem to want to copulate, but for some unknown reason they can't.

Everitt and Stacey (1987) studied the effects of medial preoptic lesions on male rats that had been trained to press a lever for access to receptive females, which dropped into

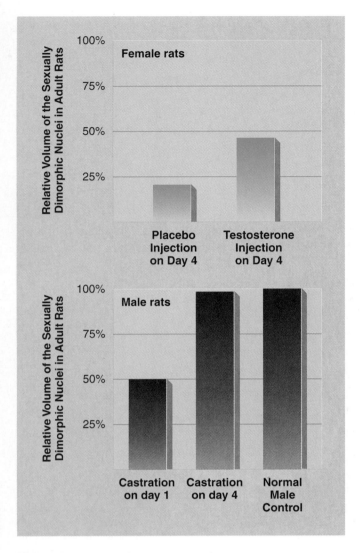

Figure 11.14 The effects of neonatal testosterone exposure on the size of the sexually dimorphic nuclei in male and female adult rats. (Adapted from Gorski, 1980.)

their test chambers through a trap door in the ceiling. Following medial-preoptic-area lesions, the male rats continued to press the lever at a high rate to receive the females, but they never managed to copulate with them. In contrast, orchidectomized males stopped pressing the lever. Apparently, orchidectomy abolishes the sexual motivation of male rats, but medial preoptic lesions do not.

Ventromedial nucleus. A hypothalamic nucleus that is involved in female sexual behavior.

Heterosexual. Sexually attracted to members of the other sex.

Homosexual. Sexually attracted to members of the same sex.

Bisexual. Sexually attracted to members of both sexes.

The medial preoptic area appears to control male sexual behavior via a tract that projects to an area of the midbrain called the *lateral tegmental field*. Destruction of this tract disrupts the sexual behavior of male rats (Brackett & Edwards, 1984). Moreover, the activity of individual neurons in the lateral tegmental field of male rats is often correlated with aspects of the copulatory act (Shimura & Shimokochi, 1990); for example, some neurons in the lateral tegmental field fire at a high rate only during intromission.

The Hypothalamus and Female Sexual Behavior

The **ventromedial nucleus** (VMN) of the hypothalamus contains circuits that are critical for female sexual behavior. Electrical stimulation of the VMN facilitates the sexual behavior of female rats, and VMN lesions reduce it (see Pfaff & Modianos, 1985). Indeed, female rats with bilateral lesions of the VMN do not display lordosis, and they are likely to attack suitors who become too ardent.

You have already learned that an injection of progesterone brings into estrus an ovariectomized female rat that received an injection of estradiol 48 hours before. Because the progesterone by itself does not induce estrus, the estradiol must in some way prime the nervous system so that the progesterone can exert its effect. This priming effect appears to be mediated by the large increase in the number of *progesterone receptors* that occurs in the VMN and surrounding area following an estradiol injection (Blaustein et al., 1988); the estradiol exerts this effect by entering VMN cells and influencing gene expression. Confirming the role of the VMN in estrus is the fact that microinjections of estradiol and progesterone directly into the VMN induce estrus in ovariectomized female rats (Pleim & Barfield, 1988).

There is evidence that the VMN mechanism that plays a role in the sexual behavior of female rats is noradrenergic. In one key experiment, levels of norepinephrine in the VMN were recorded by *cerebral dialysis* (see Chapter 5) in ovariectomized female rats (Vathy & Etgen, 1989). The mere presence of a male rat induced a massive release of norepinephrine in the VMH of ovariectomized female rats that had been brought into estrus by injections of estradiol and progesterone.

The influence of the VMN on the sexual behavior of female rats appears to be mediated by a tract that descends to the *periaqueductal gray (PAG)* of the tegmentum. Destruction of this tract eliminates female sexual behavior (Hennessey et al., 1990), as do lesions of the PAG itself (Sakuma & Pfaff, 1979).

In summary, research on rodents suggests that tracts that run from the hypothalamus to the mesencephalon play important roles in sexual behavior. Male sexual behavior is influenced by a tract that runs from the medial preoptic area to the lateral tegmental field, and female sexual behavior is influenced by a tract that runs from the ventromedial nucleus to the periaqueductal gray (see Figure 11.15).

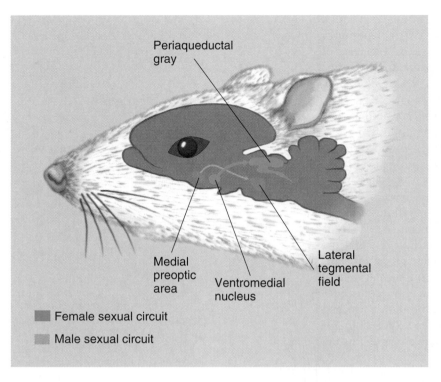

Figure 11.15 The hypothalamus-tegmentum circuits that play a role in female and male sexual behavior.

Periaqueductal gray

Medial preoptic area

Ventromedial nucleus

Lateral tegmental field

■ Female sexual circuit
■ Male sexual circuit

11.5   Sexual Orientation, Hormones, and the Brain

So far, this chapter has avoided the issue of sexual orientation. As you know, some people are **heterosexual** (sexually attracted to members of the other sex), some are **homosexual** (sexually attracted to members of the same sex), and some are **bisexual** (sexually attracted to members of both sexes). A discussion of recent research on sexual orientation is a fitting conclusion to this chapter because it brings together its hormone, hypothalamus, exception-proves-the-rule, and anti-mamawawa themes.

Sexual Orientation, Genes, and Hormones

Research has shown that differences in sexual orientation have a genetic basis. For example, Bailey and Pillard (1991) studied a group of male homosexuals who had twin brothers, and they found that 52% of the monozygotic twin brothers and 22% of the dizygotic twin brothers were homosexual. Moreover, a gene that seems to play a role in the development of sexual orientation has been located near one end of the X chromosome (Hamer et al., 1993). To keep these findings in perspective, it is important to remember that if differences in sexual orientation were determined solely by genes, the concordance rate for homosexuality would be 100% between monozygotic twins. It is also important to recognize that almost all of the research on human homosexuality has focused on males.

Many people mistakenly assume that homosexuals have lower levels of sex hormones. They don't: Heterosexuals and homosexuals do not differ in their levels of circulating hormones. Moreover, orchidectomy reduces the sexual behavior of both heterosexual and homosexual males, but it does not redirect it; and replacement injections simply reactivate the preferences that existed prior to surgery.

Efforts to determine whether perinatal hormone levels influence the development of sexual orientation have focused on nonhuman species for ethical reasons. A consistent pattern of findings has emerged from this research (see Ellis & Ames, 1987). In rats, hamsters, ferrets, pigs, zebra finches, and dogs, perinatal castration of males or testosterone treatment of females has been shown to induce same-sex preferences (see Adkins-Regan, 1988; Baum et al., 1990).

On the one hand, prudence should be exercised in applying the results of experiments on laboratory species to the development of sexual preferences in humans. It would be a mistake to ignore the profound cognitive and emotional components of human sexuality, which have no counterpart in laboratory animals; in general, the sexual behavior of humans and other primates is more influenced by experience than is the sexual behavior of other mammals (e.g., Goy, 1978). On the other hand, it would also be a mistake to think that a pattern of results that runs so consistently through so many mammalian species has no relevance to humans.

Do perinatal hormone levels influence the sexual orientation of adult humans? Although directly relevant evidence is sparse, there are some indications that the answer is yes. The strongest support for this view comes from the quasiexperimental study of Ehrhardt and her colleagues (1985). They interviewed adult women whose mothers had been exposed to *diethylstilbestrol* (a synthetic estrogen) during pregnancy. The subjects' responses indicated that they were significantly more sexually attracted to women than was a group of matched control subjects. Ehrhardt and her colleagues concluded that perinatal estrogen exposure does encourage homosexuality and bisexuality in women but that its effect is relatively weak: The sexual behavior of all but 1 of the 30 subjects was primarily heterosexual.

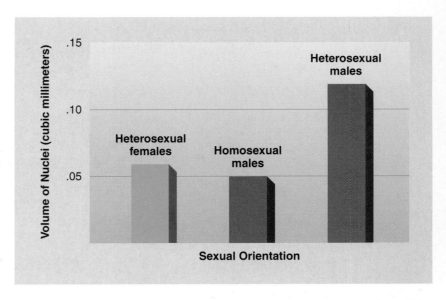

Figure 11.16 The size of the third interstitial nucleus of the anterior hypothalamus (INAH 3) in heterosexual males and females and in homosexual males. (LeVay, 1991)

Is There a Difference in the Brains of Homosexuals and Heterosexuals?

LeVay (1991) published the results of a postmortem study that may prove to be a major breakthrough in the study of human sexual orientation. He compared the neuroanatomy of three groups of subjects: heterosexual men, homosexual men, and women (who were assumed to be heterosexual). Reports of gender differences in the anterior and preoptic areas of the hypothalamus of various species, including humans, focused LeVay's research on these areas. LeVay confirmed a previous report (Allen et al., 1989) that the *third interstitial nucleus of the anterior hypothalamus (INAH 3)* is more than twice as large in heterosexual men as it is in women. In addition, he found that it is more than twice as large in heterosexual men as it is in homosexual men (see Figure 11.16). LeVay's report created a kerfuffle (fuss) in both the popular and the scientific media (Byne, 1994; LeVay & Hamer, 1994).

To put LeVay's finding in proper perspective, you should ask yourself two questions about it. First: Is it reliable? You

should remain a bit skeptical about any finding until it has been replicated, preferably by a different group of investigators; this is particularly true in an emotion-charged area of research such as the study of homosexuality. Second: What does it mean? LeVay's finding does not prove, as implied in many newspaper articles, that homosexuality results from a small INAH 3. Like all correlations, LeVay's observation is subject to a variety of causal interpretations. Being a homosexual may cause small INAH 3s, rather than vice versa, or some unrecognized third factor may be responsible for the correlation.

LeVay considered a third factor that might have led to the correlation, but he ruled it out: the possibility that AIDS was responsible for the correlation. Many of the homosexual brains in LeVay's study came from men who had died of AIDS, which is why LeVay was able to obtain such a large sample of male homosexual brains and why he did not include female homosexuals in his study. However, even when LeVay considered only those subjects who had died of other causes, there was still a weak correlation between sexual orientation and the size of the INAH 3.

Despite the fact that LeVay's study has proved nothing about the neural mechanisms of homosexuality or its causes, it is potentially of great importance. By locating a difference in the brains of male heterosexuals and homosexuals, in a part of the brain that is important for both hormonal regulation and sexual behavior, LeVay may have provided a focus for the next generation of research on human sexual orientation.

Chapter 11 Hormones and Sex

CONCLUSION

The primary purpose of this chapter was to describe the role of hormones in sexual development and behavior. First, you were introduced to the principles of neuroendocrine function (11.1). Then, the effects of sex hormones on developing (11.2) and sexually mature individuals (11.3) were reviewed. Finally, the neural and hormonal factors in sexual behavior (11.4) and orientation (11.5) were discussed.

Two important subthemes ran through this chapter: (1) that exceptional cases play a particularly important role in testing scientific theory and (2) that the men-are-men and women-are-women attitude is a misleading perspective from which to consider sexual matters. If you now appreciate why exceptional cases have been so important in the study of hormones and sex, you have learned a fundamen-

tal principle that has relevance to all fields of scientific inquiry. If you now are better able to resist the seductive appeal of the men-are-men and women-are-women attitude, you are leaving this chapter a more tolerant and understanding person than when you began it. I hope you now have an abiding appreciation of the fact that maleness and femaleness are slight, multidimensional, and at times ambiguous variations of each other.

Some stories are too good not to be told; the following is one of them. I just can't end a chapter about sex without telling it. It is about my friend's aunt, a right proper English lady. She was puzzled by "this oral sex thing" that she had been reading about in a magazine. "Good heavens," she exclaimed. "Whatever do they talk about?"

FOOD FOR THOUGHT

1. Over the last century and half, the onset of puberty has changed from age 15 or 16 to age 11 or 12, but there has been no corresponding acceleration in psychological and intellectual development. Precocious puberty is like a loaded gun in the hand of a child. Discuss.

2. Do you think sex-change operations should be permitted? Explain.

3. What should be done about the current epidemic of anabolic steroid abuse? Would you make the same rec-

ommendation if a safe anabolic steroid were developed? If a drug that would dramatically improve your memory were developed, would you take it?

4. Discuss LeVay's report of a difference in the brains of heterosexual and homosexual men. Discuss with respect to the physiological-or-psychological and the learned-or-innate dichotomies, which were criticized in Chapter 2.

KEY TERMS

Exocrine glands *(p. 269)*
Endocrine glands *(p. 269)*
Hormones *(p. 269)*
Amino acid derivative hormones *(p. 269)*
Peptide hormones *(p. 269)*
Protein hormones *(p. 269)*
Steroid hormones *(p. 270)*
Gonads *(p. 270)*
Testes *(p. 270)*
Ovaries *(p. 270)*
Copulation *(p. 270)*
Zygote *(p. 270)*
Sex chromosomes *(p. 270)*
Androgens *(p. 270)*
Estrogens *(p. 270)*
Testosterone *(p. 270)*
Estradiol *(p. 270)*
Progestins *(p. 271)*
Progesterone *(p. 271)*
Adrenal cortex *(p. 271)*
Gonadotropins *(p. 271)*
Posterior pituitary *(p. 271)*
Pituitary stalk *(p. 271)*
Anterior pituitary *(p. 271)*

Menstrual cycle *(p. 272)*
Vasopressin *(p. 273)*
Oxytocin *(p. 273)*
Paraventricular nuclei *(p. 273)*
Supraoptic nuclei *(p. 273)*
Hypothalamopituitary portal system *(p. 273)*
Releasing factors *(p. 273)*
Inhibitory factors *(p. 273)*
Thyrotropin-releasing hormone *(p. 274)*
Thyrotropin *(p. 274)*
Releasing hormones *(p. 274)*
Gonadotropin-releasing hormone *(p. 274)*
Follicle-stimulating hormone (FSH) *(p. 274)*
Luteinizing hormone (LH) *(p. 274)*
Negative feedback *(p. 274)*
Positive feedback *(p. 274)*
Ovulation *(p. 274)*
Follicle *(p. 274)*

Pulsatile hormone release *(p. 275)*
H-Y antigen *(p. 275)*
Wolffian system *(p. 276)*
Müllerian system *(p. 277)*
Müllerian-inhibiting substance *(p. 277)*
Scrotum *(p. 277)*
Ovariectomy *(p. 278)*
Orchidectomy *(p. 278)*
Gonadectomy *(p. 278)*
Genitals *(p. 278)*
Aromatization *(p. 279)*
Dihydrotestosterone *(p. 279)*
Alpha fetoprotein *(p. 279)*
Masculinizes *(p. 280)*
Defeminizes *(p. 280)*
Lordosis *(p. 280)*
Feminizes *(p. 280)*
Demasculinizes *(p. 280)*
Intromission *(p. 280)*
Ejaculation *(p. 280)*
Proceptive behaviors *(p. 280)*

Secondary sex characteristics *(p. 280)*
Growth hormone *(p. 280)*
Adrenocorticotropic hormone *(p. 280)*
Androstenedione *(p. 281)*
Androgenic insensitivity syndrome *(p. 283)*
Adrenogenital syndrome *(p. 283)*
Ablatio penis *(p. 284)*
Replacement injections *(p. 285)*
Impotent *(p. 285)*
Estrus *(p. 286)*
Estrous cycle *(p. 287)*
Anabolic steroids *(p. 287)*
Medial preoptic area *(p. 288)*
Sexually dimorphic nucleus *(p. 288)*
Ventromedial nucleus *(p. 290)*
Heterosexual *(p. 291)*
Homosexual *(p. 291)*
Bisexual *(p. 291)*

ADDITIONAL READING

The following text provides an introduction to the general field of behavioral neuroendocrinology:

Becker, J. B., Breedlove, S. M., and Crews, D. (Eds.). (1992). *Behavioral endocrinology.* Cambridge, MA: MIT Press.

The following is an excellent review of the development of sex differences in the human brain:

Breedlove, S. M. (1994). Sexual differentiation of the human brain. *Annual Review of Psychology, 45,* 389–418.

The following article is a review of clinical cases of abnormal sexual development and what they tell us about the factors that influence the development of sexual identity and preference:

Money, J. (1987). Sin, sickness, or status? Homosexual gender identity and psychoneuroendocrinology. *American Psychologist, 42,* 384–399.

The following two articles provide coverage of research on the development of sexual orientation in males; there is no comparable research in females:

Byne, W. (1994, May). The biological evidence challenged. *Scientific American, 270,* 50–55.

LeVay, S., & Hamer, D. H. (1994, May). Evidence for a biological influence in male homosexuality. *Scientific American, 270,* 44–49.

Sleep, Dreaming, and Circadian Rhythms

12.1 The Physiological and Behavioral Correlates of Sleep

12.2 REM Sleep and Dreaming

12.3 Why Do We Sleep?

12.4 Circadian Sleep Cycles

12.5 Effects of Sleep Deprivation

12.6 Recuperation and Circadian Theories of Sleep Combined

12.7 Neural Mechanisms of Sleep

12.8 The Circadian Clock: Neural Mechanisms

12.9 Hypnotic and Antihypnotic Drugs

12.10 Sleep Disorders

12.11 The Effects of Sleep Reduction

Most of us have a fondness for eating, drinking, and sex—the three highly esteemed motivated behaviors discussed in Chapters 10 and 11. But the amount of time devoted to these three behaviors by even the most amorous gourmands pales in comparison to the amount of time spent sleeping: Most of us will sleep for well over 175,000 hours in our lifetimes.

This extraordinary commitment of time implies that sleep fulfills a critical biological function. But what is it? And what about dreaming: Why do we spend so much time dreaming? And why do we tend to get sleepy at about the same time every day? Answers to these questions await you in this chapter.

Almost every time I give a lecture about sleep, somebody asks, "How much sleep do we need?" and each time, I provide the same unsatisfying answer. I explain that there are two fundamentally different answers to this question, but that neither has emerged a clear winner. One answer stresses the presumed health-promoting and recuperative powers of sleep and suggests that people need as much sleep as they can comfortably get. The other answer is that many of us sleep more than we need to and are consequently sleeping part of our lives away. Just think how your life could change if you slept 5 hours per night instead of 8. You would have an extra 21 waking hours each week, a mind-boggling 10,952 hours each decade.

As I prepared to write this chapter, I began to think of some of the personal implications of the idea that we get more sleep than we need. That is when I decided to do something a bit unconventional. While I write this chapter, I am going to be your subject in a sleep-reduction experiment. I am going to try to get no more than 5 hours of sleep per night—11:00 P.M. to 4:00 A.M.—until this chapter is written. As I begin, I am excited by the prospect of having more time to write but a little worried that this extra time might be obtained at a personal cost that is too dear.

It is the next day now—4:50 Saturday morning to be exact—and I am just beginning to write. There was a party last night, and I didn't make it to bed by 11:00; but considering that I slept for only 3 hours and 35 minutes, I feel quite good. I wonder what I will feel like later in the day. In any case, I will report my experiences to you at the end of the chapter.

The following case study challenges several common beliefs about sleep. Ponder its implications before proceeding into the body of the chapter:

Miss M ... is a busy lady who finds her ration of twenty-three hours of wakefulness still insufficient for her needs. Even though she is now retired she is still busy in the community, helping sick friends whenever requested. She is an active painter and has recently finished a biography of William Morris, the British writer and designer. Although she becomes tired physically, when she needs to sit down to rest her legs, she does not ever report feeling sleepy. During the night she sits on her bed ... reading, writing, crocheting or painting. At about 2:00 A.M. she falls asleep without any preceding drowsiness often while still holding a book in her hands. When she wakes about an hour later, she feels as wide awake as ever. It would be wrong to say that she woke refreshed because she did not complain of tiredness in the first place.

To test her claim we invited her along to the laboratory. She came willingly but on the first evening we hit our first snag. She announced that she did not sleep at all if she had interesting things to do, and by her reckoning a visit to a university sleep laboratory counted as very interesting. Moreover, for the first time in years, she had someone to talk to for the whole of the night. So we talked.

In the morning we broke into shifts so that some could sleep while at least one person stayed with her and entertained her during the next day. The second night was a repeat performance of the first night.... Things had not gone according to plan. So far we were very impressed by her cheerful response to two nights of sleep deprivation, but we had very little by way of hard data to show others.

In the end we prevailed upon her to allow us to apply EEG electrodes and to leave her sitting comfortably on the bed in the bedroom. She had promised that she would co-operate by not resisting sleep although she claimed not to be especially tired.... At approximately 1:30 A.M., the EEG record showed the first signs of sleep even though ... she was still sitting with the book in her hands....

The only substantial difference between her sleep and what we might have expected from any other seventy-year-old lady was that it was of short duration.... [After 99 minutes], she had no further interest in sleep and asked to be allowed to leave the bedroom so that she could join our company again. (Meddis, 1977, pp. 42–44)[1]

12.1 The Physiological and Behavioral Correlates of Sleep

Many changes occur in the body during sleep. This section of the chapter introduces you to the major ones.

The Three Standard Psychophysiological Measures of Sleep

There are major changes in the human EEG during the course of a night's sleep (Loomis, Harvey, & Hobart, 1936).

Although the EEG waves that accompany sleep are generally high-voltage and slow, there are periods throughout the night that are dominated by low-voltage, fast waves similar to those of waking subjects. In 1953, Aserinsky and Kleitman

---

[1]From *The Sleep Instinct* (pp. 42–43) by R. Meddis. Copyright © 1977, Routledge & Kegan Paul, London. Reprinted by permission.

discovered that *rapid eye movements (REMs)* occur under the closed eyelids of sleeping subjects during these periods of low-voltage, fast EEG activity. And in 1962, Berger and Oswald discovered that there is also a loss of electromyographic activity in the neck muscles during these same sleep periods. Subsequently, the **electroencephalogram (EEG)**, the **electrooculogram (EOG)**, and the neck **electromyogram (EMG)** became the three standard psychophysiological bases for defining stages of sleep (Rechtschaffen & Kales, 1968).

Figure 12.1 depicts a subject participating in a sleep experiment. A subject's first night's in the sleep laboratory is often fitful. That is why it is the usual practice to have each subject sleep several nights in the laboratory before commencing a study. The disturbance of sleep observed during the first night in a sleep laboratory is called the **first-night phenomenon.** It is well known to markers of introductory psychology examinations because of the creative definitions of it that are offered by students who forget that it is a sleep-related, rather than a sex-related, phenomenon.

Figure 12.1 A subject participating in a sleep experiment.

Four Stages of Sleep EEG

There are four stages of sleep EEG: stage 1, stage 2, stage 3, and stage 4. Examples of each are presented in Figure 12.2 on page 298.

After the eyes are shut and a person prepares to go to sleep, **alpha waves**—waxing and waning bursts of 8-to-12-Hz EEG waves—begin to punctuate the low-voltage, high-frequency EEG of active wakefulness. Then, as the person falls asleep, there is a sudden transition to a period of stage 1 sleep EEG. The stage 1 sleep EEG is a low-voltage, high-frequency signal that is similar to, but slower than, that of active wakefulness.

There is a gradual increase in EEG voltage and a decrease in EEG frequency as the person progresses from stage 1 sleep through stages 2, 3, and 4. Accordingly, the stage 2 sleep EEG has a slightly higher amplitude and lower frequency than the stage 1 EEG; in addition, it is punctuated by two characteristic wave forms: K complexes and sleep spindles. Each **K complex** is a single large negative wave (upward deflection) followed immediately by a single large positive wave (downward deflection). Each **sleep spindle** is a 1-to-2-second waxing and waning burst of 12-to-14-Hz waves. The stage 3 sleep EEG is defined by the occasional presence of **delta waves**—the largest and slowest EEG waves, with a frequency of 1 to 2 Hz—whereas the stage 4 sleep EEG is defined by a predominance of delta waves.

Once subjects reach stage 4 EEG sleep, they stay there for a time, and then they retreat back through the stages of sleep to stage 1. However, when they return to stage 1, things are not at all the same as they were the first time through. The first period of the stage 1 EEG during a night's sleep (**initial stage 1 EEG**) is not marked by any striking electromyographic or electrooculographic changes, whereas subsequent periods of the stage 1 sleep EEG (**emergent stage 1 EEG**) are accompanied by REMs and by a loss of tone in the muscles of the body core.

Electroencephalogram (EEG). A measure of the electrical activity of the brain, commonly recorded through scalp electrodes.

Electromyogram (EMG). A measure of the electrical activity of muscles.

Electrooculogram (EOG). A measure of eye movement.

First-night phenomenon. The sleep disturbances experienced during the first night that a subject sleeps in a laboratory.

Alpha waves. 8-to-12-Hz EEG waves that commonly punctuate the EEG of human subjects just before they fall asleep.

K complexes. The large, biphasic EEG waves that are characteristic of the stage 2 sleep EEG.

Sleep spindles. The 1-to-2-second bursts of 12-to-15-Hz EEG waves characteristic of stage 2 sleep.

Delta waves. The largest, slowest EEG waves.

Initial stage 1 EEG. The period of the stage 1 EEG that occurs at the onset of sleep and that is not associated with dreaming.

Emergent stage 1 EEG. All periods of stage 1 sleep EEG except initial stage 1.

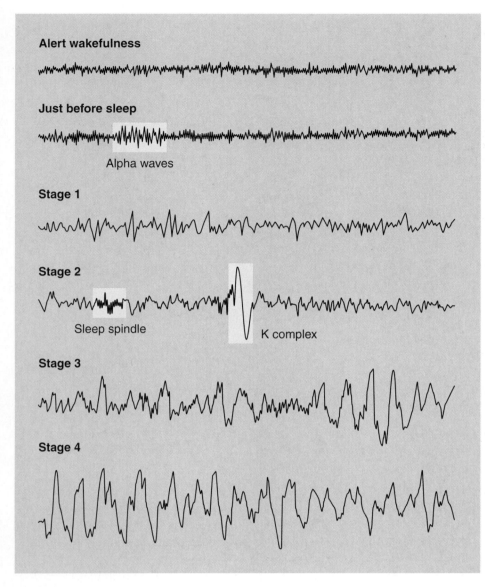

Figure 12.2 The EEG of alert wakefulness, the EEG that precedes sleep onset, and the four stages of sleep EEG. Each trace is about 10 seconds long.

periods during the night when the subject is awake; these periods of wakefulness are usually not remembered in the morning.

Let's pause here to get some sleep-stage terms straight. The sleep associated with emergent stage 1 EEG is often called **paradoxical sleep** because the EEG signal itself and the associated autonomic changes are similar to those of wakefulness, and the sleep associated with stages 3 and 4 sleep EEG is often called **delta sleep** (after the delta waves that characterize stages 3 and 4 sleep EEG). In this chapter, I follow the common practice of referring to the sleep characterized by rapid eye movements, loss of core muscle tone, and emergent stage 1 EEG as **REM sleep** and referring to stages 2, 3, and 4 together as **slow-wave sleep (SWS).**

REMs, loss of core muscle tone, and a low-amplitude, high-frequency EEG are not the only physiological correlates of REM sleep. Cerebral activity (e.g., oxygen consumption, blood flow, and neural firing) increases to waking levels in many structures, and there is a general increase in autonomic nervous system activity (e.g., in blood pressure, pulse, and respiration). Also, the muscles of the extremities occasionally twitch, and there is always some degree of clitoral or penile erection.

After the first cycle of sleep EEG—from initial stage 1 to stage 4 and back to emergent stage 1—the rest of the night is spent going back and forth through the stages. Figure 12.3 illustrates the EEG cycles of a typical night's sleep and the close relation between emergent stage 1 sleep, REMs, and the loss of tone in core muscles. Notice that each cycle tends to be about 90 minutes long and that, as the night progresses, more and more time is spent in emergent stage 1 sleep and less and less time is spent in the other stages, particularly in stage 4. Notice also that there are brief

Figure 12.3 The course of EEG stages during a typical night's sleep and the relation of emergent stage 1 EEG to REMs and lack of tone in core muscles.

Nathaniel Kleitman's laboratory was an exciting place in 1953. Kleitman's students had just discovered REM sleep, and they were driven by the fascinating implication of their discovery. With the exception of the loss of tone in the core muscles, all of the other measures suggested that REM sleep episodes were emotion-charged. Could REM sleep be the physiological correlate of dreaming? Could it provide researchers with a window into the subjective inner world of dreams? The researchers began by waking a few subjects in the middle of REM episodes and asking them if they had been dreaming. The results were remarkable:

> The vivid recall that could be elicited in the middle of the night when a subject was awakened while his eyes were moving rapidly was nothing short of miraculous. It [seemed to open] ... an exciting new world to the subjects whose only previous dream memories had been the vague morning-after recall. Now, instead of perhaps some fleeting glimpse into the dream world each night, the subjects could be tuned into the middle of as many as ten or twelve dreams every night. (Dement, 1978, p. 37)[2]

Strong support for the theory that REM sleep is the physiological correlate of dreaming came from the observation that 80% of awakenings from REM sleep, but only 7% of awakenings from NREM (non REM) sleep, led to dream recall. The phenomenon of dreaming, which for centuries had been the subject of wild speculation, was finally rendered accessible to scientific investigation. The following anecdote related by Dement (1978) communicates some of the excitement felt by those involved in the discovery:

> I decided to be a subject primarily out of envy; having listened with amazement and awe as many subjects recounted their dreams, I wished to enjoy the experience myself.... On the first night I felt like an actor preparing for a performance as I sat in front of the mirror donning my "makeup" of electrodes. I will never forget this "opening night."...
>
> A hastily trained medical student ... was monitoring the EEG and supervising my arousals. I went to sleep prepared for an exciting night and woke up with a certain

Paradoxical sleep. The sleep that accompanies emergent stage 1 EEG, so called because the physiological changes associated with this stage are similar to those of wakefulness.

Delta sleep. Stages of sleep that are punctuated by delta waves (stages 3 and 4).

REM sleep. The stage of sleep characterized by rapid eye movements, loss of core muscle tone, and emergent stage 1 EEG.

Slow-wave sleep (SWS). Sleep stages 2, 3, and 4.

urgency.... I searched my mind... I could remember nothing.... So I went back to sleep and was suddenly aware of being wrenched from the void once again. This time I could remember nothing except a very, very vague feeling of a name or a person. Disappointed but sleepy, I dozed off again.

> The next time I was jolted awake—still unable to recall anything—I began to worry. Why didn't I remember a dream? I had expected to dazzle the medical student with my brilliant recall! After a fourth and fifth awakening with exactly the same results, I was really upset. What in the world was wrong? I began to doubt the whole REM-dreaming hypothesis....
>
> The experience had left me exhausted and extremely puzzled, and I was anxious to look at the polygraphic record of my miserable night. Upon examining the record I discovered, to my utter delight and relief, that the medical student had been mistakenly arousing me in NREM. Not once had I awakened during a REM period....
>
> The next night, with additional instruction, ..., the medical student hit the REM periods right on the button, and vivid recall flooded my mind with each awakening. (pp. 38–39)[3]

Testing Common Beliefs about Dreaming

The high correlation between REM sleep and dream recall provided an opportunity to test some common beliefs about dreaming. The following are five such beliefs that have been subjected to empirical tests.

1. Many people believe that external stimuli can become incorporated into their dreams. Dement and Wolpert (1958) sprayed water on sleeping subjects after they had been in REM sleep for a few minutes, and a few seconds after the spray, each subject was awakened. In 14 of 33 cases, the water was incorporated into the dream report. The following narrative was reported by a subject who had been dreaming that he was acting in a play:

   > I was walking behind the leading lady when she suddenly collapsed and water was dripping on her. I ran over to her and water was dripping on my back and head. The roof was leaking.... I looked up and there

[2]From *Some Must Watch while Some Must Sleep* by William E. Dement, published by Portable Stanford Books, Stanford Alumni Association, Stanford University. Reprinted by permission.

[3]From *Some Must Watch while Some Must Sleep* by William E. Dement, published by Portable Stanford Books, Stanford Alumni Association, Stanford University. Reprinted by permission.

was a hole in the roof. I dragged her over to the side of the stage and began pulling the curtains. Then I woke up. (p. 550)

2. Some people believe that dreams last only an instant, but research suggests that dreams run on "real time." In one study (Dement & Kleitman, 1957), subjects were awakened 5 or 15 minutes after the beginning of a REM episode and asked to decide on the basis of the duration of the events in their dreams whether they had been dreaming for 5 or 15 minutes. They were correct in 92 of 111 cases.

3. Some people claim that they do not dream. However, these people have just as much REM sleep as normal dreamers. Moreover, they report dreams if they are awakened during REM episodes (Goodenough et al., 1959), although they do so less frequently than do normal dreamers.

4. Penile erections are commonly assumed to be indicative of dreams with sexual content. However, erections are no more complete during dreams with frank sexual content than during those without it (Karacan et al., 1966). Even babies have REM-related penile erections.

5. Most people believe that sleeptalking and **somnambulism** (sleepwalking) occur during dreams. This is not so; sleeptalking and somnambulism occur least frequently during dreaming, when core muscles tend to be totally relaxed. They occur most frequently during stage 4 sleep.

The Interpretation of Dreams

The idea that dreams are disguised messages has a long history. For example, the Bible describes how a dream of seven lean cattle following and devouring seven fat cattle warned that seven years of famine would follow seven years of plenty. It was Freud's theory of dreams that refined this view of dreams and gave it legitimacy. Freud believed that dreams are triggered by unacceptable repressed wishes, many of a sexual nature. He argued that because dreams represent unacceptable wishes, the dreams we experience (our *manifest dreams*) are merely disguised versions of our real dreams (our *latent dreams*): An unconscious censor disguises and subtracts information from our real dreams so that we can endure them. Freud thus concluded that one of the keys to understanding people and dealing with their psychological problems is to expose the meaning of their latent dreams through the interpretation of their manifest dreams.

There is no convincing evidence for the Freudian theory of dreams; indeed, the brain science of the 1890s, which served as its foundation, is now universally regarded as obsolete. Nevertheless, the Freudian theory of dreams has been the basis for many an interesting story; as a result, it continues to be widely disseminated to the general public through the entertainment and communication media as if

it were fact. Consequently, even today, the Freudian theory of dreams is deeply ingrained in many people's thinking. Many accept the notion that dreams bubble up from a troubled subconscious and that they represent repressed thoughts and wishes.

The modern alternative to the Freudian theory of dreams is Hobson's (1989) activation-synthesis theory. It is based on the observation that, during REM sleep, many brain stem circuits become active and bombard the cerebral cortex with neural signals. The essence of the **activation-synthesis theory** is that the information supplied to the cortex during REM sleep is largely random and that the resulting dream is the cortex's effort to make sense of these random signals.

Activation-synthesis theory does not deny that dreams have meaning, but it differs from Freudian theory in terms of where that meaning lies. Hobson's dreamers reveal themselves by what they add to the random jumble of brain stem signals in order to create a coherent story, not by the painful hidden message of their dreams.

Lucid Dreams

The reality of dreams is usually quite distinct from the reality of consciousness (see Williams et al., 1992). However, there are dreams, called **lucid dreams,** in which this distinction becomes blurred. These are dreams in which the dreamer is aware at the time that she or he is dreaming and can influence the course of the dream. The experience of a lucid dream is something like being awake in a dream (see Blackmore, 1991). The existence of lucid dreams has been proved by experiments in which sleeping subjects signaled to the experimenter from their dreams by a prearranged means that they were aware that they were dreaming—for example, by moving their eyes back and forth eight times (Hearne, 1978; LaBerge, 1986).

In various surveys, about 50% of respondents report having had at least one lucid dream (e.g., Gackenbach & LaBerge, 1988). However, because the concept of lucid dreaming is a difficult one to grasp, these figures are likely to be overestimates.

Because many people find lucid dreams to be a positive experience, several techniques have been devised for training people to have them. One such technique involves sig-

> **Somnambulism.** Sleepwalking.
>
> **Activation-synthesis theory.** The theory that dream content reflects the cerebral cortex's inherent tendency to make sense of and give form to the random signals that it receives from the brain stem during REM sleep.
>
> **Lucid dreams.** Dreams in which the dreamer is aware that she or he is dreaming and can influence the course of the dream.

naling to the sleeping subject each time he or she is dreaming; a mild shock is administered to the wrist at the start of each REM period (Hearne, 1990).

People who regularly have lucid dreams have recently been used to study dreaming: It is like having a conscious person in a dream who can relay information about the dream to the conscious world. For example, in one study, the subject was instructed to draw large triangles with his right arm as soon as he got into a dream and to signal to the experimenter with eye movements just before he drew each triangle. EMG activity that was consistent with triangle drawing was recorded from the right forearm each time the eye-movement signal was received (Schatzman, Worsley, & Fenwick, 1988). In another study, a woman who could create various positive sexual encounters in her lucid dreams was shown to experience real physiological orgasms (LaBerge, Greenleaf, & Kedzierski, 1983) during each dream encounter.

12.3   Why Do We Sleep?

We humans have a tendency to think that most of what we do has a special, higher-order function. For example, it has been suggested that sleep helps us reprogram our complex, computerlike brains, or that it permits some kind of emotional release to maintain our mental health. However, all mammals and birds sleep, and their sleep is much like ours—characterized by high-amplitude, low-frequency EEG waves punctuated by periods of low-amplitude, high-frequency activity (see Winson, 1993). Even fish, reptiles, amphibians, and insects go through periods of inactivity and unresponsiveness that are similar to mammalian sleep.

Recuperation and Circadian Theories

The fact that sleep is so common in the animal kingdom suggests that it serves a critical survival-related function, but there is no consensus on what that function is. There are two general theoretical approaches to the function of sleep: recuperation theories and circadian theories. The essence of the *recuperation theories* is that being awake disrupts the *homeostasis* (internal stability) of the body in some way and that sleep is required to restore it. In contrast, the *circadian theories* argue that sleep has evolved to keep animals inactive during those times of the day when they do not need to be engaging in activities necessary for their survival. According to circadian theories, prehistoric humans had enough time to get their eating, drinking, and reproducing out of the way during the daytime; and their strong motivation to sleep at night evolved to conserve their energy resources and to make them less susceptible to mishap—e.g., predation—in the dark. In essence, recuperation theories view sleep as a nightly repairman who fixes damage produced by wakefulness, while circadian theories regard sleep as a strict parent who demands inactivity because it keeps us out of trouble.

Choosing between the recuperation and circadian approaches to sleep is the logical first step in the search for the physiological basis of sleep. Is the sleep system run by a biological clock that produces compelling urges to sleep at certain times of the day to conserve energy and protect us from mishap, or is it a homeostatic system whose function is to correct some adverse consequence of staying awake?

Table 12.1 illustrates the average number of hours per day that various mammalian species spend sleeping.

TABLE 12.1

The Average Number of Hours Slept per Day by Various Mammalian Species

Mammalian Species	Hours of Sleep per Day
Giant sloth	20
Opossum, brown bat	19
Giant armadillo	18
Owl monkey, nine-banded armadillo	17
Arctic ground squirrel	16
Tree shrew	15
Cat, golden hamster	14
Mouse, rat, gray wolf, ground squirrel	13
Arctic fox, chinchilla, gorilla, raccoon	12
Mountain beaver	11
Jaguar, vervet monkey, hedgehog	10
Rhesus monkey, chimpanzee, baboon, red fox	9
Human, rabbit, guinea pig, pig	8
Gray seal, gray hyrax, Brazilian tapir	6
Tree hyrax, rock hyrax	5
Cow, goat, elephant, donkey, sheep	3
Roe deer, horse	2

Explaining the large between-species differences in daily sleep time is one of the central challenges that must be met by any successful theory of sleep. Why do cats tend to sleep about 14 hours a day and horses only about 2?

Circadian theories have done a better job than recuperation theories of explaining the substantial between-species differences in sleep times. Recuperation theories predict that species that expend more energy should sleep longer, but there is no apparent correlation between a species' sleep time and its level of activity, its body size, or its body temperature. The fact that giant sloths sleep 20 hours per day is a strong argument against the theory that sleep is a compensatory reaction to energy expenditure. In contrast, circadian theories correctly predict that the daily sleep time of each species is related to how vulnerable it is while it is asleep and how much time it must spend each day to feed itself and to take care of its other survival requirements. For example, zebras must graze almost continuously to get enough to eat and are extremely vulnerable to predatory attack when they are asleep. In contrast, African lions often sleep more or less continuously for 2 or 3 days after they

Figure 12.4 Sleeping lions. After gorging themselves on a kill, African lions sleep almost continuously for 2 or 3 days. And where do they sleep? Anywhere they want.

have gorged themselves on a kill. The photograph in Figure 12.4 says it all.

The next two sections of this chapter deal with two topics that have a bearing on the question of whether sleep is fundamentally circadian or recuperative: circadian sleep cycles and sleep deprivation.

12.4 Circadian Sleep Cycles

The world in which we live cycles from light to dark and back again once every 24 hours, and most surface-dwelling species have adapted to this regular change in their environment by developing a variety of so-called **circadian rhythms** (see Rusak & Bina, 1990; Takahashi, 1991). (*Circadian* means "lasting about 1 day.") For example, most species display a regular circadian sleep-wake cycle. Humans take advantage of the light of day to take care of their biological needs, and then they sleep for much of the night; *nocturnal animals,* such as rats, sleep for much of the day and stay awake at night.

Although the sleep-wake cycle is the most obvious circadian rhythm, "it is virtually impossible to find a physiological, biochemical, or behavioral process in animals which does not display some measure of circadian rhythmicity" (Groos, 1983, p. 19). Each day, our bodies adjust themselves in a variety of ways to meet the demands of the two environments in which we live: light and dark.

Our circadian cycles are kept on their once-every-24-hours schedule by cues in the environment. The most important of these cues for the regulation of mammalian circadian rhythms is the daily cycle of light and dark; environmental cues that can *entrain* (control the timing of) circadian rhythms are called **zeitgebers** (pronounced "ZITE gay bers"), a German word that means "time givers." In controlled laboratory environments, it is possible to lengthen or shorten circadian cycles by adjusting the duration of the light-dark cycle; for example, when exposed to alternating 10-hour periods of light and 10-hour periods of dark, subjects' circadian cycles begin to conform to a 20-hour day.

Free-Running Circadian Sleep-Wake Cycles

In a world without 24-hour cycles of light and dark, other regular cues in the environment can entrain circadian cycles. For example, the circadian sleep-wake cycles of hamsters living in continuous darkness or in continuous light can be entrained by regular daily bouts of social interaction (Mrosovsky, 1988), hoarding (Rusak et al., 1988), eating (Jilge, 1991; Mistlberger, 1990), or exercise (Mistlberger, 1991). Hamsters display particularly clear circadian sleep-wake cycles and are the favorite subjects of circadian cycle researchers.

What happens to circadian rhythms in an environment that is devoid of *zeitgebers*? Remarkably, under conditions

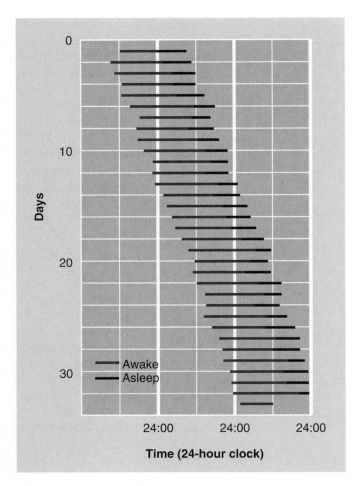

Figure 12.5 A typical free-running circadian sleep-wake cycle 25.3 hours in duration. Each day, the subject went to sleep approximately 1.3 hours later than he had the day before. (Adapted from Wever, 1979, p. 30.)

in which there are absolutely no temporal cues, humans and other animals maintain all of their circadian rhythms. Circadian rhythms in constant environments are said to be **free-running rhythms,** and their duration is called the **free-running period.** Free-running periods vary in length from subject to subject, are of relatively constant duration within a given subject, and are usually longer than 24 hours—about 25 hours in most humans. It seems that we all have an internal *biological clock* that habitually runs a little slow unless it is entrained by time-related cues in the environment. A typical free-running circadian sleep-wake cycle is illustrated in Figure 12.5 (Wever, 1979). Notice its regularity. Without any external cues, this man fell asleep approximately every 25.3 hours for an entire month.

The fact that the regularity of free-running circadian sleep-wake cycles is maintained despite day-to-day variations in physical and mental activity provides strong support for the dominance of circadian factors over recuperative factors in the regulation of sleep. Figure 12.6 on page 304 provides an extreme illustration of this point: A full 24 hours of sleep deprivation on day 24 had little effect on the subsequent free-running circadian sleep-wake cycle of this rat.

Perhaps the most remarkable characteristic of free-running circadian cycles is that they do not have to be learned. Even rats that are born and raised in an unchanging laboratory environment (in continuous light or in continuous darkness) display regular free-running sleep-wake cycles of about 25 hours (Richter, 1971).

The correlation between the length of a period of wakefulness and the length of the following period of sleep is negative, even when the cycle is free-running. In other words, on those occasions when a subject stays awake longer than usual, the following sleep tends to be shorter than usual (Wever, 1979). Humans appear to be programmed to have sleep-wake cycles of approximately 24 hours; hence, in contradiction of the main prediction of recuperation theories, the longer we stay awake during a particular cycle, the less we sleep. Recuperative theories of sleep incorrectly predict that longer periods of wakefulness will be followed by longer periods of sleep.

Many animals display a circadian cycle of body temperature that is related to their circadian sleep-wake cycle: They tend to sleep during the falling phase of their circadian body temperature cycle and awaken during its rising phase. However, when subjects are housed in constant laboratory environments, their sleep-wake and body temperature cycles sometimes break away from one another. This phenomenon is called **internal desynchronization.** For example, in one case, the free-running sleep-wake and body temperature periods of a human subject were initially both 25.7 hours; then, for some unknown reason, there was an increase in the free-running period of the sleep-wake cycle to 33.4 hours and a decrease in the free-running period of the body temperature cycle to 25.1 hours. The potential for the simultaneous existence of two different free-running periods suggests that there is more than one circadian timing mechanism.

Jet Lag and Shift Work

Modern industrialized societies are faced with two different disruptions of circadian rhythmicity: jet lag and shift work.

Circadian rhythms. Diurnal (daily) cycles of body function.

Zeitgebers. Environmental cues, such as the light-dark cycle, that entrain circadian rhythms.

Free-running rhythms. Circadian rhythms that do not depend on environmental cues to keep them running on a regular schedule.

Free-running period. The duration of one cycle of a free-running rhythm.

Internal desynchronization. The cycling on different schedules of the free-running circadian cycles of two different processes.

Figure 12.6 The effect of 24 hours of sleep deprivation on the free-running activity-rest circadian rhythm of a rat. Colored bars indicate periods of activity; thus long blank spaces are generally indicative of sleep. On day 24, the rat was totally deprived of sleep, yet the timing of its 25.3-hour free-running circadian rest-activity cycle was unaffected.

Jet lag occurs when the *zeitgebers* that control the phases of various circadian rhythms are accelerated during eastern flights (*phase advances*) or decelerated during western flights (*phase delays*). In *shift work,* the zeitgebers stay the same but workers are forced to adjust their natural sleep-wake cycles in order to meet the demands of changing work schedules. Both of these disruptions produce sleep disturbances, fatigue, general malaise, and deficits on tests of physical and cognitive function. The disturbances can last for many days; for example, it typically takes about 10 days

to completely adjust to a Tokyo-to-Boston flight—a phase advance of 10.5 hours.

What can be done to reduce the disruptive effects of jet lag and shift work? Two approaches have been proposed for the reduction of jet lag. One is the common-sense approach of gradually shifting one's sleep-wake cycle in the days prior to the flight (see Hobson 1989). The other is administering treatments after the flight that promote the required shift in the circadian rhythm. For example, exposure to intense light early in the morning has been shown to promote phase advances (Czeisler et al., 1989); Daan and Lewy (1984) used this method to accelerate the adaptation of a subject to the 9-hour phase advance that resulted after a flight from the United States to Europe. The results of a study of hamsters (Mrosovsky & Salmon, 1987) suggest that a good workout early in the morning of the first day after an eastern flight might promote adaptation to the resulting phase advance; hamsters that engaged in one 3-hour bout of wheel running 7 hours before their usual period of activity adapted quickly to an 8-hour advance in their light-dark cycle (see Figure 12.7).

Companies that employ shift workers have had great success in improving the productivity and job satisfaction of their shift workers by scheduling phase delays rather than phase advances; whenever possible, shift workers are transferred from their current schedule to one that begins later in the day (see Coleman, 1986). It is much more difficult to go to sleep 4 hours earlier and get up 4 hours earlier (a phase advance) than it is to go to sleep 4 hours later and get up 4 hours later (a phase delay).

12.5 Effects of Sleep Deprivation

Recuperation and circadian theories of sleep make different predictions about the effects of sleep deprivation. Because recuperation theories are based on the premise that sleep is a response to the accumulation of some debilitating effect of wakefulness, they predict (1) that long periods of wakefulness will produce physiological and behavioral disturbances, (2) that these disturbances will grow steadily worse as the sleep deprivation continues, and (3) that after a period of deprivation has ended, much of the missed sleep will be regained. In contrast, the circadian theories predict (1) that there will be no debilitating effects of sleep deprivation other than those that can be attributed to an increase in the tendency to fall asleep, (2) that the increase in the desire to

sleep that is produced by sleep deprivation will be greatest during the phases of the circadian cycle when the subjects normally sleep, and (3) that there will be little or no compensation for the loss of sleep once the period of deprivation has ended. Think about these predictions for a moment. On which side do you think the scientific evidence falls?

Sleep-Deprivation Studies in Humans

Kleitman's (1963) description of one of the earliest sleep-deprivation studies, which he conducted in 1922, and Dement's (1978) widely publicized case study of Randy Gardner provide strong support for the circadian theory.

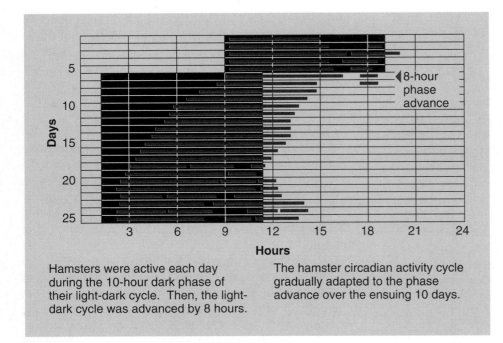

Hamsters were active each day during the 10-hour dark phase of their light-dark cycle. Then, the light-dark cycle was advanced by 8 hours.

The hamster circadian activity cycle gradually adapted to the phase advance over the ensuing 10 days.

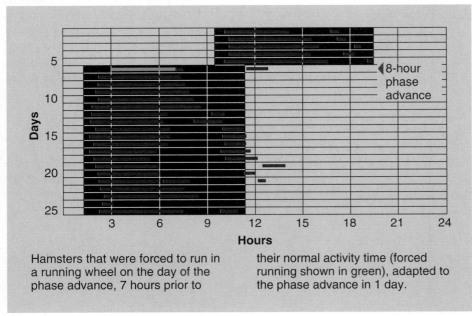

Hamsters that were forced to run in a running wheel on the day of the phase advance, 7 hours prior to

their normal activity time (forced running shown in green), adapted to the phase advance in 1 day.

Figure 12.7 A period of exercise (shown in red) accelerates adaptation to an 8-hour phase advance in the circadian light-dark cycle. (Adapted from Mrosovsky & Salmon, 1987.)

Kleitman's Classic Sleep-Deprivation Study

While there were differences in the many subjective experiences of the sleep-evading persons, there were several features common to most.... [D]uring the first night the subject did not feel very tired or sleepy. He could read or study or do laboratory work, without much attention from the watcher, but usually felt an attack of drowsiness between 3 A.M. and 6 A.M.... Next morning the subject felt well, except for a slight malaise which always appeared on sitting down and resting for any length of time. However, if he occupied himself with his ordinary daily tasks, he was likely to forget having spent a sleepless night. During the second night ... reading or study was next to impossible because sitting quietly was conducive to even greater sleepiness. As during the first night, there came a 2–3 hour period in the early hours of the morning when the desire for sleep was almost overpowering.... Later in the morning the sleepiness diminished once more, and the subject could perform routine laboratory work, as usual. It was not safe for him to sit down, however, without danger of falling asleep, particularly if he attended lectures....

The third night resembled the second, and the fourth day was like the third.... At the end of that time the individual was as sleepy as he was likely to be. Those who continued to stay awake experienced the wavelike increase and decrease in sleepiness with the greatest drowsiness at about the same time every night. (Kleitman, 1963, pp. 220–221)

The Case of Randy Gardner

As part of a 1965 science fair project, Randy Gardner and two classmates, who were entrusted with keeping him awake, planned to break the then world record of 260 hours of consecutive wakefulness. Dement read about the project in the newspaper and, seeing an opportunity to collect some important data, joined the team, much to the comfort of Randy's worried parents. Randy proved to be a friendly and cooperative subject, although he did complain vigorously when his team would not permit him to close his eyes for more than a few seconds at a time. However, in no sense could Randy's behavior be considered abnormal or disturbed. Near the end of his vigil, Randy held a press conference attended by reporters and television crews from all over the United States, and he conducted himself impeccably. When asked how he had managed to stay awake for 11 days, he replied politely, "It's just mind over matter." Randy went to sleep exactly 264 hours and 12 minutes after his alarm clock had awakened him 11 days before. And how long did he sleep? Only 14 hours the first night, and thereafter he returned to his usual 8-hour sched-

Jet lag. The adverse effects on body function of zeitgebers being accelerated during eastern flights or decelerated during western flights.

ule. Although it may seem amazing that Randy did not have to sleep longer to "catch up" on his lost sleep, the lack of substantial recovery sleep is typical of such cases.

Mrs. Maureen Weston has since supplanted Randy Gardner in the *Guinness Book of World Records*. During a rocking-chair marathon in 1977, Mrs. Weston kept rocking for 449 hours (18 days, 17 hours)—an impressive bit of "rocking around the clock." By the way, my own modest program of sleep reduction is now in its 10th day.

Many studies of human subjects have been conducted for the purpose of documenting the debilitating physiological effects of long-term wakefulness that are predicted by the recuperation theories of sleep. In view of the variety of physiological, motor, and cognitive tests that have been employed in these studies, their results have been remarkably consistent. Karadžić (1973), after reviewing the studies of the physiological effects of sleep deprivation (including studies of heart rate, respiration rate, blood pressure, skin conductance, body temperature, body weight, EMG, EEG, and evoked responses), reached the following conclusion: "There is little evidence that sleep deprivation, for periods even exceeding 200 hours, produces any marked physiological alterations" (p. 173), a conclusion later echoed by Horne (1983) and Martin (1986).

One might expect complex cognitive abilities to be particularly sensitive to disruption by sleep deprivation; however, this has not been found to be the case. Subjects deprived of sleep for one night displayed no deficits whatsoever on a battery of abstract reasoning, spatial relations, logical reasoning, and comprehension tests that were written under demanding time constraints (Percival, Horne, & Tilley, 1983).

However, the same cannot be said of passive, boring, easy tests of cognitive ability (see Meddis, 1977; Webb, 1968). The performance of such tests—particularly those requiring long periods of continuous attentiveness (e.g., see Brendel et al., 1990)—is particularly susceptible to disruption by sleep deprivation. For example, a reduction of the previous night's sleep by 3 or 4 hours is enough to produce deficits on a vigilance test that requires subjects to follow a moving light on a computer screen and to respond each time it flickers.

The fact that the performance of passive, boring, easy tasks is more susceptible to disruption by sleep deprivation than is the performance of active difficult tasks has led to the hypothesis that many of the behavioral deficits associated with sleep deprivation result from the subject's inability to stay awake; rather than from the hypothesized decline of function during wakefulness. After 2 or 3 days of sleep deprivation, it becomes very difficult for subjects to avoid microsleeps during the performance of passive tasks. **Microsleeps** are brief periods of sleep, typically about 2 or 3 seconds long, during which the eyelids droop and the subjects become less responsive to external stimuli, even though they remain sitting or even standing.

At first, the failure to observe substantial increases in sleep time following long periods of sleep deprivation was a major challenge to the theory that sleep serves a recuperative func-

tion. However, it is now clear that the brain compensates for sleep deprivation not by increasing the duration of subsequent sleeps but by increasing their efficiency. The evidence indicates that it is slow-wave sleep (SWS) in particular, rather than sleep in general, that serves the recuperative function and that the brain compensates for sleep deprivation by increasing the proportion and quality of SWS.

Following are the findings that support the theory that SWS, rather than sleep in general, serves a recuperative function: (1) Although subjects regain only a small proportion of their total lost sleep after a period of sleep deprivation, they regain most of their lost stage 4 sleep (e.g., Borbély et al., 1981; Horne, 1976). (2) Subjects who have reduced their usual sleep time get less stage 1 and stage 2 sleep, but the amount of their stage 3 and 4 sleep remains the same as before (Mullaney et al., 1977; Webb & Agnew, 1975). (3) Short sleepers normally get as much stage 3 and 4 sleep as long sleepers (e.g., Jones & Oswald, 1966; Webb & Agnew, 1970). (4) If subjects are asked to take an extra nap in the morning after a full night's sleep, it contains little stage 3 or 4 sleep, and it does not reduce the duration of the following night's sleep (e.g., Åkerstedt & Gillberg, 1981; Hume & Mills, 1977; Karacan et al., 1970). (5) After sleep deprivation, the SWS EEG of both humans (Borbély, 1981; Borbély et al., 1981) and rats (Mistlberger, Bergmann, & Rechtschaffen, 1987) is characterized by a higher proportion of slow waves.

Sleep-Deprivation Studies in Laboratory Animals

Studies using a **carousel apparatus** (see Figure 12.8) to deprive rats of sleep suggest that sleep deprivation may not be

Figure 12.8 The carousel apparatus. It is used to deprive an experimental rat of sleep while a yoked control rat is exposed to the same number and pattern of disk rotations. The disk on which both rats rest rotates every time the experimental rat has a sleep EEG. If the sleeping rat does not awaken immediately, it is deposited in the water. (Adapted from Rechtschaffen et al., 1983.)

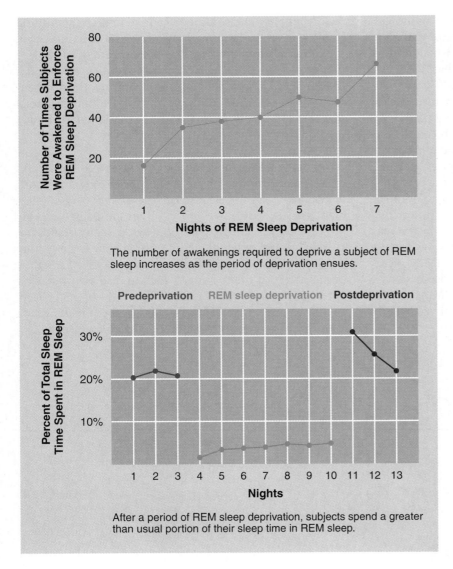

The number of awakenings required to deprive a subject of REM sleep increases as the period of deprivation ensues.

Predeprivation   REM sleep deprivation   **Postdeprivation**

After a period of REM sleep deprivation, subjects spend a greater than usual portion of their sleep time in REM sleep.

Figure 12.9 The two effects of REM-sleep deprivation.

plunged into water while sleeping kills the experimental rats not because it keeps them from sleeping but because it is stressful and physically damaging. This interpretation is consistent with the pathological symptoms that were revealed in the experimental rats by postmortem examination: swollen adrenal glands, collapsed lungs, fluid in the lungs, gastric ulcers, internal bleeding, skin lesions, scrotal damage, swollen limbs, and enlarged bladders.

REM-Sleep Deprivation

Because of its association with dreaming, REM sleep has been the subject of intensive investigation. In an effort to reveal the particular functions of REM sleep, sleep researchers have specifically deprived sleeping subjects of REM sleep by waking them up each time a bout of REM sleep begins.

REM-sleep deprivation has been shown to have two consistent effects (see Figure 12.9). First, with each successive night of deprivation, there is a greater tendency for subjects to initiate REM sequences. Thus, as REM-sleep deprivation proceeds, subjects have to be awakened more and more frequently to keep them from accumulating significant amounts of REM sleep. For example, during the first night of REM-sleep deprivation in one experiment (Webb & Agnew, 1967), the subjects had to be awakened 17 times to keep them from having extended periods of REM sleep; but during the seventh night of deprivation, they had to be awakened 67 times. Second, following REM-sleep deprivation, subjects have more than their usual amount of REM sleep for the first two or three nights (Brunner et al., 1990).

The compensatory increase in REM sleep following a period of REM-sleep deprivation suggests that the amount of REM sleep is regulated separately from the amount of slow-wave sleep, and it thus suggests that REM sleep serves a function different from that of slow-wave sleep. Numerous theories of the functions of REM sleep have been proposed (see Webb, 1973; Winson, 1993). Most of them fall into one of three categories: (1) those that hypothesize that

as inconsequential as the research on human subjects suggests. Two rats, an experimental rat and its yoked control, are placed in separate chambers of the apparatus. Each time the EEG activity of the experimental rat indicates that it is sleeping, the disk, which serves as the floor of half of both chambers, starts to slowly rotate. As a result, if the sleeping experimental rat does not awaken immediately, it gets shoved off the disk into a shallow pool of water. The yoked control is exposed to exactly the same pattern of disk rotations; but if it is not sleeping, it can easily avoid getting dunked by walking in the direction opposite to the direction of disk rotation. In one study using the carousel apparatus (Rechtschaffen et al., 1983), the experimental rats died after several days, while the yoked control animals stayed reasonably healthy.

The fact that human subjects have been sleep-deprived for similar periods of time without dire consequences argues for caution in interpreting the results of the carousel sleep-deprivation experiments. It may be that repeatedly being awakened by the moving platform or, worse yet, being

Microsleeps. Brief periods of sleep that occur in sleep-deprived subjects while they remain sitting or standing.

Carousel apparatus. An apparatus used to study the effects of sleep deprivation in laboratory rats.

REM sleep is necessary for the maintenance of an individual's mental health, (2) those that hypothesize that REM sleep is necessary for the maintenance of normal levels of motivation, and (3) those that hypothesize that REM sleep is necessary for the processing of memories.

However, none of these theories has emerged a clear winner. Early reports that REM-sleep deprivation produces a variety of personality and motivational problems (e.g., Dement, 1960) have not proved replicable, and more recent reports that REM-sleep deprivation produces memory deficits for certain kinds of material learned the preceding day (e.g., Karni et al., 1994), while promising, have yet to be adequately assessed. The main challenge faced by any theory of the function of REM sleep is to explain why **tricyclic antidepressant drugs** are not severely debilitating. Because tricyclic antidepressants selectively block REM sleep, patients who regularly take large doses (for depression or REM-sleep-related disorders) get little REM sleep for months at a time—and yet they experience no side effects that can be attributed to their REM-sleep loss.

In summary, the studies of compensatory responses to sleep deprivation have made two important points. First, the compensatory increase in the proportion of REM sleep following REM-sleep deprivation suggests that the amount of REM sleep is separately regulated. Second, the compensatory increase in the proportion of SWS following total sleep deprivation indicates that the regulation of SWS takes precedence over the regulation of REM sleep.

It is an appropriate point, here at the end of the section on sleep deprivation, for me to file a brief progress report. It has now been 2 weeks since I began my 5-hours-per-night sleep schedule. Generally, things are going well. My progress on this chapter has been faster than usual. I am not having any difficulty getting up on time or in getting my work done, but I am finding that it takes a major effort to stay awake in the evening. If I try to read or watch a bit of television after 10:30, I experience attacks of microsleep. Luckily for me, my so-called friends delight in making sure that my transgressions last no more than a few seconds.

12.6 Recuperation and Circadian Theories of Sleep Combined

If you began this chapter thinking of sleep as a recuperative process, as most people do, you were probably surprised to learn that sleep is closely regulated by circadian factors and that sleep deprivation has relatively few adverse effects. However, it is important not to overreact to this evidence. Although recuperative factors may be somewhat less important in controlling sleep than you first thought, and circadian factors somewhat more important, it is not necessarily an all-or-none issue; circadian and recuperation models are not mutually exclusive.

Borbély (1984) has proposed a model of sleep that integrates the effects of both circadian and sleep-deprivation factors. This two-process model is illustrated in Figure 12.10. The postulated circadian sleep-promoting factor is assumed to take the form of a sine wave with a minimum at about 4:00 P.M. and a maximum at about 4:00 A.M. The postulated sleep-promoting effects of wakefulness

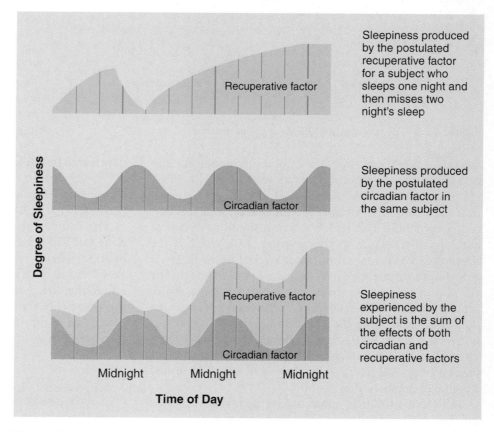

Figure 12.10 A model of how circadian factors and recuperative factors interact to determine the motivation to sleep. (Adapted from Borbély, 1984.)

Before you proceed to the next section of the chapter, complete the following exercise to consolidate what you have learned so far. The correct answers are provided at the bottom of this page. Before proceeding, review material related to your errors and omissions.

1. The three most commonly studied psychophysiological correlates of sleep are the EEG, EMG, and _____.

2. Stage 4 sleep EEG is characterized by a predominance of _____ waves.

3. _____ stage 1 EEG is accompanied by neither REM nor loss of core muscle tone.

4. Dreaming occurs during _____ sleep.

5. The modern alternative to Freud's theory of dreaming is Hobson's _____ theory.

6. Environmental cues that can entrain circadian rhythms are called _____, or time givers.

7. In contrast to the prediction of the recuperation models of sleep, when a subject stays awake longer than usual under free-running conditions, the following period of sleep tends to be _____

8. The most convincing evidence that REM-sleep deprivation is not debilitating comes from the study of patients taking _____.

9. After a lengthy period of sleep deprivation (e.g., several days) a subject's first night of sleep is only slightly longer than usual, but it contains a much higher proportion of _____ waves.

10. _____ sleep in particular, rather than sleep in general, appears to play the major recuperative role.

are illustrated for a subject who slept one night between 11:00 P.M. and 6:00 A.M. and then missed the next two nights' sleep. The bottom trace illustrates how the effects of the circadian and wakefulness factors hypothetically combine to influence this subject's sleepiness.

The answers are (1) EOG, (2) delta, (3) Initial, (4) REM, (5) activation-synthesis, (6) zeitgebers, (7) shorter, (8) tricyclic antidepressants, (9) slow (or delta), and (10) Slow-wave (or Stage 3 and 4).

Tricyclic antidepressant drugs. A class of drugs that are commonly prescribed for the treatment of depression and for some REM-sleep-related disorders because they selectively suppress REM sleep.

The first influential theory of the physiology of sleep was proposed by Bremer in 1936. He hypothesized that sleep is caused by a reduction of sensory input to the forebrain. To test his hypothesis, he severed the brain stems of cats between their *inferior colliculi* and *superior colliculi* in order to disconnect their forebrains from ascending sensory input (see Figure 12.11) This surgical preparation is called a **cerveau isolé preparation** (pronounced "ser-VOE ees-o-LAY"—literally "isolated forebrain"). As you might well imagine, cerveau isolé preparations are not too useful for the study of behavior because the subjects are paralyzed below the level of the transection, but the preparations can be used to assess neurophysiological responses of the forebrain in the absence of ascending influences.

In support of his hypothesis, Bremer found that the cortical EEG of the isolated cat forebrains was indicative of almost continuous slow-wave sleep. Only when strong visual or olfactory stimuli were presented (the cerveau isolé has intact visual and olfactory input) could the continuous high-amplitude, slow-wave activity be changed to a **desynchronized EEG**—a low-amplitude, high-frequency EEG. However, this arousing effect barely outlasted the stimuli. Bremer's theory is classed as a *passive theory of sleep* because it postulated no mechanism of active sleep regulation; it viewed sleep as a passive consequence of a decline in sensory input to the forebrain.

Reticular Activating System Theory of Sleep

Bremer's passive sensory theory of sleep regulation was gradually replaced by the theory that sleep is actively regulated by an arousal mechanism in the *reticular formation*. This hypothetical arousal mechanism was the **reticular activating system.** Three findings contributed to the wide acceptance of the reticular activating system theory of sleep (see Figure 12.11). The first finding came from a study of the **encéphale isolé preparation** (pronounced on-say-FELL ees-o-LAY)—an experimental preparation in which the brain is disconnected from the rest of the nervous system by a transection of the caudal brain stem. Despite cutting most of the same sensory fibers as the cerveau isolé transection, the encéphale isolé transection did not disrupt the normal cycle of sleep EEG and wakefulness EEG (Bremer, 1937). This suggested that a mechanism for maintaining wakefulness was located somewhere in the brain stem between the two transections. The second finding was that partial transections at the cerveau isolé level disrupted normal sleep-wake cycles of cortical EEG only when they severed the reticular activating system core of the brain stem; when the partial transections were restricted to more lateral areas, which contain the ascending sensory tracts, they had little

effect on the cortical EEG (Lindsey, Bowden, & Magoun, 1949). The third finding was that electrical stimulation of the reticular formation of sleeping cats awakened them and produced a lengthy period of EEG desynchronization (Moruzzi & Magoun, 1949). On the basis of these three early findings, Moruzzi and Magoun (1949) proposed that low levels of activity in the reticular formation produce sleep and that high levels produce wakefulness.

Three Important Discoveries about the Neural Basis of Sleep

The wave of research that was stimulated by the reticular activating system theory led to several discoveries. The following three are particularly important (see Steriade & Hobson, 1976).

Sleep is not a state of neural quiescence   Because the body is inactive during sleep, it had long been assumed that sleep is a state of general neural quiescence. Single-unit recording studies have revealed that this is not the case. Many neurons in the brain are less active during slow-wave sleep than they are during relaxed wakefulness, but the reduction in their firing rate rarely exceeds 10%—a far cry from the total inactivity that was initially assumed. Moreover, during REM sleep, many neurons are even more active than they are during relaxed wakefulness.

There are sleep-promoting circuits in the brain   The reticular activating system theory of sleep suggested that sleep is a consequence of low levels of activity in circuits whose primary role is the maintenance of wakefulness. This view was altered by the discovery that brain stimulation can induce sleep and that brain lesions can disrupt it. Both of these findings suggest that there are structures in the brain whose function is the promotion of sleep. One such sleep-promoting structure appears to be in the caudal

---

Cerveau isolé preparation. An experimental preparation in which the forebrain is disconnected from the rest of the brain by a midcollicular transection.

Desynchronized EEG. Low-amplitude, high-frequency EEG.

Reticular activating system. The hypothetical arousal system in the reticular formation.

Encéphale isolé preparation. An experimental preparation in which the brain is separated from the rest of the nervous system by a transection of the caudal brain stem.

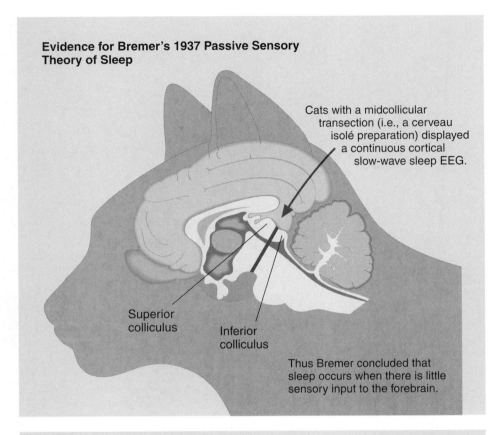

Evidence for Bremer's 1937 Passive Sensory Theory of Sleep

Cats with a midcollicular transection (i.e., a cerveau isolé preparation) displayed a continuous cortical slow-wave sleep EEG.

Superior colliculus

Inferior colliculus

Thus Bremer concluded that sleep occurs when there is little sensory input to the forebrain.

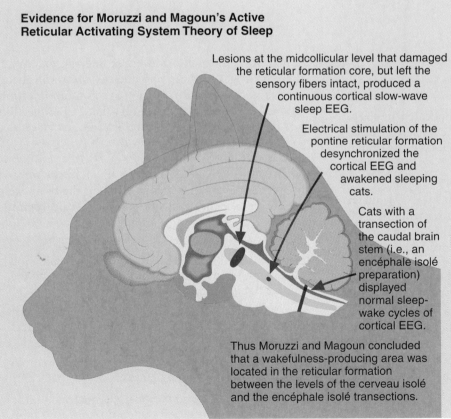

Evidence for Moruzzi and Magoun's Active Reticular Activating System Theory of Sleep

Lesions at the midcollicular level that damaged the reticular formation core, but left the sensory fibers intact, produced a continuous cortical slow-wave sleep EEG.

Electrical stimulation of the pontine reticular formation desynchronized the cortical EEG and awakened sleeping cats.

Cats with a transection of the caudal brain stem (i.e., an encéphale isolé preparation) displayed normal sleep-wake cycles of cortical EEG.

Thus Moruzzi and Magoun concluded that a wakefulness-producing area was located in the reticular formation between the levels of the cerveau isolé and the encéphale isolé transections.

Figure 12.11 Evidence for the sensory theory of sleep (a passive theory) and the reticular activating system theory (an active theory).

brain stem (i.e., in the pons and medulla). Anesthetizing (Magni et al., 1957) or cooling (Berlucchi et al., 1964) the caudal brain stem causes sleeping cats to awaken immediately.

The various correlates of sleep are dissociable Most neurophysiological theories of sleep have treated REM sleep and slow-wave sleep as if each were a unitary entity. However, evidence has accumulated that the physiological changes that go together to define REM sleep sometimes break apart and go their separate ways—and the same is true of the changes that define slow-wave sleep. For example, during REM-sleep deprivation, penile erections, which normally occur during REM sleep, begin to occur during slow-wave sleep. And during total sleep deprivation, slow waves, which normally occur only during slow-wave sleep, begin to occur during wakefulness. This suggests that REM sleep, slow-wave sleep, and wakefulness are not each controlled by a single mechanism; each state seems to result from the interaction of a variety of mechanisms that are capable under certain conditions of operating independently of one another.

The classic example of the dissociation between the behavioral and EEG indexes of slow-wave sleep is the study of Feldman and Waller (1962), who compared the effects of lesions to the cat midbrain reticular formation with those of lesions to the adjacent posterior hypothalamus. The hypothalamic lesions produced behavioral sleep that persisted even when the cats' desynchronized cortical EEG suggested that they were awake. In contrast, the midbrain reticular formation lesions produced a high-amplitude slow-wave cortical EEG that persisted even when the cats were fully alert (see Vanderwolf & Robinson, 1981).

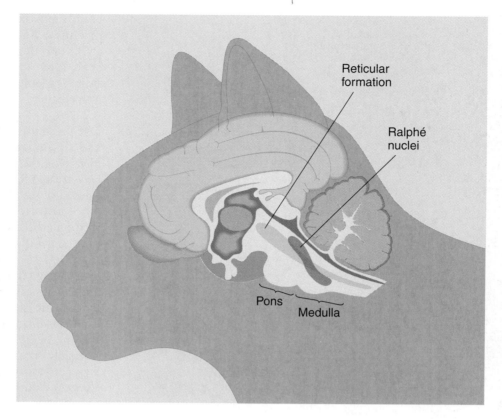

Figure 12.12 The location of the raphé nuclei in the caudal reticular formation.

Brain Areas That Have Been Implicated in Sleep and Dreaming

Several areas of the brain have been implicated in sleep. The following are three of them: the raphé nuclei, the basal forebrain region, and the REM-sleep circuits in the caudal reticular formation.

Raphé nuclei The **raphé** (pronounced "ra-FAY") **nuclei** are a cluster of serotonin-producing nuclei running in a thin strip down the midline of the caudal reticular formation (see Figure 12.12). Lesions that destroyed 80 to 90% of the raphé nuclei in cats produced complete insomnia for 3 or 4 days, and then there was a partial recovery that never exceeded more than 2.5 hours of sleep per day, all slow-wave sleep (Jouvet & Renault, 1966). Cats normally sleep about 14 hours per day, which is why they are favored as subjects in sleep experiments.

The theory that the raphé nuclei promote sleep received support from the observation that an injection of **parachlorophenylalanine (PCPA)**—a chemical that temporarily blocks the synthesis of serotonin—produced temporary insomnia in cats (Mouret, Bobillier, & Jouvet, 1968). However, when PCPA was injected every day, both REM sleep and slow-wave sleep eventually recovered to 80% of their normal levels despite the fact that serotonin levels

remained low (Dement, Mitler, & Henriksen, 1972). Further challenges to the raphé nucleus–serotonin theory of sleep came from the discovery that serotonin injections do not induce sleep and the discovery that PCPA injections do not disrupt sleep in species other than cats (see Vanderwolf, 1988).

Basal forebrain region Although much of the research on the physiology of sleep has focused on the brain stem, there is some evidence that the **basal forebrain region**—

Raphé nuclei. A cluster of serotonin-producing nuclei running in a thin strip down the midline of the caudal reticular formation.

Parachlorophenylalanine (PCPA). A chemical that blocks the synthesis of serotonin and produces insomnia in cats.

Basal forebrain region. The area of the forebrain just in front of the hypothalamus.

Locus coeruleus. A noradrenergic nucleus of the caudal reticular formation that is thought to inhibit REM sleep.

Dorsal raphé nuclei. Serotonergic nuclei of the dorsal raphé, which are thought to inhibit REM sleep.

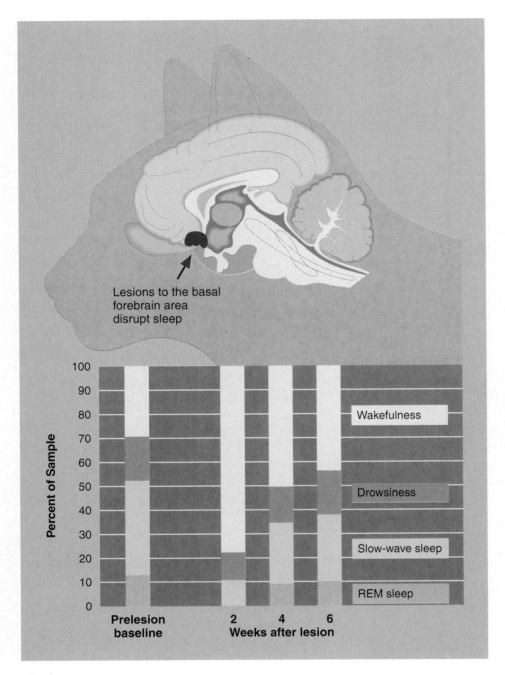

Figure 12.13 The effects of basal forebrain lesions on the sleep of cats. (Adapted from McGinty & Sterman, 1968.)

site is responsible for controlling one of the major indexes of REM sleep (Siegel, 1983; Vertes, 1983) —a site for the reduction of core muscle tone, a site for EEG desynchronization, and a site for rapid eye movements, and so on. The approximate location in the caudal brain stem of each of these putative REM-sleep centers is illustrated in Figure 12.14 on page 316.

The coordinated activation of the REM-sleep centers is controlled by cholinergic mechanisms in the pontine portion of the caudal reticular formation. Microinjections of cholinergic agonists into this site elicit immediate and prolonged REM sleep in cats (Qualtrochi et al., 1989). In sleeping human subjects, the intravenous infusion of cholinergic agonists increases REM sleep, and the intravenous infusion of cholinergic antagonists decreases REM sleep (Sitaram, Moore, & Gillin, 1978).

In contrast, neurons in two areas of the caudal reticular formation seem to play a role in inhibiting REM sleep: the *noradrenergic neurons* of the **locus coeruleus** (Lydic, McCarley, & Hobson, 1983) and the *serotonergic neurons* of the **dorsal raphé nuclei** (Trulson & Jacobs, 1979). Neurons in both areas are active during slow-wave sleep but are almost totally quiescent during REM sleep. This finding has contributed to the view (see Hobson, 1989) that the recurring cycle of REM sleep is controlled in the caudal reticular formation by a reciprocal interaction between excitatory cholinergic neurons and inhibitory noradrenergic and serotonergic neurons.

the area of the forebrain just in front of the hypothalamus—is also involved. As Figure 12.13 shows, bilateral lesions of this area in cats produce a substantial reduction of daily sleep time that is maximal 2 weeks after the lesion and recovers somewhat thereafter (McGinty & Sterman, 1968). However, LoPiccolo (1977) found no indication that basal forebrain stimulation promotes sleep in cats.

Caudal reticular formation REM-sleep circuits
REM sleep appears to be controlled from a variety of sites scattered throughout the caudal reticular formation. Each

In summary, we now understand that the cycles of REM sleep are controlled by interactions among circuits in the caudal reticular formation. However, our understanding of the circuits that cause us to fall asleep is less developed. The theory that sleep results from a general decrease in reticular activating system activity is out of step with the current knowledge of the intricacy and specificity of reticular formation circuits, and support for hypothetical basal forebrain and raphé sleep mechanisms has been inconsistent.

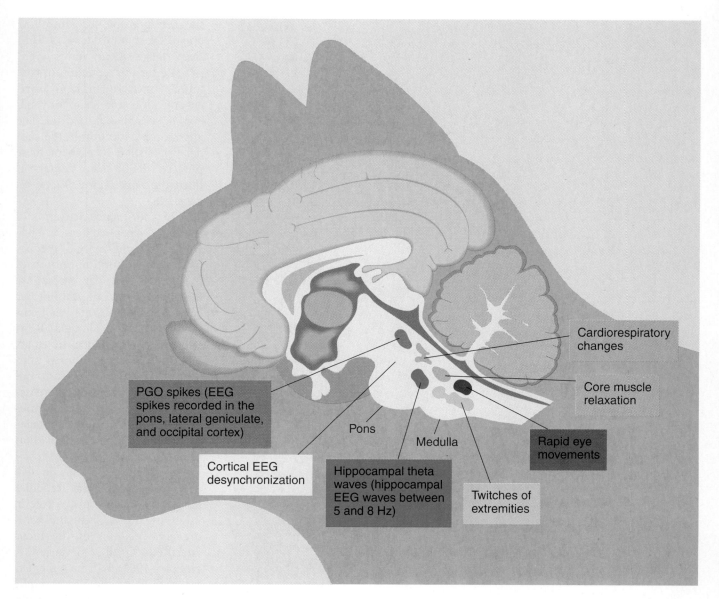

Figure 12.14 A sagittal section of the brain stem of the cat illustrating the areas that control the various physiological indexes of REM sleep. (Adapted from Vertes, 1983.)

Image labels:
- PGO spikes (EEG spikes recorded in the pons, lateral geniculate, and occipital cortex)
- Cortical EEG desynchronization
- Pons
- Hippocampal theta waves (hippocampal EEG waves between 5 and 8 Hz)
- Medulla
- Twitches of extremities
- Rapid eye movements
- Core muscle relaxation
- Cardiorespiratory changes

12.8   The Circadian Clock: Neural Mechanisms

The fact that circadian sleep-wake cycles persist in the absence of circadian signals from the environment indicates that the physiological systems that regulate sleep are controlled by an internal timing mechanism—the **circadian clock.** Where is this timing mechanism?

Location of the Circadian Clock in the Suprachiasmatic Nuclei

The first breakthrough in the search for the circadian clock was Richter's 1967 discovery that large medial hypothala-

mic lesions disrupt circadian cycles of eating, drinking, and activity in rats. Next, in the early 1970s, the **suprachiasmatic nuclei (SCN)** were identified as the specific medial hypothalamic structures that controlled circadian cycles of adrenal hormone release (Moore & Eichler, 1972), drinking, and activity (Stephan & Zucker, 1972). By the late 1970s, the SCN had been shown to control all kinds of circadian rhythms, including the sleep-wake cycle (Ibuka, Inouye, & Kawamura, 1977; Rusak, 1979; Rusak & Zucker, 1979).

Most of the early studies of the SCN were demonstrations that bilateral SCN lesions abolish various circadian cycles, even in the presence of a circadian light-dark cycle. For example, although SCN lesions do not reduce the amount of time mammals spend sleeping (e.g., Coindet, Chouvet, & Mouret, 1975; Stephan & Nunez, 1977), they do abolish its circadian periodicity.

Further support for the conclusion that the suprachiasmatic nuclei contain a circadian timing mechanism comes from the observation that the nuclei display circadian cycles of electrical, metabolic, and biochemical activity (e.g., Moore, 1982)—and that they do so even when they have been surgically isolated from the rest of the brain by circular knife cuts (Groos & Hendricks, 1982; Inouye & Kawamura, 1982). Figure 12.15 shows that the suprachiasmatic nuclei of rats take up less radioactive 2-deoxyglucose during the night than they do during the day, when the rats normally sleep (Schwartz & Gainer, 1977). Also, electrical stimulation of the SCN has been shown to produce phase shifts in free-running rhythms (Rusak & Groos, 1982; Zatz & Herkenham, 1981).

If there was any lingering doubt about the location of the circadian clock, it was eliminated by the brilliant experiment of Ralph and his colleagues (1990). They removed the SCN from the fetuses of a strain of mutant hamsters that had an abnormally short (20-hour) free-running sleep-wake cycle. Then, they transplanted these SCN into normal adult hamsters whose free-running sleep-wake cycles of 25 hours had been abolished by SCN lesions. These transplants restored free-running sleep-wake cycles in the recipients; but, remarkably, the cycles were about 20 hours long rather than the original 25 hours. Transplants in the other direction—that is, from normal hamster fetuses to SCN-lesioned adult mutants— had the complementary effect: They restored free-running sleep-wake cycles that were about 25 hours long rather than the original 20 hours.

Although the suprachiasmatic nuclei are unquestionably the major circadian clocks, they are not the only ones. Evidence for this conclusion comes from two sources. First, under certain conditions, bilateral SCN lesions have been shown to leave some circadian rhythms unaffected while abolishing others (e.g., Boulos & Terman, 1980). Second, bilateral SCN lesions do not eliminate the ability of all environmental stimuli to entrain circadian rhythms; for example, in hamsters, SCN lesions block entrainment by light but not by food or water availability (Abe & Rusak, 1992; Mistlberger, 1993; Stephan, 1992a, 1992b).

We still do not understand how the neural circuits of the SCN are capable of generating accurate circadian signals (see Aréchiga, 1993). However, it has been assumed that

Figure 12.15 Autoradiographs illustrating the increased uptake of radioactive 2-deoxyglucose by the rat SCN during the day. (From Schwartz & Gainer, *Science, 197* (1977): pages 1089–1091. Copyright 1977 by the AAAS.)

this ability must in some way result from the interactions among individual neurons. This assumption has been challenged by the discovery that individual neurons separated from the eye of a mollusk and kept alive in tissue culture maintained their circadian rhythm of neural activity (Michel et al., 1993). This discovery suggests that circadian timing may be mediated by molecular mechanisms within individual neurons rather than by interactions among neurons.

Genetics of Circadian Rhythms

Per, a gene that controls circadian rhythms in fruit flies, was located in the early 1970s (see Takahashi, 1992); but research on the genetics of circadian rhythms in mammals has progressed more slowly. The first breakthrough in the study of the genetics of mammalian circadian rhythms was the discovery in 1988 that a mutation in a single gene called *tau* shortened the circadian cycle of hamsters (Ralph & Menaker, 1988). However, very little progress has been made in the location and characterization of tau, because there is so little background information about the hamster genome.

The recent discovery of a mouse mutation with a longer-than-normal free-running circadian activity rhythm

Circadian clock. An internal timing mechanism that is capable of maintaining daily cycles of physiological change, even when there are no temporal cues from the environment.

Suprachiasmatic nuclei (SCN). Nuclei of the hypothalamus that control the circadian cycles of various body functions.

has created much excitement (Vitaterna et al., 1994) because mice are the favorite mammalian subjects of genetic research. The general location of this mutated mouse gene, which is called *clock* (for "circadian locomotor output cycles kaput"), has already been discovered; and there is good reason to believe that it will soon be cloned and its base sequence determined. There is always great excitement about the imminent possibility of cloning a mammalian gene that influences a complex behavioral attribute (see Kyriacou, 1994).

Mechanisms of Entrainment

How does the 24-hour light-dark cycle entrain the sleep-wake cycle and other circadian rhythms? To answer this question, researchers began at the obvious starting point: the eyes. They tried to identify and track the specific neurons that left the eyes and carried the information about light and dark that entrained the biological clock. Cutting the *optic nerves* before they reached the *optic chiasm* eliminated the ability of the light-dark cycle to entrain circadian rhythms; however, when the *optic tracts* were cut at the point where they left the optic chiasm, the ability of the light-dark cycle to entrain circadian rhythms was unaffected. As Figure 12.16 illustrates, these two findings indicated that visual axons critical for the entrainment of circadian rhythms branch off from the optic nerve in the vicinity of the optic chiasm. This finding led to the discovery of the *retinohypothalamic tracts,* which leave the optic chiasm and project to the adjacent suprachiasmatic nuclei (Hendrickson, Wagoner, & Cowan, 1972; Moore & Lenn, 1972).

The nature of the molecular mechanism by which activity in the retinohypothalamic tracts influences circadian

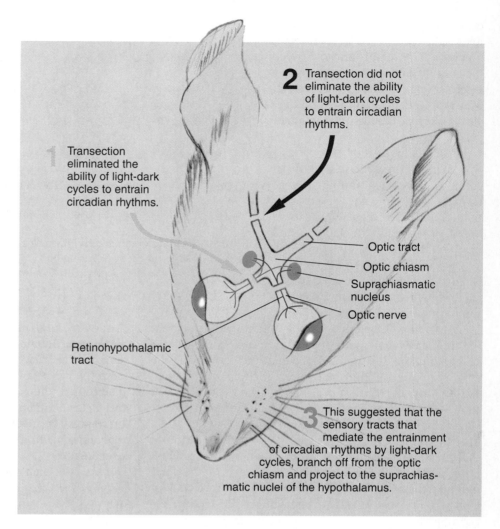

Figure 12.16 The discovery of the retinohypothalamic tracts. Neurons from each retina project to both suprachiasmatic nuclei.

rhythms was revealed by Rusak and his colleagues (1990). They studied the mechanism by which 30 minutes of intense artificial light during the night initiates a phase advance in the circadian sleep-wake cycles of rats and hamsters. They found that exposure of their subjects to light at times that induced phase advances triggered the immediate and transient expression of a gene called *c-fos* in the SCN. *C-fos* controls the production of *fos* protein, which in turn regulates the expression of other genes. This finding suggests that activation of the retinohypothalamic tracts influences circadian rhythms by controlling gene expression in the SCN (see also Ginty et al., 1993).

Most drugs that influence sleep fall into two different classes: hypnotic and antihypnotic. **Hypnotic drugs** are drugs that increase sleep; **antihypnotic drugs** are drugs that reduce sleep.

Hypnotic Drugs

The **benzodiazepines** (e.g., Valium and Librium) were developed and tested for the treatment of anxiety, yet they are the most commonly prescribed hypnotic medications. In the short term, they increase drowsiness, decrease the time it takes to fall asleep, reduce the number of awakenings during a night's sleep, and increase total sleep time. Thus they can be effective in the treatment of occasional difficulties in sleeping.

Although benzodiazepines can be effective therapeutic hypnotic agents in the short term, their prescription for the treatment of chronic sleep difficulties is ill-advised. Still, they are commonly prescribed for this purpose—primarily by general practitioners. Following are four complications associated with the chronic use of benzodiazepines as hypnotic agents: First, tolerance develops to the hypnotic effects of benzodiazepines; thus patients must take larger and larger doses to maintain their efficacy. Second, cessation of benzodiazepine therapy after chronic use causes *insomnia* (sleeplessness), which can exacerbate the very problem that the benzodiazepines were intended to correct. Third, chronic benzodiazepine use is addictive. Fourth, benzodiazepines distort the normal pattern of sleep: They increase the duration of sleep by increasing the duration of stage 2 sleep, but they actually decrease the duration of stage 4 and REM sleep.

Evidence that the raphé nuclei play a role in sleep suggested that serotonergic drugs might be effective hypnotics.

Efforts to demonstrate the hypnotic effects of such drugs have focused on **5-hydroxytryptophan (5-HTP)**—the precursor of serotonin—because 5-HTP, but not serotonin, readily passes through the blood-brain barrier. Injections of 5-HTP reverse the insomnia produced in cats (Pujol et al., 1971) and rats (Laguzzi & Adrien, 1980) by the serotonin antagonist, PCPA. However, they are of no therapeutic benefit in the treatment of human insomnia (see Borbély, 1983).

Antihypnotic Drugs

There are two main classes of antihypnotic drugs: *stimulants* (e.g., cocaine and amphetamine) and *tricyclic antidepressants*. Both stimulants and antidepressants increase the activity of catecholamines (norepinephrine, epinephrine, and dopamine) either by increasing their release, by blocking their reuptake from the synapse, or by both mechanisms. From the perspective of the treatment of sleep disorders, the most important property of antihypnotic drugs is that they act preferentially on REM sleep. They can totally suppress REM sleep even at doses that have little effect on total sleep time.

Using stimulant drugs to treat chronic excessive sleepiness is a risky proposition. Most are highly addictive, and they produce a variety of adverse side effects, such as loss of appetite. Moreover, unless stimulants are taken at just the right doses and at just the right times, there is a danger that they will interfere with normal sleep.

Endogenous Sleep Factors

There has been a revival of the old idea that sleep is caused by the buildup of sleep-inducing chemicals in the body. Chemicals that have been hypothesized to function as sleep inducers are referred to as **endogenous sleep factors.**

Delta sleep-inducing peptide (DSIP) is one putative endogenous sleep factor. Its effects were first demonstrated using a **parabiotic preparation**—a preparation in which two subjects share one physiological system. Monnier et al. (1975) connected the circulatory systems of two rabbits and found that when the thalamus of one was stimulated at a frequency that elicited cortical slow waves, both rabbits tended to fall asleep. This suggested that a sleep factor in the blood of the stimulated rabbit was affecting both rabbits. DSIP was subsequently isolated from the blood of stimulated rabbits, its structure characterized, and methods for synthesizing it developed.

Although DSIP has been shown to promote sleep in several experiments (e.g., Scherschlicht, 1983; Schneider-Hel-

Hypnotic drugs.　Sleep-promoting drugs.

Antihypnotic drugs.　Sleep-reducing drugs.

Benzodiazepines.　A class of anxiolytic drugs that are often prescribed as sleeping pills.

5-hydroxytryptophan (5-HTP).　The precursor of serotonin.

Endogenous sleep factors.　Hypothetical sleep-inducing chemicals produced in the body.

Delta sleep-inducing peptide.　A hypothetical endogenous sleep factor.

Parabiotic preparation.　A physiological preparation in which two subjects share one physiological system.

mert, 1985; Shoenenberger & Graf, 1985), its role in sleep induction is still not widely accepted (see Graf & Kastin, 1984), primarily for two reasons. One is that demonstrations of the sleep-promoting effects of DSIP have been unsystematic and inconsistent. The other is that DSIP produces a variety of physiological effects (e.g., hyperthermia), which raises the possibility that sleep might be a secondary consequence of one of DSIP's other effects.

12.10 Sleep Disorders

Many sleep disorders fall into one of two complementary categories: insomnia and hypersomnia. **Insomnia** includes all disorders of initiating and maintaining sleep, whereas **hypersomnia** includes disorders of excessive sleep or sleepiness. A third major class of sleep disorders includes all those disorders that are specifically related to REM sleep dysfunction.

In various surveys, approximately 30% of the respondents report significant sleep-related problems. However, it is important to recognize that complaints of sleep problems often come from people whose sleep appears normal in laboratory sleep tests. For example, many people who complain of insomnia actually sleep a reasonable amount (e.g., 6 hours a night), but they believe that they should sleep more (e.g., 8 hours a night). As a result, they spend more time in bed than they should and have difficulty getting to sleep. Often, the anxiety associated with their inability to sleep makes it even more difficult for them to sleep. Such patients can often be helped by counseling that convinces them to go to bed only when they are very sleepy (see Anch et al., 1988). Others with disturbed sleep face more serious problems.

Insomnia

Many cases of insomnia are **iatrogenic**—physician created. Paradoxically, sleeping pills (e.g., benzodiazepines) prescribed by well-intentioned physicians are a major cause of insomnia. At first, hypnotic drugs are effective in increasing sleep, but soon the patient is trapped in a rising spiral of drug use, as *tolerance* to the drug develops and progressively more drug is required to produce its original hypnotic effect. Soon, the patient cannot stop taking the drug without running the risk of experiencing *withdrawal symptoms,* which include insomnia. The following case study illustrates this problem:

> Mr. B. was studying for a civil service exam, the outcome of which would affect his entire future. He was terribly worried about the test and found it difficult to get to sleep at night. Feeling that the sleep loss was affecting his ability to study, he consulted his physician for the express purpose of getting "something to make me sleep." His doctor prescribed a moderate dose of barbiturate at bedtime, and Mr. B. found that this medication was very effective ... for the first several nights. After about a week, he began having trouble sleeping again and decided to take two sleeping pills each night. Twice more the cycle was repeated, until on the night before the exam he was taking four times as many pills as his doctor had prescribed. The next night, with the pressure off, Mr. B. took no medication. He had tremendous difficulty falling asleep, and when he did, his sleep was terribly disrupted.... Mr. B. now decided that he had a serious case of insomnia, and returned to his sleeping pill habit. By the time he consulted our clinic several years later, he was taking approximately 1,000 mg sodium amytal every night, and his sleep was more disturbed than ever.... Patients may go on for years and years—from one sleeping pill to another—never realizing that their troubles are caused by the pills. (Dement, 1978, p. 80)[4]

Sleep apnea is another common cause of insomnia. In sleep apnea, the patient temporarily stops breathing many times each night. Each time, the patient awakens, begins to breathe again, and drifts back to sleep. Sleep apnea usually leads to a sense of having slept poorly, and is thus often diagnosed as insomnia. However, some patients are totally unaware of their multiple awakenings and instead complain of excessive sleepiness during the day, which leads to a diagnosis of *hypersomnia.*

Sleep apnea disorders are thought to be of two types: (1) those resulting from obstruction of the respiratory passages by muscle spasms or *atonia* (lack of muscle tone), and (2) those resulting from the failure of the central nervous system to stimulate respiration. Obstructive apnea is most common in overweight people; the prevalence of CNS apnea increases with age (see Mendelson, 1987).

Two other causes of insomnia—nocturnal myoclonus and restless legs—both involve the legs. **Nocturnal myoclonus** is a periodic twitching of the body during sleep, primarily a periodic twitching of the legs. Most patients suffering from this disorder are unaware of the nature of their problem, and they generally complain of poor sleep and daytime sleepiness. In contrast, people with **restless legs** are all too aware of their problem. They complain of a hard-to-describe tension or uneasiness in their legs that keeps them from falling asleep. Benzodiazepines are often prescribed in cases of nocturnal myoclonus and restless legs because of their hypnotic, *anxiolytic* (antianxiety),

---

[4]From *Some Must Watch while Some Must Sleep* by William E. Dement, published by Portable Stanford Books, Stanford Alumni Association, Stanford University. Reprinted by permission.

muscle relaxant, and anticonvulsant properties; however, they are rarely effective.

In one study, insomniacs claimed to take an average of 1 hour to fall asleep and to sleep an average of only 4.5 hours per night; but when they were tested in a sleep laboratory, they were found to have an average sleep latency of only 15 minutes and an average nightly sleep duration of 6.5 hours. It used to be common medical practice to assume that people who claimed to suffer from insomnia but slept more than 6.5 hours per night were neurotic. However, this practice stopped when some of those diagnosed as neurotic *pseudoinsomniacs* were subsequently found to be suffering from sleep apnea, nocturnal myoclonus, or other sleep-disturbing problems. Insomnia is not necessarily a problem of too little sleep; it is often a problem of too little undisturbed sleep.

Hypersomnia

Complaints of hypersomnia are often the consequence of an unrecognized sleep disturbance or of a boring lifestyle. An exception is the hypersomnia associated with narcolepsy. **Narcolepsy** is a characterized by repeated, brief (10-to-15-minute) daytime sleep attacks. Narcoleptics typically sleep only about an hour per day more than average; it is the inappropriateness of their sleep episodes that defines their condition. Most of us occasionally fall asleep on the beach, in front of the television, or in the most *soporific* (sleep-promoting) of all daytime sleep sites: the large, dimly lit lecture hall. But narcoleptics fall asleep in the middle of a conversation, while eating, while making love, or even while scuba diving. Narcolepsy is treated with stimulants, taken in the morning.

REM-Sleep-Related Disorders

As well as being a disorder of hypersomnia, narcolepsy is classed as a *REM-sleep-related disorder*. The fact that narcoleptics, unlike normal people, go directly into REM sleep when they fall asleep (Rechtschaffen et al., 1963) has led to the view that narcolepsy is a disorder in which REM-sleep phenomena encroach on wakefulness.

Cataplexy, another REM-sleep-related disorder, is often associated with narcolepsy. Cataplexy is characterized by recurring losses of muscle tone during wakefulness, often triggered by emotional experiences. In its mild form, it may simply require that the patient sit down for a few seconds until it passes. It its extreme form, the patient drops to the ground as if shot and remains there for a minute or two, fully conscious. An attack of cataplexy occurs when the lack of core muscle tone, which normally accompanies REM sleep, occurs during wakefulness.

Research on the mechanisms of cataplexy has focused on the cells of the caudal reticular formation that control muscle relaxation during REM sleep: the cells of the **nucleus magnocellularis.** Recently, Siegel et al. (1991) recorded the activity of these cells in dogs that experienced cataplectic attacks when they became excited. Of the cells of the caudal reticular formation that were active during REM sleep, only those of the nucleus magnocellularis were also active during cataplectic attacks. This suggests that cataplectic attacks result from the encroachment of REM-related atonia into wakefulness.

Because both narcolepsy and cataplexy are disorders of REM sleep, they are often treated with *tricyclic antidepressants.* As mentioned previously, tricyclic antidepressants suppress REM sleep.

Occasionally, patients are discovered who have little or no REM sleep. Although this disorder is rare, it is important because of its theoretical implications. Lavie et al. (1984) described a patient who had suffered a brain injury that presumably involved damage to the REM-sleep generator in the pontine reticular formation. The most important finding of this case study was that the patient did not appear to be adversely affected by his lack of REM sleep. After receiving his injury, he completed high school, college, and law school and now has a thriving law practice.

Some patients experience REM sleep without core muscle atonia. It has been suggested that the function of REM-sleep atonia is to prevent the acting out of dreams. This theory receives support from case studies of people who suffer from this disorder:

> I was a halfback playing football, and after the quarterback received the ball from the center he lateraled it sideways to me and I'm supposed to go around end and cut back over tackle and—this is very vivid—as I cut back over tackle

Insomnia. Disorders of initiating and maintaining sleep.

Hypersomnia. Disorders characterized by excessive sleep or sleepiness.

Iatrogenic. Physician-created.

Sleep apnea. A condition in which sleep is repeatedly disturbed by momentary interruptions in breathing.

Nocturnal myoclonus. Periodic sleep-disrupting twitching of the legs during sleep.

Restless legs. Tension or uneasiness in the legs that keeps people from falling asleep.

Narcolepsy. A disorder of hypersomnia characterized by repeated, brief daytime sleep attacks.

Cataplexy. A disorder that is characterized by sudden losses of muscle tone during wakefulness and is often seen in cases of narcolepsy.

Nucleus magnocellularis. The nucleus of the caudal reticular formation that promotes relaxation of the core muscles during REM sleep and during cataplectic attacks.

there is this big 280-pound tackle waiting, so I, according to football rules, was to give him my shoulder and bounce him out of the way.... [W]hen I came to I was standing in front of our dresser and I had [gotten up out of bed and run and] knocked lamps, mirrors and everything off the dresser, hit my head against the wall and my knee against the dresser. (Schenck et al., 1986, p. 294).

Presumably, REM sleep without atonia is caused by damage to the nucleus magnocellularis or to an interruption of its output. Supporting this hypothesis is the fact that lesions of the caudal reticular formation often induce a similar disorder in cats:

To a naive observer, the cat, which is standing, looks awake since it may attack unknown enemies, play with an absent mouse, or display flight behavior. There are orienting movements of the head or eyes toward imaginary stimuli, although the animal does not respond to visual or auditory stimuli. These extraordinary episodes ... are a good argument that "dreaming" occurs during REM sleep in the cat. (Jouvet, 1972, pp. 236–237).

Have you ever experienced a period of paralysis or a vivid dreamlike state just as you are falling asleep or waking up? Many people have. These experiences are called **sleep paralysis** and **hypnogogic hallucinations,** respectively. Both are thought to result from the encroachment of REM-sleep phenomena into wakefulness, and both are common in cases of narcolepsy.

12.11 The Effects of Sleep Reduction

I began this chapter 4 weeks ago with both zeal and trepidation. I was fascinated by the idea that I could wring 2 or 3 extra hours of living out of each day by sleeping less, and I hoped that adhering to a sleep-reduction program while writing about sleep would create an enthusiasm for the subject that would color my writing and be passed on to you. On the other hand, I was more than a little concerned about the negative effect that losing 3 hours of sleep per night might have on me.

The research on sleep reduction suggests that my sleep-reduction objective was reasonable. There have been only two systematic studies of long-term sleep reduction. In one (Webb & Agnew, 1974), a group of 16 subjects slept for only 5.5 hours per night for 60 days, with only one detectable deficit on an extensive battery of mood, medical, and performance tests: a slight deficit on a test of auditory vigilance.

In the other systematic study of long-term sleep reduction (Friedman et al., 1977; Mullaney et al., 1977), 8 subjects reduced their nightly sleep by 30 minutes every 2 weeks until they reached 6.5 hours per night, then by 30 minutes every 3 weeks until they reached 5 hours, and then by 30 minutes every 4 weeks thereafter. After a subject indicated a lack of desire to reduce sleep further, the person slept for 1 month at the shortest duration of nightly sleep that was achieved, then for 2 months at the shortest duration plus 30 minutes. Finally, each subject slept each night for 1 year for however long the person preferred. The minimum duration of nightly sleep achieved during this experiment was 5.5 hours for 2 subjects, 5.0 hours for 4 subjects, and an impressive 4.5 hours for 2 subjects. In each of the subjects, a reduction in sleep time was associated with an increase in sleep efficiency: a decrease in the amount of time it took the subjects to fall asleep after going to bed, a decrease in the number of nighttime awakenings, and an increase in the proportion of stage 4 sleep. After the subjects had reduced their sleep to 6 hours per night, they began to experience daytime sleepiness, and this became a problem as sleep time was further reduced. Nevertheless, there were no deficits on any of the mood, medical, or performance tests given to the subjects throughout the experiment. The most encouraging result was that during a follow-up 1 year later, all subjects were sleeping less than they had previously—between 7 and 18 hours less each week—with no excessive sleepiness.

Rather than using the gradual stepwise reduction method of Friedman and his colleagues, I jumped into my 5-hours-per-night sleep schedule with both feet. This proved to be less difficult than you might think. I took advantage of a trip to the East Coast from my home on the West Coast to reset my circadian clock. While I was in the East, I got up at 7:00 A.M., which is 4:00 A.M. on the West Coast, and I just kept on the same schedule when I got home. I decided to add my extra waking hours to the beginning of my day rather than to the end so there would be no temptation for me to waste them; there are not too many distractions around this university at 5:00 A.M.

Figure 12.17 is a record of my sleep times for the 4-week period that it took me to write a first draft of this chapter. I didn't quite meet my goal of sleeping less than 5 hours every night, but I didn't miss by much: My overall mean was 5.05 hours per night. Notice that in the last week, there

Sleep paralysis. A sleep disorder characterized by attacks of paralysis just as a person is falling asleep.

Hypnogogic hallucinations. Vivid dreamlike states that some people occasionally experience just as they are falling asleep.

Figure 12.17 Sleep record of JPJP during a 4-week sleep-reduction program.

was a tendency for my circadian clock to run a bit slow; I began sleeping in until 4:30 A.M. and staying up until 11:30 P.M.

What were the positives and negatives of my experience? The main positive was the time to do things that it created: Having an extra 21 hours per week was wonderful. Furthermore, because my daily routine was out of synchrony with everybody else's, I spent little time sitting in rush-hour traffic. The only negative of the experience was sleepiness. It was no problem during the day, when I was active.

However, staying awake during the last hour before I went to bed—an hour during which I usually engaged in sedentary activities, such as reading—was at times a problem. This is when I became personally familiar with the phenomenon of microsleep, and it was then that I required some assistance in order to stay awake. Going to bed and falling asleep each night became a fleeting but satisfying experience.

I began this chapter with the question: How much sleep do we need? Then, I gave you my best professorial it-could-be-this, it-could-be-that answer. However, that was a month ago. Now, after experiencing sleep reduction firsthand, I am less inclined toward wishy-washiness on the topic of sleep. Two lines of evidence suggest that most people need about 5.5 hours of sleep per night. First, most committed subjects who are active during the day can reduce their sleep to about 5.5 hours per night without great difficulty or adverse consequences. Second, the quality of a night's sleep declines precipitously after the first 5.5 hours; there is little slow-wave sleep after this point (see Figure 12.3).

Why, then, do most of us sleep 8 to 10 hours each night? The reason may be that, as a positive incentive, sleep ranks up there with the big three motivated behaviors of Chapters 10 and 11. When food, drink, and sex are freely available, most of us partake of more than is required for survival, or even for optimal health. It seems that the same is true of sleep.

CONCLUSION

This chapter has introduced you to the fundamentals of sleep, dreaming, and circadian rhythms. It began by describing the physiological and behavioral correlates of sleep (12.1), with an emphasis on REM sleep and dreaming (12.2). Then, the next four sections introduced you to the recuperation and circadian theories of sleep (12.3); to two different lines of research that have a bearing on these theories—circadian sleep-cycle research (12.4) and sleep-deprivation research (12.5); and to a model of sleep that combines both recuperation and circadian factors (12.6). Following discussion of the recuperation and circadian theories, the chapter discussed the neural mechanisms of sleep (12.7), the neural mechanisms of the circadian clock (12.8), hypnotic and antihypnotic drugs (12.9), and sleep disorders (12.10). Finally, the chapter ended with a discussion of research on sleep reduction and its personal implications (12.11).

FOOD FOR THOUGHT

1. Do you think that your life could be improved by changing when or how long you sleep each day? In what ways? What negative effects do you think such changes might have on you?

2. Some people like to stay up late, some people like to get up early, others like to do both, and still others like to do neither. Design a sleep-reduction program that is tailored to your own biology and lifestyle and that is consistent with the research literature on circadian cycles and sleep deprivation. The program should produce the greatest benefits for you with the least discomfort.

3. How has reading about sleep research changed your views about sleep? Give three specific examples.

4. Given the evidence that the long-term use of benzodiazepines actually contributes to the problems of insomnia, why are they so commonly prescribed for its treatment?

KEY TERMS

Electroencephalogram (EEG) (p. 297)
Electrooculogram (EOG) (p. 297)
Electromyogram (EMG) (p. 297)
First-night phenomenon (p. 297)
Alpha waves (p. 297)
K complexes (p. 297)
Sleep spindles (p. 297)
Delta waves (p. 297)
Initial stage 1 EEG (p. 297)
Emergent stage 1 EEG (p. 297)
Paradoxical sleep (p. 298)
Delta sleep (p. 298)
REM sleep (p. 298)
Slow-wave sleep (SWS) (p. 298)

Somnambulism (p. 300)
Activation-synthesis theory (p. 300)
Lucid dreams (p. 300)
Circadian rhythms (p. 302)
Zeitgebers (p. 302)
Free-running rhythms (p. 303)
Free-running period (p. 303)
Internal desynchronization (p. 303)
Jet lag (p. 304)
Microsleeps (p. 306)
Carousel apparatus (p. 306)
Tricyclic antidepressant drugs (p. 308)
Cerveau isolé preparation (p. 310)
Desynchronized EEG (p. 310)

Reticular activating system (p. 310)
Encéphale isolé preparation (p. 310)
Raphé nuclei (p. 312)
Parachlorophenylalanine (PCPA) (p. 312)
Basal forebrain region (p. 312)
Locus coeruleus (p. 313)
Dorsal raphé nucleus (p. 313)
Circadian clock (p. 314)
Suprachiasmatic nuclei (SCN) (p. 314)
Hypnotic drugs (p. 317)
Antihypnotic drugs (p. 317)
Benzodiazepines (p. 317)
5-hydroxytryptophan (5-HTP) (p. 317)

Endogenous sleep factors (p. 317)
Delta sleep-inducing peptide (p. 317)
Parabiotic preparation (p. 317)
Insomnia (p. 318)
Hypersomnia (p. 318)
Iatrogenic (p. 318)
Sleep apnea (p. 318)
Nocturnal myoclonus (p. 318)
Restless legs (p. 318)
Narcolepsy (p. 319)
Cataplexy (p. 319)
Nucleus magnocellularis (p. 319)
Sleep paralysis (p. 320)
Hypnogogic hallucinations (p. 320)

ADDITIONAL READING

There are several classic introductions to the topic of sleep; the following four are my favorites:

Dement, W. C. (1978). *Some must watch while some must sleep.* New York: Norton.

Hartmann, E. L. (1973). *The functions of sleep.* Westford, MA: Murray Printing.

Hobson, J. A. (1989). *Sleep.* New York: Scientific American Library.

Meddis, R. (1977). *The sleep instinct.* London: Henley and Boston.

Drug Addiction and Reward Circuits in the Brain

13.1 Basic Principles of Drug Action

13.2 Role of Learning in Drug Tolerance and Drug Withdrawal Effects

13.3 Five Commonly Abused Drugs

13.4 Biopsychological Theories of Addiction

13.5 Reward Circuits in the Brain

13.6 Neural Mechanisms of Addiction

Drug addiction is a serious problem in most parts of the world. For example, in the United States alone, about 60 million people are addicted to nicotine, alcohol, or both; 5.5 million are addicted to illegal drugs; and many millions more are addicted to prescription drugs (see Holloway, 1991). Pause for a moment and think about the shear magnitude of the grief represented by such figures, and think about what they may mean for you personally. The incidence of drug addiction is so high that it is almost certain that you, or somebody dear to you, will be adversely affected by drugs at some point in your life. Perhaps this has happened already.

This chapter introduces you to some basic pharmacological principles and concepts; it compares the effects of five common addictive drugs; and it reviews recent research on the neural mechanisms of addiction. You likely already have strong views about drug addiction; thus, as you progress through this chapter, it is particularly important that you do not let your thinking be clouded by preconception. In particular, it is important that you do not fall into the trap of assuming that a drug's legal status has much to say about its safety. You will be less likely to assume that legal drugs are safe and illegal drugs are dangerous if you remember that most laws governing drug abuse in various parts of the world were enacted in the last century or in the early part of this one, long before there was any scientific research on the topic (see Musto, 1991).

People's tendency to equate drug legality with drug safety was recently illustrated to me in a particularly ironic fashion: I was invited to address a convention of high school teachers on the topic of drug abuse. When I arrived at the convention center to give my talk, I was escorted to a special suite, where I was encouraged to join the executive committee in a round of drug taking—the drug being a special high-proof single-malt whiskey. Later, the irony of the situation had its full impact. As I stepped to the podium under the influence of a psychoactive drug (the whiskey), I looked out through the haze of cigarette smoke at an audience of educators who had invited me to speak to them because they were concerned about the unhealthy impact of drugs on their students. The welcoming applause gradually gave way to the melodic tinkling of ice cubes in liquor glasses, and I began. They did not like what I had to say.

13.1 Basic Principles of Drug Action

This section focuses on the basic principles of drug action, with an emphasis on **psychoactive drugs**—drugs that influence subjective experience and behavior by acting on the nervous system.

Drug Administration and Absorption

Drugs are usually administered in one of four ways: by oral ingestion, by injection, by inhalation, or by absorption through the mucous membranes of the nose, mouth, or rectum. The route of administration influences the rate at which and the degree to which the drug reaches its sites of action.

Ingestion The oral route is the preferred route of administration for many drugs. Once they are swallowed, drugs dissolve in the fluids of the stomach and are carried to the intestine, where they are absorbed into the bloodstream. However, some drugs readily pass through the stomach wall (e.g., alcohol), and these take effect sooner because they do not have to reach the intestine to be absorbed. Drugs that are not readily absorbed from the digestive tract or that are broken down into inactive metabolites before they can be absorbed must be taken by some other route.

The two main advantages of the oral route of administration over other routes are its ease and relative safety. Its main disadvantage is its unpredictability: Absorption from the digestive tract into the bloodstream can be greatly influenced by such difficult-to-gauge factors as the amount and type of food in the stomach.

Injection Drug injection is common in medical practice because the effects of injected drugs are large, rapid, and predictable. Drug injections are typically made **subcutaneously (SC)**—into the fatty tissue just beneath the skin, **intramuscularly (IM)**—into the large muscles, or **intravenously (IV)**—directly into veins at points where they run just beneath the skin. Many addicts prefer the intravenous route because the bloodstream delivers the drug directly to the brain. However, the speed and directness of the intravenous route are mixed blessings; after an intravenous injection, there is little or no opportunity to counteract the effects of an overdose, an impurity, or an allergic reaction. Furthermore, many addicts develop scar tissue, infections, and collapsed veins at the few sites on their bodies where there are large accessible veins (see Figure 13.1).

Inhalation Some drugs can be absorbed into the bloodstream through the rich network of capillaries in the lungs. Many anesthetics are commonly administered by *inhalation,* as are tobacco and marijuana. The two main shortcomings of this route are that it is difficult to precisely regulate the dose of inhaled drugs, and many chronically inhaled substances damage the lungs.

Absorption through mucous membranes Some drugs can be administered through the mucous membranes of the nose, mouth, and rectum. Cocaine, for example, is commonly self-administered through the nasal membranes (snorted)—but not without damaging them.

Penetration of the Central Nervous System by Drugs

Once a drug enters the bloodstream, it is carried in the blood to the blood vessels of the central nervous system. Fortunately, a protective filter, the *blood-brain barrier,* makes it difficult for many potentially dangerous bloodborne chemicals to pass from the blood vessels of the CNS into the CNS per se.

Mechanisms of Drug Action

Psychoactive drugs influence the nervous system in many ways (see Koob & Bloom, 1988). Some of these drugs (e.g., alcohol and many of the general anesthetics) act diffusely on neural membranes throughout the CNS. Others act in a less general way: by binding to particular synaptic receptors; by influencing the synthesis, transport, release, or deactivation of particular neurotransmitters; or by influencing the chain of chemical reactions elicited in postsynaptic neurons by the activation of their synaptic receptors (see Chapter 4). Accordingly, some drugs are much more selective in their actions than others.

Drug Metabolism and Elimination

The actions of most drugs are terminated when enzymes that are synthesized by the liver stimulate their conversion to nonactive forms—a process referred to as **drug metabo-**

Figure 13.1 Scar tissue associated with chronic intravenous drug use. Many addicts who administer their drugs intravenously develop scar tissue, infections, and collapsed veins at the few sites where large veins course near the body surface.

lism. In most cases, drug metabolism eliminates a drug's ability to pass through lipid membranes so that it can no longer penetrate the blood-brain barrier. In addition, small amounts of some psychoactive drugs pass from the body in urine, sweat, feces, breath, and mother's milk before they can be metabolized.

Drug Tolerance

Drug tolerance is a state of decreased sensitivity to a drug that develops as a result of exposure to it. Drug tolerance can be demonstrated in two ways: by showing that a given dose of the drug has less effect than it had before drug exposure or by showing that it takes more of the drug to produce the same effect. In essence, what this means is that tolerance is a shift in the *dose-response curve* (a graph of the magnitude of the effect of different doses of the drug) to the right (see Figure 13.2 on page 326).

There are three important points to remember about the specificity of drug tolerance. The first is that exposure to one drug can produce tolerance to other drugs that act by the same mechanism; this is known as **cross tolerance.** The second is that tolerance often develops to some effects of a drug but not to others. Failure to understand this second point can have tragic consequences for people who think that because they have become tolerant to some effects of a drug (e.g., to the nauseating effects of alcohol or tobacco), they are tolerant to all of them. In fact, tolerance may develop to some effects of a drug while the sensitivity

Psychoactive drugs. Drugs that influence subjective experience and behavior by acting on the nervous system.

Subcutaneously (SC). Under the skin.

Intramuscularly (IM). Into a muscle.

Intravenously (IV). Into a vein.

Drug metabolism. The conversion of a drug from its active form to a nonactive form.

Drug tolerance. A state of decreased susceptibility to a drug that develops as a result of exposure to the drug.

Cross tolerance. Tolerance that develops to the effects of one drug as the result of exposure to another drug.

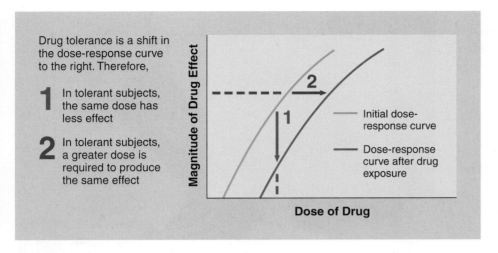

Drug tolerance is a shift in the dose-response curve to the right. Therefore,

1 In tolerant subjects, the same dose has less effect

2 In tolerant subjects, a greater dose is required to produce the same effect

Initial dose-response curve

Dose-response curve after drug exposure

Dose of Drug

Figure 13.2 Drug tolerance: A shift in the dose-response curve to the right as a result of exposure to the drug.

to other effects increases; the increases in sensitivity are called **sensitization** (Robinson, 1991). The third is that drug tolerance is not a unitary phenomenon; that is, there is no single mechanism that underlies all examples of it. When a drug is administered at active doses, many kinds of adaptive changes can occur to reduce the effect of the drug. Two categories of changes underlie drug tolerance: metabolic and functional. Drug tolerance that results from changes that reduce the amount of drug getting to its sites of action is called **metabolic tolerance.** Drug tolerance that results from changes that reduce the reactivity of the sites of action to the drug is called **functional tolerance.** Tolerance to psychoactive drugs is largely functional.

Functional tolerance to psychoactive drugs can result from several different types of neural changes. For example, exposure to a psychoactive drug can reduce the number of receptors for it, decrease the efficiency with which it binds to existing receptors, or diminish the impact of receptor binding on the activity of the cell.

Drug Withdrawal Effects and Physical Dependence

After significant amounts of a drug have been in the body for a period of time (e.g., several days), its sudden elimination can trigger an illness called a **withdrawal syndrome.** The effects of drug withdrawal are virtually always opposite to the effects of

the drug. For example, the withdrawal of anticonvulsant drugs often triggers convulsions, and the withdrawal of sleeping pills often produces insomnia. Individuals who suffer withdrawal reactions when they stop taking a drug are said to be **physically dependent** on that drug.

The fact that withdrawal effects are almost always opposite to the initial effects of the drug suggests that withdrawal effects may be produced by the same neural changes that produce drug tolerance (see Figure 13.3). According to this theory, exposure to a drug produces compensatory changes in the nervous system that offset the drug's effects and produce tolerance. Then, when the drug is eliminated from the body, these compensatory

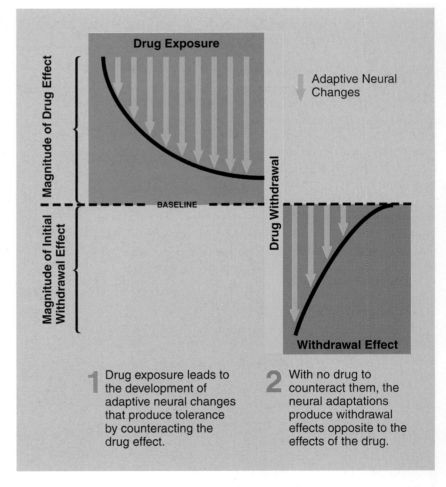

1 Drug exposure leads to the development of adaptive neural changes that produce tolerance by counteracting the drug effect.

2 With no drug to counteract them, the neural adaptations produce withdrawal effects opposite to the effects of the drug.

Figure 13.3 The relation between drug tolerance and withdrawal effects. The same adaptive neurophysiological changes that develop in response to drug exposure and produce drug tolerance manifest themselves as withdrawal effects once the drug is removed. As the neurophysiological changes develop, tolerance increases; and as they subside, the severity of the withdrawal effects decreases.

neural changes, without the drug to offset them, manifest themselves as withdrawal symptoms opposite to the initial effects of the drug.

The severity of withdrawal symptoms depends on the particular drug in question, on the duration and degree of the preceding drug exposure, and on the speed with which the drug is eliminated from the body. In general, longer exposure to greater doses followed by more rapid elimination produces greater withdrawal effects.

Addiction: What Is It?

Addicts are habitual drug users, but not all habitual drug users are addicts. **Addicts** are those habitual drug users who continue to use a drug despite its adverse effects on their health and social life and despite their repeated efforts to stop using it.

The greatest confusion about the nature of addiction concerns its relation to physical dependence. Many people equate the two: They see addicts as people who are trapped on a merry-go-round of drug taking, withdrawal symptoms, and further drug taking to combat the withdrawal symptoms. Although appealing in its simplicity, this conception of drug addiction is wrong. Addicts sometimes take drugs to prevent or alleviate withdrawal symptoms, but this is rarely the primary motivating factor in their addiction. If it were, addicts could be easily cured by hospitalizing them for a few days, until their withdrawal symptoms subsided. However, most addicts renew their drug taking even after months of enforced abstinence. This is an important issue; we will return to it later in the chapter.

When physical dependence was believed to be the major cause of addiction, the term *psychological dependence* was coined to refer to exceptions to this general rule. **Psychological dependence** was said to be the cause of any compulsive drug taking that occurred in the absence of physical dependence. However, now that it is clear that physical dependence is not the major motivating factor in addiction, there is little need for a special category of psychological dependence.

13.2   Role of Learning in Drug Tolerance and Drug Withdrawal Effects

An important line of psychopharmacologic research has shown that learning plays a major role in both drug tolerance and drug withdrawal. This research has contributed substantially to our understanding of tolerance and withdrawal, but its impact has been more far-reaching: It has emphasized that efforts to understand the effects of psychoactive drugs without considering the experience and behavior of the subjects will provide only partial answers.

Research on the role of learning in drug tolerance has focused on three phenomena: contingent drug tolerance, conditioned drug tolerance, and conditioned withdrawal effects. These phenomena are discussed in the following subsections.

Contingent Drug Tolerance

Contingent drug tolerance refers to demonstrations that tolerance develops only to drug effects that are actually experienced (see Carlton & Wolgin, 1971). Most studies of contingent drug tolerance employ the **before-and-after design** (Chen, 1968). In before-and-after experiments, two groups of subjects receive the same series of drug injections and the same series of tests, but the subjects in one group receive the drug before each test and those in the other group receive the drug after each test. At the end of the experiment, all subjects receive the same dose of the drug followed by a test so that the degree to which the drug disrupts test performance in the two groups can be compared.

My colleagues and I (Pinel, Mana, & Kim, 1989) used the before-and-after design to study contingent tolerance to the anticonvulsant effect of alcohol. In our study, two

Sensitization. An increase in the sensitivity to a drug effect that develops as the result of exposure to the drug.

Metabolic tolerance. Tolerance that results from a reduction in the amount of a drug getting to its sites of action.

Functional tolerance. Tolerance resulting from a reduction in the reactivity of the nervous system to a drug.

Withdrawal syndrome. The illness brought on by the elimination from the body of a drug on which the person is physically dependent.

Physically dependent. Being in a state from which the discontinuation of drug taking will induce withdrawal effects.

Addicts. Habitual drug users who continue to use a drug despite the adverse effects of the drug on their health and life and despite their repeated efforts to stop using it.

Psychological dependence. Compulsive drug taking that occurs in the absence of physical dependence.

Contingent drug tolerance. Drug tolerance that develops as a reaction to the experience of the effects of drugs rather than to drug exposure alone.

Before-and-after design. The experimental design used to demonstrate contingent drug tolerance in which the experimental group receives the drug before each of a series of behavioral tests and the control group receives the drug after each test.

groups of rats received exactly the same regimen of alcohol injections: one injection every 2 days for the duration of the experiment. During the tolerance development phase, the rats in one group received each alcohol injection 1 hour before a mild convulsive brain stimulation so that the anticonvulsant effect of the alcohol could be experienced on each trial. The rats in the other group received their injections 1 hour after each convulsive stimulation so that the anticonvulsant effect could not be experienced. At the end of the experiment, all of the subjects received a test injection of alcohol, followed 1 hour later by a convulsive stimulation so that the amount of tolerance to the anticonvulsant effect of alcohol could be compared in the two groups. As Figure 13.4 illustrates, the rats that received alcohol on each trial before a convulsive stimulation became almost totally tolerant to alcohol's anticonvulsant effect, whereas those that received the same injections and stimulations in the reverse order developed no tolerance whatsoever to alcohol's anticonvulsant effect.

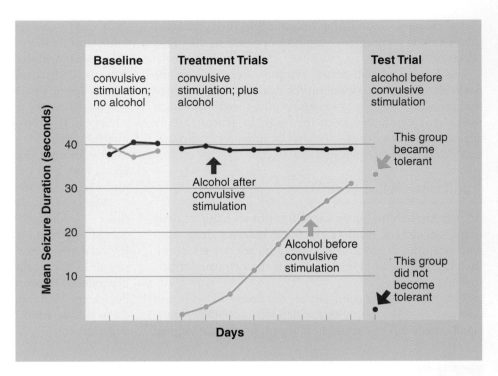

Figure 13.4 Contingent tolerance to the anticonvulsant effect of alcohol. The rats that received alcohol on each trial before a convulsive stimulation became tolerant to its anticonvulsant effect; those that received the same injections after a convulsive stimulation on each trial did not become tolerant. (Adapted from Pinel, Mana, & Kim, 1989.)

Contingent tolerance has been demonstrated for many drug effects: For example, tolerance to the disruptive effects of alcohol on the sexual behavior of male rats was greater in rats that engaged in sexual behavior after each alcohol injection (Pinel, Pfaus, & Christensen, 1991), tolerance to the anorexic effect of cholecystokinin on food consumption was greater in rats that ate after each cholecystokinin injection (Goodison & Siegel, 1995), and the disruptive effects of alcohol on maze running was greater in rats that ran the maze after each alcohol injection (Chen, 1968).

Contingent tolerance must be a very basic phenomenon indeed because it can be demonstrated even at the level of the synapse. Traynor, Schlapfer, and Barondes (1980) found that tolerance to the disruptive effect of alcohol on synaptic transmission in the abdominal ganglion of a marine snail (*Aplysia*) did not occur unless the synapse was activated during the period of alcohol exposure.

There are several different theories of contingent drug tolerance. Among them are the reinforcement-density theory, the homeostatic theory, and the drug-effect theory. The *reinforcement-density theory* (see Wolgin, 1989) is that psychoactive drugs reduce the number of reinforcements animals receive by disrupting their behavior and that the few reinforcements they do manage to obtain when they perform the disrupted behavior under the influence of the drug gradually shape behavioral changes that counteract the initial disruption. In contrast, the *homeostatic theory* (Poulos & Cappell, 1991) is that psychoactive drugs disrupt the body's homeostasis and that the experience of these disruptions initiates adaptive changes that tend to restore homeostasis by counteracting the initial drug effect. These two theories account admirably for the development of tolerance to reinforcement-reducing or homeostasis-disturbing drug effects, but they account less well for the development of tolerance to other kinds of drug effects.

The *drug-effect theory* (Pinel, Kim, & Mana, 1990) is a more general theory. According to this theory, functional drug tolerance, like all forms of neural adaptation, is triggered by the experience of disruptions of normal patterns of neural activity, whether or not the disruptions are associated with reductions of reinforcement or disruptions of homeostasis. According to this theory, tolerance develops to the drug effects that are experienced, and no tolerance develops to drug effects that are not experienced.

Conditioned Drug Tolerance

Whereas studies of contingent drug tolerance focus on what subjects do while they are under the influence of drugs, studies of conditioned drug tolerance focus on the situations in which drugs are taken. **Conditioned drug tolerance** refers to demonstrations that tolerance effects are

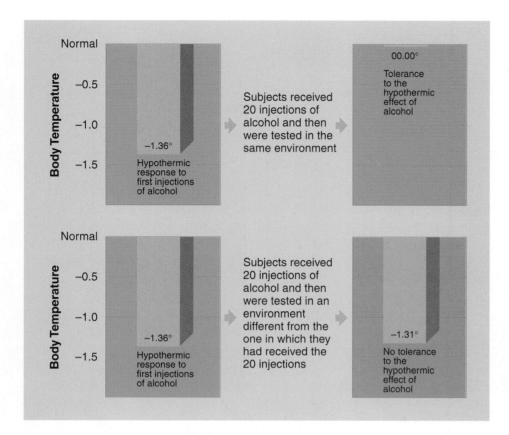

Figure 13.5 The situational specificity of tolerance to the hypothermic effects of alcohol. (Adapted from Crowell et al., 1981.)

maximally expressed only when a drug is administered in the same situation in which it has previously been administered. For example, in one demonstration of conditioned drug tolerance (Crowell, Hinson, & Siegel, 1981), two groups of rats received 20 alcohol and 20 saline injections in an alternating sequence, 1 injection every other day. The only difference between the two groups was that the rats in one group received all 20 alcohol injections in a distinctive test room and the 20 saline injections in their colony room, while the rats in the other group received the alcohol in the colony room and the saline in the distinctive test room. At the end of the injection period, the tolerance of all rats to the **hypothermic** (temperature-reducing) effects of alcohol was assessed in both environments. As Figure 13.5 illustrates, tolerance was observed only when the rats were injected in the environment that had previously been paired with alcohol administration. This *situational specificity of drug tolerance* has been demonstrated in many other experiments involving a variety of drugs (e.g., Lê, Poulos, & Cappell, 1979; Mansfield & Cunningham, 1980; Siegel, 1978).

The numerous demonstrations of the situational specificity of drug tolerance led Siegel and his colleagues to propose that addicts may be particularly susceptible to the lethal effects of a drug *overdose* when the drug is administered in a new context. Their hypothesis is that addicts become tolerant when they repeatedly self-administer their drug in the same environment and, as a result, begin taking larger and larger doses to counteract the diminution of drug effects. Then, if the addict administers the usual massive dose in an unusual situation, tolerance effects are not present to counteract the effects of the drug and there is a greater risk of death from overdose. In support of this hypothesis, Siegel and colleagues (1982) found that 96% of a group of heroin-tolerant rats died following a high dose of heroin administered in a novel environment, but only 64% died following the same dose administered in their usual injection environment. Heroin kills by suppressing respiration.

Of the several noteworthy theories that have been proposed to account for the situational specificity of drug tolerance (see Baker & Tiffany, 1985; Eikelboom & Stewart, 1982; Paletta & Wagner, 1986), Siegel's theory has been the most influential. Siegel views each incidence of drug administration as a Pavlovian conditioning trial in which various environmental stimuli that regularly predict the administration of the drug (e.g., pubs, washrooms, needles, other addicts) are conditional stimuli and the drug effects are unconditional stimuli. The central assumption of the theory is that conditional stimuli that predict drug administration come to elicit conditional responses opposite to the unconditional effects of the drug. Siegel has termed these hypothetical opposing conditional responses **conditioned compensatory responses.** The theory is that as the stimuli that repeatedly predict the effects of a drug come to elicit greater and greater conditioned compensatory responses, they increasingly counteract the unconditional effects of the drug and produce situationally specific tolerance.

Conditioned drug tolerance. Tolerance effects that are maximally expressed only when the drug is administered in situations in which it has previously been administered.

Hypothermic. Temperature-reducing.

Conditioned compensatory responses. Physiological responses opposite to the effects of a drug that are elicited by stimuli that are regularly associated with experiencing the drug effects.

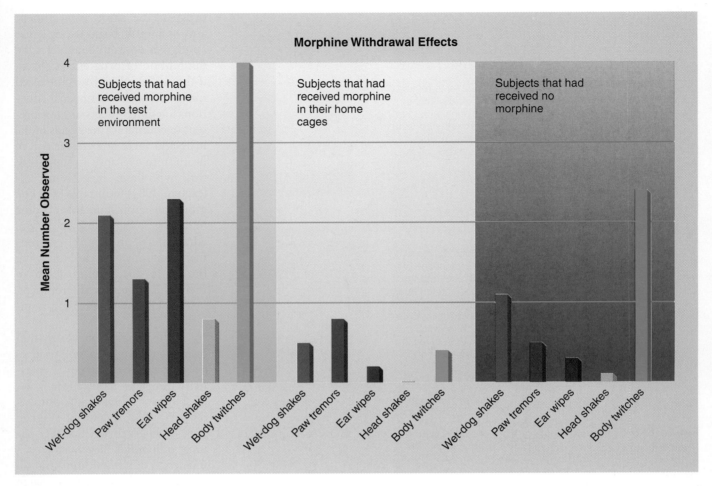

Figure 13.6 Conditioned morphine withdrawal effects in rats. Being placed in an environment in which they had previously experienced the effects of morphine elicited morphine withdrawal effects in rats. (Adapted from Krank & Perkins, 1993.)

Conditioned Withdrawal Effects

As you have just learned, Siegel's conditioned compensatory response theory suggests that when a drug is repeatedly administered in the same environment, that environment begins to elicit responses that counteract the drug effects and lead to the development of tolerance. One prediction of this theory is that in the absence of the drug, the drug environment should elicit effects opposite to the original effects of the drug. Withdrawal effects that are elicited by the drug environment or by other drug-associated cues are **conditioned withdrawal effects**.

There have been many demonstrations of conditioned withdrawal effects. For example, Krank and Perkins (1993) administered two injections each day to three groups of rats. One group of rats received a morphine injection each day in a distinctive test environment and a saline injection in their home cages; another group received saline injections in the test environment and morphine injections in their home cages; and the third group received saline injections in both the test environment and their home cages.

After 10 injection days (i.e., after 20 injections), the rats were placed undrugged in the distinctive test environment and morphine withdrawal reactions were assessed. The

Conditioned withdrawal effects. Withdrawal effects that are elicited by the drug environment or by other drug-associated cues.

Nicotine. The major psychoactive ingredient of tobacco.

Smoker's syndrome. The chest pain, labored breathing, wheezing, coughing, and heightened susceptibility to infections of the respiratory tract commonly observed in tobacco smokers.

Buerger's disease. A nicotine-produced disease in which blood flow to the legs is restricted, the ultimate result being gangrene and amputation.

Free radicals. Chemicals with one or more unpaired electrons.

results are illustrated in Figure 13.6. The rats that had received their morphine injections in the distinctive test environment displayed substantially more morphine withdrawal symptoms than did the rats that had received their morphine injections in their home cages and the rats that had received only saline injections.

13.3 Five Commonly Abused Drugs

This section is about five commonly abused drugs: tobacco, alcohol, marijuana, cocaine, and the opiates.

Tobacco

Next to caffeine, tobacco is the most widely used psychoactive drug in our society. When a cigarette is smoked, **nicotine**—the major psychoactive ingredient of tobacco—and some 4,000 other chemicals, collectively referred to as *tar*, are absorbed through the lungs. Because considerable tolerance develops to some of the immediate adverse effects of tobacco, the effects of smoking a cigarette on nonsmokers and smokers can be quite different. Nonsmokers often respond to a few puffs of a cigarette with various combinations of nausea, vomiting, coughing, sweating, abdominal cramps, dizziness, flushing, and diarrhea. In contrast, smokers report that they are more relaxed, more alert, and less hungry after a cigarette.

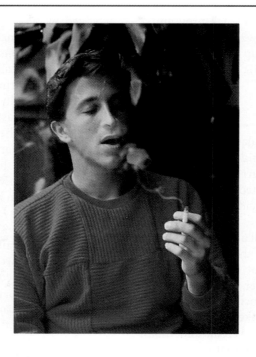

There is no question that heavy smokers are drug addicts in every sense of the word (Jones, 1987). The compulsive drug craving, which is the major defining feature of addiction, is readily apparent in any heavy smoker who has run out of cigarettes or who is forced by circumstance to refrain from smoking for several hours. Furthermore, heavy smokers who stop smoking experience a variety of withdrawal effects, such as depression, anxiety, restlessness, irritability, constipation, and difficulties in sleeping and concentrating. About 70% of all people who experiment with smoking become addicted—this figure compares unfavorably with 10% for alcohol and 30% for heroin. Moreover, only about 20% of all attempts to stop smoking are successful for 2 years or more (Schelling, 1992).

The consequences of long-term tobacco use are alarming. **Smoker's syndrome** is characterized by chest pain, labored breathing, wheezing, coughing, and a heightened susceptibility to infections of the respiratory tract. Chronic smokers are highly susceptible to a variety of potentially lethal lung disorders, including pneumonia, *bronchitis* (chronic inflammation of the bronchioles of the lungs), *emphysema* (loss of elasticity of the lung from chronic irritation), and lung cancer. Although the increased risk of lung cancer receives the greatest publicity, smoking also increases the risk of cancer of the larynx (voice box), mouth, esophagus, kidneys, pancreas, bladder, and stomach. Smokers also run a greater risk of developing a variety of cardiovascular diseases, which may culminate in heart attack or stroke. According to the Surgeon General of the United States, about 400,000 Americans die each year from smoking-related disorders (Schelling, 1992).

Sufferers from Buerger's disease provide a shocking illustration of the addictive power of nicotine. **Buerger's disease** is a condition in which the blood vessels, especially those supplying the legs, are constricted whenever nicotine enters the bloodstream:

If a patient with this condition continues to smoke, gangrene may eventually set in. First a few toes may have to be amputated, then the foot at the ankle, then the leg at the knee, and ultimately at the hip. Somewhere along this gruesome progression gangrene may also attack the other leg. Patients are strongly advised that if they will only stop smoking, it is virtually certain that the otherwise inexorable march of gangrene up the legs will be curbed. Yet surgeons report that it is not at all uncommon to find a patient with Buerger's disease vigorously puffing away in his hospital bed following a second or third amputation operation. (Brecher, 1972, pp. 215–216)

The adverse effects of tobacco smoke are unfortunately not restricted to those who smoke. There is now strong evidence that individuals who live or work with smokers are more likely to develop heart disease and cancer than those who don't. Even the unborn are vulnerable: Smoking during pregnancy increases the likelihood of miscarriage, stillbirth, and early death of the child. The levels of nicotine in the blood of breast-fed infants are often as great as those in the blood of the mother.

Because there are many active ingredients in tobacco, its mechanism of action has been difficult to identify. One current hypothesis is that free radicals are the culprits in many tobacco-related disorders. **Free radicals** are chemicals with one or more unpaired electrons; they are particularly dangerous because they can break down many biological molecules, including DNA, by *oxidation* (the removal of hydrogen atoms from a compound). Indeed, the urine of smokers has been shown to contain elevated levels of a by-product of DNA oxidation (Fischer-Nielson, Loft, & Gjervig, 1993). This raises the possibility that some of the adverse effects of smoking might be negated by *antioxidants* (compounds that block oxidation, such as vitamin C and beta-carotene). In one study, a 14-week program of beta-carotene supplements reduced by 30% the fragments of faulty genetic material coughed up by smokers (van Poppel, Spanhaak, & Ockhuizen, 1993).

Alcohol

Approximately two-thirds of the population of the United States consume alcoholic beverages, and of these about 15 million are addicted. Alcohol is currently involved in roughly 3% of all deaths in the United States, including deaths from birth defects, ill health, accidents, and violence (see Hunt, 1993).

Because alcohol molecules are small and soluble in both fat and water, they invade all parts of the body. Alcohol is classified as a **depressant** because at moderate-to-high doses it depresses neural firing; however, at low doses it can stimulate neural firing and facilitate social interaction.

At moderate doses, the alcohol drinker experiences various degrees of cognitive, perceptual, verbal, and motor impairment, as well as a loss of control that can lead to a variety of socially unacceptable actions. High doses result in unconsciousness; and if blood levels reach 0.5%, there is a risk of death from respiratory depression. The telltale red facial flush of alcohol intoxication is produced by the dilation of blood vessels in the skin; this dilation increases the amount of heat that is lost from the blood to the air and leads to a decrease in body temperature (hypothermia). Alcohol is also a **diuretic;** that is, it increases the production of urine by the kidneys.

Alcohol, like many addictive drugs, produces both tolerance and physical dependence. The livers of heavy drinkers

metabolize alcohol more quickly than do the livers of non-drinkers, but this increase in metabolic efficiency contributes only slightly to overall alcohol tolerance; most alcohol tolerance is functional. Alcohol withdrawal often produces a mild syndrome of headache, nausea, vomiting, and tremulousness, which is euphemistically referred to as a *hangover.*

A full-blown alcohol withdrawal syndrome comprises three phases. The first phase begins about 5 or 6 hours after the cessation of a long bout of heavy drinking and is characterized by severe tremors, agitation, headache, nausea, vomiting, abdominal cramps, profuse sweating, and sometimes hallucinations. The defining feature of the second phase, which typically occurs between 15 and 30 hours after cessation of drinking, is convulsive activity. The third phase, which usually begins a day or two after the cessation of drinking and lasts for 3 or 4 days, is called **delirium tremens (DTs).** The DTs are characterized by disturbing hallucinations, bizarre delusions, agitation, confusion, *hyperthermia* (high temperature), and *tachycardia* (rapid heartbeat). The convulsions and the DTs produced by alcohol withdrawal can be lethal.

Alcohol attacks almost every tissue in the body (see Anderson et al., 1993). Chronic alcohol consumption produces extensive brain damage (Hayakawa et al., 1992) and **Korsakoff's syndrome**—a neuropsychological disorder that is characterized by severe memory loss, sensory and motor dysfunction, and severe *dementia* (intellectual deterioration). It also causes extensive scarring, or **cirrhosis,** of the liver, which is the major cause of death among heavy alcohol users. Alcohol erodes the muscles of the heart and thus increases the risk of heart attack. It irritates the lining of the digestive tract and, in so doing, increases the risk of oral and liver cancer, stomach ulcers, *pancreatitis* (inflammation of the pancreas), and *gastritis* (inflammation of the stomach). And not to be forgotten is the carnage that it produces on our highways and in our homes.

Like nicotine, alcohol readily penetrates the placental membrane and affects the fetus. The result is that the offspring of mothers who consume substantial quantities of alcohol during their pregnancy frequently suffer from a disorder known as **fetal alcohol syndrome (FAS)** (see Mattson, Barron, & Riley, 1988). The FAS child suffers from some or all of the following symptoms: mental retardation, poor coordination, poor muscle tone, low birth weight, retarded growth, and physical deformity. In rats, a single day of alcohol exposure during the fetal brain growth spurt can significantly reduce adult brain weight (Goodlett, Marcussen, & West, 1990).

Alcohol has multiple mechanisms of action (see Hunt, 1993). For example, it reduces the flow of calcium into neurons by acting on calcium channels, increases the action of the inhibitory neurotransmitter GABA by acting on the GABA receptor complex, increases the number of binding sites for the excitatory neurotransmitter glutamate, reduces the effects of glutamate at some of its receptor subtypes, and interferes with second messenger systems inside neurons.

Marijuana

Marijuana is the name commonly given to the dried leaves and flowers of **cannabis sativa**—the common hemp plant. The usual mode of consumption is to smoke these leaves in a *joint* (a cigarette of marijuana) or pipe; but it is also effective when ingested orally, if first baked into an oil-rich substrate, such as a chocolate brownie, to promote absorption from the gastrointestinal tract.

The psychoactive effects of marijuana are largely attributable to a constituent called **THC** (delta-9-tetrahydrocannabinol). However, marijuana contains over 80 *cannabinoids* (chemicals of the same chemical class as THC), which may also be psychoactive (see Kephalas et al., 1976). Most of the cannabinoids are found in a sticky resin covering the leaves and flowers of the plant, which can be extracted and dried to form a dark, corklike material called **hashish**. The hashish can be further processed into an extremely potent product called *hash oil*.

Written records of marijuana use go back 6,000 years in China, where its stem was used to make rope, its seeds were used as a grain, and its leaves and flowers were used for their psychoactive and medicinal effects. One story of ancient cannabis use, whose misrepresentation has had a major impact on modern attitudes toward the drug, involved a Muslim sect headed by one Hashishin-i-Sabbah, a fanatic who tried to purge the Muslim religion of false prophets by having his followers assassinate them. Hashishin reportedly rewarded his successful assassins with a psychoactive drug, which was likely opium (Grinspoon, 1977); but the story spread that it was hashish. Both the word *assassin* and the word *hashish* were derived from his name.

In the middle ages, cannabis cultivation spread from the Middle East into Western Europe; however, in Europe, it was grown primarily for the manufacture of rope, and its psychoactive properties were largely forgotten. During the period of European imperialism, rope was in high demand for sailing vessels. In 1611, the American colonies responded to this demand by growing cannabis as a cash crop; George Washington was one of the more notable cannabis growers.

The practice of smoking the leaves of the cannabis plant and the word *marijuana* itself seem to have been introduced to the southern United States in the early part of the 1900s by Mexican immigrants; and its use gradually became popular among certain subgroups, such as the poor in city ghettos and jazz musicians. In 1926, an article appeared in a New Orleans newspaper exposing the "menace of marijuana," and soon similar stories were appearing in newspapers all over the United States under titles such as "The Evil Weed," "The Killer Drug," and "Marijuana Madness." The population was told that marijuana turned normal people into violent, drug-crazed criminals who rapidly become addicted to heroin. The old story of Hashishin was revived in a revised form, which had Hashishin giving hashish to his followers not as a reward for a job well done but to transform them into killers.

The result of the misrepresentation of the effects of marijuana by the U.S. news media was the enactment of

---

Depressant. A drug that depresses neural activity and behavior.

Diuretic. A drug that increases the production of urine.

Delirium tremens (DTs). The phase of the alcohol withdrawal syndrome characterized by hallucinations, delusions, and extremely agitated behavior.

Korsakoff's syndrome. The severe memory loss and dementia that is commonly associated with alcohol addiction.

Cirrhosis. Scarring, typically of the liver.

Fetal alcohol syndrome (FAS). A syndrome produced by prenatal exposure to alcohol and characterized by mental retardation, low birth weight, and a variety of other physical abnormalities.

Cannabis sativa. The common hemp plant and the source of marijuana.

THC. Delta-a-tetrahydrocannabinol, the main psychoactive ingedient of marijuana.

Hashish. The processed resin of Cannabis sativa.

---

many laws against the drug. In many states, marijuana was legally classified a **narcotic** (a legal term generally used to refer to opiates), and punishment was dealt out accordingly. However, the structure of marijuana and its physiological and behavioral effects bear no resemblance to those of the other narcotics; thus legally classifying marijuana as a narcotic was like passing a law that red is green.

The popularization of marijuana smoking among the middle and upper classes in the 1960s stimulated a massive program of research that has lasted a quarter of a century; yet there is still considerable confusion about marijuana among the general population. One of the difficulties in characterizing the effects of marijuana is that they are subtle, difficult to measure, and greatly influenced by the social situation:

> At low, usual "social" doses, the intoxicated individual may experience an increased sense of well-being: initial restlessness and hilarity followed by a dreamy, carefree state of relaxation; alteration of sensory perceptions including expansion of space and time; and a more vivid sense of touch, sight, smell, taste, and sound; a feeling of hunger, especially a craving for sweets; and subtle changes in thought formation and expression. To an unknowing observer, an individual in this state of consciousness would not appear noticeably different. (National Commission on Marijuana and Drug Abuse, 1972, p. 68)

Although the effects of typical social doses of marijuana are subtle, extraordinarily high doses do impair psychological functioning. Short-term memory is impaired, and the ability to carry out tasks involving multiple steps to reach a specific goal declines. Speech becomes slurred, and meaningful conversation becomes difficult. A sense of unreality, emotional intensification, sensory distortion, and motor impairment are also common. However, even after very high doses, an unexpected knock at the door can often bring about the return of a reasonable semblance of normal behavior.

In the light of the documented effects of marijuana, the earlier claims that marijuana would trigger a wave of violent crimes in the youth of America seem absurd. It is difficult to imagine how anybody could believe that the red-eyed, gluttonous, sleepy, giggling products of common social doses of marijuana would be likely to commit violent criminal acts. In fact, marijuana actually curbs aggressive behavior (Tinklenberg, 1974).

There is one effect of marijuana that warrants special mention because of its serious consequences. Marijuana-intoxicated drivers can stop as quickly as normal drivers, but they are not always as quick to notice the things for which they should stop (Moskowitz, Hulbert, & McGlothin, 1976).

What are the hazards of long-term marijuana use? The main risk appears to be lung damage. Those who regularly smoke marijuana tend to have deficits in respiratory function (e.g., Tilles et al., 1986), and they are more likely to develop a chronic cough, bronchitis, and asthma (Abram-son, 1974). Some authors list four other adverse effects of regular marijuana use; however, in each case, the evidence is either indirect, inconsistent, or incomplete (see Mendelson, 1987). First, there have been reports that chronic marijuana smoking lowers the plasma *testosterone* levels of males (e.g., Kolodny et al., 1974); but the reported reductions have been too slight to influence sexual behavior, and several studies have failed to replicate them. Second, there has been some suggestion that marijuana can adversely influence the *immune system,* but it has yet to be demonstrated that marijuana smokers are more susceptible to infection than are comparable nonsmokers. Third, because *tachycardia* (rapid heart rate) is one of the most reliable effects of marijuana, there has been some concern that chronic marijuana consumption might cause cardiovascular problems; but again there is no direct evidence for this hypothesis. Fourth, many people have hypothesized that the relaxation produced by marijuana could reach pathological proportions and produce what is generally referred to as the **amotivational syndrome.** The evidence that occasional marijuana use causes a significant amotivational syndrome is far from strong (see Mendelson et al., 1976): No significant difference was found between the grade point averages of marijuana smokers and nonsmokers in a study of 2,000 college students (Brill & Christie, 1974). Nevertheless, it seems likely that heavy marijuana use would be associated with some decline in productivity.

The addiction potential of marijuana is low. Most people who use marijuana do so only occasionally, and most who use it as youths curtail their use in their 30s and 40s. Tolerance can develop to marijuana during periods of sustained use (Babor et al., 1975). Also, withdrawal symptoms (e.g., nausea, diarrhea, sweating, chills, tremor, restlessness, sleep disturbance) can occur, but they are rare except in contrived laboratory situations in which massive oral doses are administered.

Narcotic. A legal classification of certain drugs, mostly opiates.

Amotivational syndrome. Chronic lack of motivation produced by drug use.

Cocaine hydrochloride (cocaine). A strong stimulant and analgesic that is extracted from coca paste.

Crack. The freebase form of cocaine.

Amphetamine. A stimulant drug whose effects are similar to those of cocaine.

Stimulants. Drugs that increase neural and behavioral activity.

Cocaine sprees. Binges of cocaine use.

Cocaine psychosis. Psychotic behavior observed during a cocaine spree, similar in many respects to schizophrenic behavior.

Chapter 13 Drug Addiction and Reward Circuits in the Brain

Some of the effects of marijuana have been shown to be of clinical benefit (see Cohen & Stillman, 1976). One example is marijuana's ability to block the nausea of cancer patients undergoing chemotherapy. *Nabilone,* a synthetic cannabis analogue, is now sometimes prescribed with chemotherapy (Lemberger & Rowe, 1975). Marijuana has also been shown to block seizures (Corcoran, McCaughran, & Wada, 1978), to dilate the bronchioles of asthmatics, and to decrease the severity of *glaucoma* (a disorder characterized by an increase in the pressure of the fluid inside the eye); but it is not normally prescribed for these purposes.

Because THC is fat-soluble, it was initially assumed that it influenced the brain by inserting itself directly into neural membranes. However, we now know that THC binds to receptors that are particularly dense in the basal ganglia, hippocampus, cerebellum, and neocortex (Howlett et al., 1990); presumably, it exerts most of its effects through this mechanism. The cloning of the gene for the THC receptor (Matsuda et al., 1990) triggered a search for an endogenous THC-like chemical that binds to it. Such a chemical has recently been isolated, and its structure has been characterized (Devane et al., 1992). The chemical has been named *anandamide* (which means "internal bliss") and its study is proceeding rapidly.

Cocaine

Cocaine is prepared from the leaf of the coca bush, which is found primarily in Peru and Bolivia. A crude extract called *coca paste* is usually made directly from the leaves; then, **cocaine hydrochloride (cocaine)**—the nefarious odorless white powder—is extracted from the paste. Cocaine hydrochloride is sometimes converted by abusers to its freebase form and smoked in a pipe. **Crack** is an impure freebase product that is widely used because it is relatively inexpensive.

Cocaine hydrochloride is an effective local anesthetic, and it was once widely prescribed as such until it was supplanted by synthetic analogues such as *procaine* and *lidocaine.* It is not, however, cocaine's anesthetic actions that are of interest to its users. People eat, smoke, snort, or inject cocaine in its various forms in order to experience its psychological effects. Users report being swept by a wave of well-being; they feel self-confident, alert, energetic, friendly, outgoing, fidgety, and talkative; and they have less than their usual desire for food and sleep. These effects of cocaine are similar to those of **amphetamine,** another widely abused drug.

Cocaine, amphetamine, and nicotine are **stimulants**—drugs whose primary effect is to increase neural activity. Coca-Cola is a commercial stimulant preparation consumed by many people around the world. Today, its stimulant action is attributable to caffeine, but when it was first introduced, "the pause that refreshes" packed a real wallop in the form of small amounts of cocaine.

Like alcohol, cocaine is frequently consumed in *binges* (see Gawin, 1991). Cocaine addicts tend to go on so-called **cocaine sprees,** binges in which extremely high levels of intake are maintained for periods of a day or two. During a cocaine spree, users become increasingly tolerant to the euphoria-producing effects of cocaine. Accordingly, larger and larger doses are often administered to maintain the initial level of euphoria. The spree usually ends when the cocaine is gone or when it begins to have serious toxic effects. During these binges, extremely high blood levels of cocaine are achieved, and sleeplessness, tremors, nausea, and psychotic behavior often occur.

The syndrome of psychotic behavior observed during cocaine sprees is called **cocaine psychosis.** It is similar to, and has often been mistakenly diagnosed as, *schizophrenia.* Although cocaine is extremely addictive, the withdrawal effects triggered by abrupt termination of a cocaine spree are mild (Miller, Summers, & Gold, 1993). Common cocaine withdrawal symptoms include a negative mood swing and insomnia.

During cocaine sprees, there is a risk of seizures, loss of consciousness, and death from respiratory arrest or stroke. Although tolerance develops to many effects of cocaine, repeated cocaine exposure makes subjects even more sensitive to its motor and convulsive effects (see Robinson & Berridge, 1993); this is an example of sensitization. Fatalities from cocaine overdose are most likely following

IV injection. Cocaine snorting damages the nasal membranes; and cocaine smoking damages the lungs.

Cocaine is thought to exert its behavioral effects by facilitating catecholaminergic transmission. It increases activity at catecholaminergic synapses by blocking the reuptake of *catecholamines* (dopamine, norepinephrine, and epinephrine) into presynaptic neurons.

The Opiates: Heroin and Morphine

Opium—the sap that exudes from the seeds of the opium poppy—has several psychoactive ingredients. Most notable are **morphine** and **codeine,** its weaker relative. Morphine, codeine, and other drugs that have similar structures or effects are commonly referred to as the **opiates.** The opiates have a Jekyll-and-Hyde problem of major proportions. On their Dr. Jekyll side, opiates are unmatched as **analgesics** (painkillers), and they are also extremely effective in the treatment of cough and diarrhea. But unfortunately, the kindly Dr. Jekyll always brings with him the evil Mr. Hyde—the risk of addiction.

Archeological evidence suggests that the practice of eating opium became popular in the Middle East sometime before 4000 B.C., and then it spread throughout Africa, Europe, and Asia (see Berridge & Edwards, 1981; Latimer & Goldberg, 1981). Three historic events fanned the flame of opiate addiction. First, in 1644, the Emperor of China banned tobacco smoking, and many Chinese tobacco smokers tried smoking opium and liked it. Because smoking opium has a greater effect on the brain than does eating it, many more people became addicted to opium as the practice of opium smoking slowly spread to other countries. Second, morphine, the most potent constituent of opium, was isolated from opium in 1803, and in the 1830s it became available commercially. Third, the hypodermic needle was invented in 1856, and soon injured soldiers (e.g., those of the American Civil War) were introduced to morphine through a needle; during this era, morphine addiction was known as *soldiers' disease.*

Most people are surprised to learn that until the early 1900s, opium was legally available and consumed in great quantity in many parts of the world, including Europe and North America. Opium was available in cakes, candies, and wines, as well as in a variety of over-the-counter medicinal offerings. Opium potions such as *laudanum* (a very popular mixture of opium and alcohol), *Godfrey's Cordial,* and *Dalby's Carminative* were very popular. (The word *carminative* should win first prize for making a sow's ear at least sound like a silk purse: A carminative is a drug that expels gas from the digestive tract, thus reducing stomach cramps and flatulence. *Flatulence* is the obvious pick for second prize.) There were even over-the-counter opium potions just for baby. Potions such as *Mrs. Winslow's Soothing Syrup* and the aptly labeled *Street's Infant Quietness* were popular in many households. Although pure morphine could not be purchased without a prescription in the early 1900s, it

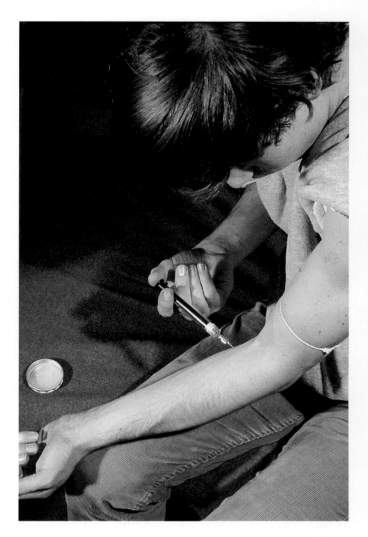

was so frequently prescribed by physicians for so many different maladies that morphine addiction was common among those who could afford doctors.

The **Harrison Narcotics Act,** passed in 1914, made it illegal to sell or use opium, morphine, or cocaine in the United States. However, the act did not include the semisynthetic opiate, **heroin.** Heroin had been synthesized in 1870 by the addition of two acetyl groups to the morphine molecule, which greatly increased its ability to penetrate the blood-brain barrier. In 1898, heroin was marketed by the Bayer Drug Company; it was freely available without prescription and was widely advertised as a super aspirin. Tests showed that it was a more potent analgesic than morphine and that it was less likely to induce nausea and vomiting. Moreover, the Bayer Drug Company, on the basis of flimsy evidence, claimed that heroin was not addictive; this is why it was not covered by the Harrison Narcotics Act.

The consequence of this omission was that opiate addicts in the United States, forbidden by law to use opium or morphine, turned to the readily available and much more potent heroin; and the flames of addiction were further fanned. In 1924, the U.S. Congress made it illegal for anybody to possess, sell, or use heroin. Unfortunately, the laws enacted to stamp out opiate addiction in the United

States have been far from successful: An estimated 2 million Americans currently use heroin, and organized crime flourishes on the proceeds.

The effect of opiates most valued by opiate addicts is the *rush* that follows intravenous injection. The *heroin rush* is a wave of intense abdominal, orgasmic pleasure that evolves into a state of serene, drowsy euphoria. Many opiate users, drawn by these pleasurable effects, begin to use the drug more and more frequently. Then, once they reach a point where they keep themselves drugged much of the time, tolerance and physical dependence develop and contribute to the problem. Opiate tolerance encourages addicts to progress to higher doses, to more potent drugs (e.g., heroin), and to more direct routes of administration (e.g., IV injection); and physical dependence adds to the already high motivation to take the drug.

Although opiates are highly addictive, their direct health hazards are surprisingly minor. The main risks are constipation, pupil constriction, menstrual irregularity, and reduced libido (sex drive). Many opiate addicts have taken large prescribed doses of pure heroin or morphine for years with no serious ill effects. In fact, opiate addiction is more prevalent among doctors, nurses, and dentists than among other professionals (e.g., Brewster, 1986):

> An individual tolerant to and dependent upon an opiate who is socially or financially capable of obtaining an adequate supply of good quality drug, sterile syringes and needles, and other paraphernalia may maintain his or her proper social and occupational functions, remain in fairly good health, and suffer little serious incapacitation as a result of the dependence. (Julien, 1981, p. 117)

> One such individual was Dr. William Steward Halsted, one of the founders of Johns Hopkins Medical School and one of the most brilliant surgeons of his day ... known as "the father of modern surgery." And yet, during his career he was addicted to morphine, a fact that he was able to keep secret from all but his closest friends. In fact, the only time his habit caused him any trouble was when he was attempting to reduce his dosage. (McKim, 1986, p. 197)

The classic opiate withdrawal syndrome usually begins 6 to 12 hours after the last dose. The first withdrawal sign is typically an increase in restlessness; the addict begins to pace and fidget. Watering eyes, running nose, yawning, and sweating are also common during the early stages of opiate withdrawal. Then, the addict often falls into a fitful sleep, which typically lasts for several hours. After the sleep is over, the original symptoms may be joined in extreme cases by chills, shivering, profuse sweating, gooseflesh, nausea, vomiting, diarrhea, cramps, pains, dilated pupils, tremor, and muscle spasms. The gooseflesh skin and leg spasms of the opiate withdrawal syndrome are the basis for the expressions "going cold turkey" and "kicking the habit." The symptoms of opiate withdrawal are typically most severe in the second or third day after the last injection, and by the seventh day they have all but disappeared.

The symptoms of opiate withdrawal are not trivial, but their severity has been widely exaggerated. Opiate withdrawal is about as serious as a bad case of the flu—a far cry from the convulsions, delirium, and risk of death associated with alcohol withdrawal:

> Opiate withdrawal is probably one of the most misunderstood aspects of drug use. This is largely because of the image of withdrawal that has been portrayed in the movies and popular literature for many years.... Few addicts ... take enough drug to cause the ... severe withdrawal symptoms that are shown in the movies. Even in its most severe form, however, opiate withdrawal is not as dangerous or terrifying as withdrawal from barbiturates or alcohol. (McKim, 1986, p. 199)

Because opiates create relatively few direct health problems for those addicts with an affordable source of pure drug, the main risks of opiate addiction are indirect. They are risks that arise out of the battle between the relentless addictive power of opiates and the attempts of governments to eradicate addiction by making drugs illegal. The opiate addicts who cannot give up their habit—treatment programs report success rates of only 10%—are caught in the middle. Because most opiate addicts must purchase their morphine and heroin from illicit dealers at greatly inflated prices, those who are not wealthy become trapped in a life of poverty and petty crime. They are poor, they are undernourished, they receive poor medical care, they are often driven to prostitution, and they run great risk of contracting AIDS and other infections from unsafe sex and unsterile needles. Moreover, they never know for sure what they are injecting: Some street drugs are poorly processed, and virtually all have been *cut* (stretched by the addition of some similar-appearing substance) to some unknown degree.

The exact number of heroin-related deaths is impossible to determine, but their number is substantial. What makes these deaths particularly tragic is that many of them seem to be caused by the very laws that were designed to prevent them.

The opiates, like marijuana, seem to exert their effects by binding to particular receptors whose normal function is to bind to *endogenous* chemicals. The endogenous chemi-

---

Opium. The sap that exudes from the opium poppy.

Morphine. The major psychoactive ingredient in opium.

Codeine. A weak psychoactive ingredient of opium.

Opiates. Morphine, codeine, heroin, and other chemicals with similar structures or effects.

Analgesics. Drugs that reduce pain.

Harrison Narcotics Act. The act, passed in 1914, that made it illegal to sell or use opium, morphine, or cocaine in the United States.

Heroin. A powerful semisynthetic opiate.

---

cals that bind to opiate receptors are called *endorphins,* and about 20 different kinds have been identified. There are three classes of opiate receptors; one of them, the *delta opioid receptor,* has been cloned and its structure characterized (Evans et al., 1992). The delta opioid receptor is a *G-protein linked receptor.*

Comparison of the Hazards of Tobacco, Alcohol, Marijuana, Cocaine, and Heroin

One way of comparing the adverse effects of tobacco, alcohol, marijuana, cocaine, and heroin is to compare the prevalence of their use in society as a whole. In terms of this criterion, it is clear that tobacco and alcohol have a far greater negative impact than do marijuana, cocaine, and heroin (see Figure 13.7).

But what about the individual drug user? Who is taking greater health risks: the cigarette smoker, the alcohol drinker, the marijuana smoker, the cocaine user, or the heroin user? You now have the information to answer this question. First, in the following Self Test, list all of the demonstrated major health hazards of each of the five drugs; be sure to focus on direct hazards of the drug, not on indirect hazards created by its legal and social status. Then, on the basis of your five lists, rank the five drugs in terms of their overall health risks. Would you have ranked the drugs in the same way before you read this chapter?

The Drug Dilemmas: Striking the Right Balance

Drug abuse is currently a serious problem. In the United States alone, recreational drugs contribute to several hundred thousand deaths each year and the public must bear the brunt of the crime and violence that is perpetrated by addicts who are forced to steal and prostitute themselves to fuel their expensive habits. Also, the public must bear the economic burdens of increased medical care, increased law enforcement, and decreased productivity—an estimated $86 billion annually (see Hunt, 1993).

Several eminent psychopharmacologists and political scientists have evaluated the U.S. approach to drug control in the light of current data; they all recommended sweeping changes (see Goldstein & Kalant, 1990; Jarvik, 1990; Nadelman, 1989). Each of these experts concluded that the

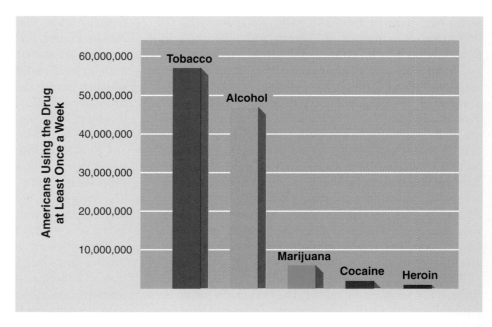

Figure 13.7 Prevalence of drug use in the United States. Figures are based on a survey of people 12 years of age and over who live in households. (Adapted from Goldstein & Kalant, 1990.)

current system of drug control is both poorly conceived and ineffective. The following quotes provide glimpses of their disenchantment with a system that treats addiction as a crime, rather than a disease, and that tries to combat it by reducing the supply and punishing the users:

> The investment of more than 70% of the federal [U.S.] drug control money into supply reduction seems misplaced.... Curtailing the supply of demanded drugs has been compared to squeezing a balloon: constrict it in one place and it expands somewhere else.... An example is the expansion of the California marijuana crop after the availability of Mexican marijuana was reduced. (Jarvik, p. 339)

> The greatest beneficiaries of the drug laws are ... drug traffickers. More than half of all organized crime revenues are believed to derive from the illicit drug business. (Nadelman, p. 941)

> Drug treatment programs remain notoriously underfunded, turning away tens of thousands of addicts seeking help even as increasing billions of dollars are spent to arrest, prosecute, and imprison illegal drug ... users. (Nadelman, p. 942)

The experts recommend a solution to the drug problem that is different than the one preferred by the American public. The experts say (1) that there is no way of stopping the supply—every major drug bust merely increases the street prices of drugs and encourages more illicit suppliers to enter the market; (2) that it makes little sense to persecute and punish the sick and the weak; and (3) that it is hypocritical to take Draconian measures against some drugs while allowing others that are more dangerous to be openly advertised. In contrast, recent surveys suggest that

List the major direct health hazards of the following five drugs. Omit indirect hazards that result from the drugs' legal or social status.

Tobacco	Alcohol	Marijuana	Cocaine	Heroin
1._____	1._____	1._____	1._____	1._____
2._____	2._____	2._____	2._____	2._____
3._____	3._____	3._____	3._____	3._____
4._____	4._____	4._____	4._____	4._____
5._____	5._____	5._____	5._____	5._____
6._____	6._____	6._____	6._____	6._____

On the basis of comparisons among your five lists, rank the five drugs in terms of the overall dangerousness of their direct health hazards.

Most Hazardous 1. _____

2. _____

3. _____

4. _____

Least Hazardous 5. _____

the U.S. public, frustrated with the drug problem and not understanding the issues, wants even more money to be spent on the approach that is currently proving so ineffective. Following are some of the specific recommendations that have been made by the experts:

1. The only way of reducing recreational drug use is by reducing the demand. Some of the billions that are currently being spent on arresting and supporting drug users in crowded jails would be better spent on education, research, and social programs.

2. More emphasis should be placed on caring for addicts than on persecuting them.

3. Unlike the current laws, the laws that govern drug use should be enforceable and should be tailored to the hazards of each drug.

4. Judges should be given greater discretion in sentencing. For example, the current 5-year minimum sentence for anybody caught sharing a small amount of heroin or cocaine is unduly harsh.

5. All cigarette and alcohol advertising should be curtailed.

6. The possession of small amounts of marijuana for personal use has been legalized in some parts of the country; the effects of this legalization should be carefully monitored. If it does not lead to a significant increase in use, other states should follow suit to allow the legal system to focus on more serious problems.

7. Experimental clinics should be established. In them, addicts, as a first step in their treatment, should be provided with small daily doses of their drug. The potential advantages of such programs are many: They would encourage addicts to enter treatment; they would bring addicts in contact with health care professionals who are experienced in dealing with the health problems of addicts (e.g., AIDS and malnutrition); they would allow some addicts who have not been able to shake their habits to live reasonably normal, productive lives; and they would reduce the amount of drug-related crime.

8. Finally, lessons should be learned from countries such as England and Holland, which have successfully taken approaches to drug control that are more in tune with the preceding recommendations.

One does not normally find a discussion of legal and social policy in a biopsychology textbook. Please excuse my digression, but I believe that the drug problem is a serious one and that biopsychologists have important things to say about it. They have a responsibility to bring the relevant research literature to the attention of policy makers and the educated public. I hope that I have interested you enough to pursue the issue further; the articles of Goldstein and Kalant (1990), Jarvik (1990), and Nadelman (1989) are a good place to start.

13.4 Biopsychological Theories of Addiction

This section of the chapter introduces two diametrically different theories of addiction: Are addicts driven to take drugs by an internal need, or are they drawn to take drugs by the anticipated pleasure? I am sure you will recognize from preceding chapters that this is the same fundamental question that has been the focus of biopsychological research on the motivation to eat, drink, and sleep.

Physical-Dependence Theories of Addiction

Early attempts to explain the phenomenon of drug addiction attributed it to physical dependence. According to the **physical-dependence theory of addiction,** physical dependence traps addicts in a vicious circle of drug taking and withdrawal symptoms. The idea was that drug users whose intake has reached a level sufficient to induce physical dependence are driven by their withdrawal symptoms to self-administer the drug each time they attempt to curtail their intake.

Early drug addiction treatment programs were based on the physical-dependence theory of addiction. They attempted to break the vicious circle of drug taking by gradually withdrawing drugs from addicts in a hospital environment. (Gradual withdrawal produces less severe withdrawal symptoms than does sudden withdrawal.) Unfortunately, once discharged, almost all detoxified addicts return to their former drug-taking habits—**detoxified addicts** are addicts who have no drugs in their bodies and who are no longer experiencing withdrawal symptoms.

The failure of detoxification as a treatment for addiction is not surprising, for two reasons. First, some highly addictive drugs, such as cocaine, do not produce severe withdrawal distress (see Gawin, 1991). Second, the pattern of drug taking routinely displayed by many addicts involves an alternating cycle of binges and detoxification (Mello & Mendelson, 1972). There are a variety of reasons for this pattern of drug use. For example, some addicts adopt it because weekend binges are compatible with their work schedules, others adopt it because they do not have enough money to use drugs continuously, others have it forced on them because their binges often land them in jail, and oth-

ers have it forced on them by their repeated unsuccessful efforts to shake their habit. However, whether detoxification is by choice or necessity, it does not stop addicts from renewing their drug-taking habits (see Robinson & Berridge, 1993).

Modern physical-dependence theories of drug addiction attempt to account for the fact that addicts frequently relapse after lengthy drug-free periods by postulating that withdrawal symptoms can be conditioned (Koob et al., 1993). According to this theory, when addicts who have remained drug-free for a considerable period of time return to a situation in which they have previously experienced the drug, conditioned withdrawal effects opposite to the effects of the drug (conditioned compensatory responses) are elicited. These effects are presumed to result in a powerful craving for the drug to counteract them.

The theory that *relapse* is motivated primarily by an attempt to counteract conditioned withdrawal effects encounters two major problems (see Eikelboom & Stewart, 1982; Zelman, Tiffany, & Baker, 1985). One is that many of the effects elicited by environments that have previously been associated with drug administration are similar to those of the drug rather than being antagonistic to them (Stewart & Eikelboom, 1982). The second is that experimental animals and addicts often display a preference for drug-predictive cues, even when no drug is forthcoming (e.g., Bozarth & Wise, 1981; Mucha et al., 1982; White, Sklar, & Amit, 1977). For example, some detoxified heroin addicts called *needle freaks* derive pleasure from sticking an empty needle into themselves. It therefore seems unlikely that conditioned withdrawal effects could be the primary motivating factor in drug relapse. In accordance with this conclusion, Krank and Perkins (1993) found that conditioned morphine withdrawal effects in rats did not increase their morphine self-administration.

Positive-Incentive Theories of Addiction

The failure of physical-dependence theories to account for the major aspects of addiction has lent support to the theory that the primary reason most addicts take drugs is not to escape or avoid the unpleasant consequences of withdrawal or conditioned withdrawal, but rather to obtain the drugs' pleasurable effects. This **positive-incentive theory of addiction** acknowledges that addicts may sometimes self-administer drugs to suppress withdrawal symptoms or to escape from other unpleasant aspects of their existence, but it holds that the primary factor in most cases of addiction is the craving for the positive-incentive (pleasure-producing) properties of the drugs (McAuliffe et al., 1986; Stewart, de Wit, & Eikelboom, 1984). Anecdotal support for this view comes from the statements of some addicts—for example:

> I'm just trying to get high as much as possible. I would have to spend $25 a day on heroin to avoid withdrawal, but I actually use about $50 worth. If I could get more money, I would spend it all on drugs. All I want is to get loaded. I just really like shooting dope. I don't have any use for sex; I'd rather shoot dope. I like to shoot dope better than anything else in the world. I have to steal something every day to get my dope.

Some of the pleasurable effects of drugs may not be direct. Most addictive drugs have been reported to have disinhibitory effects—**disinhibition** is the release from inhibition of behaviors that are not performed because of inhibitory factors that normally suppress them (Pfaus & Pinel, 1989). All you have to do is go to your local singles bar to see the ability of alcohol to release various forms of courtship behavior from inhibition. If engaging in such normally inhibited behaviors is pleasurable, it could very well be an indirect, but important, motivating factor in some cases of drug addiction, particularly during the early phases.

Two interesting positive-incentive theories of addiction are based on the idea that the positive-incentive value of addictive drugs increases with drug use. First, Krank (1989) and Tabakoff and Hoffman (1988) have suggested that the positive-incentive value of addictive drugs increases because more conditioned tolerance develops to their aversive effects than to their pleasurable effects. Second, Robinson and Berridge (1993) have suggested that in addiction-prone individuals, the use of drugs sensitizes their positive-incentive value, thus rendering the user highly motivated to consume drugs and to seek drug-associated stimuli.

A key point of Robinson and Berridge's theory deserves emphasis: They argue that it isn't the pleasure of drug taking per se that is the basis of addiction; it is the anticipated pleasure of drug taking (i.e., the drug's positive-incentive value). Initially, a drug's positive incentive value is closely tied to its pleasurable effects; but in chronic addicts, the positive-incentive value of the drug is often out of proportion with the pleasure actually derived from it: Addicts are miserable, their lives are in ruins, and the drug effects are not even that great anymore; but they still crave the drug.

13.5   Reward Circuits in the Brain

Rats (Olds & Milner, 1954), humans (Bishop, Elder, & Heath, 1963), and many other species will perform a response, such as pressing a lever, in order to administer brief bursts of electrical stimulation to specific sites in their own brains (see Figure 13.8 on page 342). This phenomenon is known as **intracranial self-stimulation (ICSS).**

Olds and Milner, the discoverers of intracranial self-stimulation, argued that the specific brain sites that mediate self-stimulation are those that normally mediate the pleasurable effects of natural rewards (e.g., food, water, and sex). Accordingly, researchers have studied the self-stimulation of various brain sites in order to map the neural circuits that mediate the experience of pleasure. Because the pleasure-producing effects of drugs are now believed to play a major causal role in addiction, this section of the chapter focuses on these cerebral pleasure circuits.

Intracranial Self-Stimulation: Fundamental Characteristics

It was initially assumed that intracranial self-stimulation was a unitary phenomenon—that is, that its fundamental properties were the same regardless of the site of stimulation. Most early studies of intracranial self-stimulation involved septal or lateral hypothalamic stimulation because the rates of self-stimulation from these sites are spectacularly high: Rats typically press a lever thousands of times

Physical-dependence theory of addiction. The theory that the main factor that motivates drug addicts to take drugs is the prevention or termination of withdrawal symptoms.

Detoxified addicts. Addicts who have none of the drug to which they are addicted in their body and who are no longer experiencing withdrawal symptoms.

Positive-incentive theory of addiction. The theory that the primary factor in most cases of addiction is a craving for the pleasure-producing effects of drugs.

Disinhibition. The release from inhibition of behaviors that are normally suppressed.

Intracranial self-stimulation (ICSS). The repeated performance of a response that delivers electrical stimulation to certain sites in the brain.

Suspending
elastic band

Lever press
activates
stimulator

Lever

Stimulator

Figure 13.8 A rat pressing a lever for rewarding brain stimulation.

the activation of natural reward circuits in the brain. Accordingly, many of the investigators who studied self-stimulation in the 1950s and 1960s viewed it as some kind of artifact—albeit a particularly interesting one. However, since then, the pendulum of opinion has swung back to its original position: The current consensus seems to be that the circuits mediating intracranial self-stimulation phenomena are reward circuits.

The return to the reward-circuit view of intracranial self-stimulation was based on four kinds of evidence. First, brain stimulation through electrodes that mediate self-stimulation often elicits natural motivated behaviors such as eating, drinking, maternal behavior, and copulation in the presence of the appropriate goal objects. This evidence led Glickman and Schiff (1967) to suggest that the activation of circuits that produce species-typical motivated behaviors is the physiological basis of reward. Second, producing increases in natural motivation (for example, by food or water deprivation, by hormone injections, or by the presence of prey objects) often increases self-stimulation rates (e.g., Caggiula, 1970). Third, lever pressing for stimulation at some brain sites (other than the lateral hypothalamus and septum, on which the early studies focused) is often quite similar to lever pressing for natural rewards (i.e., acquisition is slow, response rates are low, extinction is slow, and priming is not necessary). And fourth, it became clear that subtle differences between the situations in which rewarding brain stimulation and natural rewards were usually studied contributed to the impression that their rewarding effects are qualitatively different. For example, comparisons between lever pressing for food and lever pressing for brain stimulation are usually confounded by the fact that subjects pressing for brain stimulation are nondeprived and by the fact that the lever press delivers the reward directly and immediately. In contrast, in studies of lever pressing for natural rewards, subjects are often deprived and they press a lever for a food pellet or drop of water that they then must approach and consume to experience rewarding effects.

In a clever experiment, Panksepp and Trowill (1967) compared lever pressing for brain stimulation with lever pressing for a natural reinforcer in a situation in which the usual confounds were absent. In the absence of the confounds, some of the major differences between lever pressing for food and lever pressing for brain stimulation disap-

per hour for stimulation of these sites, stopping only after they become exhausted. However, the self-stimulation of many other brain structures has now been documented; Figure 13.9 illustrates the intracranial self-stimulation sites in the rat brain.

Early studies of intracranial self-stimulation suggested that lever pressing for brain stimulation was fundamentally different from lever pressing for natural reinforcers such as food or water. Two puzzling observations contributed to this view. First, despite their extremely high response rates, many rats stopped pressing the self-stimulation lever almost immediately when the current delivery mechanism was shut off. This finding was puzzling because high rates of operant responding are generally assumed to indicate that the reinforcer is particularly pleasurable, whereas rapid rates of extinction are usually assumed to indicate that it is not. Would you stop pressing a lever that had been delivering $100 bills the first few times that a press did not produce one? Second, experienced self-stimulators often did not recommence lever pressing when they were returned to the apparatus after being briefly removed from it. In such cases, the rats had to be **primed** to get them going again: The experimenter simply pressed the lever a couple of times, to deliver a few free stimulations, and the hesitant rat immediately began to self-stimulate at a high rate once again.

These differences between lever pressing for rewarding lateral hypothalamic or septal stimulation and lever pressing for food or water seemed to discredit Olds and Milner's original theory that intracranial self-stimulation involves

Telencephalon

1 Olfactory bulb
2 Prepyriform cortex
3 Prefrontal cortex
4 Subfornical organ
5 Cingulate cortex
6 Entorhinal cortex
7 Hippocampus
8 Septum
9 Nucleus accumbens
10 Striatum
Not shown
    Globus Pallidus
    Amygdala
    Habenula

Diencephalon

11 Fornix
12 Lateral hypothalamus
13 Ventromedial
    hypothalamus
14 Mediodorsal nucleus
    of thalamus
15 Nucleus paratenialis
    of thalamus
16 Central nucleus
    of thalamus

Mesencephalon

17 Substantia nigra
18 Ventral tegmental
    area
19 Periaqueductal gray
20 Mesencephalic
    nucleus of trigeminal
    nerve
21 Dorsal raphé
22 Median raphé

Metencephalon

23 Cerebellum
24 Superior cerebellar
    peduncle
25 Motor nucleus of
    trigeminal nerve

Myelencephalon

26 Nucleus tractus
    solitarius

Figure 13.9 The major intracranial self-stimulation sites in the rat brain. (Adapted from Phillips & Fibiger, 1989.)

peared. When nondeprived rats lever pressed to inject a small quantity of chocolate milk directly into their mouths through an intraoral tube, they behaved remarkably like self-stimulating rats: They quickly learned to lever press, they pressed at high rates, they extinguished quickly, and some even had to be primed.

The Mesotelencephalic Dopamine System and Intracranial Self-Stimulation

The mesotelencephalic dopamine system has been shown to play a particularly important role in intracranial self-stimulation. The **mesotelencephalic dopamine system** is a system of dopaminergic neurons that projects from the mesencephalon (the midbrain) into various regions of the telencephalon. As Figure 13.10 indicates, the neurons that compose the mesotelencephalic dopamine system have their cell bodies in two midbrain nuclei—the **substantia nigra** and the **ventral tegmental area;** and their axons project to a variety of telencephalic sites, including specific

Primed. Induced to resume self-stimulation by a few "free" stimulations.

Mesotelencephalic dopamine system. The ascending projections of dopamine-releasing neurons from the substantia nigra and ventral tegmental area of the mesencephalon into various regions of the telencephalon.

Substantia nigra. The midbrain nucleus of the mesotelencephalic dopamine system that is a major source of dopaminergic projections to the striatum.

Ventral tegmental area. The midbrain nucleus of the mesotelencephalic dopamine system that is a major source of dopaminergic projections to limbic and cortical structures.

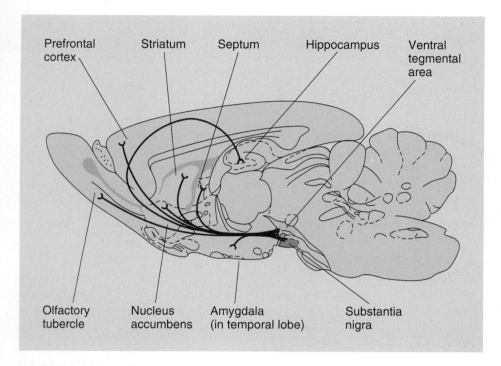

Figure 13.10 The mesotelencephalic dopamine system.

regions of the prefrontal neocortex, the limbic cortex, the olfactory tubercle, the amygdala, the septum, the striatum, and the **nucleus accumbens.**

It was originally thought that all of the dopaminergic neurons of the substantia nigra projected to the striatum and that all of those of the ventral tegmental area projected to limbic and cortical structures. However, it is now clear that there is considerable intermingling of these projections, and the original presumed distinction between the *nigrostriatal pathway* and the *mesocortical limbic pathway* has become somewhat blurred (Björkland & Lindvall, 1986). Nevertheless, it is the neurons that project from the ventral tegmental area to the nucleus accumbens that have been most frequently implicated in the effects of rewarding brain stimulation, natural rewards, and addictive drugs.

Several kinds of studies have supported the view that the mesotelencephalic dopamine system plays an important role in intracranial self-stimulation (see Chen, 1993). Prominent among these are (1) mapping studies, (2) microdialysis studies, (3) dopamine agonist and antagonist studies, and (4) lesion studies.

Mapping studies The first evidence of the involvement of the mesotelencephalic dopamine system in intracranial self-stimulation came from the discovery that many brain sites at which self-stimulation occurs are part of the mesotelencephalic dopamine system (see Routtenberg, 1978). For example, the mapping of self-stimulation sites in the mesencephalon revealed that most are located in the sub-

stantia nigra and ventral tegmental area (e.g., Routtenberg & Malsbury, 1969). Moreover, Corbett and Wise (1980) found that the mesencephalic self-stimulation sites at which the response rates were the highest and the current thresholds the lowest were those with the greatest concentrations of dopaminergic fibers.

Some self-stimulation sites do not contain large numbers of dopaminergic neurons. However, several nondopaminergic self-stimulation sites have been shown to project directly to the mesotelencephalic dopamine system (see Shizgal & Murray, 1989; Yeomans, Mathur, & Tampakeras, 1993).

Cerebral dialysis studies In *cerebral dialysis studies,* samples of extracellular fluid are continuously drawn from a particular area of the brain as the subject behaves, and the fluid is later subjected to chemical analysis. (It takes about 15 minutes to get a large enough sample for analysis.) Several investigators have used the cerebral dialysis technique to show that self-stimulation is often associated with an increase in dopamine release. For example, Phillips and colleagues (1992) found an increase in dopamine release in the nucleus accumbens when rats engaged in ventral tegmental area self-stimulation (see Figure 13.11).

Dopamine agonist and antagonist studies Several studies have shown that dopamine agonists increase self-stimulation and dopamine antagonists decrease self-stimulation. For example, microinjections of the dopamine agonist *amphetamine* into the nucleus accumbens increase lateral hypothalamic self-stimulation rates (Colle & Wise, 1988), and microinjections of the dopamine antagonist *spiroperidol* into the nucleus accumbens decrease ventral tegmental area self-stimulation rates (Mogenson et al., 1979).

Lesion studies Lesions of the mesotelencephalic dopamine system disrupt self-stimulation. For example, in one experiment (Fibiger et al., 1987), selective unilateral lesions of the mesotelencephalic dopamine system were produced by unilateral injections into the system of the selective toxin, *6-hydroxydopamine (6-OHDA).* Lesions to the ventral tegmental area ipsilateral to a stimulation electrode reduced self-stimulation, whereas lesions to the ventral tegmental

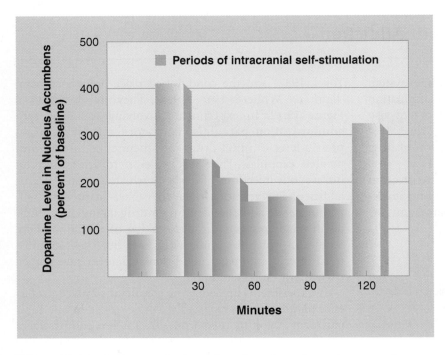

Figure 13.11 The increase in dopamine release from the nucleus accumbens during periods of intracranial self-stimulation. (Adapted from Phillips et al., 1992.)

area contralateral to a stimulation electrode did not. The fact that contralateral lesions produced no deficit indicated that general motor deficits produced by the lesions did not contribute to the decline in self-stimulation.

The Mesotelencephalic Dopamine System and Natural Motivated Behaviors

The discovery that the mesotelencephalic dopamine system plays an important role in intracranial self-stimulation stimulated interest in the role of this system in natural motivated behaviors (see Fibiger, 1993). Recent studies have measured dopamine release in the nucleus accumbens by microdialysis while rats have engaged in natural sequences of motivated behavior.

One purpose of this research has been to determine whether dopamine release is correlated with consummatory behaviors or preparatory behaviors. **Consummatory behaviors** are behaviors, such as copulation or eating, that consummate or complete a sequence of motivated behavior. **Preparatory behaviors** are behaviors, such as approaching a sex partner or searching for food, that enable an organism to perform a consummatory response. Two minor related points: (1) Preparatory behaviors are also referred to as *appetitive, instrumental,* or *anticipatory behaviors.* (2) *Consummatory* is perhaps the most frequently mispronounced of all biopsychological terms; it is pronounced "con SUHM a tor ee," not "con SUME a tor ee,"

because it is derived from the verb *consummate,* not the verb *consume.*

In an experiment by Nomikos and colleagues (see Fibiger, 1993), rats were confined for 20 minutes to one compartment of a two-compartment test box. Then, the compartment door was opened so that the rats could enter the other compartment and eat a highly palatable liquid diet. Rats received between 10 and 14 such daily training sessions. Then, on the test day, dopamine release in the nucleus accumbens was measured by cerebral dialysis during the 20-minute preparatory phase and the subsequent consummatory phase. There was no significant increase in extracellular dopamine levels during the preparatory phase, but the levels increased greatly (by 130% of the baseline) during the consummatory phase.

A similar study of male sexual behavior was conducted by Pfaus and colleagues (1990), who recorded levels of dopamine by cerebral dialysis in the nucleus accumbens of sexually experienced male rats. A male rat was first placed in a test box. Then, a receptive female rat was placed in the same box but was kept separate from the male by a mesh screen. Finally, the mesh screen was removed to permit copulation. When the female was placed in the screened chamber, there was a great increase in the male rat's preparatory behaviors (i.e., rearing, sniffing, and locomotor activity), but there was only a slight increase in the release of dopamine in the nucleus accumbens. However, when the screen was raised, the level of dopamine increased sharply (by 130% of the baseline).

The results of these two experiments indicate that dopamine release from the nucleus accumbens is related to the consummatory phase of motivated behavior but not to the preparatory phase. This observation is consistent with the view that the nucleus accumbens plays an important role in mediating the rewarding effects of natural motivated behaviors but not the incentive motivation to engage in them.

Nucleus accumbens. A major terminal of the mesencephalic dopamine system, which has been implicated in the mediation of the effects of reward.

Consummatory behaviors. Behaviors that complete (consummate) a sequence of motivated behavior.

Preparatory behaviors. Behaviors that prepare or enable an organism to perform a consummatory response.

Evidence that the mesotelencephalic dopamine system mediates the rewarding effects of intracranial stimulation and natural motivated behaviors suggests that it may also mediate the rewarding effects of addictive drugs (see Chen, 1993). And so we return to our discussion of drug addiction.

Two behavioral paradigms have been used extensively in the study of the neural mechanisms of addiction (Stolerman, 1992): the drug self-administration paradigm (see

Yokel, 1987) and the conditioned place-preference paradigm (see White & Hiroi, 1993). They are illustrated in Figure 13.12. In experiments involving the **drug self-administration paradigm,** laboratory rats or primates press a lever to inject drugs into themselves through implanted cannulas. They readily learn to self-administer intravenous injections of drugs to which humans become addicted. Furthermore, once they have learned to self-administer an addictive drug, their drug taking often mimics in major respects the drug taking of human addicts. Studies in which microinjections have been self-administered directly into particular brain structures have proved particularly enlightening.

In experiments involving the **conditioned place-preference paradigm,** rats repeatedly receive a drug in one compartment (the *drug compartment*) of a two-compartment box. Then, during the test phase, the rat is placed in the box drug-free, and the proportion of time it spends in the drug compartment, as opposed to the equal-sized but distinctive *control compartment,* is measured. Rats usually prefer the drug compartment over the control compartment when the drug compartment has been associated with the effects of drugs to which humans become addicted. The main advantage of the conditioned place-preference paradigm is that the subjects are tested drug-free, which means that the measure of the incentive value of a drug is not confounded by other effects the drug might have on behavior (see Carr, Fibiger, & Phillips, 1989; Van der Kooy, 1987).

Evidence of the Involvement of the Mesotelencephalic Dopamine System in Drug Addiction

Several lines of evidence support the view that the mesotelencephalic dopamine system—particularly its mesocortical-limbic division—mediates the rewarding effects of drugs. Most of this evidence comes from studies of morphine, cocaine, and amphetamine; however, the mesotelencephalic dopamine system has also been implicated in the rewarding effects of other drugs (e.g., alcohol, nicotine, and THC). The following are five major lines of evidence.

First, laboratory animals self-administer microinjec-

Drug Self-Administration

~ From infusion pump

The rat presses the lever to self-inject a drug, either into an area of its brain or into general circulation.

Conditioned Place Preferences

A rat repeatedly receives a drug in one of two distinctive compartments. Then, on the test, the tendency of the rat, now drug-free, to prefer the drug compartment is assessed.

Figure 13.12 Two behavioral paradigms that are used extensively in the study of the neural mechanisms of addiction: The drug self-administration paradigm and the conditioned place-preference paradigm.

Drug self-administration paradigm. A test of the addictive potential of drugs in which animals can inject drugs into themselves by pressing a lever.

Conditioned place-preference paradigm. A test that assesses an animal's preference for environments in which it has previously experienced drug effects.

tions of addictive drugs directly into various structures of the mesotelencephalic dopamine system but not usually into other brain regions. For example, laboratory animals have been shown to self-administer microinjections of morphine into the ventral tegmental area, the nucleus accumbens, and the septum (see Chen, 1993).

Second, microinjections of drugs directly into various structures of the mesotelencephalic dopamine system lead to the development of conditioned place preferences. For example, in one series of studies (see White & Hiroi, 1993), microinjections of amphetamine directly into the nucleus accumbens produced a conditioned place preference, whereas injections into other mesotelencephalic dopamine system structures (the striatum, amygdala, or olfactory tubercle) did not.

Third, addictive drugs, but not nonaddictive drugs, have been shown to increase the rewarding effects of electrical stimulation to the mesotelencephalic dopamine system (Wise et al., 1992). For example, in one study, opiates with abuse potential reduced the current threshold for self-stimulation, whereas opiates with no abuse potential did not (Kornetsky & Esposito, 1979).

Fourth, disruption of mesotelencephalic function, either by lesions or by dopamine antagonists, has been shown to reduce the rewarding effects of addictive drugs injected *systematically* (into general circulation). For example, lesions to either the ventral tegmental area (Roberts & Koob, 1982) or the nucleus accumbens (Roberts et al., 1980)—but not to the other terminal structures of the mesotelencephalic dopamine system (Roberts & Zito, 1987)—have been shown to disrupt intravenous self-administration of amphetamine. Also, both dopamine antagonists (Phillips, Spyraki, & Fibiger, 1982) and lesions to the nucleus accumbens (Kelsey, Carlezon, & Falls, 1989) have been shown to prevent the development of conditioned place preferences associated with systemic morphine injections.

Fifth, *in vivo* voltammetry and cerebral dialysis recordings from the nucleus accumbens, the striatum, and other terminals of the mesotelencephalic dopamine system have shown that the systemic self-administration of most addictive drugs is associated with increased dopamine release (see Wise, 1993). For example, in one such cerebral dialysis study, Pettit and Justice (1991) found that the levels of extracellular dopamine were elevated in the nucleus accumbens during cocaine self-administration: Larger doses of cocaine produced greater increases in the release of dopamine.

The study of the mesotelencephalic dopamine system has greatly increased our understanding of the neural basis of addiction, but what has it done for addicts? Not much, at least not yet. The challenge is to develop selective dopamine antagonists that can substantially reduce the positive-incentive value of drugs in addicts without reducing the positive-incentive value of natural motivated behaviors.

CONCLUSION

In the first four sections of this chapter, you were introduced to the basic principles of drug action (13.1), to the role of learning in drug tolerance and drug withdrawal effects (13.2), to five commonly abused drugs (13.3), and to two fundamentally different ways of thinking about drug addiction (13.4). Then, you were introduced to the reward circuit of the brain—the mesotelencephalic dopamine system and its role in intracranial self-stimulation and natural motivated behaviors (13.5). Finally, you were presented with evidence that the mesotelencephalic dopamine system mediates the rewarding effects of addictive drugs (13.6).

To illustrate in a more personal way some of the things you have learned about addiction, this chapter concludes with a series of quotations that describe the interactions of one drug addict with two drugs of abuse: cocaine and tobacco. The addict was Sigmund Freud, a man of very special significance to psychology. Freud's battles with these two drugs have sobering implications. The following excerpts are from a report written in 1972 by Edward Brecher:

> The chief ingredient in coca leaves, the alkaloid cocaine, was isolated in pure form in 1844. Little use was made of it in Europe, however, until 1883, when a German army physician ... issued it to Bavarian soldiers during their autumn maneuvers....
>
> Among those who read [the] ... account with fascination was a poverty-stricken twenty-eight-year-old Viennese neurologist, Dr. Sigmund Freud.... "I have been reading about cocaine, the essential ingredient of coca leaves, which some Indian tribes chew to enable them to resist privations and hardships," Freud wrote his fiancée, Martha Bernays, on April 21, 1884. "I am procuring some myself and will try it...."
>
> In addition to taking cocaine himself, Freud offered some to his friend and associate, Dr. Ernst von Fleischl-Marxow, who was suffering from an exceedingly painful disease of the nervous system, and who was addicted to morphine....
>
> Freud even sent some of this precious cocaine to Martha.... "[H]e pressed it on his friends and colleagues, both for themselves and their patients; he gave it to his sisters. In short, looked at from the vantage point of present knowledge, he was rapidly becoming a public menace." (pp. 272–273)

Freud's famous essay "Song of Praise," to cocaine, was published in July 1884. In this article, Freud wrote in such glowing terms about his own personal experiences with cocaine that he created a wave of interest in the drug. But within a year, there was a critical reaction to Freud's premature advocacy:

In July 1885, a German authority on morphine addiction named Erlenmeyer launched the first of a series of attacks on cocaine as an addicting drug. In January 1886 Freud's friend Obersteiner, who had first favored cocaine, reported that it produced severe mental disturbances [later called cocaine psychosis].... Other attacks soon followed; and Freud was subjected to "grave reproaches." Freud continued to praise cocaine as late as July 1887.... But soon thereafter he discontinued all use of it both personally and professionally. Despite the fact that he had been taking cocaine periodically over a three-year span, he appears to have had no difficulty in stopping. (p. 274)

Some 9 years later, in 1894, when Freud was 38, his physician and close friend ordered him to stop smoking because it was causing a heart arrhythmia. Freud was a heavy smoker; he smoked approximately 20 cigars per day:

Freud did stop for a time ... but his subsequent depression and other withdrawal symptoms proved unbearable....
  Within seven weeks, Freud was smoking again.
  On a later occasion, Freud stopped smoking for fourteen very long months....
  More than fifteen years later, at the age of fifty-five, Freud was still smoking twenty cigars a day—and still struggling against his addiction. [In a letter written at the

time, he commented on the sudden intolerance of his heart for tobacco.]
  Four years later he wrote ... that his passion for smoking hindered his analytic studies. Yet he kept on smoking.
  In February 1923, at the age of sixty-seven, Freud noted sores on his right palate and jaw that failed to heal. They were cancers. An operation was performed—the first of thirty-three operations for cancer of the jaw and oral cavity which he endured during the sixteen remaining years of his life. "I am still out of work and cannot swallow," he wrote shortly after his first operation. "Smoking is accused as the etiology [cause] of this tissue rebellion." Yet he continued to smoke.
  In addition to his series of cancers ... Freud now suffered attacks of "tobacco angina" [heart pains] whenever he smoked.... Yet he continued to smoke.
  At seventy-three, Freud was ordered to retire to a sanitarium for his heart condition. He made an immediate recovery [because he stopped smoking] ... for twenty-three days. Then he started smoking one cigar a day. Then two. Then three or four....
  In 1936, at the age of seventy-nine ... Freud had more heart trouble.... His jaw had by then been entirely removed and an artificial jaw substituted; he was in almost constant pain; often he could not speak and sometimes he could not chew or swallow. Yet at the age of eighty-one, Freud was still smoking what ..., his close friend at this period, calls, "an endless series of cigars."
  Freud died of cancer in 1939. (pp. 214–215)

FOOD FOR THOUGHT

1. There are many misconceptions about drug abuse. Describe three. What do you think are the reasons for these misconceptions?

2. A man who had been a heroin user for many years was found dead of an overdose at a holiday resort. He appeared to have been in good health, and no foul play

was suspected. What factors might have led to his death?

3. If you had an opportunity to redraft the current legislation related to drug abuse in the light of what you have learned in this chapter, what changes would you make? Explain.

Psychoactive drugs *(p. 324)*
Subcutaneously (SC) *(p. 324)*
Intramuscularly (IM) *(p. 324)*
Intravenously (IV) *(p. 324)*
Drug metabolism *(p. 325)*
Drug tolerance *(p. 325)*
Cross tolerance *(p. 325)*
Sensitization *(p. 326)*
Metabolic tolerance *(p. 326)*
Functional tolerance *(p. 326)*
Withdrawal syndrome *(p. 326)*
Physically dependent *(p. 326)*
Addicts *(p. 327)*
Psychological dependence *(p. 327)*
Contingent drug tolerance *(p. 327)*
Before-and-after design *(p. 327)*

Conditioned drug tolerance *(p. 328)*
Hypothermic *(p. 329)*
Conditioned compensatory responses *(p. 329)*
Conditioned withdrawal effects *(p. 330)*
Nicotine *(p. 331)*
Smoker's syndrome *(p. 331)*
Buerger's disease *(p. 331)*
Free radicals *(p. 331)*
Depressant *(p. 332)*
Diuretic *(p. 332)*
Delirium tremens (DTs) *(p. 332)*
Korsakoff's syndrome *(p. 332)*
Cirrhosis *(p. 332)*
Fetal alcohol syndrome (FAS) *(p. 332)*
Cannabis sativa *(p. 333)*
THC *(p. 333)*

Hashish *(p. 333)*
Narcotic *(p. 334)*
Amotivational syndrome *(p. 334)*
Cocaine hydrochloride (cocaine) *(p. 335)*
Crack *(p. 335)*
Amphetamine *(p. 335)*
Stimulants *(p. 335)*
Cocaine sprees *(p. 335)*
Cocaine psychosis *(p. 335)*
Opium *(p. 336)*
Morphine *(p. 336)*
Codeine *(p. 336)*
Opiates *(p. 336)*
Analgesics *(p. 336)*
Harrison Narcotics Act *(p. 336)*
Heroin *(p. 336)*
Physical-dependence theory of addiction *(p. 340)*

Detoxified addicts *(p. 340)*
Positive-incentive theory of addiction *(p. 341)*
Disinhibition *(p. 341)*
Intracranial self-stimulation (ICSS) *(p. 341)*
Primed *(p. 342)*
Mesotelencephalic dopamine system *(p. 343)*
Substantia nigra *(p. 343)*
Ventral tegmental area *(p. 343)*
Nucleus accumbens *(p. 344)*
Consummatory behaviors *(p. 345)*
Preparatory behaviors *(p. 345)*
Drug self-administration paradigm *(p. 346)*
Conditioned place-preference paradigm *(p. 346)*

ADDITIONAL READING

A number of paperbacks provide interesting introductions to the topic of drug abuse. The following is my favorite:

McKim, W. A. (1986). *Drugs and behavior.* Englewood Cliffs, NJ: Prentice-Hall.

The following three articles are essential reading for anybody interested in the development of more effective approaches to the drug problem:

Goldstein, A., & Kalant, H. (1990). Drug policy: Striking the right balance. *Science, 249,* 1513–1519.

Jarvik, M. E. (1990). The drug dilemma: Manipulating the demand. *Science, 250,* 387–392.

Nadelmann, E. A. (1989). Drug prohibition in the United States: Costs, consequences, and alternatives. *Science, 245,* 939–947.

For reviews of recent research on the biopsychology of addiction, I recommend the following journal issues, which are dedicated entirely to the topic:

Trends in Pharmacological Science, 13 (May 1992).

Seminars in the Neurosciences, 5 (October 1993).

Memory
and Amnesia

14.1 Amnesic Effects of Bilateral Medial Temporal Lobectomy: The Case of H.M.

14.2 Amnesia of Korsakoff's Syndrome

14.3 Memory Deficits Associated with Prefrontal Cortex Damage

14.4 Amnesia of Alzheimer's Disease

14.5 Amnesia after Concussion

14.6 Neuroanatomy of Object-Recognition Memory

14.7 Hippocampus and Memory for Space

14.8 Memory Structures of the Brain

Memory is the brain's ability to store the learned effects of its experience. It is one of the brain's most fundamental abilities; it is difficult to imagine human existence without it. Without memory, each moment would be like waking from a lifelong sleep: Each person would be a stranger, each act a new challenge, and each word incomprehensible.

Even simple invertebrate nervous systems display elementary forms of memory; however, in this chapter, the emphasis will be on the memory systems of the human brain. In particular, this chapter will focus on what has been learned about the mechanisms of human memory from the assessment of brain-damage-produced amnesia in human neuropsychological patients and in animal models of human amnesic disorders.

14.1 Amnesic Effects of Bilateral Medial Temporal Lobectomy: The Case of H.M.

Ironically, the person who has contributed more than any other to our understanding of the neuropsychology of memory is not a neuropsychologist. In fact, although he has collaborated on dozens of studies of memory, he has no formal research training and not a single degree to his name. He is H.M., a man who in 1953, at the age of 27, had the medial portions of his temporal lobes removed for the treatment of a severe case of epilepsy. Just as the Rosetta Stone has provided archaeologists with important clues to the meaning of Egyptian hieroglyphics, H.M.'s memory deficits have been instrumental in the achievement of our current understanding of the neural bases of memory.

Early Theories of Memory Storage

In order to put the scientific contributions of H.M.'s case in perspective, let's first consider two ideas about the neural bases of memory that were prominent in the 1950s, when the first reports of H.M.'s case began to appear. First, the field of memory research was reeling from Karl Lashley's fruitless search for the location of the **engram**—the hypothetical change in the brain responsible for storing a memory.

Lashley, the most influential physiological psychologist of his era, had spent 35 years (1915 to 1950) training rats, cats, and monkeys to perform complex learning tasks and then cutting, destroying, or removing specific parts of their brains in a vain attempt to erase the memory of their training. For example, in one series of studies, rats received lesions of various sizes to different parts of the cerebral cortex after they had learned a maze task. Ten days later, their retention of the task was assessed. Lashley found that only large cortical lesions disrupted retention and that the particular site of the lesion was of little consequence: Cortical lesions of equal size produced similar effects regardless of their location.

On the basis of his findings, Lashley concluded that memories for complex tasks are stored diffusely throughout the neocortex (the **principle of mass action**) and that all parts of the neocortex play an equal role in their storage (the **principle of equipotentiality**). Although Lashley conceded that certain areas of the neocortex may play a more important role than other areas in the storage of certain memories—for example, the visual cortex may play a more important role in the storage of memories of visual stimuli—he argued that memories were stored diffusely and equally throughout these functional areas. Thus one effect of Lashley's work was to discourage theories of memory that assigned specific **mnemonic** (pertaining to memory) abilities to specific parts of the brain.

The second idea about the physiological bases of memory that was prominent in the 1950s was the theory that there are two different memory storage mechanisms: a *short-term system* and a *long-term system*. According to this theory, which is still widely accepted, each memory is held in short-term storage while the physiological changes necessary for long-term storage are taking place. For example, in order to remember a new phone number, we hold it in short-term storage by actively thinking about it until its presence in short-term storage produces the physiological changes that underlie its long-term storage.

The hypothetical transfer of a memory from short-term to long-term storage is called **consolidation.** According to

Memory. The brain's ability to store the learned effects of its experiences.

Engram. The hypothetical change in the brain responsible for the storage of a memory.

Principle of mass action. Lashley's idea that memories for complex tasks are stored diffusely throughout the neocortex.

Principle of equipotentiality. Lashley's idea that all parts of the neocortex play an equal role in the storage of memories for complex tasks.

Mnemonic. Pertaining to memory.

Consolidation. The hypothetical process by which a memory is transferred from short-term storage to long-term storage.

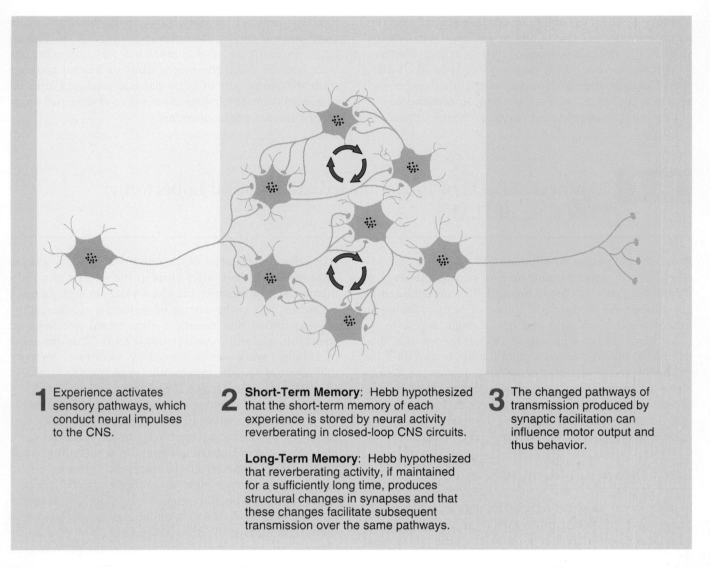

| 1 | Experience activates sensory pathways, which conduct neural impulses to the CNS. | 2 | **Short-Term Memory**: Hebb hypothesized that the short-term memory of each experience is stored by neural activity reverberating in closed-loop CNS circuits.

Long-Term Memory: Hebb hypothesized that reverberating activity, if maintained for a sufficiently long time, produces structural changes in synapses and that these changes facilitate subsequent transmission over the same pathways. | 3 | The changed pathways of transmission produced by synaptic facilitation can influence motor output and thus behavior. |

Figure 14.1 Hebb's (1949) theory of consolidation: How short-term memories were thought to be stored by reverberating neural activity that eventually becomes consolidated into long-term structural synaptic changes.

the most influential theory of consolidation (Hebb, 1949), the memory for a particular event is stored in the short-term mode by *reverberating neural activity* (neural activity that goes around and around in closed-loop circuits), which eventually produces long-term structural changes in the synapses that facilitate the later occurrence of the same pattern of activity. This structural synaptic facilitation is the putative mechanism of long-term memory storage (see Figure 14.1). The major prediction of this theory of memory is that experiences that are not held in short-term storage for a sufficient period of time by conscious consideration will not become integrated into the store of long-term memories. The classic example of this prediction is the loss of recall that is experienced by people when they are distracted just after they have looked up a new phone number.

Bilateral Medial Temporal Lobectomy

During the 11 years preceding his surgery, H.M. suffered an average of one generalized convulsion each week and many partial convulsions each day, despite massive doses of anticonvulsant medication. Electroencephalography suggested that H.M.'s convulsions arose from foci in the medial portions of both his left and right temporal lobes. Because the removal of one medial temporal lobe had proved to be an effective treatment for patients with a unilateral temporal lobe focus, the decision was made to perform a **bilateral medial temporal lobectomy**—the removal of the medial portions of both temporal lobes, including the **hippocampus,** the **amygdala,** and the adjacent cortex (see Figure 14.2). Bilateral medial temporal lobectomy had been per-

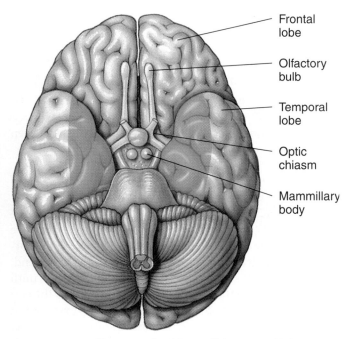

■ Tissue excised in medial-temporal lobectomy

Figure 14.2 Medial temporal lobectomy. The portions of the medial temporal lobes that were removed from H.M.'s brain are illustrated in a view of the inferior surface of the brain.

Frontal lobe

Olfactory bulb

Temporal lobe

Optic chiasm

Mammillary body

Like his intellectual abilities, H.M.'s memory for events predating his surgery remains largely intact. Although he has a mild retrograde amnesia for those events that occurred in the 2 years before his surgery, his memory for more remote events (e.g., for the events of his childhood) is normal.

In contrast to his reasonable memory for events predating his surgery, H.M. suffers from a devastating anterograde amnesia. His ability to hold information in short-term storage is well within the normal range—he has a **digit span** of six digits (Wickelgren, 1968); however, he cannot form new long-term memories. Once he stops thinking about a new experience, it is lost forever. In effect, H.M. became suspended in time on that day in 1953 when he regained his health but lost his future:

> As far as we can tell, this man has retained little if anything of events subsequent to the operation.... Ten months before I examined him, his family had moved from their old house to a new one a few blocks away on the same street. He still had not learned the new address (though remembering the old one perfectly), nor could he be trusted to find his way home alone. He did not know where objects in constant use were kept, and his mother stated that he would read the same magazines over and over again without finding their contents familiar.... [F]orgetting occurred the instant the patient's focus of attention shifted. (Milner, 1965, pp. 104–105)

formed on only a few previous occasions, but it has not been performed since. (A **lobectomy** is an operation in which a lobe, or a major part of one, is removed from the brain. A **lobotomy** is an operation in which a lobe, or a major part of one, is separated from the rest of the brain by a large cut but is not removed.)

In several respects, H.M.'s bilateral medial temporal lobectomy was an unqualified success. His generalized convulsions were all but eliminated, and the incidence of his minor seizures was reduced to one or two per day, even though the level of his anticonvulsant medication was substantially reduced. Furthermore, H.M. entered surgery a reasonably well-adjusted individual with normal perceptual and motor abilities and superior intelligence, and he left it in the same condition. Indeed, H.M.'s IQ increased from 104 to 118 as a result of his surgery, presumably because of the decline in the incidence of his seizures.

H.M.'s Postsurgery Memory Deficits

In assessing the amnesic effects of brain surgery, it is usual to administer tests of the patient's ability to remember things learned before the surgery and tests of the patient's ability to remember things learned after the surgery. Deficits on the former tests lead to a diagnosis of **retrograde** (backward-acting) **amnesia;** those on the latter tests lead to a diagnosis of **anterograde** (i.e., forward-acting) **amnesia.**

Bilateral medial temporal lobectomy. The removal of the medial portions of both temporal lobes, including the hippocampus, the amygdala, and the adjacent cortex.

Hippocampus. A structure of the medial temporal lobes that plays a role in memory for spatial location.

Amygdala. A structure of the medial temporal lobe that plays a role in the memory for the emotional significance of experiences.

Lobectomy. An operation in which a lobe, or a major part of one, is removed from the brain.

Lobotomy. An operation in which a lobe, or a major part of one, is separated from the rest of the brain by a large cut but is not removed.

Retrograde amnesia. Loss of memory for information learned before the amnesia-inducing brain injury.

Anterograde amnesia. Loss of memory for events occurring after the amnesia-inducing brain injury.

Digit span. The maximum number of random digits that a subject can successfully repeat 50% of the time—the standard measure of verbal short-term memory.

During three of the nights at the Clinical Research Center, the patient rang for the night nurse, asking her, with many apologies, if she would tell him where he was and how he came to be there. He clearly realized that he was in a hospital but seemed unable to reconstruct any of the events of the previous day. On another occasion he remarked "Every day is alone in itself, whatever enjoyment I've had, and whatever sorrow I've had." Our own impression is that … events fade for him long before the day is over. He often volunteers stereotyped descriptions of his own state, by saying that it is "like waking from a dream." His experience seems to be that of a person who is just becoming aware of his surroundings without fully comprehending the situation, because he does not remember what went before.

He still fails to recognize people who are close neighbours or family friends but who got to know him only after the operation. When questioned, he tries to use accent as a clue to a person's place of origin and weather as a clue to the time of year. Although he gives his date of birth unhesitatingly and accurately, he always underestimates his own age and can only make wild guesses as to the date.…

After his father's death, H.M. was given protected employment in a state rehabilitation centre, where he spends week-days participating in rather monotonous work, programmed for severely retarded patients. A typical task is the mounting of cigarette-lighters on cardboard frames for display. It is characteristic that he cannot give us any description of his place of work, the nature of his job, or the route along which he is driven each day, to and from the centre. (Milner, Corkin, & Teuber, 1968, pp. 216–217)

H.M. has lived in a nursing home for many years. He currently spends much of each day doing crossword puzzles; his progress on a crossword puzzle is never lost because it is written down.

Formal Assessment of H.M.'s Anterograde Amnesia

This subsection describes H.M.'s performance on seven objective tests of memory.

Digit span + 1 test H.M.'s inability to form long-term memories is illustrated by his performance on the **digit span + 1 test.** H.M. was asked to repeat 5 digits that were read to him at 1-second intervals. He repeated the sequence correctly. On the next trial, the same 5 digits were presented in the same sequence with 1 new digit added to the end. This same 6-digit sequence was presented a few times until he got it right, and then another digit was added to the end of it, and so on. After 25 trials, H.M. had not managed to repeat the 8-digit sequence. Normal subjects can repeat about 15 digits after 25 digit span + 1 trials (Drachman & Arbit, 1966).

Block-tapping memory-span test Milner (1971) demonstrated that H.M.'s amnesia was not restricted to verbal material by assessing his performance on the + 1 version of the **block-tapping memory span test.** An array of 9 blocks was spread out on a board in front of H.M., and he was asked to watch the neuropsychologist touch a sequence of them and then to repeat the same sequence of touches. H.M. had a *block-tapping span* of 5 blocks, which is in the normal range; but he could not learn to correctly touch a sequence of 6 blocks, even when the same sequence was repeated 12 times. H.M. has **global amnesia**—amnesia for information presented in all sensory modalities.

Matching-to-sample tests H.M.'s reliance on active rehearsal to remember new experiences was illustrated by a comparison of his performance on verbal and nonverbal matching-to-sample tests. On each trial of a **matching-to-sample test,** a sample item is presented. Then, after a delay, an array of test items is presented. From this array, the subject must select the one item that matches (is the same as) the sample. Sidman, Stoddard, and Mohr (1968) tested H.M. with verbal and nonverbal forms of this test (see Figure 14.3). When the stimuli were sequences of three consonants, H.M. had no difficulty at even the longest, 40-second, delay. In contrast, when the stimuli were different shapes of ellipses, H.M. could not perform at delays of more than 5 seconds. A control group of schoolchildren made almost no errors on either the verbal or the nonverbal forms of the test. Sidman and his colleagues concluded that H.M.'s verbal matching-to-sample performance was superior to his performance on the nonverbal version of the test because letters, but not ellipses, can be actively rehearsed. (There are

Digit span + 1 test. A measure of verbal memory in which each time the subject correctly repeats a sequence of digits, the next test item is the same sequence with an additional digit added to the end of it.

Block-tapping memory span test. A nonverbal equivalent of the digit span test.

Global amnesia. Amnesia for information in all sensory modalities.

Matching-to-sample test. A memory test in which a sample stimulus is momentarily presented, followed by a delay, at which point the subject must select the sample stimulus from a group of test stimuli.

Mirror-drawing test. A test in which the subject traces a star while watching her or his hand in a mirror.

Rotary-pursuit test. A test in which the subject tries to keep the end of a stylus in contact with a target rotating on a turntable.

Incomplete-pictures test. A test of memory involving the improved ability to identify fragmented figures that have been previously observed.

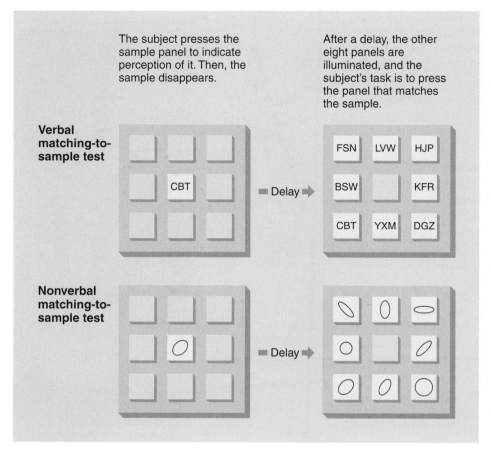

The subject presses the sample panel to indicate perception of it. Then, the sample disappears.

After a delay, the other eight panels are illuminated, and the subject's task is to press the panel that matches the sample.

Verbal matching-to-sample test

CBT

■ Delay ➡

FSN LVW HJP
BSW KFR
CBT YXM DGZ

Nonverbal matching-to-sample test

■ Delay ➡

Figure 14.3 The verbal and nonverbal matching-to-sample tests given to H.M. by Sidman, Stoddard, and Mohr (1968). Although H.M. performed the verbal form of the test without error up to the 40-second retention interval, he could not perform the nonverbal form at intervals of greater than 5 seconds, presumably because of the difficulty of actively rehearsing the nonverbal stimuli.

no English words for different ellipses that would permit their rehearsal.)

Mirror-drawing test The first indication that H.M.'s anterograde amnesia does not involve all long-term memories came from the results of a **mirror-drawing test** (Milner, 1965). H.M.'s task was to draw a line within the boundaries of a star-shaped target by watching his hand in a mirror. H.M. was asked to trace the star 10 times on each of 3 consecutive days, and the number of times that he went outside the boundaries on each trial was recorded. As Figure 14.4 on page 356 shows, H.M.'s performance improved over the 3 days, which indicates retention of the task. However, despite his improved performance, H.M. could not recall ever having seen the task before.

Rotary-pursuit test In the **rotary-pursuit test** (see Figure 14.5 on page 357), the subject tries to keep the tip of a stylus in contact with a target that rotates on a revolving turntable. Corkin (1968) found that H.M.'s performance of

the rotary-pursuit task improved significantly over 9 daily practice sessions, despite the fact that H.M. claimed each day that he had never seen the pursuit rotor before. His improved performance was retained over a 7-day retention interval.

Incomplete-pictures test The discovery that H.M. is capable of forming long-term memories for reverse mirror drawing and rotary pursuit suggested that sensorimotor tasks were the one exception to his inability to form long-term memories. However, this view was challenged by the demonstration that H.M. could also form new long-term memories for the **incomplete-pictures test** (Gollin, 1960)—a nonsensorimotor test of memory that employs five sets of fragmented drawings. Each set contains drawings of the same 20 objects, but they differ in their degree of sketchiness; set 1 contains the most fragmented drawings, and set 5 contains the complete drawings. The subject is asked to identify the 20 objects from the sketchiest set (set 1); then, those objects that go unrecognized are presented in their set 2 versions, and so on until all 20 items have been identified. Figure 14.6 illustrates the performance of H.M. on this test and his improved performance 1 hour later (Milner, Corkin, & Teuber, 1968). Despite his improved performance, H.M. could not recall previously performing the task.

Pavlovian conditioning Following a series of pairings of a tone and a puff of air to the eye, H.M. blinked each time the tone was presented (Woodruff-Pak, 1993). Two years later, he retained this Pavlovian conditioned response almost perfectly, although he had no conscious awareness of his previous training.

Scientific Contributions of H.M.'s Case

H.M.'s case is a story of personal tragedy, but its contributions to the study of the neural basis of memory have been immense. Following are six of these contributions:

1. By showing that the medial temporal lobes play a particularly important role in memory, H.M.'s case challenged the view that memory functions are diffusely and equivalently distributed throughout the brain. H.M.'s case thus renewed efforts to relate particular brain structures to particular mnemonic processes.

2. By implicating the medial temporal lobes in memory, H.M.'s case spawned a massive research effort aimed at clarifying the mnemonic functions of the hippocampus, and other medial temporal lobe structures.

3. The discovery that bilateral medial temporal lobectomy abolished H.M.'s ability to form certain kinds of long-term memories without disrupting his performance on tests of short-term memory supported the theory that there are different modes of storage for short-term and long-term memory.

4. H.M.'s case study was the first to reveal that an amnesic patient might claim no recollection of a previous experience, while demonstrating memory for it by improved performance. Conscious memories that can be expressed by declaration are **explicit** (declarative) **memories,** whereas memories that are expressed by

Figure 14.4 The learning and retention of the mirror-drawing task by H.M. Despite his good retention of the task, H.M. had no conscious recollection of having performed the task before. (Adapted from Milner, 1965.)

improved test performance without conscious awareness are **implicit** (procedural) **memories** (see Graf & Schacter, 1987; Schacter, Chiu, & Ochsner, 1993). H.M. can form new long-term implicit memories but not new long-term explicit memories.

Explicit memories. Conscious memories that can be expressed by declaration; declarative memories.

Implicit memories. Memories that are expressed by improved performance without conscious recall or recognition; procedural memories.

Figure 14.5 The rotary-pursuit task. The subject tries to keep the stylus in contact with the rotating target, and time-on-target is automatically recorded. H.M. learned and retained this task although he had no conscious recollection of the learning trials.

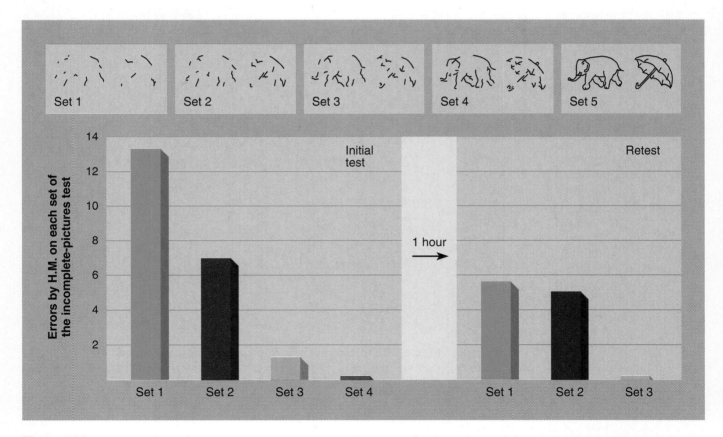

Figure 14.6 Two items from the incomplete-pictures test. H.M.'s memory for the 20 items of the test was indicated by his ability to recognize the more fragmented versions of them when he was retested. Nevertheless, he had no conscious awareness of having previously seen the items.

5. The pattern of H.M.'s memory deficits suggests that the medial temporal lobes play a role in memory consolidation. H.M.'s capacity to store short-term memories has remained intact, as has his capacity to store most of his long-term memories that were formed before his operation. His specific problem appears to be the transfer of short-term explicit memories to long-term storage.

6. The 2-year time span covered by H.M.'s retrograde amnesia challenged the notions of memory consolidation that were popular in the 1950s and 1960s. According to Hebb's consolidation theory, memories are transferred from short-term to long-term storage in a few seconds or perhaps minutes, after which they are as resistant to disruption as they are going to get. The fact that H.M.'s memory for events that occurred in the 2 years prior to his surgery was more susceptible to disruption than was his memory for more remote events suggests that the resistance of memories to disruption continues to increase for a long time after acquisition.

The Case of R.B.: Hippocampal Damage and Medial Temporal Lobe Amnesia?

Bilateral medial temporal lobectomy damages several major structures—most notably the hippocampus, the amygdala, and the adjacent cortex. However, in their original report of H.M.'s case, Scoville and Milner (1957) suggested—without good evidence—that the amnesic effects of bilateral medial temporal lobectomy are largely a consequence of the hippocampal damage. The subsequent case of R.B. supported this hypothesis (Zola-Morgan, Squire, & Amaral, 1986).

At the age of 52, R.B.'s brain was damaged during cardiac bypass surgery. An equipment malfunction interrupted the flow of blood to R.B.'s brain, and the resulting **ischemic brain damage**—brain damage produced by ischemia (an interruption of the blood supply)—left R.B. amnesic.

Although R.B.'s amnesia was not as severe as H.M.'s, it was comparable in many aspects. R.B. died in 1983 of a

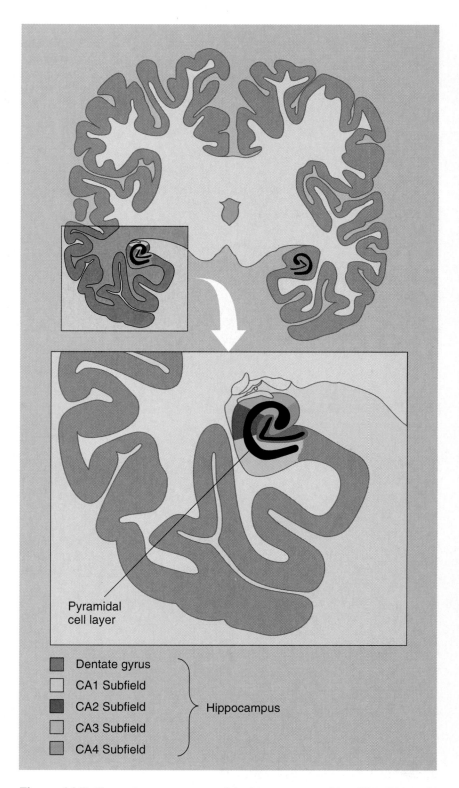

Figure 14.7 The major components of the hippocampus: CA1, CA2, CA3, and CA4 subfields and the dentate gyrus. R.B.'s brain damage appeared to be restricted largely to the pyramidal cell layer of the CA1 subfield.

heart attack, and a detailed postmortem examination of his brain was carried out with the permission of his family. Obvious brain damage was restricted largely to the

pyramidal cell layer of just one part of the hippocampus—the **CA1 subfield** (see Figure 14.7). R.B.'s case suggests that hippocampal damage by itself can produce amnesia; however, this issue is far from settled—as you will learn later in this chapter.

14.2 Amnesia of Korsakoff's Syndrome

As you have learned in previous chapters, **Korsakoff's syndrome** is a disorder of memory that is common in people who consume large amounts of alcohol. In its advanced stages, it is characterized by a variety of sensory and motor problems, extreme confusion, personality changes, and a risk of death from liver, gastrointestinal, or heart disorders. Postmortem examination typically reveals lesions to the *medial diencephalon* (the medial thalamus and the medial hypothalamus) and diffuse damage to several other brain structures, most notably the neocortex and the cerebellum.

Like H.M. and R.B., Korsakoff patients suffer from severe anterograde amnesia. However, unlike H.M. and R.B., Korsakoff patients also suffer from severe retrograde amnesia (Marslen-Wilson & Teuber, 1975). They display substantial amnesia for remote events, and their amnesia for recent events is even more severe. The retrograde amnesia for recent events is difficult to interpret because Korsakoff's syndrome has an insidious onset. It is not clear to what extent memory deficits for recent events reflect the retrograde disruption of existing memories or the gradually increasing anterograde blockage of the formation of new ones.

Like H.M. and R.B., most Korsakoff patients display normal or near normal implicit memory while exhibiting severe deficits in explicit memory. Implicit memory is most frequently assessed with a task called **repetition priming.** In one version of this test, the subjects are asked to examine a list of words and then later are presented with fragments of words that were in the list (e.g., _ S S _ S S _ _) and are asked to complete the fragments with the first words that come to mind. Korsakoff patients and other amnesic patients with damage to either the medial temporal lobe or the medial diencephalon typically complete the word fragments as well as normal subjects (e.g., ASSASSIN), thus demonstrating normal implicit memory for the original list (see Schacter, Chiu, & Ochsner, 1993). However, unlike normal subjects, they typically have little or no explicit memory for the list, that is, they typically do not recall ever having seen the list.

Ischemic brain damage. Brain damage caused by ischemia—by an interruption of the blood supply to the affected area.

Pyramidal cell layer. The major layer of cell bodies in the hippocampus.

CA1 subfield. The region of the hippocampus that is commonly damaged by cerebral ischemia.

Korsakoff's syndrome. A memory disorder that is often associated with chronic alcohol consumption.

Repetition priming. A test of implicit memory in which a list of words is presented, then fragments of the original words are presented and the subject is asked to complete the fragments with any appropriate word that comes to mind.

Mammillary bodies. A pair of hypothalamic nuclei, damage to which was originally thought to be critical for many of the memory deficits associated with Korsakoff's syndrome.

Mediodorsal nuclei. A pair of medial thalamic nuclei, damage to which is thought to be responsible for many of the memory deficits associated with Korsakoff's syndrome.

Medial Diencephalic Damage and Korsakoff Amnesia

Because the brain damage associated with Korsakoff's syndrome is so diffuse, it has not been easy to identify the portion of it that is specifically responsible for the amnesia. The first hypothesis, which was based on several small postmortem studies, was that damage to the **mammillary bodies** of the hypothalamus was responsible for the memory deficits of Korsakoff patients. However, a large-scale postmortem study by Victor, Adams, and Collins (1971) subsequently revealed several severe cases of Korsakoff's amnesia with no mammillary body damage. But in all of these cases, there was damage to another pair of medial diencephalic nuclei: the **mediodorsal nuclei** of the thalamus. The occurrence of amnesia in stroke patients with small ischemic lesions that include the mediodorsal nuclei provides additional evidence of their important mnemonic function (e.g., Graff-Radford et al., 1985; von Cramon, Hebel, & Schuri, 1985; Winocur et al., 1984). However, it is unlikely that the memory deficits of Korsakoff patients are entirely attributable to the damage of any single structure (see Butters & Stuss, 1989).

With respect to the study of amnesia, N.A. has been to the diencephalon what H.M. has been to the medial temporal lobes. After a year of junior college, N.A. joined the U.S. Air Force; he served as a radar technician until his accident in December of 1960. On that fateful day, N.A.

> was assembling a model airplane in his barracks room. His roommate had removed a miniature fencing foil from the wall and was making thrusts behind N.A.'s chair. N.A. turned suddenly and was stabbed through the right nostril. The foil penetrated the cribriform plate [the thin bone around the base of the frontal lobes], taking an upward course to the left into the forebrain. (Squire, 1987, p. 177)

> The examiners ... noted that at first he seemed to be unable to recall any significant personal, national or international events for the two years preceding the accident, but this extensive retrograde amnesia appeared to shrink.... Two-and-a-half years after the accident, the retrograde amnesia was said to involve a span of perhaps two weeks immediately preceding the injury, but the exact extent of this retrograde loss was (and remains) impossible to determine....

> During ... convalescence (for the first six to eight months after the accident), the patient's recall of day-to-day events was described as extremely poor, but "occa-sionally some items sprang forth uncontrollably; he suddenly recalled something he seemed to have no business recalling." His physicians thus gained the impression that his memory was patchy; he appeared to have difficulty in calling up at will many things that at other times emerged spontaneously....

> Since his injury, he has been unable to return to any gainful employment, although his memory has continued to improve, albeit slowly. (Teuber, Milner, & Vaughan, 1968, pp. 268–269)

A CAT scan of N.A.'s brain was taken in the late 1970s (Squire & Moore, 1979). The scan revealed a lesion in the left mediodorsal nucleus of the thalamus—the nucleus implicated in the amnesia of Korsakoff patients. Damage to other neural structures along the path of the foil was not visible.

The case of N.A. has been widely cited to support the view that the mediodorsal nuclei play an important role in memory. However, the subsequent report of a patient, B.J., with similar memory problems (Dusoir et al., 1990) suggests that the mediodorsal nuclei are not the only medial diencephalic memory structures. The case of B.J. is almost identical to that of N.A., except that it involves the left nostril rather than the right, a snooker cue rather than a fencing foil, and the mammillary bodies rather than the mediodorsal nuclei.

14.3 Memory Deficits Associated with Prefrontal Cortex Damage

The **prefrontal cortex** has traditionally been assumed to be the seat of our most complex intellectual functions. Nevertheless, neuropsychological patients with damage restricted to the prefrontal cortex often do not display deficits on conventional tests of memory (see Petrides, 1989). There are, however, two specific memory deficits that are associated with prefrontal cortex damage.

One deficit that is associated with prefrontal cortex damage is the failure to release from proactive interference. **Proactive interference** is the interfering effects of performing one task on the performance of a subsequent one. For example, normal subjects exhibit a gradual decline in their ability to learn and recall successive lists of words of the same category (e.g., lists of animal names) because of the accumulating proactive interference from learning preceding lists. However, when a list of words from a different category (e.g., a list of vegetables) is inserted in the series, the subjects display an improvement in their ability to recall these novel items. Such a release from proactive interference does not occur in patients with damage to the prefrontal cortex (Moscovitch, 1982).

The second memory deficit that has been associated with prefrontal cortex damage is a difficulty in remembering temporal sequences. For example, in a study by Corsi and Milner (see Milner, 1971), subjects were presented with a series of stimulus cards, each with a different image. Occasionally, a card with two images would appear, and the subject would be asked which of the two images had appeared previously—or, if both had appeared previously, which had appeared more recently. Patients with prefrontal damage had no problem discriminating previously presented from not previously presented images, but they had great difficulty in judging which of two familiar images had appeared more recently.

Patients with brain damage restricted to the medial temporal lobes or the medial diencephalon do not display deficits in release from proactive interference or in memory for temporal order (see Cermak, Uhly, & Reale, 1980; Squire, Nadel, & Slater, 1981). For example, both H.M. (Sagar et al., 1990) and N.A. (Squire, 1982) read 12 unrelated sentences, then 3 minutes later read another 12. Later, their ability to recognize the sentences and to recall whether they had appeared in the first or second list was assessed. Both H.M. and N.A. had difficulty recognizing the sentences that they had previously read; but when they were encouraged to guess which of the two previously read sentences had appeared in the more recent list, they performed without deficit. In contrast to H.M. and N.A., many Korsakoff patients display deficits in both release from proactive interference (Cermak, Uhly, & Reale, 1980) and memory for temporal sequence (Squire, 1982)—presumably because they usually have diffuse prefrontal cortex damage.

The prefrontal cortex is not a homogeneous structure. It is composed of numerous anatomically distinct areas, which have different connections and, presumably, different functions. The mnemonic functions of individual prefrontal areas has yet to be elucidated (see Petrides, 1994).

14.4   Amnesia of Alzheimer's Disease

Alzheimer's disease is the most common cause of *dementia* (general intellectual deterioration); close to 5% of all people over 65 suffer from it. It is terminal.

Autopsy reveals three kinds of pathological changes in the brains of Alzheimer patients: extensive neural degeneration, **neurofibrillary tangles** (threadlike tangles in the neural cytoplasm), and **amyloid plaques** (spherical clumps of scar tissue composed of degenerating neurons interspersed with an abnormal protein called *amyloid*). Although they are distributed diffusely throughout the brain, these pathological changes are particularly prevalent in the temporal, frontal, and parietal cortex; in the structures of the medial temporal lobe; and in the structures of the basal forebrain.

The first sign of Alzheimer's disease is usually a mild deterioration of memory. Then, the symptoms grow progressively more severe and diverse until a dementia develops that is so severe that the patient is incapable of most activities (e.g., eating, speaking, recognizing a spouse, or even controlling the bladder). Accordingly, efforts to understand the neural basis of Alzheimer's amnesia have focused on the testing of Alzheimer patients who have yet to reach the advanced stages of the disorder.

The memory deficits associated with predementia Alzheimer's disease are more general than those associated with medial temporal lobe damage, medial diencephalic damage, and Korsakoff's syndrome (see Butters & Delis, 1995; Carlesimo & Oscar-Berman, 1992). In addition to large anterograde and retrograde deficits in tests of explicit memory, predementia Alzheimer patients often display deficits in short-term memory and in some types of implicit memory: Implicit memory for verbal and perceptual material is deficient, whereas implicit memory for sensorimotor learning is not (see Gabrieli et al., 1993).

Early studies of the biochemistry of Alzheimer's disease focused on the large reduction in cholinergic activity that occurs in the brains of Alzheimer's patients: There is less acetylcholine, less *choline acetyltransferase* (the enzyme that stimulates the synthesis of acetylcholine), and less *acetylcholinesterase* (the enzyme that breaks down acetylcholine in synapses). This reduction of cholinergic activity results from the degeneration of neurons of the **basal forebrain,** which are the brain's major source of acetylcholine. The three main cholinergic structures of the basal forebrain are the *nucleus basalis of Meynert*, the *diagonal band of Broca*, and the *medial septal nucleus.* The nucleus basilis of Meynert projects widely to the frontal, temporal, and parietal cortexes, whereas the diagonal band of Broca and the medial septal nucleus project to the structures of the medial temporal lobe.

The reduction of acetylcholine in the brains of Alzheimer's patients suggested that the cholinergic neurons of the basal forebrain play a major role in memory. However, several findings have raised questions about this theory (see Fibiger, 1991; Zola-Morgan & Squire, 1993). For example, levels of other cerebral neurotransmitters (e.g., norepinephrine and serotonin) have also been found to be reduced in Alzheimer's patients (see Coyle, 1987); extensive damage that could account for many of the memory problems of Alzheimer patients has been found in the medial temporal lobes (see Hyman, Van Hoesen, & Damasio, 1990); cholinergic agonists have been unable to forestall the inexorable progression of Alzheimer's amnesia; and basal forebrain damage produces deficits in attention, which could easily be mistaken for memory deficits in some tests of memory (see Robbins et al., 1989). This is not to say that there is currently no support for the cholinergic theory of memory, since selective lesions to the basal forebrain area have been reported to produce memory deficits in both humans (Morris et al., 1992) and monkeys (Aigner et al., 1991).

Prefrontal cortex. The area of the frontal cortex anterior to the motor cortex, damage to which disrupts memory for temporal order and release from proactive interference.

Proactive interference. The disruptive effects of performing one task on performance of a subsequent one.

Neurofibrillary tangles. Abnormal threadlike tangles in the neural cytoplasm of patients with Alzheimer's disease.

Amyloid plaques. Scars composed of degenerating neural fibers and amyloid protein that are found in the brains of patients with Alzheimer's disease.

Basal forebrain. The cholinergic area at the base of the forebrain that is damaged in Alzheimer's disease and includes the nucleus basalis of Meynert, the diagonal band of Broca, and the medial septal nucleus.

The cholinergic theory of memory has spawned numerous attempts to show that acetylcholine agonists can function as **nootropics**—memory-improving drugs. However, despite some promising results in laboratory animals (e.g., Meck, Smith, & Williams, 1989), claims of drug-induced memory enhancement in healthy humans are best viewed with skepticism at the present time (see Thal, 1989). On the other hand, the ability of muscarinic cholinergic antagonists (e.g., scopolamine) to impair long-term object-recognition memory is well established (e.g., Aigner, Walker, & Mishkin, 1991).

14.5   Amnesia after Concussion

Blows to the head that do not penetrate the skull but are severe enough to produce *concussion* (a temporary disturbance of consciousness produced by a nonpenetrating head injury) are the most common causes of amnesia (see Levin, 1989). Amnesia following a nonpenetrating blow to the head is called **posttraumatic amnesia (PTA).**

The *coma* (a pathological state of unconsciousness) following a severe blow to the head usually lasts a few seconds or minutes, but in severe cases it can last weeks. Then, once the patient regains consciousness, there is a period of confusion. Victims of concussion are typically not tested by a neuropsychologist until after the period of confusion—if they are tested at all. Testing usually reveals that the patient has a permanent retrograde amnesia for the events that led up to the blow and a permanent anterograde amnesia for many of the events that occurred during the subsequent period of confusion.

The anterograde memory deficits that follow a nonpenetrating head injury are often quite puzzling to the friends and relatives who have talked to the patient during the period of confusion— for example, during a hospital visit. The patient may seem reasonably lucid at the time, because short-term memory is normal, but later may have no recollection whatsoever of the conversation.

Figure 14.8 summarizes the effects of a closed-head injury on memory. Note that the duration of the period of confusion and the anterograde amnesia is typically longer than that of the coma, which is typically longer than the period of retrograde amnesia. More severe blows to the head tend to produce longer comas, longer periods of confusion, and longer periods of amnesia (Levin, Papanicolaou, & Eisenberg, 1984). Not illustrated in Figure 14.8 are **islands of memory**—memories that sometimes survive for isolated events that occurred during periods that have otherwise been wiped out.

Electroconvulsive Shock and Gradients of Retrograde Amnesia

Electroconvulsive shock (ECS) is an intense, brief, seizure-inducing current that is administered to the brain through large electrodes attached to the scalp. It is used in the treat-

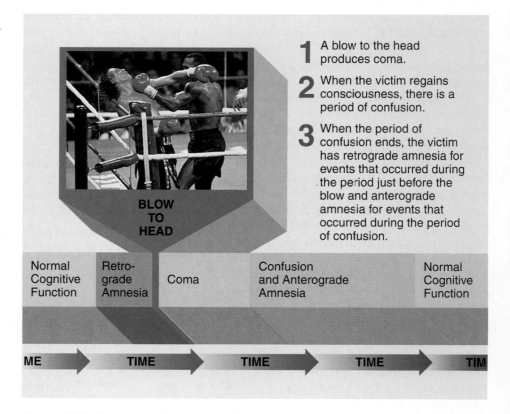

1 A blow to the head produces coma.

2 When the victim regains consciousness, there is a period of confusion.

3 When the period of confusion ends, the victim has retrograde amnesia for events that occurred during the period just before the blow and anterograde amnesia for events that occurred during the period of confusion.

BLOW TO HEAD

| Normal Cognitive Function | Retro-grade Amnesia | Coma | Confusion and Anterograde Amnesia | Normal Cognitive Function |

ME   TIME   TIME   TIME   TIM

Figure 14.8 The retrograde amnesia and anterograde amnesia that are associated with a concussion-producing blow to the head.

Chapter 14   Memory and Amnesia

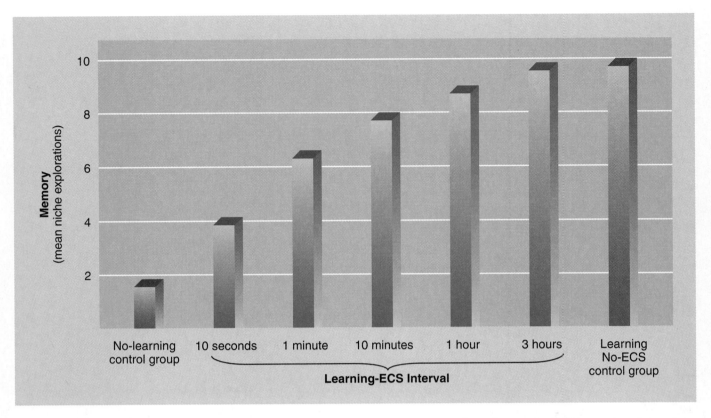

Figure 14.9 Retention of one-trial appetitive learning by control rats and by groups of rats that received ECS at various intervals after the learning trial. Only the rats that received ECS within 10 minutes of the learning trial displayed significant retrograde amnesia for it. (Adapted from Pinel, 1969.)

ment of severe depression, and one of its side effects is posttraumatic amnesia.

ECS provided a method of studying memory consolidation. The rationale was that by disrupting neural activity, ECS would erase from storage only those memories that had not yet been converted to structural synaptic changes; the length of the period of retrograde amnesia produced by an ECS would thus provide an estimate of the amount of time needed for memory consolidation.

In one such study (Pinel, 1969), thirsty rats were placed for 10 minutes on each of 5 consecutive days in a test box that contained a small niche. By the 5th of these habituation sessions, most rats explored the niche only 1 or 2 times per session. On the 6th day, a water spout was placed in the niche, and each rat was allowed to drink for 15 seconds after it discovered the spout. This was the learning trial. Then, 10 seconds, 1 minute, 10 minutes, 1 hour, or 3 hours later, each experimental rat received a single ECS. Some control rats received no learning trial, whereas others received the learning trial but no ECS. The next day, the retention of all subjects was assessed on the basis of how many times each explored the niche when the water spout was not present. The control rats that experienced the learning trial but received no ECS explored the empty

niche an average of 10 times during the 10-minute test session, thereby indicating that they remembered their discovery of water the previous day. The rats that had received ECS 1 hour or 3 hours after the learning trial also explored the niche about 10 times. In contrast, the rats that received the ECS 10 seconds, 1 minute, or 10 minutes after the learning trial explored the empty niche significantly less on the test day. This result suggested that the consolidation of the memory of the learning trial took between 10 minutes and 1 hour (see Figure 14.9).

Nootropics. Hypothetical memory-improving drugs.

Posttraumatic amnesia (PTA). Amnesia produced by a nonpenetrating head injury (e.g., by a blow to the head that does not penetrate the skull).

Islands of memory. Memories for isolated events that occurred during periods for which a person is otherwise totally amnesic.

Electroconvulsive shock (ECS). A diffuse electric shock to the brain that induces a convulsion.

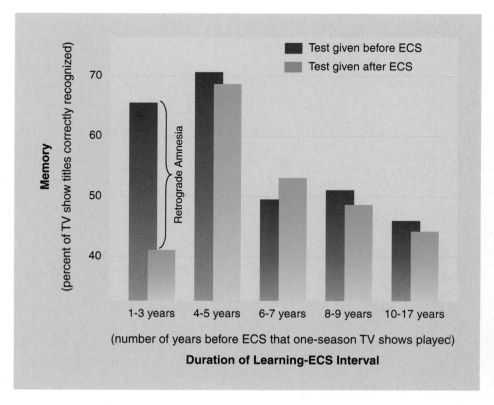

Figure 14.10 A demonstration of ECS-produced amnesia. A series of five electroconvulsive shocks produced retrograde amnesia for television shows that played for only one season in the 3 years before the shocks; however, the shocks did not produce amnesia for one-season shows that had played prior to that. (Adapted from Squire et al., 1975.)

Numerous variations of this experiment were conducted in the 1950s and 1960s, with different learning tasks, different species, and different numbers and intensities of electroconvulsive shocks. Initially, there was some consistency in the findings: Most seemed to suggest a rather brief consolidation time of a few minutes or less (e.g., Chorover & Schiller, 1965). But then things became complicated. It was reasonable to think of the neural activity resulting from an experience reverberating through the brain for a few seconds or even a few minutes; but reports of ECS gradients of retrograde amnesia covering hours, days, weeks, and even years began to appear (e.g., Squire & Spanis, 1984). These long gradients indicated that the resistance of memories to disruption by ECS can continue to increase for a very long time after learning, if not indefinitely. Thus it seems unlikely that reverberating neural activity is the mechanism of memory consolidation.

One demonstration of a long gradient of ECS-produced amnesia employed a particularly innovative test of memory. Squire, Slater and Chace (1975) measured the memory of a group of ECS-treated patients for television shows that had played for only one season in different years prior to their electroconvulsive therapy. They tested each subject twice on different forms of the test, once before they received a series of five electroconvulsive shocks and once after. The difference between the before-and-after scores served as an estimate of memory loss for the events of each year. Figure 14.10 illustrates that five electroconvulsive shocks disrupted the retention of television shows that had played in the 3 years prior to treatment but not those that had played earlier.

This chapter now moves from the discussion of human amnesia to a consideration of animal models of human amnesia. Before you make this transition, review what you have learned about human amnesia by completing the following exercise. The correct answers are provided at the bottom of this page. Before proceeding, review the material related to your errors and omissions.

1. The transfer of a memory from short-term storage to long-term storage is termed _____.

2. H.M. had his _____ temporal lobes removed.

3. The rotary-pursuit test, the incomplete-picture test, the mirror-drawing test, and the repetition-priming test are all tests of _____ memory.

4. H.M. is incapable of forming new long-term _____ memories.

5. Support for the view that hippocampal damage can by itself cause amnesia comes from the study of R.B., a subject who suffered _____ damage to the pyramidal cells of his CA1 hippocampal subfield.

6. The current view is that damage to the _____ diencephalon is responsible for most of the memory deficits of people with Korsakoff's disease.

7. N.A. had damage to the _____ nucleus of the thalamus.

8. Patients with Korsakoff's disease and patients with _____ cortex damage have difficulty remembering the temporal order of events and fail to display a release from proactive interference.

9. Alzheimer's disease is associated with the degeneration of _____ neurons in the basal forebrain.

10. Posttraumatic amnesia can be induced with _____ shock, which is used in the treatment of depression.

11. Because some gradients of retrograde amnesia are extremely long, it is unlikely that memory consolidation is mediated by _____ neural activity, as hypothesized by Hebb.

The answers are (1) consolidation, (2) medial, (3) implicit (or procedural), (4) explicit (or declarative), (5) ischemic, (6) medial, (7) mediodorsal, (8) prefrontal, (9) cholinergic, (10) electroconvulsive, and (11) reverberating.

As interesting and informative as the study of amnesic patients can be, it has major limitations. Many important questions about the neural bases of memory and amnesia cannot be answered by studying amnesic patients because controlled experiments are necessary for answering them. For example, in order to identify the particular structures of the brain that participate in various kinds of memory, it is necessary to make precise lesions in various structures and to control what and when the subjects learn, and how and when their retention is tested. Because such experiments are not feasible in human subjects, there has been a major effort to develop animal models of human brain-damage-produced amnesia to complement the study of human cases.

The first reports of H.M.'s case in the 1950s triggered a massive effort to develop an animal model of his disorder so that it could be subjected to experimental analysis. In its early years, this effort was a dismal failure; lesions of medial temporal lobe structures did not produce severe anterograde amnesia in either rats or monkeys. The failure led some researchers to suggest that the memory systems of humans differ from those of their mammalian relatives; however, this has proved not to be the case.

There were two major reasons for the initial difficulty in developing an animal model of medial temporal lobe amnesia. First, it was not initially apparent that H.M.'s anterograde amnesia did not extend to all kinds of long-term memory—that is, that it was specific to explicit (declarative) long-term memories; and virtually all animal memory tests that were widely used in the 1950s and 1960s were tests of implicit (procedural) memory (e.g., Pavlovian and operant conditioning). Second, it was incorrectly assumed that the amnesic effects of medial temporal lobe lesions were largely, if not

entirely, attributable to hippocampal damage; and most efforts to develop animal models of medial temporal lobe amnesia thus focused exclusively on hippocampal lesions.

Monkey Model of Object-Recognition Amnesia: The Nonrecurring-Items Delayed Nonmatching-to-Sample Test

H.M. does not recognize objects that he encountered for the first time after his operation. Indeed, virtually all amnesics display anterograde object-recognition deficits.

1 The monkey moves the sample object to obtain food from the well beneath it.

2 A screen is lowered in front of the monkey during the delay period.

3 The monkey is confronted with the sample object and an unfamiliar object.

4 The monkey must remember the sample object and then select the unfamiliar object to obtain the food beneath it.

Figure 14.11 The correct performance of a nonrecurring-items delayed nonmatching-to-sample trial. (Adapted from Mishkin & Appenzeller, 1987.)

Accordingly, a major breakthrough in the study of the neural mechanisms of memory was the development in the mid 1970s of a monkey model of human object-recognition deficits (Gaffan, 1974; Mishkin & Delacour, 1975).

It was discovered that bilateral medial temporal lobe lesions in monkeys produce severe deficits in the **nonrecurring-items delayed nonmatching-to-sample test.** In this test, a monkey is presented with a distinctive object (i.e., the *sample* object), under which it finds food (e.g., a banana pellet). Then, after a delay, the monkey is presented with two test objects: the sample object and an unfamiliar object. The monkey must remember the sample object so that it can select the unfamiliar object to obtain food concealed beneath it. New objects (i.e., nonrecurring items) are used on each trial. The correct performance of a trial is illustrated in Figure 14.11. Intact well-trained monkeys perform correctly on about 90% of the trials when the retention intervals are a few minutes or less.

The deficits of monkeys with bilateral medial temporal lobe lesions on the nonrecurring-items delayed nonmatching-to-sample test model the object-recognition deficits of H.M. in key respects. The monkeys' performance is normal at brief delays (delays of a few seconds); it falls off to near chance levels at delays of several minutes (see Figure 14.12); and it is extremely susceptible to the disruptive effects of distraction (see Zola-Morgan & Squire, 1984; Squire & Zola-Morgan, 1985).

Indeed, human amnesics have been tested on the nonrecurring-items delayed nonmatching-to-sample test—their rewards were coins rather than banana pellets—and their performance mirrored the performance of amnesic monkeys (Aggleton et al., 1988; Squire, Zola-Morgan, & Chen, 1988). Other tests have been used to model human object-recognition deficits in monkeys, but the nonrecurring-items delayed nonmatching-to-sample test has proved most useful.

Further support for the monkey nonrecurring-items delayed nonmatching-to-sample model comes from the demonstration that performance of the nonrecurring-items delayed nonmatching-to-sample test by monkeys is also disrupted by medial diencephalic lesions (Aggleton & Mishkin, 1983). The fact that deficits can be produced by discrete lesions of the medial dorsal nuclei (Zola-Morgan & Squire, 1985), but not by lesions of the mammillary bodies (Aggleton & Mishkin, 1983) supports the view that mediodorsal nucleus damage, rather than mammillary body damage, is the critical factor in Korsakoff's amnesia.

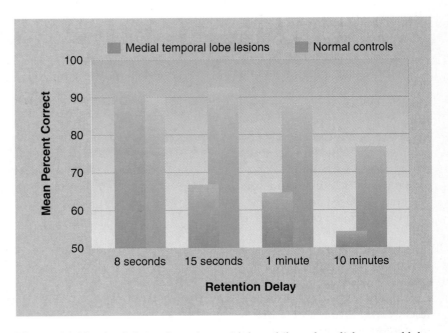

Figure 14.12 The deficits of monkeys with large bilateral medial temporal lobe lesions on the nonrecurring-items delayed nonmatching-to-sample test. There were significant deficits at all but the shortest retention interval. These deficits parallel the memory deficits of human medial temporal lobe amnesics on the same task. (Adapted from Squire & Zola-Morgan, 1991.)

Early Monkey Studies of Medial Temporal Lobe Damage and Object-Recognition Amnesia

Figure 14.13 illustrates the location in the monkey brain of three of the structures of the medial temporal lobe: the hippocampus, the amygdala, and the rhinal cortex. (The **rhinal cortex** is composed of two areas of medial temporal cortex located around the rhinal fissure: the *entorhinal cortex* and the *perirhinal cortex*.) The hippocampus, amygdala, and rhinal cortex are all severely damaged by bilateral medial temporal lobectomy. The monkey nonrecurring-items delayed nonmatching-to-sample model provided a means of testing the assumption that the resulting amnesia was specifically a consequence of the hippocampal damage.

Nonrecurring-items delayed nonmatching-to-sample test. A test in which the subject is presented with an unfamiliar sample object and then, after a delay, is presented with a choice between the sample object and another unfamiliar object—the correct choice being the nonsample object.

Rhinal cortex. The area of medial temporal cortex around the rhinal fissure; it comprises the entorhinal cortex and perirhinal cortex.

In the late 1970s and much of the 1980s, research on the monkey nonrecurring-items delayed nonmatching-to-sample model of medial temporal lobe amnesia focused on the contributions of hippocampal and amygdalar damage. Almost everybody accepted that the hippocampus played the major role in object-recognition memory, and the research focused on whether amygdalar damage contributed to the effects of hippocampal damage. To answer this question, the effects of hippocampal aspiration lesions on nonrecurring-items delayed nonmatching-to-sample tests were compared to the effects of combined hippocampal and amygdalar aspiration. The results were mixed: Some studies seemed to suggest that amygdalar damage did not contribute significantly to the amnesic effects of hippocampal damage (e.g., Mahut, Moss, & Zola-Morgan, 1981); others seemed to suggest that it contributed significantly (e.g., Squire & Zola-Morgan, 1985); and still others seemed to suggest that it played a critical role, with few memory deficits occurring unless both the hippocampus and the amygdala were aspirated (Mishkin, 1978).

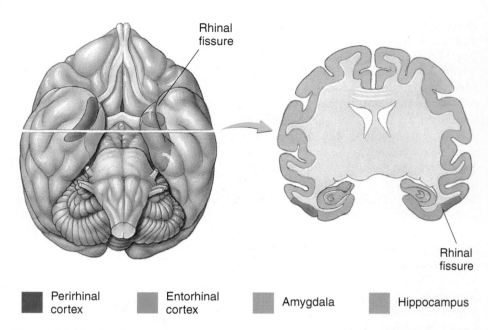

Figure 14.13 The three major structures of the medial temporal lobe, illustrated in the monkey brain: The hippocampus, the amygdala, and the rhinal cortex. The rhinal cortex is composed of the entorhinal cortex and the perirhinal cortex.

In retrospect, the source of the early confusion about the relative contributions of hippocampal and amygdalar damage to object-recognition amnesia is clear (see Murray, 1992). Until the late 1980s, the focus on the contributions of hippocampal and amygdalar damage was so great that researchers gave little consideration to the possible contributions of damage to the underlying rhinal cortex, which was always removed in order to expose the hippocampus and amygdala for aspiration. Then, in the late 1980s, two important developments took place in the study of the neural basis of object-recognition amnesia. First, researchers working with the monkey model began to assess the effects of rhinal cortex lesions. And second, a rat model of object-recognition amnesia that is directly comparable to the monkey model was developed.

Rat Model of Object-Recognition Amnesia: The Nonrecurring-Items Delayed Nonmatching-to-Sample Test

Monkeys have a major advantage over laboratory rats when it comes to modeling human brain-damage-produced amnesia: The monkey brain is more similar than the rat brain to the human brain. However, laboratory rats have two advantages of their own. The first is that it is possible to conduct large-scale studies of amnesia in rats, which is not feasible in monkeys for ethical and economic reasons. The second is that the hippocampus—the major neuroanatomical focus of research on memory—is more accessible to selective lesions in rats because of its smaller size and more dorsal location.

Figure 14.14 illustrates the usual methods of making hippocampal aspiration lesions in monkeys and rats. As a result of the size and location of the hippocampus, almost all studies of hippocampal lesions in monkeys have involved *aspiration* (suction) of large portions of the rhinal cortex in addition to the hippocampus, whereas in rats the extraneous damage associated with aspiration lesions of the hippocampus is typically limited to a small amount of parietal neocortex. Furthermore, the rat hippocampus is small enough that it can readily be lesioned electrolytically or with intracerebral neurotoxin injections; in either case there is little extraneous damage.

Several versions of the rat nonrecurring-items delayed nonmatching-to-sample test have been developed (see Aggleton, 1985; Rothblat & Hayes, 1987). The version that most closely resembles the monkey test was developed by Mumby using an apparatus that has become known as the **Mumby box.** This version of the rat nonrecurring-items delayed nonmatching-to-sample test is illustrated in Figure 14.15 on page 370.

It was once assumed that rats could not perform a task as complex as nonrecurring-items delayed nonmatching-to-sample; Figure 14.16 on page 371 indicates otherwise. Rats perform almost as well as monkeys at delays up to 1 minute (Mumby, Pinel, & Wood, 1989).

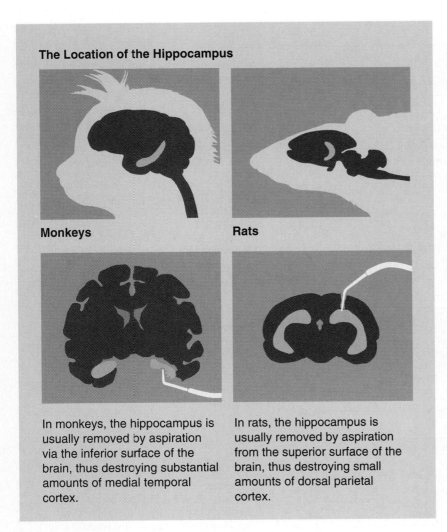

The Location of the Hippocampus

Monkeys

Rats

In monkeys, the hippocampus is usually removed by aspiration via the inferior surface of the brain, thus destroying substantial amounts of medial temporal cortex.

In rats, the hippocampus is usually removed by aspiration from the superior surface of the brain, thus destroying small amounts of dorsal parietal cortex.

Figure 14.14 Aspiration lesions of the hippocampus in monkeys and rats. Because of differences in the size and location of the hippocampus in monkeys and rats, hippocampectomy in monkeys, but not in rats, typically involves the removal of large amounts of rhinal cortex.

The validity of the rat nonrecurring-items delayed nonmatching-to-sample test has been established by studies of the effects of medial temporal lobe and mediodorsal nucleus lesions. Bilateral lesions of the rat hippocampus that also involve the amygdala and the rhinal cortex produce major retention deficits at all but the shortest retention intervals (Mumby, Wood, & Pinel, 1992), and the same is true of bilateral lesions of the mediodorsal nuclei (Mumby, Pinel, & Dastur, 1993). Thus the effects of medial temporal lobe and mediodorsal nucleus lesions on the performance of nonrecurring-items delayed nonmatching-to-sample tests is comparable in rats, monkeys, and humans.

Mumby box. An apparatus that is used to test nonrecurring-items delayed nonmatching-to-sample in rats.

Neuroanatomical Basis of the Object-Recognition Deficits Resulting from Medial Temporal Lobectomy

There is no better demonstration of the value of the comparative approach in biopsychological research than the surprising resolution to the question that has been the focus of research and speculation since the first reports of H.M.'s case: To what extent are the object-recognition deficits associated with bilateral medial temporal lobectomy a consequence of hippocampal damage? The results of experiments using the monkey and rat nonrecurring-items delayed nonmatching-to-sample models tell a consistent story that contradicts the long-held view that the hippocampus and perhaps the amygdala play the major roles in the consolidation of explicit long-term memories for objects.

The following two findings have recently emerged. First, lesions of the hippocampus that do not extend into the rhinal cortex do not produce substantial deficits in nonrecurring-items delayed nonmatching-to-sample in either monkeys or rats. In monkeys, selective lesions of the hippocampus produced a significant deficit at only the longest (10-minute) test interval (Alvarez, Zola-Morgan, & Squire, 1995); and in rats, lesions of the hippocampus and amygdala combined produced a significant deficit at only the longest (5-minute) test interval (Mumby, Wood, & Pinel, 1992). Second, lesions of the rhinal cortex that do not extend into the hippocampus or amygdala do produce major deficits in nonrecurring-items delayed nonmatching-to-sample in both monkeys (Meunier et al., 1990; Zola-Morgan et al., 1989) and rats (Mumby & Pinel, 1994). Figure 14.17 on page 371 compares the effects of rhinal cortex lesions and hippocampus plus amygdala lesions in rats.

Ischemia-Produced Brain Damage and Object-Recognition Deficits

The recent reports that object-recognition memory is severely disrupted by rhinal cortex lesions but not by hippocampal lesions have led to a resurgence of interest in the case of R.B. Earlier in this chapter, you learned that R.B. was left amnesic following an ischemic accident that occurred during heart surgery and that subsequent analysis of his brain revealed that obvious damage was restricted

The sample object is placed over one food cup at one end. An object identical to the sample object and a novel object are placed over the two food cups at the other end.

Food cup

Sample

When the sliding door is raised, exposing the sample object, a trained food-deprived rat runs down to the sample object and pushes it aside. Then, a piece of food is deposited by a food-delivery mechanism into the exposed food cup.

Food

The sample object is immediately removed by the experimenter, and the rat remains at the same end of the Mumby box until the prescribed delay period is over (e.g., 1 minute).

Then, the other sliding door is raised to expose the two objects at the other end. Trained rats, remembering their previous encounter with the sample object run to the novel object and push it aside; and food is delivered to the exposed food cup. The sliding door at the other end is lowered behind the rat.

The rat then runs to the center of the Mumby box, and the sliding door is closed behind it. Then, new objects are arranged for the next trial. One advantage of the Mumby box is that the rats do not have to be handled either during or between trials.

Figure 14.15 The Mumby box and the rat version of the monkey nonrecurring-items delayed nonmatching-to-sample paradigm.

largely to the pyramidal cell layer of his CA1 hippocampal subfield (see Figure 14.7). This result has been replicated in both monkeys and rats. In both monkeys (Zola-Morgan et al., 1992) and rats (Wood et al., 1993), cerebral ischemia produces damage to CA1 hippocampal pyramidal cells and severe deficits in nonrecurring-items delayed nonmatching-to-sample.

The relation between ischemia-produced hippocampal damage and object-recognition deficits in humans, mon-

keys, and rats seems to provide strong support for the theory that the hippocampus plays a key role in object-recognition memory. But there is a gnawing problem with this line of evidence: How can ischemia-produced lesions to one small part of the hippocampus be associated with severe deficits in nonrecurring-items delayed nonmatching-to-sample in both monkeys and rats when the deficits associated with total removal of the hippocampus are only minor?

Mumby and his colleagues (in press) conducted an experiment that appears to resolve this paradox. They hypothesized the following: (1) that the ischemia-produced hyperactivity of CA1 pyramidal cells damages neurons outside the hippocampus, possibly through the excessive release of excitatory amino acids by the hyperactive CA1 cells; (2) that this extrahippocampal damage is not readily detectable by conventional histological analysis; and (3) that this extrahippocampal damage is largely responsible for the object-recognition deficits that are produced by cerebral ischemia. Mumby and colleagues supported these hypotheses by showing that bilateral hippocampectomy actually blocks the development of ischemia-produced deficits in

Figure 14.16 A comparison of the performance of intact monkeys (Zola-Morgan, Squire, & Mishkin, 1982) and intact rats (Mumby, Pinel, & Wood, 1989) on the nonrecurring-items delayed nonmatching-to-sample task.

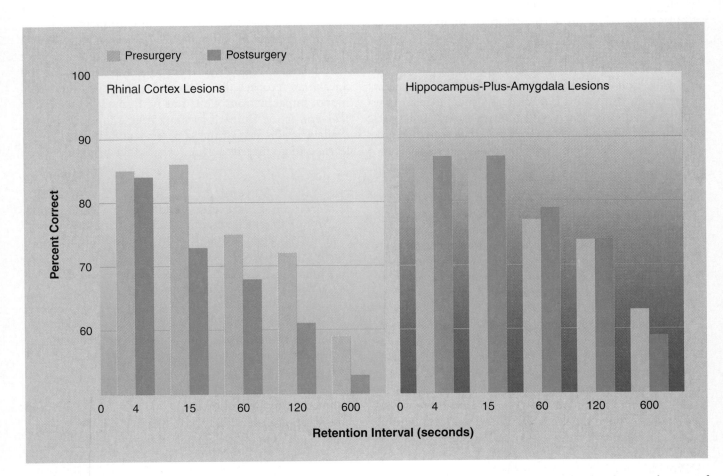

Figure 14.17 Effects of rhinal cortex lesions and hippocampus plus amygdala lesions in rats. Lesions of the rhinal cortex, but not of the hippocampus and amygdala combined, produced severe deficits in nonrecurring-items delayed nonmatching-to-sample in rats. (Adapted from Mumby, Wood, & Pinel, 1992; Mumby & Pinel, 1994.)

nonrecurring-items delayed nonmatching-to-sample. First, they produced cerebral ischemia in rats by temporarily tying off their carotid arteries. Then, one group of the ischemic rats received a bilateral hippocampectomy 1 hour later, a second group received a bilateral hippocampectomy 1 week later, and a third group received no bilateral hippocampectomy. Following recovery, the latter two groups of ischemic rats displayed severe object-recognition deficits, whereas the rats whose hippocampus had been removed 1 hour after ischemia did not. Explaining how hippocampectomy can prevent the development of the object-recognition deficits normally produced by cerebral ischemia is a major challenge to the theory that the hippocampus plays a major role in object-recognition memory.

14.7 Hippocampus and Memory for Space

Numerous studies have assessed the effects of bilateral hippocampal lesions on the performance of many kinds of memory tests by laboratory animals—primarily rats. The most consistent finding has been that hippocampal lesions disrupt the performance of tests that involve the retention of spatial locations (e.g., Jackson-Smith, Kesner, & Chiba, 1993; McDonald & White, 1993)—see O'Keefe (1993).

Rats with bilateral hippocampal lesions display deficits on two widely used tests of spatial memory: the Morris water maze test and the radial arm maze test (Jarrard, 1993). In the **Morris water maze test,** intact rats placed at various locations in a circular pool of murky water rapidly learn to swim to an invisible stationary platform just below the surface, whereas rats with hippocampal lesions learn this simple task with great difficulty or not at all. In the **radial arm maze test,** several arms (e.g., eight arms) radiate out from a central starting chamber, and the same few arms are baited with food each day. Intact rats readily learn to visit only those arms that contain food, without visiting the same arm more than once each day. Their ability to visit only the baited arms is a measure of **reference memory**—memory for the general principles and skills that are required to perform a task; and their ability to refrain from visiting an arm more than once in a given day is a measure of **working memory**—temporary memory necessary for the successful performance of tasks on which one is currently working. Rats with hippocampal lesions display major deficits on both the reference memory and the working memory measures of radial arm maze performance.

The fact that hippocampal lesions disrupt the performance of tasks that involve memory for spatial location has provided strong support for O'Keefe and Nadel's (1978) cognitive-map theory of hippocampal function. According to the **cognitive-map theory,** there are several systems in the brain that specialize in the memory for different kinds of information, and the specific function of the hippocampus is to facilitate the storage of memories for spatial location.

Providing further support for the cognitive-map theory of hippocampal function was the discovery that many rat hippocampal neurons are **place cells** (O'Keefe & Dostrovsky, 1971)—neurons that come to respond only when the animal is in a specific location (i.e., in the *place field* of the neuron). When a rat is first placed in an unfamiliar test environment, none of its hippocampal neurons have place fields for that environment; then, as the rat familiarizes itself with the environment, its hippocampal place cells acquire place fields in it. In one experiment, this took about 15 minutes (Wilson & McNaughton, 1993). Foster, Castro, and McNaughton (1989) found that hippocampal place cells do not fire when subjects are restrained and then placed in the cell's place field; this suggests that the hippocampus stores spatial information that is used to guide an animal's movement through its environment.

An ingenious experiment by O'Keefe and Speakman (1987) demonstrated that the fields of hippocampal place cells do indeed code a rat's memory for space. O'Keefe and Speakman recorded the extracellular activity of individual hippocampal neurons while rats performed in an *elevated four-arm maze.* On each learning trial, a food reward was available at the end of the same arm, and the rats quickly learned to go directly to the reward after being placed on

Morris water maze test. A widely used test of spatial memory in which rats must learn to swim directly to an invisible platform hidden just beneath the surface of a circular pool of murky water.

Radial arm maze test. A widely used test of rats' spatial ability in which the same arms are baited on each trial, and the rats must learn to visit only the baited arms only one time each on each trial.

Reference memory. Memory for the general principles and skills that are required to perform a task.

Working memory. Temporary memory necessary for the successful completion of the task on which one is currently working.

Cognitive-map theory. The theory that the main function of the hippocampus is to store memories of spatial location.

Place cells. Neurons that develop place fields—that is, that come to fire rapidly only when the subject is in a particular place in a familiar test environment.

Chapter 14   Memory and Amnesia

Rats learned to run to the end of a plus maze to obtain a food reward. The plus maze was surrounded by a curtain, and objects suspended over the maze provided the only spatial cues. Once a rat was familiar with the plus maze, the place field of one of its hippocampal pyramidal neurons was located; in this example, the neuron had a place field near the end of the arm opposite the goal arm.

Then, all the spatial cues were removed, and the rat was confined to each arm of the plus maze in sequence until the arm with its place field was located. Because there were no spatial cues, the rat had no way of knowing which arm was which. The key finding was that once the rat was released from the place field arm, the arm that it selected as the goal arm was predictable from the location of its place field; in this example, it was the arm opposite the arm that it had assumed to contain the place field. This finding indicates that hippocampal neurons encode a map of physical space that guides behavior.

Figure 14.18 An illustration of the place cell experiment of O'Keefe and Speakman (1987). Each hippocampal place cell was active only when the rat was in a particular location (i.e., in the cell's place field) of one of the four identical arms of an elevated 4-arm maze. When there were no external position cues, the activity of these units indicated where the rat "thought" it was, as indicated by the arm that it subsequently "guessed" was the goal arm.

one of the other arms of the maze. Because all arms were identical and a black curtain surrounded the apparatus, the rats had to learn to orient themselves in relation to cue objects that were pinned to the curtains. O'Keefe and Speakman found that many of the hippocampal neurons that they studied had well-defined place fields in the apparatus.

The most important result of O'Keefe and Speakman's experiment emerged during a test in which rats that had learned the task were tested in the absence of the external cue objects so that they could not tell which arm was which. First, O'Keefe and Speakman enclosed the rat in the various arms of the maze to locate the neuron's place field; then, they allowed the rat to choose a goal arm. Remarkably, in the absence of the cue objects, the location of the place field of each hippocampal neuron indicated where the rat "thought" the goal arm was. If, on the learning trials, the goal arm had been 90° to the right of the neuron's place field, during the test in the absence of the cue objects the rat "guessed" that the arm 90° to the right of the neuron's place field was the goal arm. This result is illustrated in Figure 14.18.

Although the cognitive-map theory of hippocampal function was originally based on research on rats, it has received support from the study of other species. For example, Sherry and his colleagues (see Sherry, Jacobs, & Gaulin, 1992) found that food-caching birds, which must remember the location of hundreds of food caches scattered around their territory, have a larger hippocampus than non-food-caching birds (Sherry et al., 1989). Also, a recent study of neurosurgical patients with unilateral temporal lobe and frontal lobe lesions revealed that only those patients with substantial hippocampal damage had difficulty remembering the location of objects in pictures (Pigott & Milner, 1993).

Although there is a general consensus that the hippocampus plays an important role in memory for location, not everybody agrees that it is dedicated solely to this function. Following are two alternatives to the cognitive-map theory of hippocampal function: the declarative memory theory and the configural association theory.

The *declarative memory theory* of hippocampal function is that the role of the hippocampus is the formation of all long-term declarative (explicit) memories, including memories for spatial locations (see Squire, 1992; Eichenbaum, Otto, & Cohen, 1992). Recent observations that lesions of the hippocampus that do not damage the rhinal cortex produce only minor deficits in nonrecurring-items delayed nonmatching-to-sample create problems for this theory.

The *configural association theory* of hippocampal function (Rudy & Sutherland, 1992; Sutherland & Rudy, 1989) is that the hippocampus plays a role in the long-term retention of interrelations among cues (i.e., of configural associations). According to this theory, the hippocampus is involved in the retention of the behavioral significance of combinations of stimuli but not of individual stimuli—for example, in learning that a flashing light in a particular context (i.e., at a particular location or time) signals food but not that a flashing light signals food irrespective of the context. Recently, Gallagher and Holland (1992) pitted the cognitive-map theory against the configural association theory. They compared the effects of selective hippocampal lesions on the performance of spatial and configural tasks and found that rats with hippocampal lesions were severely impaired on the Morris water maze task but were not impaired on a configural operant conditioning task.

14.8   Memory Structures of the Brain

Figure 14.19 illustrates the structures of the brain that have been implicated in memory (see Mishkin & Murray, 1994); you have already encountered most of them in this chapter. This section completes the chapter by briefly summarizing the putative mnemonic functions of each structure.

Rhinal Cortex

Recent studies of nonrecurring-items delayed nonmatching-to-sample in monkeys and rats with rhinal cortex lesions indicate that the rhinal cortex plays a major role in the formation of long-term memories for objects.

Hippocampus

Hippocampal lesions disrupt the performance of tasks that require the long-term retention of spatial information. The fact that they block the formation of new memories for spatial location but do not eliminate memories for spatial location that were acquired long before the lesions suggests that the hippocampus is involved in the consolidation of long-term memories for spatial location, not their storage. The spatial memory theory of hippocampal function has been supported by the discovery that many hippocampal neurons have place fields and by the discovery that species with well-developed spatial abilities tend to have a large hippocampus.

Amygdala

Like the hippocampus, the amygdala was initially thought to play a role in long-term object-recognition memory; however, the discovery that amygdalar lesions that do not damage the underlying rhinal cortex produce no deficits in nonrecurring-items delayed nonmatching-to-sample has challenged this theory. The current view is that the amygdala plays a specific role in memory for the emotional significance of experiences. Rats with amygdalar lesions, unlike intact rats, do not respond with fear to a neutral stimulus that has been repeatedly followed by painful electric footshocks (see LeDoux, 1992).

Inferotemporal Cortex

The retrograde amnesia produced by medial temporal lobectomy is restricted to the period immediately preceding surgery; it does not affect remote memories (see Zola-Morgan & Squire, 1990). This suggests that the medial temporal lobes play a role in the consolidation of long-term memories but are not the ultimate sites of their storage. So where in the brain are long-term memories stored? Current evidence suggests that long-term memories are stored in the cortical circuits that mediated their original experience—that is, in secondary cortex and association sensory cortex (see Roland & Gulás, 1994; Sakai & Miyashita, 1993; Tanaka, 1993).

Most of the research on the storage of long-term memories has focused on visual memories and their storage in the secondary visual cortex of the inferotemporal lobe. For example, Mishkin (1982) found that monkeys with bilateral lesions of the **inferotemporal cortex** could not perform the nonrecurring-items delayed nonmatching-to-sample task at delays greater than 1 minute—although they performed well at shorter delays, which indicates that they could still perceive the difference between the test objects and learn the principle of the task. Similarly, the *posterior*

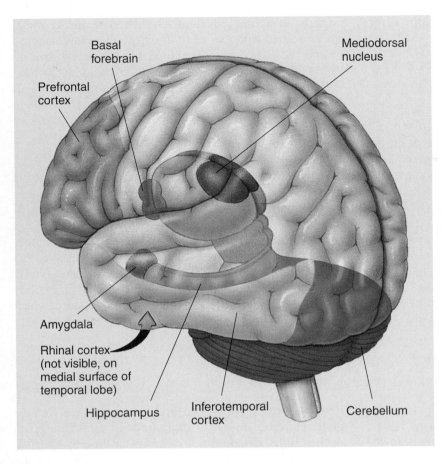

Figure 14.19 The structures of the brain that have been shown to play a role in memory.

parietal cortex is believed to store memories of spatial location, *secondary somatosensory cortex* is believed to store memories of tactile patterns, and *secondary auditory cortex* is believed to store auditory memories.

Cerebellum

Just as explicit memories of experiences are presumed to be stored in the circuits of the brain that mediated their original perception, implicit memories of sensorimotor learning are presumed to be stored in sensorimotor circuits (see Desimone, 1992). This point was demonstrated in an experiment on sensorimotor memory by Krupa, Thompson, and Thompson (1993).

Krupa and colleagues conditioned rabbits by repeatedly pairing a tone with a puff of air to the eye. Control subjects learned to blink in response to the tone and retained this Pavlovian conditioning over a series of daily test sessions. There were two experimental groups, each of which had an important structure of the eye-blink-conditioning circuit deactivated during training by microinfusions of the GABA agonist *muscimol*. The rabbits in one experimental group had their *red nuclei* deactivated; these rabbits dis-

played no behavior during conditioning; but when they were tested the next day without the muscimol, they showed that they had learned and retained the conditioning. This indicated that the memory for the conditioning was being formed at some point in the eye-blink-conditioning circuit before the red nucleus. The **cerebellum** is the structure in the eye-blink-conditioning circuit that projects to the red nucleus. The rabbits in the second experimental group had their cerebellums deactivated during the conditioning trials; and when their retention was assessed without the muscimol, they showed no retention whatsoever. Thus memories for conditioned eye-blink responses appear to be stored in the cerebellum.

Prefrontal Cortex

The prefrontal cortex is involved in memory of the temporal order of events, not of the events per se. Accordingly, monkeys with prefrontal lesions have no deficits on the nonrecurring-items delayed nonmatching-to-sample test (e.g., Bachevalier & Mishkin, 1986; Kowalska, Bachevalier, & Mishkin, 1984), but they do have difficulty performing the recurring-items delayed matching-to-sample test (Mishkin & Manning, 1978) and the delayed-alternation test (Mishkin, 1957). In the **recurring-items delayed matching-to-sample test,** the same two items are presented on each trial, and the monkeys must select the one that matches the sample; thus to chose correctly, they must remember which of the two items they have seen more recently and choose it. In the **delayed-alternation test,** the position of the reward (e.g., a food pellet) alternates from trial to trial; thus to choose correct-

Inferotemporal cortex. The area of secondary visual cortex in the inferior temporal lobe, where memories of visual images are thought to be stored.

Cerebellum. The metencephalic structure that has been shown to mediate the retention of Pavlovian eye-blink conditioning.

Recurring-items delayed matching-to-sample test. A delayed matching-to-sample test in which the same two test items are used on each trial.

Delayed-alternation test. A test in which the subject must choose between the same two items on each trial, the correct choice being the item that was wrong on the previous trial.

ly, the monkeys must remember the most recently correct position and choose the other.

Mediodorsal Nucleus

The discovery that the mediodorsal nuclei are involved in memory came from the observation that they are virtually always damaged in cases of Korsakoff's amnesia. Additional support for this view has come from two sources. First, circumscribed lesions of the mediodorsal nuclei produce nonrecurring-items delayed nonmatching-to-sample deficits in both monkeys (Aggleton & Mishkin, 1983) and rats (Mumby, Pinel, & Dastur, 1993). And second, exposure of rats to *pyrithiamine*, an antithiamin drug, produces mediodorsal nucleus damage and deficits on a variety of memory tests (Mair et al., 1991).

One theoretical issue that has been the focus of considerable debate is whether the amnesia produced by lesions of the mediodorsal nuclei and surrounding medial diencephalic structures is qualitatively different from the amnesia associated with lesions of the medial temporal lobe. So far, no consistent qualitative difference between medial diencephalic and medial temporal lobe amnesia has been delineated. This suggests that the two areas are components of the same memory circuit.

Basal Forebrain

The role of the basal forebrain in memory is controversial. The theory that it plays a role in memory is based largely on the fact that it and its cholinergic projections are invariably degenerated in Alzheimer's patients. Moreover, large lesions of this area do disrupt the performance of animals on memory tasks. However, recent evidence suggests that the structures of the basal forebrain (the medial septum, the diagonal band of Broca, and the nucleus basalis of Meynert) likely serve a variety of functions, only some of which are related to memory (see Zola-Morgan & Squire, 1993).

CONCLUSION

This chapter began by introducing you to the amnesias associated with medial temporal lobe damage (14.1), Korsakoff's syndrome (14.2), prefrontal cortex damage (14.3), Alzheimer's disease (14.4), and concussion (14.5). The study of each of these amnesic syndromes has provided important clues about the neural basis of memory, but it is the experimental study of animal models of brain-damage-produced amnesia that has led to most of the recent progress in this field. In particular, the study of animal models has led to recent advances in our understanding of the neural basis of object-recognition memory (14.6) and memory for spatial location (14.7). Current evidence suggests that the following brain structures play important roles in memory (14.8): the rhinal cortex, the hippocampus, the amygdala, the inferotemporal cortex (and other areas of secondary sensory and association cortex), the cerebellum, the prefrontal cortex, the mediodorsal nucleus, and the basal forebrain.

This chapter began with the case of H.M.; it ends with the case of another amnesic, R.M. What makes R.M.'s case particularly ironic is that he is a biopsychologist. R.M. fell on his head while skiing; and when he regained consciousness, he was suffering from both retrograde and anterograde amnesia. For several hours, he could recall little of his previous life: He could not remember if he was married, where he lived, or where he worked. Also, many of the things that happened to him in the hours after his accident were forgotten as soon as his attention was diverted from them. His was a classic case of posttraumatic amnesia. Like H.M., he was trapped in the present, with only a cloudy past and seemingly no future. The irony of the situation was that during those few hours, when R.M. could recall few of the events of his own life, his thoughts repeatedly drifted to one person—a person whom he remembered hearing about somewhere in his muddled past. Through the haze, he remembered H.M., his fellow prisoner of the present; and he wondered if the same fate lay in store for him.

R.M. is now fully recovered and looks back on what he can recall of his experience with relief and with a feeling of empathy for H.M. Unlike H.M., R.M. received a reprieve; but his experience left him with a better appreciation for the situation of those, like H.M., who are serving life sentences.

FOOD FOR THOUGHT

1. The study of the anatomy of memory has come a long way since H.M.'s misfortune. What kind of research on this topic do you think will prove to be most important in the next decade?

2. Using examples from your own experience, compare implicit and explicit memory.

3. What are the advantages and shortcomings of animal models of amnesia? Compare the usefulness of monkey and rat models.

KEY TERMS

Memory *(p. 351)*
Engram *(p. 351)*
Principle of mass action *(p. 351)*
Principle of equipotentiality *(p. 351)*
Mnemonic *(p. 351)*
Consolidation *(p. 351)*
Bilateral medial temporal lobectomy *(p. 352)*
Hippocampus *(p. 352)*
Amygdala *(p. 352)*
Lobectomy *(p. 353)*
Lobotomy *(p. 353)*
Retrograde amnesia *(p. 353)*
Anterograde amnesia *(p. 353)*
Digit span *(p. 353)*
Digit span + 1 test *(p. 354)*

Block-tapping memory span test *(p. 354)*
Global amnesia *(p. 354)*
Matching-to-sample test *(p. 354)*
Mirror-drawing test *(p. 355)*
Rotary-pursuit test *(p. 355)*
Incomplete-pictures test *(p. 355)*
Explicit memories *(p. 356)*
Implicit memories *(p. 356)*
Ischemic brain damage *(p. 358`)*
Pyramidal cell layer *(p. 359)*
CA1 subfield *(p. 359)*
Korsakoff's syndrome *(p. 359)*
Repetition priming *(p. 359)*
Mammillary bodies *(p. 359)*

Mediodorsal nuclei *(p. 359)*
Prefrontal cortex *(p. 360)*
Proactive interference *(p. 360)*
Neurofibrillary tangles *(p. 361)*
Amyloid plaques *(p. 361)*
Basal forebrain *(p. 361)*
Nootropics *(p. 362)*
Posttraumatic amnesia (PTA) *(p. 362)*
Islands of memory *(p. 362)*
Electroconvulsive shock (ECS) *(p. 362)*
Nonrecurring-items delayed nonmatching-to-sample test *(p. 367)*
Rhinal cortex *(p. 367)*

Mumby box *(p. 368)*
Morris water maze test *(p. 372)*
Radial arm maze test *(p. 372)*
Reference memory *(p. 372)*
Working memory *(p. 372)*
Cognitive-map theory *(p. 372)*
Place cells *(p. 372)*
Inferotemporal cortex *(p. 374)*
Cerebellum *(p. 375)*
Recurring-items delayed matching-to-sample test *(p. 375)*
Delayed-alternation test *(p. 375)*

ADDITIONAL READING

The following articles provide readable reviews of much of the material in this chapter:

Mishkin, M., & Murray, E. A. (1994). Stimulus recognition. *Current Opinion in Neurobiology, 4,* 200–206.

O'Keefe, J. (1993). Hippocampus, theta, and spatial memory. *Current Opinion in Neurobiology, 3,* 917–924.

Sherry, D. F., Jacobs, L. F., & Gaulin, S. J. C. (1992). Spatial memory and adaptive specialization of the hippocampus. *Trends in Neuroscience, 15,* 298–303.

Squire, L. R. (1992). Memory and the hippocampus: A synthesis of findings with rats, monkeys, and humans. *Psychological Review, 99,* 195–231.

Zola-Morgan, S., & Squire, L. R. (1993). Neuroanatomy of memory. *Annual Review of Neuroscience, 16,* 547–563.

Neuroplasticity: Development, Learning, and Recovery from Brain Damage

15.1 Phases of Neural Development

15.2 Effects of Experience on Neural Development

15.3 Neural Bases of Learning and Memory in Simple Systems

15.4 Neural Degeneration, Regeneration, and Reorganization

15.5 Neurotransplantation in the Brain

Most of us tend to think of the nervous system as a three-dimensional array of neural elements "wired" together in a massive network of circuits. The sheer magnitude and complexity of this wiring-diagram concept of the nervous system is staggering, but it sells the nervous system short by failing to capture one of its most important features. The nervous system is not a static network of interconnected elements as is implied by the wiring-diagram model. It is a plastic, living organ, which grows and changes continuously in response to its genetic programs and its interactions with its environment.

Neuroplasticity is the subject of this chapter. In it, you will learn about the neuroplastic processes involved in neural development, in learning and memory, and in recovery from brain damage. The chapter ends with a discussion of one of the most exciting fields of modern neuroscientific research: neurotransplantation.

Along with research on human subjects, you will encounter in this chapter studies that at first may appear to be strange fodder for students of biopsychology: studies of fish, frogs, salamanders, and snails. Why have some lines of research on neuroplasticity focused on such creatures? The answer in one word is "simplicity." There is an advantage in studying neuroplasticity in neural circuits that are complex enough to mediate behavioral change but simple enough to be analyzed neuron by neuron. This approach to the study of neuroplasticity is called the **simple-systems approach.**

15.1   Phases of Neural Development

In the beginning, there is a *zygote,* a single cell formed by the amalgamation of an *ovum* and a *sperm.* The zygote divides to form two daughter cells. These two divide to form four, the four divide to form eight, and so on, until a mature organism is produced. Of course, there must be more to development than this; if there were not, each of us would have ended up like a bowl of rice pudding: an amorphous mass of homogeneous cells.

To save us from this fate, three things other than cell multiplication must occur. First, cells must *differentiate;* some must become muscle cells, some must become multipolar neurons, some must become glial cells, and so on. Second, cells must make their way to appropriate sites and align themselves with the cells around them to form particular structures. And third, cells must establish appropriate functional relations with other cells. Section 15.1 describes how developing neurons accomplish these things in five phases: (1) induction of the neural plate, (2) neural proliferation, (3) migration and aggregation, (4) axon growth and synapse formation, and (5) neuron death and synapse rearrangement. These five phases of neural development are discussed in the following five subsections.

Induction of the Neural Plate

Three weeks after conception, the tissue that is destined to develop into the human nervous system becomes recognizable as the **neural plate**—a small patch of ectodermal tissue on the dorsal surface of the developing embryo. The ectoderm is the outermost of the three layers of embryo cells: *ectoderm, mesoderm,* and *endoderm.* The development of the neural plate is the first major stage of neural development.

As Figure 15.1 illustrates, the neural plate folds to form the *neural groove,* and then the lips of the neural groove fuse to form the **neural tube.** The inside of the neural tube eventually becomes the *cerebral ventricles* and *spinal canal.* By 40 days of age, three swellings are visible at the anterior end of the neural tube; these swellings ultimately develop into the *forebrain, midbrain,* and *hindbrain* (see Figure 3.21).

Prior to the development of the neural plate, each of the cells of the dorsal ectoderm is **totipotential**—having the potential to develop into any type of body cell. However, with the development of the neural plate, they lose their totipotency: Neural plate cells develop into nervous system tissue even if they are transplanted to a different part of the embryo.

The development of the neural plate is induced by chemical signals from the underlying **mesoderm layer** (see Kessler & Melton, 1994). Tissue taken from the dorsal mesoderm of one embryo (i.e., the *donor*) and implanted

Simple-systems approach. Studying the neural basis of complex processes, such as learning and memory, in simple neural systems.

Neural plate. A small patch of embryonic ectodermal tissue from which the neural groove, the neural tube, and ultimately the mature nervous system develop.

Neural tube. The tube that is formed in the embryo when the edges of the neural groove fuse; it develops into the central nervous system.

Totipotential. Capable of developing into any type of body cell if transplanted to the appropriate site of the developing embryo.

Mesoderm layer. The middle of the three cell layers in the developing embryo.

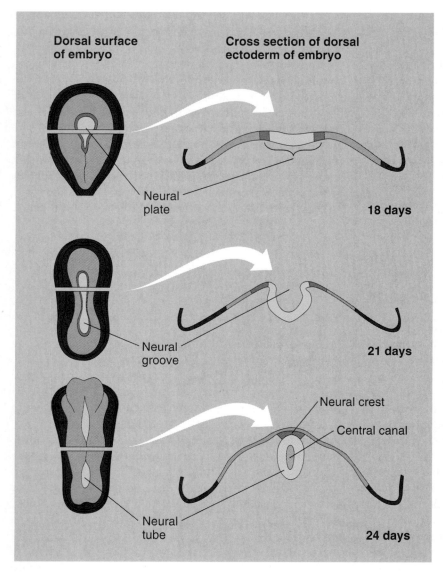

Dorsal surface of embryo

Cross section of dorsal ectoderm of embryo

Neural plate

18 days

Neural groove

21 days

Neural crest

Central canal

Neural tube

24 days

Figure 15.1 How the neural plate develops into the neural tube during the third and fourth weeks of human embryological development. (Adapted from Cowan, 1979.)

beneath the ventral ectoderm of another embryo (i.e., the *host*) induces the development of an extra neural plate on the ventral surface of the host. One of the most fanciful demonstrations of **induction** is one that may require the abandonment of the expression "as scarce as hen's teeth." Kollar and Fisher (1980) induced teeth to grow from the ectodermal cells of chick embryos by implanting beneath them a tiny piece of mouse embryo mesoderm taken from beneath the portion of the ectoderm that would have normally developed into the mouse's mouth.

Neural Proliferation

Once the lips of the neural groove have fused to create the neural tube, the cells of the tube begin to *proliferate*

(increase greatly in number). This **neural proliferation** does not occur simultaneously or equally in all parts of the tube. In each species, the cells in different parts of the neural tube proliferate in a characteristic sequence that is responsible for the pattern of swelling and folding that gives each brain its species-characteristic shape. Most cell division in the neural tube occurs in the **ventricular zone**—the region adjacent to the *ventricle* (to the fluid-filled center of the tube).

Migration and Aggregation

Migration Once cells have been created through cell division in the ventricular zone of the neural tube, they migrate to an appropriate location. During the period of **migration,** a temporary network of glial cells, called **radial glial cells** (see Figure 15.2), is present in the developing neural tube. Migrating neurons move outward along these radial glial cells to their destinations (see Hatten, 1993; Herrup & Silver, 1994).

The first neurons to be created during the phase of proliferation migrate to the *intermediate zone* of the growing neural tube (see Figure 15.3). After the intermediate zone is well established, some of the migrating cells form a layer between the *ventricular zone* and the intermediate zone. The cells that migrate to this *subventricular zone* are destined to become either glial cells or interneurons. In the forebrain, new cells begin to migrate through these layers to establish a layer of cells called the *cortical plate,* which eventually develops into the cerebral cortex. Because the cells of the deepest of the six layers of neocortex arrive at their destination first, the cells of progressively higher layers must migrate through them; this is referred to as the *inside-out pattern of cortical development.* When the migration of cells away from the ventricular zone is complete, the cells remaining there develop into *ependymal cells,* which form the lining of both the cerebral ventricles of the brain and the central canal of the spinal cord.

The **neural crest** is a structure that is situated just dorsal to the neural tube (see Figure 15.1). It is formed from cells that break off from the neural tube as it is being formed. Neural crest cells develop into the neurons and glial cells of the peripheral nervous system, and thus many of them must migrate over considerable distances. What directs them to their destinations? Their migration is directed by the media through which they travel, rather than information contained within the cells themselves. Consequently, cells transplanted from one part of the neural crest to another adopt the route characteristic of their new location.

Aggregation Once developing neurons have migrated, they must align themselves with other developing neurons that have migrated to the same area to form the structures of the nervous system. This process is called **aggregation.** Both migration and aggregation are thought to be mediated by **neural cell-adhesion molecules (NCAMs),** which are located on the surface of the neurons. Neural cell-adhesion molecules have the ability to recognize molecules on other cells and adhere to them (see Rutishauser, 1993).

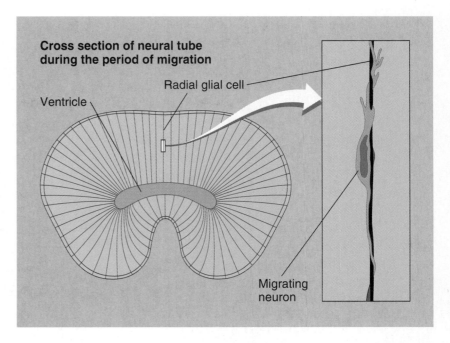

Figure 15.2 Newly created neurons migrate away from the ventricular zone along a network of radial glial cells.

Axon Growth and Synapse Formation

Once neurons have migrated to their appropriate positions and aggregated into neural structures, axons and dendrites begin to grow from them. For the nervous system to function, these neural projections must grow to appropriate targets. At each growing tip of an axon or dendrite is an amoebalike structure called a **growth cone** (see Stirling & Dunlop, 1995), which extends and retracts fingerlike cytoplasmic extensions called *filopodia* (see Figure 15.4), as if searching for the correct route. Three hypotheses have been proposed to explain how growth cones find their way to their appropriate destinations: the chemoaffinity hypothesis, the blueprint hypothesis, and the topographic gradient hypothesis.

Chemoaffinity hypothesis In 1943, Sperry conducted a classic series of experiments on the growth of axons in the frog visual system. In one of them, he cut the optic nerves of frogs, rotated their eyeballs 180°, and waited for the **retinal ganglion cells,** which compose the optic nerve, to *regenerate* (grow again). (Frogs, unlike mammals, have retinal ganglion cells that regenerate.) Once regeneration was complete, Sperry used a convenient behavioral test to assess the frogs' visual capacities (see Figure 15.5). When he dangled a lure behind the frogs, they struck forward, thus indicating that their visual world, like their eyes, had been rotated 180°. Frogs whose eyes had been rotated but whose optic nerves

Induction. The process of causing an enduring change in the nervous system.

Neural proliferation. The rapid increase in the number of neurons that occurs following the formation of the neural tube.

Ventricular zone. The zone adjacent to the ventricle in the developing neural tube; the zone where neural proliferation occurs.

Migration. The movement of cells from their site of creation in the ventricular zone of the neural tube to their ultimate location in the mature nervous system.

Radial glial cells. Glial cells that exist in the neural tube only during the period of neural migration; they form a matrix along which developing neurons migrate.

Neural crest. The structure formed by cells breaking off from the neural groove during the formation of the neural tube; it develops into the PNS.

Aggregation. The alignment of cells during development to form the various structures of the body.

Neural cell-adhesion molecules (NCAMs). Molecules on the surface of cells that have the ability to recognize specific molecules on the surface of other cells and bind to them.

Growth cone. The structure at the tip of each growing axon or dendrite that guides its growth to its appropriate target.

Retinal ganglion cells. The neurons whose axons compose the optic nerve.

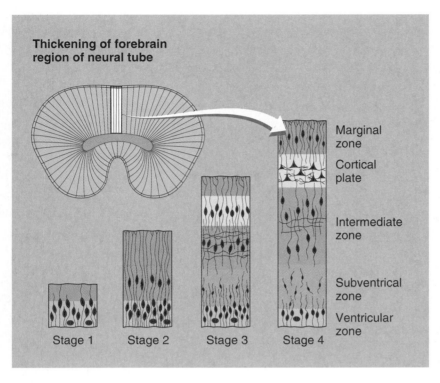

Marginal zone

Cortical plate

Intermediate zone

Subventrical zone

Ventricular zone

Stage 1 Stage 2 Stage 3 Stage 4

Figure 15.3 Neurons migrating out from the ventricular zone of the neural tube, creating new layers of cells. Illustrated here is the growth of the forebrain area of the neural tube.

The chemoaffinity hypothesis accounts for many aspects of axon growth (see Tessier-Lavigne & Placzek, 1991), but it cannot explain why targets transplanted to novel positions sometimes become incorrectly innervated. For example, when Whitelaw and Hollyday (1983) implanted an extra thigh segment in the legs of developing chick embryos so that the sequence was thigh, thigh, calf, foot—instead of the normal thigh, calf, foot—the second thigh segment became innervated by axons that normally would have innervated the calf. Also, the chemoaffinity hypothesis has difficulty explaining how some axons manage to follow exactly the same circuitous route to their target in every member of a species, rather than growing directly to the target (Bastiani et al., 1985; Kuwada, 1986).

Blueprint hypothesis The inability of the chemoaffinity hypothesis to account for certain aspects of axon development led to the proposal of the blueprint hypothesis (Singer, Nordlander, & Egar, 1979). According to the **blueprint hypothesis,** the undeveloped nervous system contains specific chemical or mechanical trails that

had not been cut responded in exactly the same way. This was strong evidence that each retinal ganglion cell had grown back to the same part of the **optic tectum** to which it had originally been connected.

On the basis of his studies of regeneration, Sperry proposed the **chemoaffinity hypothesis** of axonal development (see Sperry, 1963). He hypothesized that each postsynaptic surface in the nervous system releases a specific chemical label and that each growing axon is attracted by the label to its postsynaptic target during both neural development and regeneration. Strong support for the chemoaffinity hypothesis has come from two important discoveries. First, it has been shown that in some cases developing neurons will grow to their normal targets *in vitro* (in tissue culture) (see Bolz, 1994); this supports the chemoaffinity hypothesis because none of the spatial cues that might guide axon growth *in vivo* (in living organisms) would be present in a tissue culture. Second, chemicals that either attract (Baier & Bonhoeffer, 1994; Serafini et al., 1994) or repel (Luo, Raible, & Raper, 1993) growth cones have recently been isolated from neural tissue.

Figure 15.4 Growth Cones. The cytoplasmic fingers (the filopodia) of growth cones seem to grope for the correct route. (Courtesy of Naweed I. Syed, Ph.D., Departments of Anatomy and Medical Physiology, the University of Calgary.)

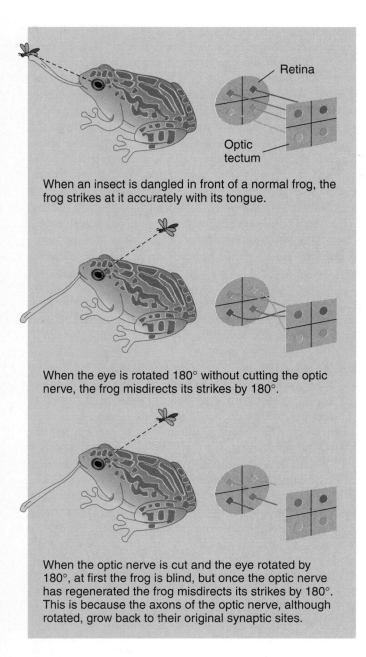

When an insect is dangled in front of a normal frog, the frog strikes at it accurately with its tongue.

When the eye is rotated 180° without cutting the optic nerve, the frog misdirects its strikes by 180°.

When the optic nerve is cut and the eye rotated by 180°, at first the frog is blind, but once the optic nerve has regenerated the frog misdirects its strikes by 180°. This is because the axons of the optic nerve, although rotated, grow back to their original synaptic sites.

Figure 15.5 Sperry's classic study of eye rotation and regeneration.

growing axons follow to their destinations. **Pioneer growth cones**—the first growth cones to travel along a particular route in a developing nervous system—are presumed to follow the correct trail by interacting with the *neural cell-adhesion molecules* of cells along the route (see Doherty & Walsh, 1992). Then, subsequent growth cones embarking on the same journey follow the routes blazed by the pioneers. The tendency of growing axons to grow along the same paths established by preceding axons is called **fasciculation**. When pioneer axons in the fish spinal cord were destroyed with a laser, subsequent axons of the same nerves

did not reach their usual destinations (Klose & Bentley, 1989; Kuwada, 1986).

Although the blueprint hypothesis can account for some aspects of axon growth, it cannot account for the ability of some developing axons to reach their correct destinations in tissue culture. Nor can it account for the ability of some developing axons to reach their correct destinations in vivo when their starting points have been surgically shifted. For example, when Lance-Jones and Landmesser (1980) cut a small portion of the spinal cord from a chick embryo, inverted it, and implanted it back into the same embryo, the axons grew out to their original target muscles despite the fact that they started from a new location (see Figure 15.6).

Topographic gradient hypothesis Much of the axonal growth in complex nervous systems involves growth from one topographic array of neurons to another. The neurons on one array project to another, maintaining the same topographic relation they had on the first; for example, the topographic map of the retina is maintained on the optic tectum (see Figure 15.7).

It was initially assumed that the integrity of topographical relations in the developing nervous system was maintained by point-to-point chemoaffinity. Although this may be the primary mechanism of axon growth in invertebrate nervous systems, research on the development of vertebrate visual systems has led to the **topographic gradient hypothesis** (Easter et al., 1985). According to this hypothesis, axons that have grown out from one sheet of cell bodies (e.g., the retina) to another (e.g., the optic tectum) arrange their synaptic terminals according to the relative positions of their cell bodies on the original sheet, as

Optic tectum. The main destination of visual neurons in lower vertebrates.

Chemoaffinity hypothesis. The hypothesis that each postsynaptic surface in the nervous system releases a specific chemical to which particular growing axons are attracted during development.

Blueprint hypothesis. The hypothesis that developing axons grow to their correct targets by following chemical or mechanical trails through the developing nervous system.

Pioneer growth cones. The first growth cones to grow along a particular route in the developing nervous system.

Fasciculation. The tendency of growing axons to follow the route of preceding axons.

Topographic gradient hypothesis. The hypothesis that axonal growth is guided by the relative position of the cell bodies on intersecting gradients, rather than by point-to-point coding of neural connections.

The pathways normally followed by the motor neuron axons growing out from the spinal cord of a chick embryo to two target muscles.

Before the motor neuron axons grew to their target muscles, Lance-Jones and Landmesser cut out a section from a developing chick spinal cord and reversed it.

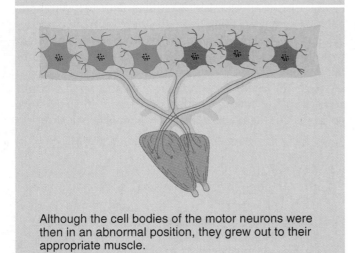

Although the cell bodies of the motor neurons were then in an abnormal position, they grew out to their appropriate muscle.

Figure 15.6 Evidence against the blueprint hypothesis. When a section of spinal cord was cut from a chick embryo, inverted, and implanted back in the same location, the motor neuron axons grew out to their original target muscles. (Adapted from Lance-Jones & Landmesser, 1980.)

defined by two intersecting right-angle gradients (e.g., an up-down gradient and a left-right gradient).

Support for the topographic gradient hypothesis has come both from studies of development and from studies of regeneration. For example, in studies of visual system development, it was found that the synaptic connections

between eyes and tectums are established long before either reach their full size; then, as the eyes and the optic tectums grow at different rates, the initial synaptic connections shift to other tectal neurons so that the retina is always faithfully mapped onto the tectum, regardless of their relative sizes (Gaze et al., 1979; Reh & Constantine-Paton, 1984).

In studies of visual system regeneration (e.g., Gaze & Sharma, 1970; Yoon, 1971), the optic nerves of mature frogs were cut and their pattern of regeneration was assessed after parts of either the retina or the optic tectum had been destroyed. In both cases, the axons did not grow out to their original points of connection (as the chemoaffinity and blueprint hypotheses predicted they would); instead they grew out to fill the available space in an orderly fashion. Axons growing from the remaining portion of a lesioned retina "spread out" in an orderly fashion to fill all of the space on an intact tectum. Conversely, axons growing from an intact retina "squeeze in" in an orderly fashion to fill the remaining space on a lesioned tectum. These results are illustrated schematically in Figure 15.7.

Axon growth and synapse formation: Conclusion
Over half a century of research on the miraculous ability of developing axons to grow to their correct targets has led to the conclusion that no single mechanism can account for all instances. The main guiding force appears to be the growth cones' attraction to specific chemical signals that are released by their targets, but there are well-documented instances in which the growth cones follow specific circuitous routes through the cellular matrix, presumably by following trails of neural cell-adhesion molecules in the substrate. Furthermore, the ability of growing axons to establish topographic gradients seems to require a spatially graded chemical signal from the target structure and a gradient-related mechanism of axon-axon interaction.

Neuron Death and Synapse Rearrangement

Neuron death Neuron death is a normal phase of neural development. Neural development operates on the principle of survival of the fittest: Many more neurons—about 50% more—are produced than are required; they compete for limited resources, and only the fittest survive.

Three findings suggest that neurons die because of their failure to compete successfully for **neurotrophins**—life-preserving chemicals that are supplied to neurons by their targets. First, the implantation of extra target sites decreases neuron death. For example, Hollyday and Hamburger (1976) grafted an extra limb on one side of a chick embryo, and fewer motor neurons on that side died. Second, destroying some of the neurons growing into an area before the period of cell death increases the survival rate of the remaining neurons (e.g., Pilar, Landmesser, & Burstein,

Figure 15.7 The regeneration of the optic nerve of the frog after portions of either the retina or the optic tectum have been destroyed: Support for the topographic gradient hypothesis.

1980). Third, increasing the number of axons that initially innervate a target decreases the proportion that survive.

Nerve growth factor (NGF) was the first neurotrophic factor to be isolated (see Levi-Montalcini, 1952, 1975). Nerve growth factor is synthesized and released by the targets of *sympathetic neurons* during the period of cell death, and it is taken up by the sympathetic neurons and promotes their survival. Since the discovery of nerve growth factor, there has been a major effort to isolate neurotrophins that promote the survival of other neurons; such

Neurotrophins. Substances that promote the survival of neurons.

Nerve growth factor (NGF). A chemical that attracts the growing axons of the sympathetic nervous system and promotes their survival.

factors may have major therapeutic value in halting the course of neurodegenerative diseases. Several substances that promote the survival of certain kinds of neurons in vitro (in tissue culture) have been identified, and work is now being directed at trying to study their actions in vivo (in living organisms)—see Nishi (1994).

Neuron death was initially assumed to be a passive process. It was assumed that the appropriate neurotrophins are needed for the survival of neurons and that without them neurons degenerate and die. However, it is now clear that cell death is an active process: The absence of the appropriate neurotrophins triggers a program inside the neurons that causes them to kill themselves (see Altman, 1992; Raff et al., 1993).

Synapse rearrangement During the period of cell death, neurons that have established incorrect connections are particularly likely to die. As they die, the space that they vacate on postsynaptic membranes is filled by the sprouting axon terminals of surviving neurons. Thus cell death results in a massive rearrangement of synaptic connections, which increases the overall accuracy of neural transmission. Synapse rearrangement focuses the output of each neuron on a smaller number of postsynaptic cells, thus increasing the selectivity of transmission (see Figure 15.8).

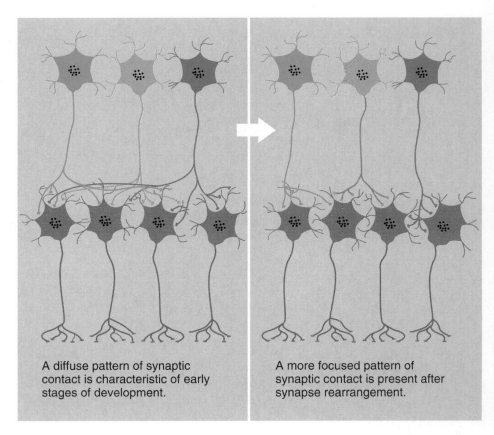

A diffuse pattern of synaptic contact is characteristic of early stages of development.

A more focused pattern of synaptic contact is present after synapse rearrangement.

Figure 15.8 The effect of neuron death and synapse rearrangement on the selectivity of synaptic transmission. The synaptic contacts of each axon become focused on a smaller number of cells.

SELF TEST

Fill in the blanks in the following chronological list of the major stages in the development of the nervous system. The correct answers are provided at the bottom of this page. Before proceeding, review material related to your errors and omissions.

1. Induction of the neural _____.

2. Formation of the _____ tube.

3. Neural _____.

4. Neural _____.

5. _____ aggregation.

6. Growth of _____.

7. Formation of _____.

8. Neuron _____ and synapse _____.

The answers are (1) plate, (2) neural, (3) proliferation, (4) migration, (5) Neural, (6) neural processes (axons and dendrites), (7) synapses, and (8) death; rearrangement.

Chapter 15   Neuroplasticity: Development, Learning, and Recovery from Brain Damage

Effects of Experience on Neural Development

Genetic programs of neural development do not act in a vacuum. Neural development unfolds through interactions between neurons and their environment. You learned in the previous section how factors in a neuron's immediate environment (e.g., neurotrophins and neural cell-adhesion molecules) can influence its development. In contrast, this section focuses on how a neuron's interactions with the external environment can influence its development. The main principle that governs the effects of experience on neural development is "use it or lose it." Neurons and synapses that are not activated by experience do not survive (see Hockfield & Kalb, 1993; Kalil, 1989).

Many of the first demonstrations of the impact of early experience on neural development came from two lines of research: from the study of the effects of early visual deprivation and from the study of early exposure to enriched environments. For example, animals reared in the dark were found to have fewer synapses (e.g., Cragg, 1975) and fewer dendritic spines (e.g., Valverde, 1971) in their primary visual cortexes, and they were found to have deficits in depth (e.g., Walk & Walters, 1973) and pattern (e.g., Tees, 1968) vision as adults. Conversely, rats that were raised in enriched (complex) group cages rather than by themselves in barren cages were found to have thicker cortexes (Bennett et al., 1964), with greater dendritic development (Greenough & Volkmar, 1973) and more synapses per neuron (Turner & Greenough, 1983).

The competitive nature of synapse development is illustrated by the disruptive effects of early monocular deprivation: The effects on the development of the visual system of depriving one eye of input are greater if the other eye is not also deprived. For example, depriving only one eye of input early in life blocks the development of vision in the deprived eye, but this does not happen if the other eye is also blindfolded.

When only one eye is blindfolded during early development, the ability of that eye to activate the visual cortex is reduced or eliminated, whereas the ability of the other eye is increased. Both these effects occur because early monocular deprivation changes the pattern of synaptic input into layer IV of the primary visual cortex. In newborn cats and monkeys, the input into layer IV from the left and right eyes is intermingled; then, during the course of normal development, it becomes segregated into equal-size alternating columns of ocular dominance (see Figure 7.19). Early monocular deprivation decreases the width of the columns of input from the deprived eye and increases the width of the columns of input from the nondeprived eye (Hata & Stryker, 1994; Hubel, Wiesel, & LeVay, 1977).

It takes only a few days of early monocular deprivation to produce significant reductions in the proportion of visual cortex neurons that can be activated by stimulation of the deprived eye. These changes were thought to be too rapid to be mediated by structural changes; however, this has proved not to be the case. Antonini and Stryker (1993) found that a few days of monocular deprivation produces a massive decrease in the axonal branching of the lateral geniculate nucleus neurons that normally carry signals from the deprived eye to layer IV of the primary visual cortex (see Figure 15.9).

The effect of neural activity on synapse rearrangement has also been demonstrated in experiments on motor neurons and muscle cells. In *neonates* (newborns), each muscle cell is normally innervated by several motor neurons, and then all but one are eliminated during the course of development. Lo and Poo (1991) developed an in vitro preparation in which one developing muscle cell was innervated by two developing motor neurons. Applying pulses of electrical stimulation to one of them caused a rapid degradation in the synaptic contacts of the other. Apparently, motor neurons compete with one another for synaptic contacts on muscle cells, and active synapses take precedence.

Figure 15.9 The effect of a few days of early monocular deprivation on the structure of axons projecting from the lateral geniculate nucleus into layer IV of the primary visual cortex. Axons carrying information from the deprived eye displayed substantially less branching. (Adapted from Antonini & Stryker, 1993.)

Some of the most remarkable demonstrations of the effects of neural activity on development come from lines of research that involve the interaction between the topographic maps of the auditory and visual systems. The following are two of them. First, Roe and colleagues (1990) caused the developing axons of ferret retinal ganglion cells to synapse in the medial geniculate nuclei of the auditory system instead of in the lateral geniculate nuclei of the visual system. Remarkably, once the ferrets matured, their auditory cortex responded to visual stimuli, and it was laid out retinotopically. Second, Knudsen and Brainard (1991) raised barn owls with vision-displacing prisms over their eyes. This led to a corresponding change in the auditory spatial map in the tectum. For example, an owl that was raised wearing prisms that shifted its visual world 23° to the right had an auditory map that was also shifted 23° to the right, so that objects were heard to be where they were seen to be (Knudsen, 1991).

15.3   Neural Bases of Learning and Memory in Simple Systems

So far, this chapter has focused on the plasticity of developing nervous systems. Now the emphasis changes to the plasticity of adult nervous systems. This section discusses how experience induces adaptive changes in adult nervous systems and how these changes are maintained and later expressed. In other words, this section focuses on the neural bases of learning and memory. Learning and memory refer to different aspects of the same neuroplastic phenomena: **Learning** is the induction of experience-produced neural changes, and **memory** is their maintenance and expression in the form of behavioral change.

This section of the chapter focuses on two influential lines of research, both of which feature the simple-systems approach. The first deals with the neural basis of learning and memory in *Aplysia*, a simple marine invertebrate; the second deals with long-term potentiation, a learning- and memory-related phenomenon of the mammalian brain.

Learning in the Aplysia Gill-Withdrawal Reflex Circuit

The **Aplysia** is a marine snail that spends its life oozing along the ocean floor eating seaweed and avoiding predation by tasting as bad as it looks (see Figure 15.10). The Aplysia *siphon* is a small, fleshy spout that is used to expel seawater and waste. When the siphon is touched, it and the adjoining gill are reflexively drawn up under a protective *mantle*. This response to touch is the Aplysia's *gill-withdrawal reflex*.

The neural circuit that mediates the Aplysia gill-withdrawal reflex is relatively simple. The skin of the siphon contains 24 sensory neurons that synapse on 6 motor neurons that are responsible for retracting the siphon and gill. The sensory neurons also activate interneurons that in turn synapse on the motor neurons. This circuit is illustrated schematically in Figure 15.11.

Nonassociative learning in Aplysia A change in behavior that results from the repeated experience of a single stimulus or of two or more different stimuli that are not spatially or temporally related is called **nonassociative learning.** The two most commonly studied forms of nonassociative learning are habituation and sensitization.

Habituation is the progressive decrease in the strength of the behavioral reaction to a stimulus that is repeatedly presented. For example, if the Aplysia siphon is touched once every 30 seconds, the gill-withdrawal reflex becomes less and less vigorous. Habituation of the Aplysia gill-withdrawal reflex lasts 2 or 3 hours following a single 10-stimulus habituation session, but several such sessions can produce habituation that lasts for weeks (Carew, Pinsker, & Kandel, 1972).

What is the neural mechanism of habituation in the Aplysia gill-withdrawal reflex circuit? The first clue came from the discovery that habituation is associated with a decline in the number of action potentials that are elicited in the gill motor neurons by each siphon touch (Castellucci et al., 1970). Because the responsiveness of the motor neurons to the neurotransmitter released by the sensory neu-

Figure 15.10 An Aplysia.

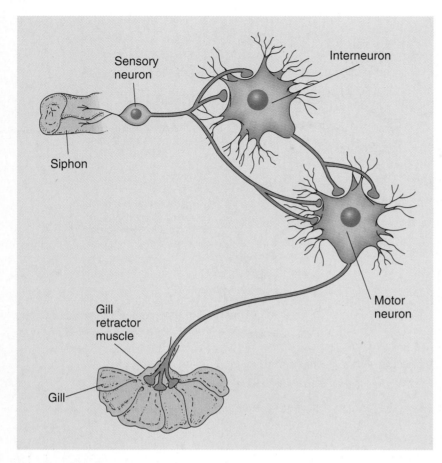

Figure 15.11 A schematic illustration of the components of the neural circuit that mediates the Aplysia gill-withdrawal reflex.

buttons that causes synaptic vesicles to fuse with the presynaptic membrane and release their contents into the synapse. It was soon established that the decrease in siphon sensory neuron neurotransmitter release during habituation of the gill-withdrawal reflex results from a decrease in the number of calcium ions entering the terminal buttons of the siphon sensory neurons in response to each action potential (Klein & Kandel, 1978; Klein, Shapiro, & Kandel, 1980).

The following theory of habituation learning in the Aplysia gill-withdrawal reflex has emerged from this line of research (see Figure 15.12 on page 390). With repeated elicitation of the gill-withdrawal reflex, each siphon touch continues to fully activate the sensory neurons, sending the same full barrage of action potentials down their axons. However, because fewer calcium ions enter the synaptic terminals in response to each successive barrage of action potentials, less and less neurotransmitter is released from the sensory neurons into the synapses, fewer and fewer action potentials are elicited in the motor neurons, and the contraction of the gill muscle in response to each siphon touch grows weaker and weaker (see Kandel, 1985).

Sensitization is the general increase in an animal's responsiveness to stimuli that occurs following a noxious stimulus. Sensitization of the Aplysia gill-withdrawal reflex lasts for several minutes

rons did not decline during habituation (Castellucci & Kandel, 1974), it was concluded that the progressive decline in the number of motor neuron action potentials must have resulted from a decline in the release of neurotransmitter from the sensory neurons.

What causes the siphon sensory neurons to release progressively less neurotransmitter in response to each successive siphon touch during the course of habituation? There are two possibilities. One is that less neurotransmitter is released because progressively fewer action potentials are elicited in the siphon sensory neurons by each successive touch; the other is that there is a decline in the amount of neurotransmitter that is released in response to each action potential. The discovery that the number of sensory neuron action potentials does not decline during the course of habituation (Castellucci & Kandel, 1974) supported the latter alternative.

Once it became clear that the habituation of the Aplysia gill-withdrawal reflex results from a decrease in the amount of neurotransmitter that is released from siphon sensory neurons in response to each of their own action potentials, researchers began the search for the mechanism of this decrease. The search focused on calcium ions because it is the influx of calcium ions into the terminal

Learning. The induction of behavior-related neural changes by sensory experience.

Memory. The maintenance and later expression as a change in behavior of experience-induced neural changes.

Aplysia. A simple marine snail whose gill-withdrawal reflex is capable of simple forms of nonassociative and associative learning.

Nonassociative learning. A change in behavior that results from the repeated experience of a single stimulus or of two or more stimuli that are not temporally or spatially related.

Habituation. The progressive decrease in the strength of the behavioral reaction to a repeatedly presented stimulus.

Sensitization. The general increase in an animal's responsiveness to stimuli following the experience of a noxious stimulus.

1 Following habituation, each touch fully activates the sensory neurons; there is no reduction in the number of action potentials.

2 However, less calcium enters the button in response to each action potential.

3 As a result, less neurotransmitter is released into the synapse in response to each action potential.

4 Consequently, each touch generates fewer action potentials in the motor neurons.

5 And ultimately, there is less contraction of the gill-retractor muscle in response to each siphon touch.

Mechanism of Habituation

1 A strong shock to the tail activates the tail sensory neurons.

2 The tail sensory neurons activate facilitatory interneurons that synapse on the buttons of sensory neurons from the siphon.

3 The barrage of action potentials from the facilitatory interneurons produces changes in the buttons of the siphon sensory neurons that cause more calcium to enter the button in response to each action potential.

4 The increased influx of calcium into the buttons of siphon sensory neurons causes more neurotransmitter to be released in response to each action potential.

5 This increases the number of action potentials generated in the motor neurons by each siphon touch.

6 And this in turn increases the strength of the gill retraction produced by each siphon touch.

Mechanism of Sensitization

Figure 15.12 Mechanisms of habituation and sensitization of the Aplysia gill-withdrawal reflex.

following a single tail shock (Carew, Castelluci, & Kandel, 1971), but it can last for weeks following a series of tail shocks administered over several days (Pinsker et al., 1973). In contrast to the mechanism of habituation, sensitization has been shown to result from an increase in the amount of neurotransmitter that is released by the siphon sensory neurons in response to their own action potentials (Castellucci & Kandel, 1976).

How does tail shock cause the siphon sensory neurons to increase their release of neurotransmitter onto the gill motor neurons? The mechanism is **presynaptic facilitation.** Sensory fibers from the Aplysia tail synapse on facilitatory *serotonergic* (serotonin-releasing) interneurons, which in turn synapse on the buttons of siphon sensory neurons (see Mercer, Emptage, & Carew, 1991). It is via these serotonergic interneurons that the tail shock changes the siphon sensory neuron buttons so that each action potential arriving there from the siphon results in a greater influx of calcium ions and a greater release of neurotransmitter onto the motor neurons (see Figure 15.12). Single brief applications of serotonin to Aplysia sensorimotor synapses in vitro produce sensitization lasting several minutes (e.g., Eliot et al., 1994), whereas multiple spaced applications produce sensitization lasting several days (e.g., Montarolo et al., 1986).

Procedures used to demonstrate discriminated Pavlovian conditioning of Aplysia gill-withdrawal reflex

When weak siphon stimulation is the CS⁺ and weak mantle stimulation the CS⁻.

Siphon stimulation CS⁻
Tail shock US
Mantle stimulation CS⁺
Time

When weak siphon stimulation is the CS⁻ and weak mantle stimulation the CS⁺.

Siphon stimulation CS⁺
Tail shock US
Mantle stimulation CS⁻
Time

Results of testing carried out 30 minutes after 15 conditioning trials

Strength of gill withdrawal elicited by CS⁺ and CS⁻

CS⁻   CS⁺

Pavlovian conditioning
Sensitization
Preconditioning baseline

Figure 15.13 Discriminated Pavlovian conditioning of the Aplysia gill-withdrawal reflex. (Adapted from Carew, Hawkins, & Kandel, 1983.)

Associative learning in Aplysia The Aplysia gill-withdrawal reflex circuit is capable of *Pavlovian conditioning*—of learning an association between a conditional stimulus and an unconditional stimulus. If a light touch of the siphon (the conditional stimulus) is paired with a strong shock to the tail (the unconditional stimulus) every few minutes for several trials, the light touch by itself begins to elicit a robust gill-withdrawal response similar to that elicited by the tail shock. The associative nature of this effect is shown by the fact that the increase in the intensity of the reflex is not nearly so great if the two stimuli are presented in an unpaired fashion (Carew, Walters, & Kandel, 1981); unpaired presentations produce sensitization but no conditioning. The conditional response is typically retained for several days after 20 conditioning trials.

The Aplysia gill-withdrawal reflex is capable of *discriminated Pavlovian conditioning*—Pavlovian conditioning to one conditional stimulus but not to another (see Figure 15.13). In an experiment by Carew, Hawkins, and Kandel (1983), two conditional stimuli were administered: mild stimulation to the mantle and mild stimulation to the siphon. Both elicited a weak gill-withdrawal response. During training, one of the conditional stimuli (called the CS⁺) was always paired with the unconditional stimulus, a severe tail shock, whereas the other conditional stimulus (called the CS⁻) was not. At the end of training, the CS⁺ elicited a strong withdrawal reaction, whereas the CS⁻

Presynaptic facilitation. The cellular mechanism thought to underlie sensitization and Pavlovian conditioning in the Aplysia gill-wirhdrawal circuit.

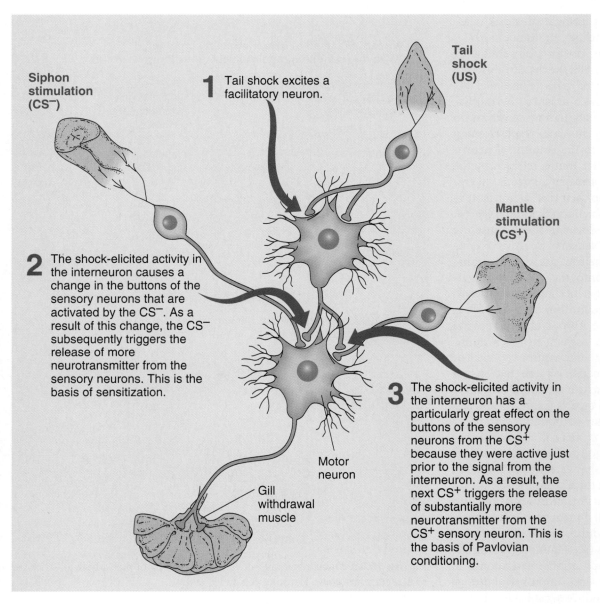

Siphon stimulation (CS⁻)

1 Tail shock excites a facilitatory neuron.

Tail shock (US)

Mantle stimulation (CS⁺)

2 The shock-elicited activity in the interneuron causes a change in the buttons of the sensory neurons that are activated by the CS⁻. As a result of this change, the CS⁻ subsequently triggers the release of more neurotransmitter from the sensory neurons. This is the basis of sensitization.

3 The shock-elicited activity in the interneuron has a particularly great effect on the buttons of the sensory neurons from the CS⁺ because they were active just prior to the signal from the interneuron. As a result, the next CS⁺ triggers the release of substantially more neurotransmitter from the CS⁺ sensory neuron. This is the basis of Pavlovian conditioning.

Motor neuron

Gill withdrawal muscle

Figure 15.14 The model that has been proposed to explain discriminated Pavlovian conditioning of the gill-withdrawal reflex. (Adapted from Kandel, 1985.)

elicited a weak withdrawal reaction. Optimal conditioning occurred when the CS⁺ preceded the unconditional stimulus by 0.5 second, and it didn't occur at all when the CS⁺ followed the unconditional stimulus.

Pavlovian conditioning of the gill-withdrawal reflex can be thought of as a special case of sensitization. In effect, it is a demonstration that tail shock has the greatest sensitizing effect on reflexes that are active during the shock. This relation between sensitization and Pavlovian conditioning is reflected in the model that has been proposed to explain Pavlovian conditioning (see Figure 15.14). Like sensitization, Pavlovian conditioning of the gill-withdrawal reflex is assumed to be mediated by the action of tail-shock-activated interneurons on the sensory neurons that normally

activate the reflex. However, unlike sensitization, Pavlovian conditioning depends on the temporal relation between the activation of the interneuron by tail shock and the activation of the sensory neuron by the CS⁺. The greatest increase in the release of neurotransmitter from the CS⁺ sensory neurons is produced following trials in which they are in the act of firing at the time when input reaches their presynaptic terminals from the tail-shock-activated interneurons. Accordingly, the synaptic facilitation that mediates this form of Pavlovian conditioning has been termed **activity-dependent enhancement** (see Glanzman, 1995).

Role of second messengers and structural changes
Earlier in this text, you learned that there are two modes of

synaptic transmission: one mode that produces rapid momentary changes in postsynaptic neurons and one that produces slow, enduring changes in postsynaptic neurons. The first mode acts through ion-channel linked receptors, and the second acts through G-protein linked receptors and second messengers. *Second messengers* are chemicals that are created inside postsynaptic neurons in response to a neurotransmitter binding to a G-protein linked receptor. Once created, second messengers can induce lasting changes in neural structure and function in a variety ways—for example, by interacting with the genetic material of the neuron. Not surprisingly, given their ability to produce lasting changes, second messengers have been implicated in memory storage (see Byrne et al., 1993; Krasne & Glanzman, 1995).

The second messenger **cyclic AMP** (cyclic adenosine monophosphate) plays a role in the sensitization of the Aplysia gill-withdrawal reflex. The tail-shock-produced release of serotonin onto the buttons of the siphon sensory neurons increases the levels of cyclic AMP in the buttons. The cyclic AMP in turn activates another enzyme, a *protein kinase*—protein kinases are a family of cellular enzymes that regulate protein synthesis. The particular protein kinase that is activated in the buttons of siphon sensory neurons by tail-shock closes many of the potassium channels in the buttons, which increases the duration of each action potential. It is this increase in the duration of each action potential that increases the influx of calcium and thus the release of neurotransmitter in response to each touch of the siphon.

Research on learning in the Aplysia gill-withdrawal reflex suggests that although long-term and short-term memories are stored at the same synapses, their mode of storage is different. Long-term storage requires that second messengers stimulate protein synthesis in the neuron cell body, whereas short-term storage does not have this requirement. Accordingly, inhibitors of protein synthesis block the formation of long-term memories but not short-term memories (see Castellucci et al., 1989). This difference suggests that short-term memories can be expressed at individual terminal buttons, whereas long-term memories, because of their reliance on the synthesis of nuclear pro-

tein, are expressed throughout the entire neuron (Emptage & Carew, 1993).

The protein synthesis that is involved in the formation of long-term memories leads to structural changes in the neuron. Bailey and Chen (1983, 1988) showed that long-term habituation and long-term sensitization induce structural changes in the synaptic terminals of the siphon sensory neurons. They labeled the siphon sensory neurons of Aplysia with horseradish peroxidase so that they could examine their synaptic terminals by electron microscopy after either habituation or sensitization. The sensory neurons of the habituated subjects had fewer active zones of neurotransmitter release, smaller active zones of neurotransmitter release, and fewer synaptic vesicles than those of control subjects. In contrast, the sensory neurons of the sensitized subjects had more active zones of neurotransmitter release, larger active zones of neurotransmitter release, and more synaptic vesicles than those of control subjects. Such structural changes cannot occur rapidly enough to account for short-term retention of sensitization and habituation; thus they are presumed to be mechanisms of long-term storage. By repeatedly applying serotonin, Glanzman, Kandel, and Schacter (1990) induced increases in the size and number of synaptic contacts in Aplysia sensory neurons that were grown in culture.

Long-Term Potentiation in Mammalian Hippocampus

Not all attempts to identify the cellular mechanisms of learning and memory have focused on learning in simple nervous systems. A different strategy has been to study neuroplastic phenomena in simple circuits that are components of complex nervous systems. Long-term potentiation is the most widely studied neuroplastic phenomenon of the mammalian nervous system.

Long-term potentiation (LTP) is the enduring facilitation of synaptic transmission that occurs following activation of a synapse by intense high-frequency stimulation of the presynaptic neurons (Bliss & Gardner-Medwin, 1973; Bliss & Lømø, 1973). Long-term potentiation has been demonstrated in many neural structures, but it has been most frequently studied at three synapses in the hippocampus: (1) the synapses of perforant path axons from the entorhinal cortex on the granule cells of the hippocampal dentate gyrus, (2) the synapses of dentate granule cell axons on the pyramidal cells of the CA3 subfield, and (3) the synapses of CA3 pyramidal cell axons on the pyramidal cells of the CA1 subfield (see Figure 15.15). LTP has been studied in freely moving animals, in anesthetized animals, and in *hippocampal slice preparations*—slices of hippocampal tissue that have been cut from a living brain and maintained alive in a saline bath.

Figure 15.16 is a demonstration of LTP in the granule cell layer of the hippocampal dentate gyrus. First, a single low-

Activity-dependent enhancement. Enhancement of synaptic transmission whose induction depends on the presynaptic neuron being active during the enhancement-inducing presynaptic input.

Cyclic AMP. Cyclic adenosine monophosphate; a second messenger involved in sensitization of the Aplysia gill-withdrawal reflex.

Long-term potentiation (LTP). The enduring facilitation of synaptic transmission that occurs following activation of a synapse by intense high-frequency stimulation of the presynaptic neurons.

intensity pulse of current was delivered to the perforant path, and the response was recorded through an extracellular multiple-unit electrode in the granule cell layer of the hippocampal dentate gyrus; the purpose of this initial stimulation was to determine the initial response baseline. Second, 10 seconds of intense high-frequency stimulation was delivered to the perforant path to induce the LTP. Third, the granule cell responses to single pulses of the low-intensity current were measured after various delays to determine their magnitude. It is apparent in Figure 15.16 that the transmission at the granule cell synapse was still potentiated 1 week after the potentiating stimulation.

Relation of LTP to learning and memory The reason long-term potentiation is one of the most widely studied neuroscientific phenomena goes back to 1949 and D. O. Hebb. Hebb argued that the facilitation of synaptic transmission is the fundamental mechanism of learning and memory. He believed that each experience triggers a unique pattern of neural activity, which reverberates through cerebral circuits. He further believed that this reverberating activity causes long-term changes in the synapses of the activated circuits and that these changes facilitate subsequent transmission across those particular synapses and store the memory of the initial experience. In this

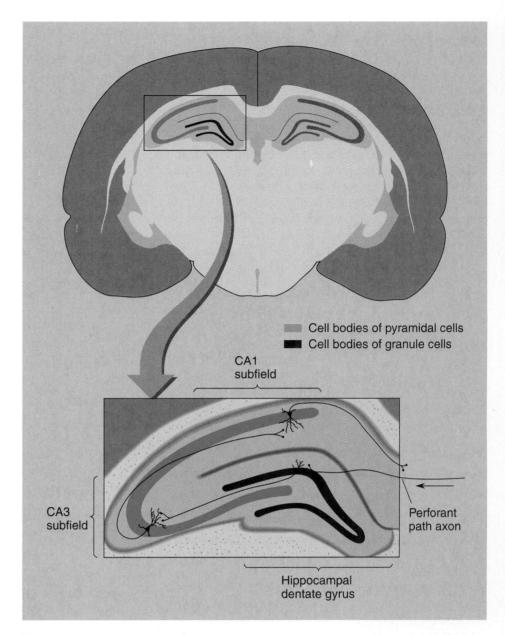

Figure 15.15 A slice of hippocampal tissue that illustrates the three synapses at which LTP is most commonly studied: (1) the dentate granule cell synapse, (2) the CA3 pyramidal cell synapse, and (3) the CA1 pyramidal cell synapse. *CA* stands for *cornu ammonis,* another name for the hippocampus.

theory, the particular synapses that are strengthened are those in which the firing of the presynaptic neuron is followed by the firing of the postsynaptic neuron. Could the synaptic changes that were hypothesized by Hebb to underlie learning and memory be related to the changes that underlie LTP?

LTP has two key properties that Hebb hypothesized to be characteristics of the physiological mechanisms of learning and memory. First, LTP can last for a long time—for many weeks after multiple stimulations (Racine & deJonge, 1988; Racine, Milgram, & Hafner, 1983). Second, LTP develops only if the firing of the presynaptic neuron is followed by the firing of the postsynaptic neuron; it does

not develop when the presynaptic neuron fires and the postsynaptic neuron does not, and it does not develop when the postsynaptic neuron fires and the presynaptic neuron does not (e.g., Kelso, Ganong, & Brown, 1986; Sastry, Goh, & Auyeung, 1986). The **co-occurrence** of firing in presynaptic and postsynaptic cells is now recognized as the critical factor in many forms of learning, and the assumption that co-occurrence is a physiological necessity for learning is often referred to as *Hebb's postulate for learning.*

Additional support for the idea that LTP is related to the neural mechanism of learning and memory has come from several observations: (1) LTP can be elicited by low levels of

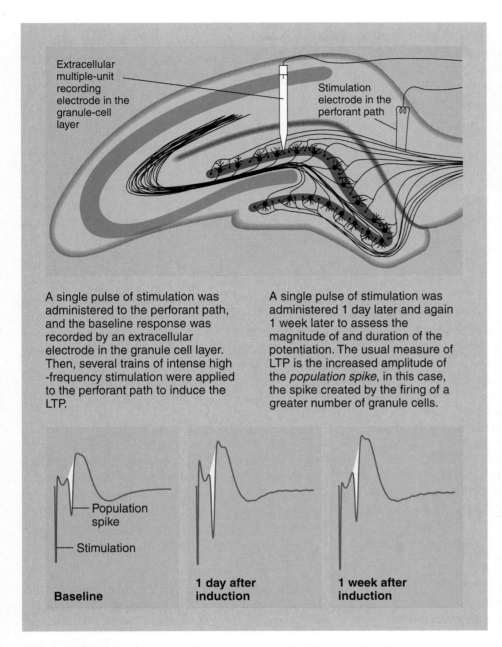

Extracellular multiple-unit recording electrode in the granule-cell layer

Stimulation electrode in the perforant path

A single pulse of stimulation was administered to the perforant path, and the baseline response was recorded by an extracellular electrode in the granule cell layer. Then, several trains of intense high-frequency stimulation were applied to the perforant path to induce the LTP.

A single pulse of stimulation was administered 1 day later and again 1 week later to assess the magnitude of and duration of the potentiation. The usual measure of LTP is the increased amplitude of the *population spike*, in this case, the spike created by the firing of a greater number of granule cells.

Population spike

Stimulation

Baseline

1 day after induction

1 week after induction

Figure 15.16 Long-term potentiation in the granule cell layer of the hippocampal dentate gyrus. (Traces courtesy of Michael Corcoran, Department of Psychology, University of Victoria, British Columbia.)

to keep in mind that LTP as induced in the laboratory by electrical stimulation is at best a caricature of the subtle cellular events that underlie learning and memory (see Eichenbaum & Otto, 1993).

Induction of LTP LTP has been studied most extensively at synapses at which the NMDA receptor is predominant. The **NMDA (N-methyl-D-aspartate) receptor** is a receptor for **glutamate**—the main excitatory neurotransmitter of the brain. The NMDA receptor has a special property. It does not respond maximally unless two events occur simultaneously: Glutamate must bind to it, and the postsynaptic neuron must be partially depolarized. This dual requirement stems from the fact that the calcium channels that are linked to NMDA receptors allow only small numbers of calcium ions to enter the neuron unless the neuron is already depolarized when glutamate binds to the receptor; it is the influx of calcium ions that triggers action potentials and the cascade of events in the postsynaptic neuron that induces LTP. The study of calcium influx has been greatly facilitated by the development of techniques for visualizing it (see Figure 15.17).

An important characteristic of the induction of LTP at glutaminergic synapses stems from the special property of the NMDA receptor and LTP's requirement for co-occurrence. This characteristic is not obvious under the usual, but unnatural, experimental condi-

stimulation that mimic normal neural activity; (2) LTP effects are most prominent in structures that have been implicated in learning and memory—structures such as the hippocampus; (3) behavioral conditioning can produce LTP-like changes in the hippocampus (e.g., Iriki et al., 1989); (4) many drugs that influence learning and memory have parallel effects on LTP (e.g., Brown et al., 1988; Skelton et al., 1987); (5) the induction of maximal LTP blocks the learning of a Morris water maze until the LTP has subsided (Castro et al., 1989); and (6) mutant mice that display little hippocampal LTP have difficulty learning the Morris water maze (Silva et al., 1992). Still, it is important

Co-occurrence. The assumption that facilitatory changes at the synapses between two neurons occur only if the firing of the presynaptic neuron causes the postsynaptic neuron to fire.

NMDA receptor. N-methyl-D-aspartate receptor; a glutamate receptor subtype that plays an important role in long-term potentiation at some synapses.

Glutamate. The main excitatory neurotransmitter of the brain.

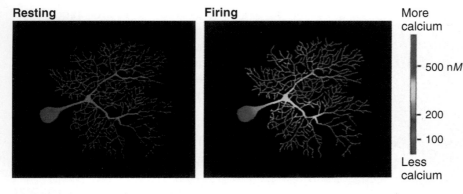

Resting   **Firing**   More calcium

500 n*M*

200

100

Less calcium

Figure 15.17 The influx of calcium into active neurons. This influx can now be visualized with microfluorometric techniques. Notice that the greatest influx occurs in the axon terminal branches. (Courtesy of Tank et al., 1988.)

tion in which LTP is induced by high-intensity, high-frequency stimulation, which always activates the postsynaptic neurons through massive temporal and spatial summation. However, when a more natural, low-intensity stimulation is applied, the postsynaptic neurons do not fire and thus LTP is not induced—unless the postsynaptic neurons are already partially depolarized so that their calcium channels open wide when glutamate binds to their NMDA receptors.

The requirement for the postsynaptic neurons to be partially depolarized when the glutamate binds to them is an extremely important characteristic of LTP because it permits neural networks to learn associations. Let me explain. If one glutaminergic neuron were to fire by itself and release its glutamate neurotransmitter across a synapse onto the NMDA receptors of a postsynaptic neuron, there would be no potentiation of transmission at that synapse because the postsynaptic cell would not fire. However, if the postsynaptic neuron were partially depolarized by input from other neurons when the presynaptic neuron fires, the binding of the glutamate to the NMDA receptors would open wide the calcium channels, calcium ions would flow into the postsynaptic neuron, and transmission across the synapses between the presynaptic and postsynaptic neuron would be potentiated. Accordingly, the requirement for co-occurrence and the dependence of NMDA receptors on simultaneous binding and partial depolarization means that, under natural conditions, synaptic facilitation records the fact that there has been simultaneous activity in at least two converging inputs to the postsynaptic neuron—such as would be produced by the simultaneous presentation of a conditional stimulus and an unconditional stimulus.

The exact mechanisms by which calcium influx induces LTP are unclear; however, there is substantial evidence that calcium exerts its effects by activating protein kinases in the neural cytoplasm (see Grant & Silva, 1994; Linden & Routtenberg, 1989). A consistent finding has been that protein kinase inhibitors block the induction of LTP (see Bashir & Collingridge, 1992). Figure 15.18 summarizes the induction of NMDA-receptor-mediated LTP.

Maintenance and expression of LTP Although there is a consensus that the chemical events that induce LTP occur in postsynaptic neurons, it is still not clear whether the mechanisms responsible for its maintenance and expression are presynaptic or postsynaptic. Do LTP maintenance and expression depend on changes in presynaptic neurons that increase their release of the neurotransmitter (see Stevens & Wang, 1994) or on changes in postsynaptic neurons that increase their responsiveness to the neurotransmitter? The difficulty in answering this question stems from the current inability to accurately measure neurotransmitter release at individual synapses (Malinow, 1994).

Although it is still not clear whether the maintenance and expression of LTP are presynaptic or postsynaptic, progress in understanding the mechanisms of maintenance and expression has recently been made on three fronts.

1. Whether LTP is presynaptic or postsynaptic, there must be some mechanism to account for the fact that its maintenance and expression are restricted to specific synapses on the postsynaptic neuron. Recent research suggests that the specificity of LTP is attributable to **dendritic spines;** calcium that enters one dendritic spine does not diffuse out of it and thus exerts its effects locally (see Harris & Kater, 1994; Stevens, 1991).

2. Whether LTP is presynaptic or postsynaptic, it seems likely that its maintenance over long intervals (weeks) would require the synthesis of neural protein. Recent

Dendritic spines. Tiny buds on dendrites, which are the location of most dendritic synapses; their function seems to be to restrict certain synaptic effects in the postsynaptic neuron to the vicinity of the synapse.

Nitric oxide. A soluable gas neurotransmitter that is thought to serve as a retrograde messenger in the production of LTP-maintaining changes in presynaptic neurons.

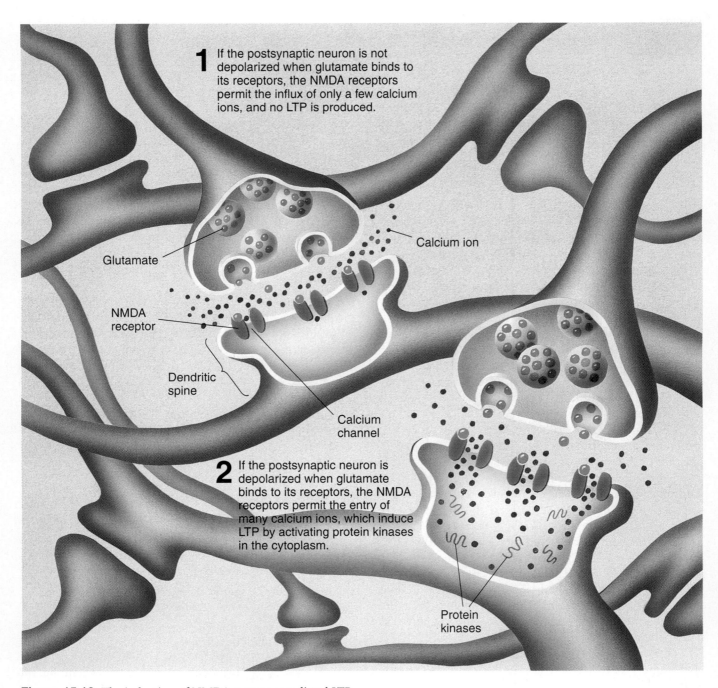

1 If the postsynaptic neuron is not depolarized when glutamate binds to its receptors, the NMDA receptors permit the influx of only a few calcium ions, and no LTP is produced.

Calcium ion

Glutamate

NMDA receptor

Dendritic spine

Calcium channel

2 If the postsynaptic neuron is depolarized when glutamate binds to its receptors, the NMDA receptors permit the entry of many calcium ions, which induce LTP by activating protein kinases in the cytoplasm.

Protein kinases

Figure 15.18 The induction of NMDA-receptor-mediated LTP.

studies of NMDA-receptor-mediated LTP have shown that blocking protein synthesis immediately after stimulation has no effect on the maintenance of LTP for 1 or 2 hours but blocks its maintenance for longer periods (e.g., Frey, Huang, & Kandel, 1993; Nguyen, Abel, & Kandel, 1994).

3. If the maintenance and expression is presynaptic while the induction is postsynaptic, there must be some signal that passes from the postsynaptic neuron back to the presynaptic neuron. Recent evidence suggests that the soluble gas neurotransmitter **nitric oxide** might serve this function; it may be synthesized in the postsynaptic neuron in response to calcium influx and then diffuse back into the presynaptic button (see Haley & Schuman, 1994; Schuman & Madison, 1994). Injection of nitric oxide inhibitors into the postsynaptic neuron during stimulation limits the maintenance of LTP to 1 hour (Haley, Wilcox, & Chapman, 1992).

This section of the chapter is about three neuroplastic responses of the nervous system to damage: degeneration, regeneration, and reorganization. Each is discussed in a separate subsection.

Neural Degeneration

After **axotomy**—the severing of an axon or bundle of axons—two kinds of neural degeneration (deterioration) occur: anterograde degeneration and retrograde degeneration. **Anterograde degeneration** is the degeneration of the **distal segment**—the segment of a cut axon between the cut and the synaptic terminals. **Retrograde degeneration** is the degeneration of the **proximal segment**—the segment of a cut axon between the cut and the cell body.

Anterograde degeneration occurs quickly following axotomy because the cut separates the distal segment of the axon from the cell body, which is the metabolic center of the neuron. The entire distal segment becomes badly swollen within a few hours, and within a few days it breaks into fragments.

The course of retrograde degeneration is different; it progresses gradually back from the cut to the cell body. In about 2 or 3 days, major changes become apparent in the cell bodies of most axotomized neurons. These early cell body changes are either degenerative or regenerative. Early degenerative changes (e.g., a decrease in size) suggest that the neuron will ultimately die. Early regenerative changes (e.g., an increase in size) indicate that the cell body is involved in a massive synthesis of the proteins that will be used to replace the degenerated axon. But early regenerative changes in the cell body do not guarantee the long-term survival of the neuron; if the regenerating axon does not manage to make synaptic contact with an appropriate target, the neuron eventually dies.

Following damage to the central nervous system (CNS), **astrologia** proliferate and absorb most of the resulting debris. This reaction is termed **phagocytosis,** and astroglia are thus referred to as *phagocytes.* In the peripheral nervous system (PNS), phagocytosis of dead neurons is largely carried out by the **Schwann cells** that compose the myelin sheaths of the degenerated axons.

Sometimes, degeneration spreads from damaged neurons to neurons that are linked to them by synapses; this is called *transneuronal degeneration.* In some cases, degeneration spreads from damaged neurons to the neurons on which they synapse; this is called **anterograde transneuronal degeneration.** And in some cases, degeneration spreads from damaged neurons to the neurons that synapse on them; this is called **retrograde transneuronal degeneration.** Neural and transneuronal degeneration are illustrated in Figure 15.19.

Neural Regeneration

Neural regeneration—the regrowth of damaged neurons—does not proceed as successfully in mammals and other higher vertebrates as it does in most invertebrates and lower vertebrates. For some reason, the capacity for accurate axon growth, which is possessed by higher vertebrates during their original development, is lost once they reach maturity. Regeneration is virtually nonexistent in the central nervous systems of adult mammals (see Bandtlow, 1993), and regeneration in their peripheral nervous systems is at best a hit-or-miss affair (see Fawcett & Keynes, 1990).

In the mammalian peripheral nervous system, regrowth from the proximal stump of a damaged nerve begins 2 or 3 days after the damage. What happens next depends on the nature of the injury (see Tonge & Golding, 1993); there are three possibilities. First, if the original Schwann cell myelin sheaths remain intact, the regenerating peripheral axons grow through them to their original targets at a rate of a few millimeters per day. Second, if the peripheral nerve is severed and the cut ends become separated by a few mil-

Axotomy. Severing an axon or a bundle of axons.

Anterograde degeneration. The degeneration of the distal segment of a cut axon.

Distal segment. The segment of a cut axon between the cut and the axon terminals.

Retrograde degeneration. Degeneration of the proximal segment of a cut axon.

Proximal segment. The segment of a cut axon between the cut and the cell body.

Astroglia. Glial cells that absorb debris at sites of neural damage in the CNS.

Phagocytosis. The act of absorbing cellular debris or foreign cells in the body.

Schwann cells. The satellite cells that compose the myelin sheaths of PNS axons and promote their regeneration.

Anterograde transneuronal degeneration. The degeneration of a neuron caused by damage to neurons that synapse on it.

Retrograde transneuronal degeneration. The degeneration of a neuron caused by damage to neurons on which it synapses.

Neural regeneration. The regrowth of damaged neurons.

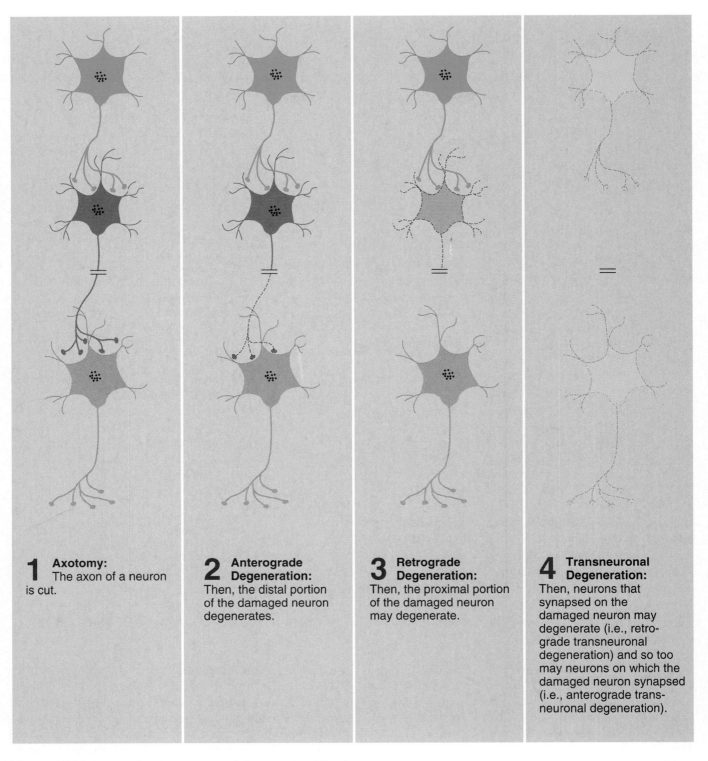

1 **Axotomy:**
The axon of a neuron is cut.

2 **Anterograde Degeneration:**
Then, the distal portion of the damaged neuron degenerates.

3 **Retrograde Degeneration:**
Then, the proximal portion of the damaged neuron may degenerate.

4 **Transneuronal Degeneration:**
Then, neurons that synapsed on the damaged neuron may degenerate (i.e., retrograde transneuronal degeneration) and so too may neurons on which the damaged neuron synapsed (i.e., anterograde transneuronal degeneration).

Figure 15.19 Neuronal and transneuronal degeneration following axotomy.

limeters, regenerating axon tips often grow into incorrect sheaths and are guided by them to incorrect destinations; that is why it is often difficult to regain the coordinated use of a limb affected by nerve damage even if there has been substantial regeneration. And third, if the cut ends of a severed mammalian peripheral nerve become widely separat-ed or if a lengthy section of the nerve is damaged, there may be no meaningful regeneration at all; regenerating axon tips grow in a tangled mass around the proximal stump, and the neurons ultimately die. These three patterns of mammalian peripheral nerve regeneration are illustrated in Figure 15.20.

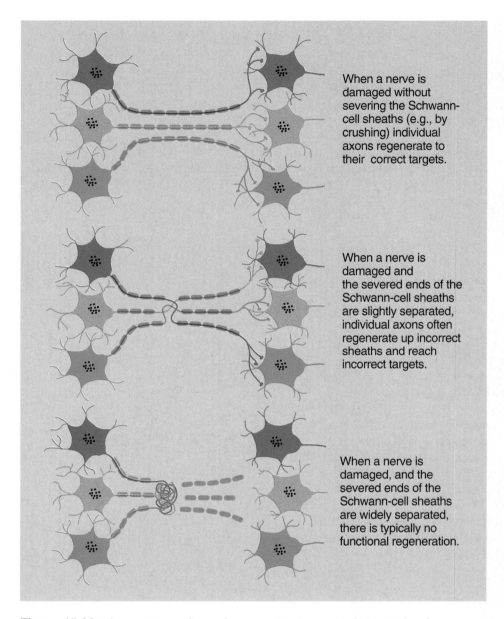

When a nerve is damaged without severing the Schwann-cell sheaths (e.g., by crushing) individual axons regenerate to their correct targets.

When a nerve is damaged and the severed ends of the Schwann-cell sheaths are slightly separated, individual axons often regenerate up incorrect sheaths and reach incorrect targets.

When a nerve is damaged, and the severed ends of the Schwann-cell sheaths are widely separated, there is typically no functional regeneration.

Figure 15.20 Three patterns of axonal regeneration in mammalian peripheral nerves.

In contrast to neural regeneration in mammals, regeneration in lower vertebrates is extremely accurate. It is accurate in both the central and peripheral nervous systems, and it is accurate even when the regenerating axons do not grow into remnant Schwann cell sheaths. The accuracy of regeneration in lower vertebrates offers hope of a medical breakthrough: If the factors that promote accurate regeneration in lower vertebrates can be identified and applied to the human brain, it might be possible to cure currently untreatable brain injuries.

When an axon degenerates, axon branches grow out from adjacent healthy axons and synapse at the sites vacated by the degenerating axon; this is called **collateral sprouting.** Collateral sprouts may grow out from the axon terminal branches or nodes of Ranvier of adjacent neurons. Collateral sprouting is illustrated in Figure 15.21.

Collateral sprouting appears to be triggered by a factor that is released from the denervated target tissue. One can induce motor neuron axons to grow collateral sprouts merely by rendering the target muscle inactive (e.g., Brown & Ironton, 1977); conversely, one can block the collateral sprouting that normally occurs from motor neuron axons following damage to adjacent axons by electrically stimulating the target muscle (Ironton, Brown, & Holland, 1978).

Neural Reorganization

It has long been assumed that the plasticity of adult mammalian nervous systems is limited to the complex functional changes that mediate learning. This assumption was supported by several influential early reports. For example,

Figure 15.21 Collateral sprouting after neural degeneration.

A | B

A | B

Axotomy of neuron A

Degeneration of neuron A and collateral sprouting of neuron B.

Hubel, Wiesel, and LeVay (1977) found that monocular deprivation influences the development of ocular dominance columns in visual cortex only if it occurs in the first few weeks of life, and they concluded that visual experience in this postnatal period puts the final touches on the organization of the primary visual cortex, which is then immutable for life. Be that as it may, it is now clear that the mature mammalian brain retains the ability to undergo significant reorganization.

Most studies of neural reorganization in adulthood have focused on the ability of adult sensory and motor systems to reorganize themselves in response to either damage or experience (see Kaas, 1991; Garraghty & Kaas, 1992). Primary sensory and primary motor cortexes are ideally suited to the study of neural reorganization because of their topographic layout.

Primary sensory cortex The reorganization of adult mammalian primary sensory cortex has been induced in three ways: by damaging sensory pathways, by damaging sensory cortex itself, or by distorting sensory experience. Examples of each of these three methods of inducing reorganization in sensory systems follow.

The following two studies illustrate the reorganization of adult primary sensory cortex that can be induced by

damaging sensory pathways. Kaas et al. (1990) assessed the effect of making a small lesion in one retina and removing the other. Several months after the retinal lesions were made, primary visual cortex neurons that originally had receptive fields in the lesioned area of the retina were found to have receptive fields in the area of the retina next to the lesion; remarkably, this change began within minutes of the lesion (Gilbert & Wiesel, 1992). In a similar study, Pons and colleagues (1991) mapped the primary somatosensory cortex of monkeys whose contralateral arm sensory neurons had been cut 10 years before. They found that the cortical face representation had systematically expanded into the original arm area. This study created a stir because the scale of the reorganization was far greater than had been assumed to be possible: The primary somatosensory cortex face area had expanded its border by well over a centimeter, likely as a consequence of the particularly long (10-year) interval between surgery and testing.

The following study illustrates the reorganization of sensory cortex that can be induced by damaging the sensory cortex itself. Jenkins and Merzenich (1987) removed the area of monkey somatosensory cortex that responded to touches of the palm of the contralateral hand. Several weeks later, they found that neurons adjacent to the lesion now responded to touches of the palm.

The following two studies illustrate the reorganization of sensory cortex that can be induced by distorting sensory experience. Recanzone and colleagues (1992) trained monkeys to detect differences in the frequency of vibrating stimuli by feeling them with their middle finger; and over several weeks, as their performance improved, the area of primary somatosensory cortex receiving input from that finger expanded. Pettet and Gilbert (1992) created the experience of a *scotoma* (a blind spot) without damaging the visual system by occluding a small area of one retina while applying visual stimulation to the remainder of the retina. Remarkably, after only several minutes of this treatment, primary visual cortex neurons with receptive fields in the occluded area had expanded the size of their receptive fields several-fold.

Primary motor cortex Reorganization of the primary motor cortex has been observed following damage to motor neurons. Sanes, Suner, and Donoghue (1990) transected the motor neurons of rats that controlled the muscles of their *vibrissae* (whiskers). A few weeks later, stimulation of the area of motor cortex that had previously elicited vibrissae movement now activated other muscles of the face. This result is illustrated in Figure 15.22.

> **Collateral sprouting.** The growth of axon branches from mature neurons, usually to postsynaptic sites abandoned by adjacent axons that have degenerated.

Primary motor cortex reorganization has also been induced by experience. Following are two examples. In one experiment (Sanes, Wang, & Donoghue, 1992), regions of adult rat primary motor cortex that did not normally produce forelimb movement when stimulated did so after the forelimb was kept extended for 30 minutes. In another (Nudo, Jenkins, & Merzenich, 1990), the area of primary motor cortex from which a particular movement could be elicited was expanded in just 1 hour by repeated elicitation of the movement with primary motor cortex stimulation.

Functions and mechanisms of neural reorganization Recent studies of neural reorganization in adult mammals have made two important points. First, either experience or neural damage can induce reorganizational changes very quickly; and second, if given sufficient time, they can induce reorganizational changes of substantial magnitude (see Gilbert, 1993; Weinberger, 1993). The current view is that the primary function of slow changes is to compensate for nervous system damage, whereas the primary function of the rapid changes is to tune the brain to changes in experience. The ability of the neocortex to rapidly expand or contract its representations of various classes of stimuli and responses depending on its experience could be one of the neural mechanisms of sensorimotor learning.

Two kinds of mechanisms have been proposed to account for the reorganization of neural circuits: a strengthening of existing connections through release from inhibition and the establishment of new connections by collateral sprouting (see O'Leary, Ruff, & Dyck, 1994). Support for the first mechanism comes from two observations: Reorganization often occurs too quickly to be explained by neural growth, and rapid reorganization never involves changes of more than 2 millimeters of cortical surface. Support for the second mechanism comes from the observation that the magnitude of long-term reorganization can be too great to be explained by changes in existing connections. Figure 15.23 illustrates how these two mechanisms account for the reorganization that occurs after damage to a peripheral somatosensory nerve.

Neural reorganization and recovery of function after brain damage The role of neural reorganization in recovery of function after brain damage is controversial (Finger et al., 1988). It seems likely that neural reorganization contributes to recovery from brain damage, but so far the only evidence for this hypothesis has been indirect. In fact, little is known for sure about recovery from brain damage. The problem is that brain damage produces a variety of changes that can easily be confused with bona fide recovery of function. For example, any improvement in the week or two after damage could reflect a decline in *cerebral edema* (brain swelling) rather than a recovery from the neural damage per se, and any gradual improvement in the months after damage could reflect the learning of new cognitive and behavioral strategies rather than the return of lost abilities.

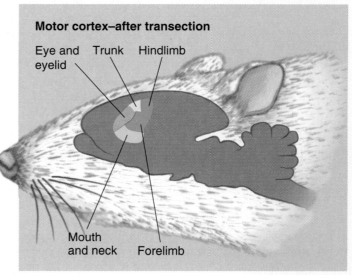

Figure 15.22 Reorganization of the rat motor cortex following transection of the motor neurons that control movements of the vibrissae. The motor cortex was mapped by brain stimulation before transection and then again a few weeks after. (Adapted from Sanes, Suner, & Donoghue, 1990.)

Despite the difficulties in studying recovery of function, three general conclusions have emerged from its investigation (Kolb & Whishaw, 1990). One is that bona fide recovery of function is less common and less complete than most people believe. Think of patient H.M. from the last chapter; his memory has not improved in over 40 years. A second is that small lesions are more likely than large lesions to be associated with recovery. And a third is that the likelihood of recovery is greater in young patients than in old patients (see Figure 15.24). The fact that neural reorganization is also greater when lesions are small (Jenkins & Merzenich, 1987) and subjects young (Gall, McWilliams, & Lynch, 1980) supports the hypothesis that neural reorganization plays a significant role in recovery of function.

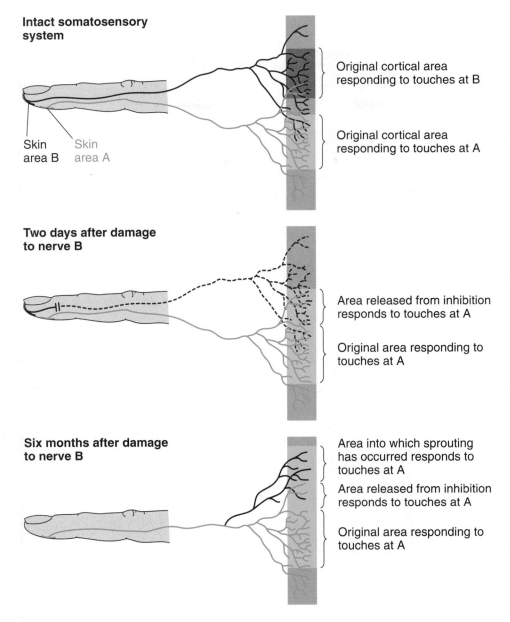

Intact somatosensory system

Skin area B
Skin area A

Original cortical area responding to touches at B

Original cortical area responding to touches at A

Two days after damage to nerve B

Area released from inhibition responds to touches at A

Original area responding to touches at A

Six months after damage to nerve B

Area into which sprouting has occurred responds to touches at A

Area released from inhibition responds to touches at A

Original area responding to touches at A

Figure 15.23 The two-stage model of neural reorganization: (1) strengthening of existing connections through release from inhibition and (2) establishment of new connections by sprouting.

15.5 Neurotransplantation in the Brain

I was introduced to the concept of brain transplantation at an early age. Perhaps you were introduced to it in the same way: by television cartoons. A common scenario in these cartoons is one in which a mad scientist places a wired helmet on the head of one animal subject and another wired helmet on the head of another animal of a different species. Then he throws a massive switch. There are some sparks, a puff of smoke, and, voilà, the brains of the two subjects have been switched. This is good for a few laughs, but the highlight of the cartoon comes when the scientist accidentally gets one of the helmets on his own head, and his brain ends up in the body of a chicken and vice versa. It is ironic that this childhood fantasy is now one of the most exciting lines of research in neuroscience. Real-life neurotransplan-

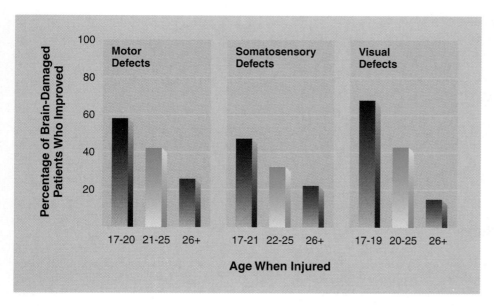

Figure 15.24 Percentage of patients showing improvement following brain injury. Teuber (1975) assessed the deficits of brain-damaged soldiers within a week of their injury and again 20 years later.

tations are not performed by the simple pull of switch, and they involve only portions of the brain, but they are no less amazing.

Modern Era of Research on Neurotransplantation

The first conclusive evidence of the survival of transplanted neural tissue in the brain of a host was published by Das and Altman in 1971. First, they radioactively labeled *thymine* (one of the four bases that constitute the genetic code of DNA) and injected it into the brains of 7-day-old *donor* rats (rats from whom transplanted tissue is removed) so that it would be incorporated into the DNA of their neurons. Then, they cut slabs of labeled cerebellum from the donor rats and transplanted them in the cerebellums of *host* rats (rats in whom transplanted tissue is implanted) of the same age. Two weeks later, autoradiographs of slides taken from the host cerebellums indicated that many of the transplanted radioactive neurons had survived.

Subsequent research has proved that rejection of *conspecific* (of the same species) CNS transplants is rare (see Nicholas & Arnason, 1992), particularly if the tissue is taken from fetal donors (see Fawcett, 1992). The optimal sites for neurotransplants are those that are highly vascularized and have sufficient growth space (Brundin & Björklund, 1987; Fine, 1986). A piece of tissue can be implanted in an existing cavity, such as the wall of a ventricle; it can be implanted in a cavity that has been surgically created; or it can be broken up into individual cells and injected into the host brain.

If fetal brain tissue is implanted at its normal site, it seems to develop normally. But what if fetal tissue from one brain site is implanted in another: Does the transplanted embryonic brain tissue develop as it would have had it been left in the donor, or is its development determined more by its site of implantation? The answer is: It depends. It depends on the age of the donor tissue; early fetal brain tissue is more likely than older brain tissue to have its development influenced by the environment into which it is transplanted. It also depends on the relation between the implanted tissue and the site into which it is transplanted. In one study, embryonic precursors of visual cortex (Jaeger & Lund, 1981) that were transplanted into the superior colliculi of neonatal rats developed into normal-appearing visual cortex tissue. However, in another study, (Schlaggar & O'Leary, 1991), embryonic precursors of visual cortex that were transplanted into the somatosensory cortex of neonatal rats developed into normal-appearing somatosensory cortex tissue.

Neural fibers grow from the host's nervous system into a neural implant, but is the pattern of projections normal? If the implant is placed in the host at the same site that it occupied in the donor, it seems to become innervated in a reasonably normal pattern. For example, superior colliculus tissue implanted in the superior colliculus became innervated by axons from both the retina and the visual cortex (Lund & Harvey, 1981). In contrast, visual cortex tissue implanted in the superior colliculus became innervated by fibers from several structures that do not normally innervate either the visual cortex or the superior colliculus (e.g., Jaeger & Lund, 1981).

Studies of the establishment of connections in the other direction—that is, from the implant to surrounding tissue—tell a similar story: An implant will develop a reasonably normal pattern of projections only if it is implanted at an appropriate site. For example, when retinal tissue was implanted in structures that do not normally receive retinal inputs, the implants survived, but no fibers grew to other structures; however, when retinal implants were positioned next to the superior colliculus—a structure to which the retinas normally project—a reasonably normal pattern of axonal projections from the implants developed (McLoon & Lund, 1980).

Raisman, Morris, and Zhou (1987) took advantage of the highly regular arrangement of cell bodies and connections in the hippocampus to study the ability of tiny hippocampal

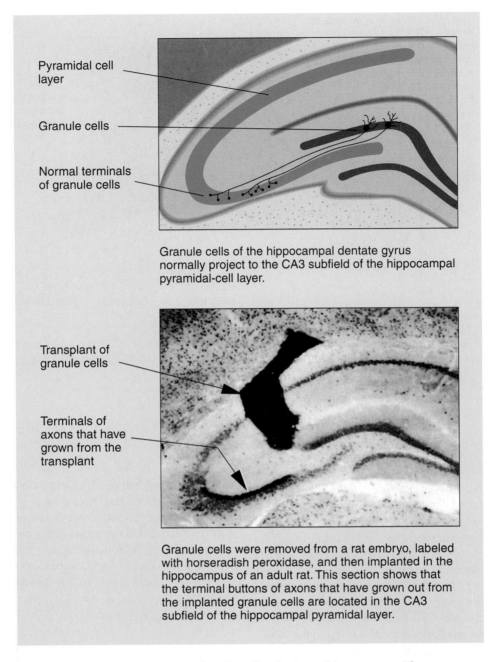

Pyramidal cell layer

Granule cells

Normal terminals of granule cells

Granule cells of the hippocampal dentate gyrus normally project to the CA3 subfield of the hippocampal pyramidal-cell layer.

Transplant of granule cells

Terminals of axons that have grown from the transplant

Granule cells were removed from a rat embryo, labeled with horseradish peroxidase, and then implanted in the hippocampus of an adult rat. This section shows that the terminal buttons of axons that have grown out from the implanted granule cells are located in the CA3 subfield of the hippocampal pyramidal layer.

Figure 15.25 Axons from a granule cell implant in the rat hippocampus. These axons grew out to their normal targets: the pyramidal cells of the CA3 hippocampal subfield.

transplants to establish normal connections. Figure 15.25 is a photograph of a slice taken through a granule cell implant that was first labeled with horseradish peroxidase. Notice that axons from the implant grew to their usual target in the CA3 subfield of the hippocampal pyramidal cell layer.

The ultimate objective of most research on CNS neurotransplantation is the development of new techniques for the treatment of CNS disorders (Lindvall, 1991). Efforts to develop neurotransplantation treatments for CNS disorders have adopted two different strategies. One strategy has been to transplant tissue that will improve the function of the patient's own damaged tissue by promoting regeneration. The other has been to transplant cells that will become integrated into the recipient's own CNS and replace damaged tissue. These two approaches are considered in the following subsections.

The optic nerve of a rat was cut. Then, a length of myelinated peripheral nerve was grafted between the stump of the optic nerve and the superior colliculus. Four months later, functional axons had grown from the eye into the superior colliculus.

Implanted Schwann-cell sheath

Stump of severed optic nerve

Superior colliculus

Regenerated axons

Figure 15.26 The stimulation and guidance of axonal regeneration from the eye to the superior colliculus by an implanted Schwann-cell sheath. (Adapted from Bray, Vidal-Sanz, & Aguayo, 1987.)

Promotion of Regeneration with Brain Transplants

Efforts to promote regeneration in the mammalian brain have focused on the question of why PNS neurons regenerate and CNS neurons do not. The obvious answer is that PNS neurons are inherently capable of regeneration while CNS neurons are not, but this answer has proved to be incorrect. CNS neurons are capable of regeneration if they are transplanted to the PNS, whereas PNS neurons are not capable of regeneration if they are transplanted to the CNS. Clearly, there is something about the environment of the PNS that promotes regeneration and something about the environment of the CNS that does not.

Schwann cells, which myelinate PNS axons, promote regeneration in the mammalian PNS by producing both neurotrophic factors and neural cell-adhesion molecules. The neurotrophic factors released by Schwann cells stimulate the growth of new axons, and the neural cell-adhesion molecules on the cell membranes of Schwann cells provide the paths along which regenerating PNS axons grow (see Bunge, 1993; Franklin, 1993). In contrast, **oligodendroglia,** which myelinate CNS axons, do not stimulate or guide regeneration; indeed, they release factors that actively block regeneration (Schwab, 1990).

The technique of implanting Schwann cell sheaths in the CNS to stimulate and guide regeneration was developed by Aguayo and his colleagues (see Guénard, Xu, & Bunge, 1993). In one study (Bray, Vidal-Sanz, & Aguayo, 1987), the optic nerve of a rat was cut, and a segment of myelinated peripheral nerve was grafted between the stump of the optic nerve and the superior colliculus. Four months later, axons of retinal ganglion cells had regenerated along the graft from the eye to the superior colliculus (see Figure 15.26), and superior colliculus neurons responded to light shone in the subjects' eyes (Keirstead et al., 1989).

Transplantation of Brain Replacement Parts

The second experimental approach to the treatment of brain damage by transplantation has been to replace damaged tissue with healthy donor tissue. Most noteworthy have been efforts to treat Parkinson's disease by transplant-

Oligodendroglia. The glial cells that myelinate CNS axons.

Autotransplantation. Transplanting of a body part to a different location in the same body.

ing dopamine-releasing cells in the striatum of the host (see Yurek & Sladeck, 1990). You may recall that the symptoms of Parkinson's disease (e.g., rigidity, tremor at rest, and lack of spontaneous movement) result from the degeneration of the dopamine-releasing neurons that project from the substantia nigra to the striatum.

The first demonstration that transplanted neural tissue can improve the behavior of brain-damaged mammals came from a study of the effects of unilateral *6-hydroxydopamine* (6-OHDA) lesions in rats (Perlow et al., 1979). First, 6-OHDA was injected into the substantia nigra, and the resulting unilateral destruction of dopaminergic neurons caused the rats to walk in circles toward the side of the lesion. Then, dopamine-releasing substantia nigra precursor cells obtained from rat embryos were implanted next to the lesion. The implants were found to reduce the circling behavior of the lesioned rats (Perlow et al., 1979); the degree of the reduction was found to be related to the number of axons growing from the implant into the striatum (Björklund & Stenevi, 1979); and the reduction was found to last for at least 6 months (Freed et al., 1980). See Björklund (1992) and Brundin and Wictorin (1993) for general reviews of this line of research.

Bilateral transplantation of fetal substantia nigra cells has proved successful in alleviating parkinsonian symptoms induced in monkeys by intramuscular injections of MPTP (Sladek et al., 1987). (You may recall that MPTP was discovered when a group of drug addicts developed Parkinson's disease after they self-administered a synthetic opiate that contained the MPTP toxin.) Fetal substantia nigra transplants survived in the MPTP-treated monkeys; they innervated adjacent striatal tissue; they released dopamine; and, most importantly, they alleviated the severe poverty of movement, tremor, and rigidity produced by the MPTP. The fact that the degree of improvement observed in each monkey was related to the degree to which dopaminergic axons from the graft invaded the striatum suggested that the innervation of the striatum by the implant was the critical factor in their improvement.

Soon after the promising effects of neurotransplants on rats and monkeys were reported, neurotransplantation was offered as a treatment for Parkinson's disease at major research hospitals in several parts of the world. The initial evaluations have been promising. The fetal substantia nigra implants have survived, and they have released dopamine into the host striatum (see Sawle & Myers, 1993). More importantly, many of the patients have improved: They have become more active, and their rigidity has declined, particularly on the side contralateral to the transplant (see Lindvall et al., 1990).

The treatment of Parkinson's disease by neurotransplantation was heralded in the popular press as a major scientific breakthrough—and it was—but the problem of Parkinson's disease is far from solved. Although the neurotransplants have significantly improved the condition of many of the patients who have had them, they are far from a total cure. Accordingly, stimulated by the promising early results in Parkinson's patients, research on the treatment of Parkinson's disease by neural transplantation has entered a new phase. Now researchers, working primarily with animal models, are trying to understand the mechanisms by which neurotransplantation influences Parkinson's disease so that they can develop more effective therapeutic protocols. It is the interplay between research on animal models and human clinical trials—not one or the other—that leads to the development of effective treatments for human brain disorders.

Autotransplantation—transplanting of tissue from one part of a patient's body to another site in the same patient—circumvents the practical and ethical problems of obtaining donor tissue for transplantation. Parkinson's disease has been treated by autotransplanting extracts of the adrenal medulla into the donor's own striatum. (Adrenal medulla extracts release small amounts of dopamine.) A positive early report stimulated considerable interest in this treatment (Madrazo et al., 1987). However, subsequent studies have found the clinical benefits of adrenal medulla autotransplants to be modest (e.g., Goetz et al., 1989), and it has been largely abandoned as an experimental therapy for Parkinson's disease, although it continues to be widely publicized.

In Chapter 6, you were introduced to the roller-coaster case of Roberto Garcia D'Orta—the Lizard. D'Orta, who suffered from Parkinson's disease, initially responded to L-DOPA therapy; but after 3 years of therapy, his condition worsened. Then he responded to treatment with a dopamine agonist, but again the improvement was only temporary. D'Orta was in a desperate state when he heard about adrenal medulla autotransplantation, and he demanded this treatment from his doctor. When his doctor refused, on the ground that the effectiveness of autotransplantation was still in doubt, d'Orta found himself another doctor—a neurosurgeon who was not nearly so cautious:

> Roberto flew to Juarez. The neurosurgeon there greeted him with open arms. As long as Roberto could afford the cost, he'd be happy to do an adrenal implant on him....
>
> Were there any dangers?
>
> The neurosurgeon seemed insulted by the question. If Señor d'Orta didn't trust him, he could go elsewhere....
>
> Roberto underwent the procedure.
>
> He flew back home two weeks later. He was no better. He was told that it took time for the cells to grow and make the needed chemicals....
>
> Then I received an unexpected call from Roberto's wife. Roberto was dead....
>
> He'd died of a stroke.... Had the stroke been a complication of his surgery? It was more than a mere possibility. (Klawans, 1990, pp. 63–64)

CONCLUSION

Neuroplasticity in its various manifestations was the subject of this chapter. This chapter described the neural changes that occur during the development of the nervous system (15.1); the effects of experience on neural development (15.2); the neural bases of learning and memory in simple neural systems (15.3); the neural degeneration, regeneration, and reorganization that occurs in adult mammals (15.4); and the phenomenon of neurotransplantation in the brain (15.5).

The final section of this chapter began with the image of a cartoon scientist running about clucking like a chicken, and the chapter ends on a similar, but less frivolous, note. It ends with the incredible experiment of Balaban, Teillet, and LeDouarin (1988). They removed from the neural tubes of chicken fetuses the segment that would have normally developed into the mesencephalon and diencephalon, and they replaced it with tissue from the corresponding segment of Japanese quail neural tubes. A few days after the chicks had hatched, Balaban and his colleagues performed a spectrographic analysis of the chicks' crowing sounds. All of the chicks made abnormal crowing sounds, and most of them made sounds unmistakably like those of Japanese quail. Transplantation of other segments of the neural tube did not have this effect. With this experiment, the cross-

After the furor died down, the rooster moved to New York and became a regular on the talkshow circuit. Dr. Woods quit his job and wandered out West, where he was arrested for making lewd comments to chickens.

species transfer of behavior by neurotransplantation has left the realm of childhood fantasy. The possibilities of this procedure boggle the imagination (see Le Douarin, 1993).

FOOD FOR THOUGHT

1. Neurotransplants are now being used in the treatment of Parkinson's disease. Suggest some other potential clinical applications of this procedure.

2. Do you think it will ever be possible to transplant memories? How might this be done? Design an experiment to demonstrate memory transplantation.

3. How has this chapter changed your concept of the brain?

KEY TERMS

Simple-systems approach
(*p. 379*)
Neural plate (*p. 379*)
Neural tube (*p. 379*)
Totipotential (*p. 379*)
Mesoderm layer (*p. 379*)
Induction (*p. 380*)
Neural proliferation (*p. 380*)
Ventricular zone (*p. 380*)
Migration (*p. 380*)
Radial glial cells (*p. 380*)
Neural crest (*p. 380*)
Aggregation (*p. 381*)
Neural cell-adhesion
molecules (NCAMs)
(*p. 381*)
Growth cone (*p. 381*)

Retinal ganglion cells
(*p. 381*)
Optic tectum (*p. 382*)
Chemoaffinity hypothesis
(*p. 382*)
Blueprint hypothesis
(*p. 382*)
Pioneer growth cones
(*p. 383*)
Fasciculation (*p. 383*)
Topographic gradient
hypothesis (*p. 383*)
Neurotrophins (*p. 384*)
Nerve growth factor (NGF)
(*p. 385*)
Learning (*p. 388*)
Memory (*p. 388*)
Aplysia (*p. 388*)

Nonassociative learning
(*p. 388*)
Habituation (*p. 388*)
Sensitization (*p. 389*)
Presynaptic facilitation
(*p. 391*)
Activity-dependent
enhancement (*p. 392*)
Cyclic AMP (*p. 393*)
Long-term potentiation
(LTP) (*p. 393*)
Co-occurrence (*p. 394*)
NMDA receptor (*p. 395*)
Glutamate (*p. 395*)
Dendritic spines (*p. 396*)
Nitric oxide (*p. 397*)
Axotomy (*p. 398*)

Anterograde degeneration
(*p. 398*)
Distal segment (*p. 398*)
Retrograde degeneration
(*p. 398*)
Proximal segment (*p. 398*)
Astroglia (*p. 398*)
Phagocytosis (*p. 398*)
Schwann cells (*p. 398*)
Anterograde transneuronal
degeneration (*p. 398*)
Retrograde transneuronal
degeneration (*p. 398*)
Neural regeneration (*p. 398*)
Collateral sprouting (*p. 400*)
Oligodendroglia (*p. 406*)
Autotransplantation (*p. 407*)

ADDITIONAL READING

The following review articles provide up-to-date readable introductions to various aspects of neuroplasticity:

Gilbert, C. D. (1993). Rapid dynamic changes in adult cerebral cortex. *Current Opinion in Neurobiology, 3,* 100–103.

Glanzman, D. L. (1995). The cellular basis of classical conditioning in *Aplysia californica*—It's less simple than you think. *Trends in Neurosciences, 18,* 30–36.

Herrup, K., & Silver, J. (1994). Cortical development and topographic maps: Patterns of cell dispersion in developing cerebral cortex. *Current Opinion in Neurobiology, 4,* 108–111.

Krasne, F. B., & Glanzman, D. L. (1995). What we can learn from invertebrate learning. *Annual Review of Psychology, 46,* 585–624.

O'Leary, D. D. M., Ruff, N. L., Dyck, R. H. (1994). Development, critical period plasticity, and adult reorganizations of mammalian somatosensory systems. *Current Opinion in Neurobiology, 4,* 535–544.

Sawle, G. V., & Myers, R. (1993). The role of positron emission tomography in the assessment of human neurotransplantation. *Trends in Neurosciences, 16,* 172–176.

16

Lateralization, Language, and the Split Brain

16.1 Lateralization of Function: Methods and Basic Findings

16.2 The Split Brain

16.3 Differences between the Left and Right Hemispheres

16.4 Cortical Localization of Language

Frontal section of the human brain, which illustrates the fundamental duality of the human forebrain.

Midsagittal section of the human brain, which illustrates the corpus callosum and other commissures.

Figure 16.1 The cerebral hemispheres and cerebral commissures.

With the exception of a few midline orifices, we have two of almost everything—one on the left and one on the right. Even the brain, which most people view as the unitary indivisible basis of self, reflects this general principle of bilateral duplication. In its upper reaches, the brain comprises two structures, the left and right cerebral hemispheres, which are entirely separate except for the **cerebral commissures** connecting them. The fundamental duality of the human forebrain and the location of the cerebral commissures are illustrated in Figure 16.1.

Although the left and right hemispheres are similar in appearance, there are major differences between them in function. This chapter is about these differences, a topic commonly referred to as **lateralization of function.** The study of **split-brain patients**—patients whose left and right hemispheres have been separated by **commissurotomy**—is a major focus of discussion. Another focus of discussion is the cortical localization of language abilities in the left hemisphere; language abilities are the most highly lateralized of all cognitive abilities.

You will learn in this chapter that your left and right hemispheres have different abilities, and you will learn that they have the capacity to function independently—to have different thoughts, memories, and emotions. Accordingly, this chapter will challenge the concept you have of yourself as a unitary being. I hope you both enjoy it.

Cerebral commissures. Tracts that connect the left and right cerebral hemispheres.

Lateralization of function. The unequal representation of a particular psychological function in the two hemispheres of the brain.

Split-brain patients. Commissurotomized patients.

Commissurotomy. Severing of the cerebral commissures.

In 1836, Dax, an unknown country doctor, presented a short report at a medical society meeting in France. It was his first and only scientific presentation. Dax was struck by the fact that of the 40 or so brain-damaged patients with speech problems whom he had seen during his career, not a single one had damage restricted to the right hemisphere. His report aroused little interest, and Dax died the following year unaware that he had anticipated one of today's most important areas of neuropsychological research.

Aphasia, Apraxia, and Left-Hemisphere Damage

One reason Dax's paper had little impact was that most of his contemporaries believed that the brain acted as a whole and that specific functions could not be attributed to particular parts of it. This view began to change 25 years later, when Paul Broca reported his postmortem examination of two aphasic patients. **Aphasia** is a brain-damage-produced deficit in the ability to produce or comprehend language.

Both of Broca's patients had a left-hemisphere lesion that involved an area in the frontal cortex just in front of the face area of the primary motor cortex. Broca at first did not realize that there was a relation between aphasia and the side of the brain damage; he had not heard of Dax's report. However, by 1864, Broca had performed postmortem examinations on seven more aphasic patients, and he was struck by the fact that, like his first two, they all had damage to the *inferior prefrontal cortex* of the left hemisphere—which by then had become known as **Broca's area** (see Figure 16.2).

In the early 1900s, another example of lateralization of function was discovered. Liepmann found that **apraxia,** like aphasia, is almost always associated with left-hemisphere damage, despite the fact that its symptoms are *bilateral* (involving both sides of the body). Apraxic patients have difficulty performing movements when asked to perform them, even though they often have no difficulty performing the same movements when they are not thinking about what they are doing.

The combined impact of the evidence that the left hemisphere plays a special role in both language and voluntary movement led to the concept of *cerebral dominance.* According to this concept, one hemisphere—usually the left—assumes the dominant role in the control of all complex behavioral and cognitive processes and the other plays only a minor role. This concept led to the practice of referring to the left hemisphere as the **dominant hemisphere** and the right hemisphere as the **minor hemisphere.**

Tests of Language Lateralization

Early research on the lateralization of language abilities compared the effects of left-hemisphere and right-hemisphere lesions. However, other techniques have now been developed for measuring language lateralization: the sodium amytal test, the dichotic listening test, and several others.

Sodium amytal test The **sodium amytal test** of language lateralization (Wada, 1949) is often given to patients prior to neurosurgery. The neurosurgeon uses the results of

Figure 16.2 The location of Broca's area. It is located in the inferior left prefrontal cortex, just anterior to the face area of the left primary motor cortex.

the test to plan the surgery; every effort is made to avoid damaging areas of the cortex that are likely to be involved in language. The sodium amytal test involves the injection of a small amount of sodium amytal into the carotid artery on one side of the neck. The injection anesthetizes the hemisphere on that side for a few minutes, thus allowing the capacities of the other hemisphere to be assessed. During the test, the patient is asked to recite well-known series (e.g., letters of the alphabet, days of the week, months of the year) and to name pictures of common objects. Then, an injection is administered to the other side, and the test is repeated. When the hemisphere that is dominant for speech, usually the left hemisphere, is anesthetized, the patient is rendered completely mute for a minute or two; then once the ability to talk returns, there are errors of serial order and naming. In contrast, when the minor speech hemisphere, usually the right, is anesthetized, mutism often does not occur at all, and errors are few.

Dichotic listening test Unlike the sodium amytal test, the **dichotic listening test** is noninvasive; thus it can be administered to healthy subjects. In the standard dichotic listening test (Kimura, 1961), three pairs of spoken digits are presented through earphones; the digits of each pair are presented simultaneously, one to each ear. For example, a subject might hear the sequence 3, 9, 2 through one ear and at the same time 1, 6, 4 through the other. The subject is then asked to report all of the digits. Kimura found that most people report more of the digits presented to the right ear than to the left, which is indicative of left-hemisphere dominance for language. In contrast, Kimura found that all the patients who had been identified by the sodium amytal test as right-hemisphere dominant for language performed better with the left ear than the right.

Why does the superior ear on the dichotic listening test indicate the dominance of the contralateral hemisphere? Kimura argued that although the sounds from each ear are projected to both hemispheres, the contralateral connections are stronger and take precedence when two different sounds are simultaneously competing for access to the same cortical auditory centers.

Other tests of lateralization Another test of lateralization is based on a comparison of the ability of subjects to identify stimuli presented in their left or right visual fields. In the language version of the test, the subject fixates on the center of a screen, and then a word is flashed on the screen for less than 0.1 second (see Figure 16.3)—just long enough to allow subjects to recognize some of the words but not long enough for eye movements to be initiated. The words are often presented vertically to control for the fact that English-speaking subjects have a tendency to scan from left to right. The usual finding of such tests is a slight tendency for words presented in the right visual field to be recognized more frequently than those presented in the

left. This right-field advantage is attributed to the fact that information in the right visual field is transmitted directly to the left hemisphere, which is the dominant language hemisphere in most subjects.

Another method of studying language lateralization is to assess the asymmetry of movements that accompany speech. Because fine movements are under contralateral control, their prevalence on one side of the body during speech indicates lateralization of speech on the other side. For example, Kimura (1973) reported that the gestures of the hands that accompany speech tend to be made with the hand contralateral to the dominant hemisphere for speech as determined by the dichotic listening test. Also, speaking subjects tend to make larger movements with the side of the mouth contralateral to the dominant language hemisphere (Wolf & Goodale, 1987; Wylie & Goodale, 1988).

Recently, lateralization of function has been studied using functional brain-imaging techniques. While the subject engages in some activity, such as reading, the activity of the brain is monitored by positron emission tomography (PET) or functional magnetic resonance imaging (functional MRI). On language tests, these functional brain-imaging techniques reveal greater activity in the left hemisphere (see Roland, 1993).

Aphasia. A disturbance in the ability to use or comprehend language.

Broca's area. The area of the inferior prefrontal cortex of the left hemisphere hypothesized by Broca to be the center of speech production.

Apraxia. A disorder in which patients have great difficulty performing movements when asked to do so out of context, but can readily perform them spontanously in natural situations.

Dominant hemisphere. A term used in the past to refer to the left hemisphere, based on the incorrect assumption that the left hemisphere is dominant in all complex activities.

Minor hemisphere. A term used in the past to refer to the right hemisphere, based on the incorrect assumption that the left hemisphere is dominant in all complex activities.

Sodium amytal test. A test of language lateralization in which each hemisphere is anesthetized with sodium amytal so that the speech abilities of the other hemisphere can be assessed.

Dichotic listening test. A test of language lateralization in which two sequences of three spoken digits are presented simultaneously to each ear and the subject is asked to report all of the digits heard.

Speech Laterality and Handedness

Two early large-scale lesion studies clarified the relation between the lateralization of speech and handedness. One study was of military personnel who suffered brain damage in World War II (Russell & Espir, 1961), and the other was of neurological patients who underwent unilateral excisions for the treatment of neurological disorders (Penfield & Roberts, 1959). In both studies, approximately 60% of **dextrals** (right-handers) with left-hemisphere lesions and 2% of those with right-hemisphere lesions were diagnosed as aphasic; the comparable figures for **sinestrals** (left-handers) were about 30% and 24%, respectively. These results indicate that the left hemisphere is dominant for language-related abilities in almost all dextrals and in the majority of sinestrals (see Benson, 1985); they also indicate that sinestrals are more variable than dextrals with respect to language lateralization (see Hellige, 1990; Joanette, 1989).

Results of the sodium amytal test have confirmed the relation between handedness and language lateralization that was first observed in early lesion studies. For example, Milner (1974) found that almost all right-handed patients without early left-hemisphere damage were left-hemisphere dominant for speech (92%), that most left-handed and ambidextrous patients without early left-hemisphere damage were left-hemisphere dominant for speech (69%), and that early left-hemisphere damage decreased left-hemisphere dominance for speech in left-handed and ambidextrous patients (30%). In interpreting these results, it is important to remember that sodium amytal tests are administered only to people who are experiencing brain dysfunction, that early brain damage can cause the lateralization of speech to shift to the other hemisphere (see Maratsos & Matheny, 1994), and that many more people are left-hemisphere dominant to start with. Considered together, these points suggest that Milner's findings likely underestimate the proportion of left-hemisphere dominant individuals among healthy members of the general population.

Sex Differences in Brain Lateralization

Interest in the possibility that the brains of females and males differ in their degree of lateralization was stimulated by McGlone's (1977, 1980) studies of unilateral stroke victims. McGlone found that male victims of unilateral strokes were three times more likely to suffer from aphasia than female victims. She found that male victims of left-hemisphere strokes had deficits on the Wechsler Adult

Dextrals. Right-handers.

Sinestrals. Left-handers.

Corpus callosum. The largest cerebral commissure.

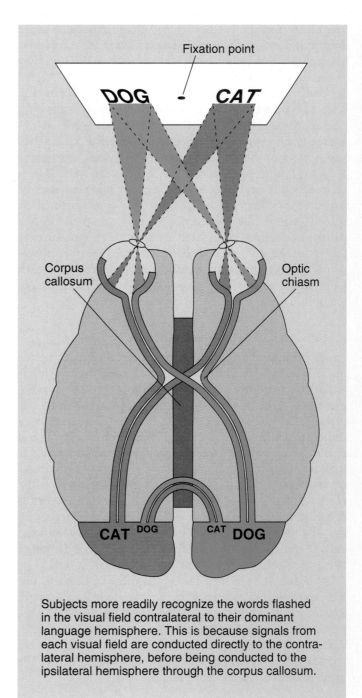

Subjects more readily recognize the words flashed in the visual field contralateral to their dominant language hemisphere. This is because signals from each visual field are conducted directly to the contralateral hemisphere, before being conducted to the ipsilateral hemisphere through the corpus callosum.

Figure 16.3 A method of studying lateralization of language abilities. Images of words are more readily recognized when they are flashed in the visual field contralateral to the dominant hemisphere for language.

Intelligence Scale (WAIS) verbal subtests, whereas male victims of right-hemisphere strokes had deficits on the WAIS performance subtests. And she found that female victims of unilateral strokes had the same deficits on the WAIS regardless of the side of the stroke. On the basis of these three findings, McGlone concluded that the brains of males are more lateralized than the brains of females.

McGlone's hypothesis of a sex difference in brain lateralization has been widely embraced, and it has been used to explain almost every imaginable behavioral difference between the sexes. Be that as it may, others have failed to confirm McGlone's findings. Indeed, Inglis and Lawson (1982) reviewed 16 studies of unilateral brain lesions and concluded that there was no evidence that left-hemisphere lesions differentially affect the performance of females and males on verbal tests. Also, Hier and Kaplan (1980) and De Renzi (1980) found the incidence of aphasia to be only slightly greater in males than in females. Kolb and Whishaw (1990) have warned that ostensible differences between females and males in brain laterality could merely reflect differences in the strategies that they used to solve problems. For example, if females tend to use verbal strategies in the solution of nonverbal problems, unilateral brain lesions would tend to have less specific effects in females than in males.

16.2   The Split Brain

In the early 1950s, the **corpus callosum**—the largest cerebral commissure—constituted a paradox of major proportions. Its size, an estimated 200 million axons, and its central position, right between the two cerebral hemispheres, implied that it performed an extremely important function; yet research in the 1930s and 1940s seemed to suggest that it did nothing at all. The corpus callosum had been cut in monkeys and in several other laboratory species, but the animals seemed no different after the surgery than they had been before. Similarly, human patients who were born without a corpus callosum seemed perfectly normal. In the early 1950s, Roger Sperry and his colleagues were attracted by this paradox.

In their experiment, Myers and Sperry trained cats to perform a simple visual discrimination. On each trial, each cat was confronted by two panels, one with a circle on it and one with a square on it. The relative positions of the circle and square (right or left) were varied randomly from trial to trial, and the cats had to learn which symbol to press in order to get a food reward. Myers and Sperry correctly surmised that the key to split-brain research was to develop procedures for teaching and testing one hemisphere at a time. Figure 16.4 illustrates the method they used to isolate visual-discrimination learning in one hemisphere of the cats. There are two routes by which visual information can cross from one eye to the contralateral hemisphere: via the

Groundbreaking Experiment of Myers and Sperry

The solution to the puzzle of the corpus callosum was provided in 1953 by an experiment on cats by Myers and Sperry. The experiment made two astounding theoretical points. First, it showed that one function of the corpus callosum is to transfer learned information from one hemisphere to the other. Second, it showed that when the corpus callosum was cut, each hemisphere could function independently; each split-brain cat appeared to have two brains. If you find the thought of a cat with two brains provocative, you will almost certainly be bowled over by similar observations about split-brain humans. But I am getting ahead of myself. Let's first consider the research on cats.

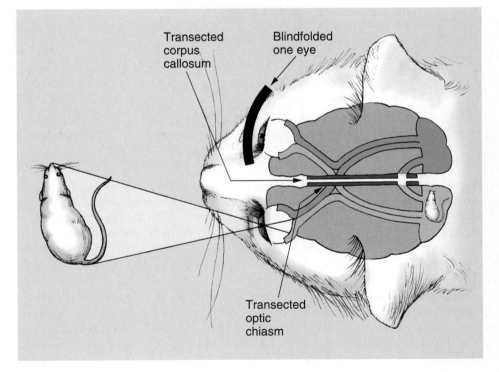

Figure 16.4 Restricting visual information in cats to one hemisphere. To restrict visual information to one hemisphere, Myers and Sperry (1) cut the corpus callosum, (2) cut the optic chiasm, and (3) blindfolded one eye. This restricted the visual information to the hemisphere ipsilateral to the uncovered eye.

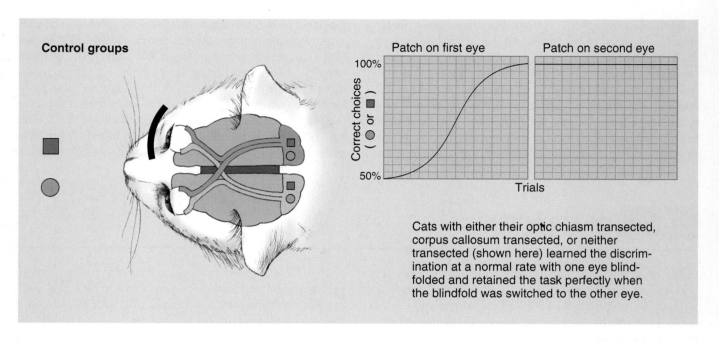

Patch on first eye   Patch on second eye

Cats with either their optic chiasm transected, corpus callosum transected, or neither transected (shown here) learned the discrimination at a normal rate with one eye blindfolded and retained the task perfectly when the blindfold was switched to the other eye.

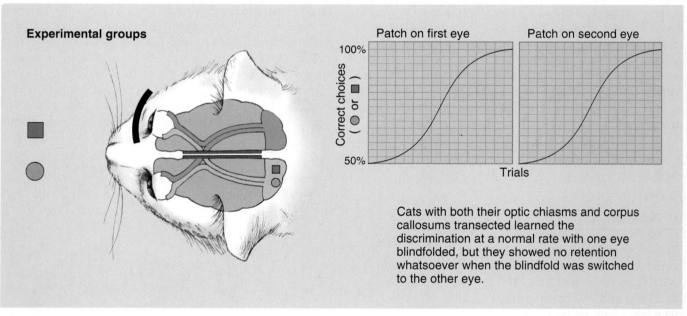

Experimental groups

Patch on first eye   Patch on second eye

Cats with both their optic chiasms and corpus callosums transected learned the discrimination at a normal rate with one eye blindfolded, but they showed no retention whatsoever when the blindfold was switched to the other eye.

Figure 16.5 Schematic illustration of Myers and Sperry's (1953) groundbreaking split-brain experiment. There were four groups: (1) the key experimental group with both the optic chiasm and corpus callosum transected, (2) a control group with only the optic chiasm transected, (3) a control group with only the corpus callosum transected, and (4) an unlesioned control group. The performance of the three control groups did not differ, so they are illustrated here as one.

corpus callosum or via the optic chiasm. Accordingly, in their key experimental group, Myers and Sperry *transected* (cut completely through) both the optic chiasm and the corpus callosum of each cat and put a patch on one eye. This restricted all incoming visual information to the hemisphere ipsilateral to the uncovered eye.

The results of Myers and Sperry's experiment are illustrated in Figure 16.5. In the first phase of the study, all cats learned the task with a patch on one eye. The cats in the key experimental group (those with both the optic chiasm and the corpus callosum transected) learned the simple discrimination as rapidly as did unlesioned control cats or control cats with either the corpus callosum or the optic chiasm transected, despite the fact that cutting the optic chiasm produced a **scotoma**—an area of blindness—in the medial half of each retina. This result suggested that one hemisphere working alone can learn simple tasks as rapidly as two hemispheres working together.

More surprising were the results of the second phase of Myers and Sperry's experiment, during which the patch was transferred to the other eye. The transfer of the patch had no effect on the performance of the intact control cats or of the control cats with either the optic chiasm or the corpus callosum transected; these subjects continued to perform the task with close to 100% accuracy. In contrast, transferring the eye patch had a devastating effect on the performance of the experimental cats. In effect, it blindfolded the hemisphere that had originally learned the task and tested the knowledge of the other hemisphere, which had been blindfolded during initial training. When the patch was transferred, the performance of the experimental cats dropped immediately to baseline (i.e., to 50% correct); and then the cats relearned the task with no savings whatsoever, as if they had never seen it before. Myers and Sperry concluded that each cat brain has the capacity to act as two separate brains and that the function of the corpus callosum is to transmit information between them.

Myers and Sperry's startling conclusions about the fundamental duality of the brain and the information-transfer function of the corpus callosum have been confirmed in a variety of species with a variety of test procedures. For example, split-brain monkeys cannot perform tasks requiring fine tactual discriminations (e.g., rough versus smooth) or fine motor responses (e.g., unlocking a puzzle) with one hand if they have learned them with the other—provided that they are not allowed to watch their hands, which would allow the information to enter both hemispheres. There is no transfer of fine tactual and motor information in split-brain monkeys because the somatosensory and motor fibers involved in fine sensory and motor discriminations are all contralateral.

Commissurotomy in Human Epileptics

In the first half of the 20th century, when the normal function of the corpus callosum was still a mystery, it was known that epileptic discharges often spread from one hemisphere to the other through the corpus callosum. This fact, and the fact that cutting the corpus callosum had proven in numerous studies to have no obvious effect on performance outside the contrived conditions of Sperry's laboratory led two neurosurgeons, Vogel and Bogen, to initiate a program of *commissurotomy* for the treatment of severe intractable cases of epilepsy. The rationale underlying this treatment—which entailed transecting the corpus callosum as well as the anterior commissure, and the hippocampal commissure—was that the severity of the patient's convulsions might be reduced if the discharges could be limited to the hemisphere of their origin. The therapeutic benefits of commissurotomy turned out to be even greater than anticipated: Despite the fact that commissurotomy is performed in only the most severe cases, many commissurotomized patients do not experience another major convulsion.

The evaluation of the split-brain patient's neuropsycho-

logical status was placed in the capable hands of Sperry and his associate Gazzaniga. First, they developed a battery of tests based on the same methodological strategy that had proved so informative in their studies of laboratory animals; that is, they developed procedures for delivering information to one hemisphere while keeping it out of the other. They could not use the same visual-discrimination procedure that had been used in studies of split-brain laboratory animals (i.e., cutting the optic chiasm and blindfolding one eye) because cutting the optic chiasm produces a scotoma. Instead, they employed the testing procedure that is illustrated in Figure 16.6. Each patient was asked to fixate on the center of a display screen; then, visual stimuli were flashed onto the left or right side of the screen for 0.1 second. The 0.1-second exposure time was long enough for the subjects to perceive the stimuli but short enough to preclude the confounding effects of eye movement. All stimuli thus presented in the left visual field were transmitted to the right visual cortex, and all stimuli thus presented in the right visual field were transmitted to the left visual cortex. Fine tactual and motor tasks were performed by the hands under a ledge so that the nonperforming hemisphere could not monitor their performance via the visual system.

The results of the tests on split-brain patients have confirmed the research with split-brain laboratory animals in one major respect, but not in another. Like split-brain laboratory animals, human split-brain patients seem to have two independent brains, each with its own stream of consciousness, abilities, memories, and emotions (e.g., Gazzaniga, 1967; Gazzaniga & Sperry, 1967; Sperry, 1964). But unlike the brains of split-brain laboratory animals, the brains of split-brain patients are far from equal in their ability to perform certain tasks. Most notably, the left hemisphere of most split-brain patients is capable of speech, whereas the right hemisphere is not.

Before I recount some of the key results of the tests on split-brain humans, let me give you some advice. Some students become confused by the results of these tests because their tendency to think of the human brain as a single unitary organ is deeply engrained. If you become confused, think of each split-brain patient as two separate subjects: Ms. or Mr. Right Hemisphere, who understands a few simple instructions but cannot speak, who receives sensory information from the left visual field and left hand, and who controls the fine motor responses of the left hand; and Ms. or Mr. Left Hemisphere, who is verbally adept, who receives sensory information from the right visual field and right hand, and who controls the fine motor responses of the right hand. In everyday life, the behavior of split-brain subjects is reasonably normal because their two brains go through life together and acquire much of the same infor-

Scotoma. An area of blindness in the visual field.

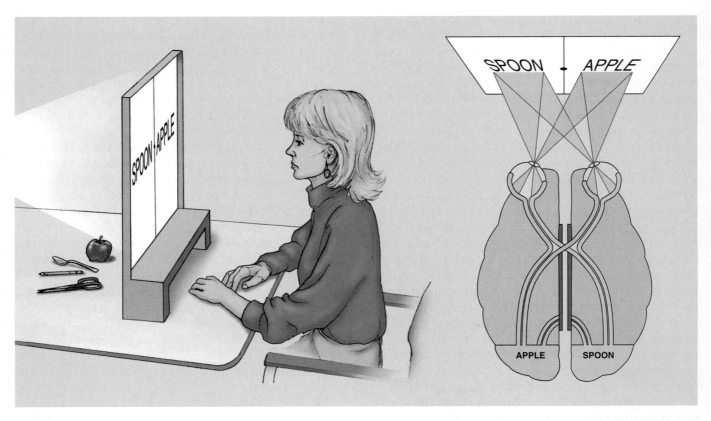

Figure 16.6 The testing procedure that was used to evaluate the neuropsychological status of split-brain patients. Visual input goes from each visual field to the contralateral hemisphere; fine tactual input goes from each hand to the contralateral hemisphere; and each hemisphere controls the fine motor movements of the contralateral hand.

mation; however, in the neuropsychological laboratory, major discrepancies in what the two hemispheres learn can be created. As you are about to find out, this situation has some interesting consequences.

Evidence That the Hemispheres of Split-Brain Patients Function Independently

If a picture of a spoon is flashed in the right visual field of a split-brain patient, the left hemisphere can do one of two things to indicate that it has received and stored the information. Because it is the hemisphere that speaks, the left hemisphere can simply tell the experimenter that it saw a picture of a spoon. Or the patient can reach under the ledge with the right hand, feel the test objects that are there, and pick out the spoon. Similarly, if the spoon is presented to the left hemisphere by being placed in the patient's right hand, the left hemisphere can indicate to the experimenter that it was a spoon either by saying so or by putting the spoon down and picking out another spoon with the right hand from the test objects under the ledge. If, however, the nonspeaking right hemisphere is asked to indicate the identity of an object that has been presented to left hemi-

sphere, it cannot do so. Although objects that have been presented to the left hemisphere can be accurately identified with the right hand, performance is no better than chance with the left hand.

When test objects are presented to the right hemisphere either visually (in the left visual field) or tactually (in the left hand), the pattern of responses is entirely different. A patient asked to name an object flashed in the left visual field is likely to claim that nothing appeared on the screen. (Remember that it is the left hemisphere who is talking and the right hemisphere who has seen the stimulus.) A patient asked to name an object placed in the left hand is usually aware that something is there, presumably because of the crude tactual information carried by ipsilateral somatosensory fibers, but is unable to say what it is. Amazingly, all the while the patient is claiming (i.e., all the while that the left hemisphere is claiming) the inability to identify a test object presented in the left visual field or left hand, the left hand (i.e., the right hemisphere) can identify the correct object. Imagine how confused the patient must become when, in trial after trial, the left hand can feel an object and then fetch another just like it from a collection of test items under the ledge, while the left hemisphere is vehemently claiming that it does not know the identity of the test object.

Cross-Cuing

Although the two hemispheres of a split-brain subject have no means of direct neural communication, they sometimes communicate with each other indirectly by a method called **cross-cuing.** An example of cross-cuing occurred during a series of tests designed to determine whether the left hemisphere could respond to colors presented in the left visual field. To test this possibility, a red or a green stimulus was presented in the left visual field, and the subject was asked to verbally report the color: red or green. At first, the patient performed at a chance level on this task (50% correct); but after a time, performance improved appreciably, thus suggesting that the color information was somehow being transferred over neural pathways from the right hemisphere to the left. However, this proved not to be the case:

> We soon caught on to the strategy the patient used. If a red light was flashed and the patient by chance guessed red, he would stick with that answer. If the flashed light was red, and the patient by chance guessed green, he would frown, shake his head and then say, "Oh no, I meant red." What was happening was that the right hemisphere saw the red light and heard the left hemisphere make the guess "green." Knowing that the answer was wrong, the right hemisphere precipitated a frown and a shake of the head, which in turn cued in the left hemisphere to the fact that the answer was wrong and that it had better correct itself! … The realization that the neurological patient has various strategies at his command emphasizes how difficult it is to obtain a clear neurological description of a human being with brain damage. (Gazzaniga, 1967, p. 27)

Learning Two Things at Once

In most of the classes that I teach, there is a student who fits the following stereotype. He sits—or rather sprawls—near the back of the class; and despite good grades, he tries to create the impression that he is above it all by making sarcastic comments. I am sure you recognize him—and it is almost always a him. Such a student inadvertently triggered an interesting discussion in one of my classes. His comment went something like this: "If getting my brain cut in two could create two separate brains, perhaps I should get it done so that I could study for two different exams at the same time."

The question raised by this comment is a good one. If the two hemispheres of a split-brain patient are capable of total independence, then they should be able to learn two different things at the same time. Can they? Indeed they can. For example, in one test two different visual stimuli appeared simultaneously on the test screen—let's say a pencil in the left visual field and an apple in the right visual field. The subject was asked to simultaneously reach into two bags—one with each hand—and grasp in each hand the object that was on the screen. After grasping the ob-

jects, but before withdrawing them, the subject was asked to tell the experimenter what was in the two hands; the subject (i.e., the left hemisphere) replied, "Two apples." Much to the bewilderment of the verbal left hemisphere, when the hands were withdrawn, there was an apple in the right hand and a pencil in the left. The two hemispheres of the split-brain subject had learned two different things at exactly the same time.

In another test in which two visual stimuli were presented simultaneously—again let's say a pencil to the left visual field and an apple to the right—the subjects were asked to pick up the presented object from an assortment of objects on a table, this time in full view. As the right hand reached out to pick up the apple under the direction of the left hemisphere, the right hemisphere saw what was happening and thought an error was being made (remember that the right hemisphere saw a pencil). On some trials, the right hemisphere dealt with this problem in the only way that it could: The left hand shot out, grabbed the right hand away from the apple, and redirected it to the pencil. This response is called the **helping-hand phenomenon.**

Yet another example of simultaneous learning in the two hemispheres involves the phenomenon of **visual completion.** As you may recall, subjects with scotomas are often unaware of them because their brains have the capacity to fill them in (to complete them) by using information from the surrounding areas of the visual field. In a sense, each hemisphere of a split-brain patient is a subject with a scotoma covering the entire ipsilateral visual field.

The ability of each hemisphere of a split-brain subject to simultaneously and independently engage in completion has been demonstrated in studies using the **chimeric figures test**—named after *Chimera,* a mythical monster composed of the combined parts of different animals. Levy, Trevarthen, and Sperry (1972) flashed photographs composed of the fused half faces of two different people onto the center of a screen in front of their split-brain subjects. The subjects were then asked to describe what they saw or to indicate what they saw by pointing to it in a series of photographs of intact faces. Amazingly, each subject (i.e., each left hemisphere) reported seeing a complete, bilaterally symmetrical face, even when asked such leading ques-

Cross-cuing. Nonneural communication between hemispheres that have been separated by commissurotomy.

Helping-hand phenomenon. The redirection of one hand of a split-brain patient by the other hand.

Visual completion. The completion or filling in of a scotoma by the brain.

Chimeric figures test. The test of visual completion in split-brain subjects that uses pictures composed of the left and right halves of two different faces.

tions as, "Did you notice anything peculiar about what you just saw?" When the subjects were asked to describe what they saw, they usually described a completed version of the half that had been presented to the right visual field (i.e., the left hemisphere). In contrast, when the subjects were asked to point out the correct face from a series of possibilities, they usually pointed to the completed version of the half that had been presented to the left visual field (i.e., the right hemisphere), regardless of which hand was used for pointing. Pointing is a crude motor response, and thus it can be controlled by either the contralateral or the ipsilateral hemisphere. Clearly, each hemisphere of a split-brain patient is capable of visual completion, and each can see a different face in exactly the same place at exactly the same time.

The Z Lens

Once it was firmly established that the two hemispheres of each split-brain patient can function independently, it became clear that the study of split-brain patients provided a unique opportunity to compare the abilities of left and right hemispheres. However, early studies of the lateralization of function in split-brain patients were limited by the fact that visual stimuli requiring more than 0.1 second to perceive could not be studied using the conventional method for restricting visual input to one hemisphere. This methodological barrier was eliminated by Zaidel in 1975. Zaidel developed a lens, called the **Z lens,** that limits visual input to one hemisphere of split-brain patients while they scan complex visual material such as the pages of a book. As Figure 16.7 illustrates, the Z lens is a contact lens that is opaque on one side. Because it moves with the eye, it permits visual input to enter only one hemisphere, irrespective of eye movement. Zaidel used the Z lens to compare the ability of the left and right hemispheres of split-brain patients to perform various tests.

The usefulness of the Z lens is not restricted to purely visual tests. For example, here is how it has been used to compare the ability of the left and right hemispheres to comprehend speech. Because each ear projects to both hemispheres, it is not possible to present spoken words to only one hemisphere. Thus, to assess the ability of a hemisphere to comprehend spoken words or sentences, Zaidel presented them to both ears, and then he asked the subject

Figure 16.7 The Z lens, which was developed by Zaidel to study functional asymmetry in split-brain patients. It is a contact lens that is opaque on one side, so that visual input reaches only one hemisphere.

to pick the correct answer or to perform the correct response under the direction of visual input to only that hemisphere. For example, to test the ability of the right hemisphere to understand the oral commands of the *token test* (see Chapter 5), the subjects were given an oral instruction (such as, "put the green square under the red circle"), and then the right hemisphere's ability to comprehend the direction was tested by allowing only the right hemisphere to observe the colored tokens while the task was being completed.

So far in this chapter, you have learned about the discovery of lateralization of function, about some of the methods used to study it, about the left-hemisphere dominance in the control of language and fine movement, and about split brains. This section takes a more systematic look at some of the differences that have been discovered between the left and right cerebral hemispheres. Because the verbal and motor abilities of the left hemisphere are readily apparent, most recent research on the lateralization of function has focused on uncovering the abilities of the right hemisphere.

Demise of the Theory of Left-Hemisphere Dominance

With the development of modern techniques for studying lateralization of function, the archaic notion of left-hemisphere dominance has been put to rest. The right hemisphere has been shown to be superior to the left in three important domains: spatial ability, emotion, and musical ability.

Spatial ability Levy (1969) placed a three-dimensional block of a particular shape in either the right hand or the left hand of her split-brain subjects. Then, after they had thoroughly *palpated* (tactually investigated) it, she asked them to point to the two-dimensional test stimulus that best represented what the three-dimensional block would look like if it were made of cardboard and unfolded. She found a right-hemisphere superiority on this task, and she found that the two hemispheres seemed to go about the task in different ways. The performance of the left hand and right hemisphere was rapid and silent, whereas the performance of the right hand and left hemisphere was hesitant and often accompanied by a running verbal commentary that was difficult for the subjects to inhibit. Levy concluded that the right hemisphere is superior to the left at spatial tasks. This conclusion is consistent with the finding that disorders of spatial perception (e.g., contralateral neglect and constructional apraxia—see Chapter 9) tend to be specifically associated with right-hemisphere damage.

Emotion According to the old concept of left-hemisphere dominance, the right hemisphere is incapable of emotion. This presumption has been proven false. Indeed, analysis of the effects of unilateral brain lesions indicates that the right hemisphere is superior to the left at perceiving both facial expression (Bowers et al., 1985) and mood (Tompkins & Mateer, 1985).

Sperry, Zaidel, and Zaidel (1979) used the Z lens to assess the behavioral reactions of the right hemispheres of split-brain patients to various emotion-charged images:

photographs of relatives; of pets; of themselves, and of political, historical, and religious figures and emblems. Their behavioral reactions were appropriate, thus indicating that right hemispheres are capable of emotional expression. In addition, there was an unexpected finding: The emotional content of images presented to the right hemisphere was reflected in the patients' speech as well as in their nonverbal behavior. This suggested that emotional information was somehow being passed from the right to the verbal left hemisphere of the split-brain subjects. The ability of emotional reactions, but not visual information, to be passed from the right hemisphere to the left hemisphere created a bizarre situation. A subject's left hemisphere often reacted with the appropriate emotional verbal response to an image that had been presented to the right hemisphere, even though it did not know what the image was.

Consider the following remarkable exchange (paraphrased from Sperry, Zaidel, & Zaidel, 1979, pp. 161–162). The patient's right hemisphere was presented with an array of photos, and the patient was asked if one was familiar. He pointed to the photo of his aunt.

Experimenter:	"Is this a neutral, a thumbs-up, or a thumbs-down person?"
Patient:	With a smile, he made a thumbs-up sign and said, "This is a happy person."
Experimenter:	"Do you know him personally?"
Patient:	"Oh, it's not a him, it's a her."
Experimenter:	"Is she an entertainment personality or an historical figure?"
Patient:	"No, just ..."
Experimenter:	"Someone you know personally?"
Patient:	He traced something with his left index finger on the back of his right hand, and then he exclaimed, "My aunt, my aunt Edie."
Experimenter:	"How do you know?"
Patient:	"By the E on the back of my hand."

Pause and think about the experiences and thoughts of these two hemispheres as each struggled to perform the task.

Musical ability Kimura (1964) compared the performance of 20 right-handers on the standard, digit version of the dichotic listening test with their performance on a ver-

> **Z lens.** A contact lens that is opaque on one side and thus allows visual input to enter only one hemisphere of a split-brain subject, irrespective of eye movement.

sion of the test involving the dichotic presentation of melodies. In the melody version of the test, Kimura simultaneously played two different melodies—one to each ear—and then asked the subjects to identify the two they had just heard from four that were subsequently played to them through both ears. The right ear (i.e., the left hemisphere) was superior in the perception of digits, whereas the left ear (i.e., the right hemisphere) was superior in the perception of melodies. This is consistent with the observation that right temporal lobe lesions are more likely to disrupt music discriminations than are left temporal lobe lesions.

Table 16.1 lists some of the abilities that have shown to be lateralized (see Kolb & Whishaw, 1990). They appear in two columns: those that are controlled more by the left hemisphere and those that are controlled more by the right hemisphere.

TABLE 16.1

Abilities That Display Cerebral Lateralization of Function

Left-Hemisphere Dominance	GENERAL FUNCTION	Right-Hemisphere Dominance
Words Letters	VISION	Geometric patterns Faces Emotional expression
Language sounds	AUDITION	Nonlanguage sounds Music
	TOUCH	Tactual patterns Braille
Complex movement	MOVEMENT	Movement in spatial patterns
Verbal memory	MEMORY	Nonverbal memory
Speech Reading Writing Arithmetic	LANGUAGE	Emotional content
	SPATIAL ABILITY	Geometry Direction Distance Mental rotation of shapes

Statistical versus All-or-None Hemispheric Differences

Studies of lateralization of function involve statistical comparisons of large groups of left-hemisphere and right-hemisphere measurements. For most measures, no statistically significant differences are found; lateralization of function is the exception rather than the rule. And when statistically significant hemisphere differences are found, they tend to be slight biases in favor of one hemisphere or the other—not absolute differences (see Brown & Kosslyn, 1993). Be that as it may, the pop psychology media inevitably portray left-right cerebral differences as absolute. As a result, it is widely believed that various abilities reside exclusively in one hemisphere or the other. For example, it is widely believed that the left hemisphere has exclusive control over language and the right hemisphere has exclusive control over emotion and creativity. The most disturbing thing about this misrepresentation is that modern educational programs are sometimes inspired by it.

Language-related abilities provide a particularly good illustration of the fact that lateralization of function is statistical rather than absolute. Language is the most lateralized of all cognitive abilities. Yet, even in this most extreme case, lateralization is far from total; there is substantial language-related activity in the right hemisphere. Following are three illustrations of this point:

1. In the dichotic listening test, the right ear tends to identify more digits than the left ear in subjects who are left-hemisphere dominant for language, but the right-ear advantage is only slight (e.g., 55% to 45%).

2. In brain-imaging studies, language-related activities usually produce greater overall activation in the left hemisphere than in the right, but there is a substantial activation in the right hemisphere (see Roland, 1993).

3. Z-lens studies of split-brain patients have shown that the right hemisphere can understand many spoken or written words, and it can also understand simple sentences (see Zaidel, 1983, 1987). Over all, the performance of the right hemisphere on various tests of language comprehension is comparable to that of a preschool child.

Neuroanatomical Asymmetries

Casual inspection suggests that the left and right hemispheres are mirror images of one another, but they are not; many anatomical differences between them have been documented. Most effort has been expended trying to document anatomical asymmetries in areas of the cortex that are important for language. Three of these areas are the planum temporale, Heschl's gyrus, and the frontal operculum (see Figure 16.8). The **planum temporale** is the area of temporal lobe cortex that lies in the posterior region of the lateral fissure; it is thought to play a role in the comprehension of language and is often referred to as *Wernicke's area*. **Heschl's gyrus** is located in the lateral fissure just anterior to the planum temporale in the temporal lobe; it is the location of primary auditory cortex. The **frontal operculum** is the area of frontal lobe cortex that lies just in front of the face area of the primary motor cortex; in the left hemisphere, it is the location of Broca's area.

Because the planum temporale, Heschl's gyrus, and the frontal operculum are all involved in language-related activities, one might expect that they would all be larger in the left hemisphere than in the right in most subjects; but they aren't. The left planum temporale does tend to be larger on the left, but only in 65% of human brains (Geschwind & Levitsky, 1968). In contrast, the cortex of Heschl's gyrus tends to be larger on the right, primarily because there are often two Heschl's gyri in the right hemisphere and only one in the left. The laterality of the frontal operculum is less clear. The area of the frontal operculum that is visible on the surface of the brain tends to be larger on the right; but when the cortex buried within sulci of the frontal operculum is considered, there tends to be a greater volume of frontal operculum cortex on the left (Falzi, Perrone, & Vignolo, 1982).

A word of caution is in order. It is tempting to conclude that the tendency for the planum temporale to be larger in the left hemisphere predisposes the left hemisphere for language dominance. Indeed, the finding that the left planum temporale is larger than the right in fetal brains (Wada, Clarke, & Hamm, 1975) is consistent with this view. However, because most studies of neuroanatomical asymmetry are conducted at autopsy, there is no evidence that people with well-developed anatomical asymmetries tend to have more lateralized language functions. In fact, there is a substantial discrepancy between the proportion of the population that has been reported to have a larger left planum temporale (about 65%) and the proportion that is left-hemisphere dominant for language (about 90%).

The recent development of brain-imaging techniques for measuring anatomical asymmetries in living humans has made it possible to study relations between anatomical and functional brain asymmetries. For example, Schlaug et al. (1995) recently used magnetic resonance imaging (MRI) to measure the asymmetry of the planum temporale and relate it to the presence of perfect pitch (the ability to

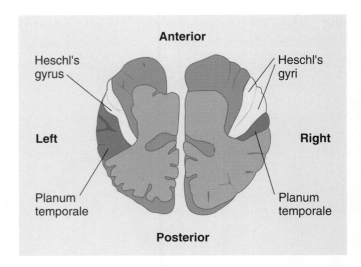

Figure 16.8 Three language areas of the cerebral cortex that display neuroanatomical asymmetry: The planum temporale (Wernicke's area), Heschl's gyrus (primary auditory cortex), and the frontal operculum (Broca's area).

identify the pitch of individual musical notes). The planum temporale was found to be more lateralized to the left hemisphere in musicians with perfect pitch than in non-musicians or in musicians without *perfect pitch* (see Figure 16.9). Because several other musical abilities have been found to be lateralized in the right hemisphere, the discovery that perfect pitch is associated with a larger left planum temporale suggests that the categories we use to think about lateralization of function—categories such as language, musical ability, and spatial ability—are too crude.

Theories of Cerebral Asymmetry

Several theories have been proposed to explain why cerebral asymmetry evolved. All of them are based on the same general premise: that it is advantageous for areas of the brain that perform similar functions to be located in the same hemisphere. One of these theories (see Levy, 1969; Sperry, 1974, 1985) is that there are two basic modes of thinking, an *analytic mode* and a *synthetic mode,* which

Planum temporale. An area of the temporal lobe that in the left hemisphere roughly corresponds to Wernicke's area.

Heschl's gyrus. The temporal lobe gyrus that is the location of primary auditory cortex.

Frontal operculum. The neuroanatomical designation for the area of prefrontal cortex that in the left hemisphere roughly corresponds to Broca's area.

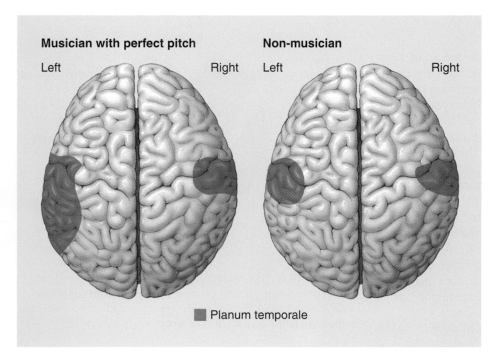

Musician with perfect pitch　Left　Right　**Non-musician**　Left　Right

■ Planum temporale

Figure 16.9 The anatomical asymmetry detected in the planum temporale of musicians by magnetic resonance imaging. In most people, the planum temporale is larger in the left hemisphere than in the right; this difference was found to be greater in musicians with perfect pitch than in either musicians without perfect pitch or control subjects. (Adapted from Schlaug et al., 1995.)

deficits in the ability to make both individual speech sounds and individual facial movements, whereas left temporal and parietal lesions produced deficits in the ability to make sequences of speech sounds and sequences of facial movements; and Wolff et al. (1990) found that subjects with reading disabilities also have difficulty performing a finger-tapping test.

Much of the debate about the evolution of cerebral lateralization of function has focused on when it evolved. Cerebral laterality was once presumed to be an exclusive feature of the hominid brain. Left-hemisphere dominance for motor control was thought to have evolved in early hominids in response to their use of tools, and then the subsequent evolution of the propensity for vocal language was thought to have evolved in the left hemisphere because of its greater motor dexterity. This theory of the evolution of laterality received initial support from reports that nonhuman primate species display no

have become segregated during the course of evolution in the left and right hemispheres, respectively. According to this theory,

> the left hemisphere operates in a more logical, analytical, computerlike fashion, analyzing stimulus information input sequentially and abstracting the relevant details, to which it attaches verbal labels; the right hemisphere is primarily a synthesizer, more concerned with the overall stimulus configuration, and organizes and processes information in terms of gestalts, or wholes. (Harris, 1978, p. 463)

Although this *analytic-synthetic theory of cerebral lateralization* has long been the darling of pop psychology, its vagueness is a problem. Because it is not possible to specify the degree to which any task requires either analytic or synthetic processing, it has been impossible to subject the analytic-synthetic theory to empirical tests.

Another theory of cerebral lateralization is the motor theory (see Kimura, 1979). According to the *motor theory of cerebral lateralization,* the left hemisphere is specialized not for the control of speech per se but for the control of fine movements, of which speech is only one category. Support for this theory comes from reports that lesions that produce aphasia also produce other motor deficits. For example, Kimura (1987) found a correlation between the disruption of language abilities by lesions and their disruption of voluntary nonspeech oral movements; Kimura and Watson (1989) found that left frontal lesions produced

Wernicke-Geschwind model. An influential cortical model of language localization.

Wernicke's area. The area of the left temporal cortex hypothesized by Wernicke to be the center of language comprehension.

Expressive. Pertaining to the generation of language, that is, pertaining to writing or talking.

Broca's aphasia. A hypothetical disorder of speech production with no associated deficits in language comprehension.

Receptive. Pertaining to the comprehension of language.

Wernicke's aphasia. A hypothetical disorder of language comprehension with no associated deficits in speech production.

Word salad. Speech that has the overall sound and flow of fluid speech but is totally incomprehensible.

Arcuate fasciculus. The major neural pathway between Broca's area and Wernicke's area.

Conduction aphasia. Aphasia that is thought to result from damage to the neural pathway between Broca's area and Wernicke's area.

consistent hand preference (see Westergard, 1991); however, MacNeilage, Studdert-Kennedy, and Lindblom (1993) have reported that hand preferences are apparent in many primate species when the nature of the responses made by each hand is considered: Several primate species prefer to manipulate objects with their right hand while holding them with their left hand. MacNeilage and his colleagues have suggested that lateralization of specialized hand use came about early in the evolution of primates when the right hand became specialized for arboreal travel, leaving the left hand free to reach for food. Also, the control of communicative vocalizations has been found to be lateralized in the left hemisphere of some nonhuman primates (see Owren, 1990), and the left hemisphere of macaque monkeys has been shown to play the dominant role in the discrimination of macaque vocalizations (Heffner & Heffner, 1984). It seems likely therefore that the evolution of cerebral lateralization preceded the evolution of hominids.

16.4 Cortical Localization of Language

So far, this chapter has focused on the functional asymmetry of the brain, with an emphasis on the lateralization of language-related functions. At this point, it shifts its focus from language lateralization to language localization. In contrast to language lateralization, which refers to the relative control of language-related functions by the left and right hemispheres, *language localization* refers to the location within the hemispheres of the circuits that participate in language-related activities.

Like most introductions to language localization, the following discussion begins with the **Wernicke-Geschwind model.** Although this model has proved to be inconsistent with the findings of many of the studies that it has spawned, it has been the single most influential theory of language localization. Because most of the research on the localization of language has been conducted and interpreted within the context of this model, reading about the localization of language without a basic understanding of the Wernicke-Geschwind model would be like watching a game of chess without knowing the rules—not a very fulfilling experience.

Historic Antecedents of the Wernicke-Geschwind Model

The history of the localization of language and the history of the lateralization of function began at the same point, with Broca's assertion that a small area in the inferior portion of the left prefrontal cortex (Broca's area) is the center for speech production. Broca hypothesized that programs of articulation are stored within this area and that speech is produced when these programs activate the adjacent area of the precentral gyrus, which controls the muscles of the face and oral cavity. According to Broca, damage restricted to Broca's area should disrupt speech production without producing deficits in language comprehension.

The next major event in the study of the cerebral localization of language occurred in 1874, when Wernicke (pronounced "VER-ni-key") concluded on the basis of 10 clinical cases that there is a language area in the left temporal lobe just posterior to the primary auditory cortex (i.e., in the left planum temporale). This second language area, which Wernicke argued was the cortical area of language comprehension, subsequently became known as **Wernicke's area.**

Wernicke suggested that selective lesions of Broca's area produce a syndrome of aphasia whose symptoms are primarily **expressive**—characterized by normal comprehension of both written and spoken language and by speech that retains its meaningfulness despite being slow, labored, disjointed, and poorly articulated. This hypothetical form of aphasia became known as **Broca's aphasia.** In contrast, Wernicke suggested that selective lesions of Wernicke's area produce a syndrome of aphasia whose deficits are primarily **receptive**—characterized by poor comprehension of both written and spoken language and speech that is meaningless but still retains the superficial structure, rhythm, and intonation of normal speech. This hypothetical form of aphasia became known as **Wernicke's aphasia,** and the normal-sounding but nonsensical speech of Wernicke's aphasia became known as **word salad.**

The following are examples of the kinds of speech that are presumed to be associated with selective damage to Broca's and Wernicke's areas (Geschwind, 1979, p. 183):

Broca's Aphasia: A patient who was asked about a dental appointment replied haltingly and indistinctly: "Yes ... Monday ... Dad and Dick ... Wednesday nine o'clock ... 10 o'clock ... doctors ... and ... teeth."

Wernicke's Aphasia: A patient who was asked to describe a picture that showed two boys stealing cookies reported smoothly: "Mother is away here working her work to get her better, but when she's looking the two boys looking in the other part. She's working another time."

Wernicke reasoned that damage to the pathway connecting Broca's and Wernicke's areas—the **arcuate fasciculus**—would produce a third type of aphasia, one that he called **conduction aphasia.** He contended that comprehension and spontaneous speech would be intact in patients with damage to the arcuate fasciculus but that there would be difficulty in repeating words that had just been heard.

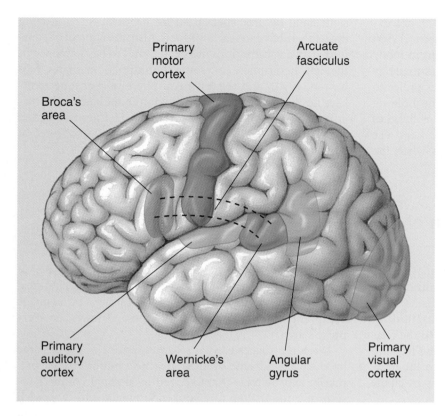

Broca's area
Primary motor cortex
Arcuate fasciculus
Primary auditory cortex
Wernicke's area
Angular gyrus
Primary visual cortex

Figure 16.10 The seven components of the Wernicke-Geschwind model.

specific neocortical areas (e.g., Freud, Head, and Marie). In fact, these advocates of the holistic approach to brain function gradually gained the upper hand, and interest in the cerebral localization of language waned. However, in 1965, Geschwind revived the old localizationist ideas of Broca, Wernicke, and Dejerine; added some new data and insightful interpretation; and melded the mix into a powerful theory: the Wernicke-Geschwind model.

Wernicke-Geschwind Model

The following are the seven components of the Wernicke-Geschwind model: primary visual cortex, angular gyrus, primary auditory cortex, Wernicke's area, arcuate fasciculus, Broca's area, and primary motor cortex—all in the left hemisphere. They are shown in Figure 16.10.

The following two examples illustrate how the Wernicke-Geschwind model is presumed to work (see Figure 16.11). First, when you are having a conversation, the auditory signals triggered by the speech of the other person are received by your primary auditory cortex and conducted to

The left **angular gyrus**—the area of left temporal and parietal cortex just posterior to Wernicke's area—is another cortical area that has been implicated in language. Its role in language was recognized in 1892 by Dejerine on the basis of the postmortem examination of one special patient. The patient suffered from **alexia** (the inability to read) and **agraphia** (the inability to write). What made this case special was that the alexia and agraphia were exceptionally pure: Although the patient could not read or write, he had no difficulty speaking or understanding speech. Dejerine's postmortem examination revealed damage in the pathways connecting the visual cortex with the left angular gyrus. He concluded that the left angular gyrus is responsible for comprehending language-related visual input, which is received directly from the adjacent left visual cortex and indirectly from the right visual cortex via the corpus callosum.

During the era of Broca, Wernicke, and Dejerine, there were many influential neuroscientists who opposed their attempts to localize various language-related abilities to

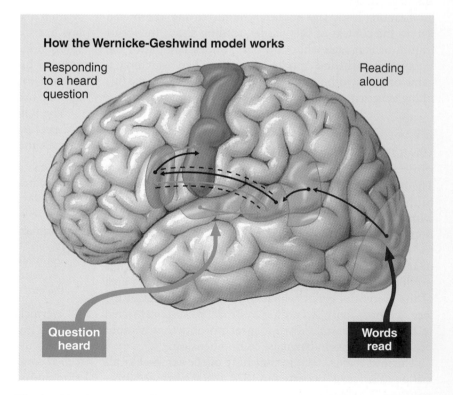

How the Wernicke-Geshwind model works

Responding to a heard question

Reading aloud

Question heard

Words read

Figure 16.11 How the Wernicke-Geschwind model works: How it responds to a heard question and how it reads aloud.

Before proceeding to the following tests of the Wernicke-Geschwind model, complete the following exercise to confirm that you understand its fundamentals. The correct answers are provided at the bottom of this page. Review material related to your errors and omissions.

According to the Wernicke-Geschwind model, the following seven areas of the left cerebral cortex play a role in language-related activities:

1. The _____ gyrus translates the visual form of a read word into an auditory code.

2. The _____ cortex controls the muscles of articulation.

3. The _____ cortex perceives the written word.

4. _____ area is the center for language comprehension.

5. The _____ cortex perceives the spoken word.

6. _____ area contains the programs of articulation.

7. The left _____ carries signals from Wernicke's area to Broca's area.

Wernicke's area, where they are comprehended. If a response is in order, Wernicke's area generates the neural representation of the thought underlying the reply, and it is transmitted to Broca's area via the left arcuate fasciculus. In Broca's area, this signal activates the appropriate program of articulation that drives the appropriate neurons of your primary motor cortex and ultimately your muscles of articulation. Second, when you are reading aloud, the signal received by your primary visual cortex is transmitted to your left angular gyrus, which translates the visual form of the word into its auditory code and transmits it to

Wernicke's area for comprehension. Wernicke's area then triggers the appropriate responses in your arcuate fasciculus, Broca's area, and motor cortex, respectively, to elicit the appropriate speech sounds.

From the foregoing description, it is apparent that the Wernicke-Geschwind model is a **serial model:** Each process that it mediates involves a chain of responses that are triggered in linear sequence, like a single line of falling dominoes. **Parallel models** are those that involve two or more simultaneous routes of activity (e.g., a dual-route model).

The answers are (1) angular, (2) primary motor, (3) primary visual, (4) Wernicke's, (5) primary auditory, (6) Broca's, and (7) arcuate fasciculus.

Angular gyrus. The gyrus of the posterior cortex at the boundary between the temporal and parietal lobes, which in the left hemisphere is thought to play a role in reading.

Alexia. A specific inability to read, one that does not result from general visual, motor, or intellectual deficits.

Agraphia. A specific inability to write, one that does not result from general visual, motor, or intellectual deficits.

Serial model. A model that involves a single chain of responses triggered in linear sequence.

Parallel models. Models involving two or more simultaneous routes of activity.

Evaluation of the Wernicke-Geschwind Model

Unless you are reading this text from back to front, you should have read the preceding description of the Wernicke-Geschwind model with some degree of skepticism. By this point in the text, you will almost certainly recognize that any model of a complex cognitive process that involves a few localized neocortical centers joined in a linear fashion by a few arrows is sure to have major shortcomings. You have learned in almost every chapter that the brain—and especially the neocortex—is not divided into neat compartments whose cognitive functions conform to vague concepts such as language comprehension, speech motor programs, and conversion of written language to auditory language. And you have learned that parallel models, rather than serial ones, are better able to account for the complexity and plasticity of human cognitive function. However, initial skepticism aside, the ultimate test of a theory's validity is the degree to which its predictions are consistent with the empirical evidence.

The remainder of the chapter focuses on empirical tests of the Wernicke-Geschwind model. Before we continue, though, three confusing points require clarification.

First, the Wernicke-Geschwind model was initially based on case studies of aphasic patients with strokes, tumors, and penetrating brain injuries. Damage in such cases is almost always diffuse, and it inevitably encroaches on sub-cortical fibers coursing through the lesion site to other areas of the brain (see Bogen & Bogen, 1976). For example, illustrated in Figure 16.12 is the extent of the cortical damage in one of Broca's two original cases (see Mohr, 1976).

Second, Broca's and Wernicke's aphasias probably do not exist in their pure forms as defined by Wernicke and Geschwind. Aphasia virtually always involves both expressive and receptive symptoms (see Benson, 1985). Accordingly, the terms *Broca's aphasia* and *Wernicke's aphasia* are commonly used to designate aphasic disorders that are largely expressive or receptive, respectively.

Third, Broca's aphasia and Wernicke's aphasia do not necessarily result from damage to Broca's and Wernicke's areas. This is a prediction of the model, not a description of the evidence.

Effects of Brain Damage on Language-Related Abilities

Surgical removal of cortical tissue In view of the fact that the Wernicke-Geschwind model grew out of the study of patients with cortical damage, it is appropriate to begin evaluating it by assessing its ability to predict the language-related deficits produced by damage to various parts of the cortex. The study of patients in whom discrete areas of cortex have been surgically removed has proved particularly informative in this regard because the location and extent of their lesions can be derived with reasonable accuracy from the surgeon's report.

The study of patients in whom the Wernicke-Geschwind language areas have been surgically removed has not confirmed the predictions of the model by any stretch of the imagination. For example, lesions that destroy all of Broca's area but little surrounding tissue typically have no lasting effects on speech (Penfield & Roberts, 1959; Rasmussen & Milner, 1975; Zangwill, 1975). There are often some speech problems after such a lesion, but their temporal course suggests that they result from postsurgical *edema* (swelling) in the surrounding neural tissue rather than from the *excision* (cutting out) of Broca's area per se. The patient typically has no speech problems immediately after Broca's area has been excised, but speech deficits develop several hours later and then gradually subside in the ensuing weeks. Similarly, permanent speech difficulties are not produced by discrete surgical lesions to the arcuate fasciculus, and permanent alexia and agraphia are not produced by surgical lesions restricted to the cortex of the angular gyrus (Rasmussen & Milner,

Figure 16.12 The extent of brain damage in one of Broca's two original patients. Like this patient, most aphasic patients have diffuse brain damage. It is thus difficult to determine from their investigation the precise location of particular cortical language areas. (Adapted from Mohr, 1976.)

Broca's area

Area of damage observed in one of Broca's subjects

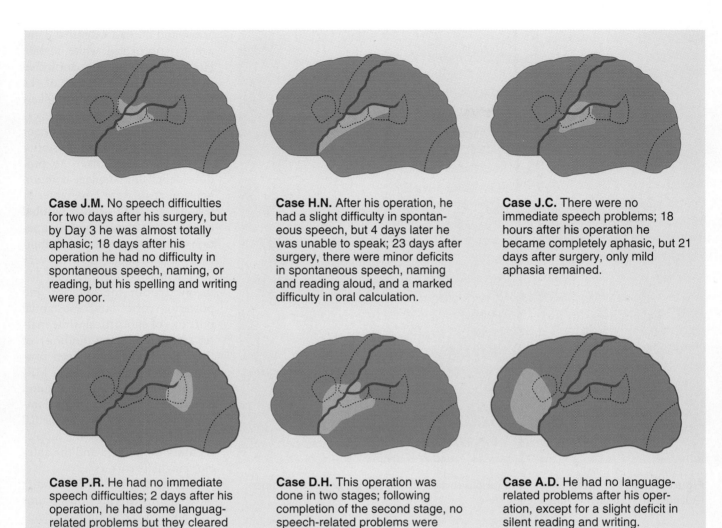

Case J.M. No speech difficulties for two days after his surgery, but by Day 3 he was almost totally aphasic; 18 days after his operation he had no difficulty in spontaneous speech, naming, or reading, but his spelling and writing were poor.

Case H.N. After his operation, he had a slight difficulty in spontaneous speech, but 4 days later he was unable to speak; 23 days after surgery, there were minor deficits in spontaneous speech, naming and reading aloud, and a marked difficulty in oral calculation.

Case J.C. There were no immediate speech problems; 18 hours after his operation he became completely aphasic, but 21 days after surgery, only mild aphasia remained.

Case P.R. He had no immediate speech difficulties; 2 days after his operation, he had some languag-related problems but they cleared up.

Case D.H. This operation was done in two stages; following completion of the second stage, no speech-related problems were reported.

Case A.D. He had no language-related problems after his operation, except for a slight deficit in silent reading and writing.

Figure 16.13 The lack of permanent disruption of language-related abilities after surgical excision of the classic Wernicke-Geschwind language areas. (Adapted from Penfield & Roberts, 1959.)

1975). The consequences of the surgical removal of Wernicke's area are less well documented; surgeons have been hesitant to remove it in light of Wernicke's dire predictions. Nevertheless, in some cases, a good portion of Wernicke's area has been removed without lasting language-related deficits (e.g., Ojemann, 1979; Penfield & Roberts, 1959). Figure 16.13 summarizes the language-related effects of six cortical excisions performed by Penfield and Roberts (1959).

Supporters of the Wernicke-Geschwind model argue that despite the precision of surgical excision, negative evidence obtained from the study of the effects of brain surgery should be discounted because the brain pathology that warranted the surgery may have reorganized the control of language by the brain.

Accidental or disease-related brain damage Hécaen and Angelergues (1964) rated the articulation, fluency, comprehension, naming ability, ability to repeat spoken sentences, reading, and writing of 214 right-handed patients with small, medium, or large accidental or disease-related lesions to the left hemisphere. The extent and location of the damage in each case was estimated by either postmortem histological examination or visual inspection during subsequent surgery. Hécaen and Angelergues found that small lesions to Broca's area seldom produced lasting language deficits and that those restricted to Wernicke's area sometimes did not. Medium-sized lesions did produce some deficits; but in contrast to the predictions of the Wernicke-Geschwind model, problems of articulation were just as likely to occur following medium-sized parietal or temporal lesions as they were following comparable lesions in

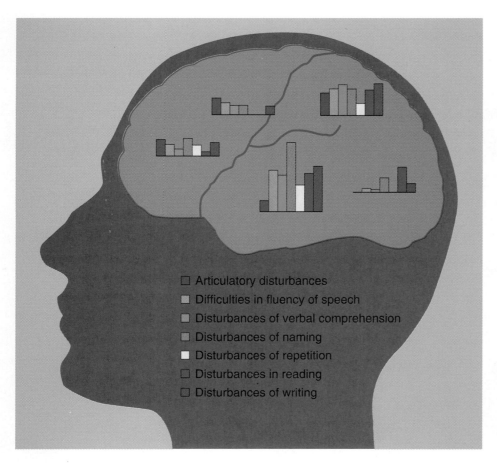

□ Articulatory disturbances
■ Difficulties in fluency of speech
■ Disturbances of verbal comprehension
■ Disturbances of naming
□ Disturbances of repetition
□ Disturbances in reading
□ Disturbances of writing

Figure 16.14 The effects of lesions to various cortical areas on language-related abilities. (Adapted from Hécaen & Angelergues, 1964.)

the vicinity of Broca's area. All other symptoms that were produced by medium-sized lesions were more likely to appear following parietal or temporal lesions than following frontal damage.

The only observation from Hécaen and Angelergues' study that is consistent with the Wernicke-Geschwind model came from the analysis of the effects of large lesions (those involving three lobes). Large lesions of the anterior brain were more likely to be associated with articulation problems than were large lesions of the posterior brain. It is noteworthy that none of the 214 subjects displayed specific syndromes of expressive aphasia (Broca's aphasia) or receptive aphasia (Wernicke's aphasia) implied by the Wernicke-Geschwind model. The effects of lesions to the frontal, temporal, parietal, or occipital lobes or to the vicinity of the central fissure are summarized in Figure 16.14.

CT and MRI scans of aphasic patients Since the development of *computed tomography (CT)* and *magnetic resonance imaging (MRI)*, it has been possible to visualize the brain damage of living aphasic patients (see Damasio, 1989). In the CT studies by Mazzocchi and Vignolo (1979) and Naeser and colleagues (1981), none of the aphasic patients had damage restricted to Broca's and Wernicke's

areas, and all had extensive damage to subcortical white matter. However, both studies confirmed that large anterior lesions of the left hemisphere were more likely to produce deficits in language expression than were large posterior lesions, and that large posterior lesions were more likely to produce deficits in language comprehension than were large anterior lesions. In both studies, **global aphasia**—an almost total elimination of all language-related abilities—was associated with very large left-hemisphere lesions that involved both the anterior and posterior cortex and substantial portions of subcortical white matter. In general, the findings of these CT studies have been confirmed by Damasio's (1989) MRI studies. However, Damasio found a few aphasic patients whose damage was restricted to the medial frontal lobes; that is, to the supplementary motor area and the anterior cingulate cortex.

Several CT and MRI studies have confirmed previous claims that aphasia can result from damage to subcortical structures (see Alexander, 1989). Aphasia can occur following damage restricted to the left subcortical white matter, the left basal ganglia, or the left thalamus (e.g., Naeser et al., 1982).

Cortical Stimulation and Localization of Language

The first large-scale brain-stimulation studies of humans were conducted by Penfield and his colleagues in the 1940s at the Montreal Neurological Institute (see Feindel, 1986). One purpose of the studies was to map the language areas of each patient's brain so that tissue involved in language could be avoided during the surgery. The mapping was done by assessing the responses of conscious patients under local anesthetic to stimulation applied to various points on the cortical surface. The description of the effects

Global aphasia. Almost total elimination of all language-related abilities.

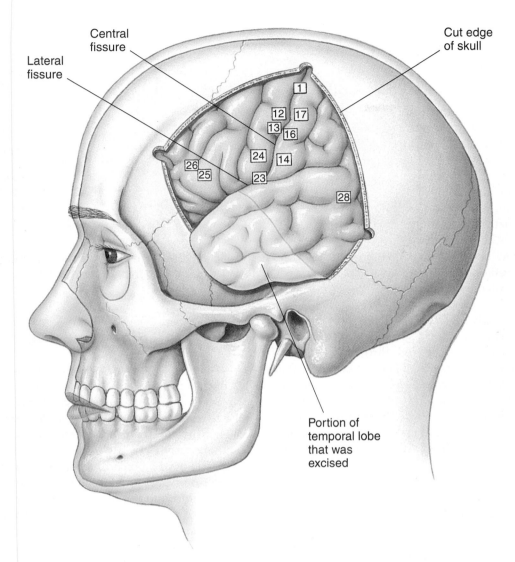

1 | Tingling in the right thumb and a slight movement

12 | Quivering of the jaw in a sidewise manner

13 | Pulling of jaw to right

14 | Sensation in the jaw and lower lip

16 | Tingling in the right side of tongue

17 | Sensation in right upper lip

23 | Stimulation applied while the patient was talking, stopped his speech. After cessation of stimulation, he said that he had been unable to speak despite trying.

24 | The patient tried to talk, his mouth moved, but he made no sound.

25 | The patient had initial difficulty, but eventually he named a picture of a butterfly.

26 | The patient said, "Oh, I know what it is" in response to a picture of a foot. "That is what you put in your shoes." After termination of the stimulation, he said, "foot."

28 | The patient became unable to name the pictures as soon as the electrode was placed here. The EEG revealed seizure activity in the temporal lobe. When the seizure discharges stopped, the patient spoke at once. "Now I can talk," he said, and he correctly identified the picture of a butterfly.

Figure 16.15 The responses of the left hemisphere of a 37-year-old epileptic to electrical stimulation. Numbered cards were placed on the brain during surgery to mark the sites where brain stimulation had been applied. (Adapted from Penfield & Roberts, 1959.)

of each stimulation were dictated to a stenographer—this was before the days of tape recorders—and then a tiny numbered card was dropped on the stimulation site for subsequent photography.

Figure 16.15 illustrates the responses to stimulation of a 37-year-old right-handed epileptic patient. He had started to have seizures about 3 months after receiving a blow to the head; and at the time of his operation, in 1948, he had been suffering from seizures for 6 years, despite efforts to control them with medication. In considering his responses, remember that the cortex just posterior to the central fissure is primary somatosensory cortex and that the cortex just anterior to the central fissure is primary motor cortex.

Because electrical stimulation of the cortex is much more localized than a brain lesion, it has been a useful method of testing predictions of the Wernicke-Geschwind model. Penfield and Roberts (1959) published the first large-scale study of the effects of cortical stimulation on speech. They found that sites at which stimulation blocked or disrupted speech in conscious neurosurgical patients were scattered throughout a large expanse of frontal, temporal, and parietal cortex, rather than being restricted to the Wernicke-Geschwind areas (see Figure 16.16). They also found no tendency for particular kinds of speech disturbances to be elicited from particular areas of the cortex: Sites at which stimulation produced disturbances of pronunciation, confusion of counting, inability to name objects, or misnaming of objects were pretty much intermingled. Right-hemisphere stimulation almost never disrupted speech.

In a more recent series of cortical stimulation studies, Ojemann and his colleagues (see Ojemann, 1983) assessed naming, reading of simple sentences, short-term verbal memory, ability to mimic orofacial movements, and the ability to recognize **phonemes**—individual speech sounds—during cortical stimulation. In contrast to the predictions of the Wernicke-Geschwind model, they found (1) that the areas of the cortex at which stimulation could disrupt language extended far beyond the boundaries of the Wernicke-Geschwind language areas, (2) that all of the specific language abilities were represented at both anterior and posterior sites, and (3) that there were major differences among the subjects in the organization of language abilities.

Because the disruptive effects of stimulation at a particular site were frequently quite specific (i.e., disrupting only a single test), Ojemann suggested that the language cortex might be organized like a mosaic, with the discrete columns of tissue performing a particular function being widely distributed throughout the language area of the cortex. However, Mateer and Cameron (1989), in yet another study of cortical stimulation, found a tendency for the cortex around the lateral fissure to be specialized for **phonological analysis** (analysis of the sound of language), leaving the other cortical speech areas to deal with **grammatical analysis** (analysis of the structure of language) and **semantic analysis** (analysis of the meaning of language).

- Sites at which stimulation produced a complete arrest of speech

- Sites at which stimulation disrupted speech, but did not block it completely

Figure 16.16 The wide distribution of left hemisphere sites where cortical stimulation either blocked speech or disrupted it. (Adapted from Penfield & Roberts, 1959.)

Parallel Processing of Language: Evidence from Dyslexia

In contrast to the Wernicke-Geschwind model, the model of reading aloud that has emerged from cognitive neuroscience research is a *dual-route parallel model*—a model in which two types of processing of the same input occur simultaneously over two different neural pathways (see Coltheart, 1985). According to the dual-route parallel model, reading aloud is simultaneously mediated by a lexical procedure and a nonlexical procedure. The **lexical procedure** is based on specific stored information that we have acquired about the written words in our vocabulary, and the **nonlexical procedure** is based on general rules of pronunciation that allow us to pronounce unfamiliar words or nonwords such as *spleemer* and *twipple*.

Evidence in support of the idea that reading aloud is mediated by parallel lexical and nonlexical pathways comes from cases of **dyslexia**—pathological reading difficulty—in which it appears that either the lexical or nonlexical procedure is impaired while the other is not (see Hinton, Plaut, & Shallice, 1993). Dyslexics in whom the lexical route appears to be dysfunctional while the nonlexical route remains functional are said to be suffering from **surface dyslexia;** conversely, dyslexics in whom the nonlexical route appears to be dysfunctional while the lexical route remains functional are said to be suffering from **deep dyslexia.**

In cases of surface dyslexia, patients have lost their ability to pronounce words based on their specific memories of the words (i.e., they have lost their lexical procedure), but they can still apply rules of pronunciation in their reading (i.e., they can still use their nonlexical procedure). Accordingly, they retain their ability to pronounce words whose pronunciation is consistent with common rules (e.g., *fish, river,* or *glass*) and their ability to pronounce nonwords according to common rules of pronunciation (e.g., *spleemer* or *twipple*); but they have great difficulty pronouncing words that do not follow common rules of pronunciation (e.g., *have, lose,* or *steak*). The errors they make often involve the misapplication of common rules of pronunciation; for example, *have, lose,* and *steak* are typically pronounced as if they rhyme with *cave, hose,* and *beak.*

In cases of deep dyslexia, patients have lost their ability to apply rules of pronunciation in their reading (i.e., they have lost their nonlexical procedure), but they can still pronounce familiar concrete words based on their specific memories of them (i.e., they can still use their lexical procedure). Accordingly, they are completely incapable of pronouncing nonwords and have difficulty pronouncing uncommon words and words whose meaning is abstract. In attempting to pronounce words, patients with deep dyslexia try to react to them by using various lexical strategies, such as responding to the overall look of the word, the meaning of the word, or the derivation of the word. This leads to a characteristic pattern of errors. A patient with deep dyslexia might say "quill" for *quail* (responding to the overall look of the word), "hen" for *chicken* (responding to the meaning of the word), or "wise" for *wisdom* (responding to the derivation of the word).

Coltheart (1980) believes that the mechanisms mediating the nonlexical procedure of reading aloud are lateralized in the left hemisphere. The most striking support for Coltheart's hypothesis has come from the study of a dyslexic patient who had a left **hemispherectomy**—removal of the left cerebral hemisphere—at the age of 14 (Patterson, Vargha-Khadem, & Polkey, 1989). Performing with only her right hemisphere, she was capable of pronouncing familiar concrete words, but she could not pronounce simple nonwords (e.g., *neg*), and her errors indicated that she was reading on the basis of the meaning and appearance of words rather than by translating letters into sounds (e.g., when presented with the word *fruit*, she responded, "Juice … it's apples and pears and … fruit"). In other words, she suffered from a severe case of deep dyslexia.

Before we leave the topic of dyslexia, I must keep a promise I made to one of my students. I promised him I would tell you about a dyslexic woman he knows who is also an insomniac and an agnostic. According to my student, this dyslexic woman stays awake every night wondering if there really is a doG.

PET Scans during Language-Related Activities

The application of modern functional brain-imaging techniques has revolutionized the study of the cerebral localization of language (see Mehler et al., 1994; Petersen & Fiez, 1993). In one particularly productive line of studies, Petersen and his colleagues have used positron emission tomography (PET) to measure the amount of blood flow to various parts of the human brain during various language-related activities. Blood flow to an area of the brain increases when the area becomes active.

The PET scan technique of Petersen and his colleagues has three noteworthy features. First, rather than injecting a radioactive gas, they inject radioactive water. The advantage of water over gas is that it quickly passes from the bloodstream, thus making it possible for several tests to be given to each subject, one every 10 minutes. Second, injections of the radioactive water are made intravenously rather than into the carotid artery. This allows the material to be dispersed equally to both hemispheres so they can be studied simultaneously. And third, Petersen and his colleagues use the *paired-image subtraction technique* to subtract the changes in blood flow during one activity from those observed during another.

In one study, Petersen et al. (1989) measured the blood flow of each subject under two sets of conditions: visual and auditory. Each set comprised four conditions of progressively increasing complexity. In the four visual conditions, the subjects were asked to do the following: (1) to fixate on (stare at) a crosshair on a blank display screen, (2) to fixate on the crosshair while printed nouns were presented on the screen, (3) to fixate on the crosshair while reading aloud the printed nouns, and (4) to fixate on the crosshair while saying an appropriate verb to go with the printed noun (e.g., cake: eat; radio: listen). The four auditory con-

Phonemes. Individual speech sounds.

Phonological analysis. Sound-related analysis of a language.

Grammatical analysis. Analysis of a language in terms of its rules of sentence structure.

Semantic analysis. Meaning-related analysis of a language.

Lexical procedure. A procedure for reading aloud that is based on information acquired about the pronunciation of specific written words.

Nonlexical procedure. A procedure for reading aloud that is based on the general rules of pronunciation of a language.

Dyslexia. A specific pathological difficulty in reading, one that does not result from general visual, motor, or intellectual deficits.

Surface dyslexia. A reading disorder in which the lexical procedure is disrupted while the nonlexical procedure is not.

Deep dyslexia. A reading disorder in which the nonlexical procedure is disrupted while the lexical procedure is not.

Hemispherectomy. The removal of one cerebral hemisphere.

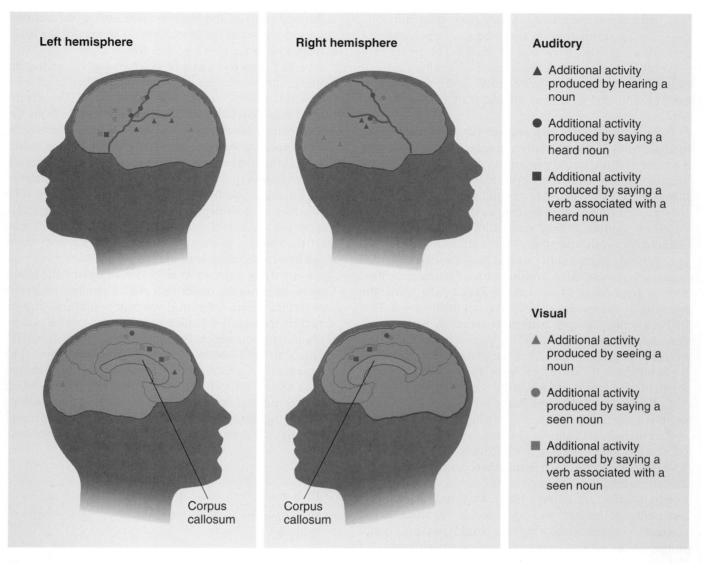

Left hemisphere

Right hemisphere

Auditory

▲ Additional activity produced by hearing a noun

● Additional activity produced by saying a heard noun

■ Additional activity produced by saying a verb associated with a heard noun

Visual

▲ Additional activity produced by seeing a noun

● Additional activity produced by saying a seen noun

■ Additional activity produced by saying a verb associated with a seen noun

Corpus callosum

Corpus callosum

Figure 16.17 A summary of the results of Petersen et al.'s (1989) PET scan study of language localization.

ditions were identical to the four visual conditions except that tape-recorded nouns were played to the subjects while they stared at the crosshair.

After the data in these visual and auditory tests had been collected, three levels of subtraction were performed on the images recorded during the tests. The activity during the fixation-only condition was subtracted from that during the passive-noun condition to get a measure of the activation produced by passively observing or hearing the nouns. The activity during the passive-noun condition was subtracted from that during the saying-noun condition to get a measure of the activation produced by saying the noun. And the activity during the saying-noun condition was subtracted from that during the verb-association condition to get a measure of the activation produced by the cognitive processes involved in forming the association.

The results of Petersen et al.'s study are summarized in Figure 16.17. First, the presentation of printed nouns added activity in the secondary visual cortex of both hemispheres, and the presentation of auditory nouns added activity in the secondary auditory cortex of both hemispheres. Second, regardless of whether the nouns were presented in printed or auditory form, repeating them aloud added activity in the somatosensory and motor areas along the central fissures of both hemispheres and along the lateral fissure of the right hemisphere. And third, regardless of whether the words were presented in a printed or auditory form, the verb-association condition added activity in the prefrontal cortex of the left hemisphere just in front of Broca's area and in the medial cortex of both hemispheres just above the front of the corpus callosum (i.e., in the cortex of the cingulate gyrus). The computer-generated images of these sub-

Chapter 16 Lateralization, Language, and the Split Brain

**Patterns of Activity
Identified by the
Three Auditory Subtractions**

**Patterns of Activity
Identified by the
Three Visual Subtractions**

Additional activity produced by
hearing a noun.

Additional activity produced by
seeing a noun.

Additional activity produced by
saying a heard noun.

Additional activity produced by
saying a seen noun.

Additional activity produced by
saying a verb assoicated with a
heard noun.

Additional activity produced by
saying a verb assoicated with a
seen noun.

Figure 16.18 PET scan computer images of the subtracted patterns of blood flow
from the experiment of Petersen et al. (1989). Each image represents a horizontal section of the brain averaged over all of the subjects in that condition. Anterior is toward
the top of the page; the right hemisphere is on your right, and the left hemisphere is on
your left. As shown by the adjacent scales, the highest levels of activity are indicated by
yellow, orange, red, and white (the very highest). (Courtesy of Steve Petersen.)

tracted patterns of cortical activation
averaged over all of the subjects are
presented in Figure 16.18.

What type of model do these
results support? Certainly not the
Wernicke-Geschwind model: There
was no evidence of the predicted activation in either Wernicke's area or in
the angular gyrus during the visual
tests; the *semantic* (meaning-related)
processing of verb association appeared to occur in lateral and medial
frontal cortex rather than in Wernicke's area; and there was considerable unpredicted activity in the right
hemisphere and in the midline areas
of both hemispheres.

Petersen and his colleagues assumed that adding a level of complexity to their behavioral tasks would
merely add additional areas of cortical
activity to those associated with the
simpler tasks. However, they found
that the activation that occurred
along the lateral fissure in the visual
and auditory noun-repetition conditions was largely absent in the respective verb-association conditions (see
Fiez & Petersen, 1993). On the basis of
this observation, they proposed the
following dual-route theory: When
subjects perform a highly practiced
verbal response, such as simply
repeating a written or spoken noun,
processing moves from sensory areas
to motor areas through the association cortex of the lateral fissure. In
contrast, when subjects are performing a verbal task that requires a more
complex analysis, such as in the verb-
association tasks, processing moves
from sensory to motor areas via
frontal and cingulate cortex. To test
this dual-route theory, Raichle and
colleagues (1991) assessed the effects
of practice on the cerebral activity
that mediated the performance of the
verb-association tasks. In support of
the theory, they found that just a few
minutes of practice producing verb
associations for the same list of nouns
changed the pattern of activation
from one involving frontal and cingulate areas to one involving areas along
the lateral fissure.

CONCLUSION

This chapter has been the story of two theories, one largely right and one largely wrong but both extremely important. On the one hand, Sperry's theory of brain duality and asymmetry has withstood the empirical challenge of the research it has generated. Study after study has confirmed and extended its basic tenets: that the two hemispheres of the human brain can function independently and that they possess different capacities that are normally integrated by the cerebral commissures. On the other hand, the empirical evidence has been less kind to the strict localizationist theories of language organization proposed by Broca, Wernicke, and Geschwind. Lesion, brain-stimulation, and brain-imaging studies have all failed to confirm their specific predictions.

The positive impact of the Wernicke-Geschwind model illustrates a frequently misunderstood point: Theories are important because they are useful, and they do not have to be right to be useful. The strengths of the Wernicke-Geschwind model lie in its clarity and testability. Because it is clear, scientists and students alike have found it to be a useful vehicle for organizing their thinking about the localization of language. And because it is so eminently testable, its predictions have stimulated and guided much of the research in the field. Considering that it was one of the first steps toward the solution of an extremely difficult problem, it is not at all surprising that it turned out to be flawed; but it is the mass of research that it has generated that will stand as the ultimate testimonial to its worth.

FOOD FOR THOUGHT

1. Design an experiment to show that it is possible for a human split-brain student to study for an English exam and a geometry exam at the same time by using the Z lens.

2. The decision to perform commissurotomies on epileptic patients turned out to be a good one; the decision to perform prefrontal lobotomies on mental patients (see Chapter 1) turned out to be a bad one. Was this just the luck of the draw? Discuss.

KEY TERMS

Cerebral commissures
(p. 411)
Lateralization of function
(p. 411)
Split-brain patients (p. 411)
Commissurotomy (p. 411)
Aphasia (p. 412)
Broca's area (p. 412)
Apraxia (p. 412)
Dominant hemisphere
(p. 412)
Minor hemisphere (p. 412)
Sodium amytal test (p. 412)
Dichotic listening test
(p. 413)

Dextrals (p. 414)
Sinestrals (p. 414)
Corpus callosum (p. 415)
Scotoma (p. 416)
Cross-cuing (p. 419)
Helping-hand phenomenon
(p. 419)
Visual completion (p. 419)
Chimeric figures test
(p. 419)
Z lens (p. 420)
Planum temporale (p. 423)
Heschl's gyrus (p. 423)
Frontal operculum (p. 423)

Wernicke-Geschwind model
(p. 425)
Wernicke's area (p. 425)
Expressive (p. 425)
Broca's aphasia (p. 425)
Receptive (p. 425)
Wernicke's aphasia (p. 425)
Word salad (p. 425)
Arcuate fasciculus (p. 425)
Conduction aphasia (p. 425)
Angular gyrus (p. 426)
Alexia (p. 426)
Agraphia (p. 426)
Serial model (p. 427)
Parallel models (p. 427)

Global aphasia (p. 430)
Phonemes (p. 432)
Phonological analysis
(p. 432)
Grammatical analysis
(p. 432)
Semantic analysis (p. 432)
Lexical procedure (p. 432)
Nonlexical procedure
(p. 432)
Dyslexia (p. 432)
Surface dyslexia (p. 432)
Deep dyslexia (p. 432)
Hemispherectomy (p. 433)

ADDITIONAL READING

The following papers provide reviews of some of the current issues in the study of cerebral laterality and language localization:

Brown, H. D., & Kosslyn, S. M. (1993). Cerebral lateralization. *Current Opinion in Neurobiology, 3,* 183–186.

Fiez, J. A., & Petersen, S. E. (1993). PET as part of an interdisciplinary approach to understanding processes involved in reading. *Psychological Science, 4,* 287–293.

MacNeilage, P. F., Studdert-Kennedy, M. G., & Lindblom, B. (1993, January–February). Hand signals: Right side, left brain, and the origin of language. *The Sciences,* 32–37.

Maratsos, M., & Matheny, L. (1994). Language specificity and elasticity: Brain and clinical syndrome studies. *Annual Review of Psychology, 45,* 487–516.

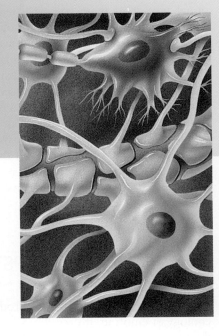

CHAPTER 17

Biopsychology of Emotion, Stress, and Mental Illness

17.1   Biopsychology of Emotion

17.2   Fear, Defense, and Aggression

17.3   Stress and Health

17.4   Schizophrenia

17.5   Affective Disorders: Depression and Mania

17.6   Anxiety Disorders

Conscious experience is saturated with emotion. The emotional impact of major personal events—such as getting married, being in a car accident, moving to a new city, or a friend dying—can be overwhelming. But even relatively minor experiences can trigger strong emotional reactions. Think of how you felt the last time you misplaced your keys, met somebody you really liked, "aced" an exam, bought a bouquet of flowers, or argued with a friend. Notice how just thinking about such past events can rekindle some of the original emotional experience. Biopsychological research on emotions is the glue that binds this chapter together.

The chapter begins with a general introduction to biopsychological research on emotions, but it soon begins to concentrate on the darker end of the emotional spectrum: fear and anxiety. Biopsychological research on emotions has concentrated on these negative *affective* (emotional) states, not because biopsychologists are a perverse lot but because of the major impact that these states have on our health and well-being. The stress associated with fear and anxiety can increase our susceptibility to a wide range of physical diseases, including ulcers and infections, and to numerous psychological disorders (see Stout & Nemeroff, 1994), including the three that you will learn about in this chapter: schizophrenia, affective disorders, and anxiety disorders.

17.1 Biopsychology of Emotion

This section provides a general introduction to the biopsychology of emotion. It describes several of the classic early discoveries, and then it discusses the role of the autonomic nervous system in emotional experience, the facial expression of emotion, and the effects of cortical damage on emotion.

Early Progress in the Biopsychological Study of Emotion

Many of the early advances in the biopsychological study of emotion were related to the following topics: Darwin's theory of the evolution of emotion, the James-Lange and Cannon-Bard theories of emotion, sham rage, the limbic system, and the Kluver-Bucy syndrome.

Darwin's theory of the evolution of emotion The first major event in the study of the biopsychology of emotion was the publication in 1872 of Darwin's book *The Expression of Emotions in Man and Animals*. In it, Darwin argued, largely on the basis of anecdotal evidence, that particular emotional responses, such as human facial expressions, tend to accompany the same emotional states in all members of a species.

Darwin believed that expressions of emotion, like other behaviors, are products of evolution; he therefore tried to understand them by comparing them in different species. From such interspecies comparisons, Darwin developed a theory of the evolution of emotional expression that was composed of three main ideas: (1) that expressions of emotion evolve from behaviors that indicate what an animal is likely to do next; (2) that if the signals provided by such behaviors benefit the animal that displays them, they will evolve in ways that enhance their communicative function, and their original function may be lost; and (3) that opposite messages are often signaled by opposite movements and postures (the *principle of antithesis*).

Consider how Darwin's theory accounts for the evolution of *threat displays*. Originally, facing one's enemies, rising up, and exposing one's weapons were the components of the early stages of combat. But once enemies began to recognize these behaviors as signals of impending aggression, a survival advantage accrued to attackers that could communicate their aggression most effectively and intimidate their victims without actually fighting. As a result, elaborate threat displays evolved and actual combat declined.

To be most effective, signals of aggression and submission must be clearly distinguishable; thus they tended to evolve in opposite directions. For example, gulls signal aggression by pointing their beaks at one another and submission by pointing their beaks away from one another, and primates signal aggression by staring and submission by averting their gaze. Figure 17.1 is a reproduction of the actual woodcuts that Darwin used in his 1872 book to illustrate this principle of antithesis in dogs.

James-Lange and Cannon-Bard theories The first physiological theory of emotion was proposed independently by James and Lange in 1884. According to the **James-Lange theory**, emotion-inducing sensory stimuli are received and interpreted by the cortex, which triggers changes in the visceral organs via the autonomic nervous system and in the skeletal muscles via the somatic nervous system. Then, the autonomic and somatic responses trigger the experience of emotion in the brain. In effect, what the James-Lange theory did was to reverse the usual common sense way of thinking about the causal relation between the experience of emotion and its expression. James and Lange argued that the autonomic activity and behavior that are triggered by the emotional event (e.g., rapid heartbeat and running away) produce the feeling of emotion, not vice versa.

Figure 17.1 Two woodcuts from Darwin's 1872 book, *The Expression of Emotions in Man and Animals,* that he used to illustrate the principle of antithesis. The aggressive posture of dogs features ears forward, back up, hair up, and tail up; the submissive posture features ears back, back down, hair down, and tail down.

In the early 1900s, Cannon proposed an alternative to the James-Lange theory of emotion, and it was subsequently extended and promoted by Bard. According to the **Cannon-Bard theory,** emotional stimuli have two independent excitatory effects: They excite both the feeling of emotion in the brain and the expression of emotion in the autonomic and somatic nervous systems. Accordingly, the Cannon-Bard theory, in contrast to the James-Lange theory, views emotional experience and emotional expression as parallel processes that have no direct causal relation.

The James-Lange and Cannon-Bard theories make different predictions about the role of feedback from autonomic and somatic nervous system activity in emotional experience. According to the James-Lange theory, emotional experience depends entirely on feedback from autonomic and somatic nervous system activity; according to the Cannon-Bard theory, emotional experience is totally independent of such feedback. Both extreme positions have proved to be incorrect. On the one hand, it seems that the autonomic and somatic feedback is not necessary for the experience of emotion: Human patients whose autonomic and somatic feedback has been largely eliminated by a broken neck are capable of a full range of emotional experiences (e.g., Lowe & Carroll, 1985). On the other hand, there have been numerous reports—some of which you will soon encounter—that autonomic and somatic responses to emotional stimuli can influence emotional experience. Failure to find unqualified support for either the James-Lange or the Cannon-Bard theory has led to the view that each of the three principal factors in an emotional response—the perception of the emotion-inducing stimulus, the autonomic and somatic responses to the stimulus, and the experience of the emotion—influences the other two (see Figure 17.2 on page 440).

Sham rage In the late 1920s, Bard (1929) discovered that **decorticate** cats—cats whose cortex has been removed—respond aggressively to the slightest provocation: After a light touch, they arch their backs, erect their hair, growl, hiss, and expose their teeth. The aggressive responses of decorticate animals are abnormal in two respects: They are inappropriately severe, and they are not directed at particular targets. Bard referred to the exaggerated, poorly directed aggressive responses of decorticate animals as **sham rage.**

Sham rage can be elicited in cats whose cerebral hemispheres have been removed down to, but not including, the hypothalamus; but it cannot be elicited if the hypothalamus is also removed. On the basis of this observation, Bard concluded that the hypothalamus is critical for the expression of aggressive responses and that the function of the cortex is to inhibit and direct these responses.

Limbic system and emotion In 1937, Papez (pronounced "Payps") proposed that emotional expression is controlled by several interconnected neural structures that

James-Lange theory. The theory that emotional experience results from the brain's perception of the pattern of autonomic and somatic nervous system responses elecited by emotional stimuli.

Cannon-Bard theory. The theory that emotional experience and emotional expression are parallel processes that have no direct causal relation.

Decorticate. Lacking a cortex.

Sham rage. The exaggerated, poorly directed aggressive responses of decorticate animals.

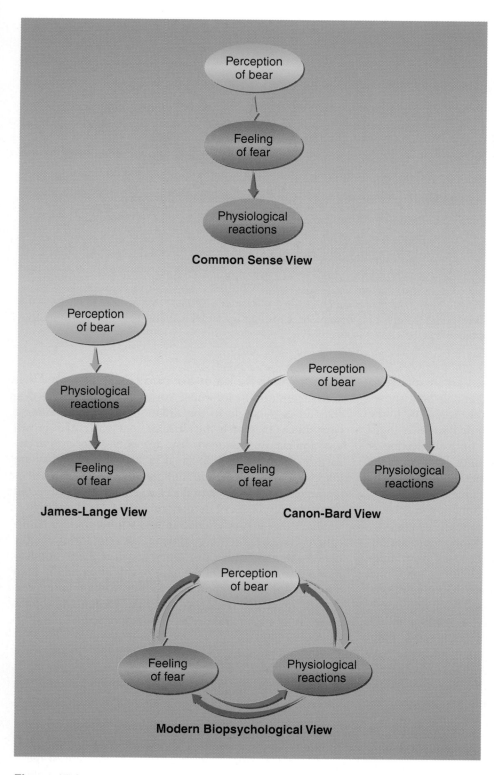

Figure 17.2 Four ways of thinking about the relations among the perception of emotion-inducing stimuli, the autonomic and somatic responses to the stimuli, and the emotional experience.

campus, fornix, cingulate cortex, septum, olfactory bulb, and hypothalamus (see Macchi, 1989). Papez proposed that emotional states are expressed through the action of the other limbic structures on the hypothalamus and that they are experienced through the action of the limbic structures on the cortex.

Kluver-Bucy syndrome In 1939, Kluver and Bucy observed a striking *syndrome* (pattern of behavior) in monkeys that had had their anterior temporal lobes removed. This syndrome, which is commonly referred to as the **Kluver-Bucy syndrome,** includes the following behaviors: the consumption of almost anything that is edible, increased sexual activity often directed at inappropriate objects, a tendency to repeatedly investigate familiar objects, a tendency to investigate objects with the mouth, and a lack of fear. Monkeys that could not be handled before surgery were transformed by bilateral anterior temporal lobectomy into tame subjects that showed no fear whatsoever—even in response to snakes, which terrify normal monkeys. In primates, most of the symptoms of the Kluver-Bucy syndrome appear to result from amygdala damage.

The Kluver-Bucy syndrome has been observed in several species. Following is a description of the syndrome in a human patient with a brain infection:

> He exhibited a flat affect, and although originally restless, ultimately became remarkably placid. He appeared indifferent to people or situations. He spent much time gazing at the television, but never learned to turn it on; when the set was off, he tended to watch reflections of others in the room on the glass screen. On occasion he became facetious, smiling inappropriately and mimicking the gestures and actions of others. Once initiating an imitative series, he would perseverate copying all movements made by another for extend-

he referred to as the limbic system. The **limbic system** is a collection of nuclei and tracts that borders the thalamus (*limbic* means "border"). Figure 17.3 illustrates some of its key structures: the amygdala, mammillary body, hippo-

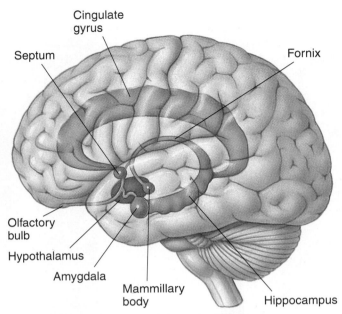

Figure 17.3 The location of the major limbic system structures in a midline ring around the thalamus. (See also Figure 3.30.)

ed periods of time.... He engaged in oral exploration of all objects within his grasp, appearing unable to gain information via tactile or visual means alone. All objects that he could lift were placed in his mouth and sucked or chewed....

Although vigorously heterosexual prior to his illness, he was observed in hospital to make advances toward other male patients.... [H]e never made advances toward women, and, in fact, his apparent reversal of sexual polarity prompted his fiancée to sever their relationship (Marlowe, Mancall, & Thomas, 1985, pp. 55–56).

Emotions and the Autonomic Nervous System

Research on the role of the autonomic nervous system (ANS) in emotion has focused on two issues: the degree to which specific patterns of ANS activity are associated with specific emotions and the effectiveness of ANS measures in polygraphy.

Emotional specificity of the autonomic nervous system The James-Lange and Cannon-Bard theories differ in their views of the emotional specificity of the autonomic nervous system. The James-Lange theory is that different emotional stimuli induce different patterns of ANS activity and that these different patterns produce different emotional experiences. In contrast, the Cannon-Bard theory is that all emotional stimuli produce the same general pattern of sympathetic activation, which prepares the organism for action (i.e., increased heart rate, increased blood pressure, pupil dilation, increased flow of blood to the mus-

cles, increased respiration, and increased release of epinephrine and norepinephrine from the adrenal medulla).

The experimental evidence suggests that the specificity of ANS reactions lies somewhere between the extremes of total specificity and total generality. There is ample evidence that not all emotions are associated with the same pattern of ANS activity (see Ax, 1955); however, there is insufficient evidence to make a strong case for the view that each emotion is characterized by a different pattern of ANS activity.

Polygraphy **Polygraphy** is a method of interrogation that employs autonomic nervous system indexes of emotion to infer the truthfulness of the subject's responses. Polygraph tests administered by skilled examiners can be useful additions to normal interrogation procedures, but they are not infallible (Iacono & Patrick, 1987).

The main problem in evaluating the effectiveness of polygraphy is that it is rarely possible in real-life situations to know for certain whether the suspect is guilty or innocent. Consequently, many studies of polygraphy have employed the *mock-crime procedure:* Volunteer subjects participate in a mock crime and are then subjected to a polygraph test by an examiner who is unaware of their "guilt" or "innocence." The usual interrogation method is the **control-question technique.** In this technique, the physiological response to the target question (e.g., Did you steal that purse?) is compared with the responses to control questions whose answers are known (e.g., Have you ever been in jail before?). The assumption is that lying will be associated with greater sympathetic activation. The average success rate in various mock-crime studies using the control-question technique is about 80%.

Despite being commonly referred to as *lie detection,* polygraphy detects emotions, not lies. Consequently, in real life situations, questions such as "Did you steal that purse?" are likely to elicit a reaction from all suspects, regardless of their guilt or innocence, making it difficult to detect decep-

Limbic system. A collection of interconnected nuclei and tracts that circles the thalamus and plays a role in emotion.

Kluver-Bucy syndrome. The syndrome of behavioral changes (e.g., lack of fear and hypersexuality) that is induced in primates by bilateral damage to the anterior temporal lobes.

Polygraphy. A method of interrogation in which autonomic nervous system indexes of emotion are used to infer the truthfulness of the responses.

Control-question technique. A lie-detection technique in which the polygrapher compares the responses to target questions with the responses to control questions.

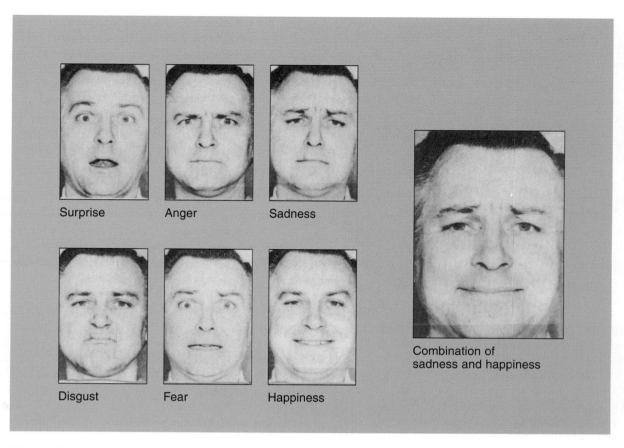

Figure 17.4 Examples of the six facial expressions that Ekman and Friesen (1975) considered to be primary: surprise, anger, sadness, disgust, fear, and happiness. All other emotional facial expressions were considered to be combinations of these six. For example, shown here on the right is an expression you might make while visiting a sick friend; it is a combination of sadness in the upper half of the face and happiness in the lower half.

tion. Lykken (1959) developed the **guilty-knowledge technique** to circumvent this problem. In order to use this technique, the polygrapher must have a piece of information concerning the crime that would be known only to the guilty person. Rather than attempting to catch the suspect in a lie, the polygrapher simply assesses the suspect's reaction to a list of actual and contrived details of the crime. Innocent parties, because they have no knowledge of the crime, react to all such details in the same way; the guilty react differently.

In one study of the guilty-knowledge technique (Lykken's, 1959), subjects waited until the occupant of an office went to the washroom. Then, they entered her office, stole her purse from her desk, removed the money, and left the purse in a locker. The critical part of the interrogation went something like this: "Where do you think that we found the purse? In the washroom?... In a locker? ... Hanging on a coat rack? ..." Even though electrodermal activity was the only measure of ANS activity used in this study, 88% of the mock criminals were correctly identified and more importantly none of the innocent parties was judged guilty.

Emotions and Facial Expression

Ekman and his colleagues have been preeminent in the study of facial expression (see Ekman, 1992, 1993). They began in the 1960s by analyzing hundreds of films and photographs of people experiencing various real emotions. From these, they compiled an atlas of the facial expressions that are normally associated with different emotions (Ekman & Friesen, 1975). The facial expressions in Ekman and Friesen's atlas are not photographs of people experiencing genuine emotions. They are photographs of models who were instructed to contract specific facial muscles on the basis of Ekman and Friesen's analysis. For example, to produce the facial expression for surprise, models were instructed to pull their brows upward so as to wrinkle their forehead, to open their eyes wide so as to reveal white above the iris, to slacken the muscles around their mouth, and to drop their jaw. Try it.

Universality of facial expression Despite Darwin's assertion that people in all parts of the world make similar facial expressions, it was widely believed that facial expres-

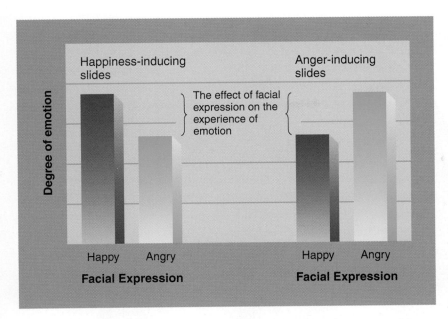

Figure 17.5 The effects of facial expression on the feeling of emotion. Subjects reported feeling more happy and less angry when they viewed slides while making a happy face, and less happy and more angry when they viewed slides while making an angry face. (Adapted from Rutledge & Hupka, 1985.)

sions are learned and culturally variable. Then, several empirical studies showed that people of different cultures do indeed make similar facial expressions in similar situations and that they can correctly identify the emotional significance of facial expressions displayed by people of other cultures (e.g., Ekman, Sorenson, & Friesen, 1969; Izard, 1971). The most convincing of these studies was a study of the members of an isolated New Guinea tribe who had had little or no contact with the outside world (Ekman & Friesen, 1971). Although these findings support Darwin's view of the universality of facial expressions, they do not deny the possibility of minor cultural differences.

Primary facial expressions   Ekman and Friesen concluded that the facial expressions of the following six emotions are primary: surprise, anger, sadness, disgust, fear, and happiness. They further concluded that all other facial expressions of genuine emotion are composed of predictable mixtures of the six primaries. In Figure 17.4, Ekman himself illustrates the six primary facial expressions and their combination to form a nonprimary expression.

Facial feedback   Is there any truth to the old idea that putting on a happy face can make you feel better? Recent research suggests that there is (see Adelmann & Zajonc, 1989). The hypothesis that our facial expressions influence our emotional experience is called the **facial feedback hypothesis.**

In a test of the facial feedback hypothesis, Rutledge and Hupka (1985) instructed subjects to assume one of two patterns of facial contractions while they viewed a series of slides; the patterns corresponded to happy or angry faces,

although the subjects were unaware of it. The subjects reported that the slides made them feel more happy and less angry when they were making happy faces, and less happy and more angry when they were making angry faces (see Figure 17.5). Why don't you try it? Pull your eyebrows down and together; raise your upper eyelids and tighten your lower eyelids, and narrow your lips and press them together. Now, hold this expression for a few seconds. If it makes you feel slightly angry, you have just experienced the effect of facial feedback.

Voluntary control of facial expression
Because we can exert voluntary control over our facial muscles, it is possible to inhibit true facial expressions and to substitute false ones. There are many reasons for choosing to put on a false facial expression. Some of them are positive (e.g., putting on a false smile to reassure a worried friend), and some are negative (e.g., putting on a false smile to disguise a lie). In either case, it is difficult to fool an expert.

There are two ways of distinguishing true expressions from false ones (Ekman, 1985). First, *microexpressions* (brief facial expressions) of the real emotion often break through the false one. Such microexpressions last only about 0.05 second, but with practice they can be detected without the aid of slow-motion photography. Second, there are often subtle differences between genuine facial expressions and false ones that can be detected by skilled observers.

The most widely studied difference between a genuine and a false facial expression was first described by the French anatomist Duchenne in 1862. Duchenne said that the smile of enjoyment could be distinguished from deliberately produced smiles by consideration of the two facial muscles that are contracted during genuine smiles: *orbicularis oculi*, which encircles the eye and pulls the skin from the cheeks and forehead toward the eyeball, and *zygomaticus major*, which pulls the lip corners up (see Figure 17.6). According to Duchenne, the zygomaticus major can be controlled voluntarily, whereas the orbicularis oculi is normally contracted only by genuine pleasure. Thus inertia of

Guilty-knowledge technique. A lie-detection technique in which the polygrapher records autonomic nervous system responses to control and crime-related information known only to the criminal and the examiners.

Facial feedback hypothesis. The hypothesis that our facial expressions can influence how we feel.

the orbicularis oculi in smiling unmasks a false friend—a fact you would do well to remember. Ekman named the genuine smile the **Duchenne smile** (see Ekman & Davidson, 1993).

Not all emotions are accompanied by changes in facial expression—as any good poker player will tell you. However, *facial electromyography (EMG)* can detect changes in the motor input to facial muscles that are too slight to produce observable changes in muscle contraction (see Tassinary & Cacioppo, 1992). For example, Cacioppo and colleagues (1986) recorded the EMG activity of several facial muscles while the subjects viewed slides. Although facial expressions were seldom evoked, the EMG activity was related to how much the subjects reported that they liked each slide. For example, the smile muscles—the orbicularis oculi and the zygomaticus major—tended to be more active while the subjects were viewing slides that they judged to be pleasant.

Orbicularis occuli

Zygomaticus major

Figure 17.6 The orbicularis oculi and zygomaticus major, two muscles that contract during genuine (Duchenne) smiles. Because the lateral portion of the orbicularis oculi is difficult for most people to contract voluntarily, fake smiles usually lack this component.

Effects of Cortical Damage on Human Emotion

The pop psychology industry has spread the view that human emotion is a single faculty that resides exclusively within the right hemisphere. The incorrectness of this view is illustrated by the effects of cortical damage on both the perception and the expression of emotions (see Pizzamiglio, Caltagirone, & Zoccaoloti, 1989).

Cortical damage and perception of emotional stimuli It is difficult to imagine how anybody could function effectively in this world without being able to recognize the emotions of others. There is evidence (see Etcoff, 1989; Bowers et al., 1987) of right-hemisphere dominance for the perception of facial expression and **prosody** (emotional tone of voice); for example, right-hemisphere lesions tend to disrupt the perception of facial expression and prosody more than left-hemisphere lesions. However, this does not mean that the left hemisphere does not play a role. Kolb and Taylor (1988) found that right temporal and right frontal cortical lesions disrupted the perception of facial expression, but so too did left frontal lesions (see Figure 17.7).

Cortical damage and expression of emotion A few studies of patients with unilateral brain damage have found a right-hemisphere dominance for emotional ex-

Duchenne smile. A genuine smile, one that includes contraction of the orbicularis oculi muscles.

Prosody. Emotional tone of voice.

Fear. The emotion that is normally elicited by the presence or expectation of threatening stimuli.

Defensive behaviors. Behaviors whose primary function is protection from threat or harm.

Aggressive behaviors. Behaviors whose primary function is to threaten or harm other organisms.

Ethoexperimental research. The systematic analysis of behavioral sequences in seminatural laboratory environments.

Alpha male. The dominant male of a colony.

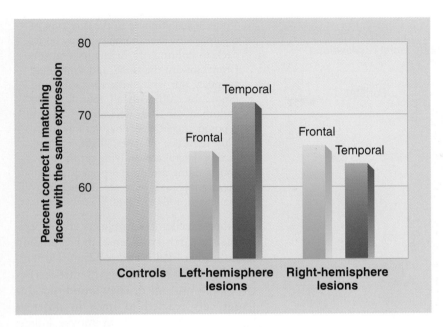

Figure 17.7 The ability of control subjects and patients with cortical damage to match photographs of faces on the basis of expression. (Adapted from Kolb & Taylor, 1988.)

pression (e.g., Caltagirone et al., 1989; Tucker, 1981), but many more have not. Studies by Kolb and his colleagues

suggest that whether or not right-hemisphere lesions disrupt emotional expression more than left-hemisphere lesions depends on the location of the lesions within the hemispheres and on the particular measure of emotional expression.

Kolb and his colleagues (Kolb & Milner, 1981; Kolb & Taylor, 1981) compared the effects of left or right frontal, parietal, or temporal lesions on two measures of emotion: the frequency of spontaneous talking and the frequency of facial expressions. The results are illustrated in Figure 17.8. There was no evidence of lateralization of facial expression, but there was evidence of localization: Frontal lobe lesions significantly reduced the number of facial expressions relative to temporal and parietal lesions irrespective of the hemisphere in which they were located. In contrast, there was evidence of both lateralization and localization of talking frequency. Patients with left frontal lesions talked less than patients with left or right temporal or parietal lesions, and patients with right frontal lesions talked more.

<table>
<tr><td>**17.2**</td><td>Fear, Defense, and Aggression</td></tr>
</table>

Biopsychological research on emotion has focused to a large degree on fear. One reason for this focus—as will become more apparent as the chapter progresses—is the major role played by chronic fear in the development of disease. **Fear** is the emotional reaction to threat; it is the motivating force for defensive behaviors. **Defensive behaviors** are behaviors whose primary function is to protect the organism from threat or harm: In contrast, **aggressive behaviors** are behaviors whose primary function is to threaten or harm.

Types of Aggressive and Defensive Behaviors

Considerable progress in the understanding of aggressive and defensive behaviors has come from **ethoexperimental research**—research that focuses on the systematic description of behavior sequences observed in controlled laboratory environments that have been structured to mimic key features of the subjects' natural environment (see Blanchard et al., 1989). Ethoexperimental research has shown that aggressive and defensive behaviors in the same species come in a variety of standard forms, each of which occurs

in different situations, serves different functions, and has different neural and hormonal bases.

The research of Blanchard and Blanchard (see 1989, 1990a, 1990b) on the *colony model of aggression and defense* is an excellent example of ethoexperimental research in the rat. Blanchard and Blanchard have derived rich descriptions of rat intraspecific aggressive and defensive behaviors by studying the interactions between the **alpha male**—the dominant male—of an established mixed-sex colony and a small male intruder:

> The alpha approaches the stranger and sniffs at its perianal area.... If the intruder is an adult male, the alpha's sniff leads to piloerection....
>
> Shortly after piloerecting, the alpha male usually bites the intruder, and the intruder runs away. The alpha chases after it, and after one or two additional bites, the intruder stops running and turns to face its attacker. It rears up on its hind legs, using its forelimbs to push off the alpha.... However, rather than standing nose to nose with the "boxing" intruder, the attacking rat abruptly moves to a lateral orientation, with the long axis of its body perpendicular to the front of the defending rat.... It moves sideways toward the intruder, crowding and sometimes pushing it off balance. If the defending rat stands solid against this "lateral

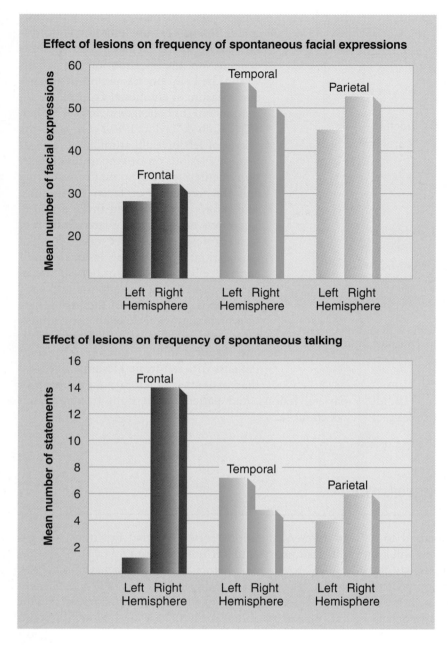

Figure 17.8 The effects of left or right frontal, temporal, or parietal lesions on the frequency of spontaneous talking and facial expressions. (Kolb & Milner, 1981; Kolb & Taylor, 1981.)

fender usually moves in the direction of the attacker's head, rolling slightly on its back to continue to orient its ventrum [front] toward the alpha, and continuing to push off with both forelimbs and hindlimbs. Although all four legs and abdomen of the defending rat are exposed, the attacker does not bite them. This sequence of bites, flight, chasing, boxing, lateral attack, lying on the back, and standing on top is repeated ... until the stranger rat is removed. (Blanchard & Blanchard, 1984, pp. 8–9)[1]

Another excellent example of ethoexperimental research on defense and aggression is the study of Pellis and colleagues (1988). They began by videotaping interactions between cats and mice. They found that different cats reacted to mice in different ways: Some were efficient mouse killers, some reacted defensively, and some seemed to play with the mice. Careful analysis of the "play" sequences led to two important conclusions. The first conclusion was that, in contrast to the common belief, cats do not play with their prey; the cats that appeared to be playing with the mice were simply vacillating between attack and defense. The second conclusion was that one can best understand each cat's interactions with mice by locating the interactions on a linear scale, with total aggressiveness at one end, total defensiveness at the other, and various proportions of the two in-between.

Pellis and colleagues tested their conclusions by reducing the defensiveness of the cats with an antianxiety drug. As predicted, the drug moved each cat along the scale toward more efficient killing. Cats that avoided mice before the injection played with them after the injection, those that played with them before the injection killed them after the injection, and those that killed them before the injection killed them more quickly after the injection. The next time you play with a cat, take the opportunity to analyze the cat's behavior in the light of Pellis's observations.

The defensive and aggressive behaviors of rats have been divided into categories on the basis of three different criteria: (1) their *topography* (form), (2) the situations that elicit

attack" movement, the alpha may make a quick lunge forward and around the defender's body to bite at its back. In response to such a lunge, the defender usually pivots on its hind feet, in the same direction as the attacker is moving, continuing its frontal orientation to the attacker. If the defending rat moves quickly enough, no bite will be made.

However, after a number of instances of the lateral attack, and especially if the attacker has succeeded in biting the intruder, the stranger rat may roll backward slowly from the boxing position, to lie on its back. The attacker then takes up a position on top of the supine animal, digging with its forepaws at the intruder's sides. If the attacker can turn the other animal over, or expose some portion of its back, ... it bites. In response to these efforts, the de-

---

[1]From "Affect and Aggression: An Animal Model Applied to Human Behavior" by D. C. Blanchard and R. J. Blanchard in *Advances in the Study of Aggression,* Vol. 1, 1984, edited by D. C. Blanchard and R. J. Blanchard. San Diego: Academic Press. Copyright 1984 by Academic Press. Reprinted by permission.

them, and (3) their apparent function. Several of these categories are described in Table 17.1.

The ethoexperimental analysis of aggressive and defensive behavior has led to the development of the **target-site concept**—the idea that the aggressive and defensive behaviors of an animal are often designed to attack specific sites on the body of another animal while protecting specific sites on its own. For example, the behavior of a socially aggressive rat (e.g., lateral attack) appears to be designed to deliver bites to the defending rat's back and to protect its own face, the likely target of a defensive attack. Conversely, most of the maneuvers of the defending rat (e.g., boxing) appear to be designed to protect the target site on its back. The emergence of the target-site concept illustrates what ethoexperimental analysis is all about. Ethoexperimentalists study the details of behavioral sequences not to accumulate libraries full of behavioral minutiae but to extract simple explanatory principles (see Pellis, 1989).

The discovery that aggressive and defensive behaviors occur in a variety of stereotypical species-common forms was the necessary first step in the identification of their neural bases. Because the different categories of aggressive and defensive behavior are mediated by different neural circuits, little progress was made in identifying these circuits before the categories were delineated (see Albert & Walsh, 1984; Davis, Rainnie, & Cassell, 1994; Kalin, 1993). For example, the lateral septum was once believed to inhibit all aggression because lateral septal lesions rendered laboratory rats notoriously difficult to handle—the behavior of the septal rats

TABLE 17.1	
Categories of Aggressive and Defensive Behavior in the Rat	

Aggressive Behaviors	
Predatory aggression	The stalking and killing of members of other species for the purpose of eating them. Rats kill prey, such as mice and frogs, by delivering bites to the back of the neck.
Social aggression	Unprovoked aggressive behavior that is directed at a conspecific for the purpose of establishing, altering, or maintaining a social hierarchy. In mammals, social aggression occurs primarily among males. In rats, it is characterized by piloerection, lateral attack, and bites directed at the defender's back.

Defensive Behaviors	
Intraspecific defense	Defense against social aggression. In rats, it is characterized by freezing and flight and by various behaviors, such as boxing, that are specifically designed to protect the back from bites.
Defensive attacks	Attacks that are launched by animals when they are cornered by threatening conspecifics or members of other species. In rats, they include lunging, shrieking, and biting attacks that are usually directed at the face of the attacker.
Freezing and flight	Responses that many animals use to avoid attack. For example, if a human approaches a wild rat, it will often freeze until the human penetrates its safety zone, whereupon it will explode into flight.
Maternal defensive behaviors	The behaviors by which mothers protect their young. Despite their defensive function, they are similar to male social aggression in appearance.
Risk assessment	Behaviors that are performed by animals in order to obtain specific information that helps them defend themselves more effectively. For example, rats that have been chased by a cat into their burrow do not emerge until they have spent considerable time at the entrance scanning the surrounding environment.
Defensive burying	Rats and other rodents spray sand and dirt ahead with their forepaws to bury dangerous objects in their environment, to drive off predators, and to construct barriers in burrows.

was commonly referred to as *septal aggression* or *septal rage*. However, we now know that lateral septal lesions do not increase experimenter-directed aggression: Rats with lateral septal lesions do not initiate more attacks at the experimenter if they are left undisturbed. However, they do initiate more defensive attacks and predatory aggression, but less social aggression.

Aggression and Testosterone

The fact that social aggression in many species occurs more commonly among males than among females is usually explained with reference to the organizational and activa-

Target-site concept. The idea that many of the species-specific sequences of attack and defense can be reduced to the fact that animals are trying to attack a specific site on the other animal's body, to protect a specific site on their own, or both.

tional effects of testosterone. The brief period of testosterone release that occurs around birth in genetic males is thought to organize their nervous systems along masculine lines and hence to create the potential for male patterns of social aggression to be activated by the high testosterone levels that are present after puberty. These organizational and activational effects have been demonstrated in many nonprimate mammalian species. For example, neonatal castration of male mice eliminates the ability of testosterone injections to induce social aggression in adulthood, and adult castration eliminates social aggression in males that do not receive testosterone replacement injections.

In contrast to the research on nonprimates, attempts to demonstrate the organizational and activational effects of testosterone on the aggressive behavior of humans have been largely negative (Meyer-Bahlburg, 1981). For example, in human males, aggressive behavior does not increase at puberty as testosterone levels increase, it is not eliminated by castration, and it is not increased by testosterone injections (see Albert, Walsh, & Jonik, 1993). A few studies have found that violent criminals tend to have slightly higher testosterone levels than nonviolent criminals; however, this weak correlation likely reflects the fact that aggressive encounters increase testosterone, rather than vice versa (see Archer, 1991).

The fact that human aggression is testosterone-independent could mean that its hormonal and neural regulation differs from the regulation in nonprimate mammalian species. However, Albert, Walsh, and Jonik (1993) believe that the evidence favors a different conclusion. They contend that the confusion has arisen because the researchers who study human aggression often fail to appreciate the difference between defensive aggression and social aggression. Most aggressive outbursts in humans are overreactions to real or perceived threat, and they are thus more appropriately viewed as defensive attack than social aggression. Consequently, the failure to find positive correlations between human aggressive behavior and testosterone levels is consistent with the failure to find positive correlations between defensive attack and testosterone levels in other species.

Neural Mechanisms of Conditioned Fear

Efforts to identify the neural mechanisms of fear have focused on the study of **fear conditioning.** In the usual fear-conditioning experiment, the subject, typically a rat, hears a tone and then receives a mild electric shock to its feet. After several pairings of the tone conditional stimulus and the shock unconditional stimulus, the rat responds to the tone with a variety of defensive behaviors (e.g., freezing and increased susceptibility to startle) and sympathetic nervous system responses (e.g., increased heart rate and blood pressure). LeDoux and his colleagues have mapped

the neural system that mediates this form of auditory fear conditioning (see LeDoux, 1994, 1995).

LeDoux and his colleagues began their search for the neural mechanisms of auditory fear conditioning by making lesions in the auditory pathways. They found that bilateral lesions to the *medial geniculate nucleus* (the auditory relay nucleus of the thalamus) blocked fear conditioning to a tone but that bilateral lesions to auditory cortex did not. This indicated that for auditory fear conditioning to occur it is necessary for signals elicited by the tone to reach the medial geniculate nucleus, but not the auditory cortex. It also indicated that a pathway from the medial geniculate nucleus to a structure other than the auditory cortex plays a key role in fear conditioning. This pathway proved to be the pathway from the medial geniculate nucleus to the amygdala. Lesions of the amygdala, like lesions of the medial geniculate nucleus, blocked fear conditioning. The amygdala receives input from all sensory systems, and it is believed to be the structure in which the emotional significance of sensory signals is learned and retained.

Several pathways carry signals from the amygdala to structures that control the various emotional responses. For example, a pathway to the periaqueductal gray of the midbrain elicits appropriate defensive responses (see Bandler & Shipley, 1994), whereas another pathway to the lateral hypothalamus elicits appropriate sympathetic responses.

The fact that auditory cortex lesions do not disrupt fear conditioning to simple tones does not mean that the auditory cortex is not involved in auditory fear conditioning. There are two pathways from the medial geniculate nucleus to the amygdala: the direct one, which you have already learned about, and an indirect one that projects via the auditory cortex (Romanski & LeDoux, 1992). Both routes are capable of mediating fear conditioning to simple sounds; if only one is destroyed, conditioning progresses normally. However, only the cortical route is capable of mediating fear conditioning to complex sounds (Jarrell et al., 1987).

Figure 17.9 illustrates the circuit of the brain that is thought to mediate fear conditioning to auditory conditional stimuli (see LeDoux, 1994). Sound signals from the medial geniculate nucleus of the thalamus reach the amyg-

Fear conditioning. Establishing fear of a neutral conditional stimulus by repeatedly pairing it with an aversive unconditional stimulus.

Extinction. The process by which the strength of a conditional response is reduced by repeated exposure to the conditional stimulus in the absence of the unconditional stimulus.

Stress. The physiological response to physical or psychological threat.

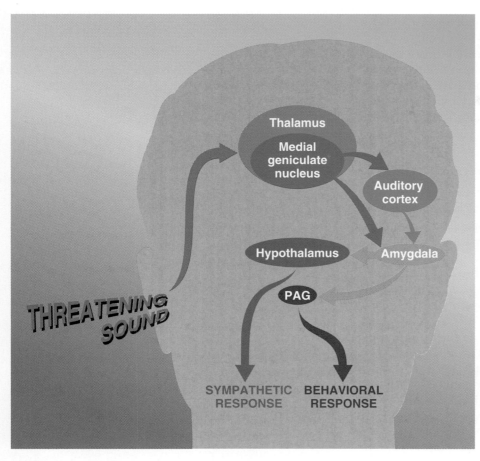

Figure 17.9 The structures that are thought to mediate the sympathetic and behavioral responses conditioned to an auditory conditional stimulus.

conditional stimulus, such as a shock. Fear responses are notoriously difficult to extinguish; nevertheless, lesions of auditory or visual cortex, which have no effect on fear conditioning to simple auditory or visual stimuli, respectively, greatly prolong the extinction of fear responses conditioned to them (e.g., Teich et al., 1989). Lesions of medial prefrontal cortex have a similar effect (Morgan et al., 1995). This suggests that the fear conditioning mediated by the amygdala is relatively indelible and that extinction of conditioned fear might be a process by which the cerebral cortex inhibits its expression.

Human Aggression, the Amygdala, and Psychosurgery

The discovery that lesions of the amygdala reduce defensive behaviors in many species (see Aggleton, 1993) led to the prescription of *amygdalectomy* (surgical destruction of the amydala) for the psychosurgical treatment of human violence. Amygdalectomy has proven effective in reducing violent behavior in some patients; nevertheless, there are good reasons for questioning its use (see Aggleton, 1993). One reason is that amygdalectomy does not always reduce violent behavior—it is difficult to justify the removal of a substantial portion of a person's brain unless the probability of a significant therapeutic effect is nearly 100%. Another reason is that amygdalectomy does not act only on violent behavior; it produces a general blunting of emotional reaction, which makes some amygdalectomized patients appear to be sedated. It may ultimately prove possible to selectively abolish violent outbursts by targeting specific nuclei in the amygdala, but this is a goal that has not yet been realized.

dala either directly or via the auditory cortex. The amygdala assesses the emotional significance of the sound on the basis of previous encounters with it, and then the amygdala activates the appropriate sympathetic and behavioral response circuits in the hypothalamus and periaqueductal gray, respectively.

Because excessive conditioned fear is thought to contribute to a variety of psychological disorders (e.g., phobias, panic, posttraumatic stress), the extinction of conditioned fear is a phenomenon of major clinical relevance. **Extinction** is the process by which the strength of a conditional response is reduced by repeated exposure to the conditional stimulus, such as a tone, in the absence of the un-

17.3 Stress and Health

When the body is exposed to harm or threat, the result is a cluster of physiological changes that is generally referred to as **stress.** All stressors, whether psychological (e.g., dismay at the loss of one's job) or physical (e.g., long-term expo-

sure to cold), produce the same core pattern of physiological changes; however, it is the stress associated with chronic fear that is of greatest relevance in this chapter. The magnitude of the stress response depends upon the stressor, the individual, and the strategies that the individual adopts to cope with the stress (McEwen, 1994). For example, in a study of women awaiting surgery for possible breast cancer, the levels of stress were lower in those who had convinced themselves that they could not possibly have cancer, that their prayers were certain to be answered, or that it was counterproductive to worry about it (Katz et al., 1970).

The Stress Response

Hans Selye (pronounced "SELL-yay") first described the stress response in the 1950s, and he quickly recognized its dual nature. In the short term, it produces adaptive changes that help the animal respond to the stressor (e.g., mobilization of energy resources, inhibition of inflammation, and resistance to infection); in the long term, however, it produces changes that are maladaptive (e.g., enlarged adrenal glands, gastric ulcers, and increased susceptibility to infection).

Selye attributed the stress response to the activation of the *anterior pituitary adrenal cortex system*. He concluded that stressors stimulate the release of **adrenocorticotropic hormone (ACTH)** from the anterior pituitary, that the ACTH in turn triggers the release of **glucocorticoids** from the **adrenal cortex,** and that the glucocorticoids produce many of the effects of the stress response. The level of circulating glucocorticoids is the most commonly employed physiological measure of stress.

With his emphasis on the role of the anterior pituitary adrenal cortex system in stress, Selye largely ignored the contributions of the sympathetic nervous system. Stressors also activate the sympathetic nervous system, which increases the release of epinephrine and norepinephrine from the **adrenal medulla.** Most modern theories of stress (see Stanford & Salmon, 1993) acknowledge the major roles of both systems (see Figure 17.10).

From the perspective of psychological science, the major contribution of Selye's discovery of the stress response was that it provided a mechanism by which psychological factors can influence physical illness: All kinds of common psychological stressors (e.g., losing a job, preparing for an examination, ending a relationship) are associated with high circulating levels of glucocorticoids, epinephrine, and norepinephrine (see Burns, 1990); and these in turn have been implicated in many physical disorders (e.g., hypertension, strokes, and diabetes). The following two sections describe two such *psychosomatic disorders* (disorders whose symptoms are primarily physical but whose causes are partially psychological): gastric ulcers and infections.

Stress and Gastric Ulcers

Gastric ulcers are painful lesions to the lining of the stomach and duodenum. In the United States alone, 500,000 new cases are reported each year (see Livingston & Guth,

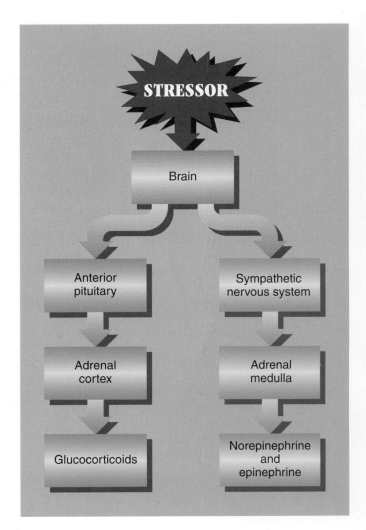

Figure 17.10 The two-system view of the stress response.

1992). Gastric ulcers are particularly prevalent in people who live in stressful situations, and high levels of stress can induce ulcers in otherwise healthy individuals. For example, gastric ulcers can be induced in rats merely by confining them to a restraint tube for a few hours.

Gastric ulcers are caused by the sufferers' own gastric secretions. Each day, the average human adult produces 2 to 3 liters of gastric secretions, the major constituent of which is *hydrochloric acid*. The function of the hydrochloric acid is to break down food during digestion, and it is normally present in concentrations that can dissolve some metals. Some cases of gastric ulcers are associated with abnormally high concentrations of hydrochloric acid. Indeed, most of the drugs currently used in the treatment of ulcers are *histamine antagonists,* which reduce hydrochloric acid secretion.

The fact that many gastric ulcer sufferers do not have abnormally high concentrations of hydrochloric acid while many nonsufferers do suggests that excess hydrochloric acid is not the only causal factor. Indeed, stress promotes the formation of gastric ulcers both by increasing hydrochloric acid secretion and by weakening the gastrointestinal tract's defenses against it. These defenses include a mucus lining that inhibits the penetration of hydrochloric acid into the wall of the gastrointestinal tract and a network of blood vessels in the mucus that quickly removes any acid molecules that do penetrate it. The sympathetic activation that is associated with each stressful episode weakens the gastrointestinal tract's defense against hydrochloric acid by shunting blood away from the gastrointestinal tract to the skeletal muscles, thus decreasing the efficiency of the mucus barrier. Then, the parasympathetic rebound following each period of stress increases hydrochloric acid secretion.

The study of the mechanisms of stress-induced gastric ulcers has focused on the amygdala because of the key role it plays in responses to threat (see Henke, 1992). Electrical stimulation of some areas of the amygdala increases the release of hydrochloric acid and decreases blood flow in the gastric mucus. As a result, stimulation of these areas of the amygdala for only a few hours can produce gastric ulcers.

Psychoneuroimmunology: Stress and Infections

A major breakthrough in the study of stress and health came with the discovery that stress can reduce a person's resistance to infection. The theoretical and clinical implications of this finding are so great that the discovery led to the emergence of a new field of biopsychological research in the early 1980s. That field is **psychoneuroimmunology**—the study of interactions among psychological factors, the nervous system, and the immune system (see Maier, Watkins, & Fleshner, 1994). Psychoneuroimmunological research has focused on three important questions, which will be discussed later in this section; but first is an introduction to the immune system.

Immune system Microorganisms of every description revel in the warm, damp, nutritive climate of your body. Your **immune system** keeps your body from being overwhelmed by these invaders. Before it can take any action against an invading microorganism, the immune system must have some way of distinguishing foreign cells from body cells. That is why **antigens**—protein molecules on the surface of a cell that identify it as native or foreign—play a major role in specific immune reactions.

Immune system barriers to infection are of two sorts. First, there are nonspecific barriers: barriers that act generally against most invaders. These barriers include mucus membranes, which destroy many foreign microorganisms, and **phagocytosis**—the process by which foreign microorganisms and debris are consumed and destroyed by *phagocytes* (specialized body cells that consume foreign microorganisms and debris)—see Figure 17.11 on page 452. Second, there are specific barriers: barriers that act specifically against particular strains of invaders. The specific barriers are of two types—cell-mediated and antibody-mediated—each defended by a different class of lymphocytes. **Lymphocytes** are specialized white blood cells that are produced in bone marrow and are stored in the lymphatic system. **Cell-mediated immunity** is directed by **T cells** (T lymphocytes); **antibody-mediated immunity** is directed by **B cells** (B lymphocytes).

The cell-mediated immune reaction begins when a **macrophage**—a type of large phagocyte—ingests a foreign microorganism. The macrophage then displays the microorganism's antigens on the surface of its cell membrane (see Figure 17.11), and this attracts T cells. Each T cell has

Adrenocorticotropic hormone (ACTH). The anterior pituitary hormone that triggers the release of glucocorticoids from the adrenal cortex.

Glucocorticoids. Steroid hormones that are released from the adrenal cortex in response to stressors.

Adrenal cortex. The cortex of the adrenal glands, which releases glucocorticoids in response to stressors.

Adrenal medulla. The core of the adrenal glands, which releases epinephrine and norepinephrine in response to stressors.

Gastric ulcers. Lesions to the lining of the stomach or duodenum, a common consequence of stress.

Psychoneuroimmunology. The study of interactions among psychological factors, the nervous system, and the immune system.

Immune system. The system that protects the body against infectious microorganisms.

Antigens. Proteins on the surface of cells that identify them as native or foreign.

Phagocytosis. The consumption of dead tissue and invading microorganisms by specialized body cells (phagocytes).

Lymphocytes. Specialized white blood cells that play important roles in the body's immune reactions.

Cell-mediated immunity. The immune reaction by which T cells destroy invading microorganisms.

T cells. T lymphocytes; lymphocytes that bind to foreign microorganisms and cells that contain them and, in so doing, destroy them.

Antibody-mediated immunity. The immune reaction by which B cells destroy invading microorganisms.

B cells. B lymphocytes; lymphocytes that manufacture antibodies against antigens they encounter.

Macrophage. A large phagocyte that plays a role in cell-mediated immunity.

Figure 17.11 Phagocytosis: A macrophage hunts down and destroys a bacterium.

body cells that have been infected by the invaders. Also created are long-lasting T cells, called *memory T cells*, that enable the immune system to react more rapidly to the same antigen if it is encountered again.

The antibody-mediated immune reaction begins when a B cell binds to a foreign antigen for which it contains an appropriate receptor. This causes the B cell to multiply and to synthesize a lethal form of its receptor molecules. These lethal receptor molecules, called **antibodies**, are released into the intracellular fluid, where they bind to the foreign antigens and destroy or deactivate the microorganisms that possess them. Memory B cells for the specific antigen are also produced during the process; these cells have a long life and accelerate antibody-mediated immunity if there is a subsequent infection by the same organism.

Cell-mediated immunity and antibody-mediated immunity are illustrated in Figure 17.12. Both processes take several days the first time a particular foreign antigen is recognized, but responses to subsequent invasions of microorganisms with the same antigen are much faster thanks to the memory T cells and B cells. This is why *inoculation* (the injection of small samples of an infective microorganism into healthy individuals) is often an effective preventive measure against the effects of subsequent infection.

Now that you have been introduced to the immune system, it is time to turn to a consideration of psychoneuroimmunological research. It has focused on the following three questions.

Does stress disrupt immune function? Numerous studies have documented the adverse effects of stress on various aspects of immune function, both in humans and in laboratory animals (see Maier, Watkins, & Fleshner, 1994; O'Leary, 1990). In laboratory animals, electric shocks, social defeat, overcrowding, the odor of stressed conspecifics, loud noise, and maternal separation have all been shown to depress immune function. In humans, the list includes final examinations, sleep deprivation, divorce, bereavement, and caring for an Alzheimer's patient.

Are stress-related decreases in immune function large enough to be of clinical significance? Although stress has been shown to suppress many aspects of immune function, it has been harder than you might think to prove that these effects are large enough to increase the rate or

two kinds of receptors on its surface, one for molecules that are normally found on the surface of macrophages and other body cells and one for a specific foreign antigen. There are millions of different receptors for foreign antigens on T cells, but there is only one kind on each T cell and there are only a few T cells with each kind of receptor. After the microorganism has been ingested and its antigens have been displayed, a T cell with a receptor for the foreign antigen binds to the surface of the infected macrophage, which initiates a series of reactions. Among these reactions is the multiplication of the bound T cell, which creates an army of T cells with the specific receptor necessary to destroy all invaders that contain the target antigens and all

Cell–Mediated Immunity

Antigen Macrophage T cell

Microorganism Receptor

Macrophages ingest the micro-organism and display its protein on their cell membranes.

T cells with an appropriate recep-tor bind to the macrophage.

The bound T cells proliferate and develop into a form that kills body cells that have been infec-ted by the microorganism.

Antibody–Mediated Immunity

B cell

Antibodies

Antigen Microorganism

Foreign antigens are bound by B cells with an appropriate receptor.

The B cells replicate and develop into a form that releases anti-bodies to the antigen.

The antibodies bind to the anti-gens and kill or deactivate the microorganism.

Figure 17.12 Specific barriers to infection: Cell-mediated immunity and antibody-mediated immunity. In cell-mediated immunity, microorganisms or body cells that they have invaded are killed by T cells; in antibody-mediated immunity, microorganisms are killed by antibodies produced by B cells.

severity of infectious diseases in humans. True, numerous studies have reported positive correlations between stress and ill health in human subjects; for example, students in one study reported more respiratory infections during their final examination period (Glaser et al., 1987). How-ever, the causal interpretation of such correlations is never straightforward: Stressed subjects may report more illness during times of stress because they expect to be more ill, because the experience of illness during times of stress is more unpleasant, or because the stress caused illness-inducing changes in their behavior (e.g., changes in diet, drug use, or sleep patterns)—see Watson & Pennebaker, 1989. Be that as it may, the causal effect of stress on the sus-ceptibility to infectious diseases has been demonstrated in many well-controlled experiments on laboratory animals. Together the two lines of evidence—the human correla-

tional studies and the controlled animal experiments—leave little doubt that stress does increase our susceptibility to infectious diseases.

What is the mechanism by which stress influences immune function? Given that stress produces wide-spread neural and hormonal activity through the anterior pituitary adrenal cortex system and the sympathetic adren-

Antibodies. Proteins that bind specifically to anti-gens on the surface of invading microorganisms and in so doing promote the destruction of the micro-organisms.

Before proceeding to a discussion of stress and psychological disorders, review your introduction to emotion, fear, and stress by filling in the following blanks with the most appropriate term. The correct answers are provided at the bottom of this page. Review material related to your errors and omissions.

1. The theory that the subjective experience of emotion is triggered by ANS responses is called the _____ theory.

2. The pattern of aggressive responses observed in decorticate animals is called _____.

3. Between the amygdala and the fornix in the limbic ring is the _____.

4. A Duchenne smile, but not a false smile, involves contraction of the _____.

5. Aggression directed by the alpha male of a colony at a male intruder is called _____ aggression.

6. The usual target site of rat defensive attacks is the _____ of the attacking rat.

7. Bilateral lesions of the medial geniculate nuclei or the _____ block fear conditioning to auditory conditional stimuli.

8. The _____ of the midbrain elicits the appropriate behavioral responses to fear-inducing stimuli.

9. Glucocorticoids are released from the _____ as part of the stress response.

10. Stressors increase the release of epinephrine and norepinephrine from the _____.

11. The study of the interactions among psychological factors, the nervous system, and the immune system is called _____.

12. T cells and B cells are involved in cell-mediated and _____ immune reactions, respectively.

al medulla system, there are innumerable mechanisms by which stress could influence immune function. For example, both T cells and B cells have receptors for glucocorticoids, which are released by the adrenal cortex, and for norepinephrine, which is released both by sympathetic neurons and by the adrenal medulla. Hypothalamic lesions,

which disrupt the visceral responses to fear, also disrupt immune function (see Maier et al., 1994).

Psychoneuroimmunology: Conclusion The discovery that stress can increase a person's susceptibility to infectious diseases is an important one. It suggested that the adverse effects of stress on health are much greater and more diverse than previously appreciated. But this is not the end of the story of stress's adverse effects on health. In the final sections of this chapter, you will learn that stress is also a causal factor in psychological dysfunction.

The answers are (1) James-Lange, (2) sham rage, (3) hippocampus, (4) orbicularis oculi, (5) social, (6) face, (7) amygdala, (8) periaqueductal gray, (9) adrenal cortex, (10) adrenal medulla, (11) psychoneuroimmunology, and (12) antibody-mediated.

Psychiatric disorders that are serious enough to require hospitalization or some comparable form of care are called **psychoses;** those that are less severe are called **neuroses.**

The remainder of this chapter focuses on two major classes of psychosis, schizophrenia and affective disorders, and on one class of neurosis, anxiety.

17.4   Schizophrenia

The term **schizophrenia** means the splitting of psychic functions. It was coined in the early 1900s to describe what was assumed to be the primary symptom of the disorder: the breakdown of integration among emotion, thought, and action. It is the disease that is most commonly associated with the concept of madness. It attacks about 1% of all races and cultural groups, typically beginning in adolescence or early adulthood.

The major difficulty in studying and treating schizophrenia is accurately defining it. Its symptoms are complex and diverse; they overlap greatly with those of other psychiatric disorders, and they frequently change during the progression of the disorder (see Andreasen, 1994; Heinrichs, 1994). As a result, there have been many attempts to break the diagnosis of schizophrenia down into several disorders, but none of these attempts has proved successful. The following are the symptoms of schizophrenia, but none of them appears in all cases; indeed, the recurrence of only one of them is grounds for the diagnosis of schizophrenia:

Bizarre delusions. Delusions of being controlled (e.g., "Martians are making me think evil thoughts"), delusions of persecution (e.g., "My mother is trying to poison me"), delusions of grandeur (e.g., "Michael Jordan admires my sneakers").

Inappropriate affect. Failure to react with an appropriate level of emotionality to positive or negative events.

Hallucinations. Imaginary voices telling the person what to do or commenting negatively on the person's behavior.

Incoherent thought. Illogical thinking, peculiar associations among ideas, or belief in supernatural forces.

Odd behavior. Long periods with no movement, a lack of personal hygiene, talking in rhymes, avoiding social interaction.

Causal Factors in Schizophrenia

In the first half of the 20th century, the cloak of mysticism began to be removed from mental illness by a series of studies that established schizophrenia's genetic basis. First, it was discovered that although only 1% of the population develops schizophrenia, the probability of schizophrenia occurring in a close biological relative (i.e., in a parent, child, or sibling) of a schizophrenic is about 10%, even if

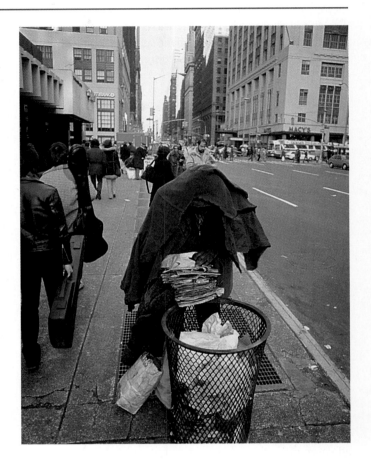

the relative was adopted shortly after birth by a healthy family (e.g., Kendler & Gruenbert, 1984; Rosenthal et al., 1980). Then, it was discovered that the concordance rates for schizophrenia are higher in identical twins (45%) than in fraternal twins (10%)—see Holzman and Matthysse (1990) and Kallman (1946).

Psychoses. Psychological disorders that are serious enough to require hospitalization or some comparable form of care.

Neuroses. Psychological disorders that are not serious enough to require hospitalization or some comparable form of care.

Schizophrenia. A psychosis that is characterized by the recurrence of any of the following symptoms: bizarre delusions, inappropriate affect, hallucinations, incoherent thought, and odd behavior.

The fact that the concordance rate for schizophrenia in identical twins is substantially less than 100% indicates that differences in experience contribute significantly to differences among people in the development of schizophrenia. The current view is that some people inherit a potential for schizophrenia, which may or may not be activated by experience. Supporting this view is a recent comparison of the offspring of a large sample of identical twins who were themselves discordant for schizophrenia (i.e., one had the disorder and one did not); the incidence of schizophrenia was as great in the offspring of the nonschizophrenic twins as in the offspring of the schizophrenic twins (Gottesman & Bertelsen, 1989).

Several types of experience have been hypothesized to play a key role in activating schizophrenic symptoms in people with an inherited susceptibility; however, much of the recent evidence has implicated exposure to stress as the major factor. Several studies have found that exposure to stressors is common just before a schizophrenic attack, and several have found correlations between the severity of the stressors and the severity of the resulting schizophrenic symptoms (see Norman & Malla, 1993).

Discovery of the First Antischizophrenic Drugs

The first major breakthrough in the study of the biochemistry of schizophrenia was the accidental discovery in the early 1950s of the first antischizophrenic drug, **chlorpromazine.** Chlorpromazine was developed by a French drug company as an antihistamine. Then, in 1950, a French surgeon noticed that chlorpromazine given prior to surgery to counteract swelling had a calming effect on some of his patients, and he suggested that it might have a calming effect on difficult-to-handle psychotic patients. His suggestion proved to be incorrect, but the clinical trials it triggered led to the discovery that chlorpromazine alleviates schizophrenic symptoms: Agitated schizophrenics were calmed by chlorpromazine, and emotionally blunt schizophrenics were activated by it. Don't get the idea that chlorpromazine cures schizophrenia. It doesn't. But in many cases it reduces the severity of schizophrenic symptoms enough to allow institutionalized patients to be discharged.

Shortly after the antischizophrenic action of chlorpromazine was first documented, an American psychiatrist became interested in reports that the snakeroot plant had long been used in India for the treatment of mental illness. He gave **reserpine**—the active ingredient of the snakeroot plant—to his schizophrenic patients and confirmed its antischizophrenic action. Reserpine is no longer used in the treatment of schizophrenia because it produces a dangerous decline in blood pressure at antischizophrenic doses.

Although the chemical structures of chlorpromazine and reserpine are dissimilar, their antischizophrenic effects are similar in two major respects. First, the antischizophrenic effect of both drugs is manifested only after a patient has been medicated for 2 or 3 weeks. Second, the onset of the antischizophrenic effect of the medication is usually associated with motor effects similar to the symptoms of Parkinson's disease: tremors at rest, muscular rigidity, and a general decrease in voluntary movement. These similarities suggested to researchers that chlorpromazine and reserpine were acting through the same mechanism, one that was related to Parkinson's disease.

Dopamine Theory of Schizophrenia

Paradoxically, the next major breakthrough in the study of schizophrenia came from research on Parkinson's disease. In 1960, it was reported that the *striatums* (caudates plus putamens) of persons dying of Parkinson's disease had been depleted of dopamine (Ehringer & Hornykiewicz, 1960). This finding suggested that a disruption of dopaminergic transmission might produce Parkinson's disease; and because of the relation between Parkinson's disease and the antischizophrenic effects of chlorpromazine and reserpine, it suggested that antischizophrenic drug effects might be produced in the same way. Thus was born the *dopamine theory of schizophrenia*—the theory that schizophrenia is caused by too much dopamine and, conversely, that antischizophrenic drugs exert their effects by decreasing dopamine levels.

Lending instant support to the dopamine theory of schizophrenia were two already-well-established facts. First, the antischizophrenic drug reserpine was known to deplete the brain of dopamine and other monoamines by breaking down their synaptic vesicles. Second, drugs, such as amphetamine and cocaine, which can trigger schizophrenic episodes in normal subjects, were known to increase the extracellular levels of dopamine and other monoamines in the brain.

An important step in the evolution of the dopamine theory of schizophrenia came in 1963, when Carlsson and Lindqvist assessed the effects of chlorpromazine on extracellular levels of dopamine and its *metabolites* (molecules that are created when another molecule is broken down). They expected to find that chlorpromazine, like reserpine, depletes the brain of dopamine; but they didn't. The extracellular levels of dopamine were unchanged by chlorpromazine, and the extracellular levels of its metabolites were increased. They concluded that both chlorpromazine and reserpine antagonize transmission at dopamine synapses but that they do it in different ways—reserpine by depleting the brain of dopamine and chlorpromazine by binding to dopamine receptors. They argued that chlorpromazine is a **false transmitter** (receptor blocker) at dopamine synapses—that is, that it binds to dopamine receptors without activating them and that, in so doing, keeps dopamine from activating them (see Figure 17.13). They further

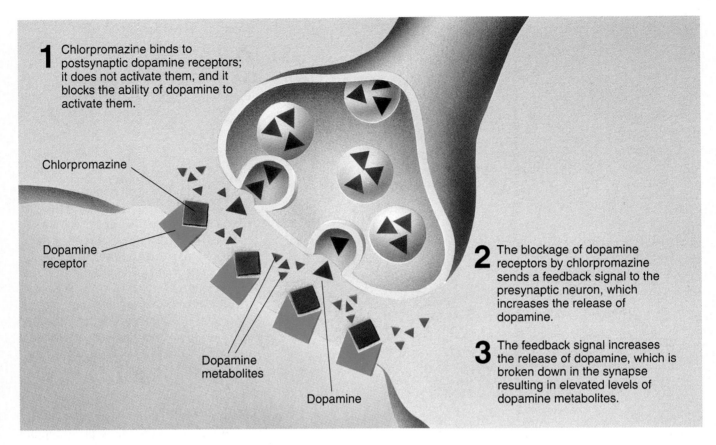

Figure 17.13 Chlorpromazine, a false transmitter at dopamine synapses.

1 Chlorpromazine binds to postsynaptic dopamine receptors; it does not activate them, and it blocks the ability of dopamine to activate them.

Chlorpromazine

Dopamine receptor

Dopamine metabolites

Dopamine

2 The blockage of dopamine receptors by chlorpromazine sends a feedback signal to the presynaptic neuron, which increases the release of dopamine.

3 The feedback signal increases the release of dopamine, which is broken down in the synapse resulting in elevated levels of dopamine metabolites.

postulated that the lack of activity at postsynaptic dopamine receptors sent a feedback signal to the presynaptic cells that increased their release of dopamine, which was broken down in the synapses. This explained why dopaminergic activity was reduced while extracellular dopamine levels stayed about the same and the extracellular levels of its metabolites were increased. Carlsson and Lindqvist's findings led to an important revision of the dopamine theory of schizophrenia: Rather than high dopamine levels per se, the main factor in schizophrenia was presumed to be high levels of activity at dopamine receptors.

In the mid 1970s, Snyder and his colleagues (Creese, Burt, & Snyder, 1976; Snyder, 1976) assessed the degree to which the various antischizophrenic drugs that had been developed by that time bind to dopamine receptors. First, they added radioactively labeled dopamine to samples of dopamine-receptor-rich neural membrane obtained from calf striatums. Then, they rinsed away the unbound dopamine molecules from the samples and measured the amount of radioactivity left in them to obtain a measure of the number of dopamine receptors. Next, in other samples, they measured each drug's ability to block the binding of radioactive dopamine to the sample, the assumption being that the drugs with a high affinity for dopamine receptors would leave fewer sites available for the dopamine. In gen-

eral, they found that chlorpromazine and the other effective antischizophrenic drugs had a high affinity for dopamine receptors, whereas ineffective antischizophrenic drugs had a low affinity. There were, however, several major exceptions, one of them being haloperidol. Although **haloperidol** was one of the most potent antischizophrenic drugs of its day, it had a relatively low affinity for dopamine receptors.

A solution to the haloperidol puzzle came with the discovery that dopamine binds to more than one receptor subtype. It turned out that chlorpromazine and the other

Chlorpromazine. The first antischizophrenic drug.

Reserpine. The first monoamine antagonist to be used in the treatment of schizophrenia; it is the active ingredient of the snakeroot plant.

False transmitter. A receptor blocker, a chemical that binds to a synaptic receptor without activating it and, in so doing, blocks the action of the neurotransmitter.

Haloperidol. A butyrophenone antischizophrenic drug.

Schizophrenia

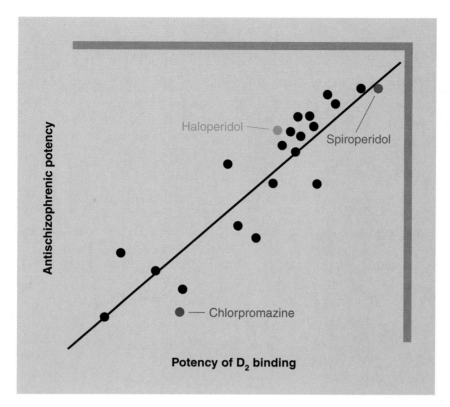

Figure 17.14 The positive correlation between the ability of various neuroleptics to bind to D_2 receptors and their clinical potency. (Adapted from Snyder, 1978.)

Although the evidence implicating D_2 receptors in schizophrenia is strong, the dopamine theory as it currently stands is not the whole story—far from it. Following are five questions about the neural basis of schizophrenia that have been the focus of recent research.

Are D_2 receptors the only receptors involved in schizophrenia? The development of *atypical neuroleptic drugs* (antischizophrenic drugs that are not D_2 receptor blockers) has challenged the view that D_2 receptors are the only receptors involved in schizophrenia. For example, **clozapine** is effective in the treatment of schizophrenia; yet, unlike conventional neuroleptics, it does not have a high affinity for D_2 receptors or produce parkinsonian side effects (see Meltzer et al., 1990). The effectiveness of clozapine and other atypical neuroleptics suggests that D_2 receptors are not the only receptors involved in schizophrenia; clozapine has a high affinity for D_1 receptors, D_4 receptors, and several serotonin receptors.

antischizophrenic drugs in the same chemical class (the **phenothiazines**) all bind effectively to both D_1 and D_2 receptors, whereas haloperidol and the other antischizophrenic drugs in its chemical class (the **butyrophenones**) all bind effectively to D_2 receptors, but not to D_1 receptors.

This discovery of the selective binding of butyrophenones to D_2 receptors led to an important revision in the dopamine theory of schizophrenia. It suggested that schizophrenia is caused by hyperactivity specifically at D_2 receptors, rather than at dopamine receptors in general. Snyder and his colleagues (see Snyder, 1978) subsequently confirmed that the degree to which **neuroleptics**—antischizophrenic drugs—bind to D_2 receptors is highly correlated with their effectiveness in suppressing schizophrenic symptoms (see Figure 17.14). For example, they found that the butyrophenone *spiroperidol* had the greatest affinity for D_2 receptors and the most potent antischizophrenic effect.

The D_2 receptor version of the dopamine theory is currently the most widely recognized theory of the neural basis of schizophrenia. The major events in its development are summarized in Table 17.2.

TABLE 17.2	
The Key Events That Led to the Development and Refinement of the Dopamine Theory of Schizophrenia	
Early 1950s	The antischizophrenic effects of both chlorpromazine and reserpine were documented and related to their parkinsonian side effects
Late 1950s	The brains of recently deceased Parkinson's patients were found to be depleted of dopamine.
Early 1960s	It was hypothesized that schizophrenia was associated with excessive activity at dopaminergic synapses.
1960s and 1970s	Chlorpromazine and other clinically effective neuroleptics were found to act as false transmitters at dopamine synapses.
Mid 1970s	The affinity of neuroleptics for dopamine receptors was found to be only roughly correlated with their antischizophrenic potentcy.
Late 1970s	The binding of existing antischizophrenic drugs to D_2 receptors was found to be highly correlated with their antischizophrenic potency.

Why does it take several weeks of neuroleptic therapy to affect schizophrenic symptoms? The dopamine theory of schizophrenia has difficulty explaining why it takes several weeks of neuroleptic therapy to alleviate schizophrenic symptoms when dopaminergic transmission is effectively blocked within hours. This discrepancy indicates that the blockage dopamine receptor is not the specific mechanism by which schizophrenic symptoms are alleviated. It appears that blocking dopamine receptors triggers some slow-developing compensatory change in the brain that is the key factor in the therapeutic effect.

What parts of the brain are involved in schizophrenia? Computed tomography (CT) and magnetic resonance imaging (MRI) of the brains of schizophrenics often reveal diffuse brain pathology. This pathology appears to be full-blown in the early stages of the disorder, which is consistent with the view that schizophrenia is a disorder of brain development that lies fallow until activated by experience (see Andreasen, 1994; Winn, 1994). The abnormalities in the brains of schizophrenics are diffuse, but they are most prevalent in the prefrontal cortex, the temporal cortex, the basal ganglia, the thalamus, and the hippocampus.

Why are neuroleptics effective against only some schizophrenic symptoms? Neuroleptics are more effective in the treatment of *positive schizophrenic symptoms* (such as incoherence, hallucinations, and delusions), which are assumed to be caused by increased neural activity, than they are in the treatment of *negative schizophrenic symptoms* (such as blunt affect and poverty of speech), which are assumed to be caused by decreased neural activity. Accordingly, it has been suggested that positive schizophrenic symptoms are produced by D_2 hyperactivity and that negative symptoms are produced by structural pathology (Roberts, 1990; Suddath et al., 1990).

By what mechanism does stress activate schizophrenic symptoms? Stress activates dopaminergic projections to the prefrontal cortex, which dampen responses to stress in other circuits. One theory is that the abnormal development of prefrontal cortex that occurs in many schizophrenics (Winn, 1994) results in exaggerated responses to stressors, and in so doing, contributes to the activation of schizophrenic symptoms (Jaskiw & Weinberger, 1992).

17.5 Affective Disorders: Depression and Mania

All of us have experienced depression. Depression is a normal reaction to grievous loss such as the loss of a loved one, the loss of self-esteem, the loss of personal possessions, or the loss of health. However, there are people whose tendency toward depression is out of proportion. These people repeatedly fall into the depths of despair, often for no apparent reason; and their depression can be so extreme that it is almost impossible for them to meet the essential requirements of their daily lives—to keep a job, to maintain social contacts, or even to maintain an acceptable level of personal hygiene. It is these people who are said to be suffering from clinical **depression.**

Phenothiazines. A class of antischizophrenic drugs that binds effectively to both D_1 and D_2 receptors.

Butyrophenones. A class of antischizophrenic drugs that bind primarily to D_2 receptors.

Neuroleptics. Drugs that alleviate schizophrenic symptoms.

Clozapine. An antischizophrenic drug that does not produce many of the side effects of conventional neuroleptics and does not bind to D_2 receptors.

Depression. A normal reaction to grievous loss; when depression is excessive, disruptive, and recurring, it is classified as a psychiatric disorder.

Many people who suffer from clinical depression also experience periods of mania. **Mania** is at the other end of the scale of mood. During periods of mild mania, people are talkative, energetic, impulsive, positive, and very confident. In this state, they can be very effective at certain jobs and can be great fun to be with. But when mania becomes extreme, it is a serious clinical problem. The florid manic often awakens in a state of unbridled enthusiasm, with an outflow of incessant chatter that careens nonstop from topic to topic. No task is too difficult. No goal is unattainable. This confidence and grandiosity, coupled with high energy, distractibility, and a leap-before-you-look impulsiveness, result in a continual series of disasters: Mania leaves behind it a trail of unfinished projects, unpaid bills, and broken relationships. Depression and mania are considered to be disorders of *affect* (emotion).

Depression is often divided into two categories: **reactive depression,** which is triggered by an obvious negative experience, and **endogenous depression,** which is not. Not all depressive patients experience periods of mania. Those that do not are said to suffer from **unipolar affective disorder;** those that do are said to suffer from **bipolar affective disorder.** Approximately 6% of people suffer from unipolar affective disorder at some point in their lives, and about 1% suffer from bipolar affective disorder. Unipolar affective disorder is twice as prevalent in women as in men, but there is no sex difference in the incidence of bipolar affective disorder. About 10% of those suffering from affective disorders commit suicide—which provides an indication of how devastating these disorders can be.

Causal Factors in Affective Disorders

Genetic factors contribute to differences among people in the development of affective disorders. Twin studies of affective disorders suggest a concordance rate of about 60% for identical twins and 15% for fraternal twins, whether they are reared together or apart (Winokur, 1978). Although there are many exceptions, there is a tendency for affected twins to suffer from the same disorder, unipolar or bipolar; and the concordance rates for bipolar disorders tend to be higher than those for unipolar disorders.

Because the concordance rate for affective disorders in identical twins is less than 100%, it is clear that differences in experience contribute to differences among people in the development of affective disorders. Most of the research on experience and affective disorders has focused on the role of stress in the etiology of depression. For example, Brown (1993) found that over 84% of a large sample of depressed patients had experienced severe stress in the preceding year, in comparison to 32% of a group of control subjects. Anisman and Zacharko (1982) have suggested that the depletion of certain neurotransmitters (e.g., of dopamine, serotonin, and norepinephrine) that is associated with stress may leave an individual sensitized to subsequent

stress and thus less capable of coping with it. They view the inability to cope effectively with stress as a major predisposing factor in depression.

Discovery of Antidepressant Drugs

Four classes of drugs have been developed for the treatment of affective disorders: monoamine oxidase inhibitors, tricyclic antidepressants, lithium, and selective serotonin-reuptake inhibitors.

Monoamine oxidase inhibitors Iproniazid, the first antidepressant drug, was originally developed for the treatment of tuberculosis, and as such it proved to be a dismal flop. However, interest in the antidepressant potential of the drug was kindled by the observation that iproniazid left patients with tuberculosis less depressed about their disor-

Mania. An affective disorder in which the patient is impulsive, overconfident, highly energetic, and distractible.

Reactive depression. Depression that is precipitated by a negative experience.

Endogenous depression. Depression that appears not to have been triggered by a negative experience.

Unipolar affective disorder. A depressive disorder in which the patient does not experience periods of mania.

Bipolar affective disorder. A disorder of emotion in which the patient experiences periods of mania interspersed with periods of depression.

Iproniazid. The first antidepressant drug, a monoamine oxidase inhibitor.

MAO inhibitors. Drugs that increase the level of monoamine neurotransmitters by inhibiting the action of monoamine oxidase.

Cheese effect. The surges in blood pressure that occur when individuals taking MAO inhibitors consume tyramine-rich foods.

Tricyclic antidepressants. Drugs with an antidepressant action and a three-ring structure.

Imipramine. The first tricyclic antidepressant drug.

Lithium. A metallic ion that is used in the treatment of bipolar affective disorder.

Prozac. The trade name of fluoxetine, the widely prescribed selective serotonin-reuptake inhibitor that is effective against depression and various anxiety disorders.

der. As a result, iproniazid was tested on a mixed group of psychiatric patients and was found to be effective against depression. It was first marketed as an antidepressant drug in 1957.

Iproniazid is a monoamine agonist; it increases the levels of monoamines by inhibiting the activity of *monoamine oxidase (MAO),* the enzyme that breaks down monoamine neurotransmitters in the cytoplasm of the neuron. **MAO inhibitors** have several side effects; the most dangerous is known as the **cheese effect.** Foods such as cheese, wine, and pickles contain an amine called *tyramine,* which is a potent elevator of blood pressure. Normally, these foods have little effect on blood pressure because tyramine is rapidly metabolized in the liver by MAO. However, people who take MAO inhibitors and consume tyramine-rich foods run the risk of strokes caused by surges in blood pressure.

Tricyclic antidepressants The **tricyclic antidepressants** are so named because of their antidepressant action and because their chemical structures include a three-ring chain. **Imipramine,** the first tricyclic antidepressant, was initially thought to be an antischizophrenic drug. However, when its effects on a mixed sample of psychiatric patients were assessed, its antidepressant effect was immediately obvious. Tricyclic antidepressants block the reuptake of both serotonin and norepinephrine, thus increasing their levels in the brain. They are a safer alternative to MAO inhibitors.

Lithium The discovery of the ability of **lithium**—a simple metallic ion—to block mania is yet another important pharmacological breakthrough that was made by accident. Cade, an Australian psychiatrist, mixed the urine of manic patients with lithium to form a soluble salt; then he injected the salt into a group of guinea pigs to see if it would induce mania. As a control, he injected lithium into another group. Instead of inducing mania, the urine solution seemed to calm the guinea pigs; and because the lithium control injections had the same effect, Cade concluded that lithium, not uric acid, was the calming agent. In retrospect, Cade's conclusion was incredibly foolish. We now know that at the doses used by Cade, lithium salts produce extreme nausea. To Cade's untrained eye, his subjects' inactivity may have looked like calmness. But the subjects weren't calm; they were sick. Be that as it may, flushed with what he thought was the success of his guinea pig experiments, in 1954 Cade tried lithium on a group of 10 manic patients, and it proved remarkably effective.

There was little immediate reaction to Cade's report. Few scientists were impressed by Cade's scientific credentials, and few drug companies were interested in spending millions of dollars to evaluate the therapeutic potential of a metallic ion, which could not be protected by a patent. Accordingly, the therapeutic potential of lithium was not fully appreciated until the late 1960s, when it was discovered that lithium is effective against depression as well as mania (Angst et al., 1970; Baastrup & Schou, 1967) . Today, lithium is the treatment of choice for bipolar affective disorder, but the effects of lithium on the brain are still largely a mystery.

Selective serotonin-reuptake inhibitors *Fluoxetine,* which is marketed under the name **Prozac,** is an offspring of the tricyclic antidepressants. It is a slight structural variation of tricyclic antidepressants that selectively blocks serotonin reuptake, rather than blocking both serotonin and norepinephrine reuptake (see Figure 17.15 on page 462). Accordingly, Prozac and other drugs of its class are called *selective serotonin-reuptake inhibitors.*

Prozac was introduced for clinical use in the 1980s. Although it is no more effective against depression than imipramine, it has already been prescribed for more than 10 million people. There are two reasons for its remarkable popularity (see Barondes, 1994). First, it has few side effects; and second, it has proved effective against a wide range of psychological disorders other than depression. Because Prozac is so effective against disorders that were once considered to be the exclusive province of psychotherapy (e.g., lack of self-esteem, fear of failure, excessive sensitivity to criticism, and inability to experience pleasure), it has had a major impact on the fields of psychiatry and clinical psychology.

Neural Mechanisms of Depression

The search for the neural mechanisms of affective disorders has focused on depression; however, the fact that lithium is effective against both depression and mania suggests that the mechanisms of the two are closely related. The dominant theory of depression is the *monoamine theory.* It is based on the fact that monoamine oxidase inhibitors, tricyclic antidepressants, and selective serotonin-reuptake inhibitors all block the reuptake of monoamines, particularly serotonin and norepinephrine. The monoamine theory of depression is that depression is associated with underactivity at serotonergic and noradrenergic synapses. The effectiveness of Prozac against depression might imply that the mechanisms of depression are specifically serotonergic, but depression is also alleviated by some selective norepinephrine-reuptake inhibitors.

The following are four problems with the monoamine theory of depression. First, it is inconsistent with the time course of antidepressant drug effects. Monoamine oxidase inhibitors, tricyclic antidepressants, and selective serotonin-reuptake inhibitors all increase monoamine levels within hours of the onset of drug therapy, but it takes weeks for the first therapeutic effects to be experienced. This suggests that some slow-developing consequence of the monoamine reuptake blockade is the key antidepressant effect. Second, some drugs that block monoamine reuptake (e.g., cocaine) do not have antidepressant effects. Third, lithium does not

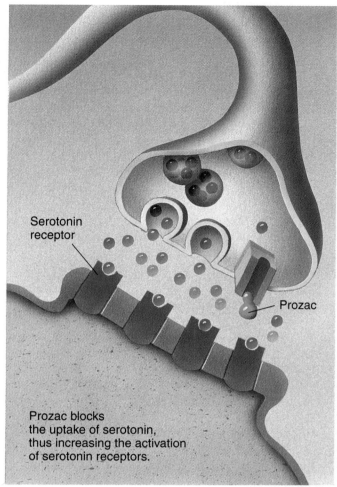

Serotonin

Serotonin is deactivated in the synapse by reuptake into the presynaptic neuron.

Serotonin receptor

Prozac

Prozac blocks the uptake of serotonin, thus increasing the activation of serotonin receptors.

Figure 17.15 Blockade of serotonin reuptake by fluoxetine (Prozac).

block monoamine reuptake but is an effective antidepressant. And fourth, measurements of monoamines and their metabolites in depressed patients have not provided support for the theory.

An alternative theory of depression focuses on the hypothalamic anterior pituitary adrenal cortex system. It is based on the finding that injections of *dexamethasone*, a synthetic glucocorticoid, do not reduce glucocorticoid release in depressed patients as they do in normal subjects. This suggests that the lack of appropriate negative feedback

Dexamethasone suppression test. A test of feedback in the hypothalamic anterior pituitary adrenal cortex system; an injection of dexamethasone, a synthetic glucocorticoid, normally suppresses subsequent glucocorticoid release.

Anxiety. Fear that persists in the absence of direct threat.

Anxiety disorder. Anxiety that is so extreme and so pervasive that it disrupts normal functioning.

Generalized anxiety disorders. Anxiety disorders that are not precipitated by any obvious event.

Phobic anxiety disorders. Anxiety disorders characterized by extreme, largely irrational fears of specific objects or situations.

Panic disorders. Anxiety disorders characterized by recurring rapid-onset attacks of extreme fear that are often associated with choking, heart palpitations, and shortness of breath.

Obsessive-compulsive disorders. Anxiety disorders characterized by recurring uncontrollable thoughts and impulses.

Benzodiazepines. The major class of anxiolytic drugs, including chlordiazepoxide (Librium) and diazepam (Valium).

Buspirone. A serotonin agonist that is an effective anxiolytic drug.

mechanisms in the hypothalamic anterior pituitary adrenal cortex system may be a factor in depression (see Barden, Reul, & Holsboer, 1995). Support for this theory comes from the finding that antidepressant therapy often restores the normal response in the **dexamethasone suppression test.** However, lack of dexamethasone suppression is not specific to affective disorders; it is also common in cases of dementia.

17.6 Anxiety Disorders

Anxiety—chronic fear that persists in the absence of any direct threat—is a common psychological correlate of stress. Anxiety is adaptive if it motivates effective coping behaviors; however, when it becomes so severe that it disrupts normal functioning, it is referred to as an **anxiety disorder.** All anxiety disorders are associated with feelings of anxiety (fear, worry, despondency) and with a variety of physiological stress reactions—for example, *tachycardia* (rapid heartbeat), *hypertension* (high blood pressure), nausea, breathing difficulty, sleep disturbances, and high glucocorticoid levels. Anxiety disorders are the most prevalent of all psychiatric disorders; in Great Britain, for example, 1 in 5 women and 1 in 10 men take antianxiety medication each year (Dunbar, Perera, & Jenner, 1989).

The four major classes of anxiety disorders are generalized anxiety disorders, phobic anxiety disorders, panic disorders, and obsessive-compulsive disorders. **Generalized anxiety disorders** are characterized by stress responses and extreme feelings of anxiety that occur in the absence of any obvious precipitating stimulus. **Phobic anxiety disorders** are similar to generalized anxiety disorders except that they are triggered by exposure to particular objects (e.g., birds, spiders) or situations (e.g., crowds, darkness). **Panic disorders** are characterized by rapid-onset attacks of extreme fear and severe symptoms of stress (e.g., choking, heart palpitations, shortness of breath); they are often components of generalized anxiety and phobic disorders, but they also occur as separate disorders. **Obsessive-compulsive disorders** are characterized by frequently recurring, uncontrollable, anxiety-producing thoughts (obsessions) and impulses (compulsions). Responding to them—for example, by repeated compulsive hand washing—is a means of dissipating the anxiety associated with them.

Pharmacological Treatment of Anxiety Disorders

Two classes of drugs are effective against anxiety disorders: benzodiazepines and serotonin agonists.

Benzodiazepines **Benzodiazepines** such as *chlordiazepoxide* (Librium) and *diazepam* (Valium) are widely prescribed for the treatment of anxiety disorders. They are also prescribed as hypnotics (sleep-inducing drugs), anti-

convulsants, and muscle relaxants. Indeed, benzodiazepines are the most widely prescribed psychoactive drugs; approximately 10% of adult North Americans are currently taking them. The benzodiazepines have several adverse side effects: sedation, ataxia (disruption of motor activity), tremor, nausea, addiction, and a withdrawal reaction that includes rebound anxiety.

The behavioral effects of benzodiazepines are thought to be mediated by their agonistic action on the GABA$_A$ receptor. Benzodiazepines bind to the GABA$_A$ receptor at a different site than the one at which GABA molecules bind and, in so doing, increase the binding of GABA molecules to the receptor (see Figure 4.20). The GABA$_A$ receptor is distributed widely throughout the brain.

Serotonin agonists **Buspirone** is a recent addition to the drugs available for the clinical treatment of anxiety disorders. Unlike the benzodiazepines, buspirone is a serotonin agonist; it acts selectively on one serotonin receptor subtype, the 5-HT$_{1A}$ receptor. The main advantage of buspirone is that it produces *anxiolytic* (antianxiety) effects without producing ataxia, muscle relaxation, or sedation—which are common side effects of benzodiazepines. Presumably, the selectivity of its behavioral effects is attributable to its selective pattern of binding. Other serotonin-agonists (e.g., monoamine oxidase inhibitors, tricyclic antidepressants, and selective serotonin-reuptake inhibitors) also have anxiolytic effects.

Animal Models of Anxiety

Animal models of anxiety have played an important role in the study of anxiety and in the assessment of the anxiolytic potential of new drugs (see Green, 1991; Treit, 1985). These models typically involve animal defensive behaviors, the implicit assumption being that defensive behaviors are motivated by fear and that fear and anxiety are similar states. Three animal behaviors that model anxiety are elevated-plus-maze performance, defensive burying, and risk assessment.

In the *elevated-plus-maze test*, rats are placed on a four-armed plus-sign-shaped maze that is 50 centimeters above the floor. Two arms have sides and two arms have no sides, and the measure of anxiety is the proportion of time the rats spend in the enclosed arms, rather than venturing onto the exposed arms (see Pellow et al., 1985).

In the *defensive-burying test* (see Figure 5.26), rats are shocked by a wire-wrapped wooden dowel mounted on the wall of a familiar test chamber. The measure of anxiety is the amount of time the rats spend spraying bedding material from the floor of the chamber at the shock source with forward thrusting movements of their head and forepaws (see Treit et al., 1993).

In the *risk-assessment test*, after a single brief exposure to a cat on the surface of a laboratory burrow system, rats flee to their burrows and freeze. Then, they engage in a variety of risk-assessment behaviors (e.g., scanning the surface from the mouth of their burrow or exploring the surface in a cautious stretched posture) before their behavior returns to normal (see Blanchard, Blanchard, & Rodgers, 1991; Blanchard et al., 1990). The measures of anxiety are the amounts of time that the rats spend in freezing and in risk assessment.

The elevated-plus-maze, defensive-burying, and risk-assessment models of anxiety have all been validated by demonstrations that benzodiazepines reduce the various indexes of anxiety in these models, whereas nonanxiolytic drugs do not. There is a potential problem with this line of evidence, however. The potential problem stems from the fact that many cases of anxiety do not respond well to benzodiazepine therapy. Accordingly, existing animal models of anxiety may be models of benzodiazepine-sensitive anxiety rather than of anxiety in general, and thus the models may not be sensitive to anxiolytic drugs that act by a different (i.e., a non-GABAergic) mechanism. For example, the atypical anxiolytic buspirone does not have an anxiolytic effect in the elevated-plus-maze test.

Neural Bases of Anxiety Disorders

Like current theories of the neural bases of schizophrenia and depression, current theories of the neural bases of anxiety disorders rest heavily on the analysis of the effects of therapeutic drug effects. The fact that many anxiolytic drugs are agonists at either $GABA_A$ receptors (e.g., the benzodiazepines) or serotonin receptors (e.g., buspirone and Prozac) has focused attention on the possible role in anxiety disorders of deficits in both GABAergic and serotonergic transmission. However, there is little additional evidence to support either mechanism.

Recent speculations about the brain structures involved in anxiety disorders have focused on the amygdala because of the central role it plays in conditioned fear (see LeDoux, 1995). In support of the involvement of the amygdala in anxiety disorders are the following findings: The amygdala has a high concentration of $GABA_A$ receptors, local infusion of benzodiazepines into the amygdala produces anxiolytic effects in animals, and local injections of GABA antagonists into the amygdala can block the anxiolytic effects of *systemic* (into general circulation) injections of benzodiazepines (see Davis, Rainnie, & Cassell, 1994).

CONCLUSION

In this chapter, you have learned about the biopsychology of emotions, with an emphasis on fear and anxiety and the accompanying stress. The chapter began with a general overview of some of the major early research on the biopsychology of emotion (17.1), before focusing on the study of fear, defense, and aggression (17.2). Then, the focus shifted to the negative impact on health of stress and anxiety, first on physical disorders such as ulcers and infections (17.3) and finally on three major classes of psychological disorders: schizophrenia (17.4), affective disorders (17.5), and anxiety disorders (17.6). Emotions are involved in psychological disorders in two ways: Stress and anxiety can precipitate psychological disorders in individuals with an inherited predisposition, and emotional dysfunction is a prominent symptom of most psychological disorders.

It is fitting for me to be writing the last few words of a chapter about emotion at a time that is such an emotional one. I feel relieved to be finishing the project that I began several years ago, and I am excited by the prospect of being able to speak through my writing to so many students like you. You must also feel relieved to be finishing this book; still, I hope that you feel a tiny bit of regret that our time together is over. We have experienced much together, but our mutual experiences have transcended space and time. Right now, I am sitting at my desk looking out over the Pacific Ocean, as the neighborhood finches celebrate the completion of this book with a song. It is 8:00 A.M., on Saturday, May 20, 1995. Where and when are you?

FOOD FOR THOUGHT

1. With practice, you could become an expert in the production and recognition of facial expressions. How could you earn a living with these skills?

2. Does the concept of target sites have any relevance to human aggression, defense, and play fighting?

3. Blunder often plays an important role in scientific progress. Discuss this with respect to the development of drugs for the treatment of psychiatric disorders.

4. The mechanism by which a disorder is alleviated is not necessarily opposite to the mechanism by which it was caused. Discuss this with respect to current theories of schizophrenia, depression, and anxiety.

KEY TERMS

James-Lange theory (*p. 438*)
Cannon-Bard theory (*p. 439*)
Decorticate (*p. 439*)
Sham rage (*p. 439*)
Limbic system (*p. 440*)
Kluver-Bucy syndrome (*p. 440*)
Polygraphy (*p. 441*)
Control-question technique (*p. 441*)
Guilty-knowledge technique (*p. 442*)
Facial feedback hypothesis (*p. 443*)
Duchenne smile (*p. 444*)
Prosody (*p. 444*)
Fear (*p. 445*)
Defensive behaviors (*p. 445*)
Aggressive behaviors (*p. 445*)
Ethoexperimental research (*p. 445*)
Alpha male (*p. 445*)
Predatory aggression (*p. 447*)

Social aggression (*p. 447*)
Intraspecific defense (*p. 447*)
Defensive attacks (*p. 447*)
Freezing and flight (*p. 447*)
Maternal defensive behaviors (*p. 447*)
Risk assessment (*p. 447*)
Defensive burying (*p. 447*)
Target-site concept (*p. 447*)
Fear conditioning (*p. 448*)
Extinction (*p. 449*)
Stress (*p. 449*)
Adrenocorticotropic hormone (ACTH) (*p. 450*)
Glucocorticoids (*p. 450*)
Adrenal cortex (*p. 450*)
Adrenal medulla (*p. 450*)
Gastric ulcers (*p. 450*)
Psychoneuroimmunology (*p. 451*)
Immune system (*p. 451*)
Antigens (*p. 451*)
Phagocytosis (*p. 451*)
Lymphocytes (*p. 451*)

Cell-mediated immunity (*p. 451*)
T cells (*p. 451*)
Antibody-mediated immunity (*p. 451*)
B cells (*p. 451*)
Macrophage (*p. 451*)
Antibodies (*p. 452*)
Psychoses (*p. 454*)
Neuroses (*p. 454*)
Schizophrenia (*p. 454*)
Chlorpromazine (*p. 456*)
Reserpine (*p. 456*)
False transmitter (*p. 456*)
Haloperidol (*p. 457*)
Phenothiazines (*p. 458*)
Butyrophenones (*p. 458*)
Neuroleptics (*p. 458*)
Clozapine (*p. 458*)
Depression (*p. 459*)
Mania (*p. 460*)
Reactive depression (*p. 460*)
Endogenous depression (*p. 460*)

Unipolar affective disorder (*p. 460*)
Bipolar affective disorder (*p. 460*)
Iproniazid (*p. 460*)
MAO inhibitors (*p. 461*)
Cheese effect (*p. 461*)
Tricyclic antidepressants (*p. 461*)
Imipramine (*p. 461*)
Lithium (*p. 461*)
Prozac (*p. 461*)
Dexamethasone suppression test (*p. 463*)
Anxiety (*p. 463*)
Anxiety disorder (*p. 463*)
Generalized anxiety disorders (*p. 463*)
Phobic anxiety disorders (*p. 463*)
Panic disorders (*p. 463*)
Obsessive-compulsive disorders (*p. 463*)
Benzodiazepines (*p. 463*)
Buspirone (*p. 463*)

ADDITIONAL READING

The following seven articles provide excellent up-to-date reviews of research on the biopsychology of emotion, stress, and mental illness:

Albert, D. J., Walsh, M. L., & Jonik, R. H. (1993). Aggression in humans: What is its biological foundation? *Neuroscience and Biobehavioral Reviews, 17,* 405–425.

Andreasen, N. C. (1994). The mechanisms of schizophrenia. *Current Opinion in Neurobiology, 4,* 245–251.

Barondes, S. H. (1994). Thinking about Prozac. *Science, 263,* 1102–1104.

Blanchard, D. C., Blanchard, R. J., & Rodgers, R. J. (1991). Risk assessment and animal models of anxiety. In B. Olivier, J. Mos, & J. L. Slangen (Eds.), *Animal models in psychopharmacology: Advances in pharmacological sciences* (pp. 117–174). Basel: Birkhauser Verlag.

Ekman, P. (1993). Facial expression and emotion. *American Psychologist, 48,* 384–392.

LeDoux, J. E. (1994, June). Emotion, memory, and the brain. *Scientific American, 270,* 50–57.

Maier, S. R., Watkins, L. R., & Fleshner, M. (1994). Psychoneuroimmunology: The interface between behavior, brain, and immunity. *American Psychologist, 49,* 1004–1017.

EPILOGUE

Biopsychology is a fascinating discipline. I have tried to convince you of this by peeling away its complexities and serving up its fundamentals with big helpings of clear writing, good humor, and personal implications. If you liked my approach, let your instructor know so that it can benefit future students at your university.

Like good friends, we have shared good times and bad. We have shared the fun and wonder of Rhonda, the dexterous cashier; the Nads basketball team; people who rarely sleep; the mamawawa theme; split brains, Freddie the Finn, and brain transplantation. And together we have been touched by the personal tragedies of Alzheimer's disease, MPTP poisoning, the lost mariner, H.M., and the man who mistook his wife for a hat. Thank you for allowing me to share *Biopsychology* with you. I hope you have found it to be an enriching experience.

If you have any comments or suggestions, write to me at the Department of Psychology, University of British Columbia, Vancouver, B.C., Canada V6T 1Z4, or send me E-mail (jpinel@cortex.psych.ubc.ca)—or better yet, if you are ever on campus, stop by for a visit.

APPENDICES

APPENDIX I   The Autonomic Nervous System

APPENDIX II   The Cranial Nerves

APPENDIX III   Functions of the Cranial Nerves

APPENDIX IV   Nuclei of the Thalamus

APPENDIX V   Nuclei of the Hypothalamus

APPENDIX VI   Some of the Peptides That Have Been Found in Mammalian Neurons

APPENDIX VII   Phases of the Human Menstrual Cycle

The Autonomic Nervous System

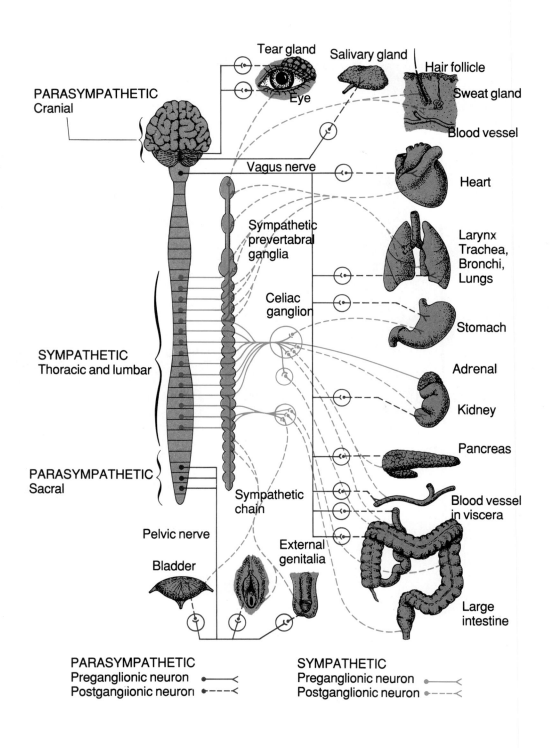

PARASYMPATHETIC
Cranial

Tear gland

Salivary gland

Hair follicle

Sweat gland

Eye

Blood vessel

Vagus nerve

Heart

Sympathetic
prevertabral
ganglia

Larynx
Trachea,
Bronchi,
Lungs

Celiac
ganglion

Stomach

SYMPATHETIC
Thoracic and lumbar

Adrenal

Kidney

Pancreas

PARASYMPATHETIC
Sacral

Blood vessel
in viscera

Sympathetic
chain

Pelvic nerve

External
genitalia

Bladder

Large
intestine

PARASYMPATHETIC
Preganglionic neuron ●——<
Postganglionic neuron ●----<

SYMPATHETIC
Preganglionic neuron ●——<
Postganglionic neuron ●----<

The Cranial Nerves

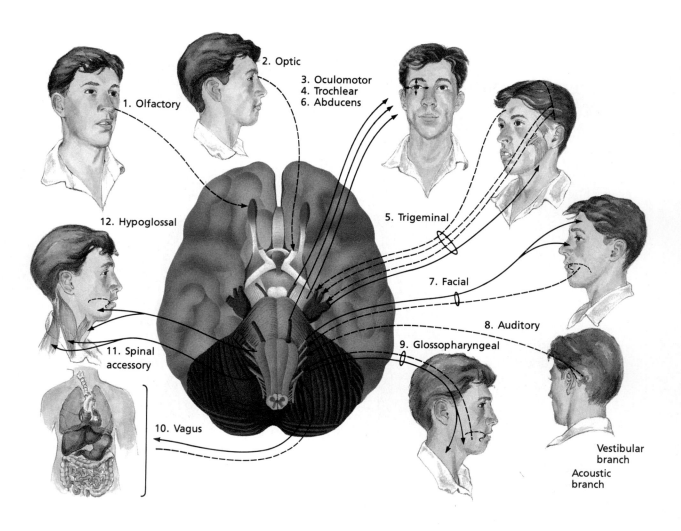

1. Olfactory
2. Optic
3. Oculomotor
4. Trochlear
6. Abducens
5. Trigeminal
7. Facial
8. Auditory
9. Glossopharyngeal
10. Vagus
11. Spinal accessory
12. Hypoglossal

Vestibular branch
Acoustic branch

APPENDIX III

Functions of the Cranial Nerves

Number	Name	General Function	Specific Functions
1	**Olfactory**	Sensory	Smell
2	**Optic**	Sensory	Vision
3	**Oculomotor**	Motor	Eye movement and pupillary constriction
		Sensory	Sensory signals from certain eye muscles
4	**Trochlear**	Motor	Eye movement
		Sensory	Sensory signals from certain eye muscles
5	**Trigeminal**	Sensory	Facial sensations
		Motor	Chewing
6	**Abducens**	Motor	Eye movement
		Sensory	Sensory signals from certain eye muscles
7	**Facial**	Sensory	Taste from anterior two-thirds of tongue
		Motor	Facial expression, secretion of tears, salivation, cranial blood vessel dilation
8	**Auditory-Vestibular**	Sensory	Audition; sensory signals from the organs of balance in the inner ear
9	**Glossopharyngeal**	Sensory	Taste from posterior third of tongue
		Motor	Salivation, swallowing
10	**Vagus**	Sensory	Sensations from abdominal and thoracic organs
		Motor	Control over abdominal and thoracic organs and muscles of the throat
11	**Spinal Accessory**	Motor	Movement of neck, shoulders, and head
		Sensory	Sensory signals from muscles of the neck
12	**Hypoglossal**	Motor	Tongue movements
		Sensory	Sensory signals from tongue muscles

Nuclei of the Thalamus

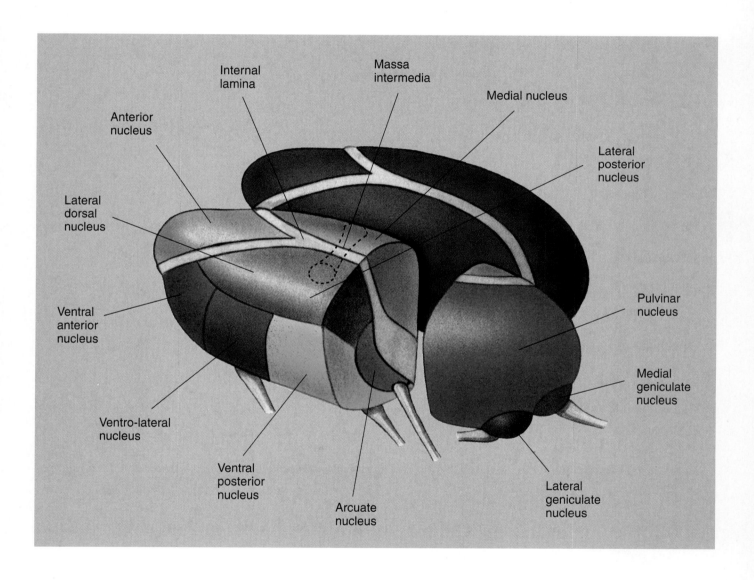

Nuclei of the Hypothalamus

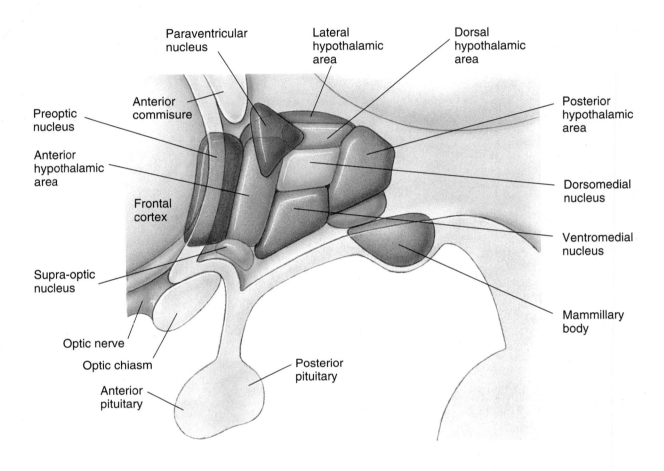

APPENDIX VI

Some of the Peptides That Have Been Found in Mammalian Neurons

Major Neuropeptides

Pituitary Peptides

Corticotropin

Growth hormone

Lipotropin

α-Melanocyte stimulating hormone

Oxytocin

Prolactin

Vasopressin

Gut Peptides

Cholecystokinin

Gastrin

Motilin

Pancreatic polypeptide

Secretin

Substance P

Vasoactive intestinal polypeptide

Miscellaneous Peptides

Angiotensin

Bombesin

Bradykinin

Carnosine

Glucagon

Insulin

Neuropeptide Y

Neurotensin

Proctolin

Hypothalamic Peptides

Luteinizing hormone-releasing hormone

Somatostatin

Thyrotropin-releasing hormone

Endorphins

Dynorphin

β-Endorphin

Met Enkephalin

Leu Enkephalin

Phases of the Human Menstrual Cycle

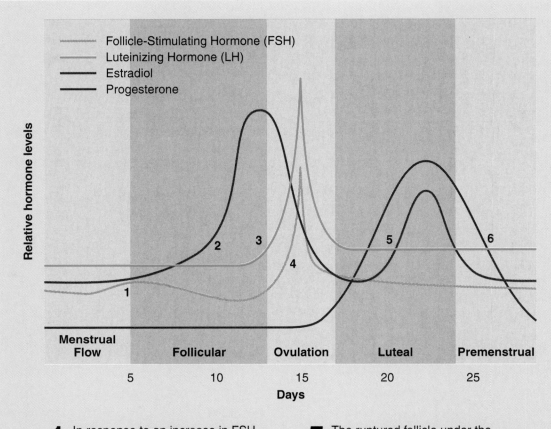

1. In response to an increase in FSH, small spheres of cells called ovarian follicles begin to grow around individual egg cells (ova).

2. The follicles begin to release estrogens such as estradiol.

3. The estrogens stimulate the hypothalamus to increase the release of LH and FSH from the anterior pituitary.

4. In response to the LH surge, one of the follicles ruptures and releases its ovum.

5. The ruptured follicle under the influence of LH develops into a corpus luteum (yellow body) and begins to release progesterone, which prepares the lining of the uterus for the implantation of a fertilized ovum.

6. Meanwhile, the ovum is moved into the fallopian tube by the rowing action of ciliated cells. If the ovum is not fertilized, progesterone and estradiol levels fall and the walls of the uterus are sloughed off as menstrual flow and the cycle begins once again.

Abe, H., & Rusak, B. (1992). Anticipatory activity and entrainment of circadian rhythms in Syrian hamsters exposed to restricted palatable diets. *American Journal of Physiology, 263,* 116–124.

Abramson, H. A. (1974). Editorial: Respiratory disorders and marijuana use. *Journal of Asthma Research, 11,* 97.

Acker, W., Ron, M. A., Lishman, W. A., & Shaw, G. K. (1984). A multivariate analysis of psychological, clinical and CT scanning measures in detoxified chronic alcoholics. *British Journal of Addiction, 79,* 293–301.

Adamec, R. (1990). In J. A. Wada, (Ed.), *Kindling 4* (pp. 329–341). New York: Plenum Press.

Adelmann, P. K., & Zajonc, R. B. (1989). Facial efference and the experience of emotion. *Annual Review of Psychology, 40,* 249–280.

Adkins-Regan, E. (1988). Sex hormones and sexual orientation in animals. *Psychobiology, 16,* 335–347.

Aggleton, J. P. (1985). One-trial object recognition by rats. *Quarterly Journal of Experimental Psychology, 37b,* 279–294.

Aggleton, J. P. (1993). The contribution of the amygdala to normal and abnormal emotional states. *Trends in Neurosciences, 16,* 328–333.

Aggleton, J. P., & Mishkin, M. (1983). Visual recognition impairment following medial thalamic lesions in monkeys. *Neuropsychologia, 21,* 189–197.

Aggleton, J. P., Nicol, R. M., Huston, A. E., & Fairbairn, A. F. (1988). The performance of amnesic subjects on tests of experimental amnesia in animals: Delayed matching-to-sample and concurrent learning. *Neuropsychologia, 26,* 265–272.

Agnati, L. F., Bjelke, B., & Fuxe, K. (1992). Volume transmission in the brain: Do brain cells communicate solely through synapses? *American Scientist, 80,* 362–373.

Aigner, T. G., Mitchell, S. J., Aggleton, J. P., DeLong, M. R., Struble, R. G., Price, D. L., Wenk, G. L., Pettigrew, K. D., & Mishkin (1991). Transient impairment of recognition memory following ibotenic-acid lesions of the basal forebrain in Macaques. *Experimental Brain research, 86,* 18–26.

Aigner, T. G., Walker, D. L., & Mishkin, M. (1991). Comparison of the effects of scopolamine administered before and after acquisition in a test of visual recognition memory in monkeys. *Behavioral and Neural Biology, 55,* 61–67.

Aizawa, H., Inase, M., Mushiake, H., Shima, K., Tanji, & J. (1991). Reorganization of activity in the supplementary motor area associated with motor learning and functional recovery. *Experimental Brain Research, 84,* 668–671.

Åkerstedt, T., & Gillberg, M. (1981). The circadian variation of experimentally displaced sleep. *Sleep, 4,* 159–169.

Albert, D. J., Jonik, R. H., & Walsh, M. L. (1992). Hormone-dependent aggression in male and female rats: Experiential, hormonal, and neural foundations. *Neuroscience and Biobehavioral Reviews, 16,* 1–16.

Albert, D. J., Petrovic, D. M., Jonik, R. H., & Walsh, M. L. (1991). Enhanced defensiveness and increased food motivation each contribute to aggression and success in food competition by rats with medial hypothalamic lesions. *Physiology & Behavior, 49,* 13–19.

Albert, D. J., & Walsh, M. L. (1984). Neural systems and the inhibitory modulation of agonistic behavior: A comparison of mammalian species. *Neuroscience and Biobehavioral Reviews, 8,* 5–24.

Albert, D. J., Walsh, M. L., & Jonik, R. H. (1993). Aggression in humans: What is its biological foundation? *Neuroscience and Biobehavioral Reviews, 17,* 405–425.

Alexander, M. P. (1989). Clinical-anatomical correlations of aphasia following predominantly subcortical lesions. In H. Goodglas (Ed.), *Handbook of neuropsychology, II, part 2.* New York: Elsevier.

Allegretta, M., Nicklas, J. A., Sriram, S., & Albertini, R. J. (1990). T cells responsive to myelin basic protein in patients with multiple sclerosis. *Science, 247,* 718–720.

Allen, L. S., Hines, M., Shryne, J. E., & Gorski, R. A. (1989). Two sexually dimorphic cell groups in the human brain. *Journal of Neuroscience, 9,* 497–506.

Altman, J. (1992). Programmed cell death: The paths to suicide. *Trends in Neurosciences, 15,* 278–280.

Alvarez, P., Zola-Morgan, S., & Squire, L. R. (1995). Damage limited to the hippocampal region produces long- lasting memory impairment in monkeys. *Journal of Neuroscience, 15,* 3796–3807.

Anand, B. K., & Brobeck, J. R. (1951). Localization of a "feeding center" in the hypothalamus of the rat. Proceedings of the *Society for Experimental Biology and Medicine, 77,* 323–324.

Anch, A. M., Browman, C. P., Mitler, M. M., & Walsh, J. K. (1988). *Sleep: A scientific perspective.* Englewood Cliffs, NJ: Prentice Hall.

Anderson, P., Cremona, A., Paton, A., Turner, C., & Wallace, P. (1993). The risk of alcohol. *Addiction, 88,* 1493–1508.

Anderson, R. H., Fleming, D. E., Rhees, R. W., & Kinghorn, E. (1986). Relationships between sexual activity, plasma testosterone, and the volume of the sexually dimorphic nucleus of the preoptic area in prenatally stressed and non-stressed rats. *Brain Research, 370,* 1–10.

Andreasen, N. C. (1994). The mechanisms of schizophrenia. *Current Opinion in Neurobiology, 4,* 245–251.

Andreassi, J. L. (1989). *Psychophysiology: Human behavior and physiological response.* Hillsdale, NJ: Erlbaum.

Andrews, K. M., McGowan, M.K., Gallitano, A., & Grossman, S. P. (1992). Water intake during chronic preoptic infusions of osmotically active or inert solutions. *Physiology & Behavior, 52,* 241–245.

Angrist, B., Rotrosen, J., & Gershon, S. (1980). Responses to apomorphine, amphetamine, and neuroleptics in schizophrenic subjects. *Psychopharmacology, 72,* 17–19.

Angst, J., Weis, P., Grof, P., Baastrup, P. G., & Schou, M. (1970). *Lithium prophylaxis in recurrent affective disorders.* British Journal of Psychiatry, 116, 604–614.

Anisman, H., & Zacharko, R. M. (1982). Depression: The predisposing influence of stress. *The Behavioral and Brain Sciences, 5,* 89–137.

Annett, J. (1985). Motor learning: A review. In H. Heuer, U. Kleinbeck, & K. H. Schmidt (Eds.), *Motor behavior: Programming, control, and acquisition* (pp. 188–212). Berlin: Springer-Verlag.

Antonini, A., & Stryker, M. P. (1993). Rapid remodeling of axonal arbors in the visual cortex. *Science, 260,* 1819–1821.

Archer, J. (1991). The influence of testosterone on human aggression. *British Journal of Psychology, 82,* 1–28.

Aréchiga, H. (1993). Circadian rhythms. *Current Opinion in Neurobiology, 3,* 1005–1010.

Aserinsky, E., & Kleitman, N. (1953). Regularly occurring periods of eye motility and concomitant phenomena, during sleep. *Science, 118,* 273–274.

Ashe, J., & Ugurbil, K. (1994). Functional imaging of the motor system. *Current Opinion in Neurobiology, 4,* 832–839.

Auerbach, S. H., Allard, T., Naeser, M., Alexander, M. P., & Albert, M. L. (1982). Pure word deafness: Analysis of a case with bilateral lesions and a defect at the prephonemic level. *Brain, 105,* 271–300.

Ax, A. F. (1955). The physiological differentiation between fear and anger in humans. *Psychosomatic Medicine, 15,* 433–442.

Baastrup, P. C., & Schou, M. (1967). Lithium as a prophylactic agent. *Archives of General Psychiatry, 16,* 162–172.

Babor, T. F., Mendelson, J. H., Greenberg, I., & Kuehnle, J. C. (1975). Marijuana consumption and tolerance to physiological and subjective effects. *Archives of General Psychiatry, 32,* 1548–1552.

Bachevalier, J., & Mishkin, M. (1986). Visual recognition impairment follows ventromedial but not dorsolateral prefrontal lesions in monkeys. *Behavioral Brain Research, 20,* 249–261.

Baier, H., & Bonhoeffer, F. (1994). Attractive axon guidance molecules. *Science, 265,* 1541–1542.

Bailey, C. H., & Chen, M. C. (1983). Morphological basis of long-term habituation and sensitization in Aplysia. *Science, 220,* 91–93.

Bailey, C. H., & Chen, M. C. (1988). Long-term memory in Aplysia modulates the total number of varicosities of single identified sensory neurons. *Proceedings of the National Academy of Sciences (USA), 85,* 2373–2377.

Bailey, M. J., & Pillard, R. C. (1991). A genetic study of male sexual orientation. *Archives of General Psychiatry, 48,* 1089–1096.

Baizer, J. S., Ungerleider, L. G., & Desimone, R. (1991). Organization of visual inputs to the inferior temporal and posterior parietal cortex in Macaques. *Journal of Neuroscience, 11,* 168–190.

Baker, B. J., & Booth, D. A. (1989). Preference conditioning by concurrent diets with delayed proportional reinforcement. *Physiology & Behavior, 46,* 585–590.

Baker, T. B., & Tiffany, S. T. (1985). Morphine tolerance as habituation. *Psychological Review, 92,* 78–108.

Balaban, E., Teillet, M. A., & Le Douarin, N. (1988). Application of the quail-chick chimera system to the study of brain development and behavior. *Science, 241,* 1339–1342.

Ballard, P. A., Tetrud, J. W., & Langston, J. W. (1985). Permanent human parkinsonism due to 1-methyl-4-phenyl-1,2,3,6-tetrahydropyridine (MPTP): Seven cases. *Neurology, 35,* 949–956.

Bancroft, J., Sanders, D., Davidson, D., & Warner, P. (1983). Mood, sexuality, hormones and the menstrual cycle: III. Sexuality and the role of androgens. *Psychosomatic Medicine, 45,* 509–516.

Bandler, R., & Shipley, M. T. (1994). Columnar organization in the midbrain periaqueductal gray: Modules for emotional expression? Trends in *Neurosciences, 17,* 379–389.

Bandtlow, C. E. (1993). Axonal regeneration in the adult vertebrate CNS. *Seminars in the Neurosciences, 5,* 391–399.

Bard P. (1929). The central representation of the sympathetic system. *Archives of Neurology and Psychiatry, 22,* 230–246.

Barden, N., Reul, J. M. H. M., & Holsboer, F. (1995). Do antidepressants stabilize mood through actions on the hypothalamic-pituitary-adrenocortical system? *Trends in Neurosciences, 18,* 6–10.

Barnstable, C. J. (1993). Glutamate and GABA in retinal circuitry. *Current Opinion in Neurobiology, 3,* 520–525.

Barondes, S. H. (1994). Thinking about Prozac. Science, 263, 1102–1104.

Bartoshuk, L. M., & Beauchamp, G. K. (1994). Chemical senses. *Annual Review of Psychology, 45,* 419–449.

Basbaum, A. I., Clanton, C. H., & Fields, H. L. (1976). Opiate and stimulus-produced analgesia: Functional anatomy of a medullospinal pathway. *Proceedings of the National Academy of Sciences (USA), 73,* 4685–4688.

Basbaum, A. I., & Fields, H. L. (1978). Endogenous pain control mechanisms: Review and hypothesis. *Annals of Neurology, 4,* 451–462.

Bashir, Z. I., & Collingridge, G. L. (1992). Synaptic plasticity: long-term potentiation in the hippocampus. *Current Opinion in Neurobiology, 2,* 328–335.

Baskin, D. G., Woods, S. C., West, D. B., van Houten, M., Posner, B. I., Dorsa, D. M., & Porte, D., Jr. (1983). Immunocytochemical detection of insulin in rat hypothalamus and its possible uptake from cerebrospinal fluid. *Endocrinology, 113,* 1818–1825.

Bastiani, M. J., Doe, C. Q., Helfand, S. L., & Goodman, C. S. (1985). Neuronal specificity and growth cone guidance in grasshopper and Drosophilia embryos. *Trends in Neurosciences, 8,* 257–266.

Baum, M. J., Erskine, M. S., Kornberg, E., & Weaver, C. E. (1990). Prenatal and neonatal testosterone exposure interact to affect differentiation of sexual behavior and partner preference in female ferrets. *Behavioral Neuroscience, 104,* 183–198.

Beal, M. F. (1992). Role of excitotoxicity in human neurological disease. *Current Opinion in Neurobiology, 2,* 657–662.

Becker, J. B., Breedlove, S. M., & Crews, D. (Eds.) (1992). *Behavioral endocrinology.* Cambridge, MA: MIT Press.

Beecher, H. K. (1959). *Measurement of subjective responses: Quantitative effects of drugs.* New York: Oxford University Press.

Bell, D. S. (1973). The experimental reproduction of amphetamine psychosis. *Archives of General Psychiatry, 29,* 35–40.

Belliveau, J. W., Kennedy, D. N., McKinstry, R. C., & Buchbinder, B. R. (1991). Functional mapping of the human visual cortex by magnetic resonance imaging. *Science, 254,* 621–768.

Bennett, E. L., Diamond, M. C., Krech, D., & Rosenzweig, M. R. (1964). Chemical and anatomical plasticity of brain. *Science, 146,* 610–619.

Benson, D. F. (1985). Aphasia. In K. M. Heilman & E. Valenstein (Eds.), *Clinical neuropsychology* (pp. 17–47). New York: Oxford University Press.

Benson, D. F., & Zaidel, E. (Eds.). (1985). *The dual brain: Hemispheric specialization in humans.* London: The Guilford Press.

Benton, A. (1985). Visuoperceptual, visuospatial, and visuoconstructive disorders. In K. M. Heilman and E. Valenstein (Eds.), *Clinical neuropsychology* (pp. 15–185). New York: Oxford University Press.

Benton, A. L. (1994). Neuropsychological assessment. *Annual Review of Psychology, 45,* 1–23.

Berger, R. J., & Oswald, I. (1962). Effects of sleep deprivation on behaviour, subsequent sleep, and dreaming. *Journal of Mental Science, 106,* 457–465.

Berkley, M., & Stebbins, W. (Eds.). (1990). *Comparative Perception, Vol. II: Communication.* New York: Wiley & Sons.

Berlucchi, G., Maffei, L., Moruzzi, G., & Strata, P. (1964). EEG and behavioral effects elicited by cooling of medulla and pons. In A. Mosso, V. Aducco, & G. Moruzzi (Eds.), *Archives Italiennes de biologie, 102,* (pp. 373–392). Pisa: Universita Degli Studi.

Bernstein, I. L., & Webster, M. M. (1980). Learned taste aversion in humans. *Physiology & Behavior, 25,* 363–366.

Berridge, V., & Edwards, G. (1981). *Opium and the people: Opiate use in nineteenth-century England.* New York: St. Martin's Press.

Bishop, M. P., Elder, S. T., & Heath, R. G. (1963). Intracranial self-stimulation in man. *Science, 140,* 394–396.

Bishop, P. O., & Pettigrew, J. D. (1986). Neural mechanisms of binocular vision. *Vision Research, 26,* 1587–1600.

Björklund, A. (1992). Dopaminergic transplants in experimental parkinsonism: Cellular mechanisms of graft-induced functional recovery. *Current Opinion in Neurobiology, 2,* 683–689.

Björklund, A., & Lindvall, O. (1986). Catecholaminergic brainstem regulatory systems. In V. B. Mountcastle, F. E. Bloom, & S. R. Geiger (Eds.), *Handbook of physiology: The nervous system* (Vol. 4, pp. 155–236). Bethesda, MD: American Physiological Society.

Björklund, A., & Stenevi, U. (1979). Reconstruction of the nigrostriatal dopamine pathway by intracerebral nigral transplants. *Brain Research, 177,* 555–560.

Blackmore, S. (1991). Lucid dreaming: Awake in your sleep? *Skeptical Inquirer, 15,* 362–370.

Blaha, C. D., Coury, A., Fibiger, H. C., & Phillips, A. G. (1990). Effects of neurotensin on dopamine release and metabolism in the rat striatum and nucleus accumbens: Cross-validation using in vivo voltammetry and microdialysis. *Neuroscience, 34,* 669–705.

Blaha, C. D., & Jung, M. E. (1991). Electrochemical evaluation of stearate-modified graphite paste electrodes: Selective detection of dopamine is maintained after exposure to brain tissue. *Journal of Electroanalytical Chemistry, 310,* 317–334.

Blanchard, D. C., & Blanchard, R. J. (1984). Affect and aggression: An animal model applied to human behavior. In D. C. Blanchard & R. J. Blanchard (Eds.), *Advances in the study of aggression* (pp. 1–62). Orlando, FL: Academic Press.

Blanchard, D. C., & Blanchard, R. J. (1988). Ethoexperimental approaches to the biology of emotion. *Annual Review of Psychology, 39,* 43–68.

Blanchard, D. C., & Blanchard, R. J. (1990a). Behavioral correlates of chronic dominance-subordination relationships of male rats in a seminatural situation. *Neuroscience and Biobehavioral Reviews, 14,* 455–462.

Blanchard, D. C., Blanchard R. J., & Rodgers, R. J. (1991). Risk assessment and animal models of anxiety. *Animal Models in Psychopharmacology: Advances in Pharmacological Sciences.* Basel: Birkhauser Verlag.

Blanchard, D. C., Blanchard, R. J., Tom, P., & Rodgers, R. J. (1990). Diazepam changes risk assessment in an anxiety/defense test battery. *Psychopharmacology, 101,* 511–518.

Blanchard, R. J., & Blanchard, D. C. (1989). Anti-predator defensive behaviors in a visible burrow system. *Journal of Comparative Psychology, 103,* 70–82.

Blanchard, R. J., & Blanchard, D. C. (1990b). Anti-predator defense as models of animal fear and anxiety. In P. F. Brain, S. Parmigiani, R. J. Blanchard, and D. Mainardi (Eds.), *Fear and defense* (pp. 89–108). New York: Harwood Academic Publishers.

Blanchard, R. J., Brain, P. F., Blanchard, D. C., & Parmigiani, S. (Eds.). (1989). *Ethoexperimental approaches to the study of behavior.* Dordrecht, The Netherlands: Kluwer Academic Publishers.

Blass, E. M., & Epstein, A. N. (1971). A lateral preoptic osmosensitive zone for thirst in the rat. *Journal of Comparative and Physiological Psychology, 76,* 378–394.

Blass, E. M., & Hall, W. G. (1976). Drinking termination: Interactions between hydrational, orogastric and behavioral controls in rats. *Psychological Review, 183,* 356–374.

Blaustein, J. D., King, J. C., Toft, D .O., & Turcotte, J. (1988). Immunocytochemical localization of estrogen-induced progestin receptors in guinea pig brain. *Brain Research, 474,* 1–15.

Bliss, T. V. P., & Gardner-Medwin, A. R. (1973). Long-lasting potentiation of synaptic transmission in the dentate area of the unanaesthetized rabbit following stimulation of the perforant path. *Journal of Physiology, 232,* 357–374.

Bliss, T. V. P., & Lømø, T. (1973). Long-lasting potentiation of synaptic transmission in the dentate area of the anaesthetized rabbit following stimulation of the perforant path. *Journal of Physiology, 232,* 331–356.

Bloch, G. J., & Gorski, R. A. (1988). Cytoarchitectonic analysis of the SDN-POA of the intact and gonadectomized rat. *Journal of Comparative Neurology, 275,* 604–612.

Block, M. L., & Fisher, A. E. (1970). Anticholinergic central blockade of salt-aroused and deprivation-induced thirst. *Physiological Behavior, 5,* 525–527.

Bogen, J. G., & Bogen, G. M. (1976). Wernicke's region—Where is it? *Annals of the New York Academy of Science, 280,* 834–843.

Bolles, R. C. (1980). Some functionalistic thought about regulation. In F. M. Toates & T. R. Halliday (Eds.), *Analysis of motivational processes* (pp. 63–75). London: Academic Press.

Bolz, J. (1994). Cortical circuitry in a dish. *Current Opinion in Neurobiology, 4,* 545–549.

Booth, D. A. (1981). The physiology of appetite. *British Medical Bulletin, 37,* 135–140.

Booth, D. A., Fuller, J., & Lewis, V. (1981). Human control of body weight: Cognitive or physiological? Some energy-related perceptions and misperceptions. In L. A. Cioffi (Ed.), *The body weight regulatory system: Normal and disturbed systems* (pp. 305–314). New York: Raven Press.

Booth, J. E. (1977). Sexual behaviour of male rats injected with the anti-oestrogen MER-25 during infancy. *Physiology & Behavior, 19,* 35–39.

Borbély, A. A. (1981). The sleep process: Circadian and homeostatic aspects. *Advances in Physiological Sciences, 18,* 85–91.

Borbély, A. A. (1983). Pharmacological approaches to sleep regulation. In A. R. Mayes (Ed.), *Sleep mechanisms and functions in humans and animals* (pp. 232–261). Wokingham, England: Van Nostrand Reinhold.

Borbély, A. A. (1984). Sleep regulation: Outline of a model and its implications for depression.

In A. Borbély & J. L. Valatx (Eds.), *Sleep mechanisms* (pp. 272–284). Berlin: Springer-Verlag.

Borbély, A. A., Baumann, F., Brandeis, D., Strauch, I., & Lehmann, D. (1981). Sleep deprivation: Effect on sleep stages and EEG power density in man. *Electroencephalography and Clinical Neurophysiology, 51,* 483–493.

Bouchard Jr., T. J. (1994). Genes, environment, and personality. *Science, 264,* 1700–1701.

Bouchard, T. J. (Jr.), Lykken, D. T., McGue, M., Segal, N. L., & Tellegen, A. (1990). Sources of human psychological differences: The Minnesota study of twins reared apart. *Science, 250,* 223–228.

Boulos, Z., & Terman, M. (1980). Food availability and daily biological rhythms. *Neuroscience and Biobehavioral Reviews, 4,* 119–131.

Bowers, D., Bauer, R. M., Coslett, H. B., & Heilman, K. M. (1985). Processing of face by patients with unilateral hemisphere lesions. I. Dissociations between judgements of facial affect and facial identity. *Brain Cognition, 4,* 258–272.

Bowers, D., Coslett, H. B., Bauer, K. M., Speedie, L. J., & Heilman, K. M. (1987). Comprehension of emotional prosody following unilateral hemispheric lesions: Processing defect versus distraction defect. *Neuropsychologia, 25,* 317–328.

Bozarth, M. A., & Wise R. A. (1981). Heroin reward is dependent on a dopaminergic substrate. *Life Sciences, 29,* 1881–1886.

Brackett, N. L., & Edwards, D. A. (1984). Medial preoptic connections with the midbrain tegmentum are essential for male sexual behavior. *Physiology & Behavior, 32,* 79–84.

Brady, J. V. (1993). Behavior analysis applications and interdisciplinary research strategies. *American Psychologist, 48,* 435–440.

Bray, G. A. (1992). Pathophysiology of obesity. *American Journal of Clinical Nutrition, 55,* 488–494.

Bray, G. M., Vidal-Sanz, M., & Aguayo, A. J. (1987). Regeneration of axons from the central nervous system of adult rats. In F. J. Seil, E. Herbert, & B. M. Carlson (Eds.), *Progress in brain research* (Vol. 71, pp. 373–378). New York: Elsevier.

Brecher, E. M. (1972). Licit and illicit drugs. Boston: Little, Brown & Co.

Breedlove, S. M. (1992). Sexual differentiation of the brain and behavior. In J. B. Becker, S. M. Breedlove, and D. Crews (Eds.), *Behavioral endocrinology* (pp. 39–70). Cambridge, MA: MIT Press.

Breedlove, S. M. (1994). Sexual differentiation of the human nervous system. *Annual Review of Psychology, 45,* 389–418.

Breitner, J. C. S. (1990). Life table methods and assessment of familial risk in Alzheimer's disease. *Archives of General Psychiatry, 47,* 395–396.

Bremer, F. (1936). Nouvelles recherches sur le mécanisme du sommeil. *Comptes Rendus de la Société de Biologie, 22,* 460–464.

Bremer, J. (1959). *Asexualization.* New York: Macmillan Publishing Co.

Brendel, D. H., Reynolds III, C.F., Jennings, J. R., Hoch, C.C., Monk, T. H., Berman, S. R., Hall, F. T., Buysse, D. J., & Kupfer, D. J. (1990). Sleep stage physiology, mood, and vigilance responses to total sleep deprivation in healthy 80-year-olds and 20-year-olds. *Psychophysiology, 27,* 677–685.

Brewster, J. M. (1986). Prevalence of alcohol and other drug problems among physicians. Journal of the American *Medical Association, 255,* 1913–1920.

Bridgeman, B., Van der Heijden, A. H. C., & Velichkovsky, B. M. (1994). A theory of visual stability across saccadic eye movements. *Behavioral and Brain Sciences, 17,* 247–292.

Brill, N. Q., & Christie, R. L. (1974). Marihuana use and psychosocial adaptation. *Archives of General Psychiatry, 31,* 713–719.

Brime, J. I., Lopez-Sela, P., Bernado, R., Costales, M., Diaz, F., Marin, B., & Vijande, M. (1991). Psychological aspects of insulin-induced thirst. *Physiology & Behavior, 49,* 153–154.

Brinkman, C. (1984). Supplementary motor area of the monkey's cerebral cortex: Short- and long-term deficits after unilateral ablation and the effects of subsequent callosal section. *Journal of Neuroscience, 4,* 918–929.

Broberg, D. J., & Bernstein, I. L. (1989). Cephalic insulin release in anorexic women. *Physiology & Behavior, 45,* 871–875.

Brou, P., Sciascia, T. R., Linden, L., & Lettvin, J. Y. (1986, September). *The colors of things.* Scientific American, 255, 84–91

Brooks, V. B. (1986). *The neural basis of motor control.* New York: Oxford.

Brown, G. W. (1993). The role of life events in the aetiology of depressive and anxiety disorders. In S. C. Stanford & S. Salmon (Eds.) *Stress: From Synapse to Syndrome* (pp. 23–50). San Diego: Academic Press.

Brown, H. D., & Kosslyn, S. M. (1993). Cerebral lateralization. *Current Opinion in Neurobiology, 3,* 183–186.

Brown, M. C., & Ironton, R. (1977). Motor neurone sprouting induced by prolonged tetrodotoxin block of nerve action potentials. *Nature, 265,* 459–461.

Brown, T. H., Chapman, P. F., Kairiss, E. W., & Keenan, C. L. (1988). Long-term synaptic potentiation. *Science, 242,* 724–728.

Brownell, K. D., & Rodin, J. (1994). The dieting maelstrom: Is it possible and advisable to lose weight. *American Psychologist, 49,* 781–791.

Brundin, P., & Björklund, A. (1987). Survival, growth and function of dopaminergic neurons grafted to the brain. In F. J. Seil, E. Herbert, & B. M. Carlson (Eds.), *Progress in brain research* (Vol. 71, pp. 293–307). New York: Elsevier.

Brundin, P., & Wictorin, K. (1993). Neuronal transplantation in rat models of Parkinson's and Huntington's diseases. *Seminars in the Neurosciences, 6,* 413–421.

Brunner, D. P., Dijk, D.-J., Tobler, I., & Borbély, A. A. (1990). Effect of partial sleep deprivation on sleep stages and EEG power spectra: Evidence for non-REM and REM sleep homeostasis. *Electroencephalography and Clinical Neurophysiology, 75,* 492–499.

Buggy, J., Fisher, A. E., Hoffman, W. E., Johnson, A. K., & Phillips, M. I. (1975). Ventricular obstruction: Effect on drinking induced by intracranial injection of angiotensin. *Science, 190,* 72–74.

Bunge, R. P. (1993). Expanding roles for the Schwann cell: Ensheathment, myelination, trophism and regeneration. *Current Opinion in Neurobiology, 3,* 805–809.

Burns, R. S., Chiueh, C. C., Markey, S. P., Ebert, M. H., Jacobowitz, D. M., & Kopin, I. J. (1983). A primate model of Parkinsonism: Selective destruction of dopaminergic neurons in the pars compacta of the substantia nigra by N-methyl-4-phenyl-1,2,3,6-tetrahydropyridine. *Proceedings of the National Academy of Sciences (USA), 80,* 4546–4550.

Burns, S. L. (1990). *How to survive unbearable stress.* Huntington Beach, CA: I-MED Press.

Butters N., & Stuss, D. T. (1989). Diencephalic amnesia. In F. Boller & J. Grafman (Eds.), *Handbook of neuropsychology, 3* (pp. 107–148). New York: Elsevier.

Butters, N., & Delis, D. C. (1995). Clinical assessment of memory disorders in Amnesia and Dementia. *Annual review of Psychology, 46,* 493–523.

Butterworth, R. F., Kril, J. J., & Harper, C. G. (1993). Thiamine-dependent enzyme changes in the brains of alcoholics: Relationship to the Wernicke-Korsakoff syndrome. *Alcoholism: Clinical and Expermental Research, 17,* 1084–1088.

Byne, W. (1994, May). The biological evidence challenged: Even if genetic and neuroanatomical traits turn out to be correlated with sexual orientation, causation is far from proved. *Scientific American, 270,* 50–55.

Byrne, J. H. (1987). Cellular analysis of associative learning. *Physiological Reviews, 67,* 329–437.

Byrne, J. H., Zwartjes, R., Homayouni, R., Critz, S. D., & Eskin, A. (1993). Roles of second messenger pathways in neuronal plasticity and in learning and memory: Insights gained from Aplysia. In S. Shenolikar and A.C. Nairn (Eds.) *Advances in Second Messenger and Phosphoprotein Research* (Vol. 27, pp. 47–108). New York: Raven Press.

Cabanac, M. (1971). Physiological role of pleasure. *Science, 173,* 1103–1107.

Cabanac, M. (1990). Taste: The maximization of multidimensional pleasure. In E. D. Capaldi & T. L. Powley (Eds.), *Taste, experience, & feeding* (pp. 28–42). Washington, DC: American Psychological Association.

Cacioppo, J. T., Petty, R. E., Losch, M., & Kim, H. S. (1986). Electromyographic activity over facial muscle regions can differentiate the valence and intensity of emotional reactions. *Journal of Personality and Social Psychology, 50,* 260–268.

Cade, J. F. J. (1949). Lithium salts in treatment of psychotic excitement. *Medical Journal of Australia, 2,* 349–352.

Caggiula, A. R. (1970). Analysis of the copulation-reward properties of posterior hypothalamic stimulation in male rats. *Journal of Comparative and Physiological Psychology, 70,* 399–412.

Cain, D. P. (1986). The transfer phenomenon in kindling. In J. A. Wada, (Ed.), *Kindling 3* (pp. 231–245). New York: Raven Press.

Calles-Escandon, J., & Horton, E. S. The thermogenic role of exercise in the treatment of morbid obesity: A critical evaluation. *American Journal of Clinical Nutrition, 55,* 533S–537S.

Calne, S., Schoenberg, B., Martin, W., Uitti, J., Spencer, P., & Calne, D. B. (1987). Familial Parkinson's disease: Possible role of environmental factors. *Canadian Journal of Neurological Sciences, 14,* 303–305.

Caltagirone, C., Zoccolotti, P., Originale, G., Daniele, A., & Mammucari, A. (1989). Autonomic reactivity and facial expression of emotion in brain damaged patients. In G. Gainotti and C. C. Caltagirone (Eds.), *Emotion and dual brain.* New York: Springer Verlag.

Campfield, L. A., Brandon, P., & Smith, F. J. (1985). On-line continuous measurement of blood glucose and meal pattern in free-feeding rats: The role of glucose in meal initiation. *Brain Research Bulletin, 14,* 605–616.

Campfield, L. A., & Smith, F. J. (1990). Transient declines in blood glucose signal meal initiation. *International Journal of Obesity, 14 (Supplement 3),* 15–33.

Cannon, W. B., & Washburn, A. L. (1912). An explanation of hunger. *American Journal of Physiology, 29,* 441–454.

Capaldi, E. D., & Powley, R. L. (Eds.), (1990). *Taste, experience, and feeding.* Washington, DC: American Psychological Association.

Capecchi, M. R., (1994, March). Targeted gene replacement. *Scientific American, 270,* 52–59.

Carew, T. J., Castellucci, V. F., & Kandel, E. R. (1971). Analysis of dishabituation and sensitization of the gill-withdrawal reflex in Aplysia. *International Journal of Neuroscience, 2,* 79–98.

Carew, T. J., Hawkins, R. D., & Kandel, E. R. (1983). Differential classical conditioning of a defensive withdrawal reflex in Aplysia californica. *Science, 219,* 397–400.

Carew, T. J., Pinsker, H. M., & Kandel, E. R. (1972). Long-term habituation of a defensive withdrawal reflex in Aplysia. *Science, 175,* 451–454.

Carew, T. J., Walters, E. T., & Kandel, E. R. (1981). Associative learning in Aplysia: Cellular correlates supporting a conditioned fear hypothesis. *Science, 211,* 501–503.

Carlesimo, G.A., & Oscar-Berman, M. (1992). Memory deficits in Alzheimer's patients: Comprehensive review. *Neuropsychology, 3,* 119–169.

Carlson, N. R. (1991). *Physiology of behavior* (4th ed.). Boston, MA: Allyn and Bacon.

Carlsson, A., & Linqvist, M. (1963). Effect of chlorpromazine or haloperidol on formation of 3-methoxytyramine and normetanephrine in mouse brains. *Acta Pharmacologica et Toxicologica, 20,* 140–144.

Carlton, P. L., & Wolgin, D. L. (1971). Contingent tolerance to the anorexinergic effects of amphetamine. *Physiology & Behavior, 7,* 221–225.

Carr, G. D., Fibiger, H. C, & Phillips, A. G. (1989). Conditioned place preference as a measure of drug reward. In J. M. Liebman & S. J. Cooper (Eds.), *The neuropharmacological basis of reward* (pp. 264–319). Oxford: Clarendon Press.

Carroll, D. (1984). *Biofeedback in practice.* New York: Longman Group.

Castellucci, V., & Kandel, E. R. (1974). A quantal analysis of the synaptic depression underlying habituation of the gill-withdrawal reflex in Aplysia. *Proceedings of the National Academy of Sciences (USA), 71,* 5004–5008.

Castellucci, V., & Kandel, E. R. (1976). Presynaptic sensitization as a mechanism for behavioral

sensitization in Aplysia. *Science, 194,*
1176–1178.

Castellucci, V., Pinsker, H., Kupfermann, I., &
Kandel, E. R. (1970). Neuronal mechanisms
of habituation and dishabituation of the
gill-withdrawal reflex in Aplysia. *Science,
167,* 1745–1748.

Castellucci, V. F., Blumenfeld, H., Goelet, P., &
Kandel, E. R (1989). Inhibitor of protein
synthesis blocks long-term behavioral
sensitization in the isolated gill-withdrawal
reflex of Aplysia. *Journal of Neurobiology, 20,*
1–9.

Castro, C. A., Silbert, L. H., McNaughton, B. L., &
Barnes, C. A. (1989). Recovery of spatial
learning deficits after decay of electrically
induced synaptic enhancement in the
hippocampus. *Nature, 342,* 545–548.

Cermak, L. S., Uhly, B., & Reale, L. (1980).
Encoding specificity in the alcoholic
Korsakoff patient. *Brain and Language, 11,*
119–127.

Chan-Ling, T., & Stone, J. (1991). Factors
determining the morphology and
distribution of astrocytes in the cat retina:
A "contact-spacing" model of astrocyte
interaction. *The Journal of Comparative
Neurology, 303,* 387–399.

Changeux, J.-P. (1993, November). Chemical
signaling in the brain. *Scientific American,
269,* 58–62.

Chen, C. S. (1968). A study of the alcohol-
tolerance effect and an introduction of a
new behavioral technique.
Psychopharmacology, 12, 433–440.

Chen, J. (1993). Dopaminergic mechanisms and
brain reward. *Seminars in the Neurosciences,
5,* 315–320.

Cheney, D. L., & Seyfarth, R. M. (1992). Précis of
how monkeys see the world. *Behavioral and
Brain Sciences, 15,* 135–182.

Choi, D. W. (1992). Bench to bedside: The
glutamate connection. *Science, 258,* 241–243.

Chorover, S. L., & Schiller, P. H. (1965). Short-
term retrograde amnesia in rats. *Journal of
Comparative and Physiological Psychology,
59,* 73–78.

Clapham, D. E. (1994). Direct G protein activation
of ion channels. *Annual Review of
Neuroscience, 17,* 441–464.

Clements, J. D., Lester, R. A. J., Tong, G., Jahr,
C. E., & Westbrook, G. L. (1992). The time
course of glutamate in the synaptic cleft.
Science, 258, 1498–1501.

Cohen, S., & Stillman, R. C. (Eds.) (1976). *The
therapeutic potential of marihuana.* New
York: Plenum Medical Book Company.

Coindet, J., Chouvet, G., & Mouret, J. (1975).
Effects of lesions of the suprachiasmatic
nuclei on paradoxical sleep and slow wave
sleep circadian rhythms in the rat.
Neuroscience Letters, 1, 243–247.

Colebatch, J. G., Deiber, M.-P., Passingham, R. E.,
Friston, K. J., & Frakowiak, R. S. J. (1991).
Regional cerebral blood flow during
voluntary arm and hand movements in
human subjects. *Journal of Neurophysiology,
65,* 1392–1401.

Coleman, R. M. (1986). *Wide awake at 3:00 A.M.*
New York: W. H. Freeman.

Colle, L. M., & Wise, R. A. (1988). Effects of
nucleus accumbens amphetamine on lateral
hypothalamic brain stimulation reward.
Brain Research, 459, 361–368.

Collier, G. (1986). The dialogue between the house
economist and the resident physiologist.
Nutrition and Behavior, 3, 9–26.

Collier, G. H. (1980). An ecological analysis of
motivation. In F. M. Toates & T. R. Halliday
(Eds.), *Analysis of motivational processes*
(pp. 125–151). London: Academic Press.

Coltheart, M. (1980). Deep dyslexia: A right
hemisphere hypothesis. In M. Coltheart,
K. Patterson, and J. C. Marshall (Eds.), *Deep
dyslexia* (pp. 326–380). London: Routledge.

Coltheart, M. (1985). Cognitive neuropsychology
and the study of reading. In M. I. Posner &
O. S. M. Marin (Eds.), *Attention and
performance: Vol. 11* (pp. 3–37). Hillsdale,
NJ: Erlbaum.

Conover, K. L., Collins, S. M., & Weingarten, H. P.
(1989). Gastric emptying changes are
neither necessary nor sufficient for
CCK-induced satiety. *American Journal of
Physiology, 256,* 56–62.

Cooper, R. M., & Zubek, J. P. (1958). Effects of
enriched and restricted early environments
on the learning ability of bright and dull
rats. *Canadian Journal of Psychology, 12,*
159–164.

Cooper, S. J., & Dourish, C. T. (1990). Multiple cholecystokinin (CCK) receptors and CCK-monoamine interactions are instrumental in the control of feeding. *Physiology & Behavior, 48,* 849–857.

Coppens, Y. (1994, May). East side story: The origin of humankind. *Scientific American, 270,* 88–95.

Corbett, D., & Wise, R. A. (1980). Intracranial self-stimulation in relation to the ascending dopaminergic systems of the midbrain: A moveable electrode mapping study. *Brain Research, 185,* 1–15.

Corbetta, M., Marzi, C. A., Tassinari, G., & Aglioti, S. (1990). Effectiveness of different task paradigms in revealing blindsight. *Brain, 113,* 603–616.

Corbetta, M., Miezin, F. M., Dobmeyer, S., Shulman, G. L., & Petersen, S. E. (1990). Attentional modulation of neural processing of shape, color, and velocity in humans. *Science, 248,* 1556–1559.

Corcoran, M. E., McCaughran, J. A., Jr., & Wada, J. A. (1973). Acute anti-epileptic effects of D9-Tetrahydrocannabinol in rats with kindled seizures. *Experimental Neurology, 40,* 471–483.

Corcoran, M., McCaughran Jr., J. A., & Wada, J. A. (1978). Antiepileptic and prophylactic effects of tetrahydrocannabinols in amygdaloid kindled rats. *Epilepsia, 19,* 47–55.

Corder, E. H., Saunders, A.M., Strittmatter, W. J., Schmechel, D. E., Gaskell, P. C., Small, G. W., Roses, A. D., Haines, J. L., & Pericak-Vance, M. A. (1993). Gene dose of apolipoprotein E type 4 allele and the risk of Alzheimer's disease in late onset families. *Science, 261,* 921–923.

Corkin, S. (1968). Acquisition of motor skill after bilateral medial temporal-lobe excision. *Neuropsychologia, 6,* 255–265.

Corkin, S., Milner, B., & Rasmussen, R. (1970). Somatosensory thresholds. *Archives of Neurology, 23,* 41–59.

Corsi, P. I. (1991). *The enchanted loom: Chapters in the history of neuroscience.* New York: Oxford.

Corwin, J. T., & Warchol, M. E. (1991). Auditory hair cells. *Annual Review of Neuroscience, 14,* 301–333.

Costall, B., & Naylor, R. J. (1977). Mesolimbic and extrapyramidal sites for the mediation of stereotyped behaviour patterns and hyperactivity by amphetamine and apomorphine in the rat. In E. H. Ellinwood, Jr. & M. M. Kilbey (Eds.), *Cocaine and other stimulants* (pp. 47–76). New York: Plenum Press.

Cowan, W. M. (1979). The development of the brain. *Scientific American, 241,* 113–133.

Cowey, A., & Stoerig, P. (1991). The neurobiology of blindsight. *Trends in Neurosciences, 14,* 140–145.

Cox, D. R., Green, E. D., Lander, E.S., Cohen, D., & Myers, R. M. (1994). Assessing mapping progress in the human genome project. *Science, 265,* 2031–2032.

Coyle, J. T. (1987). Alzheimer's disease. In G. Adelman (Ed.), *Encyclopedia of neuroscience* (pp. 29–31). Boston: Birkhäuser.

Coyle, J. T., & Puttfarken, P. (1993). Oxidative stress, glutamate, and neurodegenerative disorders. *Science, 262,* 689–295.

Cragg, B. G. (1975). The development of synapses in kitten visual cortex during visual deprivation. *Experimental Neurology, 46,* 445–451.

Creese, I., Burt, D. R., & Snyder, S. H. (1976). Dopamine receptor binding predicts clinical and pharmacological potencies of antischizophrenic drugs. *Science, 192,* 481–483.

Crews, D. (1988). The problem with gender. *Psychobiology, 16,* 321–334.

Crowell, C. R., Hinson, R. E., & Siegel, S. (1981). The role of conditional drug responses in tolerance to the hypothermic effects of ethanol. *Psychopharmacology, 73,* 51–54.

Cumming, G. D. (1978). Eye movements and visual perception. In E. C. Carterette & M. P. Friedman (Eds.), *Handbook of perception* (Vol. 9, pp. 221–255). New York: Academic Press.

Currier, R. D., & Eldridge, R. (1982). Possible risk factors in multiple sclerosis as found in a national twin study. *Archives of Neurology, 39,* 140–144.

Czeisler, C. A., Kronauer, R. E., Allan, J. S., Duffy, J. F., Jewett, M. E., Brown, E. N., & Ronda,

J. M. (1989). Bright light induction of strong (Type O) resetting of the human circadian pacemaker. *Science, 244,* 1328–1333.

Daan, S., & Lewy, A. J. (1984). Scheduled exposure to daylight: A potential strategy to reduce "jet lag" following transmeridian flight. *Psychopharmacology Bulletin, 20,* 566–568.

Daly, M., & Wilson, M. (1983). *Sex, Evolution, and Behavior.* Boston, MA: Allard Grant Press.

Damasio, A. R., Tranel, D., & Damasio, H. (1990). Face agnosia and the neural substrates of memory. *Annual Review of Neuroscience, 13,* 89–109.

Damasio, H. (1989). Neuroimaging contributions to the understanding of aphasia. In F. Boller & J. Grafman (Eds.), *Handbook of neuropsychology, Vol. 2* (pp. 3–46). New York: Elsevier.

Dartnall, H. J. A., Bowmaker, J. K., & Mollon, J. D. (1983). Microspectrophotometry of human photoreceptors. In J. D. Mollon & L. T. Sharpe (Eds.), *Colour vision: Physiology and psychophysics* (pp. 69–80). New York: Academic Press.

Darwin, C. (1872). *The expression of emotions in man and animals.* New York: Philosophical Library.

Das, G. D., & Altman, J. (1971). Transplanted precursors of nerve cells: Their fate in the cerebellums of young rats. *Science, 173,* 637–638.

Davidson, J. M. (1980). Hormones and sexual behavior in the male. In D. T. Krieger and J. C. Hughes (Eds.), *Neuroendocrinology* (pp. 232–238). Sunderland, MA: Sinauer Associates.

Davidson, J. M., Kwan, M., & Greenleaf, W. J. (1982). Hormonal replacement and sexuality in men. *Clinics in Endocrinology and Metabolism, 11,* 599–623.

Davis, H. P., Rosenzweig, M. R., Becker, L. A., & Sather, K. J. (1988). Biological psychology's relationships to psychology and neuroscience. *American Psychologist, 43,* 359–371.

Davis, M., Rainnie, D., & Cassell, M. (1994). Neurotransmission in the rat amygdala related to fear and anxiety. *Trends in Neurosciences, 17,* 208–214.

De Camilli, P., & Jahn, R. (1990). Pathways to regulated exocytosis in neurons. *Annual Review of Physiology, 52,* 625–645.

De Jonge, F. H., Louwerse, A. L., Ooms, M. P., Evers, P., Endert, E., & van de Poll, N. E. (1989). Lesions of the SDN-POA inhibit sexual behavior of male Wistar rats. *Brain Research Bulletin, 23,* 483–492.

de Kruif, P. (1945). *The male hormone.* New York: Harcourt, Brace and Co.

De Renzi, E. (1980). The influence of sex and age on the incidence and type of aphasia. *Cortex, 16,* 627–630.

De Renzi, E. (1982). *Disorders of space exploration and cognition.* New York: Wiley.

Dement, W. C. (1960). The effect of dream deprivation. *Science, 131,* 1705–1707.

Dement, W. C. (1978). *Some must watch while some must sleep.* New York: W. W. Norton.

Dement, W. C., & Kleitman, N. (1957). The relation of eye movement during sleep to dream activity: An objective method for the study of dreaming. *Journal of Experimental Psychology, 53,* 339–553.

Dement, W. C., Milter, M., & Henriksen, S. (1972). Sleep changes during chronic administration of parachorophenylalanine. *Revue Canadianne de Biologie, 31,* 239–246.

Dement, W. C., & Wolpert, E. A. (1958). The relation of eye movements, body motility and external stimuli to dream content. *Journal of Experimental Psychology, 55,* 543–553.

Demotes-Mainard, J., Vernier, P., & Vincent, J.-D. (1993). Hormonal control of neural function in the adult brain. *Current Opinion in Neurobiology, 3,* 989–996.

Dennerstein, L., & Burrows, G. D. (1982). Hormone replacement therapy and sexuality in women. *Clinics in Endocrinology and Metabolism, 11,* 661–679.

Desimone, R. (1992). The physiology of memory: Recordings of things past. *Science, 258,* 245–246.

DeValois, R. L., & DeValois, K. K. (1988). *Spatial Vision.* New York: Oxford University Press.

Devane, W. A., Hanuš, L., Breuer, A., Pertwee, R. G., Stevenson, L. A., Griffin, G., Gibson, D., Mandelbaum, A., Etinger, A., & Mechoulam, R. (1992). Isolation and structure of a brain constituent that binds to the cannabinoid receptor. *Science, 258,* 1946–1949.

Dewsbury, D. A. (1990). Contemporary issues in comparative psychology. Sunderland, Massachusetts: Sinauer.

Dewsbury, D. A. (1991). Psychobiology. *American Psychologist, 46,* 198–205.

Di Pelligrino, G. D., & Wise, S. P. (1991). Neurophysiological comparison of three distinct regions in the primate frontal lobe. *Brain, 114 ,* 951–978.

Diamond, J. (1982). Modelling and competition in the nervous system: Clues from sensory innervation of skin. *Current Topics in Developmental Biology, 17,* 147–205.

Diamond, M. C. (1986). I want a girl just like the girl.... *Discover, 7,* 65–68.

Dicker, S. E., & Nunn, J. (1957). The role of antidiuretic hormone during water deprivation in rats. *Journal of Physiology, 136,* 235–248.

Dobelle, W. H., Mladejovsky, M. G., & Girvin, J. P. (1974). Artificial vision for the blind: Electrical stimulation of visual cortex offers hope for a functional prosthesis. *Science, 183,* 440–444.

Doherty, P., & Walsh, F. S. (1992). Cell adhesion molecules, second messengers and axonal growth. *Current Opinion in Neurobiology, 2,* 595–601.

Doty, R. L. (1986). Gender and endocrine-related influences on human olfactory perception. In H. Meiselman & R. S. Rivlin (Eds.), *Clinical measurement of taste and smell* (pp. 377–413). New York: Macmillan Publishing Co.

Doty, R. L., Ford, M., Preti, G., & Huggins, G. R. (1975). Changes in the intensity and pleasantness of human vaginal odors during the menstrual cycle. *Science, 190,* 1316–1318.

Doty, R. L., Green, P. A., Ram, C., & Yankell, S. L. (1982). Communication of gender from human breath odors: Relationship to perceived intensity and pleasantness. *Hormones and Behavior, 16,* 13–22.

Doty, R. L., Snyder, P. J., Huggins, G. R., & Lowry, L. D. (1981). Endocrine, cardiovascular, and psychological correlates of olfactory sensitivity changes during the human menstrual cycle. Journal of *Comparative and Physiological Psychology, 95,* 45–60.

Doupe, A. J. (1993). A neural circuit specialized for vocal learning. Current Opinion in *Neurobiology, 3,* 104–110.

Dourish, C. T., Rycroft, W., & Iversen, S. D. (1989). Postponement of satiety by blockade of brain cholecystokinin (CCK-B) receptors. *Science, 245,* 1509–1511.

Drachman, D. A., & Arbit, J. (1966). Memory and the hippocampal complex. *Archives of Neurology, 15,* 52–61.

Dum, R. P., & Strick, P. L. (1992). Medial wall motor areas and skeletomotor control. *Current Opinion in Neurobiology, 2,* 836–839.

Dunant, Y., & Israël, M. (1985, April). The release of acetylcholine. *Scientific American, 252,* 58–66.

Dunbar, G. C., Perera, M. H., & Jenner, F. A. (1989). Patterns of benzodiazepine use in Great Britain as measured by a general population survey. *British Journal of Psychiatry, 155,* 836–841.

Dusoir, H., Kapur, N., Byrnes, D. P., McKinstry, S., & Hoare, R. D. (1990). The role of diencephalic pathology in human memory disorder. *Brain, 113,* 1695–1706.

Duvoisin, R. C., Heikkila, R. E., Nicklas, W. J., & Hess, A. (1986). Dopaminergic neurotoxicity of MPTP in the mouse: A murine model of parkinsonism. In S. Fahn, C. D. Marsden, P. Jenner, & P. Teychenne (Eds.), *Recent developments in Parkinson's disease* (pp. 147–154). New York: Raven Press.

Easter, S. S., Jr., Purves, D., Rakic, P., & Spitzer, N. C. (1985). The changing view of neural specificity. *Science, 230,* 507–511.

Edwards, D. A. (1969). Early androgen stimulation and aggressive behavior in male and female mice. *Physiology & Behavior, 4,* 333–338.

Ehrhardt, A. A., Epstein, R., & Money, M. (1968). Fetal androgens and female gender identity in the early-treated androgenital syndrome. *Johns Hopkins Medical Journal, 122,* 160–167.

Ehrhardt, A. A., & Meyer-Bahlberg, H. F. L. (1981). Effects of prenatal sex hormones on gender-related behavior. *Science, 211,* 1312–1317.

Ehrhardt, A. A., Meyer-Bahlburg, H. F. L., Rosen, L. R., Feldman, J. F., Veridiano, N. P., Zimmerman, I., & McEwen, B. S. (1985). Sexual orientation after prenatal exposure to exogenous estrogen. *Archives of Sexual Behavior, 14*, 57–77.

Ehringer, H., & Hornykiewicz, O. (1960). Verteilung von Noradrenalin und Dopamin (3-Hydroxytyramin) im gehirn des Menschen und ihr Verhalten bei Erkrankungen des Extrapyramidalen Systems. *Klinische Wochenschrift, 38*, 1236–1239.

Eichenbaum, H., & Otto, T. (1993). LTP and memory: Can we enhance the connection? *Trends in Neurosciences, 16*, 163–164.

Eichenbaum, H., Otto, T., & Cohen, N. J. (1992). Review: The hippocampus—what does it do? *Behavioral and Neural Biology, 57*, 2–36.

Eidelberg, E. (1987). Flexion reflexes. In G. Adelman (Ed.), *Encyclopedia of neuroscience, I*, (pp. 431–432). Boston, MA: Birkhauser.

Eikelboom, R., & Stewart, J. (1982). Conditioning of drug-induced physiological responses. *Psychological Review, 89*, 507–528.

Ekman, P. (1985). *Telling lies.* New York: Norton.

Ekman, P. (1992). Facial expressions of emotion: New findings, new questions. *Psychological Science, 3*, 34–38.

Ekman, P. (1993). Facial expression and emotion. *American Psychologist, 48*, 384–392.

Ekman, P., & Davidson, R. J. (1993). Voluntary smiling changes regional brain activity. *Psychological Science, 4*, 342–345.

Ekman, P., & Friesen, W. V. (1971). Constants across cultures in the face and emotion. *Journal of Personality and Social Psychology, 17*, 124–129.

Ekman, P., & Friesen, W. V. (1975). *Unmasking the face: A guide to recognizing emotions from facial clues.* Englewood Cliffs, NJ: Prentice-Hall.

Ekman, P., Sorenson, E. R., & Friesen, W. V. (1969). Pan-cultural elements in facial displays of emotions. *Science, 164*, 86–88.

Eliot, L.S., Hawkins, R. D., Kandel, E. R., & Schacher, S. (1994). Pairing-specific presynaptic facilitation at Aplysia sensory-motor neuron synapses in isolated cell culture. *Journal of Neuroscience, 14*, 368–383.

Ellis, L., & Ames, M. A. (1987). Neurohormonal functioning and sexual orientation: A theory of homosexuality-heterosexuality. *Psychological Bulletin, 101*, 233–258.

Emptage, N. J., & Carew, T. J. (1993). Long-term synaptic facilitation in the absence of short-term facilitation in Aplysia neurons. *Science, 262*, 253–256.

Epstein, A. N. (1982). The physiology of thrist. In D. W. Pfaff (Ed.), *The physiological mechanisms of motivation* (pp. 165–214). New York: Springer-Verlag.

Epstein, A. N. (1987). Drinking behavior. In G. Adelman (Ed.), *Encyclopedia of neuroscience* (pp. 340–342). Boston: Birkhäuser.

Etcoff, N. L. (1989). Asymmetries in recognition of emotion. In F. Boller and J. Grafman (Eds.), *Handbook of neuropsychology, 3*, (pp. 363–402).

Evans, C. J., Keith Jr., D. E., Morrison, H., Magendzo, K., & Edwards, R. H. (1992). *Science, 258*, 1952–1955.

Everitt, B. J., & Herbert, J. (1972). Hormonal correlates of sexual behavior in sub-human primates. *Danish Medical Bulletin, 19*, 246–258.

Everitt, B. J., Herbert, J., & Hamer, J. D. (1971). Sexual receptivity of bilaterally adrenalectomized female rhesus monkeys. *Physiology & Behavior, 8*, 409–415.

Everitt, B. J., & Stacey, P. (1987). Studies of instrumental behavior with sexual reinforcement in male rats (Rattus norvegicus): II Effects of preoptic area lesions, castration, and testosterone. *Journal of Comparative Psychology, 101*, 407–419.

Fadem, B. H., & Barfield, R. J. (1981). Neonatal hormonal influences on the development of proceptive and receptive feminine sexual behavior in rats. *Hormones and Behavior, 15*, 282–288.

Falk, J. L. (1964). Production of polydipsia in normal rats by an intermittent food schedule. *Science, 133*, 195–196.

Falzi, G., Perrone, P., & Vignolo, L. A. (1982). Right-left asymmetry in anterior speech region. *Archives of Neurology, 39*, 239–240.

Farah, M. J. (1990). *Visual agnosia: Disrders of object recognition and what they tell us about normal vision.* Cambridge, MA: MIT Press.

Fawcett, J. W. (1992). Intrinsic neuronal determinants of regeneration. *Trends in Neurosciences, 15,* 5–8.

Fawcett, J. W., & Keynes, R. J. (1990). Peripheral nerve regeneration. *Annual Review of Neuroscience, 13,* 43–60.

Feder, H. H. (1981). Perinatal hormones and their role in the development of sexually dimorphic behaviors. In N. T. Adler (Ed.), *Neuroendocrinology of reproduction: Physiology & Behavior* (pp. 127–157). New York: Plenum Press.

Feder, H. H. (1984). Hormones and sexual behavior. *Annual Review of Psychology, 35,* 165–200.

Feindel, W. (1986). Electrical stimulation of the brain during surgery for epilepsy—historical highlights. In G. P. Varkey (Ed.), *Anesthetic considerations for craniotomy in awake patients* (pp. 75–87). Boston: Little, Brown and Company.

Feldman, S. M., & Waller, H. J. (1962). Disassociation of electrocortical activation and behavioral arousal. *Nature, 196,* 1320–1322.

Fentress, J. C. (1973). Development of grooming in mice with amputated forelimbs. *Science, 179,* 704–705.

Fetz, E. E. (1993). Cortical mechanisms controlling limb movement. Current Opinion in Neurobiology, 3, 932–939.

Fibiger, H. C. (1991). Cholinergic mechanisms in learning, memory and dementia: A review of recent evidence. *Trends in Neurosciences, 14,* 20–223.

Fibiger, H. C. (1993). Mesolimbic dopamine: An analysis of its role in motivated behavior. *Seminars in the Neurosciences, 5,* 321–327.

Fibiger, H. C., LePiane, F. G., Jakubovic, A., & Phillips, A. G. (1987). The role of dopamine in intracranial self-stimulation of the ventral tegmental area. *Journal of Neuroscience, 7,* 3888–3896.

Fields, H. L., & Basbaum, A. I. (1984). Endogenous pain control mechanisms. In P. D. Wall & R. Melzack (Eds.), *Textbook of pain* (pp. 142–152). Edinburgh: Churchill Livingstone.

Fiez, J. A., & Petersen, S. E. (1993). PET as part of an interdisciplinary approach to understanding processes involved in reading. *Psychological Science, 4,* 287–293.

Fillion, T. J., & Blass, E. M. (1986). Infantile experience with suckling odors determines adult sexual behavior in male rats. *Science, 231,* 729–731.

Fine, A. (1986, August). Transplantation in the central nervous system. *Scientific American, 255,* 52–58.

Finger, S., Le Vere, T. E., Almli, C. R., & Stein, D. G. (1988). *Brain injury and recovery: Theoretical and controversial issues.* New York: Plenum.

Fischer-Nielson, S., Loft, S., & Gjervig Jensen, K. (1993). Effect of ascorbate and 5-aminosalicylic acid on light-induced 8 hydroxydeoxyguanosine formation in V79 Chinese hamster cells. *Carcinogenesis, 14,* 2431–2433.

Fitzsimons, J. T. (1961). Drinking by rats depleted of body fluid without increase in osmotic pressure. *Journal of Physiology, 159,* 297–309.

Fitzsimons, J. T. (1972). Thirst. *Physiological Reviews, 52,* 468–561.

Fitzsimons, J. T., Epstein, A. N., & Johnson, A. K. (1978). Peptide antagonists of the renin-angiotensin system in the characterisation of receptors for angiotensin-induced drinking. *Brain Research, 153,* 319–331.

Fitzsimons, J. T., & LeMagnen, J. (1969). Eating as a regulatory control of drinking in the rat. *Journal of Comparative and Physiological Psychology, 67,* 273–283.

Fitzsimons, J. T., & Simons, B. J. (1969). The effect on drinking in the rat of intravenous infusion of angiotensin, given alone or in combination with other stimuli of thirst. *Journal of Physiology, 203,* 45–57.

Foster, T. C., Castro, C. A., & McNaughton, B. L. (1989). Spatial selectivity of rat hippocampal neurons: Dependence on preparedness for movement. *Science, 244,* 1580–1582.

Franklin, R. J. M. (1993). Reconstructing myelin-deficient environments in the CNS by glial cell transplantation. *Seminars in the Neurosciences, 5,* 443–451.

Freed, W. J., Perlow, M. J., Karoum, F., Seiger, A., Olson, L., Hoffer, B. J., & Wyatt, R. J. (1980). Restoration of dopaminergic function by grafting of fetal rat substantia nigra to the caudate nucleus: Long-term behavioral, biochemical, and histochemical studies. *Annals of Neurology, 8,* 510–519.

Freeman, W. J. (1991, February). The physiology of perception. *Scientific American, 264,* 78–85.

Frey, U., Huang, Y.-Y., & Kandel, E. R. (1993). Effects of cAMP simulate a late stage of LTP in hippocampal CA 1 neurons. *Science, 260,* 1661–1664.

Friedman, J., Globus, G., Huntley, A., Mullaney, D., Naitoh, P., & Johnson, L. (1977). Performance and mood during and after gradual sleep reduction. *Psychophysiology, 14,* 245–250.

Funder, J. W. (1993). Mineralocorticoids, glucocorticoids, receptors and response elements. *Science, 259,* 1132–1133.

Gabrieli, J. D. E., Corkin, S., Mickel, S. F., & Growdon, J. H. (1993). Intact acquisition and long-term retention of mirror-tracing skill in Alzheimer's disease and in global amnesia. *Behavioral Neuroscience, 107,* 899–910.

Gackenbach, J., & LaBerge, S. (Eds.). (1988). *Conscious mind, sleeping brain.* New York: Plenum.

Gaffan, D. (1974). Recognition impaired and association in the memory of monkeys after transection of the fornix. *Journal of Comparative and Physiological Psychology, 86,* 1100–1109.

Galef, B. G. (1989). Laboratory studies of naturally- occurring feeding behaviors: Pitfalls, progress and problems in ethoexperimental analysis. In R. J. Blanchard, P. F. Brain, D. C. Blanchard, & S. Parmigiani (Eds.), *Ethoexperimental approaches to the study of behavior* (pp. 51–77). Dordrecht, The Netherlands: Kluwer Academic Publishers.

Galef, B. G., & Sherry, D. F. (1973). Mother's milk: A medium for transmission of cues reflecting the flavor of mother's diet. *Journal*

of Comparative and Physiological Psychology, 83, 374–378.

Galef, B. G., Jr., Attenborough, K. S., & Whiskin, E. E. (1990). Responses of observer rats (rattus norvegicus) to complex, diet-related signals emitted by demonstrator rats. *Journal of Comparative Psychology, 104,* 11–19.

Gall, C., McWilliams, R., & Lynch, G. (1980). Accelerated rates of synaptogenesis by "sprouting" afferents in the immature hippocampal formation. Journal of *Comparative Neurology, 193,* 1047–1061.

Gallagher, M., & Holland, P.C. (1992). Preserved configural learning and spatial learning impairment in rats with hippocampal damage. *Hippocampus, 2,* 81–88.

Gallup, G. G. (Jr.) (1983). Toward a comparative psychology of mind. In R. L. Mellgren (Ed.), *Animal cognition and behavior* (pp. 473–505). New York: North-Holland Publishing.

Garcia, J., & Koelling, R. A. (1966). Relation of lcue to consequence in avoidance learning. *Psychonomic Science, 4,* 123–124.

Garraghty, P. E., & Kaas, J. H. (1992). Dynamic features of sensory and motor maps. *Current Opinion of Neurobiology, 2,* 522–527.

Gawin, F. H. (1991). Cocaine addiction: Psychology and neurophysiology. *Science, 251,* 1580–1586.

Gaze, R. M., Keating, M. J., Ostberg, A., & Chung, S. H. (1979). The relationship between retinal and tectal growth in larval Xenopus: Implications for the development of the retino-tectal projection. *Journal of Embryology and Experimental Morphology, 53,* 103–143.

Gaze, R. M., & Sharma, S. C. (1970). Axial differences in the reinnervation of the goldfish optic tectum by regenerating optic nerve fibres. *Experimental Brain Research, 10,* 171–181.

Gazzaniga, M. S. (1967, August). The split brain in man. *Scientific American, 217,* 24–29.

Gazzaniga, M. S., Fendrich, R., & Wessinger, C. M. (1994). Blindsight reconsidered. *Current Directions in Psychological Science, 3,* 93–95.

Gazzaniga, M. S., & Sperry, R. W. (1967). Language after section of the cerebral commissure. *Brain, 90,* 131–148.

Geiselman, P. J. (1987). Carbohydrates do not always produce satiety: An explanation of the appetite- and hunger-stimulating effects of hexoses. *Progress in Psychobiology and Physiological Psychology, 12,* 1–46.

Georgopoulos, A. P. (1991). Higher order motor control. *Annual Review of Neuroscience, 14,* 361–377.

Georgopoulos, A. P., Ashe, J., Smyrnis, N., & Taira, M. (1992). The motor cortex and the coding of force. *Science, 256,* 1692–1694.

Geschwind, N. (1965). The organization of language and the brain. *Science, 170,* 940–944.

Geschwind, N. (1979, September). Specializations of the human brain. *Scientific American, 241,* 180–199.

Geschwind, N., & Levitsky, W. (1968). Human brain: Left-right asymmetries in temporal speech region. *Science, 161,* 186–187.

Gibbs, J., Young, R. C., & Smith, G. P. (1973). Cholecystokinin decreases food intake in rats. *Journal of Comparative and Physiological Psychology, 84,* 488–495.

Gilbert, C. D. (1993). Rapid dynamic changes in adult cerebral cortex. *Current Opinion in Neurobiology, 3,* 100–103.

Gilbert, C. D., & Wiesel, T. N. (1992). Receptive field dynamics in adult primary visual cortex. *Nature, 356,* 150–152.

Gilliam, T. C., Gusella, J. F., & Lehrach, H. (1987). Molecular genetic strategies to investigate Huntington's disease. *Advances in Neurology, 48,* 17–29.

Gilman, A. (1937). The relation between blood osmotic pressure, fluid distribution and voluntary water intake. *American Journal of Physiology, 120,* 323–328.

Ginty, D. D., Kornhauser, J. M., Thompson, M. A., Bading, H., Mayo, K. E., Takahashi, J. S., & Greenberg, M. E. (1993). Regulation of CREB phosphorylation in the suprachiasmatic nucleus by light and a circadian clock. *Science, 260,* 238–241.

Glanzman, D. L. (1995). The cellular basis of classical conditioning in *Aplysia californica*—it's less simple than you think. *Trends in Neurosciences, 18,* 30–36.

Glanzman, D. L., Kandel, E. R., & Schacher, S. (1990). Target-dependent structural changes accompanying long-term synaptic facilitation in Aplysia neurons. *Science, 249,* 799–802.

Glaser, R., Rice, J., Sheridan, J., Fertel, R., Stout, J., Speicher, C., Pinsky, D., Koture, M., Post, A., Beck, M., & Kiecolt-Glaser, J. K. (1987). Stress-related immune suppression: Health implications. *Brain, Behavior & Immunity, 1,* 7–20.

Glickman, S. E., & Schiff, B. B. (1967). A biological theory of reinforcement. *Psychological Review, 74,* 81–109.

Glickstein, M. (1992). The cerebellum and motor learning. *Current Opinion in Neurobiology, 2,* 802–806.

Goate, A., Chartier-Harlin, M-C., Mullan, M., Brown, J., Crawford, F., Fidani, L., Giuffra, L., Haynes, A., Irving, N., James, L., Mant, R., Newton, P., Rooke, K., Roques, P., Talbot, C., Pericak-Vance, M., Roses, A., Williamson, R., Rossor, M., Wen, M., & Hardy, J. (1991). Segregation of a missense mutation in the amyloid precursor protein gene with familial Alzheimer's disease. *Nature, 349,* 704–706.

Goddard, G. V., McIntyre, D. C., & Leech, C. K. (1969). A permanent change in brain function resulting from daily electrical stimulation. *Experimental Neurology, 25,* 295–330.

Goedert, M. (1993). Tau protein and the neurofibrillary pathology of Alzheimer's disease. *Trends in Neurosciences, 16,* 460–465.

Goetz, C. G., Olanow, C. W., Koller, W. C., Penn, R. D., Cahill, D., Morantz, R., Stebbins, G., Tanner, C. M., Klawans, H. L., Shannon, K. M., Comella, C. L., Witt, T., Cox, C., Waxman, M., & Gauger, L. (1989). Multicenter study of autologous adrenal medullary transplantation to the corpus striatum in patients with advanced Parkinson's disease. *The New England Journal of Medicine, 320,* 337–341.

Gold, R. M., Jones, A. P., Sawchenko, P. E., & Kapatos, G. (1977). Paraventricular area: Critical focus of a longitudinal neurocircuitry mediating food intake. *Physiology & Behavior, 18,* 1111–1119.

Goldman, B. (1984). *Death in the locker room: Steroids and sports.* South Bend, IN: Icarus Press.

Goldman-Rakic, P. S., Bates, J. F., & Chafee, M. V. (1992). The prefontal cortex and internally generated motor acts. *Current Opinion in Neurobiology, 2,* 830–835.

Goldman-Rakic, P. S., & Selemon, L. D. (1990). New frontiers in basal ganglia research. *Trends in Neurosciences, 13,* 241–244.

Goldstein, A., & Kalant, H. (1990). Drug policy: Striking the right balance. *Science, 249,* 1513–1521.

Goldstein, G. W., & Betz, A. L. (1986, September). The blood-brain barrier. *Scientific American, 255,* 74–83.

Gollin, E. S. (1960). Developmental studies of visual recognition of incomplete objects. *Perceptual Motor Skills, 11,* 289–298.

Gollinick, P. D., & Hodgson, D. R. (1986). The identification of fiber types in skeletal muscle: A continual dilemma. *Exercise and Sport Sciences Reviews, 14,* 81–104.

Goodale, M. A. (1993). Visual pathways supporting perception and action in the primate cerebral cortex. *Current Opinion in Neurobiology, 3,* 578–585.

Goodale, M. A., & Milner, A. D. (1992). Separate visual pathways for perception and action. *Trends in Neurosciences, 15,* 20–25.

Goodale, M. A., Milner, A. D., Jakobson, L.S., & Carey, D. P. (1991). A neurological dissociation between perceiving objects and grasping them. *Nature, 349,* 154–156.

Goodenough, D. R., Shapiro, A., Holden, M., & Steinschriber, L. (1959). A comparison of "dreamers" and "nondreamers": Eye movements, electroencephalograms, and the recall of dreams. *Journal of Abnormal and Social Psychology, 59,* 295–303.

Goodglass, H., & Kaplan, E. (1979). Assessment of cognitive deficit in the brain-injured patient. In M. S. Gazzaniga (Ed.), *Handbook of behavioral neurobiology: Vol. 2. Neuropsychology* (pp. 3–22). New York: Plenum Press.

Goodison, T., & Siegal, S. (1995). Learning and tolerance to the intake suppressive effect of Cholecystokinin in rats. *Behavioral Neuroscience, 109,* 62–70.

Goodlett, C. R., Marcussen, B. L., & West, J. R. (1990). A single day of alcohol exposure during the brain growth spurt induces brain weight restriction and cerebellar Purkinje cell loss. *Alcohol, 7,* 107–114.

Gorski, R. A. (1971). Gonadal hormones and the perinatal development of neuroendocrine function. In L. Martini & W. F. Ganong (Eds.), *Frontiers in neuroendocrinology* (pp. 237–290). New York: Oxford University Press.

Gorski, R. A. (1980). Sexual differentiation in the brain. In D. T. Krieger & J. C. Hughes (Eds.). *Neuroendocrinology* (pp. 215–222). Sunderland, MA: Sinauer.

Gorski, R. A. (1985). The 13th J. A. Stevenson Memorial Lecture: Sexual differentiation of the brain: Possible mechanisms and implications. *Canadian Journal of Physiology and Pharmacology, 63,* 577–594.

Gorski, R. A., Gordom, J. H., Shryne, J. E., & Southam, A. M. (1978). Evidence for a morphological sex difference within the medial preoptic area of the rat brain. *Brain Research, 148,* 333–346.

Gottesmann, I. I., & Bertelsen, A. (1989). Confirming unexpressed genotypes for schizophrenia. *Archives of General Psychiatry, 46,* 867–872.

Gottlieb, D. I. (1988, February). GABAergic neurons. *Scientific American, 258,* 82–89.

Gould, S. J. (1980). *The Panda's thumb: More reflections in natural history.* New York: W. W. Norton.

Gould, S. J. (1991). *Bully for Brontosaurus: Reflections in natural history.* New York: W. W. Norton.

Goy, R. W. (1970). Experimental control of psychosexuality. *Philosophical Transactions of the Royal Society of London, (B), 259,* 149–162.

Goy, R. W. (1978). Development of play and mounting behaviour in female rhesus virilized prenatally with esters of testosterone or dihydrotestosterone. In D. J. Chivers & J. Herbert (Eds.), *Recent advances in primatology* (pp. 449–462). London: Academic Press.

Goy, R. W., & McEwen, B. S. (1980). *Sexual differentiation of the brain.* Cambridge, MA: MIT Press.

Grady, K. L., Phoenix, C. H., & Young, W. C. (1965). Role of the developing rat testis in differentiation of the neural tissues mediating mating behavior. *Journal of Comparative and Physiological Psychology, 59,* 176–182.

Graf, M. V., & Kastin, A. J. (1984). Delta-sleep-inducing peptide (DSIP): A review. *Neuroscience and Biobehavioral Reviews, 8,* 83–93.

Graf, P., & Schacter, D. J. (1987). Selective effects of interference on implicit and explicit memory for new associations. *Journal of Experimental Psychology: Learning, Memory, and Cognition, 13,* 45–53.

Graff-Radford, N., Damasio, H., Yamada, T., Eslinger, P. J., & Damasio, A. R. (1985). Nonhaemorrhagic thalamic infarction. *Brain, 108,* 485–516.

Grant, P. R. (1991, October). Natural selection and Darwin's finches. *Scientific American, 265,* 82–87.

Grant, S. G. N., & Silva, A. J. (1994). Targeting learning. *Trends in Neurosciences, 17,* 71–79.

Graybiel, A. M., Aosaki, T., Flaherty, A. W., & Kimura, M. (1994). The basal ganglia and adaptive motor control. *Science, 265,* 1826–1831.

Graziano, M. S. A., Yap, G. S., & Gross, C. G. (1994). Coding of visual space by premotor neurons. *Science, 266,* 1054–1056.

Green, S. (1991). Benzodiazepines, putative anxiolytics and animal models of anxiety. *Trends in Neurosciences, 14,* 101–103.

Greenough, W. T., & Volkmar, F. R. (1973). Pattern of dendritic branching in occipital cortex of rats reared in complex environments. Experimental *Neurology, 40,* 491–504.

Grillner, S. (1985). Neurobiological bases of rhythmic motor acts in vertebrates. *Science, 228,* 143–149.

Grinspoon, L. (1971). Marihuana reconsidered. Cambridge, MA: Harvard University Press.

Groos, G. (1983). Regulation of the circadian sleep-wake cycle. *Sleep 1982, 6th European Congress on Sleep Research* (Zurich, 1982) (pp. 19–29). Basel: Karger.

Groos, G., & Hendricks, J. (1982). Circadian rhythms in electrical discharge of rat suprachiasmatic neurones recorded in vitro. *Neuroscience Letters, 34,* 283–288.

Grosof, D. H., Shapley, R. M., & Hawken, M. J. (1993). Macaque V1 neurons can signal "illusory" contours. *Nature, 365,* 550–552.

Gross, C. G., Desimone, R., Albright, T. X., & Schwarz, E. L. (1985). Inferior temporal cortex and pattern recognition. In. C. Chagas, R. Gattass, & C. Gross (Eds.), *Pattern recognition mechanisms* (pp. 179–201). Berlin: Springer-Verlag.

Gross, C.G., & Sergent, J. (1992). Face recognition. Current Opinion in Neurobiology, 2, 156–161.

Grossman, S. P. (1990). *Thirst and sodium appetite: Physiological basis.* New York: Academic Press, Inc./Harcourt Brace Jovanovich.

Grudin, J. T. (1983). Error patterns in skilled and novice transcription typing. In W. E. Cooper (Ed.), *Cognitive aspects of skilled typewriting* (pp. 121–144). New York: Springer.

Grunt, J. A., & Young, W. C. (1952). Differential reactivity of individuals and the response of the male guinea pig to testosterone propionate. *Endocrinology, 51,* 237–248.

Guénard, V., Xu, X. M., & Bunge, M. B. (1993). The use of Schwann cell transplantation to foster central nervous system repair. Seminars in the *Neurosciences, 5,* 401–411.

Gur, R. C., Mozley, L. H., Mozley, P. D., Resnick, S. M., Karp, J. S., Alavi, A., Arnold, S. E., & Gur, R. E. (1995). Sex differences in regional cerebral glucose metabolism during a resting state. *Science, 267,* 528–531.

Guyton, A. C. (1987). *Human physiology and mechanisms of disease* (4th ed.) Philadelphia, PA: W. B. Saunders.

Haber, S., Barchas, P. R., & Barchas, J. D. (1981). A primate analogue of amphetamine-induced behavior in humans. *Biological Psychiatry, 16,* 181–195.

Haley, J.E., & Schuman, E. M. (1994). Involvement of nitric oxide in synaptic plasticity and learning. Seminars in the *Neurosciences, 6,* 11–20.

Haley, J.E., Wilcox, G. L., & Chapman, P. F. (1992). The role of nitric oxide in hippocampal synaptic potentiation. *Neuron, 8,* 211–216.

Halsband, U., & Freund, H.-J. (1993). Motor learning. Current Opinion in *Neurobiology, 3*, 940–949.

Hamer, D. H., Hu, S., Magnuson, V. L., Hu, N., & Pattatucci, A. M. L. (1993). A linkage between DNA markers on the chromosome and male sexual orientation. *Science, 261,* 321–327.

Hammond, P. H., Merton, P. A., & Sutton, G. G. (1956). Nervous gradation of muscular contraction. *British Medical Bulletin, 12,* 214–218.

Han, P. J., Feng, L. Y., & Kuo, P. T. (1972). Insulin sensitivity of pair-fed, hyperlipemic, hyperinsulinemic, obese hypothalamic rats. *American Journal of Physiology, 223,* 1206–1209.

Hannah, J., & Hansen, B. C. (1990). Food intake and meal patterns in rhesus monkeys: Significance of chronic hyperinsulinemia. *Physiology & Behavior, 48,* 519–522.

Haqq, C. M., King, C.-Y., Ukiyama, E., Falsafi, S., Haqq, T. N., Donahoe, P. K., & Weiss, M. A. (1994). Molecular basis of mammalian sexual determination: Activation of müllerian inhibiting substance gene expression by SRY. *Science, 266,* 1494–1500.

Harris, G. W. (1955). *Neural control of the pituitary gland.* London: Edward Arnold (Pub.) Ltd.

Harris, G. W., & Jacobsohn, D. (1952). Functional grafts of the anterior pituitary gland. *Proceedings of the Royal Society of London (B), 139,* 1951–1952.

Harris, G. W., & Levine, S. (1965). Sexual differentiation of the brain and its experimental control. *Journal of Physiology, 181,* 379–400.

Harris, K. M., & Kater, S. B. (1994). Dendritic spines: Cellular specializations imparting both stability and flexibility to synaptic function. *Annual Review of Neuroscience, 17,* 341–371.

Harris, L. J. (1978). Sex differences in spatial ability: Possible environmental, genetic, and neurological factors. In M. Kinsbourne (Ed.), *Asymmetrical function of the brain* (p. 463). Cambridge: Cambridge University Press.

Harris, L. J., Clay, J., Hargreaves, F. J., & Ward, A. (1933). Appetite and choice of diet: The ability of the vitamin B deficient rat to discriminate between diets containing and lacking the vitamin. *Proceedings of the Royal Society of London, (B), 113,* 161–190.

Hartmann, E. L. (1973). *The functions of sleep.* Westford, MA: Murray Printing Company.

Harvey, P. H., & Krebs, J. R. (1990). Comparing brains. *Science, 249,* 140–145.

Hata, Y., & Stryker, M. P. (1994). Control of thalamocortical afferent rearrangement by postsynaptic activity in developing visual cortex. *Science, 265,* 1732–1735.

Hatten, M. E. (1993). The role of migration in central nervous system neuronal development. *Current Opinion in Neurobiology, 3,* 38–44.

Haupt, H. A., & Revere, G. D. (1984). Anabolic steroids: A review of the literature. *American Journal of Sports Medicine, 12,* 469–484.

Hayakawa, K., Kumagai, H., Suzuki, Y., Furusawa, N., Haga, T., Hoshi, T., Fujiwara, Y., & Yamaguchi, K. (1992). MR imaging of chronic alcoholism. *Acta Radiologica, 33,* 201–206.

Hearne, K. (1978). Lucid dreams: An electrophysiological and psychological study. Unpublished Ph.D. thesis, University of Hull, Hull, England.

Hearne, K. (1990). *Lucid Dreams.* London: Hamish Hamilton.

Hebb, D. O. (1949). *The organization of behavior.* New York: John Wiley & Sons, Inc.

Hécaen, H., & Angelergues, R. (1964). Localization of symptoms in aphasia. In A. V. S. de Reuck & M. O'Connor (Eds.), *CIBA foundation symposium on the disorders of language* (pp. 222–256). London: Churchill Press.

Heffner, H. E., & Heffner, R. S. (1984). Temporal lobe lesions and perception of species-specific vocalizations by macaques. *Science, 226,* 75–76.

Heffner, H. E., & Heffner, R. S. (1988). Effect of bilateral auditory cortex lesions in monkeys on sound localization. *Abstracts of the Eleventh Midwinter Meeting of the Association for Research in Otolaryngology, 85.*

Heffner, H. E., & Masterton, R. B. (1990). Sound localization in mammals: Brainstem mechanisms. In M. Berkley and W. Stebbins (Eds.), *Comparative perception, Vol. I: Discrimination.* New York: Wiley & Sons.

Heinrichs, R. W. (1993). Schizophrenia and the brain: Conditions for a neuropsychology of madness. *American Psychologist, 48,* 221–233.

Hellige, J. B. (1990). Hemispheric asymmetry. *Annual Review of Psychology, 41,* 55–80.

Hendrickson, A. E., Wagoner, N., & Cowan, W. M. (1972). Autoradiographic and electron microscopic study of retinohypothalamic connections. *Zeitschrift für Zellforschung und Mikroskopische Anatomie, 125,* 1–26.

Henke, P. G. (1992). Stomach pathology and the amygdala. In J.P. Aggleton (Ed.) *The Amygdala: Neurobiological Aspects of Emotion, Memory, and Mental Dysfunction* (pp. 323–338). Wiley-Liss, Inc.

Hennessey, A. C., Camak, L., Gordon, F., & Edwards, D. A. (1990). Connections between the pontine central gray and the ventromedial hypothalamus are essential for lordosis in female rats. *Behavioral Neuroscience, 104,* 477–488.

Herrup, K., & Silver, J. (1994) Cortical development and topographic maps: Patterns of cell dispersion in developing cerebral cortex. *Current Opinion in Neurobiology, 4,* 108–111.

Herzberg, C. & Diamond, A. (1993). Impaired contrast sensitivity in children with treated PKU, presumably due to dopaminergic deficiency. *Society for Neuroscience Abstracts, 19,* 772.

Hetherington, A. W., & Ranson, S. W. (1940). Hypothalamic lesions and adiposity in the rat. *Anatomical Record, 78,* 149–172.

Hier, D. B., & Kaplan, J. (1980). Are sex differences in cerebral organization clinically significant? *Behavioral and Brain Sciences, 3,* 238–239.

Hinton, G. E., Plaut, D. C. & Shallice, T. (1993, October). Simulating brain damage. *Scientific American, 269,* 76–82.

Hirst, W., Spelke, E. S., Reaves, C. C., Canarack, G., & Neisser, U. (1980). Dividing attention without alteration or automaticity. *Journal of Experimental Psychology: General, 109,* 98–117.

Hobson, J. A. (1989). *Sleep.* New York: Scientific American Library.

Hockfield, S., & Kalb, R. G. (1993). Activity-dependent structural changes during neuronal development. *Current Opinion in Neurobiology, 3,* 87–92.

Hofman, M. A., & Swaab, D. F. (1989). The sexually dimorphic nucleus of the preoptic area in the human brain: A comparative morphometric study. *Journal of Anatomy, 164,* 55–72.

Holloway, M. (1991, March). Rx for addiction. *Scientific American, 264,* 95–103.

Hollyday, M., & Hamburger, V. (1976). Reduction of the naturally occurring motor neuron loss by enlargement of the periphery. *Journal of Comparative Neurology, 170,* 311–320.

Holm, H., Hustvedt, B. E., & Løvø, A. (1973). Protein metabolism in rats with ventromedial hypothalamic lesions. *Metabolism, 22,* 1377–1387.

Holtzman, P. S., & Matthyse, S. (1990). The genetics of schizophrenia: A review. *American Psychological Society, 1,* 279–286.

Horne, J. A. (1976). Recovery sleep following different visual conditions during total sleep deprivation in man. *Biological Psychology, 4,* 107–118.

Horne, J. A. (1983). Mammalian sleep function with particular reference to man. In A. R. Mayes (Ed.), *Sleep mechanisms and functions in humans and animals* (pp. 262–312). Wokingham, England: Van Nostrand Reinhold.

Howlett, A. C., Bidaut-Russell, M., Devane, W. A., Melvin, L. S., Johnson, M. R., & Herkenham, M. (1990). The cannabinoid receptor: Biochemical, anatomical and behavioral characterization. *Trends in Neurosciences, 13,* 420–423.

Hubel, D. H., & Wiesel, T. N. (1979, September). Brain mechanisms of vision. *Scientific American, 249,* 150–162.

Hubel, D. H., Wiesel, T. N., & LeVay, S. (1977). Plasticity of ocular dominance columns in the monkey striate cortex. *Philosophical Transactions of the Royal Society of London, 278,* 377–409.

Hubel, D. H., Wiesel, T. N., & Stryker, M. P. (1977). Orientation columns in macaque monkey visual cortex demonstrated by the 2-deoxyglucose autoradiographic technique. *Nature, 269,* 328–330.

Hughes, J., Smith, T. W., Kosterlitz, H. W, Fothergill, L. A., Morgan, B. A., & Morris, H. R. (1975). Identification of two related pentapeptides from the brain with potent opiate agonist activity. *Nature, 258,* 577–581.

Hume, K. I., & Mills, J. N. (1977). Rhythms of REM and slowwave sleep in subjects living on abnormal time schedules. *Waking and Sleeping, 1,* 291–296.

Hunt, W. A. (1993). Neuroscience research: How has it contributed to our understanding of alcohol abuse and alcoholism? *A review. Alcoholism: Clinical and Experimental Research, 17,* 1055–1065.

Hurlbert, A. (1991). Deciphering the colour code. *Nature, 349,* 191–193.

Hustvedt, B. E., & Løvø, A. (1972). Correlation between hyperinsulinemia and hyperphagia in rats with ventromedial hypothalamic lesions. Acta Physiologica Scandinavica, 84, 29–33.

Hutchison, J. B. (1991). Hormonal control of behaviour: Steroid action in the brain. *Current Opinion in Neurobiology, 1,* 562–572.

Hyman, B. T., Van Hoesen, G. W., & Damasio, A. R. (1990). Memory-related neural systems in Alzheimer's disease: An anatomic study. *Neurology, 40,* 1721–1730.

Iacono, W. G. (1985). Psychophysiologic markers in psychopathology: *A review. Canadian Psychology, 26,* 96–111.

Iacono, W. G., & Koenig, W. G. R. (1983). Features that distinguish the smooth-pursuit eye-tracking performance of schizophrenic, affective-disorder, and normal individuals. *Journal of Abnormal Psychology, 92,* 29–41.

Iacono, W. G., & Patrick, C. J. (1987). What psychologists should know about lie detection. In I. B. Weiner & A. K. Hess (Eds.), *Handbook of forensic psychology* (pp. 460–489). New York: John Wiley & Sons.

Iadecola, C. (1993). Regulation of the cerebral microcirculation during neural activity: Is nitric oxide the missing link? *Trends in Neurosciences, 16,* 206–214.

Ibuka, N., Inouye, S. I., & Kawamura, H. (1977). Analysis of sleep-wakefulness rhythms in male rats after suprachiasmatic nucleus lesions and ocular enucleation. *Brain Research, 122,* 33–47.

Ichikawa, S., & Fujii, Y. (1982). Effect of prenatal androgen treatment on maternal behavior in the female rat. *Hormones and Behavior, 16,* 224–233.

Inglis, J., & Lawson, J. S. (1982). A meta-analysis of sex- differences in the effects of unilateral brain damage on intelligence test results. *Canadian Journal of Psychology, 36,* 670–683.

Inouye, S. I., & Kawamura, H. (1982). Characteristics of a circadian pacemaker in the suprachiasmatic nucleus. *Journal of Comparative Psychology, 146,* 153–160.

Iriki, A., Pavlides, C., Keller, A., & Asanuma, H. (1989). Long-term potentiation in the motor cortex. *Science, 245,* 1385–1387.

Ironton, R., Brown, M. C., & Holland, R. L. (1978). Stimuli to intramuscular nerve growth. *Brain Research, 156,* 351–354.

Iversen, S. D., & Koob, G. F. (1977). Behavioral implications of dopaminergic neurons in the mesolimbic system. In E. Costa & G. L. Gessa (Eds.), *Nonstriatal dopaminergic neurons: Advances in biochemical psychopharmacology* (pp. 209–214). New York: Raven.

Izard, C. E. (1971). *The face of emotion.* New York: Appleton-Century-Crofts.

Jackson-Smith, P., Kesner, R. P. & Chiba, A. A. (1993). Continuous recognition of spatial and nonspatial stimuli in hippocampal-lesioned rats. *Behavioral and Neural Biology, 59,* 107–119.

Jacobs, W., Blackburn, J. R., Buttrick, M., Harpur, T. J., Kennedy, D., Mana, M. J., MacDonald, M. A., McPherson, L. M., Paul, D., & Pfaus, J. G. (1988). *Observations. Psychobiology, 16,* 3–9.

Jaeger, C. B., & Lund, R. D. (1981). Transplantation of embryonic occipital cortex to the brain of newborn rats: A Golgi study of mature and developing transplants. *Journal of Comparative Neurology, 200,* 213–230.

Jahn, R., & Südhof, T. C. (1994). Synaptic vesicles and exocytosis. *Annual Review of Neuroscience, 17,* 219–246.

Jänig, W., & McLachlan, E. M. (1992). Characteristics of function-specific pathways in the sympathetic nervous system. *Trends in Neurosciences, 15,* 475–481.

Janosky, D. S., Huey, L., & Storms, L. (1977). Psychologic test responses and methylphenidate. In E. H. Ellinwood, Jr. & M. M. Kilbey (Eds.), *Cocaine and other stimulants* (pp. 675–688). New York: Plenum Press.

Jarrard, L. E. (1993). On the role of the hippocampus in learning and memory in the rat. *Behavioral and Neural Biology, 60,* 9–26.

Jarrell, T. W., Gentile, C. G., Romanski, L. M., McCabe, P. M., & Schneiderman, N. (1987). Involvement of cortical and thalamic auditory regions in retention of differential bradycardia conditioning to acoustic conditioned stimuli in rabbits. *Brain Research, 412,* 285–294.

Jarvik, M. E. (1990). The drug dilemma: Manipulating the demand. *Science, 250,* 387–392.

Jaskiw, G. E., & Weinberger, D. R. (1992). Dopamine and schizophrenia—a cortically corrective perspective. *The Neurosciences, 4,* 179–188.

Jenkins, W. M., & Merzenich, M. M. (1987). Reorganization of neocortical representations after brain injury: A neurophysiological model of the bases of recovery from stroke. *Progressive Brain Research, 71,* 249–266.

Jilge, B. (1991). Restricted feeding: A nonphotic zeitgeber in the rabbit. *Physiology & Behavior, 51,* 157–166.

Joanette, Y. (1989). Aphasia in left-handers and crossed aphasia. In F. Boller and J. Grafman (Eds.), *Handbook of neuropsychology, Vol. 2* (pp. 176–183). New York: Elsevier.

Johnson, P. (1984). The acquisition of skill. In M. M. Smith & A. M. Wing (Eds.), *The psychology of human movement* (pp. 215–240). London: Academic Press.

Johnston, T. D. (1987). The persistence of dichotomies in the study of behavioral development. *Developmental Review, 7,* 149–182.

Jones, H. S., & Oswald, I. (1966). Two cases of healthy insomnia. *Electroencephalography and Clinical Neurophysiology, 24,* 378–380.

Jones, H. W., & Park, I. J. (1971). A classification of special problems in sex differentiation. In D. Bergsma (Ed.) *The clinical delineation of birth defects. Part X: The endocrine system* (pp. 113–121). Baltimore: The Williams and Wilkins Company.

Jones, R. T. (1987). Tobacco dependence. In H. Y. Meltzer (Ed.), *Psychopharmacology: The third generation of progress* (pp. 1589–1596). New York: Raven Press.

Jost, A. (1972). A new look at the mechanisms controlling sex differentiation in mammals. *Johns Hopkins Medical Journal, 130,* 38–53.

Jouvet, M. (1972). The role of monoamines and acetylcholine-containing neurons in the regulation of the sleep-waking cycle. *Ergebnisse der Physiologie, 64,* 166–307.

Jouvet, M., & Renault, J. (1966). Insomnie persistante aprés lésions des noyaux du raphé chez le chat. *Comptes Rendus de la Société de Biologie (Paris), 160,* 1461–1465.

Julesz, B. (1986). Stereoscopic vision. *Vision Research, 26,* 1601–1612.

Julien, R. M. (1981). *A primer of drug action.* San Francisco: W. H. Freeman.

Jung, L. J., & Scheller, R. H. (1991). Peptide processing and targeting in the neuronal secretory pathway. *Science, 251,* 1330–1335.

Kaas, J. H. (1991). Plasticity of sensory and motor maps in adult mammals. *Annual Review of Neuroscience, 14,* 137–167.

Kaas, J. H. (1992). Do humans see what monkeys see? *Trends in Neurosciences, 15,* 1–3.

Kaas, J. H., Krubtzer, L. A., Chino, Y. M., Langston, A. L., Polley, E. H., & Blair, N. (1990). Reorganization of retinotopic cortical maps in adult mammals after lesions of the retina. *Science, 248,* 229–231.

Kaas, J. H., Nelson, R. J., Sur, M., & Merzenich, M. M. (1981). Organization of somatosensory cortex in primates. In F. O. Schmitt, F. G. Worden, G. Adelman, & S. G. Dennis (Eds.), *The organization of the cerebral cortex* (pp. 237–261). Cambridge, MA: MIT Press.

Kaku, D. A., Giffard, R. G., & Choi, D. W. (1993). Neuroprotective effects of glutamate antagonists and extracellular acidity. *Science, 260,* 1516–1517.

Kalaska, J. F., & Crammond, D. J. (1992). Cerebral cortical mechanisms of reaching movements. *Science, 255,* 1517–1523.

Kalil, R. E. (1989, December). Synapse formation in the developing brain. *Scientific American, 261,* 76–85.

Kallman, F. J. (1946). The genetic theory of schizophrenia: An analysis of 691 schizophrenic twin index families. *American Journal of Psychiatry, 103,* 309–322.

Kalm, N. H. (1993, May). The neurobiology of fear. *Scientific American, 268,* 94–101.

Kandel, E. R. (1985). Cellular mechanisms of learning and the biological basis of individuality. In E. R. Kandel & J. H. Schwartz (Eds.), *Principles of neural science* (pp. 816–833). New York: Elsevier.

Kandel, E. R., & Schwartz, J. H., (Eds). (1991). *Principles of neural science,* (2nd ed.) New York: Elsevier.

Karacan, I., Goodeneough, D. R., Shapiro, A., & Starker, S. (1966). Erection cycle during sleep in relation to dream anxiety. *Archives of General Psychiatry, 15,* 183–189.

Karacan, I., Williams, R. L., Finley, W. W., & Hursch, C. J. (1970). The effects of naps on nocturnal sleep: Influence on the need for stage-1 REM and stage-4 sleep. *Biological Psychiatry, 2,* 391–399.

Karadžić, V. T. (1973). Physiological changes resulting from total sleep deprivation. *1st European Congress on Sleep Research* (Basal, 1972), (pp. 165–174). Basel: Karger.

Karni, A., Tanne, D., Rubenstein, B. S., Askenasy, J. J. M., & Sagi, D. (1994). Dependance on REM sleep of overnight improvement of a perceptual skill. *Science, 265,* 679–682.

Karsch, F. J. (1987). Central actions of ovarian steroids in the feedback regulation of pulsatile secretion of luteinizing hormone. *Annual Review of Physiology, 49,* 365–382.

Katz, J. L., Ackamn, P., Rothwax, Y., Sachar, E. J., Weiner, H., Hellman, L., & Gallagher, T. F. (1970). Psychoendocrine aspects of cancer of the breast. *Psychosomatic Medicine, 32,* 1–18.

Kavanagh, G. L., & Kelly, J. B. (1987). Contribution of auditory cortex to sound localization by the ferret (*Mustela putorius*). *Journal of Neurophysiology, 57,* 1746–1765.

Kavanagh, G. L., & Kelly, J. B. (1988). Hearing in the ferret (*Mustela putorius*): Effects of primary auditory cortical lesions on thresholds for pure tone detection. *Journal of Neurophysiology, 60,* 879–888.

Keesey, R. E., & Powley, T. L. (1986). The regulation of body weight. *Annual Review of Psychology, 37,* 109–133.

Keirstead, S. A., Rasminsky, M., Fukuda, Y., Carter, D. A., Aguayo, A. J., & Vidal-Sanz, M. (1989). Electrophysiologic responses in hamster superior colliculus evoked by regenerating retinal axons. *Science, 246,* 255–257.

Kelsey, J. E., Carlezon, W. A., Jr., & Falls, W. A. (1989). Lesions of the nucleus accumbens in rats reduce opiate reward but do not alter context-specific opiate tolerance. *Behavioral Neuroscience, 103,* 1327–1334.

Kelso, S. R., Ganong, A. H., & Brown, T. H. (1986). Hebbian synapses in hippocampus. *Proceedings of the National Academy of Sciences U.S.A., 83,* 5326–5330.

Kendler, K. S., & Gruenberg, A. M. (1984). An independent analysis of the Danish adoption study of schizophrenia: VI. The relationship between psychiatric disorders as defined by DSM-III in the relatives and adoptees. *Archives of General Psychiatry, 41,* 555–564.

Kephalas, T. A., Kiburis, J., Michael, C. M., Miras, C. J., & Papadakis, D. P. (1976). Some aspects of cannabis smoke chemistry. In G. G. Nahas (Ed.), *Marihuana: Chemistry, biochemistry, and cellular effects* (pp. 39–49). New York: Springer-Verlag.

Kessler, D. S., & Melton, D. A. (1994). Vertebrate embryonic induction: Mesodermal and neural patterning. *Science, 266,* 596–604.

Kimble, G. A. (1989). Psychology from the standpoint of a generalist. *American Psychologist, 44,* 491–499.

Kimelberg, H. K., & Norenberg, M. D. (1989, April). Astrocytes. *Scientific American, 260,* 66–76.

Kimura, D. (1961). Some effects of temporal-lobe damage on auditory perception. *Canadian Journal of Psychology, 15,* 156–165.

Kimura, D. (1964). Left-right differences in the perception of melodies. *Quarterly Journal of Experimental Psychology, 16,* 355–358.

Kimura, D. (1973, March). The asymmetry of the human brain. *Scientific American, 228,* 70–78.

Kimura, D. (1979). Neuromotor mechanisms in the evolution of human communication. In H. E. Steklis & M. J. Raleigh (Eds.), *Neurobiology of social communication in primates* (pp. 197– 219). New York: Academic Press.

Kimura, D. (1987). Sex differences, human brain organization. In G. Adelman (Ed.), *Encyclopedia of neuroscience, Vol. II.* Boston: Birkhäuser.

Kimura, D., & Watson, N. (1989). The relation between oral movement control and speech. *Brain and Language, 37,* 565–690.

King, A. J., & Moore, D. R. (1991). Plasticity of auditory maps in the brain. *Trends in Neurosciences, 14,* 31–37.

King, A. P., & West, M. J. (1990). Variation in species-typical behavior: A contemporary issue for comparative psychology. In D. A. Dewsbury (Ed.), *Contemporary issues in comparative psychology,* (pp. 321–339). Sunderland, MA: Sinauer.

Klawans, H. L. (1990). *Newton's madness: Further tales of clinical neurology.* New York: Harper & Row.

Klein, M., & Kandel, E. R. (1978). Presynaptic modulation of voltage-dependent Ca^{2+} current: Mechanism for behavioral sensitization in Aplysia californica. *Proceedings of the National Academy of Sciences (USA), 75,* 3512–3516.

Klein, M., Shapiro, E., & Kandel, E. R. (1980). Synaptic plasticity and the modulation of the Ca_{2+} current. *Journal of Experimental Biology, 89,* 117–157.

Kleitman, N. (1963). *Sleep and wakefulness.* Chicago: University of Chicago.

Klose, M., & Bentley, D. (1989). Transient pioneer neurons are essential for formation of an embryonic peripheral nerve. *Science, 245,* 982–984.

Kluver, H., & Bucy, P. C. (1939). Preliminary analysis of the temporal lobes in monkeys. *Archives of Neurology and Psychiatry, 42,* 979–1000.

Knoth, R. L., & Mair, R. G. (1991). Response latency and accuracy on a pretrained nonmatching-to-sample task in rats recovered from pyrithiamine-induced thiamine deficiency. *Behavioral Neuroscience, 105,* 375–385.

Knudsen, E. I. (1981, December). The hearing of the barn owl. *Scientific American, 245,* 113–125.

Knudsen, E. I. (1991). Dynamic space codes in the superior colliculus. *Current Opinion in Neurobiology, 1,* 628–632.

Knudsen, E. I., & Brainard, M. S. (1991). Visual instruction of the neural map of auditory space in the developing optic tectum. *Science, 253,* 85–87.

Kolb, B. (1989). Brain development, plasticity, and behavior. *American Psychologist, 44,* 1202–1212.

Kolb, B., & Milner, B. (1981). Performance of complex arm and facial movements after focal brain lesions. *Neuropsychologia, 19,* 491–503.

Kolb, B., & Taylor, L. (1981). Affective behavior in patients with localized cortical excisions: Role of lesion site and side. *Science, 214,* 89–91.

Kolb, B., & Taylor, L. (1988). Facial expression and the neocortex. *Society for Neuroscience Abstracts, 14,* 219.

Kolb, B., & Whishaw, I. Q. (1990). *Fundamentals of human neuropsychology* (3rd ed.). New York: Freeman.

Kollar, E. J., & Fisher, C. (1980). Tooth induction in chick epithelium: Expression of quiescent genes for enamel synthesis. *Science, 207,* 993–995.

Kolodny, R. C., Masters, W. H., Kolodner, R. M., & Toro, G. (1974). Depression of plasma testosterone levels after chronic intensive marihuana use. *New England Journal of Medicine, 290,* 872–874.

Konishi, M. (1993, April). Listening with two ears. *Scientific American, 268,* 66–73.

Koob, G. F., & Bloom, F. E. (1988). Cellular and molecular mechanisms of drug dependence. *Science, 242,* 715–723.

Koob, G. F., Markou, A., Weiss, F., & Schulteis, G. (1993). Opponent process and drug dependence: Neurobiological mechanisms. *Seminars in the Neurosciences, 5,* 351–358.

Koolhaas, J. M., Schuurman, T., & Wierpkema, P. R. (1980). The organization of intraspecific agonistic behaviour in the rat. *Progress in Neurobiology, 15,* 247–268.

Koopmans, H. S. (1981). The role of the gastrointestinal tract in the satiation of hunger. In L. A. Cioffi, W. B. T. James, & T. B. Van Italie (Eds.), *The body weight regulatory system: Normal and disturbed mechanisms* (pp. 45–55). New York: Raven Press.

Kornetsky, C. (1977). Animal models: Promises and problems. In I. Hanin & E. Usdin (Eds.), *Animal models of psychiatry and neurology* (pp. 1–7). Oxford: Pergamon Press.

Kornetsky, C., & Esposito, R. U. (1979). Euphorigenic drugs: Effects on the reward pathways of the brain. *Federation Proceedings, 38,* 2473–2476.

Kosambi, D. D. (1967, February). Living prehistory in India. *Scientific American, 216,* 105–114.

Kosslyn, S. M., & Andersen, R. A. (1992). *Frontiers in cognitive neuroscience.* Cambridge, MA: MIT Press.

Koutalos, Y., & Yau, K.-W. (1993). A rich complexity emerges in phototransduction. *Current Opinion in Neurobiology, 3,* 513–519.

Kowalaska, D. M., Bachevalier, J., & Mishkin, M. (1984). Inferior prefrontal cortex and recognition memory. *Society for Neuroscience Abstracts, 10,* 385.

Kowler, E. (Ed.). (1990). *Eye movements and their role in visual and cognitive processes.* New York: Elsevier.

Krank, M. D. (1989). Environmental signals for ethanol enhance free-choice ethanolconsumption. *Behavioral Neuroscience, 101,* 365–372.

Krank, M. D., & Perkins, W. L. (1993). Conditioned withdrawal signs elicited by contextual cues for morphine administration. *Psychobiology, 21,* 113–119.

Krasne, F. B., & Glanzman, D. L. (1995) What we can learn from invertebrate learning. *Annual Review of Psychology, 46,* 585–624.

Krupa, D. J., Thompson, J. K., & Thompson, R. F. (1993). Localization of a memory trace in the mammalian brain. *Science, 260,* 989–991.

Kuczmarski, R. J. (1992). Prevalence of overweight and weight gain in the United States. *American Journal of Clinical Nutrition, 55,* 495S–502S.

Kuffler, S. W. (1953). Discharge patterns and functional organization of mammalian retina. *Journal of Neurophysiology, 16,* 37–68.

Kurata, K. (1992). Somatotopy in the human supplementary motor area. *Trends in Neurosciences, 15,* 159–160.

Kuwada, J. Y. (1986). Cell recognition by neuronal growth cones in a simple vertebrate embryo. *Science, 233,* 740–746. @REFS-MS = LaBerge, S. (1985). *Lucid dreaming.* Los Angeles: Tarcher.

Kyriacou, C. P. (1994). Working round the clock with mouse 25. *Trends in Neurosciences, 17,* 313–314.

LaBerge (1986). *Lucid dreaming.* New York: Ballantine.

LaBerge, S., Greenleaf, W., & Kedzierski, B. (1983). Physiological responses to dreamed sexual activity during lucid REM sleep. *Psychophysiology, 20,* 454–455.

Lacquaniti, F. (1992). Automatic control of limb movement and posture. *Current Opinion in Neurobiology, 2,* 807–814.

Laguzzi, R., & Adrien, J. (1980). Effets des antagonistes de la serotonine sur le cycle veille-sommeil au rat. *Journal de Physiologie et Pathalogie, 76,* 20A.

Lance-Jones, C., & Landmesser, L. (1980). Motoneuron projection patterns in the chick hind limb following early partial spinal cord reversals. *Journal of Physiology, 302,* 559–580.

Land, E. H. (1977, April). The retinex theory of color vision. *Scientific American, 237,* 108–128.

Langston, J. W. (1985). MPTP and Parkinson's disease. *Trends in Neurosciences, 8,* 79–83.

Langston, J. W. (1986). MPTP-induced parkinsonism: How good a model is it? In S. Fahn, C. P. Marsden, P. Jenner, & P. Teychenne (Eds.), *Recent developments in Parkinson's disease* (pp. 119–126). New York: Raven Press.

Langston, J. W., Forno, L. S., Robert, C. S., & Irwin, I. (1984). Selective nigral toxicity after systemic administration of 1-methyl-4-phenyl-1,2,3,6-tetrahydropyridine (MPTP) in the squirrel monkey. *Brain Research, 292,* 390–394.

Lashley, K. S. (1941). Patterns of cerebral integration indicated by the scotomas of migraine. *Archives of Neurology and Psychiatry, 46,* 331–339.

Latimer, D., & Goldberg, J. (1981). *Flowers in the blood.* New York: Franklin Watts.

Lavie, P., Pratt, H., Scharf, B., Peled, R., & Brown, J. (1984). Localized pontine lesion: Nearly total absence of REM sleep. *Neurology, 34,* 1118–1120.

Lawrence, D. G., & Kuypers, H. G. J. M. (1968a). The functional organization of the motor system in the monkey: I. The effects of bilateral pyramidal lesions. *Brain, 91,* 1–14.

Lawrence, D. G., & Kuypers, H. G. J. M. (1968b). The functional organization of the motor system in the monkey: II. The effects of lesions of the descending brain-stem pathways. *Brain, 91,* 15–36.

Le Douarin, N. M. (1993). Embryonic neural chimaeras in the study of brain development. *Trends in Neurosciences, 16,* 64–72.

Lê, A. D., Poulos, C. X., & Cappell, H. (1979). Conditioned tolerance to the hypothermic effects of ethyl alcohol. *Science, 206,* 1109–1110.

LeDoux, J. E. (1992). Brain mechanisms of emotion and emotional learning. *Current Opinion in Neurobiology, 2,* 191–197.

LeDoux, J. E. (1994, June). Emotion, memory and the brain. *Scientific American, 270,* 50–57.

LeDoux, J. E. (1995). Emotion: Clues from the brain. *Annual Review of Psychology, 46,* 209–235.

Leech, C. K., & McIntyre, D. C. (1976). Kindling rates in inbred mice: An analog to learning? *Behavioral Biology, 16,* 439–452.

Leibowitz, S. F. (1992). Neurochemical-neuroendocrine systems in the brain controlling macronutrient intake and metabolism. *Trends in Neurosciences, 15,* 491–497.

Leibowitz, S. F., Hammer, N. J., & Chang, K. (1981). Hypothalamic paraventricular nucleus lesions produce overeating and obesity in the rat. *Physiology & Behavior, 27,* 1031–1040.

Leiner, H. C., Leiner, A. L., & Dow, R. S. (1993). Cognitive and language functions of the human cerebellum. *Trends in Neurosciences, 16,* 444–454.

Lemberger, L., & Rowe, H. (1975). Clinical pharmacology of nabilone, a cannabinol derivative. *Clinical Pharmacology and Therapeutics, 18,* 720–726.

Lennox, W. G. (1960). *Epilepsy and related disorders.* Boston: Little, Brown and Co.

Lester, G. L. L., & Gorzalka, B. B. (1988). Effect of novel and familiar mating partners on the duration of sexual receptivity in the female hamster. *Behavioral and Neural Biology, 49,* 398–405.

LeVay, S. (1991). A difference in hypothalamic structure between heterosexual and homosexual men. *Science, 253,* 1034–1037.

LeVay, S., & Hamer, D. H. (1994, May). Evidence for a biological influence in male homosexuality. *Scientific American, 270,* 44–49.

LeVay, S., Hubel, D. H., & Wiesel, T. N. (1975). The pattern of ocular dominance columns in Macaque visual cortex revealed by a reduced silver stain. *Journal of Comparative Neurology, 159,* 559–576.

Levi-Montalcini, R. (1952). Effects of mouse motor transplantation on the nervous system. *Annals of the New York Academy of Science, 55,* 330–344.

Levi-Montalcini, R. (1975). NGF: An uncharted route. In F. G. Worden, J. P. Swazey, & G. Adelman (Eds.), *The neurosciences: Paths of discovery* (pp. 245–265). Cambridge, MA: MIT Press.

Levin, H. S. (1989). Memory deficit after closed-head injury. *Journal of Clinical and Experimental Neuropsychology, 12,* 129–153.

Levin, H. S., Papanicolaou, A., & Eisenberg, H. M. (1984). Observations on amnesia after non-missile head injury. In L. R. Squire & N. Butters (Eds.), *Neuropsychology of memory* (pp. 247–257). New York: Guilford Press.

Levy, J. (1969). Possible basis for the evolution of lateral specialization of the human brain. *Nature, 224,* 614–615.

Levy, J., Trevarthen, C., & Sperry, R. W. (1972). Perception of bilateral chimeric figures following hemispheric deconnection. *Brain, 95,* 61–78.

Linden, D. J., & Routtenberg, A. (1989). The role of protein kinase C in long-term potentiation: A testable model. *Brain Research Reviews, 14,* 279–296.

Linden, W., & Estrin, R. (1988). Computerized cardiovascular monitoring: Method and data. *Psychophysiology, 25,* 227–234.

Linder, M. E., & Gilman, A. G. (1992, July). G proteins. *Scientific American, 267,* 56–65.

Lindsay, P. H., & Norman, D. A. (1977). *Human information processing* (2nd ed.). New York: Academic Press.

Lindsey, D. B., Bowden, J., & Magoun, H. W. (1949). Effect upon the EEG of acute injury to the brain stem activating system. *Electroencephalography and Clinical Neurophysiology, 1,* 475–486.

Lindvall, O. (1991). Prospects of transplantation in human neurodegenerative diseases. *Trends in Neurosciences, 14,* 376–384.

Lindvall, O., Brundin, P., Widner, H., Rehncrona, S., Gustavi, B., Frackowiak, R., Leenders, K. L., Sawle, G., Rothwell, J. C., Marsden, C. D., & Björklund, A. (1990). Grafts of fetal dopamine neurons survive and improve motor function in Parkinson's disease. *Science, 247,* 574–577.

Lishman, W. A. (1990). Alcohol and the brain. *British Journal of Psychiatry, 156,* 635–644.

Livingston, E. H., & Guth, P. H. (1992). Peptic ulcer disease: Wounds in the walls of the stomach develop only after elaborate cellular and molecular defensive mechanisms are breached. *American Scientist, 80,* 592–598.

Livingstone, M. S., & Hubel, D. H. (1984). Anatomy of physiology of a color system in the primate visual cortex. *Journal of Neuroscience, 4,* 309–356.

Livingstone, M. S., & Hubel, D. S. (1988). Segregation of form, color, movement, and depth: Anatomy, physiology, and perception. *Science, 240,* 740–749.

Llinás, R., & Welsh, J.P. (1993). On the cerebellum and motor learning. *Current Opinion in Neurobiology, 3,* 958–965.

Lo, Y-J. & Poo, M-M. (1991). Activity-dependent synaptic competition *in vitro:*

Heterosynaptic suppression of developing synapses. *Science, 254,* 1019–1022.

Loomis, A. L., Harvey, E. N., & Hobart, G. (1936). Electrical potentials of the human brain. Journal of Experimental *Psychology, 19,* 249–279.

LoPiccolo, M. A. (1977). Behavioral and neuronal effects of EEG synchronizing stimuli in the cat. *Unpublished doctoral dissertation.* McMaster University, Hamilton.

Lowe, J., & Carroll, D. (1985). The effects of spinal injury on the intensity of emotional experience. *British Journal of Clinical Psychology, 24,* 135–136.

Lowe, M. R.. (1993). The effects of dieting on eating behavior: A three-factor model. *Psychological Bulletin, 114,* 100–121.

Lucas F., & Sclafani, A. (1989). Flavor preferences conditioned by intragastric fat infusions in rats. *Physiology & Behavior, 46,* 403–412.

Lund, R. D., & Harvey, A. R. (1981). Transplantation of tectal tissue in rats: I. Organization and transplants and pattern of distribution of host afferents within them. *Journal of Comparative Neurology, 201,* 191–209.

Luo, Y., Raible, D., & Raper, J. A. (1993). Collapsin: A protein in brain that induces the collapse and paralysis of neuronal growth cones. Cell, 75, 217–227.

Luria, A. R. (1972). *The history of a brain wound. The man with a shattered world.* Cambridge, MA: Harvard University Press.

Lydic, R., McCarley, R. W., & Hobson, J. A. (1983). The time-course of dorsal raphé discharge, PGO waves, and muscle tone averaged across multiple sleep cycles. *Brain Research, 274,* 365–370.

Lykken, D. T. (1959). The GSR in the detection of guilt. *Journal of Applied Psychology, 43,* 385–388.

Macchi, G. (1989). Anatomical substrate of emotional reactions. In F. Boller and J. Grafman (Eds.), *Handbook of neuropsychology, Vol. 3,* (pp. 283–304). New York: Elsevier.

Macdonald, R. L., & Olsen, R. (1994). $GABA_A$ receptor channels. *Annual Review of Neuroscience, 17,* 569–602.

MacLusky, N. J., & Naftolin, F. (1981). Sexual differentiation of the central nervous system. *Science, 211*, 1294–1302.

MacNeilage, P. F., Studdert-Kennedy, M. G., & Lindblom, B. (1993, Jan/Feb). Hand signals: Right side, left brain and the origin of language. *The Sciences*, 32–37.

MacNichol, E. F., Jr. (1964, December). Three-pigment color vision. *Scientific American, 211*, 48–67.

Madison, D. V. (1994). Nitric oxide and synaptic function. *Annual Review of Neuroscience, 17*, 153–184.

Madrazo, I., Drucker-Colín, R., Díaz, V., Martínez-Mata, J., Torres, C., & Becerril, J. J. (1987). Open microsurgical autograft of adrenal medulla to the right caudate nucleus in two patients with intractable Parkinson's disease. *New England Journal of Medicine, 316*, 831–834.

Magni, F., Moruzzi, G., Rossi, G. F., & Zanchetti, A. (1957). EEG arousal following inactivation of the lower brain stem by selective injection of barbiturate into the vertebral circulation. *Archives Italiennes de Biologie, 95*, 33–46.

Mahut, H., Moss, M., & Zola-Morgan, S. (1981). Retention deficits after combined amygdalo-hippocampal and selective hippocampal resections in the monkey. *Neuropsychologia, 19*, 201–225.

Maier, S. R., Watkins, L. R., & Fleshner, M. (1994). Psychoneuroimmunology: The interface between behavior, brain, and immunity. *American Psychologist, 49*, 1004–1017.

Mair, R. G., Knoth, R. L., Rabenchuk, S. A., & Langlais, P. J. (1991). Impairment of olfactory, auditory, and spatial serial reversal learning in rats recovered from pyrithiamine-induced thiamine deficiency. *Behavioral Neuroscience, 105*, 360–374.

Mair, R. G., Otto, T. A., Knoth, R. L., & Langlais, P. J. (1991). Analysis of aversively conditioned learning and memory in rats recovered from pyrithiamine-induced thiamine deficiency. *Behavioral Neuroscience, 105*, 351–359.

Malinow, R. (1994). LTP: Desperately seeking resolution. *Science, 266*, 1195–1196.

Malmo, R. B., & Malmo, H. P. (1979). Responses of lateral preoptic neurons in the rat to hypertonic sucrose and NaCl. *Electroencephalography and Clinical Neurophysiology, 46*, 401–408.

Malsbury, C. W. (1971). Facilitation of male rat copulatory behavior by electrical stimulation of the medial preoptic area. *Physiology & Behavior, 7*, 797–805.

Malsbury, C. W., & Pfaff, D. W. (1974). Neural and hormonal determinants of mating behavior in adult male rats. A review. In L. V. DiCara (Ed.), *Limbic and autonomic nervous system research* (pp. 85–136). New York: Plenum Press.

Mansfield, J. G., & Cunningham, C. L. (1980). Conditioning and extinction of tolerance to the hypothermic effects of ethanol in rats. *Journal of Comparative and Physiological Psychology, 94*, 962–969.

Maratsos, M., & Matheny, L. (1994). Language specificity and elasticity: Brain and clinical syndrome studies. *Annual Review of Psychology, 45*, 487–516.

Mark, V. H., Ervin, F. R., & Yakolev, P. I. (1962). The treatment of pain by stereotaxic methods. 1st International Symposium on Stereoencephalotomy (Philadelphia, 1961), *Confina Neurologica, 22*, 238–245.

Marks, W. B., Dobelle, W. H., & MacNichol, E. F. (1964). Visual pigments of single primate cones. *Science, 143*, 1181–1183.

Marler, P. (1991). Song learning behavior: The interface with neuroethology. *Trends in Neurosciences, 14*, 199–206.

Marler, P., & Nelson, D. (1992). Neuroselection and song learning in birds: Species universals in a culturally transmitted behavior. *Seminars in the Neurosciences, 4*, 415–423.

Marlowe, W. B., Mancall, E. L., & Thomas, J. J. (1985). Complete Kluver-Bucy syndrome in man. *Cortex, 11*, 53–59.

Marshall, F. H. A. (1937). On the changeover in the oestrous cycle in animals after transference across the equator, with further observations on the incidence of the breeding seasons and the factors controlling sexual periodicity. *Proceedings of the Royal Society of London, (B), 122*, 413–428.

Marslen-Wilson, W. D., & Teuber, H. L. (1975). Memory for remote events in anterograde amnesia: Recognition of public figures from newsphotographs. *Neuropsychologia, 13,* 353–364.

Martin, B. J. (1986). Sleep deprivation and exercise. In K. B. Pandolf (Ed.), *Exercise and Sport Sciences Reviews* (pp. 213–229). New York: Macmillan Pub. Co.

Martin, J. B. (1987). Molecular genetics: Applications to the clinical neurosciences. *Science, 238,* 765–772.

Martin, R. J., White, B. D., & Hulsey, M. G. (1991). The regulation of body weight. *American Scientist, 79,* 528–541.

Martin, R. L., Roberts, W. V., & Clayton, P. J. (1980). Psychiatric status after a one-year prospective follow-up. *Journal of the American Medical Association, 244,* 350–353.

Masoro, E. J. (1988). Minireview: Food restriction in rodents: An evaluation of its role in the study of aging. *Journal of Gerontology, 43,* 59–64.

Masterton, R. B. (1992). Role of the central auditory system in hearing: The new direction. *Trends in Neurosciences, 15,* 280–285.

Mateer, C. A., & Cameron, P. A. (1989). Electrophysiological correlates of language: Stimulation mapping and evoked potential studies. In F. Boller and J. Grafman (Eds.) *Handbook of neuropsychology, Vol. 2* (pp. 91–116). New York: Elsevier.

Matsuda, L. A., Lolait, S. J., Brownstein, M. J., Young, A. C., & Bonner, T. I. (1990). Structure of a cannabinoid receptor and functional expression of the cloned DNA. *Nature, 346,* 561–564.

Matteoli, M., & De Camilli, P. (1991). Molecular mechanisms in neurotransmitter release. *Current Opinion in Neurobiology, 1,* 91–97.

Matthews, P. B. C. (1991). The human stretch reflex and the motor cortex. *Trends in Neurosciences, 3,* 87–91.

Mattson, S. N., Barron, S., & Riley, E. P. (1988). The behavioral effects of prenatal alcohol exposure. In K. Kuriyama, A. Takada, & H. Ishii (Eds.), *Biomedical and social aspects of alcohol and alcoholism* (pp. 851–853). Tokyo: Elsevier.

Maunsell, J. H. R. (1992). Functional visual streams. *Current Opinion in Neurobiology, 2,* 506–510.

Mazzocchi, F., & Vignolo, L. A. (1979). Localisation of lesions in aphasia: Clinical-CT scan correlations in stroke patients. *Cortex, 15,* 627–654.

McAuliffe, W. E., Feldman, B., Friedman, R., Launer, E., Magnuson, E., Mahoney, C., Santangelo, S., Ward, W., & Weiss, R. (1986). Explaining relapse to opiate addiction following successful completion of treatment. In F. M. Tims & C. G. Leukefield (Eds.), *Relapse and recovery in drug abuse: National Institute on Drug Abuse Research Monograph Series* (Vol. 72, pp. 136–156). Rockville, MD.

McCann, T. S. (1981). Aggression and sexual activity of male southern elephant seals, Mirounga leonina. *Journal of Zoology, 195,* 295–310.

McClintock, M. K. (1971). Menstruation synchrony and suppression. *Nature, 229,* 244–245.

McDonald, R. J., & White, N. M. (1993). Triple dissociation of memory systems: Hippocampus, amygdala, and dorsal striatum. *Behavioral and Neural Biology, 59,* 107–119.

McDonald, W. I. (1984). Multiple sclerosis: Epidemiology and HLA associations. *Annals of the New York Academy of Sciences, 436,* 109–117.

McEwen, B. (1994). Introduction: Stress and the nervous system. *Seminars in the Neurosciences, 6,* 195–196.

McEwen, B. S. (1983). Gonadal steroid influences on brain development and sexual differentiation. In R. O. Greep (Ed.), *Reproductive physiology IV.* Baltimore, MD: University Park Press.

McEwen, B. S. (1987). Sexual differentiation. In G. Adelman (Ed.), *Encyclopedia of neuroscience, Vol. II* (pp. 1086–1088). Boston, MA: Birkhäuser.

McEwen, B. S., Davis, P. G., Parsons, B., & Pfaff, D. W. (1979). The brain as a target for steroid hormone action. *Annual Reviews in Neuroscience, 2,* 65–112.

McEwen, B. S., Lieberburg, I., Chaptal, C., & Krey, L. C. (1977). Aromatization: Important for sexual differentiation of the neonatal rat brain. *Hormones and Behavior, 9,* 249–263.

McFarland, H. F., Greenstein, J., McFarlin, D. E., Eldridge, R., Xu, X. H., & Krebs, H. (1984). Family and twin studies in multiple sclerosis. *Annals of the New York Academy of Sciences, 436,* 118–124.

McGinty, D. J., & Sterman, M. B. (1968). Sleep suppression after basal forebrain lesions in the cat. *Science, 160,* 1253–1255.

McGlone, J. (1977). Sex differences in the cerebral organization of verbal functions in patients with unilateral brain lesions. *Brain, 100,* 775–793.

McGlone, J. (1980). Sex differences in human brain asymmetry: A critical survey. *Behavioral and Brain Sciences, 3,* 215–263.

McHugh, P. R., & Moran, T. H. (1985). The stomach: A conception of its dynamic role in satiety. In J. M. Sprague & A. N. Epstein (Eds.), *Progress in psychobiology and physiological psychology, 11,* 197–232.

McKim, W. A. (1986). *Drugs and behavior: An introduction to behavioral pharmacology.* Englewood Cliffs, NJ: Prentice-Hall.

McLoon, S. C., & Lund, R. D. (1980). Identification of cells in retinal transplants which project to host visual centers: A horseradish peroxidase study in rats. *Brain Research, 197,* 491–495.

Meaney, M. J., & Stewart, J. (1981). Neonatal androgens influence the social play of prepubescent rats. *Hormones and Behavior, 15,* 197–213.

Meck, W. H., Smith, R. A., & Williams, C. L. (1989). Organizational changes in cholinergic activity and enhanced visuospatial memory as a function of choline administered prenatally or postnatally or both. *Behavioral Neuroscience, 103,* 1234–1241.

Meddis, R. (1977). *The sleep instinct.* London: Routledge & Kegan Paul.

Mehler, J., Dupoux, E., Pallier, C., & Dehaene-Lambertz, G. (1994). Cross-linguistic approaches to speech processing. *Current Opinion in Neurobiology, 4,* 171–176.

Mello, N. K., Mendelson, J. H. (1972). Drinking patterns during work-contingent and noncontingent alcohol acquisition. *Psychosomatic Medicine, 34,* 139–165.

Mello, N. K., Mendelson, M. P., Bree, M. P., & Lukas, S. E. (1989). Buprenorphine suppresses cocaine self-administration by rhesus monkeys. *Science, 245,* 859–862.

Meltzer, H. Y. (Ed.). (1987). *Psychopharmacology: The third generation of progress.* New York: Raven Press.

Meltzer, L. D. et al. (1990). Clinical efficacy of clozapine in the treatment of schizophrenia. *Clinical Neuropharmacology, 13, supplement 2,* 259–260.

Melzack, R. (1992, April). Phantom limbs. *Scientific American, 266,* 120–126.

Melzack, R., & Wall, P. D. (1965). Pain mechanisms: A new theory. *Science, 150,* 971–979.

Melzack, R., & Wall, P. D. (1982). *The challenge of pain.* Harmondsworth, England: Penguin Books.

Mendelson, J. H. (1987). Marijuana. In H. Y. Meltzer (Ed.), *Psychopharmacology: The third generation of progress* (pp. 1565–1571). New York: Raven Press.

Mendelson, J. H., Kuehnle, J. C., Greenberg, I., & Mello, N. K. (1976). The effects of marihuana use on human operant behavior: Individual data. In M. C. Braude and S. Szara (Eds.), *The pharmacology of marihuana* (pp. 643–653). New York: Raven Press.

Mercer, A. R., Emptage, N. J., & Carew, T. J. (1991). Pharmacological dissociation of modulatory effects of serotonin in Aplysia sensory neurons. *Science, 254,* 1811–1813.

Merigan, W. H., & Maunsell, J. H. R. (1993). How parallel are the primate visual pathways? *Annual Review of Neuroscience, 16,* 369–402.

Meunier, M., Murray, E. A., Bachevalier, J., & Mishkin, M. (1990). Effects of perirhinal cortical lesions on visual recognition memory in rhesus monkeys. *Society for Neuroscience Abstracts, 17,* 337.

Meyer-Bahlburg, H. F. L. (1981). Androgens and human aggression. In P. F. Brain & D. Benton (Eds.), *The biology of aggression* (pp. 263–290). Alpen ann den Rijn: Sijthoff & Noordhoff.

Michel, S., Geusz, M. E., Zaritsky, J. J., & Block, G. D. (1993). Circadian rhythm in membrane conductance expressed in isolated neurons. *Science, 259*, 239–241.

Middleton, F. A., & Strick, P. L. (1994). Anatomical evidence for cerebellar and basal ganglia involvement in higher cognitive function. *Science, 266*, 458–461.

Miller, N. E., Bailey, C. J., & Stevenson, J. A. F. (1950). Decreased "hunger" but increased food intake resulting from hypothalamic lesions. *Science, 112*, 256–259.

Miller, N. S., Summers, G. L., & Gold, M.S. (1993). Cocaine dependence: Alcohol and other drug dependence and withdrawal characteristics. *Journal of Addictive Diseases, 12*, 25–35.

Miller, R. L., & Baum, J. (1987). Naloxone inhibits mating and conditioned place preference for an estrous female in male rats soon after castration. *Pharmacology Biochemistry & Behavior, 26*, 781–789.

Miller, T. M., & Heuser, J. E. (1984). Endocytosis of synaptic vesicle membrane at the frog neuromuscular junction. *The Journal of Cell Biology, 98*, 685–698.

Milner, B. (1962). Laterality effects in audition. In V. B. Mountcastle, (Ed.), *Interhemispheric relations and cerebral dominance.* (pp. 177–195). Baltimore, MD: The Johns Hopkins Press.

Milner, B. (1965). Memory disturbances after bilateral hippocampal lesions. In P. Milner & S. Glickman (Eds.), *Cognitive processes and the brain* (pp. 104–105). Princeton, NJ: D. Van Nostrand Co. Inc.

Milner, B. (1971). Interhemispheric differences in the localization of psychological processes in man. *British Medical Bulletin, 27*, 272–277.

Milner, B. (1974). Hemispheric specialization: Scope and limits. In F. O. Schmitt & F. G. Worden (Eds.), *The neurosciences: Third study program* (pp. 75–89). Cambridge, MA: MIT Press.

Milner, B., Corkin, S., & Teuber, H. L. (1968). Further analysis of the hippocampal amnesic syndrome: 14-year follow-up study of H. M. *Neuropsychologia, 6*, 317–338.

Milner, D., & Goodale, M. A. (1993). Visual pathways to perception and action. *Progress in Brain Research, 95*, 317–337.

Milner, P. M. (1993, January). The mind and Donald O. Hebb. *Scientific American, 268*, 124–129.

Milner, P. M., & White, N. M. (1987). What is physiological psychology? *Psychobiology, 15*, 2–6.

Mink, J. W., & Thach, W. T. (1993). Basal ganglia intrinsic circuits and their role in behavior. *Current Opinion in Neurobiology, 3*, 950–957.

Mishkin, M. (1957). Effects of small frontal lesions on delayed alternation in monkeys. *Journal of Neurophysiology, 20*, 615–622.

Mishkin, M. (1978). Memory in monkeys severely impaired by combined but not by separate removal of amygdala and hippocampus. *Nature, 273*, 297–298.

Mishkin, M. (1982). A memory system in the monkey. *Philosophical Transactions of the Royal Society of London [Biol.], 298*, 85–95.

Mishkin, M., & Appenzeller, T. (1987). The anatomy of memory. *Scientific American, 256*, 80–89.

Mishkin, M., & Delacour, J. (1975). An analysis of short-term visual memory in the monkey. *Journal of Experimental Psychology: Animal Behavior Processes, 1*, 326–334.

Mishkin, M., & Manning, F. J. (1978). Nonspatial memory after selective prefrontal lesions in monkeys. *Brain Research, 143*, 313–323.

Mishkin, M., & Murray, E. A. (1994). Stimulus recognition. *Current Opinion in Neurobiology, 4*, 200–206.

Mistlberger, R. E. (1990). Circadian pitfalls in experimental designs employing food restriction. *Psychobiology, 18*, 23–29.

Mistlberger, R. E. (1991). Scheduled daily exercise of feeding alters the phase of photic entrainment in Syrian hamsters. *Physiology & Behavior, 50*, 1257–1260.

Mistlberger, R. E. (1993). Circadian properties of anticipatory activity to restricted water access in suprachiasmatic-ablated hamsters. *American Journal of Physiology, 263*, 22–29.

Mistlberger, R., Bergmann, B., & Rechtschaffen, A. (1987). Period-amplitude analysis of rat electroencephalogram: Effects of sleep deprivation and exercise. *Sleep, 10,* 508–522.

Mogenson, G. J., Takigawa, M., Robertson, A., & Wu, M. (1979). Self-stimulation of the nucleus accumbens and ventral tegmental area of Tsai attenuated by microinjections of spiroperidol into the nucleus accumbens. *Brain Research, 171,* 247–259.

Mohr, J. P. (1976). Broca's area and Broca's aphasia. In H. Whitaker & H. A. Whitaker (Eds.), *Studies in neurolinguistics: Volume 1* (pp. 201–235). New York: Academic Press.

Money, J. (1975). Ablatio penis: Normal male infant sex-reassigned as a girl. *Archives of Sexual Behavior, 4,* 65–186.

Money, J. (1987). Sin, sickness, or status? Homosexual gender identity and psychoneuroendocrinology. *American Psychologist, 42,* 384–399.

Money, J., & Ehrhardt, A. A. (1972). *Man & woman, boy & girl.* Baltimore: Johns Hopkins University Press.

Money, J., Schwartz, M., & Lewis, V. G. (1984). Adult erotosexual status and fetal hormonal masculinization and demasculinization: 46, XX congenital virilizing adrenal hyperplasia and 46, XX androgen-insensitivity syndrome compared. *Psychoneuroendocrinology, 9,* 405–414.

Monnier, M., Dudler, L., Gaechter, R., Maier, P. F., Tobler, H. J., & Schoenenberger, G. A. (1975). The delta sleep inducing peptide (DSIP): Comparative properties of the original and synthetic nonapeptide. *Experientia, 33,* 548–552.

Montarolo, P. G., Goelet, P., Castellucci, V. F., Morgan, J., Kandel, E. R., & Schacher, S. (1986). A critical period for macromolecular synthesis in long-term heterosynaptic facilitation in Aplysia. *Science, 234,* 1249–1254.

Moonen, C. T. W., van Zijl, P. C. M., Frank, J. A., Le Bihan, D., & Becker, E. D. (1990). Functional magnetic resonance imaging in medicine and physiology. *Science, 250,* 53–61.

Moore, R. Y. (1982). The suprachiasmatic nucleus and the organization of a circadian system. *Trends in Neurosciences, 5,* 404–407.

Moore, R. Y., & Eichler, V. B. (1972). Loss of a circadian adrenal corticosterone rhythm following suprachiasmatic lesions in the rat. *Brain Research, 42,* 201–206.

Moore, R. Y., & Lenn, N. J. (1972). A retino-hypothalamic projection in the rat. *Journal of Comparative Neurology, 146,* 1–14.

Moran, J., & Desimore, R. (1985). Selective attention gates visual processing in the extrastriate cortex. *Science, 229,* 782–784.

Morgan, M. A., Romanski, L. M., & Ledoux, J. E. (1995). Extinction of emotional learning: Contribution of medial prefrontal cortex. *Neuroscience Letters, 163,* 109–113.

Morgan, T. H., Sturtevant, A. H., Muller, H. J., & Bridges, C. B. (1915). *The mechanism of Mendelian heredity.* New York: Henry Holt.

Mori, N., & Wada, J. A. (1990). Does electrical and excitatory amino acid kindling share a common neurobiological mechanism? In J. A. Wada, (Ed.), *Kindling 4* (pp. 209–222). New York: Plenum Press.

Morris, M. K., Bowers, D., Chatterjee, A., & Heilman, K. M. (1992). Amnesia following a discrete basl forebarin lesion. *Brain, 115,* 1827–1847.

Morris, N. M., Udry, J. R., Khan-Dawood, F., & Dawood, M. Y. (1987). Marital sex frequency and midcycle female testosterone. *Archives of Sexual Behavior, 16,* 27–37.

Morris, R. G. M. (1981). Spatial localization does not require the presence of local cues. *Learning and Motivation, 12,* 239–260.

Moruzzi, G., & Magoun, H. W. (1949). Brain stem reticular formation and activation of the EEG. *Electroencephalography and Clinical Neurophysiology, 1,* 455–473.

Moscovitch, M. (1982). Multiple dissociations of function in amnesia. In L. S. Cermak (Ed.), *Human memory and amnesia* (pp. 337–370). Hillsdale, NJ: Erlbaum.

Moskowitz, H., Hulbert, S., & McGlothin, W. H. (1976). Marihuana: Effects on simulated driving performance. *Accident Analysis and Prevention, 8,* 45–50.

Mountcastle, V. B., & Powell, T. P. S. (1959). Neural mechanisms subserving cutaneous sensibility with special references to the role of afferent inhibition in sensory perception and discrimination. *Bulletin of Johns Hopkins Hospital, 105,* 201–232.

Mouret, J., Bobillier, P., & Jouvet, M. (1968). Insomnia following parachlorophenylalanin in the rat. *European Journal of Pharmacology, 5,* 17–22.

Mrosovsky, N. (1988). Phase response curves for social entrainment. *Journal of Comparative Physiology, 162,* 35–46.

Mrosovsky, N., & Salmon, P. A. (1987). A behavioral method for accelerating re-entrainment of rhythms to new light-dark cycles. *Nature, 330,* 372–373.

Mucha, R. F., Van der Kooy, D., O'Shaughnessy, M., & Bucenieks, P. (1982). Drug reinforcement studied by the use of place conditioning in rat. *Brain Research, 243,* 91–105.

Mullaney, D. J., Johnson, L. C., Naitoh, P., Friedman, J. K., & Globus, G. G. (1977). Sleep during and after gradual sleep reduction. *Psychophysiology, 14,* 237–244.

Mumby, D. G., & Pinel, J. P. J. (1994). Rhinal cortex lesions impair object recognition in rats. *Behavioral Neuroscience, 108,* 11–18.

Mumby, D. G., Pinel, J. P. J., & Dastur, F. N. (1993). Mediodorsal thalamic lesions and onject recognition in rats. *Psychobiology, 21,* 27–36.

Mumby, D. G., Pinel, J. P. J., & Wood, E. R. (1989). Nonrecurring items delayed nonmatching-to-sample in rats: A new paradigm for testing nonspatial working memory. *Psychobiology, 18,* 321–326.

Mumby, D. G., Wood, E. R., Duva, C. A., Kornecook, T. J., Pinel, J. P. J., & Phillips, A. G. (in press). Ischemia induced object-recognition deficits are attenuated by hippocampal ablation before or soon after ischemia. *Behavioral Neuroscience.*

Mumby, D. G., Wood, E. R., & Pinel, J. P. J. (1992). Object-recognition memory is only mildly impaired in rats with lesions of the hippocampus and amygdala. *Psychobiology, 20,* 18–27.

Murphy, M. R., & Schneider, G. E. (1970). Olfactory bulb removal eliminates mating behavior in the male golden hamster. *Science, 157,* 302–304.

Murray, E. A. (1992). Medial temporal lobe structures contributing to recognition memory: The amygdaloid complex versus the rhinal cortex. In J. Aggleton (Ed.), *The amygdala: Neurobiological aspects of emotion, memory, and mental dysfunction,* (pp. 453–470). New York: Wiley & Sons.

Mushiake, H., Inase, M., & Tanji, J. (1991). Neuronal activity in the primate motor, supplementary and precentral motor cortex during visually guided and internally determined sequential movements. *Journal of Neurophysiology, 66,* 705–718.

Musto, D. F. (1991, July). Opium, cocaine and marijuana in American history. *Scientific American, 265,* 40–47.

Myers, R. E., & Sperry, R. W. (1953). Interocular transfer of a visual form discrimination habit in cats after section of the optic chiasma and corpus callosum. *American Association of Anatomists: Abstracts of Papers from Platform,* p. 351.

Nadelman, E. A. (1989). Drug prohibition in the United States: Costs, consequences, and alternatives. *Science, 245,* 939–947.

Naeser, M. A., Alexander M. P., Helm-Estabrooks, N., Levine, H. L., Laughlin, S. A., & Geschwind, N. (1982). Aphasia with predominantly subcortical lesion sites. *Archives of Neurolinguistics, 39,* 2–14.

Naeser, M. A., Hayward, R. W., Laughlin, S. A., & Zatz, L. M. (1981). Quantitative CT scan studies in aphasia. *Brain and Language, 12,* 140–164.

Nathans, J. (1989, February). The genes for color vision. *Scientific American, 260,* 42–49.

National Commission on Marijuana and Drug Abuse (1972). R. P. Schafer, Chairman. *Marijuana: A signal of misunderstanding.* New York: New American Library.

Nauta, W. J. H., &. Feirtag, M. (1986). *Fundamental neuroanatomy.* New York: W.H. Freeman.

Neher, E., & Sakmann, B. (1992, March). The patch clamp technique. *Scientific American, 266,* 44–51.

Netter, F. H. (1962). *The CIBA collection of medical illustrations: Vol. 1. The nervous system.* New York: CIBA.

Newman, E. A., & Hartline, P. H. (1982, March). The infrared "vision" of snakes. *Scientific American, 246,* 116–127.

Newsom-Davis, J., & Vincent, A. (1991). Antibody- medicated neurological disease. *Current Opinion in Neurobiology, 1,* 430–435.

Nguyen, P.V., Abel, T., & Kandel, E. R. (1994). Requirement of a critical period of transcription for induction of a late phase of LTP. *Science, 265,* 1104–1106.

Nicholas, M.K., & Arnason, B. G. W. (1992). Immunologic responses in central nervous system transplantation. *Seminars in the Neurosciences, 4,* 273–283.

Nicolaïdis, S., & Rowland, N. (1975). Regulatory drinking in rats with permanent access to a bitter fluid source. *Physiology & Behavior, 14,* 819–824.

Nicolaïdis, S., & Rowland, N. (1977). Intravenous self-feeding: Long-term regulation of energy balance in rats. *Science, 195,* 589–591.

NIH Guide for the Care and Use of Laboratory Animals. National Institutes of Health, Publication No. 85–23 (Revised 1985), 9000 Rockville Pike, Besthesda, MD 20892.

Nishi, R. (1994). Neurotrophic factors: Two are better than one. *Science, 265,* 1052–1053.

Nordeen, K. W., & Nordeen, E. J. (1992). Auditory feedback is necessary for the maintenance of stereotyped song in adult zebra finches. *Behavioral and Neural Biology, 57,* 58–66.

Norman, R. M. G., & Malla, A. K. (1993). Stressful life events and schizophrenia I: A review of the research. *British Journal of Psychiatry, 162,* 161–166.

Nottebohm, F. (1991). Reassessing the mechanisms and origins of vocal learning in birds. *Trends in Neurosciences, 14,* 206–211.

Novin, D. (1964). The effects of insulin on water intake in the rat. In M. J. Wayner (Ed.), *Proceedings of the 1st international symposium in the regulation of body water* (pp. 177–184). Oxford: Pergamon Press.

Nudo, R. J., Jenkins, W. M., & Merzenich, M. M. (1990). Repetitive microstimulation alters the cortical representation of movements in adult rats. *Somatosensory Motor Research, 7,* 463–483.

O'Banion, M. K., Coleman, P. D., & Callahan, L. M. (1994), Regional neuronal loss in aging and Alzheimer's disease: A brief review. Seminars in the *Neurosciences, 6,* 307–314.

O'Callaghan, M. A. J., & Carroll, D. (1982). *Psychosurgery: A scientific analysis.* Ridgewood, NJ: George A. Bogdaen & Son, Inc.

O'Keefe, J. (1993). Hippocampus, theta, and spatial memory. *Current Opinion in Neurobiology, 3,* 917–924.

O'Keefe, J., Dostrovsky, J. (1971). The hippocampus as a spatial map. Preliminary evidence from unit activity in the freely-moving rat. *Brain Research, 34,* 171–175.

O'Keefe, J., & Nadel, L. (1978). *The hippocampus as a cognitive map.* Oxford: The Clarendon Press.

O'Keefe, J., & Speakman, A. (1987). Single unit activity in the rat hippocampus during a spatial memory task. *Experimental Brain Research, 68,* 1–27.

O'Leary, A. (1990). Stress, emotion, and human immune function. *Psychological Bulletin, 108,* 363–382.

O'Leary, D. D. M., Ruff, N. L., Dyck, R. H. (1994) Development, critical period plasticity, and adult reorganization of mammalian somatosensory systems. *Current Opinion in Neurobiology, 4,* 535–544.

O'Neill, L., Murphy, M., & Gallager, R. B. (1994). What are we? Where did we come from? Where are we going? *Science, 263,* 181–184.

Ohzawa, I., DeAngelis, G. C., & Freeman, R. D. (1990). Stereoscopic depth discrimination in the visual cortex: Neurons ideally suited as disparity detectors. *Science, 249,* 1037–1040.

Ojeda, S. R., Kalra, P. S., & McCann, S. M. (1975). Further studies on the maturation of the estrogen negative feedback on gonadotropin release in the female rat. *Neuroendocrinology, 18,* 242–255.

Ojemann, G. A. (1979). Individual variability in cortical localization of language. *Journal of Neurosurgery, 50,* 164–169.

Ojemann, G. A. (1983). Brain organization for language from the perspective of electrical stimulation mapping. *Behavioral and Brain Sciences, 2,* 189–230.

Olds, J., & Milner, P. (1954). Positive reinforcement produced by electrical stimulation of septal area and other regions of rat brain. *Journal of Comparative and Physiological Psychology, 47,* 419–427.

Oliveras, J.-L., Besson, J.-M., Guilbaud, G., & Liebeskind, J. C. (1974). Behavioral and electrophysiological evidence of pain inhibition from midbrain stimulation in the cat. *Experimental Brain Research, 20,* 32–44.

Olney, J. W., Labruyere, J., Wang, G., Wozniak, D. F., Price, M. T., & Sesma, M. A. (1991). NMDA antagonist neurotoxicity: Mechanism and prevention. *Science, 254,* 1515–1518.

Olton, D. S., & Samuelson, R. J. (1976). Remembrance of places: Spatial memory in rats. *Journal of Experimental Psychology: Animal Behavior Processes, 2,* 97–116.

Owren, M. J. (1990). Acoustic classification of alarm calls by vervet monkeys (*Cercopithecus aethiops*) and humans (*Homo sapiens*): II. Synthetic calls. *Journal of Comparative Psychology, 104,* 29–40.

Paletta, M. S., & Wagner, A. R. (1986). Development of context specific tolerance to morphine: Support for a dual-process interpretation. *Behavioral Neuroscience, 100,* 611–623.

Panksepp, J. (1975). Metabolic hormones and regulation of feeding: A reply to Woods, Decke, and Vaselli. *Psychological Review, 82,* 158–164.

Panksepp, J., & Trowill, J. A. (1967). Intraoral self-injection: II. The simulation of self-stimulation phenomena with a conventional reward. *Psychonomic Science, 9,* 407–408.

Papez, J. W. (1937). A proposed mechanism of emotion. *Archives of Neurology and Psychiatry, 38,* 725–743.

Parker, S. T., Mitchell, R. W., & Boccia, M. L. (1994). *Self-awareness in animals and humans: Developmental perspectives.* New York: Cambridge University Press.

Patterson, K., Vargha-Khadem, F., & Polkey, C. E. (1989). Reading with one hemisphere. *Brain, 112,* 39–63.

Peck, J. W., & Novin, D. (1971). Evidence that osmoreceptors mediating drinking in rabbits are in the lateral preoptic area. *Journal of Comparative and Physiological Psychology, 74,* 134–147.

Pellis, S. M. (1989). Fighting: The problem of selecting appropriate behavior patterns. In R. J. Blanchard, P. F. Brain, D. C. Blanchard, and S. Parmigiani (Eds.), *Ethoexperimental approaches to the study of behavior.* Dordrecht: Kluwer Academic Publishers.

Pellis, S. M., O'Brien, D. P., Pellis, V. C., Teitelbaum, P., Wolgin, D. L., & Kennedy, S. (1988). Escalation of feline predation along a gradient from avoidance through "play" to killing. *Behavioral Neuroscience, 102,* 760–777.

Pellow, S., Chopin, P., File, S. E., & Briley, M. (1985). Validation of open:closed arm entries in an elevated plus-maze as a measure of anxiety in the rat. *Journal of Neuroscience Methods, 14,* 149–167.

Penfield, W., & Boldrey, E. (1937). Somatic motor and sensory representations in cerebral cortex of man as studied by electrical stimulation. *Brain, 60,* 389–443.

Penfield, W., & Rasmussen, T. (1950). *The cerebral cortex of man: A clinical study of the localization of function.* New York: Macmillan Pub. Co.

Penfield, W., & Roberts, L. (1959). *Speech and brain mechanisms* (pp. 133–191). Princeton, NJ: Princeton University Press.

Percival, J. E., Horne, J. A, & Tilley, A. J. (1983). Effects of sleep deprivation on tests of higher cerebral functioning. *Sleep 1982. 6th European Congress on Sleep Research* (Zurich, 1982). (pp. 390–391). Basel: Karger.

Perenin, M.-T. & Vighetto, A. (1988) A specific disruption in visuomotor mechanisms. I. Different Aspects of the deficit in reaching for objects. *Brain, 111,* 643–674.

Perlow, M. J., Freed, W. J., Hoffer, B. J., Seiger, A., Olson, L., & Wyatt, R. J. (1979). Brain grafts reduce motor abnormalities produced by destruction of nigrostriatal dopamine system. *Science, 204,* 643–647.

Pert, C. B., Snowman, A.M., & Snyder, S. H. (1974). Localization of opiate receptor binding in presynaptic membranes of rat brain. *Brain Research, 70,* 184–188.

Peterhans, E., & von der Heydt, R. (1991). Subjective contours—bridging the gap between psychophysics and physiology. *Trends in Neurosciences, 14,* 112–119.

Petersen, S. E., & Fiez, J. A. (1993). The processing of single words studied with positron emission tomography. *Annual Review of Neuroscience, 16,* 509–530.

Petersen, S. E., Fox, P. T., Mintun, M. A., Posner, M. I., & Raichle, M. E. (1989). Studies of the processing of single words using averaged positron emission tomographic measurements of cerebral blood flow change. *Journal of Cognitive Neuroscience,* Vol. 1, pp. 153–170.

Petersen, S. E., Fox, P. T., Posner, M. I., Mintun, M., & Raichle, M. E. (1988). Positron emission tomographic studies of the cortical anatomy of single-word processing. *Nature, 331,* 585–589.

Petrides, M. (1989). Frontal lobes and memory. In F. Boller and J. Grafman (Eds.) *Handbook of neuropsychology, Vol. III,* (pp. 75–90). New York: Elsevier.

Petrides, M. (1994). Frontal lobes and behavior. *Current Opinion in Neurobiology, 4,* 207–211.

Petrinovich, L. (1990). Avian song development: Methodological and conceptual issues. In D. A. Dewsbury (Ed.), *Contemporary Issues in Comparative Psychology,* (pp. 321–339). Sunderland, MA: Sinauer.

Pettet, M. W., & Gilbert, C.D. (1992). Dynamic changes in receptive field size in cat primary visual cortex. *Procedures of the National Academy of Sciences, USA, 89,* 8366–8370.

Pettit, H. O., & Justice, Jr. J. B. (1991). Effect of dose on cocaine self-administration as studied by in vivo microdialysis. *Pharmacology Biochemistry & Behavior, 34,* 899–904.

Pfaff, D., & Modianos, D. (1985). Neural mechanisms of female reproductive behavior. In N. Adler, D. Pfaff, and R. W. Goy (Eds.), *Handbook of behavioral neurobiology, Vol. 7,* Reproduction (pp. 423–493). New York: Plenum Press.

Pfaus, J. G., Damsma, G., Nomikos, G. G., Phillips, A. G., & Fibiger, H. C. (1990). Sexual behavior enhances central dopamine transmission in the male rat. *Brain Research, 530,* 345–348.

Pfaus, J. G., & Pinel, J. P. J. (1989). Alcohol inhibits and disinhibits sexual behavior in the male rat. *Psychobiology, 17,* 195–201.

Pfeiffer, C. A. (1936). Sexual differences of the hypophyses and their determination by the gonads. *American Journal of Anatomy, 58,* 195–225.

Phelps, M. E., & Mazziotta, J. C. (1985). Positron emission tomography: Human brain function and biochemistry. *Science, 288,* 782–799.

Phillips, A. G., Coury, A., Fiorino, D., LePiane, F. G., Brown, E., & Fibiger, H. C. (1992). Self-stimulation of the ventral tegmental area enhances dopamine release in the nucleus accumbens: A microdialysis study. *Annals of the New York Academy of Sciences, 654,* 199–206.

Phillips, A. G., & Fibiger, H. C. (1989). Neuroanatomical bases of intracranial self-stimulation: Untangling the Gordian knot. In J. M. Leibman & S. J. Cooper (Eds.), *The neuropharmacological basis of reward* (pp. 66–105). Oxford: Clarendon Press.

Phillips, A. G., Spyraki, C., & Fibiger, H. C. (1982). Conditioned place preference with amphetamine and opiates as reward stimuli: Attenuation by haloperidol. In B. G. Hoebel & D. Novin (Eds.), *The neural basis of feeding and reward* (pp. 455–464). Brunswick, MN: Haer Institute.

Phillips, D. P. (1989). Neurobiology relevant to some central auditory processing disorders. *Journal of Speech-Language Pathology and Audiology (Human Communication Canada), 13,* 17–34.

Phillips, M. I., & Felix, D. (1976). Specific angiotensin II receptive neurons in the cat subfornical organ. *Brain Research, 109,* 531–540.

Phoenix, C. H., Goy, R. W., Gerall, A. A., & Young, W. C. (1959). Organizing action of prenatally administered testosterone proprionate on the tissues mediating mating behavior in the female guinea pig. *Endocrinology, 65,* 369–382.

Pigott, S., & Milner, B. (1993). Memory for different aspects of complex visual scenes after unilateral temporal- or frontal-lobe resection. *Neuropsychologia, 31,* 1–15.

Pilar, G., Landmesser, L., & Burstein, L. (1980). Competition for survival among developing ciliary ganglion cells. *Journal of Neurophysiology, 43*, 233–254.

Pinel, J. P. J. (1969). A short gradient of ECS-produced amnesia in a one-trial appetitive learning situation. *Journal of Comparative and Physiological Psychology, 68*, 650–655.

Pinel, J. P. J. (1981). Spontaneous kindled motor seizures in rats. In J. A. Wada (Ed.), *Kindling 2* (pp. 179–192). New York: Raven Press.

Pinel, J. P. J., Jones, C. H., & Whishaw, I. Q. (1992). Behavior from the ground up: Rat behavior from the ventral perspective. *Psychobiology, 20*, 185–188.

Pinel, J. P. J., Kim, C. K., & Mana, M. J. (1990). Contingent tolerance to the anticonvulsant effects of drugs on kindled convulsions. In J. A. Wada, (Ed.) *Kindling 4* (pp. 283–297). New York: Plenum Press.

Pinel, J. P. J., & Mana, M. J. (1989). Adaptive interactions of rats with dangerous inanimate objects: Support for a cognitive theory of defensive behavior. In R. J. Blanchard, P. F. Brain, D. C. Blanchard, & S. Parmigiani (Eds.), *Ethoexperimental approaches to the study of behavior* (pp. 137–150). Dordrecht, The Netherlands: Kluwer Academic Publishers.

Pinel, J. P. J., Mana, M. J., & Kim, C. K., (1989). Effect-dependent tolerance to ethanol's anticonvulsant effect on kindled seizures. In R. J. Porter, R. H. Mattson, J. A. Cramer, & I. Diamond (Eds.), *Alcohol and seizures: Basic mechanisms and clinical implications* (pp. 115–125). Philadelphia: F. A. Davis.

Pinel, J. P. J., Pfaus, J. G., & Christensen, B. K. (1991). Contingent tolerance to the disruptive effects of alcohol on the copulatory behavior of male rats. *Pharmacology Biochemistry & Behavior, 41*, 133–137.

Pinel, J. P. J., & Rovner, L. I. (1977). Saccharin elation effect. *Bulletin of the Psychonomic Society, 9*, 275–278.

Pinel, J. P. J., Symons, L. A., Christenson, B. K., & Tees, R. C. (1989). Development of defensive burying in rattus norvegicus: Experience and defensive responses. *Journal of Comparative Psychology, 103*, 359–365.

Pinel, J. P. J., & Treit, D. (1978). Burying as a defensive response in rats. *Journal of Comparative and Physiological Psychology, 92*, 708–712.

Pinsker, H. M., Hening, W. A., Carew, T. J., & Kandel, E. R. (1973). Long-term sensitization of a defensive withdrawal reflex in Aplysia. *Science, 182*, 1039–1042.

Pizzamiglio, L., Caltagirone, C., & Zoccaoloti, P. (1989). Facial expression of emotion. In F. Boller and J. Grafman (Eds.), *Handbook of neuropsychology, 3*, (pp. 383–402). New York: Elsevier.

Plapinger, L., McEwen, B. S., & Clemens, L. E. (1973). Ontogeny of estradiol-binding sites in rat brain. II. characteristics of a neonatal binding macromolecule. *Endocrinology, 93*, 1129–1139.

Pleim, E. T., & Barfield, R. J. (1988). Progesterone versus estrogen facilitation of female sexual behavior by intracranial administration to female rats. *Hormones and Behavior, 22*, 150–159.

Plomin, R. (1990). *Nature and nurture: An introduction to human behavioral genetics.* Pacific Grove, CA: Brooks/Cole.

Plomin, R., & Neiderhiser, J. M. (1992). Genetics and experience. *Current Directions in Psychological Science, 1*, 160–163.

Plomin, R., Owen, M. J., & McGuffin, P. (1994). The genetic basis of complex human behaviors. *Science, 264*, 1733–1739.

Pons, T. P., Garraghty, P. E., Friedman, D. P., & Mishkin, M. (1987). Physiological evidence for serial processing in somatosensory cortex. *Science, 237*, 417–420.

Pope, H. G., & Katz, D. L. (1987). Bodybuilder's psychosis. *Lancet, 1(8537)*, 863.

Poppelreuter, W. (1917). *Die psychischen Schädigungen durch Kopfschuss im Kriege 1914–1916: die Störungen der niederen und höheren Sehleistungen durch Verletzungen des Okzipitalhirns.* Leipzig: Voss.

Porte, D., Jr., & Woods, S. C. (1981). Regulation of food intake and body weight by insulin. *Diabetologia, 20*, 274–280.

Posner, M. I., & Raichle, M. E. (1994). *Images of the mind.* New York: Scientific American Library.

Post, R. M., Weiss, S. R. B., Clark, M., Nakajima, T., & Pert, A. (1990). Amygdala versus local anesthetic kindling: Differential anatomy, pharmacology, and clinical implications. In J. A. Wada (Ed.), *Kindling 4* (pp. 357–369). New York: Plenum Press.

Poulos, C. X., & Cappell, H. (1991). Homeostatic theory of drug tolerance: A general model of physiological adaptation. *Psychological Review, 98*, 390–408.

Powers, J. B., Newman, S. W., & Bergondy, M. L. (1987). MPOA and BNST lesions in male Syrian hamsters: Differential effects on copulatory and chemoinvestigatory behaviors. *Behavioral Brain Research, 23*, 181–195.

Powley, T. L., Opsahl, C. A., Cox, J. E., & Weingarten, H. P. (1980). The role of the hypothalamus in energy homeostasis. In P. J. Morgane & J. Panksepp (Eds.), *Handbook of the Hypothalamus—3A: Behavioral studies of the hypothalamus* (pp. 211–298). New York: Marcel Dekker Inc.

Price, R. A., & Gottesman, I. I. (1991). Body fat in identical twins reared apart: Roles for genes and environment. *Behavioral Genetics, 21*, 1–7.

Pritchard, R. M. (1961, June). Stabilized images on the retina. *Scientific American, 204*, 72–78.

Pujol, J. F., Buguet, A., Froment, J. L., Jones, B., & Jouvet, M. (1971). The central metabolism of serotonin in the cat during insomnia: A neurophysiological and biochemical study after administration of P-chlorophenylalanine or destruction of the raphé system. *Brain Research, 29*, 195–212.

Qualtrochi, J. J., Mamelak, A. N., Madison, R. D., Macklis, J. D., & Hobson, J. A. (1989). Mapping neuronal inputs to REM sleep induction sites with carbachol- fluorescent microspheres. *Science, 245*, 984–986.

Racine, R. J. (1972). Modification of seizure activity by electrical stimulation: II. Motor seizure. *Electroencephalography and Clinical Neurophysiology, 32*, 281–294.

Racine, R. J. (1978). Kindling: The first decade. *Neurosurgery, 3*, 234–252.

Racine, R. J., & Burnham, W. M. (1984). The kindling model. In P. A. Schwartzkroin & H. Wheal (Eds.), *Electrophysiology of epilepsy* (pp. 153–171). London: Academic Press.

Racine, R. J., Burnham, W. M., Gartner, J. G., & Levitan, D. (1973). Rates of motor seizure development in rats subjected to electrical brain stimulation: Strain and interstimulation interval effects. *Electroencephalography and Clinical Neurophysiology, 35*, 553–556.

Racine, R. J., & deJonge, M. (1988). Short-term and long-term potentiation in projection pathways and local circuits. In P. W. Landfield & S. A. Deadwyler (Eds.), *Long-term potentiation: From biophysics to behavior* (p. 167). New York: Liss.

Racine, R. J., Livingston, K., & Joaquin, A. (1975). Effects of procaine hydrochloride, diazepam, and diphenylhydantoin on seizure development in cortical and subcortical structures in rats. *Electroencephalography and Clinical Neurophysiology, 38*, 355–365.

Racine, R. J., Milgram, N. W., & Hafner, S. (1983). Long-term potentiation phenomena in the rat limbic forebrain. *Brain Research, 260*, 217–233.

Rafal, R. D. (1994). Neglect. *Current Opinion in Neurobiology, 4*, 231–236.

Raff, M. C., Barres, B. A., Burne, J. F., Coles, H. S., Ishizaki, Y., & Jacobson, M. D. (1993). Programmed cell death and the control of cell survival: Lessons from the nervous system. *Science, 262*, 695–700.

Raichle, M. E. (1994, April). Visualizing the mind. *Scientific American, 2*, 58–64.

Raichle, M. E., Fiez, J., Videen, T. O., Fox, P. T., Pardo, J. V., & Petersen, S.E. (1991). Practice-related changes in human brain functional anatomy. *Society for Neuroscience Abstracts, 17*, 21.

Raisman, G., & Field, P. M. (1971). Sexual dimorphism in the neuropil of the preoptic area of the rat and its dependence on neonatal androgens. *Brain Research, 54*, 1–29.

Raisman, G., Morris, R. J., & Zhou, C. F. (1987). Specificity in the reinnervation of adult hippocampus by embryonic hippocampal transplants. In F. J. Seil, E. Herbert, & B. M. Carlson (Eds.), *Progress in Brain Research* (Vol. 71, pp. 325–333). New York: Elsevier.

Rakic, P. (1979). Genetic and epigenetic determinants of local neuronal circuits in the mammalian central nervous system. In F. O. Schmitt, and F. G. Worden (Eds.), *The Neurosciences: Fourth Study Program*. Cambridge, MA: MIT Press.

Ralph, M. R., Foster, T. G., Davis, F. C., & Menaker, M. (1990). Transplanted suprachiasmatic nucleus determines circadian period. *Science, 247*, 975–978.

Ralph, M. R.. & Menaker, M. (1988). A mutation of the circadian system in golden hamsters. *Science, 241*, 1255–1227.

Ramachandran, V. S. (1992, May). Blind spots. *Scientific American, 260*, 86–91.

Ramsay, D. J., Rolls, B. J., & Wood, R. J. (1977). Body fluid changes which influence drinking in the water deprived rat. *Journal of Physiology, 266*, 453–469.

Rasmussen, T., & Milner, B. (1975). Excision of Broca's area without persistent aphasia. In K. J. Zulch, O. Creutzfeldt, & G. C. Galbraith (Eds.), *Cerebral localization* (pp. 258–263). New York: Springer-Verlag.

Ratliff, F. (1972, June). Contour and contrast. *Scientific American, 226*, 90–101.

Ratnasuriya, R. H., Eisler, I., Szmukler, G. I., & Russell, G. F. M. (1991). Anorexia nervosa: Outcome and prognostic factors after 20 years. *British Journal of Psychiatry, 158*, 495–502.

Reame, N., Sauder, S. E., Kelch, R. P., & Marshall, J. C. (1984). Pulsatile gonadotropin secretion during the human menstrual cycle: Evidence for laltered frequency of gonadotropin releasing hormone secretion. *Journal of Clinical Endocrinology and Metabolism, 59*, 328.

Rebec, G. V., & Bashore, T. R. (1984). Critical issues in assessing the behavioral effects of amphetamine. *Neuroscience and Biobehavioral Reviews, 8*, 153–158.

Recanzone, G. H., Merzenich, M. M., Jenkins, W. M., Kamil, A. G., & Dinse, H.R. (1992). Topographic reorganization of the hand representation in cortical area 3b of owl monkeys trained in a frequency-discrimination task. *Journal of Neurophysiology, 67*, 1031–1056.

Rechtschaffen, A., Gilliland, M. A., Bergmann, B. M., & Winter, J. B. (1983). Physiological correlates of prolonged sleep deprivation in rats. *Science, 221*, 182–184.

Rechtschaffen, A., & Kales, A. (1968). *A manual of standardized terminology, techniques and scoring systems for sleep stages of human subjects*. Washington, DC: U. S. Government Printing Office.

Rechtschaffen, A., Wolpert, E. A., Dement, W. C., Mitchell, S. A., & Fisher, C. (1963). Nocturnal sleep of narcoleptics. *Electroencephalography and Clinical Neurophysiology, 15*, 599–609.

Redd, M., & de Castro, J. M. (1992). Social facilitation of eating: Effects of social instruction on food intake. *Physiology & Behavior, 52*, 749–754.

Reh, T. A., & Constantine-Paton, M. (1984). Retinal ganglion cell terminals change their projection sites during larval development of Rana pipiens. *Journal of Neuroscience, 4*, 442–457.

Revusky, S. H., & Garcia, J. (1970). Learned associations over long delays. In G. H. Bower & J. T. Spence (Eds.), *The psychology of learning and motivation* (Vol. 4, pp. 1–85). New York: Academic Press.

Reynolds, D. V. (1969). Surgery in the rat during electrical analgesia induced by focal brain stimulation. *Science, 164*, 444–445.

Richter, C. P. (1967). Sleep and activity: Their relation to the 24-hour clock. *Proceedings of the Association for Research on Nervous and Mental Disorders, 45*, 8–27.

Richter, C. P. (1971). Inborn nature of the rat's 24-hour clock. *Journal of Comparative and Physiological Psychology, 75*, 1–14.

Rindi, G. (1989). Alcohol and thiamine of the brain. *Alcohol & Alcoholism, 24*, 493–495.

Ringwald, M., Baldock, R., Bard, J., Kaufman, M., Eppig, J. T., Richardson, J. E., Nadeau, J. H., & Davidson, D. (1994). A database for mouse development. *Science, 265*, 2033–2034.

Robbins, T. W., Everitt, B. J., Ryan, C. N., Marston, H. M., Jones, G. H., & Page, K. J. (1989). Comparative effects of quisqualic and ibotenic acid-induced lesions of the substantia innominata and globus pallidus on attentional function in the rat: Further implications for the role of the cholinergic neurons of the nucleus basalis in cognitive processes. *Behavioral Brain Research, 35,* 221–240.

Roberts, D. C. S., & Koob, G. F. (1982). Disruption of cocaine self-administration following 6-hydroxydopamine lesions of the ventral tegmental area in rats. *Pharmacology Biochemistry & Behavior, 17,* 901–904.

Roberts, D. C. S., Koob, G. F., Klonoff, P., & Fibiger, H. C. (1980). Extinction and recovery of cocaine self-administration following 6-hydroxydopamine lesions of the nucleus accumbens. *Pharmacology Biochemistry & Behavior, 12,* 781–787.

Roberts, D. C. S., & Zito, K. A. (1987). Interpretation of lesion effects on stimulant self-administration. In M. A. Bozarth (Ed.), *Methods of assessing the reinforcing properties of abused drugs* (pp. 87–103). New York: Springer-Verlag.

Roberts, G. W. (1990). Schizophrenia: The cellular biology of a functional psychosis. *Trends in Neurosciences, 13,* 207–211.

Robinson, T. E. (1991). Persistent sensitizing effects of drugs on brain dopamine systems and behavior: Implications for addiction and relapse. In J. Barchas and S. Korenman (Eds.), *The biological basis of substance abuse and its therapy.* New York: Oxford University Press.

Robinson, T. E., & Berridge, K. C. (1993). The neural basis of drug craving: An incentive-sensitization theory of addiction. *Brain Research Reviews, 18,* 247–291.

Robinson, T. E., & Justice, J. B., Jr. (Eds.). (1991). *Microdialysis in the Neurosciences. Vol. 7, Techniques in the neural and behavioral sciences.* Elsevier: Amsterdam.

Robitaille, R., Adler, E. M., & Charlton, M. P. (1990). Strategic location of calcium channels at transmitter release sites at frog neuromuscular synapses. Neuron, 5, 773–779.

Rodin, J. (1985). Insulin levels, hunger, and food intake: an example of feedback loops in body weight regulation. *Health Psychology, 4,* 1–24.

Roe, A. W., Pallas, S. L., Hahm, J-O., & Sur, M. (1990). A map of visual space induced in primary auditory cortex. *Science, 250,* 818–820.

Rogers, P. J., & Blundell, J. E. (1980). Investigation of food selection and meal parameters during the development of dietary induced obesity. *Appetite, 1,* 85–88.

Roland, P. (1992). Cortical representation of pain. *Trends in Neurosciences, 15,* 3–5.

Roland, P. E. (1993). *Brain activation.* New York: Wiley-Liss.

Roland, P. E., & Gulyás, B. (1994). Visual imagery and visual representation. *Trends in Neurosciences, 17,* 281–297.

Rolls, B. J. (1986). Sensory-specific satiety. *Nutrition Reviews, 44,* 93–101.

Rolls, B. J. (1990). The role of sensory-specific satiety in food intake and food selection. In E. D. Capaldi and T. L. Powley (Eds.), *Taste, experience, & feeding* (pp. 28–42). Washington, DC: American Psychological Association.

Rolls, B. J., & Rolls, E. T. (1982). *Thirst.* Cambridge: Cambridge University Press.

Rolls, B. J., Rolls, E. T., Rowe, E. A., & Sweeney, K. (1981). Sensory specific satiety in man. *Physiology & Behavior, 27,* 137–142.

Rolls, B. J., Wood, R. J., & Rolls, R. M. (1980). Thirst: The initiation, maintenance, and termination of drinking. In J. M. Sprague and A. N. Epstein (Eds.). *Progress in psychology and physiological psychology.* New York: Academic Press.

Rolls, B. J., Wood, R. J., & Stevens, R. M. (1978). Effects of palatability on body fluid homeostasis. *Physiology & Behavior, 20,* 15–19.

Rolls, B. J., Wood, R., Rolls, E. T., Lind, H., Lind, R., & Ledingham, J. G. (1980). Thirst following water deprivation in humans. *American Journal of Physiology, 239,* 476–482.

Rolls, E. T. (1981). Central nervous mechanisms related to feeding and appetite. *British Medical Bulletin, 37,* 131–134.

Rolls, E. T., & Rolls, B. J. (1982). Brain mechanisms involved in feeding. In L. M. Barker (Ed.), *The psychobiology of human food selection* (pp. 33–65). Westport, CT: AVI Pub. Co.

Romanski, L. M., & LeDoux, J.E. (1992). Equipotentiality of thalamo-cortico-amygdala projections as auditory conditioned stimulus pathways. *Journal of Neuroscience, 12,* 4501–4509.

Rose, G. A., & Williams, R. T. (1961). The psychobiology of meals. *British Journal of Nutrition, 15,* 1-9.

Rosenthal, D., Wender, P. H., Kety, S. S., Welner, J., & Schulsinger, F. (1980). The adopted-away offspring of schizophrenics. *American Journal of Psychiatry, 128,* 87–91.

Ross, J., Morrone, M. C., & Burr, D. C. (1989). The conditions for the appearance of Mach bands. *Vision Research, 29,* 669–715.

Rothblat, L. A., & Hayes, L. L. (1987). Short-term object recognition memory in the rat: Nonmatching with trial-unique junk stimuli. *Behavioral Neuroscience, 101,* 587–590.

Rothman, S. M. (1994). Excitotoxic neuronal death: Mechanisms and clinical relevance. *Seminars in the Neurosciences, 6,* 315–322.

Rothwell, J. C., Traub, M. M., Day, B. L., Obeso, J. A., Thomas, P. K., & Marsden, C. D. (1982). *Manual motor performance in a deafferented man. Brain, 105,* 515–542.

Rothwell, N. J., & Stock, M. J. (1982). Energy expenditure derived from measurements of oxygen consumption and energy balance in hyperphagic, "cafeteria"-fed rats. *Journal of Physiology, 324,* 59–60.

Routtenberg, A. (1978, November). The reward system of the brain. *Scientific American, 239,* 154–164.

Routtenberg, A., & Malsbury, C. (1969). Brainstem pathways of reward. *Journal of Comparative and Physiological Psychology, 68,* 22–30.

Rowland, N. (1981). Glucoregulatory feeding on cats. *Physiology & Behavior, 26,* 901–903.

Rowland, N., & Nicolaïdis, S. (1976). Metering of fluid intake and determinants of ad libitum drinking in rats. *American Journal of Physiology, 231,* 1–8.

Rowland, N. E. (1990a). On the waterfront: Predictive and reactive regulatory descriptions of thirst and sodium appetite. *Physiology & Behavior, 48,* 899–903.

Rowland, N. E. (1990). Sodium appetite. In E. D. Capaldi and T. L. Powley (Eds.), *Taste, experience, and feeding* (pp. 94–104). Washington, DC: American Psychological Association.

Rudomin, P. (1990). Presynaptic inhibition of muscle spindle and tendon organ afferents in the mammalian spinal cord. *Trends in Neurosciences, 13,* 499–505.

Rudy, J. W., & Sutherland, R. J. (1992). Configural and elemental associations and the memory coherence problem. *Journal of Cognitive Neuroscience, 4,* 208–216.

Rummelhart, D. E., & Norman, D. A. (1982). Simulating a skilled typist: A study of skilled cognitive motor performance. *Cognitive Science, 6,* 1–36.

Rusak, B. (1979). Neural mechanisms for entrainment and generation of mammalian circadian rhythms. *Proceedings of the Federation of American Societies for Experimental Biology, 38,* 2589–2595.

Rusak, B., & Bina, K. G. (1990). Neurotransmitters in the mammalian circadian system. *Annual Review of Neuroscience, 13,* 387–401.

Rusak, B., & Groos, G. (1982). Suprachiasmatic stimulation phase shifts rodent circadian rhythms. *Science, 215,* 1407–1409.

Rusak, B., & Zucker, I. (1979). Neural regulation of circadian rhythms. *Psychological Reviews, 59,* 449–526.

Rusak, B., Mistlberger, R. E., Losier, B., & Jones, C. H. (1988). Daily hoarding opportunity entrains the pacemaker for hamster activity rhythms. *Journal of Comparative Physiology, 164,* 165–171.

Rusak, B., Robertson, H. A., Wisden, W., & Hunt, S. P. (1990). Light pulses that shift rhythms induce gene expression in the suprachiasmatic nucleus. *Science, 248,* 1237–1240.

Russell, W. R., & Espir, M. I. E. (1961). *Traumatic aphasia—a study of aphasia in war wounds of the brain.* London: Oxford University Press.

Rutishauser, U. (1993). Adhesion molecules of the nervous system. *Current Opinion in Neurobiology, 3,* 709–715.

Rutledge, L. L., & Hupka, R. B. (1985). The facial feedback hypothesis: Methodological concerns and new supporting evidence. *Motivation and Emotion, 9,* 219–240.

Sacks, O. (1985). *The man who mistook his wife for a hat and other clinical tales.* New York: Summit Books.

Sagar, H. J., Gabrieli, J. D. E., Sullivan, E. V., & Corkin, S. (1990). Recency and frequency discrimination in the amnesic patient H. M. *Brain, 113,* 581–602.

Sager, R. (1989). Tumor suppressor genes: The puzzle and the promise. *Science, 246,* 1406–1412.

Sakai, K., & Miyashita, Y. (1993). Memory and imagery in the temporal lobe. *Current Opinion in Neurobiology, 3,* 166–170.

Sakuma, Y., & Pfaff, D. W. (1979). Mesencephalic mechanisms for the integration of female reproductive behavior in the rat. *American Journal of Physiology, 237,* 285–290.

Sanders, D., & Bancroft, J. (1982). Hormones and the sexuality of women—the menstrual cycle. *Clinics in Endocrinology and Metabolism, 11,* 639–659.

Sanes, J. N., Suner, S., & Donoghue, J. P. (1990). Dynamic organization of primary motor cortex output to target muscles in adult rats. I. Long-term patterns of reorganization following motor or mixed peripheral nerve lesions. *Experimental Brain Research, 79,* 479–491.

Sanes, J. N., Wang, J., & Donoghue, J. P. (1992). Immediate and delayed changes of rat motor cortical output representation with new forelimb configurations. *Cerebral Cortex, 2,* 141–152.

Sastry, B. R., Goh, J. W., & Auyeung, A. (1986). Associative induction of posttetanic and long-term potentiation in CA1 neurons of rat hippocampus. *Science, 232,* 988–990.

Sawchenko, P. E., Eng, R., Gold, R. M., & Simson, E. L. (1977). *Effects of selective subdiaphragmatic vagotomies on knife cut induced hypothalamic hyperphagia.* Paper presented at the Sixth International Conference on the Physiology of Food and Fluid Intake, Paris, France.

Sawle, G. V., & Myers, R. (1993) The role of positron emission tomography in the assessment of human neurotransplantation. *Trends in Neurosciences, 16,* 172–176.

Schacter, D. L., Chiu, C.-Y. P., & Ochsner, K. N. (1993). Implicit memory: A selective review. *Annual Review of Neuroscience, 16,* 159–182.

Schally, A. V. (1978). Aspects of hypothalamic regulation of the pituitary gland. *Science, 202,* 18–28.

Schally, A. V., Kastin, A. J., & Arimura, A. (1971). Hypothalamic follicle-stimulating hormone (FSH) and luteinizing hormone (LH)-regulating hormone: Structure, physiology, and clinical studies. *Fertility and Sterility, 22,* 703–721.

Schatzman, M., Worsley, A., & Fenwich, P. (1988). Correspondence during lucid dreams between dreamed and actual events. In J. Gackenbach and S. LaBerge (Eds.), *Conscious mind, sleeping brain* (pp. 67–103). New York: Plenum.

Schellenberg, G. D., Bird, T. D., Wijsman, E. M., Orr, H. T., Anderson, L., Nemens, E., White, J. A., Bonnycastle, L., Weber, J. L., Alonso, M. E., Potter, H., Heston, L. L., & Martin, G. M. (1992). Genetic linkage evidence for a familial Alzheimer's disease locus on chromosome 14. *Science, 258,* 668–672.

Schelling, T. C. (1992). Addictive drugs: The cigarette experience. *Science, 255,* 430–433.

Schenck, C. H., Bundlie, S. R., Ettinger, M. G., & Mahowald, M. W. (1986). Chronic behavioral disorders of human REM sleep: A new category of parasomnia. *Sleep, 9,* 293–308.

Scherschlicht, R. (1983). Pharmacological profile of delta sleep-inducing peptide (DSIP) and a phosphorylated analogue, (Ser-PO_4) DSIP. *Sleep 1982, 6th European Congress for Sleep Research, Zurich, 1982* (pp. 109–111). Basel, Karger.

Scherschlicht, R., & Marias, J. (1983). Effects of oral and intravenous midazolam, trizolam and flunitrazepam on the sleep-wakefulness cycle of rabbits. *British Journal of Clinical Pharmacology, 16* (Supplement 1), 29S–35S.

Schieber, M. H. (1990). How might the motor cortex individuate movements? *Trends in Neurosciences, 13,* 440-445..

Schieber, M. H., & Hibbard, L.S. (1993). How somatotopic is the motor cortex hand area? *Science, 261,* 489–492.

Schiffman, S. S., & Erikson, R. P. (1980). The issue of primary tastes versus a taste continuum. *Neuroscience and Biobehavioral Reviews, 4,* 109–117.

Schlaggar, B. L., & O'Leary, D. D. M. (1991). Potential of visual cortex to develop an array of functional units unique to somatosensory cortex. *Science, 252,* 1556–1560.

Schlaug, G., Jäncke, L., Huang, Y., & Steinmetz, H. (1995). *In vivo* evidence of structural brain asymmetry in musicians. *Science, 267,* 699–701.

Schleidt, M., Hold, B., & Attili, G. (1981). A cross-cultural study on the attitude towards personal odors. *Journal of Chemical Ecology, 7,* 19–31.

Schlundt, D. G., & Johnson, W. G. (1990). *Eating disorders: Assessment and treatment.* Boston, MA: Allyn and Bacon.

Schnapf, J. L., & Baylor, D. A. (1987, April). How photoreceptor cells respond to light. *Scientific American, 256,* 40–47.

Schneider, L. H., Cooper, S. J., & Halmi, K. A. (1989). *The psychology of human eating disorders: Preclinical and clinical perspectives.* New York: New York Academy of Sciences.

Schneider-Helmert, D. (1985). Clinical evaluation of DSIP. In A. Wauquier, J. M. Gaillard, J. M. Monti, & M. Radulovacki (Eds.), *Sleep: Neurotransmitters and neuromodulators* (pp. 279–289). New York: Raven Press.

Schoenenberger, G. A., & Graf, M. V. (1985). Effects of DSIP and DSIP-P on different biorhythmic parameters. In A. Wauquier, J. M. Gaillard, J. M. Monti, & M. Radulovacki (Eds.), *Sleep: Neurotransmitters and neuromodulators* (pp. 265–277). New York: Raven Press.

Schofield, P. R., Shivers, B. D., & Seeburg, P. H. (1990). The role of receptor subtype diversity in the CNS. Trends in *Neurosciences, 13,* 8–11.

Schreiner, C. E. (1992). Functional organization of the auditory cortex: Maps and mechanisms. *Current Opinion in Neurobiology, 2,* 516–521.

Schuman, E.M., & Madison, D.V. (1994). Nitric oxide and synaptic function. *Annual Review of Neurosciences, 17,* 153–183.

Schwab, M. E. (1990). Myelin-associated inhibitors of neurite growth and regeneration in the CNS. Trends in *Neurosciences, 13,* 452–456.

Schwartz, W. J., & Gainer, H. (1977). Suprachiasmatic nucleus: Use of 14-C-labelled deoxyglucose uptake as a functional marker. *Science, 197,* 1089–1091.

Sclafani, A. (1990). Nutritionally based learned flavor preferences in rats. In E. D. Capaldi and T. L. Powley (Eds.), *Taste, experience, and feeding* (pp. 139–156). Washington, DC: American Psychological Association.

Scott, T. R., & Giza, B. K. (1990). Coding channels in the taste system of the rat. *Science, 249,* 1585–1587.

Scoville, W. B., & Milner, B. (1957). Loss of recent memory after bilateral hippocampal lesions. *Journal of Neurology, Neurosurgery and Psychiatry, 20,* 11–21.

Searle, L. V. (1949). The organization of hereditary maze-brightness and maze-dullness. *Genetic Psychology Monographs, 39,* 279–325.

Segal, N.L. (1993). Twin, sibling, and adoption methods: Tests of evolutionary hypotheses. *American Psychologist, 48,* 943–956.

Seitz, R. J., Roland, P. E., Bohm, C., Greitz, T., & Stone-Elanders, S. (1990). Motor learning in man: A positron emission tomographic study. *NeuroReport, 1,* 17–20.

Selkoe, D. J. (1991, November). Amyloid protein and Alzheimer's. *Scientific American, 265,* 68–78.

Selmanoff, M. K., Brodkin, L. D., Weiner, R. I., & Siiteri, P. K. (1977). Aromatization and 5-alpha-reduction of androgens in discrete hypothalamic and limbic regions of the male and female rat. *Endocrinology, 108,* 841–848.

Serafini, T., Kennedy, T. E., Galko, M. J., Mirzayan, C., Jessel, T. M., & Tessier-Lavigne, M. (1994). The netrins define a family of axon outgrowth-promoting proteins homologous to C. elegans UNC-6. *Cell, 78,* 409–424.

Shapiro, B. H., Levine, D. C., & Adler, N. T. (1980). The testicular feminized rat: A naturally occurring model of androgen independent brain masculinization. *Science, 209,* 418–420.

Sherry, D. F., Jacobs, L. F., & Gaulin, S. J. C. (1992). Spatial memory and adaptive specialization of the hippocampus. *Trends in Neurosciences, 15,* 298–303.

Sherry, D. F., Vaccarino, A. L., Buckenham, K., & Herz, R. S. (1989). The hippocampal complex of food-storing birds. *Brain, Behavior and Evolution, 34,* 308–317.

Sherwin, B. B. (1985). Changes in sexual behavior as a function of plasma sex steroid levels in post-menopausal women. *Maturitas, 7,* 225–233.

Sherwin, B. B. (1988). A comparative analysis of the role of androgen in human male and female sexual behavior: Behavioral specificity, critical thresholds, and sensitivity. *Psychobiology, 16,* 416–425.

Sherwin, B. B., Gelfand, M. M., & Brender, W. (1985). Androgen enhances sexual motivation in females: A prospective cross-over study of sex steroid administration in the surgical menopause. *Psychosomatic Medicine, 47,* 339–351.

Shimura, T., & Shimokochi, M. (1990). Involvement of the lateral mesencephalic tegmentum in copulatory behavior of male rats: Neuron activity in freely moving animals. *Neuroscience Research, 9,* 173–183.

Shizgal, P., & Murray, B. (1989). Neuronal basis of intracranial self-stimulation. In J. M. Liebman & S. J. Cooper (Eds.), *The neuropharmacological basis of reward* (pp. 106–163). Oxford: Clarendon Press.

Shouse, M. N., King, A., Langer, J., Vreeken, T., King, K., & Richkind, M. (1990). The ontogeny of feline temporal lobe epilepsy: Kindling a spontaneous seizure disorder in kittens. *Brain Research, 525,* 215–224.

Sidman, M., Stoddard, L. T., & Mohr, J. P. (1968). Some additional quantitative observations of immediate memory in a patient with bilateral hippocampal lesions. *Neuropsychologia, 6,* 245–254.

Siegel, J. M. (1983). A behavioral approach to the analysis of reticular formation unit activity. In T. E. Robinson (Ed.), *Behavioral approaches to brain research* (pp. 94–116). New York: Oxford University Press.

Siegel, J. M., Nienhuis, R., Fahringer, H. M., Paul, R., Shiromani, P., Dement, W. C., Mignot, E., & Chui, C. (1991). Neuronal activity in narcolepsy: Identification of cataplexy-related cells in the medial medulla. *Science, 252,* 1315–1318.

Siegel, S. (1978). Tolerance to the hyperthermic effect of morphine in the rat is a learned response. *Journal of Comparative and Physiological Psychology, 92,* 1137–1149.

Siegel, S., Hinson, R. E., Krank, M. D., & McCully, J. (1982). Heroin "overdose" death: Contribution of drug- associated environmental cues. *Science, 216,* 436–437.

Silva, A. J., Paylor, R., Wehner, J. M., & Tonegawa, S. (1992). Impaired spatial learning in α-calcium-calmodulin kinase II mutant mice. *Science, 257,* 206–211.

Simpson, J. B., Epstein, A. N., & Camardo, J. S. (1978). Localization of receptors for the dipsogenic action of angiotensin II in the subfornical organ of rat. *Journal of Comparative and Physiological Psychology, 92,* 581–608.

Simpson, J. B., & Routtenberg, A. (1973). Subfornical organ: Site of drinking elicitation by angiotensin II. *Science, 181,* 1172–1175.

Simpson, J. B., & Routtenberg, A. (1974). Subfornical organ: Acetylcholine application elicits drinking. *Brain Research, 79,* 179–184.

Singer, J. (1968). Hypothalamic control of male and female sexual behavior. *Journal of Comparative and Physiological Psychology, 66,* 738–742.

Singer, M., Nordlander, R. H., & Egar, M. (1979). Axonal guidance during embryogenesis and regeneration in the spinal cord of the newt: The blueprint hypothesis of neuronal pathway patterning. *Journal of Comparative Neurology, 185,* 1–22.

Sitaram, N., Moore, A. M., & Gillin, J. C. (1978). Experimental acceleration and slowing of REM sleep ultradian rhythm by cholinergic agonist and antagonist. *Nature, 274,* 490–492.

Skelton, R. W., Scarth, A. S., Wilkie, D. M., Miller, J. J., & Phillips, A. G. (1987). Long-term increases in dentate granule cell responsivity accompany operant conditioning. *Journal of Neuroscience, 7,* 3081–3087.

Sladek, J. R., Jr., Redmond, D. E., Jr., Collier, T. J., Haber, S. N., Elsworth, J. D., Deutch, A. Y., & Roth, R. H. (1987). Transplantation of fetal dopamine neurons in primate brain reverses MPTP induced parkinsonism. In F. J. Seil, E. Herbert, & B. M. Carlson (Eds.), *Progress in brain research* (Vol. 71, pp. 309–323). New York: Elsevier.

Slaunwhite, W. R., III, Goldman, J. K., & Bernardis, L. L. (1972). Sequential changes in glucose metabolism by adipose tissue and liver of rats after destruction of the ventromedial hypothalamic nuclei: Effect of three dietary regimes. *Metabolism, 21,* 619–631.

Smith, F. J., & Campfield, L. A. (1993). Meal initiation occurs after experimental induction of transient declines in blood glucose. *American Journal of Physiology, 265,* 1423–1429.

Smith, G. P., Gibbs, J., Stohmayer, A. J., & Stokes, P. E. (1972). Threshold doses of 2-deoxy-D-glucose for hyperglycemia and feeding in rats and monkeys. *American Journal of Physiology, 217,* 77–81.

Snyder, S. H. (1976). The dopamine hypothesis of schizophrenia: Focus on the dopamine receptor. *American Journal of Psychiatry, 133,* 197–202.

Snyder, S. H. (1978). Neuroleptic drugs and neurotransmitter receptors. *Journal of Clinical and Experimental Psychiatry, 133,* 21–31.

Snyder, S. H. (1985, October). The molecular basis of communication between cells. *Scientific American, 253,* 132–141.

Snyder, S. H., & Bredt, D. S. (1992, May). Biological roles of nitric oxide. *Scientific American, 266,* 68–77.

Spector, R., & Johanson, C. E. (1989, November). The mammalian choroid plexus. *Scientific American, 261,* 68–74.

Sperry, R. W. (1963). Chemoaffinity in the orderly growth of nerve fiber patterns and connections. *Proceedings of the National Academy of Sciences (USA), 50,* 703–710.

Sperry, R. W. (1964, January). The great cerebral commissure. *Scientific American, 210,* 42–52.

Sperry, R. W. (1974). Lateral specialization in the surgically separated hemispheres. In F. O. Schmitt & F. G. Worden (Eds.), *The neurosciences: Third study program* (pp. 5–19). Cambridge, MA: MIT Press.

Sperry, R. W. (1985). Consciousness, personal identity, and the divided brain. In D. F. Benson & E. Zaidel (Eds.), *The dual brain: Hemispheric specialization in humans* (pp. 11–26). New York: Guilford Press.

Sperry, R. W., Zaidel, E., & Zaidel, D. (1979). Self recognition and social awareness in the deconnected minor hemisphere. *Neuropsychologia, 17,* 153–166.

Spillman, L., & Werner, J. S. (1990). *Visual perception: The neurophysiological foundations,* New York: Academic Press.

Spitzer, H., Desimone, R., & Moran, J. (1988). Increased attention enhances both behavioral and neuronal performance. *Science, 240,* 338–340.

Squire, L. R. (1982). Comparisons between forms of amnesia: Some deficits are unique to Korsakoff's syndrome. *Journal of Experimental Psychology: Learning, Memory, and Cognition, 8,* 560–571.

Squire, L. R. (1987). *Memory and brain* (p. 139). New York: Oxford University Press.

Squire, L. R. (1992). Memory and the hippocampus: A synthesis from findings with rats, monkeys, and humans. *Psychological Review, 99,* 195–231.

Squire, L. R., & Moore, R. Y. (1979). Dorsal thalamic lesion in a noted case of human memory dysfunction. *Annals of Neurology, 6,* 503–506.

Squire, L. R., Nadel, L., & Slater, P. C. (1981). Anterograde amnesia and memory for temporal order. *Neuropsychologia, 19,* 441–445.

Squire, L. R., Slater, P. C., & Chace, P. M. (1975). Retrograde amnesia: Temporal gradient in very long term memory following electroconvulsive therapy. *Science, 187,* 77–79.

Squire, L. R., & Spanis, C. W. (1984). Long gradient of retrograde amnesia in mice: Continuity with the findings in humans. *Behavioral Neuroscience, 98,* 345–348.

Squire, L. R., & Zola-Morgan, S. (1985). The neuropsychology of memory: New links between humans and experimental animals. *Annals of the New York Academy of Sciences, 444,* 137–149.

Squire, L. R., & Zola-Morgan, S. (1991). The medial temporal lobe memory system. *Science, 253,* 1380–1386.

Squire, L. R., Zola-Morgan, S., & Chen, K. (1988). Human amnesia and animal models of amnesia: Performance of amnesic patients on tests designed for the monkey. *Behavioral Neuroscience, 102,* 210–221.

Stanford, S. C., & Salmon, P. (1993). *Stress: From synapse to syndrome.* London: Academic Press.

Stea, R. A., & Apkarian, A. V. (1992). Pain and somatosensory activation. *Trends in Neurosciences, 15,* 250–251.

Stellar, J. R. (1990). Investigating the neural circuitry of brain stimulation reward. *Progress in psychobiology and physiology, 14,* 235–294.

Stephan, F. K. (1992a). Resetting of a circadian clock by food pulses. *Physiology & Behavior, 52,* 997–1008.

Stephan, F. K. (1992b). Resetting of a feeding-entrainable circadian clock in the rat. *Physiology & Behavior, 52,* 985–995.

Stephan, F. K., & Nunez, A. A. (1977). Elimination of circadian rhythms in drinking, activity, sleep, and temperature by isolation of the suprachiasmatic nucleus. *Behavioral Biology, 20,* 1–16.

Stephan, F. K., & Zucker, I. (1972). Circadian rhythms in drinking behaviour and locomotor activity of rats are eliminated by hypothalamic lesions. *Proceedings of the National Academy of Science (USA), 60,* 1583–1586.

Steriade, M., & Hobson, J. A. (1976). Neuronal activity during the sleep-waking cycle. *Progress in Neurobiology, 6,* 155–376.

Stevens, C.F. (1991). Bristling with teeth: Dendritic spines may act as calcium isolation compartments and therefore play a part in triggering long-term potentiation. *Neural Signalling, 1,* 369–371.

Stevens, C.F., & Wang, Y. (1994). Changes in reliability of synaptic function as a mechanism for plasticity. *Nature, 371,* 704–707.

Stewart, J., de Wit, H., & Eikelboom, R. (1984). Role of unconditioned and conditioned drug effects in the self-administration of opiates and stimulants. *Psychological Review, 91,* 251–268.

Stewart, J., & Eikelboom, R. (1982). Conditioned drug effects. In L. L. Iversen, S. D. Iversen, & S. H. Snyder (Eds.), *Handbook of psychopharmacology: Volume 19. New directions in behavioral pharmacology* (pp. 1–57). New York: Plenum Press.

Stirling, R. V., & Dunlop, S. A. (1995). The dance of the growth cones—where to next? *Trends in Neurosciences, 18,* 111–115.

Stoerig, P. (1993). Sources of blindsight. *Science, 261,* 493–494.

Stolerman, I. (1992). Drugs of abuse: Behavioural principles, methods and terms. *Trends in Neurosciences, 13,* 170.

Stout, S. C., & Nemeroff, C. B. (1994). Stress and psychiatric disorders. *Seminars in the Neurosciences, 6,* 271–280.

Strange, P. G. (1992). *Brain biochemistry and brain disorders.* Oxford: Oxford University Press.

Strick, P. L., & Preston, J. B. (1983). Input-output organization of the primate motor cortex. In J. E. Desimone (Ed.). Motor control mechanisms in health and disease (pp. 321–327). New York: Raven Press.

Stricker, E. M. (1973). Thirst, sodium appetite, and complementary physiological contributions to the regulation of intravascular fluid volume. In A. N. Epstein, H. R. Kissileff, & E. Stellar (Eds.), *The neuropsychology of thirst: New findings and advances in concepts* (pp. 73–98). Washington, DC: Winston.

Strubbe, J. H., & Steffens, A. B. (1977). Blood glucose levels in portal and peripheral circulation and their relation to food intake in the rat. *Physiology & Behavior, 19,* 303–307.

Suddath, R. L., Christison, G. W., Torrey, E. F., Casanova, M. F., & Weinberger, D. R. (1990). Anatomical abnormalities in the brains of monozygotic twins discordant for schizophrenia. *The New England Journal of Medicine, 322,* 789–794.

Susman, R. L. (1994). Fossil evidence for early hominid tool use. *Science, 265,* 1570–1573.

Sutherland, R. J., & Rudy, J. W. (1989). Configurational association theory: The role of the hippocampal formation in learning, memory, and amnesia. *Psychobiology, 17*, 129–144.

Sutton, S., & Ruchkin, D. S. (1984). The late positive complex: Advances and new problems. In R. Karrer, J. Cohen, and P. Teuting (Eds.), *Brain and information: Event-related potentials* (pp. 1–23). In Annals of the New York Academy of Sciences, Vol. 425. New York: New York Academy of Sciences.

Svaetichin, G. (1956). Spectral response curves from single cones. *Acta Physiologica Scandinavica, 39*, 17–46.

Swaab, D. F., & Fliers, E. (1985). A sexually dimorphic nucleus in the human brain. *Science, 188*, 1112–1115.

Swanson, L. W., & Sharpe, L. G. (1973). Centrally induced drinking: Comparison of angiotensin II- and carbachol-sensitive sites in rats. *American Journal of Physiology, 225*, 566–573.

Sweeney, M. E., Hill, P.A., Baney, R., & DiGirolamo, M. (1993). Severe vs. moderate energy restriction with and without exercise in the treatment of obesity: Efficiency of weight loss. *American Journal of Clinical Nutrition, 57*, 127–134.

Szmukler, G. I., Eisler, I., Gillies, C., & Hayward, M. E. (1985). The implications of anorexia nervosa in a ballet school. *Journal of Psychiatric Research, 19*, 177–181.

Tabakoff, B., & Hoffman, P. L. (1988). Tolerance and the etiology of alcoholism: Hypothesis and mechanism. *Alcoholism: Clinical & Experimental Research, 12*, 184–186.

Takahashi, J. S. (1991). Circadian rhythms: From gene expression to behavior. *Current Opinion in Neurobiology, 1*, 556–561.

Takahashi, J. S. (1992). Circadian clock genes are ticking. *Science, 258*, 238–240.

Talbot, J. D., Marrett, S., Evans, A. C., Meyer, E., Bushnell, M. C., & Duncan, G. H. (1991). Multiple representations of pain in human cerebral cortex. *Science, 251*, 1355–1358.

Tanaka, A. (1972). A progressive change of behavioral and electroencephalographic response to daily amygdaloid stimulations in rabbits. *Fukuoka Acta Medica, 63*, 152–163.

Tanaka, K. (1993). Neuronal mechanisms of object recognition. *Science, 262*, 685–688.

Tank, D. W., Sugimori, M., Connoer, J. A., & Llinás, R. R. (1988). Spatially resolved calcium dynamics of mammalian Purkinje cells in cerebellar slice. *Science, 242*, 773–777.

Tanzi, R. E. (1991). Genetic linkage studies of human neurodegenerative disorders. *Current Opinion in Neurobiology, 1*, 455–461.

Tassinary, L. G., & Cacioppo, J. T. (1992). Unobservable facial actions and emotion. *Psychological Science, 3*, 28–33.

Taylor, J. R., Elsworth, J. D., Roth, J. R., Sladek, J. R., Jr., & Redmond, D. E., Jr., (1990). Cognitive and motor deficits in the acquisition of an object retrieval/detour task in MPTP-treated monkeys. *Brain, 113*, 617–637.

Tees, R. C. (1968). Effect of early visual restriction on later visual intensity discrimination in rats. *Journal of Comparative and Physiological Psychology, 66*, 224–227.

Teich, A. H., McCabe, P. M., Gentile, C.C., Schneiderman, L.S., & Winters, R. W., Liskowsky, D. R., & Schneiderman, N. (1989). Auditory cortex lesions prevent the extinction of Pavlovian differential heart rate conditioning to tonal stimuli in rabbits. *Brain Research, 480*, 210–218.

Teitelbaum, P. (1957). Random and food-directed activity in hyperphagic and normal rats. *Journal of Comparative and Physiological Psychology, 50*, 486–490.

Teitelbaum, P. (1961). Disturbances in feeding and drinking behavior after hypothalamic lesions. In M. R. Jones (Ed.), *Nebraska Symposium on Motivation* (pp. 39–69). Lincoln, NB: University of Nebraska Press.

Teitelbaum, P., & Epstein, A. N. (1962). The lateral hypothalamic syndrome: Recovery of feeding and drinking after lateral hypothalamic lesions. *Psychological Review, 69*, 74–90.

Terman, G. W., Shavit, Y., Lewis, J. W., Cannon, J. T., & Liebeskind, J. C. (1984). Intrinsic mechanisms of pain inhibition: Activation by stress. *Science, 226*, 1270–1277.

Tessier-Lavigne, M., & Placzek, M. (1991). Target attraction: Are developing axons guided by chemotropism? *Trends in Neurosciences, 14*, 303–310.

Tetrud, J. W., & Langston, J. W. (1989). The effect of deprenyl (Selegiline) on the natural history of Parkinson's disease. *Science, 245,* 519–522.

Teuber, H.-L., Battersby, W. S., & Bender, M. B. (1960). Recovery of function after brain injury in man. In *Outcome of severe damage to the nervous system.* Ciba Foundation Symposium 34. Amsterdam: Elsevier North-Holland.

Teuber, H.-L., Battersby, W. S., & Bender, M. B. (1960). *Visual field defects after penetrating missile wounds of the brain.* Cambridge, MA: Harvard University Press.

Teuber, H.-L., Milner, B., & Vaughan, H. G., Jr. (1968). Persistent anterograde amnesia after stab wound of the basal brain. *Neuropsychologia, 6,* 267–282.

Thal, L. J. (1989). Pharmacological treatment of memory disorders. In F. Boller and J. Grafman, (Eds.), *Handbook of neuropsychology, Vol. 3.,* (pp. 247–267). New York: Elsevier.

Thorne, A. G., & Wolpoff, M. H. (1992, April). The multiregional evolution of humans. *Scientific American, 266,* 76–83.

Thureson-Klein, A. K., & Klein, R. L. (1990). Exocytosis from neuronal large dense-cored vesicles. *International Review of Cytology, 121,* 67–126.

Tilles, D., Goldenheim, P., Johnson, D. C., Mendelson, J. H., Mello, N. K., & Hales, C. A. (1986). Marijuana smoking as cause of reduction in single-breath carbon monoxide diffusing capacity. *American Journal of Medicine, 80,* 601–606.

Timberlake, W. (1993). Animal behavior: A continuing synthesis. *Annual Review of Psychology, 44,* 675–708.

Tinbergen, N., & Perdeck, A. C. (1950). On the stimulus situation releasing the begging response in the newly hatched herring gull chick (*Larus argentatus argentatus* Pont). *Behavior, 3,* 1–39.

Tinklenberg, J. R. (1974). Marijuana and human aggression. In L. L. Miller (Ed.), *Marijuana, effects on human behavior* (pp. 339–358). New York: Academic Press.

Toates, F. M. (1981). The control of ingestive behaviour by internal and external stimuli—A theoretical review. *Appetite, 2,* 35–50.

Tompkins, C. A., & Mateer, C. A. (1985). Right hemisphere appreciation of intonational and linguistic indications of affect. *Brain and Language, 24,* 185–203.

Tonge, D. A., & Golding, J. P. (1993). Regeneration and repair of the peripheral nervous system. *Seminars in the Neurosciences, 5,* 385–390.

Tranel, D., & Damasio, A. R. (1985). Knowledge without awareness: An autonomic index of facial recognition by prosopagnosics. *Science, 228,* 1453–1454.

Traynor, A. E., Schlapfer, W. T., & Barondes, S. J. (1980). Stimulation is necessary for the development of tolerance to a neural effect of ethanol. *Journal of Neurobiology, 11,* 633–637.

Treit, D. (1985). Animal models for the study of anti-anxiety agents: A review. *Neuroscience and Biobehavioral Reviews, 9,* 203–222.

Treit, D. (1987). RO 15-1788, CGS 8216, picrotoxin, pentylenetetrazol: Do they antagonize anxiolytic drug effects through an anxiogenic action? *Brain Research Bulletin, 19,* 401–405.

Treit, D., Robinson, A., Rotzinger, S., & Pesold, C. (1993). Anxiolytic effects of serotonergic interventions in the shock-probe burying test and the elevated plus-maze test. *Behavioural Brain Research, 54,* 23–34.

Trotter, Y., Celebrini, S., Stricanne, B., Thorpe, & Imbert, M. (1992). Modulation of neural stereoscopic processing in primate area V1 by the viewing distance. *Science, 257,* 1279–1281.

Trulson, M. E., & Jacobs, B. L. (1979). Raphe unit activity in freely moving cats: Correlation with level of behavioral arousal. *Brain Research, 163,* 135–150.

Tryon, R. C. (1934). Individual differences. In Moss, F. A. (Ed.), Comparative Psychology (pp. 409–448). New York: Prentice-Hall Inc.

Tucker, D. M. (1981). Lateral brain function, emotion, and conceptualization. *Psychological Bulletin, 89,* 19–46.

Turkenburg, J. L., Swaab, D. F., Endert, E., Louwerse, A. L., & van de Poll, N. E. (1988). Effects of lesions of the sexually dimorphic nucleus on sexual behavior of testosterone-treated female Wistar rats. *Brain Research Bulletin, 329,* 195–203.

Turner, A. M., & Greenough, W. T. (1983). Synapses per neuron and synaptic dimensions in occipital cortex of rats reared in complex, social, or isolation housing. *Acta Stereologica, Vol. 2, Suppl. 1,* 239–244.

Ulrich, R. E. (1991). Animal rights, animal wrongs and the question of balance. *Psychological Science, 2,* 197–201.

Ulrich, R. E. (1991). Commentary: Animal rights, animal wrongs and the question of balance. *Psychological Science, 2,* 197–201.

Ungerleider, L. G., & Haxby, J. V. (1994). "What" and "where" in the human brain. *Current Opinion in Neurobiology, 4,* 157–165.

Ungerleider, L. G., Mishkin, M. (1982). Two cortical visual systems. In D. J. Ingle, M. A. Goodale, & R. J. W. Mansfield (Eds.), *Analysis of visual behavior* (pp. 549–586). Cambridge, MA: MIT Press.

Valenstein, E. S. (1973). *Brain control.* New York: John Wiley and Sons.

Valenstein, E. S. (1980). *The psychosurgery debate: Scientific, legal, and ethical perspectives.* San Francisco: W. H. Freeman and Co.

Valenstein, E. S. (1986). *Great and desperate cures: The rise and decline of psychosurgery and other radical treatments for mental illness.* New York: Basic Books.

Vallee, R. B., & Bloom, G. S. (1991). Mechanisms of fast and slow axonal transport. *Annual Review of Neuroscience, 14,* 59–92.

Valverde, F. (1971). Rate and extent of recovery from dark rearing in the visual cortex of the mouse. *Brain Research, 33,* 1–11.

Van der Kooy, D. (1987). Place conditioning: A simple and effective method for assessing the motivational properties of drugs. In M. A. Bozarth (Ed.), *Methods of assessing the reinforcing properties of abused drugs* (pp. 229–240). New York: Springer-Verlag.

Van Essen, D. C., Anderson, C. H., & Felleman, D. J. (1992). Information processing in the primate visual system: An integrated systems perspective. *Science, 255,* 419–423.

van Poppel, G., Spanhaak, S., & Ockhuizen, T. (1993). Effect of b-carotene on immunological indexes in healthy male smokers. *The American Journal of Clinical Nutrition, 57,* 402–407.

Vanderwolf, C. H. (1988). Cerebral activity and behavior: Control by central cholinergic and serotonergic systems. *International Review of Neurobiology, 30,* 225–340.

Vanderwolf, C. H., & Robinson, T. E. (1981). Reticulo- cortical activity and behavior: A critique of the arousal theory and a new synthesis. *Behavioral and Brain Sciences, 4,* 459–514.

Vathy, I. U., & Etgen, A. M. (1989). Hormonal activation of female sexual behavior is accompanied by hypothalamic norepinephrine release. *Journal of Neuroendocrinology, 1,* 383–388.

Vaughan, H. G., Jr., & Arezzo, J. C. (1988). The neural basis of event-related potentials. In T. W. Picton (Ed.), *Human event-related potentials: Handbook of electroencephalography and clinical neurophysiology, Vol. III.* Amsterdam: Elsevier.

Verma, A., Hirsch, D. J., Glatt, C. E., Ronnett, G. V., & Snyder, S. H. (1993). Carbon monoxide: A putative neural messenger. *Science, 259,* 381–384.

Vertes, R. P. (1983). Brainstem control of the events of REM sleep. *Progress in Neurobiology, 22,* 241–288.

Vessie, P. R. (1932). On the transmission of Huntington's Chorea for 300 years—the Bures family group. *The Journal of Nervous and Mental Disease, 76,* 553–573.

Vicario, D. S. (1991). Neural mechanisms of vocal production in songbirds. *Current Opinion in Neurobiology, 1,* 595–600.

Victor, M., Adams, R. D., & Collins, G. H. (1971). *The Wernicke syndrome* (p. 22). Philadelphia: F. A. Davis.

Vitaterna, M. H., King, D. P., Chang, A.-M., Korhauser, J. M., Lowrey, P. L., McDonald, J. D., Dove, W. J., Pinto, L. H., Turek, F. W., & Takahashi, J. S. (1994). Mutagenesis and mapping of a mouse gene, Clock, essential for circadian behavior. *Science, 264,* 719–725.

von Cramon, D. Y., Hebel, N., & Schuri, U. (1985). A contribution to the anatomical basis of thalamic amnesia. *Brain, 108,* 993–1008.

Wada, J. A. (1949). A new method for the determination of the side of cerebral speech dominance. *Igaku to Seibutsugaku, 14,* 221–222.

Wada, J. A. (1990a). Erosion of kindled epileptogenesis and kindling-induced long-term seizure suppressive effect in primates. In J. A. Wada, (Ed.), *Kindling 4* (pp. 382–394) New York: Plenum Press.

Wada, J. A. (Ed.). (1990b). *Kindling 4.* Plenum Press: New York.

Wada, J. A., Clarke, R., & Hamm, A. (1975). Cerebral hemispheric asymmetry in humans. *Archives of Neurology, 32,* 239–246.

Wada, J. A., & Sato, M. (1974). Generalized convulsive seizures induced by daily electrical stimulation of the amygdala in cats: Correlative electrographic and behavioral features. *Neurology, 24,* 565–574.

Wada, J. A., Sato, M., & Corcoran, M. E. (1974). Persistent seizure susceptibility and recurrent spontaneous seizures in kindled cats. *Epilepsia, 15,* 465–478.

Wald, G. (1964). The receptors of human color vision. Science, 145, 1007–1016.

Walk, R. D., & Walters, C. P. (1973). Effect of visual deprivation on depth discrimination of hooded rats. *Journal of Comparative and Physiological Psychology, 85,* 559–563.

Watson, D., & Pennebaker, J. W. (1989). Health complaints, stress, and distress: Exploring the central role of negative affectivity. *Psychological Review, 96,* 234–254.

Watson, J. B. (1930). *Behaviorism.* New York: W. W. Norton.

Wauquier, A., Ashton, D., & Melis, W. (1979). Behavioral analysis of amygdaloid kindling in beagle dogs and the effects of clonazepam, diazepam, phenobarbital, diphenylhydantoin, and flunarizine on seizure manifestion. *Experimental Neurology, 64,* 579–586.

Webb, W. B. (1968). *Sleep: An experimental approach.* New York: Macmillan Company.

Webb, W. B. (1973). Selective and partial deprivation of sleep. In W. P. Koella & P. Levin (Eds.), *Sleep: Physiology, biochemistry, psychology, pharmacology, clinical implications* (pp. 176–204). Basel: Karger.

Webb, W. B., & Agnew, H. W. (1967). Sleep cycling within the twenty-four hour period. *Journal of Experimental Psychology, 74,* 167–169.

Webb, W. B., & Agnew, H. W. (1970). Sleep stage characteristics of long and short sleepers. *Science, 163,* 146–147.

Webb, W. B., & Agnew, H. W. (1974). The effects of a chronic limitation of sleep length. *Psychophysiology, 11,* 265–274.

Webb, W. B., & Agnew, H. W. (1975). The effects on subsequent sleep of an acute restriction of sleep length. *Psychophysiology, 12,* 367–370.

Weinberg, R. A. (1991). Tumor suppressor genes. *Science, 254,* 1138–1145.

Weinberger, N. M. (1993). Learning-induced changes of auditory receptive fields. *Current Opinion in Neurobiology, 3,* 570–577.

Weingarten, H. P. (1983). Conditioned cues elicit feeding in sated rats: A role for learning in meal initiation. *Science, 220,* 431–433.

Weingarten, H. P. (1984). Meal initiation controlled by learned cues: Basic behavioral properties. *Appetite, 5,* 147–158.

Weingarten, H. P. (1985). Stimulus control of eating: Implications for a two-factor theory of hunger. *Appetite, 6,* 387–401.

Weingarten, H. P. (1990). Learning, homeostasis, and the control of feeding behavior. In E. D. Capaldi and T. L. Powley (Eds.), *Taste, experience, and feeding* (pp. 14–27). Washington, DC: American Psychological Association.

Weingarten, H. P., Chang, P. K., & Jarvie, K. R. (1983). Reactivity of normal and VMH-lesion rats to quinine-adulterated foods: Negative evidence for negative finickiness. *Behavioral Neuroscience, 97,* 221–233.

Weingarten H. P., & Kulikovsky, O. T. (1989). Taste-to-postingestive consequence conditioning: Is the rise in sham feeding with repeated experience a learning phenomenon? *Physiology & Behavior, 45,* 471–476.

Weintraub, S., & Mesulam, M.-M. (1989). Neglect: Hemispheric specialization, behavioral components and anatomical correlates. In F. Boller, and J. Grafman (Eds.), *Handbook of Neuropsychology, 2.* New York: Elsevier Science Publishers.

Weisinger, R. S. (1975). Conditioned and pseudo-conditioned thirst and sodium appetite. In G. Peters, J. T. Fitzsimons, & L. Peters-Haefeli (Eds.), *Control Mechanisms of Drinking* (pp. 149–154). New York: Springer-Verlag.

Weiskrantz, L., Warrington, E. K., Sanders, M. D., & Marshall, J. (1974). Visual capacity in the hemianopic field following a restricted occipital ablation. *Brain, 97,* 709–728.

Wekerle, H. (1993). Experimental autoimmune encephalomyelitis as a model of immune-mediated CNS disease. *Current Opinion in Neurobiology, 3,* 779–784.

Weller, A., Smith, G. P., & Gibbs, J. (1990). Endogenous cholecystokinin reduces feeding in young rats. *Science, 247,* 1589–1590.

Westergaard, G. C. (1991). Hand preference in the use and manufacture of tools by Tufted capuchin (*Cebus apella*) and Lion-tailed Macaque (*Macaca silenus*) monkeys. *Journal of Comparative Psychology, 105,* 172–176.

Westerink, B. H. C., & Justice, J. B. Jr. (1991). Microdialysis compared with other in vivo release models. In T. E. Robinson and J. B. Justice, Jr. (Eds.), *Microdialysis in the neurosciences. Vol. 7, Techniques in the neural and behavioral sciences* (pp. 23–43). Amsterdam: Elsevier.

Wever, R. A. (1979). *The circadian system of man.* Andechs: Max-Planck-Institut fur Verhaltensphysiologie.

Wexler, N. S., Rose, E. A., & Housman, D. E. (1991). Molecular approaches to hereditary diseases of the nervous system: Huntington's disease as a paradigm. *Annual Review of Neuroscience, 14,* 503–529.

Whalen, R. E., & Rezek, D. L. (1974). Inhibition of lordosis in female rats by subcutaneous implants of testosterone, androstenedione or dihydrotestosterone in infancy. *Hormones and Behavior, 5,* 125–128.

Whishaw, I. Q., Kolb, B., & Sutherland, R. J. (1983). The analysis of behavior in the laboratory rat. In T. E. Robinson (Ed.), *Behavioral approaches to brain research* (pp. 141–211). New York: Oxford University Press.

White, N., Sklar, L., & Amit, Z. (1977). The reinforcing action of morphine and its paradoxical side effect. *Psychopharmacology, 52,* 63–66.

White, N. M., & Hiroi, N. (1993). Amphetamine conditioned cue preference and the neurobiology of drug seeking. *Seminars in the Neurosciences, 5,* 329–336.

Whitelaw, V., & Hollyday, M. (1983). Position-dependent motor innervation of the chick hindlimb following serial and parallel duplications of limb segments. *Journal of Neuroscience, 3,* 1216–1225.

Whittaker, D. G., & Cummings, R. W. (1990). Foveating saccades. *Vision Research, 30,* 1363–1366.

Wickelgren, W. A. (1968). Sparing of short-term memory in an amnesic patient: Implications for strength theory of memory. *Neuropsychologia, 6,* 235–244.

Wilhelm, P. (1983). *The Nobel prize.* London: Springwood Books.

Willett, W. C. (1994). Diet and health: What should we eat? *Science, 264,* 532–537.

Williams, J., Merritt, J., Rittenhouse, C., & Hobson, J. A. (1992). Bizarreness in dreams and fantasies: Implications for the activation-synthesis hypothesis. *Consciousness and Cognition, 1,* 172–185.

Willing, A. E., Walls, E. K., & Koopmans, H. S. (1990). Insulin infusion stimulates daily food intake and body weight gain in diabetic rats. *Physiology & Behavior, 48,* 893–898.

Wilson, A. C., & Cann, R. L. (1992, April). The recent African genesis of humans. *Scientific American, 266,* 68–73.

Wilson, J. D., & Griffin, J. E. (1980). The use and misuse of androgens. *Progress in Endocrinology and Metabolism, 29,* 1278–1295.

Wilson, J. D., George, F. W., & Griffin, J. E. (1981). The hormonal control of sexual development. *Science, 211,* 1278–1284.

Wilson, M. A., & McNaughton, B. L. (1993). Dynamics of the hippocampal ensemble code for space. *Science, 261,* 1055–1058.

Winn, P. (1994). Schizophrenia research moves to the prefrontal cortex. *Trends in Neurosciences, 17,* 265–268.

Winocur, G., Oxbury, S., Roberts, R., Agnetti, V., & Davis, C. (1984). Amnesia in patients with bilateral lesions to the thalamus. *Neuropsychologia, 22,* 123–143.

Winokur, G. (1978). Mania and depression: Family studies and genetics in relation to treatment. In M. A. Lipton, A. DiMascio, & K. F. Killam (Eds.), *Psychopharmacology: A generation of progress* (pp. 1213–1221). New York: Raven Press.

Winson, J. (1993). The biology and function of rapid eye movement sleep. *Current Opinion in Neurobiology, 3,* 243–248.

Wirtshafter, D., & Davis, J. D. (1977). Set points, settling points, and the control of body weight. *Physiology & Behavior, 19,* 75–78.

Wise (1993). In vivo estimates of extracellular dopamine and dopamine metabolite levels during intravenous cocaine or heroin self-administration. *Seminars in the Neurosciences, 5,* 337–342.

Wise, R. A., Bauco, P., Carlezon, Jr. W. A., & Trojniar, W. (1992). Self-stimulation and drug reward mechanisms. *Annals of the New York Academy of Science, 654,* 192–198.

Witelson, S. F. (1991). Neural Sexual mosaicism: Sexual differentiation of the human temporo-parietal region for functional asymmetry. *Psychoneuroendocrinology, 16,* 133–153.

Wodak, A., Richmond, R., & Wilson, A. (1990). Thiamin fortification and alcohol. *The Medical Journal of Australia, 152,* 97–99.

Wolf, M. E., & Goodale, M. A. (1987). Oral asymmetries during verbal and non-verbal movements of the mouth. *Neuropsychologia, 25,* 375–396.

Wolff, P. H., Michel, G. F., Ovrut, M., & Drake, C. (1990). Rate and timing precision of motor coordination in developmental dyslexia. *Developmental Psychology, 26,* 349–359.

Wolgin, D. L. (1989). The role of instrumental learning in behavioral tolerance to drugs. In A. J. Goudie and M. W. Emmett-Olglesby (Eds.), *Psychoactive Drugs: Tolerance and Sensitization* (pp. 17–114). Clifton, New Jersey: Humana Press.

Wood, E. R., Mumby, D. G., Pinel, J. P. J., & Phillips, A. G. (1993). Impaired object recognition memory in rats following ischemia-induced damage to the hippocampus. *Behavioral Neuroscience, 107,* 51–62.

Wood, R. J., Rolls, B. J., & Ramsay, D. J. (1977). Drinking following intracarotid infusions of hypertonic solutions in dogs. *American Journal of Physiology, 1,* R88–R91.

Woodruff-Pak, D. S. (1993). Eyeblink classical conditioning in H. M.: Delay and trace paradigms. *Behavioral Neuroscience, 107,* 911–925.

Woods, S. C. (1991). The eating paradox: How we tolerate food. *Psychological Review, 98,* 488–505.

Woods, S. C., & Gibbs, J. (1989). The regulation of food intake by peptides. The psychobiology of human eating disorders: Preclinical and clinical perspectives. *Annals of the New York Academy of Sciences, 75,* 236–242.

Woods, S. C., Lotter, E. C., McKay, L. D., & Porte, D., Jr. (1979). Chronic intracerebroventricular infusion of insulin reduces food intake and body weight of baboons. *Nature, 282,* 503–505.

Woods, S. C., & Porte, D., Jr. (1977). Relationship between plasma and cerebrospinal fluid insulin levels of dogs. *American Journal of Physiology, 233,* E331–E334.

Woods, S. C., & Strubbe, J. H. (1994). The psychology of meals. *Psychonomic Bulletin & Review, 1,* 141–155.

Wurtman, R. J. (1985, January). Alzheimer's disease. *Scientific American, 252,* 62–74.

Wylie, D. R., & Goodale, M. A. (1988). Left-sided oral asymmetries in spontaneous but not posed smiles. *Neuropsychologia, 26,* 823–832.

Yaqub, B. A., Gascon, G. G., Al-Nosha, M., & Whittaker, H. (1988). Pure word deafness (acquired verbal auditory agnosia) in an Arabic speaking patient. *Brain, III,* 457–466.

Yeomans, J. S., Mathur, A., & Tampakeras, M. (1993). Rewarding brain stimulation: Role of tegmental cholinergic neurons that activate dopamine neurons. *Behavioral Neuroscience, 107,* 1077–1087.

Yeung, J. C., & Rudy, T. A. (1978). Sites of antinociceptive action of systemically injected morphine: Involvement of suspraspinal loci as revealed by intracerebroventricular injection of naloxone. *Journal of Pharmacology and Experimental Therapeutics, 215,* 626–632.

Yokel, R. A. (1987). Intravenous self-administration: Response rates, the effects of pharmacological challenges, and drug preference. In M. A. Bozarth (Ed.), *Methods of assessing the reinforcing properties of abused drugs* (pp. 1–33). New York: Springer-Verlag.

Yoon, M. (1971). Reorganization of retinotectal projection following surgical operations on the optic tectum in goldfish. *Experimental Neurology, 33,* 395–411.

Yurek, D. M., & Sladek, J. R., Jr. (1990). Dopamine cell replacement: Parkinson's disease. *Annual Review of Neuroscience, 13,* 415–440.

Zaidel, E. (1975). A technique for presenting lateralized visual input with prolonged exposure. *Vision Research, 15,* 283–289.

Zaidel, E. (1983). Disconnection syndrome as a model for laterality effects in the normal brain. In J. B. Hellige (Ed.), *Cerebral hemisphere asymmetry: Method, theory, and application* (pp. 95–151). New York: Praeger Press.

Zaidel, E. (1987). Language in the disconnected right hemisphere. In G. Adelman (Ed.), *Encyclopedia of Neuroscience* (pp. 563–564). Cambridge, MA: Birkhäuser.

Zangwill, O. L. (1975). Excision of Broca's area without persistent aphasia. In K. J. Zulch, O. Creutzfeldt, & G. C. Galbraith (Eds.), *Cerebral localization* (pp. 258–263). New York: Springer-Verlag.

Zatz, M., & Herkenham, M. A. (1981). Intraventricular carbachol mimics the phase-shifting effect of light on the circadian rhythm of wheel-running activity. *Brain Research, 212,* 234–238.

Zeki (1993a). *A vision of the brain.* Oxford: Blackwell Scientific Publication.

Zeki, S. (1993b). The visual association cortex. *Current Opinion in Neurobiology, 3,* 155–159.

Zeki, S., Watson, J. D. G., Lueck, C. J., Friston, K. J., Kennard, C., & Frackowiak, R. S. J. (1991). A direct demonstration of functional specialization in human visual cortex. *Journal of Neuroscience, 11,* 641–649.

Zelman, D. C., Tiffany, S. T., & Baker, T. B. (1985). Influence of stress on morphine induced pyrexia: Relevance to a pavlovian model of tolerance development. *Behavioral Neuroscience, 99,* 122–144.

Zimitat, C., Kril, J., Harper, C. G., & Nixon, P. F. (1990). Progression of neurological disease in thiamin- deficient rats is enhanced by ethanol. *Alcohol, 7,* 493–501.

Zivin, J. A., & Choi, D. W. (1991, July). Stroke therapy. *Scientific American, 265,* 56–63.

Zola-Morgan, S., & Squire, L. R. (1984). Preserved learning in monkeys with medial temporal lesions: Sparing of motor and cognitive skills. *Journal of Neuroscience, 4,* 1072–1085.

Zola-Morgan, S., & Squire L. R. (1985). Medial temporal lesions in monkeys impair memory on a variety of tasks sensitive to human amnesia. *Behavioral Neuroscience, 99,* 22–34.

Zola-Morgan, S. M., & Squire, L. R. (1990). The primate hippocampal formation: Evidence for a time-limited role in memory storage. *Science, 250,* 288–290.

Zola-Morgan, S., & Squire, L. R. (1993). Neuroanatomy of memory. Annual *Review of Neuroscience, 16,* 547–563.

Zola-Morgan, S., Squire, L. R., & Amaral, D. G. (1986). Human amnesia and the medial temporal region: Enduring memory impairment following a bilateral lesion limited to field CA1 of the hippocampus. *Journal of Neuroscience, 6,* 2950–2967.

Zola-Morgan, S. M., Squire, L. R., Amaral, D. G., & Suzuki, W. A. (1989). Lesions of perirhinal and parahippocampal cortex that spare the amygdala and hippocampal formation produce severe memory impairment. *Journal of Neuroscience, 9,* 4355–4370.

Zola-Morgan, S., Squire, L. R., & Mishkin, M. (1982). The neuroanatomy of amnesia: Amygdala-hippocampus versus temporal stem. *Science, 218,* 1337–1339.

Zola-Morgan, S., Squire, L. R., Rempel, N.L., Clower, R. P., & Amaral, D. G. (1992). Enduring memory impairment in monkeys after ischemic damage to the hippocampus. *Journal of Neuroscience, 12,* 2582–2596.

Zusho, H. (1983). Posttraumatic anosmia. *Archives of ontolaryngology, 4,* 252–256.

CREDITS

Illustration Credits

NAME INDEX

A

Abe, H., 315
Abel, T., 397
Abramson, H. A., 334
Acker, W., 7
Adamec, R., 145
Adams, R. D., 359
Adelmann, P. K., 443
Adkins, Regan, E., 291
Adler, E. M., 93
Adler, N. T., 280
Adrian, E., 9
Adrien, J., 317
Aggleton, J. P., 367, 368, 376, 449
Agnati, L. F., 92
Agnew, H. W., 306, 307, 320
Aguayo, A. J., 406
Aigner, T. G., 361, 362
Aizawa, H., 215
Åkerstedt, T., 306
Albert, D. J., 126, 447, 448, 465
Albertini, R. J., 142
Alexander, M. P., 430
Allegretta, M., 142
Allen, L. S., 288, 292
Altman, J., 385, 404
Alvarez, P., 369
Alvarez-Buylla, A., 44
Amaral, D. G., 358
Ames, M. A., 291
Amit, Z., 340
Anand, B. K., 245–246
Anch, A. M., 318
Andersen, R. A., 21
Anderson, R. H., 288
Andreasen, N. C., 455, 459, 465
Andreassi, J. L., 17
Andrews, K. M., 256
Angelergues, R., 429–430
Angrist, B., 146
Angst, J., 461
Anisman, H., 460
Anne S., 282–283
Annett, J., 232
Antonini, A., 387
Apkarian, A. V., 198
Appenzeller, T., 366

Arbit, J., 354
Archer, J., 448
Aréchiga, H., 315
Arezzo, J. C., 110
Arimura, A., 274
Arnason, B. G. W., 404
Aserinsky, E., 296–297
Ashe, J., 215
Ashton, D., 145
Attenborough, K. S., 241
Attili, G., 201
Auerbach, S. H., 193
Aunt Betty, 197–198
Auyeung, A., 394
Ax, A. F., 441
Axelrod, J., 9

B

Baastrup, P. C., 461
Babor, T. F., 334
Bachevalier, J., 375
Baier, H., 382
Bailey, C. H., 393
Bailey, C. J., 245
Bailey, M. J., 291
Baizer, J. S., 186
Baker, B. J., 241
Baker, T. B., 329, 340
Balaban, E., 408
Ballard, P. A., 148
Bancroft, J., 287
Bandler, R., 448
Bandtlow, C. E., 398
Barchas, J. D., 146
Barchas, P. R., 146
Bard, P., 439
Barden, N., 463
Barfield, R. J., 280, 290
Barnstable, C. J., 154
Barondes, S. H., 461, 465
Barondes, S. J., 328
Barron, S., 332
Bartoshuk, L. M., 201
Basbaum, A. I., 199, 200
Bashir, Z. I., 396

Bashore, T. R., 146–147
Baskin, D. G., 250
Bastiani, M. J., 382
Bates, J. F., 212, 214
Battersby, W. S., 183
Baum, J., 285
Baum, M. J., 291
Baylor, D. A., 178
Beal, M. F., 133
Beauchamp, G. K., 201
Becker, J. B., 294
Becker, L. A., 18
Beecher, H. K., 199
Békésy, G. von, 9
Bell, D. S., 146
Belliveau, J. W., 108
Bender, M. B., 183
Bennett, E. L., 43, 387
Benson, D. F., 414, 428
Bentley, D., 383
Benton, A., 212
Benton, A. L., 10
Bergmann, B., 306
Bergondy, M. L., 289
Berkley, M., 192
Berlucchi, G., 311
Bernays, M., 347
Bernstein, I. L., 127, 265
Berridge, K. C., 335, 340, 341
Berridge, V., 336
Berry, K., 2, 132, 142
Bertelsen, A., 456
Betz, A. L., 54
Bierschwale, D., 22
Bina, K. G., 302
Bishop, M. P., 341
Bishop, P. O., 168
B.J., 360
Bjelke, B., 92
Björkland, A., 344, 404, 407
Blackburn, J. R., 129
Blackmore, S., 300
Blaha, C. D., 118
Blanchard, D. C., 125, 445–446, 464, 465
Blanchard, R. J., 125, 445–446, 464, 465

Blass, E. M., 201, 256, 261
Blaustein, J. D., 290
Bliss, T. V. P., 393
Bloch, G. J., 288
Block, M. L., 260
Bloom, F. E., 97, 325
Bloom, G. S., 92
Blundell, J. E., 243
Bobillier, P., 312
Boccia, M. L., 21
Bogen, G. M., 428
Bogen, J., 417
Bogen, J. G., 428
Boldrey, E., 216–217
Bolles, R. C., 240
Bolz, J., 382
Bonhoeffer, F., 382
Booth, D. A., 240, 241, 244, 251
Borbély, A. A., 306, 308, 317
Bouchard, T. J., Jr., 47
Boulos, Z., 315
Bowden, J., 310
Bowers, D., 421, 444
Bowmaker, J. K., 173
Bozarth, M. A., 340
Brackett, N. L., 290
Brady, J. V., 9
Brainard, M. S., 388
Brandon, P., 245
Bray, G. A., 235
Bray, G. M., 406
Brecher, E. M., 331, 347, 348
Bredt, D. S., 98, 104
Breedlove, S. M., 278, 294
Breitner, J. C. S., 143
Bremer, F., 310, 311
Bremer, J., 285
Brendel, D. H., 306
Brender, W., 287
Brewster, J. M., 337
Bridgeman, B., 13
Brill, N. Q., 334
Brime, J. I., 261
Brinkman, C., 215
Brobeck, J. R., 245–246
Broberg, D. J., 265
Broca, P., 412, 425, 426, 428, 436
Brooks, V. B., 232
Brou, P., 174, 176, 178
Brown, G. W., 460
Brown, H. D., 422, 436
Brown, M. C., 400
Brown, T. H., 394, 395
Brownell, K. D., 235, 250, 267
Brundin, P., 404, 407
Brunner, D. P., 307
Bucy, P. C., 440
Buggy, J., 260
Bunge, M. B., 406

Bunge, R. P., 406
Burnham, W. M., 145
Burns, R. S., 147
Burns, S. L., 450
Burr, D. C., 164
Burrows, G. D., 287
Burstein, L., 384–385
Burt, D. R., 457
Butters, N., 359, 361
Butterworth, R. F., 12
Buttrick, M., 129
Byne, W., 292, 294
Byrne, J. H., 393

C
Cabanec, M., 241
Cacioppo, J. T., 444
Cade, J. F. J., 461
Caggiula, A. R., 342
Cain, D. P., 145
Callahan, L. M., 143
Calles-Escandon, J., 264
Calne, S., 140
Caltagirone, C., 444, 445
Camardo, J. S., 259
Cameron, P. A., 432
Campfield, L. A., 244–245
Cann, R. L., 48
Cannon, W. B., 248, 249, 439
Capaldi, E. D., 267
Capecchi, M. R., 39
Cappell, H., 328, 329
Carew, T. J., 388, 391, 393
Carlesimo, G. A., 361
Carlezon, W. A., Jr., 347
Carlson, N. R., 17
Carlsson, A., 456–457
Carlton, P. L., 327
Carr, G. D., 346
Carroll, D., 15, 17, 439
Cassell, M., 447, 464
Castellucci, V. F., 388, 389, 391, 393
Castro, C. A., 372, 395
Cermak, L. S., 360, 361
Chace, P. M., 364
Chafee, M. V., 212, 214
Chang, K., 247
Chang, P. K., 245
Changeux, J.-P., 94, 104
Chan-Ling, C., 58, 59
Chapman, P. F., 397
Charlton, M. P., 93
Chen, C. S., 327, 328
Chen, J., 344, 346, 347
Chen, K., 367
Chen, M. C., 393

Cheney, D. L., 21
Chevreul, M., 164
Chiba, A. A., 372
Chiu, C.-Y. P., 356, 359
Choi, D. W., 133, 134
Chorover, S. L., 364
Chouvet, G., 315
Christensen, B. K., 328
Christie, R. L., 334
Chun, J. J. M., 60, 61
Clanton, C. H., 200
Clapham, D. E., 95
Clarke, R., 423
Clayton, P. J., 287
Clemens, L. E., 279
Clements, J. D., 96
Cohen, N. J., 374
Cohen, S., 9, 335
Coindet, J., 315
Colebatch, J. G., 215
Coleman, P. D., 143
Coleman, R. M., 304
Colle, L. M., 344
Collier, G., 242
Collier, G. H., 240
Collingridge, G. L., 396
Collins, G. H., 359
Collins, S. M., 249
Coltheart, M., 432, 433
Conover, K. L., 249
Constantine-Paton, M., 384
Coolidge, C., 6
Coolidge, G., 6
Cooper, R., 118
Cooper, R. M., 43
Cooper, S. J., 249, 267
Coppens, Y., 29, 48
Corbett, D., 344
Corbetta, M., 184, 206
Corcoran, M., 335, 395
Corcoran, M. E., 146
Corder, E. H., 144
Corkin, S., 196, 197, 354–356
Corsi, P., 360
Corsi, P. I., 21, 79
Corwin, J. T., 189
Costall, B., 147
Cowan, W. M., 316, 380
Cowey, A., 184
Cox, D. R., 39
Coyle, J. T., 133, 361
Cragg, B. G., 387
Crammond, D. J., 209
Creese, I., 457
Crews, D., 276, 294
Crowell, C. R., 329
Cumming, G. D., 158
Cummings, R. W., 158
Cunningham, C. L., 329

Currier, R. D., 142
Czeisler, C. A., 304

D

Daan, S., 304
Dale, H., 9
Daly, M., 26
Damasio, A. R., 187, 361
Damasio, H., 187, 430
Dartnall, H. J. A., 173
Darwin, C., 23–26, 32–33, 438, 439, 442, 443
Das, G. D., 404
Dastur, F. N., 369, 376
Davidson, J. M., 285, 286, 289
Davidson, R. J., 444
Davis, H. P., 4, 18
Davis, J. D., 251
Davis, M., 447, 464
Dax, M., 412
D.B., 184
DeAngelis, G. C., 168
DeCamilli, P., 92, 93
de Castro, J. M., 243
Dejerine, J., 426
De Jonge, F. H., 288–289
deJonge, M., 394
de Kruif, P., 286
Delacour, J., 367
Delgado, J., 14–15
Delis, D. C., 361
Dement, W. C., 299–300, 304, 308, 312, 318, 322
Demotes-Mainard, J., 270
Dennerstein, L., 287
Denton, D., 176
De Renzi, E., 193, 415
Descartes, R., 20, 21
Desimone, R., 186, 205, 375
DeValois, K. K., 170, 171, 178
DeValois, R. L., 170, 171, 178
Devane, W. A., 335
de Wit, H., 341
Dewsbury, D. A., 10–11, 17, 18, 48
D.F., 187
Di Pelligrino, D. G., 213
Diamond, A., 44
Diamond, J., 285
Diamond, M. C., 201
Dicker, S. E., 261
Dobelle, W. H., 161, 173
Doherty, P., 383
Donoghue, J. P., 401, 402
d'Orta, R. G., 81, 100, 140, 148, 407
Dostrovsky, J., 372
Doty, R. L., 201

Doupe, A. J., 45
Dourish, C. T., 249
Dow, R. S., 219
Dr. P., 180–181, 187
Drachman, D. A., 354
Duchenne, 443–444
Dum, R. P., 214
Dunant, Y., 104
Dunbar, G. C., 463
Dunlop, S. A., 381
Dusoir, H., 360
Duvoisin, R. C., 147
Dyck, R. H., 402, 409

E

Easter, S. S., Jr., 383
Eccles, J., 9
Edwards, D. A., 280, 290
Edwards, G., 336
Egar, M., 382
Ehrhardt, A. A., 283, 284, 292
Ehringer, H., 456
Eichenbaum, H., 374, 395
Eichler, V. B., 314
Eidelberg, E., 228
Eikelboom, R., 329, 340, 341
Einstein, A., 30
Eisenberg, H. M., 362
Ekman, P., 442–444, 465
Elder, S. T., 341
Eldridge, R., 142
Eliot, L. S., 391
Ellis, L., 291
Emptage, N. J., 391, 393
Epstein, A. N., 246, 256, 259, 260
Epstein, R., 284
Erickson, R. P., 203
Erlanger, J., 9
Erlenmeyer, 348
Ervin, F. R., 195
Espir, M. I. E., 414
Esposito, R. U., 347
Estrin, R., 113
Etcoff, N. L., 444
Etgen, A. M., 290
Euler, U. von, 9
Evans, C. J., 338
Everitt, B. J., 287, 289–290

F

Fadem, B. H., 280
Falk, J. L., 262
Falls, W. A., 347
Falzi, G., 423
Farah, M. J., 186

Fawcett, J. W., 398, 404
Feder, H. H., 279
Feindel, W., 430
Feirtag, M., 61, 79
Feldman, S. M., 311
Felix, D., 259
Fendrich, R., 185
Feng, L. Y., 246
Fentress, J. C., 232
Fenwich, P., 301
Fetz, E. E., 209
Fibiger, C., 119
Fibiger, H. C., 127, 343–347, 361
Field, P. M., 288
Fields, H. L., 199, 200
Fiez, J. A., 433, 435, 436
Fillion, T. J., 201
Fine, A., 404
Finger, S., 402
Fischer-Nielson, S., 332
Fisher, A. E., 260
Fisher, C., 380
Fitzsimons, J. T., 256, 258, 259, 261
Fleischl-Marxow, E. von, 347
Fleshner, M., 451, 452, 454, 465
Fliers, E., 288
Fölling, A., 43
Foster, T. C., 372
Franklin, R. J. M., 406
Freed, W. J., 407
Freeman, R. D., 168
Freeman, W., 15
Freeman, W. J., 201
Freud, S., 300, 347–348, 426
Freund, H.-J., 211
Frey, U., 397
Friedman, J., 320
Friesen, W. V., 442, 443
Frisch, K. Von, 9
Fujii, Y., 280
Fuller, J., 251
Funder, J. W., 270
Fuxe, K., 92

G

Gabrieli, J. D. E., 361
Gackenbach, J., 300
Gaffan, D., 367
Gainer, H., 315
Galef, B. G., 241
Galef, G. B., 201
Gall, C., 402
Gallagher, M., 374
Gallup, G. G., Jr., 21, 22
Ganong, A. H., 394
Garcia, J., 127

Gardner, R., 304–306
Gardner-Medwin, A. R., 393
Garraghty, P. E., 401
Gasser, H., 9
Gaulin, S. J. C., 373, 377
Gawin, F. H., 335, 340
Gaze, R. M., 384
Gazzaniga, M. S., 123, 185, 417, 419
Geiselman, P. J., 244
Gelfand, M. M., 287
George, F. W., 277
Georgopoulos, A. P., 217, 232
Gershon, S., 146
Geschwind, N., 423, 425–430, 436
Gibbs, J., 248–249
Giffard, R. G., 134
Gilbert, C. D., 401, 402, 409
Gillberg, M., 306
Gilliam, T. C., 140
Gillin, J. C., 313
Gilman, A., 256
Gilman, A. G., 94, 95, 104
Ginty, D. D., 316
Girvin, J. P., 161
Giza, B. K., 201
Gjervig Jensen, K., 332
Glanzman, D. L., 392, 393, 409
Glaser, R., 453
Glickman, S. E., 342
Glickstein, M., 219
G.O., 210
Goate, A., 143–144
Goddard, G. V., 145
Goedert, M., 143
Goetz, C. G., 407
Goh, J. W., 394
Gold, M. S., 335
Gold, R. M., 246
Goldberg, J., 336
Golding, J. P., 398
Goldman, B., 288
Goldman, J. K., 246
Goldman-Rakic, P. S., 212, 214, 219
Goldstein, A., 338, 340, 349
Goldstein, G. W., 54
Golgi, C., 9, 58
Gollin, E. S., 355
Gollinick, P. D., 224
Goodale, M. A., 186–187, 413
Goodenough, D. R., 300
Goodglass, H., 123
Goodison, T., 328
Goodlett, C. R., 332
Gorski, R. A., 279, 288–290
Gorzalka, B. B., 6–7
Gottesman, I. I., 264, 456

Gottlieb, D. I., 104
Gould, S. J., 48, 275
Goy, R. W., 280, 292
Grady, K. L., 280
Graf, M. V., 318
Graf, P., 356
Graff-Radford, N., 359
Granit, R., 9
Grant, P. R., 25
Grant, S. G. N., 396
Graybiel, A. M., 219
Graziano, M. S. A., 215
Green, S., 464
Greenleaf, W., 301
Greenleaf, W. J., 285, 286
Greenough, W. T., 387
Griffin, J. E., 277, 288
Grillner, S., 231
Grinspoon, L., 333
Groos, G., 302, 315
Grosof, D. H., 185
Gross, C. G., 188, 215
Grossman, S. P., 260, 267
Grudin, J. T., 232
Gruenberg, A. M., 455
Grunt, J. A., 286
Guénard, V., 406
Guilleman, R., 9, 274
Gulyás, B., 374
Guo, N., 119
Gur, R. C., 278
Gusella, J. F., 140
Guth, P. H., 450

H

Haber, S., 146
Hafner, S., 394
Hagg, 275–276
Haley, J. E., 397
Hall, W. G., 261
Halmi, K. A., 267
Halsband, U., 211
Halsted, W. S., 337
Hamburger, V., 384
Hamer, D. H., 291, 292, 294
Hamer, J. D., 287
Hamm, A., 423
Hammer, N. J., 247
Hammond, P. H., 14
Han, P. J., 246
Hannah, J., 250
Hansen, B. C., 250
Haqq, C. M., 275–276
Harper, C. G., 12
Harpur, T. J., 129
Harris, G. W., 272, 273, 279

Harris, K. M., 91, 396
Harris, L. J., 242, 424
Hartline, H., 9
Hartline, P. H., 152
Hartmann, E. L., 322
Harvey, A. R., 404
Harvey, E. N., 296
Harvey, P. H., 30
Hashishin-i-Sabbah, 333
Hata, Y., 387
Hatten, M. E., 380
Haupt, H. A., 287, 288
Hawken, M. J., 185
Hawkins, R. D., 391
Haxby, J. V., 186
Hayakawa, K., 332
Hayes, L. L., 368
Head, H., 426
Hearne, K., 300, 301
Heath, R. G., 341
Hebb, D. O., 3, 352, 358, 394
Hebel, N., 359
Hécaen, H., 429–430
Heffner, H. E., 191, 193, 425
Heffner, R. S., 193, 425
Heinrichs, R. W., 455
Hellige, J. B., 414
Helmholtz, H. von, 172
Hendricks, J., 315
Hendrickson, A. E., 316
Henke, P. G., 451
Hennessey, A. C., 290
Henriksen, S., 312
Herbert, J., 287
Hering, E., 172–173
Herkenham, M., 78
Herkenham, M. A., 315
Herrup, K., 380, 409
Herzberg, C., 44
Hess, W., 9
Hetherington, A. W., 245
Heuser, J. E., 92, 94
Hibbard, L. S., 217
Hier, D. B., 415
Hinson, R. E., 329
Hinton, G. E., 432
Hiroi, N., 346, 347
Hirst, W., 232
H.M., 351–358, 360, 366, 367, 369, 376, 402
Hobart, G., 296
Hobson, J. A., 300, 304, 310, 313, 322
Hockfield, S., 387
Hodgkin, A., 9, 83–85
Hodgson, D. R., 224
Hoffman, P. L., 341
Hofman, M. A., 288

Hold, B., 201
Holland, P. C., 374
Holland, R. L., 400
Holloway, M., 324
Hollyday, M., 382, 384
Holm, H., 246
Holsboer, F., 463
Holtzman, P. S., 455
Hornykiewicz, O., 456
Horton, E. S., 264
Housman, D. E., 140
Howland, B., 176
Howlett, A. C., 335
Huang, Y.-Y., 397
Hubel, D. H., 9, 165, 166,
        168–170, 176–178, 387, 401
Huey, L., 146
Hughes, J., 199
Hulbert, S., 334
Hulsey, M. G., 250, 267
Hume, K. I., 306
Hunt, W. A., 332, 338
Hupka, R. B., 443
Hurlbert, A., 173
Hustvedt, B. E., 246
Hutchison, J. B., 270
Huxley, A., 9, 83–85
Hyman, B. T., 361

I

Iacono, W. G., 10, 441
Iadecola, C., 109
Ibuka, N., 314
Ichikawa, S., 280
Inase, M., 215
Inglis, J., 415
Inouye, S. I., 314, 315
Iriki, A., 395
Ironton, R., 400
Israël, M., 104
Iversen, S. D., 147, 249
Iwasaki, C., 287
Izard, C. E., 443

J

Jackson, H., 138
Jackson-Smith, P., 372
Jacobs, B. L., 313
Jacobs, L. F., 373, 377
Jacobs, W. J., 121, 129
Jacobsohn, D., 272
Jaeger, C. B., 404
Jahn, R., 93, 96
James, S. P., 438, 439

Jänig, W., 51
Janosky, D. S., 146
Jarrard, L. E., 372
Jarvie, K. R., 245
Jarvik, M. E., 338, 340, 349
Jaskiw, G. E., 459
Jenkins, W. M., 401, 402
Jenner, F. A., 463
Jilge, B., 302
Jimmie G., 2–3, 7, 12, 122, 136
Joanette, Y., 414
Joaquin, A., 146
Johanson, C. E., 53
Johnson, A. K., 259
Johnson, P., 232
Johnson, W. G., 267
Johnston, T. D., 23, 48
Jones, H. S., 306
Jones, H. W., 282
Jones, J. McA., 107
Jones, R. T., 331
Jonik, R. H., 448, 465
Jost, A., 277, 278
Jouvet, M., 312, 320
Julesz, B., 153
Julien, R. M., 337
Jung, L. J., 93
Jung, M. E., 118
Justice, J. B., Jr., 118, 347

K

Kaas, J. H., 186, 196, 401
Kaku, D. A., 134
Kalant, H., 338, 340, 349
Kalaska, J. F., 209
Kalb, R. G., 387
Kales, A., 297
Kalil, R. E., 387
Kallman, F. J., 455
Kalm, N. H., 447
Kalra, P. S., 279
Kandel, E. R., 104, 233, 388, 389,
        391–393, 397
Kaplan, E., 123
Kaplan, J., 415
Karacan, I., 300, 306
Karadžić, V. T., 306
Karni, A., 308
Karsch, F. J., 275
Kastin, A. J., 274, 318
Kater, S. B., 91, 396
Katz, B., 9
Katz, D. L., 288
Katz, J. L., 450
Kavanagh, G. L., 192, 193
Kawamura, H., 314, 315

Kedzierski, B., 301
Keesey, R. E., 250
Keirstead, S. A., 406
Kelly, J. B., 192, 193
Kelsey, J. E., 347
Kelso, S. R., 394
Kendler, K. S., 455
Kennedy, D., 129
Kephalas, T. A., 333
Kesner, R. P., 372
Kessler, D. S., 379
Keynes, R. J., 398
Kim, C. K., 146, 327, 328
Kimble, G. A., 23
Kimelberg, H. K., 58
Kimura, D., 121, 413, 421–422,
        424
King, A. J., 191
King, A. P., 44
Klawans, H. L., 81, 135, 149,
        197–198, 407
Klein, M., 389
Klein, R. L., 93
Kleitman, N., 296–297, 299, 300,
        304–305
Klitenick, M., 119
Klose, M., 383
Kluver, H., 440
Knoth, R. L., 12
Knudsen, E. I., 192, 388
Koelling, R. A., 127
Koenig, W. G. R., 10
Kolb, B., 5, 10, 17, 121, 128, 129,
        233, 402, 415, 422, 444–446
Kollar, E. J., 380
Kolodny, R. C., 334
Konishi, M., 192
Koob, G. F., 147, 325, 340, 347
Koolhaas, J. M., 275
Koopmans, H. S., 248, 250
Kornetsky, C., 144–145, 347
Korsakoff, S. S., 12
Kosambi, D. D., 199
Kosslyn, S. M., 21, 422, 436
Koutalos, Y., 161
Kowalska, D. M., 375
Kowler, E., 158
Krank, M. D., 330, 340, 341
Krasne, F. B., 393, 409
Krebs, J. R., 30
Kril, J. J., 12
Krupa, D. J., 375
Kuczmarski, R. J., 264
Kuffler, S. W., 165
Kulikovsky, O. T., 243
Kuo, P. T., 246
Kurata, K., 215
Kuwada, J. Y., 382, 383

Kuypers, H. G. J. M., 224
Kwan, M., 285, 286
Kyriacou, C. P., 316

L

LaBerge, S., 300, 301
Lacquaniti, F., 210
Laguzzi, R., 317
La Mettrie, J. O. de, 21
Lance-Jones, C., 383, 384
Land, E. H., 174–175, 178
Landmesser, L., 383–385
Lange, C. G., 438, 439
Langston, J. W., 147, 148
Lashley, K., 184, 351
Latimer, D., 336
Lavie, P., 319
Lawrence, D. G., 224
Lawson, J. S., 415
Lê, A. D., 329
Le Douarin, N., 408
LeDoux, J. E., 374, 448, 464, 465
Leech, C. K., 145
Lehrach, H., 140
Leibowitz, S. F., 247, 249, 267
Leiner, A. L., 219
Leiner, H. C., 219
Le Magnen, J., 261
Lemberger, L., 335
Lenn, N. J., 316
Lennox, W. G., 138–139
Lester, G. L. L., 6–7
Lettvin, J. Y., 176, 178
LeVay, S., 168, 292, 294, 387, 401
Levi-Montalcini, R., 9, 385
Levin, H. S., 362
Levine, D. C., 280
Levine, S., 279
Levitsky, W., 423
Levy, J., 419, 421, 423
Lewis, V., 251
Lewis, V. G., 284
Lewy, A. J., 304
Liepmann, H., 412
Lima, A., 15, 16
Lindblom, B., 425, 436
Linden, D. J., 396
Linden, L., 178
Linden, W., 113
Linder, M. E., 94, 95, 104
Lindqvist, M., 456–457
Lindsay, P. H., 157
Lindsley, D. B., 310
Lindvall, O., 344, 406, 407
Lishman, W. A., 12
Livingston, E. H., 450

Livingston, K., 146
Livingstone, M. S., 166, 176, 177
Llinás, R., 219
Lo, Y.-J., 387
Loewi, O., 9
Loft, S., 332
Lømø, T., 393
Loomis, A. L., 296
LoPiccolo, M. A., 313
Lorenz, K., 9
Løvø, A., 246
Lowe, J., 439
Lowe, M. R., 240
Lucas, F., 241
Lund, R. D., 404
Luo, Y., 382
Luria, A. R., 131
Lydic, R., 313
Lykken, D. T., 442
Lynch, G., 402

M

Macchi, G., 440
MacDonald, M. A., 129
Mach, E., 164
MacLusky, N. J., 286
MacNeilage, P. F., 425, 436
MacNichol, E. F., Jr., 173
Madison, D. V., 98, 397
Madrazo, I., 407
Magni, F., 311
Magoun, H. W., 310, 311
Mahut, H., 368
Maier, S. R., 451, 452, 454, 465
Mair, R. G., 12, 376
Malinow, R., 396
Malla, A. K., 456
Malmo, H. P., 256
Malmo, R. B., 256
Malsbury, C. W., 289, 344
Mana, M. J., 128, 129, 146, 327, 328
Mancall, E. L., 441
Manning, F. J., 375
Mansfield, J. G., 329
Maratsos, M., 414, 436
Marcussen, B. L., 332
Marie, P., 426
Mark, V. H., 195
Marks, W. B., 173
Marler, P., 44
Marlowe, W. B., 441
Marshall, F. H. A., 272
Marslen, W. D., 359
Martin, B. J., 306
Martin, J. B., 140

Martin, J. R., 250, 267
Martin, R. L., 287
Masoro, E. J., 250
Masterton, R. B., 188, 190, 191
Mateer, C. A., 421, 432
Matheny, L., 414, 436
Mathur, A., 344
Matsubara, J., 62, 119
Matsuda, L. A., 335
Matteoli, M., 92
Matthews, P. B. C., 228
Matthyse, S., 455
Mattson, S. N., 332
Maunsell, J. H. R., 186
Mazziotta, J. C., 108
Mazzocchi, F., 430
McAuliffe, W. E., 341
McCann, S. M., 279
McCann, T. S., 26
McCarley, R. W., 313
McCaughran, J. A., Jr., 335
McClintock, M. K., 201
McDonald, R. J., 372
McDonald, W. I., 142
McEwen, B., 450
McEwen, B. S., 274, 279, 280, 288
McFarland, H. F., 142
McGinty, D. J., 313
McGlone, J., 414–415
McGlothin, W. H., 334
McGuffin, P., 43
McHugh, P. R., 249
McIntyre, D. C., 145
McKim, W. A., 17, 337, 349
McLachlan, E. M., 51
McLoon, S. C., 404
McNaughton, B. L., 372
McPherson, L. M., 129
McWilliams, R., 402
Meaney, M. J., 280
Meck, W. H., 362
Meddis, R., 296, 306, 322
Mehler, J., 433
Mellgren, R. L., 21n
Mello, N. K., 127, 340
Melton, D. A., 379
Meltzer, H. Y., 9
Meltzer, L. D., 458
Melzack, R., 198n, 199–201
Menaker, M., 315
Mendel, G., 33–34
Mendelson, J. H., 318, 334
Mendelson, M. P., 340
Mercer, A. R., 391
Merigan, W. H., 186
Merton, P. A., 14
Merzenich, M. M., 401, 402
Mesulam, M. M., 212

Meunier, M., 369
Meyer-Bahlburg, H. F. L., 284, 448
Michel, S., 315
Middleton, F. A., 219
Milgram, N. W., 394
Miller, N. E., 18, 245
Miller, N. S., 335
Miller, R. L., 285
Miller, T. M., 92
Mills, J. N., 306
Milner, A. D., 186–187
Milner, B., 196, 353–356, 358, 360,
        373, 414, 428, 429, 445, 446
Milner, P., 78, 341, 342
Milner, P. M., 3
Mink, J. W., 219
Mishkin, M., 186, 362, 366–368,
        371, 374–377
Miss C., 198
Mistlberger, R. E., 302, 306, 315
Mitchell, R. W., 21
Mitler, M., 312
Miyashita, Y., 374
Mladejovsky, M. G., 161
Modianos, D., 290
Mogenson, G. J., 344
Mohr, J. P., 354, 355, 428
Mollon, J. D., 173
Mondrian, P., 175
Money, J., 283, 284, 294
Money, M., 284
Moniz, E., 9, 15–17
Monnier, M., 317
Montarolo, P. G., 391
Moonen, C. T., 108
Moore, A. M., 313
Moore, D. R., 191
Moore, R. Y., 314–316, 360
Moran, J., 205
Moran, T. H., 249
Morgan, M. A., 449
Morgan, T. H., 34–35
Mori, N., 145
Morris, M. K., 361
Morris, N. M., 287
Morris, R. G. M., 128
Morris, R. J., 404–405
Morrone, M. C., 164
Moruzzi, G., 310, 311
Mos, J., 465
Moscovitch, M., 360
Moskowitz, H., 334
Moss, M., 368
Mountcastle, V. B., 196
Mouret, J., 312, 315
Mr. B., 318
Mr. R., 10
Mrosovsky, N., 302, 304, 305

Mrs. S., 212
Mucha, R. F., 340
Mullaney, D. J., 306, 320
Mumby, D. G., 368, 369, 371–372,
        376
Murphy, M. R., 201
Murray, B., 344
Murray, E. A., 368, 374
Mushiake, H., 215
Musto, D. F., 324
Myers, R., 407, 409
Myers, R. E., 415–417

N

N.A., 360
Nadel, L., 360, 372
Nadelmann, E. A., 338, 340, 349
Naeser, M. A., 430
Naftolin, F., 286
Nathans, J., 161, 178
Nauta, W. J. H., 61, 79
Naylor, R. J., 147
Neher, E., 104
Neiderhiser, J. M., 47
Nelson, D., 44
Nemeroff, C. B., 438
Netter, F. H., 79, 162
Newman, E. A., 152
Newman, S. W., 289
Newsom-Davis, J., 136
Nguyen, P. V., 397
Nicholas, M. K., 404
Nicklas, J. A., 142
Nicolaïdis, S., 261, 262
Nishi, R., 385
Nissl, F., 58
Nomikos, G. G., 345
Nordeen, E. J., 45
Nordeen, K. W., 45
Nordlander, R. H., 382
Norenberg, M. D., 58
Norman, D. A., 157, 232
Norman, R. M. G., 456
Nottebohm, F., 44, 45
Novin, D., 256, 261
Nudo, R. J., 402
Nunez, A. A., 315
Nunn, J., 261

O

O'Banion, M. K., 143
Obersteiner, 348
O'Callaghan, M. A. J., 15
Ochsner, K. N., 356, 359

Ockhuizen, T., 332
Ohzawa, I., 168
Ojeda, S. R., 279
Ojemann, G. A., 429, 432
O'Keefe, J., 372–373, 377
Olds, J., 78, 341, 342
O'Leary, A., 452
O'Leary, D. D. M., 402, 404, 409
Oliveras, J.-L., 200
Olivier, B., 465
Olney, J. W., 134
Olton, D. S., 127
Oscar-Berman, M., 361
Oswald, I., 306
Otto, T., 374, 395
Otto, T. A., 12
Owen, M. J., 43
Owren, M. J., 425

P

Paletta, M. S., 329
Panksepp, J., 249, 342
Papanicolaou, A., 362
Papez, J. W., 439–440
Park, I. J., 282
Parker, S. T., 21
Patrick, C. J., 441
Patterson, K., 433
Paul, D., 129
Pavlov, I., 9
Peck, J. W., 256
Pellis, S. M., 446, 447
Pellow, S., 126, 464
Penfield, W., 195–196, 216–217,
        414, 428–432
Pennebaker, J. W., 453
Percival, J. E., 306
Perdeck, A. C., 21
Perenin, M. T., 186
Perera, M. H., 463
Perkins, W. L., 330, 340
Perlow, M. J., 407
Perrone, P., 423
Pert, C. B., 99
Peterhans, E., 185
Petersen, S. E., 124, 433–436
Petrides, M., 360, 361
Petrinovich, L., 44
Pettet, M. W., 401
Pettigrew, J. D., 168
Pettit, H. O., 347
Pfaff, D. W., 289, 290
Pfaus, J. G., 129, 328, 341, 345
Pfeiffer, C. A., 279
Phelps, M. E., 108
Phillips, A. G., 127, 343–347

Phillips, D. P., 192
Phillips, M. I., 259
Phoenix, C. H., 279–280
Pigott, S., 373
Pilar, G., 384–385
Pillard, R. C., 291
Pinel, J. P. J., 128, 146, 262, 327,
    328, 341, 363, 368, 369, 371,
    376
Pinkster, H. M., 388, 391
Pizzamiglio, L., 444
Placzek, M., 382
Plapinger, L., 279
Plaut, D. C., 432
Pleim, E. T., 290
Plomin, R., 43, 47, 48
Polkey, C. E., 433
Pons, T. P., 196, 401
Poo, M.-M., 387
Pope, H. G., 288
Poppel, G., 332
Poppelreuter, W., 212
Porte, D., Jr., 249–250
Posner, M. I., 124, 129, 207
Post, R. M., 145
Poulos, C. X., 328, 329
Powell, T. P. S., 196
Powers, J. B., 289
Powley, T. L., 246, 250, 267
Preston, J. B., 217
Price, R. A., 264
Pritchard, R. M., 158
Pujol, J. F., 317
Purkinje, J. E., 158
Puttfarcken, P., 133

Q

Qualtrochi, J. J., 313

R

Racine, R. J., 145, 146, 394
Rafal, R. D., 212
Raff, M. C., 385
Raible, D., 382
Raichle, M. E., 109, 124, 129, 207,
    435
Rainnie, D., 447, 464
Raisman, G., 288, 404–405
Rakic, P., 73
Ralph, M. R., 315
Ramachandran, V. S., 154, 178
Ramón y Cajal, S., 9
Ramsay, D. J., 256, 260, 261
Ransom, S. W., 245

Raper, J. A., 382
Rasmussen, R., 196
Rasmussen, T., 216, 428, 429
Ratliff, F., 164, 165, 178
Ratnasuriya, R. H., 265
R.B., 358–359, 369–370
Reale, L., 360, 361
Reame, N., 275
Rebec, G. V., 146–147
Recanzone, G. H., 401
Rechtschaffen, A., 297, 306, 307,
    319
Redd, M., 243
Reh, T. A., 384
Renault, J., 312
Reul, J. M. H. M., 463
Revere, G. D., 287, 288
Revusky, S. H., 127
Reynolds, D. V., 199
Rezek, D. L., 279
Richmond, R., 12
Richter, C. P., 303, 314
Riley, E. P., 332
Rindi, G., 12
Ringwald, M., 39
R.M., 376
Robbins, T. W., 361
Roberts, D. C. S., 347
Roberts, G. W., 459
Roberts, L., 414, 428, 429, 431, 432
Roberts, W. V., 287
Robertson, W. D., 106, 133, 135
Robinson, T. E., 118, 129, 311,
    326, 335, 340, 341
Robitaille, R., 93
Rodgers, R. J., 464, 465
Rodin, J., 235, 250, 264, 267
Roe, A. W., 388
Rogers, P. J., 243
Roland, P. E., 198, 207, 217–219,
    233, 374, 413, 422
Rolls, B. J., 244, 247, 256, 258,
    260–262
Rolls, E. T., 240, 247, 258, 260
Rolls, R. M., 260, 262
Romanski, L. M., 448
Rose, E. A., 140
Rose, G. A., 264
Rosenthal, D., 455
Rosenzweig, M. R., 18
Ross, J., 164
Rothblat, L. A., 368
Rothman, S. M., 133
Rothwell, J. C., 210
Rothwell, N. J., 250
Rotrosen, J., 146
Routtenberg, A., 259, 260, 344,
    396

Rovner, L. I., 262
Rowe, H., 335
Rowland, N. E., 241, 244, 261, 262
Ruchkin, D. S., 110
Rudomin, P., 91
Rudy, J. W., 374
Rudy, T. A., 200
Ruff, N. L., 402, 409
Rummelhart, D. E., 232
Rusak, B., 302, 314–316
Russell, W. R., 414
Rutishauser, U., 381
Rutledge, L. L., 443
Rycroft, W., 249

S

Sacks, O., 3n, 21–22, 149,
    180–181, 212
Sagar, H. J., 360
Sager, R., 132
Sakai, K., 374
Sakmann, B., 104
Sakuma, Y., 290
Salmon, P., 450
Salmon, P. A., 304, 305
Salyer, K. E., 136
Samuelson, R. J., 127
Sanders, D., 287
Sanes, J. N., 401, 402
Sastry, B. R., 394
Sather, K. J., 18
Sato, M., 145, 146
Sawchenko, P. E., 246
Sawle, G. V., 407, 409
Schacter, D. J., 356
Schacter, D. L., 356, 359
Schacter, S., 393
Schally, A. V., 9, 274
Schatzman, M., 301
Scheller, R. H., 93
Schelling, T. C., 331
Schenck, C. H., 320
Scherschlicht, R., 317
Schieber, M. H., 217
Schiff, B. B., 342
Schiffman, S. S., 203
Schiller, P. H., 364
Schlaggar, B. L., 404
Schlapfer, W. T., 328
Schlaug, G., 423, 424
Schleidt, M., 201
Schlundt, D. G., 267
Schneider, G. E., 201
Schneider, L. H., 267
Schneider-Helmert, D., 317–318
Schoenenberger, G. A., 318

Schofield, P. R., 94
Schou, M., 461
Schreiner, C. E., 191
Schuman, E. M., 397
Schuri, U., 359
Schuurman, T., 275
Schwab, M. E., 406
Schwartz, J. H., 104, 233
Schwartz, M., 284
Schwartz, W. J., 315
Sciascia, T. R., 178
Sclafani, A., 241
Scott, T. R., 201
Scoville, W. B., 358
Searle, L. V., 43
Seeburg, P. H., 94
Seitz, R. J., 232
Selemon, L. D., 219
Selkoe, D. J., 143
Selye, H., 450
Sergent, J., 188
Seyfarth, R. M., 21
Shallice, T., 432
Shapiro, B. H., 280
Shapiro, E., 389
Shapley, R. M., 185
Sharma, S. C., 384
Sharpe, L. G., 260
Sherrington, C., 9
Sherry, D. F., 201, 241, 373, 377
Sherwin, B. B., 286, 287
Shimokochi, M., 290
Shimura, T., 290
Shipley, M. T., 448
Shivers, B. D., 94
Shizgal, P., 344
Shouse, M. N., 146
Sidman, M., 354, 355
Siegel, J. M., 313, 319
Siegel, S., 328, 329
Silva, A. J., 395, 396
Silver, J., 380, 409
Simon, H., 9
Simons, B. J., 258
Simpson, J. B., 259, 260
Singer, J., 289
Singer, M., 382
Sitaram, N., 313
Skelton, R. W., 395
Sklar, L., 340
Sladeck, J. R., Jr., 407
Sladek, J. R., 407
Slangen, J. L., 465
Slater, P. C., 360, 364
Slaunwhite, W. R., III, 246
Smith, F. J., 244–245
Smith, G. P., 240, 248–249
Smith, R. A., 362

Snowman, A. M., 99
Snyder, S. H., 98, 99, 104, 457, 458
Sorenson, E. R., 443
Spanhaak, S., 332
Spanis, C. W., 364
Speakman, A., 372–373
Spector, R., 53
Sperry, R. W., 9, 381–383,
    415–417, 419, 421, 423, 436
Spillman, L., 185
Spitzer, H., 205
Spyraki, C., 347
Squire, L. R., 358, 360, 361, 364,
    367–369, 371, 374, 376, 377
Sriram, S., 142
Stacey, P., 289–290
Stanford, S. C., 450
Stea, R. A., 198
Stebbins, W., 192
Steffens, A. B., 244
Stellar, J. R., 127
Stenevi, U., 407
Stephan, F. K., 314, 315
Steriade, M., 310
Sterman, M. B., 313
Stevens, C. F., 396
Stevens, R. M., 261
Stevenson, J. A. F., 245
Stewart, J., 280, 329, 340, 341
Stillman, R. C., 335
Stirling, R. V., 381
Stock, M. J., 250
Stoddard, L. T., 354, 355
Stoerig, P., 184
Stolerman, I., 346
Stone, J., 58
Storms, L., 146
Stout, S. C., 438
Strange, P. G., 104
Strick, P. L., 214, 217, 219
Stricker, E. M., 257
Strubbe, J. H., 242, 244, 267
Stryker, M. P., 170, 387
Studdert-Kennedy, M. G., 425, 436
Stuss, D. T., 359
Suddath, R. L., 459
Südhof, T. C., 96
Summers, G. L., 335
Suner, S., 401, 402
Sutherland, R. J., 121, 129, 374
Sutton, G. G., 14
Sutton, S., 110
Svaetichin, G., 174
Swaab, D. F., 288
Swanson, L. W., 260
Sweeney, M. E., 264
Syed, N. I., 382
Szmukler, G. I., 265

T

Tabakoff, B., 341
Takahashi, J. S., 302, 315
Talbot, J. D., 199
Tampakeras, M., 344
Tanaka, A., 145
Tanaka, K., 374
Tanji, J., 215
Tank, D. W., 396
Tanzi, R. E., 144
Tassinary, L. G., 444
Taylor, J. R., 147
Taylor, L., 444–446
Tees, R. C., 387
Teich, A. H., 449
Teillet, M. A., 408
Teitelbaum, P., 245, 246, 247
Terman, G. W., 200
Terman, M., 315
Tessier-Lavigne, M., 382
Tetrud, J. W., 147, 148
Teuber, H.-L., 183, 354, 356, 359,
    360, 404
Thach, W. T., 219
Thal, L. J., 362
Thomas, J. J., 441
Thompson, J. K., 375
Thompson, R. F., 375
Thorne, A. G., 48
Thureson-Klein, A. K., 93
Tiffany, S. T., 329, 340
Tilles, D., 334
Tilley, A. J., 306
Tinbergen, N., 9, 21
Tinklenberg, J. R., 334
Toates, F. M., 240
Tompkins, C. A., 421
Tonge, D. A., 398
Tranel, D., 187
Traynor, A. E., 328
Treit, D., 128, 464
Trevarthen, C., 419
Trotter, Y., 153
Trowill, J. A., 342
Trulson, M. E., 313
Tryon, R. C., 42
Tucker, D. M., 445
Turkenburg, J. L., 289
Turner, A. M., 387
Twain, M., 23

U

Uhly, B., 360, 361
Ulrich, R. E., 5, 18
Ungerleider, L. G., 186
Urgurbil, K., 215

V

Valenstein, E. S., 14–15, 17
Vallee, R. B., 92
Valverde, F., 387
Van der Heijden, A. H. C., 13
Van der Kooy, D., 346
Vanderwolf, C. H., 311, 312
Van Essen, D. C., 185
Van Hoesen, G. W., 361
Vargha-Khadem, F., 433
Vathy, I. U., 290
Vaughan, H. G., 110
Vaughan, H. G., Jr., 360
Velichkovsky, B. M., 13
Verma, A., 98
Vernier, P., 270
Vertes, R. P., 313, 314
Vessie, P. R., 140
Vicario, D. S., 45
Victor, M., 359
Vidal-Sanz, M., 406
Vighetto, A., 186
Vignolo, L. A., 423, 430
Vincent, A., 136
Vincent, J.-D., 270
Vincent, S., 60, 142
Vitaterna, M. H., 316
Vogel, P., 417
Volkmar, F. R., 387
von Cramon, D. Y., 359
von der Heydt, R., 185

W

Wada, J. A., 121, 145, 146, 335, 412, 423
Wagner, A. R., 329
Wagoner, N., 316
Wald, G., 9, 173
Walk, R. D., 387
Walker, D. L., 362
Wall, P. D., 198n, 199
Waller, H. J., 311
Walls, E. K., 250
Walsh, F. S., 383
Walsh, M. L., 447, 448, 465
Walters, C. P., 387
Walters, E. T., 391
Wang, J., 402
Warchol, M. E., 189
Washburn, A. L., 248, 249
Washington, G., 333
Watkins, L. R., 451, 452, 454, 465
Watson, D., 453
Watson, J. B., 20
Watson, N., 424
Wauquier, A., 145
Webb, W. B., 306, 307, 320

Webster, M. M., 127
Weinberg, R. A., 132
Weinberger, D. R., 459
Weinberger, N. M., 402
Weingarten, H. P., 240, 242, 243, 245, 249
Weintraub, S., 212
Weisel, T., 9
Weisinger, R. S., 261
Weiskrantz, L., 184
Wekerle, H., 142
Weller, A., 249
Welsh, J. P., 219
Werner, J. S., 185
Wernicke, C., 425–430, 436
Wessinger, C. M., 185
West, J. R., 332
West, M. J., 44
Westergaard, G. C., 425
Westerink, B. H. C., 118
Weston, Mrs. M., 306
Wever, R. A., 303
Wexler, N. S., 140
Whalen, R. E., 279
Whishaw, I. Q., 5, 10, 17, 121, 129, 233, 402, 415, 422
Whiskin, E. E., 241
White, B. D., 250, 267
White, N., 340
White, N. M., 3, 346, 347, 372
Whitelaw, V., 382
Whittaker, D. G., 158
Wickelgren, W. A., 353
Wictorin, K., 407
Wiepkema, P. R., 275
Wiesel, T. N., 165, 166, 168–170, 177, 178, 387, 401
Wilcox, G. L., 397
Willett, W. C., 241
Williams, C. L., 362
Williams, J., 300
Williams, R. T., 264
Willing, A. E., 250
Wilson, A., 12
Wilson, A. C., 48
Wilson, J. D., 277, 288
Wilson, M., 26
Wilson, M. A., 372
Winn, P., 459
Winocur, G., 359
Winokur, G., 460
Winson, J., 301, 307
Wirtshafter, D., 251
Wise, R. A., 340, 344, 347
Wise, S. P., 213
Witelson, S. F., 288
Wodak, A., 12
Wolf, M. E., 413

Wolff, P. H., 424
Wolgin, D. L., 327, 328
Wolpert, E. A., 299
Wolpoff, M. H., 48
Wong, J., 128
Wong, Y., 396
Wood, E. R., 368, 369, 370, 371
Wood, R. J., 256, 260–262
Woodruff-Pak, D. S., 356
Woods, S. C., 242, 249–250, 267
Worsley, A., 301
Wurtman, R. J., 143
Wylie, D. R., 413

X

Xu, X. M., 406

Y

Yakolev, P. I., 195
Yap, G. S., 215
Yaqub, B. A., 193
Yau, K.-W., 161
Yeomans, J. S., 344
Yeung, J. C., 200
Yokel, R. A., 346
Yoon, M., 384
Young, R. C., 248–249
Young, T., 172, 173
Young, W. C., 280, 286
Yurek, D. M., 407

Z

Zacharko, R. M., 460
Zaidel, D., 421
Zaidel, E., 421, 422
Zajonc, R. B., 443
Zangwill, O. L., 428
Zasetsky, L., 131
Zatz, M., 315
Zeki, S., 176, 178, 182, 183, 185–187
Zelman, D. C., 340
Zhou, C. F., 404–405
Zimitat, C., 12
Zito, K. A., 347
Zivin, J. A., 133, 134
Zola-Morgan, S., 358, 361, 367–371, 374, 376, 377
Zubek, J. P., 43
Zucker, I., 314
Zusho, H., 204

SUBJECT INDEX

The boldfaced page numbers are those on which the key terms are defined in boxes in the margin.

A

Abducens nerve, 473
Ablatio penis, 284–285
Absolute refractory period, **89**
Absorption spectrum, 159–**161**, 173
Absorptive phase, **237**, 238
Accommodation (in vision), **152**
Acetylcholine, 96–98, 224, 361
Acetylcholine receptors, 102, 103
Acetylcholinesterase, **96**, 98, 361
Achromatic colors, **172**
Acquired immune deficiency syndrome (AIDS), 292
ACTH (adrenocorticotropic hormone), **280**, 450, **451**
Action potentials (APs), **86**–91, 109, 388–389, 391, 393, 395
  recording, 116, 117
Activation-synthesis theory (of dreams), **301**
Activity-dependent enhancement, 392, **393**
Acuity (in vision), **152,** 154, 156
Addiction, 324, 327, 331–341, 346–347. *See also* Drug abuse; Drug tolerance; Drug withdrawal *entries*
Addicts, **327,** 340, 341
Adenine nucleotide base, 37
Adenosine monophosphate, cyclic, 393
ADH (antidiuretic hormone), **257,** 256–258. *See also* Vasopressin
Adiposity, 249
Adipsia, **246,** 247
Adoption studies. *See* Twin studies
Adrenal cortex, **271,** 450, **451**
Adrenal gland, 270, 271

Adrenal medulla, 269, 450, **451**
Adrenaline (epinephrine), 93, 98, 269
Adrenergic neurons, 97
Adrenocorticotropic hormone (ACTH), **280,** 450, **451**
AEPs (average evoked potentials), 110, 111
Affect in schizophrenia, 455
Affective disorders, 459–463
Afferent (sensory) nerves, **50,** 51
Afferent (sensory) neurons, 227, 388–389, 391, 393
Age-limited learning, 44, 45
Ageusia, **204**
Aggregate field, **168**
Aggregation (of neurons), **381**
Aggressive behaviors, **444**–449
  controlling, Delgado's research on, 14–15
  in decorticate cats, 439
  and pheromones, 201
  predatory, 447
  and psychosurgery, 449
  septal, 447
  signals of, 438, 439
  social, 447–448
  tests of, 125
Agnosias, **187**–188, 197–198
Agonists, 100, **101**
  cholinergic, 313
  dopamine, 344, 407
  GABA, 102, 375, 463, 464
  monoamine, 461
  serotonin, 462–464
Agraphia, **427,** 426–429
AIDS (acquired immune deficiency syndrome), 292
Alcohol
  as anticonvulsant drug, 327–328
  brain damage from, 12, 136, 332
  temperature-reducing effects of, 329
  use and abuse of, 332, 338
Alcoholics, quasiexperimental study of, 7

Aldosterone, 258, **259**
Alexia, **427,** 426–429
All-or-none hemispheric differences, 422
All-or-none responses, **86,** 87
Alpha fetoprotein, **279**
Alpha males, 125, **444**–446
Alpha waves, **109,** 110, **297,** 298
Alzheimer's disease, **143,** 142–144, 361–362, 376
Amacrine cells (in retina), 154, **155**
Amenorrhea, 288
Amino acid derivative hormones, **269**
Amino acid neurotransmitters, 97, 98
Amino acids, 38, **39,** 97, 98, 236, **237**
  excitatory, 133–135, 139
Amnesia
  of Alzheimer's disease, 361–362
  anterograde, 353–356, 362
  after concussion (posttraumatic), 362–364
  global, 354
  of Korsakoff's syndrome, 359–360, 367, 376
  from medial temporal lobectomy, 351–359, 366–372, 374–375
  object-recognition, 366–372, 374
  retrograde, 353, 362–364, 374–375
Amotivational syndrome, **334**
AMP (adenosine monophosphate), cyclic, 393
Amphetamine model of schizophrenia, 146–147
Amphetamine psychosis, **146**–147
Amphetamines, **334,** 335, 344
  abuse of, 146, 147
Amphibians, **27,** 31
Amplitude of sound waves, 188

Amygdala, 74–76, 352, **353**
  in Alzheimer's disease, 143
  in anxiety disorders, 464
  and benzodiazepines, 102
  damage to, 440, 448–449. *See also* lesions of, *below*
  electrical stimulation of, 451
  lesions of, 116, 371, 448–449
  and memory, 374
  of monkeys, 367, 368
Amygdalectomy, 449
Amyloid, **143**
Amyloid plaques, 142, 143, **361**
Anabolic steroids, **286**–288
Analgesics, 99, 199–200, 336, **337**. *See also* Opiate *entries*
Analytic mode of thinking, 423–424
Analytic-synthetic theory of lateralization, 423–424
Anandamide, 335
Anatomical directions, 62–63
Androgenic insensitivity syndrome, **282**–283
Androgenital syndrome, **282**–284
Androgens, 270, **271**, 276, 280–281, 287. *See also* Dihydrotestosterone; Estrogens; Testosterone
Androstenedione, **280**, 281
Aneurysms, **133**
Angiograms, 133
Angiography, 106–107
Angiotensin II, **259**, 258–260
Angular gyrus, 426, **427**, 435
Animal behavior. *See also specific entries, e.g.:* Aggressive behaviors; Defensive behaviors
  biopsychological paradigms of, 125–128
  study of (ethology), 21
Animal conditioning paradigms, 126–127
Animal learning paradigms, 127–128
Animal models
  of anxiety, 464
  of bilateral medial temporal lobe amnesia, 366–372
  homologous, isomorphic, and predictive, 145
  of neuropsychological diseases, 144–147
Animals. *See also specific entries, e.g.:* Canaries, birdsong in; Primates
  brain surgery on, 114–116, 415–417. *See also* Aspira-

tion; Lesion *entries;* Stereotaxic surgery
  multiple sclerosis induced in, 142
  nocturnal, 302
  research on, 113–117. *See also specific entries, e.g.:* Monkeys; Rats
Anne S., case of, 282–283
Anorexia nervosa, 235, **264**–266
Anosmia, **204**
Anosognosia, 198, **199**
ANS. *See* Autonomic nervous system
Antagonistic excitatory and inhibitory areas, 196, 198
Antagonistic muscles, **225**, 230
Antagonists, 100, **101**
  cholinergic, 313
  dopamine, 344
  histamine, 450
  opiate, 199–200, 285
Anterior cingulate cortex, **199**
Anterior (rostral) direction, **62**, 63
Anterior forebrain pathway, 45
Anterior hypothalamus, third interstitial nucleus of, 292
Anterior pituitary, **271**–273, 276, 280
Anterior pituitary adrenal cortex system, 450
Anterior temporal lobe damage, 440
Anterograde amnesia, **353**–356, 362
Anterograde degeneration, **398**, 399
Anterograde memory deficits, 361
Anterograde tracing methods, 61
Anterograde transneuronal degeneration, **398**, 399
Anterolateral system, **194**–196
Antianxiety (anxiolytic) drugs, 102, 126, 128, 462–464. *See also* Benzodiazepines
Antibodies, 118–119, 136, 452, **453**
Antibody-mediated immunity, **451**–453
Anticipatory behaviors, 345
Anticonvulsant drugs, 102, 140, 146, 327–328
Antidepressants, 460–462. *See also* Monoamine oxidase inhibitors
  tricyclic, 308, 309, 317, 319, 460, 461

Antidiuretic hormone (ADH), **257**, 256–258. *See also* Vasopressin
Antidromic conduction, **90**
Antigens, 118, **451**, 452
Antihypnotic drugs, **317**
Antipsychotic drugs, 136
Antischizophrenic drugs, 146, 147, 456–459
Antithesis principle (Darwin), 438, 439
Antithiamine drug, 376
Anxiety, **462**–464
Anxiety disorders, **462**–464
Anxiolytic (antianxiety) drugs, 102, 126, 128, 462–464. *See also* Benzodiazepines
AP (action potential), **86**–91, 101, 388–389, 391, 393, 395
  recording, 116, 117
Apes, evolution of, 28, 29. *See also* Primates
Aphagia, **245**–247
Aphasia, **413**, 412–415
  and brain-imaging techniques, 430
  Broca's, 424, 425, 428, 430
  conduction, 424–426
  global, 430
  Wernicke's, 424, 425, 428, 430
Apical dendrites, 72, 78
Aplysia, **389**, 388–393
Appetitive behaviors, 345
Appetizer effect, **242**, 243
Applied research, **8**, 9
Apraxia, 212, **213**, 412, **413**, 421
Arachnoid membrane, **52**, 53
Arcuate fasciculus, **424**–427
Arithmetic subtest of WAIS, 122
Aromatization, **279**, 280
Arterial blood pressure. *See* Blood pressure *entries*
Arterioles, 113
Arteriosclerosis, **133**
Asomatognosia, **21**–22, **197**–198
Aspartate, 97, 98
Aspiration, 114, **115**, 368
Assassin, derivation of, 333
Association cortex, **181**, 180–183, 185
  dorsolateral prefrontal, 211–214
  posterior parietal, 196, 210–212
  sensorimotor, 211–214
Associative learning, 391–392
Astereognosia, **197**, **217**
Astroglia (astrocytes), **58**, 59, **398**
Ataxia, 142, **143**
Atonia, 318
Atrophy of brain, 107

Atropine, **102**
Atypical neuroleptic drugs, 458
Auditory canal, 189, 190
Auditory cortex, 190–193, 375, 426, 448–449
Auditory evoked potentials, 110, 111
Auditory fear conditioning, 448–449
Auditory nerves, **189**–191
Auditory system, 188–193, 388
Auditory tests of language-related activities, 433–435
Auditory-vestibular nerve, 189, 473
Aunt Betty, case of, 197–198
Auras, epileptic, 138, 139
Australopithecus, 29, 30
Autoimmune disorders, 136, 142, 143
Automatisms, 138, 139
Autonomic nervous system (ANS), 10, **11, 50,** 51, 471
  activity of, measuring, 109, 112–113
  and emotions, 441–442
  neurons of, 65
Autoradiography, 118, **119**
Autoreceptors, **96**
Autotransplantation, **406,** 407
Average evoked potentials (AEPs), 110, 111
Axillary (underarm) hair, 280, 281
Axoaxonal synapses, 91
Axodendritic synapses, 91
Axon hillocks, 55, **86,** 90
Axonal conduction, 90
Axons, 54, 55
  growth of, 381–385
  myelinated, 90
  regeneration of, 58
  string-of-beads, 97
  varicosities of, 97
Axosomatic synapses, 91
Axotomy, **398,** 399

B

B cells (B lymphocytes), **451**–454
Bacterial infections of brain, 135
Ballistic movements, 210
Barn owl sound localization, 191–192
Baroreceptors, **256**–258
Basal forebrain, **361,** 376
Basal forebrain region, **312**–313
Basal ganglia, 73–76, 219
Basilar membrane, **189,** 190

Before-and-after design, **327**–328
Behavior(s)
  aggressive. *See* Aggressive behaviors
  animal. *See* Animal behavior
  anticipatory, 345
  appetitive, 345
  biology of. *See* Biopsychology
  brain interaction with, 5
  consummatory, 345
  copulatory, 289–290. *See also* Lordosis
  defensive, 125–126, 444–448, 464. *See also* Defensive burying *entries*
  disinhibition of, 341
  eating, 241–244
  and evolution, 26–27
  genetic versus learned, 20–21, 23. *See also* Nature-nurture issue
  instinctive, 21
  instrumental, 345
  natural motivated, 345
  odd, in schizophrenia, 455
  open-field, 146
  preparatory, 345
  proceptive, 280
  reproduction-related, 285–287
  selective breeding in, 42–43
  sexual. *See* Sexual behavior
  species-common, 125–126
Behavioral biology. *See* Biopsychology
Behavioral development and perinatal hormones, 279–280
Behavioral methods of cognitive neuroscience, 124–125
Behavioral neuroscience. *See* Biopsychology
Behavioral ontogeny, 42–47
Behavioral paradigms, 120–**121**
Behavioral research methods, 120–128
Behavioral stereotypies, 146–147
Behaviorism (Watson), 20
Belladonna, 102
Benign tumors, 132, **133**
Benzodiazepines, **102,** 126, **317**–319, **462**–464
Between-subjects design, 6, **7**
Betz cells, **221**
Biceps, 225, 226
Bilateral lesions, 15, 351–359, 372–374. *See also* Lesion methods of brain surgery
Bilateral medial temporal lobectomy, **353,** 351–359, 366–372, 374–375

Bimodal cells, 215
Binges of cocaine use, 334, 335, 340
Binocular, defined, **167**
Binocular cortical cells, 167–168
Binocular disparity, **152,** 153
Biology of behavior. *See* Biopsychology
Biopsychological paradigms of animal behavior, 125–128
Biopsychology, **3**
  converging operations in, **11**–13
  dichotomies in, 20–23
  divisions of, 8–11
  genetics in. *See* Genetics
  modern model of, 23, 24. *See also* Genetics, modern model of
  as neuroscience discipline, 2, 3
  versus other neuroscience disciplines, 4
  research characterizing. *See* Research
  scientific inference in, 12–14
  study of, 2–3
Bipolar affective disorder, **460,** 461
Bipolar cells, 154, **155,** 174
Bipolar electrodes, 116
Bipolar neurons, **54,** 57
Bipolar recording in EEG, 109
Bipotential precursor, 278
Birdsong development, 44–45
Bisexuality, **290,** 291
B.J., case of, 360
Bladder, 255
Blind spots (scotomas), 154, **155,** 182–184, 401, 416, 417, 419
Blindness, 161
  color, 35
Blindsight, **184**–185
Blobs, **176,** 177
Block-design test, 122, 123, 212
Block-tapping memory span test, **354**
Blood
  volume of, 113, 254, 255, 257–259
  water in, 254
Blood-brain barrier, **52**–54, 259, 325
Blood flow, 133, 433–435
Blood-flow receptors, **256,** 257
Blood flow studies of cerebral cortex, 217–219
Blood glucose, 244–245, 264
Blood pressure
  high, 112, 113, 463
  and MAO inhibitors, 460, 461
  measuring, 113

Blood pressure receptors, 256–258
Blood supply to brain, disruption of, 132–135
Blood vessel dilation and blockage, 133
Blueprint hypothesis, **383,** 382–384
Body fat, 249–253
Body fluid regulation, 254–266
Body hair. *See* Hair *entries*
Body temperature, 303, 329, 332
Body weight. *See* Weight *entries*
Boluses, 125
Brain. *See also* Cerebral *entries*
 abnormal development of, 43–44
 abnormalities in, 459
 appearance of, 2
 areas of, in sleep and dreams, 312–314
 atrophy of, 107
 bleeding in, 132–135
 blood flow to, 133, 433–435
 blood supply to, disruption of, 132–135
 chemical activity of, 118
 chemical protection of (blood-brain barrier), 52–54, 259, 325
 complexity of, 2
 divisions and structures of, 65–76. *See also specific entries, e.g.:* Brain stem; Myelencephalon (medulla)
 edema in, 402, 428
 evolution of, 30–33
 of homosexuals, 292
 infections of, 135–137, 440–441
 lateralization in. *See* Lateralization
 memory structures of, 374–376
 neurotransmitters and receptors in, 118–120
 replacement parts for, 406–407
 reward circuits in, 341–345
 sexual differentiation of, 278–279, 414–415
 and sexual orientation, 291–292
 size and weight of, and intelligence, 30
 sleep-promoting circuits in, 310–311
 swelling of, 402
Brain-behavior interaction, 5
Brain damage
 accidental and disease-related, 429–430
 from alcohol, 12, 136, 332
 to amygdala, 440, 448–449

 to anterior temporal lobes, 440
 asomatognosia from, 21–22
 to auditory cortex, 192–193, 448–449
 to Broca's area, 425
 causes of, 131–137
 to cerebral cortex, 12
 and chemical senses, 204
 closed-head, 134–135
 effects of, studying, 131–148
 and emotions, 444–446
 and facial expression, 444–446
 to frontal lobes, 123
 to hippocampus, 368–372
 to inferotemporal cortex, 186, 188
 ischemic, 358–359, 369–372
 of Jimmie G., 2–3, 7, 12
 in Korsakoff's syndrome, 12, 13, 332, 333, 359–360, 367, 376
 and language-related abilities, 428–430
 to left hemisphere, 412, 414, 429–430
 through lesions. *See* Lesion *entries*
 to medial diencephalon, 359–360, 367
 neural reorganization after, 402, 404
 to posterior parietal cortex, 186
 to posterior parietal lobes, 197–198
 to prefrontal cortex, 360–361
 to prefrontal lobes, 44
 to prestriate cortex, 187, 188
 to primary auditory cortex, 192–193
 to primary motor cortex, 217
 to primary somatosensory cortex, 196
 to secondary auditory cortex, 192
 to secondary visual cortex, 187
 to sensory system, 180–181
 testing for, 121–123
 treating, with replacement parts, 406–407
 visualizing. *See* Brain-imaging techniques
Brain hemispheres. *See* Cerebrum (cerebral hemispheres, telencephalon); Lateralization; Left hemisphere; Right hemisphere; Split brain *entries*
Brain-imaging studies, 422

Brain-imaging techniques, 106–111, 124–125, 423, 430
 and hemispheric asymmetry, 423, 424
 during language-related activities, 433–435
 in lateralization studies, 413
 and pain localization, 199
 and schizophrenia, 459
 and secondary visual cortex, 186
Brain lesions. *See* Lesion *entries*
Brain-mind dualism (Descartes), 20, 21
Brain stem, **31, 65**–70. *See also* Ventromedial cortico–brain stem–spinal tract
 evolution of, 30–33
 structures of, 221–222
Brain stimulation, 14–15
 electrical. *See* Electrical brain stimulation
Brain surgery, 449. *See also specific entries, e.g.:* Lobectomy; Lobotomy
 on animals, 114–116, 415–417
 for epilepsy, 140
 lesion methods of, 114–116. *See also* Aspiration; Lesion *entries*
 stereotaxic, 114, 115
Brain tissue, sections of, 62, 63
Brain transplantation, 403–407
Brain tumors, 131–132
Breeding, selective, 42–43
Bregma, 114, **115**
Broca's aphasia, **424,** 425, 428, 430
Broca's area, 412, **413,** 423, 425–430, 434
Bronchitis from smoking, 331
Buerger's disease, **330,** 331
Bulimia nervosa, 235, **264,** 265
Burying, defensive. *See* Defensive burying *entries*
Buspirone, **462**–464
Buttons (of axon branches), 55
Butyrophenones, 458, **459**

C

CA1 subfield, **359**
Cafeteria diet, **242**–244
Calcium channels, 93
Calcium ions, 389, 391, 393, 395, 396
Canaries, birdsong in, 44, 45

Cancer, 195, 331. *See also* Tumors (neoplasms)
Cannabinoids, 333
Cannabis sativa, **333**
Cannon-Bard theory (of emotions), **439**–441
Cannulas, **117**
Carbachol, **260**
Carbohydrates, complex, 236, 237
Carbon monoxide, 98
Cardiovascular activity measures, 112–113
Carminatives, 336
Carotid artery, 108
Carousel apparatus, 306–**307**
Cartesian dualism, 20, **21**
Case studies, **7**–9
Castration (gonadectomy), 278, 279
Cataplexy, **319**
Catecholamines, 97, 98, 101, 317, 336
Cats
   decorticate, aggression in, 439
   and mice, interactions between, 446
   split-brain, 415–417
Caudal (posterior) direction, 62, 63
Caudal reticular formation REM-sleep circuits, 313
Caudate nucleus, 14–15, 75, 76
CCK (cholecystokinin), **248**–249
Cell bodies (somas), 55, 91
Cell-mediated immunity, **451**–453
Cell membranes of neurons, 54, 55, 57
Cells. *See also* Tumors (neoplasms)
   amacrine, 154, 155
   B (B lymphocytes), 451–454
   Betz, 221
   bimodal, 215
   binocular cortical, 167–168
   bipolar, 154, 155, 174
   color-coding and brightness-coding, 172–173
   complex, 167–168
   dual-opponent color, 176–177
   egg (ova), 34–36, 270, 379
   ependymal, 380
   fetal substantia nigra, 407
   glial, 58, 380–381. *See also* Astroglia (astrocytes); Oligodendroglia (oligodendrocytes)
   hair, 189, 190
   horizontal, 154, 155
   membrane potential of, 81–85

memory T, 452
monocular cortical, 167
muscle, 387
of nervous system, 54–59. *See also* Neural *entries;* Neurons
on-center and off-center, 166, 167
place, 372, 373
pyramidal, 72, 73, 78, 359
radial glial, 380, 381
Renshaw, 230
of retina, 154–156, 174
retinal ganglion, 154–157, 166, 381–383, 388
satellite, 58
Schwann, 58, 59, 398, 400, 407
simple, 167, 168
sperm, 34–36, 270, 379
stellate, 72, 73
T (T lymphocytes), 451–454
in visual cortex, 167–168
Cellular dehydration, **254**–259
Central canal, **52**
Central fissure, 71, 72, 76
Central nervous system (CNS), **50,** 51
   disorders of, neurotransplantation for, 406
   drug penetration of, 325
   myelin of, 142
   myelin stains in, 60
   neural structures in, 54, 58, 59
   protectors of, 52–53
   spinal cord of, 64–65, 194–195, 227, 379
Central sensorimotor programs, 231–**232**
Cephalic phase, **237,** 238
Cerebellum, 67, 76, 219, **375**
Cerebral abscesses, 135
Cerebral angiography, **106,** 107
Cerebral aqueduct, **52,** 53, 68, 76
Cerebral asymmetry theories, 423–425
Cerebral commissures, 71, **411.** *See also* Corpus callosum
Cerebral computed tomography, 106, 107. *See also* Computed tomography
Cerebral cortex, **8,** 9, 70–73, 76
   blood flow studies of, 217–219
   damage to, 12
   development of, 380
   sensorimotor areas of, 211–219
   sensory areas of, 180–182
Cerebral dialysis, 118, **119,** 290
Cerebral dialysis studies, 344
Cerebral dominance, 412, 413

Cerebral edema, 402, 428
Cerebral hemispheres. *See* Cerebrum (cerebral hemispheres, telencephalon)
Cerebral hemorrhages, 132, **133**
Cerebral ischemia, **133,** 132–135, 358–359, 369–372
Cerebral localization of language, 425–435
Cerebral ventricles, **52,** 53, 379
Cerebrospinal fluid (CSF), **52,** 53, 254
Cerebrovascular disorders, 123, 132–135. *See also* Strokes
Cerebrum (cerebral hemispheres, telencephalon), **31,** 65, 70–76
   in Alzheimer's disease, 143
   evolution of, 30–33
   lateralization of function in. *See* Lateralization; Left hemisphere; Right hemisphere; Split brain *entries*
   outer layer of. *See* Cerebral cortex
   removal of, 199, 433
   as self-stimulation site, 343
   of split-brain patients, 418
Cerveau isolé preparation, **310,** 311
Cervical region of spinal cord, 194
C-fos gene, 316
Channel proteins, 54, 57
Cheese effect, **460,** 461
Chemical lesions of brain, 117
Chemical senses, 201–204. *See also* Taste *entries*
Chemically activated ion channels, 94, **95**
Chemoaffinity hypothesis, 381–**383**
Chimeric figures test, **419**–420
Chimpanzees, 22–23, 29
Chlordiazepoxide, 102, 462, 463
Chlorpromazine, **457,** 456–458
Cholecystokinin (CCK), **248**–249
Cholesterol, 270
Choline acetyltransferase, 361
Cholinergic agonists, 313
Cholinergic antagonists, 313
Cholinergic neurons, 98
Cholinergic theory of memory, 361–362
Chordates, **27**
Chorea, 140
Choroid plexuses, **52,** 53
Chromatic colors (hues), **172**–177
Chromatographs, 118

Chromosomes, **35,** 34–40. *See also* DNA *entries;* Gene *entries;* Genetic *entries;* RNA
  in Alzheimer's disease, 143–144
  crossing over of, 35, 37
  in Down syndrome, 136, 137
  mapping, 35, 39, 41
  number of, 136–137, 270
  replication of, 38–40
  sex, 35, 270, 271
  structures of, 37, 38
  X and Y, 270, 271
Ciliary (eye) muscles, **152**
Cingulate cortex, 74–76, 199
Cingulate gyrus, 74, 76
Cingulate motor areas, 214
Circadian clock, **315,** 314–316
Circadian rhythms, **303,** 302–304, 315–316
Circadian sleep-wake cycles, 302–304, 316. *See also* Sleep deprivation
Circadian theories of sleep, 301–302, 304, 308–309
Cirrhosis, 332, **333**
Clitoris, 278
Clonus in seizures, 138, 139
Closed-head injuries, 134–135
Clozapine, 458, **459**
CNS. *See* Central nervous system
Cocaine (cocaine hydrochloride), **101, 334**–336, 338, 340, 347–348
Cocaine psychosis, **334,** 335
Cocaine sprees (binges), **334,** 335, 340
Cocaine withdrawal symptoms, 335
Cochlea, **189,** 190
Cochlear nuclei, 190–191
Cocktail-party phenomenon, **206**
Cocontraction (of muscles), **230**
Codeine, 336, **337**
Codes of ethics, 6
Codons, **39,** 40
Coexistence (of neurotransmitters), **93**
Cognitive-map theory (of hippocampal function), **372**–374
Cognitive neuroscience, 124–**125**
Cognitive processes, constituent, 124, 125
Collateral sprouting (of axon branches), **401,** 400–403
Colliculi, 68, 76
Colloids, 257
Colony-intruder paradigm, **125**–126

Colony model of aggression and defense, 445–446
Color agnosia, 187
Color blindness, 35
Color cells, dual-opponent, 176–177
Color constancy, **175,** 174–177
Color vision (perception), 172–177
Colors
  achromatic, 172
  chromatic, 172–177
  complementary, 172–173
  in electromagnetic spectrum, 151–152, 172–177
  of eyes, 152
Columnar organization
  of neocortex, 72, 73
  of primary visual cortex, 168–170
Commissurotomy, **411,** 417–419
Comparative approach, **5,** 32, **33**
Comparative psychology, 10–**11**
Complementary colors, **172**–173
Completion (by visual system), 154–**155, 184,** 419–420
Complex carbohydrates, 236, 237
Complex cells, **167**–168
Complex partial seizures, 138–**139**
Complexity of sound waves, 188
Component processing theory of taste, 203
Component theory (of color vision), **172**–174
Comprehension subtest of WAIS, 122
Computed tomography (CT), **106,** 107, 430, 459
Concentration gradients, 82
Concordance rates. *See* Twin studies
Concussions, **135,** 362–364
Conditional response, 126, 449
Conditional stimulus, 126, 242, 391, 392, 448, 449
Conditioned compensatory responses, **329**
Conditioned defensive burying paradigm, **128**
Conditioned drug tolerance, 328–**329,** 341
Conditioned fear, 448–449
Conditioned place-preference paradigm, **346**
Conditioned taste aversion, **126,** 127, 201
Conditioned withdrawal effects, **330**–331, 340

Conditioning
  fear, 448–449
  of hunger, 242
  Pavlovian. *See* Pavlovian conditioning *entries*
Conditioning paradigms, 126–127
Conduction aphasia, **424**–426
Cone vision, 155
Cones, **155**–159, 173–174
Configural association theory of hippocampal function, 374
Confounded variables, 6–**7**
Consolidation (of memories), **351**–352, 358, 363–364
Consolidation theory, 351–352, 358
Conspecifics, **27**
Constituent cognitive processes, 124, **125**
Constructional apraxia, 212, **213,** 421
Consummatory behaviors, **345**
Consumption. *See* Drinking; Eating
Contingent drug tolerance, **327**–328
Contralateral, defined, **69**
Contralateral neglect, 198, **199,** 212, **213,** 421
Contrast enhancement, 163–**165**
Contrast X-ray techniques, **106**–107
Contrecoup injuries, 134, **135**
Control-question technique, **441**
Contusions, 134–**135**
Convergence
  of eyes, 152–153
  of rods and cones, 156–157
Converging operations, 11–**13,** 129
Convolutions (on cerebrum), **31**
Convulsions, 138, **139**
Co-occurrence, **395,** 394–396
Coolidge effect, 6–**7**
Copulation, 270, **271**
Copulatory behavior, 289–290. *See also* Lordosis; Reproduction-related behavior
Coronal sections of brain tissue, 62, 63
Corpus callosum, 8, 71, **414**–418
Cortex
  adrenal, 271, 450, 451
  association. *See* Association cortex
  auditory, 190–193, 375, 426, 448–449
  cerebral. *See* Cerebral cortex
  cingulate, 74–76, 199

development of, inside-out pattern of, 380
electrical stimulation of, 430–432
entorhinal, 143, 367, 368
gustatory, 203, 204
hypothalamic anterior pituitary adrenal, 462–463
inferior prefrontal, 412, 413
inferotemporal, 186, 188, 374–375
lacking, 439
motor. *See* Motor cortex
neo-, 71–73, 76, 380
occipital, 183
orbitofrontal, 202–203
pain not represented in, 198–199
parietal, 183
perirhinal, 367, 368
posterior parietal. *See* Posterior parietal cortex
prefrontal. *See* Prefrontal cortex
premotor, 214, 215, 219
prestriate, 182, 183, 186–188
of primordial gonads, 275–278
pyriform, 202
rhinal, 143, 367–369, 371, 374
sensory. *See* Sensory cortex
somatosensory. *See* Somatosensory cortex
visual. *See* Visual cortex
Cortical damage. *See* Brain damage
Cortical mechanisms of vision, 183–188
Cortical plate, 380
Cortisol, 283–284
Courtship displays in evolution, 26–27
Crack, **334,** 335
Crackpot, 136
Cranial nerves, **50,** 51, 203, 204, 472, 473
Cresyl violet, 58, 60
Cribriform plate, 202
Cross-cuing, **419**
Cross-fostering control procedure, 42
Cross sections, **62,** 63
Cross tolerance, **325**
Crossing over (of chromosomes), **35,** 37
Cryogenic blockades, 115–116
Cryoprobes, 115
CSF (cerebrospinal fluid), **52,** 53, 254
CT (computed tomography), **106,** 107, 430, 459

Curare, 14, **102,** 165
Cutaneous (skin) receptors, 192–194
Cyanosis, 139
Cyclic AMP (cyclic adenosine monophosphate), **393**
Cyclic GMP (guanosine monophosphate), 160, 161
Cytochrome oxidase, **176,** 177
Cytoplasm, 39, 56
Cytosine nucleotide base, 37

D

D$_1$ and D$_2$ receptors, 458, 459
Darwin's theory of evolution of emotional expression, 438, 439, 442, 443
D.B., case of, 184
Deafness, 192, 193
Declarative memory theory of hippocampal function, 374
Decorticate, defined, **439**
Decussation, **69,** 195
Deep dyslexia, 432, **433**
Defeminization, **280**
Defensive attacks, 447, 448
Defensive behaviors, 125–126, **444**–448, 464
Defensive burying, 447
Defensive burying paradigm, 128
Defensive-burying test, 464
Dehydration, 254–259
Delayed-alternation test, **375**–376
Delayed matching-to-sample task, 213–214
Delirium tremens (DTs), 332, **333**
Delta opioid receptor, 338
Delta sleep, 298, **299**
Delta sleep-inducing peptide, **317**–318
Delta waves, **297**
Delusions in schizophrenia, 455
Demasculinization, **280**
Dementia, **135**
from alcohol, 332
in Alzheimer's disease, 143
in Huntington's disease, 140
Dendrites, 55
apical, 72, 78
growth of, 381
Dendritic spines, **90,** 91, **396**
Dendrodendritic synapses, 91
2-deoxyglucose (2-DG), 108, **109,** 118
Deoxyribonucleic acid. *See* DNA *entries*
Dependent variables, 6, **7**

Depolarization, **84**–88, 396
Deprenyl, 146, **147**
Depressants, 332, **333**
Depression, **459**–463
drugs treating. *See* Antidepressants
neural mechanisms of, 461–463
Deprivation-induced drinking, 255–260
Depth of focus, 152
Dermatomes, **194**
Descending motor pathways, 45, 221–224
Desynchronized EEG, **310**
Detector mechanism, 239
Detoxified addicts, 340, **341**
Dexamethasone, 462–463
Dexamethasone suppression test, **462,** 463
Dextrals (right-handers), **414**
D.F., case of, 187
2-DG (2-deoxyglucose), 108, **109,** 118
Diagonal band of Broca, 361
Diastoles, 113
Diazepam, 102, 146, 317, 462, 463
Dichotic listening test, **121, 413,** 421–422
Dichotomous traits, **33,** 34
Diencephalon, 65, 68–70, 76
damage to, 359–360, 367
as self-stimulation site, 343
Diet in phenylketonuria, 44
Diet-induced thermogenesis, **251,** 264
Dietary restriction effects, 250
Diethylstilbestrol, 279, 292
Difference image, 124
Differential diagnosis, 137
Digestion, **235**–238. *See also* Gastrointestinal tract
Digit span, **353**
Digit-span test, 122, **123**
Digit span + 1 test, **354**
Digit-symbol test, 122
Dihydrotestosterone, **279,** 286
Dilantin (diphenylhydantoin), 146
Dimorphic, defined, 275
Dipsogens, 258, **259**
Directed synapses, 92, **93**
Discriminated Pavlovian conditioning, 391–392
Disinhibition (of behaviors), **341**
Distal segments, **398,** 399
Diuretics, 332, **333**
Dizygotic (fraternal) twins, **46.** *See also* Twin studies
DNA (deoxyribonucleic acid), 37–40

DNA-binding proteins, 38–**39**
DNA oxidation, 332
Dominant genes, 137
Dominant hemisphere, **413,**
    412–414, 421–422,
    424–425
Dominant traits, **33,** 34
Dopamine, 97, 98
    in brain lesions, 117
    in Parkinson's disease, 81, 140,
        147, 407
    in phenylketonuria, 43
    release of, measuring, 118
    and sexual behavior, 345
Dopamine agonists, 344, 407
Dopamine antagonists, 344
Dopamine receptors, 456–457
Dopamine theory of schizophre-
    nia, 456–459
Dopamine-releasing neurons,
    343–347
Dorsal-column medial-lemniscus
    system, **194**–195
Dorsal columns, **194**–195
Dorsal direction, **62,** 63
Dorsal horns, 64, **65**
Dorsal raphé nucleus, **312,** 313
Dorsal root, 64–65, 194, 227
Dorsal root ganglia, 65
Dorsal stream, 186–**187**
Dorsolateral corticorubrospinal
    tract, **221,** 223–224
Dorsolateral corticospinal tract,
    221, 222, 224
Dorsolateral motor pathway,
    221–224
Dorsolateral prefrontal association
    cortex, **213,** 211–214
Dose-response curve, 325, 326
Down syndrome, 38, 136, **137,** 144
Dr. P, case of, 180–181, 187
Dreams, 299–301. *See also* Sleep
    entries
    brain areas in, 312–314
    latent, 300
    lucid, 301–302
Drinking
    and angiotensin II, 258–260
    complete cessation of, 246, 247
    deprivation-induced, 255–260
    excessive, 262, 263
    and satiety, 261–262
    sham, 260–262
    spontaneous, 260, 261
    and thirst and body fluid regu-
        lation, 254–266
    and water deficits, naturally
        occurring, 260

without water deficits, 260, 261
Drug abuse
    of alcohol, 332, 338
    of amphetamines, 146, 147
    of cocaine, 334–336, 338, 340,
        347–348
    of marijuana, 333–335, 338
    of opiates, 334, 336–338
    in Parkinson's disease symp-
        toms, 147, 148
    of tobacco, 330–332, 338, 347,
        348
Drug addiction, 324, 327,
    331–341, 346–347
Drug addicts, 327, 340, 341
Drug control, 336–340
Drug-effect theory of contingent
    drug tolerance, 328
Drug metabolism, **325.** *See also*
    Metabolic tolerance
Drug self-administration para-
    digm, **126,** 127, **346**
Drug tolerance, 318, **325**–329
    to alcohol, 332
    to cocaine, 335
    conditioned, 328–329, 341
    to marijuana, 334
    to opiates, 337
Drug withdrawal effects, 318,
    326–327, 330–334, 337,
    340, 341
Drug withdrawal programs, 340
Drug withdrawal syndrome, 326,
    327, 332, 333, 337
Drugs
    absorption of, 324–325
    action of, principles of,
        324–327
    administration of, 117, 324–325
    analgesic, 99, 199–200, 336, 337.
        See also Opiate *entries*
    anticonvulsant, 102, 140, 146,
        327–328
    antidepressant, 460–462. *See*
        also Monoamine oxidase
        inhibitors
        tricyclic, 308, 309, 317, 319,
            460, 461
    antihypnotic, 317
    antipsychotic, 136
    antischizophrenic, 146, 147,
        456–459
    antithiamine, 376
    as anxiety disorder treatment,
        463–464
    anxiolytic (antianxiety), 102,
        126, 128, 462–464. *See also*
        Benzodiazepines

cutting, 337
dependence on
    physical, 326–327, 332, 337,
        340, 341. *See also* Drug
        withdrawal *entries*
    psychological, 327
depressant, 332, **333**
diuretic, 332, 333
elimination of, 325
emetic, 127
hypnotic, 317, 318, 463
ingestion of, 324
inhalation of, 324
injection of, 324, 325
legality versus safety of, 324
memory-improving, 362, 363
narcotic, 334. *See also* Opiate
    entries
neuroleptic, 458–459
in neurological disorder treat-
    ment, 136
neurotoxic effects of, 136
opiate. *See* Opiate *entries*
overdose of, 329, 335–336
problem of, solution to,
    338–340
psychoactive, 101–103, 324,
    331–340, 462–464. *See*
    also specific entries,
    e.g.: Cocaine (cocaine
    hydrochloride);
    Tobacco
research methods using,
    117–120
sensitization to, 326, 327, 335
serotonergic, 317
sleep influence of, 317–319
stimulant. *See* Amphetamines;
    Stimulant drugs
    and synaptic transmissions,
        99–103
in ulcer treatment, 450
use of, prevalence of, 338
DTs (delirium tremens), 332,
    333
Dual-opponent color cells,
    176–177
Dual-route parallel models, 432
Duchenne smile, **444**
Duck-billed platypus, 29
Duodenum, **248**
Duplexity theory of vision, **155**
Dura mater, **52,** 53
Dynamic contraction (of mus-
    cles), **225**
Dynamic phase (of VMH syn-
    drome), **245**
Dyslexia, 432–**433**

E

Ear, anatomy of, 189–190. *See also* Auditory *entries*
Eardrum (tympanic membrane), 189, 190
Eating
    complete cessation of, 245–247
    drinking associated with, 261
    excessive, 245–247
    and hunger
        and body weight, 235–253
        theories of, 239–244, 250–253
    sham, 242–243
Eating behavior determinants, 241–244
Eating disorders, 235, 263–266
ECG (electrocardiogram), **112,** 113
ECS (electroconvulsive shock), **363,** 362–364
Ectoderm layer, 379, 380
Edema in brain, 402, 428
Edge perception, 163–171
EEG, sleep, stages of, 297–299
EEG waves during sleep, 296–298. *See also* Slow-wave sleep
EEGs. *See* Electroencephalo-*entries*
Effector mechanism, 239
Efferent nerves, **50,** 51
Efflux, 85
Egg cells (ova), 34–36, 270, 379
Ejaculation, **126, 280**
EKG (electrocardiogram), **112,** 113
Electrical brain stimulation, 116, 126, 127, 145
    and language localization, 430–432
    and pain control, 199, 200
    and ulcers, 451
Electrocardiogram (ECG, EKG), **112,** 113
Electroconvulsive shock (ECS), **363,** 362–364
Electrode holders, 114, 115
Electrodermal activity measures, 112
Electrodes, bipolar, 116
Electroencephalograms (EEGs), 10, **11,** 109, **297**
    desynchronized, 310
    in epilepsy diagnosis, 138, 139
    invasive recording with, 116, 117
Electroencephalographs, 109

Electroencephalography, **109**–111
Electromagnetic spectrum, 151–152, 172–177
Electromyograms (EMGs), 111, 112, **297**
Electromyography (EMG), **111,** 112, 444
Electron microscopy, **60,** 61
Electrooculograms (EOGs), 111, **297**
Electrooculography, **111**–112
Electrophysiological recording methods, 116, 117
Electrostatic pressure, 82–85
Elevated four-arm maze, 372–373
Elevated plus maze, **126**
Elevated-plus-maze test, 464
Embolism, **133**
Embolus, 133
Emergent stage 1 EEG, **297**
Emetic drugs, 127
EMGs. *See* Electromyograms; Electromyography
Emotions. *See also* Fear
    and autonomic nervous system, 441–442
    and brain damage, 444–446
    disorders of, 459–463
    expression of, 438, 439, 442–445
    and hemispheric dominance, 421
    and limbic system, 439–441
    and pain, 199
    physiological measures of, 112–113
    research on, 438–446
    theories of, 438–441
Emphysema from smoking, 331
Empirical (observational) methods, 12
Encapsulated tumors, **131**–132
Encéphale isolée preparation, **310**
Encephalitis, **135**
Encephalomyelitis, 142, 143
Endocrine glands, **269,** 270
Endoderm layer, 379, 380
Endogenous chemicals, 337–338
Endogenous depression, **460**
Endogenous neurotoxins, 136
Endogenous sleep factors, **317**–318
Endoplasmic reticulum, 56
Endorphins, 98–99, **199,** 285, 338
Energy flow and digestion, 235–238
Energy metabolism, 237–238
Energy set point, 239

Energy utilization and food intake, 250–251
Engrams, **351**
Enriched environments, 387
Entorhinal cortex, 143, 367, 368
Entrainment, 302
    of circadian rhythms, 316
Environment. *See* Experience
Enzymatic degradation, **96**
Enzymes, **96**
EOGs. *See* Electrooculograms; Electrooculography
Ependymal cells, 380
Epidemiology, 142, **143**
Epilepsy, **137**–140
    development of, 145–146
    and electrical brain stimulation, 431–432
    kindling model of, 145–146
    treatment for, 417–418
Epileptic auras, 138, **139**
Epileptogenesis, **145**–146
Epinephrine, 97, 98, 269
Epiphyses, 284
EPSPs (excitatory postsynaptic potentials), **84**–88
Equipotentiality principle, 127, 351
ERPs (event-related potentials), **109**–110
Estradiol, 270, **271,** 290
    testosterone converted to, 279, 280
Estrogen replacement therapy, 287
Estrogens, 270, **271,** 276, 286
    synthetic (diethylstilbestrol), 279, 292
Estrous cycle, **286,** 287
Estrus, **286**–287, 290
Ethics, codes of, 6
Ethoexperimental research, **444**–447
Ethological research, **11**
Ethology, 21. *See also* Animal behavior
Etiology, 145
Event-related potentials (ERPs), **109**–110
Evoked potentials, 109–111
Evolution, **23**–33, 424–425
    of emotional expression, 438, 439, 442, 443
Excision, 428
Excitatory amino acids, 133–135, 139
Excitatory areas, antagonistic, 196, 198
Excitatory postsynaptic potentials (EPSPs), **84**–88

Exercise and weight loss, 264
Exocrine glands, **269**
Exocytosis, **93,** 94
Experience
 in affective disorder development, 460
 and genetics, 20–21, 23, 24, 42–47. *See also* Nature-nurture issue
 in learning and memory, 388–397
 and neural development, 387–388
 and schizophrenia, 456
Experimental autoimmune encephalomyelitis, 142, **143**
Experimental psychology, 20–21
Experiments in research, 5–7
Explicit memories, **356,** 359, 361
Expression of Emotions in Man and Animals, The (Darwin), 438, 439
Expressivity, **424,** 425
Extensors, **225,** 226
External reproductive organs, 278, 279
Exteroceptive sensory systems, 180, **181**
Exteroceptive system, 193
Extinction, 219, **448,** 449
Extracellular fluid compartments, 254, 255
Extracellular unit recording, 116, 117
Extrafusal muscle (skeletal muscle), **227,** 226–228
Eye-blink-conditioning circuit, 375
Eye movement, 13–14
Eye muscles, 152
Eyes. *See also* Vision; Visual *entries*
 anatomy of, 152, 153. *See also specific entries, e.g.:* Cones; Retina *entries*
 color of, 152
 control of, 210–212
 convergence of, 152–153
 coordinated, 152–153
 light entering, 151–153
 measuring, 111–112
 rapid, 297–298. *See also* REM *entries*
 and receptive field research, 165
 in vision, 158–159

F

Faces
 in chimeric figures test, 419–420

recognizing, 187–188
Facial electromyography, 444
Facial expression
 and cortical damage, 444–446
 and emotions, 442–444
 and right hemisphere, 421
Facial feedback hypothesis, **443**
Facial nerves, 203, 204, 473
False transmitters, 456, **457**
Far-field potentials, 110, **111**
FAS (fetal alcohol syndrome), 332, **333**
Fasciculation, **383**
Fast muscle fibers, 224
Fasting phase, **237**–238
Fats (lipids), 236–237. *See also* Body fat
Fatty acids, 238
Fear, **444.** *See also* Anxiety *entries*
 conditioned, 448–449
 research on, 445–449
Fear conditioning, **448**–449
Feminization, **280**
Fertility, 286–287
Fertilization of ova, 34–36
Fetal alcohol syndrome (FAS), 332, **333**
Fetal hormones, 275–278
Fetal substantia nigra cells, 407
Filopodia, 381, 382
Finches
 birdsong in, 44, 45
 evolution of, 25
Finger maze test, 218–219
Finger-tapping test, 424
First messengers, 95
First-night phenomenon, **297**
Fissures of telencephalon, 71, 72, 76
Fitness (in natural selection), **25**
Flavor, **200,** 201, 261
Flexors, **225,** 226
Flight and freezing, 447
Fluid, body, regulation of, 254–266
Fluid compartments, 254, 255
Focus, depth of, 152
Follicle-stimulating hormone (FSH), **274**
Follicles, **274**
Forebrain, 65, 66, 379, 382
 anterior, 45
 basal. *See* Basal forebrain *entries*
Fornix, 74, 76
Fos protein, 316
Fourier analysis, **171,** 189
Fovea, **155,** 154–158, 161, 166
Fraternal (dizygotic) twins, **46.** *See also* Twin studies

Freddie the Finn, 235, 238
Free fatty acids, **238**
Free nerve endings, **192,** 193
Free radicals, **330**–332
Free-running circadian sleep-wake cycles, 302–303, 316
Free-running period, **303**
Free-running rhythms, **303**
Freezing and flight, 447
Frequency of sound waves, 188
Freudian theory of dreams, 300
Frontal eye field, **210**–212
Frontal lobe (of telencephalon), 71, 72, 76
Frontal lobe damage, 123
Frontal operculum, **423**
FSH (follicle-stimulating hormone), **274**
Functional approach (to research), 32, **33**
Functional MRI, 108, **109,** 124–125, 413
Functional segregation, **181,** 182, 185–187, 209
Functional tolerance, 326, **327**

G

G protein, 95
G-protein linked receptors, **95,** 94–96, 161, 338, 393
GABA (gamma-aminobutyric acid), 97, 98, 154
GABA agonists, 102, 375, 463, 464
GABA receptor, 463, 464
Gametes, 34, **35**
Gamma-aminobutyric acid. *See* GABA *entries*
Ganglia, **54.** *See also* Retinal ganglion cells
 basal, 73–76, 219
 dorsal root, 73–76, 219
Gastric ulcers, 450–**451**
Gastritis, 332
Gastrointestinal tract, 235, 236. *See also* Digestion
 in hunger and satiety, 248–250
 ulcers in, 450–451
Gate-control theory, **199**
Gene expression, 38–**39**
Gene maps, 35, 39, 41
Gene mutations, 38, 39, 43
General paresis, **135**
Generalizability, **8**
Generalized anxiety disorders, **462,** 463
Generalized epilepsy, 138, 139
Generalized seizures, 138, **139**

Genes, **33.** *See also* Chromosomes
abnormal, 38, 39
in affective disorders, 460
in Alzheimer's disease, 143–144
in brain damage, 136–137
in circadian rhythms, 315–316
dominant and recessive, 137
in Huntington's disease, 140–141
in multiple sclerosis, 142
operator, 38–39
and schizophrenia, 456
and sexual orientation, 291–292
structural, 38–40
tumor suppressor, 132
Genetic code, 38–40
Genetic metabolic disorders, 43–44
Genetic traits, 33–35
Genetics
and experience, 20–21, 23, 24, 42–47. *See also* Nature-nurture issue
Mendelian, 33–34
modern model of, 23, 24, 32–47
and personality, 46, 47
of psychological development, 45–47
Genitals, 278, **279.** *See also* Reproductive organs
Genome mapping, 39, 41
Genotypes, **33**
Gill-withdrawal reflex in Aplysia, 388–393
Glabrous skin, **192,** 193
Glands, 269, 270. *See also* Hormones
adrenal, 270, 271
endocrine, 269, 270
exocrine, 269
mammary, 27
pituitary. *See* Pituitary gland
sweat, 112
Glans, 278
Glaucoma and marijuana, 335
Glial cells, **58,** 380–381. *See also* Astroglia (astrocytes); Oligodendroglia (oligodendrocytes)
Global amnesia, **354**
Global aphasia, **430**
Globus pallidus, 75, 76
Glossopharyngeal nerves, 203, 204, 473
Glucagon, **237,** 238
Glucocorticoids, 450, **451**
Gluconeogenesis, **238,** 246
Glucose, **237,** 236–238
blood, 244–245, 264

Glucostatic theory, 239–**241,** 244
Glutamate, 97, 98, **133, 395**–396
in brain damage, 133–135
in retina, 154, 161
Glycine, 97, 98
Glycogen, 236–237
GMP, cyclic (guanosine monophosphate), 160, 161
G.O., case of, 210
Golgi complex, 56, 92, **93**
Golgi stain, **58,** 60, 78
Golgi tendon organs, **225**–226
Gonadal hormones, 270–272, 275, 276, 285–288
in females, 286–287
in males, 285–286
Gonadectomy, 278, **279**
Gonadotropin release, 279, 288
Gonadotropin-releasing hormone, **274**–275
Gonadotropins, **271,** 276
Gonads, 270, **271,** 275–276
Graded responses, **84,** 85
Grammatical analysis, 432, **433**
Grand mal seizures, **139**
Gray matter, 64, 65
Growth cones, **381**–385
Growth hormone, **280**
Guanine nucleotide base, 37
Guanosine monophosphate (cyclic GMP), 160, 161
Guilty-knowledge technique, 442, **443**
Gustation, 201
Gustatory afferents, 203, 204
Gustatory cortex, 203, 204
Gustatory deficits, 204
Gustatory pathways, 203, 204
Gustatory system, 201, 203–204
Gut peptides, 476
Gut satiety peptides, 248–250
Gynecomastia, 288
Gyri
angular, 426, 427, 435
cingulate, 74, 76
Heschl's, 423
hippocampal dentate, 393–395
postcentral, 71, 72, 76, 195
precentral, 71, 72, 76, 216
superior temporal, 71, 72, 76
of telencephalon, 71, 72, 76

H

H-Y antigen, **274**–276
Habituation, **389,** 388–390, 393
Hair
axillary (underarm), 280, 281

excessive growth of, 288
pubic, 280, 281
Hair cells, **189,** 190
Hairless skin, 192, 193
Hallucinations, 320, 455
Haloperidol, **457**–458
Handedness, 414–425
Hangovers, 332
Harrison Narcotics Act, 336, **337**
Hash oil, 333
Hashish, **333**
Head holders, 114, 115
Health and stress, 449–455
Heart rate measures, 112, 113
Hebb's postulate for learning, 394
Helping-hand phenomenon, **419**
Hematomas, 134, **135**
Hemianopsic patients, **184**
Hemiretinas, 156, 157, 161, 162
Hemispherectomy, 199, **433**
Heritability estimates, **46,** 47
Heroin, **337,** 336–338
overdose of, 329
synthetic, and Parkinson's symptoms, 147, 148
Heroin rush, 337
Herpes virus, 136
Heschl's gyrus, **423**
Heterosexuality, **290**–292
Heterozygous organisms, **33**
Hierarchical organization, **181,** 180–183, 209–210
Hierarchy of social dominance, 26
High-acuity vision, 154, 156
Hindbrain, 65, 66, 379
Hippocampal dentate gyrus, 393–395
Hippocampal slice preparations, 393
Hippocampal transplants, 404–405
Hippocampus, 71, 73, 74, 76, 352, **353**
in Alzheimer's disease, 143
components of, 358–359
damage to, 368–372
lesions of, 371–374
long-term potentiation in, 393–397
and memory for space (location), 372–374
of monkeys, 367, 368
Hircismus, 112
Hirsutism, 288
Histamine antagonists, 450
H.M., case of, 351–358, 360, 366, 367, 369, 376, 402
Homeostasis, **238,** 239
and sleep, 301–302

Homeostatic theory of contingent drug tolerance, 328
Hominids, **29**
  evolution of, 29–31, 424, 425
Homo erectus, **29**
Homo sapiens, 29–30
Homologous animal models, **145**
Homosexuality, **290**–292
Homozygous organisms, **33**
Horizontal cells (in retina), 154, **155**
Horizontal sections (of brain tissue), **62,** 63
Hormones, **269.** *See also* Androgens
  categories of, 269–270
  replacement injections of, 285–286, 291
  and secondary sex characteristics, 280–281
  and sex, 269–292
  and sexual development, 275–285
  and sexual orientation, 291–292
  types of. *See specific entries, e.g.:* Hypothalamic hormones; Sex hormones
5-HT (5-hydroxytryptamine), 97, 98
5-HTP (5-hydroxytryptophan), **317**
Hues, 172–177
Human genome project, **39,** 41
Human subjects in research, 5
Hunger
  blood glucose in, 244–245
  conditioning of, 242
  defined, 239
  and eating
    and body weight, 235–253
    theories of, 239–244, 250–253
  gastrointestinal tract in, 248–250
  hypothalamus in, 245–248
  neural mechanisms of, 244–250
  premeal, 242
Huntington's disease (chorea), 137, **140**–141
Hybrid RNA, 120
Hybridization, in situ, 119–120
Hydrocephalus, 53
Hydrochloric acid, 450–451
6-hydroxydopamine (6-OHDA), 117, 344, 407
5-hydroxytryptamine (5-HT), 97, 98

5-hydroxytryptophan (5-HTP), **317**
Hyperinsulinemia, **246**
Hyperphagia, **245**–247
Hyperpolarization, **84**–89
Hypersomnia, 318, **319**
Hypertension, **112,** 113, 463
Hyperthermia, 332
Hypertonic solutions, **254,** 255
Hypnogogic hallucinations, **320**
Hypnotic drugs, **317,** 318, 463
Hypoglossal nerve, 473
Hypothalamic anterior pituitary adrenal cortex system, 462–463
Hypothalamic hormones, 8
Hypothalamic peptides, 476
Hypothalamic releasing hormones, 273–274, 276
Hypothalamopituitary portal system, **272,** 273
Hypothalamus, 69–70, 76
  anterior, third interstitial nucleus of, 292
  and fear conditioning, 449
  in hunger and satiety, 245–248
  lateral preoptic area of, 256
  male versus female, 288–291
  medial preoptic area of, 288–290
  nuclei of, 475
  and pituitary gland, 272–274, 276
  and sexual behavior, 288–291
  sexual differentiation of, 279
  ventromedial and lateral, 245–247
Hypothermic, defined, **329**
Hypotonic solutions, **254,** 255
Hypovolemia, **254,** 255, 257–259
Hypoxia, **139**
Hysterectomy, 287

I

I-want-a-girl-just-like-the-girl-who-married-dear-old-dad phenomenon, 201
Iatrogenic disorders, 318, **319**
Ibotenic acid, 117
ICSS (intracranial self-stimulation), **341**–345
Identical (monozygotic) twins, **46.** *See also* Twin studies
IM (intramuscular) drug administration, 117, 324, **325**
Imipramine, **460,** 461

Immune function and stress, 453–454
Immune reaction, 118
Immune system, 334, **451**–454
Immunity, antibody- and cell-mediated, 451–453
Immunocytochemistry, 118–**119**
Implicit memories, **356,** 359, 361
Impotence, **285**
In situ hybridization, **119**–120
In vivo voltammetry, 118, **119**
INAH 3 (third interstitial nucleus of anterior hypothalamus), 292
Incoherent thought in schizophrenia, 455
Incomplete-pictures test, **354**–357
Incus, 189, 190
Independent variables, 6, **7**
Indolamines, 97, 98
Induction, 379–**381**
  of long-term potentiation, 395–397
Infections
  of brain, 135–137, 440–441
  and stress, 451–454
Inferior, defined, **62**
Inferior colliculi, 68, 76, **191**
Inferior prefrontal cortex, 412, 413
Inferotemporal cortex, 143, **182,** 183, 186, 188, 374–**375**
Infiltrating tumors, 132, **133**
Influx, 85
Infrared waves, 152
Inhibition, release from, 402, 403
Inhibitory areas, antagonistic, 196, 198
Inhibitory factors, **272**–274
Inhibitory postsynaptic potentials (IPSPs), **84**–88
Initial stage 1 EEG, **297,** 298
Inside-out pattern of cortical development, 380
Insomnia, 317–**319**
Instinctive behaviors, **21**
Instrumental behaviors, 345
Insulin, **237**–238
  and body fat, 249–250
  and drinking, 261
  and eating, 244, 246
  and obesity, 264
Insulin receptors, 250
Integration (of postsynaptic potentials), **86,** 87
Intelligence
  and brain size and weight, 30
  twin studies of, 46–47
Intelligence quotient (IQ), 121, 122

Intelligence tests, 121, 122. *See also* Wechsler Adult Intelligence Scale
Intermediate zone of neural tube, 380
Internal desynchronization, **303**
Interneurons, **54,** 57, 380, 391
Interoceptive system, 193
Interstitial fluid, 254
Intracellular fluid compartments, 254, 255
Intracellular unit recording, 116, 117
Intracranial self-stimulation (ICSS), **341**–345
Intrafusal motor neuron, 226, **227**
Intrafusal muscle, 226, **227**
Intralaminar nuclei, 195, 196
Intramuscular (IM) drug administration, 117, 324, **325**
Intraperitoneal (IP) drug administration, 117
Intraspecific defense, 447
Intravenous (IV) drug administration, 117, 324, **325**
Intromission, **126, 280**
Intruders in colony-intruder paradigm, 125
Invasive EEG recording, 116, 117
Ion-channel linked receptors, **95,** 94–96, 393
Ion channels, **82,** 83
    chemically activated, 94, 95
    voltage-activated, 88–89
Ionic basis
    of action potentials, 88–89
    of resting potentials, 82–85
Ions, **82**–85
    calcium, 389, 391, 393, 395, 396
IP (intraperitoneal) drug administration, 117
Iproniazid, **460**–461
Ipsilateral, defined, **69**–70
IPSPs (inhibitory postsynaptic potentials), **84**–88
IQ (intelligence quotient), 121, 122. *See also* Intelligence *entries*
Irises, 152
Ischemic brain damage, 358–**359,** 369–372
Islands of memory, 362, **363**
Isometric contraction (of muscles), **225**
Isomorphic animal models, **145**
Isotonic solutions, **254,** 255
IV (intravenous) drug administration, 117, 324, **325**

J

Jacksonian seizures, 138, 139
James-Lange theory (of emotions), 438–441, **439**
Jet lag, 303–**305**
Jimmie G., case of, 2–3, 7, 12
Joints (of marijuana), 333

K

K complexes, **297,** 298
Kainic acid, 117
Ketones, **238**
Kidneys
    hormone from, 258, 259
    water and sodium regulation by, 255–257
Kindling model of epilepsy, 145–146
Kindling phenomenon, **145**
Kluver-Bucy syndrome, 440–**441**
Knife cuts in brain surgery, 115
Korsakoff's syndrome, 12, **13,** 332, **333, 359**–360, 367, 376

L

Labia majora, 278
Labia minora, 278
Labioscrotal swellings, 278
Laboratory animals. *See* Animal *entries*
Language
    analysis of, 432, 433
    comprehension of, 412–415, 424, 425, 428, 430
    parallel processing of, 432–433
    use of, 412–415
Language ability tests, 123
Language lateralization tests, 121, 412–415
Language localization, 425–435
Language-related abilities
    brain damage affecting, 428–430
    elimination of, 430
    hemispheric asymmetries in, 423–425
    lateralization of, 414, 422
Language-related activities, brain-imaging techniques during, 433–435
Latent dreams, 300
Lateral bodies, 278
Lateral communication in retina, 154

Lateral direction, **62,** 63
Lateral fissure, 71, 72, 76, 191, 192, 203, 204
Lateral geniculate nuclei, 69, 76, **161**–162, 166, 186
Lateral hypothalamus (LH), **245**–247
    pathway to, 448, 449
Lateral inhibition (mutual inhibition), 164–**165**
Lateral lemniscus, 191
Lateral plexus, 164, **165**
Lateral preoptic area of hypothalamus, 256
Lateral superior olives, 191
Lateral tegmental field, 290
Lateralization. *See also* Cerebrum (cerebral hemispheres, telencephalon); Left hemisphere; Right hemisphere; Split brain *entries*
    evolution of, 424–425
    of function, **411**–436
    of language, tests of, 121, 412–415
    sex differences in, 414–415
    of speech, 414
    statistical versus all-or-none, 422
    theories of, 423–424
Laudanum, 336
L-DOPA, 81, 97, **140,** 407
Lead as neurotoxin, 136
Leaky-barrel model, **251,** 252
Learned behavior versus genetics, 20–21, 23. *See also* Experience; Nature-nurture issue
Learned taste preferences and aversions, 241–242
Learning, 388, **389**
    age-limited and open-ended, 44, 45
    associative, 391–392
    and drinking, 261
    Hebb's postulate for, 394
    and long-term potentiation, 394–395
    neural bases of, 388–397
    nonassociative, 388–391
    sensorimotor, 219
    and sensorimotor control, 210–211
    simultaneous, 419–420
    visual-discrimination, 415–417
Learning paradigms, 126–128. *See also* Conditioning *entries*
Left-handers, 414

Left hemisphere. *See also* Lateralization
  damage to, 412, 414, 429–430
  as dominant, 412–414,
    421–422, 424–425
  electrical stimulation of,
    431–432
  and language, 121
  perceptual-motor testing of,
    123
  versus right hemisphere,
    421–425
Lens
  of eye, 152, 153
  Z, 420–422
Lesion methods of brain surgery,
  114–116. *See also* Aspiration
Lesion studies
  of fear conditioning, 448
  of intracranial self-stimulation,
    344–345
  of speech lateralization and
    handedness, 414
Lesions
  amygdala, 371
  bilateral, 15, 351–359, 372–374
  of Broca's area, 425
  through chemicals, 117
  in corpus callosum, 415–418
  in cortex, 428–429
  hippocampal, 371–374
  mediodorsal nucleus, 369
  in optic chiasm, 416–417
  for pain treatment, 195
  rhinal cortex, 371
  septal, 126
Leucotome, **15**
Leucotomy. *See* Lobotomy
Lexical procedure, 432–**433**
LH (lateral hypothalamus),
  245–247
LH (lateral hypothalamus) syndrome, 246
LH (luteinizing hormone), **274**
Librium, 102, 317, 462, 463
Lidocaine, 335
Lie detection (polygraphy),
  441–442
Ligands, 118, **119**
Light
  brightness of, 157–158,
    163–167
  converted into neural signals,
    159–161
  defined, 151
  intensity of, 152, 157–158,
    170–171
  reaching retina, 152–161

refraction of, 152
theories of, 151
wavelengths of, 151–152,
    157–158, 163–167, 172–177
Light perception, 151–153,
    157–158, 163–167
Limbic system, 73–76, 439–**441**
Linkage (of genetic traits), 34–**35**
Lipectomy, **252**, 253
Lipid bilayer, 54, 57
Lipids (fats), 236–**237**. *See also*
  Body fat
Lipogenesis, **246**
Lipolysis, **246**
Lipostatic theory, 240, **241**
Lissencephalic brains, 70
Lithium, **460**–462
Liver scarring, 332, 333
Lizard, The (Klawans), 81
Lobectomy, **353**, 351–359,
    366–372, 374–375
Lobes
  anterior temporal, 440
  frontal, 71, 72, 76, 123
  medial temporal, 143, 367, 368
  posterior parietal, 196–198
  prefrontal, 15, 44
  of telencephalon, 71, 72, 76
Lobotomy, **353**
  prefrontal, 15–17, 199
  transorbital, 15, 16
Localization of language, 425–435
Location, memory for, 372–374.
    See also Spatial *entries*
Locus coeruleus, **312**, 313
Long-term memory, 351–352, 393
Long-term potentiation (LTP),
    393–397
Longitudinal fissure, 71, 76
Lordosis, 6, **7, 126, 280,** 286–287,
    290
Lordosis quotient, **126**
Loudness, 188
LTP (long-term potentiation),
    393–397
Lucid dreams, **301**–302
Lumbar region of spinal cord, 194
Lung cancer from smoking, 331
Lung damage from marijuana use,
    334
Luteinizing hormone (LH), **274**
Lymphocytes, **451**

M

M layers (magnocellular layers),
    161–162, 166
M pathway, 162, 186

Mach bands, 164
Macrophages, **451**–452
Mad Hatter, 136
Magnetic resonance imaging
    (MRI), **106**–109, 124–125
  brain damage visualized by, 430
  and hemispheric asymmetry,
    423, 424
  in lateralization studies, 413
  and schizophrenia, 459
Magnocellular layers (M layers),
    161–162, 166
Malignant tumors, 132, **133**
Malleus, 189, 190
Mamawawa (men-are-men and
    women-are-women) atti-
    tude, 269, 275, 276, 285
Mammals, **27**
  evolution of, 27–31
  hippocampus of, long-term
    potentiation in, 393–397
  neural regeneration in, 398–401
  sleep of, hours of, 301
Mammary glands, 27
Mammillary bodies, 69, 70, 76,
    359, 360
Man with a Shattered World, The
    (Luria), 131
Mania, **460,** 461
Manifest dreams, 300
Mantle of Aplysia, 388, 392
MAO (monoamine oxidase), 146,
    147
MAO (monoamine oxidase)
    inhibitors, 146, **147,**
    460–461
Marijuana use and abuse,
    333–335, 338
Masculinization, **280**
Mass action principle, 351
Massa intermedia, 69, 76
Matching-to-sample task, delayed,
    213–214
Matching-to-sample test, **354**–355
Maternal defensive behaviors, 447
Maze-bright and maze-dull rats,
    42–43
Meals, 239
Mechanical stimuli, 193
Medial diencephalon damage,
    359–360, 367
Medial direction, **62,** 63
Medial dorsal nuclei, **202**
Medial geniculate nuclei, 69, 76,
    191, 448–449
Medial lemniscus, **194,** 195
Medial preoptic area (of hypothal-
    amus), **289,** 288–290
Medial septal nucleus, 361

Medial superior olives, 191
Medial temporal lobe, 143, 367, 368
Medial temporal lobectomy, 351–359, 366–372, 374–375
Mediodorsal nuclei, **359,** 360, 369, 376
Medulla
  of brain (myelencephalon), 65–67, 76, 343
  of primordial gonads, 275–278
Medullary pyramids, 221
Medullary relay nucleus, 202, 203
Meiosis, **35,** 34–37
Membrane potentials, **81**–91
Memory(ies), **351,** 388, **389**
  cholinergic theory of, 361–362
  consolidation of, 351–352, 359, 363–364
  declarative, 374
  explicit, 356, 359, 361
  implicit, 356, 359, 361
  islands of, 362, 363
  long-term, 351–352, 393
  and long-term potentiation, 394–395
  neural bases of, 388–397
  object-recognition, 366–372, 374
  reference, 372
  sensorimotor, 375
  short-term, 122, 351–352, 393
  for space (location), 372–374
  tests of, 121–123, 354–357
  working, 372
Memory deficits. *See also* Amnesia; Korsakoff's syndrome
  anterograde and retrograde, 361
  from bilateral medial temporal lobectomy, 351–359, 366–372, 374–375
  from predementia Alzheimer's disease, 361
  from prefrontal cortex damage, 360–361
Memory fields, 213
Memory-improving drugs, 362, 363
Memory storage theories, 351–352. *See also* Memory(ies), long-term; Memory(ies), short-term
Memory structures of brain, 374–376
Memory T cells, 452
Men-are-men and women-are-women (mamawawa) attitude, 269, 275, 276, 285

Mendelian genetics, 33–34
Meninges, **52,** 53
Meningiomas, **131**–132
Meningitis, **135**
Menstrual cycle, **272,** 275, 477
Menstruation, cessation of, 288
Mental illness and prefrontal lobotomy, 15–17. *See also* Psychiatric disorders
Mental retardation and phenylketonuria, 43–44
Mercury as neurotoxin, 136
Merkel's disks, 193
Mesencephalon (midbrain), 65, 66, 68, 76, 343, 379
Mesocortical limbic pathway, 344
Mesoderm layer, **379**–380
Mesotelencephalic dopamine system, **343**–347
Messenger RNA, **39,** 40, 119–120
Metabolic disorders, genetic, 43–44
Metabolic tolerance, 326, **327.** *See also* Drug metabolism
Metabolites, 456
Metastatic tumors, 132, **133**
Metencephalon, 65, 67, 76, 343
Mice and cat interactions, 446
Microelectrode pullers, 81, 82
Microelectrodes, **81**–82
Microexpressions, 443
Microsleeps, 306, **307**
Microspectrophotometry, **172,** 173
Microtubules, 56, 92
Midbrain (mesencephalon), 65, 66, 68, 76, 343, 379
Midsagittal section, 62
Migraine-induced scotoma, 184
Migration (of neurons), **381,** 380–382
Mind-brain dualism (Descartes), 20, 21
Minerals, diet selection for, 241–242
Minnesota Study of Twins Reared Apart, 46–47
Minor hemisphere, 412, **413**
Mirror-drawing test, **354**–356
Miss G., case of, 198
Miss M., sleep study of, 296
Mitochondria, 56
Mitosis, **35,** 34–36
Mnemonic abilities, **351**
Mock-crime procedure, 441
Mondrians, 175
Monkeys
  ischemia in, 370–372
  New-World and Old-World, 28, 29

object-recognition amnesia in, 366–367
  split-brain, 417
Monoamine agonists, 461
Monoamine neurotransmitters, 97, 98
Monoamine oxidase (MAO), 146, 147
Monoamine oxidase (MAO) inhibitors, 146, **147, 460**–461
Monoamine reuptake blockage, 461–462
Monoamine theory of depression, 461–462
Monoamines, 97, 98
Monocular, defined, **167**
Monocular cortical cells, 167
Monocular deprivation, 387, 401
Monopolar recording in EEG, 109
Monozygotic (identical) twins, **46.** *See also* Twin studies
Morgan's Canon, 14, **15**
Morphine, 200, 336, **337**
Morphine withdrawal effects, 330–331
Morris water maze, **128,** 395
Morris water maze test, **372,** 374
Motion perception, 13–14
Motivated behaviors, natural, 345
Motor control dominance by left hemisphere, 424–425
Motor cortex
  primary. *See* Primary motor cortex
  secondary, 211, 212, 214–215
Motor disorders, 140–141. *See also* Parkinson's disease
Motor end-plate, 224, **225**
Motor homunculus, 216, **217**
Motor neurons, 8, 90, 387
  action potentials of, 388–389, 391, 393
  intrafusal, 226, 227
Motor output, 210
Motor pathways, 45, 221–224
Motor pool, 224, **225**
Motor seizures, 138, 139
Motor theory of lateralization, 424
Motor units, 224, **225**
Movement agnosia, 187
MPTP, **146**–148, 407
MPTP model of Parkinson's disease, 146–148, 407
Mr. B., case of, 318
MRI. *See* Magnetic resonance imaging

Mrs. Byrne's Dictionary of Unusual, Obscure, and Preposterous Words, 112
Mrs. S., case of, 212
MS (multiple sclerosis), 136, 142, **143**
Müllerian-inhibiting substance, **277**
Müllerian system, **277**, 278
Multiple sclerosis (MS), 136, 142, **143**
Multiple-unit recording, 116, 117
Multipolar neurons, **54**, 57
Mumby box, **369**, 368–371
Mumps, 136
Muscarinic receptors, 102, 103
Muscle cells, 387
Muscle-spindle feedback circuits, 226, 227, 229
Muscle spindles, **225–227**
Muscle tension measures, 110–112
Muscle tone, lack of, 318
Muscles and muscle fibers, 113, 152, 224–230
Musical ability, 421–422
Mutations, 38, **39**, 43
Mutual inhibition (lateral inhibition), 164–165
Myelencephalon (medulla), 65–67, 76, 343
Myelin, 55, 58, 59, 142
Myelin stains, **60–61**
Myelinated axons, 90

N

N.A., case of, 360
Nabilone, 335
Naloxone, 199–200, 285
Naltrexone, 199–200
Narcolepsy, **319**
Narcotics, **334.** *See also* Opiate *entries*
Nasal hemiretina, **156,** 157, 161, 162
Natural motivated behaviors, 345
Natural selection, 25–26
Nature-nurture issue, 20–**21**, 23, 47, 284
NCAMs (neural cell-adhesion molecules), **381**, 383
Needle freaks, 340
Negative feedback, **274**, 275, 462–463
Negative feedback systems, **238**, 239
Negative schizophrenic symptoms, 459

Neocortex, 71–73, 76, 380
Neonates, 387
Neophobia, 127
Nephrectomized rats, **256–258**
Nephrons, 255, 257
Nerve endings, free, 192, 193
Nerve growth factor (NGF), **385**
Nerves, **54.** *See also* Neural *entries;* Neuro- *entries*
  afferent (sensory), 50, 51
  auditory, 189–191
  cranial, 50, 51, 203, 204, 472, 473
  efferent, 50, 51
  facial, 203, 204, 473
  glossopharyngeal, 203, 204, 473
  optic, 69–70, 316, 384, 385, 473
  parasympathetic, 50, 51, 471
  spinal, 64, 65
  sympathetic, 50, 51, 471
  vagus, 203, 204, 246, 473
Nervous system
  cells of, 54–59. *See also* Neurons
  divisions of, 50–51
    autonomic. *See* Autonomic nervous system
    central. *See* Central nervous system
    peripheral, 50–51, 54, 58, 59
    somatic, 50–51, 65, 109–112
  electrical activity of, recording, 116, 117. *See also* Electroencephalo- *entries*
  layout of, 50–54
  studying, methods of, 106–120
  of vertebrates, directions in, 62–63
  viral infections of, 135–137
Neural activity, reverberating, 352
Neural bases
  of anxiety disorders, 464
  of learning and memory, 388–397
  of schizophrenia, 458–459
Neural cell-adhesion molecules (NCAMs), **381**, 383
Neural circuits for birdsong, 45
Neural crest, 380–**381**
Neural degeneration, 398, 399
Neural development
  and experience, 387–388
  phases of, 379–386
Neural grooves, 379, 380
Neural mechanisms
  in circadian clock, 314–316
  of conditioned fear, 448–449
  of depression, 461–463
  of drug addiction, 346–347
  of hunger and satiety, 244–250
  of sleep, 310–316

Neural plate, **379–380**
Neural proliferation, 380, **381**
Neural regeneration, **398–401**, 406
Neural reorganization, 400–403
Neural signals, light converted to, 159–161
Neural tube, **379–382**
Neuroanatomical asymmetries between hemispheres, 423–425
Neuroanatomical techniques, 58, 60–62, 78
Neuroanatomy, 4, **5**
  of object-recognition amnesia, 366–372, 374
Neurochemistry, 4, **5**
Neuroendocrine system, 269–276
Neuroendocrinology, 4, **5**
Neurofibrillary tangles, 143, **361**
Neuroleptics, 458–**459**
Neurological disorders, drug treatment of, 136
Neurologists, 121
Neuromodulators, 99
Neuromuscular junctions, **102**, 224
Neurons, 2, **3**, 31
  adrenergic, 97
  afferent (sensory), 227, 388–389, 391, 393
  aggregation of, 381
  in Alzheimer's disease, 143
  anatomy of, 54–57
  bipolar, 54, 57
  cell membranes of, 54, 55, 57
  cholinergic, 98
  death of, 384–386
  dopamine-releasing, 343–347
  inter-, 54, 57, 380, 391
  migration of, 380–382
  motor. *See* Motor neurons
  multipolar, 54, 57
  polarization of, 82–85
  polarized, 82–85
  postsynaptic, 133–134, 395–397
  presynaptic, 396–397
  resting potential of, 82–85
  of somatic and autonomic nervous system, 65
  sympathetic, 385
  synaptic transmission between. *See* Synapses; Synaptic *entries*
  tonically active, 219
  unipolar, 54, 57
Neuropathology, 4, **5**
Neuropeptides, 97–99
Neuropharmacology, 4, **5**
Neurophysiology, 4, **5**

Neuroplasticity, 379–408
Neuropsychological diseases, 137–144. *See also* Brain damage
  animal models of, 144–147
Neuropsychological testing, 121–123
Neuropsychologists, 121
Neuropsychology, **8**–10, 12
Neuroscience, **3**, 2–4
  behavioral. *See* Biopsychology
  biopsychology as discipline of, 2, 3
  cognitive, 124–125
Neurosecretory cells, 273
Neuroses, **455**
Neurotoxins, **117**, 136. *See also* MPTP
Neurotransmitter molecules
  receptor activation by, 94–96
  release of, 93, 94, 100–101
  reuptake, enzymatic degradation, and recycling affecting, 96
  synthesis, packaging, and transport of, 92–93, 100–101
Neurotransmitters, 56, 85
  amino acid, 97, 98
  in Aplysia learning, 388–389, 391, 393
  blocking, 456, 457
  in brain, locating, 118–120
  in brain damage, 133–135
  classes of, 97–99
  coexistence of, 93
  drugs affecting, in research, 117–120
  monoamine, 97, 98
  peptide, 93, 95, 96
  putative, 98
  small-molecule, 93, 95–96
  soluble-gas, 97, 98
Neurotransplantation in brain, 403–407
Neurotrophins, 384, **385**
Neurotropic infections, 135–**137**
NGF (nerve growth factor), **385**
Nicotine, **330**, 331, 335. *See also* Tobacco
Nicotinic receptors, 102, 103
Nigrostriatal pathway, **140**, 344
Nimiety, 265
Nissl stain, **58**, 60, 78
Nitric oxide, 98, 109, **396**, 397
NMDA (N-methyl-D-aspartate) receptor blockers, 134
NMDA (N-methyl-D-aspartate) receptors, 134, **135**, **395**–397

Nobel Prize winners, 8, 9
Nociceptive stimuli, 193
Nocturnal animals, 302
Nocturnal myoclonus, 318–**319**
Nodes of Ranvier, 55, **90**
Noise
  in cognitive testing, 125
  in EEGs, 110
Nonassociative learning, **389**, 388–391
Nondecremental conduction of action potentials, 89
Nondirected synapses, 92, **93**
Nonexperimental studies, 5, 7–8
Nonhuman subjects in research, 5. *See also* Animal *entries*
Nonlexical procedure, 432–**433**
Nonrecurring-items delayed non-matching-to-sample test, **367**, 366–372, 374, 375
Nootropics, 362, **363**
Norepinephrine (noradrenaline), 97, 98, 117, 290
Noun-repetition conditions, 435
Nuclei, **54**, 56
  caudate, 14–15, 75, 76
  cochlear, 190–191
  intralaminar, 195, 196
  lateral geniculate, 69, 76, 161–162, 166, 186
  medial dorsal, 202
  medial geniculate, 69, 76, 191, 448–449
  medial septal, 361
  mediodorsal, 359, 360, 369, 376
  medullary relay, 202, 203
  parafascicular, 195, 196
  paraventricular, 246–248, 272, 273
  raphé, 312, 313
  red, 68, 76, 221, 375
  sensory relay, 69
  sexually dimorphic, 288–290
  solitary, 202, 203
  suprachiasmatic, 314–315
  supraoptic, 272, 273
  thalamic. *See* Thalamic nuclei
  ventral posterior, 69, 76, 194, 195, 203, 204
  ventromedial, 290, 291
  vestibular, 222, 223
Nucleotide bases, 37–39
Nucleus accumbens, 344, **345**
Nucleus basalis of Meynert, 361
Nucleus magnocellularis, **319**, 320
Nuscimol, 375
Nutritive density, **242**, 243

O

Obesity
  as eating disorder, 263–265
  and hypothalamus, 245–247
  impact of, 235
Object agnosia, 187
Object-assembly test, 122
Object-recognition amnesia, 366–372, 374
Observational (empirical) methods, 12
Obsessive-compulsive disorders, **462**, 463
Occipital cortex in vision, 183
Occipital lobe of telencephalon, 71, 72, 76
Oculomotor nerve, 473
Odd behaviors in schizophrenia, 455
Off-center cells, 166, **167**
6-OHDA (6-hydroxydopamine), 117, 344, 407
Old-World monkeys, 28, 29
Olfaction, 201
Olfactory bulbs, **202**
Olfactory deficits, 204
Olfactory mucosa, **202**
Olfactory nerve, 473
Olfactory pathways, 202–203
Olfactory receptors, 201–202
Olfactory system, 201–204
Olfactory tract, 202
Oligodendroglia (oligodendrocytes), **58**, 59, **406**
Ommatidia, 164, **165**
On-center cells, 166, **167**
Ontogeny, **43**, 42–47
Open-ended learning, 44, 45
Open-field behavior, 146
Open-field tests, **125**
Operant conditioning paradigm, **126**–127. *See also* Conditional *entries;* Conditioned *entries;* Conditioning *entries*
Operator genes, 38–**39**
Opiate analgesics, 199
Opiate antagonists, 199–200, 285
Opiate receptors, 338
Opiate tolerance, 337
Opiate withdrawal syndrome, 337
Opiates, 98–99, 334, **337**, 336–338
Opioid peptides, 476
Opium, 336, **337**
Opponent-process theory (of color vision), **172**–174
Optic chiasm, 69–70, 76, 316
  lesions in, 416–417

Optic nerves, 69–70, 316, 384, 385, 473
Optic tectum, 68, **383,** 382–384
Optic tracts, 316
Orbicularis oculi, 443–444
Orbitofrontal cortex, **202**–203
Orchidectomy, 278, **279,** 285, 290, 291
Organ of Corti, **189,** 190
Orthodromic conduction, **90**
Oscilloscopes, **82,** 83
Osmoreceptors, **256**–257
Osmotic pressure, **254,** 255
Ossicles, **189,** 190
Ova, 34–36, 270, 379
Oval window, **189,** 190
Ovariectomy, 278, **279,** 287, 290
Ovaries, 270, **271**
    development of, 275–277
    removal of, 278, 279, 287, 290
Ovulation, **274**
Owl sound localization, 191–192
Oxidation, 332
Oxytocin, **272,** 273

P

P layers (parvocellular layers), 161–162
P pathway, 162, 186
P300 wave, 110, **111**
Pacinian corpuscles, **192,** 193
PAG. *See* Periaqueductal gray
Pain
    adaptiveness of, 198
    paradoxes of, 198–200
    perception of, 193
Pain control, 199–200. *See also* Analgesics
Paired-image subtraction technique, 124, **125,** 433–435
Palpation, 421
Pancreatitis, 332
Panic disorders, **462,** 463
Pantropic infections, 135–**137**
Papillae, 203
Parabiotic preparation, **317**
Parachlorophenylalanine (PCPA), **312**
Paradoxes of pain, 198–200
Paradoxical sleep, 298, **299**
Parafascicular nuclei, 195, 196
Parallel models, **427,** 428
    dual-route, 432
Parallel processing, **182**
    of language, 432–433
Parallel systems, 182
Paraplegics, 17

Parasympathetic nerves, **50,** 51, 471
Paraventricular nuclei, **246**–248, **272,** 273
Parietal cortex in vision, 183
Parietal lobe of telencephalon, 71, 72, 76
Parkinson's disease, **140**
    and basal ganglia, 75
    dopamine in, 81, 140, 147, 407
    d'Orta case of, 81, 100, 140, 148, 407
    MPTP model of, 146–148, 407
    symptoms of, and drugs, 147, 148, 456
    treating, 81, 97, 140, 406–407
Partial epilepsy, 138–139
Partial seizures, 138–**139**
Parvocellular layers (P layers), **161**–162
Passive theory of sleep, 310, 311
Patellar tendon reflex, 226, **227**
Pavlovian conditioning, 242, 391–392
Pavlovian conditioning paradigm, **126,** 127
Pavlovian conditioning test, 356
PCPA (parachlorophenylalanine), **312**
Pea plants, genetics in, 33–34
Penis, accidental destruction of, 284–285
Peptide hormones, **269**–270
Peptide neurotransmitters, 93, 95, 96
Peptides, 92, **93,** 476
    delta sleep-inducing, 317–318
    gut, 476
    gut satiety, 248–250
    hypothalamic, 476
    neuro-, 97–99
    opioid, 476
    pituitary, 476
Per gene, 315
Perception, **181**
    color, 172–177
    edge, 163–171
    light, 151–153, 157–158, 163–167
    mechanisms of, 180–206
    motion, 13–14
    of pain, 193
    spacial, disorders of, 421
    speech, difficulty of, 192, 193
    of temperature, 193
    three-dimensional, 152–153
    visual, of subjective contours, 184, 185

Perceptual-motor function tests, 123
Perfect pitch, 423, 424
Performance subtests of WAIS, 122
Periaqueductal gray (PAG), 68, 76, **199**–200, 290, 291
    pathway to, 448, 449
Perimetry test, **182,** 183
Perinatal androgens, 278–279
Perinatal hormones, 278–280, 291–292
Peripheral nervous system (PNS), **50**–51, 54, 58, 59
Perirhinal cortex, 367, 368
Peritoneum, 256, 257
Personality, twin studies of, 46, 47
PET. *See* Positron emission tomography
Petit mal seizures, **139**
Phagocytes, 398, 451–452
Phagocytosis, **398, 451**–452
Phantom limbs, **200**–201
Phase advances and delays, 304
Phenothiazines, 458, **459**
Phenotypes, **33**
Phenylalanine, 43, 44
Phenylalanine hydroxylase, 43
Phenylketonuria (PKU), **43**–44, 137
Phenylpyruvic acid, **43**
Pheromones, **200,** 201
Phobic anxiety disorders, **462,** 463
Phonemes, 432, **433**
Phonological analysis, 432, **433**
Photons, 151
Photopic spectral sensitivity curve, **156**–159
Photopic vision, **155**
Phyla, 27
Phylogeny, 42, **43**
Physical dependence on drugs, 326–**327,** 332, 337, 340, 341. *See also* Drug withdrawal *entries*
Physical-dependence theories of addiction, 340, **341**
Physiological-psychological dichotomy, 20–23
Physiological psychology, **8**–9, 12
Physiological research methods, 113–117
Pia mater, **52,** 53
Picture-arrangement tests, 122
Picture-completion tests, 122
Pigments, 158–161
Pioneer growth cones, **383**
Pitch, 188
    perfect, 423, 424

Pituitary gland, 69, 70, 76, 271, 276
 anterior, 271–273, 276, 280
 posterior, 271, 273, 276
Pituitary peptides, 476
Pituitary stalk, **271,** 273
PKU (phenylketonuria), **43**–44, 137
Place cells, **372,** 373
Place fields, 372
Placental barrier, 279
Planum temporale, **423,** 424
Plethysmography, **112,** 113
Pneumoencephalograms, 107
Pneumoencephalography, **106**–107
PNS (peripheral nervous system), **50**–51, 54, 58, 59
Polarized neurons, 82–85
Polydipsia, 262, 263
Polygraphy (lie detection), **441**–442
Pons, 67, 76
Positive feedback, **274,** 275
Positive-incentive properties of drinks, 261
Positive-incentive theories, **241, 341**
 of addiction, 340, 341
 of hunger and eating, 240–241, 244
Positive-incentive value, 240, **241**
Positive schizophrenic symptoms, 459
Positron emission tomography (PET), 108–**109,** 124–125
 and cortical localization of pain, 199
 in hemispheric asymmetry measurement, 423, 424
 during language-related activities, 433–435
 in lateralization studies, 413
 secondary visual cortex identified by, 186
Postcentral gyrus, 71, 72, 76, 195
Posterior (caudal) direction, **62,** 63
Posterior parietal association cortex, 196, **210**–212
Posterior parietal cortex, **182,** 183, 195–197
 in Alzheimer's disease, 143
 association, 196, 210–212
 damage to, 186
 and memory, 374–375
Posterior parietal lobe, 196–196
Posterior pituitary, **271,** 273, 276
Postsynaptic inhibition, **90**–92

Postsynaptic neurons, 133–134, 395–397
Postsynaptic potentials, 84–88, 109
Posttraumatic amnesia (PTA), **363,** 362–364
Precentral gyrus, 71, 72, 76, 216
Predatory aggression, 447
Predictive animal models, **145**
Prefrontal cortex, 360–**361**
 in Alzheimer's disease, 143
 damage to, 360–361
 dorsolateral association, 211–214
 inferior, 412, 413
 and memory, 375–376
 and schizophrenia, 459
Prefrontal lobes, **15,** 44
Prefrontal lobotomy, **15**–17, 199
Pregnancy
 alcohol during, 332, 333
 smoking during, 331
Premotor cortex, 214, **215,** 219
Preparatory behaviors, **345**
Prestriate cortex, **182,** 183, 186–188
Presynaptic facilitation, **391**
Presynaptic inhibition, **90**–92
Presynaptic neurons, 396–397
Primary auditory cortex, 190–193, 426
Primary gustatory cortex, 203, 204
Primary motor cortex, 212, 214, 216–**217,** 219
 damage to, 217
 reorganization of, 401–402
 in Wernicke-Geschwind model, 426, 427
Primary sensory cortex, **181,** 180–183, 401
Primary somatosensory cortex, 195–198
Primary visual cortex, **161**–162, 166, 183–187, 387
 columnar organization of, 168–170
 damage to, 183–185
 organization of, 176–177, 401
 in Wernicke-Geschwind model, 426, 427
Primates, **29**
 evolution of, 28–31, 424–425
Priming (for self-stimulation), 342, **343**
Primordial gonads, 275–278
Principle of antithesis (Darwin), 438, 439
Principle of equipotentiality, 127, **351**

Principle of mass action, **351**
Proactive interference, 360, **361**
Procaine, 335
Proceptive behaviors, **280**
Proceptivity, 286–287
Progesterone, **271,** 286, 290
Progesterone receptors, 290
Progestins, **271,** 276
Proof, defined, 275
Proprioceptive system, 193
Prosimians, 28, 29
Prosody, **444**
Prosopagnosia, **187**–188
Protein hormones, **269**–270
Protein kinase, 393
Protein synthesis in long-term memory, 397
Proteins, 38–**39**
 alpha feto-, 279
 channel, 54, 57
 DNA-binding, 38–39
 in energy storage, 236, 237
 fos, 316
 G, 95. *See also* G-protein linked receptors
 signal, 54, 57
Proximal segments, **398,** 399
Prozac, **460**–462
Pseudoinsomniacs, 319
Psychiatric disorders, 455–464
Psychoactive drugs, 101–103, 324, **325,** 331–340, 462–464. *See also specific entries, e.g.:* Cocaine (cocaine hydrochloride); Tobacco
Psychobiology. *See* Biopsychology
Psychological dependence on drugs, **327**
Psychological development, genetics of, 45–47
Psychological disorders and conditioned fear, 449
Psychological-physiological dichotomy, 20–23
Psychology
 comparative, 10–11
 experimental, 20–21
 neuro-, 8–10, 12
 physiological, 8–9, 12
Psychomotor attacks, 138–**139**
Psychoneuroimmunology, **451**–454
Psychopharmacological research methods, 117–120
Psychopharmacology, **8,** 9
Psychophysiological activity measures, 109–113, 296–297
Psychophysiology, 10, **11**
Psychoses, **455**
 toxic, 136, 137

Psychosomatic disorders, 450–454
Psychosurgery. *See* Brain surgery
PTA (posttraumatic amnesia), **363,** 362–364
P300 wave, 110, **111**
Puberty, 275, 280–281
Pubic hair, 280, 281
Pulsatile hormone release, **274,** 275
Punch-drunk syndrome, **135**
Punishment, 126
Pupils, 152
Pure research, **8,** 9
Purkinje effect, **158**
Putamen, 75, 76
Putative neurotransmitters, 98
Pyloric sphincter, 248
Pyramidal cell layer, **359**
Pyramidal cells, 72, 73, 78
Pyriform cortex, **202**
Pyrithiamine, 376

Q

Quasiexperimental studies, **7,** 9

R

Rabies, 136
Radial arm maze, **126**–128
Radial arm maze test, **372**
Radial glial cells, 380, **381**
Radio-frequency lesions, 114–115
Radio-opaque substances, 106–107
Rage
    septal, 447
    sham, 439
Random motion (in resting potential), 82–83
Raphé nuclei, **312,** 313
Rapid eye movements. *See* REM *entries*
Rats
    aggression and defense among, 445–447
    anxiety modeling by, 464
    behavioral testing of, 125–126
    electrical brain stimulation in, 145
    ischemia in, 370–372
    maze-bright and maze-dull, 42–43
    nephrectomized, 256–258
    object-recognition amnesia in, 368–369
    thigmotaxic, 125–126

R.B., case of, 358–359, 369–370
Reactive depression, **460**
Reading aloud, procedures for, 432–433
Reading problems
    from alexia, 426–429
    from dyslexia, 432–433
Receptive fields (of visual neurons), **165**–170, 215
Receptivity (language), **424,** 425
Receptivity (sexual), 286–287
Receptor blockers, **101,** 456, 457
Receptor molecules of B cells, 452
Receptor subtypes, 94, **95**
Receptors, 94, **95,** 155
    acetylcholine, 102, 103
    activation of, by neurotransmitter molecules, 94–96
    auto-, 96
    blood-flow, 256, 257
    blood pressure (baro-), 256–258
    in brain, locating, 118–120
    cutaneous (skin), 192–194
    D_1 and D_2, 458, 459
    dopamine, 456–457
    G-protein linked, 94–96, 161, 338, 393
    GABA, 463, 464
    insulin, 250
    ion-channel linked, 94–96, 393
    muscarinic, 102, 103
    nicotinic, 102, 103
    NMDA, 134, 135, 395–397
    olfactory, 201–202
    opiate, 338
    osmo-, 256–257
    progesterone, 290
    in sensory systems, 180–182
    serotonin, 458
    T cell, 452
    taste, 203
    tendon and muscle, 225–228
    visual, 154–156
Recessive genes, 137
Recessive traits, **33**–35
Reciprocal innervation, 229–230
Recuperation theories of sleep, 301–302, 304, 308–309
Recurrent collateral inhibition, **230,** 231
Recurring-items delayed matching-to-sample test, **375**
Red nuclei, 68, 76, 221, 375
Reference memory, **372**
Reflexes
    sensorimotor, 230–231
    stretch, 226–229
    withdrawal, 228–230

Reflexive (unconditional) response, 126
Refraction of light, 152
Refractory periods (of action potentials), 89
Regeneration
    of axons, 58
    neural, 398–401, 406
    of optic nerves, 384, 385
    of retinal ganglion cells, 381–382
Reinforcement, 126
Reinforcement-density theory of contingent drug tolerance, 328
Relapses by drug addicts, 340
Relative refractory period, **89**
Releasing factors, 272–274
Releasing hormones, **274**
REM sleep, **299,** 298–301, 311–314, 317
REM-sleep circuits, 313
REM-sleep deprivation, 307–308
REM-sleep-related disorders, 319–320
REMs (rapid eye movements), 297–298
Renaissance, 20
Renal arteries, 255, 256
Renal veins, 255, 256
Renin, 258, **259**
Renshaw cells, 230
Repetition priming, **359**
Replacement injections (of hormones), **285**–286, 291
Replication (of DNA), **39,** 38–40
Repolarization of action potential, 89
Reproduction-related behavior, 285–287. *See also* Copulatory behavior; Proceptive behavior; Sexual behavior
Reproductive ducts, 276–278
Reproductive organs
    external, 278, 279
    and fetal hormones, 275–278
Reptile evolution, 27, 31
Research
    approaches to, 5, 32, 33
    errors in, 14–17
    subjects in, 5
    types of, 5–9, 11, 444–447
Research methods, 105–120
    behavioral, 120–128
    brain-imaging, 106–111
    in cognitive neuroscience, 124–125
    invasive, 113–117
    nervous system, 106–120

neuropsychological, 121–123
pharmacological, 117–120
physiological, 113–117
psychophysiological, 109–113
Reserpine, 456, **457**
Response-chunking hypothesis, **232**
Resting potential (of neurons), **82**–85
Restless legs, 318–**319**
Reticular activating system, **310**
Reticular formation, 66–68, 76, 195, 196, 222, **223**. *See also* Caudal reticular formation REM-sleep circuits
Retina, 384
  blind spots on (scotomas), 154, 155, 182–184, 401, 416, 417, 419
  cells of, 154–156, 174
  fovea of, 154–158, 161, 166
  light reaching, 152–161
Retina-geniculate-striate pathway, **161**–162, 166, 167, 173–174
Retinal ganglion cells, **155**, 154–157, 166, **381**–383, 388
Retinal images, 13–14, 158–159
Retinex theory (of color vision), **175**
Retinocentric visual receptive fields, 215
Retinohypothalamic tracts, 316
Retinotopic organization, **161, 189**
Retrograde amnesia, **353**, 362–364, 374–375
Retrograde degeneration, **398**, 399
Retrograde memory deficits, 361
Retrograde tracing methods, 61–62
Retrograde transneuronal degeneration, **398**, 399
Reuptake, **96**
Reverberating neural activity, 352
Reversible lesions, 116
Reward circuits in brain, 341–345
Rey-Osterrieth Complex Figure Test, **123**
Rhinal cortex, 143, **367**–369, 371, 374
Rhodopsin, **158**–161
Ribonucleic acid. *See* RNA (ribonucleic acid)
Ribosomes, **39,** 40, 56, 92
Right-handers, 414
Right hemisphere. *See also* Lateralization
  abilities of, 421–425

and language, 121
versus left hemisphere, 421–425
as minor, 412, 413
perceptual-motor testing of, 123
Rigidity in seizures, 138, 139
Rising phase of action potential, 89
Risk assessment in defense, 447
Risk-assessment test, 464
R.M., case of, 376
RNA (ribonucleic acid), **39,** 40
  hybrid, 120
  messenger, 39, 40, 119–120
  transfer, 39, 40
Rod vision, 156
Rods, **155**–161
Rostral (anterior) direction, 62, 63
Rotary-pursuit test, **354,** 355, 357
Ruffini endings, 193

S

Saccades, **158**
Saccharin elation effect, 262, **263**
Sacral region of spinal cord, 194
Sagittal sections (of brain tissue), **62,** 63
Salt and thirst, 255–256
Saltatory conduction, **90**
Saralasin, 259
Satellite cells, **58**
Satiety, 239, **242**
  blood glucose in, 244–245
  and drinking, 261–262
  gastrointestinal tract in, 248–250
  hypothalamus in, 245–248
  neural mechanisms of, 244–250
  sensory-specific, 244, 245, 262
  social influences on, 243
Satiety peptides, 248–250
SC (subcutaneous) drug administration, 117, 324, **325**
Scalp electroencephalography. *See* Electroencephalo- *entries*
Scanning electron microscope, 60, 61
Schedule-induced polydipsia, 262, **263**
Schizophrenia, **455**–459
  amphetamine model of, 146–147
  and brain-imaging techniques, 459
  causal factors in, 455–456
  versus cocaine psychosis, 335
  dopamine theory of, 456–459

  drug treatment of, 456–459
  neural basis of, research on, 458–459
  and stress, 456, 459
  and visual tracking, 10
Schizophrenic symptoms, positive and negative, 459
Schwann cells, **58,** 59, **398,** 400, 407
Science, bad, 14–17
Scientific inference, **13,** 12–14
Scientific method, 12
Scintillation counters, 217
SCL (skin conductance level), **1 12**
SCN (suprachiasmatic nuclei), 314–**315**
Scotomas (blind spots), 154, 155, **182**–184, 401, 416, **417,** 419
Scotopic spectral sensitivity curve, **156**–159
Scotopic (rod) vision, **156**
SCR (skin conductance response), **112**
Scrotum, **277,** 278
Second messengers, **95,** 392–393
Secondary auditory cortex, 191, 192, 375, 434
Secondary gustatory cortex, 203, 204
Secondary motor cortex, 211, 212, 214–**215**
Secondary sensory cortex, 205
Secondary sex characteristics, **280**–281
Secondary somatosensory cortex, 195–197, 375
Secondary visual cortex, 183–187, 206, 434
Sedatives, 102
Seizures, epileptic, 137–140, 417
Selective attention, **204**–206
Selective breeding, 42–43
Selective serotonin-reuptake inhibitors, 460–462
Self-awareness studies, 21–23
Self-stimulation, intracranial, 341–345
Self-stimulation paradigm, **126,** 127
Semantic analysis, 432, **433**
Semantic processing of verb association, 435
Semicircular canals, 190, **191**
Seminal vesicles, 277
Seminatural animal learning paradigms, 127–128
Sensation, **181**

Sensitive period (of development), **44**
Sensitivity (in vision), **152**
Sensitization, 389–393
  to drugs, 326, **327**, 335
Sensorimotor areas of cerebral cortex, 211–219
Sensorimotor association cortex, 211–214
Sensorimotor control and learning, 210–211
Sensorimotor function, principles of, 209–211
Sensorimotor function tests, 123
Sensorimotor learning, 219
Sensorimotor memory, 375
Sensorimotor phase (of birdsong development), **44**–45
Sensorimotor programs, central, 231–232
Sensorimotor reflex, 230–231
Sensorimotor spinal circuits, 224–231
Sensorimotor system, 209–233
  hierarchical organization of, 209–210
  versus sensory systems, 209–210
Sensory cortex
  primary, 180–183, 401
  secondary, 205
Sensory deficits, 180–181
Sensory evoked potentials, **109**–110
Sensory feedback, **210**
Sensory input, 210
Sensory (afferent) nerves, 50, 51
Sensory (afferent) neurons, 227, 388–389, 391, 393
Sensory relay nuclei, 69
Sensory-specific satiety, 244, **245**, 262
Sensory systems
  exteroceptive, 180, 181
  organizational principles of, 180–182
  versus sensorimotor system, 209–210
Sensory theory of sleep, 310, 311
Septal aggression (rage), 447
Septal lesions, 126
Septum, 74–76
Serial models, **427**, 428
Serial sensory system organization, 182
Serotonergic drugs, 317
Serotonergic interneurons, 391
Serotonin (in memory storage), 397

Serotonin agonists, 462–464
Serotonin receptors, 458
Serotonin-reuptake inhibitors, 460–462
Set-point assumption, 239
Set-point mechanism, 239
Set-point theories
  of drinking, 261, 262
  of hunger and eating, 239–240, 242–244, 250–253
  and obesity, 264
Settling points, **251**
  in body weight regulation, 250–253, 264
Sex and hormones, 269–292
Sex chromosomes, **35**, 270, **271**
Sex drive
  of men, 286
  of women, 287
Sex hormones. *See* Steroid hormones
Sex-linked traits, **35**
Sex reassignment, 284–285
Sex-related side effects of anabolic steroids, 287–288
Sex steroids, 270–271
Sexual attractiveness, 287
Sexual behavior
  and dopamine, 345
  and endorphins, 285
  and hypothalamus, 288–291
  and pheromones, 201
  and testosterone, 285–286
  tests of, 126
Sexual development
  exceptional cases of, 282–285
  and hormones, 275–285
Sexual differentiation
  of brain, 278–279, 414–415
  of hypothalamus, 279
Sexual intercourse, 270, 271. *See also* Lordosis
Sexual orientation, 290–292
Sexual pheromones, 201
Sexually dimorphic nucleus, **289**, 288–290
SFO (subfornical organ), **259**–260
Sham drinking, **260**–262
Sham eating, **242**–243
Sham rage, **439**
Shift work, 303–304
Short-term memory, 122, 351–352, 393
Signal averaging, 110, **111**, 124, 125
Signal integration in EMG, 111, 112
Signal proteins, 54, 57
Signal-to-noise ratio, 125

Signals in EEGs, 110
Similarities subtest of WAIS, 122
Simple cells, **167**, 168
Simple partial (Jacksonian) seizures, 138, **139**
Simple-systems approach, **379**
Simultaneous learning, 419–420
Sine-wave grating, 170, **171**
Sine waves, 188–189
Sinestrals (left-handers), **414**
Sinuses, 53
Siphon of Aplysia, 388–389, 391–393
Situational specificity of drug tolerance, 329
Skeletal muscle (extrafusal muscle), **227**, 226–228
Skin, glabrous (hairless), 192, 193
Skin conductance level (SCL), **112**
Skin conductance response (SCR), **112**
Skin receptors, 192–194
Sleep. *See also* Dreams
  brain areas in, 312–314
  delta, 298, 299
  drugs and chemicals influencing, 317–319, 463
  EEG waves during, 296–298
  excessive, 318, 319
  micro-, 306, 307
  neural mechanisms of, 310–316
  paradoxical, 298, 299
  psychophysiological measures of, 296–297
  REM. *See* REM *entries*
  slow-wave, 298, 299, 306
    EEGs during, 310, 311, 313
  theories of, 301–302, 304, 308–311
Sleep apnea, 318, **319**
Sleep deprivation, 304–308
Sleep disorders, 318–320
Sleep EEG stages, 297–299
Sleep factors, 317–318
Sleep paralysis, **320**
Sleep-promoting brain circuits, 310–311
Sleep reduction effects, 320–321
Sleep spindles, **297**, 298
Sleep-wake cycles, 302–304, 310. *See also* Sleep deprivation
Sleepiness, excessive, 318, 319
Sleeping pills, 318
Sleeplessness, 317–319
Sleeptalking, 300
Sleepwalking, 301
Slow muscle fibers, 224

Slow-wave sleep (SWS), 298, **299,** 306
  EEGs of, 310, 311, 313
Small-molecule neurotransmitters, 93, 95–96
Smell, 200–204
Smiling, 444
Smoker's syndrome, **330,** 331. *See also* Tobacco
Smoking, 331–332, 338, 347, 348. *See also* Nicotine
SNS (somatic nervous system), **50**–51, 65, 109–112
Social aggression, 447–448
Social dominance hierarchy, 26
Society for Neuroscience, 4, **5**
Sodium, kidney regulation of, 255–257
Sodium amytal test, **413, 121,** 412–414
Sodium deficiency, 241
Sodium-potassium pumps, **84,** 85
Soldier's disease, 336
Solitary nucleus, **202,** 203
Soluble-gas neurotransmitters, 97, 98
Soluble gases, 97, 98
Solutes, 254
Somas (cell bodies), 55, 91
Somatic nervous system (SNS), **50**–51, 65, 109–112
Somatosensation, 193
Somatosensory agnosias, 197–198
Somatosensory cortex, 195–201
  primary, 195–196
  secondary, 195–197, 375
Somatosensory homunculus, 196, **197**
Somatosensory system, 193–201
  pathways of, 194–196
Somatotopic maps, 216–217
Somatotopic organization, 196, **197,** 214, **215**
Somnambulism, **301**
Song-control brain structures, 45
Soporifics, 319
Sound localization, 191–192
Sound waves, 188
Sounds, 188. *See also* Auditory system
Space, memory for, 372–374
Spatial abilities, 126–128, 421
Spatial-frequency theory, 170–**171**
Spatial perception disorders, 421
Spatial summation, **86,** 87
Species, **27**–31
Species-common behaviors, **125**–126

Spectral sensitivity curves, 156–159
Speech
  and brain damage, 428–429
  and electrical brain stimulation, 432
  movements accompanying, 413
Speech disorder (Broca's aphasia), 424, 425, 428, 430
Speech lateralization, 414
Speech lateralization test, 121
Speech perception difficulty, 192, 193
Speech production center (Broca's area), 412, 413, 423, 425–430, 434
Speech sounds (phonemes), 432, 433
Sperm cells, 34–36, 270, 379
Sphincter muscles, 113
Sphygmomanometer, 113
Spike-and-wave discharges, 3-per-second, 139
Spinal accessory nerve, 473
Spinal circuits, sensorimotor, 224–231
Spinal cord, 64–65, 194–195, 227, 379
Spinal nerves, 64, 65
Spindle afferent neurons, **227**
Spinorectal tract, 195, 196
Spinoreticular tract, 195, 196
Spinothalamic tract, 195, 196
Spiroperidol, 344
Split brain, 415–425
Split-brain cats, 415–417
Split-brain monkeys, 417
Split-brain patients, **411,** 418
Spontaneous drinking, **260,** 261
Spontaneous talking, 445, 446
Stabilized retinal images, **158**–159
Stapes, 189, 190
Static phase (of VMH syndrome), **245**
Statistical hemispheric differences, 422
Stellate cells, 72, 73
Stereognosis, **194, 217**
Stereotaxic atlases, 114, **115**
Stereotaxic instruments, 114, **115**
Stereotaxic surgery, 114, 115
Sterility, 286
Steroid hormones, 54, 270–**271,** 279, 286–288, 291. *See also* Glucocorticoids; Sex, and hormones
Stimulant drugs, 146, 147, 317, **334,** 335. *See also specific*

entries, e.g.: Amphetamines; Cocaine (cocaine hydrochloride); Nicotine
Stomach contractions, 248, 249
Stress, **448**
  in anxiety disorders, 463
  and depression, 460
  and health, 449–455
  and infections, 451–454
  and schizophrenia, 456, 459
Stress response, 450
Stretch reflex, **227,** 226–229
Striate cortex. *See* Primary visual cortex
Striatum, 75, 76, **140**
String-of-beads axons, 97
String-of-beads synapses, 92
Strokes, **133,** 123, 132–135, 414, 461
Structural genes, **39,** 38–40
Subarachnoid space, **52,** 53
Subcutaneous (SC) drug administration, 117, 324, **325**
Subdural space of skull, 134, 135
Subfornical organ (SFO), **259**–260
Subjective contours, **184,** 185
Submission, signals of, 438, 439
Subsongs, 44
Substantia nigra, 68, 76, 81, **140,** **343**–344, 407
Subventricular zone of neural tube, 380
Suicide, 460
Sulci, 71
Superior, defined, **62**
Superior colliculi, 68, 76, 191
Superior olives, **191**
Superior temporal gyrus, 71, 72, 76
Supplemental motor area, 214, **215**
Suprachiasmatic nuclei (SCN), 314–**315**
Supraoptic nuclei, **272,** 273
Surface dyslexia, 432–**433**
Surface interpolation, 155
Sutures of skull, 14
Sweat glands, 112
SWS. *See* Slow-wave sleep
Sympathetic nerves, **50,** 51, 471
Sympathetic neurons, 385
Synapses, 55
  development of, 387
  formation of, 381–385
  rearrangement of, 385–387
  structure of, 91–93

Synaptic transmission between
neurons, 91–96
drugs affecting, 99–103
and long-term potentiation,
393–397
second messengers in, 392–393
Synaptic vesicles, 56, 92–**93**, 96
Syndromes, defined, 440
Synergistic muscles, **225**
Synthetic mode of thinking,
423–424
Syphilis, 135
Syrinx (voice box), 45
Systemic injection of morphine,
200
Systoles, 113

T

T cells (T lymphocytes), **451**–454
Tachycardia, 332, 334, 463
Talking, spontaneous, 445, 446
TANS (tonically active neurons),
219
Tardive dyskinesia (TD), 136, **137**
Target-site concept, **447**
Tars in tobacco, 331
Taste, 200–204
Taste aversions, 126, 127, 201,
241–242
Taste buds, **202,** 203
Taste preferences, 241–242, 261
Taste receptors, 203
Tau gene, 315
TD (tardive dyskinesia), 136, **137**
Tectorial membrane, **189,** 190
Tectum, 68, 76, 195, 196, 222,
223
optic, 382–384
Tegmentum, 68, 76
Telencephalon. *See* Cerebrum
(cerebral hemispheres,
telencephalon)
Temperature
body, 303, 329, 332
perception of, 193
Temporal cortex
inferior, 143
in vision, 183
Temporal hemiretina, **156,** 157,
161, 162
Temporal integration in visual
system, 158–159
Temporal lobe epilepsy, 138–139
Temporal lobe of telencephalon,
71, 72, 76
Temporal summation, **86**–88

Tendons, 224
receptors of, 225–228
Testes, 270, **271**
development of, 275–277
removal of (orchidectomy),
278, 279, 285, 290, 291
Testicular atrophy, 288
Testosterone, 270, **271,** 276
and aggression, 447–448
in behavioral development,
279–280
converted to estradiol, 279, 280
and marijuana, 334
and reproduction-related
behavior, 285–286
secretion of, 277, 278
and sexual behavior, 285–286
as steroid, 287
Testosterone replacement therapy,
285–286
Thalamic nuclei, 474
lateral geniculate, 69, 76,
161–162, 166, 186
medial geniculate, 69, 76, 191,
448–449
relay, 180–182
medial dorsal, 202
ventral posterior, 69, 76, 194,
195, 203, 204
Thalamus, 68–69, 76, 202, 203
THC (delta-a-tetrahydrocannabinol), **333,** 335
Thermal stimuli, 193
Thermogenesis, diet-induced, 251,
264
Thiamin (vitamin B$_1$). *See also*
Pyrithiamine
deficiencies of, 12, 241, 242
metabolism of, 136
Thigmotaxic rats, **125**–126
Thinking. *See also* Cognitive
entries
incoherent, in schizophrenia,
455
modes of, 423–424
Third interstitial nucleus of anterior hypothalamus (INAH
3), 292
Thirst
and cellular deprivation,
255–259
and drinking and body fluid
regulation, 254–266
and hypovolemia, 257–259
Thoracic region of spinal cord,
194
Threat display evolution, 438,
439

Three-dimensional perceptions in
visual system, 152–153
3-per-second spike-and-wave dis-
charges, **139**
Threshold of excitation, **86**
Thrombosis, **133**
Thrombus, 133
Thymine, 404
Thymine nucleotide base, 37
Thyrotropin, **274**
Thyrotropin-releasing hormone,
274
Timbre, 188
Tobacco, 330–332, 338, 347, 348
Token test, **123,** 420
Tolerance to drugs. *See* Drug tol-
erance
Tone of voice, 444
Tongue, 203
Tonic-clonic convulsions, 139
Tonically active neurons (TANs),
219
Tonotopic organization, **189**
Tonus in seizures, 138, 139
Topographic gradient hypothesis,
383–385
Topographic maps of auditory
and visual systems, 388
Topography, 446
Totipotentiality, **379**
Touch, identification by, 194, 197,
217
Toxic psychosis, 136, **137**
Tracts, **54**
Transduction, **158,** 159, 161
Transection, 416
Transfer RNA, 39, 40
Transneuronal degeneration, 398,
399
Transorbital lobotomy, **15,** 16
Tremors in seizures, 138, 139
Triceps, 225, 226
Trichromatic theory (of color
vision), 172–174
Tricyclic antidepressants, 308, **309,**
317, 319, **460,** 461
Trigeminal nerve, 194, 195, 473
Trochlear nerve, 473
Tropic hormones, 271
True-breeding lines, **33,** 34
Tryptophan, 97
Tumor suppressor genes, 132
Tumors (neoplasms), **131**–133.
See also Cancer
Twin studies, 46–47
of affective disorders, 460
of homosexuality, 291
of intelligence, 46–47

of multiple sclerosis, 142
of obesity, 264
of personality, 46, 47
of schizophrenia, 455–456
Twins, identical (monozygotic) and fraternal (dizygotic), 46
Tympanic membrane (eardrum), **189**, 190
Tyramine, 461
Tyrosine, 43, 97, 269

U

Ulcers, 450–451
Unconditional (reflexive) response, 126
Unconditional stimulus, 126, 391, 392, 448, 449
Underarm (axillary) hair, 280, 281
Unipolar affective disorder, **460**
Unipolar neurons, **54**, 57
Uracil nucleotide basis, 39
Ureters, 255, 256
Urethral folds, 278

V

Vagus nerves, 203, 204, 246, 473
Valium, 102, 146, 317, 462, 463
Variables, types of, 6–7
Varicosities of axons, 97
Vas deferens, 277
Vasopressin, **272**, 273
Ventral direction, **62**, 63
Ventral horns, 64, **65**, 227
Ventral noradrenergic bundle, 246
Ventral posterior nuclei, 69, 76, **194**, 195, 203, 204
Ventral root, 64, 65
Ventral stream, 186–**187**
Ventral tegmental area, **343**–344
Ventricles, 380
Ventricular zone (of neural tube), **381**, 380–382
Ventromedial cortico–brain stem–spinal tract, **221**–224
Ventromedial hypothalamus (VMH), **245**–247
Ventromedial motor pathways, 221–224
Ventromedial nucleus (VMN), **290**, 291
Verb association, semantic processing of, 435

Verb-association condition, 434
Verbal subtests of WAIS, 122, 414
Verbal test performance, sex differences in, 414–415
Vertebrate evolution, 27–31
Vertebrate nervous system, directions in, 62–63
Vertebrates, **27**
Vestibular nucleus, 222, **223**
Vestibular system, 190, **191**
Viral infections of nervous system, 135–137
Vision
    acuity in, 152, 154, 156
    color, 172–177
    cortical mechanisms of, 183–188
    duplexity theory of, 155
    eye movement in, 158–159
    photopic (cone), 155
    scotopic (rod), 156
    sensitivity and accommodation in, 152
Visual agnosia, **187**–188
Visual completion, 154–155, 184, **419**–420
Visual cortex, 183–188
    aggregate field of, 168
    cells in, 167–168
    and fear conditioning, 449
    functional segregation in, 185–187
    primary (striate). See Primary visual cortex
    secondary, 183–187, 206, 434
    spatial-frequency theory of, 170–171
Visual-discrimination learning, 415–417
Visual edges, 163–171
Visual field area blindness (scotomas), 154, 155, 182–184, 401, 416, 417, 419
Visual field stimuli, 413
Visual fields, receptive, 165–170
Visual illusions, 151
Visual perception of subjective contours, 184, 185
Visual receptive fields, 165–170, 215
Visual receptors, 154–156, 164, 165
Visual system, 151–177
    and auditory system, 388
    color-coding and brightness-coding cells in, 172–173
    completion by, 154–155, 184, 419–420

development of, 384, 385
    and electromagnetic spectrum, 151–152
    motion perception in, 13–14
    research on, 165–166
    temporal integration in, 158–159
    three-dimensional perceptions in, 152–153
Visual tests of language-related activities, 433–435
Visual transduction, 159–161
Vitamins, diet selection for, 241–242. *See also* Thiamin (vitamin B$_1$)
VMH (ventromedial hypothalamus), **245**–247
VMH syndrome, 245
VMN (ventromedial nucleus), **290**, 291
Vocabulary subtest of WAIS, 122
Voice, tone of, 444
Voice box, 45
Voltage-activated ion channels, 88–**89**
Voltammetry, in vivo, 118, 119
Voluntary movement, 224

W

WAIS (Wechsler Adult Intelligence Scale), 46, **121**–123, 414
Walking as sensorimotor reflex, 230–231
Water deficits, 260, 261
Water deprivation, 256
Wavelengths of light, 151–152, 157–158, 163–167, 172–177
Wechsler Adult Intelligence Scale (WAIS), 46, **121**–123, 212, 414
Weight-gain programs, 251
Weight-loss programs, 250–251, 264
Weight regulation, 235–353, 264
Wernicke-Geschwind model, **424**–432
Wernicke's aphasia, **424**, 425, 428, 430
Wernicke's area, **424**, 423–429, 432, 435
White matter, 64, 65
Wisconsin Card Sorting Test, 122–**123**
Withdrawal effects, 318, 326–327, 330–334, 337, 340, 341

Withdrawal programs, 340
Withdrawal reflex, **229,** 228–230
Withdrawal syndrome, 326, **327,**
    332, 333, 337
Within-subjects design, 6, **7**
Wolffian system, **277,** 276–278
Word-association test, 124
Word deafness, **192,** 193
Word salad, **424,** 425
Working memory, **372**
Writing problems (agraphia),
    426–429

X

X chromosomes, 270, 271
X-ray photography, 106–107. *See
    also* Computed tomogra-
    phy
Xenon 133, 217

Y

Y chromosomes, 270, 271

Z

Z lens, **421,** 420–422
Zebra finches, birdsong in, 44, 45
Zeitgebers, **303,** 302–304
Zeitgeist, 20, **21**
Zygomaticus major, 443, 444
Zygotes, **35,** 34–36, 270, **271,** 379